T3-BNY-125

Ralph Volney Harlow

Revised by NELSON BLAKE

Syracuse University

HENRY HOLT AND COMPANY • *New York*

THE UNITED STATES:

From Wilderness to World Power

Third Edition

Library of Congress Catalog Card
Number: 57—5713
February, 1959

23467–0617

Printed in the United States of America

PREFACE TO THIRD EDITION

At Dr. Harlow's request I undertook the assignment of preparing the present revision—a task that he himself would have performed with his usual thoroughness, had his health permitted. The last three chapters have been my particular responsibility. For events through 1952 I have tried to preserve as much as possible of Dr. Harlow's own point of view by condensing and rearranging material from the 1953 edition. The final chapter on the Eisenhower administration is entirely my own. I have also extended the list of Selected Readings to include some of the significant recent literature.

Before his death on October 3, 1956, Dr. Harlow had read most of my manuscript and given it his general approval. But he was too weak to give me the benefit of his criticism on matters of detail. I can only hope that my contribution reflects in some way the affectionate memory in which I hold this fine scholar under whose department chairmanship I served for several years and whom I have always been proud to call my friend.

N. M. B.

Syracuse, New York
November 18, 1956

PREFACE TO FIRST EDITION

This book is designed to provide basic, essential material for the one-year college course in American history. It is full enough to include an account of the most important developments, and at the same time brief enough to allow considerable time for collateral reading. No text book is expected to be a general reference work, still less a small encyclopedia. It should be a guide to the student, something which will explain briefly what he needs to know and tell him where he can find additional information and different interpretations. The text itself should meet the first aim while the reading lists should help in meeting the second.

Probably no two teachers would agree completely on the selection of material for a text. Certainly every specialist will feel that any text gives insufficient emphasis to his particular area of study. And yet a comparison of standard texts will show considerable uniformity in selection and emphasis. The subject matter of this one, the over-all plan, the organization, and the manner of presentation have been derived from a continuous teaching experience of thirty-five years. It is hoped that the book will appeal to both teachers and students. When a student likes his text the work of the instructor is immeasurably easier.

Every general survey must come down as close to the immediate present as the mechanics of publication permit. Contemporary history however is full of peculiarly difficult problems. All the material is controversial in character, and developments which bulk large in the current news may or may not have lasting significance. For example when the final chapters of this book were being written the "cold war" between the Soviet Union and the Western powers suggested the possibility of serious trouble. But the historical pattern into which this contest will fall cannot be known for several years.

A book of this size does not provide space for many illustrations, certainly not enough to suggest the amazing variety of available pictures in this field. In selecting those which are included the guiding principle was to use something interesting and also something which has not become too common by repeated use in other texts. Also, because Americans have so often observed their public affairs with the saving grace of humor, it seemed desirable to recognize this tendency by putting in a few cartoons.

Perhaps there should be a brief personal note about my own concept of history. I have never been able to find any factors or forces in history except those which have been created by human beings. Human behavior falls into recognizable patterns, patterns which are persistent but at the same time continuously subject to change. History is the study of these patterns and changes. It is easy to talk about cause and effect—about which we know considerably less than we like to admit—and about trends, as though words and terms in themselves constitute explanations. Trends would seem to be not molds which predetermine the shape of human affairs, but simply the result of numerous decisions, made from day to day. Such decisions, repeated often enough, do create conditions which make certain policies practically inevitable. But a series of radically different decisions, which would have been possible at one time, would have made entirely different decisions equally inevitable. I have never been able to see justification for any purely mechanistic interpretation of history, such as economic determinism or any other determinism. History is selected material taken from the sum total of human behavior. If there is any one single formula which provides the key to complete understanding of this behavior, that formula has eluded all who have hunted for it.

R. V. H.

Westbrook, Connecticut
January 3, 1949

CONTENTS

LIST OF MAPS

Chapter 1

THE FIRST ENGLISH COLONY

Beginnings of American History

THIS volume is a summary of the history of the United States. Its purpose is to trace the growth of our nation from seemingly inauspicious and simple beginnings at scattered points along a part of the Atlantic coast to the vast country and complex social structure which we know today. Actually these beginnings were not simple. Any examination of the background would show how many different forces, each one the result of a long process of growth, combined to make America a going concern. Because this study is a summary, many of the earlier steps must be omitted. There is no space here for the explorations which first brought America to the attention of Europeans. Nor is there room for any account of the rise of the Spanish Empire, a far-flung entity already a century old when the English settled Jamestown.

Omission of the story of Spain in America is regrettable because Spanish activity here has had important and lasting influences on the history of the United States. The danger of Spanish aggression in the South helps to explain the establishment of the colony of Georgia. During the American Revolution Spanish leaders tried to prevent the United States from occupying any part of the Mississippi valley. Subsequently Spanish activity in the South and Southwest was a source of almost continuous trouble for the new American government. When the Latin American nations became independent, their relations with the United States proved to be important in shaping American policy. And as the United States expanded, former Spanish American territory and Spanish-speaking inhabitants were brought within the jurisdiction of this country. From the latter part of the sixteenth century to the present day there has never been a time when this Spanish or Latin American influence could be ignored.

As students of the history of the United States we can never overlook the importance of the Spanish colonial empire, but the limitations of space confine us to the beginnings of the English colonies. The people whose activities constitute the history of this country were not natives. They were immigrants from Europe. These newcomers found the so-called Indians here and either used them for their own purposes, after the manner of the Spaniards in Mexico and South America, or drove them out or killed them off as the English did in what is now the United States. To be sure, the Indians contributed something, but surprisingly little, to American history. They introduced the Europeans to new agricultural products—of which the most important were beans, maize, potatoes, squash, and tobacco—to a new game bird—the wild turkey—and to the buffalo or bison of the western plains. The English language received a few additions in the form of Indian words, and our maps still carry some Indian place names. Indian contributions to American history have been so slight that one is justified in suggesting that they might be omitted entirely without appreciably altering the main trend of development.

The Beginnings of American History in Europe and England

American history began therefore not with the Indians but with the arrival of the first Europeans. For that part of North America included in the United States, the significant part of history began with the coming of the English. As compared with the meager contributions of the Indians, the English brought a complex, well-developed civilization. Among other cultural traits they brought their language, both oral and written, and fastened it so firmly that later, non-English immigrants have never succeeded in displacing it. They brought the arts and crafts of agriculture, shipping, commerce, and primitive manufacturing. Along with these came the all-important institutions of government, judicial procedure, and law, still the bases of our democracy today. They also gave us our forms of religious worship.

English Culture

The processes by which these English institutions were established here are the real beginnings of American history, and there should be at least a mention of the origin of these institutions. English culture came from Europe, and European culture was composed of numerous elements fused together at different times into beliefs, practices, and institutional behavior. The English language is a composite product derived from at least three different tongues: Germanic, Latin, and French. English religious beliefs came from the Near East and Europe by way of the ancient Hebrews and Greeks, and they were then put into familiar form by the medieval Catholic Church and by Protestant reformers of the sixteenth century. Many of the basic principles of government and law had been contributed by the ancient Romans. The foundations of science and mathematics had been built by the Greeks and later by the Moslems. Then the British added numerous contributions of their own. From these diverse origins came the civilization which was transplanted to the new environment in America.

John Cabot

Even before the end of the fifteenth century Spain and Portugal had planned to divide the New World between themselves, and in doing so they gave little thought to England. Englishmen, however, showed considerable interest in the New World. In 1497 King Henry VII issued a commission to a Genoese sailor, John Cabot, for a voyage of discovery. Cabot came upon the continent of North America, thereby securing to his employer a title to nearly half the western hemisphere. For this service the frugal Tudor bestowed upon the explorer the sum of £10, the equivalent of perhaps $400 in modern purchasing power. What his self-indulgent son, Henry VIII, might have done in North America had he not been disturbed by other interests was never made known. As it was, he got himself so deeply involved in theological controversy, ecclesiastical reorganization, and matrimonial troubles that the New World made little appeal to him.

But whatever may be alleged against Henry VII for his downright stinginess or against Henry VIII for his extravagances, there is no doubt that these Tudor kings laid the foundations of English prosperity and of English maritime greatness. Henry VII had been interested in shipbuilding as well as in exploration, even going so far as to offer bounties for the construction of large vessels. Moreover, he built the first dry dock in England—at Portsmouth. Henry VIII displayed an even livelier concern in English sea power. In 1545 he established the Navy Board, and he founded the training school for pilots, known as Trinity House, which is still in existence. These proceedings explain where the seamen of the next generation, the famous Elizabethan sea dogs, got their start.

English economic development during the Tudor period differed radically from that of Spain. Spanish wealth depended not on the cultivation of Spanish resources but on the systematic exploitation of the New World. Spain was receiving much and, from the economic standpoint, giving little. In the case of England, on the other hand, colonial development was preceded, in fact was really forced, by the remarkable industrial growth and commercial expansion within the nation itself.

English Industry and Trade

By the middle of Elizabeth's reign, about 1580, progress was evident in the whole range of manufacturing. Most of the older crafts were enjoying a much larger market. Builders were kept busy in supplying the demands for new dwellings. Artisans in the textile trades were trying to provide the varied and expensive fabrics which fashion required the social leaders to wear. Both men and women were equally anxious to move just ahead of rapidly changing styles and, in their efforts to beautify their persons, they called upon the lacemakers and jewelers to aid the tailors. In addition to the steadily increasing activity in the old trades, new ones were becoming more important. The discovery of the art of printing called for large numbers of skilled craftsmen: paper makers, bookbinders, press makers and type founders. Map makers and instrument makers put the new discoveries of science at the disposal of merchants and sailors.

Industrial development is partly the cause and partly the result of increasing activity on the part of the merchants, those who buy and sell what others produce. As their trade increased, the merchants began to save money. This accumulating capital made possible larger and more extensive business operations as well as the rise of a class of promoters, men who were on the lookout for new chances to make money. Both manufacturers and merchants became interested in wider markets. This wave of prosperity was also due in part to the increasing volume of money in Europe. The gold and silver which the Spaniards imported from America could not be confined within the boundaries of Spain; they had to pay it out for supplies. Merchants and nobles in other countries got some of it and used it to buy goods. When people want to buy, any increase in the amount of money available encourages business activity. Men who made more money than they needed for direct living expenses and for amusement put their surplus to work. They invested it in manufacturing or in trade and so increased their profits.

In order to carry on the expanding trade to the best advantage, merchants formed joint-stock companies in which each member invested what he could afford and from which, when there were profits, he drew a share in proportion to his investment. These companies were given charters by the government, assuring them a monopoly of the trade with some specific part of the world. The oldest of these companies, the Merchants Adventurers, had been organized for the purpose of handling the sale of English woolen cloth in the Netherlands. By the time of Queen Elizabeth, the Merchants Adventurers were taking an active part in a general export trade. Englishmen went abroad, not only to sell British products but to buy goods for the English markets. Other companies were organized to trade with the Baltic States, Russia, Turkey, Morocco, Africa, and the Far East. The profits of these companies averaged not 6 or 10 percent but from 100 to 400 percent or even more. In 1622, one shipment of goods from India which cost £386,000 sold in England for £1,915,000.

Anglo-Spanish Rivalry

During part of the sixteenth century, English progress continued without bringing on any conflict with the rapidly growing Spanish Empire. But sooner or later the lines of development of these two nations were bound to cross, particularly so if the British should presume to encroach upon Spanish trade or Spanish colonial possessions. In addition to rivalry over imperial and economic interests, a growing contest over religion might put an end to English peace. Spain was still a Catholic country, and the Spanish King, Philip II, regarded himself as the great lay champion of his faith. He had been the husband of Elizabeth's predecessor, Mary Tudor, so he had some interest in England. He was prepared to overthrow Protestantism, if he could, wherever it prevailed, and England seemed to demand special efforts on his part. No Spaniard could forget the treatment which Catherine of Aragon had received at the hands of Henry VIII, and no Catholic could forgive the repudiation of papal authority which Elizabeth had approved. There had been cause enough to act before 1570 when Elizabeth was excommunicated by the Pope; after that it became a religious duty to deprive her of her throne, if not of her life. Philip therefore was ready to encourage plots against the Queen in order to give her place to the more orthodox Mary Stuart. In defending their religion, Englishmen were well aware that they were defending not only their ruler but their whole system of government. The underlying issues in the contest between England and Spain were therefore commercial interests, which involved colonies and sea power; Protestantism; and national independence.

For fully twenty years before England and Spain went to war, the feeling of each nation toward the other grew steadily more bitter, while minor conflicts in various parts of the world foretold the approach of the crisis. Among these early manifestations of increasing hostility were the activities of the Elizabethan seamen. These daring adventurers, of whom John Hawkins and Francis Drake were the most famous, set out deliberately to defy the power of Spain and to seek their fortunes in the trade of her Empire.

Sir John Hawkins specialized in the African slave trade, and he found his market in the forbidden area of Spanish America. In 1562 he fitted out a small expedition to buy Negro slaves in Africa for sale to Spanish planters in the West Indies. Spanish law prohibited such business; nevertheless, Hawkins disposed of his first cargo advantageously in Santo Domingo. In spite of official Spanish protests, Hawkins made repeated visits to the West Indies, clearing a profit of 60 percent or more on his investment. The planters wanted slaves, law or no law, and Hawkins was glad to risk official displeasure to help the planters and to increase his own fortune.

Hawkins and Drake

Francis Drake, a young relative of Hawkins, had nothing in particular to sell to the Spaniards, but he was fired by a holy hatred of their faith as well as by a deep-seated hunger for vengeance. As a youth he had been sailing in Hawkins's service when the Spaniards nearly succeeded in putting an end to both their promising careers. Beginning in 1572 and using the West Indies as a base of supplies, Drake seized Spanish ships, burned Spanish colonial towns, and actually robbed a Spanish mule train bringing gold and silver from Peru to the Atlantic coast. On the way home he captured a Spanish treasure ship. In 1577, bent on more plunder, Drake took out a fleet of five ships manned by a force of 150 men. This time he passed through the Straits of Magellan, losing all but one ship. With this single vessel he sailed north along the western coast of South America, robbing the Spaniards as he went. News traveled so slowly in those days that he could move from port to port before his next victims had any warning that he was in their part of the world. Afraid to return home by the same route because of the danger of falling into Spanish hands, he struck boldly westward across the Pacific. After an absence of two years, he reached England by way of the Far East. His cargo was worth $4,000,000.

The audacity of these Englishmen compels admiration even now, and it did then, everywhere but in Spain. When the Spanish ambassador complained bitterly to Queen Elizabeth, she assured him that she knew nothing of these men. But when Drake returned, the Queen herself conferred knighthood upon him, and she seems to have been well taken care of in the division of his spoils. The exploits of these enterprising seamen and the attitude of the virgin Queen toward them were not the only grievances which Philip could list in his indictment of England. When his Dutch subjects rebelled against Spanish rule, Elizabeth sent them secret encouragement and subsequently open help in money and men.

While Drake was threatening the security of the Spaniards on the sea, another famous Englishman, Sir Walter Raleigh, proposed to break down Spanish claims on land. In 1584, under authority of a charter granted by the

Queen, he sent a small exploring expedition to North America. In July 1584, Raleigh's agents entered Pamlico Sound and landed on Roanoke Island, now a part of North Carolina. These Englishmen were most enthusiastic over their discoveries. Queen Elizabeth named the country Virginia, the Land of the Virgin Queen.

In the following year, 1585, Raleigh sent Captain Ralph Lane to this same region to decide upon the proper site for the colony. Then in May

Raleigh's Experiment

1587, Raleigh sent out a real colonizing expedition, consisting of three ships and 150 colonists. This group included twenty-five women and children; the governor and leader was John White, artist and explorer. The colony was started on Roanoke Island. Toward the end of the summer White returned to England for supplies. Because of growing trouble with Spain he was unable to return until 1591. When he came the colonists had disappeared. Their cabins were still there, but these and a single word, "Croatan," carved on a tree were all that remained of the settlement. The fate of the colonists still remains a mystery. Raleigh spent £40,000 without founding a permanent settlement, but his money was not thrown away. His example inspired others to undertake the work of colonization, and, once the troubles with Spain were over, England acquired a real hold in North America.

Unsuccessful as it was, this attempt to violate the Spanish claim to North America was another goad to Philip, already infuriated over the commercial situation. Then, when Elizabeth ordered the execution of Mary Stuart, Philip decided that there was nothing left but the appeal to force. The only way that his commercial structure could be saved was to conquer England.

The most spectacular part of the war came in the beginning. Philip planned to overwhelm England with a single, crushing blow and to that

War with Spain

end he organized the great Armada. He mobilized a fleet of 130 vessels, with a total force of 30,000 men. Over half of these were soldiers, and the fleet carried the necessary material for a successful war on land, including even horses, mules, and carts.

Philip underestimated the strength of his foes. He expected that his own shores at least would be safe from attack, but, even before the Armada left port, Sir Francis Drake sailed into the harbor at Cadiz, destroyed some of the Spanish ships, and captured Spanish treasure. Philip counted on an English people divided by religious controversy, but, however much they might quarrel among themselves, Protestants and Catholics stood together against the foreign danger. He counted on the superior power of both the Spanish army and the Spanish navy, but Philip's military forces never had a chance because they could not get ashore. As for the navy, English ships under the command of Lord Howard of Effingham, Sir John Hawkins, and Sir Francis Drake proved more seaworthy and were better handled than the Spanish galleons. The English guns were better and their gunners more accurate than the Spanish. Even the elements fought against

Spain. To the disturbing currents of the English Channel, never easy for any but the best of pilots, there were added unfavorable winds and severe storms. The Armada was almost annihilated. Two thirds of the ships were wrecked, and nearly three quarters of the men were killed. A few vessels straggled back to Spain by way of northern Ireland, but these had lost all effectiveness as fighting units. The English lost not a single ship and only sixty men.

The destruction of Spanish ships and men could easily have been made good, but not so the loss in pride and morale. Spanish sea power was broken. By 1591 the English had captured more than 800 Spanish ships, and five years later Lord Howard captured and plundered Cadiz itself. This succession of defeats did not mark the end of the Spanish Empire, which lasted for 200 years more, but it left the Spanish treasury bankrupt and it put a stop to Spanish expansion. Since that time the history of Spain has been one of decline.

Factors in English Colonization

The Anglo-Spanish war ended in 1604. Two years later a group of enterprising Englishmen formulated plans which led to the first permanent English settlement in North America. In doing so they were taking advantage of those conditions and circumstances which combined to encourage colonization. First were the financial resources of the merchants, resources which had been accumulating during a century or more of commercial prosperity. British traders were well acquainted with the record of Spanish colonial development and they looked forward to equally gratifying returns on their own investments. They were willing to risk their fortunes in the hope of making larger ones, and their help was essential. It cost money to hire ships, provide food and supplies, and pay the costs of transporting colonists and their goods to the New World. The government might have assumed the responsibility and the risk, as the Spanish authorities had done, but the English way was different. Englishmen preferred to make colonizing a matter of private enterprise and private profit. At the same time, these British capitalists counted on the government to provide military and naval protection for the colonists. Thanks to the victory over Spain, the government was in a position to meet this demand.

At the opening of the seventeenth century England had a large class of sufferers from a prolonged economic depression. They were interested in colonies because of the chance to make a better living. Their economic difficulties were the results of a change in the English farming system. Down to the fifteenth century the small farmers, whether owners or tenants, raised wheat, horses, cattle, and sheep, thus producing what they needed for their own families and possibly a surplus for sale. But by the sixteenth century sheep raising had largely taken the place of general farming because the large landholders found heavy profits in wool. Tenant farmers and laborers were no longer needed to till the soil, so they formed an army of the unemployed. The landowners and the woolen manufacturers who sided with them were so politically powerful that they were even allowed to take over the common lands on which the farmers had kept their livestock, and turn these into pasture land for sheep. Since the care of sheep required little labor, this policy left thousands of farmers and farm laborers with no means of support. Sometimes the inhabitants of a whole village had to leave their homes, only to become common beggars. This process had been going on for perhaps a hundred years before Elizabeth came to the throne.

Thus while English merchants and manufacturers enjoyed unusual prosperity, the dispossessed victims of the wool growers were facing privation. Moreover, the war with Spain had made the lot of the poor even worse than before. This contest and other wars on the Continent interrupted commerce, cut down the market for English woolen cloth, and consequently spread the depression to spinners and weavers. By the end of Elizabeth's reign economic conditions had settled into what looked like a permanent depression. The most discouraging feature of this situation was the lack of hope of improvement in England. Men turned to America as a possible solution for their troubles. As early as 1574, Sir Humphrey Gilbert wrote: "We might inhabit some part of these countries [America] and settle there those needy people of our country which now trouble the commonwealth and through want here at home are enforced to commit outrageous offences whereby they are dayly consumed with the gallows." And in 1611, the Spanish minister to England wrote: "Their [referring to the English] principle reason for colonizing these parts is to give an outlet to so many idle, wretched people as they have in England, and thus prevent the dangers that might be feared of them."

Land and Religion

The unemployed Englishman needed land, and America had land in abundance. Here was a chance to exchange abject poverty for economic security. In addition to its economic advantages the ownership of land had a social and sentimental appeal. Landholders were a privileged class, the possessors of political as well as economic power. They alone could vote for members of Parliament. The country gentry dominated their tenants and neighbors. As for the nobility, their status was determined by their great estates. These considerations helped to shape the thought of many Englishmen; they knew that the acquisition of a farm in America would not make every man a lord, but it would bring tangible advantages.

Promoters of colonies and merchants, as distinguished from prospective settlers, could see other advantages in North American land, the chief of which was timber. As a growing commercial and manufacturing country England needed timber, and the domestic supply was rapidly disappearing. In those days all ships were built of wood, and they were made watertight by means of products of the forests, particularly tar and pitch. Wood was still the fuel used in smelting iron. Even the textile manufacturers needed wood for the construction of their spinning wheels and looms. Explorers in the New World all reported on the abundance of timber in North America. Here, then, was a natural resource which would amply repay a large investment in colonial enterprise.

Another of the forces that encouraged English colonization in America was religious unrest. Although the Church of England had been established during the reign of Elizabeth, and although this Church satisfied the majority of Englishmen, there were two groups who did not like it. On one side were the Roman Catholics, who were prevented by their creed from accepting any but their own Church; on the other were the Dissenters who wanted a more complete break with the past. These extreme Protestants were ready to leave England if they could establish colonies dedicated to their own particular theories of religion. Besides these questions of freedom of worship, both Catholics and Protestants saw an opportunity to bring Christianity to the heathen, thereby saving them from eternal punishment.

The London Company and the First English Colony

Colonial Charters

In 1606 King James I granted charters to two new joint-stock trading companies, organized to exploit economic opportunities in North America. To the London Company the king's charter granted the territory between the 34th and the 41st degrees of latitude, and to the Plymouth Company that between the 38th and the 45th, with the provision that in the region where the grants overlapped, there must be a gap of at least a hundred miles between settlements of the two companies. Each company received authority "to deduce a Colony" into America. This was an important provision because under English law no Englishman could emigrate without official permission. These charters granted permission to all who might go under company auspices.

In addition to granting the land, the Crown provided for a simple plan of government for the proposed colonies. Each colony was to have a council of thirteen members to govern in accordance with royal orders; the members of these bodies were to be appointed by the king. In addition, there was created the "Council of Virginia" in England to have general oversight of both colonies. The charters also made provision for the legal rights of prospective settlers; they and their descendants were promised "all Liberties, Franchises, and Immunities, within any of our other Dominions, to all Intents and Purposes, as if they had been abiding and born, within this our Realm of *England,* or any other of our said Dominions."

Rights of Englishmen

In subjecting these charters to modern interpretation it is well to remember that the rights and liberties granted were those which Englishmen of that day enjoyed. Certain principles had been firmly established. First was the doctrine of constitutional government—that is, a government resting upon a recognized body of law. This law was binding not only upon citizens and subjects but also upon government officials themselves, even upon the king. The English nobility had compelled King John to acquiesce in this principle when he approved the Great Charter. Under this same principle of constitutional government, individual citizens were protected

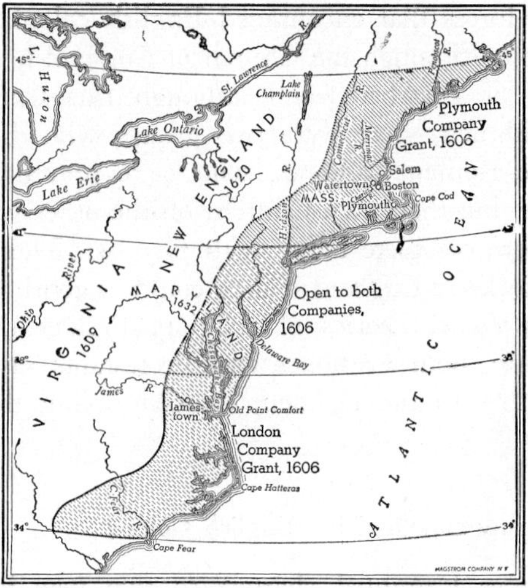

Map 1. Early Limits of English Colonies in North America

against the arbitrary exercise of governmental authority; they had certain rights which the government must respect. Englishmen could not be arrested without a warrant, nor kept in prison without adequate reason. The right of habeas corpus was recognized in both mother country and colonies. Then the principle of trial by jury was an established safeguard against arbitrary decisions by the judges. These rights of the individual before the law were carried to America.

The London Company which founded the first colony at Jamestown had a total membership of 659 persons, of whom 110 were merchants and 282 were described as "citizens." There were also representatives of the upper classes, known as "gentlemen." A majority of the members belonged to the middle class, and the project was a middle-class venture. According to the plans of the promoters, the colony was thought of as a plantation to be worked by the settlers, who in turn were servants of the company. The primary purpose, like that of the older joint-stock companies, was to make money for the stockholders. Virginia was not started as an experiment in democracy or popular government.

Jamestown

The first settlers arrived in Virginia in 1607 and unwisely decided to make their homes on the banks of the James River. Here a combination of brackish water, lack of adequate drainage, and malarial mosquitoes soon brought on sickness. It was partly this unfavorable location and partly a combination of circumstances which neither the company nor the colonists could control that account for the hardships of the early years. The first settlers were of all kinds: gentlemen, artisans, and laborers, a good average lot of Englishmen. Their environment, however, was anything but average. Any group of civilized human beings, no matter how intelligent and able they may be, will find it difficult to adjust themselves to life in a wilderness.

These colonists were 3000 miles away from their base of supplies. Because they could not begin to raise their food at once, they had to import it from England. Some of the supplies which the company shipped over spoiled in transit, while some were bad when they started. The colonists did not succeed in raising even maize until 1609.

In the course of a few months the poor health of the colony was alarming. Poor food combined with disease (probably dysentery and malaria) left the men weak and discouraged. At one time during that desolate first year only six well persons could be found in the colony. The settlers were so ill that "some of them would eat their fish raw, rather than they would go a stones cast to fetch wood and dresse it." One of the first settlers wrote a pathetic but vivid account of these early sufferings:

> There were never Englishmen left in a foreign country in such miserie as we were in this new discovered Virginia. We watched every three nights, lying on the bare ground, what weather soever came—which brought our men to be most feeble wretches . . . it would make . . . hearts bleed to heare the pitiful murmurings and outcries of our sick men without reliefe, every night and day for the space of sixe weekes; in the morning their bodies being trailed out of their cabines like Dogges, to be buried.

Captain John Smith

By the end of the first year only thirty-eight settlers remained alive. Probably the colony would have failed completely if it had not been for the courage and determination of Captain John Smith, who contrived to get food from the Indians. He compelled the settlers to work. He explored the back country. He defended the little village of Jamestown against the hostile savages. When an accident forced him to return to England, the colony barely escaped destruction.

In addition to these reasons for discouragement, the very system on which the colony was founded made success impossible. The aim of the company was dividends, to be derived from the labor of the settlers. The colonists were not independent farmers but merely the servants of the company. With the company as the sole land owner it is not surprising that the men were lazy; whatever they made went to enrich the company instead of themselves. The greatest stimulus to activity, the opportunity for private gain, was absent.

Changes in Government

In 1609 the promoters of the colony applied for a new charter in order that a better system of control might be installed. This second charter ended all connection between the London and the Plymouth Companies and abolished the council which had resided in the colony. The new charter also changed the name of the concern to the Virginia Company. Under the new system there was to be only one council, resident in England, with a treasurer as a managing director. This body was given full power to make all laws and regulations necessary for the government of Virginia, provided that such laws were not inconsistent with those of England, and received authority to rule over the settlers. In Virginia, the authority of the company was vested in a governor, appointed by the council in England. The charter was so drawn that the treasurer could act as the executive head of both council and colony. At the same time the company planned to send out families, instead of individual male adventurers.

In 1611, on the strength of this charter, the council placed the colony under martial law. Everything was organized on a military basis. The men not only carried arms when they went to work but marched back and forth in true military style. The regulations, known as Dale's Laws, under which this system was carried into effect, were drawn up by the council in England and enforced, perhaps not very strictly, by Sir Thomas Dale, the governor. Toward the end of 1618, after about seven years of this rigorous government, the colony numbered about 600 souls. The company had spent £80,000 and, far from being able to pay dividends, was about £5000 in debt.

What the colony needed was economic reform rather than a mere change of government, and Governor Dale made a small beginning in this direction. In 1611 he started the practice of granting small tracts of land to individuals, with permission to keep for themselves any profits they might make from these grants. Five years later the company extended the practice, first limiting the individual grants to three acres, and then later increasing the area to fifty. From that time on the ambitious colonist had an incentive to work.

Tobacco and Slavery

The next need was a "money crop," a product which would command a good price in England. This crop proved to be tobacco. In 1614 John Rolfe discovered a new method of curing the leaf—that is, preparing it for market—and so made it commercially profitable. This luxury was already becoming a necessity to fashionable England, and the new method of curing it solved Virginia's problem. Within six years the colony was showing unmistakable signs of prosperity. Every farmer in Virginia was raising tobacco. Virginia exported 20,000 pounds of tobacco in 1617, 60,000 in 1624, and 500,000 in 1627. These figures mean little by themselves but, interpreted in terms of growth, they are significant. This extraordinary increase meant more plantations, more settlers, a greater colony in every way. In the course of seven years from 1622 to 1629, the population increased from fewer than 1000 to nearly 3000. From then on to the end of the seventeenth century, from 1500 to 2000 new immigrants arrived each year. At last Virginia was able to produce something that the rest of the world was eager to buy, and by 1630 prosperity was assured.

Quantity production of tobacco required cheap labor. A solution of this problem was found in the use of indentured servants. These were persons who sold themselves into labor service for a specified number of years, usually five. The owner of the contract could sell it at any time, so the servant might be transferred from employer to employer. But at the expiration of the term the servant became completely free.

At first these indentured servants were white immigrants from the British Isles, but in 1619, according to the record, a Dutch "man of warre" brought "twenty negars" into the colony. The government itself bought their services and then sold the contracts to individual farmers. These first Negroes in Virginia were not slaves but indentured servants and after they had worked out their time they became free; some of them became landowners. During the early history of Virginia the number of Negroes increased slowly; in 1649 there were only 300 and in 1671 they numbered 2000. The first formal recognition of Negro slavery, as distinguished from indentured labor, came in 1656, and slavery was regularly provided for by law in 1661.

First American Legislature

These economic developments were accompanied by equally significant changes in government. In 1618 Sir Edwin Sandys became treasurer of the Virginia Company. He was a liberal in politics. In those days liberalism meant opposition to the theories of divine right professed by King James I; English liberals were trying to make Parliament the most important branch of the government. Sandys objected to the system of absolutism in the government of Virginia, and in 1618, under his direction, the company put into effect a "charter of grants and liberties." This provided for a representative assembly in the colony, to meet once a year. This House of Burgesses, the first representative lawmaking body in America, met in July 1619.

In an ordinance of 1621 the company outlined more clearly the framework of government for Virginia. The governor represented the company and served as chief executive in the colony. Associated with him in his executive work was a council of state, appointed by the company. Next came the House of Burgesses, made up of two representatives from every town or "hundred" in the colony. According to this ordinance every free male inhabitant, seventeen years of age or older, could vote. The property qualification for voting was introduced in 1670. The governor, council, and house could make laws for the colony, but the measures passed by the assembly were subject to the veto of the governor, and even if he approved a measure, it might still be set aside by the company in England. Furthermore, the ordinance provided that the laws made in Virginia must not be inconsistent with the laws of England.

End of the Charter

In spite of hardship and suffering, malnutrition, disease, and an appalling death rate, the colony of Virginia survived. Tobacco and the system of individual land grants made the new settlement a going concern. The Virginia Company, on the other hand, as distinguished from the colony, became more and more deeply involved in difficulties. In 1622 an Indian massacre wiped out a number of settlers and so raised the question of the capacity of the company to defend its property and the lives of the colonists. The company itself was weakened by factional controversies among its own members. As a corporation it was deeply in debt, so that bankruptcy and liquidation had become inevitable. To make matters worse, King James I was trying to cultivate the good will of Spain, and Spanish agents were working to discredit Virginia. Spain had no desire to see a powerful English colony within range of her own American empire. Again there was a long dispute between the king and the company over the control of the tobacco trade. In 1624 King James revoked the charter, and the English government took over the management of the colony of Virginia. For the future the king appointed the governor and the members of the council. But the House of Burgesses was not destroyed and it remained as the representative body of the planters. The net result of the revocation of the charter, therefore, was the transfer of control from a corporation to the king.

Economic Conditions

By 1630 the colony revealed the political, social, and economic characteristics which lasted until the close of the seventeenth century. In the main Virginia was a community of small farmers, the great majority of whom—some 90 percent—not only owned but cultivated their land. Before 1705 the average farm or plantation was about 370 acres. Large estates were rare. According to the careful estimates of Professor Wertenbaker, there were relatively few indentured servants and slaves; the average number of such workers per farm was only 1.5. It was not until the heavy importation of slaves in the eighteenth century altered this balance that Virginia ceased to be an agricultural democracy. The landed aristocrats, such as Colonel William Byrd of Westover, were few in number.

Although these Virginia farms were relatively small, certainly in comparison with some of the great estates which were built up during the eighteenth century, they were large enough to prevent the growth of anything approaching town life in Virginia. The county therefore became the unit of local government. The scattering of the population had certain important consequences in the arrangements for recreation, education, and religion.

The history of Virginia was not one of uninterrupted progress and prosperity. Shortly before 1660 the planters began to suffer from a serious economic depression, and the hard times lasted until 1682. During this interval the colonists were disturbed still further by Indian warfare and by armed rebellion against the established government. The depression was due to a sharp drop in the price of the basic crop, tobacco. In 1667 the secretary of the colony, Thomas Ludwell, reported that the average farmer in Virginia was getting only 50 shillings for his year's crop. Out of this small income he had to buy manufactured goods for his home and clothing for himself and his family. In 1680 the governor and council reported that "the people of Virginia are generally, some few excepted, extremely poor, not being able to provide against the pressing necessities of their families." There was no lack of food because at that period the farmers raised their own and the fertile soil of Virginia produced an ample supply. But the loss of income from tobacco resulted in serious hardship to large numbers of people. This condition was due to a glut of the market, brought about in large part by British regulations and restrictions on the tobacco trade (see Chapter 6).

The Indian troubles began in the summer of 1675, when some Indians murdered two Virginia farmers. In revenge Virginia militiamen killed the murderers and several more Indians for good measure. For the remaining part of the year there were numerous attacks by the Indians upon the whites, and early in 1676 there was a serious Indian uprising.

Bacon's Rebellion

At this time the governor of Virginia was the old and conservative Sir William Berkeley, loyal supporter of King Charles I and of his son. The House of Burgesses which had been elected in 1661 was conservative too; in fact, Berkeley liked the members so well that he would not order a new election for fourteen years. The majority of the members had lost touch with their constituents, and they regularly upheld the governor. Berkeley himself was interested in the fur trade along the frontier and therefore wanted to retain the good will of the Indians. He refused to do anything effective to protect the people from the Indians. The legislature did appropriate money for building forts, but the most obvious result of this policy was to increase the burden of taxes on a people already desperate for lack of funds. The depredations of the Indians continued.

Unable to get help from the regular authorities, some of the planters chose one of their own number, Nathaniel Bacon, as a new leader. In the spring of 1676 he organized a small force and successfully attacked one group of Indians. Berkeley proclaimed Bacon and his whole band rebels against the government, because Bacon had taken the field without a commission from the governor. But Bacon had the support of a majority of the people, and they forced the governor to provide for a new election. Berkeley even went so far as to pardon Bacon, readmit him to the council, and then commission him to lead a campaign against the Indians. Once Bacon left Jamestown, however, Berkeley repudiated his agreement, revoked Bacon's commission, and ordered the militia to go out and arrest him.

Backed by most of the people in the colony, Bacon proceeded to organize a rival government. He called the legislature into session and again marched against the Indians. Berkeley, who had fled from Jamestown, returned to the capital and tried to re-establish his authority. Then Bacon attacked the capital itself and burned the principal buildings. Shortly afterward he died, and Berkeley recovered control. Although King Charles II ordered an amnesty for all the rebels, Berkeley ignored the order and executed thirteen of Bacon's followers. For this unnecessary severity Berkeley—characterized as an "old fool" by the king—was deprived of his post and ordered back to England.

Between 1676 and 1682 the Virginians continued to suffer from the combined evils of unsatisfactory government and economic depression. After this time the price of tobacco rose again, and with the return of prosperity political difficulties attracted less attention. The Indian troubles were temporarily settled by a treaty signed in 1676.

Chapter 2

NEW COLONIES—NEW ENGLAND TO GEORGIA

WHILE the London Company was working on its colony in Virginia, its associate, the Plymouth Company, started a settlement at Sagadoc, at the mouth of the Kennebec River. After a two-year struggle with frontier hardships, the Indians, and illness, the colony ended in failure. In 1620 the Plymouth Company transferred its rights to the New England Council, headed by Sir Ferdinando Gorges. The council did not found any colonies but in 1621 it granted land to the Pilgrims at Plymouth. Eight years later the council granted part of what is now New Hampshire to Captain John Mason. Gorges himself tried to start a new colony in Maine. In 1635 the New England Council went out of existence.

Puritan Occupation of New England

The major drive behind settlements in New England was not these two ineffective companies, but the Puritan movement in England. Puritans were religious dissenters, opposed to the organization, forms of worship, and beliefs of the Church of England. The Puritans were also radicals in politics, opposed to the king. They tried to make Parliament the supreme authority in England and they were determined to make themselves supreme in Parliament. Because of this political activity King Charles I dismissed Parliament in 1629; it did not meet again until 1640. During this period many Puritans became so discouraged with the prospect of reform in England that they determined to settle in America.

English Puritans

In addition to its religious and political implications, English Puritanism was a class or social movement. The merchants with their allies, the artisans and shopkeepers, represented the growing power of business enterprise. They were the ones who built up and dominated the increasingly profitable commercial enterprises of their time. They furnished the money and the talent for the joint-stock trading companies and they made English colonization a reality. In spite of their wealth and their contributions to English well-being, the Puritan merchants lacked both political power and social prestige, then the monopolies of the landowning class. When the Puritans attempted to secure power for themselves, they were stigmatized as upstarts and climbers, interlopers who were trying to overturn the social and political structure which God had founded. It is plain now that

Puritanism was one of those explosive forces which have appeared from time to time and which have brought about fundamental alterations in prevailing thought and customs.

Among these English dissenters was a small group of religious and political radicals known as Separatists, because they demanded complete freedom to manage their own church affairs; sometimes they were called Brownists, because of the prominence of one of their leaders, Robert Browne. They encountered so much opposition in England that they fled to Holland. After ten years in Holland they decided to leave. The cause of their withdrawal may have been the well-grounded fear that their children would lose their identity as Englishmen, or it may have been the outbreak of the Thirty Years' War, which threatened to engulf all Europe. Whatever the reason, the Separatists decided to settle in America.

Plymouth

After giving due consideration to the Dutch colonies of Guiana and New Netherlands, they decided to remove to English North America, or Virginia. This name seems to have been loosely used to include not only the region assigned to the London Company but territory to the north and east as well. They could not secure a charter from the king, but unofficially he agreed not to molest them. The Separatists themselves could not finance the enterprise so they borrowed £7000 from some London merchants. They set sail in 1620 on the *Mayflower* and in November landed on Cape Cod, approximately where Provincetown is now located. The sand dunes of the Cape looked anything but inviting, so after exploring the region they moved across the bay and settled at a harbor which John Smith had already named Plymouth. There were only 101 pioneers in this enterprise.

Before landing from the *Mayflower* they drew up a formal agreement or compact by which they agreed to form "a civill body politick." Announcing that they had "undertaken, for the glorie of God, and advancement of the Christian faith, and honour of our king and countrie, a voyage to plant the first colonie in the Northerne parts of Virginia," they proposed to make their own laws "for the generall good of the colonie," and they promised due obedience to these laws. Instead of being subject to the control of a commercial company 3000 miles away, as the settlers of Jamestown were at the time, they managed their own government.

Legally they had a right to enter into this Compact because they found themselves in a part of the British possessions where no government existed. But this was merely an agreement among themselves, not between them and the king. The Compact could not and did not free them from the operation of the laws of England or from the English government. They were squatters with no rights which the English government was bound to respect. They did not wish to separate completely from England, otherwise they would have picked some part of the world for their colony which was not owned by the English Crown. They were not long in realizing that their situation was precarious, and in 1621 they secured a patent from the New England Council. In 1630 they got a second patent from the same organization in order to have their territorial limits more clearly defined. This was necessary because of the ambitious plans of the newly formed Massachusetts Bay Company.

Numerically the Pilgrim colony was not important. Four years after the settlement there were only 123 inhabitants in Plymouth. By 1630 there were between 250 and 300 persons. As late as 1691, when Plymouth was annexed to Massachusetts, the population numbered approximately 9000, and many of these had entered the colony not directly from England but indirectly by way of Massachusetts. In the course of a few years the colony of Massachusetts Bay largely overshadowed the Plymouth colony. But Plymouth had the distinction of being the second permanent British colony in the New World.

Massachusetts Bay

Preparations for another settlement in New England began as early as 1624. Under the leadership of the Reverend John White, an Anglican clergyman, a company of 100 members was organized at Dorchester, England, to promote the fisheries off the coast of Newfoundland. This group started a settlement on Cape Ann in Massachusetts with Roger Conant as governor. Two years later the Dorchester Company went into bankruptcy; Conant with a few settlers moved a short distance south and settled at Salem. Then in 1628 a group of London merchants formed the New England Company, and according to their own statement secured from the New England Council a grant of land between two lines drawn westward from points on the Atlantic coast, one three miles north of the Merrimac, the other three miles south of the Charles. John Endicott took Conant's place as governor. In 1629, because of disputes over the title to this grant, the promoters asked for and secured a charter directly from King Charles I. This charter created the Massachusetts Bay Company and gave it the same territory previously granted to the New England Company. There has always been a mystery about the granting of this charter; evidently it was "surreptitiously . . . obtained" with neither the knowledge nor the consent of the New England Council.

As originally established, the Massachusetts Bay Company was a commercial enterprise, the primary purpose of which was to make money through trade. Then the management of the concern passed into the hands of men interested in founding a Puritan colony in America. Those members not interested in going to Massachusetts resigned; the others signed the Cambridge Agreement, by which they bound themselves to emigrate to the colony. John Winthrop joined the company at this time.

The charter provided for the usual officials of any joint-stock trading corporation. There was a governor, a deputy governor, and eighteen assistants to be chosen by the freemen or members of the company. These terms applied originally not to any colony but merely to the company. If the charter were translated into modern English, the words president, vice-president, directors, and stockholders would be substituted for those listed above.

The official business of the company was to be transacted in a so-called General Court, to meet four times a year, consisting of the governor, the assistants, and the freemen. This joint meeting of the stockholders and directors, for that is exactly what the original General Court was, received authority to admit new freemen, to elect the governor, deputy governor, and assistants, and "to establish all manner of wholesome and reasonable orders, lawes, statutes, and ordinances . . . not contrarie to the laws of . . . England." In addition they might create the necessary administrative offices.

When the final draft of the charter passed the seals, there was a curious but very important omission. Ordinarily every such document specified the place of meeting of the company created, but no place was named in this one. Consequently, so the assistants reasoned, the company was free to meet where it pleased, and the managers decided to move both company and charter to America. On March 29, 1630, the company set sail with the charter. By this simple expedient an ordinary joint-stock company was transformed into a colony, and the system provided for transacting company business became the form of government for the colony. The London Company had remained in England, and from there governed Virginia as a subsidiary enterprise. In the case of the Massachusetts Bay Company, the company itself went to the colony and governed it on the ground. Actually this process of transferring the charter to America was illegal, but the promoters were not deterred by this technicality.

Settlement at Boston

The first group of settlers, over 900 in number, including the company, went first to Salem and then to Boston. In the course of 1630 about 2000 more came over. The leading laymen, such as Governor Winthrop and others, were "gentlemen." The clergy were all Puritans. The rank and file of the settlers were small merchants, farmers, and artisans, some of whom left England because of hard times, some because of persecution. The great majority were men of humble birth. It is interesting to find that hardly a fifth of the Massachusetts settlers were church members.

Although the leaders of this enterprise were Puritans interested in establishing a Puritan commonwealth, they did not emphasize this fact in their efforts to secure settlers. In fact, their advertising was almost silent on the subject of religion, but they said a great deal about the economic possibilities of New England. In one pamphlet of twelve pages written for the purpose of encouraging settlers to go to Massachusetts, there were only twelve lines devoted to religion. The following quotation gives an idea of the main drift of the argument:

> Great pity is it to see so much ground for corn and for grass as any is under the heavens, to be altogether unoccupied, when so many honest men and their families in old England, through the populousness thereof, do make shift to live one by the other. . . . As for wood, a poor servant may have more timber and fuel than could many a nobleman in England . . . and as for fresh water the country is full of dainty springs and some great rivers and some lesser brooks.

The first governor of the Bay Colony, John Winthrop, wrote enthusiastically of the advantages of New England:

. . . the country is exceeding good and the climate very like our own. . . . For the country itself, I can discern little difference between it and our own. We have had only two days, which I have observed more hot than in England. Here is as good land as I have seen there, but none so bad as there. Here is sweet air, fair rivers, and plenty of springs, and the water better than in England. Here can be no want of any thing to those, who bring means to raise out of the earth and sea.

Puritan Government

The government which the company set up in Massachusetts was at first an oligarchy, or a "theocracy" as someone described it. John Winthrop himself was no liberal, and neither he nor his associates had the remotest intention of setting up a republic or a democracy. The attitude of this close corporation was well expressed by Winthrop himself, in discussing the unwisdom of referring important questions "to the body of the people, because the best part is always the least, and of that best part the wiser part is always the lesser." In the original group of over 900 colonists, there were only twelve freemen all told, and even by autumn, when the number of settlers had more than doubled, the number of freemen still remained the same. These twelve men, with Winthrop at their head, had full legal authority to "correct, govern, punish, pardon, and rule" the whole body of colonists. During that time the General Court consisted of those twelve men and no others. The colonists had no voice in the election of the freemen, no way of making laws for themselves. They were just as much under the arbitrary will of the company as the first settlers in Virginia had been under the London Company. The mere fact that the company resided in the colony did not make its rule any less absolute.

The Massachusetts Bay Company was no more tolerant in religion than it was in government. The settlement was a Puritan commonwealth. Settlers of all kinds were welcome, provided they would accept the system and keep quiet. Theological disputes were kept down to a minimum by the simple expedient of banishing or deporting heretics. The Puritans had come over to secure not toleration but freedom for the exercise of their own religion.

In England, during the twenty-seven years which preceded the founding of the Bay Colony, criticism of the arbitrary Stuart policy had steadily increased, and political liberalism became fashionable in England. It was impossible to keep these liberal ideas out of Massachusetts; the colony received a number of logical individuals who could see little difference between the underlying philosophy of John Winthrop and that of Charles Stuart. Sooner or later, the Winthrop system was sure to encounter criticism and opposition, and eventually the Puritan leaders had to decide whether they would emulate the king or admit the dissatisfied to share in the government.

The first effort to liberalize the government came in October 1630, before the colony was a year old. A group of 109 settlers raised the whole issue by asking to be made freemen—that is, admitted to membership in the company. The request was peculiarly embarrassing to Winthrop and his associate rulers. If it should be granted, they might lose their authority. On the other hand, if they refused to grant it, they knew that some of the settlers would go elsewhere, and Massachusetts needed colonists. Then the request raised another problem. The first freemen had been stockholders—that is, investors in the company's stock. These new applicants did not wish to invest; they merely wanted to vote.

Limited Reform

The way out of the dilemma which Winthrop discovered showed that life in the New World had not dulled Puritan wits. The 109 were admitted as freemen, but Winthrop informed them that the freemen enjoyed no power except the right to elect the assistants. The new freemen had never seen the charter, and Winthrop took care that they did not see it for four years; during this time they did not know that the governor was guilty of a flagrant violation of their legal rights.

The next difficulty arose in 1632, when certain residents of the settlement at Watertown objected to being taxed by the assistants. For the time being nothing happened. In 1634, however, the freemen mustered up sufficient courage to demand a sight of the charter; then they learned for the first time how they had been deprived of their rights for four full years. This time the ruling powers had to surrender. From then on, arrangements were made for four meetings of the General Court each year. The first, at which all the freemen were to be present in a body, was to elect the governor, deputy governor, and assistants. The other three were to be representative, and at these general legislative business was to be transacted. This arrangement necessitated the development of a representative system, whereby each town was authorized to send two freemen to the legislature. For the first few years the representatives met with the assistants, but in 1644 a two-chambered legislature was provided for.

All these changes meant a more general participation in political affairs, but the number of freemen necessarily remained small. The freemen constituted a close corporation, and they themselves fixed the qualifications for membership in their own select circle. Under the charter, strictly interpreted as it always was, violated outright as it could be and was for years at a time, there was not much room for democracy. The right to vote was limited to church members, and approved church members at that. In 1670, when the population of the colony had increased to 25,000 persons, there were only 1100 freemen.

It is not surprising that affairs in this Puritan theocracy should have attracted the attention of the government in England. The Plymouth Colony had been left alone because it had made itself neither conspicuous nor troublesome. The Bay Colony challenged British authority and almost invited investigation. Among those who demanded an inquiry into the

English Investigations

affairs of Massachusetts was Sir Ferdinando Gorges, who insisted that the Bay Colony charter was a direct violation of his own proprietary rights. He suggested that the charter be brought before the Privy Council. In 1634, partly as a result of his complaints, the Privy Council appointed a commission, with Archbishop Laud at the head, to check further Puritan emigration and to revoke charters "surreptitiously and unduly obtained." This same commission was likewise authorized to make laws for the government of the English colonies, to remove colonial governors, and to hear and decide complaints from the colonies.

In 1635 the commission secured a writ of quo warranto against the Massachusetts Bay Company, but because of the growing trouble in England the writ was never served. There is little doubt that the approach of the Civil War in England saved the life of the Massachusetts Bay Company. It was not until after 1660 that the Privy Council was able to turn its attention once more to Massachusetts, and during that long interval the foundations of the Puritan commonwealth were solidly laid.

Expansion and Confederation in New England

Roger Williams

Among the more conspicuous critics of the established order in Massachusetts was a clergyman, Roger Williams. As an independent in religion he opposed the ecclesiastical system of the Bay Colony, and as a democrat in politics he found fault with the arbitrary government there. Williams really believed that the people were the source of authority. He also found fault with the land system. He argued that the settlers should have bought the land of the Indians.

Ordered out of Massachusetts, in the winter of 1635-36, Williams moved to Narragansett Bay and founded a settlement at Providence. There he put his liberal principles into practice. His associates controlled the government under an agreement similar to the Mayflower Compact, and they worshiped as they pleased. There was no established church, and consequently no compulsory attendance and no forced contributions for church support.

Mrs. Hutchinson

The second of the Rhode Island settlements, the Portsmouth Colony on Rhode Island proper, was started by another heretic and refugee from Massachusetts, Mrs. Anne Hutchinson, who was one of the most conspicuous of the early radicals. She objected to the theology expounded in the Boston church and to the government instituted by John Winthrop. Her criticism was not merely negative, and therein lay her offense. She evolved a religious system of her own based, as she said, upon direct divine revelation. To have anyone question the soundness of Puritan government and Puritan theology was bad enough, but to have a woman lay claim to divine inspiration was sin against the Holy Ghost. Any critic of an established order can always get a following, and some of Mrs. Hutchinson's admirers were among the most prominent men in the colony. Something had to be done, so she was placed on trial before the General Court, with

Governor Winthrop presiding. The defendant had little chance of a fair hearing. Her case was settled beforehand. The Court emphasized "the troublesomeness of her spirit, and the danger of her course amongst us, which is not to be suffered," and decreed that she should be banished and imprisoned until she could be sent away. Banishment from the colony was followed by excommunication from the church.

A third settlement in Rhode Island was started in 1639 at Newport and a fourth in 1643 at Warwick. Samuel Gorton, the founder of the latter colony, was a notorious heretic. After a brief sojourn in a number of towns in Massachusetts, he betook himself to Providence, only to be banished from that place of refuge for the unadaptable. No system would suit him but one of his own making, and it may be that only sheer weariness of spirit made him stay in his own colony.

Union in Rhode Island

With such antecedents, these four little colonies could hardly be expected to display a spirit of cooperation, and for more than a century "separatism" was the sign that marked the true Rhode Islander. And yet existing circumstances forced them into some sort of working union. In 1643 Roger Williams secured a patent for the first three towns, possibly as a means of protection against the impending New England Confederation. By this document the settlers were given the rights of self-government, provided that they kept their laws in harmony with those of England. In 1647 Warwick, Gorton's colony, was admitted and a systematic form of government was worked out. The plan provided for a president, a board of four assistants, and an elective assembly. But the Rhode Islanders would not delegate too much power to their own chosen representatives. In order to safeguard their "rights," they instituted an interesting form of initiative and referendum. The voters of any one town could propose laws, which the legislature might accept or reject, while each town had full power to accept or reject any act of the legislature.

Williams's patent answered the purpose of a fundamental law until something more substantial could be secured. In 1663, after the trouble between Cavaliers and Roundheads had been settled in England, the colony of Rhode Island secured a formal charter. This document, like several others of a similar nature, is an interesting commentary on the theories and philosophy of the king who granted it, Charles II. It guaranteed religious freedom, something which Charles had suggested for England in his Declaration of Breda but something which Parliament had refused to grant. "All and every person and persons," so reads the charter, "may . . . freely and fully have and enjoy his and their own judgments and consciences, in matters of religious concernments, throughout the tract of land hereafter mentioned."

Furthermore, this same Charles II, customarily depicted as a clever, scheming absolutist in England, confirmed the Rhode Island principle of representative government. The voters were authorized to elect a governor, deputy governor, and ten assistants. Likewise they elected a general assembly, consisting of six representatives from Newport, four each from Providence, Portsmouth, and Warwick, plus two from each additional town. Thus the United Colony of Rhode Island and Providence Plantations was solidly established, and, except for three years, the charter granted by Charles II remained the fundamental law of Rhode Island until 1842.

While the Rhode Island Dissenters and Separatists were learning some of the essentials of cooperation, other groups of settlers were moving into the fertile Connecticut valley. These ventures were, if possible, more typical of the normal westward drift of the Americans than the Providence and Warwick experiments. The leaders, Thomas Hooker and John Haynes, found scant room for their abilities in a community ruled by John Winthrop and John Wilson. Furthermore, they needed better and more abundant pasturage for their cattle. But above everything else was the lure of greater opportunity in the west.

Connecticut and New Haven

In 1636 men from Cambridge, Dorchester, and Watertown moved out beyond the bounds of Massachusetts and settled the river towns: Hartford, Wethersfield, and Windsor, while Roxbury pioneers were settling in Springfield, Massachusetts. This significant advance was observed with wrath by the Dutch, who had already established fur-trading posts in the same section, and with apprehension by the Indians, who were not slow to realize the meaning which these new colonies had for them. After the Puritan manner, the freemen in the river towns organized a representative government similar in its main outlines to those in Massachusetts and Rhode Island. Other Puritans, under the leadership of Lord Saye and Sele, had already settled Saybrook at the mouth of the Connecticut River, and Saybrook became part of Connecticut.

In 1638 another group of Puritans from England, led by John Davenport and Theophilus Eaton, set up their "Bible Commonwealth" at New Haven. In this model settlement the Scriptures were to be the guide for individuals and for the government, and only church members were allowed to vote. The voters proceeded to select seven godly men to rule over them. In true American fashion New Haven sent out offshoots, of which Milford and Guilford were among the earliest. With this expansion, a representative assembly became necessary, and one was duly created. In 1662 the Connecticut colony secured a charter, which provided for a union of New Haven and Connecticut. This charter continued the representative system; because it was quite satisfactory, it lasted until 1818.

Still other settlements were started, in New Hampshire, which was generally controlled by Massachusetts until 1679, and in Maine which was a part of Massachusetts until 1820.

New England Confederation

The processes by which the Rhode Island and Connecticut settlements were evolved—expansion and fusion—are typical of American history. And, if individual towns found it wise to unite to promote the general welfare, it was equally desirable to bring about further cooperation by combining the governments themselves into a still larger union. Connecticut, especially, was awake to the dangers of her isolated situation and to the need of support. The river towns, frontier outposts in New England, were in the very heart of the Indian territory, and the attitude of the Indians was becoming daily more menacing. Also, the Dutch had never recognized the right of the Puritans to settle near their fur-trading posts, and the Connecticut people knew that only the lack of power prevented the Dutch from driving them out. Finally, the French from Quebec and Montreal, who found it convenient to use the Connecticut River, were not at all pleased at the prospect of English farms along one of their main highways.

If the logic of events pointed toward confederation, so too did the common interests and ideals, especially of Massachusetts, Connecticut, and Plymouth. Connecticut, as the colony most in need of help, made the first suggestion of union as early as 1637; and, undiscouraged by the indifference of her neighbors, she renewed her proposals in 1638, 1639, and 1642. By 1642 the government of Massachusetts Bay had become more receptive. From various quarters reports were current concerning an impending Indian uprising. Conditions in England too made cooperation necessary in New England. If the threatened war between the king and the Parliamentarians should really come, it might spread to America, and the Puritans needed to be prepared. No matter which way the war should result, a confederation would have its advantages. If the colonists should be left to their own devices, they wanted to be able to use their power effectively and wisely. On the other hand, if the king should be successful they would need to organize for defense.

In 1643 commissioners from Plymouth, New Haven, and Connecticut met with a committee of the General Court in Boston for the purpose of working out a formal basis for federation. Difficulties were numerous, such as local jealousy and local pride, but these were compromised and an agreement was signed. The Confederation included the four colonies which took part in the conference at Boston—and only those. Maine was left out because of its heretical and democratic tendencies. Rhode Island tried to join, both in 1644 and again in 1648, but admission was refused unless the Rhode Islanders would acknowledge the jurisdiction of either Massachusetts or Plymouth. This, at least, was the reason alleged for rejecting the Rhode Island petitions. Perhaps the real reason is to be found in the supreme contempt of the authorities in Massachusetts for their neighbors. "Concerning the Islanders," wrote Winthrop, "we have no conversing with them, nor desire to have, further than necessity or humanity may require." And, when he was compelled to contaminate his pen by referring to them, he described their colony sometimes as a "sink," sometimes as a "sewer."

The Articles of Confederation, twelve in number, bound the four colonies together under the name of "The United Colonies of New England." Under the Articles, each colony was left in control of its own local affairs; but common interests were put in the hands of a central board of eight commissioners, who were empowered to decide upon all questions of war and peace, to fix the respective contributions in men and money, and to pass upon applications of other colonies for admission to the Confederation. Six members of the board constituted a quorum. So the four members were all on the same level as regards influence, in spite of the fact that the Bay Colony had a population of 15,000, while the others had not over 3000 each. Again Massachusetts agreed to furnish 100 men for military purposes for every 45 furnished by each of the others. Only one concession was made to the largest and wealthiest of the four members: that two meetings out of every five should be held in Boston, an empty honor, when Massachusetts could be bound by the action of the three smaller members.

It is significant that the Articles contain no reference to the English government. The dominant part of New England had really taken its affairs into its own hands, regardless of king or Parliament. And when some of the English authorities criticized the New England governments for forming the Confederation, their agent Winslow had an unanswerable argument: "If we in America should forbear to unite for offence and defence against a common enemy till we have leave from England, our throats might be all cut before our messenger would be half seas through."

During the troublous times of the Civil War and the Commonwealth, Massachusetts ignored English authority. In 1644 the General Court voted to punish anyone who should attempt to raise troops for the king. And the Bay Colony was just as ready to flaunt the power of Parliament as that of the Stuarts. In 1651 Parliament suggested that the Massachusetts Charter be surrendered in return for a new one properly issued by the new government. The only reply ever made was that the men of Massachusetts were quite content to live under a governor and magistrates of their own choosing and under laws of their own making. Further proof, if any were needed, of the independent attitude of the colony came in 1653, when the authorities in Massachusetts refused to permit any public proclamation of the elevation of Cromwell to the office of Lord Protector.

The Confederation handled such matters as relations with the Indians and with the Dutch along with boundary and tariff disputes among the members themselves. During the period of King Philip's War its work was decidedly important. But the Articles had been in force less than ten years when the first serious manifestations of weakness occurred. In 1652, in spite of the opposition of Massachusetts, the commissioners voted for war against the Dutch. The Bay Colony thereupon refused to provide any forces for the campaign, and the minor members had no way of coercing their recalcitrant neighbor. This breakdown in the functioning of the Confederation could never be repaired, and, although the commissioners continued to meet regularly until 1684 and irregularly thereafter, they accomplished little.

After the Restoration in England, the Confederation was weakened still more by the consolidation of two of the members, Connecticut and New Haven. Moreover, Charles II was not unwilling to show favors to Rhode Island and Connecticut in order to offset the growing power of Massachusetts, and these two colonies in turn were ready to assist in the process of humbling the Puritan stronghold.

Although the Confederation was only a partial success, its history cannot be overlooked because it epitomizes so much of American growth. The forces which were destined to create the United States were present and at work in connection with the Confederation. Expansion, the sense of need of common action, compromise, and a written agreement to work together were typical of the later stages of American development. So too were the differences among the members, and the tendency, sometimes revealed, for one member to go its own way regardless of the others. In fact, the chief weakness of the Confederation was the refusal of Massachusetts to pay due regard to the needs of her neighbors.

The Growing British Empire

While these developments were going on in New England, colonists from England were occupying wide areas of land in the West Indies and in North America. By 1640 nearly 20,000 settlers had come to New England, and this was less than one third of the total number of emigrants. During this time the population of Virginia increased to 8000. Thousands more went to the British West Indies: more than 18,000 to Barbados, 12,000 to St. Kitts, 4000 to Nevis. Englishmen had become colonial-minded, and they showed their confidence in America by going there.

While Virginia was developing its system of prosperous tobacco farms, Maryland, another agricultural colony, was founded immediately to the north. The promoter of this enterprise was George Calvert, Lord Baltimore. **Maryland** As a secretary of state he had been able to keep in touch with the growing interest of the government in the Virginia colony. His own enthusiasm for colonial projects can be seen in his membership in both the London and the Plymouth Companies. He succeeded in securing the promise of a charter from Charles I, but he died before the document was ready. In 1632 his son, Cecil Calvert, received the charter and prepared to carry out his father's plans.

The territory conveyed included the land between the northern boundary of Virginia and the 40th parallel of latitude. The proprietor was given authority to make laws with the advice and consent of the freemen or their deputies. These laws must not be inconsistent with the laws of England, and the charter expressly provided that no interpretation should be placed upon it which would limit the allegiance to the king. These two limitations would tend to keep both the proprietor and his legislature from getting too far away from English control.

With reference to religion, Calvert (Lord Baltimore) was given the patronage of all churches, with the express provision that they were to be "dedicated and consecrated according to the Ecclesiastical Laws of our Kingdom of England"—that is, the charter called for the establishment of

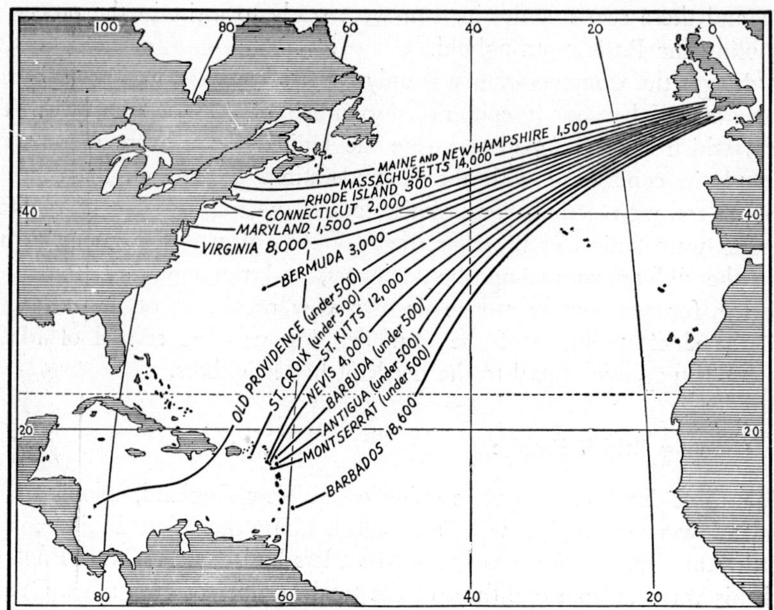

From Savelle's *The Foundation of American Civilization*

Map 2. English Migrations to the Americas, 1607-40

the Anglican Church in the colony. But Baltimore reasoned that the document did not prohibit the introduction of other churches; hence he permitted Catholic priests to conduct Roman Catholic services.

It seems that the leading motive in George Calvert's mind had been a desire to found a great family estate in Maryland; his son Cecil, however, was interested in providing a place of refuge for persecuted Catholics. When he inherited his father's title, the two motives were joined. But the English laws against Catholics were very severe at that time, and any open attempt to found a Catholic colony would have aroused enough protest to cause the revocation of the charter. Of his settlers, probably 75 percent were Protestants, and they could not be offended with impunity, especially in matters of religion. Cecil Calvert sent his brother Leonard as the first governor, and in his instructions he defined his religious policy as one of toleration. The officials were to be careful "to preserve unity & peace amongst all of the Protestants." Moreover, "all Acts of Romane Catholique Religion" were "to be done as privately as may be." All Catholics were ordered to "be silent upon all occasions of discourse concerning matters of Religion," and the governor was warned to "treate the Protestants with as much mildness and favor as Justice will permitt."

When the colonists reached Maryland in 1634, their actions showed that Lord Baltimore had profited from the experience of Virginia. The site selected for the first settlement—St. Mary's on the Potomac—was satisfactory, especially in regard to health. Again, while Jamestown had been settled in May, Baltimore's first colony was so timed that it would be started in February in ample time for spring planting. Special efforts were made to begin food production without delay, and both corn and tobacco were planted that first season. In Maryland there was no fruitless search after gold, and consequently no "starving time."

Any list of the builders of the United States, of the men whose solid constructive work contributed greatly to the development of the growing nation, should give an important place to the name of Charles II. His colonial interests were wide and varied. In addition to granting liberal charters to two of the New England colonies, he was actively concerned in promoting new enterprises in the unsettled regions along the Atlantic coast, thereby linking the English colonies together. His work was an essential preliminary to any plan of union in British North America.

Charles II

When the Stuarts and their Cavalier friends returned to England after their exile in Scotland and France, their most pressing need, both as individuals and as a class, was to restore their wrecked fortunes. Eager as they were to fill their own pockets, they were equally alert to find revenue for the public treasury. This responsibility fell upon the king, who was still the head of the executive department. Parliament might restrict him in his plans for taxation and in his expenditures, but Parliament had not at that time taken full charge of public finance.

The most promising source of wealth was the New World. Englishmen knew something of the profits in tobacco and in the fur trade, and they could see no reason why other economic interests should not be developed. Moreover, the colonies belonged to the king, so that Parliament, which had already upset some of the royal plans for England, could not interfere. Thus it happened that both Charles II and his brother James, the Duke of York, turned their attention to founding new colonies and to reorganizing some of those already established. Associated with the Stuart brothers in this work were Clarendon, the king's devoted follower and minister, noted for his *History*—and for the sound moral advice which he wasted upon his master —and Anthony Ashley Cooper, Earl of Shaftesbury, one of the founders of the Whig party. John Locke, the philosopher, also helped to establish colonies which were destined in time to use his own philosophy to justify their fight for independence. Less famous perhaps, but equally interested were Carteret and Berkeley, who were concerned in both Carolina and New Jersey. Likewise there was the king's cousin, Prince Rupert, the brilliant cavalry leader of the Cavaliers. The principle on which these promoters worked was simple: through the development of the commercial possibilities in various new regions they could make their own fortunes, and at the same time, by imposing tariff duties on the articles of this new commerce, the government could provide itself with revenue.

The first venture of the Restoration speculators was in the region south of Virginia, called Carolina, in honor of the chief patron of the enterprise. The king granted the area to a group of proprietors, including Clarendon,

Shaftesbury, Berkeley, and Carteret. Their aim was to make the Carolinas and the Bahamas centers of trade in semitropical products, such as almonds, silk, and wine. There were two charters granted, one in 1663 and another in 1665, although the second charter did little beyond enabling the proprietors to incorporate in their colony the offshoots from Virginia in the Albemarle district of North Carolina.

Carolina

The charter provided for a government under the direction of the propri etors, with the assistance of a representative assembly. Likewise, as in the case of Rhode Island and Connecticut, it contained a guarantee of religious toleration, provided that the people who enjoyed these "indulgences and dispensations" should declare their loyalty to the king and should "not in any wise disturb the peace and safety . . . or scandalize or reproach the Church of England or its adherents."

The proprietors did not succeed in sending colonists to Carolina until 1670, and in 1672 their settlement numbered only 400 persons. Compared with the rapid growth of Massachusetts, this slow progress was discouraging. The failure to develop was not due to any lack of effort on the part of the promoters. Both Shaftesbury and Locke worked hard to build up the enterprise, but they could not overcome the odds against them. The crops which had been depended upon to bring prosperity would not grow, and it took time to find out what could be produced with profit. The South Carolina farmers raised food, for export to the West Indies and incidentally to supply the pirates who were flourishing in those days, but there was no real prosperity until rice culture was undertaken in the eighteenth century. The system of proprietary control lasted until 1719; then, after ten years of confusion, the Crown purchased a seven-eighths interest in the Carolina title, and organized two royal colonies, North and South Carolina.

During the first half of the seventeenth century, while the English were consolidating their hold in Virginia and in New England, the Dutch West India Company began to occupy the middle region of the Atlantic coast, particularly Manhattan Island and the valley of the Hudson River. By 1660 they had a flourishing settlement on Manhattan, which they called New Amsterdam, and an important post for the fur trade at Fort Orange, where Albany now stands. The Dutch disputed unsuccessfully the right of the Puritans to settle near the Connecticut River. Checked in this quarter toward the east, the Dutch then worked toward the south and west and made small settlements in the valley of the Delaware River. In the meantime, Puritans from Connecticut moved across the Sound to Long Island, and a few Englishmen settled west of the Hudson, two regions which were at that time claimed by the Dutch.

New York

Of all the Restoration colonial projects the seizure of this Dutch colony of New Netherlands was the most important, both for strategic and for economic reasons. The Dutch title was based partly on purchase and partly on priority of occupation. But the English government claimed the whole continent of North America by virtue of John Cabot's discovery in 1497.

Charles II never recognized the validity of the Dutch title, and oddly enough his theory was upheld by an American court some two hundred years after his death. In 1889 a court in New York State held that the Dutch had been trespassers and that the English had really owned the land continuously after 1497.

These Dutch settlements in North America were peculiarly valuable. New Amsterdam had the best harbor on the Atlantic coast, while the Hudson and Mohawk Rivers constituted one of the few comparatively easy roads into the interior to the fur-trading territory. In 1664, the king granted the whole territory of the Dutch in North America to his brother and changed its name to New York. As an excuse for the seizure, the king alleged that the Dutch were carrying Virginia tobacco to Continental ports and so interfering with the proper regulation of the tobacco trade. Unfortunately for the Dutch, the charge was true. But the real reason for the grant was the desire to eliminate the Dutch and to destroy their trade. In 1667, afer a short war, the Dutch surrendered their claim. They resumed possession in 1673, but in the following year they finally surrendered both land and title to the English.

For the government of New York, James and his associates put into effect a code known as the Duke's Laws, based upon laws already in operation in Massachusetts and New Haven. In 1683 provision was made for a legislature, similar to those in the other colonies, but when James became king this was abolished. In 1691 it was re-established on a permanent basis. Unlike the Carolinas, New York grew rapidly.

In 1664 the Duke of York ceded a part of his grant, the territory later called New Jersey, to two of the Carolina proprietors, Berkeley and Carteret. Even before the grant was made, there were a number of English settlers already located there in addition to the Dutch who had claimed it as a part of New Netherlands. In the southern part there were a number of Swedish colonists. The history of the Jersey settlements is too complicated to be told here. English Quakers became interested in the province, even before William Penn secured his grant in Pennsylvania, and in 1674 a group of them bought Berkeley's share. After a good many vicissitudes, the two parts of the territory, east and west, were united to form the royal province of New Jersey (1702).

Pennsylvania

The colony of Pennsylvania was founded by William Penn, an intimate friend of many members of the court circle. He was the son of Admiral Penn, who had spent a large personal fortune fighting for Charles I. William Penn had for some time been interested in the theoretical aspects of government, and these speculations became bound up with a desire to help his fellow Quakers. The indebtedness of Charles II to Admiral Penn enabled the young Quaker to put his theories into practice. In 1680 William Penn asked for a grant of land in America, not in settlement of the debt but merely in consideration of the circumstances in which the debt had placed him. The charter was granted in March 1681.

In the earlier charters almost no provisions had been inserted for British supervision of colonial officials. In fact, the only restriction had been that colonial laws must not be inconsistent with the laws of England, and even this was left without any provision for enforcement. As a result some of the colonies, notably Massachusetts, had attended to their affairs as they pleased regardless of the wishes or the interests of England. As the system of commercial regulations was gradually extended, it became more and more difficult to secure due observance when the majority of local officials were not responsible to the Crown. The Pennsylvania charter was framed to meet these problems and to keep the colony tied closely to the growing empire.

Among other things the charter required the proprietor to keep a resident agent of the colony in London, ready to answer queries or complaints concerning the nonobservance of the laws of trade. This agent was required to pay within a year any damages awarded by the courts. Failure to do so would give the Crown full right to annul the charter and to take over the government of the colony. All Pennsylvania laws had to be submitted to the Privy Council, and that body could disallow them any time within six months after they arrived. Furthermore, the charter reserved to Parliament the right to levy taxes in Pennsylvania.

Penn and his heirs received the necessary authority to make laws with the consent of the freemen or of their deputies meeting in a representative assembly. But the proprietor was empowered to issue ordinances without the consent of the freemen in case it should be inexpedient to call the representatives together. Fortunately for the colony, the first proprietor was not the man to take advantage of this privilege. William Penn planned to interpret his charter as liberally as possible, and at the very beginning he promised prospective colonists that they should live under laws of their own making.

Penn himself came to his colony in October 1682 and personally supervised the work of laying out the capital city, Philadelphia. He made a treaty of peace and friendship with the Indians and organized the colonial government. He did not seem disturbed when in the following year, the assembly drew up a new system of its own and adopted it. Penn let them do it their way, realizing that there was very little difference between the new form and his own.

The new colony was well advertised, and its prospective advantages were soon known all over western Europe. By 1685 there were 8000 settlers in Pennsylvania, a motley collection including Swedes, Danes, Finns, Dutch, Germans, Welsh, Scottish, Irish and a few French. Only half the inhabitants were English. Penn's colony, therefore, was the first one to be made up of the mixture of races destined to become the population of the United States.

Delaware was originally a part of Pennsylvania, sometimes referred to as "the three lower counties." In 1702 it became a separate colony with its own legislature, although it still remained within the jurisdiction of the governor of Pennsylvania.

The last of the thirteen continental colonies, Georgia, was not founded until 1732. Along the coast this valuable territory between South Carolina and Florida had been partially settled by the Spaniards. The Spaniards had also investigated the rumors of possible mineral wealth in the mountains, while the French, working up from Mobile Bay, were beginning to realize the advantages in the Indian trade. The English also had sent various exploring parties into the region even before 1730.

Georgia

The plans for settlement called for the establishment of a sort of combination barrier colony and philanthropic enterprise. The new colony might serve to ward off possible Spanish danger from the south, and to receive the worthy poor who cared to try their fortunes in the New World. Georgia was started as a proprietary colony, although the board of trustees named in the charter were prohibited from receiving any profits and all financial accounts were to be submitted to the British government. The charter gave the company power to make laws and to enforce them; it made no provision for a representative assembly. All officials, except revenue officers, were to be appointed by the company, although the governor had to be approved by the king. The system of proprietary government was not satisfactory, and in 1752 Georgia was added to the list of royal colonies.

By 1732 therefore the British Empire on the continent of North America included thirteen separate colonies, extending from Massachusetts to Georgia. In addition England had Nova Scotia, acquired from France in 1713, and Newfoundland. In the West Indies, England owned Barbados, Nevis, St. Kitts, and Jamaica, all prosperous colonies. Here were thriving farms, villages, and towns, successful communities of energetic, self-reliant people.

The Growing Empire

Although some of these colonies had the misfortune of a relatively slow development at the start, once they began to grow they increased rapidly in population and in economic prosperity. In 1607, before the founding of Jamestown, the white population was, of course, zero. The following table shows what happened during the next century and a half.

Comparison of Population

	1689	*1760*
New England	80,000	473,000
Middle Colonies	45,000	405,000
Southern Colonies......	95,000	718,000 *

* Nearly 300,000 of these were Negro slaves.

The figures for 1760 would suggest that the American people were moving into new territory away from the seaboard. As a matter of fact, the process of colonization was only begun when the seaboard colonies were established. Beyond the tidewater regions lay the so-called piedmont. In this section, running from Maine through Vermont, New York, and Pennsylvania southward to Georgia, there was gradually built up a new society, farther removed from Europe, both in distance and in mental attitude, and still further modified by American conditions.

The same causes sent settlers into this upland region which had sent the first Virginians beyond Jamestown. People were attracted by cheap land and by the hope of freedom. Reports concerning the value of this back country were circulated through the colonies by fur traders and by official explorers sent out by colonial governors or by colonial land companies. Almost on the heels of the explorers followed the cattlemen, in search of free grazing lands, just beyond the established settlements.

Throughout the eighteenth century there was a steady migration from the older colonies and from Europe into the back country. In 1690, beginning at the north, there were settlements only along the rivers in what is now the state of Maine, while Vermont was still unsettled. In New Hampshire there was no occupied country beyond a line drawn twenty-five miles from the coast. Massachusetts had one block of settlements reaching fifty miles westward from the coast and another in the Connecticut River valley. By 1760 central Massachusetts and the Berkshires were occupied, New Hampshire was filling up, and Vermont had numerous towns. This region was typical frontier country during the generation before the Revolution. Land grants were made by the governors of both New Hampshire and New York, and two groups of settlers, one from each of these older colonies, carried on a small-scale war to clear up their titles. Taking the law into their own hands, "Green Mountain Boys" threatened, flogged, and occasionally shot the "Yorkers." When the Revolution came, the Vermonters set up a state government of their own, and for the next fifteen years vainly petitioned Congress for recognition. In New York the settlements followed the Mohawk valley westward toward the Great Lakes, and in Pennsylvania the piedmont filled rapidly, especially after 1725.

Scotch-Irish and Germans

In the South there were two lines of settlement. Pioneers from the tidewater colonies and newcomers from Europe passed on through the occupied territory to the open spaces beyond. Then thousands of Scotch-Irish and Germans entering at Philadelphia moved first into the upland regions of Pennsylvania and from there southward, up the Shenandoah valley in Virginia and on into the Carolinas and Georgia.

Moved by political, economic, or religious discontent, the Germans came in large numbers; by 1730 there were over 20,000, mostly in the western part of Pennsylvania. By 1756, about 75,000 Germans had arrived. Some followed the valleys into the South, while others remained in Pennsylvania, where their descendants, incorrectly labeled "Pennsylvania Dutch," live to this day.

At about the same time, in 1715, a heavy emigration started from Ireland, consisting both of Protestants of Scottish ancestry and of Catholic Irish from the Ulster counties. Irish farmers found their prosperity threatened, if not ruined, by British commercial regulations, and artisans complained about

British restrictions on woolen manufactures. Furthermore, neither Catholics nor Presbyterians cared to support the Anglican Church in Ireland. Part of this stream moved on away from the coast, to settle in Worcester, Warren, and Pelham, Massachusetts. Some followed the Connecticut valley toward the north, and occupied Windsor and Orange Counties in Vermont and Grafton County in New Hampshire. Larger numbers went to Pennsylvania, taking up land in the Susquehanna valley and then spreading out over the western sections of the colony. The Scotch-Irish began moving up the Shenandoah valley. Some settled in what is now West Virginia. Others drifted on, and between 1740 and 1760 they made widely scattered settlements from Virginia to the mountains of northern Georgia.

By 1750, stretching from Maine to Georgia, there was a back-country district territorially distinct from the tidewater. In this region could be found a population radically different from that in many of the older sections. Here were people of slender means, hardened by contact with an untamed environment, tilling their small farms with their own hands. They were independent of labor, either slave or hired, and even more independent of the conventionalities of civilization. Even this early some of the Westerners were inclined to be resentful of eastern control. It was a democratic society, with the members on the same level, tolerant of much that the aristocratic commercial centers spurned, made up of self-reliant, self-respecting frontiersmen.

Chapter 3

ECONOMIC AND SOCIAL LIFE IN THE COLONIES

THE founding of new colonies and the occupation of the frontier would suggest that settlers in the New World were able to make a living. They were, and some of them became wealthy. For the man of average physical strength who was willing to work, the colonies offered better economic opportunities than were to be found in England, and American history shows how these opportunities were used. In some respects this business of making a living was the most important part of our early development; without it there would have been no story worth telling.

Colonial Agriculture

Among all economic activities, farming is basic and indispensable. In a new country, particularly if they want to eat, people need to be close to the land. For this reason nearly all the American colonists had to be farmers, and 95 percent of them were. The conditions under which farming was carried on and the kind of crops raised depended on soil, climate, local needs, and outside demands. Because these factors differed widely in the various colonies, agriculture developed along several lines.

Farming in South Carolina

In South Carolina the early settlers found profit in raising Indian corn, hogs, and cattle. To their farm produce they soon added the products and by-products of the forest—lumber, tar, and turpentine, the ships' stores so much in demand. South Carolina did not become prosperous until rice culture was introduced. Rice was first grown there about 1690, and the experimenters soon realized that the low lands along the coast were peculiarly favorable for the successful development of the crop. It became profitable almost from the start, so much so that the planters sometimes trebled their capital every three years. In 1700 the colony exported a few hundred barrels of grain, and from that time on to the American Revolution the rice trade brought economic prosperity. The table below gives

Barrels of Rice Exported

Year	Barrels
1720	17,000
1730	43,000
1740	91,000
1750	48,000
1755	96,000
1761	101,000
1774	125,000

the figures for the increase in production. It should be noted that between 1740 and 1750 the size of the barrel was enlarged but there was an increase in the quantity exported in spite of the decrease in the number of barrels. The larger barrel was regularly used after 1750.

About fifty years after rice culture was started, the daughter of an English army officer learned that indigo would flourish in South Carolina. Since chemists had not yet discovered the art of making dyestuffs in the laboratory, textile manufacturers had to depend on vegetable coloring matter. So indigo had a high commercial value and became a second money crop. Cotton, which became the most important southern crop after the Revolution, was not raised in commercial quantities before 1775.

Away from the coast and beyond the range of cornfields, the pioneers in Carolina used the unoccupied land as pastures for livestock. Grazing was free and food was abundant. Horses, cattle, and hogs could almost take care of themselves. It cost little to raise horses for export, and to produce meat for both local use and trade. Salt beef and salt pork should be listed among the important products of the Carolinas.

Tobacco Colonies

For a time the economic interests of North Carolina, Virginia, and Maryland were so much alike that these three colonies may be treated as a unit. Farming was their chief industry, and during the seventeenth century their most important crop was tobacco. Tobacco's popularity created an immense demand which the Americans were able to satisfy. Tobacco had saved the first settlements in Virginia from failure, and tobacco brought a continuous income to the communities which raised it. The conditions under which the crop was produced exerted a definite influence on the mode of life. The planters needed plenty of land because the cultivation of tobacco soon exhausted the fertility of the soil, and modern methods of maintaining productivity by means of commercial fertilizers were yet to be discovered.

Middle Colonies

The soil of Pennsylvania, New Jersey, and New York was unusually rich, so rich that farmers could raise crops of wheat year after year on the same land without going to the trouble and expense of putting in fertilizer. When the land was worn out it could lie fallow—that is, remain uncultivated—until grass began to grow. Then it could be used for pastures, for there was still more land available for farming. In this region there was less specialization than in the South. Wheat was the most important crop, and the land produced twenty-five to thirty bushels per acre. Middle colony farmers also raised corn, barley, rye, oats, and buckwheat. Favorable soil and climate gave the people here an abundance of fruit—apples, peaches, pears, and cherries—as well as such luxuries as melons. Outside the lower Hudson valley in New York, where the Dutch had left a tradition of large estates, the average agricultural unit in the middle colonies was the small farm. Most of the owners worked on their own lands, and, while there were some slaves in Pennsylvania, free labor was the rule.

Over large areas in New England the land was rocky and the soil thin. Then as now, poor land demanded more work than good land, and hired labor was expensive. The farmers therefore kept their holdings down to what they could cultivate themselves. Besides wheat and corn, the New England farms produced oats, barley, and rye. They raised the Indian vegetables—pumpkins, squash, beans—and such imported food crops as carrots, turnips, and peas. Fruit trees, including apples, pears, cherries, and plums, thrived. Peaches would grow in parts of Connecticut and Massachusetts. The New England farmer kept one or two horses, a yoke of oxen, ten to fifteen head of cattle, a few hogs, and possibly a few sheep. He made his own butter and cheese, killed and salted his own meat, cut his own fuel from his own farm, and provided himself with practically all necessities except a little iron and such luxuries as sugar, coffee, tea, and rum.

New England Farms

In New England the colonial governments granted land under approximately similar conditions. A group of proprietors would secure from the legislature an area containing about thirty or forty square miles. This would comprise a town. The proprietors then divided the land among themselves, so distributing it that each individual received a share of meadow for raising grass, a portion of good tillage land for general farming, some upland pasture, and a woodlot. With this arrangement, each proprietor was as well placed as his neighbor. Many of the farmhouses in New England were grouped around a village green, close to the church, with the farmland, pasture, and woodlots stretching back away from the settlements.

American Commerce

Although agriculture is the one economic activity essential to the maintenance of life itself, trade is necessary for civilized living. People may exist without trade for generation after generation, as southern mountaineers did for so many years before the coming of the automobile and good roads. But they have few comforts and none of the luxuries which make life pleasant. Just as soon as a farmer can raise more of anything than he needs, he can sell his surplus—if there are nonfarmers somewhere who want food—and use the proceeds to buy something which he needs but cannot raise. The real value of rice to the Carolinian, or tobacco to the Virginian, was not in the crop itself but in the readiness of people to buy these crops. Commerce—the exchange of goods—enabled the colonial Americans to enjoy a number of luxuries which they could not produce and in doing so helped to bring wealth and prosperity to the whole community.

Export Trade

In South Carolina the farms and forests provided materials for a flourishing export trade. With fair regularity the Charleston dealers sold provisions to coasting vessels plying up and down the seaboard or between the continent and the West Indies. Less frequently, but often enough to deserve mention, they did the same thing for pirate vessels, then common in Atlantic and West Indian waters. In the West Indies they found a market for their salt beef and pork, corn, and also for their tar and lumber. The South

Carolinians owned few ships, so their exports were carried largely in English vessels. These in turn brought imports from England.

Because of the popularity of tobacco the Americans were able to send large quantities of this crop abroad. In 1649 Virginia alone exported 1,500,000 pounds of the leaf, and in 1753 nearly 54,000,000 pounds. In six months of 1692, 136 ships laden with tobacco entered English ports. These came from Virginia and Maryland. In 1706 a single fleet of nearly 300 vessels went to English ports from the tobacco colonies.

Just as the general mode of life in Virginia was influenced by the conditions under which tobacco was produced, so too were various economic customs shaped by the conditions under which it was sold. Here is an example: The colonists received little or no actual money in return for their tobacco. It was customary for the planters to ship their crop to English merchants "on account." During the year—also "on account"—they bought whatever English supplies they wanted. As long as the planter lived, the books were rarely closed. They might show a profit for him one year and a loss for another, but in any case the account was carried along. As a result of this unsystematic arrangement, the planters always bought their supplies in England—clothes, furniture, table silver, wine, and other luxuries—and they were not infrequently in debt. English merchants sometimes lost their patience over these slipshod methods. In 1756 one of these merchants, a mild-mannered Quaker, wrote to a planter in Virginia:

> Have yours of the 25th, 10th. month, and continue to admire at the excuses thou make. . . . As to remittances thou may think them out of the question, however for forms sake I enclose thy account current balance still due £74 6s 5d; to be out of temper with thee is not worth while . . . however, perhaps, an honest fit may take thee and if it should, pray remember thy old friend.

The planters were not entirely to blame for their inability to pay their bills. After 1700 the price of tobacco was almost always low. Heavy taxes were levied on tobacco when it arrived in England, taxes that had to be paid out of small profits. Restrictions imposed by the British government prevented the Americans from shipping their tobacco directly to the continent of Europe, although 80 percent of it eventually went there. It had to go to England first so that duties could be collected on it. This alone would have handicapped the planters even if they had no other difficulties.

Since, as an effect of all these causes, there was never enough money in circulation in Virginia to meet ordinary needs, tobacco was used as a measure of value, and warehouse receipts for tobacco in storage circulated like money. The salaries of public officials, even of clergymen, were fixed in pounds of tobacco rather than in pounds sterling. The price of tobacco fluctuated from year to year, and so too did the salaries measured in tobacco.

The export trade from the middle colonies furnished an excellent index to the economic interests of the people. From the farms came wheat and corn, exported both as grain and as flour and meal. There was also salt meat of various kinds—corned beef, salt pork, ham and bacon—and a smaller quantity of butter and cheese. Pennsylvania and New York also sent out livestock, both horses and cattle. From the forests came lumber, some of which was exported in the form of staves for making barrels and hogsheads for the sugar and rum trade. Most of the exports from these middle colonies went to the West Indies, which were largely dependent on the British North American colonies for their supplies of food. With the money derived from this export trade in foodstuffs, livestock, and lumber, the merchants of New York and Philadelphia bought English manufactured goods for sale throughout the middle group.

The merchants of the coast towns in New England exported grain, salt meat, and salt fish to the West Indies. Their ships returned with cargoes of sugar and molasses, a by-product of the sugar business. In New England, the molasses was allowed to ferment and was then distilled to make rum. Distilleries were important in the economic life of the day. Newport, Rhode Island, had twenty-two of them at one time, and there were others in Medford, Boston, and Providence. In 1750 Massachusetts alone produced 1,500,000 gallons of rum. Some of this was used for domestic consumption, but more of it went to Africa, where it was exchanged for slaves. From the profits of this commerce with the West Indies and with Africa the New England merchant was able to import cloth, glass, china, silver, tea, and wine from England. In addition to this trade, the merchant might run a peddling business up and down the coast, trading in kitchenware, cutlery, notions, and trinkets.

As a result of this active commerce, shipbuilding became an important industry in both the middle colonies and New England. Between 1727 and 1766 there were 1650 ships registered in Pennsylvania, and of these 737 were built in Philadelphia. The pioneers in Massachusetts built and launched their first ship, *The Blessing of the Bay,* in 1631; by 1675 more than 700 ships had been built in Massachusetts alone. This activity in turn called for the growth of related industries such as sailmaking, ropemaking, and the manufacture of ship's hardware.

The frequent references to the West Indies suggest that the North American colonies transacted much more business with them than with England. Aside from tobaco, naval stores, and a part of the rice, which did go to England, most of the exports from these colonies went to the West Indies. Most American products were wanted neither in the British Isles nor in Europe, so the West Indian market was essential. Even the New England fishermen looked to the West Indies for their prosperity, since the poorer grades of salt fish were shipped there to be fed to the slaves. The better grades found a market in Europe. Perhaps the most striking feature of this colonial commercial structure is the relatively small place which England occupied in it. Manufactured goods and luxuries came from her ports to the colonies, but the bulk of American exports went elsewhere. Not so many years were to elapse before some colonists became convinced that they could get along better outside than within the British economic system.

Before the American Revolution, economic life in the colonies depended almost entirely on what the colonists could "extract" from natural resources —lumber, furs, fish, and agricultural products. Manufacturing was slow to develop, partly because there seemed to be more profit in exploiting natural resources and partly because labor was costly. Men would not work for wages as low as the European level when with only a little trouble they could become independent farmers and landowners. And yet, even before 1760, there were signs of growing industrial activity, particularly in New England. Distilleries, as we have seen, were numerous in Providence and in Boston. Gristmills, sawmills, and tanneries were to be found throughout the back country. In all the colonies, homespun cloth was being made for domestic use and, within limited areas, for sale. This textile business, carried on in the homes, had already reached an important level by 1705. In that year the English governor of New York, writing to the Board of Trade in England, reported the amount of cloth, both linen and woolen, which was being made. He commented significantly: "As for the woolens they are already too good; the colonials are making coarse cloth; good serges are being made. I fear that England will not long be needed to supply cloth for this colony." Three years later a writer in Boston declared that in the country districts not one person in forty wore anything but homespun. By 1750 the colonists were making the larger part of their own cloth, and Englishmen saw the market for one of their most important products slipping away.

Industry

After 1720, especially in the middle colonies and in southern New England, a variety of iron products was made and sold. Iron ore was discovered in Pennsylvania and in New York, while Connecticut, Massachusetts, and Rhode Island had deposits of "bog iron" profitable enough to work. Local slitting and rolling mills made iron rods which the farmers bought and worked up into nails, hoops, and tires. Chains and anchors were made for the local shipbuilders. The casting of pots, kettles, and other iron household utensils became a prosperous though small business.

Social Classes

Aristocrats and Laborers

Diverse economic interests and varying degrees of success in making a living sooner or later result in the rise of social classes. In older communities these classes are in large part the product of tradition, but in the colonies of the seventeenth and eighteenth centuries tradition exerted little or no influence. Classes were determined by occupation, by the amount and kind of property owned, and by income. During the first few years of colonial history classes were not clearly defined. By 1725, however, Virginia had developed an aristocracy based upon ability, land, and wealth; during the next fifty years the members of this group dominated public life in this colony. These owners of the larger plantations in the tidewater area duplicated as far as possible the mode of life of the country gentry in England. The home of Colonel William Byrd at Westover, on the James River not far from Richmond, is still one of the most beautiful country houses in the South. Here, with an estate of thousands of acres of land, plenty of slaves, and all the known luxuries of the day, Colonel Byrd could entertain in princely fashion. His table was well provided with fine linen, glass, china, and silver. He and his friends had time for hunting, horse racing, dancing, and cards.

These plantations in Virginia were the big business enterprises of the South. George Washington's plantation at Mount Vernon, which was developed toward the end of this period, was a typical example. Here Washington had about 300 slaves to furnish the necessary labor. A surprising amount of detail was involved in the organization and administration of one of these great farms. At Mount Vernon, for example, there were brickmakers, masons, carpenters, coopers to make barrels, spinners, weavers, millers, and blacksmiths. Washington kept large herds of cattle and many horses. Aside from the luxuries which came from England and the salt used for preserving meat, practically all the necessities for the whole plantation, including cloth for the slaves, could be raised or made at home. A well-managed plantation was almost independent of the outside world.

Charleston, South Carolina, was another center of colonial aristocracy. An unidentified writer of the mid-eighteenth century found much to admire in this place:

> The town is regularly and pretty strongly fortified both by nature and by art; the streets are well cut; the houses are large and well built, and rent extremely high. The church is spacious, and executed in a very handsome taste, exceeding everything of that kind which we have in America. . . . It [the town] contains about eight hundred houses, and is the seat of the governor and the meeting place of the assembly. Several handsome equipages are kept here. The planters and merchants are rich and well bred; the people are showy and expensive in their dress and way of living; so that every thing conspires to make this by much the liveliest and politest place, as it is one of the richest too, in all America.

In New York, there was still another landed aristocracy with interests similar in many respects to those of its contemporaries in Virginia. The Van Cortlandt estate of 15,000 acres, Livingston Manor, the grant to the Van Rensselaer family, and numerous others enabled their owners to enjoy both the pleasures of this world and a political influence in keeping with their social position.

Aside from these manorial lords in New York, the aristocracy of the middle and northern colonies was made up almost entirely of wealthy merchants. Some of these northern aristocrats had homes which compared favorably with those of planters in Virginia. Benning Wentworth of New Hampshire kept up the social prestige of his section in one of the finest houses in America, a palatial establishment with more than fifty rooms.

Next in line below these leaders in wealth, social life, and politics came the small farmers. By the middle of the eighteenth century they were in numbers the most important, and in many respects they were the strongest and most typically American segment of the whole population. They tilled the land in New England, in parts of New York, and quite generally in the middle colonies, and they were becoming increasingly influential in the back country or piedmont region of the South.

In the cities and large towns there was still a third group: the laborers, artisans, mechanics, and small shopkeepers. They built the ships and made rope and cordage, sail cloth, and some of the ships' hardware. They made candles and soap, ran the slaughterhouses, served as blacksmiths, millers, bakers, brewers, distillers, and did all the work necessary to enable the merchants to make money. Perhaps this group should be stretched to include the free laborers on the farms and the sailors who manned the whalers and merchant vessels registered in American ports.

In a class by themselves were the fishermen of the New England coast, those resourceful and hardy men who won their living from the sea. From all accounts they were not very different from their successors at Gloucester, Marblehead, or Martha's Vineyard today. If the fishermen constituted the middle class of the seafaring population, the ship captains were the aristocracy. They too have left their memorials in the form of the fine substantial old houses which still give beauty and distinction to villages, towns, and cities along the New England coast.

Next to the bottom of the social scale were the white indentured servants, men who had voluntarily put themselves under contract to work for a specified number of years to pay the expenses of their journey to America. Below them were the Negro slaves who did the work in the tobacco fields of Virginia and in the rice swamps of South Carolina. Fortunately for the owners, most of the slaves were not discontented enough to rebel. If their masters cared for them properly and fed them well—and this was generally the case except in the rice fields—they remained happy and reasonably contented with their lot. Their work was no harder than that of the independent small farmers, and they were secure in the knowledge that the ordinary necessities of life, shelter, clothing, and food, would be provided by their owners. On the other hand, slavery was inconsistent with the social and political system which was taking shape in America, a system based upon freedom and equality. Although few early Americans foresaw it, here was a source of future trouble.

Colonial Folkways

Religion

In Virginia and in Massachusetts, as in England, church affairs were carefully controlled by the government. In Virginia the Church of England was established by law, and all inhabitants were legally required to attend its services. In Massachusetts the Congregational Church occupied a similarly privileged position. In both cases the ministers were paid by the government. There seems to have been less trouble over heresy in the southern colonies than in New England, but even in Virginia there was no law for religious toleration until 1699. In Massachusetts all who questioned the authority of the established church were severely punished. Roger Williams and Mrs. Anne Hutchinson were banished from the colony. The treatment accorded the Quakers shows what happened to persistent heretics. By 1659 the authorities in Massachusetts had publicly whipped forty of these people, imprisoned sixty-four, cut off the ears of three, and hanged four. This extreme penalty was inflicted because the victims had refused to obey orders and leave the colony.

Maryland and Rhode Island promised religious toleration, and all the English colonies founded in North America after 1660 allowed freedom in religious matters, with the result that a variety of denominations appeared. In New York there were so many forms of religious belief that any policy except one of broad toleration would have given rise to serious controversy. When the Dutch ruled New York, there were Roman Catholics, Puritans, Lutherans, Dutch Reformed, Jews, and in addition "many Atheists and other servants of Baal among the English under this government who conceal themselves under the name of Christians." After the English took possession of New York, laws provided for the establishment of a church under the control of the government, but there was no requirement that this church be patterned after any particular denomination. It was Protestant in its theology. It was supported by public taxation, and the ministers received their authority from the governor. Under this arrangement the Church of England had a place, but not the only place, and the Dutch kept their Dutch Reformed creed and clergymen. According to the proclamation issued by the Duke of York, "liberty of conscience is allowed, provided such liberty is not converted to licentiousness or the disturbance of others in the exercise of the Protestant religion."

In 1683 Thomas Dongan, a Roman Catholic governor of New York, made some interesting comments:

> Here bee not many of the Church of England; few Roman Catholicks; abundance of Quakers preachers, men and Women especially; Singing Quakers; Ranting Quakers; Sabbatarians; Antisabbatarians; some Jews; in short of all sorts of opinion there are some, and the most part of none at all. . . . The most prevailing opinion is that of the Dutch Calvinists.

Morals and Law

In early Virginia the church wardens were required to report for trial "all who led profane and ungodly lives, common swearers and drunkards." It would seem, however, that considerable discretion was allowed, and people who lived respectably had no trouble with the authorities. But in Puritan Massachusetts, the legislature laid down strict rules regarding conduct, and for a time most of these were enforced. In 1631 the General Court decreed "that all persons that have cards, dice, or [card] tables in their houses, shall make away with them before the next court." Three years later the same body decreed "that noe person shall take tobacco publiquely . . . nor privately, in his own house, or in the house of another." Then in 1637, the authorities tried to tell the women how to dress, or rather how they must not dress. "The court, taking into consideration the great superfluous, and unnecessary expenses occasioned by reason of some new and immodest fashions, as also the wearing of silver, golde, and silk laces, girdles, hatbands, etc., hath therefore ordered that noe person . . . shall hereafter make or buy any apparell . . . with any lace on it, silver, golde, silke, or thread." These masculine lawmakers also decreed that "hereafter no garments shall be made with short sleeves, whereby the nakedness of the arme may be discovered in the wearing thereof."

During the period of Dutch supremacy in New York, the official attitude toward morals went to the opposite extreme from that in Massachusetts. In 1648 even the clergy, according to one complaint, "are very ignorant in regard to true religion, and very much given to drink. To this they are led by the seventeen tap-houses here," certainly a generous allowance for the total population of 600. Pennsylvania tried to strike a balance between religious toleration on the one side and a degree of supervision of public morals on the other. In 1682 the assembly abolished alehouses, horse racing, bear baiting, cockfighting, cards, dice, lotteries, and the theater.

After 1689 or 1700 these extremes in the combined fields of religion and morals became less striking. Even in Massachusetts, both the Church of England and the Quakers secured a measure of toleration. The laws designed to regulate personal habits and customs broke down. The use of tobacco became common, and women dressed as they pleased. Young men and young women fell into the habit of going to walk on Sunday afternoons instead of attending church. The more tolerant spirit in religion and in morals shocked the conservatives who looked upon any departure from the old standards as wrong. In 1734 Jonathan Edwards, then a Congregational minister of Northampton, Massachusetts, declared that many people in his neighborhood were "very insensible of the things of religion, and engaged in other cares and pursuits." Clergymen were delighted when a widespread religious revival, the Great Awakening, swept through the colonies. This began in 1734. But in spite of temporary success, the reformers could not restore the religious and moral severity which had been the custom of earlier days.

Education

The first public school system in British America was authorized by an act of the General Court of Massachusetts in 1647. Education was necessary to enable the people to understand the religion and the laws and, more particularly, to prepare a sufficiently large number of boys for Harvard College. According to this first law, each town of fifty families was expected to appoint a teacher of reading and writing. In towns of a hundred families there was to be a grammar school capable of fitting boys for college. Towns failing to comply with this law were subject to a fine.

The first school in New York was established in 1638, at New Amsterdam. About twenty years later a Latin School was opened there. By 1664 the majority of the Dutch communities in America had schools, so that they were as well off in this respect as was New England. In Pennsylvania, provision was made for public education as early as 1683, although here the schools were not supported by taxation. The parents of children in school paid the teachers. The first colleges established in colonial America followed English precedent. After the manner of Oxford and Cambridge, Harvard, William and Mary, and Yale [1] all went back to the Middle Ages for their courses of study. Five more, established about 1750, followed similar customs: Princeton, King's College (later renamed Columbia), Brown, Rutgers, and Dartmouth. The Greek and Latin classics furnished the foundation for the work which was supplemented with mathematics, logic, a very little science, and what the ministers called "moral philosophy."

The first great change in this academic program appeared in 1755, when Benjamin Franklin and some of his associates organized the College of Philadelphia, later the University of Pennsylvania. Here students could get the traditional medieval training if they wanted it, but they could also study mathematics, surveying, navigation, physics, chemistry, agriculture, and, most important of all, history, government, economics, and international law. The founding of this college with its rich and varied curriculum was part of a revolution in the history of American thought.

Before 1760 the leading commercial ports had the small beginnings of public libraries. Boston seems to have been the first town in the British colonies to have a collection of books open to the public. Philadelphia and Charleston came next, with New York the last of the group. Benjamin Franklin again showed his originality as in his plans for the university. He liked to read, but for a number of years he was too poor to buy the books he wanted; so he organized a club of poor young men like himself who loved books and who wished to increase their store of practical knowledge. With every member contributing a small amount regularly they could read the best books at little cost to anyone.

Freedom of the Press

Newspapers began to appear soon after the opening of the eighteenth century. The first was *The Boston News-Letter,* established in 1704. In 1719 *The American Weekly Mercury* appeared in Philadelphia. By the time the Revolution broke out, every colony but Delaware and New Jersey had weekly newspapers. In addition to news, these journals carried political discussion, some of which stirred the colonial governors to protest against what they considered disrespect of authority.

In spite of official disapproval, the newspapers flourished and continued to give expression to the American point of view. The principle of the freedom of the press was soundly established. In this respect America was far ahead of England. In 1733 John Peter Zenger, publisher of the *New-York Weekly*

[1] These institutions were founded respectively in Massachusetts in 1636, Virginia, 1639, and Connecticut, 1701.

Journal, accused the governor of making corrupt politics his guide in appointing judges. Zenger was promptly arrested, charged with libel, and kept in prison several months to await trial. When his case came before the court, Zenger was defended by Andrew Hamilton of Philadelphia, one of the best-known lawyers of his day. According to English law a person might be punished for libel even if his statements were entirely true. Hamilton urged the jury to ignore the law, and his plea stands as one of the great landmarks of American liberty:

> The question before the court, and you, gentlemen of the jury, is not of small or private concern; it is not the cause of a poor printer, not of New York alone. . . . It is the cause of liberty, and I have no doubt that your upright conduct this day will not only entitle you to the love and esteem of your fellow citizens, but every man who prefers freedom to a life of slavery will bless and honor you, as men who have baffled the attempt of tyranny, and who by an impartial and uncorrupt verdict, have laid a noble foundation for securing to ourselves, our posterity, and our neighbors, that to which nature and the laws of our country have given us a right—the liberty of exposing and opposing arbitrary power . . . by speaking and writing the truth!

The jury brought in a verdict of not guilty.

Thanks to these various agencies—church, school, university, books, and the press—the American colonists were well informed. According to Benjamin Franklin, a surprisingly large proportion of the people knew how to read. More important still, they knew how to think, particularly in regard to politics and government. The general level of literacy in America was probably as high as it was in England. It is true that America produced no great poets or playwrights before the Revolution, but it is also true that American political documents of the mid-eighteenth century take high rank. The newspapers published in the leading commercial centers analyzed clearly and intelligently the weaknesses in the arguments by which English officials sought to justify British supremacy over America. Americans had learned how to express themselves well. The Declaration of Independence reveals a literary quality possessed by few state papers of any time.

Chapter 4

AMERICAN GOVERNMENT AND BRITISH POLICY

In the foregoing summary of British colonial development there have been numerous references to government in the colonies and to the British authority from which these American governments were derived. With the exception of Plymouth, which was allowed generally to operate under its own regime until 1691, all the colonies had legislative bodies established under a grant from the Crown; after the Restoration this was true even of the self-governing republics of Rhode Island and Connecticut. In the formative years American institutions developed within limits laid down by Great Britain and under the influence of established British customs. No matter how eloquently American leaders proclaimed their right to independence in 1776, they could not blot out the record of history. This record showed how the colonies had evolved and grown, not as independent entities but as parts of an expanding empire and always within a framework of English precedents. As colonial systems went in those days, that of the English was surprisingly liberal, and under it Americans acquired and enjoyed a remarkable degree of self-government. Nevertheless, the principles of the British regulatory system and the agents of the British government were always present. It would therefore be misleading to discuss American government without showing its relation to the imperial system.

Colonial Government

Pattern of Government

The framework of American government was fundamentally the same in all the colonies. There were two interests—English and American—concerned in appointing officers and in making legal rules, and both interests were represented. In each of the royal colonies—those under the direct supervision of the king—there were a governor, appointed by the king; a council, also appointed by the king; and a representative assembly, elected by the voters. In the proprietary colonies—Maryland, Pennsylvania, and Delaware—the forms were the same, but the proprietors instead of the king named the governors and members of the councils. Rhode Island and Connecticut received charters from King Charles II which made them practically self-governing republics. In both these colonies the voters chose the governors and councils as well as the elective assemblies.

In each of the colonies the governor was the chief executive. He could call the members of the assemblies together and dismiss them. He commanded the military forces in his colony and he enforced the laws. In all the colonies except Connecticut and Rhode Island, he was the connecting link between his colony and England. The majority of colonial governors were Englishmen, although occasionally prominent Americans might be appointed. The council in each royal colony was made up of men prominent in local affairs, usually twelve in number. This body served as an advisory cabinet for the governor and as the supreme court in the colony. It was also the upper house when the colonial legislature was in session. The council therefore represented both English and American interests, because, while the members were Americans, they owed their places to the king.

American Legislatures

Following the council came the elective branch of the legislature, the lower house, virtually the same in all the colonies in spite of the different names attached to it: House of Burgesses in Virginia, Assembly in New York, or House of Representatives in Massachusetts. This was the body representing not the people but the voters—in other words, the property owners. Suffrage qualifications were not uniform in the various colonies, but not more than a sixth of the population voted in any, and probably the average was about one tenth. These elective assemblies shared with the councils the right of initiating legislation except financial, which custom reserved to the lower house alone. All legislation passed by the colonial assemblies was subject to the governor's veto and, if it passed him, to disallowance by the Privy Council in England.

The key to colonial constitutional history during the eighteenth century is to be found in a shifting of the balance of power within the framework just described. In all the colonies the elective branch of the legislature increased in power at the expense of the governor and council. During the seventeenth and eighteenth centuries, the colonial legislatures were undergoing a rapid and interesting growth. Beginning as mere borough assemblies, they developed into miniature parliaments with a sense of power and of pride in their achievements. In fact, the members of these bodies came to look upon them as virtually the equals of the House of Commons. In 1691 the House of Burgesses instructed its agent in England "to supplicate their majesties to confirm to Virginia the authority of the Gen'l assembly consisting of the Governor, Council, and Burgesses as near as may be to the model of the Parliament of England." The very statement of this concept of the House of Burgesses is significant, and it was widely at variance with English official views.

According to British theory, the Burgesses owed their existence to a grant made by the Virginia Company and after the revocation of the charter to a similar grant made by the king. Other legislatures which were founded later derived their powers from a royal charter or from some other royal act. In the beginning this royal power was limited only by the inadequately defined principles of the unwritten British constitution. In practice the king issued commissions to the royal governors, in which he defined the governors' authority and made clear his superiority to the local assembly. Royal power over the colonies was reaffirmed in the instructions drawn up for the guidance of the governors. In fact the whole system of royal government for the colonies was put into definite form in these documents. In 1747 the attorney general of the British government declared that the right of the Americans to send representatives to their assemblies was founded on the commissions and instructions given to the governors.

This legal definition which placed all American legislative bodies under the power of the Crown was not in conformity with prevailing practice.

Growing Powers

By virtue of custom and prescriptive right, these elective assemblies had raised themselves to a position superior to that of both governor and council, so that they became the dominant factors in colonial government. The results of this growth were never clearly appreciated in England, but they were fully apparent to colonial political leaders. From their point of view the local assemblies were just as important, each in its own field, as was Parliament in England. In the colonies, as in England, this legislative supremacy was the result of long contests with the executive power. The steps in this evolutionary process are fairly clear. In general, colonial leaders aimed at frequent elections, so that the legislators could be kept in close touch with the voters. In Massachusetts and Pennsylvania, for example, there were annual elections, in North and South Carolina biennial; the other colonies tried to secure triennial elections at least. Along with frequent elections, the colonial legislatures insisted upon their right to pass judgment on the qualifications of their own members. By doing so they could refuse to seat representatives chosen by corrupt methods, and they could keep out candidates whom the governors might try to work in by political chicanery.

More important still in the process of legislative advancement was the effective use made of financial power. Following a course parallel with that of Parliament, the American assemblies secured control over taxation. They then began the process of making specific appropriations, so that they controlled expenditures. Furthermore, the legislatures aimed at a large measure of administrative control, especially in financial matters. Several of the colonial legislatures got control of the colonial treasurers. Virginia did this in 1704, New York in 1715, and New Jersey, Pennsylvania, and the Carolinas before 1750. Sometimes the speaker of the assembly was made the treasurer of the colony. Control over expenditures gave the legislatures vast powers. Merely by refusing to act, they could bring the whole system to a standstill. It was an unusual governor who would oppose a determined group of legislators when he knew that they could stop payments from the treasury and so ruin his administration. He was more likely to yield to pressure and sign the bills which the assembly wanted, even though he had to ignore his instructions from the king.

In England the promoters of parliamentary supremacy soon discovered that some sort of organization was necessary to enable them to function smoothly without executive leadership. The Cabinet met this need. In similar fashion the colonial legislatures evolved a form of organization which enabled them to make their power effective. In a number of assemblies—notably those of Massachusetts, New York, Virginia, and North Carolina—self-constituted, informal committees, consisting of leaders in the legislature, assumed control of the governments. The operations of such a group can be clearly traced in Massachusetts just before the Revolution. A dozen men, with Samuel Adams in the lead, decided upon the legislative program and also upon what the executive officials should be allowed to do.

Self-government

In New York an informal joint committee held frequent meetings during the session. This group made out the list of legislative business, dictated the appointment of officials, controlled the payment of salaries, and dominated the whole government in its executive as well as its legislative branches. In Virginia the determination of the tidewater planters to run the government seriously hampered the executive, but he obeyed their orders. After one of his contests with the House of Burgesses, Governor Dinwiddie, somewhat the worse for the encounter, retired with the complaint that "such wrong headed People (I thank God) I never had to do with before."

In North Carolina there was another joint committee, self-appointed like the one in New York, busily engaged in directing the government. The royal governor was helpless in a contest with this group. The members forced their measures upon him in spite of his opposition by putting them in as riders on appropriation bills, and through their control of salaries they had a firm grip on the administration. In both colonies, although there was no official institutional basis for such a thing, miniature cabinets were in full operation. As time went on, the governors were brought more and more completely under the control of their legislatures. That is how the representatives of the voters in America rather than the agents of the king in England became the real rulers in the colonies. This transfer of power from English governors to American leaders was a great help in preparing the colonies for independence. The voters themselves learned at first hand how governments were managed and how to use power. This practical knowledge gave confidence both to the leaders and to the voters who elected them. Out of this experience in self-government the Americans put their ideas and beliefs together into a political philosophy. They argued that these American legislatures were just as important for the colonies as Parliament was for England. They contended that if new laws or new taxes were needed, American assemblies could make the necessary decisions better than anybody else. After a time they came to believe that they alone had a right to do these things and that the king and Parliament must not interfere.

In the lower ranks of government there were additional opportunities for gaining experience in politics and public affairs. In New England, town meetings looked after local business, and these town meetings were carried on almost independently of royal officials. In somewhat similar fashion, county and parish organizations in the middle and southern colonies taught the American people the art of government and gave the leaders practical training.

One more force strengthened the American belief in their right to govern themselves. Large numbers of the first settlers and many of their successors came to America because they were dissatisfied with conditions at home. This was particularly the case with some of the Puritans from England and with the Germans and Scotch-Irish. In the New World they expected freedom. These dissenters passed on to their descendants a tradition of self-reliance and of impatience with unnecessary restraints, and their attitude toward outside authority became widespread. In his famous speech on conciliation with America, Edmund Burke referred to this American state of mind as the very "dissidence of dissent."

The British Colonial System

By way of contrast with the American doctrine that Americans possessed full authority in the areas of local and provincial government, English officials and legislators still insisted upon the principle of British supremacy. After 1681 all new colonial statutes had to be submitted to the king's advisory body, the Privy Council. In case of disapproval the Privy Council could declare them null and void or, in official terminology, "disallow them." By this procedure the effects of the governor's surrender to legislative pressure might be overcome. The Privy Council disallowed laws because they were inconsistent with laws of England, because they conflicted with certain principles of colonial administration, or because they ran counter to English economic interests. This power the Privy Council exercised sparingly, but it was in reserve in case of need.

British Controls

The principle of British supremacy was proclaimed in numerous statements designed to set forth the authority of Parliament over the colonies and in acts of Parliament itself. In 1650 Cromwell's Parliament asserted its power to legislate for the colonies:

> Whereas the islands and other places in America, where any English are planted, are and ought to be subject to and dependent upon England and both ever since the planting thereof, have been and ought to be subject to the laws, orders, and regulations as are and shall be made by the parliament.

In 1720, the chief justice of the Court of Common Pleas in England ruled that the colonies "may be bound by Laws, made respectively for them by an English Parliament." The purport of these British statements is obvious: American legislatures did not possess sole power in their respective localities; Parliament also had power.

Important though it was, the question of who should make laws for the colonies was not the only problem in the growing tangle of Anglo-American relations. There were the more comprehensive issues of policy or guiding principles, of legislation needed to put the policy into actual practice, and of administrative regulations designed to make the policy work. British officials took the initiative in the effort to solve these problems.

Mercantilism

During the first part of the seventeenth century England had neither practical experience nor political theory to serve as a guide in making colonial policies. But there was a popular doctrine of economics known as mercantilism, and in accordance with this theory the system of colonial control was evolved. The aim of mercantilism was economic self-sufficiency —that is, each state aimed to become mistress of all her resources and to prevent rivals from participating in any of her economic interests. Mercantilism demanded the development of a favorable balance of trade; in other words, the nation should try to sell more than it bought. Such a balance of trade would bring gold into the country. Colonies were desirable in the system, because they could furnish raw materials and supplies which could not be produced at home. Mercantilism did not contemplate the establishment of self-governing colonies, because such units might contribute nothing to the parent state. The idea of colonies as markets for home manufacture did not take definite form until the middle of the eighteenth century.

Once the colonies were established, it became necessary to regulate their trade so that other nations could have no part in it and so that it would bring profit to the parent state. Throughout this whole philosophy runs the idea of colonies both politically and economically dependent upon the colonizing power. But the superior government did not want to ruin the economic life of the colonies; it wished merely to prevent the colony from developing interests which might compete with those already established at home. That was the negative side. On the positive side, the parent state tried to develop and foster those economic interests which were suited to the colony. Each part of the empire was expected to specialize in those products and commodities which nature had designed for it.

Navigation System

These principles were applied first to the tobacco trade of Virginia. In 1621 the Privy Council ordered the Virginia colonists to ship all their tobacco to English ports; then it prohibited both the importation of foreign tobacco and the raising of tobacco in England. Foreign merchants were forbidden to bring American colonial tobacco to England. These regulations restricted the market of the Virginia planters to the British Empire, and thereby limited the profits of the colonists. On the other hand, Americans were given a monopoly of the English market. This provision was at the time ample compensation for the other, because it forced Englishmen to smoke Virginia tobacco, if they smoked at all, when many would have bought the Spanish product if left to their own choice.

Before Cromwell's time not much more was done in the way of formulating colonial policy, partly because the colonies were small, partly because of trouble in England. Cromwell was greatly interested in the whole colonial and commercial problem. He found one serious obstacle in the way of English development: the Dutch grip on the carrying trade of the world. These enterprising people built ships more cheaply than their rivals, and they were able to charge lower rates than the merchants of other countries. Cromwell wished to capture this Dutch trade for English merchants.

In 1651, apparently under the direct influence of Cromwell, Parliament passed a Navigation Act designed to close English trade to the Dutch. This measure provided: that goods imported into England from Asia, Africa, or America were to be brought only in English ships; that goods from Europe could be brought in English ships, or in the ships of the country where the goods were produced or manufactured; and that goods for the English colonies in America could be carried there only in English ships.

The purpose of the law was to create an English commercial monopoly, the benefits of which were confined to English subjects. For the purposes of this act, ships built in the English *colonies* were on the same level with ships built in England, so that the American shipping interests could profit from it. Under the protection of the act, American shipping steadily increased, and before the end of the seventeenth century Boston, Newport, New York, and Philadelphia became important mercantile centers. Cromwell therefore conferred an inestimable advantage upon colonial-built ships by freeing them from all competition except that of England. The later Navigation Acts interfered with colonial commerce, but this first one was a powerful stimulus.

When the Cavaliers came back into power in 1660 they saw great advantages in the Cromwellian Navigation Act. To remove doubt as to its validity, they had it re-enacted with important additions. The new measure provided that certain specified colonial products must be carried directly to England. These, the "enumerated commodities," were sugar, cocoa, tobacco, cotton, and dyewoods. As in the tobacco regulations of 1621, colonial producers were given a monopoly of the English market by way of compensation for the loss of possible markets on the Continent.

By continuing and making permanent the old restrictions on the tobacco trade, this Navigation Act of 1660 resulted in serious loss for some of the American colonies. The low price of tobacco caused trouble in Virginia, and the resulting hard times were one of the causes of Bacon's Rebellion in 1676. For nearly twenty-five years these British regulations kept the tobacco planters close to poverty. The enumeration of the other five commodities would have had serious consequences for the commercial colonies if the restrictions had been strictly enforced. American merchants had found profit in carrying West Indian products to the ports of Continental Europe, and by 1660 this trade had attained such proportions that British merchants were complaining bitterly of American competition. On their return trips American shippers carried European products to America without routing them through British ports. Thus the British merchants lost trade and the British government lost revenue. The new Navigation Act was designed to stop these American practices. Fortunately for American welfare, the new measure was never effectively enforced except during the Andros regime in New England. Then the results were described as disastrous.

In 1663 still another Navigation Act provided that all European commodities shipped to the American colonies must first be landed in some British port so that duties might be collected. By this means the American practice of carrying European goods directly to American ports could be discouraged. Because violations continued and enforcement became increasingly difficult, in 1672 Parliament passed one more measure, providing that, in case the carrier did not give bonds to carry his cargo of enumerated commodities to England, he must pay a duty of one penny per pound at the port of clearance.

Administrative Organization

As the regulations increased in number, administrative machinery was created to provide enforcement. In 1660 the king appointed a Privy Council Committee for Foreign Plantations, with two subordinate councils, one for plantations and one for trade. This committee was expected to familiarize itself with conditions in the colonies, to keep in touch with colonial governors, and especially to secure copies of new colonial laws. Incidentally, it was to try to secure greater uniformity in the systems of government of the colonies. In 1674 this committee gave way to a standing committee of the Privy Council of twenty-four members, known as the Lords of Trade. This new committee served as a bureau of information on colonial affairs. It collected and kept on file material pertaining to the colonies. It drafted all the instructions for the royal governors, considered plans for new colonies, suggested candidates for colonial positions, and passed upon the new laws enacted in the colonial legislatures. All complaints from the colonies were referred to it, and it investigated charges brought against a specified colony.

Along with the development of these organs of control in England, the policy of commercial regulation necessitated the appointment of new officials in the colonies. In American ports there soon appeared surveyors, collectors of customs, naval officers, tidewaiters, and various other agents of the English Customs Board. These men collected the duties provided for in the Navigation Acts and tried to prevent smuggling. Sometimes they were assisted by vessels of the royal navy.

In 1696 Parliament passed a new Navigation Act, an administrative measure designed to eliminate weaknesses in the colonial system. In order to bring the chartered colonies within the range of royal regulation this new measure provided that governors in these colonies must be approved by the king. Next the governors themselves were required to take oaths binding them to uphold the acts of trade. The penalty for neglect of duty in this respect made the offender liable to dismissal from office and a fine of £1000. Furthermore, the act empowered either the Lords of the Treasury or the Commissioners of Customs to station customs officials anywhere in the colonies. The customs service itself was reorganized. Then a regular system of vice-admiralty courts in charge of royal officials was established in the colonies. Thus the requirements of administration made necessary the evolution of a complex official structure in the colonies, all of which was placed beyond the legal reach of the Americans.

Also in 1696, a royal order created the Board of Trade to succeed the Lords of Trade and to have general oversight of all colonial commercial questions. This new board was composed of eight ministers, who were ex officio members, and eight active members not connected with the ministry, who did most of the work. The Board passed upon all instructions issued to the colonial governors, and kept on file for study and reference all reports sent in from the colonial executives. Furthermore, it examined all new laws passed by the colonial legislatures, and advised the Privy Council with reference to its action regarding them. It was supposed to be the body from which the Privy Council, the Cabinet, the various boards, and any interested individuals could get information about the colonies.

From 1700 to 1760 there were no changes in the basic principles of colonial administration. The defects of the system, if it can be called a system, are obvious. No part of this complicated machinery had been planned solely with reference to colonial needs. The Board of Trade was concerned with the commerce of the whole British Empire and with manufacturing as well. The Board might lose sight of colonial matters in its efforts to solve larger problems. Moreover, as the "plantations" of the seventeenth century grew into the prosperous colonies of the eighteenth, British officials rceognized no change in their legal status. In the beginning there had been no doubt of the authority of the Privy Council to regulate colonial affairs. This was true even in Massachusetts. Although the Puritans ignored England, they had been able to do so only because circumstances in England made interference in America practically impossible. As the colonies grew, their legislators were converted to the belief that their authority was final. Eventually the colonial theory of autonomy was bound to clash with the British theory of supremacy.

In addition to the king, the Privy Council, and the Board of Trade, there were various other groups of officials in England which had a hand in regulating American affairs. Problems of colonial defense on land were handled by the War Office. The members of this group planned military operations and directed the movement of troops. The Admiralty looked after defense on the sea, and also supervised all British and colonial ocean-going commerce.

As new administrative problems developed, or when new gaps appeared in the system of British control, Parliament would enact new laws to solve the problems. Among these was the Molasses Act of 1733, a supplement to the navigation system, designed to stop the importation of French West Indian molasses into the colonies and to bring larger profits to the sugar planters in the British West Indies. The French islands furnished a profitable market for fish, lumber, meat, grain, and livestock, and the planters

Molasses Act

there were glad to sell molasses at a low price in exchange. The molasses trade with the French West Indies was looked upon with disfavor by influential interests in England. Many West Indian planters had gone back to England, where they used their influence in Parliament to promote their own financial well-being with little regard for that of other fortune hunters. Because of French competition, prices for English sugar and molasses remained low, and the English growers turned to Parliament for a remedy. They pointed out the value of West Indian products to England and emphasized the need of proper encouragement. In spite of the arguments of the New England shipping interests to the effect that their West Indian trade alone gave them specie to purchase English manufactures, the West Indian planter interests carried the day. The Molasses Act imposed heavy duties on all foreign sugar, rum, and molasses imported into the British Empire. The tax on molasses, sixpence per gallon, was designed to be prohibitive. Fortunately for New England, the measure was not enforced until after 1758, so the old trade continued to flourish with little interruption by British officials.

British Restrictions

Parliament also passed laws to restrict manufacturers in the colonies. In 1699, the colonists were forbidden to export manufactured woolen goods. This measure did not interfere with the making of homespun for home use or local sale. Parliament merely wished to prevent the development in the colonies of competition with the important woolen industry in England. Here again the doctrines of mercantilism were clearly evident. Fifty percent of British exports were in the category of woolen goods, and the number of persons in England directly interested in the woolen business was considerably larger than the total population in the British colonies. The law was drawn in the interest of the larger number of people concerned.

In 1732, under the influence of the London Company of Felt Merchants, a law was passed to restrict the making of hats in America. In 1750 Parliament prohibited certain branches of iron manufacture and tried to prevent the establishment of any new plants for manufacturing iron in the colonies. None of these restrictions on colonial industry was designed to prevent the Americans from making goods for their own use. They were designed only to protect established industries in England from colonial competition. In every case the British government acted on the theory that economic activities in America should supplement those in England and not enter into rivalry with them. For twenty years or more, before 1682, the restrictions seriously hurt the tobacco planters. Yet, with a few exceptions, one of which will be described below, the British system was not so burdensome as one might think, because it was not strictly enforced. In spite of the Molasses Act of 1733, American merchants continued to import French molasses, and the British customs officers winked at the regular violation of the law. This flexible system of enforcement left the Americans contented for the time being.

The Dominion of New England

Before 1756, when the Seven Years' War demonstrated the need of more vigorous control, British authorities made only one serious attempt to enforce their regulatory system against the shipping interests of the commercial colonies. This one attempt centered in Massachusetts. Even there the issue was not strictly drawn between colony and mother country because the proposed British reforms were designed in part to protect the non-Puritan group in the Bay Colony against the tyrannical control of the Puritan ruling class. Massachusetts had been a problem from the start. It was the largest colony and also the most persistent in ignoring English regulations.

Defiance in Massachusetts

Between 1630 and 1691 there were various developments in Massachusetts which illustrated both the need of an effective colonial policy and the difficulty of making such a policy work. English officials were in an embarrassing dilemma: if they did not assert their authority, they might lose their colonies by default; if they did assert it, they might drive the Americans into open rebellion. They were bound to have trouble in either case. From the beginning of the Massachusetts Bay Colony in 1630 the independent-minded Puritans had ignored the authorities in England, acting as though they were and ought to be free from British control.

Sometimes the Puritan rulers came close to open defiance. In 1646, when the colony was only sixteen years old, the legislature of Massachusetts claimed for itself and for officials under the charter "absolute power of government," with full power to "make laws, to erect all sorts of magistracy, to correct, punish, pardon, govern, and rule the people absolutely," without the supervision of any outside authority. They denied the right of appeal to English courts, and they would not admit any obligation to answer complaints made against them in England. "Our allegiance binds us not to the laws of England," they declared, "any longer than while we live in England, for the laws of the Parliament of England reach no further, nor do the king's writs under the great seal." The merchants of Massachusetts also demonstrated their independent spirit by their consistent violation of the Navigation Acts, particularly by bringing goods from Europe directly to America without first stopping at British ports to pay duty on them. In 1660 some of the Puritan leaders in Massachusetts were opposed to recognizing Charles II as king and were advocating complete independence for their colony.

Here were sufficient reasons for British complaint against Massachusetts, but there were still more. By 1660 Massachusetts had among its colonists a number of non-Puritans, some of whom were Quakers, some members of the Church of England. Many of these Anglicans were prominent citizens, men of wealth and standing. But because they were not members of the Congregational Church they could not vote. Their complaints reached

England and served further to convince the authorities that the Puritan rulers of Massachusetts needed to be called to account.

Shortly after his accession to the throne, King Charles II began to give serious consideration to these reports from Massachusetts. In 1661, he appointed a committee of the Privy Council to investigate the situation in New England and especially to consider the case of Massachusetts. As a result of this investigation, the king made certain demands upon the colony. He ordered the officials to broaden the franchise by giving the right to vote to all respectable landowners even though they were not members of the Puritan Church. Next he ordered them to permit the Church of England to hold services in Massachusetts. These two demands were in harmony with the policy of Charles II in other colonies, and they were designed to undermine the political and religious absolutism of the Bay Colony. The king then ordered that the colony administer justice in his name and compel all the inhabitants to swear allegiance to him. The Puritan officials in Massachusetts did not obey these orders.

Investigations

In 1664 the king appointed a special committee of investigation to go to Massachusetts and to make a careful survey of the situation. The commission was ordered to look into the Indian problem, to capture the regicides, to enforce obedience to the Navigation Act, and to secure the establishment of liberty of conscience for all. These were the avowed aims. In addition the committee received secret instructions, with orders to secure from the General Court a law or laws empowering the king to nominate the governor of Massachusetts, to control the militia, and to pass upon the laws enacted in the province. In general the committee was expected to "dispose the people to an entire submission and obedience to the king's government."

When the commissioners arrived, the authorities in Massachusetts would permit no interference with the government or with the courts, and they denied the validity of the royal commission. They garrisoned the fort in the harbor and made plans for defense. When the king's representatives tried to hold a public inquiry, the people were officially warned to ignore them. The report of the committee was not favorable to Massachusetts, and one of its recommendations was that the king strengthen his hold, by force if necessary. The proposed solution was the abrogation of the charter. At the time, however, the king took no action.

Beginning in 1674 the Lords of Trade began work on a policy designed to strengthen the authority of British officials over all the colonies. This program devoted special attention to Massachusetts. In 1676 the Lords of Trade sent over an investigator, Edward Randolph, with instructions to find out what laws in the colony were at variance with the laws of England, and to see how the Navigation Acts were being observed. In 1681 Randolph received a commission as collector of customs in New England. The government of Massachusetts placed every obstacle in his way. He himself was not allowed to work, while his deputies were fined and imprisoned. Recalcitrant merchants, smarting under penalties imposed for violating the laws of trade, sued the collector's agents for damages in the local courts. Randolph's report was very unfavorable to Massachusetts.

Upon the strength of Randolph's representations, the Crown ordered the issue of a writ of quo warranto as the first step in annulling the charter, but legal technicalities prevented the completion of the process. Then, in 1684, under a writ of *scire facias,* the charter was revoked, and Joseph Dudley was named the first royal governor. If this action seems inconsistent with the liberal policy which Charles II had pursued elsewhere, the fact remains that the king waited over twenty years before bringing action, and during that time he received two full reports showing that the authorities in Massachusetts had violated their own charter, besides ignoring some of the reasonable orders of the king.

Dominion of New England

During the first part of the reign of Charles II, the Council for Foreign Plantations had advised the fusion of all northern colonies into a single dominion. The Lords of Trade had never been able to win the approval of Charles II for their plan, but James II was more responsive. In 1686 the plans were worked out. These called for the union under a single government of all the colonies north of Pennsylvania. For the governor of this new dominion Sir Edmund Andros was selected. Andros was forty-nine years old, a soldier, with considerable experience in administrative work; a man of ability with an honorable record, but somewhat lacking in the qualities of the diplomat. He was sent over to execute a policy formulated by the Lords of Trade; he had no discretion regarding the form of government to be established. His position in New England was certain to be difficult, for, while he was in sympathy with the plan, the New Englanders were not.

Andros was appointed in May 1686 and entered Boston the following December. His administration was a constant succession of disputes. The new governor came with extensive powers. The General Court was abolished. With the assistance of an appointive council of forty-two members Andros had authority to make laws, levy taxes, and establish new courts of justice. He was empowered to grant religious toleration. Then, most important of all, he was instructed to enforce the Navigation Acts.

Upon his arrival Andros had intended to continue the old revenue laws until he and his council could make a careful study of the question of taxation. The Puritan authorities ruined this plan; under their direction the final session of the General Court repealed all tax laws. In attempting to work out a new law the governor antagonized both the landowners and the merchants. Actually neither the taxes nor the laws were in themselves burdensome, but the Puritans looked upon them as dangerous violations of American rights. The non-Puritans were not seriously disturbed because they had no voice in the government of Massachusetts anyway; they were no worse off under the tyranny of Andros than under the tyranny of the Puritans. Andros also worked to establish religious freedom, particularly so that members of the Church of England might enjoy their own form of worship. Under his auspices work was started on King's Chapel, the first Anglican Church to be built in Boston. Here again he antagonized the Puritans.

Still acting under instructions, Andros tried other policies which were equally objectionable to non-Puritans and Puritans alike. He announced that the title deeds under which the inhabitants held their land were defective and that new ones would have to be secured. These new deeds would all provide for payment of quitrents to the king. All landowners were incensed over this decree because any such wholesale attack upon their titles could result only in confusion and in expensive lawsuits.

Worse still, Andros enforced the Navigation Acts. He actually put an end to illegal trade with Europe, but the results were deadly. For nearly three years business was ruined, shops were closed, and prominent merchants went into bankruptcy. With this policy Andros again antagonized both Puritans and non-Puritans and so prepared the way for his own downfall. In 1689 reports of the revolution against King James II in England reached Massachusetts. Taking advantage of the disturbance in England, local leaders deposed and imprisoned Andros and then sent him back to England. This ended the combined plans of consolidation of the colonies and their arbitrary control by the British government. Local legislatures resumed their work, land titles were secure again, the Navigation Acts were no longer enforced, illegal trade with the French and Spanish West Indies was resumed, and prosperity returned to New England.

New Charter

The overthrow of Andros made necessary a new form of government for Massachusetts. In 1691, after the accession of William and Mary, a new charter was granted under which Massachusetts became a modified royal colony. According to this arrangement, Massachusetts Bay, Plymouth, Maine, and, for a short time, Nova Scotia were all combined into a single colony. The new charter provided for a governor appointed by the king, a House of Representatives elected by the voters, and a council chosen by the General Court. Under this odd arrangement councilors could vote to continue themselves in office. Because there was legally no General Court in existence when the system went into effect, the first councilors were named in the charter. The governor, with the consent of the council, had power to appoint the judges, sheriffs, marshals, and certain other officials in the colony, and to adjourn or dissolve the General Court at will. Courts of justice might be established by act of the General Court, but parties to all important suits were given the right of appeal to England.

This new charter for Massachusetts, like the one granted to William Penn ten years earlier, attempted to reconcile the conflicting interests of the imperial government and the colonists. Actually it created an institutional basis for bitter disputes. The Americans already had well-defined ideas concerning the rights of their legislatures. This new charter placed the General Court of Massachusetts under limitations which were inconsistent with these alleged rights. The governor could interpose his authority with a veto after the legislature had acted, or he could even prevent action by dissolving the legislature. Again the charter provided no legal relief from the burdensome features of the Navigation Acts. The new authorities merely winked at their violation; more conscientious officials in England might at any time insist upon enforcement as vigorous as that carried out during the regime of Sir Edmund Andros.

Chapter 5

BACKGROUND OF THE REVOLUTION

While the British colonial empire was growing along the Atlantic seaboard in North America, the French were building colonies in the St. Lawrence valley and in Louisiana. Quebec was founded in 1608, St. Louis in 1682, New Orleans in 1718. French plans for expansion called for control of the Great Lakes and also of the Ohio River. By the eighteenth century the English were also interested in the Ohio valley. Old rivalries in Europe plus friction in the New World resulted in a series of Anglo-French wars. These lasted, off and on, from 1689 to 1815. There were intervals of peace between these dates, but they were only truces during which the combatants prepared for the next struggle. Americans were directly involved in every one of these wars.

New France

Anglo-French Rivalry and the Seven Years' War

One of these contests, known as the Seven Years' War in Europe (1756-63) or as the French and Indian War in America, had important results for the colonists. By that time the points of friction where French and English interests clashed were widely scattered over the world: India, Africa, Europe, the Caribbean, and, most important of all from our point of view, North America. The French had a naval base at Louisburg, Cape Breton Island, while the English had one not far away at Halifax, Nova Scotia. The French had a fort at Crown Point, New York, the English had bases at Saratoga and Oswego.

Between 1745 and 1755 the real center of interest in North America was the Ohio valley. The westward movement, which had already accounted for the settlement of the piedmont in Virginia, was bringing the more enterprising Americans into the territory beyond the Alleghenies. As early as 1716, Governor Spotswood of Virginia led an exploring expedition into the West, and in a report sent to England he urged that settlements be established on Lake Erie and that special efforts be made to fortify and defend the mountain passes. His proposals were not carried out, but numbers of American explorers and fur traders and even some prospective settlers had crossed the Allegheny barriers before the Seven Years' War began.

Anglo-French Rivalry

In 1747 a combination of wealthy Virginia planters and British financiers, known as the Ohio Company, petitioned for 500,000 acres on the upper Ohio. The Board of Trade gave its approval. The company began operations at once. Surveyors were sent to map the country; trade with the Indians was started; and efforts were made to found settlements there. But the government of Virginia was opposed to the projects of the company, not because it disapproved of plans for opening the West but because prominent officials in Virginia were already planning to exploit the region for themselves. In 1745 John Robinson, speaker of the House of Burgesses, with some of his associates received a grant of 100,000 acres; by 1757 the government of Virginia had granted about 2,000,000 acres to prospective settlers and speculators in the Ohio valley. Promoters in other colonies were becoming interested in the West. Philadelphia merchants, unwilling to see Virginia monopolize the new territory, were planning to send fur traders into the valley, and Benjamin Franklin urged the establishment of new colonies there.

The French in Canada also had interests in this same Ohio valley, and they were in no mood to stand by and watch the English occupy this region. They saw that, if successful, the English thrust westward through the Ohio valley would be a constant menace to the French hold on the Lakes, if not to Canada itself. In 1749 Duquesne, the governor of Canada, sent a small force to seize the disputed territory. By the spring of 1753, the French planned to occupy the strategic point at the junction of the Monongahela and the Allegheny Rivers, the beginning of the Ohio.

Alarmed at these measures, and urged on by a letter from the British Secretary of State for the colonies, Governor Dinwiddie of Virginia decided to act. In November 1753 he sent George Washington to protest against this move of the French. Washington spent the winter on this journey, which took him as far north as Lake Erie. He brought back nothing but a courteous announcement that the French would not withdraw. In the meantime, Dinwiddie sent a small force to build a fort at the beginning of the Ohio. In the spring of 1754 these Virginians were defeated by the French, who finished the fort themselves, calling it Fort Duquesne. Washington went to the rescue of the Virginians, but after a preliminary victory he was compelled to surrender to the French.

Albany Congress

In the meantime, the Board of Trade had been gathering information about these developments in North America and trying to formulate an effective policy with reference to them. In September 1753 the Board directed the governors of New Hampshire, Massachusetts, New York, New Jersey, Pennsylvania, Maryland, and Virginia to arrange for a meeting with representatives of the Six Nations, the powerful Indians in New York. The purpose of the proposed conference was an alliance between the colonies and the Indians. On June 19, 1754, delegates from the colonies named above except New Jersey and Virginia, plus delegates from Rhode Island and Connecticut, met at Albany, New York. The events of that very spring furnished the clearest proof that action was needed: by the time the Albany Congress assembled, Washington had already been defeated at the forks of the Ohio and the French were securely established at Fort Duquesne.

The question of an alliance with the Indians was connected with the issue of colonial defense, while adequate defense in turn called for colonial union. These topics were discussed at the Congress, but the delegates did not have authority to act. Those from Massachusetts alone were empowered to enter the proposed union; the others were authorized to discuss Indian affairs only. But thanks to the efforts of Benjamin Franklin and Governor Shirley of Massachusetts, a plan of union was approved by the Congress.

Plan of Union

This Albany plan provided for a chief executive over the colonies, known as the president-general, to be appointed and supported by the Crown. Then there was to be a legislature, or Grand Council consisting of forty-eight members chosen by the colonial legislatures. The basis of representation was population and wealth. The Council was to exercise general oversight of Indian affairs and of war; it was to have authority to raise and pay troops, build forts, and equip a colonial navy, to make the necessary laws, and to levy the necessary taxes for putting its policies into effect.

The plan had certain merits, not the least of which was the arrangement for the participation of both the interested parties, England and the colonies, but there were also defects. The Albany plan would place upon the colonies a much greater portion of the cost of their own defense than they had ever carried before, and they demurred. What was the use of spending their own money when the English taxpayers might pay for this war as they had paid for the others? Furthermore, the notion of delegating to any authority any measure of control over taxation was contrary to American political theory. The center of the colonial constitutional system was the local legislature, and it required a revolution in more senses than one before the idea of a central government could even be tolerated. The colonial legislatures refused to ratify this part of the work of the Albany Congress and so refused to take the most obvious step in the direction of adequate defense. As a result concerted action became practically impossible; because the Americans did not approve the Albany plan, the British took no action on it.

This same attitude of unwillingness to undergo expense even in the face of serious danger was demonstrated in the action of individual colonies. Early in 1754 the General Court of Massachusetts called Governor Shirley's attention to the advance of the French and urged him to ask for British help. In the same year the legislature of Connecticut asked the British government to send arms for defense. Two years later the same colony proposed that the king send over a fully equipped regiment to be stationed in Connecticut. Evidently the cost of this help would be met by the British. The General Court of Massachusetts suggested that the American governments might advance some of the money, but they were to be reimbursed by the British after the war was over. The Virginians were equally desirous of having British troops sent to aid them and equally frank in their readiness to shift the cost to British taxpayers.

Seven Years' War

After the Albany Congress finished its sessions, the British Cabinet worked out plans for the coming war. These called for the capture of Forts Duquesne, Niagara, and Crown Point, and the elimination of French adherents in Nova Scotia. At the same time, the navy was to be used to prevent French reinforcements from reaching Canada. Admiral Boscawen's failure in this part of the campaign came dangerously near to presenting the French with the Ohio. As it was, the English suffered serious reverses in the early part of the war.

The first of these defeats—that of General Braddock—occurred in 1755 not far from Fort Duquesne. Braddock's campaign antedated the formal declaration of war between England and France. The slow-moving British force, trying to conduct its campaign after the manner approved in Europe, was caught in a forest battle with the French and Indians. Braddock himself was killed; quantities of supplies were destroyed; and of the force of 1900 men fewer than 500 came through uninjured. The enemy lost about twenty-five. The defeat opened up to Indian attacks the whole frontier back of Pennsylvania, Maryland, and Virginia, along a line 350 miles in length. Not a single British settler or trader remained west of the mountains, and Indian raiding parties burned, scalped, and massacred almost at will. To make matters worse, in the summer of 1755 English and colonial attacks on Crown Point and Niagara also failed.

After the formal declaration of war in 1756 the struggle became world-wide, but the formal declaration did not put an end to British reverses in North America. In 1756, the English lost Oswego, and in 1757 an expedition against Louisburg failed dismally. The French also seized Fort William Henry on Lake George. At that point Prime Minister William Pitt came to the rescue. He was convinced that he alone could save England and he took full charge. Pitt had the knack of inspiring others with his own energy and enthusiasm and under his driving power the English began to push the French back. Pitt appointed new generals, among whom were Amherst and Wolfe, and by 1758 the value of the new management was demonstrated. Louisburg was taken, next Duquesne, and then Fort Frontenac on Lake Ontario, all in this one year. The capture of Fort Frontenac cut the main line of communication between Canada and the French posts in the West, and thus the chain of French forts in the Ohio valley had to yield. By the end of 1758 French power in the West was broken. In 1759 Wolfe won lasting fame by the capture of Quebec, the strongest of all French positions in the New World. The capture of Montreal in 1760 destroyed French power in Canada, as that of Fort Frontenac had already done in the West. So far as North America was concerned, the war was over.

In the West Indies and in Europe hostilities continued until 1763. Spain entered the war in 1762, and the English seized Cuba. Hampered by the peace policy of the new king, George III, and full of wrath at the bungling of the king's chief adviser, the Earl of Bute, Pitt had resigned in 1761. Two years later the war was brought to an end by the Peace of Paris. England secured Canada and the French possessions east of the Mississippi River. She likewise received the West Indian islands of Tobago, Dominica, Grenada, and St. Vincent. France was permitted to keep her West Indian islands of Guadaloupe, Martinique, and Haiti. France also kept two little islands off Newfoundland, St. Pierre and Miquelon, used for drying fish.

England restored Cuba to Spain but kept Florida. Then France gave the whole colony of Louisiana to Spain. The Peace of Paris marked the end of the long contest between Great Britain and France for the control of North America.

New Imperial Problems

The expulsion of the French from North America was an event of unusual significance; so too was the great increase in the size of the British Empire. But even more important was the effect of the war on the relations between the British government and the continental British colonies. Before 1760 the colonists had felt the need of British protection against the constant danger of a French attack. This feeling of dependence had kept the Americans within bounds. Once the French menace disappeared, one of the chief bonds between colonies and empire suddenly disappeared.

Colonial Attitude

Furthermore the Seven Years' War brought to light certain weaknesses in British colonial policy. The colonies were not qualified to engage in extensive military enterprises. The question of voting even a small sum of money or of raising a handful of troops regularly resulted in weeks of debate in the colonial assembly and, more often than not, in a long dispute between governor and assembly over constitutional issues.

According to British plans, the colonists had been expected to furnish provisions for the British troops in North America and to assist in quartering troops and in equipping forts. It fell to the colonial governors to see that the necessary action was taken. Of all the colonies Massachusetts alone, under the inspiration of Governor William Shirley, really did as much as could reasonably be expected. Connecticut and Rhode Island were both afraid of doing more than their share. Of the group of New England colonies, New Hampshire was the most backward, and much of the assistance finally given came too late to be of any value. The action of the New Hampshire legislature is a good illustration of the attitude of many of the governments toward the war. The leaders in the legislature looked upon the struggle with France as an opportunity to subject the governor still more completely to their control. For example, in 1756, the assembly voted £30,000 for the Crown Point campaign, but in the bill appropriating the money it appointed its own agents to go to New York to supervise the expenditure of the funds.

Massachusetts, Connecticut, and New York furnished 70 percent of the total number of colonial forces, and New York stood fourth in the amount of money appropriated on account of the war. During the first part of the struggle New York's contributions were so hedged with restrictions, like those described in New Hampshire, that the help given was nearly worthless. Toward the end, after the governor had surrendered to the assembly, the grants were more liberal. New Jersey, one of the smaller colonies, did fairly well and considerably better than Maryland or the Carolinas.

In Pennsylvania, one of the largest and wealthiest of the colonies, the struggle between the assembly and the proprietary governor took precedence over the war itself. In 1754 a small grant of £5000 was made, but it was placed at the disposal of a committee of the legislature. During the rest of 1754 and the whole of the critical year of 1755 nothing else was done. Thus, while the French were building Fort Duquesne and Braddock was moving toward defeat and death, the Pennsylvanians hardly turned a hand to ward off the danger. They preferred to let the French and Indians overrun the whole frontier rather than to cooperate in any general plan of defense. Even when Braddock's men were getting under way, it was difficult to secure conveyance for the troops, and certain Pennsylvania merchants, including some members of the assembly, sold powder and other supplies to the French and Indians.

In Maryland little was done. The Maryland assembly put all local troops under the direction of a committee of its own choosing and specified the time, place, and under what commanders they should serve. When Loudoun was the British commander in chief in North America, the legislature demonstrated its lack of cooperation by refusing to allow any Maryland troops to serve under him.

Because of her interest in western lands, Virginia had more at stake in the contest over the Ohio valley than any other single colony. Governor Dinwiddie was aware of this interest, and in 1753 and 1754 he tried to arouse in the House of Burgesses an appreciation of the seriousness of the coming crisis. His efforts to secure appropriations were constantly thwarted by his opponents in the House, and his plans for striking a vigorous blow at the French had to be abandoned. In 1754 he did succeed in getting an appropriation of £10,000, placed, however, not in his hands but in those of a committee of the House. The following year brought no change in the situation, and the governor dissolved the House, characterizing the members as "very mutinous and unmannerly." However, as in the case of Maryland, once a more compliant governor than Dinwiddie came over, the House of Burgesses became fairly liberal. The contributions of North and South Carolina were negligible. Evidently the American leaders trusted to the British army and navy to win the war, while they themselves seemed more interested in winning victories over the royal or proprietary governors.

In these circumstances British charges of American ingratitude and indifference were not surprising. According to English officials, the only solution of the difficulty was a larger measure of parliamentary control, supported by parliamentary taxation; this would necessarily call for a revision of existing relationships between colonies and empire. So the war raised the question of imperial reorganization, with special reference to the needs of defense.

The question of imperial reorganization was raised again by the continuance during the war of the trade between the commercial colonies and the French West Indies. The merchants had been so long accustomed to selling to the French and to buying and smuggling French molasses that they continued it as a matter of course. Likewise the French West Indies had become so dependent upon North American food supplies that they were inclined to rely upon the same source in spite of war. Trade with the enemy had been made illegal by act of Parliament and by act of some of the colonial legislatures, notably those of Pennsylvania and New York. These laws were completely ineffective. Part of the trade with the enemy was carried on with Canada. The French forces there were supplied with beef, pork, and flour, chiefly from Pennsylvania, New York, and New England. Some of these provisions were sent overland, some by way of Cape Breton. At Cape Breton, New England skippers could pick up French molasses and sugar for their return cargoes. According to Governor Dinwiddie, the French expeditions into the Ohio valley in 1755 were made possible by these supplies from the English colonies. In other words, New York and Pennsylvania furnished the means whereby the French defeated Braddock.

Trade with the French

Those who were especially interested in defeating the French tried to stop illegal trade. Governor Dinwiddie urged that provisions be placed upon the list of enumerated commodities, so that export outside the British Empire might be forbidden. The English government was unwilling to go that far, but it did order the navy to break up the trade. The trade went on. The Rhode Islanders were notorious for their open commerce with the French. Loudoun wrote Pitt that the traders there were "a lawless set of smugglers, who continually supply the Enemy with what provisions they want, and bring back their Goods in Barter for them." In 1757, the year after the formal declaration of war, Parliament passed a law prohibiting the export of provisions to any ports outside the British Empire.

The passage of this law had no appreciable effect, and trade with the French continued without interruption until 1761. French officials were glad to sanction the trade, even going so far as to license American ships to protect them from the French navy. Some of the commerce was carried on openly, some under thin disguises. American merchant vessels carried passes to the French islands under flags of truce, theoretically for the exchange of prisoners of war, actually for commercial purposes. Before the war was over these flag-of-truce passes became an open scandal. Governor Denny of Pennsylvania made a practice of selling for £20 apiece passes in blank that could be filled in by the purchaser. Protected by such passes, colonial captains were free to sail for any French port and to trade openly with the enemy. Sometimes a captain had the forethought to take one or two prisoners of war for the sake of form. By this subterfuge American merchants turned the war into a profitable financial venture for themselves and for the farmers whose produce they sold. In these enterprises Rhode Island and Pennsylvania were the most active. In 1759 and 1760 the Delaware River at Philadelphia swarmed with vessels unloading cargoes received from the French in exchange for provisions.

But the Philadelphians were not alone in their illegal trade. Prominent merchants in Boston, Providence, Newport, and New York had a hand in it. When Pitt complained of this trade and called upon the local authorities to stop it, the general response was a profession of ignorance. A committee of the council of Massachusetts reported that they could find nc evidence of any commercial connection between their colony and the French islands. Governor Fitch of Connecticut wrote in similar vein. Governor Hopkins of Rhode Island was more honest: he admitted that trade was going on but justified it on grounds of economic necessity. This plea was not entirely ingenuous. To be sure, these merchants had relied upon French West Indian commerce for normal profits in time of peace, but the war had increased the demand and raised the price of foodstuffs in the English colonies so trade with the enemy was not essential.

There was also a flourishing trade between New England ports and the French, carried on through the neutral Spanish port of Monte Cristi. This town was in Santo Domingo, just over the border from Haiti, and although its political connections were Spanish its economic and commercial connections were French. All the exports from Monte Cristi were French, all the imports destined for the French. Monte Cristi imported from British North America such commodities as grain, meat, fish, horses, lumber, British manufactured goods, and even war supplies. On one day, February 5, 1759, there were twenty-eight vessels in Monte Cristi harbor: seven from New York, eight from Rhode Island, eight from Massachusetts, four from Connecticut, and one from Virginia. During one week in 1760, an average of fifty vessels a day put in to that port, almost all of them from the British North American colonies. Occasionally there were as many as a hundred vessels, all from the same ports, in the harbor in one day.

The results of the trade were evident. The regular export of provisions in large quantities so drained the colonies that the English armies operating there had to be supplied in part from England. Thus the illicit American commerce added considerably to the difficulty and the expense of prosecuting the war. Provisions were actually more plentiful in the French West Indies than in the English islands.

With this help secured from American merchants the French could supply their privateers—a constant menace to English commerce. Not only were the French West Indies enabled to hold out, but, according to no less an authority than Pitt himself, the war lasted three years longer than necessary because American merchants frustrated the work of the British navy. Thus the commercial colonies were in the anomalous position of fighting the French in Canada and feeding them in the West Indies.

Writs of Assistance

In 1760 William Pitt sent a circular letter to the colonial governors urging them to bring to judgment all merchants implicated in illegal trade. British prize courts condemned vessels which were caught in it, and the British navy made attempts to check it, but still the trade continued. In this connection Pitt also ordered the customs officers to enforce the Molasses Act of

My Book and Heart
Must never part.
Job feels the Rod,
Yet blesses GOD.
Proud Korah's Troop
Was swallow'd up.
Lot fled to Zoar,
Saw fiery Show'r
On Sodom pour.
Moses was he
Who Israel's Host
Led thro' the Sea.
N
O
P
Q
R
Noah did view
The old World and new.
Young Obadias,
David, Josias,
All were pious.
Peter deny'd
His Lord and cry'd.
Queen Esther sues,
And saves the Jews.
Young pious Ruth,
Left all for Truth.
Young Samuel dear,
The Lord did fear.
Aabcdefghijklmnopq
rstuvwxyz& aeiou
ABCDEFGHIJKLMNOPQ
aeiou
da de di do du
Will be done on Earth
daily Bread; and forgive us our
Trespasses
lead us not into Temptation, but
from Evil. Amen.

THE NEW ENGLAND PRIMER *(above) was the third book published in New England (about 1690) and the first schoolbook in the colonies. Education then was inseparably connected with religion, and the child who learned his alphabet from the* PRIMER *absorbed sound moral principles along with much Biblical information. (Bottom) The horn book was more widely used than the* PRIMER *because it could be made at home. At first, letters were scratched on a wood paddle; later, letters and maxims were written on parchment or paper, protected by a piece of transparent horn. (Courtesy, New York Public Library)*

Numb. II.

THE New-York Weekly JOURNAL.

Containing the freshest Advices, Foreign, and Domestick.

MUNDAY November 12, 1733.

Mr. *Zenger.*

INcert the following in your next, and you'll oblige your Friend,

CATO.

Mira temporum felicitas ubi sentiri quæ velis, & quæ sentias dicere licit.

Tacit.

THE Liberty of the Press is a Subject of the greatest Importance, and in which every Individual is as much concern'd as he is in any other Part of Liberty: therefore it will not be improper to communicate to the Publick the Sentiments of a late excellent Writer upon this Point. such is the Elegance and Perspicuity of his Writings, such the inimitable Force of his Reasoning, that it will be difficult to say any Thing new that he has not said, or not to say that much worse which he has said.

There are two Sorts of Monarchies, an absolute and a limited one. In the first, the Liberty of the Press can never be maintained, it is inconsistent with it; for what absolute Monarch would suffer any Subject to animadvert on his Actions, when it is in his Power to declare the Crime, and to nominate the Punishment? This would make it very dangerous to exercise such a Liberty. Besides the Object against which those Pens must be directed, is their Sovereign, the sole supream Magistrate; for there being no Law in those Monarchies, but the Will of the Prince, it makes it necessary for his Ministers to consult his Pleasure, before any Thing can be undertaken: He is therefore properly chargeable with the Grievances of his Subjects, and what the Minister there acts being in Obedience to the Prince, he ought not to incur the Hatred of the People; for it would be hard to impute that to him for a Crime, which is the Fruit of his Allegiance, and for refusing which he might incur the Penalties of Treason. Besides, in an absolute Monarchy, the Will of the Prince being the Law, a Liberty of the Press to complain of Grievances would be complaining against the Law, and the Constitution, to which they have submitted, or have been obliged to submit; and therefore, in one Sense, may be said to deserve Punishment, So that under an absolute Monarchy, I say, such a Liberty is inconsistent with the Constitution, having no proper Subject in Politics, on which it might be exercis'd, and if exercis'd would incur a certain Penalty.

But in a limited Monarchy, as *England* is, our Laws are known, fixed, and established. They are the streight Rule and sure Guide to direct the King, the Ministers, and other his Subjects: And therefore an Offence against the Laws is such an Offence against the Constitution as ought to receive a proper adequate Punishment; the severa

Constit

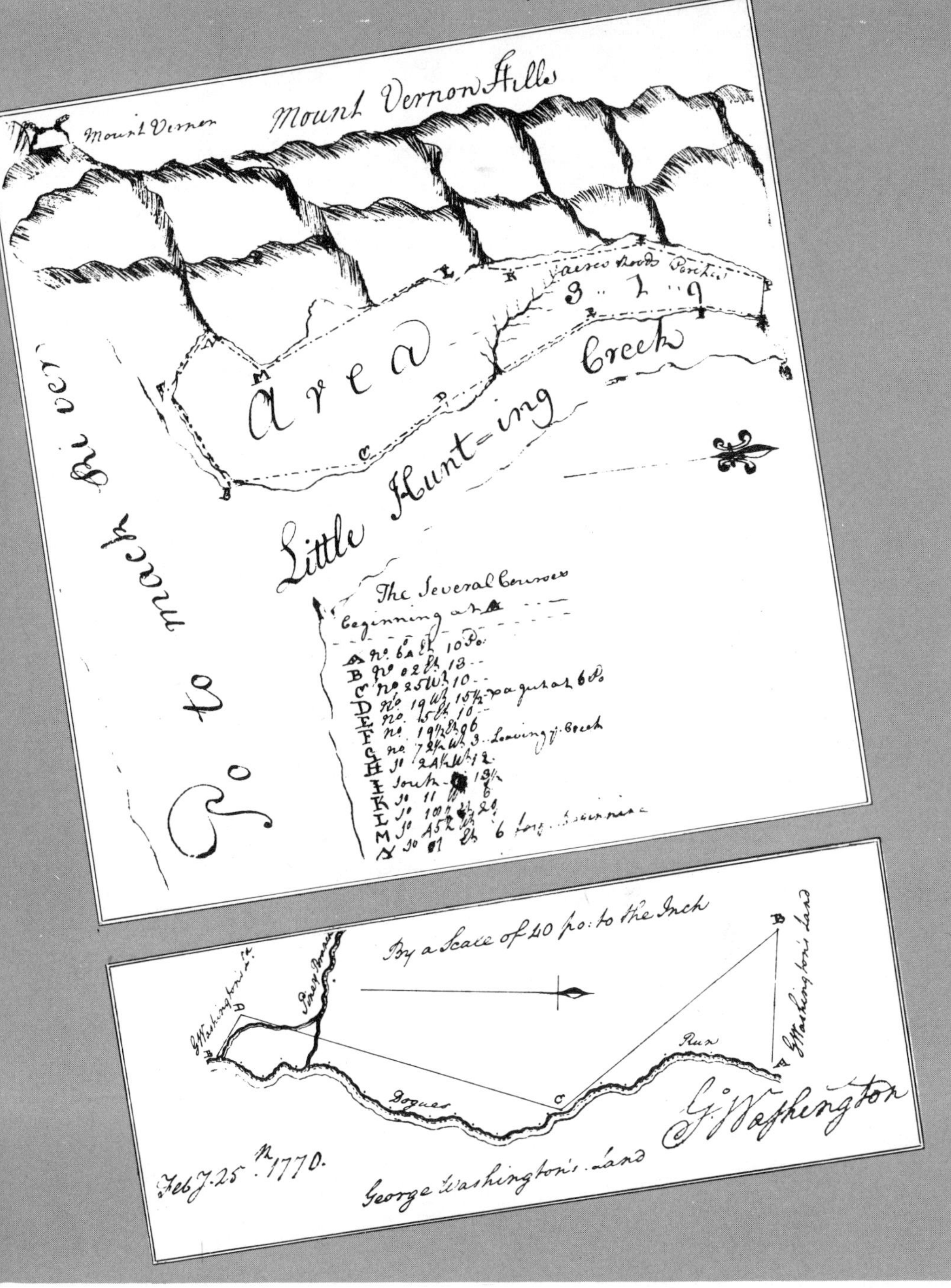

THE NEW-YORK WEEKLY JOURNAL began publication, November 5, 1733, to attack Governor William Cosby's political practices. The resulting libel suit, won by John Peter Zenger, editor and publisher, established the principle of freedom of the press. (Opposite) Issue No. 2. (Above) Two surveys by George Washington. Sketch of Mount Vernon area is apparently an early work; survey below shows considerably more experience. (Courtesy, New York Public Library)

"THE Repeal. Or the Funeral Procession of Miss Americ-Stamp" is typical of eighteenth-century British cartooning, full of allusions which were obvious to newspaper readers of that day. The two skulls carry dates of the pro-Stuart, or Jacobite, uprisings; man with coffin is George Grenville, promoter of the Stamp Act; chief mourner is Sejanus. (In Roman lore Sejanus was a horse which brought nothing but misfortune to all who had anything to do with the beast.) Last two marchers are the Archbishops of York and Canterbury; ships are named for the three Whig leaders of parliamentary majority for repeal. British merchants had opposed the law from the beginning and were as enthusiastic over repeal as the Americans. (Courtesy, New York Public Library)

1733. Here he achieved a degree of success, the measure of which may be observed partly in the reports to the Treasury and partly in the intensity of opposition created by the policy. Between 1734 and 1755 the total revenue collected under this law was only £5686. During the years of the war, thanks to Pitt's efforts, the collections amounted to £4375. But this enforcement led to friction between the merchants and the customs officers, and the local courts of justice showed marked consideration for those merchants who habitually broke the law.

In Boston Pitt's efforts at enforcement led to a contest between merchants and British officials which is sometimes described as one of the early stages of the Revolution. In searching for smuggled goods the customs men used writs of assistance, or general search warrants. The ordinary warrant was worthless because it had to specify both the place to be searched and the goods supposed to be there. By the time the officials succeeded in getting in, the place would be empty. With a writ of assistance officials could go anywhere. In 1759 and 1760 the Boston merchants tried to have the Superior Court of Massachusetts declare such writs illegal. Two Boston lawyers, Oxenbridge Thacher and James Otis, argued the case for the merchants. Otis made a vivid appeal to the emotions of his hearers, but in spite of that he lost his case, and writs of assistance were used until the Revolution.

Imperial Problems

In addition to demonstrating weaknesses in the British colonial system, the Seven Years' War left certain problems that called for immediate solution. Canada in the north and Florida in the south, recently incorporated in the Empire by means of conquest, were inhabited by French and Spanish aliens. These people were not only unfamiliar with English ways but in many respects hostile to them. A form of government was needed which would arouse the least possible new bitterness and which would nevertheless enable English officials to assert their authority if necessary.

Along with this problem of government for Canada and Florida there was the larger question of the West, the area lying between Canada and western Florida and between the Alleghenies and the Mississippi. Here too there were problems of government, including the important matter of additional funds to meet the costs of administration and defense against attack. Britain had come out of the Seven Years' War with impressive territorial gains, but much time would be required to make these regions economically profitable. Unable to provide for their own defense, they were dependent for this service upon other parts of the Empire. Somebody had to provide substantial sums of money.

There was also the problem of American rivalry in the West. Several of the older colonies had overlapping claims in this region. The Virginians were there, actually at work before 1755, and in 1763 they proceeded to pick up the threads of their interests which the war had compelled them to drop. First the Virginia troops to whom Governor Dinwiddie had promised land grants in the Ohio valley united to promote their claims, and in this work they had the energetic support of George Washington. Under his leadership they sent a petition to the king, which the Board of Trade began to consider in March 1763. The Ohio Company then sent a special agent to London to make sure that their interests were not overlooked. Next, in June 1763 the Mississippi Company was founded. This included promoters from Virginia and Maryland, prominent among whom were George Washington, the Lees of Virginia, the Fitzhughs, and others. This new concern sought to obtain from the Crown a grant of 2,500,000 acres on the Mississippi River, of which each one of the adventurers was to get 50,000 acres for himself. In September 1763 this company sent a memorial to the king.

These American efforts to exploit the coveted region were observed with considerable concern in England. Official opinion there was divided. One group, including the influential Hudson's Bay Company, advocated a policy somewhat like that of the French—that is, development of the fur trade; they opposed settlements beyond the Alleghenies. Another group urged the promotion of populous colonies to serve as markets for British manufactures. But while this second group was interested in developing the new regions, it was opposed to giving the Americans a free hand there. If exploitation was to take place, let it be under the auspices of the whole Empire, rather than of one or two especially favored colonies.

Indian Policy

These important questions could not be considered solely on their own merits. In England there were political entanglements which stood in the way of an impartial solution, while in America the question of western policy was bound up with the Indian problem. The Indians realized that English control of the Ohio valley would mean something very different from the French fur-trading system. It was the custom of the English to stay, to cut up the country into farms, and to drive out the game, the fur-bearing animals, and the Indians too. Beside this fundamental source of friction, there was the attitude of the British traders; they were always ready to rob the Indians. Then the French encouraged the Indians in their hostile attitude; they spread reports that the English could not hold the West and that the French would soon be restored to power.

It might have been good policy for the English to conciliate the natives, but instead of doing so the military men in charge chose the opposite course. General Amherst did not believe in bribing the Indians to remain quiet, so he cut off the presents which they had been receiving. He also prevented them from getting supplies of powder and lead, and he tried to deprive them of rum. Ordinarily a humane and respectable gentleman, Amherst seems to have adopted the traditional slogan of the frontier that the only good Indian is a dead Indian. In any case he wrote to one of his agents: "You will do well to try to inoculate the Indians by means of blankets [that is, try to spread smallpox among them] as well as to try every other method that can serve to extirpate this execrable race. I should be very glad your scheme for hunting them down by dogs could take effect."

The Indians became restless and then hostile. The first impetus to revolt was given by the chief Pontiac. On May 7, 1763, the Indians started the uprising known as Pontiac's Conspiracy. They had planned a surprise attack on Detroit, but this failed because the English received warning in time. But the Indians captured and massacred all other garrisons west of Niagara, and during the summer of 1763 the whole Northwest was in an uproar. It appeared for a time that neither the American colonists nor the English government would have any control over the region. But superior resources began to tell, and in October Pontiac asked for terms. Peace was restored in the following spring.

Pontiac's Conspiracy

British Policies and American Attitudes

This Indian war, which threatened to deprive the British Empire of some of its most valuable gains under the Peace of Paris, made necessary a definite, precise statement of the western and Indian policies of the British government. Indian affairs had to be organized, but there were serious differences of opinion as to method. Some members of the Cabinet advocated the creation of a strong, independent department for the management of all Indian affairs; others preferred to leave the whole question of Indian control to the military department; a third group suggested that the British government ignore the Indian question and leave it to the colonists.

Pontiac's Conspiracy emphasized still another aspect of the problem: the necessity of protection against similar outbursts in the future. Who should pay the taxes needed to uphold British authority? If the experience of the Seven Years' War counted for anything, the Americans would not assume the burden voluntarily; during the Conspiracy they refused again to pay more than was absolutely required. In the spring of 1763 the three New England colonies of New Hampshire, Massachusetts, and Rhode Island refused to comply with specific requests for help from the English commanders. Leaders in Virginia asked the British government for British garrisons on the frontier. Benjamin Franklin seems to have been alone among the colonists in suggesting that the Americans would really profit in the long run from any expense incurred in guarding their own frontiers. Closely connected with the Indian problem was the question of white settlement beyond the mountains. A boundary line was needed to separate the Indian country from regions open to white pioneers.

Most of these issues were dealt with in the Proclamation of 1763. The boundaries of the newly acquired regions were defined. Next came a plan of government for the same areas. There were three of these provinces on the continent: Quebec, East Florida, and West Florida; a fourth, called Grenada, included the West Indian islands recently acquired from France. As soon as the population should be large enough to warrant its introduction, the government was to be of the ordinary type in operation in the royal colonies already established. Until that time, the royal governor was to have supreme authority, without any elective legislature.

Proclamation of 1763

With reference to the Indian problem, the Proclamation fixed the line

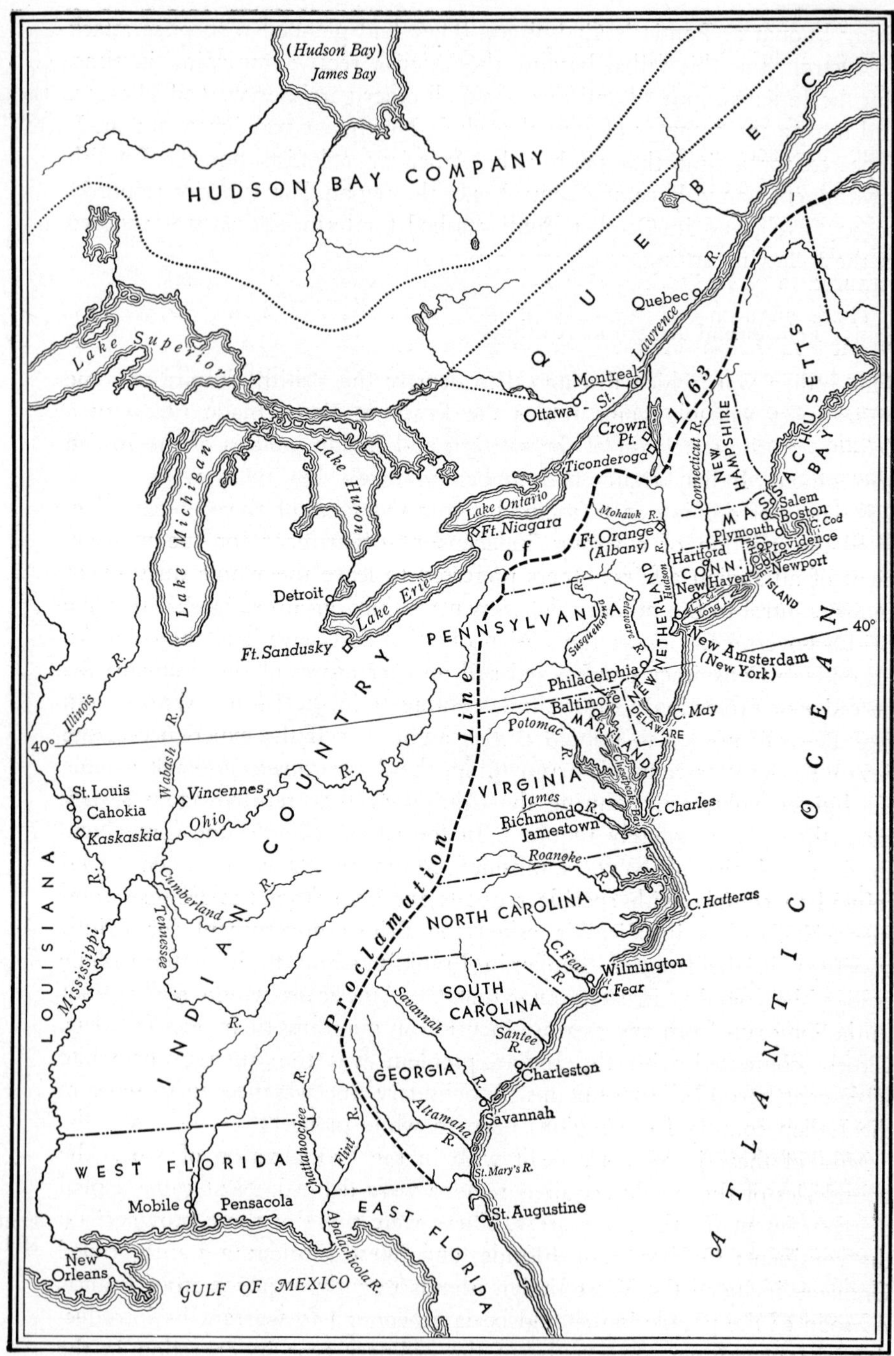

Map 3. The Proclamation Line of 1763

between Indian territory and the region open for settlement at the Appalachian divide. Everything beyond was a great Indian reservation, in which white settlement was not allowed. Private purchases of land from the Indians were prohibited, and the governors in all the colonies, old and new, were forbidden to make any land grants within the territory set apart for the red men. Settlers already located in the region were ordered out. The proclamation placed the control of the Indian trade in the hands of the imperial government, and, in addition to being licensed, every trader was required to bind himself to observe any rules that might be made.

There were certain specific blunders in the Proclamation, the chief of which was the provision that English law was to prevail in the new provinces. An English attorney general characterized this as "an act of the grossest and absurdest and cruelest tyranny, that a conquering nation ever practiced over a conquered country." This blunder was rectified in the Quebec Act, eleven years later.

In the colonies there was uncertainty or bitterness over the possible effect of the Proclamation on the westward movement, but this feeling was due to misunderstanding. The king's ministers looked upon the establishment of the Indian boundary line as a tentative measure; they hoped to guide settlements into the eastern part of the new provinces, and then, gradually by purchase, to extinguish the Indian title in the reservation. The obstruction of the westward advance would be only temporary, but, in accordance with the approved principles of diplomacy, the Indians had to be assured that the policy was permanent and that the line would stay. Whatever the Indians may have been led to believe, the American colonists assumed that they were to be permanently excluded from the West.

Who Should Pay?

There is still one more phase of this new western policy to be considered —that of taxation and finance. In English official circles there was a growing conviction that a share of the additional administrative costs should be carried by the Americans. They had a direct stake in the profitable development of the West; if they would not assume the burden voluntarily, Parliament might fall back upon its latent power and compel them to contribute.

This suggestion supplies another reason for attributing so much importance to the Proclamation of 1763. Out of the need of funds to make it effective came George Grenville's revenue measures of 1764 and 1765—the Sugar and Stamp Acts. The new plans for taxing the colonies were the product not of any policy of tyranny but of the financial requirements growing out of the needs of the West. It is rather curious that around these revenue measures, which in England were looked upon simply as incidents in the great general problem of imperial organization, there should have developed the first spectacular repudiation of its authority which the British government had encountered.

While the problems which had come to light during the Seven Years' War were being settled, colonial leaders had occasion to look carefully into the whole question of the colonial status, particularly into those aspects of it which emphasized the subordination of Americans to British authority. Reference has been made to the attack upon the customs service in Massachusetts occasioned by the newly formed decision to enforce the old Molasses Act and to Otis's speech against the writs of assistance. Otis was not an advocate of independence but of autonomy. On the basis of autonomy he denied the legality of the writs and by so doing he raised the issue of the nature and extent of British control.

The Parson's Cause

In 1763 another American lawyer, Patrick Henry of Virginia, denied the right of the Privy Council to disallow a colonial law. Henry's argument was made in a legal dispute over a clergyman's salary, and therefore the episode is referred to under the name of the Parson's Cause. In Virginia clergymen of the established church were public officials, paid by the colony. Under laws in force until 1758, each minister received 17,280 pounds of tobacco, regardless of the size of his parish, his own abilities, or the current price of tobacco. Since the price varied from one penny to sixpence per pound, the clergymen fared well in good years. In 1758, when tobacco was high, the Virginia legislature passed a law, ordering payment of these salaries in money, at the rate of twopence per pound of tobacco. The market price that year was about three times as much, so the clergymen felt that they were being cheated. The effect of the law was to reduce the real salary, in terms of pounds sterling, from £400 to £144. The clergy therefore carried their grievances to the Crown, and the Privy Council disallowed the law. Then some of the clergy sued the government for back pay. The most famous of these suits was brought by Reverend James Maury in the court of Hanover County. The vestry retained Patrick Henry to defend its interests against the rector. Legally the colony owed back pay to the rector, but Henry made such a clever appeal to the jury that instead of giving the clergyman the amount to which the law clearly entitled him, they gave him one penny. The basis of Henry's argument was a flat denial of the right of the Privy Council to disallow acts of the colonial legislature. The statute under discussion had been passed to meet an emergency, and Henry insisted that the local legislature had full authority to act. On the strength of this speech to the jury he was elected to the House of Burgesses. Both in Massachusetts and in Virginia, therefore, the two lawyers who had come out strongly in opposition to certain forms of British authority found themselves clothed with new power as members of their respective colonial assemblies.

Colonial Politics

In addition to these specific denials of the principle of British supremacy, there were other forces at work in American politics and government which might have a bearing on any dispute between the Empire and the colonies. Out of the contest between the merchants and the customs officers in Massachusetts there developed a sort of bloc in the legislature, the members of which made political capital out of their opposition to the royal officials. The size of this group fluctuated from time to time in accordance with the ebb and flow of feeling over new British policy. A minority until 1765, it became a majority then and remained in control of the General Court until

1771. The leaders of this party in Massachusetts were James Otis, Samuel Adams, and John Hancock. This group will be described more fully later.

In Pennsylvania there was another type of contest, different from that in Massachusetts but equally favorable for the capitalization of any dispute over British power. In this proprietary colony the dominant group in the government, corresponding to the tidewater planters in Virginia, was composed of the Quakers in the three eastern counties: Philadelphia, Chester, and Bucks. The opposition included the Germans and Scotch-Irish in the western counties and workingmen in the city of Philadelphia. The western farmers found that their natural economic outlet was the Susquehanna, which connected them with the city of Baltimore in Maryland rather than with Philadelphia, and this tended to widen the gap. Then the Philadelphia artisans, who did not enjoy the right to vote, felt that they were ill treated and oppressed by the Quaker aristocracy. Thus a common grievance tied these two dissimilar factions together.

The issues in the dispute between the aristocracy and their opponents were the important matters of taxation and representation. From 1760 to 1776 the struggle between the two continued, and then it was merged into the larger controversy of the Revolution. In the matter of representation, the grievance of the western counties was genuine enough. As these newer regions increased in population, they had not been granted representation in the legislature commensurate with their numbers. The older counties, in power at the beginning, determined to keep what they had by the simple, undemocratic method of ignoring the just claims of the West.

The three eastern counties, including the city of Philadelphia, had 26 representatives for 16,221 taxable inhabitants, while the five western counties had only 10 representatives for 15,443 taxables. This was the situation in 1760, and it remained unchanged until 1769, in spite of the fact that the five newer counties were steadily increasing in population. In 1771, 1772, and 1773 a new county was organized each year, with one representative each, so there was no change in principle until 1776. No further explanation is needed to show why the Quaker aristocracy of the East was meeting with bitter opposition. In trying to restrict the power of the eastern leaders, the Scotch-Irish and Germans in the western counties evolved a political organization which, if necessary, could be used to oppose British authority.

For these and other reasons the Seven Years' War and the attempt to solve problems resulting from it proved to be the turning point in relations between the American colonies and the British Empire. British efforts at administrative reform stirred the Americans first to protest and then to revolt. Under the circumstances political organizations such as those in Massachusetts and Pennsylvania played an important part.

Chapter 6

THE RISE OF AMERICAN OPPOSITION

As British officials studied colonial attitudes during the Seven Years' War and analyzed postwar problems, they came to a logical but disastrous conclusion. If the colonial system was not working satisfactorily, make it work well. Make imperial control a fact. Pass laws and create administrative machinery to bring the colonies under control. The Cabinet tried to put this policy into effect. Leadership in this thankless job fell to George Grenville, at the time Chancellor of the Exchequer. Grenville has been aptly described as "the fingers rather than the soul of good government"—that is, a small-minded man whose interest in mechanical efficiency blinded him to the fact that persons affected by administrative measures are human beings.

Grenville's Reforms

New Policies

Beginning in 1764 Grenville started to make all officials more efficient. To this end he issued an order directed to all appointees holding colonial offices: they must either go to their posts and begin work or resign. This order was revolutionary. Men received these colonial jobs not in the expectation of doing work—that could be handled by subordinates—but in the hope of drawing salaries. In other words, the appointments were part of the system of political patronage of that day. Grenville's specific aims were to strengthen the customs service in America and to enforce the Navigation Acts.

Also in the interests of efficiency Grenville proposed to make some British officials in the colonies independent of the local assemblies. If British agents could look to the British Treasury for support, they would be less responsive to the pressure of local American politicians. Grenville also proposed to raise money for the defense of the West, and he determined to have Americans pay a share of this cost. He figured that 10,000 soldiers were needed on the frontier, and this number would call for an appropriation of £30,000. He counted on getting one third of this sum from the Americans. Grenville then called upon Parliament for the necessary legislation. Laws were passed to increase the authority of the customs officials, and to make smuggling more difficult. Powers of the admiralty courts were increased and stricter regulations were imposed regarding the registration of merchant ships.

The next measure in Grenville's program was the Revenue Act of 1764, often referred to as the Sugar Act. This law reduced the import duty on French molasses from sixpence to threepence per gallon; the difficulty was that the sixpenny duty had rarely been collected, so ordinarily it was not burdensome. The new duty would be collected; this was one of the purposes of the Grenville reforms. The net effect was to impose a new tax. The same measure imposed other import duties on coffee and on wine from the Azores, which hitherto had come in free. Then lumber and iron were added to the list of enumerated commodities. Cases arising under the law would be tried in the admiralty courts without a jury. Then came the section which aroused bitter complaint: all duties under the law were to be paid in specie, rather than in colonial paper money.

Sugar Act

Had Grenville been a statesman, he would have looked into that molasses trade which he was so ready to tax. In doing so, he would have discovered what every intelligent American merchant and many of the royal governors understood clearly: that the prosperity of the middle and northern colonies depended on this very trade in foreign molasses. The British islands could not begin to supply the demand. Their entire output was only slightly over 50 percent of the quantity carried into Rhode Island alone, while all the colonies together used about eight times as much as the English islands produced. Moreover, the British sugar planters charged anywhere from 25 to 40 percent higher prices than those charged in the French islands. The trade was too important to be treated ignorantly.

If Grenville had pushed his investigations a little further, he would have learned that colonial authorities considered a threepenny tax too high. They were convinced that a one penny tax was all the trade could stand. As a matter of fact in 1766 the English authorities admitted the soundness of the argument by reducing the tax to that figure. But Grenville's mind was not interested in any such subtleties of economics, so he learned none of these things before his measure became law.

American Protests

After its enactment he learned that colonial merchants had deep convictions on the subject of colonial revenue. This fact in itself should have made him go slowly because the merchants were not troublemakers. They had a keen appreciation of the benefits accruing to them from their membership in the British Empire. They knew that they were protected from foreign competition in the carrying trade by the first Navigation Act. This advantage alone was more than enough to outweigh the restrictive measures of the other Navigation Acts, especially since they could be easily evaded. Then, at a time when piracy was a factor in maritime activity, the merchants knew that they were enjoying the full benefits of protection by the British navy, without paying a penny for it. They knew that in their Mediterranean trade they were protected from the depredations of the Barbary corsairs by payments made by the British government. Finally, they had enjoyed a flourishing trade before the Seven Years' War, and the British conquests held out bright hopes for a steady increase in their commerce. Serious protests from the merchants really meant something.

The Sugar Act had no effect on the plantation colonies of the South, but it called out strong protests from the merchants of the North. In New York the merchants met and appointed a committee to petition the assembly asking that body to call upon Parliament for a repeal. Merchants in Philadelphia and Boston, in fact in all the commercial centers, were equally active. In the summer of 1764 some merchants in Boston signed an agreement to restrict the use of British cloth and to encourage the local textile industry in an effort to bring pressure to bear upon the British.

The merchants aimed at reform, and they urged merely the repeal of the objectionable bill. The most famous protests were those written by James Otis of Massachusetts, the lawyer who had assisted the merchants in their campaign against the writs of assistance; by Stephen Hopkins of Rhode Island, a merchant deeply interested in the West Indian trade; and by John Dickinson of Philadelphia, a lawyer in close touch with the mercantile interests of that city. These critics of Grenville's plan tried to make plain the vital importance of the West Indian trade, with reference not only to the merchants and to the distillers but also to the farmers who depended upon the West Indian market for the sale of their surplus products. In addition, James Otis characterized the new taxes imposed by Parliament as a violation of "natural law" and consequently null and void.

The Sugar Act brought hard times to the colonies. From Boston there were complaints that the number of vessels engaged in the West Indian trade had dropped to one fifth of those in it the preceding year. The merchants generally agreed that business was bad and getting worse. Similar complaints poured in from all the commercial colonies.

The protests of the merchants were based on economic facts. Other protests were the result of local political activity. In Massachusetts, for example, the Otis group in the House of Representatives used the Sugar Act as a political issue to strengthen themselves and to weaken their opponents. The debate over the Sugar Act made Samuel Adams famous. He drafted one of the protests against the measure, and as a reward the Boston voters put him into the House of Representatives.

The Stamp Act

More Revenue

Undeterred by colonial protests against the Sugar Act, Grenville went ahead with his program. In 1764 he had announced that revenue measures in addition to the Sugar Act would be necessary, and he had suggested a series of stamp taxes. Before putting the measure before Parliament, however, he gave the colonial legislatures an opportunity to provide the desired revenue by other means. Since they took no action the Stamp Act was passed in March 1765 to go into effect the following November. During its course through Parliament, this ill-fated measure attracted almost no attention, and outside of Parliament there were few warnings of impending trouble. Not even William Pitt, supposedly the friend of the colonies, paid any attention to the bill. When it passed he was temporarily out of public life, ill with gout, but he was constantly writing letters on all sorts of issues, and if he had been interested in the Stamp Act, he probably would have said so.

There were others in London at the time who saw no great harm in the Stamp Act. Benjamin Franklin anticipated no trouble, and according to report he applied, in behalf of his son, for one of the positions as stamp distributor. In Virginia Richard Henry Lee did the same thing for himself, much to his embarrassment when colonial opposition broke loose. It required considerable explaining to tell why he was ready to serve in that capacity.

The Stamp Act provided for stamp duties on a variety of documents, such as ship clearance papers, licenses, deeds, bonds, and leases, and also upon playing cards, dice, newspapers, pamphlets, and advertisements. In one respect the Stamp Act resembled the Sugar Act: cases arising under the law would be tried in admiralty courts. The proceeds, so the law made clear, were to pay for English troops on the frontier. Thus the money raised would all be spent in America. If the Proclamation of 1763 had not set up a barrier to settlement, the money would have been spent for purposes beneficial to all colonies interested in the West. In any case, the older colonies would profit from having the frontier adequately guarded. Viewed simply as the answer to a problem in economics and in defense, the Stamp Act was sound. But the American colonists did not consider the measure with complete objectivity. The merchants had already been stirred by the Sugar Act, while artisans and laborers were uneasy over the prevailing economic depression. Furthermore, the new measure bore heavily upon two other groups—the printers and the lawyers, who were in a position to make their protests heard.

Patrick Henry's Resolves

All that was needed was someone to give point to the feeling of resentment. The man who did it was Patrick Henry of Virginia. On May 29, 1765, in spite of the opposition of the conservatives, the House of Burgesses passed some resolutions which he had introduced. In the first four of these resolutions Henry declared that all British subjects in America were entitled to all the liberties and privileges of Englishmen. One of the distinguishing characteristics of British freedom was the privilege of the citizen to participate, through his elected representatives, in levying taxes and making laws. In the fifth he declared that the general assembly of Virginia had the sole and exclusive right to tax the inhabitants, and that any attempt to vest such power elsewhere would have a tendency to destroy both British and American freedom. Next he argued that the inhabitants of Virginia were not obliged to obey any tax law unless the local legislature passed it. In the seventh and last he characterized as an enemy to his country any person who should proclaim the binding force of any tax law passed by any legislature outside the colony.

There is some question as to how many of these resolutions were passed. The *Journal* of the House of Burgesses lists only the first four as being adopted, while Henry himself wrote that the first five were passed. But the formal action of the legislature was not a matter of great importance. The newspapers printed all but the third as the Virginia Resolves, so Patrick Henry was hailed as the American leader who denied the authority of Parliament over the colonies. Evidently feeling ran high in the House on that memorable occasion. A French traveler who happened to be present at the time reported "very hot Debates" over the Stamp Act. Some of the members, so he continued, "were for shewing their resentment to the highest."

In Massachusetts the first formal action came on June 8, when the House of Representatives sent out an appeal for a meeting of delegates from the various colonies at New York to formulate a united protest against the Stamp Act. The time suggested was the following October, the month before the Stamp Act was to go into effect. At the appointed time delegates from nine of the colonies met in the Stamp Act Congress in New York, but weeks before that plans were being worked out to defeat the measure.

Inspired by the Virginia Resolutions, the opponents of the Stamp Act in Massachusetts began a vigorous campaign. In that colony there were two riots, on August 14 and August 26, the first of which had the appearance of being not the work of irresponsible troublemakers but a deliberately planned demonstration. As a result, the stamp distributor of Massachusetts, Andrew Oliver, was compelled to resign. On August 26 the mob broke loose again, this time with more appearance of spontaneity. After a number of minor depredations, they wound up with an attack on the home of Lieutenant Governor Hutchinson, one of the most conspicuous of the conservative politicians in the province.

Attacks on Distributors

Violence in Massachusetts set the fashion for mobs elsewhere. In New York the stamp distributor was a Scottish merchant by the name of James McEvers. Upon receipt of the news from Boston he handed in his resignation. Everywhere in the thirteen colonies the distributors resigned before November 1. Rioting broke out in such widely separated colonies as New York, Virginia, and North Carolina.

On October 7, after a summer of political unrest, twenty-seven delegates from nine colonies met in the Stamp Act Congress at New York.[1] The Congress adopted a declaration of rights and grievances and sent petitions to the king, Lords, and Commons in England. In the declaration the Congress asserted that it was an "undoubted right of Englishmen, that no taxes be imposed on them but with their own consent, given personally or by their representatives." Then the delegates challenged the right of Parliament to tax the colonies: "The only representatives of the people of these colonies are persons chosen therein by themselves, and . . . no taxes ever have been or can be constitutionally imposed on them, but by their respective legislatures." Subsequently these resolutions were approved by those colonial assemblies which had sent no delegates to the Congress.

Stamp Act Congress

[1] Massachusetts, Rhode Island, Connecticut, New York, New Jersey, Pennsylvania, Delaware, Maryland, South Carolina.

Sons of Liberty

In their efforts to defeat the Stamp Act the leaders tried experiments with new political organizations, the most important of which was the Sons of Liberty. The name seems to have been used first in Connecticut, whence it spread eastward to Boston and then west and south through New York to the Carolinas. This organization opposed both the Stamp Act and the privileged classes in the colonies. In New York in January 1766 the Sons of Liberty tried to prevent anyone from using the stamps. In February the New York Sons of Liberty appointed a committee to write to leading opponents of the Act in other parts of British North America. They opened correspondence with all the colonies from New Hampshire to South Carolina. This step was soon followed by the logical suggestion of a Congress representing all the Sons of Liberty, but before this enterprising plan could be carried out the repeal of the Stamp Act made further proceedings unnecessary.

In Boston the opponents of the Stamp Act followed the example of their fellows in New York and organized a local branch of the Sons of Liberty. The most prominent members were merchants and businessmen, one of the publishers of the *Boston Gazette,* and some political leaders, of whom Samuel Adams was the most conspicuous. Of those who were known to be members of the Sons of Liberty, several were likewise prominent leaders in the Boston Caucus Club, Samuel Adams's political machine.

Repeal

American leaders had worked deliberately to nullify the Stamp Act, and they succeeded. By the early part of 1766 business was proceeding as usual without stamps. Newspapers were published without stamps; customs officials issued clearance papers without them; and even lawyers and courts of justice transacted their business almost as though the law had never been passed. During November and December 1765 the leading merchants in America signed agreements to import no more goods from England until the Stamp Act should be repealed. This protest had considerable influence on English merchants and manufacturers. When these Englishmen joined the Americans in demanding the repeal of the objectionable measure, action became inevitable. In Parliament, prominent members like William Pitt and Edmund Burke—who a few years later made the famous speech on conciliation—took the American side. Benjamin Franklin, who was then in England as agent for his colony, used his influence to help repeal. On March 21, 1766, Parliament voted the repeal, and the American victory seemed complete. The colonies had nullified a British-made law and had compelled the mother country to surrender. And Parliament also reduced the threepenny duty on molasses to one penny so that this tax was no longer a burden. News of the repeal of the Stamp Act reached the colonies in May 1766. It was received with widespread, unrestrained, and perhaps indecorous enthusiasm. In the towns the shops were closed—but not the taverns—and there were public bonfires, dinner parties, and celebrations generally.

In their satisfaction over their victory the Americans hardly noticed another act of Parliament, passed on March 18, 1766, just three days before the repeal of the Stamp Act. This measure, the Declaratory Act, had the following sinister title: "An Act for Better Securing the Dependency of His Majesty's Dominions in America upon the Crown and Parliament of Great Britain." One paragraph of the act asserted that "the said colonies and plantations in *America* have been, are, and of right ought to be, subordinate unto and dependent upon the imperial Crown and parliament of Great Britain," and the king and Parliament "had, hath, and of right ought to have, full power and authority" to make laws "of sufficient force and validity to bind the colonies and people of America, subjects of the Crown of Great Britain, in all cases whatsoever."

The contest between mother country and colonies over the Stamp Act started talk of independence. The French visitor in the House of Burgesses wrote:

> . . . this Country Can not be long subject to great Britain, nor Indeed to any Distant power, its extent is so great the Daily Increase of its Inhabitants So considerable, and haveing everything necessary within themselves for their Own Defence, that no Nation whatsoever seems beter Calculated for independency, and the Inhabitants are already Intirely Disposed thereto and talk of Nothing more than it.

If the contest over the Stamp Act had been the only episode of its kind, the solidarity of the empire need not have been seriously threatened. England might perhaps have kept the colonies if she had let them have their way in legislation and taxation. This was the lesson of the Stamp Act. British officials, however, could not bring themselves to admit it.

The Townshend Acts and Nonimportation

External Taxes

In 1767, the year following the repeal of the Stamp Act, the Cabinet worked out a new program of colonial taxation. From time to time the Americans had paid duties levied on commerce. Some of these, notably the tax on molasses, had aroused protest, but none of them had stirred up any such storm as that over the Stamp Act. The new Chancellor of the Exchequer, Charles Townshend, reasoned that additional external taxes (as he called them) might be made to produce considerable revenue. The Townshend Acts dealt with a number of important phases of colonial finance and administration. First there were new tariff duties to be collected on paint, paper, glass, and tea. The revenue derived from these taxes was to be used primarily to pay the salaries of colonial judges, governors, and other royal officials in the colonies, thereby freeing them from their dependence upon American legislatures. Any surplus which might remain after the salaries were paid would be used to pay troops on the frontier.

The Townshend program also provided for a reorganization of the customs service in America. A new American Board of Customs Commissioners was created. From its headquarters in Boston the Board would have full charge of all customs business in North America, including the service in Bermuda and the Bahamas. To expedite the trial of smuggling cases, courts of vice-admiralty were set up in Boston, Philadelphia, and Charleston. Townshend, therefore, provided the necessary administrative organization for the collection of the new taxes and an effective judicial system for punishing violators of the law.

Another important section of the Townshend program was punitive in purpose. The New York Assembly had failed to comply with certain provisions of the Mutiny Act which placed upon colonial legislatures the obligation to furnish provisions and quarters for royal troops stationed in the colonies. One of Townshend's laws prohibited the Assembly from meeting until the members would agree to vote the supplies required. In taking this action Parliament assumed a position of superiority over American legislatures which the Americans had hitherto refused to accept.

This program was considerably more ambitious than Grenville's, especially in the scheme for reforming colonial government. Townshend's purpose was to free British officials in the colonies, particularly the governors, from their dependence on American legislatures, and by so doing to reestablish executive authority. American leaders resented his threat to the power of their legislatures. If Townshend had his way, so the Americans reasoned, not only would all their victories be nullified but the very means by which they had won their successes would be lost.

Nonimportation

In their efforts to defeat the Townshend program, colonial leaders planned to bring economic pressure on English merchants and manufacturers. The first formal action seems to have been that taken by the Boston town meeting of October 28, 1767. At that time an agreement was adopted by which the signers bound themselves not to purchase a long list of imported articles. As a part of the same program, efforts were made to encourage local manufacturing.

The success of a self-denying policy of this kind depended upon the hearty cooperation of all the commercial colonies. If the Boston merchants should act alone, they would merely throw increased business to their competitors in Rhode Island or New York. In December 1767 Providence adopted a nonconsumption agreement, and Newport followed a little later. The other commercial centers were in no hurry to act.

In the spring of 1768 the Boston merchants agreed to a general nonimportation plan, provided the merchants elsewhere would join with them, but the Philadelphians refused their consent. As a result the plan for a general, intercolonial policy of nonimportation had to be abandoned. For the time being it seemed that effective opposition would collapse.

In the meantime the Boston political leaders had the satisfaction of compelling the newly established Board of Customs Commissioners to leave town and to take refuge in Castle William down the harbor. Shortly after this disturbance word came that the ministry had decided to station troops in Boston to exercise a restraining influence on the population there. If the Cabinet had been consciously working to create more ill feeling than already existed, it could not have devised a more effective means. The idea of British troops in town was opposed by thousands, where the Townshend Acts had aroused perhaps a few hundred. British officials thus played directly into the hands of colonial leaders.

The first important result of this news was a revival of the nonimportation policy. In August 1768 the Boston merchants signed an unconditional agreement, binding themselves to import no British goods, with the exception of a few necessities, between January 1, 1769, and January 1, 1770. It appears that many of the signers were not merchants but shopkeepers, and of the merchants who signed, reports were current that they had taken the precaution of stocking up beforehand with goods enough to carry them through the lean year. On October 1, 1768, the New York merchants adopted a nonimportation agreement, while Philadelphia held off until March 1769. But at last, by the fall of 1769, some sort of nonimportation plan had been adopted in every colony but New Hampshire.

It is at first sight rather surprising to find approval for a nonimportation measure in Virginia, the leading plantation colony, in which the only merchants were English and Scotch agents whose business had hardly been affected by the Townshend duties. As a matter of fact, the merchants had nothing to do with the project; the active leaders were George Washington, Patrick Henry, Richard Henry Lee, Thomas Jefferson, and Peyton Randolph. Under their direction, in May 1769, members of the dissolved House of Burgesses adopted a nonimportation agreement. It met with general approval, except among the merchants. The promoters of this nonimportation movement in Virginia were the leaders of the newer political groups in the piedmont, men who for one reason or another were opposed to the older political machine. Their economic interests had not been seriously affected by the Townshend Acts, and they would hardly have felt the new taxes. It may be that they joined the commercial colonies in this form of protest simply because they disapproved of the principle of British taxation. It is also possible that in the Townshend Acts they found a political issue which they could turn to account.

In the commercial colonies recalcitrant merchants who refused to join in the nonimportation movement were first blacklisted, then threatened, tarred and feathered, and even exiled. The leaders effectively enforced their program. In Massachusetts, in 1769, English imports fell off nearly 50 percent. In New York the agreement was well enforced, and imports from England were practically stopped. In Philadelphia the record was somewhat less satisfactory, but there is no doubt that commerce suffered.

Massachusetts Circular Letter

The campaign against the Townshend Acts was accompanied by both formal protests and by sharp statements defining American political theory. In the circular letter which he prepared for the House of Representatives in Massachusetts Samuel Adams proclaimed

> . . . that in all free states the constitution is fixed, and as the supreme legislative derives its power and authority from the constitution, it cannot overleap the bounds of it without destroying its own foundation . . . that it is an essential, unalterable right, in nature, engrafted into the British constitution, as a fundamental law, and ever held sacred and irrevocable by the subjects within the realm, that what a man has honestly acquired is absolutely his own, which he may freely give, but cannot be taken from him without his consent.

According to Adams the Americans looked upon the Townshend Acts as "infringements of their natural and constitutional rights."

The constitutional doctrine of the circular letter was in direct contradiction to the principle of the Declaratory Act. If the Americans should choose to stand irrevocably upon one and the British upon the other, a clash was inevitable. Evidently Lord Hillsborough, Secretary of State for the Colonies, realized this danger when he ordered the House of Representatives in Massachusetts to rescind its vote for approving and transmitting the letter to the other colonies. By a vote of 92 to 17 the House refused to follow his orders. Thereupon Governor Bernard declared the House dissolved.

John Dickinson

Among other famous protests against the alleged right of parliamentary taxation, those of John Dickinson, a young lawyer of Philadelphia, should be given a prominent place. Published in the *Pennsylvania Chronicle* under the heading "Letters from a Farmer," they constituted an impressive exposition of American constitutional theory. Dickinson was particularly vehement in attacking the British order which suspended the Assembly of New York. This colony, he wrote, had been punished "in a manner pernicious to American freedom, and justly alarming to all the colonies." If Parliament could order the indefinite suspension of an American legislature, Americans had no rights which were safe from British aggression. As for parliamentary taxation, Dickinson flatly denied the power of Parliament to levy any taxes whatever, external or internal, upon the Americans. Evidently Dickinson had never read the charter of his own colony on this point.

Conservatives *v.* Radicals

Another American Victory

In 1770 Parliament repealed all the Townshend taxes except the threepenny duty on tea. At this time Lord Hillsborough explained to the colonial governors that the Cabinet "entertained no design to propose or consent to the laying of any further taxes on America for the purpose of raising a revenue." This announcement was an abandonment, practically, of Grenville's policy of raising revenue in the colonies and also of the principle of the Declaratory Act. Hillsborough's purpose was to restore the situation which had existed before 1763. But the controversy over taxation had generated forces which prevented any restoration of former conditions. By 1770 a group of radical leaders had come into power in the colonies, leaders who did not shrink at the suggestion of independence. They had risen to power by opposing British policy. Acceptance of Hillsborough's plan of reconciliation, therefore, would threaten their plans with ruin.

Two Schools of Thought

Between the end of the nonimportation controversy in 1770 and the dispute over the Tea Act in 1773, there were two contradictory currents in the history of the colonies. The more conspicuous of these was the determined effort of the radical leaders to keep the Anglo-American dispute alive. The other was the effort made by the conservatives to restore good feeling and to forget the unpleasantness caused by the Grenville and Townshend schemes of taxation. The contests over British policy had separated the radical from the conservative elements; hence by the end of 1770 the party alignment in the colonies had become fairly clear. In the commercial colonies the conservatives included some professional politicians—that is, the royal officials; many other officeholders dependent upon them; nearly all the merchants; and a considerable portion of the rural population. The radicals included a few merchants; many lawyers, shipworkers, and other artisans in the towns; certain newspaper publishers; and the advocates of independence. In 1770 the radicals seem to have been inferior in numbers to the conservative group, but they succeeded in making an impression inversely proportioned to their numerical strength.

Samuel Adams, who won the fame of bringing the dispute to a definite climax, was by temperament a crusader. The son of a politician, he was brought up in the midst of the political quarrels of the 1730's and 1740's, and in early life he developed an active hatred of England. After graduating from Harvard he tried his hand first at the law, then at business. In the meantime he entered politics by way of the Boston Caucus Club, the organization that controlled town meetings and managed elections, and held various offices in Boston. More and more he devoted himself to his one real interest—politics. In the controversy over the Sugar Act in 1764 he had taken such an important part that he was rewarded with a place in the House of Representatives, where he immediately became a leader.

In New York the radicals included the unfranchised elements together with some men who for one reason or another had fallen out with the local ruling aristocracy. In Pennsylvania the radicals were the workingmen in Philadelphia, with leaders from the upper classes, such as Charles Thomson, and the dissatisfied farmers in the western counties. In Virginia they were the piedmont planters, such as George Washington and Thomas Jefferson, together with the lawyers who worked with them, such as Patrick Henry. These Virginia radicals were men of larger property interests than many of their associates in the other colonies.

Many colonial leaders had acquired a chronic suspicion of the British government so that the mere repeal or moderation of tax laws failed to satisfy them. They felt the weight of the British imperial system so keenly that they would not think of reconciliation on the basis of the old order. When public opinion threatened to become quiet and indifferent, they kept it active and alert. Sometimes the absence of specific issues hampered them seriously, but sometimes an event occurred which made their work easier.

One of these disturbances was the Boston Massacre of March 5, 1770. Late in the summer of 1768 British troops had been sent to Boston to uphold the authority of the new Board of Customs Commissioners. The radicals hated the troops and complained constantly of their presence. Because of these protests, the governor had the General Court meet in Cambridge instead of in Boston. For a year and a half the troops had remained in town without becoming involved in any disturbance. Realizing the delicacy of the situation, the officers kept the privates under the strictest discipline. The Boston populace, on the other hand, was under no such restraint, and irrepressible individuals amused themselves by trying to find out how much abuse the redcoats would stand.

Boston Massacre

On March 2, 1770, some of the Boston ropemakers provoked an altercation with the soldiers on guard, and the resulting dispute developed into a kind of running skirmish, lasting off and on for three days. On the evening of March 5 a much larger crowd gathered, and the dispute became serious. Led by a Negro sailor, Crispus Attucks by name, part of the crowd set upon one of the sentries and handled him so roughly that he called for help. Captain Preston came out with a corporal's guard, but the mob became even more threatening. Suddenly one of the soldiers fired into the crowd, and in the excitement seven others followed. The result was five men killed and six wounded.

Instantly the town was in an uproar. The danger of an attack upon the troops was so serious that responsible citizens went on guard to prevent a small-scale war. Samuel Adams insistently demanded that the redcoats be sent out of town. After a series of dramatic interviews with Adams, Governor Hutchinson ordered both regiments down to the Castle William.

In considering the question of responsibility for the Massacre, it is well to consider the facts in connection with subsequent judicial proceedings. Captain Preston and his seven privates were placed on trial for murder, in a local Massachusetts court, before a local jury, in a community roused to fury over the casualties of the evening of March 5. Their lawyers were two prominent young radicals, Josiah Quincy and John Adams. It would be difficult to imagine a situation more unfavorable for the defendants. And yet in spite of these adverse factors Captain Preston and five of the privates were entirely acquitted, while the other two were convicted of manslaughter and let off with a merely nominal penalty. The evidence produced in court, in spite of the efforts of the prosecution and the desire of the jury to convict, placed the responsibility upon Crispus Attucks, one of the victims, and upon the Boston mob.

Another incident which served to inflame opinion was the burning of the *Gaspee* in 1772. The *Gaspee* was a vessel of the royal navy, employed off the Rhode Island coast in enforcing the trade laws. Lieutenant Dudingston, in command, stopped and searched all vessels entering Narragansett

Bay. According to the charges of the merchants, he seized vessels on insufficient evidence. Be that as it may, he was probably the most hated man anywhere within reach of Rhode Island. On June 9 the *Gaspee* ran aground a few miles from Providence. At night eight boats put out from the town, full of armed men. They reached the *Gaspee* before daybreak, boarded her, and took possession. They made a prisoner of Dudingston, who had been wounded in the encounter, and then set the crew ashore. These formalities completed, they burned the *Gaspee* to the water's edge. The British government appointed a special commission to investigate the affair, but, in spite of the fact that almost everybody in Providence knew who the guilty parties were, not a man could be convicted, and no one was ever punished.

Burning the "Gaspee"

At about the same time, in Massachusetts, a dispute was started over the plan of the British government to pay salaries of the judges and other officials out of the royal treasury. The radicals vigorously opposed this policy; they realized that if it should be generally adopted, the local legislatures would lose the means of influencing royal governors.

Conservative Reaction

The three years following the collapse of the nonimportation movement were years of unusual economic prosperity, and active opposition to British authority almost came to an end. The merchants were eager to make up for profits lost during the Townshend disputes. Moreover, the conservative classes generally looked with horror at the steady development of radicalism among the unprivileged classes. To their minds the danger of mob control, or even a government managed by the "lower" classes, had become a serious menace. Prominent officials wrote of the spread of "levelling principles," or of the growing importance of the "lower sort of people." As one of them put it, a gentleman no longer met "what used to be called common civility." Among the merchants this sort of thing took the place of complaints against the British government.

The repeal of the Stamp Act and the Townshend duties had removed the fears of the merchants, and they had been delighted when the import duty on molasses was reduced to a penny a gallon. The threepenny duty on tea still remained, but for the three years preceding the famous "Tea Party" there was little complaint against it. The British government had gone far in arranging a satisfactory settlement. The conservatives were well pleased. Beginning with the fall of 1770, a pronounced conservative reaction set in. One manifestation of it has already been mentioned, namely, the collapse of the nonimportation movement. The merchants were already restive under Adams's leadership; when they saw their chance they dropped him entirely.

This reversion to a more conservative course is delightfully portrayed in the case of John Rowe, whose diary records his own growing sense of the dangers of radicalism. Rowe was a substantial Boston merchant with an interest in politics, a fondness for fishing, and a love of social festivities. Inclined to be cosmopolitan in his associations and friendships, he was in close touch with everybody from Governor Hutchinson to Samuel Adams.

As a result there was not a better informed man in all New England. He had been one of the most active leaders in the nonimportation movement, but as it became more violent he became alarmed. The leaders could continue to place him on their committee of enforcement, but they could not prevent him from going fishing on the days of their most important meetings. His change of attitude in this issue was typical of many of his class.

Rowe found a general desire to forget the dispute with England, and, if he and those like him had their way, cordial relations would have been restored. In June 1770, for example, Rowe and a group of prominent Bostonians spent the evening at "Province House," drinking the king's health. "A great many gentlemen attended this Public Mark of Loyalty to his majesty & Family." Again, on January 18, 1771, the queen's birthday, Rowe spent the evening at a very elaborate celebration, with "a very grand assembly," including the governor, lieutenant governor, officers of the royal army and navy, in fact as he put it, "all the best people in town a general coalition so that harmony, peace, & friendship will once more be established in Boston."

If this conservative turn had been confined merely to social affairs, it would have had little historical significance, but it was manifested in other directions. In the Council, or upper house in the General Court, a number of members began to work with the governor, something they had not done since 1765. Prominent politicians were deserting the radicals and going over to the other side.

Radicals also lost ground in the House of Representatives. In the fall of 1770 Samuel Adams and his party met defeat for the first time in more than four years. Then in the elections of 1771 the conservatives secured a majority. Adams's party split into fragments, and some of his most active supporters either dropped temporarily out of politics, as John Adams did, or went over to the conservative side, after the manner of John Hancock. The latter was peculiarly successful in keeping himself in the front rank of the dominant group; in 1773 he was again working with Samuel Adams. In New York, the years from 1770 to 1773 were exceptionally quiet and peaceful. The lower classes were prosperous and contented, the Sons of Liberty were no longer heard of, and relations with England were cordial. There, as in Massachusetts, the dispute seemed to be over. Similar conditions prevailed in the other colonies.

Samuel Adams

The radical politicians, however, would not accept defeat. Instead of welcoming the conservative reaction, they set themselves to check it and to restore the condition of tense excitement and bitterness which had prevailed before 1770. To Samuel Adams the re-establishment of good feeling was an unmixed calamity. After it started he spent the busiest three years of his life in an effort to combat it, and the war that came was a tribute to his success. The brighter the conservative prospects appeared, the more vigorously he worked. By means of newspaper articles, political campaigning, and direct personal appeals, he sought to bring back the heated emotions of Stamp Act times. His purpose was to inspire others with his own bitter hatred of Great Britain.

Adams was successful in this campaign. Signs of renewed unrest soon became visible. But propaganda alone is never enough to bring on revolution. An organization is needed to complete the process. The leaders must have something by means of which they can guide and direct the opinion they have created into the proper channels. Adams realized this need of organization, and by September 1771 he was considering plans for it. He aimed at a system of committees in all the colonies, so tied together by common aims and leadership that they could operate as a single unit. The Sons of Liberty had given him the idea in 1766.

Committees of Correspondence

After discussing the project with his friends, Adams picked the fall of 1772 to carry his plan into effect. He proposed the appointment of a committee of correspondence to keep in touch with similar committees to be appointed in other towns. At a second meeting held a few days later, the Boston committee was appointed. The next step was to induce the leading towns in the province to follow suit, and by July 1773 almost every town in Massachusetts had its committee of correspondence. The radical leaders in Massachusetts had created a political party devoted to the cause of American rights. Accounts of this activity were reported to radicals elsewhere, particularly to Richard Henry Lee of Virginia. In March 1773, under the leadership of Patrick Henry and Richard Henry Lee, the House of Burgesses of Virginia appointed a committee to correspond with other American legislatures. Within the next twelve months eleven of the thirteen colonies—all but Pennsylvania and North Carolina—had legislative committees of correspondence at work. The framework of the radical organization was thus enlarged to include most of the colonies.

To consolidate this new political party, the leaders began to talk about an intercolonial convention similar to the Stamp Act Congress. Writing in April 1773, Thomas Cushing of Massachusetts reported to Arthur Lee of Virginia, then in London: "Some imagine if the colonies are not soon relieved, a congress will grow out of this measure." And in the following October Governor Hutchinson of Massachusetts wrote: "They give out openly that they must have another Convention of all the Colonies."

During the short period from the spring of 1770 to the spring of 1773, no one could tell which of the two currents in American thought and opinion—radical or conservative—would prevail. Samuel Adams in Massachusetts, John Morin Scott in New York, Richard Henry Lee in Virginia, and Christopher Gadsden, one of Adams's friends in South Carolina, were all vigorously at work on the radical side; on the other were many less conspicuous but wealthy and influential leaders. As we look back on the situation, it is easy to see that Adams and his associates were aided by a growing conviction in the minds of the rank and file of the Americans that they no longer needed the help of the British government. The radicals were allied with the stronger cause.

Chapter 7

THE BREAK WITH GREAT BRITAIN

At the beginning of 1773 it would have been difficult for any observer to tell which of the two political currents, radical or conservative, would become dominant. Then new developments brought drastic changes, and by the spring of 1775 the thirteen colonies were in open rebellion against the British government. The war began in Massachusetts, so events there need careful examination. Trouble started with the Tea Act of 1773.

The Tea Act and Its Results

In that year the British Cabinet was more concerned with problems in India than with the situation in North America. The East India Company was close to financial ruin. In an effort to help it, Lord North had Parliament pass a law under which the British government itself acquired more power in Indian affairs. As part of his program Lord North tried to give the East India Company a more profitable market for its tea. The company's warehouses were heavily stocked, having some 17,000,000 pounds in all. If a substantial portion of the amount could be turned into cash, the company might be saved from bankruptcy. Out of this situation came the Tea Act of 1773; passed without evil intent toward the North American colonies, it had important and unforeseen repercussions.

The Tea Act

The Tea Act permitted the East India Company itself to export tea directly to the colonies and to establish branch offices there, thus giving it a monopoly of the tea business in America. Hitherto the Company had been required by law to sell to English merchants, who in turn sold to American importers. The new law eliminated both the English and the American wholesale dealers, two sets of middlemen. The American consumer would henceforth pay only two profits, one to the local shopkeeper, the other to the company. In addition, the company received back from the Treasury the tariff duties paid when the tea was imported into England. The only tax which the Americans would pay was the threepenny duty imposed by the Townshend Acts of 1767 and continued in force when the other taxes were repealed.

These were the chief provisions of the law. There is an old legend that George III and his advisers favored the measure because it afforded an opportunity for trying the question with America. This statement was probably not the king's. He did, however, wish to continue some form of parliamentary taxation to uphold the principle of the Declaratory Act. Writing to Lord North after he received word of colonial protests against the Tea Act, the king declared: "I am clear there must always be one tax to keep up the right, and as such I approve of the Tea Duty." There was no need of trying the question. The chief complaints against the threepenny duty had come during the nonimportation movements, and after these ended in 1770 merchants in several of the colonies imported tea regularly and paid the duty without recorded protests. The government was not dependent upon subterfuge to inveigle the Americans into paying the tax.

Had North's measure been passed at any time before 1760 it might have attracted little attention. But in 1773 conditions were different; the people were keyed up to a high pitch of excitement. It was therefore easy to represent the Tea Act as a serious grievance. In the commercial colonies the basis of protest was the monopoly of the tea trade given to the East India Company. In Massachusetts the radical politicians made an issue of the threepenny tax; the leader in this campaign was Samuel Adams.

Opposition in Massachusetts

By 1773 Samuel Adams had definite opinions about taxation by Parliament. He believed that the colonial legislature was supreme in all matters of legislation and taxation pertaining to the colony. Parliament had no right to pass laws or to levy taxes for the colonies. This theory was the center of the talk about "no taxation without representation." The Americans had complained about the various schemes of taxation not so much because they were not represented in Parliament but because these taxes had been imposed by a body other than the local assembly.

Inspired by this feeling, Samuel Adams made up his mind that colonial rights must be put upon a solid, permanent basis. Just how to achieve this objective he had not decided. He could arouse in others the same state of mind for which he himself was noted, but it takes more than political emotionalism to arouse a people to rebellion. There was, of course, the possibility that rebellion would not be necessary. If the British government could be caught in such a predicament that it would pay any price in return for help, the *quid pro quo* might be made the formal guarantee of American rights—that is, complete, absolute, legislative autonomy.

In the summer of 1773 the opportunity came. Adams received a letter from Arthur Lee, agent for some of the colonies in England, to the effect that another general European war was imminent and that the situation might be used to compel the English government to grant the demands of American radicals. Adams knew enough English history to appreciate the value of the suggestion. It was exactly by this means, taking advantage of royal need, that Parliament had won its victories over the king. Adams hoped to force the British authorities to relinquish their assumed right to tax the colonies, in return for American help in this prospective war. Then the colonies could demand and get the guarantees they desired.

The Massachusetts Legislative Committee of Correspondence was summoned, to consider and to agree upon action concerning any requisitions that might be made in case of war. Adams himself wrote the call for the meeting. He urged the radicals to withhold all help until their rights were firmly established. And while Adams was urging all interested parties to present a united front to England, he insisted upon the necessity of avoiding any settlement based upon compromise. Adams hoped to compel the consignees—agents of the East India Company—to resign, but they refused. Thereupon the radicals voted that the tea should not be landed. On November 9, Samuel Adams wrote to Arthur Lee: "One cannot foresee events; but from all the observation I am able to make, my next letter will not be upon a trifling subject."

Boston Tea Party

Shortly before the tea arrived the consignees proposed a compromise plan whereby the offending commodity might be landed and stored, under guard of a town committee, until they could get orders from the company. This proposal the radicals rejected because it would involve payment of what Adams called "the tribute." On November 28 the tea ships arrived. The radicals refused to permit the cargoes to be landed, and Governor Hutchinson refused to permit the ships to clear for the return trip. By so doing he played directly into Adams's hands. The deadlock continued until December 16, when, under the law, the customs officials would be obliged to seize the tea for nonpayment of duty. At this point men disguised as Indians boarded the vessels and dumped the tea into the harbor.

Although the merchants resented the provision of the Tea Act which granted a monopoly to the East India Company, they probably would not have arranged for the "Tea Party." Samuel Adams seems to have been largely responsible for it. Certainly the objectionable cargoes were handled with less violence in other commercial centers. Even if Hutchinson's stubbornness prevented the consignees from letting it go back to England, as New York and Philadelphia consignees did, it might have been stored as it was in Charleston—not in damp cellars but in warehouses. In 1776 the Charleston tea was auctioned off for the benefit of the Revolutionary government. Because of the less extreme methods used in those other commercial centers, there were no coercive acts for them.

Samuel Adams looked upon the destruction of the tea as a brilliant victory, but not all Americans agreed with him. Benjamin Franklin, then serving as agent for the Massachusetts House of Representatives in England, wrote:

> I am truly concern'd as I believe all considerate Men are with you, that there should seem to any a Necessity for carrying Matters to such Extremity, as, in a Dispute about Publick Rights, to destroy private Property. . . . I cannot but wish & hope that before any compulsive Measures are thought of here, our General Court will have shewn a Disposition to repair the Damage and made Compensation to the Company.

Many of the Boston merchants sided with Franklin rather than with Adams. The conservative property owners and importers had no wish to see a revival of the mob spirit of 1765, nor could they see any gain in provoking British authorities into making drastic reprisals. Since 1770 the

The Port Act

British had been moderate and conciliatory and the conservatives were prepared to cooperate with them. As for the British Cabinet officials, they were placed in an uncomfortable situation. The "Tea Party" was a challenge to them. They were compelled either to make an ignominious surrender or to use force at a time when the radicals in Massachusetts were flushed with pride at the success of their demonstration.

North's first response was crushing. This was the Boston Port Act, to go into effect in June 1774. It provided for the transfer of both the capital and the customhouse from Boston to Salem and prohibited all commercial navigation in Boston harbor. The port would be reopened when the town paid the East India Company for the tea, valued at approximately £15,000. So intense was the feeling against Massachusetts that members of the House of Commons who had hitherto been outspoken in defense of the colonies voted for the bill.

More Coercive Acts

Next on the program of retribution was the Act for the Impartial Administration of Justice, providing for the trial of civil and military officials for capital offenses. The purpose was to protect British officials who might become involved in difficulties in America. If a fair trial could not be secured in the colony, the defendants might be tried in England. Another measure made important changes in the system of government for Massachusetts. Henceforth the council was to be appointed by the king, according to the practice in all other royal colonies; it will be recalled that the charter of 1691 had given the General Court power to elect the councilors. Next the Massachusetts Government Act provided that jurors would be chosen by the sheriffs. Then the Government Act prohibited all town meetings, except one each year for the election of town officers, without the permission of the governor. Governor Hutchinson was removed from office, and his place was given to General Thomas Gage.

One more measure adopted by Parliament in 1774, habitually but mistakenly grouped with the Coercive Acts, was the Quebec Act. It had nothing to do with North's plan for punishing the Bostonians. Its purpose was to remedy certain defects in the Proclamation of 1763. The boundaries of Quebec were extended to the Ohio River, with the proviso that no rights previously granted were to be affected by the change. This measure automatically removed the prohibition against settlement in the region, but at the same time it placed the territory under Canadian control. Here is to be found one basis of American resentment against the law. The Act also guaranteed to the French Catholic subjects the right to worship as they pleased and arranged for the trial of civil cases in accordance with the principles of French rather than English law. With reference to government, there was to be a royal council but no elective assembly. Here were additional grounds of complaint. Extreme Protestants objected to any sign of toleration for Roman Catholics, while the provision for lawmaking was regarded as tyrannical.

If Parliament had purposely planned to drive the colonies out of the

Empire, it could have found no better instrument than the Boston Port Act. The law spelled ruin for the second largest port in North America. The shipyards, ropewalks, docks, and warehouses would become nothing but historical curiosities. If Parliament could legislate people out of their living in such fashion, American rights were a mere fiction. Hitherto there had been doubt as to the wisdom of carrying opposition to England to extremes. After the Port Act much of this doubt disappeared.

Plans of Opposition

In their plans for independence, the Massachusetts radicals needed an issue on which they could appeal to the other colonies for help. The issue was furnished by Lord North in his coercive policy. American leaders immediately started to work for the adoption of an all-inclusive nonintercourse agreement, something so complete and far-reaching that all trade with Great Britain, both import and export, could be stopped. The Massachusetts Committee of Correspondence laid the proposal before legislative leaders in other colonies. Realizing the desirability of haste, so that action might be taken before popular animosity should have a chance to cool, Samuel Adams expressed the hope that nonimportation agreements might be made at once, without waiting for a congress. A silversmith of Boston, Paul Revere, carried the letters to New York and Philadelphia.

The First Continental Congress

Political leaders in other colonies realized the dangerous implications in Lord North's coercive program, but they were not prepared to adopt a general nonimportation policy. Most of them agreed that the situation called for a clear statement of American rights and for action to uphold these rights. But instead of urging a nonimportation policy upon their respective legislatures, as Adams had requested them to do, they advocated an American congress. There was difference of opinion as to the best method of getting results, but there was also widespread agreement on the necessity of making common cause with Massachusetts. A convention at Philadelphia resolved that the Boston Port Act was "unconstitutional, oppressive to the inhabitants of that town, [and] dangerous to the liberties of the British colonies. . . ." The same convention declared that Boston was "suffering in the common cause of America." These Pennsylvanians advocated a congress of all the colonies. They also appointed a committee to collect money for the relief of suffering Bostonians.

In New York a similar convention declared that any attempt to invade the liberties of one colony "is immediately an attack upon the liberties and constitution of all the British colonies." This body characterized the Port Act as "highly unconstitutional, and subversive of the commercial rights of the inhabitants of this continent." The New York group favored a congress. A meeting in Virginia took substantially the same action. Lord North's attempt to punish the Bostonians gave a powerful impetus to the cause of colonial union.

During the summer of 1774 the twelve colonies from New Hampshire to South Carolina appointed delegates to an American, or continental, congress.

Delegates to Congress

Georgia was not represented. Because the proposed gathering was irregular, if not extralegal, there was no uniformity in the method of selecting the representatives. In one case—that of Rhode Island—the appointment was made legally and officially by the whole legislature. In some others the elective branch acted alone, and in some cases special committees made the selection.

To a certain extent the purposes of the promoters of the Congress were revealed in the instructions which they drew up for the delegates. In the majority of cases the delegates were ordered to obtain redress of American grievances and to establish American rights on a secure, permanent footing. Four of the colonies—New Hampshire, Massachusetts, Pennsylvania, and Virginia—expressly told their representatives to work for the restoration of harmony and good will in their relations with England. In only two cases—Maryland and Virginia—was there any direct reference to the primary purpose of the Congress, that of working out a nonimportation agreement. Some of the delegates came with full power to act; some were authorized merely to consult and advise with the other delegates; while those from New York and New Jersey came with no formal powers whatever.

The Congress was scheduled to begin its sessions on September 5, 1774, at Philadelphia. Many of the delegates had never been outside their own respective colonies before this time; for them the journey was a thrilling adventure. By September 1, twenty-five delegates had arrived at Philadelphia, and they all had dinner together. On the next day the Virginians came in. John Adams wrote that they "appear to be the most spirited and consistent of any." Two days later Adams dined with Mr. Joseph Reed, the lawyer, and a party of several delegates; "an elegant supper, and we drank sentiments till eleven o'clock." After the formal sessions began, Adams continued to dine out; Mr. and Mrs. Fisher "provided us the most costly entertainment; ducks, hams, chickens, beef, pig, tarts, creams, custards, jellies, fools, trifles, floating islands, whipped sillabubs, &c; &c. Parmesan cheese, punch, wine, porter, beer, &c." One of the delegates from Connecticut, Silas Deane, wrote to his wife that he was "engaged to dine out every day this week."

These brief excerpts from the records do not sound like the early stages of revolution. Nevertheless, the round of dinners should not be ignored. Most of the delegates were strangers to each other, and they needed to get acquainted. Furthermore they had to reconcile local differences and overcome local jealousies. These preliminaries were conducted under favorable auspices in the comfortable homes of wealthy Philadelphians.

When the Congress opened there were two factions among the delegates, one radical, one conservative. The radicals wanted independence; the others hoped to keep the colonial status, but under new and adequate guarantees of American rights. Although the two groups were almost equal in numerical strength, the radicals had a slight advantage. They selected the meeting place, and they chose the secretary, Charles Thomson, a Philadelphia radical who had failed to secure an election as delegate.

The aim of the Massachusetts leaders, Samuel Adams, John Adams, Elbridge Gerry, and Robert Treat Paine, was to win approval of the Boston plan of nonintercourse. They were actively supported in this policy by the Virginians and by Christopher Gadsden of South Carolina. But the Bostonians encountered opposition because of their extreme radicalism, and they had to proceed with unusual care. John Adams has left an interesting account of their methods. "We have had numberless prejudices to remove here. We have been obliged to keep ourselves out of sight, and to feel pulses and sound depths, to insinuate our sentiments, designs, and desires by means of other persons, sometimes of one province, sometimes of another." A conservative member from Maryland put the situation somewhat more bluntly: "Adams and his crew, and the haughty sultans of the South, juggled the whole conclave of the delegates."

Suffolk Resolves

Early in its sessions Congress approved a stirring set of resolutions on American rights, known as the "Suffolk Resolves." This declaration had been drawn up in Boston, under the supervision of Dr. Joseph Warren. Paul Revere carried the document to the Continental Congress. Its formal approval transformed it from expression of local opinion into an American political creed. After denouncing the recent acts of Parliament as an "unparalleled usurpation of unconstitutional power," the Resolves urged that the new laws be rejected "as the attempt of a wicked administration to enslave America." Then the Resolves advised the people to meet for military training at least once a week and announced that they would act on the defensive "so long as such conduct may be vindicated by reason and the principles of self-preservation, but no longer."

Galloway's Plan

Next the radicals defeated the Galloway Plan, the only constructive suggestion made by the conservatives. Joseph Galloway, a prominent lawyer of Philadelphia, proposed to safeguard American rights by means of a new basis of imperial union. His plan called for the continuation of the existing colonial governments for all local matters. For problems affecting two or more colonies, however, he proposed a chief executive to be appointed by the king and a legislative council to be chosen by the various colonial assemblies. This body would act in all matters in which Great Britain and the colonies, or the colonies as a whole, or any two or more colonies might be interested. Up to this point the Galloway Plan was in its main outlines similar to the Albany Plan of 1754. But there was a unique feature in Galloway's proposal which stamps him as a genius. The Grand Council was to have the standing of a branch of Parliament. Measures pertaining to the colonies might originate either in Parliament or in the Council, and the approval of both bodies was necessary before an act could become effective. Galloway's proposal had certain obvious advantages: it provided for the badly needed central authority, but at the same time it preserved the colonial legislatures. Parliament would lose its power to impose an unsatisfactory law upon the colonies. The Congress set apart a day for discussing the plan and then, after discussion, defeated it by the vote of a single colony.

The third major action of Congress was the adoption of the Continental Association. This recommended that after December 1, 1774, all imports of British goods should cease and that, with few exceptions, there be no more purchases from Great Britain. After September 10, 1775, all exports to England and to the West Indies were to stop. The Congress advised every county, city, and town throughout the colonies to appoint committees with authority to blacklist all who refused to comply with the Association. Then, on October 14, the Congress approved a statement of American rights: the "Declaration and Resolve." The Congress sent letters to the people of Quebec, to the people of Great Britain, and to the officials in England. Taken together, the state papers prepared by this First Continental Congress are an excellent exposition of the American theory of government.

The Association

Although some of the delegates brought with them instructions to restore normal relations between the colonies and England, the adoption of the Suffolk Resolves might have been interpreted as a threat of war. It is difficult to determine how far the delegates went in talking about the possibility of rebellion and war, but they gave some consideration to the subject. In reporting progress to his friends at home, Samuel Adams wrote:

Possibility of War

> I have been assured, in private conversation, with individuals, that, if you should be driven to the necessity of acting in the defence of your lives or liberty, you would be justified by their constituents, and openly supported by all the means in their power.

On the other hand, John Adams seemed to find a somewhat different emphasis in talks upon this delicate subject of possible war:

> If it is a secret hope of many, as I suspect it is, that the congress will advise to offensive measures, they will be mistaken. I have had opportunities enough, both public and private, to learn with certainty the decisive sentiments of the delegates and others upon this point. They will not, at this session, vote to raise men or money, or arms or ammunition. Their opinions are fixed against hostilities and rupture, except they should become absolutely necessary; and this necessity they do not yet see. They dread the thoughts of an action.

Early in October 1774 the Congress heard reports that General Gage was extending fortifications in Massachusetts. The Congress sent him a formal warning that the delegates approved the conduct of the Bostonians in opposing British laws, and they called the general's attention to "the determined resolution of the colonies, for the preservation of their common rights, to unite in their opposition to those acts." Then they urged Gage to consider carefully how his policy might "irritate & force a free people, however well disposed to peaceable measures, into hostilities . . . & may involve us in the horrors of a civil war." Then the Congress advised the

Bostonians to conduct themselves peaceably toward Gage and his troops "as far as can possibly be consistent with their immediate safety, and the security of the town."

In this same connection John Dickinson wrote that the Congress had taken so definite a stand as to compel Great Britain to modify her policy "or inevitably involve herself in a civil war." And he went on: "The first act of violence on the part of Administration in America, or the attempt to reinforce General Gage this winter or next year, will put the whole Continent in arms, from Nova Scotia to Georgia." Subsequently Joseph Galloway reported that after the official work of the Congress was finished, "the Republicans adjourned to a tavern in order to concert the plan which was necessary to be pursued by their party, throughout the Colonies for raising a military force." The majority of delegates were prepared to support Massachusetts in case she should suffer further at the hands of Great Britain, but they would not authorize an attack upon the British forces.

The Move toward War

In all the colonies there were committees of correspondence or similar bodies, prepared to enforce the Association, and they lost no time in going to work. Figures reported on the importation of British goods into America show a decline in 1775 of almost 97 percent. No British regulation of American trade had ever been as vigorously enforced as was this extra-legal Continental Association.

In adopting the Association, the Congress had hoped to move the British merchants to action, so that they would compel Parliament to repeal the coercive acts. The English merchants were keenly aware of this loss of American trade, and during the first few months of 1775 they urged Parliament to change its policy toward America. When Parliament met early in 1775, it was almost swamped with petitions from English businessmen, all urging moderation in the policy toward America. The Cabinet, however, did not act in time to prevent hostilities.

Tension in Massachusetts

While the Continental Congress was in session and afterward, the people in Massachusetts cut the remaining ties that bound them to the British system. They did this with comparative ease, and the transition from colony to commonwealth was soon almost complete. Towns held their meetings, regardless of the Act of Parliament prohibiting them; county conventions were held; and in October a provincial congress met. Under the directions of this body the towns raised and trained their militia, while the provincial congress itself appointed committees of safety and supply. Once aroused, the country towns were impatient at the delay and anxious to begin hostilities. Samuel Adams, however, hoped to throw upon General Gage the odium of making the first move, and during the winter he and other leaders held the towns in check.

By the end of 1774 British power had been almost divorced from Massachusetts. The new council had no influence, the old General Court had passed out of existence, and Governor Gage's authority did not reach beyond Boston and the British forces under his command. Even the courts of justice ceased to function. John Adams wrote: "Not a court of justice has sat since . . . September. Not a debt can be recovered, nor a trespass redressed, nor a criminal of any kind be brought to punishment." All contemporary reports reveal increasing tension between British officials and the local population.

Among the observers of this delicate situation was an officer of the British army whose diary is an excellent commentary on the situation. In January 1775 he reported an altercation between some of the officers and the town watch in Boston. General Gage ordered a court of inquiry. He was "much displeased" with the conduct of his officers, because he was "anxious to prevent just cause of complaint on the part of the townspeople." On January 30, 1775, the officer reported that the daily routine of the troops "is done with the utmost strictness, as the ferment among the people has by no means subsided. We have a free intercourse with the Country," he continued, "but the people are evidently making every preparation for resistance. They are taking every means to provide themselves with Arms."

General Gage

In these circumstances Gage had to keep his men ready for instant action. In February 1775 he began to send them on practice marches into the country with full arms and equipment. The people feared "that something particular is concealed under these movements, and there are always some persons appointed to Watch the motions and direction of the Troops." Although they were uneasy, the Bostonians and their neighbors made no attempt to interfere with the regular marches of the troops, but they never relaxed their watchfulness. "I am of opinion that, if once General Gage should lead his troops into the country," wrote Dr. Joseph Warren, "with design to enforce the late Acts of Parliament, Great Britain may take her leave, at least of the New-England colonies, and, if I mistake not, of all America."

Occasionally something happened to show how close the explosion was and how little would be needed to set it off. On March 6, 1775, the leaders in Boston arranged for a service in the Old South Church to commemorate the Boston Massacre. Dr. Warren was the orator of the day. Several British officers attended, ready to protest against any aspersions on the king's troops. The townspeople "certainly expected a Riot, as almost every man had a short stick, or bludgeon, in his hand." Both sides were looking for trouble, and a single blow might have started hostilities. The blow did not come, but the tension continued. During these tense days both Lord Dartmouth in England, Secretary of State for the Colonies, and General Gage in Boston became convinced, as Gage put it, "that, if a respectable force is seized, and a pardon proclaimed for all others, government will come off victorious." Gage therefore prepared to move against the radicals and so precipitated the crisis.

On April 14 the provincial congress of Massachusetts adjourned for a month. Gage, who had been watching proceedings carefully, felt that the time had come to arrest John Hancock and Samuel Adams, and incidentally to seize or destroy some of the military stores which the committee of supply had been collecting. Rumors of his proposed move were soon afoot, and on April 18 the local leaders sent out a hurried call for the provincial congress to reassemble. On this very same day General Gage ordered a detachment of troops to be ready at ten o'clock that night on the shore of the Charles River opposite Cambridge. This news was in circulation on the water front as early as two o'clock in the afternoon. That night Gage started his famous expedition on its way to Lexington and Concord. The countryside was warned by William Dawes and Paul Revere. The British failed to capture Hancock and Adams, but they did destroy supplies. Then, pursued by steadily increasing bands of "minute men," they retreated under fire to Boston. The long-expected war was on.

Lexington and Concord

The news was carried rapidly from place to place, reaching New York on Sunday, April 23, Philadelphia at five in the afternoon on April 24, Virginia April 30, Charleston May 8, and from all quarters came reports of a determination to stand by Massachusetts. On May 10, 1775, the Second Continental Congress assembled in Philadelphia. This meeting was not the result of the fighting at Lexington and Concord but of a resolution adopted at the First Continental Congress.

Although hostilities started in April, time was needed to enable the revolutionists in the different colonies to get possession of their provincial governments. In New York, for example, the provincial congress did not secure control until the end of May. In Virginia the complete break with the royal government did not come until October 1775. There was one curious illustration of the difficulty of transmitting news to outlying posts in the interior. At Fort Ticonderoga, New York, there was a small force of only forty-eight British troops. No report of the fighting at Lexington and Concord reached them. But the Revolutionary government in Connecticut sent a militia force under Benedict Arnold into Vermont, where it joined a handful of Vermonters under Ethan Allen. Leaving these forces in the woods, Allen rode casually up to the fort and asked the commanding officer to let him hire some of the British regulars to work on the lake. He got the men and by nightfall had them helplessly drunk. Then he demanded and received the surrender of the fort. Here the Americans found valuable stores of ammunition and twenty pieces of artillery.

Organizing for War

Any attempt to summarize the causes of a movement as complex as the American Revolution is bound to be unsatisfactory, and the conclusions are generally open to criticism at some point. Perhaps the most important single cause is the growth of the colonies, which gave them a steadily increasing sense of their own importance. This is especially true in connection with the constitutional development centering in the colonial legislatures. By 1760 the Americans had become politically self-sufficient, and any en-

Causes of the Revolution

croachment on the field of their legislatures was bitterly resented. Therefore the change in British policy with reference to colonial revenue ran counter to one of the main lines of colonial development. The formula of "no taxation without representation" was simply the objective statement of this feeling regarding the pre-eminence of the local assemblies. The commercial colonies were complaining of and opposing the customs service. American leaders wanted liberty—that is, complete autonomy for the colonial governments.

It is difficult to explain the Revolution in terms of geographical distance from England or in accordance with any theory of inevitability or in terms of the oppressive character of British policy. Point is given to this suggestion by the refusal of Nova Scotia to join the revolt. Here was a royal colony, inhabited by British subjects commercially in close touch with ports in New England. Cultural ties were close because during the 1760's settlers from Massachusetts and Connecticut had moved into Nova Scotia. Nova Scotia had been a victim of the Stamp Act, the Townshend Acts, and the Tea Act, but these measures inspired little if any talk of revolt there. When some of the recent arrivals from New England attempted to propagate radical doctrines they were driven out of the colony. The legislature at Halifax seems to have had a less exalted sense of its own importance than those of Massachusetts and Virginia, while political leadership in Nova Scotia was very conservative.

Chapter 8

MILITARY OPERATIONS AND THE FRENCH ALLIANCE

THE Americans appeared to be poorly prepared for the war which began on April 19, 1775. They lacked an effective central government, a navy, and a trained army. The Continental Congress met in May 1775, but the members had to learn how to conduct a war by the process of trial and error. On June 15, 1775, the Continental Congress appointed George Washington as commander in chief of the army. He did not reach Cambridge to take command of the American forces near Boston until July 3, 1775.

From Bunker Hill to Independence

Bunker Hill

A short time before his arrival, on June 17, American and British forces clashed in the first formal engagement of the war, the battle of Bunker Hill. American troops had occupied the lower of two hills on the Charlestown peninsula. On the two sides were the Mystic and the Charles Rivers. The narrow causeway connecting the peninsula with the mainland was so close to sea level that it was sometimes flooded. To the west were the hills of Somerville, commanding Charlestown, while Dorchester Heights commanded Boston. The British might have adopted any of several courses. By occupying the high ground at Somerville and Dorchester they could have compelled the Americans to evacuate the whole area of Boston. Or by placing a small force on the causeway they could have starved the Americans in Charlestown into surrender. Again they could try a frontal attack up the hill. In spite of the protests of his officers, General Gage decided upon this course.

Charles Francis Adams described the battle as "one of the most singular examples on record of what might be called the 'balancing of blunders' between opposing sides." Then, thanks to what he called "the superior capacity for blundering of the British commanders," the battle was actually a moral victory for the Americans. The Americans drove back two successive attacks; when the third came they had no more powder. The British lost heavily—1000 men—more than twice the number of American losses.

Washington's Problems

After the battle of Bunker Hill, Washington tried to transform his untrained forces into an army, but he encountered unexpected obstacles. In the course of two months he dismissed a colonel and two captains for cowardice and three more captains for other offenses; besides these, he had five other officers under arrest. By the end of August 1775, he wrote:

"I have made a pretty good slam among such kind of officers as the Massachusetts government abound in."

Discipline, or the lack of it, was only one of Washington's problems. Lack of supplies was even more serious.

> My situation is inexpressibly distressing [he wrote] to see the winter fast approaching upon a naked army, the time of their service within a few weeks of expiring, and no provision yet made for such important events. . . . The military chest is totally exhausted; the paymaster has not a single dollar in hand; the commissary general assures me that he has strained his credit, for the subsistence of the army, to the utmost. The quartermaster general is in precisely the same situation.

And most of the troops were close to mutiny.

Some of these difficulties resulted from civilian greed. The commander in chief was shocked by the willingness of businessmen to make money out of the army. Washington wrote about the evils of "speculators, various tribes of money makers, and stock jobbers of all denominations." With these troubles on his hands the General alternately prayed and cursed:

> Such a dearth of public spirit, and want of virtue, such stock-jobbing, and fertility in all the low arts to obtain advantages of one kind or another . . . I never saw before, and pray God I may never be witness to again. . . . Such a dirty, mercenary spirit pervades the whole that I should not be at all surprised at any disaster that may happen.

While Washington was trying to hold his own army together, he organized and sent off two expeditions for an attack upon Canada, one under Benedict Arnold against Quebec by way of the Maine wilderness, and the other under Richard Montgomery against Montreal by way of Lake Champlain. On December 3 Montgomery joined Arnold before Quebec, but the hardships of campaigning in that wild country had reduced their combined strength to 1000 men. In spite of heavy odds, on New Year's Day 1776, they attacked the city. Montgomery was killed, Arnold wounded, and the fight was lost. During the spring Congress sent reinforcements to Arnold, and on June 8, 1776, he risked another battle. But the Americans were again defeated and compelled to retreat to Lake Champlain.

Capture of Boston

During this same winter the situation at Boston remained unchanged. Washington had practically no powder and could not risk an attack upon the British. On the other hand, General Howe, who had succeeded Gage in command of the British forces in Boston, was so lacking in energy that he made no trouble for the Americans. In March 1776 Washington was able to break the deadlock. By this time he had received the artillery and supplies captured ten months earlier at Ticonderoga. He fortified Dorchester Heights, thereby making Boston untenable. On March 16 the British forces, accompanied by nearly 1000 Loyalists, evacuated the city and embarked for Halifax.

By the end of the first year of hostilities some of the major problems of the war were becoming clear. One weakness was lack of public support. Out of the total population of 2,500,000 people, not more than one third actively upheld the American side. Another third gave full support to the British, while the other third was indifferent. Even those who openly took the American side were none too eager to serve in the army. With at least 250,000 men of military age available in this group of professed friends of the Revolution, the American army could never count more than 90,000 with the colors. In 1779-80, the American forces dropped to a total of 45,000 men.

Debate on Independence

In spite of these discouragements the leaders of the Revolution found the logic of events pointing clearly toward independence. For a time the lack of numerical strength and the hesitant attitude of some Americans prevented the Congress from adopting this logical policy. At the beginning of the winter of 1775-76 not a single colony was ready officially to sanction a formal break with Great Britain and even in the following spring, after the British had left Boston, there was still vigorous opposition. From the beginning the Tories were determined to prevent a separation or, if that should prove impossible, to stave it off as long as possible. In that group were to be found not only former royal officeholders and the Anglican clergy but large numbers of conservative individuals: merchants, professional men, and others who saw more to lose in abandoning the empire than there was to gain in proclaiming independence.

The Loyalists were opposed by the organized radicals, men in charge of the committees of correspondence and provincial congresses; these extra-legal bodies had picked up the reins of government where they had been dropped by officials of the old order. Because these leaders controlled the machinery of government and the various organs of publicity, they were able to make a deeper impression than the conservatives. Furthermore, the course of events was working on their side. The efforts of the British government to suppress the rebellion led inevitably to acts which roused even moderate Americans to align themselves with the radicals.

To the growing sentiment in favor of separation a tremendous impetus was added by the publication of Thomas Paine's pamphlet, "Common Sense." Paine was somewhat like Voltaire in the clearness with which he phrased his obvious, self-evident criticisms of the established order. Although he was a recent arrival from England, Paine ridiculed the theory of kingship; he even made light of the English constitution. Then, appealing to that pride in the coming greatness of the country which characterized every true American, Paine pointed out the absurdity in having a whole continent controlled by a little island 3000 miles away. The pamphlet sold by the hundred thousand copies, and its effect was soon evident in the more determined stand taken by the promoters of independence.

The immediate problem was to win over the Continental Congress, where sentiment against independence was strong. The five middle colonies had instructed their delegates to oppose independence, and the winter had passed before a single government officially sanctioned the step. During May and June sentiment in behalf of independence developed rapidly. The radicals were able politicians, and arousing public sentiment was the work for which they were best trained. They did this by working through their customary agents, the local committees, and by bringing personal pressure upon their hesitant colleagues. One of the strong arguments used was the need of foreign help. Both union and independence were essential if such help were to be secured. On June 7, 1776, in compliance with instructions from his state, Richard Henry Lee made the motion "That these united colonies are, and of right ought to be free and independent states." Even then the conservative delegates, especially from the middle colonies, held back; they knew that public sentiment in their own states was still lagging far behind Virginia and New England. As a result the radicals had to agree to a delay of three weeks, although in the interim a committee was set to work on the form of a declaration. During this interval, opportunely for the advocates of independence, news came from England that King George III had arranged to buy the services of 20,000 German troops to be used in subduing the Americans. This policy aroused bitter resentment in America. On July 2 the Congress committed itself to a resolution of independence. On July 4 this resolution was approved by twelve states, New York being the one to stand out.

The Declaration

The document known as the Declaration of Independence was drawn up by a committee of Congress, although Thomas Jefferson did most of the work. Its purpose was to arouse enthusiasm for the cause. Even more effectively than Paine, Jefferson put into enduring phrases the convictions of the revolutionary party. Under his handling, thoughts which had long been the common property of the radicals were transformed into slogans for the nation. With the Declaration the country reached the climax toward which strict logicians like Samuel Adams had been pushing it for years. Ending as it did the lingering hopes of the moderates for a peaceful reconciliation, it forced them into the decision which they had hoped to avoid. Henceforth lines between Patriots and Loyalists were drawn more sharply, and opposition to the radicals was automatically transformed into treason to the country. In New York the Loyalist element was especially strong, and its hopes were continually buoyed up by promises of immediate and effective help from Great Britain. But on July 9, 1776, the New York provincial congress approved the Declaration of Independence, thereby creating at least the appearance of American unity.

Military Activities

During the three months after General Howe's evacuation of Boston the British were perfecting plans for a new campaign. These made New York the next scene of action. In broad outline the policy called for the separation of New England from the other colonies. Then New England could be starved into submission. After the campaign around Boston came to an end, Washington sent his troops on to New York. He arrived there in April 1776. Shortly before July 1, General Howe's transports appeared off Sandy Hook, followed by a second expedition in charge of his brother, Lord Howe. Actual fighting, however, did not begin until August. The delay was due to Lord Howe's attempt to bring about a reconciliation. But with the Declaration of Independence still new, the leaders were in no mood to consider peace on any terms that Howe could offer. When the Howe brothers once understood this, real operations were begun.

Battle of Long Island

General Howe was to capture New York City, while General Carleton was to come down from Canada and seize Lake Champlain, Lake George, and the upper Hudson. Howe's part of the work was not especially difficult. The British forces numbered nearly 25,000 men, well-trained and equipped and supported by a powerful fleet, while Washington was obliged to rely upon an ill-trained, poorly organized army of some 18,000. The American commander unwisely tried to protect New York by holding Brooklyn Heights on Long Island. With a superior navy this plan might have been feasible; without a fleet, the American forces ran a grave risk of being left in isolation on Long Island.

The battle of Long Island began on August 22, 1776. The British general, Sir Henry Clinton, landed on Long Island in the rear of the American army. In the first engagement the British captured a third of Washington's men. Then, on the night of August 29, thanks to the help of a light fog, the American commander and his men ferried from Brooklyn to Manhattan and so escaped from the trap. But superior British forces drove him from the city, and from that time until the end of the war the British retained possession of New York.

But the capture of New York was only part of the British plan of campaign for 1776. General Carleton moved south from Canada, following Arnold's troops. In this retreat Arnold revealed the extraordinary vigor and resourcefulness which stamped him as one of the ablest commanders in the American cause. Carleton succeeded in reaching Fort Ticonderoga, but instead of continuing the fight he turned his back to the Americans and returned to Canada. This part of the British campaign was a flat failure.

Washington's forces in the meantime were almost at General Howe's mercy. The American commander left New York and retreated to New Jersey. During this campaign in New Jersey the British found widespread Loyalist sentiment. Prepared to pay for their supplies with gold, the invaders had little difficulty in procuring the provisions and horses they needed. Washington's forces were steadily dwindling, and the Jersey population showed no inclination to enlist under him, but they were ready to join the British. The British commander offered full pardon to all the inhabitants who would take an oath of allegiance to the king, and nearly 3000 people availed themselves of the privilege. Had it not been for the atrocities committed by British and Hessian forces, there would have been an even more emphatic manifestation of loyalty.

Trenton and Princeton

The situation was bad for the Americans, and even Washington felt that if a new army could not be enlisted, "the game is pretty nearly up." And yet instead of yielding to discouragement, Washington determined to try the effect of a surprise attack.

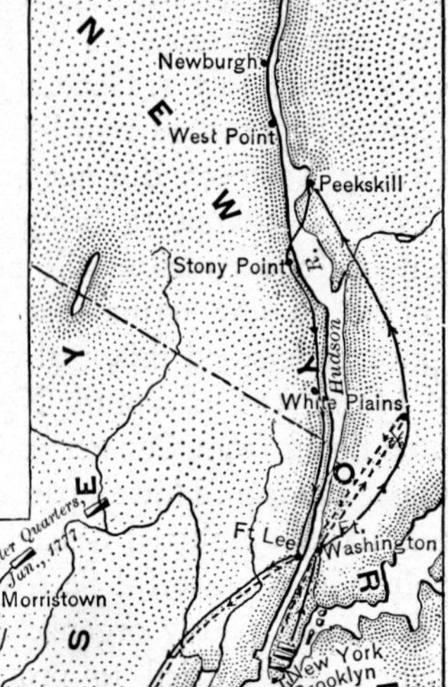

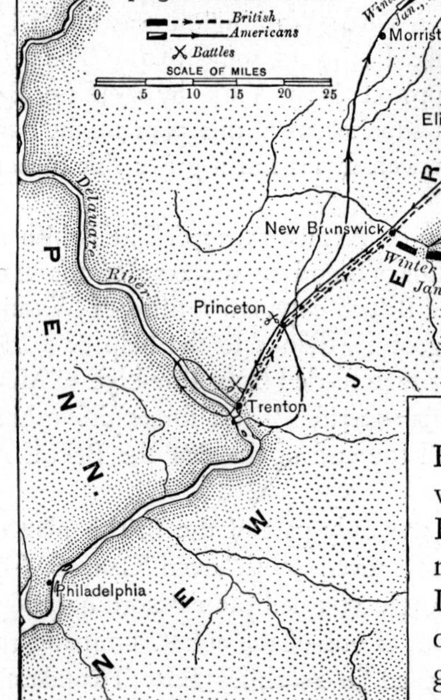

Map 4. Campaign in Middle States

He planned to recross the Delaware and strike at the center of Howe's line at Trenton. Christmas night was the time chosen. It proved to be so stormy that only one third of his army could get over and even that work consumed ten hours. Then, after a nine-mile march through the storm, his little division of 2500 men took the town completely by surprise. Unable to offer any effective defense, the enemy, mostly Hessians, were driven out of town and then compelled to surrender. Washington's troops took over 1000 prisoners.

This brilliant victory aroused the flagging interest of the Americans, and men began to re-enlist. On December 29 the American commander was able to cross the river again and occupy Trenton. Cornwallis hurried out from New York and, picking up a force from the British camp at Princeton, tried to capture Washington. Neatly outmaneuvering Cornwallis, Washington attacked the remaining British forces at Princeton, and then retired to spend the winter at Morristown, New Jersey, safe from the enemy but unfortunately subjected to almost every hardship except attack.

Washington's exploit at the beginning of winter deprived the British of their gains of the preceding summer and fall, with the exception of New York City. More important still, American courage and hope were renewed The Hessians, with a sensible eye to the advantages of being on the winning side, began to desert to the American standard. As for the Loyalists who had taken the oath of allegiance to the king, they found themselves left to the none too tender mercies of the American troops. Washington forced all who had taken the British oath to take a new one to the United States or retire to the British lines.

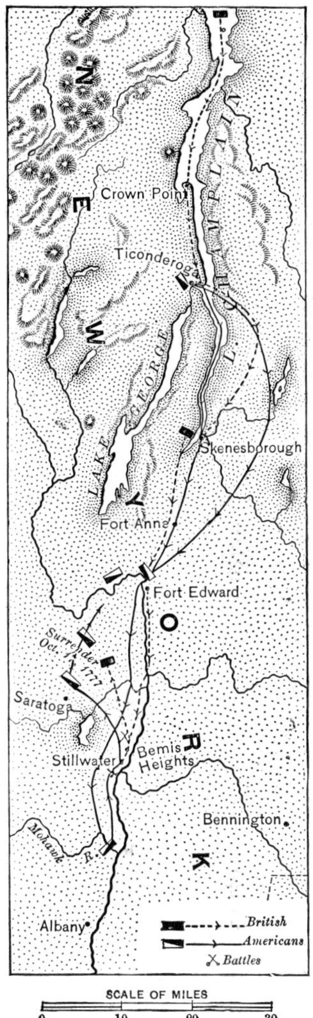

Map 5. Burgoyne's Campaign

Campaign against Albany

In the spring of 1777 the British authorities decided to renew their efforts to separate New England from the other states. This time they made preparations for a more effective campaign. General Burgoyne was picked to lead an army of 8000 men down from Canada along the traditional route past Crown Point and Ticonderoga to Albany. Colonel St. Leger was to take a force to Oswego and then work eastward through the Mohawk valley to meet Burgoyne at Albany. General Howe was to move his army of 25,000 men up the Hudson to join St. Leger and Burgoyne. These complex operations in the wilderness were to be directed by the War Office in London, 3000 miles distant.

Early in June Burgoyne started south, and in the course of a month he had reached and captured Ticonderoga. After leaving Ticonderoga the British troubles began. Because of the distance from Canada, Burgoyne was dependent upon the surrounding country for supplies. These, however, were removed as he advanced toward Fort Edward. As his wants became serious, he determined to send an expedition over to Bennington to seize American supplies stored there. This gave General John Stark, under a New Hampshire commission, an opportunity to make himself famous. The British and German raiding party was beaten, and New England farmers began to hurry toward New York, hoping to capture Burgoyne's whole force.

In July St. Leger started from Oswego, intending to march toward Albany by way of Fort Stanwix. He encountered various difficulties, though none were insuperable until he got almost within striking distance of a small force under Benedict Arnold. By a clever ruse on the part of Arnold, St. Leger's army was thrown into a panic and virtually disbanded. With a few followers the Colonel made his way back to Montreal. Thus the expected union of the two northern forces failed to take place, and Burgoyne's situation became dangerous. If he had been a free agent, with power to move his troops in accordance with his own needs, he would have retired to Fort Edward, but orders from England compelled him to push on toward Albany to join Howe.

And where was Howe? Nowhere near Albany but down on Chesapeake Bay moving toward Philadelphia from the south. Early in June he had received from the ministry the plan of the northern campaign without any specific instructions for himself. His own plan of capturing Philadelphia had been approved previously, so he took 14,000 men to carry out his own campaign. On August 25 he received the first intimation that he had been expected to join Burgoyne.

When Howe left New York for Philadelphia, Washington was within ten days' march of Albany. If he had taken his forces north, the combined American armies might have compelled Burgoyne to surrender in September. Instead of trying this expedient, Washington took his men south and tried to hamper Howe's march from Chesapeake Bay to Philadelphia. At Germantown he missed an opportunity to defeat the British. Howe in the meantime captured Philadelphia and secured control of the lower part of the Delaware River.

Burgoyne's Surrender

Burgoyne had been cornered at Saratoga, so he had to surrender. On October 14 he asked for terms, and three days later the "convention" was signed. According to the terms of this agreement, the British army was to go to Boston, and from there to England, under promise not to serve again. Congress, however, violated the agreement, and the troops were not allowed to go home. They remained for almost a year at Boston, and then were transferred to Virginia. By 1783 this British force had practically dissolved.

After indecisive battles near Philadelphia—at Brandywine and Germantown—Washington went into winter quarters at Valley Forge. Because of the shortcomings and incompetence of the commissary department, ample supplies were held up for want of transportation. As a result Washington's 3000 men almost starved. The surprising thing is that they endured as much as they did. Perhaps the absence of mutiny or absolute disintegration of the army can be explained by the continuous change of regiments, as one short-term enlistment gave way to another. But in spite of the difficulties, Baron Steuben used the winter to give the men something which many had never received before—regular army training.

The American commander was fortunate in having the advice and assistance of several other experienced soldiers from Europe. The young Marquis de Lafayette came to America before his own country entered the war and served on Washington's staff. More important than Lafayette were two officers from Poland, Count Pulaski and Thaddeus Kosciusko, who gave their services to the task of building an army in America. Washington was able to stand guard over the British in New York and to prevent them from gaining control of any more territory in the north.

Valley Forge

The victory at Saratoga was not the only important success won by the Americans. In 1778 and 1779 there were victories in the West which gave the United States a valid claim to the whole Northwest Territory. This military success was the logical outcome of the westward movement itself. As early as 1768 Daniel Boone in Kentucky and James Robertson in Tennessee were laying the foundations of new states, although these settlements did not grow to maturity until after the war. In 1775 other pioneers had laid the foundations of a new colony south of the Ohio, to be known as Transylvania. Others planned to found still another new colony east and northeast of Transylvania, to be known as Westsylvania. In 1780 Robertson moved on still farther west in Tennessee and settled Nashborough, or Nashville as it came to be called.

Clark in the West

In these cases, as in all others, the threat of white settlements aroused the Indians, and the British were only too glad to encourage them in attacks on the frontier. To put an end to this danger, George Rogers Clark determined to carry the war into the West. Under a commission granted by Virginia, Clark raised a small force of volunteers, all frontiersmen, with a sprinkling of outlaws who could have struck terror into any community. In the spring of 1778 he captured Kaskaskia. The French residents were well disposed to the Americans and aided them in getting control of the next objective, Vincennes. This was captured in 1779.

Alliance with France

The American success at Saratoga ended the British hope of separating New England from the other states. It also had important consequences in the field of diplomacy and foreign affairs. The Americans had actually beaten a British army in the field. This victory convinced the skeptical officials of the French government that England could be defeated and so encouraged the French to come openly to the support of the United States. French help in turn proved to be one of the decisive factors in winning the war.

French Help

In order to understand the willingness of France to encourage rebellion and representative government, it is necessary to go back to the Peace of Paris of 1763. Formerly the greatest power on the Continent, France had been beaten, stripped of most of her empire, and humiliated. The war was hardly over when French leaders began to think of revenge, and reports of growing dissatisfaction in the American colonies suggested the means.

France might encourage the Americans to rebel and so make serious trouble for her English enemy. With this idea in mind Choiseul, French minister for foreign affairs, sent over a number of investigators to report on conditions in America. They furnished information about fortifications, artillery, topography, depth of harbors and rivers, and the number and conditions of roads—in other words the essential information for an invading army.

When the American war started, Vergennes was the French foreign minister. He too was glad to make trouble for England. The most important reports to Vergennes concerning Anglo-American relations came not from agents in America but from Baron de Beaumarchais. In 1775 Beaumarchais was in London on a secret diplomatic mission for the French government. At the British capital he fell in with Arthur Lee of Virginia, still acting as agent for his own colony and at the same time representing the Continental Congress. Lee convinced Beaumarchais that the Americans could win their war, and Beaumarchais saw a fine opportunity for France to crush England. He urged Vergennes to give secret help to the Americans.

In the latter part of 1775 Vergennes sent an unofficial agent to America. Without giving specific pledges to the Americans, this agent assured the members of Congress that France was well disposed toward them. He evidently gave the impression that they might count on some assistance from France. More important still, he intimated that France had no plans for recovering control of Canada or Louisiana.

Some time afterward, probably in December 1775, Vergennes urged the French king to help the American cause. "England is the natural enemy of France," so Vergennes wrote, "an enemy greedy, ambitious, unjust, and false." Therefore it would be desirable to encourage the Americans to make all possible trouble for this enemy. At first help could be given surreptitiously; then in case the Americans should win any impressive victories, France could come openly to their assistance. Maurepas, the chief minister, went even further than Vergennes. He advocated an open offensive against England "to strengthen France, to weaken England, and to secure peace on the Continent, which was constantly disturbed by English intrigues and English money."

Vergennes submitted his arguments for helping America to the king of Spain, and although the Spanish minister for foreign affairs was not wholly in favor of giving encouragement to rebellion in America—Spain had a large empire there—nevertheless the Spanish authorities were ready to assist France in making trouble for England. In May 1776, the two governments agreed that each should advance the sum of 1,000,000 livres ($200,000) to help the Americans.

In December 1775, as a result of hints from France, the Congress appointed two committees to negotiate with foreign governments and to take

Silas Deane

charge of foreign trade. In March 1776, Congress commissioned Silas Deane to go to France in the dual capacity of commercial agent and secret diplomatic envoy. Deane also acted as representative of a group of merchants who planned to buy supplies for the American army and also to trade on their own account. This effort to combine public business, private trade, and diplomacy involved Deane in such a tangle that subsequently Congress professed utter inability to understand just what he had done.

In July 1776 Deane reached Paris, where he found preparations for American aid actually in progress. He was promptly put in touch with Beaumarchais, who was already acting as the agent through whom French assistance was being extended to America. When Deane and Beaumarchais once got together not only were supplies forthcoming in large quantities but loans were also available. Because of official French policy already decided upon, the success of the mission to Paris was assured.

The plan of Beaumarchais, carried out with the approval of both Vergennes and Louis XVI, was to establish a commercial firm under the Spanish name of Roderique Hortalez. The business of this firm was to act as a secret channel through which the French government could send military supplies to America. During the lifetime of the firm Beaumarchais paid out more than $4,000,000. He collected cannon, muskets, and gunpowder, together with clothing and tents for 25,000 men. Most of these supplies came directly from military warehouses of the French government. The first installments reached the United States in time for the summer campaigns of 1777 and so contributed powerfully to the American victory at Saratoga.

In the course of the whole war France gave to the United States outright sums of money amounting to $1,996,500 and made loans to the amount of $6,352,500. Spain gave this country the equivalent of nearly $4,000,000 and lent nearly $250,000. Subsequently Congress, Beaumarchais, and Deane disagreed as to the terms under which this help was supplied. Arthur Lee had assured Congress that France would expect no reimbursement whatever. Deane and Beaumarchais counted on payment for the military equipment. Congress preferred to accept Lee's interpretation and this body refused to settle Deane's accounts. It also refused to pay anything to Beaumarchais. Beaumarchais himself died in poverty, but in 1831 the United States paid something to his heirs. Deane also died in poverty. In 1842 Congress made belated amends by paying $37,000 to his heirs.

Franco-American Alliance

After the Declaration of Independence the Americans hoped for a formal alliance with France. To this end Congress drafted a tentative treaty and appointed a commission to negotiate with the French foreign office. The commission consisted of Silas Deane, Arthur Lee, and Benjamin Franklin. At first not even Franklin's popularity and cleverness could induce Vergennes to commit himself to a formal treaty. The king was anxious to avoid giving offense to England, so anxious that he would not allow Vergennes to receive the American commissioners officially. Then in the fall of 1776, when news of Washington's defeat on Long Island reached France, the foreign office became excessively cool. Even Beaumarchais became alarmed, not only for the cause of French help but for his own personal safety. "My government," he told Franklin, "will cut my throat as if I was a sheep."

In December 1777, Paris heard the news of Burgoyne's surrender at Saratoga. At once the attitude of Vergennes changed from cool indifference to enthusiastic cordiality. Vergennes's secretary, Gerard, came to Franklin's residence to congratulate the Americans. Before the end of the year Vergennes assured the Americans that his government would enter into a formal treaty with them. In February 1778, representatives of France and the United States signed not one but two treaties, one dealing with commerce, the other providing for common action in the war. The commercial treaty provided for the regulation of Franco-American trade on a basis of "the most perfect equality and reciprocity." The treaty of alliance guaranteed the independence of the United States. It provided for mutual help, under specified conditions, in case of defensive war and outlined the arrangements to be made in case either party should conquer British territory. France renounced all claim to her former possessions on the continent of North America. With reference to peace, the following paragraph from the treaty is of special interest:

> Neither of the two parties shall conclude either truce or peace with Great Britain without the formal consent of the other first obtained; and they mutually engage not to lay down their arms until the independence of the United States shall have been formally or tacitly assured by the treaty or treaties that shall terminate the war.

The treaty also provided that neither party should make any claim upon the other for compensation, regardless of the outcome of the war.

The alliance meant war between France and England, and when France entered the war the ultimate success of the United States was practically assured. French supplies, French troops, and above all French naval assistance proved to be invaluable. In addition to this direct help, the indirect results of the alliance proved to be almost as valuable: England could no longer concentrate her forces in North America, because she could never tell when a new European combination might strike her at home. All things considered, the agreement with France was a vitally important factor in the Revolution or rather in the achievement of American independence.

Victory for the Americans

The entrance of France into the contest was followed by that of Spain. After Spain entered the war, Congress sent John Jay to Madrid, in the hope of securing another European alliance. Jay found it impossible to get any formal treaty, although he did get some financial help. After spending nearly three years at the edge of the Spanish court, he went on to Paris; by that time he had well-defined theories concerning the true motives back of Franco-Spanish diplomacy and of its bearing on the United States.

With the entrance of Spain into the war, the contest began to take on the appearance of the customary eighteenth-century struggle for the balance of power, and this time England found herself without a single ally. She herself forced Holland into the war—on the French side—in order to cut off Dutch trade with the United States. Although the other nations did not come in, some of them joined in a commercial agreement, which proved to be almost as damaging to England as open belligerency would have been. This was the arrangement known as the "armed neutrality."

Armed Neutrality

Because of England's tendency to interpret her privileges on the seas in such fashion as to give her a hold on neutral trade, the leading neutrals began to emphasize the doctrine that free ships make free goods—that is, that noncontraband, belligerent-owned cargoes on neutral vessels were not subject to seizure. Both Catherine of Russia and Frederick the Great of Prussia became interested in this principle. Frederick was well disposed toward France and bitter against England because of her treatment of him during the Seven Years' War. Therefore he persuaded Catherine to head the combination of neutrals. Denmark, Sweden, Russia, Prussia, and the Holy Roman Empire all agreed to protect their commerce against British seizures.

In England the American victory over Burgoyne made just as profound an impression as it did in France. North's ministry realized that the thirteen colonies might soon be lost entirely, even if they were not lost already. Only the most generous concessions to American demands would save them, and the time for concessions might have passed. North had been working on a program of conciliation for some time, but he was dilatory and Parliament was not in the habit of acting on short notice. On December 10, 1777, the prime minister announced that he would offer measures looking toward reconciliation, but he did not introduce the necessary bills for this purpose until February 17, 1778, after the Franco-American treaties had been signed.

Carlisle's Mission

Parliament authorized the appointment of five commissioners to submit North's offer to the Americans. North appointed Lord Carlisle, William Eden, George Johnstone, and the two Howe brothers, the general and the admiral; these last two were already in America. The first three reached America in June 1778, just as General Howe was moving his army from Philadelphia back to New York.

Briefly, the commissioners were authorized to deal with any persons in America, official or otherwise, who would give them a hearing. They were to offer concessions in various stages, stopping short only of "open and avowed Independence." All measures of Parliament relating to the colonies, passed since 1763, would be suspended, and Parliament would never again enact any measures involving taxation of the colonies, except measures necessary for the regulation of trade. The British government would even allow the Americans to appoint the customs officials stationed in American ports. Congress might be continued as a permanent part of the government. and Americans would be allowed representation in Parliament if they so desired. Full pardon would be granted to all participants in the "rebellion."

Had such proposals been offered prior to the outbreak of war they would doubtless have been accepted. But after the Declaration of Independence, Saratoga, and the French alliance the Americans would consider nothing but independence. Nothing but military defeat could bring them back into the Empire. In October 1778, the commissioners returned to England with little to report except an account of their fruitless attempts to negotiate.

The signing of the Franco-American treaties of 1778 brought France actively into the war. French officials planned to send help to America at once. On April 13, 1778, a French fleet left Toulon for active service in North American waters. On his arrival there the commander, Count D'Estaing, at first attempted to capture or destroy Admiral Howe's squadron at New York, but he could not get his ships into the harbor. Then the French planned an attack upon the English force at Newport, Rhode Island. For this enterprise the American, General John Sullivan, and the French Lafayette would cooperate with D'Estaing's warships. But Sullivan's militia forces could not be collected in time for an immediate attack, and by the time they were ready Lord Howe suddenly appeared off Newport with a strong fleet. To avoid capture D'Estaing put to sea where his ships were badly battered by a heavy storm. Then he had to run in to Boston for repairs.

French Forces in America

The only appreciable result of the campaign around Newport—apart from the damage to the French vessels—was a tremendous burst of American wrath against the French. General Sullivan and his officers published a signed statement to the effect that the D'Estaing's withdrawal from Newport was injurious to French honor, contrary to the king's instructions, and detrimental to the interests of the United States. American newspapers gave publicity to the charge. In Boston a mob attacked a group of French sailors, and one French officer died from wounds inflicted there. The New Englanders seemed to feel, as Vergennes put it later, that French help was the direct result of the merit of the recipient rather than of the generosity of the donor. This outburst of ill temper over conditions for which the French were not responsible might have broken up the alliance, but, in spite of ample justification for resentment, Count D'Estaing remained calm and courteous. He even offered to enlist as a colonel under Sullivan if by doing so he could contribute anything to the cause. Subsequently New England's wrath subsided, while D'Estaing sailed to the West Indies. There he defeated the British squadron under Admiral Byron.

American Navy

As colonists the Americans had developed a large and successful merchant marine. When the war came, Congress hoped to utilize this maritime experience in the development of a navy, but the results did not come up to expectations. In the course of the war American privateers captured some 600 English merchant ships, but this gain was more than offset by the loss of some 900 American vessels. For the small regular American navy, as distinguished from privateers, John Paul Jones made the most spectacular contributions. He was the first officer to raise the American flag on an American warship, and in 1778 he began a series of raids in British home waters. In 1779 his flagship, the *Bon Homme Richard,* won a dramatic fight with the British *Serapis*.

The next step in the process of helping America was the dispatch of Rochambeau's army to America to cooperate with Washington's troops outside of New York. This force of 5500 French veterans landed in Rhode Island in July 1780. They brought their own supplies of ammunition, clothing, tents, and even $1,600,000 in coin. The French army went into winter quarters in Rhode Island. By the end of 1780 France had spent $30,000,000 on the war with no definite results except the defeat of Byron in the West Indies. Thus by the spring of 1781 the Americans seemed no nearer to independence than they had been in 1778, while the French government had moved much closer toward bankruptcy.

British Campaign in the South

During the years 1780 and 1781 the British were trying a new plan of campaign. They still held possession of New York, but their active operations were transferred to the South. Their purpose was to cut off individual states one by one. In Georgia they actually succeeded. The engagements there were in the nature of heavy guerilla warfare. Under Morgan, Greene, "Light Horse Harry" Lee and other commanders, the Americans succeeded in gradually wearing down the British forces. In the spring of 1781 the hitherto more or less planless fighting began to approach a climax. At Guilford Courthouse, North Carolina, General Cornwallis came out with a technical victory over Greene, while Morgan defeated a British force at Cowpens. British numbers were so reduced that Cornwallis took refuge on the coast at Wilmington, North Carolina.

From Wilmington Cornwallis started on his expedition that ended the war. He determined to conquer Virginia, on the theory that it was the key to the whole South. A small army was already operating there, and he joined it with his own troops. His aim was to capture Lafayette, whose force, hardly large enough to be called an army, had been facing General Benedict Arnold, who had gone over to the British side. At first Lafayette was compelled to retreat; then reinforcements came to his rescue, and he gradually forced Cornwallis back to the coast. By the end of July 1781, Cornwallis had fortified himself at Yorktown, where he was safe from any American troops but from which there was no escape except by the sea. If the American troops should be reinforced and if the British navy should be unable to help him, he ran the risk of being starved into surrender.

In May 1781, Washington and Rochambeau met at Wethersfield, Connecticut, to plan their activities for the summer. Washington wanted to attack New York, while Rochambeau urged a campaign in Virginia, in cooperation with de Grasse, the new commander of the French fleet in American waters. Washington's plan was approved. But Rochambeau was not satisfied with the outlook, and he almost begged de Grasse to bring over more troops. Concerning the Americans Rochambeau wrote:

> I ought not to conceal from you that these people are at the end of their resources; Washington will not have half the troops he counted upon, and I believe, although he conceals the fact, that he has not now six thousand men. . . . Such is the actual picture of the lamentable condition of the forces in this country. . . . It is, therefore, of the greatest importance that you take in your ships the largest number of soldiers possible.

Victory at Yorktown

At this point, in August 1781, circumstances combined to make a campaign in Virginia essential. The British in New York received reinforcements, so Washington and Rochambeau could not safely attack there. On August 14 Washington learned that de Grasse with a large squadron was approaching Chesapeake Bay with the design of helping to drive the British from Virginia. The American commander ordered Lafayette to prevent the escape of the British forces, then he planned to take the Franco-American forces from the Hudson valley to Virginia. On September 5 they reached Philadelphia, where they learned that de Grasse was already in Chesapeake Bay. Three weeks later the combined French and American forces faced the British under Cornwallis at Yorktown while de Grasse cut off the means of escape by sea. After a siege of seventeen days Cornwallis asked for terms. On October 19, 1781, he surrendered his army.

This victory in the South wrecked British plans for that section as completely as had Burgoyne's surrender in the North four years before. More than that, the British disaster in Virginia coincided in time with discouraging news from all parts of the world. In India the English hold was seriously threatened; in America, Spain had driven the English out of Florida; in the Mediterranean, Spanish forces captured Minorca and threatened even Gibraltar itself. De Grasse had raised so much havoc in the West Indies that England had nothing left there but Jamaica, Barbados, and Antigua. Added to these outright losses there was chronic trouble in Ireland, made worse, of course, by the encouragement which the Irish got from the rapidly accumulating British disasters. To make the situation still more complex, Austria and Russia were pressing their services upon the belligerents in an effort to bring about peace by negotiation. The victory at Yorktown therefore ended the fighting.

Chapter 9

REVOLUTIONARY PROBLEMS AND THE TREATY OF PEACE

ALONG with the military activities of the Revolution there were numerous developments which had an important influence on the early history of the new nation. One of these was a tendency toward lawlessness. During the colonial period and during the early stages of the Revolution most of the leaders had come from the privileged ruling class. But in their contests with royal officials these leaders had called upon the nonvoting groups, the unprivileged artisans and farm laborers, for help. Once the workers were aroused, they decided to have an active part in the new order. In this determination they found encouragement in the prevailing revolutionary philosophy. Radical leaders had talked much of liberty, of representation, of the tyranny of government, of the horrors of servitude. All this appealed to the populace. If the colonies as a whole could throw off the rule of the Empire, why should not the citizens repudiate the authority of the old ruling class or even that of the state itself?

Revolutionary Theory and New Governments

Revolutionary Philosophy

Started as a political revolt, the war with England soon upset old social patterns. Perhaps one of the most alarming symptoms appeared in Massachusetts, the original home of the public-school system. Various observers reported that the towns were dismissing teachers because they could not keep the schools going and support the war at the same time. With the schools closed, the children were left in idleness and mischief, "given up to all evil," so Abigail Adams wrote.

John Winthrop, a descendant of the first governor, characterized the Revolution in these terms: "There is such a spirit of innovation gone forth as I am afraid will throw us into confusion. It seems as if everything was to be altered. Scarce a newspaper but teems with new projects." Observers noted a changed attitude toward religious observances. The provincial congress of Massachusetts expressed regret at this change: "Among the prevailing sins of this day, which threaten the destruction of this land, we have reason to lament the frequent profanation of the Lord's day. . . . Many spending their time in idleness and sloth, others in diversions, and others in journeyings or business, which is not necessary on said day."

Doctor Ramsay of South Carolina, one of the contemporary historians of the Revolution, soberly concluded:

War never fails to injure the morals of the people engaged in it. The American war, in particular, had an unhappy influence of this kind. . . . On the whole, the literary, political, and military talents of the citizens of the United States have been improved by the revolution, but their moral character is inferior to what it formerly was. So great is the change for the worse, that the friends of public order are loudly called upon to exert their utmost abilities, in extirpating the vicious principles and habits, which have taken deep root during the late convulsions.

Other signs of change in social attitudes were to be found in what the provincial congress of Massachusetts called the "alarming symptoms of the abatement of the sense, in the minds of some people, of the sacredness of private property." This lack of respect for the rights of property was almost inevitable. Government and property had long been bound together so that any attack upon one was certain to be accompanied by assaults on the other. Debtors were refusing to pay debts, and, when their creditors resorted to the courts, the courts were overthrown. In June 1776 a small mob of patriots, armed with clubs, prevented the court from sitting in Bristol County, Massachusetts. Courts were allowed to try cases in only two counties in the state: Essex and Middlesex. Courts of justice were the outstanding symbols of government under law, and law was being flouted. John Adams quoted a conversation with one of his clients on this subject: "Oh Mr. Adams, what great things have you and your colleagues done for us! We can never be grateful enough to you. There are no courts of justice now in this Province, and I hope there never will be another." Adams was shocked at this opinion. He feared that half the nation might hold similar views, because half the nation was in debt. "Surely we must guard against this spirit and these principles," he observed, "or we shall repent of all our conduct." In 1776, the town of Pittsfield, Massachusetts, formally petitioned the House of Representatives to order "that no person may, at present, be allowed to sue for private debts."

Property

In setting aside the rules which ordinarily control civilized communities these enthusiasts were merely endorsing the political generalities which had circulated freely at the beginning of the war. What was government anyway but an agreement between individuals? There was "no witchcraft" in it, so one amateur political scientist affirmed, while another modestly stated that there was little needed but a legislature. "I incline to think," he wrote, "that this is all the learning necessary to moddle a government." One Massachusetts town resolved that "we do not want any Govinor but the Govinor of the Universe and under him a States General to consult with the Wrest of the U.S. for the good of the whole." As for a judiciary the same town advised each town "to Chuse a Comitte . . . of judges Consisting of a number of wise understanding and Prudent Men that shall jug and Detarmin all Cases between Man and Man." Benjamin Hichborn of Boston told his contemporaries that civil liberty is "a power existing in the people at large . . . to alter or annihilate both the mode and essence of

Political Ideas

any former government . . . for any cause or for no cause at all, but their own sovereign pleasure."

The political doctrines of the Revolutionary period found expression in correspondence, in the press, and most important of all in public documents and state papers. So far as theory was concerned, the most famous statement occurs in the Declaration of Independence. Other expressions of this same doctrine were included in the state constitutions adopted during the Revolution. For instance, the Virginia Bill of Rights furnished a model for other states to follow. This document declared:

> That all power is vested in, and consequently derived from, the people; that magistrates are their trustees and servants, and at all times amenable to them.
>
> That government is, or ought to be instituted for the common benefit, protection, and security of the people, nation or community; of all the various modes and forms of government, that is best which is capable of producing the greatest degree of happiness and safety, and is most effectually secured against the danger of maladministration; and that when any government shall be found inadequate or contrary to these purposes, a majority of the community hath an indubitable, inalienable and indefeasible right to reform, alter, or abolish it, in such manner as shall be judged most conducive to the public weal.

The constitutions of Vermont and of Massachusetts proclaimed the same principle, in the very same words.

As the revolutionists reduced political theory to its lowest terms, they became suspicious of wealth and learning. Newspaper articles warned the people to beware of "men of liberal education," and to refuse to vote for lawyers, doctors, or even ministers.

> Choose men that have . . . learnt, that as government hath heretofore been administered, it was only a mere machine in the hands of the rulers to plunder the commonality. Choose men that have learnt to get their living by honest industry, and that will be content with as small an income as the generality of those who have to pay them for their service.

Public Officials

This attack upon men of wealth and learning lowered the level of ability in some legislative bodies. Certain members of the Massachusetts House of Representatives, elected in 1775, so Elbridge Gerry wrote, "might have lived till the milennium in silent obscurity, had they depended on their mental qualifications to bring them into public view." James Otis, for some time insane, in one of his lucid intervals gave forth the following terse comment on the men who were in charge in Massachusetts in 1777: "When the pot boils, the scum will arise."

For several years after the Revolution observant citizens found cause to lament the changed character of their public officials. Jeremy Belknap of New Hampshire called attention to "the deficiency of persons qualified for the various departments in the Government. . . ." And the elderly David Jarrett of Virginia declared: "My age enables me to know that the people are not now by half so peacefully and quietly governed as formerly; nor are the laws, perhaps by the tenth part, so well executed."

And yet, in spite of this spirit of anarchism, the American people made surprisingly constructive achievements. First of all they reorganized their state governments. In Massachusetts the provincial congress gave way to a new House of Representatives in 1775, and until 1780 the state was governed under the old charter of 1691. The office of governor was declared vacant, the House of Representatives was restored, and the council took charge of executive work. Before the adoption of the Declaration of Independence, New Hampshire, Virginia, and South Carolina, in addition to Massachusetts, had set up governments independent of the Crown. By 1780, when Massachusetts adopted a new constitution, eleven out of the thirteen states had put their political affairs upon a new foundation. Connecticut and Rhode Island both continued their government under their charters. They had been virtually independent republics before 1775 so there was really little need of change.

State Constitutions

So far as was possible these new governments retained the features of the old. The elective branches of the legislatures were increased in size to provide for a more equitable representation, but their powers and functions were not seriously altered. The members of the upper houses were thenceforth elected by the voters in most of the states. In Maryland they were chosen by electors, in Georgia by the lower house. The executive underwent an even greater change. In each of the New England states the governor was elected by the voters; in New York, by the wealthy voters; and in the other states by the legislatures, except in Pennsylvania where for a time they substituted a plural executive for the governor.

Theoretically the new state executives had less authority than their royal or proprietary predecessors; actually there was little difference. To be sure, the executive was carefully hedged about with restrictions so that he could never overawe the legislature. But in practice, during the later colonial period, the assemblies had gained power over the governors. What the states really did in shaping the powers of their executives was to leave them pretty much as colonial practice had made them.

Because of long political experience, these Americans had comparatively little difficulty in working out a satisfactory system of state government. The question of a national government, however, was more complicated. In the colonies there had never been any genuine, widespread, deep-rooted desire for union. The failure of the Albany Plan had illustrated this attitude. Local pride was strong, and confidence in the local legislatures even stronger. Yet at the approach of war the states made no serious efforts to organize an effective national government; the first and second Continental Congresses were legally nothing more than meetings of diplomatic agents sent out by the states.

National Government

The Second Continental Congress had convened at Philadelphia early in May 1775. Although they had no specific authority to do so, the members immediately assumed the prerogatives of a central government. They raised an army and took charge of the conduct of the war. They raised money, not by taxation but by printing notes and borrowing. They made regulations covering foreign commerce and they entered into diplomatic relations with foreign powers, particularly France.

Although Americans disliked the idea of national power because of their experience in the British Empire, they soon found that they could not conduct the war without a central government. In June 1776, Congress appointed a committee to draw up Articles of Confederation. The committee presented its report on July 12; then in November 1777, after nearly a year and a half of debate and with many misgivings, Congress submitted the Articles to the states. Ratification was not completed until 1781, the last year of active fighting.

In framing the plan, and in the subsequent discussion, American statesmen had to solve the puzzle which had been troubling the British Cabinet ever since the seventeenth century—that of the proper distribution of power. How much must the central authority have, and how little could the states manage to surrender? As the first few years after the war made plain, the Articles did not answer either of these questions satisfactorily.

Articles of Confederation

Like the state constitutions, the Articles of Confederation furnished important illustrations of Revolutionary political theory. The dominant note throughout was fear of a central government, even of one created by the Americans themselves. The purpose of the Articles, therefore, was to create a central government possessed of the minimum of power and to safeguard state rights in every possible way. Under the Articles each state retained its "sovereignty, freedom, and independence and every power, jurisdiction and right, which is not by this confederation expressly delegated" to the United States. Each state might send from two to seven delegates to the Congress, but no state could have more than one vote. The Articles gave control of foreign affairs to the Congress. The Articles also made Congress a court of last resort in disputes between two or more states. Congress could manufacture money, make rules for the Indian trade outside of state jurisdictions, operate a postal service, appoint officers, and make regulations for the Continental army and navy, and raise money—not, however, by means of taxation. For any action the vote of nine states was required, except for amendments which required a unanimous vote. This provision made legislation difficult and legal change in the Articles impossible. The Articles did not provide for a separate executive or judiciary; Congress combined in itself the functions of the three branches of government.

Loyalist Problems

As the war went on, the American governments had to do something about the Loyalists or Tories, those Americans who remained loyal to England. Bitter enough at the start, the relations between Patriots and Loyalists became steadily worse as the war continued. The open and avowed Loyalists showed their feelings by supporting the British troops whenever possible

The Tories

and by enlisting in the British army. According to Van Tyne, New York alone furnished about 15,000 men for the royal army and navy. Also Loyalist militia units were organized, and the rumor was that these companies in New York outnumbered Washington's whole army. Had the British government given more vigorous encouragement to this form of activity, the Loyalist troops might have been far more numerous.

Both the states and the Continental Congress laid down policies for destroying this sort of opposition. Although in the early days of the war attempts at conversion were common, these soon gave way to a policy of revenge and to what the Loyalists described as persecution. Those who stayed at home were subjected to careful control, deprived of suffrage rights, and refused the privileges of citizenship if they would not take the oath of allegiance. They could not hold office, and they had no rights in court. No Loyalist could bring a suit at law, serve as a guardian, make a will, buy or sell land, or serve on a jury. State legislatures passed laws prohibiting all speaking or writing against the patriot cause. It became a criminal offense to speak disrespectfully of Congress, to argue in favor of British authority in the United States, or to speak against the raising of troops. Because spies were always at work on both sides, it became necessary to identify strangers, and every traveler had to carry a certificate of Americanism from Congress or from some local committee. Innkeepers and stagedrivers were fined if they neglected to ask patrons to show their credentials. Tories could not get these certificates, so they were compelled to stay at home.

No government, if it is strong enough to suppress them, will tolerate in time of war the things which the Loyalists did. The more extreme Tories failed to appreciate the force of this principle; discreet people realized it and kept out of trouble. Some of the Tories left the states voluntarily. Others were expelled by the state governments and banished either for the duration of the war or permanently. Loyalist property was confiscated—sometimes indirectly by a system of fines and special taxation, sometimes by direct seizure.

Of the more prominent Americans who changed sides after the war had started, General Benedict Arnold was the most conspicuous. In the early

Arnold's Treason

part of the war he had made a brilliant record in fighting against overwhelming odds. When the British evacuated Philadelphia in 1778, Washington sent Arnold, temporarily incapacitated for active service, to take command in the city. While there he married a Tory wife, a society belle named Peggy Shippen. Apparently dazzled by the atmosphere of extravagance, he spent money faster than he earned it. Various accusations were brought against him, particularly to the effect that he was guilty of selling army supplies for his own private gain. It was partly because of these charges that Congress refused to allow certain claims of his in connection with his Canadian campaign early in the war, and Washington found it necessary to reprimand him.

Upset by these difficulties, Arnold deliberately determined to betray the American cause. He asked Washington for the command at West Point—the key to the American position in the North—and got it without question because Washington had confidence in his military ability. Then Arnold promised to surrender the place to the British commander, Clinton. His plans were uncovered through the capture of Major André, but owing to an unfortunate blunder Arnold himself was able to escape to the British lines. He was given a command in the British army and fought through the remaining part of the war on that side.

Paper Money and Economic Problems

Revolutionary Finance

The Loyalists were one of the major problems of the Revolution. Paper money was another. For the first five years of the war the American people transacted business under the combined advantages and disadvantages of a rapidly depreciating paper currency. Other economic activities need to be considered against this background. The Americans adopted this monetary policy because it was the easiest to follow. A mere glance at the financial situation in April 1775 will show how desperate the American case was. The total amount of ready money in the country was small, amounting perhaps to $22,000,000 in paper and something between $6,000,000 and $12,000,000 in specie. This was not enough to meet even ordinary demands of peace.

Governments have surprisingly few means of securing revenue. Taxation, the ordinary method, presupposes certain essential conditions which did not exist in the colonies in 1775; there must be an adequate volume of money in circulation together with general business prosperity so that people have incomes from which the levies may be drawn. When the Revolution broke out, the commercial sections of the country were thrown into a financial crisis because of the temporary interruption of the ordinary lines of trade. New England felt the loss of the fisheries and of the carrying trade; the middle states were shut off from their West Indian markets; and the southern states had difficulty in disposing of their tobacco, lumber, and naval stores. Suppose taxes were imposed, who could pay them?

Borrowing was at first almost as much out of the question as taxation. The business depression nearly destroyed the hope of domestic loans, while the subsequent depreciation of paper money made lending unprofitable. Then too the war was such a hazardous venture that for nearly three years no foreign government would come openly to the support of the Americans. Direct confiscation, except of course from the Loyalists, would not have been tolerated in any state at the time. Prevented from taxing, borrowing, or confiscating, the Revolutionary leaders were compelled to capitalize their single available asset: the hope of winning the war. This hope could be made financially available by means of paper money.

Moderate issues of paper would provide money for circulation; if kept within limits, no serious complications would arise. If the issues passed the limits of moderation, however, they would be automatically transformed into taxes with the widest incidence, if not into practical confiscation; depreciation would see to that. What the public might lose in depreciation would be counterbalanced by the gain to the government of means to finance the war. In this way the bitterness which heavy taxation or direct confiscation would have engendered might be diffused over a relatively long period.

Paper Money

Once the policy of paper money was started, the legislatures put out quantities of it with no definite plans for redemption. As the quantity of notes in circulation steadily increased, their value went down. Prices, of course, rose in proportion. The holders of the paper shouldered the loss. Those losses may have constituted a heavier burden of expense, in the aggregate, than would probably have been necessary under the other course, but this burden was distributed over several years and over a large part of the population. While taxation would have affected property owners primarily, depreciation and repudiation took in everybody who held a single Continental or state note. It would have been possible to devise more equitable schemes of taxation, but no plan could have been more comprehensive in incidence. Once depreciation started, every bill was worth less when paid out than when received.

During the era of paper money the Continental Congress issued approximately $191,550,000. The state of Virginia put out even more, a grand total of $224,250,000. This was the largest sum printed by any single state. Massachusetts came next with a total in the neighborhood of $66,000,000; the other states issued some. With only two minor exceptions this mass of paper was entirely unsecured. Congress planned to have the states tax the people in order to redeem the Continental notes, but the states could not even redeem their own issues.

Depreciation

Depreciation was the inevitable consequence. How early it began no one can tell exactly, but it started before the end of 1775. Depreciation in turn led to price fixing by law. Between 1776 and 1780 New England and the middle colonies experimented with statutes for holding prices down, but difficulties of enforcement proved insuperable.

As depreciation carried the value of the bills to ever lower levels, Congress and the state governments had only one expedient left—that is, repudiation. On March 18, 1780, Congress fixed the ratio of the Continental notes to specie at 40 to 1, thus reducing an obligation of $200,000,000 to a mere $5,000,000. Within a year Congress again put the ratio at 75 to 1 and shortly thereafter left the notes with no value whatever.

The losses involved in this repudiation would have been staggering had they been inflicted suddenly, but that was not the case. As the money passed from hand to hand the ordinary individual suffered little. The merchant and even the laborer could charge enough more to protect himself. The ones most seriously affected were those dependent on incomes limited to a definite number of pounds or dollars. For those who could pass on the bills of credit to another victim without delay, the paper structure was advantageous. As long as the output of bills and notes continued, there was no taxation. The governments were drawing their resources from depreciation rather than from revenue.

This fact was clearly understood in Congress and elsewhere. On three different occasions between 1779 and 1781 Franklin explained the effects of a depreciating currency. Regretting that orphans, widows, and those dependent on fixed incomes were the chief sufferers, the Pennsylvania philosopher found compensation for this loss in the benefits to society in general. The public debt, he declared,

> is proportionably diminish'd with the Depreciation; and this by a kind of imperceptible Tax; every one having paid a Part of it in the Fall of Value that took place between his receiving and Paying such Sums as pass'd thro' his hands. For it should always be remembered, that the original Intention was to sink the Bills by Taxes, which would as effectually extinguish the Debt as an actual Redemption.

A year and a half later he wrote that "so much of the public debt has in this manner been insensibly paid, that the remainder . . . does not exceed six millions sterling." After watching the experiment of financing a war with paper Franklin became enthusiastic over the policy: "This Currency, as we manage it, is a wonderful Machine. It performs its Office when we issue it; it pays and clothes Troops, and provides Victuals and Ammunition; and when we are obliged to issue a Quantity excessive, it pays itself off by depreciation."

The state notes were disposed of under laws designed to establish their value in terms of specie. At first there was a general tendency to adopt the Congressional ratio of 40 to 1, but this proved too expensive. In 1782 Virginia and Georgia decreed a legal ratio of 1000 to 1. During this same period the American people seem to have been free of all taxes except for purely local matters. Certainly Congress levied no taxes, even though before 1781 it had as much authority to tax as it had to print paper money—that is, none at all. As for the states, with a few unimportant exceptions, they seem to have raised no money by taxation before 1781. After that, with the return to a specie basis, taxation once more was made systematic.

On sober consideration the whole record of Revolutionary finance is extraordinary. At the end of a war lasting more than seven years, the national government had a total debt of $42,000,375 in coin. To this should be added the state debts incurred on account of the war which in 1789 amounted to $21,789,370, the sum actually assumed by the federal government under Hamilton's plan. Pitkin, in his *Statistical View,* estimated the total cost of the Revolution, in specie, at $135,000,000. If this figure is reasonably accurate, and it is probably as close as any estimate could be, more than half the cost of the war was borne by the people at the time.

Economic Conditions

As for economic conditions in general, during the first part of the war farmers, artisans, and merchants all suffered from hard times. During the latter part of the war most people prospered. This was especially true of the merchants. American merchants traded indirectly with England by way of the West Indies, Nova Scotia, or Holland, and in rare cases directly with British ports. There was also considerable commerce with the countries of northern Europe, with France, and with the West Indies. In addition to ordinary commercial transactions, privateering after 1779 furnished employment for sailors and the shipbuilding trades as well as income for the owners and merchants.

There was always an element of risk in this wartime commerce, but the shortage of imported goods and abnormally high prices made for heavy profits. The greatest gains went to those prepared to take a chance, generally younger traders with little experience. Some of the more conservative merchants seemed unable to adapt themselves to the situation. As a result there were numerous complaints of widespread differences in income, with some merchants getting rich and others reduced to poverty. Easy profits and paper money encouraged liberal spending and thoughtless extravagance.

In addition to much speculative overseas trade there was a profitable overland exchange of goods between New England and New York. New York provided wheat, beef, and pork, largely perhaps for the army, while Massachusetts and Connecticut sent numerous manufactured goods into New York and the middle colonies. This traffic was handled over the roads, with sometimes as many as 200 wagons in one expedition. Because of its favorable location, Hartford figured prominently in this business. Of all American commercial centers Philadelphia profited most heavily from the trade of the Revolutionary era. She had connections with both Europe and the West Indies together with a number of enterprising merchants to exploit these connections. Robert Morris, Thomas Willing, and William Bingham made themselves famous as merchants of this period.

Achievement of Independence

Plans for Peace

From the American point of view the main objective of the war was peace with independence, and in 1779 Congress appointed a committee to consider the proper terms. After six months of work, the committee submitted its first report. In this preliminary statement the members of the committee laid claim to both the Northwest and the Southwest Territories as far as the Mississippi River. Then they asked for free rights of navigation on the river and for the right of deposit at its mouth—that is, the privilege of landing and storing goods temporarily without payment of duty. Then they called for confirmation of American fishing rights off Newfoundland. Congress appointed John Adams as its agent to negotiate peace on these terms.

The French ministers at Philadelphia, first Gérard and then Luzerne, tried successfully to prevent Congress from endorsing the committee's report. In this work both French ministers admitted they did not confine themselves to methods of moral suasion. Thomas Paine, author of *Common Sense,* then serving as secretary to the Congress, had been notoriously anti-French in his writings. Gérard wrote Vergennes that in return for $1000 per year, Paine promised to use his pen to help the French cause. Then Luzerne wanted the support of General John Sullivan, who had just been elected to Congress; again, so Luzerne reported to Vergennes, the price was $1000 per year. In commenting upon his success with Sullivan, Luzerne wrote: "This delegate has shown in this affair equal patriotism and attachment for the alliance."

Concerning the fisheries the French held that it was a matter outside the range of the alliance, but they opposed American demands. Vergennes himself wrote that the rights off Newfoundland "belong exclusively to the British." Gérard explained the French position in the following words: "I told them that I was convinced that England would grant them the fisheries by the same title as that by which they had previously held them, to wit, as subjects of the British crown, but that they had no need of the aid of France for that arrangement." As for the West, Vergennes was more sympathetic with Spanish ambitions than with American.

Then, because Vergennes did not like John Adams, the French minister to the United States urged the appointment of a group of commissioners. Again Luzerne was successful. In 1781 Congress appointed a commission of five to negotiate peace: Adams, Franklin, Jay, Jefferson—who did not go to Europe in time for the negotiations—and Henry Laurens.

Because of pressure tactfully applied by the French agents, Congress modified its original demands concerning peace. When final instructions were prepared for the American commissioners, they were bound by only two specific orders: to secure recognition of independence and to preserve the French alliance. Demands for the fisheries and for western territories were dropped. But the commissioners were instructed

> . . . to make the most candid and confidential communications upon all subjects to the ministers of our generous ally, the king of France; to undertake nothing in the negotiations for peace or truce without their knowledge or concurrence; and ultimately to govern yourselves by their advice and opinions.

Negotiations at Paris

In April 1782 Franklin began informal conversations about peace with the British agent, Richard Oswald. Oswald was a retired merchant, well acquainted with American affairs, and a friend of Franklin. Unofficially Franklin made it clear that the British must grant complete independence to the thirteen states; Canada must be restricted to the St. Lawrence valley; and the British must recognize American rights to the fisheries. When the

British ministry opposed an immediate recognition of American independence, Franklin made no further advances and waited for the arrival of John Jay. He reached Paris from Spain in June 1782.

Oswald's first commission authorized him to deal with representatives of the American "colonies or plantations," thus leaving the essential matter of independence to subsequent negotiations. When Franklin and Jay consulted Vergennes on this issue, Vergennes advised them to ignore the form of Oswald's commission and to begin negotiations. Franklin was at first inclined to accept Vergennes's advice, but Jay insisted upon British recognition of independence before any discussion of other matters. Franklin and Jay together then explained to Oswald that his commission must authorize him to deal with representatives of the United States.

During his residence at Madrid Jay had learned of Spanish ambitions in the Southwest east of the Mississippi. He was convinced that Vergennes would uphold Spain. His suspicions that Vergennes would not support American claims were strengthened when the British gave him the copy of a letter from the French legation in America to Vergennes. The writer, Marbois, advised Vergennes not to endorse American claims to the Newfoundland fisheries. Next one of Vergennes's agents, Rayneval, proposed to Jay that England be left in control of all American territory west of the Alleghenies and north of the Ohio and that Spain have most of the southwest territory. Soon afterward Jay learned that Rayneval had gone to England. In view of all these indications of French support of Spain, Jay believed that Rayneval's purpose was to commit England on two policies: to exclude Americans from the fisheries and to bar them from most of the West.

Treaty of Peace

Jay put his suspicions together and decided to act. He induced an Englishman, Benjamin Vaughan, to go to England for the purpose of securing a new commission for Oswald. He argued that it would be to the advantage of England to offer liberal terms to the United States in order to break the tie between the new nation and France. Shelburne, in charge of British foreign affairs, saw the logic of the argument. He instructed his agents to treat with representatives of the United States. By November 1782 the first draft of the treaty was finished.

The terms of this draft were so favorable to the Americans that Vergennes observed: "You will remark that the English buy a peace rather than make one. Their concessions on the boundaries, the fisheries, and the loyalists, exceed all that I believed possible." Once the work was done, Vergennes's manner suggested hurt feelings rather than anger. To Luzerne he wrote:

> You, as well as I, will surely applaud the extensive advantages which our Allies, the Americans, have obtained by the peace, but certainly you will not be less surprised than I was at the action of the commissioners. . . . The American commissioners will not say that I have sought to interfere, and still less that

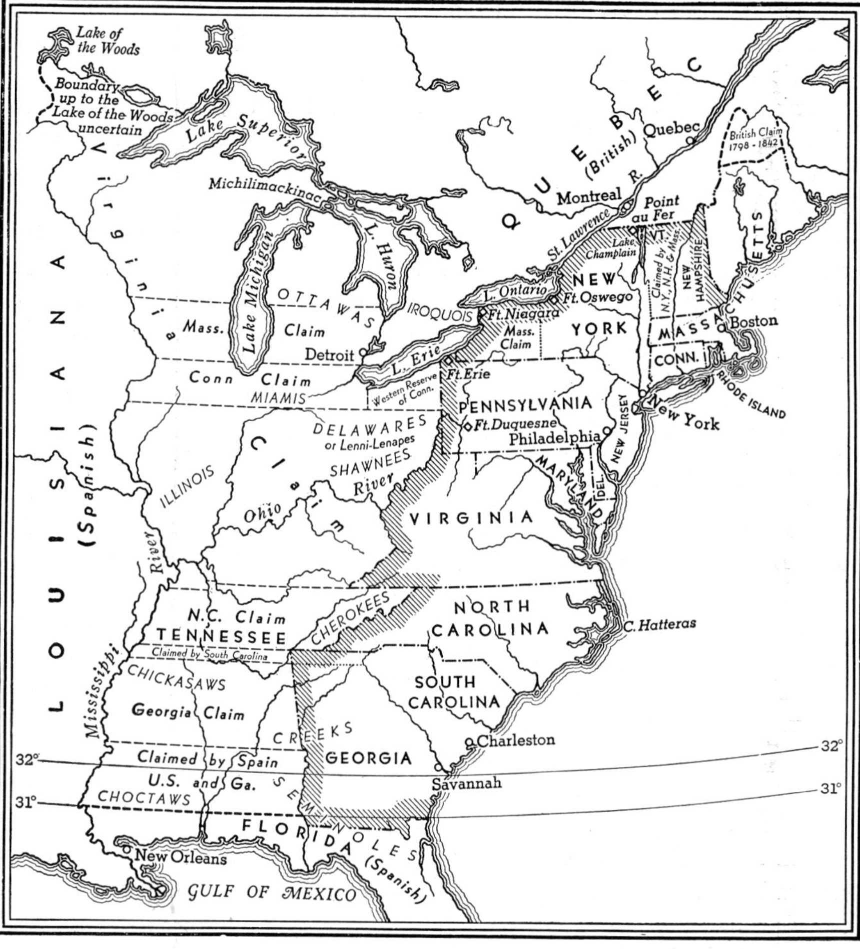

Map 6. Territory Owned or Claimed by the Thirteen States in 1783

I have wearied them with my curiosity. They hold themselves carefully aloof from me. . . . If we can judge the future by what we have just seen, we shall be poorly repaid for what we have done for the United States of America.

Next Vergennes unburdened himself to Franklin:

I am at a loss to explain your conduct and that of your colleagues on this occasion. You have concluded your preliminary articles without any communication between us, although the instructions from Congress prescribe that nothing shall be done without the participation of the king. . . .

But Vergennes had no reason for being disturbed. He had previously approved the course which the Americans followed—that is, of carrying on discussions with the British commissioner. As soon as the preliminary draft was completed, the Americans gave a copy to Vergennes. They had not made a secret peace, but had merely carried on separate negotiations.

The definitive treaty between the United States and Great Britain was signed on September 3, 1783. Because it provided the formal legal basis of American independence it is one of the most important documents in American history. Article I recognized the thirteen states as "free, sovereign and independent." Article II defined the boundaries in such a way that the United States received both the Northwest and the Southwest Territories. The western boundary was fixed at the Mississippi, the southern at the 31st parallel of latitude. The northern boundary was drawn in complicated terms, but it left Maine as a part of Massachusetts. The line then ran along the present northern borders of New Hampshire and Vermont. From Vermont it followed the 45th parallel to the junction of this line with the St. Lawrence River, thence along the river and the middle of Lakes Ontario, Erie, Huron, and Superior. From Lake Superior the boundary went to the Lake of the Woods and thence to the Mississippi. Article III gave the Americans the right to take fish not only off Newfoundland but in the Gulf of St. Lawrence and "at all other places in the sea where the inhabitants of both countries used at any time heretofore to fish." The Americans also received "liberty" to dry and cure fish on certain specified territory as long as it should remain unsettled. Article IV provided that creditors on both sides "shall meet with no lawful impediment to the recovery of the full value in sterling money, of all *bona fide* debts heretofore contracted." Article V provided that Congress "shall earnestly recommend" to the states that they restore all Loyalist rights and properties. Other provisions covered such matters as the restoration of prisoners of war and the withdrawal of British forces "with all convenient speed and without . . . carrying away any negroes or other property of the American inhabitants" from all territory awarded to the United States. The right of navigation on the Mississippi River from mouth to source was guaranteed to citizens of both countries.

The British signed separate treaties with France and with Spain. Great Britain restored Florida to Spain, but the treaty did not define the boundary. Subsequently Spain was inclined to stretch Florida so as to include a substantial portion of the Southwest Territory. Also Spain controlled the mouth of the Mississippi, therefore her agents could practically nullify the provision regarding British and American navigation of the river.

Outlook for the Future

The Treaty of 1783 gave the Americans practically all that the congressional committee had asked for in 1779: independence, the West, and the fisheries. There were possibilities of future development here which almost staggered the imagination. The Spanish ambassador to France at this time wrote:

> This federal republic is born a pigmy. A day will come when it will be a giant; even a colossus, formidable to these countries. Liberty of conscience, the facility for establishing a new population on immense lands, as well as the advantages of the new government, will draw thither farmers and artisans from

all the nations. In a few years we shall watch with grief the tyrannical existence of this same colossus.

What did France get out of the war? She had the satisfaction of seeing England lose thirteen of her colonies. But England had not been beaten as decisively as France in 1763, and relatively her losses were far less serious than those of France at that time. France came out of the struggle bankrupt, and within six years she found herself plunged into a revolution more far-reaching in its consequences than the American war.

Chapter 10

FOREIGN AND ECONOMIC PROBLEMS, 1783-89

Western Lands

THE treaties which closed the Revolutionary War defined the boundaries and established legal titles to the Northwest and Southwest Territories, but they did not settle all the problems connected with them. For a time it had seemed that these western territories might prove to be a cause of controversy among the states. Fortunately this particular danger had been removed before the end of the war. At the close of the colonial period several colonies had claims to western lands, and some of these claims overlapped. When George Rogers Clark led his men into Kaskaskia and Vincennes he was serving under a commission of the state of Virginia, not of Congress. If Virginia conquered some of the key positions in the West, and if Congress did nothing there, to whom did the region belong?

Problems and Progress in the Northwest

The states which had no western lands were jealous of those which did. The possessors of outlying territory had a rich source of revenue which would give them great advantages over their less fortunate sister states. They could keep taxes low and so attract settlers from states where taxes were high. During the early part of the Revolution the state of Maryland made an issue of this western land business, and her delegates in Congress refused to approve the Articles of Confederation until all the states should cede their western possessions to the United States. Then the national government would profit from any land sales, and the proceeds would benefit the American people as a whole. After considerable delay New York and Connecticut agreed to turn their claims over to Congress, and soon afterward Virginia gave up her lands north of the Ohio River. This action removed the fears of the Marylanders, and in 1781 Maryland ratified the Articles of Confederation. The other states gave up their claims to Congress. Thus the western territories became the common property of the United States, and this public domain furnished a powerful bond of union.

Northwest Posts

The Northwest Territory had great economic and strategic advantages. Military posts in the area were centers for the fur trade and for trade with the Indians. The posts were so located as to control the portages, the stretches of land over which trappers and Indians carried their canoes between lakes and rivers. The provisional draft of the Treaty of Peace put the Americans in possession of most of the posts. Eight of them were of outstanding importance. Two guarded the route between Montreal and

Lake Champlain: Dutchman's Point and Pointe au Fer. Three others controlled the upper St. Lawrence and Lake Ontario: Oswegatchie, Oswego, and Niagara. Fort Erie guarded the eastern end of Lake Erie, while Detroit was the key to the passage between Lakes Erie and Huron. Michilimackinac covered the entrances to Lakes Huron, Michigan, and Superior.

In 1782, before the negotiations for peace were completed, parties in Canada sent memorials to the authorities in England pointing out the advantage of the fur trade, the economic and strategic advantages of the posts, and the need of Indian help in keeping Americans out. As a result, in 1783, the governor of Canada, General Haldimand, promised to supply the Indians of the region with arms, munitions, clothing, and food, thereby making and keeping them dependent upon British agents. The posts were the only centers from which these supplies could be distributed.

Although the Treaty of Peace called for the surrender of all territory awarded to the Americans with "all convenient speed," British officials refused to withdraw. Furthermore they refused to permit agents of Congress even to talk with the Indians in the Northwest. In 1784 the British Cabinet approved Haldimand's refusal to give up the posts, justifying this amazing decision by the alleged refusal of the Americans to comply with the terms of the treaty with reference to British debts and the Loyalists. This reason was a mere pretext, because the British had decided upon the policy of holding the posts before they had any real evidence as to whether the Americans could or could not comply with their obligations under the treaty.

To make matters worse the British gave encouragement to the Indians in the Northwest in their hostile attitude toward the Americans. Then in 1787 the new governor, Lord Dorchester, received specific instructions to hold the posts at all costs. If the Americans should take them by force, Dorchester was authorized to recover them at once and to use the Indians as allies in preventing the Americans from taking possession of their own territory. The chief reason for this violation of the treaty was the fur trade, the richest single branch of commerce in North America. The center of this trade had been at Montreal. The furs themselves were secured mostly from the Indians, and more than half the annual supply came from the tribes living south of the newly established boundary. If the Americans were allowed to keep the posts much of the trade would be diverted to Albany and New York, and Canada would be ruined. So the British continued to hold the posts and also to encourage the Indians in acts of hostility against the United States.

Kentucky and Tennessee

Neither inability to secure their rights nor the threat of Indian warfare kept pioneers from going into the West. Prospective settlers were beginning to look toward the Northwest. As for the Southwest, settlement in that quarter had begun actively before the Revolution and it continued through the war and afterward. The occupation of the West was in principle similar to the building of the thirteen colonies, only it was carried out on a larger scale.

In many ways the achievements of the American people in occupying the extent of the present United States were greater than those of the English in settling the Atlantic seaboard. In fact, it would be hard to find in all history a comparable story of expansion. New settlement succeeded new settlement with bewildering rapidity, and millions of square miles of wilderness became civilized country. There is, of course, one obvious difference between this American colonial movement and that of the British during the seventeenth and eighteenth centuries. British colonies were all overseas, 3000 miles and more distant from the mother country, whereas the area of American colonization was always just beyond the range of settlements already in existence. By 1785 there were 20,000 settlers in Kentucky, and a smaller but substantial number in Tennessee.

For a time Kentucky was governed as a single county in the state of Virginia, and Tennessee as part of North Carolina. But there were indications, and strong ones, that these rich farming areas would not remain tied to the mother states indefinitely. In 1784 and 1785 the Kentuckians showed deep resentment at rumors that Congress, with Virginia's approval, might agree with Spain to deprive them of the right to use the Mississippi. At the time there was little patriotism in the sense of loyalty to the Confederation, and if Congress should be so shortsighted as to ignore the needs of Kentucky, the people of Kentucky could easily ignore Congress. There was a possibility that Kentucky and Tennessee might form a western confederacy; still another possibility was that the western Americans might join forces with Spain.

Prior to the year 1785 the westward movement had gone on without the help of an established land policy. However, as the original states gradually ceded their western land claims to Congress, a land policy became essential.

Land Ordinance

In 1785 Congress passed the Land Ordinance providing for rectangular surveys of the public lands. The surveyors first selected a line running north and south, which they called the principal meridian. The one chosen was the present boundary between Ohio and Indiana. Then they picked a base line running east and west. From points six miles apart on the meridian the surveyors ran additional lines east and west, and in similar fashion lines north and south from points six miles apart on the base line. Thus the country was blocked off into squares, each containing thirty-six square miles. Each one of these blocks or squares was called a township. The township was subdivided into thirty-six sections, each one square mile—640 acres—in area. Section No. 16 in each township would be sold to provide funds for public schools. In this same law Congress arranged for the establishment of land offices, in which records of the surveys and sales could be preserved. Provision was made for selling the land at public auction at a price not less than $1 per acre. The first surveys were made in 1785 and 1786.

Actual settlement in the Northwest Territory did not start until after the enactment of the Land Ordinance. In Boston, in 1786, a new land company known as the Ohio Associates was organized to promote settlement north of the Ohio. Most of the members were veterans of the Revolution. Some of the leading directors were General Rufus Putnam, General Samuel H. Parsons, and the Reverend Manasseh Cutler, a doctor of divinity and a Congregational clergyman. In his case theological training proved to be no barrier to successful land speculation. Before the Ohio Associates would buy western land, they insisted that Congress provide a system of government for the new territories.

For six months or more, in desultory fashion, Congress had been discussing the problem of territorial government without getting anywhere. Then Cutler appeared before Congress with an attractive offer. If his company could be assured of a satisfactory form of government, it would buy 1,000,000 acres of land. The Yankee clergyman, however, refused to offer more than 66⅔¢ an acre, a figure which Congress reluctantly accepted. But Cutler was not prepared to pay cash. He would buy the land with soldiers' certificates, which were so badly depreciated that in currency his 66⅔¢ actually was reduced to something less than 10¢.

Congress accepted the offer and then drafted a form of government. This was passed as the Northwest Ordinance of 1787. In this brilliant measure three different political stages were provided for. During the first, while the population of a given district in the Territory was small, Congress would exercise complete control. It would appoint a secretary, a governor, and judges. These officials would have full authority over the district, subject to established legal principles and to Congress. They did not have power to make laws, but they could select any laws of any of the states which might serve the needs of their district. The second stage would begin when the population of a given district should include 5000 adult male settlers. Then the voters were authorized to elect a legislature, with power to make laws and to levy taxes; the Territory could also send a delegate to Congress. The right to vote was granted to each adult male, possessed of a fifty-acre freehold, provided he had been a citizen of any of the states and had resided in the Territory for one year, or if he had resided in the Territory for two years. Aliens therefore might enjoy suffrage rights. When the total population of the Territory should reach the number of 60,000, it would be ready for the third stage: admission to statehood in the Union on terms of complete equality with the original states. The Ordinance also had a bill of rights. This section guaranteed religious freedom. It gave settlers the benefits of habeas corpus and the privilege of trial by jury. It guaranteed the right of bail; it provided for moderate fines; and it prohibited cruel and unusual punishments.

Northwest Ordinance

Here was a workable colonial system. It protected the settlers in their civil rights, and it gave them training in self-government. One of the defects of the British colonial system had been its failure to include any plan for raising the colonists from a position of inferiority to one of equality with the privileged ruling class in England. Under the American system the settlers could be sure of statehood, just as soon as their numbers warranted admission to the Union.

Cutler's own contribution to the Ordinance seems to have been not authorship but inspiration. It is hard to tell who was really responsible for the document. Many of its principles had been under discussion for several years, so the author was little more than an able compiler. Probably Nathan Dane had more to do with the form and phraseology than anyone else. He and Cutler therefore would have the distinction of turning out one of the greatest of all American laws.

There was one more important provision of the Ordinance—the prohibition of Negro slavery. It pledged the Northwest to an agricultural system based on free labor. The origin of this prohibition is not entirely clear. Nathan Dane wrote it, but Jefferson had suggested it in 1784. In fact, the hint was made at the time that in voting for the nonslavery principle, some southern members of Congress may have done so to deprive the Northwest of the advantages of slavery in order to prevent it from becoming a competitor of the South. In any case in the greater part of the old Northwest, climatic and agricultural conditions were unfavorable to slavery, so it would probably have taken no firmer hold there than it did in New York and New England. It is worth noting that in 1791 all the provisions of the Ordinance of 1787 were re-enacted by Congress in order that this colonial system might be continued by the new government. Under its satisfactory provisions, the United States spread its domain from the Appalachian Mountains to the Pacific coast.

The Ohio Associates bought 1,781,760 acres of land from Congress, and in 1788 General Putnam led the first permanent settlers into the Northwest Territory. They founded Marietta. In the same year another group bought a large tract about 200 miles farther west and started Cincinnati. Between Marietta and Cincinnati a third group of pioneers founded Chillicothe and still another laid the foundations of Cleveland, on Lake Erie. This eastern division of the Northwest Territory subsequently became the state of Ohio. Once reports were spread concerning the richness of the lands in the Ohio area, the movement of settlers became surprisingly rapid. In 1788 nearly 1000 boats carrying more than 18,000 people passed the site of Marietta on their way west.

Developments on the Frontier

Spanish-American Friction

The growth of settled communities on both sides of the Ohio River inevitably turned the attention of pioneers toward the Mississippi, the great natural highway of the central plains. The Mississippi furnished the only available route for exporting farm produce from the regions beyond the Appalachian barrier. It was actually cheaper and easier to ship goods from Pittsburgh to Philadelphia by way of the Ohio, the Mississippi, the Gulf of Mexico, and up the Atlantic coast than to send them directly east over the mountains. This was the case particularly for Kentucky and Ohio. Here was one reason why the western settlers wanted undisputed rights to use the river. Another reason was to be found in the Indian trade, still largely in the hands of the French, with headquarters at St. Louis. The change of title to lands east of the Mississippi from England to the United States, and the change of title to lands west of the Mississippi from France to Spain and back again to France in 1800, had left the French traders undisturbed. But the coming of Americans into the central valleys was bound to lead to competition, and the pioneers had no intention of leaving the French in control. As one means of protecting their growing trade with the Indians, the Americans demanded rights on the Mississippi.

American migration into the Southwest had already alarmed the Spaniards, who wanted the region for themselves. They had claimed the right to conquer it from the British, and they had been instrumental in preventing any French approval of American claims beyond the Alleghenies. In Madrid, from 1780 to 1782, John Jay had met with nothing but opposition from Spanish authorities. At the close of the Revolution England ceded Florida back to Spain, and Spain made plans to place obstacles in the way of American expansion. As early as 1782 the government of King Charles III of Spain asserted its exclusive right to control navigation on the Mississippi River, obviously with the intention of preventing its use by the Americans. In 1784 the Spanish authorities ordered the river closed to American navigation; Americans caught on the Mississippi would be placed under arrest and their goods would be confiscated.

Spanish agents also planned to bring the Indian tribes of Georgia and the Southwest under their jurisdiction. At a series of conferences between Spanish officials and three leading southern tribes—the Creeks, Chickasaws, and Choctaws—the Indians acknowledged the supremacy of Spain rather than of the United States, and they agreed to exclude all traders except those holding Spanish licenses. The aim here was to create an Indian buffer state between Spanish possessions and the United States. Nevertheless Spain did not consider her policy as one of hostility; her agents wanted Indian trade, not war with the United States. In fact, Spanish officials opposed Indian attacks upon American pioneers and refused to provide arms which the Creeks wanted for such attacks. The Creeks did make war upon settlements in Georgia and also those on the Cumberland River, but the Spaniards were not responsible for these attacks.

Jay and Gardoqui

In pursuing her policy of trade rather than war, Spain began negotiations with the United States for the purpose of settling outstanding differences. Of these the most important were boundary questions and American demands for rights of navigation on the Mississippi and of deposit at its mouth. In these negotiations Gardoqui represented Spain, while John Jay represented Congress. The two governments, however, were so far apart that agreement was impossible. Gardoqui's instructions prohibited him from granting any commercial privileges whatever to the Americans.

In 1786 Jay and Gardoqui agreed upon the draft of a treaty by which the United States surrendered not her rights on the river but the use of these rights for twenty years; in return Spain would grant limited commercial privileges. This indifference to the vital need of river transportation so angered the West and its friends that Jay did not venture to submit the document to Congress. While Congress through its representative was thus giving grave offense to the West, Spain was cautiously trying out a crafty scheme to sever the Southwest from the United States. Spanish officials decided to open the river to a few selected frontiersmen and in this way to win them over, and through them the whole population. The few men chosen were to be allowed navigation rights and the right of deposit, while their less fortunate neighbors found the river tightly closed.

In working out this program the Spanish agents had the cordial cooperation of General James Wilkinson, veteran of the American Revolution and an unscrupulous schemer. In 1788 Wilkinson became a Spanish agent and took an oath of allegiance to the king of Spain. Beginning in 1792 he received a Spanish pension of $2000 per year, and this payment continued for thirteen years. Aside from Wilkinson's own personal profits, the only result of this intrigue was to keep alive a separatist faction in the Southwest. This pro-Spanish group never became strong enough to lead an actual secession movement, but for several years it did keep Congress uneasy. The danger was not averted until Kentucky and Tennessee were admitted to the Union, in 1792 and 1796 respectively, and until, in 1795, the United States and Spain agreed to a formal treaty.

Vermont

Vermont was still another product of the colonization movement on the frontier. The early history of Vermont was influenced by a long controversy between New Hampshire and New York. In 1741 the king gave the region north of Massachusetts to New Hampshire. Then in 1764 the king declared the Connecticut River to be the eastern boundary of New York, north of Massachusetts. In the meantime settlers had moved into the region west of the Connecticut, having secured their land titles from New Hampshire. The colonial government of New York refused to recognize the validity of these titles and insisted that the Vermont farmers buy their land over again from New York. This dispute was marked by considerable local violence, in which the "Green Mountain Boys" subjected agents of New York to rough handling. In 1777 representatives of Vermont met at Windsor, adopted a state constitution, and appealed to Congress for admission to the Confederation. Congress was not strong enough to offend both New York and New Hampshire, and the Vermonters were left to their own devices. One of these was intrigue with the British.

The economic connections of Vermont resembled in principle those of Kentucky and Tennessee. The best natural outlet for her produce was by way of Montreal. Because Congress refused to give them what they asked for, the two Allen brothers carried on negotiations with the British. Like the Southwest, Vermont was one of those detached sections, ready to turn to the side which promised the more satisfactory economic advantages. Realizing how delicate the balance was, the Canadian government suggested the desirability of keeping Vermont independent and of granting favorable commercial concessions. This problem was not settled until 1791, when Vermont, the fourteenth state, was admitted to the Union.

In these frontier districts the feeling was largely the same. The United States was new, not able to command complete loyalty on the part of the original states and still less among the pioneers, whose main concern was the prosaic one of getting a living and whose patriotism would be molded by the government which would make the task as simple as possible. Unable to occupy its own territory in the Northwest, seriously threatened with the loss of Vermont and the Southwest, and tormented by Spanish claims for an enlarged Florida, the government of the Confederation struggled with problems which it was not powerful enough to solve.

Influence of the Frontier

Although the Continental Congress could do little for these various frontier communities beyond giving them the Ordinances of 1785 and 1787, the settlers contrived not only to make a living for themselves but also to create impressive new communities. In 1790 Kentucky had a population of 73,677 and Tennessee, 35,691. By 1800 Kentucky alone could boast a population of 220,995.

The frontier made important contributions to American life, particularly by promoting a stronger national feeling. In these western communities there were representatives of many states and sections of the country. Marietta and Cleveland in Ohio were founded by pioneers from New England. Cincinnati was started by settlers from the middle states, chiefly New Jersey and Pennsylvania. Still a third group in Ohio came from Virginia. This last contingent represented the small-farmer class in the piedmont rather than the great planters, Virginians who had no difficulty in adjusting themselves to the simple type of life and to the system of free labor which they found in their new homes. This mingling of Americans from all parts of the country was an important factor in breaking down the prevalent spirit of local state pride and in developing American loyalties.

Economic Adjustments

The problems of the frontier and of foreign policy were undeniably difficult. But they probably looked worse than they really were, because of unfavorable economic conditions. Before the Revolution American leaders had prophesied great prosperity just as soon as the Americans were freed from British commercial restrictions. In the long run this prediction was sound. But the advocates of freedom overlooked the temporary difficulties which were sure to accompany any change in the political structure. For a time these difficulties were peculiarly troublesome. In fact, the immediate result of political independence was economic confusion.

Commercial Problems

For a time British authorities seemed inclined to be generous in granting commercial concessions to their former subjects. In March 1783 the younger Pitt, chancellor of the exchequer, introduced a bill in Parliament for the purpose of admitting American ships and American commodities into British West Indian ports on the terms which prevailed before 1763. Pitt's bill also gave American ships their former privileges in the carrying trade. Two months later Hartley, one of the British peace commissioners at Paris, proposed that commerce between his country and the United States be established "on the most enlarged principles of reciprocal benefit to both countries." He even suggested a formal treaty providing "that all the citizens of the United States of America shall be permitted to import into, and export from, any part of his Britannic Majesty's dominions, in American ships, any goods, wares, and merchandises" which had been so imported and exported before the war.

But Pitt and his fellow liberals were opposed by a conservative group, with Lord Sheffield as its spokesman. Pointing out that the United States had become a foreign nation, Sheffield went on:

> It is the situation she herself has chosen by asserting her independence. . . . By asserting their independence the Americans have renounced the privileges, as well as the duties, of British subjects. If, in some instances, as in the loss of the carrying trade, they feel the inconvenience of their choice, they can no longer complain.

Lord Sheffield objected to Pitt's bill for readmitting Americans into the closed circle of British mercantilism. By forcing the former subjects to accept the consequences of their choice, the British could increase their own trade. If American ships were excluded from all carrying trade in the British West Indies, employment would be found for hundreds of British sloops. The Americans could not retaliate by threatening to buy their manufactured goods outside the Empire, because mere self-interest would compel them to buy in the cheapest market. Lord Sheffield also pointed out that a considerable part of American commerce before the war had been conducted with the help of long-term credit and that the British alone were in a position to grant such credit.

Lord Sheffield carried his point, and in July 1783 a new British order in council defined the status of American trade. With the exception of salt fish, American exports could be taken to the West Indies, but only in British-built and British-owned ships. West Indian products could be taken to the United States, but only in British bottoms. The exception of salt fish from the list of permissible exports to the West Indies was significant. In the Treaty of 1783 the British recognized American rights in the Newfoundland fisheries, but it was the West Indian market which made the fisheries profitable. If the British should exclude American fish from their islands, they would nullify an important provision of the Treaty of 1783.

Postwar Trade

If this order in council had been enforced it probably would have done considerable harm. But it was not strictly enforced. British planters in the

West Indies bought American goods carried in American ships. In addition to this extensive illegal trade with British islands, the Americans were allowed to trade with French Martinique and with Spanish Cuba. According to available evidence, therefore, the British order in council of 1783 did not give British ships the desired monopoly in commerce between the West Indies and North America. It did, however, arouse American wrath. Evidence of this anti-English feeling may be found in retaliatory legislation adopted in at least six of the thirteen states. Massachusetts, New Hampshire, and Rhode Island prohibited British vessels from loading any American goods or merchandise. Maryland and North Carolina imposed heavy discriminatory port charges on British ships, while both Maryland and New York placed double import duties on all goods brought in British ships. Restrictive measures of this sort have a way of reacting unfavorably upon the makers, particularly so when some shipping centers refuse to cooperate. Connecticut would not join with her associates, so she was in a position to pick up trade which the laws of her neighbors might turn away.

Much more important than these retaliatory devices were the efforts to open new lines of commerce. Even before the end of the Revolution merchants from New England were investigating opportunities in Swedish ports, and it was not long before American ships were going to Holland, Russia, Portugal, and to the German port of Hamburg. In 1784 merchants of New York sent the *Empress of China* to the Orient, and so began the extensive American ventures in Chinese and East Indian waters.

It is difficult to tell precisely how extensive this postwar commerce was because of the lack of statistical information. But the following table is probably as accurate as any to be found.

Year	*Exports from the United States*	*Imports into the United States*
1784	£ 749,345	£3,679,467
1785	893,594	2,308,023
1786	843,119	1,603,465
1787	893,637	2,009,111
1788	1,023,789	1,886,142

There seems to be no way of breaking down these totals to show the extent of trade with different ports, but it would be safe to attribute 90 percent of the imports to British sources. For purposes of comparison, it is interesting to note that in 1774, the thirteen colonies had imported goods from England to the value of £2,532,919. In 1784, therefore, American imports of British goods were some 45 percent above normal. The war was hardly finished when Americans began to stock up with British imports.

During colonial times such imports had been paid for with profits from the export trade to the West Indies, and American merchants hoped for a continuance of the old system. But the figures just given for postwar exports indicate a disproportionate decline. Imports therefore had to be paid for in specie, and the result was a temporary but acute shortage of money in some sections of the United States. The troubles of this "critical period" were due to unbalanced trade.

There is an abundance of contemporary comment in letters and newspapers in support of these general statements. Commerce was active enough to bring substantial fortunes to the new class of wartime profiteers. Money came easily and it was spent freely. This tendency accounts for the widespread complaints of luxurious living. In 1784 the *Massachusetts Centinel* of Boston warned the people of the serious consequences certain to result from

> . . . such unbounded importations of European manufactures, as have taken place since the Peace; nevertheless the rage still continues with unabating ardor. . . . Since the establishment of independence, as total a revolution has taken place in the system of our commerce, as in the administration of our government; and an entire new code of laws is now as necessary for the regulation of the one, as a new constitution was for the administration of the other.

Not long afterward the same paper published an address to the inhabitants of Massachusetts, signed "An American," of which the following was the burden of the argument:

> The general complaints among all ranks, in the city and in the village, are the scarcity of specie, and the great encrease of luxury and prodigality.—It is vanity to think of preventing our money from leaving the country, while the present inordinate consumption of foreign gewgaws continues.

Shortage of Money

As a result of these abnormal commercial conditions some of the American people were rich while others found themselves without money. Men who had been fairly well off could pay neither debts nor taxes. People complained of the high cost of government. When creditors sued their debtors they could not collect because people had no money. Lawyers, sheriffs, and even judges became unpopular because they tried to enforce the laws regarding debts and property rights. In Massachusetts, some towns petitioned the legislature either for a reduction or a complete remission of taxes; the town of Palmer described its poverty as follows:

> The great dificualties That the Inhabitants of this Commonwealth (and the Said Town of Palmer in Particular) Labours under by Reason of the grate scarsety of surculating medeam Rendors it dificualt for the said Inhabitants to Paye There Taxes and cary on there Nessessary bussiness.

One resident of Salem in 1786 found money so scarce that his church collection brought in hardly a dollar.

If there was no money, the logical thing seemed to be to print paper notes. There was no limit to the quantity which might be turned out and the greater the issues, the higher prices would go. Then the farmers could pay their debts. Seven of the thirteen states tried to cure their trouble by this means. Rhode Island not only made paper money legal tender but imposed a fine on people who should refuse to receive it. Merchants closed their shops and farmers from Massachusetts and Connecticut would not bring provisions into the state. They did not care to take their pay in worthless paper.

The Continental Congress was in no condition to help the states. Congress could not even support itself. Each state could raise some money through taxation but under the Articles of Confederation Congress could not raise a penny. Since Congress could not even pay interest on the Revolutionary War debt, the principal continued to grow year after year. When Congress appealed to the states for an amendment to the Articles so as to permit a national import duty of 5 percent, Rhode Island refused to agree. A second proposed amendment that would have given Congress the power to collect duties for only five years was killed by the action of New York. From 1781 to 1786 Congress was able to collect by means of so-called requisitions about $2,500,000, not enough to meet payments due on the foreign debt alone, with not a shadow left for either the domestic debt or for running expenses. In 1784 the total debt, foreign and domestic, amounted to about $35,000,000, and it was steadily increasing because of unpaid interest.

Rebellion and Recovery

The climax of this story of hard times was Shays's Rebellion, which occurred in Massachusetts in 1786. Even before the end of the Revolution the farmers of Massachusetts had complained of their lot. For a few years they had profited heavily, but after 1780, as prices fell and taxes steadily rose, the country people were reduced to hardship. Because of the fluctuating paper currency, their earlier prosperity had no real permanence, and they could lay by nothing to carry them through a series of lean years. The more farsighted ones had paid off their mortgages while profits remained high, but not all had been sensible enough to do that. By 1782 and 1783 the agricultural counties of the state were facing bankruptcy.

Farmers' Problems

The farmers complained because the paper-money laws had been repealed. More specifically they were bitterly opposed to the courts, in which actions for debt might be brought, to the lawyers who brought suit, and to the government officials who were drawing high salaries. The restless spirits said that the yeomanry, the very bulwark of the state, was being "Squeezed and Oppres'd, to maintain a few Lawyers . . . who grow Rich on the Ruins of their Neighbors."

Agitation against hard times had started in 1782. In March of that year the town of Hardwick, Worcester County, sent out a circular letter proposing a county convention to discuss grievances and possible remedies. Early in April thirty-four delegates came together, representing twenty-six towns. The next month a still larger convention met and repeated the stock complaints against high taxes and the use of courts of justice as debt-collecting machinery. In 1782 and 1783 Hampshire County, in the Connecticut valley, had seven county conventions called to discuss economic grievances. The leader in this area was a former clergyman, Samuel Ely. Ely made the following complaints:

Conventions of Protest

> We must throw up our constitution . . . the constitution is broke already, the Governor has too much salary, the Judges of the Superior Court have too much salary, we can get men that will ride the circuit for half the money . . . the General Court should not sit; we will pay no more respect to them than to puppies.

This agitation came to a climax in 1786. In June of that year the House of Representatives adjourned without complying with the demand for paper money. The conservative *Massachusetts Centinel* was really frightened at the probability of trouble:

> The spirit of discontent which has seized on all orders, and appears in every part of the continent, as well as in this State in particular, must create the most serious apprehensions in the breast of every real patriot— The people of property are in continual fears of such measures being adopted, either by a paper currency, tender law, or some other visionary expedient, as well destroy all Confidence not only in the State, but in one another. Those who have little to lose, and subsist wholly on speculation are equally dissatisfied with the present situation of affairs, and as no change can be for the worse, are universally wishing for the very things which are deprecated by the others as the worst of evils. A general ferment of opinion prevails, and it is not easy to predict the consequences. . . .

In August county conventions met in Worcester, Hampshire, and Middlesex counties. On August 29 a mob took possession of the courthouse at Northampton and prevented the court from sitting. The situation was so serious that Governor James Bowdoin issued a proclamation, calling attention to attacks upon the courts and to the widespread, open defiance of the authority of the government. He ordered all judges, sheriffs, grand jurors, constables, and other officers to suppress disorder, and then he authorized the use of the militia. A few days later some of the inhabitants of Boston met in Faneuil Hall, to express disapproval of the methods adopted by the discontented elements and to assure the governor of their readiness to uphold his authority.

Shays's Rebellion

Governor Bowdoin made a vigorous show of official authority and doubtless prevented the disorders from becoming more serious. In November, by way of assuring peaceful and undisturbed sessions of the Supreme Court in Cambridge, the governor stationed three regiments of infantry and three companies of artillery there. Newspapers reported that insurgents from Berkshire, Middlesex, Hampshire, and Worcester counties had collected near Worcester for an impressive march upon Cambridge, but they changed their minds when they heard of the governor's vigorous preparations to receive them. A small insurgent army of 350 did seize the courthouse in Worcester.

By this time leadership of the insurgents devolved upon Daniel Shays, a veteran of the Revolution. He had been promoted to a captaincy in that war and when peace came his fellow citizens had elected him to various local offices. He was therefore no mere upstart of a troublemaker but a respectable citizen caught in the tangle of economic depression. His participation in the revolt of 1786 indicates that conditions were serious.

Finding their plans for an attack upon Cambridge blocked by the militia, Shays and his associates turned westward toward the Connecticut valley and started for Springfield. Their objective was the arsenal which had been established during the American Revolution. The crisis came on January 25, 1787, when Shays with a force of 1200 men appeared before Springfield. The insurgents found General Shepard waiting for them with some companies of artillery. General Shepard opened fire and so forced the rebels to break ranks and retreat. Shays's Rebellion was over. The General Court passed a law imposing disabilities on all the rebels who were caught, but there were no executions, and Governor Bowdoin's successor, John Hancock, pardoned those who were still in prison. Bowdoin's course of impressive firmness in the face of attack and of wise moderation when the danger was over revealed unusual common sense on his part. By March 1787 General Lincoln reported from Pittsfield that a large number of former rebels with their household furniture and their cattle were moving into Vermont.

After the whole thing was over and peace had been restored, Barnabas Bidwell of Berkshire County wrote his impressions of the character and quality of the insurgents:

> I find the majority of the populace has been disaffected to Government measures. The Gentlemen of learning & the liberal professions, especially the Clergy, are universally for Government. Debtors are generally on the other side, and this class comprehends more than half of the people. Persons guilty of crimes, or who wish to commit crimes: Rhode Island Emigrants and almost all the denomination of Baptists; men of warm passions and but little reason; men of fickle minds, fond of every new scheme and proud of an enterprising spirit,— such have pretty generally engaged in the Insurrection. They have been joined by many, who have no attachment to any establishment, but were glad of the commotion, as it gave them something to do. They have also drawn in a large number of boys; and also of the ignorant, uninformed, but well-meaning common people, who hearing such a dreadful out cry against Government, believed there were some intolerable grievances, although they knew not what.

To the advocates of law and order this uprising of debt-ridden farmers and thoughtless boys against high taxes, debts, courts of justice, and the authority of government looked like anarchy, and they were afraid of more serious outbreaks in the future. John Jay wrote that the prevailing insecurity of property and the lack of confidence in government might lead the orderly and industrious part of the population to despair of liberty itself. The implication was that he feared the establishment of an autocratic system as the only force capable of holding disorders in check.

General Knox, who subsequently became secretary of war, feared an actual social revolution; writing of the insurgents he declared:

> Their creed is that the property of the United States has been protected from the confiscation of Britain by the joint exertions of *all,* and therefore ought to be the *common property of all;* and he that attempts opposition to this creed is an enemy to equity and justice, and ought to be swept from off the face of the earth. . . . They are determined to annihilate all debts, public and private, and have agrarian laws. . . . This dreadful situation [Knox assured Washington] has alarmed every man of principle and property in New England. . . . Our government must be braced, changed or altered to secure our lives and property.

Fortunately, a turn for the better in economic affairs removed the grounds of discontent. In most states the economic crisis had already passed before Daniel Shays led his men on that forlorn venture into Springfield, and by the summer of 1787 good times were apparent. Even in November 1786 Benjamin Franklin found the best of reasons for optimism:

Economic Recovery

> Our husbandmen, who are the bulk of the nation, have plentiful crops, their produce sells at high prices and for ready, hard money. . . . Our working people are all employed and all get high wages, are well fed and well clad. Our estates in houses are trebled in value by the rising of rents since the Revolution. Buildings in Philadelphia increase amazingly, besides small towns rising in every quarter of the country.

By 1788 the people had settled down to hard work, and they were getting full benefits from it. There were still complaints of a shortage of cash in Massachusetts, but no more talk of rebellion. When John Adams returned from England in that year he wrote: "The agriculture, fisheries, manufactures, and commerce of the country are very well, much better than I expected to find them."

As an instance of mob activity the rebellion would have had little significance for the United States as a whole, but, coming as it did in the midst of hard times and a general disinclination to respect law and the government, it assumed in the minds of men then living the sinister aspect of anarchy. Had it not been for the return of better economic conditions no one can tell how far the disorder might have spread. Thoughtful Americans of that day were alarmed over the danger to the fabric of society, while property owners were fearful of the loss of all they possessed.

Those who were most seriously affected by the dangers in the critical period, the merchants and larger property owners, men with money to lose, began seriously to contemplate revision of the Articles of Confederation, with a view to safeguarding not only their own interests but the public interests which depended upon a continuance of peace and good order. As one of them put it tersely at the time: "What is property without good government?"

There was considerably more than coincidence in the juxtaposition of Shays's Rebellion and the plans for the Federal Convention of 1787. One serious threat to good government had been confined to a single state and had been suppressed by local authorities. What if the disturbance had spread more widely and what if local governments had been unable to hold it in check? In case of such a crisis there was no superior power which could intervene. The Continental Congress had been purposely left without power over the states; it could be of no help in time of trouble. If property were worth nothing without good government, it behooved the American people to provide the government. This relationship between the threat of wide disorder and the creation of the federal Constitution justifies attention to a rebellion which failed of all its immediate objectives.

Political Results

Chapter 11

THE FEDERAL CONSTITUTION

The Drive for a New Government

Drive for a New Government

It is difficult to measure the influence of any rebel such as Daniel Shays upon the thought of his own time. He was neither a philosopher nor a writer, and he left no record beyond what appears in the newspapers and in the letters of his badly scared contemporaries. But he did frighten the well-to-do into a panic. Advocates of a new government found him a great help in their work; he could be cited as an impressive example of what might happen if the Confederation were left unchanged. He did not initiate the movement leading toward the Federal Convention, but his activities furnished the promoters with vivid arguments in favor of a change.

The unsatisfactory character of the Articles of Confederation was evident even before they had been adopted by the states. As early as 1780 Alexander Hamilton was urging a more powerful central government. By 1787 the demand for action was too strong to be resisted. James Madison was finding fault with the Confederation not so much on grounds of economics as on grounds of the inevitable ineptitude of Congress. He cited the violation of treaties, the defiance of Congress by the states, the absence of effective guarantees against domestic uprisings, the lack of coercive power in the Confederacy—all these in addition to the refusal of the states to comply with congressional requisitions for money. Madison even went so far as to propose a congressional negative on state laws. Another important factor at work was the controversy between Americans and Spaniards in the Southwest. A stronger government might compel Spain to grant American rights.

Before Shays's Rebellion had begun, a chain of events had been started which soon led to action. Virginia and Maryland were trying to work out a policy covering the navigation of the Potomac. In 1785, at Washington's invitation, commissioners from the two states met at Mount Vernon and drew up resolutions on the subject. Then Maryland suggested another conference on commercial questions and asked that both Pennsylvania and Delaware be invited. The Virginia legislature approved, and its commission, with Madison as a member, invited the other states to send delegates to a convention to meet at Annapolis in the early fall of 1786.

Call for the Federal Convention

Only five states sent representatives to the Annapolis meeting. Unable to accomplish anything because of lack of support, the Annapolis delegates proposed another convention of all the states, to meet at Philadelphia the second Monday in May 1787. There it would be possible "to devise such further provisions as shall appear to them necessary to render the constitution of the federal government adequate to the exigencies of the Union," and to report a plan for that purpose to Congress for submission to the states. Congress issued a formal invitation, calling upon the states to send delegates to a convention "for the sole and express purpose of revising the articles of confederation."

Twelve states took advantage of the opportunity to share in the deliberations; only Rhode Island, the traditional home of the otherwise-minded, refused to send delegates. The members were chosen by the state legislatures, so they were good examples of the governing class. They were conservative, alarmed at the widely prevalent signs of disorder, and anxious to provide for better enforcement of the laws. They had the benefit of practical experience in government, either as state executives, members of their local legislatures, or as members of Congress.

Businessmen wanted a stronger central government to bring about a revival of commerce. Other advocates of a strong central government who stressed economic considerations were the holders of Revolutionary paper. This paper had depreciated badly, and the Confederation held out no hope of improvement. Both bona fide holders and shrewd speculators were aware of advantages to come if the government should establish American credit. The market value of the debt would be substantially increased. Still other economic interests were agitating for a change. Alexander Hamilton and certain Americans wished to promote industrial development in America; a more powerful central government would be in a position to help them. Congress had no authority to levy a protective tariff, and without a tariff how could manufacturers hope to compete with established British interests? On the other hand, many political leaders of the Revolution still believed that any government strong enough to provide safeguards for business and for property would be a menace, not only to the liberties of the people but to the very existence of the states themselves. In this group were small farmers and debtors and a number of believers in abstract doctrines of the rights of man. These were the Anti-Federalists.

Although the Federal Convention met only eleven years after the adoption of the Declaration of Independence, the men who had signed the Declaration were conspicuously absent from the convention. Thirty-nine delegates signed the Constitution; of these only six had signed the Declaration. The old revolutionists were out of the picture. Democracy, for a time a word to conjure with, temporarily became a symbol of "Shaysism." The new leaders abandoned the doctrine that any group of people had a right to overthrow the government at will. Many delegates actually believed that popular power should be suppressed. Edmund Randolph of Virginia declared: "Our chief danger arises from the democratic parts of our constitution. . . . None of the [state] constitutions have provided sufficient checks against the democracy. The feeble Senate of Virginia is a phantom. . . ."

Political Theory

Roger Sherman of Connecticut did not believe that the people should elect members of the House of Representatives. He would have given this power to the state legislatures: "The people . . . should have as little to do as may be about the Government. They want information and are constantly liable to be misled." Elbridge Gerry of Massachusetts supported Sherman: "The evils we experience flow from the excess of democracy. The people do not want virtue; but are the dupes of pretended patriots." Randolph of Virginia explained that one cause of the prevailing unrest in the United States was to be found "in the turbulence and follies of democracy."

While some members of the Convention thus opposed democracy, others ridiculed the principle of disinterested service to the people. Alexander Hamilton argued that men must have material inducements to make them support the government. He would shape public policies so as to benefit the rich, and he would make it possible for officeholders to enrich themselves:

> A reliance on pure patriotism had been the source of many of our errors. Take mankind in general, they are vicious—their passions may be operated upon. . . . We have been taught to reprobate the danger of influence in the British government. . . . One great error is that we suppose mankind more honest than they are. Our prevailing passions are ambition and interest; and it will ever be the duty of a wise government to avail itself of those passions, in order to make them subservient to the public good—for these ever induce us to action.

Gouverneur Morris even more bluntly declared that

> . . . loaves and fishes must bribe the Demagogues. They must be made to expect higher offices under the general than the State governments. A Senate for life will be a noble bait. Without such captivating prospects, the popular leaders will oppose and defeat the plan. . . . We should remember that the people never act from reason alone.

Some of the delegates wanted to substitute the principle of national supremacy for the doctrine of states' rights. William Pinkney of Maryland introduced a motion to give the new national legislature power to annul any state laws which it should "judge to be improper." Only then could the states be kept in "due subordination to the nation." James Madison seconded the motion and observed that "an indefinite power to negative legislative acts of the States is absolutely necessary to a perfect system."

The Federal Convention therefore represented a social, economic, and political group which had little in common with the revolutionists of 1775, and the delegates spoke a language which would have been unrecognizable in the First Continental Congress. Even so, it is not necessary to jump to the conclusion that the primary motive of the Federalists in promoting the Constitution was the desire to line their own pockets. The motives shaping human behavior are not so simple. The immediate problem of the delegates was to devise a federal system with a satisfactory division of authority between the nation and the states. In the years before 1775 British officials had struggled with this same problem and they had evolved a workable federal system. The Crown and Parliament had taken charge of defense,

Federalism in the Empire

The same authorities had regulated commerce and had tried to standardize the monetary system. The same central government had provided an inter-colonial postal system. If domestic disturbances upset local authorities, British troops restored order. When any colonial legislature passed an undesirable law the Privy Council might disallow it. The House of Lords was the final court of last resort to which appeals could be carried from local colonial courts. Actually the Federal Convention had to invent very little that was new; it merely utilized existing experience.

The New Constitution

The Federal Convention was in session from May 25 to September 7, 1787. During that time fifty-five delegates attended, although they were not all present at any one time. The average attendance ranged from thirty to thirty-five. The discussions were carried on in secrecy. Theoretically the Convention had assembled to amend the Articles of Confederation, but a number of delegates, including the leaders of the Virginia delegation, drew up a plan which proved to be the framework of the Constitution itself. This Virginia plan called for the establishment of a two-chambered legislature, a national executive, and a system of national courts. The new legislature was to have power to act—to pass laws and to levy taxes.

The policy of the antinational or weak government group was embodied in the New Jersey or Paterson plan, which called merely for a revision of the Confederation. Paterson and his friends would permit Congress to levy import duties, to regulate trade, and to compel the states to pay the sums assessed against them by the central authority. In this way the two main theories concerning a proper form of government for the United States were laid before the Convention.

The Compromises

The first contest between the two groups came over the issue of representation in Congress. The Federalists wanted representation on the basis of population, while the Anti-Federalists wanted to preserve the principle of equality of states. The delegates voted that the states should be represented in the lower house on the basis of population. In the upper house, or Senate, all states were represented equally. This arrangement was often called the Connecticut Compromise, or the Great Compromise.

Several more compromises were adopted. One issue was that of direct taxes: Should Congress have power to levy them and, if so, on what basis—population or property? As the discussions proceeded, some of the conservative eastern delegates saw a chance to insure their section against a possible danger from the growing influence of the West. Congress might admit new states, and they would be represented on the basis of population. Let direct taxes be assessed on the same principle, said the Easterners. Then, even if the West should acquire a preponderating influence in the new Congress, it would have to pay for its power in direct taxes. At this point the question had to be decided whether or not, for purposes of representation and direct taxes, slaves were a part of the population. Some of the delegates suggested a ratio which had been used before—that is, the inclusion of three fifths of the slaves in the figures which would determine the number of representatives and direct taxes. This "federal ratio" was adopted.

Again there was a difference of opinion between the southern agricultural states and the middle and northern commercial centers. The mercantile interests wanted to give Congress authority to regulate trade, while the plantation interests demurred at this for fear that the power might be used to block the slave trade. The regulation of commerce was lodged in the hands of Congress with the proviso that there should be no interference with the slave trade for twenty years and no export taxes.

One of the most complicated of the compromises was that concerning the election of the President. Various proposals were offered, all derived from precedents controlling state executives. One group urged that the President be elected by Congress, while another proposed election by the voters. The Convention arranged for a semi-indirect election. The voters choose electors, and they in turn select the President. But if no candidate considered by them should secure a majority, then the House of Representatives, voting by states, would select one from the five highest on the electors' list.

These compromises reveal much of the spirit prevailing in the Convention. There were differences of opinion, and stubbornness was evident. The less conciliatory members withdrew and went home, but the majority of delegates were able to forget their personal preferences for the sake of the public welfare, and the Constitution was made possible by their efforts. While the irreconcilables went home, these others stayed and helped to make the United States a going concern. The Federal Convention finished its sessions on September 17, 1787.

Supreme Law of the Land

The Constitution made possible the creation of a national government. The Constitution itself, all federal laws passed by virtue of its authority, and all treaties made under it are "the supreme Law of the Land; and the Judges in every State shall be bound thereby, any Thing in the Constitution or Laws of any State to the contrary notwithstanding." In many ways this statement is the most significant part of the whole document. In the future no state could maintain a law contrary to the Constitution. One might think that this supremacy of federal law would need the guarantee of force, but the framers were too well acquainted with the prevailing temper to talk of force. The method which they adopted is more effective than force, and it did not arouse serious antagonism. Every state judge became an agent for upholding the Constitution, because his decisions must take account of the Constitution and the laws passed under it.

Another factor contributing to the supremacy of the Constitution was the power given to the federal government to act directly on individuals. Any person who violated the Constitution or the federal laws was liable to punishment in federal courts. No state could save its citizens from such punishment by any method short of actual rebellion. Under the Articles of Confederation the government lacked this power of dealing with offenders, because the state governments alone had jurisdiction over individuals.

This principle of national supremacy was upheld further by the power of the Supreme Court to declare an act of Congress or of a state legislature unconstitutional. It is true that this power is not named in the Constitution, and it is also true that Congress is empowered to define the appellate jurisdiction of the Supreme Court. Nevertheless, the Court has exercised this power. John Marshall advocated this power for the Court in the Virginia Convention which ratified the Constitution, and he developed it fully in one of his famous decisions as Chief Justice, in the case of *Marbury* v. *Madison*.

President and Congress

The Constitution created the office of President, with effective powers. The President was expected to enforce the laws. He was made commander in chief of the army and navy. He could veto acts of Congress unless both houses of Congress, by a two-thirds vote, should pass the measure over again. He also was empowered to direct the foreign policy of the government. To make him independent, the Constitution guaranteed him a term of four years in office, during which he could be removed only on proof of high crimes and misdemeanors. The President had become the policy-making official of the federal government.

Among the extensive powers granted to Congress, control over finance stands first. Congress is the money-raising and the money-spending branch of the government. Borrowing and taxing powers are broad. Equally important for the welfare of the people is the power to regulate interstate and foreign commerce. In other matters where uniform practices were essential, Congress received full authority to act. To prevent unfair treatment or discrimination in the case of new arrivals from other countries who should wish to become citizens, Congress was empowered to pass naturalization laws. And because business could not be confined within state limits, business troubles became the concern of Congress. To assist in the process of settling the affairs of those who could not pay their debts, Congress was allowed to pass a national bankruptcy law. Congress received full power to coin money and to regulate the value thereof.

During the colonial period the British government had inaugurated a postal service, and the Confederation continued this arrangement. The Constitution gave Congress power to provide such service for all the states. This involved the granting of contracts for carrying mail and the regulation of postal charges. To encourage inventions and to give inventors the reward due them for their work, Congress was empowered to pass laws defining the conditions under which patent rights may be issued. Once the American people turned their attention to industrial activity, the Patent Office became an extremely important branch of our government.

The Constitution conferred upon Congress the power to declare war. But once war has begun, the body which authorizes it has no power to bring it to an end. The President and the Senate do that, by virtue of their treaty-making rights. Theoretically, Congress could stop a war by refusing to raise money for it, but so far no such drastic step has been considered necessary.

In keeping with the fundamental principle of national supremacy, the Constitution imposed a number of restrictions upon the hitherto unlimited power of the states. State governments could no longer issue bills of credit—the kind of paper money which had depreciated so fast during the Revolution. (The states succeeded partly in nullifying this provision by chartering state banks which issued notes.) The states were forbidden also to collect duties on imports and to impose tonnage or other port charges on shipping. Again, state legislatures were prohibited from passing any laws that would make possible the violation of contracts.

In one other respect the Constitution reflected recent developments in the United States. Shays's Rebellion had alarmed property owners all over the country, and the alarm was peculiarly disturbing because there was no power above the state capable of interfering in this local disturbance. The Constitution provides that the President may send federal troops into a state to suppress domestic insurrection, if the legislature asks for help or, in case the legislature is not in session, if the governor so requests. Even if a state does not request help, the President may send in troops to uphold federal laws.

Checks and Balances

In its three separate branches—judicial, executive, and legislative—the new federal government could effectively transact the various kinds of business which would properly come before it. According to the theory of that day each branch needed some independence, but not too much. Therefore each branch was subject to checks by one of the others. Although the President and the Senate appointed the justices of the Supreme Court, they could not remove these important officials. Although the Supreme Court might declare an act of Congress unconstitutional, Congress could prevent such action by limiting the jurisdiction of the Court. The President as commander in chief of the army could not make himself tyrannical, because Congress could destroy the army by refusing to provide money for it. Although the President had charge of foreign policy, he had to submit treaties to the Senate for its approval, and war could not be declared except by act of Congress.

At least, this was the theory of checks and balances. In practice the executive and legislature have rarely been so completely separated as one might expect. We talk about branches of the government as though they were something impersonal, but there can be no government except through the agency of men. And men have a way of modifying customs and even constitutions. Every able President from Washington's time to the present has compelled Congress to follow his orders when he wished to do so, thereby bridging the gap which is supposed to separate the executive from the legislature.

Ratification

The Convention sent the new document to Congress and Congress sent it to the states. The members of the Convention realized that there would be vigorous opposition to the new Constitution, and they felt certain that much of the opposition was already represented in the state legislatures. To let these bodies pass on the document might prove disastrous. It was therefore proposed to entrust the work of ratification to state conventions especially chosen for this purpose. Again, since the Articles of Confederation required the approval of all thirteen states for any change in the form of government, and unanimity on a proposal to abandon the old Articles entirely could not be expected, the Convention declared that ratification by nine states would be sufficient.

The publication of the Constitution plunged the whole country into a discussion of the relative merits of the confederation *versus* the federal union. Voters were soon divided into two groups, the Federalists and the Anti-Federalists. The Federalists included the financial and commercial interests in the North, men who feared that society itself was endangered by the prevalent political thinking and by such outbreaks as Shays's Rebellion; associated with the financiers and merchants were many of the larger plantation owners in the South. The Federalists for one reason or another realized the need of a stronger central government.

Federalists and Anti-Federalists

The opposition, probably much larger numerically, included the small farmers throughout the country and some of the more important farmers in the South. In Massachusetts the followers of Daniel Shays were Anti-Federalist almost to a man. So too were the old leaders of pre-Revolutionary days, Patrick Henry, Richard Henry Lee, and, for a time, Samuel Adams. They feared the power of a remote lawmaking body like Parliament. They had helped to bring about a war to prevent the establishment of a British central government over the states; some of these men looked upon the proposed American system as almost as bad. These Anti-Federalists found certain defects in the Constitution. They found no bill of rights in it; what would happen to the freedom of the individual without a bill of rights? Then they felt that the Constitution conferred too much power upon the federal government, more than Great Britain had enjoyed and more than could safely be intrusted to any human beings.

In addition to these arguments the Anti-Federalists raised various ill-defined fears concerning the proposed system. They were afraid of arbitrary power, of the loss of their liberties, and of tyrannical domination by men of property. They complained about the ambiguous phraseology of the document itself, professing to find evidence of studied duplicity which boded ill for the common man. Again as they saw it, the new document gave too great power to the new executive.

The Federalists undertook to meet these objections. They emphasized the solid advantages, both political and economic, which would follow ratification. They held out the promise of more satisfactory relations with foreign powers; better business at home; prosperity for everybody, including the farmers; orderly government; and the security of property. The best statement of their beliefs is to be found in the series of newspaper essays signed "Federalist," written by Alexander Hamilton, John Jay, and James Madison.

Federalist Success

During the flood of popular discussion the voters of each state elected delegates to special ratifying conventions. Both parties worked hard to control these bodies. At the start the Anti-Federalists seemed to have the advantage; they were at least more numerous. But the Federalists had the benefit of greater political experience and of better leadership. They also had the prestige of George Washington on their side. With such assets they were able to overcome the superior numbers of their opponents.

Five of the states ratified quickly: Delaware (Dec. 7, 1787), Pennsylvania (Dec. 12), New Jersey (Dec. 18), Georgia and Connecticut (in the first two weeks of 1788). There was little opposition except in Pennsylvania, which was held in line by the vigorous efforts of leading Federalists. In some of the other states the opponents were strong enough to threaten defeat, but again superior leadership brought success to the Federalists.

In New Hampshire, when the convention assembled, a majority of the delegates represented constituents who were strongly opposed to ratification. This feeling seems to have been due to misunderstanding and Anti-Federalist agitation, because according to one report, few citizens of the state had any first-hand acquaintance with the document. Tobias Lear wrote to George Washington:

> I was surprised to find . . . that so little information respecting the Constitution had been diffused among the people. The valuable numbers of Publius are not known. . . . The debates of the Pennsylvania and Massachusetts Conventions have been read by but few persons; and many other pieces, which contain useful information have never been heard of.

Because of the strength of the opposition the Federalists had to utilize the strategy of delay; they secured an adjournment from February until June. By dint of much effort enough delegates were converted to the Federalist cause to risk a vote. When the test came, the convention voted for ratification by a majority of ten: 57 to 47.

When Massachusetts chose the delegates to her state convention, impressions left by Shays's Rebellion were still vivid, and Shays's followers were well represented in the convention. Benjamin Lincoln wrote to Washington:

> Many of the insurgents are in the Convention, even some of Shays's officers. We could hardly expect anything else; nor could we . . . justly suppose that those men, who were so lately intoxicated with large draughts of liberty, and who were thirsting for more would . . . submit to a Constitution which would

further take up the reins of Government, which, in their opinion, were too straight before.

For a time Samuel Adams opposed the Constitution, and he never really approved it. The most that his friends could accomplish at first was to induce him to refrain from open agitation against it; at the end he voted for ratification. John Hancock remained in doubt until he was able to see on which side the majority lay. In some sections of the state feeling against the Constitution was so strong that forty-six towns refused to send delegates to the convention. Had they been represented the outcome might have been different. The final vote in the convention was 187 for ratification, 168 opposed. Delegates from the counties where Shays had a large following voted against ratification.

In New York Hamilton estimated that more than half the people were Anti-Federalist. He, Jay, and other influential leaders secured a majority of the delegates, but their margin of victory was narrow, only 30 to 27. According to Patrick Henry three quarters of the Virginians were opposed to ratification, and in some counties the percentage was higher, up to 90. In the Virginia convention the Federalists planned every step in advance, even to the selection of all makers and seconders of Federalist motions. The speakers were chosen for their influence and reputation. By dint of the hardest work by the Federalists Virginia ratified by a vote of 89 to 79. Had it not been for the influence of such men as Madison, Marshall, and Washington the Federalists might have suffered defeat.

The contest was one of the most sharply fought and the closest in American history. In many of the states the two parties were so evenly balanced that professional politicians could not predict the outcome of the voting. John Marshall wrote later:

> Indeed it is scarcely to be doubted that in some of the adopting states a majority of the people were in the opposition. In all of them, the numerous amendments which were proposed demonstrate the reluctance with which the new government was accepted.

Two states—Rhode Island and North Carolina—did not ratify until after the new federal system was established and in operation.

Chapter 12

FEDERALIST POLICIES

Establishment of the New Government

Washington's Inauguration

On July 2, 1788, the president of the Continental Congress, sitting at New York, announced that nine states had ratified the Constitution. Congress then directed the states to arrange for the choice of Presidential electors on the first Wednesday in January 1789; the electors would cast their ballots for President and Vice President on the first Wednesday in February; the new Congress would assemble in New York on the first Wednesday in March. The electors chose George Washington for President and John Adams for Vice President.

Washington was ideally suited to be the first President. He brought to the office the prestige of a great name and the solid qualities of sound judgment. The Revolution had furnished proof of his courage and determination. He had wide experience in dealing with both men and public affairs. His success in the conduct of his plantation and his real estate was evidence of administrative ability, as a result of which he had become one of the wealthiest men in the country. He could therefore look upon public office as a public trust, not as a means of increasing his private income.

Because of the difficulties of communication and travel, several months elapsed before the new government could be installed. The new Congress was supposed to assemble on the first Wednesday in March, which happened to fall on the fourth; largely by accident, therefore, March 4 became the date for inaugurating a new administration. But on the date appointed so few Senators and Representatives had arrived in New York that neither house of Congress could organize; they did not begin work together until April 5. After that, Washington and Adams had to be notified of their election. They were inaugurated on April 30.

The most immediate need of the new federal government was revenue, and on April 8, 1789, Congress began its debate on a tariff law. But progress was slow; the bill was not signed until July 4 and went into effect August 1. In addition to providing revenue it afforded a little protection to American manufacturers. To encourage American shipping, this tariff act allowed a discount of 10 per cent on the duties of goods imported in American vessels. Then Congress passed a navigation act, levying a tax, or tonnage duty, on all ships entering American ports. This tax was collected at the rate of 6 cents per ton on American ships, 20 cents on ships built in the United States but of foreign registry, and 50 cents a ton on all others. This measure helped to revive American shipping.

With these important economic measures out of the way, Congress

The Cabinet

enacted a series of laws to complete the work of organizing the federal system. President Washington signed laws creating the Department of Foreign Affairs (later called the State Department), the War Department, and the Treasury Department. Next came the judiciary bill, authorizing the appointment of a chief justice and five associate justices of the Supreme Court. The same measure provided for three circuit courts, thirteen district courts, and an attorney general.

As head of the Department of Foreign Affairs, Washington selected Thomas Jefferson, author of the Declaration of Independence and more recently American minister to France. The headship of the War Department went to Henry Knox of Massachusetts, a veteran of the Revolution. Edmund Randolph of Virginia, one of the prominent Federalists in the recent Convention, became attorney general. The most important office of all at that time, that of secretary of the treasury, went to Alexander Hamilton, a genius in finance, government, and politics. Born in the West Indies, he had come to New York early in his youth. During the Revolution he had served on Washington's staff; the commander in chief had found him to be a man of unusual intellectual powers, abounding in energy, full of initiative and self-confidence. President Washington started the custom of using these department heads as an advisory body, and this group became known as the Cabinet.

Federalist Finance

Hamilton was the outstanding leader in Washington's Cabinet, and he did not confine his activity to executive circles. He assumed responsibility for putting the administration's program through Congress. He attended committee meetings, used his personal influence to bring members into line, and saw to it that they voted his way. Hamilton believed in the rule of the rich. Property owners, merchants, financiers, and manufacturers, so he argued, should govern the country. He thought that the government should attempt to promote the well-being of such groups by giving them definite advantages. During 1790 and 1791, Hamilton described his financial policies in a series of four great reports: two on public credit, one on banking, and one on manufactures. Then he had the specific recommendations of these reports incorporated in bills for Congress to pass.

His first proposals dealt with the payment of the public debt and the establishment of American credit. By 1790 the foreign debt, including arrears of interest, had increased to $11,710,378; and the domestic debt amounted to $42,414,085. There was little controversy over the money owed abroad; everyone agreed that it should be paid in full. But the domestic debt was different. During the Revolution the Continental Congress had issued a variety of certificates—carefully distinguished from Continental notes, or paper money—to pay for supplies and for soldiers' wages. Little or none of this paper was worth its face, or par, value when issued; by 1790, its market value had sunk to about 25 cents on the dollar.

In his first report on the public credit, Hamilton urged payment of this indebtedness at full par value, regardless of its past history. The new government needed credit to succeed; to obtain this it must prove its financial soundness and honesty by meeting all obligations. He would, therefore, call in the outstanding certificates and give in exchange United States bonds with fixed rates of interest. This arrangement was called funding.

Not all members of Congress approved of his policy. They believed that there was no excuse for giving a higher value to the certificates than they had when issued and that to do so would add unnecessarily to the financial burden of the new government. Furthermore, much of the paper had passed out of the hands of the original holders, so that those who had suffered losses on it would not get the benefit of payment at par. The only gainers would be speculators. Anti-Federalists called the plan unjust. James Madison, who had been a strong Federalist in the beginning, went over to the other side and became the Congressional leader of Hamilton's opponents. But Hamilton had his way, and the funding bill passed. Payment at par enabled numerous speculators to clear small fortunes, but it also put American credit upon a solid and enduring basis.

With the national debt out of the way, Hamilton proposed that the federal government assume that part of the state debts which had been incurred on account of the Revolution, amounting to $21,500,000. Hamilton argued that these obligations had been incurred in a common cause. Also he said that by tying the creditors to the federal government they could strengthen the national system. Then he pointed to the wisdom of clearing up the wide variety of local securities in circulation.

The Federalists supported Hamilton, and the Anti-Federalists opposed. These opponents were won over by a logrolling bargain. Congress had been discussing the location of the federal capital, and the South wanted it located on the Potomac. Hamilton cared little for that issue, but he realized that it might be used as trading material. In talking with Jefferson, he mentioned the possibility of getting northern votes for the Potomac site in return for southern votes for assumption. Jefferson called Madison into conference, the upshot of which was a dinner for the three statesmen. There an agreement was reached, the assumption plan became law, and the national capital was placed on the Potomac.

Construction: Strict or Loose?

The third project on Hamilton's list was the United States Bank, in which the government would own one fifth of the capital stock. Hamilton argued that the notes of a sound bank would furnish a substitute for gold and silver money, of which this country never seemed to have enough. Such a bank would also help the government in handling its financial problems and furnish a safe place for deposit of public funds. Hamilton's proposal started a lively debate. Jefferson argued that Congress had no authority to create the bank. He admitted that the Constitution gave Congress power to levy taxes for the purpose of paying the debts and providing for the common defense and general welfare, but he said that a bank was not necessary. As for the "elastic clause," which gives Congress authority to make all laws "necessary and proper" for carrying into effect the enumerated powers, Jefferson argued that they could be made effective without a bank, so a bank was neither "necessary" nor "proper."

Hamilton placed a different interpretation upon the "elastic clause." It was designed to give Congress implied powers, he said, which could be exercised as long as they did not conflict with specific restrictions on congressional action. These implied powers justified the establishment of the bank. Washington agreed with Hamilton and gave his approval to the theory of broad, or loose, construction of the Constitution as distinguished from Jefferson's theory of strict construction. Again Hamilton was victorious, and the Bank was established. The law authorized the issue of capital stock to the amount of $10,000,000, one fifth of which was held by the United States. The Bank could issue notes, transact ordinary banking business, and receive federal deposits.

Whisky Rebellion

In order to meet the annual installments due on the public debt, the treasury needed more revenue than the first tariff law would produce. Partly to raise more money and partly to give wider publicity to the new government, Hamilton proposed an excise law, among the provisions of which was a tax on distilled liquor. Congress passed the measure in March 1791. Hamilton favored the excise because it would increase the number of federal officials and so give publicity to the new government.

Frontiersmen did not agree with him. The pioneers always lacked adequate transportation facilities, and out of this trouble came the popularity of the private still. Corn was bulky, practically impossible for many of the frontiersmen to sell directly. Some fed it to hogs and drove the animals to market. Others made it into whisky. A farmer in western Pennsylvania, for instance, could load his horse with two 8-gallon kegs of whisky worth 50¢ a gallon at his home and take it east over the mountains where whisky sold for $1 a gallon.

This new tax on stills was very unpopular in western Pennsylvania. In 1791 and 1792 mass meetings were held, denouncing the law. In 1794, when federal revenue agents tried to serve writs on unlicensed distillers, open rebellion broke out. Acting on the advice of Hamilton, President Washington called on the governors of four states for militia forces. Fifteen thousand troops marched into the zone of trouble and scattered the rioters. Of the few who were caught, two were convicted and imprisoned, but Washington pardoned them. By suppressing the rebellion the new government proved that it could collect the taxes which it levied.

Protective Tariff

In his fourth report, on manufactures, Hamilton said that the national government must protect American industries. Newly established enterprises could not sell their goods at the low price levels of foreign manufacturers. If the government would put a high tariff on imports, foreign goods could be kept out altogether. In this way infant industries not yet able to stand on their own feet could be made strong and prosperous. Of course American consumers would have to pay higher prices, but even so, Hamilton said, the loss was not real. The growth of manufacturing towns and cities would create additional demands for foodstuffs. With a prosperous home market, the farmers would be less dependent on exports. In 1792 Congress revised the tariff in order to give additional protection to American industries. Hamilton's policy was now complete. He had started with the aim of encouraging the rich and the influential classes to support the federal government. To that end he gave the financiers the funding and assumption plans; to the businessmen he gave the bank; to the manufacturers, the tariff. To conservatives generally he gave the benefits of good government and the peace of mind that goes with security.

Another important development of this first national administration was the adoption of the Bill of Rights in the form of the first ten amendments to the Constitution. Some of the state-ratifying conventions had given their approval to the new regime with a tacit understanding that it would be improved in accordance with their demands. By the time the first Congress took up the matter, interested parties had submitted a total of 124 proposed amendments. After several weeks of discussion the Senate and the House agreed upon twelve. These twelve were submitted to the states, and ten were ratified. The first eight amendments in the Bill of Rights were designed to protect individuals from tyrannical action by the national government. Congress was forbidden to pass laws for the establishment of any religion, or for the prevention of freedom of belief or worship; Congress was not allowed to interfere with the freedom of speech or of the press, or with the right of the people to assemble and to petition for redress of grievances. Congress may not deprive the people of the right to bear arms. Amendments Four to Eight, inclusive, guarantee to the people the famous rights of Englishmen, those safeguards of individual liberty which the people had compelled the king to grant. Americans were secured against "unreasonable searches and seizures" and against illegal search warrants; they were not to be subject to illegal arrest or to loss of life, liberty, or property without due process of law; they were assured of the right of trial by jury in both criminal and civil cases; they were protected against excessive bail, excessive fines, and cruel or unusual punishments. The Ninth Amendment made it clear that the mention of certain rights should not be used to deny other rights not specifically named. The Tenth Amendment and last in this series reserved to the states and to the people the powers not delegated to the national government or prohibited to the states. These first ten amendments became effective in December 1791.

Bill of Rights

The Frontier and the Indians

The old Congress had not been strong enough to admit new states. The new government met this problem successfully. In 1791 the Kentuckians drew up a state constitution. Congress voted to admit Kentucky as a state, setting the date of admission as June 1, 1792. By this time the population

New States

had grown to 100,000. In February 1791, a few days before the vote to admit Kentucky, Congress had decided to bring Vermont into the Union, and on March 4, 1791, Vermont became the fourteenth state. In 1796 the number of states in the Union was raised to sixteen with the admission of Tennessee.

Not all the problems of the frontier could be solved so simply. In 1790 the federal government did succeed in making peace with the Creek Indians in the Southwest, but in the Northwest the relations with the Indians became steadily worse. In 1790 the American commander in the Northwest, General Josiah Harmar, suffered a humiliating defeat. The next year General St. Clair, with a force of 2000 men, was subjected to a still more decisive defeat. His men became panic-stricken; they threw away their arms and retreated a full thirty miles. Out of the 2000, fifty came through uninjured. By that time the Indians were becoming more and more bold. They made almost continuous raids upon the scattered American settlements and, encouraged by British agents, they were demanding a large slice of the Northwest Territory for themselves.

Indians and British

Realizing how critical the situation had become, Washington appointed General Wayne, the "Mad Anthony" of Revolutionary days, to take charge of the section. In 1793, after spending a year in drilling a new army, Wayne made a fruitless effort to settle the trouble without war. But British agents broke up whatever peace sentiment there might have been, and Wayne was forced to fight. Alarmed at Wayne's methodical preparations, the British established a strong outpost on the Maumee, thirty miles south of Detroit, so that, no matter what Wayne did to the Indians, he would find it difficult to attack the Northwest posts. Early in 1794 Lord Dorchester, the governor of Canada, made a speech to a delegation of Indians, in which he asserted that the Americans had no rights in the Territory and practically promised to give the Northwest Territory back to the Indians. Dorchester was officially reprimanded, but the Indians never heard of the censure, so they persisted in defying Wayne's army.

In June 1794 the American troops began to move. In August, Wayne came upon a large force of Indians assembled within two miles of the British position south of Detroit. In the battle of Fallen Timbers he won a brilliant victory and followed it up by destroying Indian supplies and property for miles around. A year later, in 1795, Wayne negotiated with the Indians the Treaty of Greenville, which ended their power in the old Northwest and opened to settlement the parts not occupied by the British. The treaty provided for a boundary line running from the Ohio to Fort Recovery, then to the Muskingum River, and thence due north to Lake Erie. The Indians agreed to stay north and west of that line. In making this agreement with the Indians, Wayne had the help of Jay's Treaty with England, in accordance with which the British prepared to give up the Northwest posts.

Problems of a Neutral—Diplomacy and Commerce

During this Indian warfare, a situation developed in Europe which profoundly affected the United States. In 1789 the French Revolution started. Because of French help in their war against England and because of the treaties of 1778, many Americans sympathized with the French and wanted to help them. "Jacobin Clubs," named after revolutionary societies in France, soon appeared in the United States. In Congress, opinion was divided between the "Jacobins," or pro-French party, and the "Anglo-men." President Washington and most of his Cabinet were sympathetic with the British, but Jefferson, the secretary of state, was pro-French. As long as the French Revolution remained within the confines of France, pro-French feeling in the United States was a matter of no great consequence. When the struggle spread beyond the French border, and particularly when the new French government went to war with England in February 1793, these divided foreign sympathies of American citizens proved dangerous.

Influence of French Revolution

One of the first problems demanding American official attention was that of the status of the new regime in France. Should the United States recognize the revolutionary government? Secretary of State Jefferson said yes. "It accords with our principles," he wrote, "to acknowledge any Government to be rightful which is formed by the will of the nation, substantially declared." The new government was recognized.

Early in 1793 Washington wrote to Jefferson: "It behooves the Government of this country to use every means in its power to prevent the citizens thereof from embroiling us with either of those powers, by endeavoring to maintain a strict neutrality." Then the President consulted his Cabinet for advice on specific issues in the Franco-American situation. Should the United States issue a formal notice of neutrality? Should the American government receive a diplomatic representative from the new government in France? Were the treaties of 1778 still in force? Washington's advisers all approved the policy of neutrality, and they agreed that Jefferson should receive the new French minister. Concerning the treaties both Hamilton and Jefferson came practically to the same conclusion, although they reached it by different lines of reasoning. Hamilton wanted a statement that the treaties were not in force; Jefferson said they were still binding, but that they could be suspended until the situation in France cleared up.

In accordance with this advice Washington issued a proclamation of neutrality. The United States would adopt an impartial course toward both belligerents. American citizens were warned to refrain from any acts which would conflict with such a course. The proclamation informed all citizens that if they participated in the war or carried contraband to the belligerents they would forfeit any claim to the protection of their own government. In the following year, 1794, Congress reinforced this executive proclamation with a neutrality law. This measure prohibited Americans from enlisting

Neutrality

in or accepting commissions in belligerent armies and from sending out military or naval expeditions from bases in this country.

These measures of 1793 and 1794 laid the foundations of a major American foreign policy, one that continued until 1915. The United States proclaimed that its interests were separate from those of Europe, that it would not be a party to the wars of Europe. Here was the policy of isolationism. But this was political isolation only, not economic. American citizens were free to carry on whatever trade they could in contraband and noncontraband alike, with both sides, subject to the power of either belligerent to stop contraband trade with the other. Noncontraband commerce was supposed to be under the protection of international law, and the United States government made an effort to uphold the rights of American citizens who took part in such trade.

Citizen Genêt

On the very day when President Washington's proclamation of neutrality was published, the administration received important news from South Carolina: Citizen Edmond Charles Genêt, minister of the First Republic of France, had arrived at Charleston two weeks earlier. The policy of neutrality had been adopted in anticipation of the French minister's arrival; it now remained to be seen how the new agent would behave. Without waiting to observe the usual amenities of diplomacy, which would have required him to proceed to Philadelphia, present his credentials, and then await formal reception by the secretary of state, the impetuous young Frenchman began work at once. Acting in accordance with his instructions, he made plans for two military expeditions, one against Louisiana, the other against Florida. Then he prepared to issue French commissions to Americans who cared to serve. Genêt violated international law and flouted the President's proclamation of neutrality.

To make sure of the necessary pro-French attitude in America, Genêt was instructed "to direct opinion by means of anonymous publications. . . . The Boston and Baltimore gazettes will be the best ones to use for distributing such publications. . . ." Genêt also commissioned privateers, which set out from American ports to prey upon British commerce. Here again the minister violated international law and the treaties of 1778, but he carried out his instructions. Genêt organized a Jacobin Club in Charleston and then started north to begin direct negotiations with the State Department. His trip became a great triumphal journey, and as he moved from place to place he took pains to stir up hostility against Great Britain. Once in Philadelphia, he was officially received with a coolness in sharp contrast to the enthusiasm shown elsewhere.

His manifold activities drove the State Department to desperation. French privateers were bringing in prizes; they even seized one vessel, the *Little Sarah,* in American waters. The State Department promptly demanded her release, but Genêt christened her *La Petite Democrate* and sent her out as a privateer. Genêt's behavior could no longer be tolerated, and in August 1793 Jefferson officially requested the French government to recall its exuberant representative. Genêt was recalled, but he never went home. He settled on Long Island, married a daughter of George Clinton of New York, and lived in retirement until 1834.

Neutral Trade

The European war created new commercial opportunities, and American merchants were quick to take advantage of them. In February 1793 France opened her colonial ports to American shipping. Holland, France, and Spain found trade with their colonies cut off unless the trade could be handled by neutral ships. The United States was well situated geographically to profit from this situation. The war turned over most of the carrying trade of the western world to American ships and created a profitable market in Europe for North American foodstuffs. Colonial products such as sugar, coffee, cocoa, pepper, spices, and indigo were carried by American merchants directly to Europe or to ports in the United States from which they could be transshipped to Europe. Manufactured goods from Europe, and particularly from England, were brought back to the United States, the West Indies, and South America. France and her colonies would pay generously for American food supplies; this demand raised the prices for agricultural products to the highest level ever reached up to that time. During the war the average price of flour was $9.12 per barrel as against an average price of $5.41 before 1791 and $5.46 in the 1820's. American tonnage engaged in overseas trade more than doubled during the war years, while in the decade from 1791 to 1801 American exports increased almost fivefold. The following table gives a vivid illustration of this result of the war.

EXPORTS FROM THE UNITED STATES, 1791-1801

Year ending Sept. 30	
1791	$19,012,041
1792	20,573,098
1793	26,109,572
1794	33,026,233
1795	47,989,472
1796	67,064,097
1797	56,850,206
1798	61,527,097
1799	78,665,522
1800	70,971,780
1801	94,115,925

International Law

Great Britain could not let this trade continue without making an effort to stop it. The Cabinet saw the work of the English navy frustrated by this neutral commerce, and British merchants uneasily watched the steady growth of a rival merchant marine. English authorities therefore insisted upon their own interpretation of international law. They held that enemy-owned goods might be seized and confiscated even if carried in neutral vessels, and they favored a broad definition of contraband. Great Britain also insisted upon the Rule of 1756, that trade closed in time of peace could not legally be opened in time of war. Officers of the royal navy stretched to an extreme their rights of visit and search and made themselves obnoxious by impressing seamen, taking both Englishmen and bona fide Americans. In June 1793 the Privy Council issued an order authorizing the seizure of all vessels laden with grain or flour. In the following November the British issued a second Order in Council, but kept it secret until their privateers and warships had time to reach West Indian waters. This order directed British naval officers to seize all ships laden with French colonial products or carrying provisions to these colonies. By March 1, 1794, 250 American ships had been seized. The British paid for what they took, but at prices fixed by themselves.

The Americans needed a legal basis for protesting against this high-handed British policy; they found one in certain principles of international law which had been proclaimed in part by the armed neutrals of the American Revolution. The Americans held that free ships made free goods—that is, belligerent-owned property, except contraband of war, carried in neutral vessels could not be legally seized. Or they held that the flag covers the cargo and so made even enemy goods safe from capture. They called attention to the doctrine of the freedom of the seas. Principles of international law, however, did not enforce themselves.

Jay's Treaty

President Washington hoped that these problems could be solved by diplomacy. With this idea in mind he sent John Jay on a special mission to England. Jay was instructed to secure from the British government formal recognition of rules covering neutral trade. Then he was ordered to insist upon indemnities for slaves illegally seized by the British during the Revolution; in return the United States would indemnify the British for losses on account of American debts owed to British merchants on the eve of the Revolution. Some of the states had placed legal obstacles in the way of the collection of such debts. Both parties would agree to a policy of disarmament for the Great Lakes. Then Jay was ordered to secure commercial privileges in the West Indies for American ships of limited tonnage. And he was expected to bring about the withdrawal of British troops from the Northwest posts. Jay arrived in England in June 1794 and went immediately to work. In spite of the weakness of his country, Jay seemed to be in a position strong enough to insist upon concessions. Wayne was moving against the Indians, and his victory at Fallen Timbers in August seriously weakened the British hold on the Northwest. Also some of the nations of northern Europe were considering the plan of a league of neutrals similar to the armed neutrality of the American Revolution. They were ready to admit the United States to this league. Such a combination might have deprived England of supplies for the continuance of her struggle with France. England had no wish to increase the number of her enemies, and she was particularly anxious not to lose her valuable export trade to the United States.

No one can tell how much Jay might have secured if he had been given proper support, but, for some reason which has never been satisfactorily explained, Hamilton ruined his chances. Jay's strongest hope lay in holding over the head of the British government the threat of American participation in the proposed league of European neutrals. But Hamilton secretly informed the British minister, Hammond, without letting even Jay know, that the United States would have nothing whatsoever to do with any European league.

Signed on November 19, 1794, Jay's Treaty provided that certain disputed points, including the New England boundary line, indemnities for shipping seized, and American debts owed to British merchants, were to be settled by joint commissions. The Northwest posts were to be evacuated by June 1, 1796. Americans were allowed free trade from Vermont with Quebec and Montreal, and the East Indian trade was opened to Americans without restrictions. For the West Indian trade, Article XII of the treaty opened it to American vessels of not over seventy tons burden on the express condition that the United States should agree to export no molasses, sugar, coffee, cocoa, or cotton, no matter where grown, to any foreign country. Concerning neutral rights on the high seas, the treaty said nothing at all.

The Senate rejected Article XII and the British government accepted the amendment, so leaving the English West Indian trade where it had been—legally, but not completely, closed to Americans. Although the treaty was not satisfactory, it was better than nothing. After considerable hesitation, Washington approved it and sent it to the Senate. It was bitterly criticized there, but it was ratified. For a time the House refused to appropriate certain sums of money called for by the treaty. In the country at large the treaty and the administration responsible for it were violently attacked, and Jay himself became the target for unmeasured abuse.

Pinckney's Treaty

Evidently Jay's Treaty created a more favorable impression in Europe than in the United States. In any case it was important enough to exert a profound influence upon Spain. That decrepit government felt grave concern at the news of the Anglo-American agreement. Visions of the loss of Florida, Louisiana, and Mexico began to trouble the Spanish foreign office, and the officials decided to curry favor with the American republic. On October 27, 1795, Thomas Pinckney obtained the Treaty of San Lorenzo. This opened the Mississippi to American navigation and granted the right of deposit. Furthermore Spain agreed to accept the 31st parallel as the boundary between Georgia and Florida. It also recognized the Mississippi as the western boundary of the United States. This treaty gave the western pioneers what they most needed—commercial privileges on the Mississippi. With those secured, there was little to be gained by intrigue with Spain or England. For the first time since the American Revolution the United States enjoyed legal guarantees against foreign aggression in the Southwest Territory. Pinckney's Treaty therefore was a major triumph for the new nation.

Politics and Parties

During Washington's administration two national political parties, Federalists and Jeffersonian Democrats, were well organized. The Federalists were conservative in outlook, believing in government by the owners of property. Businessmen of all kinds counted on funding, the assumption of state debts, and the National Bank to bring prosperity to themselves and to bring peace, order, and security to the country. Thomas Jefferson described the Federalists as

Political Parties

> . . . all the officers of the government, all who want to be officers, all timid men who prefer the calm of despotism to the boisterous sea of liberty, British merchants and Americans trading on British capitals, speculators and holders in the banks and public funds, a contrivance invented for the purposes of corruption and for assimilating us in all things, to the rotten as well as the sound parts of the British model.

The Federalists themselves realized that their work was far from finished when they ratified the Constitution; they wanted to build their principles into the foundation of the government and then manage elections so that national officials would always be well disposed to Federalist views. Because the Constitution did not in so many exact words authorize Congress to assume the states' debts, to create the bank, or to levy a protective tariff, the Federalists advocated broad, or loose, construction of the Constitution. They contended that Congress should be able to pass any law which would benefit the country unless the Constitution in so many words withheld the power. To these principles just described—friendliness to wealth and a broad interpretation of the Constitution—the Federalists added a third—that is, peace, or at least nonparticipation in the wars of Europe. The Federalists had more cordial feelings toward England than toward revolutionary France.

After Washington's inauguration, the Anti-Federalists changed their name and set themselves against the rule of the financial and mercantile interests. They would accept the new system, but they would object to the way the Federalists managed it. This group included small farmers and any laborers so fortunate as to possess the right to vote. They indignantly denied the Hamiltonian doctrine that the way to promote general well-being was to legislate for the small class at the top. They favored the common man. Just as the Federalists used the doctrine of loose construction to justify Hamilton's work, so the opposition demanded strict construction. They would have the federal legislature confine its attention to subjects specifically authorized in the Constitution.

In the South these Anti-Federalists called themselves Republicans; in the North, Democrats. Sometimes they used both terms in hyphenated form. From the beginning they had been greater in numbers than the Federalists, but they lacked organization and leadership. Thomas Jefferson gave them what they needed in both these matters. To provide an organization Jefferson encouraged the formation of clubs. By 1794 he had a network of "Democratic Societies," north and south, engaged in regular correspondence with one another. On May 12, 1794, the *Boston Gazette* reported the proceedings of a recent meeting of the local club—held at the Green Dragon tavern—known as "the Massachusetts Constitutional Society." The members heard reports of the activities of "our brethren" of Virginia, New York, Vermont, and South Carolina and examined the constitutions adopted by these organizations. The members ordered their corresponding committee to send a circular letter to all the societies in the United States which were "founded on republican principles." By means of these clubs the Jeffersonian Democrats in various parts of the country could work effectively together.

Jefferson's Clubs

The Federalists disliked these clubs. President Washington accused them of starting the "Whisky Rebellion" and asked if there could be anything "more absurd, more arrogant, or more pernicious to the peace of society" than these "self-created bodies"? He believed that Jeffersonians were unfit to take part in public affairs. "I shall not, whilst I have the honor to administer the government," he wrote, "bring any man into any office of consequence knowingly whose political tenets are adverse to the measures which the general government are pursuing; for this, in my opinion, would be a sort of political suicide."

The Democrats or Republicans established a chain of newspapers from New Hampshire to Georgia. These journals, so the Federalists complained, "have stuck at nothing, in order to deceive the public, and to destroy the government which protects them. Lie has followed Lie, in such rapid succession that Truth . . . has been lost in the multitude of its adversaries." Federalist comment on the Jeffersonian press should not be taken too seriously. The real basis of this Federalist attack was not the character of the Democratic papers but their political success. According to one writer in 1798, nine out of ten newspapers south of the Hudson were Democratic.

As early as 1792 party lines were clearly defined in the congressional elections, but it was not until 1796 that they affected a presidential contest. In that year the Federalists nominated John Adams and Thomas Pinckney, while the Democrats selected Thomas Jefferson and Aaron Burr. In this campaign foreign affairs occupied a prominent place. The French were bitter over Jay's Treaty, and the French minister, Adet, took part in the campaign with both propaganda and money. He worked for Jefferson.

Election of 1796

Hamilton, the directing head of the Federalist machine both during and after his term as secretary of the treasury, was anxious to defeat Adams, so he privately advised some Federalist electors to vote for Pinckney but not for Adams. Reports of this maneuver leaked out, and some of Adams's friends retaliated by voting for him and not for Pinckney. Adams won the Presidency with 71 electoral votes, but Pinckney fell short with only 59. The second man on the list was the Republican, Thomas Jefferson, who received

68. The country therefore would have a President of one party and a Vice President of another.

Why?

In September 1796, in a farewell address, President Washington announced that he would retire from office at the close of his second term. In this announcement he gave advice to his countrymen. He begged them to preserve their Union, the "main pillar in the edifice of your real independence, the support of your tranquillity at home, your peace abroad, of your safety, of your prosperity, of that very liberty which you so highly prize." Then he pointed out the economic advantages which each section, North, South, East, and West, derived from free trade within the Union.

Washington's Farewell Address

The retiring President urged the American people to support the national government. "Respect for its authority, compliance with its laws, acquiescence in its measures, are duties enjoined by the fundamental maxims of true liberty. . . ." Washington did not approve of political parties, and he warned the people against them. He never considered the party as a necessary device to facilitate the working of a democratic system, but always as a faction, a minority, composed of unscrupulous and "unprincipled" men. He liked the principle of checks and balances. To preserve these, he urged care upon all officials to see that they "confine themselves within their respective constitutional spheres, avoiding in the exercise of the powers of one department to encroach upon another."

Washington's advice on foreign policy has been repeated so often that it has become hackneyed, but in the repetitions one short but significant paragraph is customarily omitted. The first part is familiar: "Observe good faith and justice toward all nations. Cultivate peace and harmony with all." Then come the familiar warnings to avoid "permanent, inveterate antipathies against particular nations and passionate attachments for others. . . ." He would avoid further political commitments abroad; he would "steer clear of permanent alliances. . . ." With this statement he coupled another, which for some reason is not so widely known: "Taking care always to keep ourselves by suitable establishments on a respectable defensive posture, we may safely trust to temporary alliances for extraordinary emergencies."

Federalist "Tyranny" and Democratic Protest

One major reason for Washington's advice to his countrymen on foreign affairs was to be found in the delicate relations with France. In 1794, when Jay had been sent to England, Washington also sent James Monroe on a mission to France. Monroe had given assurances to the French foreign office that Jay would make no agreement with England inconsistent with American obligations to France. Technically Jay's Treaty did not encroach in any way upon the treaties of 1778. But Jay's Treaty did prohibit the fitting out of privateers in American ports, and the French objected to this. Furthermore under Jay's Treaty the English navy was free to seize Ameri-

French Insults

can provision ships bound for France, on condition of paying for the cargoes. French officials objected vigorously to seeing their main source of supply destroyed. By way of retaliation, the Directory declared the American alliance at an end and announced that all goods destined for England would be regarded as contraband of war. In November 1796, after the Presidential election, the Directory recalled its minister to the United States.

Monroe had already been recalled. When his successor, C. C. Pinckney, went to present his credentials, the French authorities refused to receive him; they would have nothing to do with any representative from the United States until this country should apologize for its alleged mistreatment of France. Such was the situation when John Adams became President. Adams was as eager as his predecessor to maintain peace; he was equally determined to maintain American rights.

Upon receipt of the news that France had insulted Pinckney, Adams called Congress in special session and outlined the situation. He said the speech of the president of the French Directory was even more alarming than his refusal to receive Pinckney:

> It evinces a disposition to separate the people of the United States from the government, to persuade them that they have different affections, principles and interests from those of their fellow citizens whom they themselves have chosen to manage their common concerns and thus to produce divisions fatal to our peace. Such attempts ought to be repelled with a decision which shall convince France and the world that we are not a degraded people, humiliated under a spirit of fear and sense of inferiority, fitted to be the miserable instruments of foreign influence, and regardless of national honor, character, and interest.

"XYZ" Affair

Adams closed his speech with a statement that he desired peace and that he would make one more effort to reach a satisfactory settlement by negotiation. He planned to send over a special commission of three members, consisting of Pinckney, John Marshall, and Elbridge Gerry. Pinckney was included because France had to remedy the wrongs done to him upon his arrival. John Marshall was a Federalist, one of the ablest men in his party, soon to become Chief Justice of the Supreme Court. Elbridge Gerry was a Jeffersonian Democrat from Massachusetts, a friend of President Adams. In their instructions the envoys were directed to see that "no blame or censure be directly, or indirectly, imputed to the United States." Any engagements entered into must be consistent with Jay's Treaty. The negotiations began in October 1797, and the three Americans attempted to deal with officials of the Directory. All the members of that notorious government were corrupt. Their secretary for foreign affairs was Talleyrand, formerly the Bishop of Autun, the keenest and most unscrupulous statesman in Europe. When the Americans arrived, Talleyrand refused to receive them officially. He worked through certain agents, who have come down to fame as Messieurs *X*, *Y*, and *Z*.

The first of these negotiators told the Americans that the Directory had been offended by Adams's speech to Congress and that "they should be softened." This softening process, he explained, would cost the United States $250,000. Then the Americans must make a new loan to France, a "large" loan. Furthermore the United States must agree to pay its citizens for any depredations committed by Frenchmen upon American commerce. Soon another French agent came around: "I will not disguise from you that this situation being met, the essential part of the treaty remains to be adjusted. . . . *You must pay money—you must pay* a great deal of money." Marshall and Pinckney wished to break off these interviews, but at Gerry's insistence they allowed them to continue. Failing in their efforts to extract money from the Americans, Talleyrand's agents tried to frighten them into compliance. If they counted on uniting the Americans in resistance to the French demands, they would fail:

> You are mistaken: you ought to know that the diplomatic skill of France and the means she possesses in your country are sufficient to enable her, with the French party in America, to throw the blame [for breaking off negotiations upon the Federalists]; and you may assure yourselves that this will be done.

After more fruitless exchanges, in March 1798, the three envoys at last met Talleyrand, but he was no more willing to confer than his agents had been. Marshall thereupon left France for home. Pinckney could not leave because his daughter was too ill to travel. Gerry remained in Paris to deal with Talleyrand alone. In March 1798 Adams submitted a summary of the negotiations to Congress, and the Federalists promptly demanded war with France. The Democrats, however, questioned the truth of the President's summary. This was the very thing that Adams wanted, because it called public attention to the whole proceeding. He then submitted his evidence; the story of the attempted bribery became public property, and there arose a tremendous outcry against France.

Convention of 1800

Congress immediately prepared for war. The army was increased, Washington, Hamilton, and Knox were appointed generals, and a navy department was organized. There was no official declaration of war, but each side began to seize merchant vessels belonging to the other. This state of warfare continued during 1798 and 1799. But neither Talleyrand nor Adams wanted war, and Adams determined to try the effect of a new commission. The President then named three men: William Vans Murray, Oliver Ellsworth, Chief Justice of the Supreme Court, and William R. Davie, onetime governor of North Carolina. They went at once to France. By that time Napoleon was in power, and Talleyrand had a new scheme in his mind—the recovery of Louisiana and the restoration of the French empire overseas. For the success of this policy he needed peace with the United States. On September 30, 1800, a convention was signed. This agreement abrogated the treaties of 1778 and proclaimed the principle that free ships make free goods. It did not, however, provide for any French indemnities for American shipping illegally seized. American claimants on this score would have to look to their own government for payment. But the convention removed the danger of war and gave the United States a chance to gain further strength before it entered the European struggle.

Alien and Sedition Acts

The danger of war with France gave the Federalists an opportunity for attacking the Democratic newspapers. Some of these, edited by foreigners, had been particularly bitter in opposing the Federalists. The Federalists wanted to drive these papers out of business. For this purpose, in 1798 the Federalist majority in Congress put through the Alien and Sedition Acts. By a new naturalization law they lengthened the residence requirement for citizenship from five years to fourteen. The Alien Law gave the President authority to banish aliens; the Sedition Law declared any libel of the President or any attempt to stir up disaffection against the government a crime, punishable by heavy penalties.

The Alien Law was never invoked, but several foreigners left the country for fear of what might happen. Under the Sedition Law the Federalists made, all told, twenty-five arrests, including in their haul the editors of the four most prominent Jeffersonian papers in the country: the *Independent Chronicle* of Boston, the *Argus* of New York, the *Aurora* of Philadelphia, and the *Examiner* of Richmond.

The Sedition Act was used to suppress any criticism of the President, no matter how trivial. Prominent Federalist officials combed the opposition papers for evidence, generally without finding statements dangerous enough to do more than provoke a slight smile. Some of the suits were based on flimsy charges. One of their victims, Matthew Lyon, had asserted that under President Adams "every consideration of the public welfare was swallowed up in a continual grasp for power, in an unbounded thirst for ridiculous pomp, foolish adulation, and selfish avarice." Lyon was convicted under the Sedition Act, fined $1000, and sentenced to four months in prison. One Baldwin, of Newark, New Jersey, was fined $100 for expressing a wish that the wadding of a cannon fired in honor of President Adams might hit the estimable gentleman in the broadest part of his trousers. David Brown of Dedham, Massachusetts, had been responsible for erecting a liberty pole with the following inscription upon it: "No Stamp Act, No Sedition, No Alien Bills, No Land Tax; downfall to the Tyrants of America, peace and retirement to the President, long live the Vice-President, and the Minority; may moral virtue be the basis of civil government." Brown was sentenced to eighteen months in prison and to a fine of $400. Because he could not pay his fine he stayed in prison two years until Jefferson pardoned him.

The Federalists defended their laws on the ground that drastic measures were necessary to save the government; they found authority for them in the principle of broad construction of the Constitution. The Jeffersonian Democratic-Republicans charged that the Alien and Sedition Acts were unconstitutional. To give additional weight to their protests and to make them official, the Jeffersonian leaders planned to have them endorsed by some of the state legislatures. For this purpose resolutions known as the Kentucky and the Virginia Resolutions were drafted.

Kentucky and Virginia Resolutions

The first Kentucky Resolution, adopted in November 1798, declared that the states were not united on the principle of "unlimited submission to their general government." Congress could exercise powers specially delegated to it and no others. "Whensoever the general government assumes undelegated powers, its acts are unauthoritative, void, and of no force." The resolution put the Alien and Sedition Acts in this category and announced that Kentucky would not submit to them. In a second Kentucky Resolution, adopted in November 1799, the author argued that the central government could not pass judgment on the nature and extent of its own powers. The states, however, could decide whether or not Congress had violated the Constitution; in cases of such abuse of power, "nullification by those sovereignties [the states] of all unauthorized acts done under color of that instrument is the rightful remedy." Some years later Thomas Jefferson admitted that he wrote these two documents. The Virginia Resolutions, written by James Madison, followed the same line of reasoning, although Madison did not use the word "nullification." These statements were the Democratic protest against the Federalist effort to restrict the right of free political discussion. In the northern states, where the Federalists were in power, the legislatures expressed disapproval of this doctrine of states' rights. In Democratic states the Resolutions were generally approved.

This controversy over the Sedition Act suggested that Federalist leadership had undergone a serious deterioration. Only a few years before, the party was organizing the national government, paying off the national debt, conquering the Indians, and achieving diplomatic success in dealing with Great Britain and Spain. But in 1798 the leaders were gravely stirred over the wish of an inconsequential nobody that President Adams might receive a harmless bump in the seat of his pants.

John Adams was not happy in his high office. Troubles abroad, controversies at home, and factional quarrels in his own Cabinet kept his administration in constant turmoil. The Jeffersonian Democrats found fault with everything he did, and the group of Federalists who followed Hamilton denied him his rightful place as head of his party. Adams had retained three members of Washington's Cabinet, who took their orders from Hamilton and worked against the President. The President tolerated this interference until 1800, when he reorganized his Cabinet and forced Hamilton's friends to resign. This action brought relief from immediate embarrassment, but it widened still further the rift in the Federalist Party; factional fights helped to prepare for Federalist defeat in 1800.

Hamilton had never respected Adams, and in 1800 he refused to support him for a second term. Writing on May 10, after Adams and C. C. Pinckney had been nominated by the Federalists, Hamilton asserted that

. . . *most* of the most *influential men* of that party [the Federalists] consider him as a very *unfit* and *incapable* character. . . . My mind is made up. I will never more be responsible for him by any direct support, even though the consequence should be the election of *Jefferson*. . . . If the cause is to be sacrificed to a weak and perverse man, I withdraw from the party.

Chapter 13

JEFFERSONIAN DEMOCRACY

Election of Jefferson

THE factional quarrel between the followers of Adams and Hamilton meant defeat for the Federalists in the Presidential campaign of 1800. On the other hand the Democrats could look forward confidently to their first major victory. The Federalists renominated John Adams, while the Democrats nominated Jefferson and Aaron Burr. Burr was a grandson of the clergyman, Jonathan Edwards, and the son of a president of Princeton. After serving with honor in the Revolution he devoted himself to law, politics, and feminine society. He elevated nothing which he touched. Personally he was a man of unusual charm, and he was blessed with a store of cheerfulness that never deserted him. But he lacked robust convictions about anything, and he was devoid of moral sense. "Great minds," he was fond of saying, "care little for small morals."

In the electoral vote Jefferson and Burr tied with 73 votes apiece. Adams had 65. Because of the tie, the Federalist House had to choose between Jefferson and Burr. Because of their hatred of Jefferson, many Federalist Congressmen were ready to put Burr in the President's chair. Others felt that Jefferson was the lesser evil, and they would try to neutralize his influence by bargaining for the election of a Federalist Vice President. But Hamilton, much as he disliked Jefferson, would not agree to support Burr. "I trust the Federalists will not finally be so mad as to vote for Burr," he wrote. "I speak with an intimate and accurate knowledge of his character. His elevation can only promote the purposes of the desperate and profligate." After thirty-six ballots in the House, Jefferson was chosen.

Jefferson's Politics—Theory and Practice

This election of Jefferson in 1800 is sometimes called a "revolution," but there was no such general overturn as that expression would imply. Adams lost the Presidency, partly because of weakness in the Federalist party, partly because of Burr's successful work in New York. In 1796 Adams had received all the electoral votes of that state. Had he received only half of them in 1800, he would have won the election. As it was he got none, and the New York votes elected the Democrats. The Democrats also secured control of Congress. For the first time since the ratification of the new Constitution political power passed from the men of wealth—merchants, bankers, and manufacturers—to the middle class and the farmers.

For the defeated Federalists the beginning of Jefferson's administration was a time of deep gloom. The former rulers despised the new President as a man, suspected his methods, and hated his political principles. Hamilton wrote "that he is crafty and persevering in his objects; that he is not scupulous about the means of success, nor very mindful of the truth; and that he is a contemptible hypocrite." A Federalist in Connecticut declared that the true purpose of Democratic-Republicanism was

> . . . to destroy every trace of civilization in the world, and to force mankind back into a savage state. . . . We have now reached the consummation of democratic blessedness. We have a country governed by blockheads and knaves. . . . Can the imagination paint anything more dreadful on this side of hell?

But these comments were partisan. American Presidents have rarely been as bad as the opposition party professes to believe.

The circumstances of the inauguration added to the blackness of the scene. Jefferson was the first President to be installed in office in Washington, D.C., where the unfinished capitol, the straggling boardinghouses, and the mile-long stretch of mud named Pennsylvania Avenue appeared prophetic of confusion. The eminent respectability and pleasing regularity of Philadelphia seemed far more in keeping with national dignity than this new, unkempt village on the Potomac. But the city of Washington had great possibilities even if the Federalists could not see them.

Jefferson the Man

Jefferson's personal appearance certainly did not justify these Federalist fears. Even his height—six feet, three inches—was balanced by his loose-jointed build and his slouching manner. There was no trace of cruelty or indifference to the well-being of mankind in his sunny, red, freckled face. The ordinary observer saw in him not a monster but simply a large, raw-boned farmer, careless in manner, careless in dress, but very human and genial. Perhaps geniality was the trait that most impressed itself on casual acquaintances. He could talk with enthusiasm and intelligence on nearly every subject known to man. His dinners were celebrated for their conversation.

It is simpler to describe the new President's appearance than to analyze his character. He has been accused of inconsistencies without number, but inconsistency is hardly the word. He was both a doctrinaire and a practical politician. Evidence of this divergence between Jefferson the philosopher and Jefferson the statesman appears all through his life. He could help to incite the Virginians to revolution, and he could write the Declaration of Independence, but with all of his youth and physical vigor he would not enlist in the Revolutionary army. Again the divergence appears in his strictures upon the Quebec Act and his own law for the government of Louisiana; in his talk about the benefits of frequent revolutions and in his readiness to use the army and navy in enforcing the embargo; in his protestations of friendliness for France and in his subsequent proposal for a military alliance with England. This dichotomy in his thinking rarely troubled Jefferson himself.

As the author of the Declaration of Independence Jefferson was one of the best-known Americans of his day. During the Revolution he strengthened his reputation as a liberal reformer by bringing about the abolition of the system of entail and by establishing religious liberty in Virginia. Later, as American minister to France, he gave the French revolutionists the benefit of his philosophy. He was an advocate of freedom and an opponent of arbitrary rule. On the receipt of news of Shays's Rebellion, he proclaimed his belief in the rights of the people in these flaming words: "God forbid! we should ever be twenty years without such a rebellion. . . . What country can preserve its liberties if their rulers are not warned from time to time that their people preserve the spirit of resistance?" And in another letter on the same subject he had written: "The Spirit of resistance to government is so valuable on certain occasions that I wish it to be always kept alive. It will often be exercised when wrong, but better so than not to be exercised at all. I like a little rebellion now and then. It is like a storm in the atmosphere."

Jefferson's Philosophy

In politics Jefferson favored the landed interests as opposed to the financiers and industrialists. He loved to write about the virtues of the tillers of the soil. Upon them alone, he argued, depended the security and permanence of the American system of government:

> Those who labor in the earth are the chosen people of God, if ever He had a chosen people whose breasts he has made his peculiar deposit for substantial and genuine virtue. It is the focus in which He keeps alive that sacred fire, which otherwise might escape from the face of the earth. Corruption of morals in the mass of cultivators is a phenomenon of which no age nor nation has furnished an example.

As for industrial workers in towns, Jefferson considered them a positive danger to the republic:

> While we have land to labor, then, let us never wish to see our citizens occupied at a work-bench or twirling a distaff. Carpenters, masons, smiths are wanting in husbandry; but, for the general operations of manufacture, let our workshops remain in Europe. It is better to carry provisions and materials, and with them their manners and principles. The loss by the transportation of commodities across the Atlantic will be made up in happiness and permanence of government. The mobs of great cities add just so much to the support of pure government, as sores do to the strength of the human body. It is the manners and spirit of a people which preserve a republic in vigor. A degeneracy in these is a canker which soon eats to the heart of its laws and constitution.

In a letter to James Madison, Jefferson argued that a democratic government would last

> . . . as long as we remain virtuous; and I think we shall be so, as long as agriculture is our principal object, which will be the case, while there remain vacant lands in any part of America. When we get piled upon one another in large cities, as in Europe, we shall become corrupt as in Europe, and go to eating one another as they do there.

In his inaugural address the new President showed not only excellent temper but remarkable ability in putting the thoughts of the common man into enduring words. For those Federalists who were expecting a discharge of fire and brimstone against themselves and an anarchistic attack upon government, the address was a surprise. Jefferson tried to promote good relations between the parties. "We are all Republicans, we are all Federalists," he declared. He advocated "a wise and frugal government, which shall restrain men from injuring one another, which shall leave them otherwise free to regulate their own pursuits of industry and improvement." He put in a plea for "equal and exact justice to all men"; for "peace, commerce, and honest friendship with all nations, entangling alliances with none." He would support "the state governments in all their rights, as the most competent administrations for our domestic concerns and the surest bulwarks against anti-republican tendencies." He appealed for "absolute acquiescence in the decisions of the majority." To justify this acquiescence, the will of the majority "to be rightful must be reasonable"; he warned his hearers that "the minority possesses their equal rights, which equal law must protect. . . ."

Reform Jefferson looked upon his party's victory in the late election as a mandate to carry through certain reforms. He pledged his administration to economy and to wise expenditure of public money. He would simplify the government, restrict the activities of what he regarded as dangerous institutions such as the army, navy, and the federal courts, and make the federal government really beneficial to the people.

To assist him in his work Jefferson picked his advisers with care. His long-time friend, confidant, and protégé, James Madison, became secretary of state. The treasury went to Albert Gallatin, a naturalized Swiss, perhaps the equal of Hamilton in his understanding of public finance. To make Congress function properly, Jefferson picked the floor leaders himself. For a time this honor was divided between John Randolph of Roanoke and another Virginian, William Branch Giles. When the President drafted bills, his floor leaders saw that they went through. When these legislative lieutenants failed him, as John Randolph did eventually, Jefferson made moving appeals to some of his friends to run for Congress so that they might act as his agents in the House. Through the medium of the caucus Jefferson was able to meet his party associates informally outside of Congress.

Jefferson found it desirable to fill some of the civil service positions with loyal Republicans. When he became President, all the appointive offices were in the hands of Federalists, men who hated and distrusted him and who would be only too glad to embarrass his administration. There was in addition the normal desire to reward good party workers. Actually he made comparatively few removals, but these were loudly criticized by the Federalists. He began by turning out of office the most recent Federalist beneficiaries. The next group to go were those who had been appointed after the November elections of 1800. But these removals did not create vacancies fast enough. Concerning officeholders, Jefferson ruefully complained that "few died and none resign," so he hastened the process of their retirement. But there was no clean sweep in the federal civil service, and numbers of Federalists were not disturbed in their jobs.

Economy

Gallatin planned to pay off the national debt as rapidly as possible. He hoped at the same time to reduce taxes. Hamilton's unpopular excise tax was the first to go. These plans in turn demanded economy which Gallatin effected by cutting in half the expenditures for the army and navy. In his estimates for the coming year Gallatin allowed $930,000 for the army and $670,000 for the navy. The federal army was reduced to a mere 3000 men. As for the navy, which the Jeffersonians considered a monument to Federalist extravagance and folly, he planned to lay up all the frigates in the eastern branch of the Potomac. There, as he bluntly put it, they would be "under the immediate eye of the department and would require but one set of plunderers to look after them."

Coast defense was necessary, so Jefferson urged the construction of a fleet of little gunboats, built for speed, carrying a small crew and an armament of a single gun. Congress appropriated $50,000 to build fifteen of these vessels. By 1804 Numbers 1 and 2 were finished. Number 1 was sent south to Savannah harbor. While it was there, a terrific coastal hurricane blew down church spires, carried off the roofs of houses, and raised a tidal wave of unheard-of destructiveness. When the storm was over, Gunboat Number 1 was discovered in a cornfield eight miles inland. Jefferson's "Mosquito Fleet" became the stock joke of the Federalists. At a dinner in Boston, one toast ran: "Gunboat Number 1: If our gunboats are of no use upon water, may they at least be the best upon earth."

Attack on the Judiciary

Another part of the Jeffersonian program was the attack upon the federal judiciary. In February 1801, only a few days before the end of Adams's term, Congress had passed a law to create additional district courts and six circuit courts of appeal and to authorize the appointment of more judges. A year later, Jefferson's Congress repealed the law, thus taking away places from judges whom President Adams had appointed. Congress also decreed that the Supreme Court should not meet again until February 1803.

Next, in 1803, Congress began impeachment proceedings against Associate Justice Chase of the Supreme Court. This extreme Federalist had offended the Republicans, partly through his excessive zeal in prosecuting offenders under the Sedition Act and partly through his offensive comments on Jefferson's political colleagues. The Republicans, he declared, were aiming "to take away all security for property and personal liberty." If they should succeed, he continued, "our republican constitution will sink into a mobocracy, the worst of all possible governments." Although Chase was put on trial before the Senate, his opponents could submit no proof that he had been guilty of "high crimes and misdemeanors," so he was not convicted. Then the Jeffersonians received a jolt from John Marshall. In the first session of the Supreme Court after its enforced vacation, the Chief

Justice handed down his decision in the case of *Marbury* v. *Madison*. Here he developed the doctrine that the Court could declare an act of Congress unconstitutional. This decision was a warning to the Democratic party and its leaders; the Constitution imposed limits beyond which Jefferson and his Congress could not go.

The problem of the new justices for the district courts was complicated. There was enough judicial business to warrant the expansion of the system, but Jefferson did not want the places manned by Federalists. After legislating the offices out from under Adams's appointees, Congress passed another measure restoring most of the positions it had just destroyed. Jefferson then filled them with good Democratic-Republicans.

Tripoli and Louisiana

In spite of his desire for peace Jefferson was unable to avoid war, and the contest forced upon him was, by a strange irony, a naval war. Those disreputable dependencies of the Turkish Empire, the Barbary states of Tunis, Tripoli, Algiers, and Morocco, had for generations secured their revenue by levying tribute on Mediterranean commerce. The leading maritime powers regularly bought exemption from their plundering, sometimes to the extent of $300,000 a year. Before the Revolution the Americans had been covered by the payments made by Great Britain, but after 1783 they had to pay their own tribute. The Barbary rulers were always demanding presents, seizing American ships, and holding the crews for ransom. In 1795, for example, the United States had paid nearly $800,000 to the Algerians.

War with Tripoli

In Jefferson's administration the Bashaw of Tripoli, dissatisfied with his $83,000 a year from the United States, declared war. Jefferson sent a fleet to the Mediterranean, and the contest lasted until 1805. Even after that there was trouble for the next ten years, although the pirates were beginning to show a wholesome respect for force.

Talleyrand's Program

The greatest of all the accomplishments of the Jeffersonian administration—the purchase of Louisiana—had been unforeseen during the campaign of 1800. This territory, including approximately one third of the present United States and stretching from the Gulf of Mexico to Canada and from the Mississippi to the Rocky Mountains, had been turned over to Spain in 1763. After Talleyrand took charge of the French foreign office, he began to scheme for the return of Louisiana to its former possessor. In this policy, he had the support of the new dictator of France, Napoleon Bonaparte. The Spanish government was not opposed to giving back Louisiana, provided the price were right. In the colony itself the French inhabitants favored the retrocession. Prior to 1795 the colony had not prospered; then the privileges granted to Americans in the Mississippi valley, with the right of deposit, marked the beginning of a commercial revival.

In 1795, the year that Spain and the United States signed the Treaty of San Lorenzo, France secured Santo Domingo. Talleyrand felt that Spain had made a blunder in her agreement with the United States, particularly in giving this country everything north of the 31st parallel. He wrote:

> There are no other means of putting an end to the ambition of the Americans than that of shutting them up within the limits which nature seems to have traced for them; but Spain is not in a condition to do this great work alone. She cannot, therefore hasten too quickly to engage the aid of a preponderating Power, yielding to it a small part of her immense domains in order to preserve the rest.

If Spain would only cede Florida and Louisiana to France, he continued,

> . . . from that moment the power of America is bounded by the limit which it may suit the interests and the tranquillity of France and Spain to assign her. The French Republic, mistress of these two provinces, will be a wall of brass forever impenetrable to the combined efforts of England and America.

On October 1, 1800, the French representative at Madrid signed the secret Treaty of San Ildefonso, which provided for the retrocession of Louisiana to France with the boundaries which it had in the hands of Spain. In return Talleyrand and Napoleon promised to give the Italian province of Tuscany to the Duke of Parma, a satellite of the Spanish king, a promise, by the way, which they never carried out. On March 21, 1801, France and Spain signed the definitive treaty for the retrocession, thereby completing the bargain.

Monroe's Mission

Although Jefferson showed concern over this transfer of title to Louisiana, he did not become seriously excited until the spring of 1802. Then he outlined his fears to Livingston: "The cession of Louisiana and the Floridas by Spain to France works most sorely on the United States. . . . It completely reverses all the political relations of the United States, and will form a new epoch in our political career. . . ." France had been the friend of America, but now all this was changed.

> There is on the globe one single spot, the possessor of which is our natural and habitual enemy. It is New Orleans, through which the produce of 3/8 of our territory must pass to market. . . . The day that France takes possession of New Orleans fixes the sentence which is to retain her forever within her low-water mark. From that moment we must marry ourselves to the British fleet and nation. We must turn all our attention to a maritime force.

Then the renewal of the war in Europe would be the signal for an American attack upon Louisiana.

In December 1802 Jefferson heard that the Spanish authorities in New Orleans had withdrawn the right of deposit. By this time Americans in the West were demanding war. Jefferson sent Monroe to France as a special agent to buy New Orleans and a part of West Florida. Congress appropriated $2,000,000 to defray expenses, and early in 1803 Monroe started on his mission. He was instructed to offer as high as $10,000,000 for New Orleans and the two Floridas. If France should refuse to sell, he was to ask for a renewal of the right of deposit. Failing in that, Jefferson hinted that he would probably be sent to England to negotiate a treaty of alliance. Monroe went off with Jefferson's assurance that on the success of the mission "depend the future destinies of this Republic."

During this interval Napoleon turned his attention to Haiti. The Negro population on the island, under the leadership of Toussaint l'Ouverture, had rebelled and set up a republic. For a time Napoleon's forces had been able to hold the Negroes in check, but early in 1803, as the ruler of Europe was about to take formal possession of Louisiana, he received news that wrecked his plans. Two French armies in Haiti had been wiped out, partly by war, partly by yellow fever, and the commander there was frantically calling for 35,000 more men. Napoleon could not send these reinforcements because he had already decided to renew the war in Europe. He had to leave Haiti to its fate. Then, fearing that he could not hold Louisiana without Haiti as a base, he suddenly decided to sell the province to the United States.

Purchase of Louisiana

On April 10, 1803, just before Monroe's arrival, Napoleon called in his finance minister, Marbois, for an interview. "Irresolution and deliberation are no longer in season," he announced to his astonished subordinate. "I renounce Louisiana. It is not only New Orleans that I cede; it is the whole colony, without reserve. . . . I direct you to negotiate the affair. Have an interview this very day with Mr. Livingston." Marbois informed Talleyrand of the new plan. Shortly thereafter Talleyrand came to Livingston with an offer to sell the whole of Louisiana. The American minister had received no previous hint of Napoleon's extraordinary decision, and his first reply was that his government would not be interested. Later he returned to Talleyrand and asked for terms; negotiations started at once. On Monroe's arrival the two men signed the treaty which transferred Louisiana to the United States. For the sum of $15,000,000 the United States got the territory with the same limits it had when ceded by Spain to France. Livingston and Monroe tried to get from Marbois a formal statement regarding the boundaries, and the French minister carried their request to Napoleon. That gentleman had no intention of clearing up the uncertainty. "If an obscurity did not already exist," he sagely observed, "it would perhaps be good policy to put one there." Talleyrand was as noncommittal as Napoleon on the subject, and the Americans were left free to take what they could get. Their work was a diplomatic triumph of tremendous importance. No other American negotiators ever secured so much territory for so little money. On October 21, 1803, the treaty was proclaimed in effect, while Spain was still in possession. On November 30 control passed to the hands of France, and on December 20 France turned the region over to the United States.

Although the astute trio of Marbois, Talleyrand, and Napoleon refused to inform Jefferson and Madison of their decision on the subject, these three Frenchmen had already agreed upon the bounds of Louisiana. According to specific instructions which they framed for the guidance of French officials in Louisiana, the province was bounded on the west by the Rio Grande, up

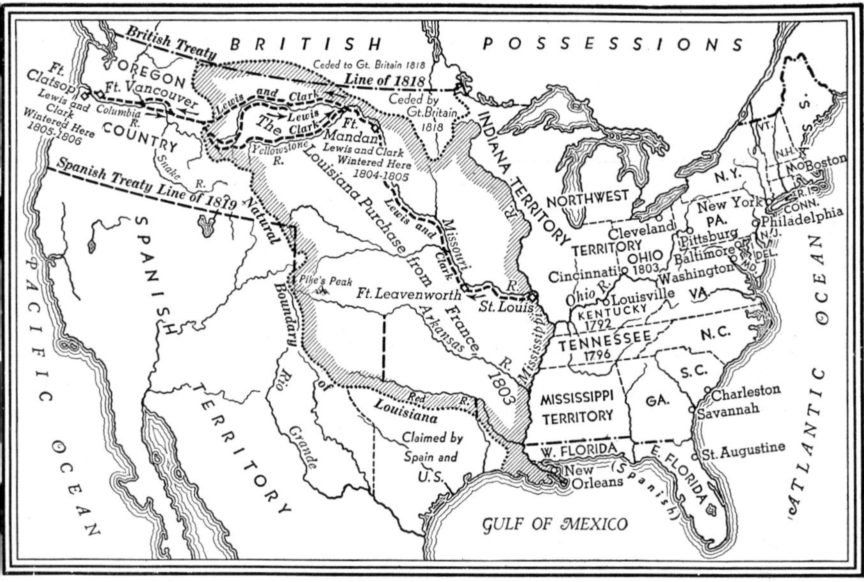

Map 7. The Louisiana Purchase in 1803

to the 30th parallel, so the French included Texas in Louisiana. On the east the boundary followed the Mississippi to the Iberville, north of New Orleans, and then to Lakes Maurepas and Pontchartrain to the Gulf. Therefore France did not include West Florida in Louisiana.

When the news of the purchase reached Jefferson, the strict-constructionist President was embarrassed. He thought at first that he would have to "appeal to the nation for an additional article to the Constitution, approving and confirming an act which the nation had not previously authorized." Then came reports of possible Federalist opposition, so Jefferson dropped his plan for getting an ex post facto amendment. With this step Jefferson virtually discarded strict construction.

The possession of new territory raised the problem of government. Jefferson and Madison drafted a bill for the purpose, which Congress passed in 1804. This measure provided for a governor, secretary, judges, and a legislative council of thirteen members, all to be appointed by the President. There was to be no elective assembly. French civil law was to remain in force. This bill was a close copy of the constitutional portions of the Quebec Act of 1774. Just how Jefferson reconciled his Louisiana Government Act with his attack upon the Quebec Act in the Declaration of Independence he never explained. This undemocratic measure was repealed in 1805, and the principles of the Ordinance of 1787 were substituted for it.

Evidently the purchase of Louisiana stimulated Jefferson's desires for expansion, and he turned his attention toward the Floridas. On the theory that the region around Mobile had been included in Louisiana, Congress established a customs district there. In 1805 Jefferson tried to seize the whole province of West Florida, but John Randolph defeated his plan. Later, when Madison was President, West Florida was seized.

Even before the purchase, while Louisiana was still in the hands of Spain, Jefferson had become interested in the region beyond the Mississippi River. He wanted to establish friendly relations with the Indian tribes living in the Missouri valley, and he was particularly anxious to bring the fur trade of that country under American control. On January 18, 1803, he urged Congress to authorize an expedition to explore the West. After securing the consent of Congress, Jefferson chose Captain Meriwether Lewis, his private secretary, and Lieutenant William Clark, a brother of George Rogers Clark, to take charge of the work. In 1804 the Lewis and Clark expedition, with a party numbering forty-five, started up the Missouri River. They spent the winter in what is now North Dakota, near the site of the present city of Bismarck. In the spring of 1805 they crossed the mountains, and by November they reached the headwaters of the Columbia River. Captain Robert Gray of Boston had entered the mouth of this river in 1793. Lewis and Clark followed the Columbia from beginning to end and spent their second winter on the Pacific coast. They returned to Washington in 1806, having covered a distance of some 8000 miles. These explorations gave the United States a valid claim to the Oregon country.

Lewis and Clark

Federalist Opposition

Jefferson's Triumph

The Federalists in New England disapproved of most of Jefferson's measures, and they found particular fault with the purchase of Louisiana. Some of them even began to talk about withdrawal, or secession, from the Union. The prime mover in the scheme was Senator Timothy Pickering of Massachusetts, who had been secretary of state in Adams's Cabinet. His principal associates were Plumer of New Hampshire and Tracy and Griswold of Connecticut. Writing in December 1803, Pickering prophesied the establishment of "a *new confederacy,* exempt from the corrupt and corrupting influence and oppression of the aristocratic democrats of the South." Convinced that the Union must be dissolved, the plotters took steps to establish the proposed new confederacy. In 1804 the Senate ratified the Louisiana Purchase Treaty, and thus intensified Federalist opposition; 1804 was also the year of a Presidential election and consequently a good time for any political action. The Federalists turned first to George Cabot of Massachusetts as the proper leader for their scheme. Cabot, however, did not favor secession.

Then the Federalist plotters had to look elsewhere for leadership, so they turned to New York. By 1804 Vice President Aaron Burr had become almost an outlaw in his own party. He was ready to accept the Federalist endorsement of his candidacy for governor of New York on one condition: he would agree to the plans for secession, but his new allies must not ask him to make any more promises. But Burr was defeated in the race for the governorship, and the Federalist plot failed. One of the men responsible for Burr's downfall was Alexander Hamilton. Burr challenged the former secretary of the treasury to a duel. On July 11, 1804, the two men met outside of Weehawken, New Jersey, and Burr killed his opponent.

In the Presidential election itself, Jefferson almost swept the country, winning 162 out of a total of 176 electoral votes. Even Massachusetts gave her votes to Jefferson. In the election of 1804, the Twelfth Amendment to the Constitution was in effect. This provided that each elector should vote separately for President and Vice President. The amendment also provided that in case no candidate should receive a majority of the electoral votes, the House of Representatives, voting by states, should choose one of the three candidates standing highest in the electoral vote.

After he killed Hamilton, Burr was indicted for murder but was not convicted. Then he left New York to rebuild his political fortunes in the West. In 1805 he appeared once more in Washington. His plans were hazy at the time and, except for his schemes of land speculation in Arkansas, they have never been cleared up; perhaps his chief purpose was to extract money from anybody stupid enough to trust him. In 1806 Burr collected a small fleet of boats on the Ohio to carry out his plans in the Southwest. In November of that year Jefferson issued a proclamation ordering his arrest on a charge of treason. He was placed on trial at Richmond, Virginia, but acquitted for lack of evidence. After acquittal, he became more completely an outcast.

Jefferson's first term was a triumph for the President and for his party. The administration kept its promises of reform, and it gave the country the unexpected advantage of the Louisiana Purchase. During much of this time the President was free from the burdens imposed upon the United States by warfare in Europe. Far from injuring the United States, the transition from Federalist to Democratic control had been beneficial.

Chapter 14

NEUTRAL TRADE AND THE WAR OF 1812

"Peaceable Coercion"

IN 1801 the belligerent powers in Europe signed the Peace of Amiens and so ended eight years of war. This cessation of hostilities had two important consequences for the United States. It ended wartime restrictions on neutral trade. It also took business away from American shippers. In 1801 exports from the United States stood at the impressive figure of $94,115,925; in 1803 they had dropped to $55,800,033. This decline of American commerce was due to the return of British shipping to its customary routes.

In 1803, two months after France signed the Louisiana Purchase Treaty, Napoleon renewed the war in Europe. It continued without interruption until 1814. For the future, therefore, Jefferson and his associates would be troubled with the problems of neutral trade which had so disturbed the Federalists. Jefferson was just as anxious to keep his country out of war as Washington and Adams had been and, as the event proved, for the duration of his own administration he was just as successful.

Commercial Profits

War in Europe was profitable to the neutral Americans, and American exports increased. England needed naval stores from the Baltic and tropical products from the West Indies. British manufacturers wished to sell their woolen goods and hardware. France needed West Indian products, foodstuffs, and manufactured goods. American shippers were glad to carry commodities to both France and England because prices were high and profits pleasing. The following table shows the development of this export trade through 1808.

EXPORTS FROM THE UNITED STATES

Year	*Domestic produce*	*Foreign produce*	*Total*
1803	$42,205,961	$13,594,072	$ 55,800,033
1804	41,467,477	36,231,597	77,699,074
1805	42,387,002	53,179,019	95,566,021
1806	41,253,727	60,283,236	101,536,963
1807	48,699,592	59,643,150	108,343,150
1808	9,433,546	12,997,414	22,430,960

Before 1805 Napoleon made extensive plans to invade England. Then the British fleet under Nelson annihilated the French navy in the Battle of Trafalgar, thus making a French attack upon England impossible. On the other side, Napoleon had defeated all his Continental enemies: Austria at the Battle of Austerlitz in 1805, Prussia at Jena in 1806, and Russia at Friedland in 1807. England was as powerless to crush Napoleon on land as he was to fight England at sea. Both parties resorted to economic warfare, and American merchants were soon in trouble.

Economic Warfare

There is no point in trying to determine which belligerent first began restrictions on neutral trade. Two rival systems of government were in conflict, and the authorities in each case were prepared to do everything possible to win. Napoleon knew that English greatness rested upon industry and commerce. If he could interrupt English trade he might reduce merchants, manufacturers, and workers to such extreme poverty that they would compel their government to end the war. On the other hand Napoleon had to import some foodstuffs and manufactured goods. If European ports could be closed to these essential supplies, the French would be compelled to beg for peace. With her navy the strongest in the world, Great Britain had a distinct advantage. She could keep her own lines of trade open, and she could close enemy ports. But to make her sea power effective she would necessarily violate the rights of neutrals.

Early in the war Napoleon ordered the seizure of British goods and ships and the arrest of British subjects in German ports which he had recently acquired. The British declared a blockade of Continental ports along the English Channel and the North Sea. Under previous regulations the British had permitted American merchants to carry West Indian goods to Europe, even though the products were of enemy origin. The only restriction was that the shipper must take them into an American port and pay American duties on them. British prize courts sanctioned this procedure in 1802 in a famous decision involving the ship *Polly*. The authorities did not concern themselves with the question as to whether or not the duties were paid back when the goods left for France. In 1805, however, in the *Essex* case the courts held that such repayment of duty restored the enemy status of the goods; since it was the intent of the shipper to take the cargoes to enemy ports, the goods were liable to seizure. Then Britain imposed additional restrictions. For the future, all commodities en route to the continent of Europe would have to go through a British port, so that the British could collect duties. Beginning in May 1806, the British government issued a series of orders in council, designed to cut off supplies from France. One declared the coast from Le Havre to Ostend under blockade and prohibited to neutrals any coasting trade between Le Havre and the Elbe River. Another, published in January 1807, declared the whole French coasting trade closed to neutrals. A third, in November 1807, put the whole European coastline under blockade from Trieste to Copenhagen. Under this last order, no neutral ship could enter any port from which British vessels were excluded, unless it had first cleared from a British port and had paid duties there.

Not to be outdone in this contest of paper blockades, Napoleon planned to exclude English commerce from continental Europe. To this end he began to bring the ports of Europe under his control. By 1807, with his Russian treaty, he had everything in his hands except Spain and Portugal. Napoleon issued a series of decrees aimed at neutral as well as British trade. In November 1806, from Berlin, he declared the British Isles under blockade and announced that no vessel clearing from any English port would be admitted to any French port. In December 1807, by the Milan decree, he proclaimed that any ship submitting to search by English officers, paying any duty to the British government, or even bound for or coming from a British port would be seized on its appearance in French waters. Thus any ship which had complied with English orders in council would be liable to confiscation if it should put into a French port. In spite of these restrictions, up to the end of September 1807, American commerce steadily expanded. Prices were so high that American merchants could afford to lose two out of three ships; if one out of three escaped capture, they would still make a profit.

Fruitless Diplomacy

Both Washington and Adams had tried to secure recognition of American rights without war. Two possible courses were open: retaliatory legislation and diplomatic negotiation. Jefferson's predecessors had tried both, and so did he. In April 1806 Congress passed a nonimportation act, providing that after the following November 1, unless in the meantime British decrees should be modified, specified British manufactured goods would be denied admission to American ports.

Next Jefferson instructed James Monroe and William Pinkney of Maryland to secure a new commercial treaty with England to take the place of Jay's Treaty. The new treaty, Jefferson hoped, would define neutral rights, provide for indemnities for goods illegally seized, and stop the British practices of impressing American sailors and searching ships in American waters. During this period the British navy maintained a virtual blockade of American ports, stopped and searched neutral merchantmen, and continued to impress seamen.

This question of impressment was troublesome. The navy was England's chief hope in the contest with Napoleon, but its efficiency was steadily undermined by wholesale desertions. Life on board a British man-of-war was nearly unbearable, with wretched quarters and miserable food. Many of the crews had been filled by press gangs, so the seamen escaped when opportunity came. Being wise, they chose American ports as the best place to make their change; then they were always sure of employment in the American merchant marine. According to one estimate, American vessels were getting every year an average of 2500 deserters from the royal navy. Search parties took back about 1000 a year, along with some bona fide American citizens.

Up to a certain point Monroe and Pinkney succeeded in their negotiations. They secured a new treaty, which allowed Americans to engage in the carrying trade between the New World and the "unblockaded" ports in Europe, provided that all commodities were first landed in an American port and the duties paid. Here was a catch that might have nullified the whole agreement, because any new order in council might declare any port in Europe under blockade. The treaty contained no mention whatever of impressment. Jefferson was so much displeased that he refused even to submit the document to the Senate.

Monroe explained that the British and American representatives had reached an unofficial agreement on impressment, which gave the United States the concessions it had asked for. He argued that his treaty was better than nothing:

> When I took into view the prosperous and happy condition of the United States, compared with that of other nations: that, as a neutral power they were almost the exclusive carriers of the whole world; and that, in commerce, they flourished beyond example, notwithstanding the losses, which they occasionally suffered, I was strong in the opinion, that these blessings ought not to be hazarded, in such question.

Unwarranted Aggression

In 1807 a new episode threatened to bring Jefferson's peaceful policy to an end. For four years British naval officers had been overbearing but not actually hostile. This year they overstepped the line. In June the American frigate, *Chesapeake,* Captain Barron commanding, started off for a cruise in the Mediterranean. According to rumor she had on board a deserter from the British navy, one Ratford. As the American vessel put out to sea, she was followed by the British frigate, *Leopard.* Once outside American waters, the *Leopard* hailed the *Chesapeake.* When the *Chesapeake* hove to, the British commander demanded the right to search her for deserters. This demand would have been permissible in case of a merchant vessel, but in the case of a man-of-war it was an arrogant insult. Barron properly refused to comply, whereupon the British ship immediately opened fire.

The *Chesapeake* was not ready for action. Her guns had not been fitted to their carriages, her gun deck was piled up with supplies for the voyage, and her ammunition was inaccessible on short notice. Completely at the mercy of the *Leopard,* Barron surrendered after his crew had succeeded in firing a single shot. The British then searched the vessel, found Ratford, and carried him off. They also took three other seamen, all American citizens, but like Ratford deserters from the British navy. News of this indefensible proceeding aroused a demand for war.

Jefferson would have no war. He found just as urgent reasons for maintaining peace after 1807 as before 1801. Federal revenue was largely derived from English imports. No official desired to face a war, the first result of which would be to cut off the income essential to its successful prosecution. If the two Federalist Presidents had been justified in their efforts to preserve peace, Jefferson's decision was sound. Realizing that war would be no remedy, he began to ponder a scheme of economic warfare. He knew how eager both France and England were to secure American foodstuffs and raw materials. Suppose American exports were entirely cut off; would not the haughty Europeans sue for terms?

In his annual message to Congress in December 1807, the President outlined his plans for "peaceable coercion." He asked for an embargo on all exports, and Congress passed the bill. This Embargo Act prohibited the sailing of any American vessel from any port of the United States to any foreign port. Foreign ships could sail only in ballast. Ships engaged in the coasting trade were required to furnish bonds, double the value of the cargo, that they would land their commodities only in American ports. So Europe would be deprived of supplies, and France and England would be starved into respect for the maritime rights of the United States. Actually the embargo was not felt in France, and, while it did cause embarrassment in England, it had no appreciable influence on public policy.

Embargo Act

Failing to achieve the purpose for which it had been designed, Jefferson's embargo destroyed the trade it was supposed to protect. A glance at the table given above shows how export trade fell off, almost $86,000,000 in a single year. In New England, where one third of the ships engaged in the carrying trade were owned, there was serious hardship. Some ships remained away from American ports. Those in port were left to rot at the wharves, shipyards and warehouses were empty, sailors were idle, farmers lost their markets, and commodity prices were cut in half. National revenue diminished at least 50 percent.

Because the law was being violated at every opportunity, Jefferson urged Congress to enact a drastic enforcement measure. This was done in January 1809. The bond for coasting vessels was raised to six times the combined value of the vessel and the cargo. Collectors were authorized to refuse clearance papers, if to their minds there appeared any intention to violate the law, and they could use the army and navy to compel obedience.

The wrath of New England flared up into fury. Where in the Constitution did the author of the Kentucky Resolutions find any warrant for the embargo? Congress had power to regulate trade, but regulation did not mean ruin. Furthermore, when had the Federalists ever perpetrated anything so tyrannical as the Enforcing Act of 1809? In the winter of 1809, distressed at the destruction wrought by the embargo and disturbed at the uproar in New England, the President retired to Monticello.

Politics and War

Madison for President

If the Federalist party had not been weakened beyond repair, it would have taken advantage of Jefferson's blunder. In 1808 any strong opposition could have made political capital out of the ruin. But the country was through with the Federalist party, and nothing would induce the voters to give it another trial. Jefferson followed the custom started by Washington by refusing a third term, but he chose his successor. At least he made known his desire to have his secretary of state, James Madison, as the next

President. In the election, Madison secured 122 electoral votes against 47 for the Federalist candidate, C. C. Pinckney.

In personal appearance the new executive was pretty much everything that Jefferson was not. The "little Virginian" was only five and a half feet tall and of nervous temperament. On inauguration day he was literally half sick with fright. In the Federal Convention, in Congress, and in the State Department, where extensive and exact knowledge was much needed, Madison had been comfortable and unusually competent. But in the President's chair, which demands a combination of keenness in practical politics, farsightedness in public problems, and vigor in execution, Madison was deficient. He had every reason to be dizzy and pale at his inaugural reception. The party organization was the creation of his predecessor. Even Jefferson had found it hard at times to make his following stay with him. Madison found it impossible. The machine had made him President, and it expected him to obey orders.

In Madison's first term the most important issue was that of the United States Bank, the charter of which was due to expire on March 4, 1811. The bank had been profitable, it had been soundly managed, and it had rendered a distinct service to the government. Madison, Gallatin, and William H. Crawford of the Senate, an able financier, all three loyal Jeffersonians, favored a recharter. But the bank had been established by the Federalists, and most of the Democrats had consistently railed against it as unconstitutional. Therefore, the party which had accepted the constitutionality of the Louisiana Purchase, the embargo, and the Enforcing Act now reverted to strict construction and refused to continue the bank.

Diplomacy of Desperation

Madison inherited Jefferson's foreign policy, which had resulted in no change in English or French policies but which did create bitter resentment at home. Just before the end of Jefferson's term, Congress had repealed the embargo, substituting for it a nonintercourse arrangement. This allowed trade with all the world except the makers of the two sets of restrictive decrees. On May 1, 1810, the first nonintercourse policy was abandoned. In its place a measure known as "Macon Bill No. 2" allowed unrestricted trade. Then, in case either Great Britain or France revoked her obnoxious decrees and the other power failed to do so, the President could restore nonintercourse with the offending nation.

During 1810 the much-harassed American export trade had begun to revive, reaching on September 30 the total of $66,757,970. Then nonintercourse was revived against England and trade declined. In 1811 and 1812 the British government began to make concessions to the United States. First it disavowed the act of the captain of the *Leopard* and made reparation for the *Chesapeake* affair.

During the winter England began to suffer from the loss of trade with the United States. She had lost practically all of her market in continental Europe and the revival of nonintercourse left her manufacturers and merchants with quantities of unsold goods. Factories had to close for lack of orders and workmen were thrown out of employment. Businessmen begged the administration to change its policy toward America. As a result of this alarming economic collapse the English Cabinet announced on June 16, 1812, that the orders in council were revoked. These concessions, however, came too late to prevent war.

War Hawks Disputes over commerce were not the only cause of war. There were other developments which had a profound influence on the Congress of the United States and which helped to account for the declaration of war. In the elections of 1810 some of the older leaders lost their places in Congress, and their seats were taken by young newcomers. Most conspicuous among them were Henry Clay of Kentucky, thirty-five years of age, and John C. Calhoun of South Carolina, then only thirty. These two and their colleagues were known as war hawks.

The new Congress met for its first session in November 1811, when the leading Democratic newspapers were insistently clamoring for war. Clay, chosen speaker of the House, placed on his committees men known to favor war. On November 29, 1811, the House Committee on Foreign Affairs, reporting on President Madison's message, made the following significant statement:

> The period has arrived when in the opinion of your committee it is the sacred duty of Congress to call forth the patriotism and resources of the country. By the aid of these, and with the blessing of God, we confidently trust that we shall be able to procure that redress which has been sought for by justice, by remonstrance, and forbearance in vain.

Clay had been urging war for two years. To punish England and at the same time to add to the grandeur of the United States, all the war hawks united in a demand for the conquest of Canada. "I trust I shall not be presumptuous," said Clay, "when I state that I verily believe that the militia of Kentucky alone are competent to place Montreal and Upper Canada at your feet." The war hawks were interested in the West, in territorial expansion, and in the Indians. They were also interested in the problems of overseas trade, because the prosperity of the West depended upon the export of foodstuffs. These factors all had an influence in bringing on war.

Indian Wars The Indian problem was peculiar. Although the Treaty of Greenville of 1795 was still in effect, the Indians had been subjected to unceasing and unscrupulous pressure by white pioneers. By 1809 the Indians had been compelled to abandon their rights to some 48,000,000 acres in the Northwest. In this year two Shawnee brothers, Tecumseh and the Prophet, made an effort to protect the Indians from further losses. They organized a new Indian confederacy and opposed further sales of Indian land. Successful in his own section, Tecumseh, in 1811, went south to form an alliance with the Creeks.

Westerners who had designs on Indian land for themselves or for white settlers interpreted the work of Tecumseh as an attack on white interests.

They found a leader in William Henry Harrison, at that time governor of Indiana Territory. Harrison in turn was certainly not restrained by the War Department. In November 1811, during Tecumseh's absence, Harrison moved into camp near the Indian village of Tippecanoe on the Wabash. Provoked by this move, the Indians attacked Harrison's force and were badly beaten. Harrison immediately became the hero of the West.

War with England

If there was any immediate cause of the War of 1812 it was probably the work of Tecumseh and the Prophet. Their activity stirred up the West and aroused the voters. Conquer Canada and end Indian wars, the argument ran. The voters in turn gave Congress a heavy majority in favor of war. It is fruitless to seek the causes of war solely in the commercial policies of the belligerent powers of Europe. The war hawks were responsible for the declaration of war. They urged freedom of the seas, territorial expansion, and the conquest of Canada. Clay talked eloquently of dictating peace at Montreal or Halifax. On June 1, 1812, after opposing war as long as he dared, Madison sent a war message to Congress; and on June 18 that body declared war. The vote in the House was 79 to 49, with a majority of New England members in the opposition.

A comparison of British and American resources made a dark picture for the United States. When the war began Congress had already (February 6, 1812) voted to recruit a force of volunteers, 50,000 strong. The regular army consisted of 6700 officers and men. Eight days after declaring war Congress voted to enlarge it to 25,000. Before March 1813, in the regular army only thirteen officers had been promoted to the rank of general. Because of age or incompetence most of these were a sorry lot. William Henry Harrison was the youngest and most competent. General Dearborn, commander in chief, was sixty-one. Thomas Pinckney was sixty-three; James Wilkinson was only fifty-five, but he was a notorious scoundrel; William Hull was sixty years old.

England had a navy of more than 800 war vessels, 230 of which were larger than any American craft. The American navy consisted of a dozen ships with a personnel of 5000. But the navy had able officers. Langdon Cheves asked Congress to appropriate $7,500,000 for the construction of twelve 74's—heavy warships—and twenty frigates, or cruisers, but the House defeated this bill. This discrepancy in naval strength was partly offset by the war in Europe. Before the latter part of 1814 England could not concentrate her forces in American waters.

The American treasury was empty, while England had an income of $70,000,000 from taxation alone. Gallatin had submitted estimates to Congress showing that the war would bring a deficit of at least $4,000,000 the first year. In June, after declaring war, Congress voted to postpone the whole question of taxes. Congress behaved as though the United States could win the war with a token army, with almost no navy, and without money.

The outcome of the first military campaigns could have been predicted from this comparison of resources. With the conquest of Canada as the primary object of the war, General Dearborn planned a campaign against Montreal along the route of Lake George and Lake Champlain. With the main attack there were to be three subsidiary movements, one from Sackets Harbor on the eastern end of Lake Ontario, one from Niagara at the western end, and one from Detroit between Lakes Erie and Huron.

Military Operations

The first advance was toward Malden, in Ontario, twenty miles from Detroit. General Hull took command of his troops at Dayton, Ohio, and started on the 200-mile march toward Detroit. Hull sent all his baggage, hospital stores, intrenching tools, and even his muster rolls and instructions by schooner to Detroit. He chose this method because of the impossibility of sending heavy supplies by land; they would not arrive in time for the campaign. What he sent by water did not arrive either; the British captured the whole consignment.

Hull crossed into Canada, and then, overcome by fear, recrossed to Detroit. Brock, the Canadian commander, followed, and, playing upon the American general's timidity, frightened him into a surrender. Brock, with a force of hardly more than 1300 men, captured an American army of 2500; with Detroit he got the whole Michigan territory. Subsequently General Hull was courtmartialed for cowardice, but he was an old man so his only punishment was loss of his command. The other campaigns planned for 1812 were not so disastrous; they were merely negative. The operations around Niagara brought no results. In northern New York General Dearborn led a large force from Plattsburg to the Canadian line; then he led them back to winter quarters.

The New Navy

In the meantime officers and men of the little American navy were giving an inspiring demonstration of what could be accomplished with proper equipment and leadership. Only three days after General Hull surrendered at Detroit, his nephew, Captain Isaac Hull, commanding the frigate *Constitution,* defeated and destroyed the British *Guerrière* off the Gulf of the St. Lawrence. Three other duels with ships of approximately the same strength resulted in equally decisive victories for the Americans.

The British navy, however, with its vast strength soon swept the American flag from the Atlantic. But the American commanders did effective work on the Great Lakes. In the winter of 1812-13, Commodore Oliver Hazard Perry built six small ships for service on Lake Erie. On September 10, 1813, he decisively defeated the British fleet on the Lake. Perry's victory enabled General William Henry Harrison, the new commander in the Northwest, to recapture Detroit. Then, in October 1813, at the battle of the Thames, Harrison won an important victory and so secured the West against further danger of British attack. During 1813, General Dearborn captured Toronto, or York as it was then called, and held it long enough to burn the public buildings. In the same year renewed efforts were made to cross over into Canada from northern and western New York.

To take command of this expedition General Wilkinson was brought

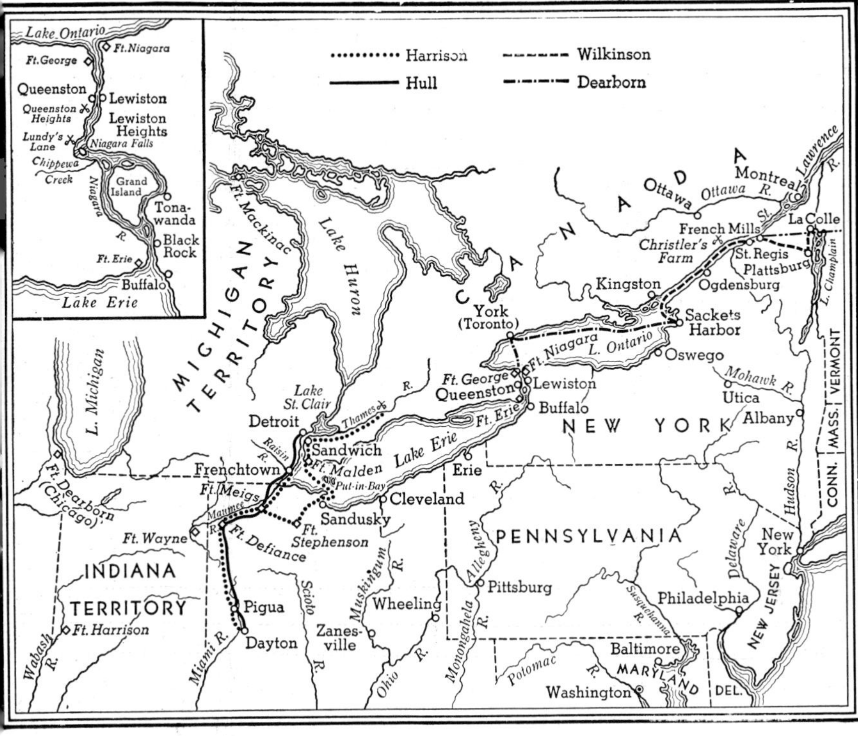

Map 8. The War of 1812

up from the South. He got his orders on May 19, 1813, at New Orleans; after proceeding leisurely by way of Washington and New York he turned up at Sackets Harbor on August 20. Wilkinson found himself in command of a force of 3483 of whom 1441 were unfit for duty. His subordinate officers were no more competent than their commander, and the enlisted men had received no training. The plan of campaign called for an attack on Montreal, and Wilkinson moved his troops down the St. Lawrence. Early in November they were on the Canadian side, some twenty miles northeast of Ogdensburg. In the first battle they were defeated and driven back to New York. In the following year, 1814, Madison appointed new generals who began to win victories. In July, Winfield Scott, recently promoted to the rank of brigadier general, defeated the British at Chippewa, and later the Americans practically won the decision at Lundy's Lane.

The last naval battle of real consequence in the war was fought on Lake Champlain. In the summer of 1814 the British planned to send 11,000 men south along the Lake over Burgoyne's old route to Albany. Captain Thomas Macdonough was in command of the few American vessels on Lake Champlain. Although he had the smaller force, he won a brilliant victory over the British. By so doing he made the proposed British invasion of New York impossible. With Macdonough's victory in the East and with Scott's work in the West, the Americans secured control of their whole northern border westward from New Hampshire.

In the South, Andrew Jackson was placed in charge of militia forces, primarily to break the Indian power in Georgia and Alabama. During the spring and summer of 1814 he was fighting the Creeks; he inflicted a decisive defeat upon them at the battle of Horseshoe Bend. This victory opened a new section of the Southwest to white settlement and consequently to cotton culture. As for Jackson himself, it brought him a major-generalship and the command in the Mobile-New Orleans district.

Final Campaigns

With the defeat of Napoleon in 1814, the British could devote more attention to the American war. In addition to the projected invasion by way of Lake Champlain already referred to, the officials planned one campaign in Chesapeake Bay and another against New Orleans. On the Chesapeake the two main objectives were Baltimore, with its shipping interests, and Washington, the federal capital.

The British fleet had been in full control of the Bay for nearly a year and a half, yet the administration had done little to provide for the defense of Washington. On August 19, 1814, General Ross landed 4000 veteran troops at Benedict, Maryland. To meet this danger, General Winder and Monroe, acting secretary of war, sent out a call to the neighboring states for militia. Then, after a hasty glance at the improvised army drawn up to guard Washington, Madison and his Cabinet drove away to take refuge in the woods of Virginia. Once in the capital, the British burned the capitol, department buildings, and the White House. This done, at the end of a week the British re-embarked. During the same summer, British forces occupied portions of Massachusetts, now in the state of Maine. By September, they were in possession of the region around the Penobscot River, and the inhabitants were required to take an oath of allegiance to George III.

The last campaign of the war, in the New Orleans district, began late in the fall of 1814. On December 23, the advance guard of the British army was within seven miles of New Orleans. General Jackson checked that force, and the British commander waited for the main army. After another preliminary encounter, in which the advantage was with the Americans, the real battle came on January 8, 1815. The British forces, veterans of seven years' experience in Europe, were completely defeated, and by the end of January they were in full retreat. This victory, however, had no effect upon the outcome of the war, because just two weeks before the battle, the treaty of peace had been signed.

Federalist Opposition

While the national administration was demonstrating its incapacity in the conduct of the war, New England Federalists were gradually moving from opposition toward treason. Federalist leaders were more concerned with opposing the national government than in fighting the British. In the years before 1812 and for many years thereafter, the stock remedy for a dissatisfied section was the doctrine of states' rights, set forth in the Kentucky and Virginia Resolutions of 1798-99. The Federalist view was ably represented in some resolutions of the Connecticut and Massachusetts legislatures, which in subject matter and tone deserve to be ranked with their more famous prototypes from the South. The Connecticut legislature declared that "the state of Connecticut is a FREE, SOVEREIGN, and INDEPENDENT state; that the United States are a confederacy of states; that we are a confederated and not a consolidated republic." In similar vein, the "Great and General Court of the free, sovereign, independent State of Massachusetts" resolved that "Whenever the national compact is violated . . . this legislature is bound to interpose its power, and wrest from the oppressor its victim. . . . This is the spirit of our Union . . . explained by the very man [Madison] who now sets at defiance all the principles of his early political life." **States' Rights**

On June 22, 1812, four days after the declaration of war, the governor of Massachusetts refused to comply with the request of the secretary of war that he call out the state militia. Four days later he issued a proclamation for a public fast day to ask God's forgiveness for the war. At the same time, the House of Representatives of Massachusetts issued an "Address to the People," urging them to "organize a *peace party* throughout your Country, and let all party distinctions vanish. . . . Express your sentiments without fear, and let the sound of your disapprobation of this war be loud and deep." On July 14, a convention of delegates from over fifty towns in the Connecticut valley met for the purpose of opposing the war.

The three states of Massachusetts, Rhode Island, and Connecticut were financially stronger than any other section of the Union, but during the war New England bought only $3,000,000 worth of federal bonds while the middle states took $35,000,000 worth. New England merchants furnished provisions to British ships operating off the coast. The following extract from a letter written by the British commander in Canada in August 1814 is an eloquent commentary on the pro-British attitude of some Americans:

> Two thirds of the army in Canada are at this moment eating beef provided by American contractors. . . . This circumstance, as well as that of the introduction of large sums of specie into this province, being notorious in the United States, it is to be expected Congress will take steps to deprive us of those resources, and under that apprehension large droves are daily crossing the lines coming into lower Canada.

In September 1814 Massachusetts withdrew her militia from federal service and placed the force—70,000 strong, well-drilled and well-equipped—under a state commander. This step was taken two weeks after the capture of Washington and one week after a portion of Maine had been overrun by the enemy. Justification was found in the necessity of providing for local defense. Connecticut had already done the same thing, and these state armies, more formidable than any federal forces, gave the President ample cause for concern. One of the best, clearest, and most logical expositions of the states' rights doctrine is to be found in a speech in the House of Representatives, delivered on December 9, 1814, against a proposed federal conscription law:

> No law professedly passed for the purpose of compelling a service in the regular army, nor any law, which under color of military draft, shall compel men to serve in the army, not for the emergencies mentioned in the Constitution, but for long periods & for the general objects of war, can be carried into effect. In my opinion, it ought not to be carried into effect. The operation of measures thus unconstitutional & illegal ought to be prevented, by a resort to other measures which are both constitutional & legal. It will be the solemn duty of the State Governments to protect their own authority over their Militia, & to interpose between their citizens & arbitrary power. These are among the objects for which the State Governments exist & their highest obligations bind them to the preservation of their own rights and the liberties of their people. . . . With the same earnestness with which I now exhort you to forbear from these measures, I shall exhort them [his constituents] to exercise their unquestionable right of providing for the security of their own liberties.

The whole speech, of which this quotation is a short extract, is a moving appeal for nullification. Neither Jefferson in 1798 and 1799 nor John C. Calhoun in the years after 1825 could put more strongly the case for state "interposition" against federal authority. In this instance the speaker was not from the South but from New England. Later he was destined to move over to the other side of the question and to deliver the most famous plea for federal supremacy ever heard in Congress: the great reply to Hayne. This speaker of December 9, 1814, was no other than Daniel Webster.

Hartford Convention

In December 1814 representatives of the disgruntled Federalists met in convention at Hartford, Connecticut. This convention reflected two distinct shades of opinion. All the members were dissatisfied with prevailing conditions, but they did not agree on a remedy. The extremists were eager for secession, but the moderates controlled the deliberations, and they were prepared to try diplomacy and negotiation before they turned to the last resort. After a secret session of three weeks, they issued a report. Part of this document consisted of quotations from Madison's own Virginia Resolutions of 1798. The report concluded with resolutions calling upon the states to adopt measures for their own protection. Their citizens were to be guarded against any federal conscription law; the states were to seek from the federal government authorization to defend their own territory, funds for which were to be derived from federal revenue collected within the states. The report also recommended seven amendments to the Constitution, designed to abolish the three-fifths clause in the matter of representation, to make admission of new states impossible without a two-thirds majority in each house of Congress, to prohibit all embargoes of longer

than sixty days, to prevent a declaration of war without a two-thirds vote, and to put an end to the Virginia monopoly of the Presidential office. If these recommendations were unheeded, the delegates promised a second convention, and the promise was accompanied by a thinly veiled threat of secession.

The convention sent a committee to Washington to lay its demands before the federal authorities. Before they arrived news of Jackson's victory at New Orleans, followed by the report of satisfactory peace negotiations, made the errand ridiculous. This news of victory and peace may have saved the Union because the New England Federalists, maddened by the ruin of their commerce, were bent upon serious business.

The Treaty of Ghent

Negotiations for Peace

Negotiations looking toward peace had been started in the first year of the war. The Czar of Russia offered mediation but, while Madison accepted, the British government rejected the proposal. In the summer of 1813 Castlereagh offered to negotiate directly, and Madison was ready to grasp any scheme for getting out of the contest. It took time to bring the two groups of commissioners together, but they began their discussions in the summer of 1814 at Ghent. The American commission was noteworthy for the ability and experience of three of its members: John Quincy Adams, Henry Clay, and Albert Gallatin.

John Quincy Adams, son of John Adams, had begun his career of public service at the age of eleven, when he acted as secretary to his father in Paris in 1778. He had represented his state in the federal Senate; later he represented his country at St. Petersburg. Clay was an able politician and a brilliant speaker, loyally devoted to his country. Gallatin was in some respects the ablest member of the commission. Even-tempered, tactful, and sensible, he assumed the responsibility of maintaining harmony. His good nature and endless patience were largely responsible for the final results.

To deal with this group of Americans, the British government sent a commission consisting of three mediocrities: Lord Gambier, Henry Goulburn, and William Adams. This work at Ghent was Lord Gambier's first venture into important public business; Goulburn was one of the under-secretaries of state for the colonies, while Adams was an admiralty lawyer. More able men could not be spared; they were with Castlereagh at Vienna, drawing the new map of Europe after Napoleon's surrender.

When negotiations began the American position was poor. On the seas the British navy was supreme, and the blockade of the American coast was steadily becoming more rigid. Every American attempt to invade Canada had failed. In New England widespread discontent was pointing toward secession. The ending of the European war enabled England to send her veterans to America. Fully cognizant of the situation, the British envoys were "arrogant, overbearing, and offensive." In October 1814 both groups of commissioners got word of the burning of Washington; the receipt of this news gave further tactical advantages to the British. When the game of negotiations started, they seemed to hold all the high cards.

Relying on the strength of their hand, the Englishmen opened with a series of terms not out of harmony with their victorious position. The greater part of the old Northwest was to be made over into an Indian state, independent but under British protection. The northern part of Massachusetts (Maine) was to be ceded to Canada. The United States must relinquish all right to maintain war vessels on the Great Lakes. Finally, the right of Great Britain to navigate the Mississippi must be renewed.

The Americans had been instructed to obtain recognition of the theories of maritime law proclaimed by the United States and abandonment by the British of their alleged right of impressment. The Americans were also to secure indemnities for illegal captures at sea and to urge the transfer of Canada to the United States. On the submission of the British demands, the Americans promptly rejected them. At this point the peculiar abilities of Henry Clay were put to work. Although innocent of experience in the game of diplomacy, he had given himself intensive training in another pastime, success in which depends upon a deep understanding of human nature: the American game of poker. Clay believed that the British commissioners were eager for peace. On the strength of his convictions, the Americans refused to continue the discussions and ostentatiously prepared to go home. Clay knew almost exactly how his adversaries would behave, and he was certain that, even if they recognized his bluff, they would not dare to call him.

He was right. The British agents made the blunder of letting Clay see how deeply disturbed they were at his procedure. Then they wrote home for new instructions—and got them. Moreover, their manner began to change. They became less arrogant and more uncomfortable as they watched the untutored Americans playing them out of their assets. The British had decided to make peace, as Clay guessed. Tired of war, the English people were uneasy at the prospect of further fighting and opposed to more expense. Moreover, if the contest lasted, there was always the danger that some European power might come to the assistance of the Americans. The risks of continuing an unnecessary war were too great.

The commissioners then began to talk business. Both sides yielded on so many issues that the treaty bore little relation to the original sets of demands or to what were supposed to be the issues of the war. Signed on December 24, 1814, the Treaty of Ghent provided for the cessation of hostilities, for the release of prisoners, for the restoration of conquests on both sides, for the ending of Indian hostilities, and for the appointment of commissioners to settle disputed boundary questions. There was no reference to impressments, blockades, right of search, or neutral rights, nothing about the fisheries, nothing about the control of the Great Lakes. It was a very different document from the one Clay had pictured back in 1812 and dic-

Treaty of Ghent

tated at Quebec or Halifax, so different that he characterized it as a "damned bad treaty." But the treaty was far from being as bad as Clay thought at the time. If the United States gained nothing by the war, she certainly lost nothing except money and men. The direct cost of the war in money was $119,624,000. In view of the downright stinginess of Congress and of the incompetence of the War Department, the outcome might have been considerably worse. The treaty was unanimously ratified by the Senate.

Some of the unsettled issues were dealt with in later negotiations. In 1815 the two governments accepted a commercial treaty, which practically revived the commercial sections of Jay's Treaty. In 1817 Great Britain and the United States agreed that neither party should maintain naval forces on the Great Lakes. As a result of this arrangement, neither Canada nor the United States has ever fortified the boundary between the two countries. In 1818 another treaty renewed American fishing rights off Newfoundland.

The War of 1812 has sometimes been called the second war for independence, but this name ignores both the causes and the results of the struggle. After the war the United States was no more independent than before. This government gained nothing which it had not previously enjoyed. The problem of impressment did not arise again. It was a war issue, and it automatically dropped out of sight with the end of the war. So too did the contest over neutral trade. Once the war was finished the seas were free, and they remained so for a hundred years. But when a new world war broke out in 1914, the whole tangle of neutral rights *versus* belligerent restrictions again arose to torment this nation.

Chapter 15

THE AMERICAN SYSTEM—INDUSTRY, COTTON, AND FOODSTUFFS

Industrial Development

Economic Nationalism

With the end of the War of 1812 and of the wars in Europe, the American people were free for the first time to devote themselves almost entirely to American affairs. Their leaders determined to make the country prosperous by promoting the development of each major section—East, South, and West—and to make it united through ties of mutual dependence. Under this plan manufacturing interests in the East were to be encouraged and protected from foreign competition by a tariff. The South could devote itself to cotton culture. The West could specialize in food production, to supply both the other sections. By making each geographical area dependent on the other two, and by making them all prosperous, the new statesmen could achieve economic as well as political independence. Another essential part of the program called for better facilities for transportation.

These were the fundamental ideas of the "American system." Henry Clay was a great popularizer of this program, but he was not the inventor of it. Like other great conceptions, it was evolved out of the meditations of a large number of active-minded Americans. It was a logical development of Hamilton's economic nationalism. One of the most elaborate expositions of the program is to be found in the farewell address of George Washington. For a time all the war hawks of 1812, including Calhoun, Lowndes, and Grundy, were associated in promoting the "American system" and in addition to them were John Quincy Adams and, somewhat later, Daniel Webster.

The industrial part of this program developed rapidly. During the colonial period and for several years after the Revolution, the American people imported most of their manufactured goods. Nevertheless there had been considerable small-scale manufacturing in the homes, particularly of linen and woolen goods. After the Revolution merchants encouraged this domestic industry by sending raw materials around to farmers' wives, and then collecting and selling the finished product. Under this arrangement not only textiles but boots and shoes were made at home. But there was no manufacturing on a large scale, partly because of the scarcity and consequent high cost of labor, partly because there was more profit to be made from the sale of products of the sea, forests, and farms. This was particularly true from 1793 to 1807 when American merchants and shippers were supplying the fighting European nations with raw materials and food.

Textile Industry

During the years of the embargo and the War of 1812 Americans had to make their own goods or go without. Thus the embargo and the war gave an important impetus to American manufacturing. As a matter of fact, the first signs of a new era in American industry had appeared in 1790. In England leaders in the textile business had been experimenting with new machines for spinning cotton yarn. These machines were so successful that the owners tried to prevent their sale outside England. One young Englishman, Samuel Slater, came over to this country, not with the machines themselves or even with designs but with a knowledge of how they were made. He tried to interest American investors in the idea of a cotton mill equipped with English machines. In 1790 he received the necessary financial backing and started a cotton mill, the first in America, at Pawtucket, Rhode Island. During the next ten years seven more mills were started; by 1808 there were fifteen cotton mills, all located in New England. These plants ran about 8000 spindles. But as soon as trade with Europe stopped, there was a remarkable increase in American industrial activity. By 1815 there were 500,000 spindles in operation.

In New England conditions were favorable for the establishment of factories. The interruption of trade with Europe left the merchants no means of investing their money, and they were glad to put it into factories. When trade fell off the farmers lost their markets, so their sons and daughters were eager for work in the mills. These people were accustomed to work, and some of them had real mechanical ingenuity. So too had some of the factory owners. As early as 1798 Eli Whitney, the inventor of the cotton gin, was running a gun shop at New Haven, Connecticut. He applied the principle of interchangeable parts to the manufacture of guns, thereby helping to bring into use one of the most important principles in American manufacturing. Another important New England resource was abundant water power. These advantages enabled Americans to develop the factory system. The first American textile factories were spinning mills, and the yarn was sent around to weavers who made the cloth at home. Although the power loom was invented in the eighteenth century, it was not made practicable until 1814. In that year Francis C. Lowell combined the two processes of spinning and weaving in his mill at Waltham, Massachusetts. The next steps of dyeing and printing were soon added.

Tariff of 1816

As long as they had no competition, these "infant industries" flourished. When the War of 1812 came to an end, British manufacturers planned to drive them out of existence and to recapture their lost markets. They sent large quantities of goods to this country and prepared to sell them at any price, no matter how low. "It is worth while," one of their representatives said in Parliament, "to incur a loss upon the first exportation in order, by a glut, to stifle in the cradle those rising manufactures in the United States which the war had forced into existence contrary to the natural course of things." In 1813 the United States imported goods to the value only of $13,000,000; by 1816 imports jumped to $147,000,000. In response to American demands Congress passed the Tariff Act of 1816. This law divided imports into three groups. For those commodities which could be produced at home in sufficient quantity to fill the demand, duties were high enough to exclude foreign-made goods; the second group, on which moderate duties were placed, included articles which could be made here, but not in sufficient quantity to take care of normal needs; the third group, carrying a tariff for revenue only, included all other imports. To provide adequate protection against low-cost East Indian yarn and cloth, the bill introduced the principle of minimum valuation. All cotton cloth which originally cost less than 25 cents per square yard was rated at 25 cents for tariff purposes. So the Democratic party, which had once fought Hamilton's plans for protection, now admitted the soundness of his philosophy.

The bill was introduced into the House by William Lowndes of South Carolina; John C. Calhoun and Henry Clay took a leading part in securing its enactment. In the final vote the representatives of the middle states and the West voted heavily in favor, those from the South divided, with 23 in favor and 34 opposed, while the New Englanders approved it by the vote of 17 to 10. These ten negative votes came from the shipping interests, which were opposed to protection.

In the same session of 1816, Congress passed another act which the businessmen wanted but which the Democrats had hitherto vigorously opposed—a law creating the second Bank of the United States. Even Henry Clay, who had opposed the bill to recharter the first bank in 1811, was now a leading advocate of the new one. The second bank had a capital of $35,000,000—Hamilton's much criticized first bank had been capitalized at only $10,000,000—one fifth of which was owned by the federal government. The President of the United States appointed five of the twenty-five directors. By this time, with the Democrats converted to so much of the old Hamiltonian program, party lines became almost invisible.

After 1816 the factory system developed in various industries: boots and shoes, clocks and watches, and the making of machines of different types.

The Factory System

In 1846 Elias Howe secured a patent for a sewing machine, a device which transferred still more work from the home to the factory. The sewing machine was responsible for the development of the ready-made clothing business on a large scale, and it helped to put the making of shoes and harness on a factory basis.

Of all American large-scale industries, cotton manufacturing developed most rapidly, and the value of the factory system with its improved machinery was quickly reflected in the falling price of cloth. In 1815 plain cotton sheeting cost 40 cents a yard, but in 1829 the price had dropped to 4½ cents. During the period from 1830 to 1860 the productive capacity of the cotton mills, as measured by the number of spindles, increased more than fourfold. The amount of raw cotton used increased more than fivefold, and the value of finished cotton goods went up from $26,000,000 in 1830 to $115,681,774 in 1860. As early as 1830 products of the woolen, cotton, and iron works in the United States exceeded the value of southern farm products by 50 percent.

The iron industry did not show as large a value for its finished product as cotton, but it furnished essential material for the rapidly increasing machine shops and railroads. Beginning in 1840 the ironworks used anthracite coal for smelting, and with this improved fuel they greatly increased their production. In 1845 American rolling mills began to make iron rails for the railroads; when the Civil War came there were over thirty mills for making rails. Pennsylvania became the center of the iron industry, just as Massachusetts had the lead in cotton. In addition to rails, American ironworkers were making castings for a variety of uses: hardware for buildings, parts for steam engines, and stoves for cooking and household heating. American ingenuity led to the invention of a number of automatic machines for making nails, tacks, pins, hairpins, bolts, rivets, and chains. Machines also turned out standardized parts for making brass clocks.

American industry has always been noted for its ingenuity in designing labor-saving devices. Two Englishmen, in writing a report to their government on American industry in 1854, commented at length upon these new devices. They were particularly impressed with American spinning machinery which made it possible for one operative to do the work of 3000 expert hand spinners. In England there had been persistent opposition to labor-saving devices, but America welcomed every mechanical improvement. Englishmen were surprised to find that even "the workmen hail with satisfaction all mechanical improvements, the importance and value of which, as releasing them from the drudgery of unskilled labor, they are enabled by education to understand and appreciate."

New Social Problems

American Labor

The rise of the factory system resulted in a large increase in the number of wage earners, and in new social conditions. Mill towns like Lowell, Fall River, or Pawtucket bore little resemblance to seaports like Salem or Philadelphia. There had been manufacturing in the ports, but the work was done in small shops or at home, not in large factories with power-driven machinery. In colonial industries the employees were nearly all men, because hard muscular labor was needed. In the factories everything was different. Few of the jobs called for physical strength, so women and children could be employed more advantageously and at lower wages than men. A visitor to the "cotton works" of Pawtucket in 1801 found that the operations of cleaning, carding, spinning, and winding cotton were left to children from four to ten years old. They were paid 12 to 25 cents a day. This factory employed more than 100 children. The hours of labor at first were those common on the farms, from sunrise to sunset, or if the working days were of uniform length throughout the year, twelve hours.

Before 1850, possibly down to 1860, these industrial wage earners—except the children—were fairly well situated. Conditions were so much better than in the mill towns of England that European visitors expressed surprise and pleasure at the contrast. Writing in 1836, the Frenchman Chevalier exclaimed: "The United States are certainly the land of promise for the laboring class. What a contrast between our Europe and America!" Writing a few years earlier, an Englishman found the American workingman too independent, lacking in a respectful regard for his employer:

> The workmen are under very little subjection: sometimes they are absent from their work for several days, to the great detriment of their employer; but should they be reprimanded, it might cause the proprietor to be insulted; and the indignation of the working people, in this land of equality, is really to be dreaded.

A wage earner who saved his money could become independent. Any able-bodied immigrant, fresh from Europe, could earn a dollar a day, at unskilled labor; his board and room would cost him $2 a week, and his clothing was not expensive. In a few months he could buy himself a farm. By contrast with European employees, the Americans were indeed well off. Nevertheless a twelve-hour working day left little time for recreation or for what is called today "adult education." Nor could the workingman with a family save enough from his wages to carry him over occasional periods of unemployment.

As for the women, they showed a decided preference for work in the factories to work as housemaids. There was no loss of dignity or social position in factory work, and the wages were adequate. In the cotton mills at Waltham, Massachusetts, about 1835, there were 500 employees, chiefly women and children. Women made $2 or $3 a week over and above their living expenses; children, $1. Some of the employees at Waltham saved enough money to pay off the mortgage on the home farm, or to send a brother to college. Sometimes the girls built their own houses in Waltham. "I saw a whole street of houses built with the earnings of the girls," one observer wrote, "some with piazzas, and green Venetian blinds; and all neat and sufficiently spacious."

By 1835 Lowell, Massachusetts, had become the leading manufacturing town in the United States. It had the largest and the best-managed factories and the richest corporations. The cotton mills at Lowell produced more yarn per spindle and more cloth per loom than any other mills in the world. The employees numbered 6000; of this total, 5000 were young women ranging in age from seventeen to twenty-four, chiefly farmers' daughters. The companies which owned the mills built boardinghouses for these girls and saw to their proper management, with good accommodations and good meals. Wages ranged between $3 and $6 per week, depending on the character of the work and the skill of the operator. Board and room at the company houses cost $1.25 per week.

For a good many years the worst features of the English textile mills were kept out of American factories. Working conditions were not bad;

living conditions were good; and the operatives well cared for and relatively happy. Charles Dickens, ordinarily a most caustic critic of things American, was delighted with conditions in Lowell:

> These girls . . . were all well dressed; and that phrase necessarily includes extreme cleanliness. . . . They were healthy in appearance, many of them remarkably so, and had the manners and deportment of young women. The rooms in which they worked were as well ordered as themselves. In the windows of some there were green plants, which were trained to shade the glass; in all, there was as much fresh air, cleanliness, and comfort, as the nature of the occupation would possibly admit of. . . . I solemnly declare, that from all the crowd I saw in the factories that day, I can not recall or separate one young face that gave me a painful impression; not one young girl whom . . . I would have removed from those works if I had had the power.

A less enthusiastic comment on the Lowell mills referred to the long working day—thirteen hours in summer and from daylight to dark in winter.

> At half-past four in the morning the factory bell rings, and at five the girls must be in the mills. . . . At seven the girls are allowed thirty minutes for breakfast, and at noon thirty minutes more for dinner, except during the first quarter of the year, when the time is extended to forty-five minutes.

By 1850 Massachusetts had a law prohibiting the employment of children under twelve years of age, and restricting the labor of those between twelve and fifteen to nine months in each year. Outside Massachusetts child labor was common. And not all mills were as well ordered as those at Lowell.

Social Experiments

Before the panic of 1837 pauperism was rare in the factory towns of New England. Partly on this account, but more because of satisfactory conditions among the workers, little was accomplished by social reformers who tried to improve the lot of American labor by customs imported from abroad. During the second quarter of the nineteenth century efforts were made to establish communistic societies here, but they were not very successful.

Between 1824 and 1850, there were at least forty experiments with some form of social organization in which the individual was supposed to live for the benefit of the community. The earliest was started in 1824 by Robert Owen. He was a wealthy cotton manufacturer of Scotland who had shown a lively interest in the welfare of his employees. Through his efforts his own factory acquired an enviable reputation for satisfactory working conditions. Owen became convinced that economic and social happiness could best be secured through the formation of independent industrial communities, operated for the welfare of the whole group, with no ambitions for private profit. Coming to America in 1824, he bought land enough for his experiment at New Harmony, Indiana. He hoped to lay the foundation of a new social system. Instead, for three years, he watched the members of his community indulge in one quarrel after another until the enterprise failed. The most widely discussed of these utopian projects was Brook Farm, outside Boston. There the members planned to support themselves on a large dairy farm. The whole enterprise would be operated for the interests of all, without private profit. Started in 1840, this community came to an end in 1846 when the buildings were destroyed by fire.

For one reason or another most of the others failed too. At that time, when there was still plenty of new land available and when natural resources were hardly touched, the rewards for individual initiative and energy were relatively high. Communal life might promise security and such necessities as food, shelter, and clothing, but it would never bring wealth. For similar reasons the early efforts to organize American laborers accomplished little. There were labor organizations in America, particularly before the panic of 1837. Skilled laborers, such as shoemakers, tailors, carpenters, and printers, began to organize "trade societies" or labor unions. Between 1833 and 1837 in Boston, New York, Philadelphia, and Baltimore, 150 unions appeared with a total membership of 25,000. During the same four years there were over 160 strikes in the United States, the majority for higher wages, although some aimed at securing a ten-hour day. Among the results of this early labor movement there was a general adoption of the ten-hour day. And some of the states, notably Massachusetts, passed laws to improve working conditions and, most important of all, to restrict child labor. Also, in 1842, in Justice Shaw's decision in the case of *Commonwealth* v. *Hunt,* the right to strike received legal sanction.

The efforts to launch a great labor movement before the Civil War did not bring impressive results. At this stage of American development, there was no permanent factory class. For those who worked in the mills, wages were high enough to give a reasonable degree of security. Conditions in many factories, even down to the end of the nineteenth century, were far from depressing. Most men and women who worked in the mills did so because they were paid relatively well. Some even liked the work.

Immigration

Europeans caught the fever of American ambition and came over by hundreds of thousands. In 1825, for the first time in American history, the number of immigrants arriving during the year passed the 10,000 mark. In 1842 the new arrivals numbered over 100,000 and in 1850 over 300,000. For the ten years before 1840 the total ran over 1,700,000.

There were three main racial groups represented in this peaceful invasion. The fifty-three Scandinavians who came into New York in 1825 were followed by thousands of their countrymen, who settled chiefly in the Northwest. Between 1830 and 1855 more than 500,000 Germans followed the Scandinavians, also going for the most part into the Northwest. Beginning in the 1840's large numbers of Irish entered the United States. While a few became farmers in the Northwest, the majority of the Irish preferred the cities of the Atlantic seaboard or the manufacturing towns of the industrial sections.

"MULTILATED BRITANNIA," an undated and unsigned cartoon, may have been published in Amsterdam as the lettering says, but the legend is in French and German, not Dutch. It registers the obvious delight of the cartoonist at the plight of England, chained to her island—so the Armed Neutrality hoped—with some of her colonies detached and her trade fettered by war. The Dutch had ample reason to hate the British, who tried to block Dutch trade with the Americans. The brooms at the mastheads apparently refer to the great Dutch naval victory over the English fleet in 1667. The cartoon may have been drawn in Paris, the source of a considerable volume of anti-British propaganda; its probable date is somewhere between 1778 and 1781. (Courtesy. New York Public Library)

July 14 one of these we occupied as a private apar
furnished with good soft beds and a neat
and tho' contracted in dimensions, was from
exceeding tidyness far pleasanter than its
exterior led one to expect. The other buil
was the family house, and more spacious, w
a wide piazza in front of the bar-room,
accommodations within for the stage passeng
who had arrived a while before us - here a
Capital supper was spread for us to which
did full justice as we had taken but a
mere luncheon at Upper Sandusky, and
latter part of the day's journey since leav
the Reserve had been very fatiguing from
badness of the road. This was our first
night in a log-cabin, and we found it ve
comfortable, it was of a better class, too, th
is generally met with in the solitudes of
Backwoods - not so much, however, in its conv
as in the scrupulous neatness & good order of
things in and around it.

Scioto Crossing. T.K.W. 1

SCIOTO Crossing was a stopover for travelers crossing Ohio from north to south. This page from the diary of Thomas K. Wharton, engineer and architect, shows the inn in 1830, the smaller log cabin where Wharton slept, the four-wheeled coach, and the stable with horses in front. (Courtesy, Manuscript Division, New York Public Library)

Cotton Culture and Slavery

In the southern states, those lying below Pennsylvania and the Ohio River, development under the "American system" was confined almost entirely to agriculture. In the older parts of the South—Maryland, Virginia, and North Carolina—tobacco continued as the great money crop, while South Carolina still depended on rice. In Louisiana the planters found sugar profitable. Upland farmers raised tobacco, corn, and hogs. They still transformed some of their corn into whisky. But all these products were destined to be overshadowed in importance by a crop new to America: this was cotton, which profoundly affected the history of the old South and of the newer Southwest and, less directly, of the country as a whole.

Southern Cotton

After 1815 cotton became the greatest export commodity; cotton shaped the plantation life throughout the new Southwest; cotton fastened the system of slave labor firmly upon the southern states. And because the South came to specialize more and more in cotton, she became increasingly dependent upon the other sections for such necessities as food, clothing, and most manufactured goods. G. S. Callender pointed out that the cotton crop was worth more to the South than gold to California, because the wealth derived from cotton was greater and more widely distributed than that derived from the gold fields.

Although the cotton plant had been cultivated in India for 2000 years, it was not grown commercially in North America until the time of the Revolution. By 1783 Georgia was raising small quantities for export. In 1791 Georgia and South Carolina together produced about 2,000,000 pounds, of which hardly a tenth was exported. So far, the plant was grown on the lowlands near the coast; this was the "long staple," "sea-island" variety, the fibers of which averaged perhaps two inches in length. But there was comparatively little territory suited to this particular crop, so its production was necessarily small.

Another kind of cotton, the upland, "short staple" variety, with a fiber averaging seven eighths of an inch, could be grown anywhere in the South except in the mountains. This type of cotton was not commercially profitable because of the high cost of separating the fiber from the seeds. In 1793 Eli Whitney of Connecticut, sojourning in Georgia, invented a machine known as the cotton gin, for separating seeds from fiber. Upland cotton became profitable, and in the course of the next forty years cotton culture spread over the South, particularly in the new states of the Southwest.

Whitney's cotton gin came into use shortly after the invention of new spinning machinery in England. In the days of the spinning wheel it had been impossible to make cotton yarn strong enough for cloth, so, while cotton had been used, it was mixed with linen or wool. With the new machinery spinners could produce cotton yarn of ample strength, and cotton cloth became popular. By 1825 the demand for cotton cloth was almost world-wide, and the bulk of the world's raw cotton came from the southern states. The value of this crop to the South itself and to the whole country may be seen in the increasing returns from the export trade. Down to 1800 tobacco had been the most important single article of export from the South, and in that year the tobacco exported was worth $6,220,000; the cotton exported was worth $5,250,000. But after that date the exports of cotton mounted rapidly: $15,108,000 in 1810; $26,309,000 in 1820; $204,128,493 in 1859. Tobacco exports in 1859 stood at $21,174,038, and this figure, it should be noted, was more than twice as high as that for any previous year.

Negro Slavery

The spread of cotton growing was accompanied by extension and commercialization of Negro slavery. With the increase in the cotton crop, the margin of profit declined, so that large-scale production became a necessity. White farmers could and did raise cotton, but the small farmer working his own farm could not compete successfully with the big plantation owner with a large force of Negro slaves. The plantation therefore became the common cotton-growing unit, with slavery for its labor system.

The spread of cotton culture gave a new lease on life to slavery. In Virginia the economic wastefulness of the institution had long been apparent, and the realization of this weakness can be traced in the establishment of abolitionist societies. Before 1830 they were more numerous in the South than in the North. But the steadily growing demand for slaves on the cotton plantations, the steady rise in the prices of "good field hands" from $200 in 1792, $250 in 1815, to $600 in 1836, tended to smother any general abolitionist sentiment which may have existed.

And yet even on the cotton plantations the profitableness of slavery steadily decreased. Slave labor was worth most on comparatively new cotton plantations. As the fertility of the soil declined, the labor of the slaves was not sufficiently valuable to maintain prices at the prevailing high level. By 1840 the value of slaves in the border states was maintained by the market for them in the new cotton country. Sooner or later that demand was bound to slacken, and the cost of maintaining slaves would become greater than the return from their labor. Just when that point would be reached was not clear, but there were signs that it might have been by 1880 or 1900. Once the economic basis had gone—and it was certainly destined to go—the institution could not survive. Had it been allowed to die a natural death, the end would probably have come before the close of the nineteenth century.

In general slaves were less efficient than free, white laborers. With proper organization and control, however, slaves could be fitted into arrangements for large-scale farming. By 1830 most Southerners were convinced that slavery and cotton were inseparable. The economies of large-scale production gave the great planters a marked advantage over the man who worked his own land. Furthermore, the men with large incomes could buy more land and more slaves and, by increasing the size of their crops, make up for any reduction in the price of cotton.

Without making apologies for the system, one may say that on the average plantation the slaves were not harshly treated. Many of the owners were kindly, humane men, and only few mistreated their slaves. Some Negroes had to be encouraged to work, but there were ways of doing this short of actual force. The following extract from the report of an overseer on a large plantation, made to his employer in 1827, shows the kind of treatment that was common. "I killed twenty-eight head of beef for the people's Christmas dinner. I can do more with them in this way than if all the hides of the cattle were made into lashes." The owner had to furnish living quarters, clothing, and food for his slaves and to provide necessary medical attention. Each family had its cabin and most slaves received two outfits of clothing each year.

During the busy season the working day ran from sunrise to sunset, with two hours at noon for rest. In this respect the slaves were on a level with farm laborers everywhere, and the plantation owners believed that the lot of the average factory worker was worse than that of most slaves. Work out of doors and on the land was at least healthful.

The economic benefits of cotton culture were not confined to the South. The planters did not raise enough food for their own communities and became dependent on farmers elsewhere, chiefly in the Northwest. Livestock, especially cattle and hogs, could be driven overland to the plantations. Other provisions, such as pork, lard, beef, butter, corn, and flour, could be shipped down the Ohio and Mississippi Rivers. Cotton therefore contributed heavily to the growing wealth of the Northwest and so might be considered an indirect cause of the rapid settlement of the states north of the Ohio. This trade with the Northwest was one factor which led to the building of one of the first railroads in the United States, the Charleston and Hamburg in South Carolina. This line was one link in a proposed through railroad from Charleston to the Ohio.

Cotton land in the new Southwest was opened for cultivation by typical pioneers who cut off the timber, cleared the land, built their cabins, and began primitive farming. In the second generation, with the land well cleared, pioneers generally sold out to cotton planters, men with money enough to buy several small farms and to operate them as a unit. The planter brought in slaves, and as he did so, many of the earlier settlers moved on to the next frontier. Pioneer shacks gave way to imposing homes of the planters and to collections of cabins for the slaves. The average planter kept between 75 and 100 slaves, although some had as many as 1000. These planters dominated society and politics. They and their friends among the lawyers held the offices, managed the state legislatures, and served as Representatives, Senators, and sometimes as members of the Cabinet at Washington.

But the planter class was never large. In 1845 the southern states had a total white population numbering perhaps 6,000,000; there were all told not more than 8000 great plantation owners. Perhaps 300,000 more owned slaves, and so qualified for membership in the privileged class. Here was an aristocracy resting on slave labor, and surrounded by several million nonslaveowning white farmers.

The southern system was not economically sound. Specialization in cotton made it seem wasteful to use land for other crops, particularly foodstuffs.

Economic Weakness

These supplies could be obtained from the Northwest, but such an arrangement made the South a dependent section. It was dependent on the North not only for foodstuffs but also for many essential services: shipping, for transportation of its staple crops; insurance, because the South itself lacked capital; banking facilities; and capital for building its railroads. The combination of slavery and the plantation prevented the accumulation of surplus capital in the South. The landowners seemed continually in need of more land, and more land required more slaves. Additional land was needed to offset the falling price of cotton: almost 30 cents per pound in 1816, 17 cents in 1820, 9 cents in 1828. As the price of cotton went down, the price of slaves went up.

By the 1850's the planters were caught in a tangle of economic problems from which escape seemed impossible. Costs of production were rising, and efforts to maintain incomes by raising more cotton forced down the price. Low prices and high costs led inevitably to debts and mortgages. Some of the farsighted planters foresaw what was coming and sold out at the peak of prosperity. Before many years had passed the buyer was almost certain to regret his purchase. By most indications the southern planters were on the road to poverty, if not ruin. This unfortunate state of affairs was not so clearly understood at the time as it is today. The planters knew that something was wrong, but they were ignorant of the causes of their trouble. Nevertheless everybody could see that wealth was not accumulating in the South as it did in the West and in the Northeast. In economic affairs the South lagged behind the other sections. There seemed to be an element of unfairness in this, especially since the South produced the most valuable single crop of the whole country. The gross value of the cotton crop was high, but the individual farmer did not receive the gross value. He received so many cents per pound and from this amount he had to deduct his cost of production. In most cases the net profit was too small to provide adequate return on the original investment plus cost of production.

Because the planter class could not understand the weaknesses in their own system, they were inclined to hold outsiders responsible for their increasing troubles. They considered the tariff on manufactured goods their chief grievance because it raised the cost of clothing for their slaves. Because they were frequently in debt they favored a liberal banking policy, one that would not be unduly burdensome to borrowers. Before the panic of 1837 the state of Louisiana borrowed $22,950,000 to promote a "satisfactory" banking system. Mississippi borrowed $7,000,000 to go into banking. The South therefore tended to become unlike the North and West. And difference led first to misunderstanding and later to actual war—the War for Southern Independence.

Agriculture in the Northwest

While industry was growing in the Northeast and cotton culture was spreading in the South, the Northwest grew rapidly into a prosperous farming region. This particular boom began about 1807, when the embargo and the War of 1812 interrupted commercial prosperity. From 1811 to 1817 especially, people living in towns along the main highways and keepers of toll gates and bridges reported an almost constant stream of emigrants moving toward the Ohio valley and the Northwest. In one month in 1811, one interested observer in western Pennsylvania counted 236 wagons passing through his town. Four of the wagons had sixty people with them, but the average per wagon was about eight. Western New York told the same story. In 1817, the keeper of one toll gate reported that 2000 families, with 16,000 people, passed him, westbound. Families who could not afford a wagon went on foot, drawing their few possessions, and occasionally small children, in a handcart. The tide flowed on, winter and summer alike.

Northwestern Prosperity

The explanation of this westward migration is the same as that given for the similar trend during the colonial period: dissatisfaction with conditions at home and hope for a more favorable environment on the frontier. Farmers found themselves confronted with the choice between more intensive agriculture, or moving out where they could get more land. For many the second alternative was the easier. Ambitious laborers looked forward to becoming independent property owners.

To what extent the opportunity was real and to what extent imaginary may be open to question. In these western communities with their primitive standard of living the requirements of social convention did not prevail. That fact alone reduced to a negligible figure the cost of raising a family. The man who was ready to begin life over again and to live for a time as his remote ancestors had done found his opportunity in the West. But for the man who appreciated the benefits and comforts of civilization, opportunities of the frontier were largely illusory. The father of a great American historian, economist, and sociologist, William Graham Sumner, who tried pioneering in this very period, came back home with the sage observation that if a man was willing to live as poorly and to educate his children as badly in the East as he would be obliged to do in the West, he could do better at home.

The movement of population into the West resulted in new states for the Union. Between 1803 and 1821 eight new states were admitted: Ohio, Louisiana, Indiana, Mississippi, Illinois, Alabama, Missouri, and Maine. The process of making the first state in the Northwest Territory differed somewhat from the procedure in Kentucky, because in the Northwest the Ordinance of 1787 had been in effect from the beginning. In April 1802 Congress passed an enabling act, authorizing the people of Ohio to draft a new constitution preparatory to admission into the Union. This step, by the way,

The Growing Nation

became a precedent followed in the creation of practically all new states thereafter, Texas and California being the chief exceptions. The enabling act provided that the proceeds from the sale of one section in each township should be set apart for education. Congress retained the title to, and consequently the right to sell, public land in the state, but 5 percent of the proceeds of these sales would be used to build roads. Before the end of the year a convention drafted a new constitution and so qualified for admission. Congress completed the process of admitting Ohio to the Union in February 1803, and in March the new state government began its work.

The next new state came from the South. In 1811 Congress passed an enabling act for the admission of Louisiana, with boundaries the same as those of the present state. At this time Josiah Quincy, one of the Federalist Representatives of Massachusetts, angrily warned his colleagues of the danger of admitting this new state. Should this ill-fated step be taken, he declared, the eastern states would be justified in withdrawing from the Union, "amicably if they can, forcibly if they must." In spite of this threat Congress admitted Louisiana in 1812, and Massachusetts did not secede from the Union.

Before other territories could acquire the population large enough to warrant their admission as states, more work was necessary in pushing the Indian barrier still farther beyond the lines of white settlement. In the Northwest, in the Wabash region, General William Henry Harrison had broken the Indian power at the battle of Tippecanoe. This was in 1811. Three years later Andrew Jackson defeated the Indians in the Southwest, at the battle of Horseshoe Bend in Alabama—then a part of Mississippi Territory—and so opened the area between Georgia and Louisiana to white advance. In 1814, with the close of the War of 1812, cotton planters were already looking for more land, and cotton planting spread rapidly and widely in response to an ever-increasing demand. In 1810 Mississippi Territory had a population of 40,352; during the next ten years the figure went up to 203,349. In 1817 Congress divided the Territory into two parts, and that same year the western part was admitted as the state of Mississippi. Indiana was admitted in 1816, Illinois two years later, and Alabama in 1819.

While the southern states were developing into the "cotton kingdom" with its white aristocracy and its system of slave labor, the Northwest was building the most prosperous agricultural region in the country. When the first pioneers were opening up the land, the casual observer would have seen little difference between Indiana and Alabama. The process of clearing the land was the same in each section, the crude cabins of the settlers were much alike, and the people themselves were not noticeably different. For the first few years the resemblance continued; then, after the crudeness of the frontier gave way to more civilized ways of living, differences began to appear. In the Northwest democracy and free labor became foundations of the political and social order. The farms remained relatively small: the quarter section—160 acres—was looked upon as the desirable average.

Before 1810 the communities in Ohio and Indiana were rural; town life had not even begun to develop. According to the census of 1810, the largest western city, New Orleans, had a population of 24,562; the other towns were hardly more than villages, and there were only three of these. Pittsburgh with 4768 ranked second to New Orleans; Lexington, Kentucky, had 4326. Cincinnati, the only approach to a commercial center in Ohio, numbered 2540. And these were all. There were of course other villages, with a few score or a few hundred inhabitants, but no urban development. These pioneers had little to sell to the outside world. Here was a region with little trade, and the absence of trade always means the absence of towns. After 1815 all this was changed. The spread of cotton culture over the Southwest made wide areas in that section dependent on the Northwest for provisions: flour, meal, salt pork, bacon, lard, salt beef, and fresh meat on the hoof. The trade in foodstuffs was as valuable to the Northwest as that in cotton was to the South. The Northwest followed a different line of development from that of the South. In one section, as in the other, the first pioneers were succeeded by farmers with capital, who bought up the original holdings, but in the Northwest the newcomers did not bring in slave labor. Frame houses appeared in place of the cabins, fields were more carefully cultivated, orchards were developed.

Towns and Trade

By the middle of the nineteenth century people in the West were interested in improved agricultural methods. Farmers were becoming aware of the necessity for crop rotation: they planted corn, oats, barley and clover or grass in successive years. They also began to use fertilizer, although not on any large scale. When cheap, rich land was abundant, it seemed poor economy to do any unnecessary work on the soil because labor cost money.

The West was the scene of a genuine agricultural revolution, one brought about by the introduction of farm machinery. Down to 1830 farmers still used hand tools, as distinguished from machines, and these tools were not very different from the ones used in ancient Assyria. Grain was sown by hand, and until 1803 it was cut with a sickle. After that date the cradle came into use. The only device for threshing was the flail, or the use of horses or donkeys on a threshing floor. Grass was cut with a scythe, raked with a hand rake, and loaded and unloaded with a hand pitchfork. Corn was planted by hand and cultivated with the hoe. The only implements deserving the name of machine—and they were simple—were the plow, the harrow, and the cart. Between 1830 and 1860 American inventors and manufacturers made available a series of machines which greatly reduced the amount of hand labor needed in farming, and so cut down the costs.

Agricultural Revolution

The first improvements were made in the plow. For centuries every plow had a wooden moldboard—that is, the surface which turns the furrow over. In 1814 Jethro Wood of New York secured a patent for a cast-iron plow made with interchangeable parts. During the next fifteen years the iron plow came into general use. After the Civil War, when steel became common and cheap, a steel moldboard took the place of iron. By 1840 farmers in the West were using horse-drawn cultivators, seed drills, and corn planters.

These machines simplified the work of preparing the soil, planting, and caring for the growing crops, but they left untouched the important problem of the harvest. There was no great advantage in being able to plant a larger acreage unless labor in gathering the crops could be reduced. In 1834 Cyrus Hall McCormick was granted a patent for a reaper. His device needed and received several improvements before it became really practicable; but by 1845 the McCormick reaper was used generally on the larger western farms. Although it merely cut the grain and did not bind it, it enabled one man to do the work of ten men using cradles. The horse rake, in use after 1830, was worth nine men with hand rakes. By the year 1855 the mowing machine for cutting grass was generally used on the western farms. These two devices helped the haymaker as the reaper helped the wheat farmer. One more great improvement came in 1836 with the invention of a practical threshing machine. With these machines a farmer could increase his output and cut his cost of production. The increasing use of machinery on the farms did not result in unemployment; it merely made it easier for men to make money from the land, and so encouraged more people than ever to try their hands at farming.

In the 1850's Southern planters were finding the problem of making a living more and more difficult. Farmers in the Northwest on the other hand were fast getting out of debt. Retired farmers had capital to invest in banks or in manufacturing. Here was the difference between prosperity and depression, apparently permanent in each case. Starting in 1800 on terms of equality, in the short period of fifty years the Northwest and the Southwest had become almost two different countries.

Between 1840 and 1860 the Northwest became more and more important as the source of food for the American people. As late as 1850 the middle Atlantic states still produced more than half of the nation's wheat. By 1860 western production more than doubled, and this section took the lead. The figures for the total production of wheat show a remarkable increase: 27,518,000 bushels in 1840; 43,842,000 bushels in 1850; and 95,004,000 bushels in 1860. During the same period the production of corn was almost quadrupled. Meat packing had always been a source of income to the American farmer, but in colonial days the business was in the hands of scattered individuals. After 1818 Cincinnati became noted for the increasing quantity of salt pork, smoked ham, and bacon.

American Traits

These new states in the West were developing new social customs as well as new farming methods. After 1815 travelers from Europe began to describe the "typical American." Before 1800 differences between the ordinary American and the ordinary European had not been so striking as to arouse comment. By the end of the War of 1812, the divergence was clear. The impressions that foreign observers carried home with them varied considerably, depending on the part of the country visited, on their own sense of humor, or lack of it, and on their power of adjustment. But in the case of those who traveled widely, there was a general agreement that the New England population around Boston differed radically from the Americans living between Harrisburg, Pennsylvania, and Cincinnati, Ohio, the region then in process of transition from frontier conditions to the normal state of civilized society.

Typical Americans

To an observing Englishman like Charles Dickens, one of the outstanding American characteristics seemed to be crudeness of bearing, manners, and customs. In the early 1840's he was amused and disgusted at the widespread prevalence of tobacco chewing with its accompaniment of spitting, regardless of time, place, or circumstance. On an Ohio River steamboat it disturbed him to find in the men's cabin no place but the floor to leave his clothes when he retired, and it did not add to his equanimity when, in the morning, he had to take them up on deck to clean off the tobacco juice deposited upon them by his fellow travelers during the night. The same signs of the habit he observed in Congress, at receptions, at inns, everywhere in fact outside of the Boston, New York, and Philadelphia aristocracy.

He also found the Westerners taciturn and lacking in humor. Many of them traveled in silence, ate their meals in silence, chewed their tobacco in silence, and spat with as much silence as possible.

> Nobody says any thing, at any meal, to any body. All the passengers are very dismal, and seem to have tremendous secrets weighing on their minds. . . . Every man sits down, dull and languid; swallows his fare as if breakfasts, dinners, and suppers were necessities of nature never to be coupled with recreation or enjoyment. . . . The people are all alike too. There is no diversity of character.

But Dickens was too severe on the West. There were admirable qualities there. These new Americans were an industrious lot, hard workers, with few if any idlers among them. They were engaged in a serious business, that of conquering a continent, and if they appeared unsociable when they traveled, they were probably tired. The frontier did not develop the social graces, it is true, but it brought out qualities which were essential to the business at hand. Moreover, these Westerners were ambitious, for themselves and even more so for their children. Every man among them hoped to give his children a better place in the world than he had succeeded in making for himself. It may be that this combination of hard work and ambition gave rise to another American quality, that nervous, hurried energy which always surprised visitors from abroad.

Another trait that distinguished the true American was his strong faith in the future greatness of his country. Americans believed that Europe, already effete, was on the decline, and for the centuries to come the United

States would be superior to any nation the world had ever seen. This conviction led naturally to boastfulness, which Europeans were inclined to ridicule.

> Other nations boast of what they are or have been, but the citizen of the United States exalts his head to the skies in the contemplation of what the grandeur of his country is going to be. Others claim respect and honor because of the things done by a long line of ancestors; an American glories in the achievements of a distant posterity. Others appeal to history; an American appeals to prophecy, and with Malthus in one hand and a map of the back country in the other he boldly defies us to a comparison with America as she is to be, and chuckles in delight over the splendors the geometrical ratio is to shed over her story. This appeal to the future is his never-failing resource. If an English traveller complains of their inns and hints his dislike to sleeping four in a bed he is first denounced as a calumniator and then told to wait a hundred years and see the superiority of American inns to British. If Shakespeare, Milton, Newton are named, he is again told to wait until we have cleared our land, till we have idle time to attend to other things; wait till 1900, and then see how much nobler our poets and profounder our astronomers and longer our telescopes than any that decrepit old hemisphere of yours will produce.

This breezy bit of satire from a London magazine of 1821 was more genial in tone than many of the criticisms of American character and probably more accurate. There is no doubt that both the faith and the bragging were carried to extremes.

Perhaps the most striking quality exhibited in these pioneer farmers was their resourcefulness, their capacity to adjust themselves to their mode of life, and supply themselves with what they needed. The life they were living drove them into adaptability. The man who could not fit himself to his environment may have gone back home, or he may have starved or frozen to death; in any case he ceased to be a pioneer. There was no charity in that sort of life. Men would help each other in misfortune and need, but they could not carry along the incompetents. Because of the necessity for doing things quickly the American became a jack-of-all-trades, and in doing so developed qualities of superficiality.

Of the lesser qualities, many foreign observers commented on the inquisitiveness of Americans. They thought nothing of asking a stranger, and especially one from abroad, where he got his clothes, how much he paid for them, how he came by his watch, whether it was a gift or a purchase, and if the latter, how much it cost and whether he wound it in the morning or at night. Then they inquired about his previous journeys, his plans for the future, and anything else that an active mind could think of. If the victim of this rapid-fire questioning seemed reserved, he was stigmatized as a conceited foreigner beneath the contempt of all true Americans.

If there is any one aspect of American history which needs to be emphasized above all others, it is the continuous growth and development of the opportunities for making a living. From the early days of the colonial period down to the beginning of the Civil War, America offered every able-bodied man of ambition a chance to improve his position in life. Not all the people took advantage of it, but the chance was there. This growth was possible because, and only because, the American people were able to use the resources which they found, to develop them, and to profit from this development. The very variety of these resources enabled Americans in different sections to produce goods for sale to each other, and also to the outside world. A steadily expanding commerce, both domestic and foreign, brought increasing wealth.

Chapter 16

IMPROVEMENTS IN TRANSPORTATION AND COMMUNICATION

Overland Travel

The First Roads

THE farsighted leaders who planned the "American System" inevitably included transportation in their program. They realized that intersectional trade and national unity both would be impossible if the various parts of the country remained physically isolated from one another. Then the rapid westward movement and the admission of new states made the need of roads and canals even more obvious and imperative. For the first American colonies along the seaboard, the Atlantic Ocean had served as the means of communication. As people moved inland numerous rivers made it possible for the pioneers to keep in touch with the older settlements. For a time these limited facilities had to serve because there was nothing else. There were no roads.

The earliest routes of overland travel in America were Indian trails. These were difficult enough for riders on horseback and completely impossible for stagecoaches and freight wagons. However, after 1650 a road was built from Boston to Providence, and before the Revolution this Post Road had been extended to New York. Another road led across New Jersey from Paulus Hook and helped to connect New York with Philadelphia. But even on these roads most of the traffic was on horseback. The first regular stagecoach route in the colonies was started in Massachusetts in 1744. Twelve years later a coach line ran from Paulus Hook to Philadelphia, but the trip took two days. In 1774 Paul Revere spent a week in going from Boston to Philadelphia on horseback, and he was doing his best to make fast time. Up to the advent of the railroads the record for speedy overland travel was held by the Roman Emperor Tiberius. Early in the first century of the Christian era he covered 200 miles in twenty-four hours. But as late as 1825 the President of the United States had to be content with fifty miles per day.

Turnpikes

Shortly before 1790 the Scotsman John L. McAdam worked out a theory of road construction which has been followed from his own day to this. He discovered that a road built of small broken stones, laid about ten inches deep, would withstand both the wear of traffic and the action of frost. McAdam's discovery led to the building of stone-surfaced roads; they marked the first real improvement in overland transportation in America. After 1790 the American people undertook a comprehensive program of road building. Practically all these early roads were constructed, not by the government, but by private enterprise. In 1790 the state of Pennsylvania chartered a company to build the Lancaster Pike, a stone-surfaced road running sixty-six miles from Philadelphia to Lancaster. This project was completed in 1794, and it brought excellent profits to the builders. By 1820 Pennsylvania alone had chartered eighty-six companies; they built nearly 2200 miles of roads. New York had 135 turnpike companies, and New England 180, all busy before the War of 1812. Evidence of the prevailing prosperity of the country may be found in the investments in road building; they amounted to $40,000,000 by 1812, a sum equal to the Continental debt in 1783.

The collection of toll charges on these roads was a legitimate part of private enterprise, but it made the costs of travel and transportation too high to suit farmers and businessmen. The average cost of hauling freight over the roads was $10 per ton for every 100 miles. Since one way of cutting these costs would be for the government to build the roads and then open them to the public free of charge, the demand developed for government road building, or, to use the language of that day, for the "construction of internal improvements at public expense."

Gallatin's Proposals

Beginning in 1803, Congress began to plan for a wagon road to connect the Ohio River with tidewater Maryland. Two years later the national government decided to build the road from Cumberland, Maryland, the head of river navigation on the Potomac, over the route followed by General Braddock in 1755 through southwestern Pennsylvania. Going south of Pittsburgh, the road would reach the Ohio River at Wheeling, then Virginia. In 1806 President Jefferson appointed a board of commissioners, three in number, to decide upon the exact route, and to get the consent of the three states through which the road would run. In 1808 Secretary Gallatin submitted to the Senate a report on roads and canals, in which he argued that internal improvements could not be profitably built with private capital because of the heavy expense involved. So, as Gallatin observed: "The general government can alone remove these obstacles." With Jefferson's approval, Gallatin justified this additional departure from the Democratic doctrine of strict construction by arguing:

> Good roads and canals will shorten distances, facilitate commercial and personal intercourse, and unite by a still more intimate community of interests, the most remote quarters of the United States. No other single operation within the power of government can more effectually tend to strengthen and perpetuate that union, which secures external independence, domestic peace, and internal liberty.

Gallatin's plan was comprehensive enough to take in the whole country. He proposed a series of canals to shorten the distance of transportation by water between various points along the Atlantic coast—that is, one across Cape Cod in Massachusetts, one to connect the Raritan and Delaware Rivers in New Jersey, another from Chesapeake Bay to Albemarle Sound. Next

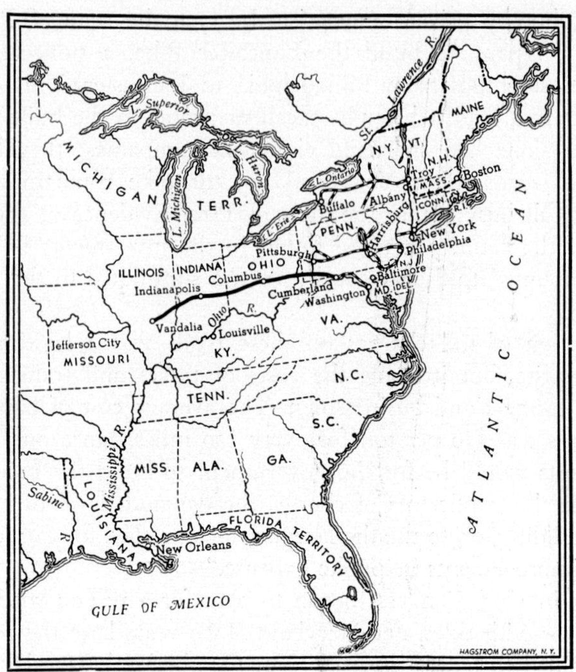

Map 9. Roads and Canals about 1830. The Cumberland Road is shown by the heavy line, the canal systems by the black and white line.

he suggested a national turnpike to run along the coast from eastern Massachusetts to Georgia. The rest of his program called for roads to connect the headwaters of some of the rivers which flowed into the Atlantic with others which joined the Mississippi.

The Cumberland Road

In 1811 the national government made the first contracts for constructing the Cumberland, or National, Road. According to congressional specifications it was to be sixty-six feet wide, with a surface of stone covered with gravel; culverts and bridges were to be of stone; grades were to be evened, after the manner of good road construction today. The original section from Cumberland to Wheeling was open for traffic in 1818. Mail from Washington could reach Wheeling in thirty hours. Immediately there was so much traffic that the eastern portions were nearly worn out before the western part was completed. Six years later plans were made to extend the road through to Columbus and Indianapolis and then to Vandalia.

For a brief period after the close of the War of 1812 nationalists in Congress advocated the extensive use of federal money for building additional national roads. John C. Calhoun was made chairman of a congressional committee to look into the matter of establishing a permanent fund for this purpose. In December 1816 he reported a bill, providing that the sum of $1,500,000, the amount paid by the Second Bank of the United States for its charter, should be used for the construction of roads and canals. The bill also provided that dividends received by the United States on its bank stock should be used for the same purpose. In arguing for the enactment of the measure, Calhoun pointed out that the great geographical extent of the United States was a threat to national unity. Good roads would serve as bonds of union. Calhoun's bonus bill passed Congress, but President Madison vetoed it because he thought it was unconstitutional. Calhoun pointed out Madison's inconsistency: "If we are restricted in the use of our money to the enumerated powers, on what principle can the purchase of Louisiana be justified?" Calhoun's argument was unanswerable, but Madison's veto stood. The Cumberland Road was the only enterprise of its kind undertaken by the national government.

Coaches, Wagons, and Inns

The advantages of the Cumberland Road encouraged local communities to improve their own roads, so that after 1825 travel by land became much more general. Turnpike companies, "plank road" companies, and town and county governments combined to make stagecoach travel and freight-wagon traffic fairly rapid. For the transportation of freight on the turnpikes, the Americans developed and used the Conestoga wagon—better known under its more famous name, the covered wagon. The wheels were built with broad rims and tires to prevent them from sinking into the mud. The body was high, and the bottom was often watertight like a boat. As streams were numerous and bridges had not entirely replaced ferries, the wagon's body might have to float over deep water. The average load pulled by four or six horses or oxen was from four to six tons of freight.

In those days of slow overland travel, inns were important. They were perhaps more widely scattered and more numerous in relation to the population than at the present time. Captain Marryat, an English traveler, was greatly pleased with the innkeepers. He found them men of high character and surprisingly honest. "I never in one instance found that I had been imposed upon," he wrote. For the hotels themselves, he could not say so much.

> There are no neat, quiet little inns as in England. It is all the "rough-and-tumble" system, and when you stop at humble inns you must expect to eat peas with a two-pronged fork, and to sit down to meals with people whose exterior is anything but agreeable, to attend upon yourself, and to sleep in a room in which there are three or four other beds (I have slept in one with nearly twenty), most of them carrying double, even if you do not have a companion of your own.

Steamboats, Clipper Ships, and Canals

Travel by Water

Thanks to the road, the stagecoach, the Conestoga wagon, and the inns, travelers and businessmen from different sections of the country were brought together in a fashion that had been rarely possible before the Revolution. These several factors helped to make the Americans a united people. And yet, important as these developments were, they were overshadowed by even more significant developments in the facilities for transportation by water. The United States has the advantage of a great system of navigable inland waterways. In the North the chain of Great Lakes is navigable for practically its whole extent, and even the most serious natural obstacle, Niagara Falls, has been circumvented by the Welland Canal. The rivers along the Atlantic coast are navigable for longer or shorter distances—longer in the South than elsewhere. The Mississippi with its tributaries is navigable for thousands of miles.

Along the Ohio and the Mississippi the pioneers moved themselves and their worldly goods in square, flat-bottomed barges, which floated downstream. Rafts and flatboats also carried local farm products down the rivers. For northbound traffic the traders used narrow keelboats, propelled by poles or oars. But upstream transportation was expensive; so many men were required to work the oars that cargo space was limited. What was needed was a craft drawing as little water as a raft, large enough to provide room for freight, and capable of being moved against the current. The Mississippi River steamboat solved this problem.

Steamboats

Before the end of the eighteenth century various experiments with steamboats had been made in this country and in Europe, and the first successful boats were the product of several different inventors. In 1786 and in 1787 John Fitch built two steamboats, neither of which proved usable. Also in 1787 James Rumsey launched a steamer at Shepherdstown, then Virginia, which made a speed of four miles per hour. In the following year Rumsey patented the water-tube boiler, the device which makes high steam pressure possible. His new type of boiler greatly increased the efficiency of the steam engine and by so doing took the steamboat out of the experimental class. In 1790 Fitch launched his third boat, which occasionally made eight miles per hour, and he ran it for 1000 miles on regular trips between Philadelphia and Trenton. His boat never became commercially profitable because it could not carry a heavy load. Prior to the launching of Robert Fulton's *Clermont,* at least sixteen steamboats had been built in the United States, and fifteen of these were regularly operated. Fulton talked with Rumsey, and he made use of Fitch's drawings.

In 1807 Fulton's boat, the *Clermont,* made the trip from New York City to Albany and back in sixty-two hours. "The morning I left New York," Fulton wrote, "there were not perhaps thirty persons in the city who believed that the boat would move one mile an hour or be of the least utility; and, while we were putting off from the wharf, which was crowded with spectators, I heard a number of sarcastic remarks." The crowd christened the new craft "Fulton's Folly." But Fulton could let them joke; his voyage opened a new era in transportation by water. In 1811 a steamer was launched on the Ohio at Pittsburgh. In 1815 a steamer made the difficult voyage upstream from New Orleans to Pittsburgh. By 1820 sixty steamboats were in service on these western rivers; this number increased to 300 by 1837 and to more than 1000 by 1860.

The Mississippi steamboat was a practical craft, built for service not beauty. She was flat-bottomed, with no keel, and drew surprisingly little water. She was propelled by a paddle wheel at the stern. This wheel was as broad as the stern itself, and so constructed, that the loss of part of a blade or even a whole blade could not prevent her from making port. These boats became famous. They inaugurated a new kind of life both on and alongside the river. Mark Twain's *Life on the Mississippi* is an excellent description of customs and persons of the steamboat period.

Charles Dickens found his two journeys on a Mississippi River steamboat anything but pleasant, especially the voyage downstream:

> The boat, proceeding at the rate of twelve or fifteen miles an hour, has to force its passage through a labyrinth of floating logs, which, in the dark, it is often impossible to see beforehand or avoid. All that night, the bell was never silent for five minutes at a time; and after every ring the vessel reeled again, sometimes beneath a single blow, sometimes beneath a dozen dealt in quick succession. . . . Looking down upon the filthy river after dark, it seemed to be alive with monsters, as these black masses rolled upon the surface.

However uncomfortable the boat trip may have been for overparticular passengers such as Dickens, the river traffic was increasingly profitable. In 1807, the produce shipped down the river to New Orleans was valued at $5,000,000. By 1840, about the time Dickens inspected the river, the shipments received at New Orleans had gone up in value to $50,000,000, and twenty years later to the figure of $185,000,000.

Steamboats had their first era of prosperity on the inland waterways. As late as 1840 the United States had no steamboats registered for ocean traffic, and in 1850 our total ocean-going steamboat tonnage stood at 44,942, as compared with a figure of 1,585,711 for sailing vessels. It was not until 1890 that steamships really superseded sailing ships on the high seas.

Clipper Ships

Possibly because of the threat of steam competition, builders of ocean-going craft designed new types of sailing vessels—freight carriers built for speed. These were the clipper ships, the first of which appeared in the early 1840's. They were built with a narrow, concave prow and carried more sail than ordinary ships. One of the earliest clippers, the *Rainbow,* made the long voyage to China and back in less time than it took the average vessel to cover half the route. But the pride of the American clipper fleet was the *Flying Cloud,* designed and built by Donald McKay at Boston. In 1851 she sailed from Boston around Cape Horn to San Francisco in seventy-nine days, beating all previous records by ten days. On this trip her best run was 374 miles in twenty-four hours; on three consecutive days she covered 992 miles. But even the *Flying Cloud* was at the mercy of the winds. Her poorest day on the record-making run was only forty miles. But in the days of wooden ships these fast freight carriers represented the final triumph of naval architects.

Where there were no rivers, the steamboat obviously was of no value.

But American initiative and enterprise constructed canals, bringing to places remote from ocean, lakes, and rivers the advantages of inexpensive transportation by water. Between 1820 and 1837 various states constructed thousands of miles of canals. The most famous and the most profitable of these man-made rivers was the Erie Canal, connecting the Hudson River with Lake Erie. Started in 1817 under Governor DeWitt Clinton, the project was completed in 1825. The Erie Canal was independent of winds, rough water, or other obstacles to regular navigation—except ice. Natural lakes and artificial reservoirs along the route were used to maintain the proper water level. Three hundred and sixty-three miles in length, it was the greatest engineering enterprise undertaken up to that time in the United States. The original cost of the Erie Canal was $8,400,000. Down to 1882, when all toll charges were abolished, the total cost of building, widening, and maintaining the canal amounted to $78,862,153; during that period the total receipts from tolls were $121,461,871. New York State consequently cleared a substantial profit from its investment.

Erie Canal

When the canal was first opened, the cost of shipping one ton of heavy freight from Buffalo to New York City dropped from $100 to less than $8, and later even this rate was lowered. Buffalo became an important commercial center, handling lumber and grain going east and manufactured goods going west. By 1827 the governor of Georgia reported that wheat from western New York sold for a lower price in Savannah than Georgia wheat because of the low cost of transportation by water. Encouraged by the success of the Erie Canal, New York State built a number of branches so that the central section of the state was served by a network of canals. By 1836 this collateral system had a total mileage of 656. Canals connected the Erie Canal with Seneca Lake and Lake Cayuga, Syracuse with Oswego, and the Hudson River with Lake Champlain.

Other Canals

One of the striking results of this new canal system was the rapid increase in the volume of traffic through New York City and the partial decline of business at Philadelphia. Before the completion of the Erie Canal the people of Pennsylvania and Maryland had profited from their virtually complete control of business with the West by way of the Cumberland Road. The Pennsylvanians, determined not to lose their commerce, began work in 1826 on a project even more ambitious than the Erie Canal: a canal and railroad over the mountains from Philadelphia to Pittsburgh, a total distance of nearly 400 miles. The highest point on the proposed route was 2300 feet above sea level. In spite of the difficulties, the work was finished in eight years. While the greater part of the distance was covered by canal, there was a thirty-seven-mile stretch over the mountains where canal building was impossible. For this section a series of inclined planes was constructed. Canal boats were run on movable platforms and hauled over the mountains. On the other side they resumed their journey by water. Pennsylvania also built an elaborate network of canals, most of which proved unprofitable.

Other states caught the fever. In 1833 Ohio opened a canal running from Cleveland on Lake Erie to Portsmouth on the Ohio, over 300 miles in length. More canals were planned and partly built, in Ohio, Indiana, and Illinois. Then interested parties in Washington, D. C., Maryland, and Virginia subscribed nearly $4,000,000 for the Chesapeake and Ohio Canal to connect Washington with Cumberland and eventually with the Ohio River. This work was never completed.

Railroads and the Telegraph

Early Railroads

When the canals were first planned, they seemed to be the long-desired solution of the problem of inland transportation. Water-borne traffic was cheap, safe, and easy to handle. Lacking the ability to see into the future, the state officials who built canals and the people who clamored for them could not know that, even while many of them were being constructed, a new invention would make most of them obsolete long before they could ever repay their costs. The first practical experiments with railroads were being made in the very midst of the era of canal building, and the railroads were destined to ruin the business of most of the canals. Indeed, by 1860 most of them had dropped out of the picture. The Pennsylvania Canal and Portage Railroad continued to function until the 1890's, and so too did the Erie Canal. In the present century New York State has constructed a successor to the Erie, the Barge Canal, which handles a substantial volume of freight business every year; but it is the only canal of any length still in operation in the United States.

When the states of Pennsylvania and Virginia began work on their canals, Baltimore faced the unpleasant possibility of losing much of her trade to her rivals. Businessmen of Baltimore determined to outdo her neighbors. They laid plans for a railroad to connect Baltimore with the Ohio River; the line would be 250 miles long, and it would have to cross a range of mountains 3000 feet high. In 1828 Maryland and Pennsylvania granted the necessary charters for the road, and the work was started on July 4, 1828. This event was celebrated with the "most splendid civic procession, perhaps, ever exhibited in America."

Although the Baltimore and Ohio was the first long-distance railroad planned for this country, it was not the first to begin operations. The merchants of Charleston, South Carolina, began to suffer lasting hard times as newer cotton lands in the Southwest entered into competition with the older cotton-producing states. Businessmen of Charleston hoped to recover some of their lost trade by diverting cotton from Savannah, Georgia, to their own port. For this purpose they planned a railroad to connect Charleston and Hamburg; this line, the first steam railroad in the United States, 136 miles in length, was completed in 1833; it ran a steam locomotive on a short section in 1830. This railroad did not, however, bring the desired commercial results. The state of Georgia refused to permit the South Carolina company to cross the Savannah River, and the Georgians began to build railroads in order to maintain their grip on their own commerce.

When part of the Baltimore and Ohio Railroad was opened for traffic in 1830, horses and sails furnished the power, but the steam locomotive, already being used experimentally, was adopted before the end of that year. As early as 1804 Oliver Evans had driven a steam-propelled vehicle through the streets of Philadelphia, and in 1820 John Stevens built a railway in Hoboken on which he ran a locomotive which pulled a train at the speed of fifteen miles an hour, but it could not run in rainy weather; when the track was wet horses took the place of locomotives.

In the North plans were made for a railroad running west from Albany, in direct competition with the Erie Canal. But no railroad could operate without a state charter, and the canal was owned by the state of New York. In its early days, therefore, the New York Central Railroad was not permitted to carry any freight whatever; beginning in 1844 it could carry freight only in the winter, when the canal was frozen. After 1851 this restriction was removed. Another early railroad was the Boston and Albany, designed to connect Boston with the Erie Canal. By 1840 the United States had 2818 miles of railroad in operation. In 1920, when railroad building came to an end in this country, the mileage had increased to 260,000.

The first railroad connection between eastern tidewater and the western lakes was furnished by the New York Central—or rather by the original short links which were eventually tied together to form the Central. In 1850 Boston established rail connection with Ogdensburg on the St. Lawrence. In 1851 the New York and Erie was opened; planned and built as a unit, it connected Lake Erie with the lower Hudson opposite New York City. In 1854 the Pennsylvania Railroad completed its line from Philadelphia to Pittsburgh. The Baltimore and Ohio, the earliest of the long lines to be started, did not reach the Ohio until 1853.

When railroads were first started, most people looked upon them not as main lines of transportation but as feeders and connecting links for rivers and canals. There were few who could foresee that waterways would ever be superseded. But in the course of thirty years it became evident that the railroads were far more effective than canal boats or steamboats. They provided service the year round, while in northern states the canals, rivers, and lakes were frozen and closed to traffic in winter. Furthermore, railroads were less expensive. It is true that transportation by rail cost more than transportation by water, but the difference was more than offset by the savings due to greater speed. Shortly before 1840 it cost one passenger more than $75 to go from Chicago to New York City; by 1850 the fare by lake and rail was $17. And the freight charge on a barrel of flour over the same route was 80 cents.

Every improvement in coach roads, turnpikes, river traffic, and railroads saved time in transportation. The Post Office Department was quick to take advantage of the new facilities to speed up the mail service. During the early history of the Post Office, rates were high because transportation was expensive. The basic charge was 6 cents for a single sheet to be carried not over thirty miles. If the distance was over 400 miles, the cost was 25 cents. In 1845 the basic charge was placed at 5 cents for a letter weighing not more than one-half ounce for 300 miles; for more than 300 miles the charge was 10 cents. After 1850 letters were carried for a flat rate regardless of distance.

Postal Service

Envelopes were not used during the early part of the nineteenth century because they would have been an unnecessary addition to the weight of a letter. The writer left a blank space on his letter sheet for the address, folded the paper to bring it in the proper place, sealed the folded sheet with wax, and put it in the mail. The recipient paid the postage. In 1847 postage stamps came into use and soon envelopes were common. With the advent of stamps and lower rates, the sender paid the charge.

While the railroad was still in its early stages of development, an ingenious inventor discovered a device for transmitting messages instantaneously over long distances—the telegraph. The inventor Samuel F. B. Morse was a portrait painter who played with electricity as a hobby. He began his experiments in 1832 and by 1838 had his telegraph in working order, but he could get no financial backing to make it commercially available. In 1843 Congress gave him $30,000 to be used for opening a telegraph line from Washington to Baltimore. It was completed in 1844, and a new era in communication began. By 1862 a transcontinental line was completed to San Francisco. The Western Union Telegraph Company was formed by consolidating a number of small, formerly independent concerns into a nation-wide system.

Telegraph and Cable

The telegraph was used by the railway systems of the country as a means of enabling train dispatchers to direct the movement of rail traffic. Newspapers realized the opportunities afforded by the telegraph to inform the public promptly of important events all over the country. When the device was new, the New York newspapers had columns headed: "Special, by Electric Telegraph." Businessmen, particularly brokers, found the telegraph indispensable in keeping themselves and their customers in touch with important changes in the market. In this particular field, however, some people complained that the telegraph was more of a nuisance than a help because bad news could be carried as rapidly as good. When the panic of 1857 started, reports of bankruptcies were spread over the land, carrying fear into every business section. Fortunately this shortsighted complaint did not retard the progress of telegraphic communication.

It is obvious now that if messages could be transmitted over great distances by land, they might also be sent over similar distances under water, provided that proper lines could be laid. In 1854 Cyrus W. Field became interested in the project of an Atlantic cable connecting the United States with England by way of Newfoundland. In 1858 Field's company laid the cable, and messages were sent across the Atlantic. But the apparatus soon ceased to work because the wires were not properly insulated. In 1866 Field had a new cable laid, and this has been in successful operation ever since.

Commercial Prosperity

The development of transportation completed the "American System." Southern planters sold their cotton, tobacco, and sugar to American merchants in the eastern states or to Europe. In return they bought food supplies from the West and manufactured goods from the East. The West sold its food products to the South and bought eastern-manufactured goods. The East bought cotton, tobacco, and sugar from the South and, eventually, food supplies from the West. As time went on shipments of western foodstuffs were divided, some going South but an increasing quantity going East to supply the steadily increasing population in the industrial sections. In 1850, for the first time, eastbound traffic over the Erie and the Pennsylvania Canals surpassed the westbound traffic in manufactured goods.

Export trade in southern staple crops and intersectional trade explain the ever-growing prosperity of the United States. Population was increasing at such a rate, and the standard of living in the new West was rising so rapidly, that there was always a demand for more goods. As long as exports moved out of our seaports and as long as there was any more West to settle, there seemed to be no limit to the possibilities of trade or to the productive enterprises which trade made possible. Both the industrial system itself and the economic doctrines of the people were built on the theory of an ever-constant increase in demand and in productive capacity.

Chapter 17

AMERICAN POLITICS, 1816-29

New Issues

Changing Political Practices

For some time after the War of 1812 the "American System" with its philosophy of economic progress and nationalism seemed to be the dominant influence on public affairs in all parts of the United States. In some ways the decline of the Federalists as a national political party could be attributed to this influence. At least the Federalists in New England had become narrow and sectional in outlook. Older members of the party could not or would not return to the Hamiltonian philosophy which had made the early Federalists strong. Young members of the party, John Quincy Adams for example, joined the opposition. So the party of Jefferson and Madison became first the majority, and then the only, party able to elect its candidates with practically no opposition. In fact, in national affairs, nomination by the Democrats was virtually equivalent to an election. Under this simple arrangement James Monroe was elected to the presidency in 1816.

During Monroe's administration there were various manifestations of a new spirit of democracy in the United States. Between 1816 and 1830 ten new state constitutions were adopted, nearly all of which provided for universal manhood suffrage. At the same time the majority of states abandoned the old plan of having presidential electors chosen by the state legislatures and turned the responsibility over to the voters. Furthermore, the presidential nominating machinery was subjected to severe criticism. The selection of candidates for the highest office in the land had been left to the party caucus. This method was now opposed on the ground that it violated the spirit of the Constitution. Further objections came from those who said the scheme of caucus nomination was undemocratic. In 1816 the caucus almost ran counter to the decision of the party leaders. Monroe was the party's choice for the nomination, but Crawford nearly got it for himself, losing by the narrow margin of 65 to 54. In 1820, in his second election, Monroe received all but one electoral vote.

The few years immediately after 1820 have sometimes been described as the "era of good feeling." This description may be correct, so far as the absence of an opposition party went, but it hardly applied to the Democratic organization: this was full of bitter disputes, carried on within the President's Cabinet. The leading members of this group were John Quincy Adams, secretary of state; John C. Calhoun of South Carolina, secretary of war; and William H. Crawford of Georgia, secretary of the treasury. All three were candidates for the Presidency in the coming election of 1824, and their official relations were marked by bitter rivalry. In addition to this Cabinet group, there was another aspirant for the Presidential chair, Henry Clay of Kentucky, speaker of the House of Representatives.

Slavery in Missouri

Among the domestic issues of Monroe's administration the problem of slavery in Missouri caused serious concern. Bitterness over this issue threatened to interrupt the trend toward national solidarity which the "American System" was developing. Legally there was little basis for a dispute. Missouri was part of the Louisiana Purchase, and slavery had been sanctioned there by both French and Spanish law. The Louisiana Purchase Treaty had clearly provided for the protection of all inhabitants in their liberty, property, and religion. By 1818 there were probably 2500 slaves in Missouri, and slaves were property. The Constitution gives Congress power to legislate for the territories, but Southerners denied that this power could be used to abolish slavery.

In 1818 Missouri asked to be admitted to the Union. While the bill for this purpose was under consideration, Tallmadge of New York moved two amendments; one to prevent the further introduction of slavery into the state, the other providing that all children born in the state should become free at the age of twenty-five. These Tallmadge amendments started a lively discussion. In the northern states mass meetings were held for the discussion of slavery, and the legislatures of five states—Pennsylvania, New York, New Jersey, Delaware, and Ohio—adopted resolutions protesting against any further spread of slavery into the West. Southern state legislatures opposed restrictions on slavery. Then President Monroe laid the question before his Cabinet. The members agreed that Congress had power to prohibit slavery in the territories, but they could not agree as to whether restrictions imposed on a territory would be binding when the territory became a state.

Congressional debate upon the amendments and upon the larger question of slavery was lively and bitter. For the antislavery side Senator Rufus King of New York argued that, under the constitutional provision granting power to make all needful rules and regulations for the territories, Congress could exclude slavery. For precedent, he cited Ohio, Indiana, and Illinois—all admitted under restrictions imposed by the Ordinance of 1787. King based his argument upon constitutional grounds, which were clear for the territories, but he overlooked or omitted the principle that a state was entirely free to legislate as it pleased on slavery. Congressional prohibition of slavery could be binding only during the territorial period because the state could repudiate it. William Pinkney of Maryland pointed out this possibility.

Missouri Compromise

The Tallmadge amendments passed the House but met defeat in the Senate. Just how the question would have been settled on the merits of the case no one knows. Fortunately the eastern counties of Massachusetts, now the state of Maine, were applying for statehood. This furnished an opportunity to preserve the balance in the Senate and to compromise the dispute. The Thomas amendment to the Missouri bill provided for slavery in Missouri, but it prohibited it in the remaining part of the Louisiana Purchase which lay to the north of the 36° 30′ line, Missouri's southern border; this was an essential part of the compromise. Thus Maine and Missouri were both admitted, one free, the other slave. Southern leaders voted for the compromise to save the Union, not because they approved of the principle.

This dispute over slavery was one of the consequences of the development of the West. Congress had settled the question of slavery for the states east of the Mississippi River in the Northwest Ordinance of 1787. But the Ordinance did not apply to the Louisiana Purchase. Northern members of Congress who believed that slavery was wrong and southern members who believed it was right both wanted the West to develop in accordance with their special views. The Missouri Compromise was designed to settle the problem so that there would be no difficulty when other territories should apply for admission. The Compromise did settle the immediate issue, but it left ugly feelings on both sides.

Latin American Problems

Latin American Independence

In the field of foreign policy Monroe and his secretary of state, John Quincy Adams, were confronted with a peculiarly difficult situation in Latin America. Out of this tangle the administration eventually emerged with an important treaty and a popular foreign policy. The treaty provided for the purchase of Florida and for an agreement upon the western boundary of the Louisiana Purchase. The foreign policy was the Monroe Doctrine. For 300 years the Spanish Empire had flourished without serious internal weakness, and then in the course of two decades the whole structure disintegrated. The real beginning of Latin American independence dates from 1807, when Napoleon took possession of the Spanish government. In order to force recalcitrant Portugal into his Continental system, Napoleon planned to control Spain and then extend his power over Portugal. To this end, he deposed both King Charles IV and his son Prince Ferdinand and gave the kingdom to Joseph Bonaparte, his own brother. But the Spanish people rebelled against this highhanded proceeding.

Spain's colonies in Latin America refused to recognize Napoleon's authority and set up governments of their own, professing allegiance to Ferdinand VII the deposed prince. By 1810 all of Spanish America except a part of Peru was in open rebellion. In 1811 Venezuela declared herself independent of both Napoleon and Ferdinand VII and proclaimed a republican form of government. Miranda, the patron saint of Latin American freedom, became the first president. But by 1812 Miranda was overthrown, given up to the Spaniards, and shipped to Spain to spend the last three years of his life in a prison in Cadiz.

In its pursuit of "legitimacy" the Congress of Vienna in 1814 restored Spain to its Bourbon rulers, and Ferdinand VII became king. The new king re-established the former system of colonial absolutism, both in government and in trade. But the colonies had enjoyed a taste of independence, with no commercial restrictions, and they objected to the restoration of the old monopoly. In 1816 Buenos Aires declared itself independent, and its example was quickly followed all the way from Chile to Mexico. Although the last battle was not fought until 1824, except in Puerto Rico and Cuba, Spanish power in America was virtually a thing of the past. During the same period the Portuguese colony of Brazil also became independent.

American Policy

This course of events raised a number of serious questions. Should the United States recognize these new republics or not? What should be the guiding principles concerning the relations between the United States and Latin America? And more important still, what should be the attitude toward the Latin American policy of Europe? Specifically, if any European nation or nations endeavored to restore Spanish power, what should the United States do? Or, if any European nation should desire to aid the Latin Americans, should the United States cooperate or not?

The United States sympathized with this movement toward independence; Latin Americans were granted full belligerent rights and Latin American vessels were welcomed in North American ports. Officially, however, the United States remained neutral, and the government hesitated for a time before recognizing the independence of these new republics. During 1811 and 1812 this government sent special agents to Argentina and Venezuela, with instructions "to explain the mutual advantages of commerce with the United States, to promote liberal and stable regulations, and to transmit seasonable information on the subject." These missions marked the opening of regular commercial relations between the United States and Latin America.

Although the government at Washington did not recognize these new governments, both Jefferson and Madison opposed the pretensions of any non-Spanish power in that quarter of the world. In 1808 Jefferson wrote that no other foreign power should be allowed to secure either political domination or commercial control there. "We consider their interests and ours the same, and that the object of both must be to exclude all European influence from this hemisphere." In 1811 President Madison urged Congress to declare "that the United States could not see without serious disquietude any part of the neighboring territory in which they have in different respects so deep and so just a concern pass from the hands of Spain into those of any other Foreign Power." Congress adopted this resolution.

Monroe hesitated to accord formal recognition, and this delay displeased the more energetic Americans, who found a leader and a spokesman in Henry Clay. For ten years Clay stood out as the great champion of recognition. In 1817 and again in 1818 he delivered speeches against American neutrality. In 1820 he forced through the House of Representatives a resolution in favor of recognition. The country at large agreed with Clay. Even though he could not compel the administration to act, he could point to the unreasonable stubbornness of the secretary of state and so discredit him with the voters. Adams and Clay both were looking forward to the Presidential election of 1824, and Clay found the Latin American issue a good one.

The issue of Latin American independence was closely related to the problem of Florida. Both Jefferson and Madison had ordered the occupation of parts of West Florida by American troops, and the Spanish government had protested against these moves. Madison also planned to seize East Florida, but when Spain broke off diplomatic relations he abandoned this project and from 1814 to 1819 the province was a constant menace to peace along the Georgia boundary. In the latter part of the War of 1812 British forces had used it as a base of operations against the United States, and after the war British officers incited Indians and fugitive Negro slaves to continue guerrilla warfare against the United States. Spanish authorities were unable to suppress this nuisance, so American forces proceeded to do so. The United States had a right to do this under the Treaty of San Lorenzo of 1796, by which Spain had bound herself to prevent the Florida Indians from making trouble for the states.

Jackson in Florida

In December 1817 President Monroe ordered General Andrew Jackson to put an end to the Indian attacks. His orders were vague and allowed Jackson ample discretion, both as to the manner and as to the extent of his operations. Jackson received his orders in Tennessee. He wrote a letter to Monroe, with the following suggestions: "Permit me to remark that the arms of the United States must be carried to any point, within the limits of East Florida, where an enemy is permitted and protected, or disgrace attends." Then Jackson advised the seizure of the whole of East Florida and promised to handle the matter so as not to implicate the administration: "Let it be signified to me through any channel (say Mr. J. Rhea) that the possession of the Floridas would be desirable to the United States, and in sixty days it will be accomplished." Jackson always asserted that he received through Rhea the assurance for which he asked. Later on Monroe insisted that he never read this letter until after Jackson was in Pensacola.

Treaty of 1819

Jackson captured the key points in northern Florida, finishing up with Pensacola in 1818. Incidentally, he executed two British subjects, Arbuthnot and Ambrister, for complicity in Indian attacks upon American forces. The Spanish government, with which diplomatic relations had recently been renewed, demanded that the posts be surrendered and that Jackson be punished. Monroe yielded on the first point, but he did not punish Jackson. Then there followed a vigorous exchange of views between the Spanish minister and John Quincy Adams. The outcome was the Treaty of 1819 by which Spain ceded the Floridas to the United States. The two powers at the same time agreed upon a western boundary for Louisiana. The line was to run from the mouth of the Sabine River, following the western bank of that river to the 32d parallel, then due north to the Red River, along it to the 100th meridian west from London, then due north to the Arkansas

River, along its southern bank to the source, then to the 42d parallel, and from there westward to the Pacific. By this treaty therefore, while the United States secured a clear title to all of Florida, it surrendered its title to Texas. Spain delayed ratification of the new treaty until October 1820, because she hoped to prevent the United States from recognizing the independence of the Latin American republics. In 1822, with the Florida treaty out of the way, Monroe informed Congress that the time for recognition had come, and he asked for an appropriation for sending ministers. In 1824 diplomatic representatives were sent to Colombia, the Argentine Republic, and Chile, and in 1826 to Mexico.

The Monroe Doctrine

If there had been no other considerations, the decision to recognize the independence of the republics might have marked the end of American concern in the problem, but there still remained the attitude of Europe. In September 1815 the powers of Russia, Prussia, and Austria signed a treaty creating the Holy Alliance. The aim of this combination was "to take for their sole guide the precepts of that holy religion, namely, the precepts of justice, Christian charity and peace." About two months later, in November 1815, Great Britain, Russia, Prussia, and Austria signed another treaty creating the Quadruple Alliance. The aim of these four powers was to prevent revolutionary disturbances in Europe. In the course of events, the more dramatic title was applied to the more important agreement, so this alliance to keep the peace became generally known as the Holy Alliance. The members of the Alliance held a series of conferences, in which they agreed to suppress revolutions in Naples, Portugal, and Spain. They then planned to restore Spanish authority over Latin America. England, however, opposed this project, and the Continental powers did not dare act in the face of British objections.

Europe and Latin America

Because of the seriousness of the situation Canning, the British foreign minister, tried to win general support for a common policy toward Latin America. He outlined his views in a note to the governments of Austria, Russia, Prussia, Portugal, Spain, the Netherlands, and the United States. The position of the English government, as defined by Canning, was that Spain could not recover control of her colonies; that recognition of the new republics could be left to a more opportune time; that no obstacle should be placed in the way of amicable negotiations between Spain and the republics; that Great Britain did not aim at the possession of any territory there, but that she could not see any of it transferred to any other power. The note closed with the suggestion that the powers might join in publicly proclaiming these items as their policy.

While the Monroe administration was trying to decide what to do with these European complications in Latin America, the President and his secretary of state were confronted by a difficulty in the Northwest. In 1821 the Czar of Russia issued an order warning all foreign vessels not to come within 100 miles of any part of the Pacific coast of America, north of the 51st parallel. The Oregon territory, then under the joint control of Great Britain and the United States, extended northward to the parallel of 54° 40′. Secretary Adams therefore announced that the United States would contest the right of Russia to *any* territorial establishment in North America, and that "we should assume distinctly the principle that the American continents are no longer subjects for *any* new European colonial establishments." Later, he announced that, outside the European colonies already established, "the remainder of both the American continents must henceforth be left to the management of American hands."

Russian Aggressio

During November 1823 Monroe's Cabinet debated the subject of foreign policy. Richard Rush, the American minister to England, had kept Monroe informed of Canning's suggestions, and Monroe had written to his two predecessors, Jefferson and Madison, for advice. Monroe himself favored joint action with England, and Jefferson and Madison agreed with him. John Quincy Adams, however, stubbornly opposed the President on this issue. "It would be more candid, as well as more dignified," he declared, "to avow our principles explicitly to Russia and France, than to come in as a cock boat in the wake of the British man of war." Adams knew that Great Britain would oppose European intervention in Latin America, no matter what the United States did. Therefore, if it came to a question of force against Europe, the United States would have the help of British power, without the disadvantage of a formal alliance. The secretary of state converted the President to his point of view.

Monroe Doctrine

The Monroe Doctrine consists of two sections of Monroe's annual message to Congress of December 2, 1823. The first part, aimed at Russia in the Northwest, declared "that the American continents by the free and independent condition which they have assumed and maintain, are henceforth not to be considered as subjects for future colonization by any European powers." The second part said that the United States would keep clear of European complications and announced that the United States would consider any attempt of the European powers to extend their system to any part of America "as dangerous to our peace and safety."

This doctrine was not new. Various prominent American leaders had expressed sentiments similar to those embodied in Monroe's message. The Monroe Doctrine therefore was a name for an old policy, an official statement of a popular principle. The doctrine was not a part of international law, nor even a rule binding on the United States. No obligation was created by it, either to Europe or to Latin America. It was neither a pledge to anybody nor an agreement with anybody. It did not have even the force of law in this country. Any administration would be as free to repudiate it as Monroe had been to proclaim it.

John Marshall and the Supreme Court

Marshall's Principles

All these developments, except the debate over slavery, reflected the rise of a strong national spirit. This spirit of nationalism was inherent in the "American system" and in the Monroe Doctrine. Still another manifestation of this growing nationalism was revealed in decisions of the Supreme Court. The more important decisions were formal assertions of national power and national supremacy. The great spokesman for the Court was Chief Justice John Marshall. From 1801 to 1835 he led the Court and dominated his colleagues. In interpreting the Constitution Marshall held that it was the work of the people, not of the states. In case of disagreement the states must yield to superior authority. Marshall also believed in an interpretation which would allow the most beneficial use of constitutional authority. And while he admitted that the government of the United States was one of limited powers, nevertheless it was supreme within those prescribed limits.

One of the most important of these decisions, *Marbury* v. *Madison,* delivered in 1803, was a warning from the Federalist Chief Justice to the Democratic President. It proclaimed the doctrine that an act of Congress which is repugnant to the Constitution is *ipso facto* null and void. The facts in the case were simple. In the closing hours of his administration, Adams had signed a commission appointing William Marbury justice of the peace. The commission was not delivered, and when the Democrats came in, Madison, the new secretary of state, refused to deliver it. Thereupon Marbury sought a writ of mandamus to compel delivery. Marshall held that the act of Congress authorizing the Supreme Court to issue that form of writ was unconstitutional. The reasoning of the Chief Justice was clear and logical. The people of the United States had the right to lay down certain guiding principles for their government, which they had done in the Constitution, therefore the Constitution determined the limits of congressional authority; the Constitution is the supreme law of the land. Then he concluded that an act of Congress which was contrary to the Constitution could not be law, or, if it could, the Constitution became a dead letter. There was no middle ground.

If Congress could not pass a law contrary to the Constitution, it logically followed that a state legislature was subject to the same limitation. This doctrine the Court declared in 1810, in *Fletcher* v. *Peck,* which annulled an act of the Georgia legislature revoking certain land grants. The Court held that the law in question was a violation of contract, therefore unconstitutional. Later, in the Dartmouth College case, decided in 1819, the Court declared again that a contract could not be impaired by state law.

The Chief Justice was as willing to assert the authority of the Supreme Court over state courts as over state legislatures. In 1809, in *United States* v. *Judge Peters,* the Court upheld the state courts of Pennsylvania against an act of the legislature. In 1816, in *Martin* v. *Hunter's Lessee,* the Supreme Court accepted an appeal from a Virginia court and reversed the decision of the local tribunal, on the ground that the state court had not kept within proper constitutional limits. Again in 1821, in *Cohens* v. *State of Virginia,* the Supreme Court asserted its right to receive appeals from state courts.

The doctrine of implied powers was set forth explicitly in *McCulloch* v. *Maryland* in 1819. The state legislature had imposed a tax on the local branch of the Second United States Bank. In upholding the rights of the bank, Marshall declared that the Constitution conferred upon Congress two kinds of powers: fundamental and derived. If the end sought was legitimate, any means not specifically prohibited might be used. Therefore, he concluded, the law creating the bank was constitutional and the tax law of Maryland was unconstitutional. Among other important decisions was that of *Gibbons* v. *Ogden*, in 1824, which declared unconstitutional an act of the New York legislature granting a monopoly of steamboat operation in New York waters. The Court declared that Congress alone had control of interstate commerce.

The Presidential Election of 1824

Rival Candidates

During President Monroe's second term the Jeffersonian Democratic-Republican party split into factions, and out of this confusion Jackson and his friends created a new Democratic party. For a time the process of establishing this new organization was slow, but during the campaign of 1824 progress was fairly rapid. The leading contestants in this campaign were three members of Monroe's Cabinet: John Quincy Adams, William H. Crawford, and John C. Calhoun. Next came two other able aspirants, both from the West: Henry Clay of Kentucky, speaker of the House, and Andrew Jackson of Tennessee, hero of New Orleans and of the enterprise in Florida. All but the last had extensive experience in public affairs. Jackson knew little of statesmanship, but he was an able soldier.

In 1816 the controlling factor in national politics had been an alliance between the Republicans of Virginia and the Democrats of New York. The Virginians could control the electoral votes of Kentucky, North Carolina, Tennessee, and usually Georgia, with a total of 59. New York had 23 votes of her own, and could usually count on those of New Jersey. This coalition could deliver 90 electoral votes out of a total of 190. According to previous arrangements the Virginians had named the President while the New Yorkers picked the Vice President. In 1822 this arrangement broke down under the weight of too many candidates: Virginia and New York supported Crawford, but Kentucky favored Clay; Tennessee wanted Jackson; North Carolina was torn by a desire to support both Calhoun and Jackson; and South Carolina favored Calhoun. Under these conditions there was bound to be considerable bargaining among the candidates and their friends. Eventually Jackson and Calhoun agreed to support each other, Jackson for President, Calhoun for Vice President.

Prior to 1819 and outside his own state Jackson had not been regarded as a Presidential possibility. But he had friends who were interested in advancing his fortunes, partly in order to advance their own. When Clay and Crawford saw signs of Jackson's increasing popularity, they determined to use his venture in Florida as a means of discrediting him. In January 1819 Jackson's enemies in the House introduced resolutions condemning his activities in Florida, particularly the execution of Arbuthnot and Ambrister and the seizure of Pensacola. Actually these efforts worked to Jackson's advantage, and the House of Representatives rejected the resolutions of criticism. Then, early in 1819, Jackson visited Baltimore, Philadelphia, and New York, where he was received enthusiastically.

like today #

Andrew Jackson

By 1822 Jackson's friends, John H. Eaton, Major William B. Lewis, and Felix Grundy, began to work for the Presidential nomination for their hero. Newspapers in Pennsylvania and Tennessee took up the cause, and the legislature of Tennessee adopted resolutions declaring that Jackson ought to be President. Scotch-Irish farmers in western Pennsylvania became enthusiastic Jackson supporters. One of their leaders, the Reverend Edward Patchell, established a newspaper, the *Alleghany Democrat,* to help Jackson. Patchell's earnestness was reflected in a letter to Jackson: "Altho' I well know that my talents were unadequate to the task, yet I depended not only in my personal courage alone, but I trusted in my God, and your God, whome hath raised you up for to be a Saviour and a deliverer for his people." Patchell tried to break down the influence of the regular Democratic politicians. As he explained it:

> I have reduced the Lousie party here from ten thousand to something less than fifty, and they are chiefly the antient and notorious wire workers, they are the office holders and office hunters, and all they can do now is grin and shew their teeth. . . . And should we fail this Election, I will pray my God to spare life until I see Andrew Jackson President of the United States, and then let me close my eyes in peace.

In this Presidential race of 1824 there is no way of discovering how the people themselves felt about the various candidates, and no way of discovering accurately what the popular vote was. In six states, containing a quarter of the total population, the electors were chosen by the legislatures, so there was no popular vote. In several other large states only a minority went to the polls. In several states, not all four candidates were before the voters; in some there were only three tickets, in some only two. Any attempt to determine the popular vote for each of the four candidates is simply a waste of time.

In the electoral vote, Jackson received 99, Adams 84, Crawford 41, and Clay 37. This outcome threw the election into the House of Representatives. Clay was out of the running, because the House was limited to the

PLAIN Sewing Done Here. Symptoms of a Locked Jaw. This cartoon by David Claypoole Johnston was published as a lithograph in 1834. Henry Clay had led the Whigs in the fight for senatorial censure of Jackson for removing deposits from the Bank of the United States. Eventually Thomas Hart Benton persuaded the Senate to rescind the censure. (Courtesy, American Antiquarian Society)

GOD AND LIBERTY!

TEMPERANCE!!

TRUTH, JUSTICE AND RIGHT: VIRTUE, LOVE AND CHARITY.

WASHINGTON, AMERICA AND UNION FOREVER.

For America, her Constitution and Union we would die,
To bind that old Serpent Prince Alcohol we will try.

☞ LOOK HERE!---Over Thirty Thousand American People Destroyed Annually by Intoxicating Drinks. ☞ To the Rescue, Sons and Daughters of Liberty.

DECLARATION

BY THE

GODDESS OF LIBERTY.

To the Congress of the United States and all the State Legis-

13. For protecting them by a mock trial from punishment, murders which they commit upon our people.

14. For imposing taxes upon us without our consent.

15. He has plundered our wives, our mothers, and our children of all the comforts and necessities of life, turned them into the streets, abused and maltreated them.

16. He has caused our people to build thousands of prisons, penitentiaries, insane and lunatic asylums, and poor-houses, and filled them with our people, besides murdering and hanging them upon

deeds, and the duty that they enjoined upon us, the love that we have for our Lord our God and for ourselves, the duty that we owe to our children and to the human family, and for the integrity, glory, honor, prosperity, and happiness of the American people, taking upon ourselves the duty and rights of American citizens, the sacred truths taught us in the Declaration of American Independence, and the sacred rights of the Constitution of the United States,—do solemnly publish and declare that Alcohol—that is, intoxicating drinks—is an evil, and a great evil, a great curse to

lums, poor-houses, and to plunder from thy people over one hundred and fifty millions of dollars annually, to murder and hang them upon the gallows,—to commit all manner of vice and crime, and to cause oceans of grief, and tears, and suffering to flow over thy country, and to destroy over thirty thousand of thy people annually. Oh! vain and foolish nation! Say unto thy nation and unto thy people, Rise up now, and drive this old Prince out of thy country, and banish him forever from they shores, and thou shalt grow and increase, and shalt be a mighty nation, and shalt

THIS Temperance broadside, approximately 15 by 30 inches, was probably printed between 1845 and 1850 at the height of the pre-Civil War campaign for temperance, to be posted on bulletin boards, trees, covered bridges—wherever there was room. It is a violent attack on "Prince Alcohol," in the manner of the Declaration of Independence's attack on George III. Intoxicating drinks, the broadside says, "rule with a more destructive tyranny over the people of these United States than George the Third ever did." (Courtesy, New York Public Library) three names highest on the list, but as speaker of the House he controlled enough votes to determine the outcome. During the preliminary campaign he had opposed both Crawford and Jackson. He had more in common, politically, with John Quincy Adams, so he threw his support to the New Englander. Adams won the election.

The Second Adams

When Clay's decision was made public, Adams's opponents, in disagreement on everything else, united in an imposing display of wrath. Clay's support, they proclaimed, was the result of a corrupt bargain by which Adams would get the Presidency, while Clay would become secretary of state, and in accordance with time-honored custom, heir apparent. This "corrupt bargain" charge first appeared in an unsigned newspaper communication and it was never proven true, but the charge placed the new President in a peculiar dilemma. If he did not appoint Clay to the State Department, the opposition would say that the exposure of his scheme had frightened him out of it; if he did, they would advertise the act as proof of their charge. Adams ignored the difficulty, and gave Clay the place.

Those who attempt to explain all American political activity in terms of economic interest have a difficult time with this era of the 1820's. Logically the South and West, interested in agriculture and trade, should have joined forces against the East, which was becoming more and more directly concerned with industry and finance. Then Calhoun, Crawford, Clay, and Jackson should have joined in opposition to Adams, Van Buren, and Webster. To be sure, Calhoun and Jackson worked together for a time but not for long, and in the main the political alignment of these leaders can be explained more satisfactorily on purely personal grounds than in terms of great economic interests. In other words, many of the political disputes of this period were personal rather than economic in character.

Administration of John Quincy Adams

President Adams urged Congress to enact laws for promoting the general welfare. He believed the national government should undertake a carefully planned program of internal improvements. He wanted a national university and a national observatory. He tried to encourage the scientific exploration of the American coastline, especially in the Northwest. He believed that the government should promote agriculture, literature, science, and art. He called attention to the need of so safeguarding the sale of public lands that the general public would benefit. In general he believed that the power and resources of the national government should be used to help the American people.

Adams's Policies

Adams's proposals never received careful consideration. At the time most Congressmen were so much interested in the next Presidential election that they had little concern for anything else. Adams himself was partly responsible for the failure of his program: he urged his projects upon Congress in spite of the known opposition in the South to any such broad extension of federal authority, and he took no effective steps to overcome this opposition. If the national government could do all the things that Adams recommended, it might some time interfere with slavery. Adams did nothing to reassure the South on this point.

Adams was no more successful in foreign affairs than in his program for the general welfare. Some Latin American leaders were planning for a Pan-American Congress at Panama, and Adams wished to send delegates. Congress opposed. Some southern leaders argued that the Pan-American Congress might take action hostile to Negro slavery. At last, in March 1826, Congress voted to comply with the President's request, but their long delay wrecked his plan. One of the Americans died on the way to Panama, and the Congress adjourned before the other arrived.

Adams had to deal with two issues, both of which carried over into the administration of his successor: the tariff and the Georgia Indian problem.

Calhoun and the Tariff

In 1824 Congress had passed a new tariff bill, which had not been satisfactory to anyone and which had been especially displeasing to the woolen interests. They had become steadily more important between 1820 and 1830, and the value of woolen products increased from $2,500,000 in 1820 to more than $15,500,000 in 1831. New England manufacturers were demanding more protection for this industry, while the sheep raisers were also pointing out their need of congressional help. In 1827 a tariff bill was introduced, providing for increased protection; it passed the House, but in the Senate it was defeated by the vote of the Vice President, Calhoun. Beaten on this bill, the protectionists went to work on another.

In the new Congress, the House committee introduced a bill so framed as to satisfy the producers of raw material and to refuse the protection desired by New England. This measure was not an honest attempt to deal with an economic problem but a crafty political scheme. Southern representatives were opposed to protection, so they drafted a measure so distasteful to New England that members from that section were expected to join with the South to defeat it. To the horror of the promoters of this "tariff of abominations" enough New Englanders voted for the bill to put it through. John Randolph said that "the bill referred to manufactures of no sort of kind, but the manufacture of a President of the United States."

Although largely responsible for drafting it, southern leaders bitterly condemned the measure. When Calhoun went home from Washington, he found his state in an uproar over the tariff. He set himself the task of working out a plan of opposition which would satisfy his constituents and enable him to retain his political following. He succeeded, although he did so at the cost of sacrificing his nationalistic philosophy. The explanation of his own change, and the shift of opinion in his own state, may be found in the falling price of cotton. In 1816 the average price of standard upland, short staple cotton in New York was almost 30 cents a pound. At that time the political leaders of South Carolina were strong nationalists, favoring the broad program of the "American System." By 1820 cotton had dropped to

20 cents and by 1824 to less than 15 cents. During these same years opinion in South Carolina turned sharply away from the "American System," and people in the state were attributing their economic hardships to the protective tariff. They demanded its repeal as unconstitutional. In 1827, when the price of cotton dropped to 9 cents, the people of South Carolina were talking of nullification. Calhoun had to change with his section; if he wished to stay in politics he had to attack the tariff. And yet, if he should do so openly, he would sacrifice political support in the middle states and in New England.

In the summer of 1828 Calhoun prepared a document, destined to see light as the report of a legislative committee. It seemed hardly expedient for the Vice President to proclaim the philosophy that he was considering. This was the South Carolina "Exposition," which for the first time put the doctrine of nullification into definite, systematic form. Arguing first that the tariff was unconstitutional, Calhoun next showed how the tariff put a heavy economic burden on the South. The plantation owners had to buy practically all of their manufactured supplies, and Calhoun argued that the tariff compelled them to purchase in an unnecessarily high market. As a remedy, he suggested nullification, the logical conclusion of the extreme states' rights doctrine. Each state, he reasoned, was entitled to determine whether or not the federal government had exceeded its constitutional authority, and to prevent the law in question from operating within its limits until three fourths of the states had declared for or against it. Calhoun hoped to provide a peaceful way to protect the states from unwarranted federal measures. Under his handling nullification developed into something more than a protest; it became a plan of action. Calhoun proposed it as an instrument to preserve the Union, but his successors used it to justify secession. what happened?

Georgia Indians

Adams's other problem was the Georgia Indians. In 1802 Georgia had ceded her unoccupied lands to the federal government in return for $1,250,000 plus the promise of the federal authorities to extinguish the Indian title throughout the state. In 1821 the government and the Indians signed the Treaty of Indian Springs by which the Creeks ceded all their land to the state. Soon after the ratification of this treaty, the Creek chief who signed it was murdered, and the entire tribe repudiated the agreement. When Governor Troup of Georgia prepared to survey the lands, President Adams warned him to wait until a new treaty could be signed. Troup refused to desist and threatened civil war in case the President should try to stop him by force.

In 1826 Adams secured a new treaty with the Creeks which ceded all but a small part of their lands and gave the Indians until January 1, 1827, to leave Georgia. Then Georgia denied the right of the federal government to reopen the question. Declaring that Georgia was sovereign on her own territory, Troup had the survey begun. Adams threatened the belligerent governor with the full weight of federal displeasure and then laid the matter before Congress. Congress did nothing. In 1827 the Cherokees in the same state declared themselves independent of all authority, state or federal. The Georgia legislature passed a law extending its jurisdiction over the Cherokee region, and the tribe appealed to Adams. His term expired before there was time to act, so these unsettled issues were handed down to the next administration.

Chapter 18

FROM JACKSON TO TYLER

Jacksonian Politics

ANDREW JACKSON's defeat in 1824 had discouraged neither the candidate nor his friends. They insisted that the "Old Hero" had not been beaten honestly; he had been counted out in a corrupt bargain. So the Presidential campaign of 1828 really began in 1825 when the House of Representatives chose John Quincy Adams. Between 1824 and 1828 Jackson's managers kept Jackson continually before the public, by means of receptions and public dinners. Jackson newspapers advertised their candidate, and local committees were organized to round up Jackson voters.

Election of 1828

There were few specific issues in the campaign of 1828. Jackson carried the Northwest, partly because of the desire of that section to defeat the eastern leaders, and partly because of his attitude toward the Indians. The West wanted the Indians removed, and Jackson was the man to do it. In the Southwest, Jackson could stand on his record against the Indians at Horseshoe Bend, against the British at New Orleans, and against the outlaws in Florida. In the older West, Kentucky, Missouri, and Tennessee, formerly Clay's bailiwick, Jackson swept the field because Clay had supported the bank and John Quincy Adams. Every electoral vote from all three sections of the West went to Jackson. In the South, the cotton sections favored Jackson because they felt that he was opposed to the tariff. Then too, his ticket was strengthened there because of the popularity of the vice-presidential candidate, Calhoun. The three other southern states, Virginia, North Carolina, and Maryland, voted for Jackson because he was supposed to favor states' rights. Maryland, however, gave 6 electoral votes to Adams.

In the middle states Jackson secured all the electoral votes of Pennsylvania, and 20 out of 36 of New York. This section was the stronghold of protectionism, and Jackson was believed to favor the tariff. His managers had convinced the people of each region that the "Old Hero" stood for the very things they wanted. The fact that he drew votes both from ardent protectionists and from violent opponents of the tariff did not bother them. In New England, Jackson got 1 electoral vote—from the state of Maine. The total vote gave Jackson 178 and Adams 83.

By the time of his inauguration in 1829 Jackson had developed into a man of courtly bearing and for the most part of an agreeable temper. He had little formal education, but he had acquired a good deal of self-discipline. Even if his state papers in their original form gave evidence of weakness in matters of spelling and grammatical construction, they gave emphatic proof of the power of clear and forcible expression. In his military career he had shown a tendency to decide quickly and to act readily; these traits stayed with him during his Presidency.

Politics and Policies

In selecting his Cabinet Jackson had two aims: to surround himself with men who would not oppose him, and to exclude all adherents of Henry Clay. For secretary of state, he picked Martin Van Buren of New York, the Democratic leader in that state, known politically as "the Little Magician." The other members were not especially distinguished. If the Cabinet was weak, it had one advantage: it had no connection with the preceding administration. Jackson himself had little confidence in his own Cabinet, and he almost discontinued the custom of holding Cabinet meetings. He fell into the habit of turning to a small group of political friends, known as the "Kitchen Cabinet," the leading members of which were William B. Lewis, Jackson's friend from Tennessee, Amos Kendall, Duff Green, and Isaac Hill. These last three were "Jackson editors," who had promoted his candidacy in 1828. In addition the new President sought advice from his nephew, Andrew J. Donelson.

Jackson's inaugural outlined the policies in which he was interested: due regard for the rights of the states; economy; the promotion of agriculture, commerce, manufactures, and internal improvements; a just and liberal treatment of the Indians; and reform in the civil service. The address was somewhat ambiguous because of Jackson's position. He had approved protection and internal improvements, but he had become the leader of a party destined to oppose both these policies.

When Jackson arrived in Washington for his inauguration, he found a small army of admirers to celebrate his victory. They were also present to look after their own interests. There was much talk about reform, about dismissing the advocates of corruption. All this meant jobs, and it behooved the hopeful to be on the ground. Jackson gave considerable thought to the problem of the civil service. He was in favor of the law which Crawford had inspired, limiting the term of all appointees in the Treasury Department to four years, with the possibility of reappointment. Jackson wanted to extend this principle to all branches of the civil service: "It is rotation in office that will perpetuate our liberty," he said.

In the first draft of his inaugural Jackson characterized the selection of federal civil servants as one of the President's most important duties. "It shall be my care," he wrote, "to fill the various offices at the disposal of the Executive with individuals uniting as far as possible the qualifications of the head and heart, always recollecting that in a free government the demand for moral qualities should be made superior to that of talents."

The Spoils System

Jackson's reference to the civil service spread terror among the officeholders. Many of them, especially in the capital, had been appointed by President Washington. On March 17, 1829, the administration began to "clean house." Clerks grown old in the service were removed. In selecting the new incumbents, only one test was considered: loyalty to Jackson. Ability, training, fitness—all went into the discard to make way for political favoritism. Jackson himself explained his policy in naïve terms. Why shouldn't he give jobs to the men who had worked for his election? "And to what motive other than the love of country and the exercise of a sound judgment could their course be ascribed?" Although the new policy brought panic into the bureaucracy, it was not a clean sweep. Not more than a third of the total lost their jobs.

After 1830 the excitement over this question disappeared, but by that time new precedents had been established. In some of the states, notably New York and Pennsylvania, it had long been customary to use state offices as rewards for political activity. Politics had become a profession demanding full time of the leaders. But not even a politician could live without income; therefore the party in power distributed jobs to the workers, with an understanding that work in the office might be left to subordinates while the holder devoted his time to political activity.

Under Jackson this spoils system was nationalized. Jackson's advisers frankly used appointments in the federal civil service to build up the growing Jacksonian Democratic party. Every postmaster and customhouse collector might be made a local agent of the new machine, devoting himself to work for his party. And, because these lieutenants made their living by grace of the organization, it became their duty to contribute a portion, perhaps 5 percent, of their salaries, to the party's campaign chest.

Many of Jackson's new appointees were no better than those displaced. One of the President's friends was horrified at conditions in the Treasury Department. "Talk of reform! The departments are full of the laziest clerks, and men are paid large salaries for neglecting the public business." These men, however, understood politics and created an effective political organization.

Break with Calhoun

The victory of the "Old Hero" in 1828 had been made possible by an alliance between Jackson and Calhoun, both leaders in their respective sections. Because of Jackson's lack of experience in politics, Calhoun expected to manage the administration for four years and then to become President in 1832. But neither Jackson nor his friends had any intention of giving Calhoun his own way. Instead of running the government, Calhoun found himself pushed into the background and eventually forced out of the party. The break between the two men occurred in the spring of 1830. Calhoun's friends were dropped from the administration, and Martin Van Buren of New York became Jackson's chief adviser. It is difficult to tell how much of this break was due to Van Buren's own maneuvering, how much to Jackson's increasing dislike of Calhoun, and how much to the affair of Mrs. John B. Eaton, better known by her maiden name of Peggy O'Neal.

Jackson had long been suspicious of the good faith of Calhoun. These suspicions were confirmed by a letter written by Crawford, asserting that Calhoun, as secretary of war, had advocated punishment for Jackson because of his high-handed proceedings in Florida. Jackson had considered

Calhoun as his friend at the time, and would have continued to do so, had it not been for the machinations of Lewis, Van Buren, and other manipulators. They wanted to bring about a break between the two men in order to ruin Calhoun's prospects for the Presidency. When Crawford's letter appeared, Jackson asked for an explanation. Calhoun could not very well give any, except to justify his stand in 1818 and to criticize Crawford for publishing a Cabinet secret. To Jackson any criticism was equivalent to a personal insult. After reading Calhoun's attempt at self-justification, he broke off relations, informing the Vice President, in words that bite even now, that "no further communication with you on this subject is necessary."

Shortly after Jackson broke with Calhoun, the Cabinet began to break up, due partly to the President's determination to get rid of Calhoun's friends, and partly to a dispute over the social status of Mrs. Eaton. She was a handsome young woman, with enough unconventionality to make her all the more alluring to her admirers. In this group were some of the best-known men in Washington, including not only Jackson but even Daniel Webster. She was the daughter of a Washington innkeeper, and her sudden elevation to the rank of Cabinet member's wife provided Washington with a delightful scandal. In such matters men, left to themselves, are considerably more charitable in their judgments than women. They could forgive a good deal in anyone so fascinating as the sprightly Peggy. This masculine tolerance may have confirmed the wives of the other Cabinet members in their determination to ostracize Mrs. Eaton. In any case they did so, and they were led by the wife of the Vice President, Mrs. John C. Calhoun. Jackson was convinced that the wife of his secretary of war was the victim of injustice, and he ordered his advisers to pay due respect to the injured beauty. Because of the danger of domestic insurrections, most of them had to refuse. Van Buren, however, was a widower, free to treat Mrs. Eaton with gallant courtesy. He won the instant and lasting regard of Jackson, while his less fortunate colleagues were soon set adrift. Even Van Buren resigned from the Cabinet, but with Jackson's approval, to become candidate for the vice-presidency. In getting rid of his first Cabinet, Jackson was able to secure men more directly in sympathy with him and his measures and, in that way, to promote party unity. The fall of Calhoun and the rise of Van Buren showed that the work of constructing a new party was nearly completed.

West Indian Trade

Although Jackson's administration was concerned primarily with American problems, there were in both his first and second terms important developments in foreign affairs. In his first term Jackson became interested in the old question of the West Indian trade. Ever since 1783 this branch of commerce, formerly so profitable to American merchants, had been closed to American shipping. During the early 1820's British and American governments both had tried, unsuccessfully, to reopen this commerce. In 1829 direct trade between the West Indies and the United States was impossible for either English or American ships.

Jackson's new minister to England began negotiations looking toward the resumption of trade relations in this area. Then in his first annual message to Congress Jackson spoke in flattering terms of Great Britain and pointed out that with her "we may look forward to years of peaceful, honorable, and elevated competition." Congress gave Jackson power to open American ports to British ships from the West Indies, on condition that British West Indian ports should be opened to American ships. At this time Huskisson in England was trying to convert the Tories to a policy of free trade, and the British were in a mood for concessions. Negotiations were successful, and in October 1830 the President announced that direct trade was reopened. This arrangement allowed American ships to carry products of the United States to the West Indies and to bring West Indian products to the United States. The new concessions proved valuable to American merchants and producers. In the course of a single year exports from the United States to the West Indies increased from a value of $140 to $1,439,593; during the same year imports from the West Indies to this country went up from $101,843 to $873,855.

States' Rights and Nullification

In domestic policy Jackson and his advisers were interested as much in political strategy as in reform. Even in dealing with internal improvements there was emphasis on politics rather than economic interests. Internal improvements had been a favorite policy in the West, but this policy was associated with the name of Henry Clay. Since any achievements in this field would redound to Clay's advantage, Jackson would not endorse internal improvements. In 1830 Congress passed a bill for constructing the Maysville road, in the state of Kentucky. Jackson vetoed this measure, and later he defeated other road and canal projects in the same way.

Some of the most important acts and discussions of Jackson's administration grew out of an unsettled major problem: the relative power of the states and the nation. First came the dispute between the Creek Indians and the state of Georgia. Governor Troup had defied the United States government, and President John Quincy Adams had been unable to call him to account. In the meantime the Cherokees had carried their troubles to the federal Supreme Court. In the case of the *Cherokee Nation* v. *Georgia,* Marshall had decided that the tribe was not a foreign nation and that it could not sue in any federal court. In an obiter dictum he described the Cherokees as a "domestic dependent nation" and declared that the courts and the states were bound to uphold acts of the federal government concerning the Cherokees. The federal government should then have protected the Indians, but Jackson refused to act.

Jackson and Georgia

A closely related issue appeared in still another dispute between Georgia and the Cherokee Indians. In December 1830 the legislature of Georgia prohibited white persons from living within the Cherokee area without a license signed by the governor. A Presbyterian missionary, more famous as a lexicographer, Worcester, was arrested for violation of this law, and sentenced to four years' imprisonment. Worcester appealed to the federal Supreme Court. In the case of *Worcester* v. *Georgia,* Chief Justice Marshall ruled that the laws of Georgia were not in effect in the Cherokee section and also that the particular statute was unconstitutional. The court then ordered the Georgia authorities to release Worcester. The state refused to comply, and President Jackson made no effort to uphold the authority of the court. "John Marshall has made his decision," Jackson is alleged to have said, "now let him enforce it!" Jackson sympathized with the state rather than with the Indians, and so did practically all of his admirers in the South and West.

Webster-Hayne Debate

In 1830 this same issue of federal authority versus states' rights, in different form, came up for discussion in the United States Senate, in the Webster-Hayne debate. The arguments on the two sides became the standard authorities, one for states' rights, the other for nationalism. As so often happens, the discussion began on a different, and apparently unrelated, subject. Late in December 1829 Senator Samuel A. Foote of Connecticut introduced a resolution designed to limit sales of public lands. Benton of Missouri promptly objected on the ground that the resolution was really an attack upon the West, designed to check the further growth of the new section. Southern Senators came to the assistance of the West in opposing the restrictionists from the East. Finally Hayne of South Carolina introduced the doctrine of states' rights, and the subject of the debate shifted from public lands to the proper status of the federal government. At this point Daniel Webster entered the contest in opposition to Hayne.

Hayne raised the question of nationalism by pointing out the dangers of consolidation and the unfairness of the tariff, basing his arguments on Calhoun's "South Carolina Exposition." This theory of states' rights and nullification, he insisted, was the traditional American doctrine, accepted in earlier years almost everywhere throughout the Union.

Webster's answer, the "Reply to Hayne," was an able exposition of federal supremacy. Taking up Hayne's theory that the states possessed the ultimate authority to decide whether or not acts of Congress were constitutional, Webster replied with an emphatic denial. Only by revolution could a state get around federal law. Between obedience and open rebellion there could be no middle ground. Then he argued that Hayne's conclusions were based upon a complete misunderstanding of the federal system. According to Hayne, the federal government was merely the agent of the states. Webster insisted that the federal government was the people's government. State legislatures, he said, were not sovereign over the people, because the people had chosen to place sovereignty elsewhere, namely, in the federal government. The Constitution therefore restricted the rights of the states, and no state could of its own accord rightfully throw off those restrictions. If the people disapproved of anything in the Constitution, they might amend it, but until they did so, the Constitution and the acts of Congress passed in accordance therewith remained the supreme law of the land.

Was it possible that Webster had forgotten the occasion, sixteen years earlier, when he had devoted his extraordinary powers to the task of opposing the conscription law for the War of 1812 and when he had openly threatened, if the proposed measure passed, to urge upon his constituents a resort to nullification? In 1814 Webster stood upon the same ground occupied by Hayne in 1830, and he used the same theories to support his position. In the meantime public opinion in New England had changed, and Webster had changed with it. Because of the growth of the West, the industrial development of the East, and the decisions of the Supreme Court, there was a new attitude toward the federal government. It had been weak in the beginning, and the states strong, but the very fact of its existence made necessary a shifting of the balance. If it was to function as a government, its measures must prevail over local opposition. For that very reason its authority continued to grow. By 1830 the point had been reached where shrewd observers were aware of the tendency, and they altered their convictions to make them fit the new situation.

Nullification

Shortly after this discussion of nationalism versus state's rights, the country was furnished with a practical demonstration of the working of the two theories. In South Carolina, where the tariff had long been a source of ill feeling, the objectionable measure of 1828 had aroused the state almost to open opposition. In 1832 a new measure was passed, an improvement over its predecessor, but nevertheless a grievance to South Carolina.

Convinced that all hope of relief from Congress had disappeared, the state determined to put Calhoun's theory of nullification or "interposition" into practice. That became the issue in the state election of 1832, and the nullifiers won. The state legislature assembled in October, and both houses passed a bill providing for a special state convention. On November 19 this body met at Columbia, with a heavy majority in favor of nullification. Five days later it adopted the Ordinance "to nullify certain acts of the Congress of the United States, purporting to be laws, laying duties and imposts on the importation of foreign commodities." This document declared the Acts of 1828 and 1832 null and void. If the federal government should attempt to use force, South Carolina threatened to secede:

> We will not submit to the application of force, on the part of the Federal Government, to reduce this State to obedience . . . we will consider the passage, by Congress, of any act authorizing the employment of a military or naval force against the State of South Carolina, her constituted authorities or citizens . . . as inconsistent with the longer continuance of South Carolina in the Union . . . the People of this State will thenceforth hold themselves absolved from all further obligation to maintain or preserve their political connection with the people of the other states, and will forthwith proceed to organize a separate

government, and to do all other acts and things which sovereign and independent States may of right do.

Jackson had the garrison at Fort Moultrie increased and on November 18 he sent General Scott to the state. On December 10, strengthened by his overwhelming majority for a second term, Jackson issued a stirring proclamation to the people of South Carolina:

> I consider the power to annul a law of the United States, assumed by one State, incompatible with the existence of the Union, contradicted expressly by the letter of the Constitution, unauthorized by its spirit, inconsistent with every principle on which it was founded, and destructive of the great object for which it was formed.

Jackson was prepared to send 40,000 troops into South Carolina.

The dispute was not permitted to reach the stage of civil war. While Congress was at work on a "force bill" giving the President authority to use the armed forces, Clay introduced a compromise tariff. This measure provided that when the duties exceeded 20 percent, the excess should be gradually reduced, one tenth in 1833, another tenth two years later, and one tenth every second year until 1841, with other reductions in 1842. With the help of Calhoun, now disturbed at the turn of affairs, the bill was passed. On the same day, March 1, the force bill became law. The South Carolina radicals, left with no support from other states, first suspended their ordinance of nullification and then repealed it. South Carolina did not nullify an act of Congress, but her policy forced a reduction in tariff rates. The federal government did not use force because South Carolina's surrender made drastic action unnecessary. Neither side won a clean-cut victory. If there was an advantage on either side, perhaps the decision would go to the federal power because it came out of the contest with increased prestige.

Jackson's Triumph

Jackson and the Bank

The attainment of party solidarity during his first term was hastened by Jackson's attitude toward the Second Bank of the United States. It provided what had heretofore been wanting, a definite issue which politicians could use to arouse the voters. Chartered in 1816, the bank had not been entirely happy during its first few years. Bad management brought embarrassments, and popular opposition seemed almost to threaten its very life. Had it not been for the Supreme Court, in its *McCulloch* v. *Maryland* decision, the bank would have been taxed to death in the southern and western states. Later on the bank became a success.

In his first annual message Jackson referred to the approaching end of the bank's charter, and remarked that both "the constitutionality and the expediency" of the institution had been seriously questioned. Both the President and his followers in the West were opposed to the bank, partly on the ground that it had been a financial success, partly because of the conservatism of the officers. Furthermore the bank was a great financial monopoly. According to rumor, zealously circulated by the "Kitchen Cabinet" group, the bank had used its influence against Jackson in the campaign of 1828. Jackson knew that some of his political foes were heavy borrowers at the bank.

Exactly when Jackson decided to make the bank an issue is not clear. He was pondering over the matter in 1829, and he raised the question again in 1831. Because of the effect of the President's questioning upon business, Biddle, the bank's president, determined to settle the controversy by applying for a new charter. He did so in January 1832. A bill for a recharter was introduced in the House in March and passed both houses in July by narrow majorities. On July 10, Jackson vetoed the bill. In 1836, when its federal charter expired, the main bank at Philadelphia continued in business under a state charter. Along with many other banks it failed and went out of business in the panic of 1837.

From the standpoint of economics the veto message was ludicrous. But Jackson did not pretend to be a financial expert; he was a popular politician, and there was political capital to be derived from an attack upon the great monopoly. As campaign strategy, the message was a remarkable document. It brought Jackson widespread Southern and Western support in the Presidential campaign of 1832 and so made Jackson's nomination for a second term inevitable. By 1832 he had a real party behind him, a new Democratic organization.

National Conventions

In the campaign of 1832 certain extraneous issues appeared, destined to leave a lasting mark on party activity. In 1826 one William Morgan, a New Yorker, had mysteriously disappeared. He had published a book purporting to reveal the secrets of Freemasonry, and the public assumed that the order had made away with him. Out of this belief there grew up a widespread opposition to secret societies of any kind. Masons, according to report, so completely controlled the judicial machinery of the country that no Mason could ever be punished for crime. No jury dared to convict, and no judge would sentence a brother of the order. Public feeling became bitter and insisted that the Masons must go. The excitement was carried over into politics, and an anti-Masonic political party was formed, dedicated to the destruction of the great fraternal organization.

This party would have achieved temporary notoriety from its attacks upon the Masons, but there was little to give it lasting strength. It did acquire fame, however, because it introduced the national party convention to take the place of the discredited and discarded caucus. On September 26, 1831, delegates of the party met at Baltimore, to nominate candidates for President and Vice President.

On December 12, 1831, a convention of so-called National Republicans met at Baltimore. They were the followers of Adams and Clay, loose constructionists who advocated a protective tariff, internal improvements, and the bank. This group nominated Henry Clay.

The Jacksonian Democrats held their first convention at Baltimore in May 1832. While Jackson's nomination was a foregone conclusion, there was doubt concerning his running mate. He preferred Van Buren. The convention was under the control of the "Kitchen Cabinet," and thanks to their foresight Van Buren received the nomination. They brought about the adoption of the two-thirds rule, which the party retained until 1936. There were various candidates for the nomination, but Van Buren was the only one able to command the necessary two thirds. In the popular vote Jackson ran nearly 160,000 ahead of Clay, while the electoral vote stood: Jackson 219, Clay 49.

This proof of support strengthened Jackson in his determination to force South Carolina to back down. It also encouraged him to attack the bank. Although the bank's charter did not expire until 1836, Jackson determined to divorce it from the government. The charter made the bank the depository of federal funds, unless the secretary of the treasury should order otherwise. Jackson planned to withdraw the deposits. Jackson had to find a new secretary of the treasury to carry out the policy, but that was easy. Late in September 1833 the Treasury announced that the Girard Bank of Philadelphia would become the first government depository. By the end of the year twenty-three banks had been selected to handle federal funds.

In the annual message of December 1833 Jackson referred to these proceedings, thereby giving Congress an opportunity to strike back at him. The Senate adopted a resolution of censure which declared that the reasons for the removal of the deposits were unsatisfactory and that the President had assumed authority not conferred by the Constitution or the laws. Jackson protested against the censure, and, after a long dispute, in January 1837, the Senate, under Benton's leadership, voted to expunge the resolutions from its *Journal*. This step closed the controversy over the bank.

Removal of the Indians

Among other measures of Jackson's second term, the Indian policy is one of the more important. Jackson had been committed to some project of removing Indians from the South and Middle West to regions beyond the Mississippi. Regretting that the step was necessary, he argued that the Indians could not be allowed to impede the progress of white settlement and civilization. In June 1834 Congress provided for the creation of an Indian territory west of the Mississippi River. The process of removal went on rapidly. In December 1835 Jackson announced that, except for two small groups in Ohio and Indiana (not more than 1500 in number) and the Cherokees, all tribes east of the Mississippi had made an agreement regarding removal. By 1837 ninety-four Indian treaties had been concluded, for the most part ceding Indian lands to the United States.

Before the end of his second term Jackson enjoyed one more triumph in foreign affairs. In 1831 the United States and France had come to an agreement by which the French government had consented to pay 25,000,000 francs, in full settlement of the claims of American citizens, while the United States was to pay 1,500,000 francs. The treaty was ratified in February 1832. The actual fulfillment of the treaty depended upon an appropriation by the French legislature, but because the treaty was unpopular this had not been made. In 1834 Jackson recommended reprisals on French property in case the French legislature still refused to act. This message caused considerable ill feeling in France, but in 1835 the legislature finally made the appropriation on condition that some of Jackson's remarks be satisfactorily explained. Jackson refused to make any apologies and again urged reprisals. He did, however, suggest that subjects in a President's message were purely domestic concerns. The French government made no further objections and paid the money. The other important foreign problem, Texas, will be dealt with later.

The Panic and the Whigs

By the end of his second term Jackson and his friends had created a powerful political party with a network of local committees and of federal officeholders extending over the whole country. Though its greatest source of strength was still the West, it had powerful adherents also in New York and Pennsylvania. The Democrats held their national convention in 1835 and nominated Martin Van Buren of New York.

New Whig Party

During this same period the various elements in the opposition were knit together into a political party. They called themselves Whigs, in imitation of eighteenth-century Englishmen and Americans who opposed King George III. From their point of view Jackson was a tyrant as dangerous to the liberties of America as George III had been in 1776. The term "Whig" was first used in this sense in 1834 in Connecticut and New York, and in this same year the Whig party was organized. The operations of the Whigs bring out some of the peculiar features in American politics. Under that caption were included a far more heterogeneous mixture than that under the Jackson banner in 1828. The nucleus of the new party was the group of national Republicans, or the Adams-Clay-Webster following, noted for their advocacy of a national bank and a protective tariff. At the other extreme were the states' rights element, which repudiated Jackson because he had threatened the South Carolina nullifiers with force. Many of the anti-Masons drifted into the Whig party. So diverse were these elements that they were never really consolidated. As a party the Whigs had few if any principles; they merely opposed Jackson. Under ordinary conditions there would have been nothing to hold the factions together, but the spoils system had brought in a new dispensation in politics, and the desire for federal jobs took the place of agreement on issues and leaders. The Whigs wanted the plums of office. Because of their internal weaknesses the Whigs did not even hold a national convention, and they could not agree upon a candidate. In Pennsylvania the Whigs nominated and voted for

William Henry Harrison; in Massachusetts the Whigs voted for Daniel Webster; in Ohio the Whig choice was Judge McLean; in North Carolina it was Willie Mangum; in Tennessee Hugh L. White. Twenty-six states took part in the election. Of the popular vote Van Buren received 762,978, while all the Whig candidates together received 736,250. Of the total electoral vote of 294, Van Buren had 170, while Harrison, the leading Whig, polled 73.

Speculation

The outstanding feature of Van Buren's term was the panic of 1837. The causes of this economic collapse are to be found partly in excessive investments by the state governments in roads and canals, in banking practices, in widespread speculation (particularly in land), and in the financial crisis in Europe. The general characteristic of the time was business on borrowed money. Men went into debt to build factories, to buy land, to buy slaves. In the prevailing enthusiasm for internal improvements state governments spent money liberally and borrowed freely. Because of the widespread demands for funds, interest rates were high, 2 or even 4 percent a month. Security for these loans was given in the form of bonds payable in thirty, forty, or fifty years. It is difficult to show how deeply the states ran into debt without giving some specific examples. In 1820, while road building was still looked on as a private enterprise, the total debt of the borrowing states amounted to only $13,000,000. By 1835 the total debt had risen to more than $66,000,000. In 1838 the debt figure stood at $170,000,000.

Many of the financial problems of the time were connected with banking methods. When the government ceased to use the Bank of the United States, it used a number of selected state banks as depositories. On the whole these seem to have been carefully managed and, in spite of the tales of favoritism and "wild-cat" methods, they were reasonably sound. But the approaching end of the national bank gave an impetus to local banks of all kinds, and many of these new ones were everything that banks ought not to be. Started with little capital and less specie, they ran riot in issuing notes and in making loans. Between 1829 and 1837 the number of banks increased from 329 to 788, while the total capitalization increased only from $110,000,000 to $290,000,000. The loans went up from $137,000,000 to $525,000,000 and their note circulation from $48,000,000 to $149,000,000.

This plunge into loose banking was both cause and effect of speculation. Money was "easy," and business on credit underwent a rapid expansion. Partly as a result of the reopening of the West Indian trade, American commerce was growing rapidly, and prices were moving upward. The public debt was entirely paid and, because income exceeded expenditures, the federal treasury was actually accumulating a surplus. To get rid of this surplus, Congress in 1836 passed an act providing for distributing it among the states. The whole amount, nearly $37,500,000, was to be paid over in the form of a loan, in four installments. The apportionment was based upon population, so that New York got the largest share, approximately $5,500,000, while Michigan and Delaware each drew a little over $380,000. Only three payments were made, however, because the panic of 1837 plunged the treasury into a deficit. Many of the states applied the money on internal improvements and then borrowed heavily to complete the work. Thus the distribution of the surplus encouraged the tendency to speculation. Nowhere was this spirit of speculation illustrated more vividly than in the sales of public land. For several years the annual receipts from public land sales had averaged about $1,880,000. In 1836 they went up to $24,877,000. Most of this business was done not with cash but with bank notes.

A man would borrow $100 in bank notes on his own personal note as security; with public land in the West selling at $1.25 per acre he would buy eighty acres. His purchase might be miles from any settlement, but that did not matter. He would lay out his land in streets and building lots, and his wild land immediately became town property worth ten times what he paid for it. Then he would go to a bank, put up his eighty acres as security, and borrow $1000. This time he would buy 800 acres; by splitting this into streets and lots, and so creating new security, he could borrow $10,000, and so on, piling up a huge inverted pyramid of bank credit without having used a cent of actual cash. In any economic crisis, the banks would find they had no real security behind their notes given by these land speculators.

In 1836 President Jackson became alarmed over these public land sales on credit. In an effort to stop it, he issued the "specie circular," which ordered the land offices to accept nothing but hard money in payment for public land. The "specie circular" put a sudden stop to business activity. The time had come for the collapse of paper credit.

Wild speculation in land was one evidence of an unhealthy condition in business. Further proof was to be found in the extravagant expenditures of ordinary citizens. One newspaper writer complained:

> We are too fond of showing off in our families; and in this way our expenses far exceed our incomes. Our daughters must be dressed off in their silks and crapes, instead of their linsey-woolsey. Our young folks are too proud to be seen in a coarse dress, and their extravagance is bringing ruin on our families. When you can induce your sons to prefer young women for their real worth rather than their show; when you can get them to choose a wife who can make a good loaf of bread and a good pound of butter to a girl who does nothing but dance about in her silks and laces; then gentlemen, you may expect to see a change for the better. We must get back to the good old simplicity of former times if we expect to see more prosperous days.

Panic of 1837

Such speculation may continue for a long time without harmful results until someone becomes frightened. But when fear starts, it spreads rapidly and the structure built on credit will go to smash. Fear began to spread in 1837. Banks entered upon a wild scramble for cash; failing to get it, they closed their doors. Confidence disappeared first in Europe, where Continental banks tried to call in money they had lent to Englishmen. English banks in turn tried to call their American loans. American banks then turned to their borrowers, who were unable to pay. In May 1837 banks in New York suspended specie payments; those in other parts of the country followed suit.

When the banks failed, everybody suffered. Manufacturers had to cut wages or discharge their employees. Landowners who rented property could not collect rents and could pay neither interest nor taxes. They could not sell land at any price. Government revenues fell off because imports decreased in volume and public land sales stopped. Specie became so scarce that not a bank in the country could pay out hard money. The price of cotton dropped suddenly from 20 to 10 cents per pound. An odd thing happened in wheat: the American crop failed entirely in 1837, so that American farmers had to import seed for their next planting. The price of flour went to $12 a barrel, an almost unheard-of figure. Therefore while the cotton planters suffered from low prices because of a glut, the wheat farmers suffered even more severely because of a scarcity. The crash came in 1837; the country did not really recover until after 1843.

In October 1837 the federal government began to issue treasury notes; between that date and 1843 these issues amounted to $47,000,000. Van Buren proposed an additional remedy, known as the independent treasury system, under which the funds of the government would be separated from the business world. All money received would be deposited in the treasury at Washington, or in various "sub-treasuries" to be established in certain selected centers. Because of opposition in Congress, the President's measure was not enacted until 1840. In 1841 the Whigs repealed it, but in 1845 the law was re-enacted.

While Van Buren and the administration were struggling with the embarrassments created by the panic, Clay, Webster, and John Quincy Adams took advantage of the depression to strengthen the Whig organization. Nothing is quite so good for the opposition party as a panic. The voters can easily be made to fasten the whole responsibility for it upon the administration in office. With that idea firmly implanted, they proceed to take vengeance in the next Presidential election.

Campaign of 1840

The Whig convention met at Harrisburg in December 1839. They were unable to agree upon any constructive program. They were also unable to agree upon either Clay or Webster, the leading candidates. Passing over them, the convention nominated William Henry Harrison. He was nearly seventy years old and he knew little about politics. For Vice President the Whigs selected John Tyler of Virginia, a follower of Calhoun and a Democrat in everything except his attitude toward Jackson.

The campaign of 1840 struck a new note in American politics. The Whigs used the methods of the circus and swept the country along in a great, hilarious uproar. Because Harrison had once worn a coonskin cap, lived in a log cabin, and drunk hard cider, coons, cabins, and cider were chosen as symbols for the party. Local conventions were held in every city, with numerous parades and demonstrations. When the Democrats held their convention in Baltimore, the Whigs organized their biggest procession of all in the same city to flaunt their strength in the eyes of their foes.

The Democrats ridiculed the enthusiasm of the Whigs and derisively referred to the Baltimore procession as an animal show. The Whigs could well afford to let the Democrats laugh. On election day Van Buren, the Democratic candidate, carried only seven states with 60 electoral votes. Harrison received 234 electoral votes. The total popular vote for all the candidates exceeded that of 1836 by about a million.

On inauguration day, Harrison was installed in office with enthusiastic applause, furnished in large measure by the swarms of office seekers who poured into Washington. The new President had little acquaintance with his responsibilities and almost no experience in politics. Consequently he turned to Henry Clay because Clay was the leader of the Whigs. Clay advised Harrison on Cabinet appointments and legislative policies. Congress was called in special session, primarily to repeal the Independent Treasury Act, to establish a new bank, to enact a higher tariff, and to provide for internal improvements. Some of these policies were popular in the East, some in the West; the southern Whigs did not like any of them. Within a month after his inauguration and nearly two months before Congress met, Harrison died. Tyler, his successor, disapproved of the major points in Clay's program.

Congress passed a bill for a bank, which the President promptly vetoed. A second met the same fate. Clay's internal improvements' plan was so altered that it was worthless. Clay then advised Tyler's Cabinet to resign. All the members did so except the secretary of state, Daniel Webster. Webster was then engaged in a series of delicate negotiations with Lord Ashburton, the British minister to the United States, and he did not wish to jeopardize the prospect of a satisfactory settlement by turning his department over to an inexperienced man.

Relations with Canada

Troublesome enough in themselves, these foreign problems had been rendered more serious by American sympathy for the Canadians in their insurrections from 1837 to 1840. There were French Canadian uprisings and republican uprisings, both aimed at the overthrow of British rule. Before the United States government could act effectively to compel neutrality, Americans along the border had participated in the disturbances. Out of this situation developed the *Caroline* affair. In 1837 military forces, fitted out in New York, stationed themselves on Navy Island in American waters near Niagara. Their supplies came from the United States, by the steamer *Caroline*. In December 1837 a detachment of Canadian militia crossed the river, set fire to the *Caroline,* and sank her in midstream. In the course of this enterprise one American was killed. In 1840 one Alexander McLeod was arrested and tried for the murder. The British government demanded his release on the ground that whatever he had done had been in the course of carrying out military orders. McLeod was being tried in a New York court, and the federal government had no authority to interfere. Such was the situation when Webster became secretary of state. Webster was able to secure McLeod's release. Then, to guard against the recurrence of such a complication, he persuaded Congress to pass a law providing that a subject of a foreign power on trial in a state court might be transferred to a federal court.

A more important controversy had grown out of the uncertainty regarding the location of the boundary line between Maine and New Brunswick. The treaty of 1783 had been anything but definite on that point, and the citizens of Maine and New Brunswick had gone almost to the point of war. The Webster-Ashburton Treaty of 1842 compromised the dispute. The territory in question was divided in such a way that Maine got the Aroostook valley and a part of the valley of the upper St. John. The United States gained possession of 7000 square miles, and Great Britain about 5000. It is possible that the general disapproval on both sides with which the treaty was received is a tribute to its fairness and justice.

Chapter 19

THE ERA OF REFORM

A Literary Revival

For the student of history who is interested in the broad aspects of human behavior as well as in economics, politics, and government, the three decades preceding 1860 are fascinating. The period has been described as "the intellectual and moral renaissance" and also as "the hot-air period in American History." Both characterizations are accurate. It was a time of awakening in literature and religion. It was also a time of humanitarian and moral reform. James Russell Lowell left a brief but vivid description of this extraordinary enthusiasm for making people better.

Perfectionists at Work

> Every possible form of intellectual and physical dyspepsia brought forth its gospel. . . . Everybody had a mission (with a capital M) to attend to everybody-else's business. No brain but had its private maggot, which must have found pitiably short commons sometimes. Not a few impecunious zealots abjured the use of money (unless earned by other people), professing to live on the internal revenues of the spirit. Some had an assurance of instant millenium so soon as hooks and eyes should be substituted for buttons. Communities were established where everything was to be common but common sense. . . . Many foreign revolutionists out of work added to the general misunderstanding their contribution of broken English in every most ingenious form of fracture. All stood ready at a moment's notice to reform everything but themselves.

Among the more lasting results of this eagerness for improvement, the literary revival might come first. Emerson, Hawthorne, Bryant, Lowell, and Whittier were in their prime then; Cooper and Poe fit into the period in its beginning, and Whitman and Longfellow at its end. The first really important American writer, apart from theologians, historians, and those who wrote of politics and statesmanship, was Washington Irving. Irving's *Sketch Book* included two famous stories, "Rip Van Winkle" and "The Legend of Sleepy Hollow," and *A History of New York from the Beginning of the World to the End of the Dutch Dynasty by Diedrich Knickerbocker* was another dip into the past, and its purpose was to entertain. This alleged history with its ponderous name was one long burlesque. In 1835 Irving published his *Tour of the Prairies,* in which he described his own experiences with an exploring party beyond the Mississippi. Next he published *The Adventures of Captain Bonneville,* which he wrote with the help of Bonneville's own journal. These works dealt with life as Irving saw it.

New Era in Literature

James Fenimore Cooper (1789-1851) did more than Irving with native American themes, although his field was the historical novel. Cooper is most famous for the five Leatherstocking Tales, and of these *The Last of the Mohicans* is the most widely read. In these stories he dealt with life on the frontier, with the relation of whites and Indians, and with the gradual disappearance of frontier customs as civilization spread over the wilderness.

The greatest literary artist of the second quarter of the nineteenth century was Edgar Allan Poe (1809-49). He was the first American to use the device of the short story. He also introduced the detective story; "The Gold Bug," "The Murders in the Rue Morgue," and "The Purloined Letter" are the best examples of this type of his work. Then Poe wrote horror stories, such as "The Black Cat" and "The Fall of the House of Usher." But Poe was also a poet, and his verse put him in the comparatively small group of internationally famous authors.

After 1840 a new trend appeared in American literature, known as transcendentalism. Trancendentalists believed that the human mind contained in itself an understanding of such principles as right and wrong, an understanding of religion and of God; that these principles did not come from experience, but from something outside of experience. Through this relationship between man's spirit and God, the human soul became one means of revealing the truth about God to man. Another means of revealing eternal truth was Nature. So the transcendentalists studied and wrote about the soul and its connections with a Higher Power, and about Nature as the mirror which reflected God. The most famous literary representative of the transcendentalists was Ralph Waldo Emerson. Another representative of the transcendental school was Henry David Thoreau.

American Poets

American literature of the mid-nineteenth century is famous for its poetry, and the list of writers is notable: Henry Wadsworth Longfellow, John Greenleaf Whittier, Walt Whitman, James Russell Lowell, Oliver Wendell Holmes, and Sidney Lanier. Longfellow's verse is like his life: pleasing, smooth, comfortable; he never stirred anyone to intense feeling, but he brought enjoyment probably to more readers than any other American author. His longer poems—"Evangeline," "The Courtship of Miles Standish," "Hiawatha"—deal with important aspects of American history. Whittier never won Longfellow's international fame, but his verse had the peculiarly great quality of making people feel life as Whittier lived it and as so many New Englanders lived it.

Although he was born on Long Island and lived most of his life in New Jersey, Walt Whitman was the best representative of the new democratic America, the America of the West. And in keeping with the new life which he described, Whitman experimented with new verse forms as more suitable means of expression. He has sometimes been described as the greatest American poet, sometimes as the most typically American poet.

Sidney Lanier, musician and poet, lived to be only thirty-nine, and in his adult life he knew little but hardship and illness. Born in Georgia, he entered the Confederate Army soon after graduation from college. Taken prisoner on a blockade runner near the end of the war, he contracted tuberculosis. The rest of his life was a struggle against disease, but, in spite of handicaps which would have silenced most men, he contrived to write some of the most musical verse in American literature.

These poets dealt with important issues of their day. Whittier was the great poet of the antislavery movement. Lowell wrote some extremely vigorous verse in dialect, condemning the government of his country for the war with Mexico; he wrote also a second series dealing with the Civil War. These *Biglow Papers* brought him wide popularity in his day, and some critics still profess to find them valuable. Oliver Wendell Holmes was the most versatile of them all—physician, teacher of anatomy, essayist, poet, and novelist. In spite of the demands of his profession, which were heavy, he produced a surprising amount of writing in which he gave lasting fame to intellectual Boston. *The Deacon's Masterpiece,* Holmes's story of the building, career, and collapse of the *Wonderful One-hoss Shay,* is a figurative description of the breakdown of the Puritan system of theology.

Novelists and Historians

Of the novelists of the period there were three, in addition to Irving and Cooper, of outstanding importance: Nathaniel Hawthorne, Harriet Beecher Stowe, and Herman Melville. In some respects Hawthorne's novels reflect as much of himself as of the times he tried to describe. He showed a gloominess and a concern with the consequences of sin that was not necessarily typical of all Puritans or their descendants. But *The Scarlet Letter* and *The House of Seven Gables* are great stories, even if they are not cheerful. Mrs. Stowe's most important work *Uncle Tom's Cabin* was the most popular book of the period. Herman Melville wrote stories of the sea, of which the best known is *Moby Dick,* the story of the white whale. For some reason Melville gained very little fame in his own day, and it was not until the twentieth century that his books became popular. *Moby Dick* is a story of the whale fishery in and out of New Bedford.

Among other writers of lasting fame were the great historians: Bancroft, Prescott, Motley, and Parkman. Bancroft wrote the history of the American colonial period and the Constitution; Prescott described the Spanish conquests of Mexico and Peru; Motley told of the rise of the Dutch republic; Parkman dealt with the French colonies in the new world and their long struggle with the English. These historians combined in remarkable fashion the elements of sound historical accuracy with great readability; their books are still entertaining reading.

Reform in Education

At the present time one of the most important and most typical of our American institutions is the free public school. Every state in the Union provides educational facilities for its children and youth, all of them through the high school and many through college as well. The idea of public schools took a practical turn in the early history of Massachusetts with a law requiring the towns to maintain schoolmasters. The first high school in English North America, the Boston Latin School, was founded in 1635, but the real development of the public school system did not come until after 1825.

The backwardness of the schools may be explained in part by the shortcomings of the American colleges of the period. If they failed to keep pace with a changing world, the few public schools would be just as conservative, because the only higher education available for teachers was that offered by the colleges. Down through the first third of the nineteenth century the course of study in American colleges was like that at Harvard in its early days, which in turn modeled its curriculum on that of the medieval universities. Students studied Latin and Greek; these were the basis of the whole educational system. Secondarily they studied rhetoric, mathematics, natural philosophy—the nearest approach to physics and chemistry available—logic, and moral philosophy. There were no modern languages, practically no history, and no science worthy of the name. There were rare exceptions to this hard and fast arrangement, notably at the Universities of Pennsylvania and Virginia, but their departures from tradition brought unfavorable comment.

Modernizing the Colleges

In the 1820's there were numerous protests against the traditional combination of classical languages, mathematics, and philosophy. On being installed as president of the University of Nashville, Tennessee, in 1825, Philip Lindsley declared: "The farmer, the mechanic, the manufacturer, the merchant, the sailor, the soldier . . . must be educated." In developing his theories of vocational education, president Lindsley called for shops, gardens, and a farm. He wished also to introduce such subjects as government, international law, commerce—he probably meant business education —and agriculture. Here was one of the earliest, most carefully thought-out plans for vocational education. The plan was not carried through at the time, but it was important as a sign of the times.

A year later, in 1826, at the University of Vermont, President James Marsh worked to introduce courses in languages, English literature, and physics and to permit students to break away from the standard curriculum. In 1827 a new type of school opened at Whitesboro, New York, near Utica: the Oneida Institute of Science and Industry. Founded on the new manual labor principle, the Oneida Institute required its students to work three and a half hours every day in agriculture or at some mechanical trade. This manual labor was designed partly to cut down the cost of education, but it was also a definite part of the educational process. The founder of the Institute proudly described this policy as "a system of education which is to introduce the Millennium." In 1834 Oneida adopted a new curriculum, with no Latin whatever and no Greek classics; in their places Hebrew and the Greek New Testament were substituted. There were also courses in "Political Economy," and in "Principles of Human Government."

In August 1833 plans were completed for establishing the Oberlin Collegiate Institute, about twenty miles south of Cleveland, Ohio. Oberlin aimed to train young men for the ministry and proposed the revolutionary and almost unheard-of notion of training young women for teaching. And Oberlin, like Oneida, adopted the manual labor principle. Furthermore, the Oberlin Institute greatly reduced the amount of Greek and Latin required.

The best evidence of the importance of this educational overturn is to be found in the effect it had on the conservatives and in their protests against it. The most famous of these protests was prepared by the faculty of Yale College in the form of a report to the trustees. In 1827 this body asked for an opinion as to the desirability of dropping Latin and Greek as essential requirements for the degree, and of substituting modern languages. They got their answer. Under the leadership of President Jeremiah Day, the Yale faculty registered a vigorous and solemn negative to the proposed change. "From different quarters we have heard the suggestion, that our colleges must be new-modelled; that they are not adapted to the spirit and wants of the age; that they will soon be deserted, unless they are better accommodated to the business character of the nation." Yale had no sympathy with these radical proposals. She would continue to train the mind, and she would have nothing to do with vocational education: "We have, on our premises, no experimental farm or retail shop, no cotton or iron manufactory." The traditional course of classical languages, mathematics, and philosophy was best adapted to mental growth. The notion that modern languages could be profitably studied without adequate training in the classics they declared to be visionary and silly. In short, Yale would have nothing to do with new departures in education. "By persevering in its present course the college has much to expect and nothing to fear: But by deserting the highroad which it has so long travelled, and wandering in lanes and bypaths, it would trifle with its prosperity, and put at hazard the very means of its support and existence." The trustees agreed with the faculty.

Public Schools

In 1826 New York's Governor DeWitt Clinton—already famous for starting the Erie Canal—gave the legislature of his state some advice on the subject of education: "The first duty, and the surest evidence of good government, is the encouragement of education. . . . I consider the system of our common schools as the palladium of our freedom for no reasonable apprehension can be entertained of its subversion so long as the great body of the people are enlightened by education." By 1860 the majority of states—except in the South—adopted the policy of public schools supported by general taxation. In Boston a new public high school for boys had been opened in 1821—and one also for girls, the first in the country in 1826. But as late as 1840 Massachusetts did not have more than twelve high schools, and this number was greater than in any other state. In 1860 Massachusetts had seventy-eight high schools, New York forty-one, and Ohio forty-eight.

The real work of educational reform began in 1837 when Massachusetts organized its first state Board of Education and appointed Horace Mann secretary. Originally a lawyer, Mann became the best-known educational reformer of his time. He found that one third of the children in the state had no chance at even an elementary school training. Mann went to work to raise money, to arouse interest in providing better facilities, and to induce the town meetings to spend money on their schools. Then he found there were too few well-trained teachers. To remedy this defect he established the first normal school in the United States in 1839 at Lexington. In 1845 Mann organized a state association of teachers. He helped to secure a new state law providing that all children under twelve years of age must spend at least six months of every year in school. Between 1837 and 1847 Massachusetts invested the substantial sum of $2,000,000 in school buildings; through Mann's efforts fifty new public high schools were started.

Up to this time the colleges in the country were privately endowed. In 1817 the territory of Michigan worked out a comprehensive plan of public education, beginning with primary schools and ending with a state university. Twenty years later, after Michigan was admitted to the Union, the state university became a reality. All the other western states sooner or later adopted similar plans.

Newspapers and the Lyceum

If the free public school is a necessity for all children in democratic governments, independent newspapers with honest, intelligent editors are equally necessary for adults. Before the days of radio, the newspaper was the only available means of keeping the citizens informed about the affairs of their government. During the period of the 1830's and 1840's American newspapers were transformed. Formerly, the primary purpose of the papers had been to print long essays on political subjects and very little current news. There were reports of the doings of Congress and the state legislatures, and there were bitter political articles, the kind of thing that most readers now would find very dull.

The first modern newspaper was the New York *Sun*. It was cheap, it was amusing, and it played up the sensational. Its editors worked on the principle that the readers wanted entertainment. But the *Sun* also printed fresh news. It introduced the editorial page, consisting of a series of short, vivid comments on public affairs or matters of general interest.

Among other up-to-date papers were the New York *Herald*, edited by James Gordon Bennett; the *Tribune*, made famous by Horace Greeley; and *The New York Times*, edited by Henry Raymond. These papers kept special correspondents in Washington to write full reports of the activities at the national capital. The *Herald* had the most alert reporters, but its editorial page, while breezy and readable, was not the equal of Greeley's in the *Tribune*. When the telegraph was made available in 1844 the newspapers were able to report widely scattered events all over the country. The new type of newspaper was not confined to New York. The *New Orleans Picayune* in the South and the *Springfield Republican* in New England are among the newspapers of the period which historians must use in trying to understand public opinion of that day.

Going further into the educational facilities of this period before the American Civil War, the student will run across numerous references to the lyceum, or public lecture. In almost every town people contributed money to hire famous men to come and talk to them. There were few great writers of the day who did not occasionally appear on the lyceum platform; some spoke hundreds of times. Theodore Parker, the famous antislavery clergyman of Boston, lectured all over New England, parts of New York, and Ohio. Edward Everett made himself famous with his lecture on "Washington and the Union." Henry Ward Beecher added to his fame as a pulpit orator by his work on the lyceum platform. This was a development which gave people in the smaller towns an opportunity to hear and see the men who were helping to form public opinion.

The Drive for a Moral Order

Evangelical Religion

During the 1830's the people of the northern part of the United States became deeply aroused over religious reform. The aims of the leaders were to improve the churches, to make the country better, to educate the people, and so to train a more desirable kind of citizen. This reforming zeal was most evident in New England, central New York, and Ohio. Here was a section with common hopes and ideals, and the leaders in the different states kept in touch with each other by means of an amazing volume of correspondence. Those who had money contributed to every good cause; others helped with speeches, writings, and prayers. The active agents in this work were the evangelical denominations, some new colleges, and many zealous individuals.

The genesis of the reform movement was religious in an evangelical, revivalistic sense. After 1800 "vital religion" with its "protracted meetings," long-drawn-out revivals, and "hopeful conversions" was a characteristic feature of the American scene. Central New York felt the impact with a revival beginning in Oneida in 1825 under the leadership of the young evangelist, Charles Grandison Finney. Spreading out from this section, it affected the whole area from New England to the Middle West.

One result of reforming zeal was manifested in theological disputes within the various religious denominations. These disputes resulted in the formation of numerous rival groups, offshoots of the parent churches. When for any reason a denominational organization failed of its purpose, the dissatisfied reformers would break away and start a new one. Each additional offshoot became another active agency for making the world better. For example, the list of Baptist denominations included the regular, orthodox, or "hardshell" Baptists, Seventh-Day Baptists, Free Baptists, Freewill Baptists, General Six-Principle Baptists, Two-Seed-in-the-Spirit Predestinarian Baptists, and some others. Methodists and Presbyterians divided in somewhat similar fashion.

This theological ferment produced a countermovement in the direction of religious unity, the very opposite of the process which threatened to split the denominations into fragments: this was the foundation of undenominational or antidenominational churches. As they moved away from sectarianism, these reformers called the fervent denominationalists anti-Christian. They would accept as members any who believed in Christ. By uniting all the faithful in each community into a single body, they hoped to work more effectively than ever for the regeneration of the country.

In New England the reform of the Congregational Church, which really dated back to the period of the Revolution, gave rise to the Unitarian movement. The old Calvinistic doctrines of predestination and infant damnation gave way to a more cheerful faith. According to the strictly orthodox believers, Unitarianism could not be described as a reform, because it denied one of the most fundamental beliefs of Christianity: the divinity of Christ. Its adherents, however, called it a "rational" faith, which attempted to separate true religion from superstition.

Latter-Day Saints

Mormons

Never before in the Christian era had there been so many different denominations; it was indeed a hard-to-please person who could neither find a place in one of them nor be content to remain quietly outside them all. But there were uneasy spirits who wanted a new religion. One new church founded at this time, 1830, was that of the Mormons or Latter-Day Saints. Its prophet and leader was Joseph Smith of Palmyra, New York. He published *The Book of Mormon,* the contents of which he claimed were miraculously revealed to him by the angel Moroni. In the course of a year the new prophet had 1000 converts, and their number increased rapidly. By 1844, when Smith was murdered, his followers numbered 15,000. Finding themselves persecuted in the states where they tried to settle—Ohio, Missouri, and Illinois—the main body of Mormons moved out to the region of the Great Salt Lake, then a part of Mexico, now in the state of Utah, the present home of their spiritual successors.

The Mormon settlement at Salt Lake City furnished an illustration of semisocialistic living. Roads, canals for irrigation, even freight service to the Missouri valley, were built and operated by the church. The members bought their supplies from the church store, and profits were used for the general welfare. To make the community independent of the outside world, the authorities planned to establish industries of all kinds, particularly woolen, cotton, and paper mills. Although actual development fell short of some of these hopes, the Mormon territory became prosperous.

Bibles and Tracts

Religious revivals were encouraged by three great organizations, the American Bible Society, the American Tract Society, and the American Sunday School Union, all of which kept up a continuous drive against the forces of sin. The Bible Society was evangelistic in aim; it undertook to provide every family with a copy of the Bible. When it celebrated its fourth anniversary, its president talked about "the delightful prospect opened up to us by the promulgation of the Gospel over the habitable earth."

But the Bible was expensive, so the reformers planned to supplement it with tracts. These little messages could be widely circulated at slight cost, and their distribution was held to be just as important as that of the Bible. "To my mind, no mode has yet been devised for diffusing religious knowledge, which proves as successful as tracts. They make their way into every class—into every occupation." So wrote one of the organizers of the New York Tract Society. In 1825 the American Tract Society was organized. At its first annual meeting, held in New York on May 10, 1826, its purpose was defined in the constitution: "to diffuse a knowledge of our Lord Jesus Christ as the Redeemer of sinners, and to promote the interests of vital godliness and sound morality, by the circulation of Religious Tracts, calculated to receive the approbation of all Evangelical Christians."

The Bible societies and the tract societies were organized for carrying on a continuous attack upon the wicked and their sins. The national organizations of these societies, their state organizations, and local branches in the counties, cities, and towns were all intimately tied in with the evangelical churches. It would be difficult to imagine a more effective device for keeping up a constant, inescapable drive upon the people. Then to make the network more complete and the religious influence still more pervasive, particularly among the children, religious reformers launched the Sunday School movement, with its own national organization: the American Sunday School Union. The Union was determined to establish Sunday Schools everywhere, and in 1827 it boasted of having over 400,000 children under regular instruction, with 60,000 teachers.

Temperance

Other earnest reformers began a drive against alcohol. Societies for the suppression of intemperance were formed in the eastern and middle states before 1820, but they did not become dynamic until the time of the great religious revival. In 1826 "the American Society for the Promotion of Temperance" was organized in Boston at the very time when the country was caught in the full sweep of evangelistic fervor. These advocates of temperance kept up a continuous attack upon their convivial neighbors and upon the men who made and sold them their drink.

For the reformers the traditional intimacy between liquor and the hotel business had long been a matter of deep regret, and some of the temperance men of the 1830's tried to break the alliance. They proposed to establish temperance taverns where the respectable traveler might put up, free from disturbing associations with the bar. The temperance hotel movement was one of a number of by-products of the campaign against liquor; it probably never had the support of a majority of the temperance men, but it was indicative of the extremes to which some reformers were running. Further evidence of this propensity for going to extremes is to be found in the following letter: "I have got beyond Temperance to the 'Cold Water Society'—no Tea, Coffee or any other slops—only pure Water to drink and coarse fare to eat."

In 1840 a new and unexpected impetus was given to the cause of temperance by the formation of the Washington Temperance Society at Baltimore. This new organization, started and largely carried on by reformed drunkards, spread over the country with surprising rapidity. It was customary for groups of "reformed inebriates" to hold temperance meetings for the purpose of winning new converts. In 1846 Maine adopted the first state law to prohibit the sale of liquor for beverage purposes, and in the course of the next ten years twelve more states followed her example. Partly because of difficulties of enforcement most of these measures were repealed. Before the close of the Civil War all the states but Maine, New Hampshire, and Vermont had abandoned this type of restriction.

The antitobacco movement never gained the headway of the antialcohol crusade, although it did inspire some interesting literature. Unhampered by limitations of exact knowledge and swept along by the zeal of their day, the enemies of smoking would go to any length of misstatement or absurdity. The same spirit of robust righteousness was carried over into the realm of dietic reform. During the 1830's Sylvester Graham, whose name has become synonymous with whole wheat flour, was the most conspicuous figure in this work. *The Graham Journal of Health and Longevity,* published in Boston by David Campbell, made its appearance in 1837. It was dedicated to the improvement of health through better diet.

While the more ambitious of these social prophets aimed at the regeneration of mankind as a whole, others limited their efforts to selected groups. There were organizations for helping the underprivileged. Among these was the American Bethel Society, organized in 1846 to provide religious instruction and moral guidance for workers on the eastern canals, particularly those in New York. It was associated with the Western Seamens Friend Society, which conducted similar work along the thousand miles of canals in Ohio, Pennsylvania, and Indiana.

Women's Rights

The issue of women's rights, including the demand for suffrage, became important during the 1850's, particularly with the work of Lucy Stone, Elizabeth Cady Stanton, and Susan B. Anthony. Premonitions of this new reform came in the 1830's, with particular reference to women's dress. The objective was greater simplicity. The most famous advocate of dress reform was Amelia Bloomer, of Seneca Falls, New York. Beginning in 1848 she published a semimonthly journal known as *The Lily*. In a printed circular describing her enterprise, Miss Bloomer promised to

> . . . labor zealously and earnestly for the emancipation of Woman from the crushing evils of Intemperance—from the cruel enactments of unjust laws made without her consent—from the destructive influences of Custom and Fashion—from mistaken views of duty and personal effort, and for her elevation to her true position in society of perfect and entire equality in all that relates to her social, civil and religious rights and duties.

With more than becoming modesty the subscription price was placed at 50 cents per year.

One more reform remains to be listed. On May 8, 1828, the American Peace Society was organized in New York "to illustrate the inconsistency of war with Christianity, to show its baleful influence on all the great interests of mankind, and to devise means for insuring universal and permanent peace." The new organization would bring peace by applying the principles of the gospel to international relations.

The Rise of the Abolitionists

To some of the more earnest advocates of social betterment, the reforms just described were merely incidental because they dealt with evils of second-rate importance. The greatest evil of the day, so they said, was slavery, therefore the greatest reform movement was abolitionism. There was logic in their position. If one were called upon to provide an all-absorbing cause for reformers, an issue which would stir them to their very depths, it would be hard to invent anything better for the purpose than slavery. Looked at from the outside and from a distance—and few abolitionists had any real, firsthand acquaintance with the institution—slavery seemed to represent the negation of every sound principle both of American democracy and of the Christian religion. As an institution it possessed an abundance of material for effective dramatization, especially in the hands of those endowed with vivid imaginations and slight regard for truth. The abolitionist picture was something like this: Man, fashioned in the image of God, was beaten by a brutal overseer, forcibly torn from his wife and children, denied the advantages of education and the protection of the law, and compelled to labor against his will. These and other woes of the slave furnished the abolitionists with material for masses of vivid newspaper stuff and for countless thundering speeches. Once the antislavery movement was well under way, other reforms did seem insignificant.

Antislavery

There had been antislavery societies before 1830. Some of the Quakers in Pennsylvania had organized one in 1775. By 1823 there were similar organizations in nine other states, six of which were in the South. By 1830 there were probably a hundred antislavery organizations. In 1816 a group of reformers founded the American Society for the Colonization of the Free People of Color of the United States. The Colonization Society planned to solve the Negro problem by shipping free Negroes to Africa. The society founded Liberia, named its capital Monrovia, in honor of President Monroe, and then looked for colonists. But in the course of ten years the Society sent only 1162 Negroes to Liberia.

During the late 1820's there was a diminution of intensity in this antislavery movement. Then suddenly it received a powerful new impetus from an obscure journalist in Boston, William Lloyd Garrison. Garrison had worked for a time with Benjamin Lundy, publisher of *The Genius of Universal Emancipation,* an antislavery paper of Baltimore. On January 1, 1831, Garrison published the first number of *The Liberator*. One reading of this issue was enough to convince anybody that the editor was a master of invective. He proclaimed his purpose in these burning words:

Garrison's "Liberator"

I shall strenuously contend for the immediate enfranchisement of our slave population—I *will be* as harsh as truth and as uncompromising as justice on this subject—I do not wish to think, or speak, or write with moderation—I am in earnest—I will not equivocate—I will not excuse—I will not retreat a single inch, and I *will be heard*.

Garrison believed that slavery was "a damning crime." With that relentless logic which is one of the chief attributes of the genuine crusader, he concluded that every slaveowner was a criminal. Concerning the Southerners he wrote:

We would sooner trust the honor of the country and the liberties of the people in the hands of the inmates of our penitentiaries and prisons, than in their hands, for safe keeping. . . . They ought not to be allowed seats in Congress. No political, no religious co-partnership should be had with them, for they are the meanest of thieves, and the worst of robbers. We should as soon think of entering into a "compact" with the convicts at Botany Bay and New Zealand . . . we do not acknowledge them to be within the pale of Christianity, of republicanism, or humanity.

American Anti-Slavery Society

In the same year, 1831, which first saw *The Liberator,* there was an uprising of slaves in Virginia, known as Nat Turner's rebellion. The Virginia legislature had an important debate on the morality of slavery. Again in this pivotal year leaders in northern Ohio, "the western reserve," launched a vigorous antislavery movement in that section. On December 4, 1833, a national antislavery convention met at Philadelphia, to organize the American Anti-Slavery Society. There were sixty delegates present from ten states. Among the most conspicuous delegates were Beriah Green of Whitesboro, New York, who presided; Arthur and Lewis Tappan of New York; William Lloyd Garrison; and the famous poet, John G. Whittier.

The temper and purpose of the new national society were defined in commissions issued to agents sent to win adherents in the various states:

Our object is, the overthrow of American slavery, the most atrocious and oppressive system of bondage that has ever existed in any country. We expect to accomplish this, mainly by showing to the public its true character and legitimate fruits, its contrariety to the first principles of religion, morals, and humanity, and its special inconsistency with our pretensions, as a free, humane, and enlightened people. . . . Insist principally on the "Sin of Slavery," because our main hope is in the consciences of men.

This American Anti-Slavery Society was upheld and supported by a large number of local and state societies: in 1835 these numbered about 200, but by 1840 there were 2000, with a total membership of 175,000. These organizations held meetings, listened to speakers, subscribed to antislavery newspapers, and did their best to inspire hatred of slavery.

It is impossible to find out how many genuine abolitionists there were in the North, but it is safe to say that before 1854 they were a small minority. Garrison's famous paper, *The Liberator,* never had a circulation of more than 1400 copies per week. *The Liberator* was the most outspoken of all the antislavery periodicals and it was widely quoted in the South, but it did not have a wide influence. Throughout the North and West there were altogether about seventy antislavery papers. In 1853 the most widely distributed of all of them, the *National Era,* had a weekly circulation of 28,000 copies. One of the editors of the *Era* was John Greenleaf Whittier.

Abolitionist Threats against the Union

Even though the abolitionists were in the minority, they stirred up a tremendous amount of bitter feeling. Many Northerners criticized them, notably businessmen who had customers in the South and political leaders who tried to encourage cordial relations between the two sections. Daniel Webster declared that the abolitionists accomplished nothing good or useful. **Divided Opinions**

By 1835 bitterness between the abolitionists and the slaveowners had gone so far that one of the agitators in New York, Gerrit Smith, actually called the contest a civil war:

> It is not to be disguised, that a war has broken out between the North and the South. Political and commercial men are industriously striving to restore peace: but the peace, which they would effect, is superficial, false, and temporary. True, permanent peace can never be restored, until slavery, the occasion of the war, has ceased.

As early as 1836 some Southerners were predicting that abolitionism, if continued, would result in open warfare between the sections. Almost precisely the same theory was expressed in the same year by Charles Grandison Finney, the evangelist of Oberlin: "We are in our present course going fast into a civil war. . . . Will not our present movements in abolition result in that? . . . Nothing is more manifest to me than that the present movement will result in this, unless your mode of abolitionizing the country be greatly modified." The only hope, as Finney saw it, was to make abolition "an appendge [*sic*] of a general revival of religion." Then he expressed his opinion of the abolitionists. Some were good men, "but there are but few of them *wise* men. Some of them are reckless. Others are so denunciatory as to kill all prayer about it. There is very little confidence and concert among many of our abolitionists."

A well-known northern lawyer and Congressman, Daniel Cady of New York, father of Elizabeth Cady Stanton, wrote practically the same thing; he could not convince himself that "preaching at the north will benefit the slaves at the south." Then he gave his views on the problem:

> When the whites at the south shall become truly pious and enlightened Christians slavery will be stripped of all its evils or cease to exist—and until a majority of the whites become Christians in the slave states, slavery will continue unless abolished by force—or unless slave labor should become unprofitable. I go for slavery rather than a civil war—and I have less faith in the conversion

of the white population of the south, than I have that machines worked by steam and electricity will yet be invented to work the level lands of the south and render slave labor unproductive—I cannot therefore be supposed to have much confidence in the speedy abolition of slavery.

These earnest workers for emancipation might have made a more pleasing impression if they had not quarreled among themselves, but some of them came to hate Garrison even more than they hated slavery. Lewis Tappan of New York described Garrison as "The Massachusetts Madman." And again Tappan wrote: "I loathe the spirit that comes from the east. Our organization is a stench in the nostrils of the nation, and the approaching meeting will increase it." Having reached the point where neither faction could think of the other without throwing all semblance of ordinary politeness and decent manners to the winds, Garrison and Tappan, with their cohorts, proceeded to part company. Their schism resulted in a division in the American Anti-Slavery Society. But Garrison had no intention of withdrawing; on the contrary he prepared for the coming seventh anniversary meeting of May 1840 by chartering a steamer and offering a free ride to New York to anybody who would go in the guise of a delegate from Massachusetts. Thanks to this foresight he turned up at the convention with some 550 "delegates," out of a total of 1008. The Garrisonian principles of women's rights, nonresistance, and antipolitical action were then endorsed by the majority, and the American Anti-Slavery Society became Garrison's instrument.

Threats of Secession

The most important difference between the Garrisonian and the non-Garrisonian abolitionists was in the matter of voting. Non-Garrisonians believed that opposition to slavery should not prevent a man from taking part in ordinary politics. Garrison argued that because the American Constitution permitted slavery, the whole system of government was necessarily bad. Therefore Garrison and his followers took no part in elections.

Garrison's next step was to advocate the separation of the free states from the slave states, and after 1842 this became one of his major policies. To his mind both the Union and the Constitution on which it rested ought to be destroyed because both sanctioned slavery. "We affirm the Union is not of heaven," he thundered in *The Liberator*. "It is a horrible mockery of freedom. In all its parts and proportions it is misshapen, incongruous, unnatural."

In 1843 he wrote the following statement and used it as the motto of *The Liberator:* "Resolved, That the compact [the Constitution] which exists between the North and the South is 'a covenant with death and an agreement with hell'—involving both parties in atrocious criminality—and should be immediately annulled." In 1844 Wendell Phillips, one of Garrison's associates, submitted the following resolution at the annual meeting of the American Anti-Slavery Society, and the resolution was adopted: *"Resolved,* That secession from the present United States Government is the duty of every abolitionist; since no one can take office under the United States Constitution without violating his anti-slavery principles, and rendering himself an abetter of the slaveholder in his sin."

Not all the abolitionists refused to vote or advocated secession from the Union. They agreed with Garrison in his hatred of slavery but they could see no wisdom in breaking up the country. Even if the northern states should withdraw, slavery would be more securely established in the South than ever. The thing to do, they insisted, was to keep up the attack upon slavery and to use the power of the federal government as an aid in the attack.

Southern Response to Abolitionism

In the South, political leaders and newspapers voiced the general resentment against Garrison's attacks upon the South and its "peculiar institution." They vehemently denied that slaveowners were habitually cruel and abusive. Southerners were just as good citizens and just as good Christians as the best people in the North. They treated their slaves well, as humane, kindly men should. From their point of view the real danger to the welfare of the United States came not from slavery but from the abolitionists who were doing their best to arouse sectional strife. There were some southerners who went as far in their direction as Garrison went in his. They would not vote in national elections and they would not hold federal office because to do so would amount to association with the criminal abolitionists. But the majority of the southern leaders preferred to work through Congress and to protect their rights through the national government.

Federal Government and Abolition

With representatives from both the proslavery and antislavery groups present at every session, Congress sometimes became the scene of bitter disputes. For several years moderate abolitionists who still recognized the national government sent petitions to Congress asking for laws against slavery. Although the Constitution guaranteed the right of petition, proslavery representatives objected to having these particular ones debated. They would vote to lay them on the table. Then in 1840 the proslavery majority was strong enough to force through the "gag rule" which made it unnecessary for Congress even to receive antislavery petitions. After a dispute lasting four years, northern representatives, led by John Quincy Adams, mustered strength enough to repeal the rule.

In view of the character of Garrison's attacks upon the southerners, they could hardly be blamed for trying to keep his journal from their homes. They did not want to read it themselves and still less did they want their slaves to see it. To be sure, not many of the slaves were able to read, but a single rebellious spirit on a plantation might cause serious trouble. During Jackson's administration some southern people complained to the postmaster general because abolitionist papers and literature were being sent through the mails. He replied that he could not order the local postmasters to refuse to deliver such mail, but he would take no action in case the postmasters themselves should refuse to deliver it. In this way the South protected itself against "dangerous" literature.

In 1840 a comparatively few abolitionists organized the Liberty party and nominated James G. Birney as the candidate for the presidency. But this was the very year of the division of the antislavery forces into two main groups, so there was little prospect of uniting even all the abolitionists on a single ticket. In the election Birney received 7069 votes in the country at large, out of a total of 2,411,185. In 1844 Birney ran again, this time receiving 62,300 votes, out of a total of 2,698,605.

Abolitionist Influence

In 1852 the *National Era* brought out Harriet Beecher Stowe's *Uncle Tom's Cabin* in serial form; the story was subsequently published in book form. In the very first year the publishers sold a million copies. This phenomenal sale might be regarded as an index to the strength of abolitionism—or a tribute to the popularity of a new American writer. Or again it is possible that Mrs. Stowe's absorbing novel created more abolitionists than all the antislavery journals combined. Regardless of its literary merits or shortcomings, the book was an astounding piece of antislavery propaganda.

One other aspect of the abolitionist movement needs to be mentioned. This was the "underground railway," the system by means of which fugitive slaves could be transported from place to place through the North until they found refuge in Canada. In so far as there was any centralized management for the work, it was handled by the Vigilance Committee of New York City. This branch of the antislavery organization, consisting of about 100 members, was created on November 20, 1835, to protect free Negroes from kidnapers or from anybody, official or unofficial, who might try to return northern Negroes to slavery. The committee furnished legal advice for Negroes arrested and threatened with servitude; incidentally it was just as ready to help fugitive slaves as bona fide freedmen. During the first year of its existence, the Vigilance Committee saved about 300 persons, fugitives and otherwise, from being carried into slavery. Abolitionists provided the fugitives with shelter and food and sometimes helped them move from place to place. While there was no specific line followed, there were several possible routes. One went from Cincinnati northward to Lake Erie. Another came up through central New York to Oswego or farther west to Rochester on Lake Ontario.

It is difficult today to explain satisfactorily either the origin or the driving power that made the abolitionist movement so bitterly dynamic. What force drove Garrison to keep up for thirty years that flood of vituperation, and of passionate, seditious appeals for disunion which characterized *The Liberator?* The person who could answer this question to the satisfaction of the psychologist could also tell why Wendell Phillips turned his back upon his traditions, social surroundings, and friends to aid Garrison, and why Theodore Parker, the clergyman, could preach the doctrine of violence and pride himself upon his success in breaking the laws of his country.

It is not enough to say simply that these men were so moved by the wickedness of slavery that they were compelled to work for its destruction. They knew nothing of slavery at first hand because not one of them had ever seen a plantation. Furthermore, slavery had been an American institution for over 200 years when Garrison came along, and never before the nineteenth century had there been such an extraordinary outcry against it as Garrison launched in *The Liberator*. Probably the extreme abolitionists were driven on by emotions stimulated by causes largely within themselves. They happened to be abolitionists because that reform was attracting attention in the section where they lived. It is a fair assumption that if they had been raised in South Carolina or Alabama, they would have been as active proponents of slavery as John C. Calhoun or William L. Yancy.

The controversy colored public life, affecting both politics and actions of the government. Congress found it increasingly difficult to discuss any question, no matter what, on the merits of the case. The first consideration was always, How would the matter affect slavery? Some economic historians have argued that, left to itself, slavery would have died naturally. They hold that even before the Civil War slave labor had ceased to be profitable in the border states and that it was becoming less profitable in the lower South. Once it became a source of actual loss, the planters would have to run away from their slaves to avoid the expense of supporting them. This opinion makes one wonder whether the abolitionists were not attacking the problem in the wrong way.

Chapter 20

TERRITORIAL EXPANSION

Manifest Destiny in Texas

NEITHER Jacksonian politics nor the drive for moral reform had interrupted the continuous American drive toward the West. By 1819 this movement had carried the cotton planters across the lower South from Georgia to Louisiana, but in that very year the federal government took action which might have interfered with any further advance. The Florida Purchase Treaty surrendered the American claim to Texas and named the Sabine River as the western boundary of "the cotton kingdom." Perhaps expansion should have stopped there, but an international frontier is an artificial barrier, especially so when a broad unoccupied expanse of fertile land lies on the other side. American pioneers were ready to cross the border and to settle in Mexico.

Americans in Texas

The history of Mexico as an independent nation was a story of revolutions—eight in eighteen years. In 1824 the Mexicans had adopted a federal constitution, based largely upon that of the United States. The first president remained in office for the full term of four years. There were revolutions in 1828, 1829, and again in 1832, the last of which brought Santa Anna into power. During this interval the government could neither maintain order at home nor fulfill its obligations abroad.

In 1820, only a year after the Florida Treaty was signed, Moses Austin, formerly of Connecticut and afterward of Missouri, asked the Spanish governor of Texas for a grant of land large enough to provide farms for 300 American families. In June 1821 Austin heard that his request had been approved. He died before he could take advantage of his good fortune, but his son Stephen F. Austin planned to occupy the grant. The Spanish authorities dealt generously with Austin. He could establish his colony wherever he chose in Texas, with as much land as he might need at no cost. His colonists must be persons of good character, willing to become Roman Catholics, and they must take an oath of allegiance to the Spanish government. In 1822 Mexico became independent, and Austin went to Mexico City to ask the new rulers for a confirmation of his title.

At this time Mexico wanted settlers from the United States and offered surprisingly liberal terms to any who would come. On January 1, 1823, the new Mexican government enacted a colonization law, providing for gifts of land either to individuals for their own use or to founders of colonies in Texas. A cotton planter might have 177 acres, and a cattle raiser 4428 acres. The head of a colony would receive for himself 360 acres of tillable land or 66,000 acres of grazing land. There were additional inducements in the way of exemption from taxes and import duties.

Reports of this measure and of a second equally liberal one passed in 1824 encouraged thousands of Americans to flock into Texas. New cotton land in the United States cost $1.25 an acre; in Texas it cost nothing. By 1825 7000 immigrants from the United States had settled in Texas and by 1830 the number had increased to 20,000. The Mexicans had wanted colonists and had urgently invited them to come. This tidal wave of settlers, however, was more than the authorities had expected, and they became alarmed, fearing that Texas would become an American province. After the damage had been done, the Mexicans tried to undo it. In 1827, following a small insurrection of some American colonists in Mexico, the Mexican government issued orders prohibiting further American immigration. This order was not enforced. In 1830, Mexico made more determined efforts. Troops were ordered to enforce Mexican regulations, recently arrived immigrants were expelled, and prospective settlers were stopped at the border. At the same time, the Mexican authorities themselves planned to colonize Texas.

Texan Rebellion

In 1833 Santa Anna became president of Mexico. It would have been difficult to find any Mexican temperamentally less fitted to deal with the Texans than he. Ambitious, selfish, unscrupulous, cruel, and vindictive, he thought of political office in terms of absolute power and financial return. For a time Santa Anna permitted some relaxation in the policy of repressing the Texans. In 1835, however, he became even more severe than his predecessors. Declaring himself dictator, he overthrew the constitution. He destroyed the rights of the states and placed them under governors appointed by himself. Next he announced that the militia should be reduced to the proportion of one man for every 500 in the population, and he ordered all inhabitants not enrolled in the militia to give up their arms. Compliance with this arrangement would have left American settlers at the mercy of the Indians and of the Mexicans recently sent into Texas. These new decrees made rebellion inevitable. Early in 1836 the Texans declared their independence and established a republic. War followed, and Santa Anna invaded Texas to suppress the rebellion. He announced that all foreigners who took up arms against him would be executed.

For a time these developments attracted little attention in the United States. Before the latter part of 1835 Texas was hardly mentioned in American newspapers. Nevertheless some inhabitants of New Orleans did become interested. They raised money and military forces to aid the Texans. Before the end of 1835 Americans in Mississippi and in Kentucky engaged in the same work. Then public meetings in widely separated cities—Baltimore, Washington, Cincinnati, Boston, and Philadelphia—passed resolutions of sympathy with the Texans. During the winter of 1835-36 three commissioners from Texas traveled from New Orleans to Washington, where, unofficially, they received "the most marked attention." Americans bought bonds of the new republic, and they gambled in Texas "scrip," paper money with theoretical landed security behind it.

The government at Washington maintained a policy of strict neutrality. The London *Times,* it is true, charged that the rebellion in Texas "was known, watched, and encouraged by the Cabinet of the day at Washington." Mexicans made the same charges. But available evidence proves that President Jackson and the State Department were meticulously careful in observing the proprieties. Federal district attorneys were warned to prevent any violation of neutrality. Even the British consul at Matamoras reported that he could find no evidence of help given by the federal government and that federal attorneys prosecuted every case of violation of the neutrality laws.

Lone Star Republic

The Mexican government was not strong enough to conquer the rebels, but Santa Anna undertook an invasion and by March 1836 had reached San Antonio. The Texan defenders, only 188 strong, shut themselves in an old chapel made over into a fort, the Alamo, and held off 2400 Mexicans for a week. Every man of the defending army was killed. At the near-by town of Goliad the Mexicans had collected nearly 500 Texan prisoners, captured by various Mexican forces. Santa Anna ordered the whole lot executed. On March 27, 1836, which happened to be Palm Sunday, the Mexicans shot one group of 300; then the Mexicans dragged out fifty wounded prisoners and murdered them. After this massacre at Goliad Santa Anna resumed his slow progress toward the Sabine. By mid-April he had reached the San Jacinto River, two thirds of the distance across Texas. Santa Anna believed that resistance had collapsed and he became careless. On the 21st General Sam Houston and the Texan army closed in for a totally unexpected attack. The Mexicans lost 630 killed, 730 prisoners, and 208 wounded, over half their army. The Texans lost 2 men killed and 23 wounded. On the next morning some Texan scouts found Santa Anna himself hiding in the grass. They brought him into camp, alive, and Houston took full advantage of his captive. He insisted that Santa Anna order his few remaining troops out of Texas. The dictator obeyed.

On May 14, 1836, still a prisoner, Santa Anna signed two treaties. In the first he agreed to end the war and to send all Mexican forces beyond the Rio Grande; in the second he promised so to arrange matters at Mexico City that Mexico would recognize Texan independence and settle the boundary line. The Texans agreed not to demand territory beyond the Rio Grande. By these two treaties the Texans won their objectives in the war. Subsequently Santa Anna admitted that he had no intention of complying with these treaties; he had signed them merely to save his own skin. The Mexican Congress announced that they would pay no attention to "any stipulations with the enemy which the President while imprisoned has made or may make, which stipulations shall be regarded as null, void and of no effect." Still later the Mexican minister at Washington made a similar statement.

The officials of the Lone Star Republic desired annexation to the United States, and they sent an agent to Washington to make the necessary arrangements. Pending annexation Texas was a sovereign power. The Jackson administration was not prepared to annex Texas, but Congress authorized the President to open diplomatic relations with the new neighbor. On March 3, 1837, Jackson appointed a minister to Texas. Recognition by France followed in 1839 and by England in 1842. Mexico, however, refused to follow these examples.

Annexation of Texas

The British had interests in Texas and hopes for the future. If the Republic should remain independent and if its government should adopt a policy of free trade, Texas could contribute to the economic prosperity of Great Britain. As the population increased there would be a profitable market for British manufactured goods. Texas could supply British cotton mills with raw cotton, so England would become progressively less dependent upon the United States. Then, too, some Englishmen were playing—not officially—with the idea of a new empire to include not only Texas but California and a generous section of the intervening region. In 1843 Lord Aberdeen urged Mexico to recognize the independence of Texas; if she would do so, "England will oppose the annexation of Texas" to the United States.

President Tyler favored annexation, and in October 1841 he suggested that Webster, his secretary of state, look into the matter. John Quincy Adams, then chairman of the House Foreign Relations Committee, came out strongly against annexation. Some abolitionists professed to believe that the Texan rebellion had been inspired by proslavery interests in the United States for the express purpose of bringing more slave states into the Union. Benjamin Lundy described the war for Texan independence as a "crusade against Mexico, set on foot and supported by slaveholders, land-speculators &c., in order to re-establish, extend, and perpetuate the system of slavery and the slave trade." Lundy had considerable influence with John Quincy Adams.

In spite of this opposition President Tyler went ahead with plans for annexation. In April 1844 a treaty for this purpose was signed. Just then another Presidential campaign was ready to open. The Whigs met in convention on May 1, 1844, and nominated their old leader Henry Clay. The platform was silent on the subject of Texas, but a few days before the convention Clay had come out strongly against annexation, calling the proposal "perfectly idle and ridiculous, if not dishonorable." On the very same day Van Buren, the leading Democratic candidate, also published a letter opposing annexation.

The Democrats met on May 27, 1844. Discarding Van Buren, chiefly because he opposed annexation, they chose James K. Polk of Tennessee. He had already put himself on record as favoring "the immediate re-annexation of Texas to . . . the United States." The Democratic platform clearly defined the attitude of the party: *"Resolved,* That our title to the whole of the territory of Oregon is clear and unquestionable; that no portion of the same ought to be ceded to England or any other power; and that the re-occupation of Oregon and the re-annexation of Texas at the earliest practicable period are great American measures."

On June 8, less than two weeks after the Democratic convention's emphatic demand for Texas, the United States Senate rejected the treaty of annexation. The adverse vote was due largely to the leadership of Henry Clay. His friends in the Senate voted against the treaty. So too did a few Democratic followers of Van Buren. These activities combined to make annexation the leading issue in the Presidential campaign, and Polk, the advocate of annexation, carried the election.

After the election the annexationists in Congress arranged to bring Texas into the United States by means of a joint resolution. They had been unable to secure the necessary two-thirds vote to ratify a treaty, but they could command the mere majority in each house requisite for a joint resolution. This arrangement provided for the admission of Texas on the following terms: Boundary questions were to be adjusted by the United States government; Texas was to cede to the United States all public buildings, ports, and harbors, and to retain both debts and public lands; with the consent of the inhabitants, additional states might be formed out of Texas. The measure passed with little difficulty, and Tyler signed it on March 1, 1845, just three days before he left office. The Texans approved, and in December 1845 Texas was admitted to the Union. The annexationists justified their policy on the ground that Texas had maintained her independence for nine years in spite of Mexican attempts at reconquest. Texan rights to independence were as good as Mexico's; both rested on revolution.

Oregon and California

A year after the annexation of Texas, the United States and Great Britain reached a satisfactory settlement of the Oregon question. This was the region lying between the Rocky Mountains and the Pacific and bounded on the north and south by the parallels 42° and 54° 40′. Spain had originally claimed the whole Pacific coast, but she never settled north of California. Russia at one time claimed the coast as far south as San Francisco, and in 1821 as far as the 51st parallel. England had a claim to the territory, based on the Nootka Sound Convention of 1790 signed by England and Spain. The claims of the United States dated back to 1792, when Captain Gray had explored a part of the Columbia River. In 1803-05 Lewis and Clark, sent out by Jefferson to look over the Louisiana Purchase, followed the Columbia toward its mouth. In 1811 John Jacob Astor, a New York fur merchant, founded Astoria in what is now Oregon. Although the British captured this trading post during the War of 1812, the Treaty of Ghent restored it to the United States. By the Florida Treaty of 1819, Spain surrendered all her rights north of California to the United States. Left in joint possession, the United States and Great Britain had not been able to agree upon a

Oregon Territory

division of the territory. In 1818 the two governments signed a treaty providing for joint occupation for ten years. During that time subjects of both powers were to be free to use the territory on equal terms. In 1824 the Russians relinquished their claims to any of the region south of 54° 40′. In 1826 Great Britain and the United States renewed negotiations for a division of the territory. The United States suggested the extension of the 49th parallel, but the British refused to agree. The following year the arrangement for joint occupation was continued indefinitely, with the understanding that it might be terminated by either party on one year's notice.

During this period the British government left Oregon to the Hudson's Bay Company. Under its auspices widely separated fur-trading posts were established and no settlement of any kind was permitted within 100 miles of any of these stations. In 1836 some American missionaries, H. H. Spaulding and Marcus Whitman, began work among the Oregon Indian tribes. Next, Senator Lewis F. Linn of Missouri introduced a bill providing for a line of forts from Missouri to Oregon and for the grant of a whole section of land to every male emigrant eighteen years of age or over. In 1843 this Linn Bill passed the Senate, by a vote of 24 to 22, but the House failed to pass it. Confidently expecting that it would go through, 1000 pioneers moved into the territory in 1843. By that time American interest in Oregon was developing, and the slogan of "fifty-four forty or fight" became popular. Although President Polk had been inclined to favor the "whole of Oregon," he authorized Secretary of State Buchanan to renew the offer of a division at the 49th parallel. The British minister refused to negotiate on this basis. Polk then advised Congress to permit him to give the necessary one year's notice for terminating the joint agreement.

Congress complied with Polk's request, and due notice was transmitted to the British government. Then the British found it expedient to meet Polk halfway. In June 1846 the British minister in Washington submitted the draft of a treaty, providing for the 49th parallel to the strait, but giving Vancouver to Great Britain. The treaty was signed, and the Senate ratified, by a vote of 41 to 14. Oregon was organized as a free territory.

California and New Mexico

During the early 1840's Americans had their eye on California and also on the wide expanse known as New Mexico. In 1845 California was not entirely empty, but empty enough to leave ample room for new arrivals. Spanish colonists from Mexico had founded mission stations there to convert the Indians to Christianity. They were followed by farmers and cattlemen. There were probably never more than 6000 Mexicans in the province. They sold local products, chiefly hides, to foreign trading ships which came to San Francisco and San Diego in violation of Spanish law. In 1842 the American minister to Mexico wrote Webster that Mexico might possibly be persuaded to sell California to the United States and that he had a high regard for the province. "As to Texas, I regard it as of very little value compared with California, the richest, the most beautiful, and the healthiest country in the world." Webster expressed interest in the prospect, but an unfortunate episode so enraged the Mexicans against the United States that the matter had to be dropped. On October 19, 1842, an American naval officer, Commodore Jones, heard a rumor that war had broken out between the United States and Mexico. He promptly seized Monterey, the Spanish capital of California, and raised the American flag. The next day, on discovering the report was false, he hauled down the flag, apologized, and withdrew. The Mexicans resented his act and refused to consider any proposal for selling California to the United States.

In the meantime, other people were looking at California. A year before Jones's exploit at Monterey, the English minister in Mexico urged his government to make California a part of the British Empire. Mexico was certain to lose control over it soon, he insisted, and His Majesty's government ought to prevent it from falling into the hands of any power but England. It took little gossip to create the belief that England was bent on organizing a great colony including Texas, New Mexico, and California. President Polk treated some of this talk seriously.

In June 1845 the small group of Americans in California declared the territory independent and prepared to fight Mexico as the Texans had done. This was the beginning of the "Bear Flag Revolt." It happened that Captain John C. Frémont of the United States Army was then in California, looking over the country. He had no lawful right to be on Mexican soil, but legal formalities carried little weight on the frontier. The "Bear Flag" rebels invited him to lead their enterprise, and he accepted, thereby giving Mexico another grievance against the United States.

With Texas and California both drawn within the range of interest of the United States, the intervening province of New Mexico could not entirely escape attention. This was an agricultural settlement with no mining and no industries. Down to 1821 it had no connections with the United States. In that year, however, regular trade was started between Santa Fé and St. Louis. Since there were not more than 40,000 inhabitants in the whole colony, this looked like another field for the operation of "manifest destiny." There was no rebellion of American pioneers here as there had been in the other two Mexican outposts, but none was necessary. New Mexico was to become one of the spoils of war.

Polk and Mexico

When President Tyler began to work for the annexation of Texas, Santa Anna had warned him that such a step would bring grave consequences: "The Mexican government will consider equivalent to a declaration of war against the Mexican Republic the passage of an act for the incorporation of Texas into the territory of the United States; the certainty of the fact being sufficient for the immediate proclamation of war." This was in August 1843. After Congress had passed the joint resolution for annexing Texas, the Mexican minister at Washington referred to it as "an act of aggression the

Mexican Threats of War

most unjust which can be found in the annals of modern history." With this parting shot, on March 6, 1845, he broke off diplomatic relations and went home. Mexican newspapers assumed that a state of war existed. The Mexican Congress passed measures for increasing the army in order to resist annexation, and the administration advised a declaration of war just as soon as the process of annexation should be completed. From the city of Mexico the American consul reported: "War with the United States seems to be the desire of all parties rather than to see Texas annexed." Such was the situation which Polk had inherited from his predecessor.

There were other difficulties, in addition to Texas, which made for ill feeling between the two governments. Various American citizens were clamoring for the payment of claims against Mexico. These were based upon property destroyed or seized and upon lives lost. A joint commission had been at work in an attempt to decide just how much Mexico owed on this account. Claims amounting to $2,000,000 had been declared valid, and there were at least as many more which had not been adjusted. On her side Mexico had a grievance against the United States on account of help given to Texans by private citizens from across the border. The dispute over the boundary between Texas and Mexico also caused trouble. Mexico claimed everything between the Rio Grande and the Sabine. The Texans, on the other hand, claimed the Rio Grande as their border, and Santa Anna had recognized this claim in the treaty of 1836—which he subsequently repudiated.

In June 1845 Polk sent General Zachary Taylor to Texas, with orders to advance to a point on or near the Rio Grande but to refrain from any action, except defensive, unless Mexico formally declared war. In January 1846, ordered to occupy a point on the Rio Grande, Taylor moved to Point Isabel, nearly opposite Matamoras. Shortly afterward the Mexican government, for the first time, named the Neuces as the boundary between Mexico and Texas.

Slidell's Mission

In spite of the unfavorable outlook, Polk tried to avoid war. He wanted to collect the claims which were due and to secure an agreement concerning the Texas boundary. More important still, he wanted a representative at Mexico City to be on the watch for possible European intrigue in New Mexico and California. However, the most important considerations in Polk's mind were his large ideas regarding territorial expansion. With the unanimous approval of his Cabinet, he was prepared to buy California and New Mexico—and to pay as high as $40,000,000.

Polk's first aim, therefore, was to renew diplomatic intercourse with Mexico City. In March 1845, less than a month after the Mexican minister had left Washington, Polk sent an unofficial agent to find out whether Mexico would receive a representative from the United States. In making these advances Polk informed the Mexicans that the annexation of Texas was a closed issue, not open for discussion. In October 1845 the Mexican government committed itself in these words:

Although the Mexican nation is deeply injured by the United States, through the acts committed by them in the department of Texas, which belongs to this nation, my government is disposed to receive the commissioner of the United States, who may come to the capital with full powers from his government to settle the dispute in a peaceable, reasonable, and honorable manner.

Polk's Cabinet agreed with him as to the desirability of resuming diplomatic relations and approved Polk's choice of a minister, John Slidell of New Orleans. Slidell's instructions were first to re-establish friendly relations between the two governments and then to take up the subject of claims. They might be settled by a cession of Mexican territory to the United States. Polk suggested that, if this could be done without endangering the success of his mission, Slidell try to purchase Upper California and New Mexico. For this territory, the United States would pay from $15,000,000 to $40,000,000 in addition to assuming the claims. Slidell was ordered to be on his guard against schemes of foreign powers, which might turn Mexico against the United States, and to prevent the cession of California either to England or to France. In a letter supplementary to the instructions, Secretary of State Buchanan ordered Slidell to drop the proposal for buying territory if it seemed to stand in the way of securing the Rio Grande boundary for Texas.

Slidell landed at Vera Cruz on November 29, 1845. A week later he was in Mexico City. The authorities refused to receive him.

The Supreme Government is advised that the agreement which it entered into to admit a plenipotentiary of the United States with special powers to treat of the affairs of Texas does not compel it to receive an Envoy Extraordinary and Minister Plenipotentiary to reside near the Government, in which character Mr. Slidell comes according to his credentials.

Slidell resented the Mexican refusal to receive him, as an insult to himself and as an affront to his government. He wrote of "the unparalleled bad faith" of the Mexican authorities, of that government's "gross falsification of the correspondence which led to my appointment, and the utter futility of the miserable sophistry by which it attempts to justify its conduct." Slidell, however, did not return home. Polk learned of the refusal to receive Slidell on January 12, 1846; on the very next day he sent orders to General Taylor to advance to the Rio Grande.

Soon afterward the Mexican government suffered another revolution. Accused of "seeking to avoid a necessary and glorious war," Herrera was overthrown by a group of Santa Anna's friends. The dictator himself was then in exile, but he selected as president one Paredes. The new Mexican executive took an oath to defend the claims of Mexico to all territory as far north as the Sabine River. This oath shows that nobody at this time, least of all the Mexicans, took seriously the notion of a boundary along the Nueces. The new administration was founded on a pledge of war against the United States. In dealing with Great Britain over the question of

Oregon, Polk had found the British authorities prepared to negotiate. He had taken the initiative in an effort to negotiate with Mexico, but his efforts were frustrated by action of the Mexican officials themselves.

By the end of April 1846 matters came to a crisis both in Washington and on the Mexican border. Shortly after General Taylor occupied Point Isabel, the Mexican commander at Matamoras ordered him to leave and threatened war if he failed to go. On April 24 a detachment of Mexican troops attacked one of Taylor's scouting parties on the north bank of the Rio Grande, killed and wounded sixteen men, and took over forty prisoners. This action had been taken under direct orders from President Paredes. The war was on, although Polk did not hear of it until May 9.

Crisis on the Border

During the last week in April and the first in May Polk and his Cabinet devoted most of their attention to the Mexican situation. Their conclusion—arrived at before hearing of the attack upon Taylor's force—was that the President should ask Congress to declare war and that the message for that purpose should be ready on Tuesday. That evening, after the Cabinet meeting, Polk learned of the Mexican attack on Taylor's men. At another Cabinet meeting on the same evening it was decided to send the war message on the following Monday, May 11, 1846.

In his request for a declaration of war Polk summarized the story of the Slidell mission, showing how his efforts to settle the difficulties had been nullified by the refusal of the Mexicans to negotiate, and at the same time making plain the fact that Mexico had made no counterproposal. Then he referred to Taylor's presence at the Rio Grande, described the attack upon his scouting party, and made the statement that "Mexico has passed the boundary of the United States, has invaded our territory and shed American blood upon the American soil." War therefore existed "by act of Mexico herself." The vote on the declaration was considerably nearer unanimity than had been the case in 1812: 173 to 14 in the House, 42 to 2 in the Senate.

Many Whigs questioned the truth of Polk's statement that hostilities had occurred on American soil. Abraham Lincoln, representing the Springfield district of Illinois, introduced a series of resolutions in the House, accusing the President of falsehood. Lincoln called attention to Mexican settlements north of the Rio Grande and insisted that the attack occurred not on American soil but in a Mexican cornfield.

In the war which followed the United States troops were always outnumbered, but they were superior in personnel and in equipment. The Americans were generally victorious, but they had plenty of heavy fighting. After the declaration of war, Taylor advanced toward Mexico. In two battles, Palo Alto and Reseca de la Palma, he drove the Mexicans out of their positions, and across the Rio Grande. In September Taylor won a three-day battle at Monterey, and in November he captured Saltillo, the capital of Tamaulipas.

In the meantime the administration decided to land an expedition at Vera Cruz, under the command of General Scott, for the purpose of capturing

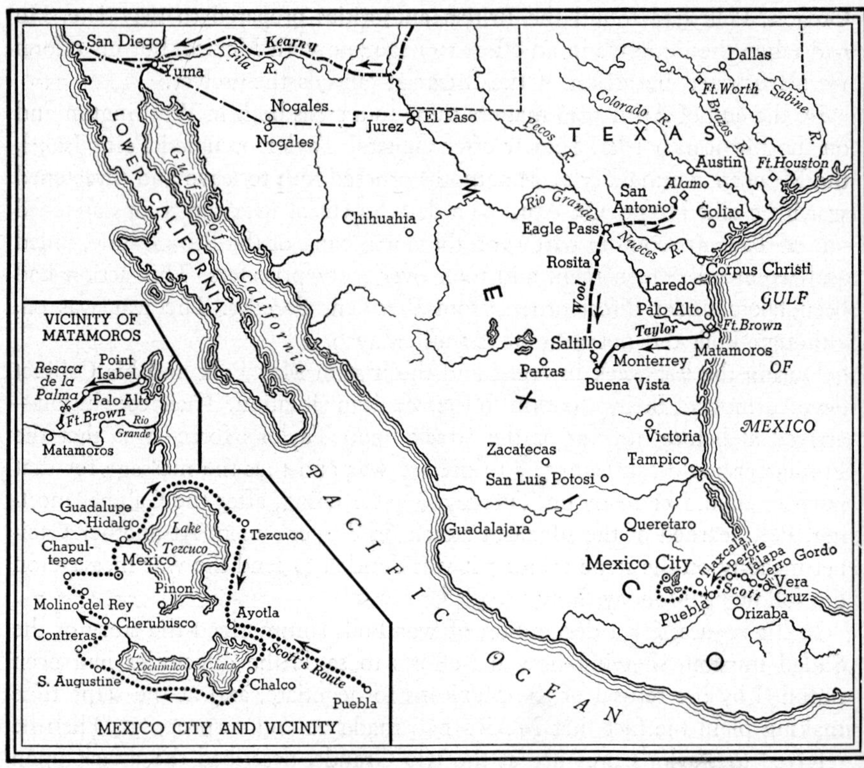

Map 10. The Mexican War

Mexico City. Some of Taylor's men were taken for the new campaign. Santa Anna, again in Mexico, learned of the Vera Cruz expedition, and, on hearing reports of Taylor's weakness, he tried to annihilate the American forces. Moving north with more than 20,000 men, he attacked Taylor with about 5000 at Buena Vista. Taylor won a brilliant victory (January 1847) and with it the war in northern Mexico was concluded. In March 1847 Scott's forces landed at Vera Cruz. On April 17 and 18, at Cerro Gordo, Scott's army of 9000 won a victory over 13,000 Mexicans. After this victory, Scott moved on toward Mexico City.

American Victories

In addition to the expeditions under the commands of Taylor and Scott the administration sent a third American force under General Kearny against California by way of New Mexico. With an army of only 1800 men he advanced upon Santa Fé, known to be defended by a Mexican force more than twice as large. On reports of Kearny's approach the Mexican army withdrew without a battle. Kearny organized a temporary government there and then, with 300 men, started for California. In October 1846 he learned that California was already in American hands. He sent two thirds of his small detachment back to Santa Fé and went on to California, reaching San Diego in December.

The United States Navy had done the greater part of the work in occupying California. In July Commodore Sloat took possession of Monterey and shortly afterward one of his captains occupied San Francisco. Other points in northern California were taken with practically no resistance. In August Commodore Stockton, Sloat's successor, seized Los Angeles. When Kearny arrived from New Mexico he organized a provisional government for California.

Because of the tense feeling aroused by the abolitionist crusade, expansion and slavery were inevitably discussed together. Texas would be a slave state, a prospect which many northern Democrats viewed with disfavor. They had been induced to approve the project of annexing Texas by the promise of the southern Democrats to work for the re-occupation of the whole of Oregon, and a bargain to this effect was made in the Democratic convention of 1844. When the Oregon issue came up, Calhoun and a number of other prominent southern Democrats supported Polk in his policy of a division along the 49th parallel. Exasperated at Calhoun's breach of faith, northern Democrats waited for revenge. Their chance came in 1846, with Polk's appeal to Congress for an appropriation of $2,000,000 "for the purpose of defraying any extraordinary expenses which may be incurred in the intercourse between the United States and foreign nations." It was common talk in Congress that money would be needed to buy the Rio Grande boundary.

David Wilmot of Pennsylvania introduced an amendment to the appropriation bill, which became famous as the "Wilmot Proviso." It read as follows:

> Provided, That, as an express and fundamental condition to the acquisition of any territory from the Republic of Mexico by the United States, by virtue of any treaty which may be negotiated between them, and to the use by the Executive of the moneys herein appropriated, neither slavery nor involuntary servitude shall ever exist in any part of said territory, except for crime, whereof the party shall first be duly convicted.

Wilmot Proviso

The Proviso passed the House, but it was still under discussion in the Senate when the session ended. Although the Proviso was never adopted by Congress, it became the guiding principle of the moderate antislavery forces. They were willing to let slavery alone in the states, but they were determined to prevent any further extension in the territories.

While Scott was moving on toward Mexico City, Polk sent one of the clerks of the State Department, Nicholas P. Trist, to Mexico to make peace. His instructions were not notably different from Slidell's. The chief difference was that Trist was to pay $5,000,000 less for New Mexico and California. On August 24, 1847, after the Mexicans had been beaten in a series of battles near Mexico City, an armistice was signed, and peace negotiations were begun. But the Mexicans refused to come to terms, and, when reports of the proceedings reached the President, he sent orders for Trist's recall. Unable to reach an agreement, the two armies resumed hostilities, with the result that on September 14 Scott occupied Mexico City. In the course of the next two months American forces occupied most of the strategic positions in Mexico. Santa Anna abdicated—although not permanently—and his successors began negotiations with Trist. Trist went ahead on the basis of his original instructions, and early in 1848 the commissioners signed a treaty of peace.

Treaty of Guadalupe-Hidalgo

This Treaty of Guadalupe-Hidalgo "adjusted" the Texan boundary in accordance with Polk's wishes. The boundary between the United States and Mexico was drawn along the Rio Grande to New Mexico, thence along the Gila River to the line between Upper and Lower California, and along this line to the Pacific. The territory thus secured for the United States included the present states of Arizona, New Mexico, Utah, Nevada, and California, as well as portions of Colorado and Wyoming. In return the United States assumed claims of American citizens against Mexico to the amount of $3,250,000 and agreed to pay Mexico the sum of $15,000,000. In March 1848 the treaty was ratified by the Senate.

In the United States there was a widespread but poorly organized feeling that Polk ought to keep all of Mexico. This conviction was especially strong in New York and in parts of the Middle West. Resolutions adopted by public meetings, newspaper articles, opinions of army and navy officials, and assertions of numerous Congressmen all united in demanding the whole country. In 1847 the New York State Democratic convention passed resolutions in favor of annexing all of Mexico. By January 1848 this agitation was well under way, and with a little more time it might have become formidable. What would have happened if Trist's treaty had not reached Washington at this point no one can tell. Its arrival, and the President's determination to accept it, prevented the demand for all of Mexico from becoming imperious. Ratification of the treaty brought the question to an end.

New American Interests

Polk's interests in foreign policy were not confined to Oregon and Mexico. For example, there was considerable talk of a Panama or Nicaragua Canal. In 1848 the United States and New Granada (as Colombia was then called) ratified a treaty covering transit on the Isthmus of Panama. New Granada guaranteed to the United States the right of way across the Isthmus, either by railroad or canal. The United States in turn guaranteed the "perfect neutrality" of the Isthmus, in order that free transit from sea to sea might continue without interruption, and, in addition, the "rights of sovereignty and property which New Granada has and possesses over the said territory." This treaty was still in force in 1903 when it was rendered void by the Panama Revolution. Under the treaty the Panama Railroad Company, an American corporation, built the Panama Railroad.

The second treaty concerning the possible canal was the Clayton-Bulwer agreement with Great Britain, signed in April 1850. This was the product of a rather complicated situation in Central America, where Great Britain seemed to be getting a secure hold. For years she had a colony there (known now as British Honduras). She also had a protectorate over the Mosquito Indians. In 1848 the British seized the port at the mouth of the San Juan River. Greytown, as the place came to be called, was the logical eastern terminus of a canal across Nicaragua. Great Britain, in actual possession of this territory, enjoyed a distinct advantage in any negotiations. The United States, with no foothold there, was asking for concessions; she hoped to induce the British to relinquish Greytown and to admit the United States to a share in the control of the canal.

Isthmian Canal

The Clayton-Bulwer Treaty provided for joint Anglo-American control over any Isthmian canal which might be constructed. Both governments bound themselves never to obtain any exclusive control over the canal, never to fortify it, or to exercise dominion over Nicaragua, Costa Rica, the Mosquito Coast, or any part of Central America, also never to make any alliance with any of these Latin American states for the purpose of securing any unequal advantages with reference to the use of the canal. The second article provided for neutralizing the canal in case of war between the contracting parties. The two governments agreed to invite other states to participate in these arrangements.

Cuba also attracted attention during this period. In 1823 John Quincy Adams had called it the "natural appendage" to the United States. The island commanded important routes of commerce while the South saw in it a possible slave state. Between 1848 and 1854 various attempts were made to instigate revolutions in Cuba for the purpose of bringing the island under American control. "Filibustering" became almost a custom. Under the leadership of the Cuban Narcisco Lopez, encouraged by the support of prominent southerners, expeditions were fitted out in American ports. In 1849 and again in 1850 Lopez tried to upset Spanish control of the island, but both ventures failed. Another attempt, in 1851, also failed; in still another, in 1854, Lopez and some of his southern backers lost their lives.

Cuba

In 1854 it appeared that President Pierce might win Cuba by conquest. An American merchant vessel, the *Black Warrior,* was seized by customs officials in Cuba for violating port regulations. The secretary of state instructed the American minister in Madrid Soulé to demand damages to the amount of $300,000. Before the orders reached him, the authorities had released the vessel. Soulé, a hot-headed expansionist, was determined to provoke war. He delivered an ultimatum to the Spanish government, so drawn as to arouse Spanish pride, and demanded a reply inside of forty-eight hours. The Spanish government declined to meet Soulé's demands, but Marcy, the secretary of state, refused to support his overzealous minister.

Not long after this episode had blown over Secretary Marcy instructed the American ministers to England, France, and Spain to meet at Ostend, a summer resort in Belgium, to discuss the Cuban question. Two of these men, John Y. Mason and Pierre Soulé, were from the South, and the third,

James Buchanan of Pennsylvania, formerly secretary of state, was on intimate terms with southern leaders. They were all expansionists, and they all wanted Cuba. The result of their deliberations was a statement known as the Ostend Manifesto. They declared that the United States ought to buy Cuba as soon as possible. If Spain should refuse to sell, "then by every law, human and divine, we shall be justified in wresting it from Spain." The secretary of state was able to drop the proposal without still further antagonizing Spain.

In spite of the desire for territorial expansion, the United States succeeded in acquiring only one additional strip. This was the Gadsden Purchase, acquired from Mexico in 1853-54. At this time there were a few matters concerning which Mexico and the United States disagreed. The Treaty of Guadalupe-Hidalgo had not been entirely clear as to the ownership of the Mesilla valley, about nine square miles in extent. Then Santa Anna, back again as dictator with the title of His Most Serene Highness, had presented claims against the United States to the amount of $40,000,000, on account of Indian depredations. Under the Treaty of Guadalupe-Hidalgo the United States was required to prevent Indians on the American side of the line from making incursions into Mexico. This obligation had not been complied with, hence the claims for damages. Furthermore the Pierce administration with Jefferson Davis, secretary of war, actually in charge, was planning for a transcontinental railway over the southern route to California by way of Texas and Santa Fé. A part of the line ran through the Gila River valley in northern Mexico. President Pierce appointed James Gadsden, a former army officer and later a rice planter and railroad president of South Carolina, as minister to Mexico. Gadsden was instructed to settle the points in dispute and to buy the land needed for the right of way for the road.

Gadsden Purchase

According to newspaper reports Gadsden had been secretly instructed to buy, if possible, the Mexican states of Chihuahua, Sonora, and Lower California. Actually the territory bought was far smaller. The draft of Gadsden's treaty provided for the settlement of a few claims, for new arrangements regarding Indian depredations, for the settlement of the boundary dispute, and for the sale of the Gila valley. American interests were given a right of way across the Isthmus of Tehuantepec, and the United States received the right to intervene there. The price to be paid was $15,000,000.

The newspapers were loud in their criticism of the territory acquired. The New York *Herald* described it as "worth just nothing at all, being simply a wild, hideous, howling, God-forsaken desert." Greeley's *Tribune* agreed with Bennett's *Herald*. Greeley called the bargain "the most unblushing swindle ever perpetrated upon the country." Greeley also found fault with the region itself: "A more heaven-forsaken piece of earth does not lie out of doors. . . . The more we have of such country, the worse we

are off." But the Senate cut the purchase price to $10,000,000 and ratified the treaty.

One of the most important treaties negotiated during this period was that signed with Great Britain in 1854, providing for Canadian reciprocity. Rights of American fishermen were more clearly defined, and Canadian fish was allowed to come into American ports free of duty. Also the Canadians were given rights of navigation on Lake Michigan, in return for which the Americans received similar rights on the St. Lawrence and the Canadian canals. This arrangement was to last for twelve years.

Perry and Japan

One important episode in the story of widening American interests, as distinguished from territorial expansion, took place on the opposite side of the globe. For a period of sixty years American merchants had carried on a flourishing trade with certain ports in China. Japan, however, had lived for two centuries in a state of isolation. But there had been causes of complaint against her, partly on account of reports of harsh treatment of American sailors who had been shipwrecked on her coast. American whaling vessels, which cruised all over the world, found fault because they could not use Japanese ports either for repairs or to get supplies. Then in 1850 Daniel Webster once more became secretary of state. Shippers from his own section had long been interested in Far Eastern trade, and he was convinced that it was time for Japan to open her doors.

In 1851 the American government planned to send an imposing mission to Japan, headed by Commodore Matthew C. Perry. Webster himself drafted the instructions which ordered Perry to secure protection for shipwrecked Americans in Japan, to arrange for opening Japanese ports to vessels in need of supplies, and if possible to secure general commercial privileges for American merchants there.

Leaving Virginia in 1852, Perry collected the largest American fleet which had ever appeared in the Far East. In July 1853 he entered the harbor of Yeddo, or Tokyo. In order to make the proper impression on the Japanese, Perry refused to let himself even be seen by subordinate officials. He represented the President of the United States, and he would talk with no one but a representative of the emperor. When the local Japanese authorities ordered him to leave the port, he did so but came back with a stronger fleet and moved his ships farther in toward the city. Then, after various preliminary talks, the emperor's agent appeared and welcomed Perry with an elaborate ceremonial.

In March 1854 Perry secured the treaty for which he had been working. It opened two ports to American commerce and permitted the United States to send a consul to reside in Japan. This marked the end of Japanese isolation. Perry's diplomatic triumph was an epoch-making achievement, the importance of which was recognized in Europe as well as in America. In 1857, in the Townsend Harris Treaty, provision was made for formal diplomatic relations between the United States and Japan. In arguing for approval of this treaty, the Japanese premier made this interesting observation: "In establishing relations with foreign countries, the object should always be kept in mind of laying a foundation for securing the hegemony over all nations." At the time few Americans paid any attention to this formula.

Chapter 21

POLITICS AND SLAVERY, 1850-57

New Problems in the West

THE hot discussion of slavery and related questions during the Mexican War was an evil omen for the two great parties. Drawing their membership from both North and South, the leaders objected to any issue which tended to weaken party solidarity. Their aim had been to keep the discussion of slavery out of Congress. Never entirely successful, they failed utterly during and after the War with Mexico, and the Wilmot Proviso pointed toward a new party alignment—northern and western against southern. Under these circumstances, the coming of the political conventions in 1848 was looked upon with grave concern.

The Democrats nominated Lewis Cass of Michigan, one of the ablest men in the party. Their platform denied the authority of Congress to interfere with domestic institutions of the states and declared that the federal government ought not to meddle with slavery. With reference to the War with Mexico the platform followed Polk in stating that it was a "just and necessary" war, begun by Mexico. It was also a war, the platform declared, "in which every American citizen should have shown himself on the side of his country." This was a slap at the Whig opposition.

Election of 1848

The Whigs came together at Philadelphia in June. Among their Presidential possibilities the most prominent was Henry Clay. Still a hero to his constituents, as he had been ever since his entry into public life, and still in some respects the best-known politician in the country, he labored under the disadvantage of his three defeats. After Clay came the two victorious generals of the Mexican War, Taylor and Scott. Fortunately for the party they were both Whigs. Of the two, Taylor had more of the vote-getting assets which politicians call "availability," and he got the nomination. Taylor was a Southerner and a slaveowner, with no definite views on public questions.

The Liberty party and other antislavery politicians nominated John P. Hale of New Hampshire. Dissatisfied Democrats of New York, with other antislavery groups, nominated Van Buren. Then Hale withdrew from the race and Van Buren fell heir to Hale's following. In the election, Taylor's popular vote was 1,360,099; Cass had 1,220,544. Van Buren's 291,263 was insignificant in itself, but over 40 percent of it came from New York. With the Democratic party in that state almost evenly divided, its electoral vote went to the Whigs. The vote of New York was enough to elect Taylor, so for the second and last time in their history the Whigs were given an opportunity to administer the federal government. Taylor and Cass each carried fifteen states, but Taylor had 163 electoral votes to 127 for Cass.

Disputes over Slavery

If it had not been for the patronage, the Whigs might well have regretted their success in the election. Never since Jefferson's time had the future held more prospects of trouble. Then the chief danger had come from abroad; now it came from the United States, in the controversy over slavery, bad enough in itself, and recently made worse because of its connection with the policy of expansion. On previous occasions the acquisition of new territory had necessitated the adoption of a rule or formula covering slavery. In 1787 the Ordinance for the Northwest Territory had prohibited slavery, leaving the Southwest free to do as it pleased. For the Louisiana Purchase, the Missouri Compromise prohibited slavery north of the 36° 30′ line, except in Missouri, and left the region to the south open to slavery. Texas came in as a slave state, while Oregon was organized as free. But there was no formula for New Mexico and California. The Wilmot Proviso had been proposed for that purpose, but it had not become law.

There were other proposals for ending the controversy. One of these would have extended the Missouri Compromise line to the Pacific. That would have given the South a smaller share than the North, as the same principle had done in the Louisiana Purchase, but many southern leaders were ready to accept it. Polk himself favored this proposal, and in doing so he had the unanimous support of his Cabinet. Others suggested that Congress should provide territorial governments for California and New Mexico, but should prohibit their legislatures from acting on slavery. Still others wanted to leave the question to the decision of the inhabitants in the territories concerned, a doctrine called by its opponents "squatter sovereignty."

Other matters in dispute needed attention, particularly the slave trade in the District of Columbia. Antislavery leaders were determined to prevent the buying and selling of slaves in the capital, if not to bring about complete abolition for the District. Southern Congressmen were insisting upon a more effective law for the rendition of fugitive slaves. The statute for this purpose, passed in 1793, had become more and more a grievance to the North and more difficult to enforce.

Danger of Secession

By 1848 feeling ran so high that some southern leaders talked of secession. One South Carolinian reported: "The abolition question must soon divide us. We are beginning to look upon it [secession] as a relief from incessant insult. I have been myself surprised at the unusual prevalence and depth of this feeling." Former Governor Hammond of the same state believed that the sooner the Union broke up, the better. In February 1850 Calhoun wrote: "Disunion is the only alternative that is left us."

In Mississippi, home of Jefferson Davis, sentiment for secession was even stronger than in South Carolina. A state convention endorsed a proposal for a southern convention, to meet at Nashville, Tennessee; the avowed purpose was to "adopt some mode of resistance," and "to provide in the last resort for their separate welfare by the formation of a compact and a Union." On March 6, 1850, the legislature of Mississippi appropriated $20,000 to send delegates to Nashville and $200,000 for "necessary measures for protecting the state . . . in the event of the passage of the Wilmot proviso." Governor Quitman was prepared "to recommend the calling of a regular convention . . . with full power to annul the federal compact." This sentiment was popular throughout the South.

Such was the situation which Taylor had to face, and there was no time for delay. The discovery of gold in California had made it necessary to organize a territorial government there at once. In January 1848, at Sutter's Mill in the lower Sacramento valley, the builder of the mill saw shining particles in the millrace. On examination they proved to be gold. From all over the country there was a rush to California, and the rapidly growing population was of the sort to be expected in such circumstances: adventurers and desperados of all kinds, together with ordinary, respectable human beings. In order to prevent anarchy, the law-abiding settlers assumed control and meted out quick justice to evildoers. California needed a constitution.

Gold and Government

Almost immediately after his inauguration President Taylor had sent agents to New Mexico and California. They urged the people to draw up constitutions and to apply for admission into the Union. California had already started proceedings before the President's representative arrived, and in September 1849 a state convention met and drew up a constitution, prohibiting slavery. In November this was adopted by the people. All that remained was for Congress to approve and to take the state in. In his annual message President Taylor called attention to California's application and urged favorable action. He also said that New Mexico might be counted on to submit her new constitution in the near future. The North and West favored the admission of California with her free-soil constitution. Southerners opposed for fear of additional loss of political power in national affairs.

The Compromise of 1850

At this point national leaders in Congress went to work on plans to satisfy the South and to save the Union. In this group the most conspicuous leaders were Henry Clay of Kentucky, Stephen A. Douglas of Illinois, and Daniel Webster of Massachusetts. Clay and Webster were rounding out forty years of service in national affairs. Douglas was a younger man but no less loyal to the Union. Late in January 1850 Clay submitted a list of proposals for compromise, designed to secure "the peace, concord, and harmony of the Union." These provided that California should be admitted with her free-state constitution, and that the remaining portion of the Mexican cession should be given territorial organization without restrictions on slavery. The dispute over the boundary between Texas and New Mexico was to be settled. If Texas would relinquish her claims on a part of New Mexico, the

Clay's Proposals

federal government would assume the Texan debt contracted before annexation. The slave trade in the District of Columbia was to be forbidden, and a more effective fugitive slave law was to be passed.

These resolutions started a debate that continued until the following September. Speaking in support of his program, Clay said that he had never been "so appalled and so anxious." He approved the admission of California as a free state and the adoption of popular sovereignty for New Mexico. "What more do you want?" he asked the antislavery enthusiasts. "You have got what is worth a thousand Wilmot provisos. You have got nature itself on your side."

Next Clay emphasized the necessity of a new fugitive slave act. Under the existing law, that of 1793, responsibility for enforcement lay with the states, and the states would not fulfill their obligations. Massachusetts, for example, had passed a law making it a penal offense for her officials to perform any duties under the law of 1793. Pennsylvania had forbidden her judicial authorities to accept jurisdiction in any fugitive slave case.

Clay had spoken in February. Calhoun announced that he would speak on March 4, but when the time came he was too ill to stand the strain. Senator Mason read the speech for him. Calhoun called attention to the great increase of northern power, an increase which had destroyed the old equilibrium between the sections. He attributed the failure of the South to keep pace with the North to the Ordinance of 1787 and to the Missouri Compromise, which had excluded slaveowners from territories belonging to the nation. Next he argued that the protective tariff and the system of internal improvements had worked regularly to the detriment of the South. To preserve the Union, Calhoun went on, the North must recognize the equal rights of the South in all recently acquired territory. Then the North must return fugitive slaves and northern people must desist from their agitation over slavery. He demanded an amendment to the Constitution which would restore to the South power to protect her interests from aggression. He opposed the admission of a free California.

By this time threats from the South had become so numerous that President Taylor had to state his position. He told members of Congress that he would use force to prevent Southern secession. At the height of this crisis, when the Union was threatened with dissolution and civil war, Daniel Webster announced that he would plead for the Union. The result was the Seventh of March Speech. Webster made no attempt to conceal the gravity of the situation and he did not try to flatter his hearers. "Necessity compels me to speak true rather than pleasing things." Then he amplified Clay's assertion that no merely human legislation was needed to settle the question of slavery in the Southwest.

Now as to California and New Mexico, I hold slavery to be excluded from those territories by a law even superior to that which admits and sanctions it in Texas. I mean the law of nature, of physical geography, the law of the formation of the earth. That law settles forever, with a strength beyond all terms of human enactment, that slavery cannot exist in California or New Mexico. . . . I would not take pains uselessly to reaffirm an ordinance of nature, nor to re-enact the will of God. I would put in no Wilmot proviso for the mere purpose of a taunt or a reproach.

Webster and the Union

Webster endorsed the proposal for a new fugitive slave act, and in doing so he expressed his opinion of the abolition societies: "I think their operations for the last twenty years have produced nothing good or valuable." Then he urged his hearers to do everything within reason to save the Union: "Never did there devolve on any generation of men higher trusts than now devolve upon us for the preservation of this constitution, and the harmony and peace of all who are destined to live under it."

At the time opinion differed as to the value of Webster's effort. Abolitionists condemned him with all the words at their command. Theodore Parker stated the abolitionist feeling: "I know no deed in American history done by a son of New England to which I can compare this but the act of Benedict Arnold." Other Americans bestowed high praise upon Webster. A group of 800 representative citizens of Boston sent Webster a message of confidence and praise, and similar addresses came to him from New York and Philadelphia. Webster's speech did much to produce a cooler temper, and it actually broke up the secessionist movement. Before he spoke, six states had appointed their delegates to the Nashville convention, all looking toward secession. But when the convention met in June, sentiment had completely changed, and its resolutions were so mild in tone as to be innocuous. As Robert C. Winthrop put it: "Webster's speech has knocked the Nashville Convention into a cocked hat." Modern students of this episode emphasize Webster's service in saving the Union and in preventing the immediate outbreak of civil war.

William H. Seward of New York spoke for the radical element of the North. He was in no mood for compromise: "I say to the slave States, you are entitled to no more stringent laws; and that such laws would be useless. . . . Has any government ever succeeded in changing the moral convictions of its subjects by force?" Then concerning the territories, he admitted that the Constitution devoted the territories "to union, to justice, to defence, to welfare, to liberty. But there is a higher law than the Constitution, which regulates our authority over the domain, and devotes it to the same noble purposes."

Terms of the Compromise

In mid April 1850 Clay's proposals were referred to a special committee of thirteen, six members from the South, six from the North, with Clay as the thirteenth. The committee arranged the proposals in three series of pairs. California was to come in free, while Utah and New Mexico would be organized without the Wilmot Proviso—that is, under the principle of popular sovereignty. The boundary of Texas would be restricted, but Texas would receive pecuniary compensation. There would be a new fugitive slave law, and the slave trade would be prohibited in the District of Columbia. In this form the compromise had the support of Clay, Webster, Cass, and Douglas. It was opposed by Seward, Chase, Jefferson Davis, and a large southern delegation. President Taylor had opposed the compromise, but he had died on July 9, 1850. His successor, Fillmore, favored the compromise and used the patronage to win support for it. After a long debate the compromise was adopted. The opposing votes were cast by northern and southern radicals, whose consciences would allow them to destroy the Union but not to save it.

Of all the provisions of the Compromise of 1850, the Fugitive Slave Act was the most unsatisfactory to the North. This law placed the responsibility for apprehending fugitive slaves upon federal marshals and judges instead of upon state officials. Heavy penalties were provided for officials responsible for the escape of a fugitive from justice.

The antislavery element denounced the Fugitive Slave Act as unconstitutional, un-Christian, and immoral and declared that they would not obey "its inhuman and diabolical provisions." These threats soon resulted in action. In 1851 the United States marshal in Syracuse, New York, arrested a Negro workingman there, William Henry, popularly known as Jerry. An enraged mob, including some of the best-known citizens of central New York, rescued Jerry from the officers and sent the Negro on to safety in Canada. In the same year a mob in Boston, composed largely of Negroes, rescued the fugitive Shadrach from federal officers. Several states passed personal liberty laws designed to protect alleged fugitives from recapture. In the South an equally rabid campaign was led by Governor Quitman of Mississippi and William L. Yancey of Alabama.

On the other hand, the moderates worked to build up popular support for the Compromise. "Union meetings" passed resolutions upholding the Compromise and demanding enforcement of the Fugitive Slave Act. In the South Clay and Crittenden of Kentucky, with Stephens, Cobb, and Toombs of Georgia, were working to allay secessionist sentiment and they won a temporary victory. A state convention drew up a "Georgia platform," declaring that the state would regard the compromise as a permanent adjustment. When Congress assembled in December 1850, its opening was far more peaceful than it had been the year before. Leaders from all sections proclaimed their loyalty to the compromise. By the fall of 1851, except for the Yancey-Quitman group, practically all influential opposition to the compromise had been beaten, both in the North and in the South.

Economic and Political Changes

Historically the Compromise of 1850 was an arrangement of primary importance for the Union. It showed what a few level-headed public servants could accomplish in the face of two groups of extremists working at cross-purposes. If the essence of politics is to adjust conflicting interests, here was politics at its best. The Compromise put off actual secession for ten years, and during those ten years the northern states reached a new high level in their economic development. In 1850 the northern states exceeded the southern states in population by approximately 4,000,000; by 1860 the margin of the North had increased to 7,000,000. In the same decade the Union states built almost twice as much new railroad mileage as the South. Industrial development, which had begun at the opening of the century, was rapidly accelerated after 1850. By 1860 the Union states produced ten times as much in manufactured goods as did the South. In any comparison of military assets, the North had acquired an impressive superiority over the South. This was evident in man power, industry, finance, shipping, sea power, and railroad transportation. Before 1850 the Mississippi River had connected the Northwest closely to the South. But much of the railroad construction between 1850 and 1860 connected the Northwest with the Atlantic coast region. These economic links proved to have definite political value when the real crisis came in 1860 and 1861. Those who grant that the preservation of the Union was desirable look upon the Compromise of 1850 as an essential step in the development of national greatness. It delayed secession until the North was able to meet the danger.

Election of 1852

With the adoption of the compromise and approval of its "finality," the two parties were able to turn to the Presidential campaign of 1852 with no major problem to embarrass them. In making their nominations, the Democrats could not agree on any one of their more prominent leaders, such as Cass, Marcy, Buchanan, or Douglas, and on the forty-ninth ballot, the convention swung to Franklin Pierce of New Hampshire. The new candidate had the sort of noncommittal record which is a valuable asset in politics. He was handsome in person, kindly in his dealings with his associates, without enemies, and eminently safe. Furthermore, he had a military record in the War with Mexico, and he was a friend of Jefferson Davis.

The Whigs were under the influence of their southern contingent and allowed the Georgians to write their platform. This was strongly states' rights in tone. For candidates the party had Fillmore, Webster, and one of the heroes of the Mexican War, General Winfield Scott. It took fifty-three ballots to convince the Whigs that nobody but Scott could get the nomination. In spite of his nomination Scott could not win the support of the southern Whigs because they doubted his loyalty to the Compromise. The Whig party broke on the issue of "finality" of the Compromise, and it never recovered. Pierce carried every state but five, getting 254 electoral votes to Scott's 42.

Although the election and inauguration of Pierce brought no change in national policies, his accession happened to coincide with an unusual change in Congress. The old leaders had largely ended their careers before March 4, 1853. Henry Clay died in June 1852, and the whole country mourned his loss. Webster followed Clay in October of the same year. Others either retired or were forced out of politics. Van Buren had retired in 1848, Winthrop of Massachusetts in 1851, and in this same year Thomas Hart Benton lost his seat in the Senate.

These men had all been unionists, and they could not be replaced. They had been trained in politics in the period after 1815, when nationalism flourished almost as a gospel, and as long as they were in Congress neither southern secessionism nor northern abolitionism could go unrebuked. Unionists remained, to be sure, but they were younger men, without the balance and the experience of Webster and Clay. Perhaps the most conspicuous of the group of younger unionists was Stephen A. Douglas of Illinois. He upheld the Compromise and he never became disturbed over slavery as an institution. No one denied his ability, but observers felt that his courage might run away with his judgment. With Douglas there were Cass of Michigan and Marcy of New York, both champions of the Compromise. Among the southern unionists were to be listed Bell of Tennessee, Crittenden of Kentucky, and Clayton of Delaware.

New Leaders

In general the younger members were more concerned with purifying the Union than with preserving it. Trained in the thirties and forties, they could not help being influenced, in one way or another, by the doctrines of radical abolitionism. Those from the North were determined that slavery should not spread into the territories. They opposed secession, but they did not oppose policies that might exasperate the South into secession. The leaders in this group of northern radicals included Chase and Wade of Ohio, Sumner of Massachusetts, and Seward of New York. Chase was a keen debater and an able politician but somewhat too selfish to make a first-rate party man. Sumner was well educated, courageous in expressing his own views, but intolerant. Wade was a fighting westerner, who plunged into the slavery dispute with Sumner's zeal, untempered by either political or legal training. Seward was an expert in politics and a man of ability.

Set off against these radical "Yankees" were the proslavery champions of the South, who agreed in placing the safety of slavery above the preservation of the Union. Angered by the steady attacks of the abolitionists, they looked upon the whole North with suspicion. They had nothing to lose because they cared little for the Union so they could be as belligerent as they pleased. Among the more extreme of these southerners, Barnwell Rhett of South Carolina, Quitman and A. G. Brown of Mississippi, were out-and-out secessionists. Even more extreme, but not a member of Congress, was William L. Yancey. After 1854 they were joined by former unionists such as Robert Toombs of Georgia and Jefferson Davis of Mississippi.

The Kansas-Nebraska Act

When President Pierce's first session of Congress opened in December 1853 it seemed that the slavery question was adequately guarded. In all federal territories the status of slavery had been clearly defined by law, and only new legislation could alter the arrangements. Such action seemed impossible. And yet, inside of a month, Congress was plunged into a new fight over slavery. The calm brought about by the Compromise was suddenly destroyed, and the country did not settle down until after the Civil War.

In December 1853 Dodge of Iowa introduced a bill to organize the Nebraska territory. This was a part of the Louisiana Purchase, lying west of Iowa and Missouri. It was for the most part still held by Indian tribes and consequently closed to white settlement. For ten years Stephen A. Douglas of Illinois, chairman of the Senate Committee on Territories, had been working for the organization of this region. There were scattered white settlements in it, many of which had been made contrary to law. The squatters wanted to become owners, but they had to wait until the territory was organized. The Wyandot Indians, who had adopted the forms of white civilization, were also clamoring for a territorial organization. Many Missourians for one reason or another were anxious to move into Nebraska and they demanded organization. Perhaps the most important force at work was the widespread interest in a transcontinental railroad. The admission of California had created a demand for better transportation facilities through the Far West. Ben Holladay started a coach line from Missouri through the Platte River valley to California, which is described vividly in Mark Twain's *Roughing It*. But this was a makeshift at best; the country wanted a railroad.

Problem of Nebraska

Douglas and his friends in Illinois wanted a line from Lake Michigan to Oregon. Benton of Missouri, working desperately to get back into Congress, demanded a line from St. Louis over the Platte trail. Jefferson Davis, the guiding director of the Pierce administration, was planning one from New Orleans through El Paso. This proposed southern line could go through organized territory, and the prospect of speedy settlements along the road would encourage capitalists to take the risk of building it. Since both of the proposed northern lines would run through unorganized territory, the promoters insisted upon organizing Nebraska.

Early debates on organizing the Nebraska territory brought out two main objections. Many southern Congressmen opposed the creation of any more free territories. Also the Texans objected, because they were eager for a southern Pacific road. If settlers were allowed to move into Nebraska, the central route might be selected after all. So the Texans amused Congress by displaying an hitherto unsuspected interest in the rights of the Indians—outside their own state. Texans tried to block the central Pacific project by keeping settlers out of the country through which it must pass. Profiting by this debate, the Committee on Territories planned to make the Dodge bill satisfactory to its opponents. To do this they would have to win southern support for the organization of a free territory. For such important concessions the price would have to be satisfactory. Possibly some arrangement regarding slavery might put the bill through.

On January 4, 1854, Douglas reported for the Committee on Territories.

He began by questioning the legal validity of the Missouri Compromise under which slavery was excluded from Nebraska. The committee, he said would not venture to pass judgment upon so delicate a subject. But he and his colleagues felt that the principles of the Compromise of 1850 were not local but general in effect, designed to cover something more than the Mexican cession. It became the duty of the committee, therefore, to perpetuate these principles. As set forth in the report, the principles were, first that all questions pertaining to slavery in the territories were to be left to the decision of the people residing therein. Next, all cases involving title to slaves were to be referred to local tribunals, with right of appeal to the federal courts.

Kansas-Nebraska Act

To make the Dodge bill conform to the principles enunciated in the report, the committee amended it by adding a new statement: "And when admitted as a State or States, the said Territory, or any part of the same shall be received into the Union, with or without slavery, as their Constitution may prescribe at the time of their admission." In the first draft nothing was said directly about the Missouri Compromise, but that was hardly necessary because the meaning of the bill was plain. Subsequently the three principles of the report were incorporated in the bill.

On January 16, Dixon of Kentucky moved an amendment to the Dodge bill, specifically repealing the restrictive section of the Missouri Compromise. On January 23, after previously securing the approval of Jefferson Davis and President Pierce, Douglas introduced a new measure, the Kansas Nebraska bill. This provided for the organization of two territories instead of one and announced that the prohibition of slavery in the Missouri Compromise had been "superseded by the principles of the legislation" of 1850 and was consequently "inoperative."

Abolitionist Opposition

After the introduction of the bill Chase and Sumner asked Douglas to postpone debate so that members of the Senate might have time to study the measure. What they really wanted was time to prepare an antislavery protest against the bill, not so much to influence the Senate as to stir up abolitionists in the North and West. The protest appeared, January 18 1854, under the heading: "The Appeal of the Independent Democrats in Congress to the People of the United States." The "Appeal" was written by Senator Chase of Ohio and signed by Chase and Charles Sumner of the Senate and by Joshua R. Giddings, Edward Wade, Alexander DeWitt, and Gerrit Smith of the House. It was published in the *National Era*.

The phraseology of the "Appeal" was more significant than its statements of alleged facts. It denounced the bill "as a gross violation of a sacred pledge [the Missouri Compromise], as a criminal betrayal of precious rights, as a part and parcel of an atrocious plot to exclude from a vast unoccupied region immigrants from the Old World and free laborers from our own States, and convert it into a dreary region of despotism inhabited by masters and slaves." The "Appeal" also reflected upon Douglas's motives: "Will the people permit their dearest interests to be thus made the mere hazards of a presidential game, and destroyed by false facts and false inferences?" The "Appeal" did consolidate opposition to the bill, and, in the words of the Annual Report of the American Anti-Slavery Society, "helped greatly to excite and to inform the public mind as to the urgency of the crisis."

The debate on the measure was more bitter than that over the Compromise of 1850. Chase and Sumner accused Douglas of aiming to let slavery into all the territories. In defense, Douglas urged the futility of legislation against slavery by showing how slaves had been held in Illinois in spite of the Ordinance of 1787 and in Nebraska in spite of the Missouri Compromise. His solution for the problem, which he called "popular sovereignty," went back, he said, to the Revolution. In spite of the efforts of the opposition the bill passed the Senate by a vote of 37 to 14. The administration made it plain that every Democrat must vote for the measure or give up hope of any share in the spoils. Thanks to the vigorous use of the patronage, the bill eventually passed the House by a vote of 113 to 100.

The question of Douglas's motive was summarily answered at the time, at least by his opponents. Chase's assertion in the "Appeal" that it was the price Douglas paid for southern support in the Democratic national convention of 1856 was widely believed. Historians have not been satisfied with that answer. For one thing, as the balloting in 1852 had shown, Douglas was more in need of votes in his own Northwest than in the South. So, if his bill were a bid for support, it was not directed at the South.

It seems more reasonable to accept the explanation of his biographer Allen Johnson. Douglas had two chief interests: the Democratic party and the Pacific railroad project. He felt that his party was in grave danger of dissolution because it had no great unifying principle to consolidate it. This lack he endeavored to supply in his doctrine of popular sovereignty. He was led to favor two territories—Kansas and Nebraska—because of the demand for them in the West. Missouri was interested in the southern part, Iowa in the northern. Moreover, if only one territory were organized, the majority of settlers would probably go into the southern part, and that would mean a central Pacific road. With two territories, there might be at least an even chance for the northern route which Douglas favored.

The Republican Party

No matter what his motive may have been, Douglas made a tremendous blunder. He failed to gauge accurately the depth of antislavery feeling or to realize how easily the whole uproar, allayed in 1850, might be revived. He might justify his doctrine of popular sovereignty with all the wealth of logical and historical argument at his command, but the abolitionists would have none of it, if it meant slavery in Kansas. On the other hand, the South would not accept the doctrine if it should threaten to make Kansas free.

It is easy now to point out one fallacy in the popular-sovereignty argument. Douglas assumed that slavery was a local issue. It had been once but that time had passed. It had become the most serious national issue confronting the country. And to northern leaders, even those who were not abolitionists, it seemed absurd to let a handful of pioneers decide a great question for the whole country. With the passing of the Kansas-Nebraska Act the storm of antislavery controversy broke out anew. The valuable results of the Compromise of 1850 had been swept away in an instant. Greeley declared that "Pierce and Douglas have made more Abolitionists in three months than Garrison and Phillips could have made in half a century."

Sectionalism in Politics

Some of the consequences of this colossal blunder had become apparent even before the bill was passed. On the last day of February 1854, a number of antislavery Whigs and Democrats met at Ripon, Wisconsin, to protest against the Kansas-Nebraska bill. If the bill should pass, they threatened to organize a new political party dedicated to the principle of the Wilmot Proviso: no further extension of slavery. One of the participants suggested the name "Republican" for the proposed party. In July the party was actually started at Jackson, Michigan. The promoters demanded the repeal both of the Kansas-Nebraska Act and of the Fugitive Slave Law. During the summer and fall of 1854, "anti-Nebraska" conventions were held in a number of states, and candidates were nominated for the fall elections. By November 1854 the Republican party was a fact.

The elections of 1854 showed what Douglas had done. In the Northwest at the time the Kansas-Nebraska bill was passed, all the Senators and 24 of the 29 Congressmen from Indiana, Illinois, Michigan, Wisconsin, and Iowa were Democrats. In 1854 new anti-Democratic coalitions of one sort or another carried four of these states, all but Illinois. The same forces carried Maine, Vermont, and New York. In the new Congress, in place of the 159 disciplined followers who put the Kansas-Nebraska bill through, the Democrats had only 75. The opposition numbered 192.

Civil War in Kansas

While political parties were feeling the impact of northern anger over the repeal of the Missouri Compromise, the territory of Kansas was giving a vivid demonstration of popular sovereignty. Ordinarily, after the organization of a territorial government, it took years to bring the population up to the point necessary for statehood. The Northwest Territory, for example, had been organized in 1787; the first state to be admitted from it, Ohio, did not enter the Union until 1803. Illinois was not admitted until 1818. Popular sovereignty might have worked there.

Popular Sovereignty

In Kansas everything was different. Congress was committed in advance to a policy which had been imposed without reference to local conditions, and the whole country had a feverish interest in proceedings there. The first migration into Kansas was similar to those which had occurred at other regions on the frontier. Settlers moved into Kansas from the Northwest, particularly from Iowa, Indiana, and Illinois, and from some southern states, particularly from Kentucky and Missouri. In addition to this type of settlement, which might be described as normal, there was considerable assisted emigration. In the reform belt of the North, and in a few cases in the South, groups were organized to promote the settlement of Kansas. Pioneers who went to the territory under these auspices were missionaries bent on making Kansas a Free Soil or a slave territory, as the case might be. It was their duty to see that popular sovereignty produced the result desired by their respective sponsors.

In the North this assisted emigration was carried on by Kansas Aid Societies, organized chiefly in Massachusetts, New York, and Ohio. The most famous of the group was the New England Emigrant Aid Company, incorporated in Massachusetts. This concern founded towns in Kansas, of which the best known is Lawrence. It provided the settlers with such essentials as gristmills and sawmills. Precisely how many settlers went to Kansas under the auspices of such organizations is not known. The manuscript records of the New England Emigrant Aid Company report a total of eighteen parties of emigrants, with 1240 settlers. None of the other companies even approached this total. From the evidence available it is safe to conclude that these assisted emigrants comprised only a minority of the population, but they were a vocal and obstreperous minority.

During these early stages Missourians sent proslavery pioneers into Kansas. Their efforts were supplemented by the work of Colonel Buford of Alabama, who raised a company of 300 men to help Kansas. Unlike the protégés of northern aid companies, this group went unarmed; the members carried Bibles instead of rifles. Upon their arrival in Kansas, however, they were promptly supplied with more worldly weapons. Although the South was interested in Kansas, it did not send as many missionaries as the North. Even so, the strength of these opposing groups was great enough to alarm thoughtful observers. In a special message to Congress in January 1856, President Pierce called attention to "the extraordinary measure of propagandist colonization of the Territory" and warned that serious trouble would follow.

Government for Kansas

As settlers came into Kansas, federal authorities took the first steps in organizing a territorial government. The newly appointed governor, Andrew H. Reeder of Pennsylvania, named November 29, 1854, for the election of a territorial delegate to Congress. On that day more than 1600 armed men from Missouri, organized in "Blue Lodges," entered the territory and voted for Whitfield, the proslavery candidate. He was elected, and Congress admitted him. In February 1855 a census was taken; this showed a total of 8601 inhabitants—with 3000 voters—over half of whom came from the South, with only 700 from New England. Had this census been taken in the preceding fall, or if it had been delayed until the following spring, the figures would probably have been different. Thousands of pioneers from the Northwest had gone into Kansas, staked out their claims, and then returned home for the winter. They were not counted.

In March 1855 Governor Reeder announced that elections to the territorial legislature would be held on the 30th of the month. He gave only a brief advance notice of the election, and of the pioneers who had gone home only those in Iowa and Missouri were able to get back in time to take part. The Kansas-Nebraska Act gave the right to vote to all free white male inhabitants, twenty-one years of age or over, actually resident in the territory. No specified length of time for residence could be named because when the act was passed there were practically no legal residents in Kansas. Governor Reeder seems to have taken what little precaution he could against fraud, but no person in his position could have done much. It was impossible to distinguish between the settler from Iowa who came in, put up a shack, and intended to stay and the Missourian who went through the same motions and intended to go home after the election. The judges of elections had to be satisfied with a declaration of intent. According to some authorities, at least 5000 armed Missourians crossed the border on election day and helped to roll up the total of 6307 ballots. But this report needs to be taken with caution. Because of the hasty return of many of the genuine settlers, the vote was inevitably larger than the census figures warranted. It is impossible to tell how much fraud there was.

Upon protest of the voters, Reeder ordered new elections in seven districts where fraud had been unusually flagrant. In the supplementary elections six antislavery men had been elected. The legislature was strongly proslavery, and these six were promptly unseated and those originally chosen, all proslavery, were admitted. By the summer of 1855 the proslavery element had full possession of the territorial government. Governor Reeder, originally proslavery in sympathy, had been disgusted at the violation of law. After he gave President Pierce a full account of the situation he was removed from office. So complete was his conversion to the antislavery group that he became their candidate for territorial representative in Congress.

Topeka Constitution

The Free Soilers in Kansas determined to ignore the territorial government, to organize a state government, and to appeal for admission as a free state. On October 23, 1855, a convention consisting only of Free Soilers met at Topeka. After passing an ordinance to prohibit any Negroes, free or slave, from entering the state, the delegates drew up a constitution. One month later the Free Soil voters elected a governor and a legislature. On December 15, 1855, the Free Soil constitution was submitted to popular referendum. Only 1731 votes were cast in favor of it. On March 4, 1856, the Topeka legislature applied to Congress for admission to the Union. During this same winter the Topeka government sent representatives to the eastern states to raise money and to stir up sentiment in support of the Free Soil cause.

With two rival governments in operation, one territorial, the other calling itself a state organization, violence was inevitable. The first outbreak, the Wakarusa War, occurred in December 1855. By the following spring the contest became worse. On May 21 a proslavery force attacked the town of Lawrence, headquarters of the Free Soil group, burned the hotel, destroyed the newspaper, pillaged a number of houses, and killed two men. Three days later a Connecticut Yankee by the name of John Brown, who had gone to Kansas by way of New York, took vengeance on the proslavery element. He led a small force to Pottawatomie Creek, pulled five proslavery men out of their beds, and had them killed on the spot. This cold-blooded murder brought him considerable notoriety. More will be heard of him later. More than 200 settlers lost their lives, and property was destroyed to the amount of $2,000,000.

Sumner and Brooks

On Senator Charles Sumner of Massachusetts this civil war in Kansas made a profound impression. On May 19 and 20, 1856, Sumner shocked his colleagues with a speech entitled "The Crime against Kansas." Lewis Cass, the oldest member of the Senate, described the speech as "the most un-American and unpatriotic that ever grated on the ears of the members of this high body." Sumner had spent weeks in preparing this speech, carefully working over every sentence and paragraph. Then for some reason he endeavored to give additional point to his remarks by reducing them to the concrete and the personal. Selecting Senator A. P. Butler of South Carolina as his special victim, and commenting on the fact that Butler was absent at the time, he covered the Senator with ridicule and insults.

Sumner went far in presuming upon his senatorial immunity from prosecution, and Butler had no legal redress. Two days later, after the Senate had adjourned, Sumner was seated at his desk, writing. While he was there Preston Brooks, a member of the House of Representatives from South Carolina and a relative of Butler, came up to Sumner. Announcing his name but without giving Sumner a chance to rise, he pounded him over the head with a heavy gutta-percha cane. Sumner broke his desk free from its fastenings and struggled to his feet, but, dazed by the heavy blows, he could do nothing to defend himself. By the time Brooks was forcibly stopped, he had beaten Sumner into insensibility. In the North, Sumner's speech was taken as a justifiable assault upon an evil institution, and the section was roused to horror over Brooks's retaliation. In the South the horror was over Sumner's speech, while Brooks was hailed as a hero.

Free Soil Victory

Civil War in Kansas with assault and battery in the United States Senate seemed to be a new southern challenge to the militant Free Soilers of the North, and they were quick to respond. In a letter published in the Syracuse *Journal,* May 31, 1856, the abolitionist Gerrit Smith called for real war upon the Missourians: "I wish the convention [one of his Radical Political

Abolitionist gatherings in Syracuse] would go with me in voting slavery to death. But I tell you, gentlemen, with all my heart, that if the convention is not ready to go with me in voting slavery to death, I am ready to go with it in putting slavery to a violent death."

In July 1856 the militant friends of Kansas held a convention at Buffalo. In the course of this meeting, Gerrit Smith submitted a series of resolutions, two of which provoked a lively discussion: "1. Resolved, that armed men must be sent to Kansas to conquer the armed men, who came against her," and 4. The attempt to force slavery upon Kansas must be defeated "at whatever cost," and "that too, whether the Administration shall, or shall not, continue to favor the nefarious attempt." In a speech supporting his resolutions, Smith urged the Free Soilers to make war upon the federal government.

Threats of War

With civil war on a small scale actually going on in Kansas, and with Northern abolitionists urging war against the federal government, the movement to aid Kansas seemed likely to ruin the United States. Advocates of military intervention talked of sending 10,000 settlers to Kansas at once, and 10,000 more men were to be enrolled in the states, officered, drilled, armed, and made ready to rendezvous in Iowa to march into Kansas in the case of another invasion from Missouri. The free-state legislatures were to be called upon for $2,000,000 to defray the cost of this operation. Then the belligerent clergyman, Thomas Wentworth Higginson, submitted a more radical plan of action. He wanted "to start a *private* organization of picked men, who shall be ready to go to Kansas in case of need, to aid the people against *any* opponent, state or federal."

End of Kansas Aid

By the end of the winter of 1856-57 the far-flung Kansas Aid Movement was practically finished. What had it done for Kansas? The New England Emigrant Aid Company did provide its settlers with sawmills and gristmills, and it did found towns. But Kansas was settled not by abolitionists from New England and New York but by pioneers from the Northwest. Emigrants from Illinois and Iowa rather than from Massachusetts and New York made Kansas a free state. Furthermore, the quality of material sent out by the Kansas aid committees was considerably below standard. William Hutchinson, a Vermonter then living at Lawrence, Kansas, had no illusions on this score. Answering a specific question as to the kind of settlers furnished by the aid groups, he said they were a mixed lot. "On the whole, I must say, that until the last party arrived, I think the individuals sent to the Territory during the last three months have not strengthened our cause, nor added to the moral stamina of our people."

Hutchinson's restrained comments on the character of some of the Free Soilers may be explained by the simple fact that he was one of them. Not all pioneers from the North were so charitable in expressing their opinions. A former resident of Boston, Massachusetts, who had lived in Kansas for two years had little respect for his new neighbors.

> The whole country abounds in unprincipled men and especially does this remark apply to Lawrence which place is a great rendezvous for rogues and horse thieves and not a suitable place for any decent person. Some of our principal men are charged with being connected with bands of horse thieves. Principle and honor is unknown here— Their motto is to make money at all hazards by fair means or foul.

If these allegations were true, the free soil agitation had not promoted the cause of sound citizenship.

The collapse of the Kansas Aid Movement in the East did not end the struggle in Kansas. President Pierce had used national power to protect the proslavery faction. James Buchanan, Democratic candidate in 1856, promised, if elected, to provide for a fair vote in Kansas. When he became President in 1857 he planned to bring peace and order to the troubled territory. His policy called for the appointment of an impartial, fearless, honest governor, who would secure a fair registration of voters, guarantee honest elections, and give the voters in the territory a genuine opportunity to decide for or against slavery.

The new governor was a man of national prominence, Robert J. Walker of Mississippi. He had been a senator from his state and secretary of the treasury under Polk. When he arrived in Kansas he found the proslavery group prepared to elect delegates to a constitutional convention. The Free Soilers, who supported the so-called state government, would not vote, so all the delegates to the convention were proslavery. Governor Walker, however, did persuade the Free Soilers to vote in the election of a new territorial legislature. By rigidly insisting upon the exclusion of all those not qualified to vote, Walker secured an honest election. This left the Free Soil party in control of the legislature, because by that time they heavily outnumbered the proslavery group.

Lecompton Constitution

The minority, however, went ahead with its constitutional convention at Lecompton and framed its constitution. Instead of submitting the whole document to the popular vote, they submitted only a single article dealing with slavery. But other parts of the document provided for the protection of slave property already in Kansas, regardless of the vote on that specific section. The Free Soil party, and the North in general, characterized the plan as a miserable trick. Governor Walker himself, a slaveowner from the lower South, told the leader in the enterprise that the scheme was "a vile fraud, a base counterfeit, and a wretched device to keep the people from voting." After the convention adjourned, Walker made a hurried trip to Washington to lay the matter before the President. He found that the President, under the influence of Jefferson Davis, had concluded to support the Lecompton constitution. Walker resigned. Buchanan's decision to approve the proslavery scheme, and to repudiate the governor whom he had promised to support, wrecked the Democratic party.

On December 21, 1857, the proslavery Kansans voted on the Lecompton constitution; it was approved by a vote of 6226 to 569. More than a third of the affirmative votes were subsequently proved illegal. Then the territorial legislature, with its antislavery majority, set a date for another vote, when the voters would be given a chance to accept or reject the whole constitution, not merely the single slavery section. In January 1858 they registered a vote of over 10,000 against the document. In spite of this showing Buchanan advised Congress to admit Kansas as a state under the Lecompton constitution. Next, the administration framed the English bill, providing for a resubmission of the constitution to the voters of Kansas on the conditions that, if they rejected it, the state would lose a part of the public land to which it was entitled, and that it could not be admitted as a state until the population equaled the ratio required for a representative in Congress. This scheme to bribe the Kansans to accept the Lecompton document and to punish them if they rejected passed Congress. In August 1858 the voters decided the question, 1926 in favor of the Lecompton constitution, 11,812 against. With this triumph for the Free Soil cause, the bitter struggle in Kansas was over, but the Democratic majority in Congress would not admit the territory into the Union.

Chapter 22

THE ROAD TO SECESSION

Major Issues in Economics and Politics

In looking back upon the troubled decade from 1850 to 1860, historians find it hard to explain the numerous crosscurrents in American action and American thought. No country in the world ever enjoyed more favorable conditions for living, and none had a more promising future. Thanks to the recent acquisitions of territory, the American people had land enough for ages to come. No other individual nation could boast so much in the way of natural resources, growing transportation facilities, expanding industry, or profitable agriculture, to say nothing of an intelligent, energetic population. The United States was safe from danger of invasion by a foreign foe; this security against military attack freed the Americans from the burden of costly armament. And yet, in spite of these advantages, the Union was close to civil war.

Prosperity and Depression

In the early part of 1857, the economic outlook was more promising than ever before. During the late 1820's and early 1830's the price of cotton had fallen steadily, with serious consequences for the older cotton states. During the 1850's, however, the price advanced, standing around 11 cents per pound for a time, and then, in 1857, going up to 14 cents. Because of a marked increase in the world-wide demand for cotton cloth, manufacturers in the United States and in Europe were using more raw cotton than ever. In 1860, the South produced 5,300,000 bales, practically 87 percent of the total world production of that year. But agricultural prosperity was not confined to the South. In 1849, the country raised 49,157,701 bushels of wheat; in 1860, the total stood at 95,004,000. Between 1849 and 1859, the price rose from $1.20 to $1.55, and there seemed to be no slackening in demand.

Heavy increases in the production of staple crops were accompanied by an increased volume of exports. American shipowners took advantage of expanding foreign trade and provided the transportation. This was the great era of the clipper ship. Between 1846 and 1857, American shipping engaged in foreign trade increased from 943,000 tons to 2,268,000. In 1857, the American merchant marine in both foreign and domestic commerce showed a total tonnage of 5,299,000, almost equal to that of Great Britain.

To offset this pleasing picture of agricultural, industrial, and mercantile expansion, the year 1857 was marked by a widespread economic depression. This crisis resembled that of 1837. It was due in part to excessive investment in railroad building, excessive in the sense that some of the mileage laid down would not become profitable for years to come. Then there were ill-advised real estate booms, as there had been in 1837. Again the banks were not adequate for the increasing volume of business. Bank notes were issued with the same prodigality which had been so evident in Jackson's administration and with the same lack of regard for security. The crash was marked by business failures and by unemployment in the industrial areas; New York City alone had 40,000 unemployed. But the panic of 1857 was only a temporary interruption of economic progress, and its effects were largely confined to northern centers. By 1860, recovery was general.

Northern Profits

There was one significant aspect of American economic activity of this period; the large profits went to the North. Producers of southern cotton and tobacco received the market price, and the commission agents who sold the products may have been located in the South, but banking, foreign exchange, and insurance were services provided chiefly by northern business firms, and northern men received the profits. Most of the shipping was owned in the North. So too were the factories. New York was the recognized financial capital of the nation. Consequently, while the South had to be satisfied with the income only of the farmer and the commission dealer, the North had the larger and more gratifying returns from other branches of business. Businessmen have always been able to charge more, proportionately, for their services than farmers have for their crops. Wealth was concentrating in the North, and relatively the South was falling behind.

Southern writers and economists convinced themselves and their associates that the South was being exploited by northern financiers. According to the southern thesis the South produced the real wealth of the nation, the basic raw materials which formed the bulk of American exports. Furthermore the South bought most of the imported goods and paid unnecessarily high prices because of the tariff. The fees, charges, and commissions paid for banking and insurance, for transactions in foreign exchange, and for shipping were all in the nature of tribute levied upon the weaker but more deserving section by unscrupulous money-grubbers who lived far away.

It is easy now to point out the fallacies in this reasoning. The North had not sprung suddenly into existence, full grown, with its manifold economic structure completely developed. On the contrary this supremacy was the composite result of the activities of many thousands of individuals, the first of whom started from scratch. In the beginning opportunities had been open to all, regardless of section. There was nothing in the eternal verities which decreed that New York rather than Charleston or Baltimore should become the financial and business center of the nation. Robert G. Albion has shown that it was neither luck nor merely geographical location which put New York at the head of all American cities. It was the enterprising spirit and superior ability of her merchants, bankers, and businessmen. They handled the cotton trade of the South because they could do it better and less expensively than the southerners themselves. Again, there was nothing in nature alone that gave the Northeast its industrial supremacy; since the 1880's the South has actually taken the lead in cotton manufacturing. The South might have achieved this distinction before 1860. In the South the men of wealth chose to devote themselves to the production of cotton, and in doing so they left the more profitable lines of business to others. To the producers of cotton went the income of producers, and no more.

Discussions in Congress did not deal with northern and southern differences in precisely these terms. There was considerable talk of the inequitable working of the protective tariff, and in 1857, under the influence of Howell Cobb, a new tariff act cut the rates to an average of 19 percent. This was the nearest approach to free trade which the country had seen since the close of the War of 1812. This low tariff did not help the South, because the tariff had not been the major factor in economic backwardness in the South. On the other hand, it did antagonize several important interests in the North and West. The lower rates on imported textiles aroused the manufacturers of New England, just as the lower duties on iron alienated many Pennsylvanians. Again the lower duties on raw wool stirred up opposition among the farmers in Vermont, Pennsylvania, and the West.

Political Issues

These matters should theoretically have been uppermost in American political discussion, both before and after the Presidential campaign of 1856. They were tied up with the major concern of all human beings, that of making a living. But men in public life devoted relatively little attention to these major economic issues. Public officials got themselves so immersed in the question of slavery, particularly the status of slavery in the territories, that any mention of this topic made them forget everything else.

Certainly the great economic questions of the day had little influence in the choice of Presidential candidates, while "bleeding" Kansas had a profound influence. The Democrats had to select a candidate who would conciliate the wavering members of their party in the North, so they dropped both Pierce and Douglas. On the seventeenth ballot they picked James Buchanan of Pennsylvania, an old, conservative, easygoing man not likely to make trouble. One of his chief assets was his absence from the country during the debate over the Kansas-Nebraska bill. He had antagonized no one, and voters might consider him safe. He had represented his country abroad, and he had been secretary of state under Polk. But his contribution to economic thought was conspicuous by its absence. The Democratic platform upheld the doctrine of popular sovereignty as the best solution of the slavery problem in spite of the unfortunate demonstration in Kansas.

The Republicans also paid more attention to politics than to economics in selecting their candidates. As a new party, composed of dissatisfied Democrats and Whigs, it could not afford to favor either wing. Chase had been too good a Democrat to satisfy the Whigs, while Seward, the ruler of the Whig machine in New York, would not draw many converts from the Democrats. The Republicans nominated John C. Frémont, the "Pathfinder," so called, whose career in California could be made to look like an asset. Frémont could never have traveled far in politics on his own merits, but the Republicans relied upon the widespread antislavery feeling to conceal his political weakness. The platform demanded the abolition of slavery in the territories and the admission of Kansas under the Topeka constitution. One of the major issues in the campaign was "bleeding Kansas."

As the Republican party steadily gathered strength in the North, the more radical southern leaders began to renew their threats of secession. If the Republicans should win, they declared, the South would leave the Union. Senator Mason of Virginia urged Jefferson Davis, the secretary of war, to provide the militia in the southern states with arms from federal arsenals. This renewed danger of disunion seriously affected the more conservative voters in the North. Buchanan was elected with 174 electoral votes to 114 for Frémont. The Democrats also secured control of both houses of Congress.

If it had not been for the dispute over slavery in the territories, Buchanan's administration might have been concerned with problems connected with the normal growth of the West. There was, for example, the demand for a railroad to the Pacific, but this project was stalled by sectional rivalry over the most feasible route. Then there was the demand for federal land grants to promote agricultural education. Senator Justin H. Morrill of Vermont introduced a bill for this purpose which passed Congress only to be defeated by Buchanan's veto. Many people in the North were calling for free land grants to settlers in the West. Congress did pass a compromise bill which reduced the price of land to 25 cents per acre, but under southern pressure Buchanan vetoed this measure, as he had the Morrill Act. He found it unconstitutional.

Slavery—From Dred Scott to John Brown

These matters might have provided the major issues for Buchanan and his opponents, but they did not. The issue of slavery in the territories took precedence over everything else. Two days after Buchanan's inauguration, the Supreme Court stirred up the whole country with its decision in the Dred Scott case. The facts of the case are simple. Dred Scott had been the slave of one Dr. Emerson, an army physician. In the course of his professional duties Dr. Emerson took Scott with him to Illinois, a free state by virtue of the Ordinance of 1787 and the state constitution, and then into the northern part of the Louisiana Purchase, made free by the Missouri Compromise. In 1838 master and slave had returned to Missouri. Emerson died in 1844, and Scott eventually became the property of one Sandford of New York. Several years later Scott brought suit in a Missouri court to secure his freedom on the ground that residence in Illinois had released him from slavery. The Missouri supreme court decided against him.

Supreme Court and Slavery

The case was then carried on appeal to the federal courts. The circuit court followed precedent and upheld the decision of the Missouri tribunal, whereupon, by another appeal, the case was carried to the federal Supreme Court. There was ample precedent covering a case of that sort, which, if followed, would have brought a mere matter-of-fact decision, upholding the previous decisions. The majority of the Court decided to follow this course, and one of the associate justices was instructed to write the decision. Then the justices learned that two of their number, Curtis and McLean, were planning to write dissenting opinions in which they would stress the legality of the Missouri Compromise. This agreement had been repealed, in oblique fashion, by the Kansas-Nebraska Act, but the antislavery forces wanted the principle restored. With Curtis and McLean determined upon their course, the Court found it expedient to go into the whole complex question of congressional authority over slavery in the territories.

Chief Justice Roger B. Taney wrote the majority opinion in the case, but every justice on the bench put in an opinion of his own. The majority agreed with the Chief Justice, although they reached their conclusions by lines of reasoning different from his. Curtis and McLean dissented. Taney upheld the lower courts in declaring that Scott was not free. Then the Chief Justice entered into a long, involved, and historically unsound dissertation upon slavery in the United States. No Negro could be a citizen, he said, because there were no Negro citizens when the Constitution was adopted, so the document applied only to whites. If he was not a citizen, Scott could not sue in the federal courts.

Once that question was settled there was nothing more to be said, but Taney kept on going. Taking up Scott's plea that residence in Illinois and in the Louisiana Purchase had released him from slavery, the Chief Justice argued that Congress had no authority to legislate against the property rights of any citizen which were duly guaranteed by the Constitution. Slavery was one of these rights, therefore the prohibition of slavery in the territories was unconstitutional and void from the date of its enactment. This final assertion had no logical place in the decision, or, as lawyers put it, it was obiter dictum, with no authority as a precedent. As for Scott's temporary residence in a free state, that did not make him permanently free because he had returned to Missouri with his master. Having done so, he resumed his status as a slave.

Associate Justice Curtis pointed out the weakness in Taney's argument. It was easy to prove that there had been Negro citizens before, during, and after 1787. The theory that Congress had no right to prohibit slavery in the territories was contrary to unbroken custom followed since 1789. Curtis concluded by asserting that the Missouri Compromise was constitutional up to 1854 when it was repealed, and that Scott had been freed by his residence on free soil. Instead of allaying bitterness over slavery, the decision, like the Kansas-Nebraska bill, made it worse than ever. Antislavery leaders pointed to it as further proof of the determination of the "slave power" to dominate all branches of the federal government.

The decision was a serious matter for the Democratic party. Douglas had tried to unite the diverse factions on the principle of popular sovereignty and seemingly he had succeeded. At least the Democrats had approved the principle during the campaign of 1856. Then the Dred Scott decision proclaimed the right of any slaveowner to take his property into any of the territories, a right obviously inconsistent with popular sovereignty. President Buchanan and the southern Democrats took the side of the Supreme Court, while Douglas and his following upheld the principles of the Kansas-Nebraska Act. This split in the ranks of the Democrats promised trouble in the coming elections of 1858 and 1860.

Lincoln-Douglas Debates

The best-advertised of the various contests in 1858 took place in Illinois. Stephen A. Douglas was campaigning for re-election to the Senate. As the author of the Kansas-Nebraska bill, he was the best-known Democrat in the country. To oppose him the Republicans picked Abraham Lincoln of Springfield. Lincoln had been prominent in local politics for years, sometimes as representative in the state legislature and for one term as representative in Congress. While there he had achieved distinction in his persistent effort to convict Polk of falsehood in describing the skirmish that preceded the Mexican War. When the Whig party was going to pieces, Lincoln became a member of the new Republican party. He was better known as a lawyer than as a politician, but as a candidate for office he had assets of peculiar value. Born in the cabin of a Kentucky mountaineer, he had given himself a remarkable education. His legal knowledge was deeper and more extensive than that of the ordinary western lawyer of his day; more important still was his extraordinary command of English, shown in the clarity and lucidity of his statements. He knew the language of the common people.

After both candidates had started their campaigns, Lincoln challenged Douglas to a series of joint debates, which would give their hearers a chance to see the two men in action on the same platform and, more important, give them an opportunity to answer each other directly. There were seven of these debates, one in every electoral district where the two had not already spoken. The first of the series was held at Ottawa on August 21, not three weeks after the Kansas voters had decisively beaten the Lecompton constitution.

The general trend of the seven debates was about the same. Each candidate tried to pick flaws in the previous statements of the other and to force the other into damaging admissions. One of the examples of this sort of fencing was Douglas's persistent charge that Lincoln was in favor of complete equality between the white and the Negro races. Lincoln's reply was characteristic; that charge, he said, was "but a specious and fantastic arrangement of words, by which a man can prove a horse-chestnut to be a chestnut horse." Later, he answered the charge in all seriousness:

> I say upon this occasion I do not perceive that because the white man is to have the superior position the negro should be denied everything. I do not understand that because I do not want a negro woman for a slave I must necessarily want her for a wife. My understanding is that I can just let her alone.

At Freeport, Lincoln asked Douglas a question, hoping to lead him into an embarrassing dilemma with reference to popular sovereignty. "Can the people of a United States Territory, in any lawful way, against the wish of any citizen of the United States, exclude slavery from its limits prior to the formation of a State Constitution?" Lincoln's aim was to force Douglas to explain popular sovereignty in the light of the Dred Scott decision. If Douglas replied in the negative, Lincoln could advertise him as a man who repudiated his foundation principle. If Douglas gave an affirmative answer, he would draw the fire of southern leaders in Congress, Jefferson Davis for example, who denied that power to people in the territories.

Political Results

Douglas tried to clear the trap with his "Freeport doctrine." Regardless of Supreme Court decisions on an abstract question, he said, the people in a territory had lawful power to introduce slavery, or to exclude it, as they preferred. Slavery could not exist without certain essential police regulations, which could be provided only by the territorial legislature. By passing the necessary laws, that body could make the existence of slavery possible; by refusing to pass them, the legislature could keep slavery out.

The final vote in the state was unusually heavy. In the contests for the state legislature which would choose the senator, the Douglas men got 174,000 votes, the Lincoln men 190,000. Had the present system of popular election of senators prevailed then, Lincoln would have won. But in spite of the popular majority of the Republicans, they secured only thirty-five seats, while the Democrats got forty. Of fifteen contested seats, the Democrats, again with a minority, got eight seats, the Republicans seven. In the final vote Douglas got fifty-four, Lincoln forty-six. The explanation of the curious discrepancy between the popular vote and the party alignment in the legislature is to be found in the use of "gerrymandering." The Democrats had been in control of the legislature before the election, and they juggled the electoral districts in such a way that the Republican vote was smothered. Lincoln failed to win a place in the United States Senate, but he made it impossible for Douglas to win the Presidency in 1860.

Militant Abolitionism

In the following year, 1859, the country was subjected to another shock over slavery. John Brown, one of the spectacular figures in the history of "bleeding" Kansas, made a sensational attack upon the government arsenal at Harpers Ferry. Kansas had attracted a number of venturesome, restless spirits, John Brown among others, whose indulgence in crime could be justified under the comforting formula of service in a good cause. Men who committed murder in Kansas, acting in the name of righteousness, were not murderers but servants of the Lord—if they were Free Soilers. Only the killing done by the Missourians was felony. On May 24, 1856, John Brown had been the leader in a peculiarly brutal, cold-blooded murder of five proslavery men at Dutch Henry's Crossing, on Pottawatomie Creek. At the time the circumstances of this exploit were not known to those eastern philanthropists who financed the Kansas aid movement, so John Brown's reputation did not suffer. As for John Brown himself, the disturbances in Kansas inspired him with a conviction that bloodshed could be used effectively in freeing the slaves. To finance his new campaign he would draw on those eastern friends who had given liberally of time and money to the Free Soil cause in Kansas.

During the winter of 1857-58 Brown's plans gradually assumed definite shape, so that he could talk about them to others and raise money for his project. Brown's financial backers included the Reverend Thomas Wentworth Higginson; the Reverend Theodore Parker; Frank B. Sanborn, a teacher of Concord, Massachusetts; George L. Stearns, a businessman of Boston; Dr. Samuel Gridley Howe (husband of Julia Ward Howe); and Gerrit Smith, the abolitionist. Brown explained to some of them that he would lead a small group of followers to a place in the Virginia mountains, from which he could make raids upon the surrounding country. As he freed the slaves they would increase the strength of his band, and then he could gradually widen the field of operations. He even had a plan of government all worked out, to use when he had freed enough territory and men.

Brown's friends contributed $4000 to his cause, and in giving money they knew that it would be used for an armed enterprise in Virginia. In July 1859 Brown rented two houses on a farm in Maryland, four miles from Harpers Ferry, Virginia. His arms were collected there. On Sunday night, October 16, 1859, with a force of eighteen men, he made his attack. He told his followers not to take life unnecessarily but not to hesitate in defending themselves. His men then cut the telegraph wires, seized the bridge over the Potomac, and captured the federal arsenal at Harpers Ferry. By midnight Brown was in full possession of the town, government property and all. Then he sent out a party to begin freeing the slaves and to seize white citizens for hostages.

Harpers Ferry

As news of the raid spread from town to town armed men poured into Harpers Ferry. By Monday noon Brown and what was left of his band were besieged in one of the government buildings. On Monday evening Colonel Robert E. Lee arrived with a detachment of marines. On the following morning Brown was captured. Ten of his band had been killed and five taken prisoners, while four got away. Brown was indicted and placed on trial for conspiracy, murder, and treason against the state of Virginia. On October 31 the jury brought in a verdict of guilty. He was sentenced to be hanged in December. On the day of his execution, mass meetings and memorial services were held in the North, funeral bells tolled, and eulogies were delivered almost without number. Writers such as Thoreau went into ecstacies over Brown's idealism and heroism.

On December 14, 1859, the United States Senate appointed a select committee to investigate the affair at Harpers Ferry and to find out "whether any citizens of the United States not present were implicated therein, or accessory thereto, by contributions of money, arms, munitions, or otherwise." This Mason Committee, as it was called, began work on January 4, 1860, and completed its investigations the following June 14, 1860.

It is plain from the record that the Mason Committee had no genuine desire to investigate the work of those men who really knew something

"POST Office, San Francisco, California. A Faithful Representation of the Crowds Daily Applying at That Office for Letters and Newspapers." (From the Phelps Stokes Collection, Courtesy, New York Public Library)

River and
Levee at New Orleans from the
North East Angle of New

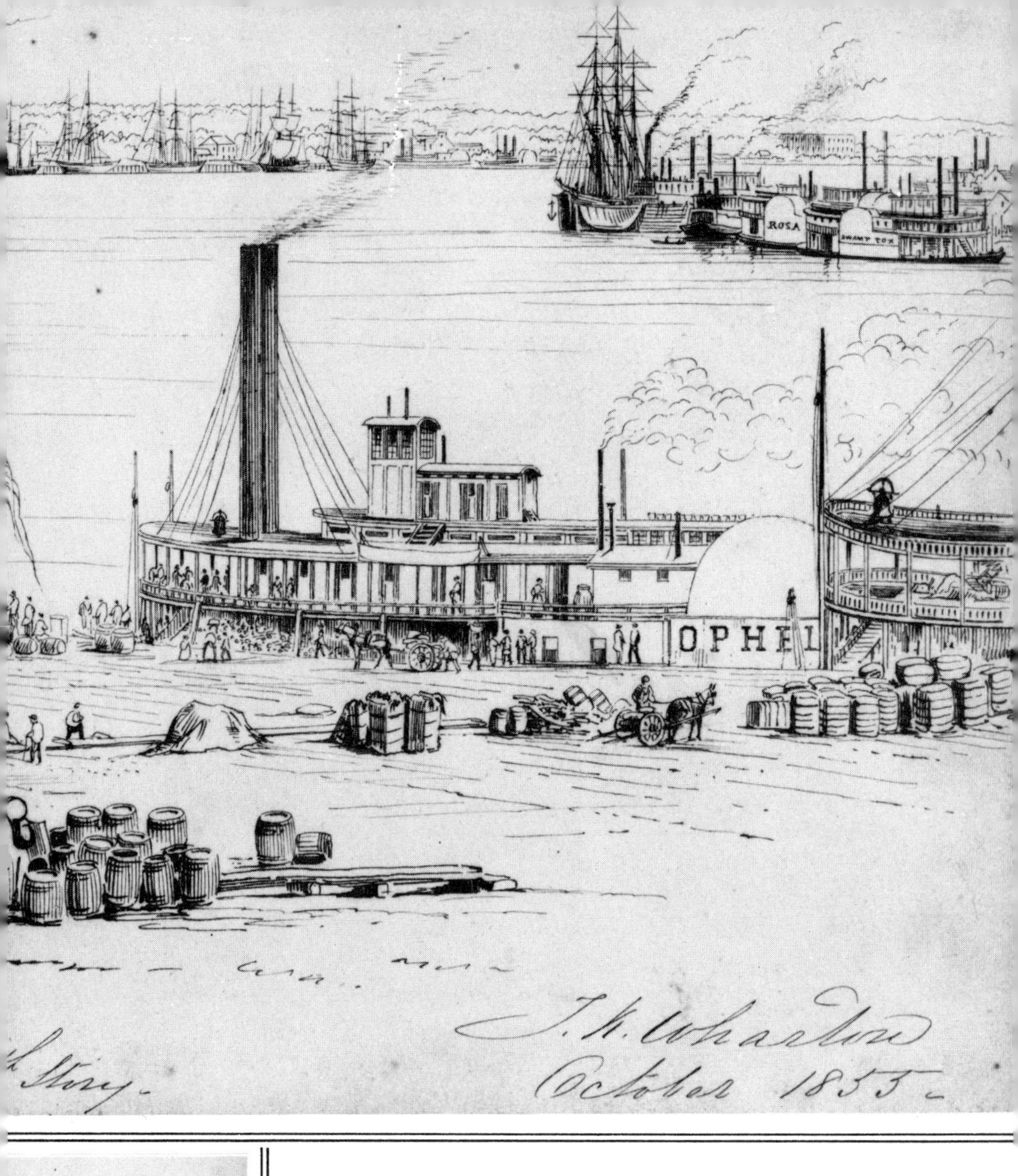

IN ADDITION *to his five-volume diary, still unpublished, Wharton made an impressive book of sketches, many of which were intended for publication in a volume of engravings. (Above) A sketch of part of New Orleans harbor from the federal customhouse which Wharton designed. Besides giving some idea of the amount of traffic on the Mississippi, it shows how extensively sailing vessels were then used. (Left) The sternwheeler on the Ohio is characteristic of Wharton's fine, detailed drawing. (Courtesy, Manuscript Division, New York Public Library)*

JOHN BROWN *by John Steuart Curry (right). Admirers of John Brown call this a cartoon rather than a portrait because it reveals only the trait of fanaticism. (From the Encyclopaedia Britannica Collection of Contemporary Painting. Copyright, William Benton.) Although the years 1835 to 1860 were the golden age of whaling, the* CHARLES W. MORGAN, *last whaler to operate under sail, completed her final voyage in 1921, after eighty years of service. "Arctic Whaling" (below) is a photograph of the mural in the Marine Museum of the Marine Historical Association, Mystic, Conn. (Courtesy, Marine Museum)*

about Brown's conspiracy. It did not wish to probe too deeply because of fear of the effect on the country if the John Brown affair were given any further publicity. Apart from the practically fruitless investigation by this committee, the federal government made no attempt whatever to investigate the Harpers Ferry affair. None of Brown's northern backers was ever punished.

Election of 1860

Democratic Schism

John Brown's raid and the debate which it provoked in Congress came as an unfortunate prelude to the Presidential campaign of 1860. At a time when the Democratic party had already begun to divide on the slavery issue, this new wave of bitterness threatened to wreck the organization beyond hope. Alarmed by Douglas's "Freeport doctrine," and fearing more antislavery raids, the South insisted upon positive congressional action in support of slavery. In the Senate, Jefferson Davis, who had become the spokesman for his section, presented the southern demands. The election of a Republican President, he said, would mean the end of the Union. As for slavery, Congress must uphold it. If a territorial legislature failed to provide adequate protection for the system, Congress must do so. Furthermore, people in a territory could not, so Davis said, pass upon the question of slavery until they drew up their state constitution. Davis proved that the South had repudiated popular sovereignty.

On April 23, 1860, the Democratic national convention met at Charleston, South Carolina. From the beginning there was bitter antagonism between southern and western delegates. The West demanded Douglas and a platform of popular sovereignty. Southern members, on the other hand, considered Douglas as bad as a Republican. The committee on resolutions had to choose between Douglas's popular sovereignty and Davis's congressional protection for slavery, and they chose the latter. But Douglas men insisted upon presenting a minority report. The southern platform announced that no territorial legislature had the power to abolish slavery or to deny the right of property in slaves; it also declared that Congress was bound to furnish adequate protection to slave interests in the territories. Douglas's minority report pledged the party to uphold the Dred Scott decision.

After a heated debate, the convention adopted the minority, or Douglas, platform. Davis's followers then withdrew from the convention. Under these conditions nominations were impossible, so after ten days the convention adjourned, to meet at Baltimore in June. The bolting delegations arranged to meet at Richmond. On May 7 a group of former Whigs and Know-Nothings, older politicians who looked with horror upon the approach of war, met at Baltimore. Calling themselves "the Constitutional Union Party," they adopted for their platform the Constitution, the Union of the states, and the enforcement of the laws. Their candidates were John Bell and Edward Everett.

One week later the Republicans met in Chicago. The wrecking of the Democratic party at Charleston was an almost certain guarantee of Republican victory, and on that account the excitement was intense. Spectators by the thousand crowded the city. From the first day it was evident that the main issue was a contest between Seward and Lincoln. Seward wanted the nomination, and because of his record as a political strategist and manipulator he had the support of machine politicians. But Seward was a radical, and not all the Republican party was out-and-out abolitionist.

Lincoln's Nomination

Before the nominations were made the platform had to be drawn. This document called for the continuance of the Union and for upholding the rights of the states. It denounced the John Brown raid "as among the gravest of crimes." It repudiated the radical southern doctrine that Congress must protect slavery in the territories and reasserted its own belief that there must be no further extension of slavery. Then the platform took up current economic issues. For the manufacturers it called for the restoration of high protective tariff rates. For the West the Republicans promised the admission of Kansas, a railroad to the Pacific, and a homestead law. The first two days had been occupied in organization and platform making, and nominations were left for the following morning. On the third ballot Lincoln received the nomination.

After the Republicans had completed their work, the Democrats, or part of them, came together at Baltimore. Douglas received the nomination of the northern wing while Breckinridge of Kentucky was selected by the secessionist group. Every ballot cast for him was a vote for southern independence.

Republican Victory

In the election the popular vote was as follows: Lincoln, 1,866,452; Douglas, 1,376,781; Breckinridge, 849,781; Bell, 588,879. The electoral vote gave Lincoln 180, Breckinridge 72, Douglas 12, Bell 39. These figures bring out some interesting facts. The total popular vote of the three candidates opposed to secession was 3,832,288, almost three million more than the secessionist candidate received and over 80 percent of the total. Four states which ultimately seceded cast anti-Breckinridge votes ranging from about 2500 in Georgia to over 18,500 in Virginia. Also, in all the states which joined the Confederacy, with the exception of South Carolina, the combined anti-Breckinridge vote was heavier than the secessionist vote. In South Carolina there was no popular vote in the presidential election. In the country at large the sentiment was overwhelmingly against secession. If the southern states had not seceded, there would have been an anti-administration majority of eight in the Senate and twenty-one in the House.

An analysis of the returns shows clearly that Lincoln's victory was due not to the schism in the Democratic party but to the strength of the Republican ticket in the North and West. Thanks to the peculiar system of electing Presidents, Lincoln carried enough states, with a popular vote in each case greater than that of his combined opponents, to give him the election. Of his total of 180 electoral votes, he owed only 15 to the schism. The Republican party had already become dominant. Lincoln's victory was not due to abolitionist influence because neither the candidate nor the Republican party had attacked slavery as the abolitionists demanded. In fact some abolitionists expressed considerable contempt for the Republican nominee.

What really did count were the Republican organizations in the states. In New York Thurlow Weed and William H. Seward carried their whole Whig machine into the Republican party, so they could deliver that state. Oliver P. Morton had brought the old Democratic organization of Indiana into the new party. Simon Cameron was the first of a long line of successful Republican bosses in Pennsylvania. In Missouri Carl Schurz was uniting the German vote with the former adherents of Thomas Hart Benton. These organizations were manned by men who had established connections with the voters and who knew how to get out the vote.

For the first time in American history a sectional party, representing the North and West, had been elected to control the national government. Before 1860 the slaveholding states had dominated the national government; they had held the office of President for more than fifty of the total of seventy-two years of federal history and for the greater part of the time had controlled either one or both houses of Congress. Some northern Presidents, Pierce and Buchanan for example, were so completely under southern control that they might well be listed as actual southerners. Throughout its whole life up to 1860, the Supreme Court always had a majority of southern justices. Federal appointments were in the hands of the President, so southerners received at least their share of positions in the civil service. Now the South faced not only loss of prestige but loss of economic position as well.

Ever since the federal government had been founded southerners had possessed relatively greater influence in the election of representatives and Presidents than their contemporaries in the North. For this privileged position they were indebted to two provisions of the Constitution, one giving each state two senators, regardless of population, and the other providing for the "federal ratio" by which representation in Congress depended on population, with three fifths of the slaves counting as part of the population. Since the slaves had no voice in political life, the arrangement for counting three fifths of their number simply added so much to the political power of the white people. In other words, the southern whites had relatively more representatives in Congress than the northern whites. In 1860 the total white population of the fifteen slave states was about 8,000,000, and these states sent thirty senators to Washington. New York State alone had a population of 4,000,000, but it had only two senators. New York, Pennsylvania, and Ohio, with a population greater than that of all the slave states combined, had only six senators. The "federal ratio" gave the southern states ninety representatives and 120 electoral votes; New York had thirty-five electoral votes. The election of 1860 showed that for the future the sheer weight in numbers of the North and West would cancel this advantage.

The Confederate States of America

South Carolinians had threatened that the election of Lincoln would lead to the disruption of the Union. In November 1860 the legislature was in session to choose presidential electors and also to take whatever action the circumstances seemed to demand. On receipt of the news of Lincoln's election, the legislature passed a bill providing for a constitutional convention to meet on December 17.

When the members of this body came together, it was a foregone conclusion that the state would secede. On December 20 the convention adopted, unanimously, an ordinance of secession. "We, the people of the State of South Carolina, in convention assembled, do declare and ordain . . . that the Union now subsisting between South Carolina and other States under the name of 'The United States of America' is hereby dissolved." Four days later the convention adopted a Declaration of Causes, modeled upon the Declaration of Independence. This asserted that the federal Constitution had been adopted as an experiment, that it had worked constantly to the detriment of South Carolina, and that the character of the government had gradually changed from a federal organization to a consolidated democracy. It announced that the election of a President by a purely sectional party had rendered it unsafe for South Carolina to remain longer in the Union.

The Union Divided

As a result of these proceedings South Carolina resumed her status as an independent, sovereign state, organized a government, and adopted a state flag. Before the end of the winter conventions in the six other cotton states had taken similar action: Mississippi, Florida, Alabama, Georgia, Louisiana, and Texas. The other slave states delayed action until after Lincoln's inauguration. When President Lincoln issued his first call for troops on April 15, North Carolina, Arkansas, and Tennessee joined the Confederacy. In Virginia the unionist element had the upper hand until after the Fort Sumter crisis, and then the radicals carried the state out of the Union. On May 23, 1861, the issue of secession was submitted theoretically to popular vote, but the polling places were guarded by Confederate troops. In counties where the vote was close, Union men were intimidated into not voting. After Virginia seceded, Richmond became the Confederate capital.

On February 4, 1861, delegates from the seven cotton states met at Montgomery, Alabama, to organize a government for the new confederacy. Anxious to complete their work before the inauguration of Lincoln, they published their provisional constitution on February 8. On March 11 they published the permanent constitution. The preamble proclaimed the "sovereign and independent character" of the states, but nowhere in the document is there a reference to the rights of nullification or secession. In most respects the Confederate constitution resembled the federal with more guarantees for the rights of the states. Of course the document provided for the legalization of slavery; although it prohibited the African slave trade, it also prohibited Congress from passing any laws impairing the right of property in slaves and insisted that both Congress and the territorial governments must protect slavery in any territories. Shortly after the provisional government had been proclaimed, the Montgomery convention chose Jefferson Davis as President and Alexander H. Stephens as Vice President of the Confederate States. Inaugurated on February 18, 1861, Davis had his government in working order before Lincoln entered office.

The South based its right to secede upon various grounds, constitutional, legal, strategic, and economic. Southerners felt that they would be better off out of the Union than in. Probably the most effective cause of secession was the deep emotional feeling of the southern leaders. Sometimes this spirit found expression in terms of contempt for the North, sometimes in a curious blending of southern patriotism with intense religious zeal. The secession convention of the state of Mississippi was opened with prayer, of which the following excerpt is a good sample:

Arguments for Secession

> Thou, Oh, God! hast seen the malign and mighty agencies which many of the sister States of this great national family have for years past employed for our annoyance, reproach, and overthrow, as equals in a Confederated Union; and how they have pursued the process of depriving us of our just rights, and destroying in our midst the institution which Thy Providence has solemnly bound us to uphold, defend and protect. . . .

Advocates of secession believed that Lincoln's election threatened their property rights in slaves, valued at three to four billion dollars, and they looked upon secession as the only possible safeguard. In this connection they relied upon cotton to bring them friends, and even actual assistance in case they were attacked. "Cotton is king" was the prevailing sentiment. Perhaps this state of mind, fairly common throughout the South, was expressed most bluntly in the words of Senator Hammond of South Carolina.

> I firmly believe that the slave-holding South is now the controlling power of the world—that no other power would face us in hostility. Cotton, rice, tobacco, and naval stores command the world; and we have sense to know it, and are sufficiently Teutonic to carry it out successfully. The North without us would be a motherless calf, bleating about, and die of mange and starvation.

This statement reveals the sort of fervor common to all revolutionary movements, beneficial in the sense that it inspires people to heroic action but dangerous because it blinds them to essential facts. There was a general tendency in the South to overlook the weakness of cotton. Cotton was worthless unless it could reach a market; when war began, the Union forces were able to interrupt the sale of cotton to American factories, and the Union blockade almost ended the sale of cotton to England and France.

Had the advocates of secession been more familiar with information available to them in print, they might have been less confident. The *London*

Economist had explained how the production of raw cotton and the manufacture of cotton cloth had temporarily exceeded the demand. Ordinarily British manufacturers kept a two-year supply of raw cotton in storage, and they planned to have enough cotton cloth in various centers to last for two years. But in 1861 the accumulated stocks of both raw cotton and cotton goods amounted to a three-year supply. Instead of being short of cotton, therefore, the British had an abundance, and they welcomed the interruption of their supply from the South. They could sell their goods at high prices. Of course Southern leaders expected foreign intervention in their behalf in case of war, a hope that proved to be without foundation. It so happened that the period of the war coincided with a period of crop failures in England and in Europe. For that reason wheat proved to be a more powerful factor in determining international relations than cotton, and during the whole war the Northwest was producing bumper crops of wheat.

There was nothing new in the underlying philosophy of secession. As Southerners were fond of arguing, the American Revolution was secession from the British Empire. During the Revolution there were curious and interesting manifestations of the same principle. Vermont seceded from New York, Berkshire County almost seceded from Massachusetts, and later Kentucky and Tennessee were threatening to secede from Virginia and North Carolina. During the constitutional period the doctrine of states' rights was widely and generally popular, and if the theory of an indissoluble union had been proclaimed in 1787 and 1788 it seems reasonably certain that the Constitution could not have been ratified. After 1789, the philosophy of states' rights and secession was not given up. The letters of the New England Federalists of the Jeffersonian period are full of the doctrine.

In view of southern theories and southern arguments, Jefferson Davis was an excellent selection for the Confederate presidency. Not a man in the

President Davis

South could argue more convincingly than he in behalf of independence. He had an extensive knowledge of historical and constitutional precedents combined with an intense emotional fervor. In his letters and in his messages to Congress he endowed the Confederate cause with the moral character essential to the conduct of war. By birth he was a Kentucky mountaineer, of the same stock and of practically the same neighborhood that produced Abraham Lincoln, but he had grown up in the lower South. As a Mississippi planter he understood the needs and difficulties of his class. He had served in both houses of Congress and he had been secretary of war in the Cabinet of President Pierce. He was a graduate of West Point and a veteran of the Mexican War. Davis knew that war with the North was possible, but he declared that the South did not want war and would not needlessly engage in it. In view of the danger of war, he urged the Confederate Congress to make adequate provision for "a well-instructed and disciplined army" and for a navy.

In making up his Cabinet Davis recognized the two leading groups in the Confederacy, the southern nationalists and the advocates of states' rights.

The State and War Departments went respectively to Robert Toombs of Georgia and L. P. Walker of Alabama, prominent southern leaders of the states' rights school. But Christopher C. Memminger, a Charleston lawyer, who became secretary of the treasury, Stephen P. Mallory of Florida, secretary of the navy, Postmaster General John H. Reagan, and Attorney General Judah P. Benjamin were all southern nationalists. They were not opposed in principle to the subordination of the states; they merely found fault with the working of the principle under the federal Constitution. Davis himself, in spite of almost endless lip and pen service to the doctrine of states' rights, became a nationalist by force of circumstances. The administration of the new government was therefore divided on an issue over which feeling was exceedingly bitter. This same line of cleavage, between the southern nationalists and the advocates of states' rights, ran through the whole Confederacy, eventually dividing both government and people into two irreconcilable factions, and so contributing heavily to the final collapse.

During these critical months seceding southerners took over federal property in their states. Customhouses, forts, even the mint at New Orleans fell into hostile hands. The "secessionists" occupied nineteen seacoast fortifications and seven arsenals; here they found hundreds of heavy guns and over 200,000 muskets. The value of this property amounted to several million dollars, exclusive of the $500,000 in coin which the seceders of Louisiana took at New Orleans. In Texas, General Twiggs, still wearing his uniform of an officer in the United States Army, deliberately arranged for the surrender of nineteen army posts to Texan authorities.

Buchanan's Indecision

President Buchanan made no attempt to interfere with this seizure of federal property. He did not believe in secession, but as an old-time Jeffersonian Democrat he could find no constitutional justification for coercing the South. There were two precedents bearing on the problem: Jackson's proclamation to South Carolina in 1833 and Taylor's general threat against possible seceders in 1850. But neither Jackson nor Taylor had been faced by a new government formed by seven states. Buchanan's problem was more difficult than those of his predecessors, and he at least could find no excuse for decisive action. In trying to deal with Buchanan's policy, the student may explain very simply what it was—that is, nothing. It was not "appeasement" because Buchanan himself made no concessions to the South; it was not bargaining because he asked nothing of the southerners, except that they resume their normal status in the Union; they asked nothing of him except what he freely gave—freedom from interference.

While this display of southern aggression and executive inaction continued, Lincoln remained only a spectator. The Constitution gives the President-elect no power during this interval, established custom bars him from any participation in official business, and the amenities of public life compel him to refrain from anything suggestive of dictation to the men still in office. Fortunately, with only this single exception, these intervals between election and inauguration have been free from serious crises, but the single exception threatened ruin to the United States. In a private letter Lincoln wrote: "He (Buchanan) is giving away the case, and I have nothing to say, and can't stop him." But Lincoln could at least formulate his own plans for subsequent official use. Before South Carolina left the Union, he declared that all the states should "be left in as complete control of their affairs respectively, and at as perfect liberty to choose, and employ, their own means of protecting property . . . as they have ever been under any administration." When secession was still only a threat, he held "that no State can in any way lawfully get out of the Union without the consent of the others; and that it is the duty of the President and other government functionaries to run the machine as it is." The day after South Carolina seceded, he asked a friend to tell General Scott, then in command of the United States Army, "confidentially, I shall be obliged to him to be as well prepared as he can to either hold or retake the forts, as the case may require, at and after the inauguration." This much indicated that executive inaction would end on March 4, 1861.

While Buchanan was drifting with the tide, Congress was busy with the forlorn hope of compromise. The Crittenden Resolutions provided that the Missouri Compromise should be restored and extended to the Pacific. This proposal was weak because the line would have crossed the State of California without the consent of the state. Once in effect, it should be made to apply to all new territory that might be acquired in the future. When these proposals came before Congress, the Republican members consulted President-elect Lincoln in order that their action might be in harmony with the policy of the incoming administration. He advised strongly against acceptance of the compromise plan, chiefly because it was inconsistent with the primary Republican principle of no further extension of slavery in the territories. His followers yielded to his wishes, and the Republicans voted against the Crittenden Resolutions.

After Crittenden's plan had been rejected, the legislature of Virginia invited the other states to send commissioners to a peace convention to meet February 4, 1861, in Washington. Former President Tyler headed the Virginia delegates. Twenty-one states accepted the invitation. The sessions lasted just a month, to March 4. The delegates worked out a plan of compromise, less satisfactory to the South than the Crittenden Resolutions and also less satisfactory to the Republicans. When submitted to Congress, it received only seven favorable votes.

Lincoln's Inaugural

On January 10, 1861, Lincoln finished his work at Springfield and moved to Washington. In his inaugural address he spoke to allay apprehension regarding his policy toward the South. Quoting from one of his own earlier speeches, Lincoln said: "I have no purpose, directly or indirectly, to interfere with the institution of slavery in the States where it exists. I believe I have no lawful right to do so, and I have no inclination to do so." Then he quoted from the Republican platform which disclaimed any intention of disturbing the right of each state to control its own affairs. Continuing, he said:

> I now reiterate these sentiments; and, in doing so, I only press upon the public attention the most conclusive evidence of which the case is susceptible, that the property, peace, and security of no section are to be in any wise endangered by the new incoming administration. I add, too, that all the protection which, consistently with the Constitution and the laws, can be given, will be cheerfully given to all the States when lawfully demanded, for whatever cause—as cheerfully to one section as to another.

He insisted upon the preservation of the Union and he denied the right of secession. Acts of violence within any state against the authority of the United States were "insurrectionary or revolutionary, according to circumstances." While giving warning that federal laws were to be enforced, he said that there would be no violence or bloodshed, unless it were forced upon the national authorities. The power granted to him would be used "to hold, occupy, and possess the property and places belonging to the government, and to collect the duties and imports. . . . In your hands, my dissatisfied fellow-countrymen, and not in mine, is the momentous issue of civil war. The Government will not assail you."

The Cabinet of the new President included men of various shades of opinion. Seward, the real leader of the Republican party down to 1860, was made seceretary of state, while Chase of Ohio, another Presidential possibility in 1860, received the Treasury. Simon Cameron of Pennsylvania, better known as an adept in party politics than as a statesman, became secretary of war. Gideon Welles, the secretary of the navy, had led the Connecticut delegation in the Republican convention of 1860. Edward Bates of Missouri, Attorney General, and Montgomery Blair of Maryland, the Postmaster General, came from slave states of doubtful loyalty to the administration. Lincoln spent the first month of his administration in trying to survey his problem—and in taking care of applicants for federal jobs. The mere fact that the Union had been broken in two and that there was more than an even chance of war did not deter the politicians from demanding their rewards.

Chapter 23

MILITARY ACTIVITIES, 1861-65

The Civil War—Issues and Resources

Fort Sumter

When the Civil War began in 1861, people in the two sections, North and South, disagreed completely about causes and responsibility. Today, more than eighty years afterward, they are still in disagreement on these matters. However, there is little difference of opinion over the episode which touched off the explosion. This was the attack on Fort Sumter. In the harbor of Charleston, South Carolina, there were three federal forts: Pinckney, Moultrie, and Sumter. Major Robert Anderson was in command at Fort Moultrie, but on December 26 he had transferred his small force to Sumter, which could be more easily defended. The South Carolina authorities ordered Anderson to return to Moultrie, and he refused. Thereupon South Carolina took possession of Forts Moultrie and Pinckney. On the same day, December 27, 1860, the collector of the port and all the customhouse officials severed their connection with the federal government. The collector became a state official, deposited funds in the state treasury, and raised the South Carolina flag over the customhouse. On December 30, under orders of the governor, state troops seized the United States arsenal with large quantities of arms and ammunition.

Because of its location in Charleston harbor and because of southern determination to control it, Fort Sumter became the immediate center of interest. President Lincoln had hardly been installed in office when he received word from Major Anderson that his provisions were nearly exhausted. Lincoln immediately instructed Secretary of War Cameron to notify General Scott "to exercise all possible vigilance for the maintenance of all the places within the military department of the United States, and to promptly call upon all the departments of the government for the means necessary to that end." On March 9, Lincoln asked Scott for a written statement as to how long Major Anderson could hold out without supplies and reinforcement. Scott advised the surrender of the fort. Five of the seven members of the Cabinet, including the secretaries of war and the navy, agreed with Scott.

On March 29, 1861, President Lincoln sent a special messenger to Charleston with the following announcement to Governor Pickens: "I am directed by the President of the United States to notify you to expect an attempt will be made to supply Fort Sumter with provisions only; and that if such an attempt be not resisted, no effort to throw in men, arms, or ammunition will be made without further notice, or in case of an attack upon the fort."

This warning was delivered on April 8 and immediately telegraphed to Montgomery.

When this message arrived, Jefferson Davis called a Cabinet meeting and laid the problem before his advisers. Robert Toombs, secretary of state, opposed any Confederate attack upon the fort:

> Mr. President, at this time it is suicide, murder, and will lose us every friend at the North. You will wantonly strike a hornet's nest which extends from mountain to ocean, and legions now quiet will swarm out and sting us to death. It is unnecessary: it puts us in the wrong; it is fatal.

In spite of this warning, Davis instructed General Beauregard to demand the evacuation of Fort Sumter and, in case of refusal, to go ahead and "reduce it." Anderson refused to surrender. On April 12 Beauregard ordered his batteries to open fire on the fort. The firing lasted all day and began again actively on the morning of the 13th. In the afternoon, with the fort in ruins, Anderson accepted terms of evacuation. **Civil War**

On receipt of the news Lincoln declared:

> I shall hold myself at liberty to repossess, if I can, like places which had been seized before the Government was devolved upon me. And in every event I shall, to the extent of my ability, repel force by force. . . . I scarcely need to say that I consider the military posts and property situated within the States which claim to have seceded as yet belonging to the Government of the United States as much as they did before the supposed secession.

On April 15 he called out 75,000 militia, to enforce the laws of the United States; on April 19 he proclaimed a blockade of Confederate ports.

During these trying six weeks Lincoln had avoided any action suggestive of aggression. He left the little United States Army where it was, scattered among the numerous military posts in the West. Apart from sending the small, and wholly ineffective, relief expeditions prepared for Fort Sumter and for Fort Pickens in Florida, he did nothing with the navy. His call for a special session of Congress was not issued until April 15 when he ordered out the militia, and even then he named July 4 for the first meeting. All this stood out in sharp contrast with the course of the Confederates, with their seizure of federal property, their open preparations for war, and their bombardment of Fort Sumter. Undoubtedly the majority of southerners would have preferred peace to war, but only on their own terms. Lincoln would have preferred peace to war too, but only on condition that the southern states recognize their allegiance to the federal government.

The Civil War was not undertaken as a drive against slavery. Lincoln found himself confronted by a rebellion; being entrusted with the responsibility of enforcing the laws, he endeavored to suppress this rebellion. To his mind, the assumed right of secession was the very negation of government. Lincoln himself was clear as to the purpose of the war. His primary object was to preserve the Union: it had become necessary, he said in May

1861, "to settle this question now, whether, in a free government, the minority have the right to break up the government whenever they choose." Congress agreed with the President. Both houses resolved that the aim of the war "was not conquest or subjugation, not to interfere with or to overthrow the rights or the established institutions of the Southern States, but to maintain the supremacy of the Constitution and to preserve the Union."

Lincoln's first call for volunteers brought him substantial support from the nonslaveholding states. At the same time it helped to clarify the situation in the border states, so that they were compelled to join one side or the other. Missouri and Kentucky were kept in the Union, partly by Lincoln's handling of the issue of slavery, partly by the quick work of a few militant leaders, but in the last analysis by the predominance of Union sentiment.

Border States

Maryland created a difficult problem. Confederate sympathy was strong throughout the state and particularly so in Baltimore; on April 19, an unruly mob there attacked the 6th Regiment of the Massachusetts militia on its way to Washington. Two days later pro-Confederate rioters cut the telegraph line and tore up the railroad tracks between Baltimore and Washington, thereby temporarily isolating the national capital. Not satisfied with these efforts to embarrass the Lincoln administration, the mayor of Baltimore and his friends destroyed railroad bridges on the lines to Philadelphia and Harrisburg. At the height of this crisis, the Maryland legislature assembled. There was danger that this body might vote to secede. Lincoln decided not to interfere with the members, unless they should vote to arm the citizens against the United States. If they should do this, he authorized General Scott to uphold federal authority.

At this time it was easier for the President to make policies than to execute them. With the Confederacy already in arms, with Maryland almost ready to secede, and with all railroad connections to the North temporarily out of commission, Lincoln had for protection practically nothing but the 6th Regiment from Massachusetts. He knew that the 7th from New York and the 8th from Massachusetts were on the way, but they were held up at Annapolis, again by pro-Confederate Marylanders. However, on April 25 the New York regiment reached Washington. By May 13 train service was resumed, and the immediate danger from Maryland was over.

The first session of the Confederate provisional Congress had adjourned on March 16, so it was not in session during the dispute over Fort Sumter. But the new government had already provided for an army of 100,000 men, and it had begun to organize a navy. After Lincoln's call for volunteers, Davis summoned his legislature for a special session to begin on April 29. When it convened, Davis submitted a long message in which he referred to Lincoln's proclamation as a declaration of war against the South. He asserted that the Confederacy desired only to be let alone, that it wanted peace "at any sacrifice save that of honor and independence." So began the struggle for southern independence.

Before the fall of Fort Sumter northern opinion had been characterized by indifference and indecision. Even so influential a molder of public sentiment as Horace Greeley of the New York *Tribune* urged that "the erring sisters" be allowed to depart in peace. The news of Sumter shocked the North into action, and men hurried to enlist to save the Union.

Resources for War

As the two governments, federal and Confederate, took stock of their respective resources, it must have seemed to the former that the war was won before it began, so great was northern superiority in all material assets. The Union consisted of twenty-three states with a population of 22,700,000, while the Confederacy had eleven states with a white population of only 5,096,000. This discrepancy in numbers was made up for in part by geographical advantages. Fighting on the defensive, the South had shorter lines of communication. Its territory was well served by rivers which facilitated Confederate movements and made obstacles for their opponents. In other respects the odds were heavily against the Confederacy. The chief source of revenue of its citizens was cotton, worthless if cut off from a market. The value of this asset was practically destroyed by the Union blockade. Manufacturing on a large scale had never developed there, and the section could not be self-sustaining. In the North there was a wide variety of manufacturing. New England and the middle states had textile mills and machine shops in numbers almost sufficient to take care even of the abnormal needs of war. Moreover, the diversified and profitable economic life of the North provided funds for a long war. When additional supplies were needed, rifles for example, the North had no difficulty in securing them from England.

Although it was fortunate in most respects, the North did not have an army ready for action. In 1860 the regular army consisted of about 16,000 officers and men. Of the 1200 officers trained at West Point, 200 felt a stronger loyalty to their states than to the government which they had taken a solemn oath to defend. They joined the Confederacy. None of the officers had ever seen service with large forces, not even during the Mexican War. When Lincoln called for 75,000 volunteers there was no one fitted by experience to handle so large an army. The War Department had no plans for moving, clothing, or feeding such a force.

Early Stages and General Strategy

The volunteers and regulars who collected in Washington remained there without any spectacular movement until midsummer. By that time the country was clamoring for an attack upon the Confederates. Their forces were just across the Potomac, almost within sight of Washington itself. Besides this army under Beauregard, there was another Confederate force under General Joseph E. Johnston in the Shenandoah valley. Both of these threatened the federal capital.

In the middle of July, against the advice of his general officers, including Scott himself, Lincoln decided that his collection of men in uniform must attack the Confederates in Virginia. The only prospect of success lay in the equality of inexperience of the enlisted men on both sides. The Battle of Bull Run started on July 21, and for a time, in spite of the inexperience of the troops, the Union commander McDowell had his plans working well. By three o'clock in the afternoon it appeared that he had won a brilliant victory. But the arrival of a fresh detachment of Johnston's army enabled the Confederates to turn the tide, and the Federal forces broke and ran. What had been an army became a panic-stricken mob. Most of the men stopped when they reached their fortifications south of the Potomac, but some crossed the river and hurried into Washington.

Bull Run

The day after the Battle of Bull Run, Lincoln called upon General George B. McClellan to take command of the forces around Washington. McClellan had been at work in the western part of Virginia. Previously he had seen some of the campaigns of the Crimean War. McClellan spent months in drilling the volunteers, and by November 1861 it seemed that this part of his work was finished. His plan was to develop a perfect fighting machine of at least 250,000 men. With that army, an overwhelming force, he counted on a march to the Confederate capital. But much to the disgust of the President and the country, he spent all the fall and winter in getting ready.

War Strategy

To understand what happened next calls for a brief analysis of Union strategy. A little study of the map will make this clear. Union forces in Virginia had two objectives: to protect the North from invasion and to capture Richmond. In the West Union forces worked, first, to secure control of the Mississippi River and, next, to capture the important railway center at Chattanooga, Tennessee, the gateway to Georgia from the west. President Lincoln showed considerable insight into the detailed problems of topography and strategy. He was one of the few to notice at the start the essential unity of the whole military and naval problem. In his mind the blockade of the ports and the campaigns in Virginia and in the Mississippi valley were not isolated ventures but intimately related parts of a single process. In January 1862 he wrote:

> I state my general idea of this war to be that we have the greater numbers, and the enemy has the greater facility of concentrating forces upon points of collision; that we must fail unless we can find some way of making our advantage an overmatch for his; and that this can only be done by menacing him with superior forces at different points at the same time, so that we can safely attack one or both if he makes no change; and if he weakens one to strengthen the other, forbear to attack the strengthened one, but seize and hold the weakened one; gaining so much.

In the Confederacy, for the first year of the war, Davis's military policy was defensive. The seizure of Fort Sumter was not an aggressive action, as he saw it; the South was merely resuming possession of its own property.

Map 12. The Scene of the Civil War

Confederate forces were stationed along the frontier not to invade the North but merely to protect the South. Inside this military barrier Davis assumed that life would go on as though there were no war. In making this decision he ran counter to the advice of one of his ablest generals, Thomas J.—better known as "Stonewall"—Jackson. In the summer of 1861 Jackson advised an invasion of Pennsylvania and Maryland.

There are few instances in history where a policy merely of defense has ever resulted in victory. It would seem that Davis's only hope lay in a smashing offensive, both in Pennsylvania and in the Mississippi valley, to overwhelm the North before its full strength was available. The Confederate policy really played into Lincoln's hands by giving the Union time to organize. Failing to realize the importance of hitting first, Davis lost his only possible chance to win the war. In 1861 enthusiasm for the Confederate cause was at its highest; war weariness, when it came, affected the South first.

During the latter part of 1861 Davis was less directly concerned with military affairs than with the establishment of the "permanent" government of the Confederacy under the new constitution. In the elections held in November, Davis and Stephens were chosen President and Vice President respectively, for a six-year term. The inaugural ceremonies were held at Richmond on February 22, 1862. In his inaugural address, Davis called attention to "the malignity and barbarity of the Northern States" in their prosecution of the war. In the Confederacy, on the other hand, "there has been no act on our part to impair personal liberty or the freedom of speech, of thought, or of the press." The final result, Davis said, was certain to favor the South; "the period is near at hand when our foes must sink under the immense load of debt which they have incurred." Even the blockade was bringing some good. It was making the Confederacy self-supporting and independent.

Peninsula Campaign

In the North General McClellan seemed just as firmly bent upon inaction and defense as Jefferson Davis, but Lincoln ordered him to attack Richmond. The assignment was difficult. Between Washington on the Potomac and Richmond on the James lie two rivers, the Rappahannock and the York, which run through marshlands, swamps, and forests. Although the shortest distance between the two capitals is hardly over 100 miles, no army could travel in a straight line. McClellan's first plan was to move his force overland, keeping it between Washington and the Confederate army. Then he suddenly changed his mind and decided to send his men by boat to the peninsula between the York and the James. That route seemed to offer fewer natural obstructions. Lincoln sanctioned the change with the express condition that Washington be fully protected meanwhile. The troop movement began on March 10, 1862. McClellan had the advantage of superior forces, and by June 1862 he was within striking distance of the Confederate capital. Generals Lee and Jackson, however, outmaneuvered McClellan. In July McClellan's army returned to Washington, and McClellan himself was removed from his command. The peninsula campaign was over, a complete failure.

Fortunately for the Union cause, other ventures were more successful. On April 19, Lincoln had announced a blockade of the Confederate coast from South Carolina to Florida. To make the blockade effective, certain permanent bases were needed on the shore. Late in August an expedition sailed from Fort Monroe for the North Carolina coast, where there were points of great strategic value for the Federal blockade. In January 1862 Union forces captured Roanoke Island, and in March they took possession of New Berne, Fort Macon, Beaufort, and other neighboring points. Enough territory was taken to enable General Burnside to establish a temporary government. In November 1861 Union forces seized Hilton Head, South Carolina, as another link in their blockading operations.

In March 1862, shortly before McClellan moved his troops to the peninsula, the Confederate navy put into service the old frigate *Merrimac,* newly made over into a great ironclad, renamed the *Virginia.* On March 8 she steamed into Hampton Roads, rammed and sank the *Cumberland,* and forced the *Congress* to surrender. That same evening a Union ironclad, the *Monitor,* arrived in Hampton Roads. She was a curious-looking craft, with her deck only a foot above water, with a round turret in the center. Although she carried only two guns, her revolving turret and mobility gave her the advantage over the lumbering *Merrimac.* On the morning of March 9, the two vessels plunged into a furious gunnery duel at close range. Neither was able to get a decisive victory, but the *Merrimac* was obliged to put back to port for repairs; although she was restored to service again, the Confederates refused to risk her in another fight.

Operations in the West and in Virginia

Unconditional Surrender Grant

In the West, during this same winter and spring of 1862, other movements were going on, strategically just as important as those in Virginia and more satisfactory to the Union. The key to these western campaigns was in the western end of Kentucky, where the state narrows down between the lower Ohio and the Tennessee boundary. The places of cardinal importance were Cairo, Illinois, just across from Kentucky, where the Ohio joins the Mississippi, and Memphis, Tennessee, an important railroad center and river port. From this strategic section there were rivers and railroads leading into the very heart of the Confederacy.

Early in 1862 Halleck was in command of the Union forces between the Mississippi and Cumberland Rivers; Buell commanded other Union troops between the Cumberland and the Alleghenies. The Confederate General Polk had seized the river terminal of one of the railroads, the Mobile and Ohio, at Columbus, Kentucky. To clinch their hold on the region and to safeguard railroads to the south, the Confederates then built two forts,

Henry, on the Tennessee River, and Donelson, on the Cumberland, both in northern Tennessee and about twelve miles apart.

One of the Union brigadier generals in the West was Ulysses S. Grant, a West Point graduate, thirty-nine years of age. He had resigned from the army in 1854 and found it difficult to get back when the war started, but he was finally placed in charge of some western regiments. Grant established his headquarters at Cairo and occupied Paducah and Smithland, at the mouths of the Tennessee and Cumberland Rivers. On February 1, 1862, Halleck authorized Grant, with the assistance of Commodore Foote and some gunboats, to move against Forts Henry and Donelson and against Island No. 10 in the Mississippi below Columbus. In strange contrast to McClellan, Grant had his forces in motion on the next day. On February 6, Fort Henry surrendered. Grant then began his attack on Fort Donelson. Should this fall, the whole of Tennessee between the Alleghenies and the Mississippi would be open to a Union advance.

On February 16 the Confederate commander at Fort Donelson asked for terms, and Grant replied, "Nothing except unconditional and immediate surrender can be accepted." The Confederates yielded to these "ungenerous and unchivalrous terms," as they called them, and Union forces took possession of Donelson. Buell entered Nashville without a fight. This victory forced the Confederates to withdraw to the next line which could be defended, that running from Memphis through Corinth to Chattanooga. By April 1862, Grant, with 45,000 men, was stationed at Pittsburg Landing, less than twenty miles from Corinth, and Buell was moving to join him with 36,000 more.

Shiloh

Once in camp at Pittsburg Landing Grant waited for Buell's arrival, not expecting a Confederate attack. By April 2, Buell's advance forces had arrived at the river, opposite Pittsburg Landing, but had not crossed. Grant's line was two miles long, and one of his divisions was five miles away. No attempt was made to throw up entrenchments, and the men were left in a position of serious danger in case the Confederates cared to move.

The Confederates at Corinth were in command of General A. S. Johnston, with Beauregard and Bragg under him. Johnston took in the situation, and on April 6, in the battle of Shiloh, he attacked the Federal line with his whole force. Grant was then having breakfast at Savannah, five miles away from the point of attack. Hearing the noise of the guns he hurried to the scene and put his men to work. The battle lasted all day. Johnston himself was killed, but Beauregard carried on the attack. By nightfall the Union line was in the hands of the Confederates. Beauregard was ready to begin again on the next day, and, confident of victory, he telegraphed to Richmond that the battle was won. Delighted with the news, only a month after the loss of the first Confederate line in Tennessee, Jefferson Davis sent a special message to his Congress: "I am able to announce to you, with entire confidence, that it has pleased Almighty God to crown the Confederate arms with a glorious and decisive victory over our invaders."

Davis, however, sent his congratulations before the end of the fighting. During the night Buell arrived with 20,000 fresh troops ready for immediate action, and Grant was able to take the offensive. Before the end of the day the Confederates were defeated, and Beauregard took his men back to Corinth and then to Memphis. By the middle of June 1862 the Federals controlled the Mississippi as far south as Vicksburg, and they had driven the Confederates out of their second line of defense in southwestern Tennessee. Vicksburg on the Mississippi and Chattanooga in southeastern Tennessee both lay open to attack.

In April 1862, less than three weeks after Grant's victory at Shiloh, Federal forces captured New Orleans. After the loss of New Orleans, the Confederates fortified Port Hudson, Louisiana, which guarded the mouth of the Red River. This was the broad highway for food supplies coming into the main part of the Confederacy from Texas and Arkansas. Between Port Hudson and Vicksburg, a distance of 125 miles, the Confederates continued to hold the Mississippi until the summer of 1863.

Army of the Potomac

From the Union point of view campaigns in the East were considerably less satisfactory than those in the West. In August 1862, the Confederate generals Lee and Jackson caught General Pope's army at the Second Battle of Bull Run and inflicted a crushing defeat upon him. With McClellan defeated on the Peninsula and with Pope beaten at the Second Bull Run, the Confederate leaders decided upon a vigorous offensive, with a great triple attack upon the North. Van Dorn was sent against the Federal forces in the Memphis-Corinth section. Bragg and Kirby Smith were sent into Kentucky to win that state and thus force the evacuation of Tennessee. Lee himself advanced into Maryland. Van Dorn accomplished nothing of any consequence. Smith succeeded in occupying Lexington, Kentucky, and sent detachments to within a few miles of Cincinnati, Ohio, while Bragg advanced toward Louisville. The actual results were negligible, and this second part of the offensive proved fruitless.

To meet the threat in the East, Lincoln restored McClellan to his command. Lee was moving north into Maryland right after harvest time, evidently determined to seize a supply of wheat. On September 17 the two armies met at Antietam. If McClellan had known how to handle an army, he might have inflicted a decisive defeat upon Lee. Instead, he let the Confederates retreat into Virginia without making any attempt to stop them. Then he gave Lee five weeks for rest and recuperation. On November 7 Lincoln again removed McClellan from his command. It took two years to rid the army of generals who did not know how to fight and to find commanders who could use the forces at their disposal.

To take McClellan's place as commander of the Army of the Potomac, the President selected General Ambrose E. Burnside. He decided to move directly against Richmond by way of Fredericksburg. On December 13, 1862, with 106,000 men, Burnside began the attack upon Lee, with 72,000. Two days later the Federals recrossed the Rappahannock, badly beaten, with a loss of over 12,000 men. This defeat at Fredericksburg cost Burnside his position. The next Union commander selected was General Joseph Hooker.

Spending the early spring in reorganizing the forces badly demoralized after Fredericksburg, Hooker was ready for action before the end of April 1863. The next battle, at Chancellorsville, lasting from May 1 to May 3, consisted largely of a series of blunders and misfortunes on Hooker's part; which predominated no one but a military expert could say, but the result was evident. Again the Federal forces were badly beaten, this time with a loss of nearly 17,000 men.

Gettysburg

In June 1863 Hooker followed McClellan and Burnside into the background, and General Meade was placed in command of the ill-fated Army of the Potomac. At this point Lee made another effort to carry the war into Union territory. By way of the Shenandoah valley he moved rapidly north, and by June 29 his forces were stretched from Chambersburg to Harrisburg, Pennsylvania. Meade had taken command of the Union army just the day before. He aimed at the control of Gettysburg in order to prevent Lee from turning south again. The attack came on July 1, and for two days the battle continued without decisive advantage to either side. On the afternoon of July 3 Lee decided to send a division of fresh troops against the center of Meade's line. The Union artillery had full command of the ground immediately in front of that point, but Lee, having acquired a habit of victory, disregarded the danger. Pickett's men, who made the charge, crossed the intervening space between the two armies in the face of deadly fire and began hand-to-hand fighting with the Federals. This time the Union line held, and the Confederates dropped back. Pickett lost two thirds of his command. This ended the heaviest fighting of the Battle of Gettysburg. Lee lost 22,000 men, or nearly 30,000 if prisoners are included—men whom he could ill spare. The Union forces lost 18,000, or over 23,000 including prisoners. On the evening of July 4, in a heavy downpour of rain, Lee took his men back to the Potomac River. Because of high water the Confederate army spent a week on the Maryland side, unable to get across. Meade wanted to attack at once, but nearly all his corps commanders advised against it, so Lee got away again.

Even though Lee escaped, the Union victory at Gettysburg marked the turning point of the war. Gettysburg represented the utmost that Lee could do, and it was not enough. For the future he was destined to find it more difficult to secure both men and supplies. He could still cause serious trouble to those Union forces engaged in the task of taking Richmond, but after the summer of 1863 the North was never again in danger of Confederate invasion. Moreover, although the end of the war was not in sight, the nature of the final outcome was certain. After the summer of 1863 the Confederacy was certain to lose.

On the same July 4 that saw Lee's rainsoaked veterans retreating to the Potomac, Grant captured Vicksburg and virtually opened the whole Mississippi to Union control. Grant's achievement was one of the most remarkable of the war and has been summarized thus:

Vicksburg

> In nineteen days Grant had crossed the great river into the enemy's territory, and marched one hundred and eighty miles through a most difficult country, skirmishing constantly, had fought and won five distinct battles, inflicting a greater loss upon the enemy than he himself sustained and capturing many cannon and fieldpieces, had taken the capital of the State and destroyed its arsenals and military manufactories, and was now in the rear of Vicksburg.

Unable to take the town by storm, Grant settled down to a siege and so starved the army and population into submission. On July 4 the place surrendered. With Vicksburg gone, Port Hudson had to yield; it surrendered on July 8. The capture of these two points gave the river to the Union, and more. It separated Texas, Arkansas, and Louisiana from the rest of the Confederacy and so cut off an important source of Confederate supplies.

Of the three main keys to the Confederacy, Richmond, Vicksburg, and Chattanooga, the Federals had full control of one. During the fall they got the second, Chattanooga. Late in the summer of 1863, Rosecrans began to move against Bragg's army in central Tennessee. Gradually pushing the Confederates back, Rosecrans was able on September 9 to occupy Chattanooga. From there he started to follow the retreating Confederates into Georgia. But they turned upon Rosecrans and at the battle of Chickamauga gave him a bad beating. Except for the stubborn stand of General Thomas, the defeat might have been decisive. As it was, Rosecrans had to go back to Chattanooga.

Final Victory for Grant and Sherman

Grant in Command

The administration sent reinforcements from the Army of the Potomac and placed Grant in full command of the Armies of the West. Grant's first step was to set Rosecrans aside and put Thomas in charge of Chattanooga. On October 23, Grant himself took charge. A month later, with the necessary reinforcements available, he was ready for work. The Battle of Chattanooga, which lasted from November 23 to November 25, was one of the most spectacular of the war. Thomas began the attack and drove the Confederates out of their first line. At midnight Sherman began to move his forces across the Tennessee River. On November 24 Hooker won the Battle of Lookout Mountain. On the 25th, Thomas's troops were ordered to take the Confederate rifle pits at the foot of Missionary Ridge. They did so, but, instead of waiting for further commands, the whole force—18,000 men—in the face of murderous artillery fire, climbed the ridge, and in "one of the greatest miracles in military history" drove the Confederates in confusion down the other side. The Battle of Chattanooga was as important as the victory at Vicksburg; it gave the Federal forces an open door into Georgia.

On February 29, 1864, Congress revived the grade of Lieutenant General, hitherto held by only two men in the United States, George Washington and Winfield Scott. Lincoln appointed Grant to the position and put him in full charge of all military operations of the war. The new commander came east to lead the ill-fated Army of the Potomac. From the start he made the defeat of Lee's army rather than the capture of Richmond his main objective, thereby endorsing a principle which Lincoln had been advocating since 1863. At the very beginning of Grant's active work in Virginia, Lincoln assured the general of his own complete approval and, except for an occasional hint, left Grant to his own devices. Grant crossed the Rapidan on May 3, 1864, and moved into a stretch of territory not far from Chancellorsville, known as the Wilderness. Halfway through this desolate fifteen-mile stretch he was attacked by Lee, whose troops had moved in by roads crossing Grant's at right angles. The two-day battle there was a draw, "a compound murdering-match" with losses approximately equal on both sides, probably about 17,000 apiece. Lee failed in his attempt to prevent Grant from passing through the Wilderness, while Grant was as far from capturing Lee as before.

Hitherto, after a contest of that sort, the Army of the Potomac had retreated for repairs and a new commander. This time it did not retreat. On the contrary, Grant's next move was toward Spotsylvania Court House, about fifteen miles distant. Again Lee refused to be passed, and again Grant plunged into heavy battles, lasting from May 8 to 18. This fighting around Spotsylvania cost Grant nearly 18,000 men. The Confederates did not report their losses, but they probably suffered just as heavily. During the first twelve days of June, in the series of engagements around Cold Harbor, Grant lost 10,000 more. Still determined to keep on, he next aimed at Petersburg, twenty miles below Richmond, the railroad center for a number of lines from the South. Unable to capture the place at once, Grant decided on a siege.

With Grant tied up before Petersburg, Lee tried the same maneuver which had wrecked McClellan's Peninsula campaign two years before: a raid down the Shenandoah valley toward Washington. General Early threatened the national capital, and then, during July and August, he sent cavalry parties into Maryland and as far north as Chambersburg, Pennsylvania. Even if Grant could not capture Lee, he was able to put a stop to that sort of activity. Sheridan was sent into the Shenandoah with a large detachment of the Army of the Potomac. On September 19 he fought Early at Winchester and again three days later at Fisher's Hill. On October 19, at the Battle of Cedar Creek, he drove the Confederates out of the valley and put an end to further threats.

Sherman at Atlanta

Although Grant kept up a constant pressure on Lee, there were no further significant developments in Virginia until the spring of 1865. The disappointment of the North was bitter and intense. Had it not been for Union successes in another part of the South, it is almost certain that Grant's failure to get decisive results would have brought about a change in the administration in the election of 1864. Fortunately, reports from Sherman came in time to restore confidence. On May 5, while Grant was involved in the Battle of the Wilderness, Sherman started from Chattanooga with Atlanta as his objective. He had about 100,000 men, while Joseph E. Johnston, the Confederate commander in Georgia, had about 64,000. This discrepancy was not great, because as Sherman advanced eastward he was obliged to leave detachments to guard his line of communications. The distance from Chattanooga to Atlanta is slightly over 100 miles with a number of natural barriers lying between. The two commanders were military geniuses.

Johnston took full advantage of local topography to impede Sherman's progress and refused to risk a general engagement. Time after time Sherman maneuvered him out of his position, whereupon he withdrew to a new one in the rear, leaving the Union forces to begin over again. By July, after eight weeks of this steady, relentless pushing, Johnston was forced across the Chattahoochee River, the last natural barrier before Atlanta. On July 17 Sherman took his own troops across, ready to attack one of the most important cities in the South. At this point Jefferson Davis removed Johnston from his command and put General John B. Hood in his place. No one was more delighted with the change than Sherman. Ever since May he had tried unsuccessfully to induce Johnston to fight. Nobody knew better than Sherman that Johnston's work during his retreat to the Chattahoochee had been of the highest order. With Hood in command Sherman's task was greatly simplified.

On July 20 the Confederates attacked. They were driven back into their trenches with a loss of 6000 men. Two days later, in the Battle of Atlanta, Hood lost 10,000 more. The Confederates held out in Atlanta until September 1. That night Hood destroyed some of the government property in the city and abandoned the place. Sherman occupied it and made it his headquarters. Sherman's capture of Atlanta ranks in importance with the capture of Memphis, Chattanooga, and Vicksburg. Hitherto it had been safe from any of the ravages of war, and the Confederates had made it into a manufacturing center, with textile mills and uniform factories. It was also an important center for cotton storage. Sherman had no intention of leaving anything in the city which would make it valuable to the Confederacy. All factories, stores, machine shops, public buildings, even the railroad station, were destroyed. If the people objected to this sort of thing, Sherman insisted that "they and their relatives must stop the war."

March to the Sea

Once in Atlanta, Sherman found himself in a peculiar situation. He did not wish to take his army back over the line to Chattanooga, and it would have been foolish to keep his magnificent force tied up with nothing but patrol work to kill time. By October he was trying to convince Grant of the feasibility of a march to Milledgeville, then the state capital, and to Savannah. "I can make this march, and make Georgia howl!" he insisted. If successful, as he confidently expected to be, this expedition would hasten the collapse of the Confederacy. Georgia had become one of the most important sources of food in the South. Besides taking care of its own population it was feeding Lee's army in Virginia.

Early in November Grant gave his consent, and Sherman prepared for the trip. All the sick and disabled were sent back to Tennessee, as well as all the baggage which could be spared. On November 12 Sherman cut his telegraph wires, so as to be free from any interference from headquarters, and four days later, with a carefully selected army of 60,000 veterans, he started toward the southeast. Covering a stretch of country sixty miles in width, in the heart of the best farming country in the South, Sherman's men destroyed everything that might be useful to the enemy. Sherman estimated the damage to the state of Georgia at $100,000,000, four fifths of which was "simple waste and destruction." For a month Sherman pushed on toward the sea; on December 13 he reached the coast and got into communication with the Union fleet offshore. His demand for the surrender of Savannah was refused, but on the night of December 20 the Confederates abandoned the city.

In February 1865 Sherman's army, still practically as strong as it had been on its arrival in Atlanta, left Savannah for South Carolina. On February 17 Sherman entered Columbia, and, in the confusion of Confederate retreat and Union advance, somebody set the town on fire. The responsibility for this act has never been definitely fixed. By March 19 Sherman reached Goldsboro in the center of North Carolina, 425 miles from Savannah. His advance to the north separated Charleston from the Confederacy, and on February 18 this important port was taken by the Federal fleet without a fight.

Confederate Collapse

Sherman's march north was one of the most important events of the war. It enabled the Union forces virtually to cut off food supplies for the Confederates, which was the heaviest blow that Lee's army of northern Virginia had received since the beginning of the war. Early in 1865, therefore, Lee was compelled to meet the relentless pressure of Grant's army in Virginia and at the same time to defend himself against Sherman's force closing in from the South. There was not sufficient strength left in the Confederacy to withstand this double attack.

During the winter of 1864-65 the Confederacy was on the verge of collapse. Military reverses in the field, the pressure of the blockade, growing shortage of food, the breakdown of internal transportation—all these combined to produce war weariness and defeat. Signs of internal weakness had begun to appear even in the summer of 1863. In August of that year the Confederate forces were seriously weakened by the large numbers of men absent without leave. Punishment was of no avail, and Davis was reduced to the extremity of begging the men to return, promising all who would come back within twenty days a general pardon. In February 1864 Davis called the attention of the Confederate Congress to a condition "already productive of serious evil." The original enthusiasm for the cause, he said, had disappeared in some sections. While many of the soldiers were showing their patriotism by re-enlisting, there was evidence outside the army of "discontent, disaffection, and disloyalty." In some sections, he went on, judges were releasing men from the army under habeas corpus proceedings. Desertion he described as "already a frightful evil." In September 1864 Davis reported that two thirds of the soldiers were absent, "most of them without leave."

In March 1865 Grant renewed his drive against Lee's army, and in a few weeks the struggle was over. On April 9 Grant and Lee met near Appomattox Court House to arrange the terms of surrender. The contrast between the two men was striking. Lee appeared in a new uniform, the very embodiment of military dignity. Grant came in the uniform of a private, with nothing but his general's stars to distinguish him from a common soldier. Always considerate and gentle in his personal dealings, the Union commander could not bring himself to refer to the occasion which brought him face to face with his great opponent. There was no trace of bitterness in his attitude, no suggestion of arrogance in his manner; those signs of littleness were as foreign to Grant as they were to Lee. The two men had met before during the Mexican War, and Grant tactfully found in this an opening for their conversation. For half an hour they chatted pleasantly about those earlier campaigns, until Lee reminded Grant of the business at hand. The terms of surrender were then drawn up and signed. At Lee's request, Grant allowed the Confederate cavalrymen and artillerymen to keep their horses; "they will need them for the spring ploughing."

Appomattox

On April 26 Johnston surrendered his army of 37,000 to General Sherman. Their agreement also included some 50,000 more troops in Georgia, subject to Johnston's orders. The surrenders of Lee and Johnston had ended the war, although Kirby Smith, the last Confederate commander in the field, did not give in until May 26 at Shreveport, Louisiana.

On April 2 the Confederate government had fled from Richmond. Davis, still clinging to the illusion that the Confederacy was a going concern, escaped to North Carolina, where he held his last Cabinet meeting. But he had waited too long. Hoping to avoid capture he moved south into Georgia with the intention of finding refuge abroad. On May 10 he was captured by Federal officers and imprisoned in Fortress Monroe. So ended the military aspects of the experiment with secession.

Chapter 24

WAR PROBLEMS—FOREIGN AND DOMESTIC

British Attitude toward the Civil War

FROM the outbreak of hostilities at Fort Sumter, President Lincoln held to the theory that the southern states were still parts of the federal government. Instead of being at war they were merely in a state of rebellion. If this theory were sound, foreign governments would have no concern with the contest. There were a number of difficulties with Lincoln's interpretation, not the least of which was the refusal of Europe to accept it. Foreign problems therefore could not be avoided.

Foreign Policy

In making Seward his secretary of state, Lincoln had been guided more by the necessities of Republican politics than by regard for the foreign service. Seward was the most powerful leader in the party, and the administration had to recognize him by giving him the highest place in the Cabinet. He proved to be an admirable man for the post, once he learned that he was not the President. Like many others he had assumed that Lincoln was an untutored country lawyer, whose elevation to the Presidency was due not to his own merits but to the peculiar situation that had prevailed in 1860. As the recognized head of the party, Seward took it for granted that he would continue to lead after March 4, 1861.

On April 1, 1861, Seward submitted to his chief a document entitled "Thoughts for the President's Consideration." In this essay he observed that no policy had yet been adopted, that the country needed one, and so he had prepared one. For a domestic policy he urged that the emphasis be shifted from slavery to union. With reference to foreign affairs, he suggested that England and Russia be called sharply to account for alleged sympathy with the Confederates. Then he pointed out that Spain was showing interest in Santo Domingo, while France had designs upon Mexico. He would forestall danger in these quarters by sending an ultimatum to each. His purpose was to prevent foreign interference in American affairs. He admitted that his program might result in war, but he believed a foreign war might reunite the American people.

Aside from the presentation of this document, Seward conducted himself well. It was his advice which led Lincoln to appoint as minister to England Charles Francis Adams, son of John Quincy Adams. The new minister arrived in London on May 13, 1861, nearly a month after hostilities had begun, and it fell to him to work against formal recognition of Confederate independence.

In the English Cabinet of the time Palmerston was prime minister, Earl

Russell secretary of state for foreign affairs, and Gladstone chancellor of the exchequer. Opinion in the country was divided. The upper classes were in sympathy with the South. The middle-class element was opposed to slavery, but it found the Union policy so lacking in energy that it hardly knew which side to take. English journalists in America were sending back reports of disunion and dissension. The correspondent of the London *Times* wrote: "Practically, so far as I have gone, I have failed to meet many people who really exhibited any passionate attachment to the Union, or who pretended to be actuated by any strong feeling of regard or admiration for the government of the United States in itself." The Continental nations usually got their information about American affairs from British sources, and at this time they were ready to let England take the initiative in dealing with the American war.

British Attitude

Jefferson Davis was convinced that cotton was his strongest weapon and that he could use it to force recognition. On May 3, 1861, two of his unofficial agents in England had an interview with Russell, looking toward recognition. A few days later, Dallas, Adams's predecessor, received what he interpreted as assurance that no action would be taken until the new minister should arrive. Both sides therefore prepared to wait a few days more. But on May 13, the very day that Adams arrived in London, the British government published its proclamation of neutrality, which recognized the Confederacy as a belligerent power. Great Britain considered the contest between North and South as an international rather than a domestic matter. The Lincoln administration interpreted the step as proof of a desire to have the status of the Confederacy settled before Adams could reach London.

The North resented this action. Feeling ran high, and the traditional bitterness against England was revived in full force. Historians, however, have been inclined to look upon the issue of the proclamation at that time as peculiarly fortunate because it forestalled further action for a considerable period. Had the British government waited a few months, until after the Battle of Bull Run, it probably would have gone further and recognized the independence of the South. But Adams felt that the British government was hostile toward the North, and in May 1861 he wrote that his mission might be terminated at any moment.

That was the situation when the *Trent* Affair threatened to bring on war between England and the Union. The Confederacy had decided to send commissioners to England and France to urge recognition and aid. James M. Mason and John Slidell were the men selected. Running the blockade, they took passage from Havana on a British mail steamer, the *Trent*. On November 8, 1861, the day after she left Havana, she was overhauled by a vessel of the American navy, the *San Jacinto*, Captain Wilkes commanding. The *San Jacinto* fired two shots to bring the *Trent* to a stop. Then a force of sailors and marines boarded her and removed Mason, Slidell, and their

"Trent" Affair

secretaries, in spite of the protests of the British officers. Wilkes took his prisoners to Fort Warren in Boston harbor.

On November 16 the news of the capture reached New York. Wilkes was welcomed with a series of receptions, dinners, and votes of thanks, some of which were adopted by the federal House of Representatives.

In England, on the other hand, the news was received with mingled feelings of wrath and amazement. An unknown Yankee naval officer had insulted the British flag. In the past England had never recognized the sanctity of any neutral flag, and on occasions without number she had violated neutral rights on the seas. A Cabinet meeting decided that the seizure was in violation of international law and that reparation must be made. Earl Russell drew up a dispatch to Lord Lyons, the British minister in Washington, which in its original form would probably have provoked war. Fortunately the message was softened at the suggestion of Queen Victoria. In its denatured phraseology it demanded the liberation of Mason and Slidell and "a suitable apology for the aggression." The government of the United States was to have seven days in which to make a reply. If none came, or if an unsatisfactory one were given, Lyons was to leave at once for London. The Admiralty prepared for war, 8000 troops were sent to Canada, and the government prohibited the export of arms and ammunition.

In this case the American government was able to act in a spirit of graciousness which contrasted sharply with the British attitude. On November 30 Seward wrote Adams that Wilkes had acted without instructions, and he hinted that his government would surrender the envoys. Adams imparted this news to Russell. Lincoln and Seward were both inclined toward moderation. "I fear the traitors will prove to be white elephants," Lincoln wrote. "We must stick to American principles concerning the rights of neutrals. We fought Great Britain for insisting by theory and practice on the right to do exactly what Captain Wilkes has done. If Great Britain shall now protest against the act and demand their release, we must give them up, apologize for the act as a violation of our doctrines, and thus forever bind her over to keep the peace in relation to neutrals, and so acknowledge that she has been wrong for sixty years." On December 26, 1861, Seward announced the surrender of Mason and Slidell. American opinion in general supported the administration. Wilkes had done practically what British commanders had done during the period before the War of 1812, and the United States had always condemned such proceedings. The British demand for the surrender of Mason and Slidell was justified by American interpretations of international law.

Confederate Navy

As the war progressed other causes of friction arose between England and the United States. Unable to provide themselves with commerce raiders, the Confederates turned to British shipbuilding firms. Vessels were constructed in British yards, equipped in or from British ports, and started on their careers of destruction from neutral harbors. Adams kept the British officials fully informed of these matters, and they could have prevented the ships from leaving port. In March 1862 the *Florida* was allowed to leave Liverpool, where she had been built for the Confederate service. After she got away Justice Cockburn said that she should have been detained; British authorities were not using due diligence in fulfilling their duties as a neutral. Before the British authorities made up their minds to act decisively, a second raider, the *Shenandoah,* embarked upon her career.

The most famous case was that of the *Alabama,* which like the *Florida,* was constructed in Liverpool for the Confederacy. It was common knowledge that the vessel would be fitted out and equipped from a British base, and Adams laid evidence to prove it before the British foreign office. He demanded that the boat be seized before she left port. Had it not been for a regrettable combination of factors, the *Alabama* would have been detained, but before the order to seize the ship arrived she slipped out to sea. She received her armament and supplies from British vessels and promptly began to destroy Union merchant shipping. After the war was over the British government paid heavily for her depredations.

In the summer of 1863 it seemed that an even more serious situation might arise. Adams learned that the Laird firm at Liverpool was building some ironclad rams for the Confederacy. As usual, he submitted his evidence and asked that they be detained. On September 1 Earl Russell, who had been none too friendly toward the Union, announced that he could find no proof that the boats were being built for the Confederacy. Nevertheless, even though proof was wanting, the British Cabinet decided to prevent the departure of the rams. Before Adams was informed of this decision, he had read a sharp lesson to the foreign secretary. Warning Russell against letting any more vessels for the Confederate navy escape from English ports, Adams concluded: "It would be superfluous in me to point out to your lordship that this is war." This time the vessels were seized before they could get away.

The decision of the foreign office to keep the rams in port marked the end of British violations of international law in that particular field. By the summer of 1863 there was visible a marked change in British opinion. Hitherto sympathy with the South had been strong, and its strength was based in part upon the early manifestations of Confederate power. The Davis government seemed to be on the way toward victory. But after Gettysburg and Vicksburg the ultimate supremacy of the Union became certain. From that time until the end of the war, British opinion was decisively with the North. As Owen Wister ironically put it: "The London *Times* and the *Saturday Review* had lately been quoting the Bible as sanction for slavery; for England dearly loves the Bible, but now many voices in London became sure that slavery was wicked; for England dearly loves success."

Further evidence of changing sentiment in England was to be seen in the official attitude toward Mason, the Confederate agent. By 1863 British official circles had become noticeably cool, and Mason himself became increasingly ill at ease. In his message to the Confederate Congress on January 12, 1863, Davis characterized the policy of neutrality adopted by all the European states as "an actual decision against our rights and in favor of the groundless pretensions of the United States." The refusal to recognize the independence of the Confederacy was both unjust and injurious. If the governments of Europe had granted recognition, "the moral effect of such action would have been to dispel the delusion under which the United States have persisted in their efforts to accomplish our subjugation," and the war would have been shortened. Davis also complained because the British government recognized the legality of the blockade.

Blockade Running

Throughout the war there were always difficulties connected with the blockade. In the Confederacy there was a steady and increasingly insistent demand for manufactured goods and successful blockade-runners were sure of good profits. Moreover, with cotton at 42 cents a pound outside the Confederacy, even the small cargoes which a blockade-runner could carry promised handsome returns. In spite of the steadily increasing efficiency of the Federal navy, blockade running continued almost until the end of the war.

It was common for traders engaged in supplying the Confederacy to carry clearance papers for Nassau in the Bahamas or for Matamoras in Mexico. They might put into those ports, or they might not. In any case the Confederacy was their ultimate destination. In order to stop the practice, vessels of the Union navy began to seize boats bound for Nassau, provided there was reason to believe that their clearance papers did not tell the whole truth and that their cargoes were really going to some southern port. To justify the seizure of such vessels, the United States Supreme Court revived the doctrine of continuous voyage. In deciding whether a cargo ought to be condemned or not, the determining factor was the ultimate destination rather than the place named in the ship's papers. A large consignment of arms, cleared for Nassau, was destined for the Confederacy because Nassau was at peace. Among the cases that reached the Supreme Court, the *Dolphin* and *Bermuda* furnished important precedents, because the Court sanctioned the seizure of both vessel and cargo. In the case of the *Springbok* the cargo was condemned, while the vessel was freed because there was no evidence of fraudulent action on the part of the owners.

The French in Mexico

Relations between the Confederacy and France were no more satisfactory to Davis than were those with Great Britain. Napoleon III expressed sympathy for the South and in 1862 he proposed that his own government, with England and Russia, join in proposing an armistice for six months. The British authorities refused to participate, and Napoleon III would not make the venture alone. Early in 1863, according to Slidell, Napoleon himself suggested a complicated arrangement whereby ironclad vessels might be constructed for the Confederacy in French ports. The work was begun with the Emperor's knowledge and approval but without formal contracts. These would be signed when the Emperor gave his verbal assurance that the vessels would be permitted to leave port under the Confederate flag. But the Union victories of 1863 made the French ruler a bit more cautious, and he never gave the assurance. The Confederacy did not get the ships.

These difficulties were only a part of the burden which Seward had to carry during the war. Napoleon III caused trouble when he began to experiment with a colonial scheme in Mexico, and the story of his puppet Maximilian is an interesting episode in the career of the adventurer of the Revolution of 1848.

Unrest in Mexico

The preference which Mexico had for revolution as a substitute for orderly elections has been mentioned before, in connection with Texas. By 1857 she had a record of thirty-six different governments in as many years, and nearly all of them had been preceded by revolution. In 1857, after the final disappearance of Santa Anna, the Mexicans adopted a new constitution, and a president was elected with almost no opposition. He was duly inaugurated on December 1 for a term of four years. Inside of a month he had been driven from the country. According to the constitutional provision covering presidential vacancies, the next in line for the office was Benito Juarez. Juarez was an Indian, an able leader who had a genuine interest in the Mexican people. He was unable to restore order, and for two years Mexico was plunged in confusion. Outrages against American citizens and personal insults to Forsyth, the American minister, compelled the United States to sever diplomatic relations. These were restored in 1859, and from that year to 1867 the United States recognized the Juarez government.

In December 1860 Juarez captured Mexico City and began a series of attacks upon the strong clerical party. In addition to his domestic difficulties, Juarez was troubled with foreign problems. His predecessors had borrowed money from any banker who would lend to them. Their understanding of public finance was that whatever they got they spent to keep themselves in power, and then passed the obligations to pay over to their successors. After the volume of this indebtedness had piled up to a point where the prospect of payment looked dubious, the foreign bankers appealed to their governments for help.

By 1861 Great Britain, Spain, and France were insisting upon a settlement of various claims against Mexico. England and Spain complained that debts remained unpaid and that claims for property damaged or destroyed received no attention. The French grievances were less substantial. One claim was based upon $15,000,000 in bonds issued through a Swiss banking firm. For bonds to that amount, the thrifty Swiss house had turned over to one of the ephemeral Mexican governments the sum of $750,000. Then the bonds were taken by French bankers, and the French government insisted upon the payment of the whole $15,000,000. In addition, claims to the extent of $12,000,000 more were trumped up for alleged injuries to French subjects.

Financial Problems

Juarez was in no position to meet these claims; in fact he was inclined to question the binding force of all financial arrangements made by his predecessors. In making the loans the bankers knew that they were indulging in wild gambling; Mexico had never enjoyed enough lasting stability to justify expectations of payment. And yet these Europeans gravely declared that Mexico must play the game according to the rules accepted among firmly established governments. According to these rules the Mexican republic, not merely the ruling group of revolutionary adventurers, was responsible for these debts.

In July 1861 Juarez decreed that payments to all foreign bankers be suspended for two years. The British and French ministers demanded an immediate revocation of the order, and when Juarez refused they broke off diplomatic relations. The Spanish government had already taken this step. This threat of a European triple alliance against Mexico boded ill for the Monroe Doctrine, and Seward tried to ward off actual intervention. He suggested to Juarez that the United States would assume responsibility for paying the interest on the whole debt of Mexico for five years, provided certain securities were given. These, Seward said, should be a mortgage on the public lands and mineral rights in Lower California, Chihuahua, Sonora, and Sinaloa. If Mexico should not reimburse the United States within six years, the American title to these properties would become absolute.

The validity of this arrangement was made conditional upon a British and French agreement not to enforce payment, provided the Senate would ratify Seward's plan. But the European governments looked upon the proposal as a thinly veiled arrangement for the seizure of Mexican territory by the United States, and they were determined to have a hand in any such profitable game. Furthermore, the United States Senate looked coldly upon Seward's plan for mortgaging Mexico into good financial behavior.

The rejection of Seward's plan left the parties where they were in the beginning. Thereupon, in October 1861, Great Britain, Spain, and France agreed upon intervention in Mexico. They announced that they were seeking no acquisition of territory and no special advantages. They also said that they had no intention of impairing the sovereignty of Mexico. They asked the United States to acquiesce in their proposed measures, but they made it plain that their action would be in no way influenced by an unfavorable reply. Seward said that his government could not become a party to the agreement. He did not deny the right of the three powers to intervene, and he expressed satisfaction at the assurance that there was no intention of impairing the sovereignty of Mexico.

Early in 1862 a combined English, French, and Spanish force took possession of Vera Cruz. According to the original plan, only the coast cities were to be seized, but, once French troops had landed, Napoleon III proposed to capture Mexico City. After a month the English and Spanish governments withdrew from the enterprise and left the French a clear field. By the summer of 1863 French troops, heavily reinforced, had occupied Mexico City. Then the French summoned a carefully picked convention of prominent white Mexicans, representing chiefly the powerful clerical party. The convention announced that Mexico desired a monarchy with a Catholic emperor for a sovereign. An aspirant for the post was found in Maximilian of Austria, the brother of Francis Joseph. The Mexican people—that is, the Indians—were not consulted as to their preferences in the matter, but they rarely had been in previous overturns. Maximilian was installed by a faction, as his predecessors had been, but in this particular case the faction had the backing of Napoleon III.

Emperor Maximilian

Maximilian himself entered Mexico in 1864, and the presence of 35,000 French troops inspired fear, if not respect. He had widespread support among the white groups but not among the Indians. From 1864 to 1867 Juarez kept up constant guerilla warfare, but he was not strong enough to recover control of the government. At the close of the American war Seward informed Napoleon that French troops could no longer be tolerated in Mexico. The Emperor agreed to take them out if the United States would recognize Maximilian. Seward refused. Napoleon then, in 1866, agreed to withdraw them all by the following year, and he did so. When Francis Joseph hinted at Austrian support for his brother, Seward silenced him by a plain threat of war. When the French troops left, Maximilian might have saved his life by going with them, but he felt that he owed something to his associates. His decision to remain put him at the mercy of Juarez, and on June 19, 1867, he was shot.

This attempt to establish a French protectorate over Mexico was the first serious challenge to the Monroe Doctrine. The episode attracted widespread attention, and protests against France were registered in newspapers, party platforms, and in congressional resolutions. Fortunately, the test happened to come at a time when the United States was able to resort to vigorous action. Because of the seriousness of the principle at stake, the country was justified in its feeling of elation at Seward's victory. The prospect of a renewal of European control over Latin America had been decisively checked.

In 1862 and 1863, when Confederate officials were still hoping for French intervention in their own cause, they made a point of endorsing Napoleon's policy in Mexico, even going so far as to express approval of Maximilian. In his message to Congress of December 1863, Davis referred to the "lively interest" felt in this venture.

> Although preferring our own Government and institutions to those of other countries, we can have no disposition to contest the exercise by them of the same right of self-government which we assert for ourselves. If the Mexican people prefer a monarchy to a republic, it is our plain duty cheerfully to

acquiesce in their decision and to evince a sincere and friendly interest in their prosperity.

But Napoleon III had lost interest in the Confederacy, and Maximilian refused to receive a minister from Davis's government.

Wartime Finance

Paying for the War

During the Civil War, as in wars generally, the government found it easier to keep the ranks filled with men than to raise the necessary funds. Congress at first preferred loans to taxes so that war costs could be shifted to later generations. In July 1861 Chase, the secretary of the treasury, was authorized to borrow $250,000,000. At the same time Congress levied a direct tax of $20,000,000, imposed an income tax of 3 percent on incomes above $800, and increased the tariff rates. From time to time Congress either raised the rates on taxes already in existence, such as the tariff, or imposed new taxes in the form of stamp duties. In 1862 the income tax was raised to 3 percent on incomes from $600 to $10,000 and to 5 percent on higher incomes; later these rates were raised again to 5 and 10 percent, respectively. It took time to realize the returns from these various sources, and in 1863 Congress bridged the gap by authorizing the issue of legal tender, noninterest-bearing treasury notes. These were known as green backs. The amount issued at first was $150,000,000, but before the end of the war the volume outstanding had been increased to $449,000,000. Throughout the war they fluctuated in value, as reports from the front were favorable or otherwise.

In the course of the war the government raised approximately $667,000,000 in taxes and $2,140,000,000 in loans. Because the bonds did not sell rapidly, in February 1863 Chase induced Congress to pass the National Banking Act. This provided for federal incorporation of banks. These national banks could issue notes, which were secured by government bonds. Every national bank was required to purchase bonds equal in amount to at least one third of its paid-up capital. These were deposited with the treasurer of the United States and held by him. Then the banks were allowed to issue notes equal in amount to 90 percent of the market value of the bonds. This measure provided currency, and at the same time created a dependable market for the bonds. In 1865 state bank notes were driven out of circulation with a 10 percent tax.

Wartime Prosperity

The success of federal finance was made possible by the extraordinary business "boom" which the North enjoyed during the war. Business entered upon a period of expansion that was not checked until the panic of 1873. Prosperity extended to all parts of the Union and affected every phase of economic life. The nation was still primarily agricultural, and there were good harvests every year, especially of wheat and corn. In 1862 and 1863 there were "bumper crops" of wheat. In 1862 the Union States raised

177,000,000 bushels of wheat, 4,000,000 more than the whole country had raised in its best year before the war.

This agricultural activity was made possible by a number of factors. There was no serious shortage of labor because of the widespread introduction of labor-saving machinery. With the help of the machines, women could take the place of men in the fields and they did so, especially in the West. Markets for the heavy agricultural output were found in various quarters. The army required more food than would have been necessary for the same number of men in civil life. There were also increasing demands for American wheat abroad. In 1861 crops failed all over Europe, while England suffered a second failure the next year. In 1862 the United States exported 60,000,000 bushels of wheat, three times as much as the average annual export for the preceding ten years.

Every branch of industry expanded to meet wartime demands. The woolen mills were apparently the most flourishing of all. They were rushed to fullest capacity, and for those days the profits were enormous. One manufacturer said he was then making $2000 a day. The dividends paid by the woolen mills ranged from 10 to 40 percent.

In Pennsylvania and the other states where iron-manufacturing plants were located, there were signs of prosperity equaling those in the woolen centers. The demand for farm implements, farm machines, textile machinery, and, of course, munitions kept them busy. In Philadelphia fifty-eight new factories were built in 1862, fifty-seven in 1863, sixty-five in 1864. Other cities reported equally interesting figures. During the war years more patents were issued than ever before in the history of the Union. Five thousand were issued in 1864 alone, as against forty-two in the Confederacy.

This expansion in agriculture and in industry, added to the activity of the War Department in transporting troops and supplies, meant an equally big gain for the railroads. Every year of the war, railroad journals reported a steady increase in traffic and dividends. Companies paid off their indebtedness and made good profits besides. On a number of lines between 1860 and 1865 freight and passenger traffic was doubled.

Confederate Problems

The Confederacy presented a very different picture. Never self-sufficing either agriculturally or industrially before the war, and partly cut off from its sources of manufactures and food, its people had to familiarize themselves with a new type of farming and with manufacturing. Factories were built, notably in Atlanta, and machine shops were constructed to provide tools and munitions, but there was nothing like the profitable economic expansion just described in the North.

Because of the absence of accumulated capital and the dislocation of economic life in the Confederacy, Jefferson Davis's task of financing the war was much more difficult than Lincoln's. The Confederate Treasury started with about $20,000,000 in specie, a quarter of which was the federal money seized in the mints and customhouses when the war began; the rest was secured from the banks in the first loan. This amount was soon spent in purchasing munitions and supplies abroad, and when it was gone the government depended upon unsecured note issues, amounting, all told, to $1,000,000,000. The notes were legal tender and they were convertible at par into 8 percent Confederate bonds. The bonds were payable in coin, theoretically; as a matter of fact they were never paid at all. At the beginning of 1863 the Confederate paper dollar was worth 33 cents in gold, by the end of that year 5 cents, and in April 1865, 1 6/10 cents. Flour cost $1000 a barrel, coffee $40 a pound, wood $5 a stick. When the farmers refused to sell produce for this worthless paper, the government seized the supplies it needed. This rapid decline of Confederate credit was revealed again in the market value of the bond issues. The first loan of $15,000,000 was quoted at 90 in 1862, and at 5 or lower in 1864. Early in 1863 the Confederate Secretary of the Treasury Memminger arranged through the banking house of Emile Erlanger in Paris for a loan of $15,000,000 at 7 percent. The principal was to be paid in New Orleans cotton six months after the end of the war. Erlanger bought the bonds at 77 and sold them in England at 95½. So enthusiastic were the English friends of the Confederacy that they oversubscribed the loan three times in two days. After Chattanooga the bonds dropped to 37, and with the final Union victory they dropped to 0. As Lord Salisbury put it, the English nobility had bet their money on the wrong horse.

In this effort to find means for prosecuting the war, the Confederate Congress enacted two laws providing for the confiscation of property. The first of these, passed in March 1863, authorized President Davis to appoint commissioners for each state; these officials were empowered to fix prices for all commodities bought by the government. The second, passed a month later, authorized a tax in kind of one tenth of all farm produce in the Confederacy. Even Davis himself, in his message of December 1863, described this system of supplying the army as "unequal in its operation, vexatious to the producer, injurious to the industrial interests, and productive of . . . discontent among the people."

Arbitrary Power

Aside from military and financial problems, both governments had to contend with difficulties that rarely if ever trouble a country in time of peace.

Suppressing Disloyalty

The federal government underwent a vast increase in power. Congress levied direct taxes, endowed agricultural colleges, and gave the Union Pacific Railroad its start. Furthermore, Lincoln ordered the suspension of the privilege of habeas corpus, and disloyal citizens were arrested. But there was no suppression of Congress, and the members of that body were just as free to criticize the administration as ever. Except in the border states, there was no interference with elections, and there were no executions of political prisoners.

From the beginning of the war, when the pro-Confederate mob in Baltimore fired upon the 6th Regiment from Massachusetts and the governor of Kentucky tried to proclaim neutrality between the belligerents, the administration had to evolve a policy for checkmating the enemies of the Union within the Union itself. Opposition was not confined to the border states. Throughout the North there were scattered elements of a peace party. In this group were to be found objectors to war in general, because of ethical or religious convictions, and objectors to this particular war, on the ground that the federal government had no right to coerce the states. Finally there were the "Copperheads," who were openly sympathetic with the Confederacy.

By their attack upon troops in federal service, the zealous Marylanders had come dangerously close to treason. Lincoln felt that they had sacrificed all claim to the protection of the law, and he prepared to invoke extraordinary powers to restrain them. In 1861 he authorized General Scott to suspend the writ of habeas corpus along the line of troop movements between Washington and Bangor, Maine. On September 24, 1862, Lincoln issued a proclamation, declaring that "disloyal persons are not adequately restrained by the ordinary process of law from hindering the enlistment of troops and from giving aid and comfort in various ways to the insurrection." Consequently, he declared, all rebels and insurgents in the Union, and all persons who interfered with the enrollment of troops, should be subject to martial law and liable to trial by military tribunal; also that the writ of habeas corpus should be suspended in respect to all persons imprisoned by military authority.

The President found justification for these orders in the Constitution, which gives a negative power to suspend the writ of habeas corpus. There was, however, considerable fault-finding, especially by those who felt that Congress alone could set aside legal safeguards. In March 1863 Congress gave the President authority to do what he already had done. Strengthened by this legislative approval, Lincoln, on September 14, 1863, proclaimed a suspension of the writ of habeas corpus in case of all prisoners held as spies, aiders or abettors of the enemy, deserters from Union forces, resisters of military conscription, or "for any other offense against the military or naval service."

Lincoln's Defense

This removal of time-honored safeguards of individual liberty laid Lincoln open to bitter adverse criticism. In denying the rights of free speech and a free press, his opponents said, he was guilty of destroying the very foundations on which the government rested. Fortunately for the cause of the Union, Lincoln was not disturbed by these complaints and always found convincing arguments to justify his own course.

Let the Union be destroyed, he declared, and not only would the Constitution fall with it, but also the privileges about which the peace party was so insistent. By a temporary encroachment on some of those rights he might save the Union and the whole structure of privileges erected upon it. His duty, as he saw it, was to preserve "by every indispensable means, that government—that nation of which the Constitution was the organic law." Under conditions then existing, "Measures otherwise unconstitutional might become lawful by becoming indispensable to the preservation of the Constitution through the preservation of the nation." Measures which the President could not take in time of peace became permissible in time of war, because, as he saw it, "the Constitution invests its Commander in Chief with the law of war in time of war." And again, he declared that "certain proceedings are constitutional when, in cases of rebellion or invasion, the public safety requires them, which would not be constitutional when, in absence of rebellion or invasion, the public safety does not require them."

Lincoln assumed that the safety of the state required the incarceration of a number of people, and they were promptly arrested. These arrests were made without warrants by federal marshals or military officials, and in many cases no formal charges were ever brought and no trial took place. The length of imprisonment depended upon circumstances. These imprisonments were made on grounds of suspected treason, aiding the Confederacy, acting as Confederate spies, and harboring deserters. "Disloyalty" was the reason given for imprisoning certain prominent Democrats.

Arbitrary Arrests

Altogether more than 13,000 individuals were subjected to arbitrary arrest. Many of the victims were inconspicuous, but there was one striking exception. Clement F. Vallandigham of Ohio, nationally known Democratic politician, had made himself notorious by his attacks upon Lincoln's war policy. As long as he was a member of Congress he could talk with impunity, but his term expired in 1863. In May of that year General Burnside ordered his arrest on the charge of obstructing enlistment in the army. Vallandigham was tried by court-martial, found guilty, and sentenced to imprisonment for the duration of the war. Immediately he became the hero of the disaffected. Then, when the political enemies of the administration and the peace party were preparing to capitalize Vallandigham's martyrdom, Lincoln ruined their scheme by making their victim ridiculous. Instead of keeping the man in prison, the President sent him under a flag of truce into the Confederate lines. With the cordial cooperation of his new hosts, Vallandigham left the South and retired to Canada, entirely free, but more of a joke than a hero. Then he became the Democratic candidate for governor of Ohio and directed his campaign from Canada. Perhaps the attitude of his state can best be seen in the 100,000 majority which it rolled up against him. After this failure he returned home.

When a meeting of Democrats in New York censured the President for punishing Vallandigham, Lincoln replied that the man had been punished because he had endeavored to prevent the raising of troops and to encourage desertion from the army. Desertion in time of war, he declared, must be punished by death. "Must I shoot a simple-minded soldier boy who deserts, while I must not touch a hair of a wily agitator who induces him to desert? . . . I think that . . . to silence the agitator and save the boy is not only Constitutional but withal a great mercy."

The most extreme cases of suppression of individual freedom occurred in Maryland early in the war. In July 1861 the administration ordered the arrest of the police commissioner of Baltimore. When the national House of Representatives asked the President for a statement of his reasons for this measure, he replied: "I have to state that it is judged to be incompatible with the public interest at this time to furnish the information called for by the resolution." The following September, under orders of Secretary of War Cameron, General Dix arrested ten members of the legislature of Maryland and one member of Congress. Subsequently, General Banks arrested nine more Maryland legislators. In Maryland, Missouri, and Kentucky troops supervised elections to discourage disloyal voters.

This policy inevitably brought complaint against Lincoln, but he was convinced that his course was right. As he told his opponents, his primary task was to save the government. The existing war imposed extraordinary responsibilities upon him, but at the same time it gave him extraordinary powers. As he wrote to Governor Seymour of New York, who had protested against the new policy of conscription: "My purpose is to be in my action just and constitutional, and yet practical, in performing the important duty with which I am charged—of maintaining the unity and the free principles of our common country."

Other manifestations of arbitrary power were to be found in the censorship of telegrams and newspapers. Newspapers were forbidden to carry important news regarding proposed troop movements, but sometimes they did so in spite of the obvious impropriety. Papers which indulged in too severe criticism of the President were suppressed, and sometimes the editors were arrested; in other cases mailing privileges were denied. Occasionally generals in command assumed the responsibility of stopping publications. Altogether between three and four hundred papers were suppressed.

Censorship

This limited application of censorship raises the question as to what the government did in the way of propaganda—that is, efforts designed to create and maintain a favorable opinion. Beyond the speeches of Lincoln and his associates in the government and in Congress, there seems to have been very little that was official. But private agencies took up the work of spreading the Union cause. The best-known organization of this sort was the Union League, which was put into operation at Philadelphia in 1862. In the course of a few months leagues were organized in Baltimore and Washington, New York and Boston, and as far west as San Francisco. Before long there were branches in eighteen states. The purpose of the Union League was to promote "unconditional loyalty to the Government of the United States . . . unwavering support of its efforts to suppress the Rebellion, and to spare no endeavor to maintain unimpaired the National Unity, both in principle and territorial boundary."

Lincoln's critics found the crowning example of arbitrary power in the Conscription Act of 1863. Under this measure men between the ages of eighteen and forty-five were declared eligible for military service, except post office and railroad officials, clergymen, teachers, and those physically disabled. The system of drawing was peculiar. Every congressional district had to supply a certain quota. If enough men in a district volunteered to fill this number, none were drafted. Where volunteering was not sufficient, the names of all those liable to service, on separate strips of paper, were put into a box, and those drawn were required to serve. But a drafted man was permitted to hire a substitute, the cost of which ranged from $300 to $1500. Insurance companies were ready to insure men against draft and did so until the government put a stop to the practice. This draft law aroused severe criticism, and in New York it was the occasion of serious riots lasting several days. There were minor riots in Jersey City and in Boston. Elsewhere the work of enrollment was carried through without difficulty.

Conscription

In the Confederacy President Davis found himself confronted by many similar problems, and necessity drove him into policies at least as arbitrary as any of those adopted in the Union. His government suspended the writ of habeas corpus, adopted conscription laws, and authorized the seizure of private property for military purposes. These measures resulted in widespread criticism of the Confederate administration.

Disloyalty in the South

These critics complained of the destruction of states' rights and of the establishment of a military despotism. Then there were certain influential newspapers, particularly the *Charleston Mercury* and the *Richmond Examiner*, which regularly opposed the administration. To these foes of the government there should be added some of the local political leaders, who placed the preservation of states' rights above the Confederate cause. These leaders who continually harassed Davis found almost solid backing in the upland region of the South. The mountaineer whites, individualistic in their political philosophy, had never been any too well disposed toward the Confederacy. In western Virginia and eastern Tennessee Union sentiment had predominated when the war began. Later, in parts of North Carolina, Georgia, and even in Davis's own state of Mississippi, the traditional hostility of the small farmer toward the great plantation owner reasserted itself in open defiance of the Confederacy. Wearied by war, embittered over the confiscation of their property, and maddened by conscription, these men expressed their feelings in the slogan: "It's a rich men's war but a poor men's fight."

The Freeing of the Slaves

While Lincoln found himself attacked from one quarter by those who resented his policy of dealing with hostile criticism, he was attacked from another by the abolitionists. They looked upon the war as an opportunity for ending slavery and they resented Lincoln's unwillingness to move fast enough. There was at the same time an anti-abolition group, so large and influential that Lincoln could not ignore it. The Republican party was not agreed upon abolitionism, and the Cabinet was divided. Lincoln's position became even more uncomfortable when some of the Union generals began to set slaves free. General Frémont tried this experiment first in Missouri. Lincoln asked Frémont, privately, to withdraw his proclamation on slavery. Frémont refused to comply with the request, so Lincoln relieved Frémont of his command.

Abolitionist Policies

In May 1862 General Hunter, in command at Port Royal, South Carolina, followed Frémont's example and declared all the slaves in Georgia, Florida, and Louisiana "forever free." Lincoln curtly declared that "no commanding general shall do such a thing . . . without consulting me." He followed this announcement with a general order, declaring Hunter's proclamation "altogether void." If circumstances should make emancipation desirable as a war measure, he said, the commander in chief, not the generals in the field, would issue the necessary regulations.

Lincoln could annul these orders of Frémont and of Hunter, but the problem of slavery still remained. During the first year of the war, by stressing the cause of the Union, the President had been able to keep emancipation in the background. But by 1862 he could do this no longer. The abolitionists had their adherents among the newspapers, in the army, and in Congress; as the war continued they became more and more insistent. Slavery must go. This group may have been a minority in the country at large, but its facilities for making itself heard were more than sufficient to compensate for any inferiority in numbers. Again, as long as emancipation was not one of Lincoln's main objectives, the North could never be certain of English sympathy. But once he decided to overthrow slavery, the President would secure the important moral support of the powerful antislavery liberal group in that country. Against these possible gains, Lincoln had to consider the almost certain loss of support in the very quarters where his advocacy of the Union had brought him strength. Not all the northern states were abolitionist in sentiment, while the border states were still proslavery. These were practical considerations which the abolitionists could overlook; the President could not ignore them.

Horace Greeley, generally an extremist, who had urged the country to let the southern states go in peace, now came out as one of the leaders of the immediate emancipation group. In August 1862 he addressed an open letter to the President, calling it "The Prayer of Twenty Millions":

> On the face of this wide earth, Mr. President, there is not one disinterested, determined, intelligent champion of the Union cause who does not feel that all attempts to put down the rebellion, and at the same time uphold its exciting cause, are preposterous and futile; that the rebellion, if crushed out tomorrow, would be renewed within a year if slavery were left in full vigor; that army officers who remain to this day devoted to slavery can at best be but halfway

loyal to the Union; and that every hour of deference to slavery is an hour of added and deepened peril to the Union.

Lincoln's reply was characteristic:

> My paramount object is to save the Union, and not either to save or destroy slavery. If I could save the Union without freeing any slave, I would do it; if I could save it by freeing all the slaves, I would do it; and if I could save it by freeing some and leaving others alone, I would also do that.

Compensated Emancipation

Lincoln himself had given as much careful thought to emancipation as any man in the country. Being a conservative lawyer, he recognized the legal validity of the master's title to his slaves; this vested interest, he felt, should not be arbitrarily annulled. It might, however, be purchased by the state, and then the state could free the slaves. With this end in view, on March 6, 1862, he submitted a special message to his "fellow-citizens of the Senate and House of Representatives," recommending the adoption of the following joint resolution:

> That the United States, in order to cooperate with any State which may adopt gradual abolishment of slavery ought to give such State pecuniary aid, to be used by such State, in its discretion, to compensate for the inconvenience, public and private, produced by such change of system.

Payment for the slaves might be made at the rate of $400 each. Congress adopted the recommendation, but the border states refused to take advantage of it.

Again and again Lincoln reverted to this idea of compensated emancipation. In his second annual message, December 1862, he urged Congress to adopt an amendment to the Constitution, promising compensation to any state which should abolish its slaves at any time prior to January 1, 1900. The long period, he said, would spare "both races from the evils of sudden derangement, in fact, from the necessity of any derangement"; it would save the slaves from the "destitution which must largely attend immediate emancipation in localities where their numbers are very great." Finally, as late as February 6, 1865, Lincoln proposed compensation for those states which would cease their resistance to federal authority by April 1, next. His Cabinet, however, unanimously disapproved, whereupon compensation dropped out of the picture.

Emancipation Proclamation

After the first failure of the plan for buying the freedom of the slaves, Lincoln had given thought to another method of conciliating the abolitionists. He had no legal nor constitutional right to proceed against slavery in any state but, as head of the army, he could use his war power in any way that might embarrass the enemy. He planned, therefore, to announce freedom for all slaves in those parts of the country still in rebellion. For this purpose he worked out a carefully phrased proclamation, the first draft of which was written early in July 1862. At the end of the month, after Congress had adjourned, he showed it to his Cabinet. Seward suggested that public announcement of this proclamation be held up until after a military victory for the Union. Lincoln published it on September 22 after McClellan had succeeded in checking Lee's progress at Antietam. It was to go into effect January 1, 1863. The gist of the proclamation was contained in the following sentence: "All persons held as slaves within any state or designated part of a state the people whereof shall be in rebellion against the United States shall be then, thenceforward, and forever free."

Even a casual reading of the document makes it plain that the Emancipation Proclamation did not immediately emancipate a single slave. It applied neither to the border states nor to those portions of the Confederacy then held by Union forces. It could not be made effective in the Confederacy. Lincoln's famous document therefore was designed not to free the slaves but to announce a policy for the future, and to please politicians like Chase and Frémont and editors like Greeley. Lincoln himself admitted that it had "no constitutional or legal justification, except as a military measure."

In December 1863 a member of Congress introduced in the House a Thirteenth Amendment to the Constitution, providing for the final and absolute prohibition of slavery everywhere within the jurisdiction of the United States. But this Amendment did not win the approval of Congress until January 1865. By the following December, it was ratified by the necessary three quarters of the state legislatures, and put into effect.

Politics during the War

Political Issues

At the time it was issued, the Emancipation Proclamation was politically unpopular. By 1862, when the congressional elections came around, Lincoln knew that many Democrats who had upheld him in 1861 would vote against his party, and he knew that his party itself was torn with serious factional differences. In the Republican camp there were the radicals who insisted upon immediate abolition and the conservatives who placed the preservation of the Union above everything else. In the President's Cabinet these factions were led respectively by Chase and Seward. Some Democrats supported Lincoln during the war, as for example Stanton and Andrew Johnson. Others, like McClellan, approved of the war but disapproved of the Lincoln administration. Still others, the "copperheads," tried to block enlistments, encouraged desertion, and when possible sent military information to the Confederate authorities. In prosecuting the war, Lincoln had to keep this complex political situation in mind. Every new measure and proposal had to be considered not on its merits but with reference to its effect on his own party and upon the opposition. Next to winning victories in the field it was essential to retain a majority in Congress.

The issues in this congressional campaign of 1862 were the wartime policies of the administration, particularly the suspension of habeas corpus, arbitrary arrests, and emancipation of the slaves. The Republicans lost New York, Pennsylvania, Ohio, Indiana, Illinois, and Wisconsin. New Jersey, which had gone against the Republicans in 1860, did the same in 1862. The administration majority in Congress was cut down to the narrowest margin.

This outcome made the administration somewhat nervous as the Presidential campaign of 1864 approached. Disappointment over Grant's failure to bring the war to a speedy close found expression among the Republicans in criticism of Lincoln and in demands for a more vigorous prosecution of the war. The radicals of the Chase-Frémont school were especially outspoken in their desire for a new executive. This group attempted to carry the whole party with it by calling a convention of its own. Meeting at Cleveland, they drew up a platform advocating, among other things, a constitutional amendment to prohibit slavery, congressional rather than executive control of reconstruction, and the confiscation of Confederate property. For their candidate they picked their first standard bearer, John C. Frémont. In September, however, Frémont dropped out of the campaign.

The regular Republicans, laying emphasis upon their wartime title of "the Union party," met at Baltimore in June. They agreed with the radicals in calling for the Thirteenth Amendment, but disagreed with them in their attitude toward Lincoln. Lincoln got all the votes except those of Missouri on the first ballot. For Vice President the convention selected one of the conspicuous pro-war Democrats, Andrew Johnson of Tennessee. At the time his choice seemed to be an excellent piece of political strategy because it made the ticket acceptable to other Democrats.

Lincoln's Victory

The Democrats planned to make capital out of Lincoln's failure to end the war, and they postponed their convention until August 29. Their platform characterized the conduct of the war as a failure and demanded a change in administration, but the Democrats did not advocate peace on southern terms. However, the permanent chairman was a peace Democrat of New York, Horatio Seymour, and the notorious Vallandigham wrote the platform. It took the party twenty years to recover from the effects of such leadership. The Democratic nominee was General McClellan. On September 1 the Democrats adjourned, prepared to go before the country with their war-is-a-failure platform, even though their candidate would not stand on it. On September 2 the first reports of Sherman's capture of Atlanta began to arrive. Before the end of the month Sheridan won his victories in the Shenandoah valley, and Farragut had won another in Mobile Bay. The Republican newspapers ridiculed the Democratic platform, and Lincoln became more popular. In the election he carried all but three states, Kentucky, Delaware, and New Jersey, getting 212 electoral votes to 21 for McClellan. His popular plurality was nearly half a million. But his success was due largely, if not entirely, to the sudden change for the better in the field.

By March 4, 1865, when Lincoln was inaugurated for his second term, the end of the war was in sight, and the President's popularity was assured. On April 11, two days after Lee's surrender, Lincoln participated in a general celebration and delivered his last public address. The end of the war, he said, made immediate plans for reconstruction imperative. But the whole subject was full of difficulty. In the South there was no organized authority to deal with. "We simply must begin with and mold from disorganized and discordant elements. Nor is it a small additional embarrassment that we, the loyal people, differ among ourselves as to the mode, manner, and measure of reconstruction." Some of his critics, he said, were finding fault with him because he had not decided definitely whether the seceded states were in the Union or out of it. He did not intend to argue the point; on the contrary, as he told his hearers, he felt that discussion of such a "pernicious abstraction" could work nothing but harm.

> We all agree that the seceded States, so called, are out of their proper practical relation with the Union, and that the sole object of the Government, civil and military, in regard to those States, is to again get them into that proper relation. I believe that it is not only possible, but, in fact, easier, to do this without deciding or even considering whether these States have ever been out of the Union, than with it. Finding themselves safely at home, it would be utterly immaterial whether they had ever been abroad.

In his last Cabinet meeting, held on April 14, 1865, Lincoln made a strong plea for lenience toward the South:

> I hope there will be no persecution, no bloody work after the war is over. None need expect me to take any part in hanging or killing them. . . . Enough lives have been sacrificed. We must extinguish our resentment if we expect harmony and union.

Murder of Lincoln

That same evening Lincoln and a small party went to a play in Ford's Theater. Shortly before the end of the performance, John Wilkes Booth, an actor, gained access to the President's box. Before anyone was aware of the interruption, he placed a pistol directly against Lincoln's head and shot him. Then he leaped to the stage, breaking his leg in the fall, but because of the general confusion he succeeded in making his escape. He took refuge in Virginia, but his hiding place was discovered, and upon his refusal to come out and surrender he was shot. His fellow conspirators were tried, convicted of conspiracy to commit murder, and hanged. Booth's crime solved no problems. On the contrary, it deprived the people of their ablest leader at a time when his services were most urgently needed.

Chapter 25

RECONSTRUCTION

Conditions in the South

Economic Collapse

WHEN Lee accepted Grant's terms of surrender at Appomattox, the Civil War was over and the Confederate States of America ceased to exist as a government. Interest in reconstruction took the place of interest in the war, and for the next twelve years this subject dominated American politics and government. The Lincoln administration had not entered upon the war for the purpose of destroying slavery, and the end of the war found slavery still in existence in the border states. The Emancipation Proclamation had foretold the end of the peculiar institution, and the war had practically destroyed slavery in the Confederacy. The Thirteenth Amendment designed to abolish it completely, was even then in process of ratification by the states. The adoption of this Amendment would bring about a complete change in the relation of whites and Negroes. The close of the Civil War therefore found the South facing a double problem: recovery from the effects of the fighting and the establishment of a new status for former slaves.

For the northern states, reconstruction was relatively simple. The military forces had to be demobilized and the civil courts restored to full authority but that was practically all. In the South, on the other hand, the war had brought general disaster. Even in the areas untouched by actual fighting economic activity had come almost to a standstill. For the regions of actual warfare the status was one not of stagnation but of chaos. In many case fields on the farms had remained uncultivated for periods of from one to four years, so that they were grown up to briers and underbrush. Livestock had been killed for food or confiscated by the armies. Fences, fruit trees buildings, and roads were damaged or destroyed. Farm tools had worn out and there had been no means of replacement during the war. Even seed and fertilizer for new crops were wanting. In Georgia, throughout the are covered by Sherman's march, sixty miles in width, destruction of farms wa almost complete. Confederate veterans who came straggling home to ruine farms were in no position to support themselves and their families, to sa nothing of their former slaves.

Adequate transportation facilities might have made the situation less bac but the war almost ruined these facilities. The destruction of railroad prop erty had been widespread and effective. On some lines the rival armies ha torn up the tracks, burned the crossties, wrecked the locomotives, and ruine the rolling stock. On others the roadbeds were overgrown with briers wooden bridges, buildings, and water tanks were partly or wholly in ruin

One serious obstacle to recovery was the absence of capital and the lack of credit. Southerners had invested their funds in Confederate bonds. Hard money had given way to Confederate paper. Bonds and paper money were both worthless at the end of the war. For the farsighted individuals who had put their money into real estate, there was no immediate relief because there was no sale for land. Thousands of acres were actually deserted by their owners because they had neither the means nor the labor to cultivate them.

The Freedmen

To complete the picture of ruin, the labor system of the South had broken down. The former slaves, numbering approximately 4,000,000, had represented a market value of more than $2,000,000,000. This investment was completely wiped out. More important still, the customs of the country which had been built upon slavery were suddenly rendered obsolete. The Negroes were not all free when the war came to an end, but in December 1865 the Thirteenth Amendment went into effect, and this ended slavery for all time. In anticipation of this measure, even before the end of the struggle, some Negroes had begun to drift into the army camps. Others left the plantations and wandered into the nearest towns. Settlements of Negro fugitives were started along the seacoast and at points on the Mississippi. Although these groups of vagrants and refugees were numerous, they included only a fraction of the Negroes; most of them remained on the plantations. Here they were a burden to their former owners, who, in spite of good intentions, could not find enough food for them.

But the problem of the freedmen was not simply a matter of food, clothing, and shelter. New legal, social, and economic regulations were necessary. Under slavery the Negroes had received all necessities of life from their owners. Freedom cut the Negro loose from security and left him stranded with no means of supporting himself and with no legal rights. When the federal government gave freedom, it gave that and nothing more. The ordinary Negro possessed no property; not even the clothes which he wore belonged to him. He had received no training to fit him for the responsibilities of freedom, and he had no experience as an independent laborer or farmer. In the circumstances there was bound to be unrest, but most of the Negroes proved loyal and anxious to cooperate. However, some Negroes were bewildered by the change in their station in life, and they became uneasy. Vagrancy and petty thievery were bound to develop, particularly in view of the generally disorganized state of society and the difficulty in procuring food. In general the problem was to define the place of the Negroes in the new economic and social structure. What were their rights before the law, in the schools, in churches, in public buildings, and on common carriers? Under what conditions should they be allowed to own land or to enjoy the privileges associated with freedom?

As for the southern whites, they seemed ready to cooperate with federal officials and to accept the fact of freedom for the Negroes. No single statement will describe their attitude because attitudes varied widely with different individuals. On the basis of his observations General Grant believed that "the mass of thinking men of the South accept the present situation of affairs in good faith. . . . The citizens of the Southern States are anxious to return to self-government within the union as soon as possible . . . they are in earnest in wishing to do what is required by the government."

Plans of Lincoln and Johnson

The need of a policy of reconstruction had first appeared when Union forces conquered parts of the Confederacy while the war was still in progress. In the summer of 1862 President Lincoln had worked out the details of a program for Louisiana. The specific terms under which parts of the South might be restored to the Union were listed in the President's proclamation of 1863. To those southerners who would take a prescribed oath, the terms of which called for obedience to the federal Constitution and for acceptance of all acts of Congress and of all executive proclamations regarding slavery, Lincoln promised pardon and restoration of citizenship. During the war the privilege of taking the oath was denied to those holding important positions in the Confederate army, navy, or government, as well as to those who had resigned places in the federal government to join the Confederacy. Then, if loyal citizens could be found to the number of at least 10 percent of the voters in a state, according to the census of 1860, they might proceed to establish state governments. Lincoln promised to recognize these as legal. By 1864 there were three governments organized under this 10-percent plan: Louisiana, Tennessee, and Arkansas.

Ten-percent Plan

In applying this 10-percent plan, Lincoln's primary purpose was reconciliation. He hoped that normal conditions could be promptly restored, and he did not intend to impose further burdens on the South. According to his theory the southern white people were the ones best fitted to reorganize state governments in their section. Lincoln did not share the abolitionist notion that the Negroes should be elevated at once to full rights of citizenship. Privately he suggested that a few of them might be given the vote but he made no provision for them in any of his official plans. He had no intention of turning southern society upside down.

For various reasons Lincoln's plan of reconstruction failed to satisfy Congress. The leaders in Congress then evolved a policy of their own, in a bill framed by Henry Winter Davis and Benjamin F. Wade. The Wade-Davis bill declared the southern states outside the Union. As a condition of readmission a clear majority of the voters in any given state would be required to take an oath of allegiance. The state would then be required to abolish slavery and to repudiate the Confederate debt. The law denied the privilege of voting and of holding office to officials of the Confederate government and to Confederate military officers above the rank of colonel. Congress sent this measure to the President on July 4, 1864, which happened to be the day of adjournment. Lincoln refused to sign it, so it was killed by a pocket veto. Nothing further was done to reorganize southern state governments until after the end of the war.

In the next session of Congress the leaders acted to improve conditions among the Negroes. For this purpose Congress passed a law creating the Freedmen's Bureau, a part of the War Department. The Bureau had branches all over the South. It had charge of charitable work for both Negroes and destitute whites; it arranged for the distribution of supplies and land among the Negroes; it laid down regulations regarding labor; and it exercised certain judicial functions in cases involving Negroes.

President Johnson

On April 15, following the assassination of Lincoln, Andrew Johnson became President. Like so many other men in public life, he was a poor boy who became famous. Apprenticed to a tailor at the age of ten, he never went to school for a single day, but he learned to read, and after he was married his wife taught him to write. He entered politics at the age of twenty, and after he had gained experience in local offices his neighbors sent him to Congress. Later he was elected governor of Tennessee for two successive terms, and in 1857 he became a member of the United States Senate. Refusing to follow his state in secession, he became a loyal supporter of the Lincoln administration, and it was due to Lincoln's insistence, in part, that he became a candidate for the vice-presidency in 1864.

Because of his defeat in the contest with Congress over reconstruction and because of the efforts of his opponents to discredit him, Johnson's reputation suffered among his contemporaries; to make matters worse, some of the earlier historians of this period based their estimates of Johnson on the misrepresentations of his foes. They helped to perpetuate the unfounded notion that Johnson was little better than a chronic inebriate. His biographer Winston has effectively refuted this unjust aspersion.

The major task of Johnson's administration was to complete the process of reconstruction. Johnson began where Lincoln left off and continued the 10-percent program. On May 29, 1865, he issued an amnesty proclamation, similar to Lincoln's except that it excluded from its benefits all former Confederates who owned property to the value of $20,000, provided they had voluntarily taken part in the "rebellion." But Johnson promised clemency and pardon in individual cases, and he was generous in carrying out this promise. He went on to appoint governors for the remaining southern states and to authorize them to arrange for constitutional conventions.

By the time Congress assembled in December the states had nearly completed the process of reorganization. After their constitutional conventions had made the needed amendments to their constitutions, they provided for the election of legislatures and state officials and chose representatives and senators to Congress. By the end of 1865 the work had been completed in all the Confederate states with the exception of Texas; this state was reconstructed a few months later.

In some respects the most puzzling task confronting these new southern legislatures was that of providing for the needs of the Negroes and fitting them into their new place in society. For the white part of the population these matters were already settled, but for the Negroes the law had to be remade. Southern law had recognized and provided for slavery, but the slave codes had been rendered obsolete by the Thirteenth Amendment. Southern legislators did not intend to give Negroes all the rights which abolitionists thought the race deserved. Furthermore, because the Negroes had been the laboring class in the South, the new laws contained numerous regulations regarding labor.

Black Codes

These new "black codes" defined the domestic relations of the Negroes—that is, the position and legal rights of husbands, wives, and children. Then they set forth the rights of the Negroes in court, questions of jury trial, and property rights, particularly with reference to land. Then there was the problem of labor, the responsibilities of the employer and the employed. Some of the codes decreed that vagrants and those convicted of petty crime should be bound out to labor for specified lengths of time. The new laws gave the southern Negroes rights and privileges which they had never possessed before, but they stopped far short of racial equality.

From the northern point of view these "black codes" constituted the chief count in the indictment of the newly established southern governments. Northern critics declared that the laws were designed to circumvent the Thirteenth Amendment and to restore slavery. Added to the wrath over the specific provisions of these laws was the deep moral indignation of the abolitionists over the refusal to grant equality to the Negroes. The abolitionists condemned the whole body of this legislation. Unfortunately for the South the war had put an end temporarily to the principle of local self-government. Southerners could no longer regulate their social customs as they wished. Northern leaders were determined to show the South who had won the war and to put the beaten "rebels" in their place.

On August 20, 1866, President Johnson proclaimed the restoration of peace, order, tranquillity, and civil authority throughout the United States. From his point of view reconstruction was completed. Johnson was mistaken; far from being completed, reconstruction had hardly begun. The Lincoln-Johnson 10-percent governments with their "black codes" were nothing but a temporary interlude. Months before the summer of 1866 a group of congressional leaders and their supporters, known to history as the Radical Republicans, were already at work on their plan for an entirely different policy of reconstruction.

Plans of Congress

Economic Issues

President Lincoln's program for the South had been planned as a genuine policy of reconstruction. The state governments were to be rebuilt and empowered to work out the new social order for whites and Negroes alike—with the whites in control. Lincoln had no intention of forcing his own concept of a new social order on the South. Still less was the President concerned with reconstruction as a means of safeguarding the economic interests of important classes in the North. In Congress, on the other hand, influential leaders looked upon the protection of these northern interests as the most important duty of the national government, and they were determined to make reconstruction promote these ends.

For an understanding of this congressional program it is necessary to recall some of the significant economic consequences of the Civil War. Heavy bond issues, amounting to a total of $2,621,000,000, resulted in the establishment of new vested interests. Interest rates were liberal, averaging 6 or 7 percent. Many of the bonds had been paid for with depreciated paper money, in some cases at 50 cents on the dollar. If the bonds should be redeemed at par, in gold, the holder would profit heavily. The bonds themselves provided for payment of interest only in gold; legally the principal could have been paid in paper. But the investors wanted gold for their bonds. Safeguarding the bonds and the investors therefore became one of the primary concerns of Congress.

Even before the end of the war Charles Sumner was pleading for Negro suffrage as a means of protecting the bonds. Without Negro votes, he argued, southern Democrats would dominate the southern governments "and menace the national credit by assailing the national debt." Later, in 1866, Sumner explained that only with the help of Negro votes "can you save the national debt from the inevitable repudiation which awaits it" if a combination of southern and northern Democrats should recover control in Congress. This connection between Negro suffrage and northern financial interests was one of the commonplaces of radical northern doctrine. "I could easily convince any man," wrote Elizur Wright, a former abolitionist, "that it will probably make a difference of at least $1,000,000,000 in the development of the national debt, whether we reconstruct on the basis of loyal white and black votes, or on white votes exclusively." Johnson opposed the radicals on this issue.

Closely related to this question of the bonds was the National Banking Act of 1863, authorizing the issue of national bank notes against federal bonds as security. In 1865 Congress passed a supplementary measure imposing a tax of 10 percent on all state bank notes, thereby driving them out of circulation. The radicals feared that a combination of northern and southern Democrats might overthrow this banking system, so they were determined to prevent any restoration of Democratic control.

During the Civil War the Republicans had not only restored the old Federalist and Whig policy of high protection for American manufacturers but they had gone far beyond their predecessors. In 1857 the average level of tariff rates stood at 19 percent, but by 1864 the level had been raised to 47 percent. But the manufacturers remembered that the old combination of northern and southern Democrats had been strong enough to hold the rates down before the war, and there was no doubt that the same combination would favor a similar policy for the future. Here was one more reason for compelling the former Confederate states to protect Republican policies.

Another part of the Republican program—that of generous land grants—had been temporarily blocked by Democratic opposition before the Civil War, but it had been solidly established during the war itself. In addition to the Homestead Act, which promised a farm to anybody who would live on it, Congress had given land to railroad corporations. A Democratic majority would probably put an abrupt stop to this generosity, and the best safeguard for the policy was steady Republican control of Congress.

As long as the war lasted Republican policies were safe, but under the Presidential plan of reconstruction southern Democrats were coming back into power. Worse yet, the ratification of the Thirteenth Amendment put an abrupt end to the old "federal ratio" under which only three fifths of the slaves had been counted in determining the basis of southern representation in Congress. With slavery a thing of the past, southern delegations in Congress would be larger than before the war, and unless the Republicans did something, these delegates would be Democratic.

Radical Republicans

These considerations were clearly evident to the Republicans in Congress in 1865. They planned to ruin the executive plan of reconstruction by refusing to seat the recently elected representatives and senators from the South. Then they would give the vote to the Negroes, make them loyal Republicans, and so save the results of the war. Leaders in this program were Thaddeus Stevens and Benjamin F. Butler in the House and Charles Sumner in the Senate.

As it was gradually unfolded, the radical program of reconstruction destroyed the recently established 10-percent governments in the South, disfranchised the southern whites, gave the vote to the southern Negroes, and extended a large measure of federal control over local affairs in the states of the former Confederacy. To accomplish these objectives the radicals had to dominate Congress, the President, and the Supreme Court. On December 1, 1865, before Congress opened, the Republican caucus bound the majority to a resolution denying admission to representatives and senators from the South. When Congress assembled three days later, the clerk of the House omitted the names of all members-elect from the states of the former Confederacy. Next the radical majority appointed a joint committee on reconstruction of fifteen, of which Thaddeus Stevens was the dominant member. This committee spent a year in collecting evidence on conditions in the South and in shaping the various measures of the congressional program.

The refusal to admit the southern members was a proceeding of doubtful constitutionality. Each house does have the right of passing on the qualifications of its members, but this right did not justify the denial of representation to eleven states. Even Stevens and Sumner felt the force of this argument, and they invented strange fictions to excuse their course. Stevens held that the states in question were no longer states but conquered provinces. Sumner argued that the seceding states had committed suicide and so lost their status under the Constitution.

Protection for Negroes

In February 1866 Congress passed the first of its measures in the new plan of reconstruction. This extended the life and enlarged the powers of the Freedmen's Bureau. The measure provided for the appointment of a large number of agents and gave them extensive powers. It guaranteed military protection for the freedmen whenever they were deprived by state law of any rights enjoyed by the whites. The agents of the Bureau were given jurisdiction over cases involving freedmen. Then the act authorized the construction of schools for the freedmen and arranged for a more systematic policy of leasing land to them.

President Johnson found this proposed law unconstitutional and vetoed it; this veto ended the prospect of cooperation between executive and legislature in reconstructing the South. Johnson found fault with the bill because trials under the law would take place without a jury and without any of the recognized rules of law or evidence. The safeguards which English and American law had so laboriously constructed for the protection of the individual against arbitrary decisions were set aside. At the time Congress could not muster sufficient votes to pass the measure over the President's veto, although it did so later.

The next measure on the congressional program was the Civil Rights Act, passed over Johnson's veto. This measure declared the Negroes citizens of the United States and made the rights enjoyed by white citizens the measure of rights for all. Any denial of equal rights carried penalties of fine and imprisonment, and federal courts were given jurisdiction over cases arising under the law. Federal officials, including those of the army and navy, were given power to enforce this act.

Fourteenth Amendment

To make sure that no subsequent Congress would repeal the provisions of this Civil Rights Act, the radicals planned to supplement it with an amendment to the federal Constitution. This amendment, the Fourteenth, was approved by Congress and sent to the states in June 1866. Like the Civil Rights Act, it declared the Negroes citizens of the United States. Then it went on: "No State shall make or enforce any law which shall abridge the privileges or immunities of citizens of the United States; nor shall any State deprive any person of life, liberty, or property, without due process of law; nor deny to any person within its jurisdiction the equal protection of the laws." Next the amendment decreed that if the right to vote should be denied to any adult male citizens, twenty-one years of age, or over, except for the commission of crime, the offending state should have its representation in Congress diminished in proportion to the number of citizens so injured. The third section prohibited those who had taken part in the Confederacy from holding office in state and federal governments until Congress should restore their rights of citizenship. This section temporarily excluded most southern leaders from public affairs. Then the national and state governments were both prohibited from paying the Confederate debt.

Soon after the submission of the Fourteenth Amendment, Congress made public the report of the Joint Committee of Reconstruction. This document asserted that the southern people, by their voluntary act in leaving the Union and engaging in war against it, had sacrificed all constitutional rights; "the conquered rebels were at the mercy of the conquerors." Before they could be restored to citizenship and to their constitutional rights, they must give guarantees that they were qualified to resume their former status. The authority to decide upon the proper measures of restoration rested not with the President alone but with the whole federal government. The so-called governments set up under executive proclamations had no legal standing. During this same summer of 1866 Congress passed the Freedmen's Bureau bill over the President's veto. The Bureau was the foundation upon which the congressional majority built the Republican party in the South.

Election of 1866

By this time the differences between the President and Congress were sharply defined, and there was no possibility of compromise. This conflict developed at the beginning of the campaign for the election of a new Congress. The radicals hoped to secure a two-thirds majority in each house, so that they could override executive vetoes. Johnson hoped for a vote of confidence. Unfortunately for the President, developments occurred during the campaign which convinced many voters that Congress was right. In New Orleans, a combination of radicals and Negroes planned to reopen a state constitutional convention which had completed its work and ended its existence two full years earlier. The purpose was to adopt the principle of Negro suffrage. Before the delegates assembled there was talk of violence. On July 30, the day of opening, the conservatives, aided by the city firemen, police, and a mob, carried through a deliberately planned attack on the convention hall. At least forty people were killed and four times as many wounded. This attack upon the radicals and their Negro allies was widely advertised as typical of the attitude of southern whites toward Republicans and Negroes.

Johnson undertook an extensive speaking tour, known as "the swing around the circle." He visited the leading cities in the East and the Middle West. In his speeches he expressed his opinion of his congressional opponents in blunt, uncompromising terms. These extemporaneous speeches were often marred by bad taste. This was unfortunate because it gave the country a false impression of the President. In the meantime, with the exception of Tennessee, the southern legislatures uniformly rejected the Fourteenth Amendment, thereby furnishing the radicals with one more excuse for proceeding against them. To make matters worse, Johnson himself had advised these legislatures to reject the amendment. All these factors combined to defeat Johnson, and the radicals were successful in securing the desired majority.

Completion of the Congressional Plan

Made confident by this evidence of popular support, the radicals did not wait for the new Congress to assemble. The short session of the Thirty-ninth Congress began in December 1866 just after the elections were over, and the radicals prepared to enact their program. The first of the series of congressional acts of reconstruction, dated March 2, 1867, was entitled: "An Act to Provide for the More Efficient Government of the Rebel States." Its preamble was a simple lie: "Whereas no legal state governments or adequate protection for life or property now exists in the rebel states. . . ." In order to provide proper protection for life and property, Congress re-established military rule in the South—two years after the close of the war. The ten states—Tennessee had ratified the Fourteenth Amendment and had been reconstructed—were organized into five military districts, subject to the military authority of the federal government. Each district was put into the hands of a major general. The measure gave suffrage to the Negroes and took it away from all southern whites who had participated in the Confederacy. Under the supervision of the generals, the voters might frame new state constitutions, which, upon approval by a majority of the voters and of Congress, might go into effect. These new constitutions must provide for Negro suffrage. Once these requirements had been met, civil governments could be organized. The new legislatures must ratify the Fourteenth Amendment. After all this, if Congress approved, the states might be readmitted to the Union. The measure became law over Johnson's veto. At the same time Congress passed another measure which put these major generals directly under the control of General Grant, so that President Johnson could not restrict their activities.

Congressional Reconstruction

This first Reconstruction Act was unconstitutional, and Johnson's veto message (prepared by former Attorney General Beach and Attorney General Stanbery) was cogently reasoned proof of this fact. Pointing out that the alleged purpose of the bill was not the real one, Johnson described the measure as a device for "coercing the people into the adoption of principles and measures to which it is known that they are opposed, and upon which they have an undeniable right to exercise their own judgment." He found the law "in palpable conflict with the plainest provisions of the Constitution, and utterly destructive to those great principles of liberty and humanity for which our ancestors . . . have shed so much blood and expended so much treasure."

Next Congress passed a supplementary Reconstruction Act under which the military commanders were instructed to register the voters, to arrange for the election of delegates to state constitutional conventions, and to make sure that new constitutions were framed. Once this work was done the constitutions were submitted to the voters and then forwarded to Congress.

Although he had vetoed all these measures, Johnson attempted to enforce them once they became law. Because of their peculiar features, constitutional and otherwise, Johnson turned for advice on legal matters to his attorney general, Stanbery. The latter held that the district commanders in the South were not free to ignore the existing governments. The radicals thereupon accused Johnson of attempting to undermine their laws, and in order to restrict the President still further they passed another Reconstruction Act, the purpose of which was to define the "true intent and meaning" of the two previous laws. This new measure placed the southern governments definitely under the control of the generals. Both the generals and their subordinates were freed from the necessity of recognizing "the opinion of any civil officer of the United States."

Congress and Johnson

Along with the first Reconstruction Act Congress had passed two other measures designed to hamper the President. By the Tenure of Office Act he was forbidden to remove any civil official without the consent of the Senate. From the earliest days of the republic Presidents had made removals without consulting the Senate, and their right to do so had never been denied by any competent authority. The Tenure of Office Act therefore violated precedents of seventy-five years' standing. The other measure prohibited the President from giving orders directly to the army; he must give them through General Grant. And the President was forbidden to remove Grant from his command or to station him outside of Washington except at his own request or with the consent of the Senate. Johnson vetoed the Tenure of Office Act, but he could not veto the army act without rejecting the appropriation bill of which it was a part.

Sixty years later, in the Myers case, the Supreme Court upheld the President's power of removal and declared the Tenure of Office Act unconstitutional. The net result of these Reconstruction Acts of Congress was the establishment of a party dictatorship with complete control over Congress, the President, and the South. The radical majority in Congress did all this, not because the country was in danger but for the purposes of imposing additional punishment upon the beaten Confederates and of consolidating the Republican party's hold on the national government and on the South.

Impeachment

The next ambition of the radicals was to remove Johnson from the Presidency. They had carried all their points in spite of his objections, but he had forced them to pass measures over his vetoes. Actually the movement to impeach Johnson began before the enactment of the first Reconstruction Act. Early in January 1867 the House passed a resolution which called for an investigation of Johnson's record, with impeachment as the ultimate objective. The Judiciary Committee of the House recommended impeachment, but the House itself could find no legitimate excuse for such action. Later Johnson asked for the resignation of Stanton, the secretary of war. Stanton worked with the radicals in Congress, and his continuance in the Cabinet was an intolerable nuisance to the President. He refused to resign, so Johnson removed him, and the radicals accused the President of violating the Tenure of Office Act. It is true that Johnson dropped Stanton without the approval of the Senate, but even some of the radicals themselves had admitted previously that in passing the law they did not intend to have it apply to Lincoln's appointees in Johnson's Cabinet. Nevertheless the radicals used the Stanton case as an excuse for impeachment.

In February 1868 the House, by a vote of 126 to 47, passed a resolution "That Andrew Johnson, President of the United States, be impeached of high crimes and misdemeanors in office." It is a striking commentary on the purposes of the radicals that they adopted the resolution to impeach before they had framed any formal charge whatever. It is also significant that the resolution was referred not to the Judiciary Committee but to the Committee on Reconstruction, of which Thaddeus Stevens was chairman. The House adopted eleven articles of impeachment. When stripped of their superfluous verbiage, the articles accused Johnson of removing Stanton, asserting his constitutional prerogative as commander in chief of the army, and of making speeches offensive to Congressmen.

The trial of the President before the Senate, with Chief Justice Chase presiding, lasted from March 30 to May 26, 1868. The President did not appear in person before his accusers, but he was represented by some of the ablest lawyers in the United States. They made short work of the charges and proved that Johnson was guilty of no impeachable offense. But the Senators were not trying Johnson on the charges; these were merely a means of removing him. The vote therefore was an expression of opinion as to whether Johnson should or should not continue to serve as President. The vote stood 35 to 19, just one short of the two thirds needed for conviction. Johnson therefore finished out his term.

Supreme Court and Reconstruction

There have been times when the Supreme Court has exerted considerable influence upon national policy, particularly by opposing congressional legislation. What was the Court doing in the period of congressional reconstruction? The answer is, surprisingly little. In the Milligan case, decided before Congress passed its first Reconstruction Act, the Court declared against the use of military tribunals where regular judicial process was available. This decision disturbed the radicals almost as much as Johnson did later by some of his vetoes. The congressional acts of reconstruction ignored this decision and set up military tribunals in time of peace. Milligan had been tried and condemned to death by a military tribunal in Indiana. He appealed to the United States Supreme Court. Justice Davis declared that the principle at issue "involves the very framework of the government and the fundamental principles of American liberty." The Court held that Milligan was entitled to the protection afforded by the Constitution, and it declared: "One of the plainest constitutional provisions was, therefore, infringed when Milligan was tried by a court not ordained and established by Congress." If the principle of this decision had been recognized, the congressional plan of reconstruction should not have been passed.

In January 1867, in *Cummings v. the State of Missouri,* the Supreme Court declared unconstitutional the provision in a Missouri statute requiring the taking of a test oath. In this case and in a somewhat similar one, Ex parte *Garland,* the Court laid down principles contrary to those on which the majority in Congress was proceeding. As a result Congress began to consider plans for curbing the Court. Wendell Phillips urged the abolition of the Court. This was the situation when the McCardle case attracted general attention. McCardle, a newspaper editor in Mississippi, had been more truthful than discreet in publishing unfavorable comments concerning the congressional program. Arrested under military authority, he was placed on trial before a military tribunal. Attempts were made, under habeas corpus proceedings, to have the case brought before the Supreme Court, and the officer who had charge of McCardle refused to surrender him. The Supreme Court had this part of the affair under consideration when in March 1868 Congress stepped in with a law which took from the Supreme Court jurisdiction in appeals from lower courts involving habeas corpus proceedings. Schenck of Ohio, speaking for the radicals, explained that the purpose was to discredit and weaken the Supreme Court. "And I hold it to be not only my right, but my duty as a Representative of the people, to clip the wings of that court." In depriving the Supreme Court of jurisdiction over the McCardle case, Congress proclaimed its purpose to protect its whole reconstruction program from any danger of judicial review.

In 1869, in the case of *Texas* v. *White,* the Supreme Court had an opportunity to define its attitude toward the congressional policy of reconstruction, but the Chief Justice and a majority of the Court refused to meet the issue. Chief Justice Chase was content to say that the Court saw no reason to question the constitutionality of the Reconstruction Acts. These important laws were never formally passed upon by the Court.

The New Order in the South

In the South congressional reconstruction turned the social order upside down, deprived the former ruling class of any voice in public affairs, and saddled upon the property owners a load of debt largely representing corruption and waste. The major generals took command at once, and the southern people were moved back to the status prevailing at the close of the war. Then the commanders and their subordinates began to register the voters. The registrars made an effort to disfranchise the largest possible number of southern whites, and the men who were best acquainted with local conditions were excluded from public life.

Carpetbaggers and Negroes

With the southern whites out, responsibility for operating the new governments went to the newcomers: military officers, agents of the Freedmen's Bureau, and the carpetbaggers. These were northerners who had taken up their residence in the South, some of whom were honest, respectable citizens, while others were adventurers. These individuals went South to exploit the country and its people. Associated with them were southerners who chose to join the new ruling class. Some of these natives had honestly opposed the Confederacy, and they welcomed the chance to wreak vengeance upon members of the old aristocracy. Others, men with little principle, found profit on the winning side.

In these circumstances political leadership passed to men devoid of experience in southern public life. At the same time the right to vote was conferred liberally upon the Negroes. There were more than 700,000 of these enfranchised freedmen, and in Alabama, Florida, Louisiana, Mississippi, and South Carolina they formed a majority of the electorate. Through no fault of their own they were incapable of exercising the powers thrust upon them. Even the few who could read knew nothing of politics and government. Many of them did not know the name of the county in which they lived, and some had no idea of their own age. Large numbers had only one name. Others assumed names which were supposed to carry weight. Oberholtzer reported that the voting lists of the city of Charleston contained sixty-three Abraham Lincolns, forty-six George Washingtons, and over thirty Andrew Jacksons. Some registered in several different places. These made up the new electorate, and they would have an important influence in making laws, in the administration of justice, in formulating policies of taxation, and in deciding upon expenditures.

The first task of the voters in each state was to elect delegates to a constitutional convention. Every convention had a radical majority; in South Carolina and Louisiana the majority was Negro. In many cases the men chosen were unfit for the work. The Negroes were ignorant and lacking in experience; some carpetbaggers were unscrupulous and corrupt. In Alabama only two of the Negro delegates could write. In South Carolina, out of a total of 128 delegates, only 17 paid any taxes whatever.

Between 1868 and 1870 the voters in the southern states, acting under the congressional reconstruction policy, finished the work of framing and approving their constitutions. Then they elected governors and legislatures and re-established state governments. But they were still not entirely reconstructed. Before they could be admitted to the Union they were required to ratify the Fourteenth Amendment. This requirement was only one of the many peculiarities of the congressional policy. According to the Constitution amendments are to be ratified by states. In this case ratification was insisted upon as a prerequisite to statehood.

In June 1868 Congress decreed that six of the southern states had complied with all requirements, and they were readmitted. Georgia was one of the six, but the Georgia legislature took the impolitic step of unseating the Negroes elected to the legislature, so Congress deferred the act of restoration until the Georgians should prove more amenable to discipline. By 1870 all southern states were reconstructed. Before the process was finished, Congress had sent out still another amendment to the Constitution, the Fifteenth, providing that the right to vote should not be denied by the United States or by any state on account of race, color, or previous condition of servitude. This Amendment was proclaimed in effect in 1870.

Of the seven states restored before the end of 1868, the majority were governed by carpetbaggers. Ten of the fourteen federal senators, twenty of the thirty-five representatives, and four of the seven governors were carpetbaggers. The new leaders therefore took the choice posts for themselves and left the others for Negroes. These carpetbag-Negro governments were controlled by the Republican party. The Freedmen's Bureau with its local branches was the nucleus of the party. Officials of this organization had helped not only to register the voters but to indoctrinate them firmly in Republican principles.

Republican Machines

Closely connected with the Freedmen's Bureau was the Union League, a carpetbag and Negro political machine. After congressional reconstruction began, branches of the League were established in the South, and the organization became a political machine to control the Negro vote. By 1868 its local units, known as councils, were as common as branches of the Freedmen's Bureau. Each state had its grand council, while the National Grand Council had its headquarters in New York. The League was a secret society with the ceremonial of a great fraternal order. According to its announced purposes it aimed to preserve liberty, perpetuate the Union, uphold the laws and the Constitution, protect all loyal men from harm, elevate the laboring man, and teach the duties of citizenship.

The League's officials enforced the strictest discipline among the members. The League nominated candidates for office and all members were bound by oath to vote for these nominees. Members who voted Democratic were harshly dealt with. Representatives of the League examined the ballots of Negro voters before they were placed in the boxes or if necessary marked the ballots themselves. Sometimes the votes were paid for. In Florida the League directed the activities of organized gangs of voters, who moved from precinct to precinct, voting at each place under assumed names. The chief purpose of the League was to carry elections.

Financial Corruption

Lacking in previous political experience and deprived of all tutelage except that provided by the Freedmen's Bureau and the League, many Negro politicians were corrupt and extravagant. The administration of government became a tragic farce in which disfranchised whites who paid most of the taxes could do nothing but look on. The New York *Nation* described the state officials of Georgia as "probably as bad a lot of political tricksters and adventurers as ever got together in one place." Protected from molestation by federal military forces, they scrambled for "places of trust and profit, by means of nearly every device known to the gambling-house, the mock-auction room and the thimble-rigger's table." Conditions in other states were equally bad. If any scheme of transferring public funds from state treasuries to private pockets was left untried, the omission was due to simple ignorance not to design. It should be stated, however, that graft and corruption were also to be found in many places in the North at that time, and the Tweed Ring in New York was as skilled in chicanery as any group of carpetbaggers. Rhodes described the administration of Louisiana under carpetbag rule as "a sickening tale of extravagance, waste, corruption, and fraud." Votes were openly bought and sold. The carpetbag governor had a salary of $8000 per year, out of which he cleared $100,000 during his first year. He held the job for four years, and he was supposed to have accumulated at least $500,000 before he retired.

The extravagances of South Carolina during this period were no more extensive than those in other states, but they were perhaps a bit more spectacular. The legislators of South Carolina set up a refreshment room next to the representatives' chamber, the cost of which ran to $125,000 for a single session. The list of statehouse supplies bought with state funds included the most expensive wine, liquor, and cigars. Along with these refreshments was an imposing list of fancy groceries, ranging from such staples as butter, cheese, and salt to imported mushrooms, brandied cherries, and imported biscuits. Then the legislators spent $200,000 for furniture, of which perhaps $17,000 worth went into the statehouse. The rest of it went to the homes of members of the legislature or of administrative officials. The state bought horses, mules, harness, wagons, and carriages, used to stock the farms of Republican politicians. State officials had clothing for themselves and their wives paid for out of the state treasury. Household supplies and farm equipment were provided in the same way.

This carpetbag regime piled up state expenses without bringing adequate return for the money. Offices were increased in number, and the principal duty of the incumbents was that of drawing their salaries. Costly public building programs or public works such as railroads were started, many of which left no record of their existence except the payments made on their account. By 1872 the indebtedness of the eleven states of the Confederacy had increased by the appreciable sum of $131,717,777. In South Carolina the bonds representing the state debt were issued in violation of state law. Taxes were increased. During the five years from 1869 to 1874 Mississippi saw her tax rate multiplied fourteen times. Responsibility for this episode rests directly on the Radical Republican leaders in Congress. They interrupted the work of reconstruction and turned the South over to greedy political adventurers.

Ku Klux Klan

This regime of extravagance and plunder stirred the southern whites to action. They furnished most of the money which the carpetbaggers spent so freely, but they could not vote. The situation demanded a remedy, and the only remedy lay outside the law; the injured parties therefore resorted to violence. The best-known agency for opposing the carpetbaggers and their Negro allies was the Ku Klux Klan. This secret organization had started as a form of harmless sport in 1866 at Pulaski, Tennessee. Its origin therefore had been entirely independent of congressional reconstruction. But in 1867 the members adopted a constitution and made it an instrument for driving the Negroes out of politics.

Membership in the Klan was denied to Radical Republicans, members of the Loyal, or Union, League, and members of the Grand Army of the

Republic. The organization was opposed to the principle of racial equality, and it was devoted to the policy of making the South a white man's country. Klansmen were expected to work for the restoration of political rights and for the protection of the white people. The titles of the officers and the robe of the order were designed to strike fear into the minds of superstitious Negroes. At first the klansmen relied largely upon harmless terrorism. With white-robed, silent klansmen patrolling the neighborhood all night, the Negroes found it expedient to remain at home. But terrorism was not all harmless. Flogging, torture, or even death would show that the Klan meant business. Observers sometimes noted desirable results. The Negroes became orderly and stopped wandering around the countryside at night. Petty thievery became less common. The Klan marked the beginning of the restoration of white supremacy.

Such at least is the most charitable view of the order. But a secret society, operating outside the law and pledged to violence, was bound to attract the lovers of crime for its own sake. Oberholtzer summarized the work of the Klan as "a reign of outrage and crime which, taken together, forms a record of wrong among the most hideous in the history of any modern state." Conditions became so bad that in 1871 Congress appointed a committee of investigation. Its findings were published in thirteen bulky volumes which contain a jumble of gossip, wild rumor, and unassailable facts.

In Louisiana the Knights of the White Camellia performed functions similar to those of the Ku Klux Klan. The order was so successful politically that a Republican majority of 26,000 recorded in the spring elections of 1868 was in the following November transformed into a Democratic majority of 46,000. The congressional investigating committee reported that just before the election over 2000 people had been killed or wounded.

To meet this situation Congress planned to combat violence with federal authority. In May 1870 Congress passed the first of a series of three measures designed to restore order in the South. This "force bill" prohibited, under heavy penalties, any use of force, bribery, or intimidation for the purpose of keeping loyal citizens away from the polls. The President was authorized to use the army and navy to uphold federal power, and federal courts were given jurisdiction over cases arising under the law. A second "force bill" passed the following year provided for still heavier penalties for the commission of any of the offenses named in the first measure. This law called for the appointment of federal supervisors of elections in the South. The third measure in this series, generally known as the Ku Klux Act, became law in 1871. It provided that operations of unlawful organizations might be declared rebellion against the government of the United States. In case of such rebellion the President was authorized to suspend the privilege of habeas corpus and to proclaim martial law. Acting under this Ku Klux measure, President Grant declared nine counties in South Carolina in a state of rebellion, and in two years the courts recorded more than 1000 convictions.

Force Acts

Gradually the system of radical reconstruction was overthrown, and white supremacy was re-established. The first states to recover from carpetbag control were Tennessee, Virginia, North Carolina, and Georgia. By 1876 there were only three states still in the hands of carpetbaggers, who had to be upheld by the federal army. They were restored to the whites in 1877. The first steps in this process of recovery were in many cases extralegal if not criminal, but the southern whites justified them on grounds of necessity. Intimidation of Negro voters, violence, stuffing the ballot boxes, or flagrant falsification of returns were common. The work of rebuilding a white man's party in the South had been greatly simplified in 1872 when Congress passed an Amnesty Act, restoring citizenship and voting privileges to 150,000 former Confederates.

White Supremacy

By that time the North itself was tiring of the whole contest. As the Civil War became a thing of the past, a degree of sympathy with the traditional policy of local self-government could be revived. All the Southerners needed was freedom from interference by the national authorities, and such interference became less and less frequent. In the North there had never been enough sympathy with Negro suffrage to give Negroes unrestricted voting rights there. In 1867 Negroes were allowed to vote in New England—with the exception of Connecticut—and in New York, and that was all. Before 1869 nine northern states voted down proposals to give the vote to Negroes. It is not surprising therefore that the southern states should have been given the same privilege of granting and withholding suffrage.

Furthermore the Republican hold upon the South was weakened by factional disputes sometimes among the radicals themselves, sometimes between the more disreputable carpetbaggers and the respectable element among southern Republicans. As the leaders quarreled among themselves and as the Negroes withdrew from politics, radicalism in the South was doomed. In 1869 the radical delegations from the southern states in Congress numbered sixty-four; by 1877 this number had been reduced to six.

In 1877 the last federal troops were withdrawn from the South, and congressional reconstruction became a matter of history. The white man's party, uniformly Democratic, was in power in all southern states. In the beginning the exclusion of the Negroes from the polls had been accomplished by means of dubious legality, and there was no legal barrier to their return to power. The southerners therefore proceeded to adopt new measures, the purpose of which was the permanent abolition of the Negro vote. This objective was achieved by means of constitutional amendments. In the framing of these new regulations southern legislators and constitutional conventions had to circumvent the Fifteenth Amendment, but this was easy. All the states adopted literacy tests, requiring the prospective voter to be able to read the state or the federal Constitution, or both. Some states called for sufficient knowledge of constitutional law to enable the applicant to explain and interpret the Constitution. Few Negroes—and few college students either for that matter—could explain satisfactorily the meaning of

The Solid South

ex post facto laws or of bills of attainder. Other amendments required the applicant to make out and sign his own application. Then there were property qualifications and residence requirements; poll tax requirements necessitated the payment of a poll tax months before election. In order to vote the citizen had to be able to show his receipt. States disfranchised citizens convicted of crimes such as larceny, vagrancy, bigamy, and receiving stolen goods. When these obstacles threatened to exclude ignorant white Democrats as well as Negro Republicans, six of the states added "grandfather clauses" to their constitutions, providing that, even though an applicant could not meet the legal requirements, he could vote provided he or his father or grandfather had voted in 1860. The following examples show how effective these various measures were. At the close of the nineteenth century Mississippi, with a Negro population of voting age of 147,000, had 8615 registered Negro voters; Louisiana had 127,000 Negroes old enough to vote, with 5300 actual voters; Alabama with 130,000 possible Negro voters had about 5000 on the voting lists. The southern states disfranchised the Negroes as completely as though the Fifteenth Amendment did not exist. And the punitive clause of the Fourteenth Amendment has never been applied.

Congressional reconstruction showed how government should not be conducted. An irresponsible majority, motivated by hatred or by a desire to promote selfish economic interests, set out to punish the greater part of southern society. Federal officials deliberately overrode legal safeguards which had been established to protect individuals and minorities. The consequences of the congressional policy were far-reaching. Bryce, in the *American Commonwealth,* concluded that reconstruction "determined and explained the whole subsequent course of events and the present attitude . . . of the Southern people." One of the peculiar phenomena of American politics, the "solid South," is the direct consequence of reconstruction. The great majority of southern whites are not only Democratic, but they remain united by one single factor regardless of all other issues. They insist upon the maintenance of white supremacy.

Reconstruction in Agriculture

For the southern people the most immediate problems of reconstruction were concerned not with politics and government but with the processes of making a living. The primary essential was to bring the land back under cultivation and to produce cotton, for cotton had been the primary means of support. By 1869, four years after the end of the war, the worst of the economic difficulties were over. By that year the major southern crops brought in a gross return of $300,000,000, of which cotton accounted for five sixths of the total. In 1871 cotton alone accounted for a gross return of nearly $435,000,000. Also in 1869 southern purchases in northern markets reached the figures for 1859.

These figures show that the southern people were again in a position not only to take care of themselves but to make money, but they do not reveal the economic transformation which was taking place in southern agriculture. One of the major changes was the increasing number of small farms.

The great plantations of pre-Civil War days were split into smaller units. In the decade from 1860 to 1870 the number of farms in Tennessee increased from approximately 82,000 to 118,000; in South Carolina from 33,000 to 52,000; in Mississippi from 43,000 to 68,000; and in Louisiana from 17,000 to 28,000. The rural population which operated these farms was divided into three fairly well-defined classes. First there were the owners, men who operated their own farms, or who rented land to tenant farmers. Next came the tenants, those who hired land in return for a fixed money rental. Like the owners, they assumed the responsibilities of management. Third in the scale came the share croppers. The owner furnished the land and generally the necessary adjuncts: fertilizer, seeds, and tools; the cropper provided the labor. At the end of the season the owner would take his share of the crop, agreed upon in advance, and the cropper had what was left.

An inseparable feature of the post-Civil War farming was the crop-mortgage system, a device used by owners and tenants alike. One of the chief obstacles in the way of the resumption of ordinary living in the South was the lack of both money and credit. The crop mortgage solved the problem. In order to provide himself with fertilizer for his land and with clothing and other necessities for his family, the farmer would buy what he needed on credit from the local storekeeper. The merchant carried the farmer through the season, and, by way of security for these advances, the farmer gave a mortgage on his growing crop. At the end of the season the merchant would sell the crop and balance his books. If the crop brought a profit for the farmer over and above the advances, the merchant would carry the amount on his books in preparation for the next season. If there was a loss, it was charged against the farmer in hope of better luck the coming year. The merchant did not actually charge interest because his prices were high enough to cover all his costs. According to one estimate the charge amounted to interest at rates varying from 40 to 100 percent.

In addition to its exorbitant cost the crop mortgage had other consequences. It tied the farmer to one particular merchant because as long as he was in debt the farmer could not borrow from any other lender. The crop mortgage also tended to fasten the single-crop system on the South, and the single crop was cotton. It had numerous advantages as security. It had no value whatever until ripe, and the harvested crop was hard to conceal. Most important of all there was always a market for it; regardless of what happened to the borrower, therefore, the lender would do better than to break even. The crop-mortgage system lasted until the federal government began to lend money to the farmers at low rates of interest, but this new financing was not available until after World War I.

Industrial Progress

Economic development in the new South was not confined to recovery in agriculture. Beginning in 1878 businessmen and newspaper editors began a planned campaign of publicity to encourage the local manufacture of cotton. The results came up to expectations. In the course of the next twelve years the number of spindles and looms almost trebled. Between 1880 and

1910 the number of spindles in southern cotton mills increased from 610,000 to 4,298,000; by 1915 the figure stood at 12,711,000, with a total of 19,396,000 in states outside the South. This shifting of the cotton textile business from New England to the South was one of the major economic readjustments of the period.

During the latter part of the nineteenth century and in that part of the twentieth before World War I, southern manufacturers enjoyed distinct advantages over their competitors in the older industrial sections. Land for both factories and tenement houses was cheaper than in the North. Taxes were lower, building costs were lower, and fuel was cheaper and more abundant. Furthermore, the labor question presented few problems. Wages themselves were lower, and, because the mills were new, there was no permanent factory class. The sons and daughters of the small farmers in the South, lowland and upcountry alike, found in the mills a new and pleasing way of making a living. Wages seemed generous in comparison with previous earnings. Then, because industry was new, the states had no restrictions on hours of labor or on the employment of children. Here was a situation similar in some respects to that of New England in the 1830's.

In some southern states the manufacture of tobacco became a thriving business, particularly in Virginia, North Carolina, and Kentucky. By 1880 North Carolina alone had 118 tobacco factories. During the same period Tennessee and Alabama began the manufacture of iron and steel. In 1870 the site of Birmingham, Alabama, was a cotton field. Founded in 1871, the "Pittsburgh of the South" by 1890 had a population of 26,000. Between 1880 and 1890 fifty new blast furnaces were opened in the South. In some respects the social implications of this industrial growth were as important as the economic. Mill operatives and miners added new elements to the population, and poor whites of the upland areas found new opportunities for employment.

Southern Politics

Economic transformation and social change in turn had important political consequences. Before the Civil War the ruling class in the South was made up of the great planters, the more important landowners, and the professional groups: clergy, physicians, and lawyers. These men had held the local offices, and they represented their states in Congress, the Cabinet, and in the Supreme Court. But the new order of things was different. The small farmers and industrial laborers had votes and great potential strength. All they needed was leadership and organization. So it happened that in many cases the new type of southern politician was the man who built his political machine on the foundation of small farmers and other men whom the old regime had overlooked and neglected. The first southern leader of the new type was Tillman of South Carolina, who flourished in the 1880's and 1890's.

One problem resulting from the Civil War and reconstruction the South has not solved—the Negro question. Even the use of the word "problem" conveys a false impression. The Negro question is a complex social situation, including a variety of issues differing widely in various communities. The situation is difficult to describe because it is so full of contradictions and because it is bound up with so much tense emotion. Southern whites are sensitive on this topic. The basic problem is the refusal of the whites to admit Negroes to the status of equality.

The Color Line

The Negro is indispensable in the economic structure of the South. He furnishes about 90 percent of the unskilled labor, both on the cotton fields and in the towns. He does the more arduous work around the factories and warehouses. All domestic work for hire is performed by Negroes. In many cases they operate small service shops—bakeries and barber shops, for example. Much of the small retail trade is in their hands. Thousands of Negroes have had professional training so that they are physicians, lawyers, clergymen and teachers.

To the outsider the most striking characteristic in the relationship of the two classes is the drawing of the color line—not the fact that the line is there, but the way it is drawn. White families who can afford it always have Negro housemaids and Negro nurses for the children. In the homes the relationship on both sides is one of affectionate regard. A Negro nurse may accompany her white charges anywhere, even in hotels and Pullman cars. Intimacy is not the issue; it is the ever-present drive against equality. If the same Negro nurse should venture into such places alone she would be unceremoniously ejected. White people will patronize Negro bakeries and barber shops—provided the trade is limited to the whites—but white customers would promptly stop coming if Negroes were served. Negro ministers and teachers work with their own people, and only with them. No southern white would teach in a Negro school, and northern whites who go South to teach Negroes are ostracized by their white neighbors. A white physician may have both white and black patients, but a Negro physician serves only those of his own race.

In public places, hotels, railroad trains, steamboats, railroad and boat stations, the color line is sharply drawn. The Negro is not admitted to hotels which receive white guests except as an employee. Of course the same thing is true in many places in the North. The South provides the Jim Crow car on railroads, a phenomenon unknown in the North. Negroes find it impossible to buy space in Pullman cars anywhere in the South. Thus the South has prescribed a place for Negroes in the scheme of southern society. In most cases the Negro accepts this place. As long as the place is accepted without question the two races have no friction. Negroes who find it impossible to accept their status in this social structure may migrate to colored communities in northern cities where they enjoy all the privileges of equality with their own people.

Thoughtful southern whites realize how indispensable the Negro is and make every effort to maintain comfortable relations between the two groups. When serious friction develops, it usually comes between the Negroes and the poorer class of southern whites, the class which feels most keenly the fact of Negro competition in economic matters. Unskilled laborers and share croppers are the ones most likely to cause trouble. Educated Negroes resent the status of inferiority which has been imposed upon their race, without its consent, and they have tried, unsuccessfully so far, to find a solution of the problem.

Chapter 26

PRESIDENT GRANT

Corruption at Washington

Election of 1868

DURING Johnson's administration the Radical Republican majority in Congress had dominated national politics, and the leaders hoped to have their power continued by the elections of 1868. To make sure of success they needed a candidate who could draw votes in his own right. They chose General Grant. Grant had been closely associated with the radicals in administering their policy of reconstruction, and he was in full sympathy with it. Knowing little of politics himself, he was ready to rely upon the advice of those who did. With such a man in the White House the radicals would not be disturbed continually by executive vetoes as they had been under Johnson.

The people knew little of Grant's career just before the Civil War. A failure in business, with a well-established taste for liquor, he was almost down and out. The war had rescued him from this fate. Party leaders and people alike overlooked Grant's complete lack of political experience. He had voted for President only once in his life, and that was for Buchanan in 1856; in 1860 he did not vote, but he had favored Douglas. It required considerable stretching of the imagination to see Grant as a good Republican, but his cordial cooperation with the Radicals had wiped out any previous errors of political judgment.

In their platform the Republicans expressed approval of their policy of reconstruction with special reference to Negro suffrage for the South. The Democratic platform recited a long list of Republican violations of law and the Constitution. The election itself was notorious for naturalization frauds in New York, for shameless repeating at the polls in the same state, and for violence and disorder in Louisiana. But Democratic efforts were unavailing. Grant polled a popular vote of 3,012,833, against 2,703,249 for Seymour; the electoral vote gave Grant 214 and Seymour 80.

Grant's Appointments

In making up his Cabinet Grant gave the State Department to a friend and former patron, Elihu Washburne of Galena, Illinois, but the appointment was designed to give Washburne the necessary prestige so that he could be sent as minister to one of the European governments. Washburne's successor in the State Department was Hamilton Fish of New York, who brought real distinction to his own department and stood out sharply as one of the few redeeming features of the Grant administration. There were two other good appointments: Jacob D. Cox in the Department of the Interior and E. Rockwood Hoar as attorney general. The other Cabinet appointments were not noteworthy. Grant's appointments to the foreign posts were generally poor.

For the federal civil service Grant and his friends undertook a thoroughgoing purge. Those tainted with friendliness toward Andrew Johnson and those who had been connected with the Democratic party were dropped. In filling the vacancies thus created, Grant was led into some grave blunders; the *Nation* described his appointments as "probably some of the worst ever made by a civilized Christian government." He removed men indiscriminately, even those who carried the routine work of the departments, and in their places he appointed incompetent and corrupt plunderers. The Treasury in particular, according to the *Nation,* became a "hotbed of low jobbery."

In making these appointments Grant relied upon the advice of the leaders in his party. Under their persuasion he removed an able collector from the New York customhouse, and thereby found room for one Thomas Murphy. General Horace Porter, one of Grant's secretaries, instructed Murphy as to his responsibilities: "I only hope you will distribute the patronage in such a manner as will help the Administration." When Attorney General Hoar refused to cooperate in this prostitution of the offices, Grant summarily dismissed him, and he did the same with Cox of the Interior. Grant's own private secretary was General Orville E. Babcock, one of the most influential figures in the administration. He had wide contacts with a variety of corrupt forces; one commentator declared that he "fished for gold in every stinking cesspool." Like the carpetbaggers of the South, if Babcock missed a chance to turn a dishonest dollar, the oversight was due to ignorance not intent. No evidence has ever been uncovered to show that Grant himself made any personal gain from the schemes of his associates.

President Grant did little in shaping public policy. But there were developments which occurred during his eight years in office that require mention; some of these affected his administration because they concerned his friends and associates.

The Gold Corner

First on the list, in 1869, was the attempt of Jay Gould and James Fisk to corner the available supply of gold. At the time the country was still on a depreciated paper basis, but there was generally a supply of gold available for use in settling foreign trade balances. This fund averaged about $20,000,000 in amount, and the price fluctuated along with that of all commodities. The federal government always kept gold in the Treasury. This supply varied in quantity from $65,000,000 to $100,000,000. When the price of gold rose too high—that is, the price measured in greenbacks—the government would sell enough to stabilize the market. Because of these factors there was constant trading in gold, and the gold room was as lively a place as the stock exchange. These transactions in gold were of two kinds: straight business buying and selling, and speculative ventures. The legitimate transactions usually amounted to $5,000,000 or $10,000,000 daily. In these circumstances a man possessing adequate financial resources and plenty of nerve might conceivably buy the full amount of gold in circulation. Then, if he could induce the federal Treasury to stop the sale of gold, he could put the price where he pleased.

For the successful execution of such a scheme there had to be a combination of different factors. The cornerer must discover some plausible, convincing reasons powerful enough to prevent the government from selling its own gold. Here Gould's fertile mind did the trick. He reasoned that the domestic price of wheat was determined by fluctuations in the price of greenbacks measured in gold. But these local fluctuations would not affect the price of wheat in the world market. Therefore, if the value of greenbacks could be lowered by raising the price of gold, other commodity prices would rise too. This rise in prices would stimulate business activity.

Gould's next problem was to sell the idea to President Grant. The President's brother-in-law Abel Rathbone Corbin, a retired operator in the stock market, was living in New York, and Gould was successful in cultivating his acquaintance. He impressed upon Corbin the desirability of raising prices, and Corbin tried to bring Grant around. When Grant visited New York, Gould was invited to meet him. Gould and James Fisk ostentatiously entertained Grant, thereby convincing watchful observers of their friendliness with the President. At first, when Gould brought up his plan for raising prices, Grant was opposed, but by September 1869 he was converted to Gould's way of thinking. Grant wrote to Secretary of the Treasury Boutwell, explaining the need of holding up the price of gold in the interest of moving the crops. Boutwell thereupon wrote to Butterfield, the official in charge of the subtreasury in New York, privately instructing him not to sell gold without specific instructions from Washington. At this point Gould, the master conspirator, confided to his associate Fisk: "This matter is all fixed up. Butterfield is all right. Corbin has got Butterfield all right, and Corbin has got Grant fixed all right, and in my opinion they are all interested together."

Gould had already established connections with members of the Tweed Ring, the organization in charge of the government of New York City, and through them he had a hold on some of the judges in the New York courts. Gould also controlled a bank in New York, so that he could be sure of ample credit. By the second week in September Gould seemed to have all the necessary factors under complete control. Then he began to buy gold. And in buying Gould did not think of himself alone. He bought gold for Horace Porter, then serving as Grant's secretary, but Porter had the good sense to reject the favor. Gould also bought gold for Corbin and for Butterfield, and they were not only interested but receptive. Corbin made $25,000 on the deal without running the slightest risk.

At this point Grant began to suspect that some reprehensible project was under way, and he wrote to Corbin to keep clear of the gold market. Gould was promptly informed of this untoward development, and he saw at once that he was beaten. Without informing his associate Fisk that he was pulling out, he quietly sold his gold on the rising market. Fisk in the meantime continued to buy. On September 24 the price of gold touched 162, thirty points above normal. Businessmen were wild with worry. With the gold room in turmoil, the stock market close to a panic, and business facing collapse, the Treasury issued the order to sell gold. At once the price dropped to 135. Gould had disposed of all his purchases with a profit estimated at $11,000,000. Fisk was left with heavy purchases, contracted for at the high prices of "Black Friday." But Fisk was not disturbed. He repudiated his contracts and let his broker go into bankruptcy. Congress conducted an investigation and collected a mass of evidence which, according to Henry Adams, "it dared not probe, and refused to analyze."

Pacific Railroad Bills

The story of the Crédit Mobilier, which came to light during Grant's administration, did not concern the President himself, but it did involve the activities of Grant's political associates. From the angle of the government the episode was one of simple bribery, but the whole affair was typical of the ethical standards of that day in both government and business. The first chapter in this affair opened in 1861 when Collis P. Huntington of California spent the winter in Washington, D. C., lobbying for a Pacific railroad bill. He carried $200,000 with him, and in the course of the winter he sent his partners in California such informing messages as these: "I believe with $200,000, we can pass our bill." And again: "It has cost money to fix things." In 1862 Congress passed the first Pacific railroad bill. This act provided for a government loan to the builders of the prospective road in the form of $55,000,000 in 6-percent government bonds. In addition the government promised to give the builders ten square miles of public land for every mile of track laid down. At this point the Central Pacific of California joined forces with the Union Pacific of Boston and New York. As it turned out the Central Pacific built the road running east from California, while the Union Pacific ran west from Omaha.

In 1863 Thomas C. Durant of Boston, representing Union Pacific interests, spent a winter in Washington. Durant paid out more than twice as much money as Huntington, and he was twice as successful. In 1864 Congress passed the second Pacific railroad bill. This measure permitted the builders of the Pacific railroad to issue bonds to the amount of the government loan, namely $55,000,000. It gave the road a right of way 200 feet wide, with authority to take construction material from the public domain, and it doubled the land grant to twenty square miles for each mile of track. In the end the two railroad companies received from the government approximately 23,000,000 acres of land. Estimates of the value varied from $50,000,000 to $100,000,000.

Crédit Mobilier

The promoters of the road planned to let the contracts for actual construction to themselves, so that they could enjoy any profits which might accrue to the builders. By charging exaggerated prices for construction, the profits would be high. To make this part of the plan work, the railroad companies needed dummy corporations. Durant, vice president of the Union Pacific, discovered a defunct corporation in Pennsylvania, the Pennsylvania Fiscal Agency, with a charter giving it sufficiently broad powers to suit his purpose. He bought it for $26,645 and induced the legislature of Pennsylvania to change its name to the Crédit Mobilier. He then increased the capital stock to $2,500,000, most of which he and his associates kept for the time being. The Union Pacific let the contracts for building the road to the Crédit Mobilier. In California the Central Pacific did the same sort of thing with the Contract and Finance Company.

In 1867 Oakes Ames and his brother Oliver bought stock in both the Union Pacific and in the Crédit Mobilier and took an active part in building the road. The record of padding the costs of construction is too involved to give in full, but according to fair estimates the actual cost of building the Union Pacific from Omaha to Promontory Point, Utah, was $44,000,000, whereas the Crédit Mobilier charged $94,000,000. The Central Pacific cost $43,000,000, and the price charged was $79,000,000. These figures give some idea of the purposes of the promoters. Even though the railroad should show no profit on its freight and passenger traffic for years, the builders would be amply reimbursed. Perhaps, as their friends alleged, this was the only expedient which made it possible to build the road.

In the session of Congress which began in December 1867, C. C. Washburn, who later won fame as a flour manufacturer, introduced a bill to regulate rates on the Union Pacific. Oakes Ames, also a member of the House, became frightened over the prospect of a legislative investigation into the affairs of his associated companies. He knew that the public would find it difficult to understand many of the matters connected with the enactment of the two Pacific railroad bills or the curious contracts under which the road was being constructed. Being a practical man, Ames distributed shares of Crédit Mobilier stock among Congressmen, where, as he wrote, "they will do us the most good." If Congressmen could not afford to buy the stock, Ames carried it for them and allowed them to pay for it out of dividends. In the single year of 1868 Crédit Mobilier paid dividends in cash and in stocks and bonds worth altogether at actual market prices $341.85 on each share of stock. The total profits distributed in legislative circles ran up to more than $33,000,000.

During the Presidential campaign of 1872 some of the newspapers published charges implicating several prominent Republican leaders in bribery and corruption in this Crédit Mobilier matter. The accusations were so damaging that Congress could not avoid an order for an investigation. When it came, the results were vividly described in the *Nation:* a "total loss, one Senator; badly damaged and not serviceable to future political use, two Vice Presidents and eight Congressmen. The condition of Ames's reputation language is inadequate to describe." Ames himself was censured by the House, a penalty which he regarded as unjustifiably cruel. After all, when so many members of Congress had been tarred with the Pacific railroad stock, it did seem that Ames was singled out for invidious distinction. Among those involved, according to the investigation, was James A. Garfield. But the question of his guilt or innocence in the matter resolved itself into a question of the relative veracity of Ames and Garfield. Garfield convinced himself and his biographer T. C. Smith of his innocence.

Other Scandals

One might think that the session of Congress which uncovered proof of such extensive bribery would have been careful to avoid questionable practices, but instead Congress passed the "salary grab." This measure, sponsored by Benjamin F. Butler, raised the President's salary from $25,000 to $50,000 per year. The Constitution prohibits the President from approving a bill to raise his salary during his term. On March 3 Grant signed the bill doubling his salary for the term beginning on March 4. Congressmen also raised their own salaries from $5000 per year to $7500. And they made this increase retroactive from March 4, 1871, so that at the close of the session each Congressman was entitled to the comfortable sum of $5000 in back salary. On this occasion both the press and the public protested so vehemently that in 1873 Congress repealed the measure.

During Grant's second term details of the Belknap scandal were published. According to law the secretary of war had the privilege of appointing the traders at the army posts. These men had a profitable monopoly on the sale of all goods on military reservations. Evidence showed that beginning in 1870 the trader at Fort Sill had paid $6000 to $12,000 annually to be allowed to retain his post. The evidence also showed with absolute certainty that Secretary of War Belknap or his wife had received at least $40,000 of these payments. In 1872 the New York *Tribune* had published convincing testimony on this matter, and the commanding officer at Fort Sill had corroborated the charges. The officer who reported the facts was dismissed from the service with Grant's knowledge and approval. In 1876 a congressional committee brought out the proof, and the Senate prepared to impeach Belknap. To avoid impeachment he resigned. Grant not only accepted his resignation but wrote him a letter expressing confidence in him. Although Belknap was no longer an official of the government and therefore not subject to impeachment, the House instituted proceedings, but the Senate would not vote him guilty because of lack of jurisdiction, and Grant did his best to hamper Belknap's accusers.

During this same period there were damaging disclosures concerning the "Whisky Ring," a combination of distillers and collectors of internal revenue. The distillers found it cheaper to bribe officials than to pay the tax. The manager of the ring was General John A. McDonald, Grant's appointee as supervisor of internal revenue in Missouri; Babcock, Grant's secretary, looked after the ring's interests at Washington. The ring operated throughout the whole Mississippi valley, and its profits were handsome. In 1874 the government was defrauded of $1,200,000 in St. Louis alone, and the distillers there were only a small minority. In 1874 McDonald paid the hotel bill of President Grant and his party during a ten-day visit in St. Louis.

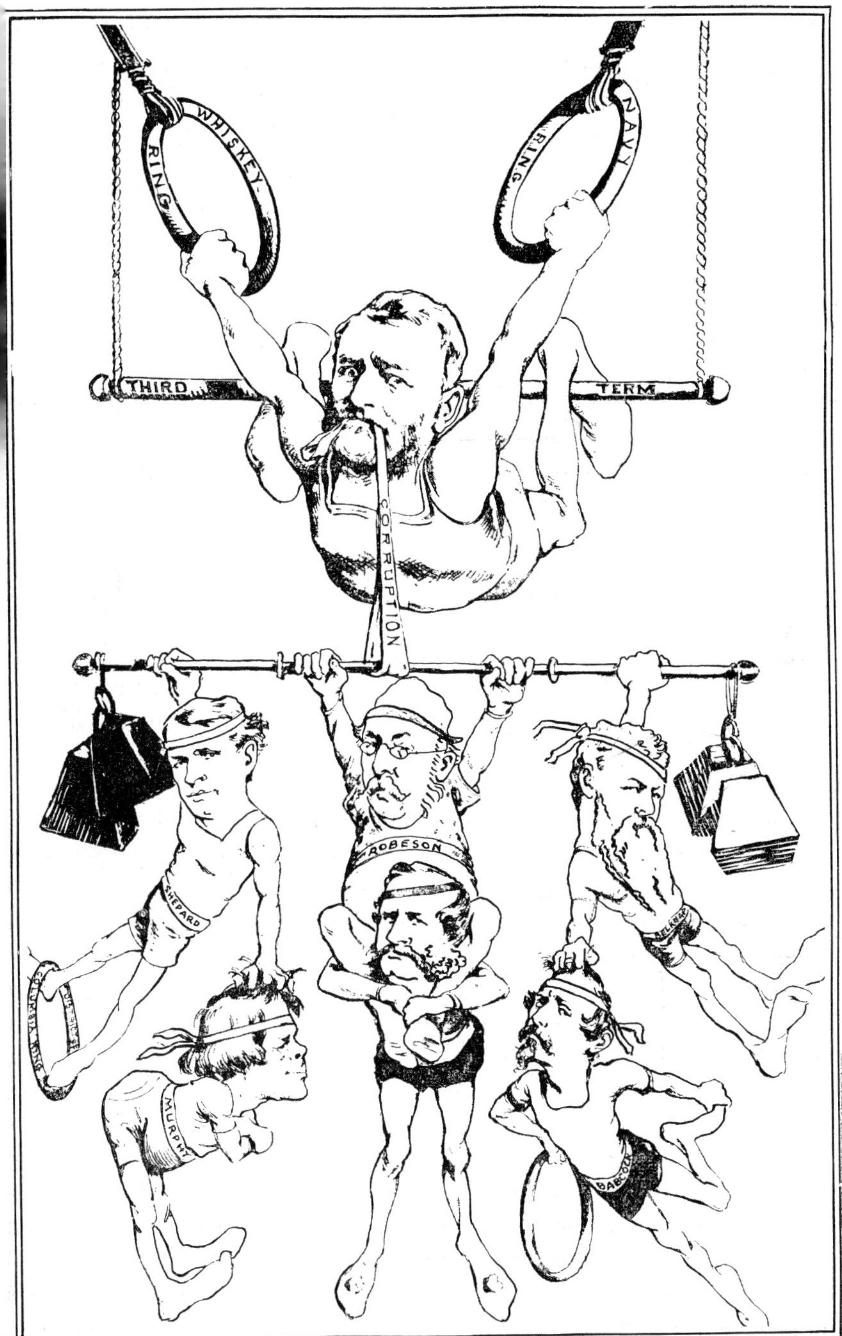

In 1880, when some Republican leaders revived a third-term boom for President Grant, this cartoon by Joseph Keppler was published in the February 4 issue of *Puck*. Grant is pictured as a strong man, supporting Shepard (correctly, Shepherd), who had been in charge of the rebuilding of Washington, D. C., Robeson, Grant's secretary of the navy, Belknap, secretary of war, Murphy, collector of customs in New York, Williams, attorney general, and Babcock, Grant's private secretary—a vivid reminder of the famous scandals of the Grant administrations. (Courtesy, New York Public Library.)

But in this very year Grant's new secretary of the treasury, Benjamin H. Bristow, began to collect evidence concerning the ring. At once the whole crew of disreputable hangers-on in the administration, with Babcock at the head, began a concerted drive to force Bristow out of office. But Bristow stayed in long enough to uncover the frauds and to name those responsible for them. He found that McDonald and Babcock were deeply involved, with McDonald standing out as the unquestioned leader. As the cases came to trial, member after member of the ring was convicted and sentenced. McDonald was put behind the bars. Early in 1876 Babcock himself was indicted and put on trial, but he was saved from conviction by Grant's active help. The President then gave Babcock a good job in the District of Columbia. And Secretary Bristow, who had uncovered and helped punish the ring, was forced to resign from the Cabinet.

Greenbacks, Politics, and Depression

Paper Money or Gold

In Grant's first term the pressure of both businessmen and political leaders forced the administration to do something about the problem of the greenbacks. By the close of the Civil War the Treasury had put into circulation a total of $428,000,000 of these notes; together with the national bank notes they were practically the only money in circulation. The greenbacks had never reached par, and their fluctuations encouraged the prevailing spirit of speculation. They had been issued to meet the emergencies of the war, with a tacit understanding that they would be redeemed as soon as possible after the close of hostilities. But they could not be withdrawn suddenly without a sharp drop in prices which, in turn, would bring widespread business depression. In financial circles there was a demand for the gradual retirement of the greenbacks and for a restoration of the gold standard. Farmers and debtors, on the other hand, opposed retirement. They advocated the retention of the notes as a permanent financial policy.

Secretary of the Treasury McCulloch believed that the gold standard must be restored as soon as possible. In 1866 Congress authorized the secretary to retire the greenbacks gradually, and in less than two years the Treasury cut the greenback circulation to $356,000,000. By that time inflationist sentiment had become so strong that in January 1868 Congress passed another law putting an end to the policy of gradual retirement. Then in the campaign of 1868 the Democrats came to the defense of the greenbacks. Their policy called for an increase in the volume of notes in circulation and for the payment of both principal and interest of the bond issues in paper.

In March 1869, after Grant became President, Congress provided for the payment of both interest and principal of the bonds in gold—even though the later issues did not specifically promise redemption in gold. Investors who had bought bonds with heavily depreciated paper therefore made a profit of 50 percent on the principal in addition to the substantial profit from interest payments in gold. This same law held out the hope of redemption of the greenbacks in coin.

In 1870, in the midst of the discussion of financial problems, the Supreme Court handed down an important decision with reference to the greenbacks. In the case of *Hepburn* v. *Griswold* the Court declared unconstitutional that part of the law of 1862 which made the greenbacks legal tender; this decision applied only to debts contracted before the law was passed. At that time there were two vacancies on the bench, and President Grant named two new Justices, Strong and Bradley. Subsequently the legal tender question was reopened, and in a new decision, May 1871, the Court reversed its opinion as handed down in the Hepburn case. By so doing the Court restored the legal tender clause for all contracts, regardless of their date.

Following the Panic of 1873 there were insistent demands for an increase in the volume of greenbacks. In 1874 Congress provided for new issues to bring the total up to $400,000,000. Grant vetoed this "inflation bill" and thereby won the reputation of being a friend to sound money. Subsequently the total was raised to $382,000,000 without serious protest. In 1875 the Republican majority in Congress worked out a temporary solution of this troublesome question by providing for ultimate redemption of the greenbacks in gold. According to this measure, on and after January 1, 1879, the Treasury would exchange the paper for gold at par. The law also provided for the gradual reduction of the quantity of greenbacks to $300,000,000 and for an increase in national bank notes to prevent any possibility of deflation.

Liberal Republicans

By the fourth year of Grant's first term the President and his political intimates had demonstrated their unfitness for public office. Some of the evidence on this matter was already public property; additional disclosures were soon to come. The situation called for leadership capable of creating interest in a more honest and efficient government. A group of newspaper men appreciated both the need and the opportunity. Greeley of the *Tribune,* Godkin of the *Nation,* William Cullen Bryant of the New York *Evening Post,* Samuel Bowles of the Springfield *Republican* in Massachusetts, Carl Schurz and B. Gratz Brown of Missouri, together with Charles Francis Adams, the former minister to England, and other honest political leaders—all these were demanding reform within the Republican party. By reform they meant honesty and respectability in public office. For specific policies, they called for a more moderate policy toward the South and a reduction of tariff rates. They advocated civil service reform to eliminate the crowd of incompetent and dishonest incumbents of the customhouses and the departmental offices in Washington. Calling themselves Liberals, this group hoped to capture the regular Republican organization and to nominate one of the reformers for the Presidency. Against this threat the regular Republicans prepared to use their well-organized machine. Every local worker and every committee was ordered to hold the party together solidly for Grant. These forces were so firmly established that the reformers could make no impression upon them, so they decided upon a third party with a candidate of their own.

The Liberal Republican convention assembled at Cincinnati. The delegates included old idealists and also old professional politicians who for one reason or another had fallen out with the Grant regulars and so lost their jobs. Then there were doctrinaires, including some of the journalists and civil service reformers, men with excellent intentions but lacking in practical experience.

Greeley against Grant

If the Liberals could have found leadership commensurate with their ability, they might have made a strong appeal to the country. But they passed over their strongest candidate, Charles Francis Adams, and, stampeded by the professional politicians, they nominated their weakest candidate, Horace Greeley, editor of the New York *Tribune*. Greeley was a great newspaper man, but he was not endowed with the qualities usually demanded of a President. From the point of view of political expediency the nomination was comic. The only hope of Liberal success lay in winning a substantial share of the Democratic vote, so the strategy called for the nomination of a candidate for whom the Democrats could vote without losing self-respect. But Greeley had spent the greater part of his adult life in one long editorial campaign against the Democratic party, and he had done so with a venom which had made him famous. Nevertheless the Liberals presented him to the Democrats as a candidate deserving of their support. The Democrats were still discredited by the attitude of some of their associates during the war, and they had no prospect of winning with their own candidate. Consequently, in spite of the absurdity of their actions, they endorsed Greeley.

The regular Republicans nominated Grant for a second term. For Vice President they nominated Henry Wilson of Massachusetts, abolitionist and colleague of Charles Sumner in the United States Senate. Never before in American history had a party gone before the country with a candidate so vulnerable at so many points. And yet, in spite of his own record and that of his associates, Grant swept the country, carrying thirty-one states to Greeley's seven, with a plurality of more than 700,000.

Panic of 1873

Apart from such scandals as the Belknap affair and the Whisky Ring, there was little to bring distinction to Grant's second term. The outstanding development was the panic of 1873. Because of the closely integrated connections and far-reaching influence of private investments, banking relationships, and foreign trade, any financial stringency in one important country was bound to affect all others, and any real crisis would develop into a world-wide depression. In both Europe and the United States large amounts of capital were tied up in railroads, in many cases in projects which could not pay dividends for years to come. In the United States railroad construction for the years 1865 to 1873 reached the total of 35,000 miles of track. Railroad construction stimulated excessive activity in related industries: coal, iron, steel, rolling stock, and building materials. Wages were high, profits were generous, and business was active. In American railroads alone investors had put in approximately $3,000,000,000, half of which came from Europe. Railroad securities were, moreover, so watered by stock manipulators that some of the stock was worthless. Speculation on the stock exchange had sunk to sheer gambling.

The crash came in September 1873. Brokerage houses in New York failed and security prices dropped sharply. On September 18 the great banking firm of Jay Cooke and Company closed its doors. The shock to the business world could hardly have been greater had the United States government itself become bankrupt. Jay Cooke was the best known and one of the most successful of those businessmen who had found profit in the Civil War, and his bank was supposed to be impregnable. Two days after the Cooke failure the stock exchange in New York closed, not to reopen for ten days. Bankruptcies spread from brokers and bankers to ordinary businessmen. In 1874 the number of bankruptcies reached 5830; in 1875, 7740; in 1878, 10,478. Commodity prices dropped along with securities. In 1872 the price of pig iron was $53 per ton; in 1878 it stood at $16.50. Construction work stopped on the railroads, and thousands of laborers were thrown out of work. Railroad employees lost their jobs or suffered substantial cuts in wages. Steel mills, machine shops, textile mills, and other manufacturing enterprises had to slow down or close entirely. By 1878 over half the iron and steel mills were closed. Even for those lucky enough to be employed, wages were cut. Buying power fell off with the loss of jobs and wages, and the importation of luxuries from Europe diminished by a third. The impact of the depression was not confined to any one group, but the large class of industrial wage earners seemed to be the hardest hit.

The Disputed Election of 1876

Political Tactics

The depression had important results in American politics. In the congressional elections of 1874 the voters chose a Democratic majority. Republican prospects for the Presidential campaign of 1876 were gloomy. To make matters worse, the recent disclosures concerning Grant's political associates had damaged the party, and no one could tell how much more corruption would be uncovered before November. The dictates of strategy left only one course for the Republicans, and that was to fall back on the emotions of the Civil War. If they could only revive the hatred of that era and stigmatize the Democrats as the party of rebellion, the voters might give the Republicans another chance. One of the most conspicuous exponents of this policy, called "waving the bloody shirt," was James G. Blaine, a prominent contender for the Republican nomination.

As a counterattack against this "bloody shirt" technique the Democrats exposed Blaine's own business ventures. He had been active in selling securities of the Little Rock and Fort Smith Railroad, a short land-grant line in Arkansas. Blaine himself took advantage of his position as speaker of the House to save the land grant for the Little Rock and Fort Smith, thereby rendering distinctive service. In May 1876 a congressional committee dominated by Democrats began to investigate Blaine's relationship with the Little Rock and Fort Smith. Blaine himself categorically denied any improper connection.

Then James Mulligan, former clerk of a Boston broker, appeared in Washington. The committee learned that Mulligan had letters in his possession written by Blaine to Mulligan's former employer, Warren Fisher, which would reveal the nature of Blaine's connection with the road. Blaine called upon Mulligan at his hotel and induced him to surrender the letters. Then Blaine announced that he would read the letters to the House. What he did was to read selections from them and to accompany the selections with a running comment of interpretation. The evidence was plain that Blaine had saved the land grant and that he had played upon his official position as speaker to induce his patrons to buy the bonds of his road. Today the disclosure of such a blunted sense of propriety would ruin a public career. The Mulligan letters did help to ruin Blaine's chances for the Republican nomination.

Among other Republican aspirants there was Roscoe Conkling, who had wide political influence by virtue of his work as chief dispenser of federal patronage. Then there was talk of a third term for Grant. The House of Representatives disposed of his candidacy by passing a resolution, with a vote of 233 to 18, to the effect that any departure from the established precedent limiting a President to two terms "would be unwise, unpatriotic, and fraught with peril to our free institutions." Then there was Governor Rutherford B. Hayes of Ohio; on the seventh ballot he received the nomination. He had a good war record; he was an advocate of the gold standard and so was satisfactory to the businessmen; and he had made an excellent impression as governor of his own state. To oppose Hayes the Democrats nominated Samuel J. Tilden, a prominent lawyer of New York. Both candidates were men of distinction.

The real excitement came when the newspapers unofficially tabulated the electoral returns. Tilden had a substantial plurality of the popular vote, at least 250,000 more than Hayes. There were 369 electoral votes, and the successful candidate would therefore need 185 to win. At first Tilden seemed to have a clear majority. Then leaders at Republican headquarters persuaded friendly newspapers to claim the election for Hayes; they reiterated the claim so often that they may have come to believe it themselves. Tilden had 184 certain votes, his beyond the possibility of any doubt. Hayes had an equally clear title to 165, but he needed the remaining 20 to win. The Republicans laid claim to all these 20.

To one vote in this group the Republicans had a clear title. In Oregon the majority was Republican, and the three electors of course belonged to the majority. But one of these three was a postmaster and constitutionally ineligible to serve. The governor, a Democrat, thereupon named the candidate who stood fourth in the election; he was a Democrat. The Republicans insisted that the will of the voters should prevail and that the three electoral votes of Oregon must be Republican.

Republican claims to the remaining nineteen votes were not so plausible. In South Carolina bands of armed Democrats toured the state breaking up Republican meetings; most of the Negroes dropped out of politics. The Democrats elected the governor, a majority of the state legislature, and Democratic presidential electors. A state canvassing board, controlled by Republicans, acquiesced in the Democratic victory for state officials and state legislators, but it threw out the presidential electors and certified to the election of seven Republicans. In Florida, too, the Democrats polled a majority vote, but a Republican returning board certified the Republican electors.

Disputed Returns

In Louisiana, on the face of the returns, the Democratic electors had a majority of 9000 votes. The Republicans claimed that this success was due either to padding the returns or to the intimidation of Republican voters. The returning board transformed the Democratic majority of 9000 into a Republican majority of 4000. In doing so it threw out 13,000 Democratic votes.

The opposing factions in Louisiana were not left alone to settle the tangle. Visiting statesmen, so called, representing both national parties, went to Louisiana to look after their respective interests. Among the more prominent members of the Republican delegation were John Sherman and James A. Garfield, both of Ohio. The returning boards in both Florida and Louisiana were subjected to something more than moral suasion, and the Republican title to the electoral votes of these states was open to question. But not all the bargaining was carried on by Republicans. According to a collection of cipher telegrams, Manton Marble, editor of the New York *World,* and Colonel William T. Pelton, Tilden's son-in-law and campaign manager, had some illuminating correspondence with southern politicians. These cipher dispatches were eventually decoded by editors of the New York *Tribune.* These telegrams prove that up to a certain time some of the votes were for sale. The telegrams also prove that the Democrats failed to buy them, not necessarily because of scruple but because of lack of funds or undue care in trying to make a bargain that would hold. The Republicans eventually secured every one of the doubtful votes.

The next move in this extraordinary election had to be taken by Congress. According to the Constitution, the electoral votes are cast in the various states and then the returns are forwarded to Congress. This body meets in joint session and counts the votes. But the Constitution does not state specifically who shall count the votes. If the president of the Senate had the power to do so, he would have counted all the doubtful votes for Hayes because he was a Republican. The speaker of the House, on the other hand, was a Democrat, and he would have used his power to elect Tilden. There was no recognized way out of this impasse, so some compromise had

The Electoral Commission

to be evolved. The solution was the creation of the Electoral Commission. Congress provided for this body of fifteen; five Senators, five Representatives, and five Justices of the Supreme Court. The Senate named three Republicans and two Democrats; the House two Republicans and three Democrats; four of the judges, two Democrats and two Republicans, were named in the bill creating the Commission, and they were empowered to select the fifth. There was a general understanding that they would select Judge David Davis, who had been Lincoln's agent in the Republican National Convention of 1860 and who had joined the Liberal Republican movement in 1872. He was supposed to be independent in politics. But at this point the Democratic legislature of Illinois elected him to the United States Senate, and Davis accepted. The other judges were all Republicans, so the Commission was composed of eight Republicans and seven Democrats.

When Congress met in joint session to count the electoral votes, the members agreed to the customary poll of states in alphabetical order. Where there was no dispute, Congress itself could record the returns as usual. Then the four states with disputed returns could be turned over to the Electoral Commission. Florida was the first one to reach the Commission, and by a vote of eight to seven the Commission gave Florida to the Republicans. South Carolina and Louisiana went Republican, in the same way. Incidentally, after Hayes had made John Sherman secretary of the treasury, the members of the Louisiana returning board and their secretaries received positions in the Treasury Department at Washington.

The Democrats talked of opposing the inauguration of Hayes, but before the crisis was reached there was a series of conferences between influential leaders of both parties. It was agreed that, if the Democrats would permit Hayes to be inaugurated, he would remove the troops from Florida, South Carolina, and Louisiana. Such action would give these states to the Democrats for the election of 1880. With this final issue cleared up, Hayes was inaugurated without further opposition.

New Issues in Foreign Policy

For a number of years before the Civil War American foreign policy found expression in what the leaders called "manifest destiny." The war interrupted this trend, but the desire for a greater United States still remained. William H. Seward, secretary of state during the administration of Lincoln and Johnson, was one of the ardent believers in territorial expansion. It so happened that his opportunity to acquire additional territory for his country was not of his own making but was made possible by the decision of a foreign power. As early as 1857 officials of the Russian government had raised the question of selling their American colony of Alaska to the United States, but nothing was done. Then in 1860 the Russian minister to the United States, Edward de Stoeckl, reported that President Buchanan was

Buying Alaska

interested and that he was willing to pay $5,000,000 for the colony. The outbreak of the Civil War interrupted negotiations.

In 1866, when Stoeckl was in Russia, the Russian government decided to sell Alaska to the United States. Stoeckl was sent back to Washington to negotiate the sale. His instructions ordered him to get at least $5,000,000; other details were left to his discretion. The Russian minister arrived in the United States in 1867. He found Secretary Seward so eager to buy that he raised his asking price to $7,000,000. Seward agreed to this figure and to an additional $200,000, which, so Stoeckl said, would cover the cost of exchange. On March 30, 1867, the treaty providing for the sale at the price agreed upon —$7,200,000—was signed. Even at this higher price the United States got a bargain. The Senate ratified the treaty in April, and in October the United States formally took possession.

One further formality remained over which Seward had no control. Russia turned over the territory before she received any money, and the United States acquired full possession without advancing a cent. During the spring and summer of 1867 Congress was busy with reconstruction, and the members of the House paid no attention to the obligation to Russia. Stevens, Republican leader in the House, had promised to see the appropriation through, but he was in no hurry. Stoeckl wrote home for instructions, suggesting that he thought of telling Seward that Russia had fulfilled her part of the bargain and if the United States should refuse to pay she could take the province for nothing. The minister for foreign affairs promptly wrote back to do nothing of the sort. It would be imprudent, he said, to expose American cupidity to any such temptation.

Perhaps the reference to American cupidity gave Stoeckl the cue for his next maneuver. In any case he hired two influential lobbyists, Robert J. Walker and John W. Forney. Walker was taken on early in May 1868. On the 18th of that month the House Committee of Foreign Relations reported a bill; this became law in July. Stoeckl reported that it had cost a large sum of money to secure the enactment of this bill.

Seward's desire to annex additional territory had not been confined to Alaska. Even before Stoeckl had broached this subject, the secretary of state had been negotiating for the purchase of the Danish West Indies. In October 1867 the Danish government agreed to sell St. Thomas and St. John for $7,500,000. The inhabitants were in favor of the transfer to the United States, and in 1868 a treaty providing for the sale was ratified by the Danish Parliament. But the United States Senate refused to ratify the treaty, and the sale was not completed. Nearly fifty years later the United States did buy the islands at double the price agreed upon in this treaty.

"Alabama" Claims

During this period the most serious matters within the jurisdiction of the State Department had to do with British relations. Seward had never forgiven the British foreign office for its recognition of the belligerency of the Confederacy. Bitterness on this score was intensified by the work of the English-built commerce raiders during the Civil War and by the inability of the British and American governments to effect a settlement of the claims growing out of this destruction. In 1865 Earl Russell had flatly refused to submit these claims to arbitration. Subsequent changes in the British Cabinet, however, led to a more conciliatory attitude, and early in 1869 representatives of the two governments agreed upon a formula for ending this troublesome dispute, but the Senate refused to approve it.

In Grant's first term Secretary Fish secured a new agreement with the English government. All points at issue between the two governments were to be submitted to a joint commission; the commission was authorized to embody its recommendations for a settlement in the form of a treaty. During the winter and early spring of 1871 this commission of ten members —five from each government—met in Washington. In addition to the *Alabama* claims, there was the San Juan water boundary in Puget Sound, the desire of New England fishermen for a renewal of their privilege to fish in Canadian waters, and the hope of middle western interests for navigation rights on the St. Lawrence and its canals. These matters were all dealt with in the Treaty of Washington, signed on May 8, 1871. The treaty provided for a settlement of the *Alabama* claims, and the British expressed regret for the escape of the *Alabama* and other vessels and for their depredations. The amount to be paid to the United States would be determined by a board of arbitration, but in making its award the board would recognize three rules which were included in the treaty itself. The rules declared that a neutral government was bound to use due diligence to prevent the fitting out or equipping of any vessel within its jurisdiction if there was any reason to believe that it was to be used in war against a friendly power. The neutral must not permit a belligerent to make use of its ports or waters for hostile purposes. The government must exercise due diligence to prevent the violation of these rules. These principles were not in the recognized body of international law at the time, but they were now put in force and made retroactive to the period of the Civil War.

The Treaty of Washington provided also that Canadian fishing privileges would be opened to American fishermen for a limited term of years, and in return the United States agreed to open its coastal fisheries north of the 39th parallel of latitude to Canadian and British fishermen. The United States consented to admit Canadian fish into American ports free of duty. The San Juan boundary near Vancouver Island was to be submitted to the arbitration of the emperor of Germany. American citizens received free rights of navigation of the St. Lawrence, and British subjects received similar privileges on three rivers in Alaska. Each government agreed to recommend to the states concerned and to the Dominion of Canada that reciprocal use be granted to both Canadians and Americans of the canals on the Great Lakes waterway. The Senate ratified this treaty. The tribunal for arbitrating the *Alabama* claims met at Geneva and worked from December 1871 to September 1872. It awarded the United States the lump sum of $15,500,000 in gold, and this sum was duly paid.

Before Secretary Fish had begun to make headway in settling the disputed questions with Great Britain, President Grant became involved in a scheme for the annexation of Santo Domingo. The initiative seems to have come from two adventurers in New York, William L. Cazneau and Joseph W. Fabens. They aimed to secure control of a substantial portion of the public lands in Santo Domingo. They could get these properties for nothing, but if the United States should take possession the land would acquire great value. The two men were also interested in mining, transportation, harbor facilities, and even in banking. All these enterprises would become profitable in the event of annexation by the United States. Grant and his secretary, Babcock, fell in with the scheme, and Babcock actually secured a treaty of annexation. This treaty never had a chance of ratification in the Senate.

Santo Domingo and Cuba

In 1868, six months before the close of Johnson's administration, Cuban rebels started a revolution against Spanish rule. This struggle lasted ten years. The United States was interested, partly because of the geographical position of the island, partly because of the activities of a Cuban revolutionary organization in New York City. This body worked to arouse American sympathy for the rebels, and it sent out filibustering expeditions to give them help. In 1869 the United States offered its services to Spain to assist in ending the dispute on the basis of Cuban independence, but the Spanish government would not talk of peace so long as the insurgents were still under arms.

In 1873 a Spanish naval vessel seized the *Virginius,* bound for Cuba on a filibustering expedition from the United States. The ship was flying the American flag, and her papers—obtained under false pretenses—showed that she had an American registry. She had a crew of fifty-two officers and men, chiefly American and British citizens. The passengers, over one hundred in number, were nearly all Cubans. The Spanish authorities took her into the harbor of Santiago, Cuba, and entered upon a course of summary justice. They executed fifty-three persons, including "General" Ryan, an Irish advocate of Cuban freedom, some Englishmen, some Americans, and a number of Cubans. Further executions were stopped when the commander of an English naval vessel, Captain Lorraine, prepared to bombard the city. Here was a major crisis in diplomacy.

In the United States the newspapers, the public, and the administration raised loud protests over the insult to the American flag. The incident might easily have resulted in war between Spain and the United States, but Secretary Fish worked for a satisfactory settlement by peaceful means. Evidence showed conclusively that the *Virginius* had no right to her papers and that she was illegally flying the flag of the United States. Fish secured the release of the vessel and of the surviving members of her crew and passenger list. The Spanish government formally disclaimed any intent to insult the flag of the United States and subsequently paid an indemnity to the families of American citizens who had been illegally executed.

Chapter 27

DEVELOPMENT OF THE WEST

Mining, Cattle Raising, and Farming

New States

ONE significant feature of American history has been the ability of the people to make constructive achievements in spite of shortcomings at Washington. This feature is especially evident in the history of the West. In 1865 the region beyond the Mississippi consisted of two narrow strips of partly settled country, separated from each other by nearly a thousand miles of plains and mountains. On the eastern side the occupied area reached a line running along the western borders of Minnesota and Iowa, across central Nebraska and Kansas, along the western border of Arkansas and through central Texas. On the western fringe, California and Oregon had already been admitted as states. Then the exigencies of national politics rather than the size of the population had brought Nevada into the Union in 1864—the Republicans needed two Senators from the state.

Between 1865 and the present time much of the habitable part of the million square miles in the West was settled. The list of states admitted to the Union during this time is impressive. Colorado was admitted in 1876. In 1889 the four large states of Montana, the two Dakotas, and Washington were admitted. Idaho and Wyoming followed the next year. Utah was kept out until 1896; when the Church of the Latter-Day Saints officially disavowed the doctrine of plural marriage, Utah was admitted. Oklahoma joined in 1907, and New Mexico and Arizona in 1912. According to the census of 1870 the area included in these eleven states admitted to the Union after the Civil War had a population of 311,030; by 1930 the population for this same area was 8,943,861, an increase of nearly 3000 percent.

Silver Mining

The first white settlers in this vast area were the miners; by 1861 they were systematically at work on the rich deposits in Colorado and Nevada. "Pikes Peak or Bust" became a familiar slogan of west-bound treasure hunters. Denver, which had been a mere Indian village in 1859, developed during the next five years into a thriving town of 4000 inhabitants. Miners went into Arizona in 1863 and into Idaho and Montana in 1864. In the region of the richer deposits, west of Denver in Colorado and along the Comstock Lode in Nevada, scores of mining towns and villages came into existence and then disappeared. Among the most famous centers were Central City, Colorado, and Virginia City, Nevada. Mark Twain gave lasting notoriety to the latter in *Roughing It.* At the height of their prosperity these mining towns were among the busiest places in the United States, and probably the most picturesque. Virginia City reached its peak in population in 1878 with 38,000 inhabitants. As a thriving metropolis it could boast of

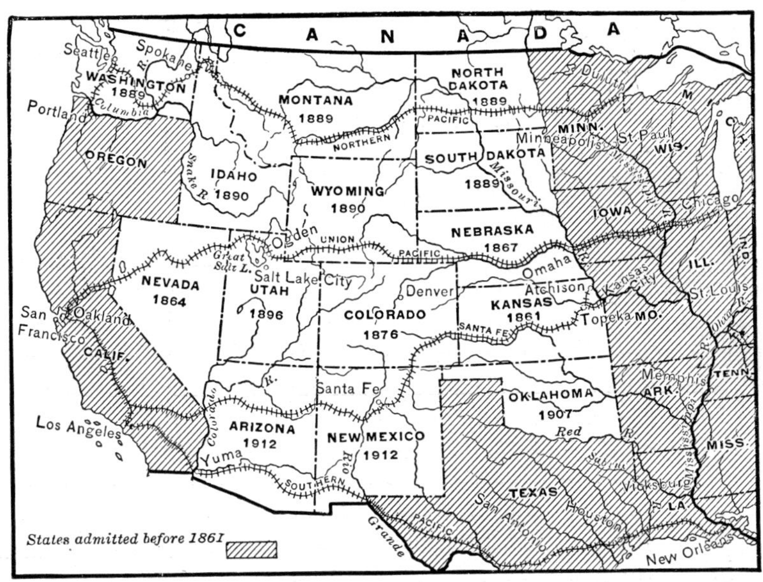

Map 13. The New West

twenty laundries, fifty dry-goods merchants, six churches, one hundred and fifty places for selling liquor, eighteen barbers, four banks, and several gambling houses. It had daily passenger train service at the rate of one train every fifteen minutes. But with the exhaustion of the more easily worked ores, the Comstock Lode became less profitable, and population declined rapidly in Virginia City. By 1900 it was down to 2695, and by 1940 to 600 or less. But even as a ghost town Virginia City has a charm for the tourist.

Between 1859 and 1880 the various companies operating on the Comstock Lode took out silver ore to the value of $306,000,000. The mines there have never been abandoned, and by 1941 the total value of both gold and silver taken from that one area was approximately $1,000,000,000. Fortunes came easily but they went quickly, and miners and stockholders alike found that silver was an unstable foundation to build upon. Heavy overproduction along the Comstock Lode and at other mines forced the price down, while the adoption of the gold standard of currency by the leading countries of the world depressed the price still farther.

Cattle Kings and Farmers

Another episode of western American life of this period, just as picturesque as that of the silver mining camps and almost as transitory, was the cattle business on the great plains. In 1866 the discovery was made that beef cattle could be fattened for market on the plains, and almost at once the cow country became famous. This region stretched from Canada to Texas and from Kansas on the east to the Rocky Mountains on the west. During the winter the cattle grazed on state-owned land in Texas. There were no fences and no effort was made to keep the stock of various owners separate. In the spring an annual roundup enabled the cowboys to sort out the property. The young calves followed their mothers, and they were caught and branded with the owner's mark. Stray calves were divided among the owners on a pro rata basis. After branding, the calves were turned loose again. The steers, which had been branded the year before, were taken in charge by the cowboys for the "long drive." Working north as hot weather dried up the pasturage, the cowboys eventually brought their charges to one of the new railroad lines. Then the animals were taken to Kansas City, Omaha, or Chicago, the meat-packing centers.

For a period of twenty years, until the farmers broke up the plains into small, individually owned holdings, western cattlemen enjoyed the benefits of free grazing land. At the same time the development of improved methods of refrigeration made it possible to ship fresh beef to any part of the United States. The discovery of better processes of canning gave an even wider scope to the operations of the meat packers. This combination of factors drove eastern producers of beef out of business.

The primitive era of free pasturage lasted only a few years. The barbed wire of the farmers made the long drive across the plains impossible. And the cattlemen themselves contributed to their own downfall. They overstocked the plains so that pasturage became relatively scarce, and they glutted the market with an excessive number of steers. Then the producers found themselves at the mercy of the railroads and of the packers, who managed to keep cattle prices down. Thereafter the business of producing beef cattle was carried on not on the great plains but on ranches, privately owned and of restricted size.

The coming of the farmers marked another stage in the settlement of the West, and at this point the federal government made important contributions. To facilitate the transfer of the public domain into private hands Congress adopted three important land grant policies; these measures help to account for the greatest mass movement of population in all history.

National Land Policy

For several years before the Civil War advocates of a new federal land policy had been calling for free land. President Buchanan was opposed to free land and he prevented any action during his administration. In 1860 the Republican party included in its platform the demand for a "complete and satisfactory homestead measure." In 1862 Congress enacted such a law. It provided that any person, twenty-one years of age or older, who was a citizen of the United States or who had declared his intention of becoming one, might occupy and use a piece of public land, not over 160 acres in extent. If he should live on the land for five years and put up a habitation on it, he could become the owner, on payment of $10.

Another land grant act developed out of the new agricultural outlook in the West. In that area the day of the old-fashioned farmer, working his land with hand tools, was rapidly becoming a thing of the past. The new order called for large-scale farming operations carried on with machinery. This change in turn made a new type of training necessary, and there were calls for government help in promoting agricultural education. Shortly before the Civil War several states, particularly Pennsylvania, Michigan, Iowa, and Minnesota, had organized state colleges of agriculture. In 1857 Justin S. Morrill of Vermont, chairman of the House Committee on Agriculture, introduced a bill providing for grants of public land to promote agricultural education. The measure passed Congress, only to be defeated by Buchanan's veto. In 1862 this Morrill bill was revived and enacted. It provided that the federal government should give public land to the various states, in the ratio of 30,000 acres or the equivalent thereof in "land scrip" for each representative and senator in Congress. New York, for example, received the equivalent of 990,000 acres of public land under this law.

In addition to the Homestead Act and the Morrill Act there were the various grants to railroad companies. To encourage the construction of the first transcontinental railroad Congress gave the companies which built it public land, first of ten and then twenty square miles for each mile of track. Congress was equally generous in its grants to other companies. Between 1862, the date of the first Pacific Railroad Act, and 1871, when Congress terminated this policy, the federal government gave the railroads 127,628,000 acres. The plan was to grant the land in alternate sections on each side of the track; if any of this area happened to be already occupied, alternative grants were provided in a zone fifteen miles in width on each side of the track. In addition to these direct grants from the federal government, the roads received 4,797,574 acres which the federal government had previously given to some of the states.

For some reason the Homestead Act received greater publicity than the other land-grant policies, but prior to 1890 the government gave title to only 48,225,736 acres under this law. The railroads received more than twice as much. In 1888 the government stopped selling land, and thereafter grants under the Homestead Act showed a rapid increase. Between 1890 and 1910 the government gave deeds to approximately 70,500,000 acres; between 1910 and 1933 grants under the Homestead Law reached a total of 118,177,232 acres.

Machinery and Grain

The most obvious and also the most important result of this generous federal land policy was an increase in the area of land brought under cultivation. Between 1860 and 1870 the improved farm land of the United States increased by 25,810,379 acres and in the following decade, by almost 96,000,000; from 1880 to 1900 another 129,727,445 acres were added. Most of these new farms produced grain of one kind or another: wheat, corn, oats, and barley. Both the land and the crops were suited to the use of improved farm machinery, which diminished the need for human labor at harvest time something like 2000 percent. The McCormick reaper which had come into general use on the western farms before the Civil War had merely cut the grain. In 1878 John F. Appleby of Wisconsin invented the twine binder as an addition to the reaper. This device did more than any other thing to speed up the process of harvesting wheat, and from this point of view it

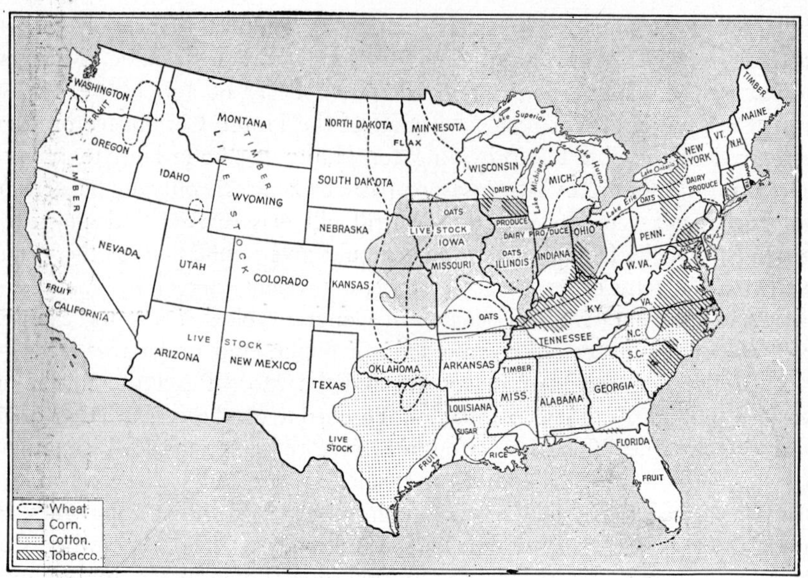

Map 14. Principal Agricultural Areas in the United States

might be regarded as one of the most significant of all the inventions of this period. In 1885 a practicable combine was put on the market, a machine which combined the processes of harvesting and threshing. Between 1890 and 1900 the increasing use of gasoline engines diminished still further the need of human labor in the grain fields.

The rapid increase in the quantity of grain produced in the United States upset the grain markets of the whole world. The amount raised was no more than the world needed, but it was more than people could afford to buy at good prices. Between 1860 and 1910 the output of barley increased ten times, oats six times, and wheat four times. The barley was used largely in brewing, the oats as food for horses, and the wheat for human beings. During these same years the population of this country increased less than threefold. The effect of these increases upon prices is obvious. Between 1865 and 1893 the price of wheat fluctuated from year to year but the general trend was downward. In 1866 wheat had sold for $1.60 per bushel; in 1894 it dropped to 67 cents.

Frontier Myth

As one stage in a continuous process of national development, the occupation of the West was an important episode in American history. The increase in the number of farms and farmers, the rapid advance in the quantity of grain produced, and the transformation of the prairies from wild areas to civilized communities—all these were matters of record. No student of American history would think of ignoring this part of the story. But some writers on the subject—notably Frederick Jackson Turner and his school—were not satisfied to stop at this point. They saw in the development of the West not a portion of American history but the most important factors in American history, the factors which gave significance and meaning to all other aspects of national development. In their enthusiasm some of them gave currency to generalizations which went considerably beyond available facts. One of the most common of these might be called the myth of the closing of the frontier. The basis of this myth was a statement in the census of 1890: "the unsettled area has been so broken into by isolated bodies of settlement that there can hardly be said to be a frontier line." Such was the record of "the passing of the frontier" in American history. It was easy to conclude from the words in the census report that by 1890 most of the public land had been occupied, and that the whole West was filled with settlers. Such was not the case. The land grants under the Homestead Act after 1890 show how rapidly settlement continued. But the most important conclusion drawn from this simple statement was the one which assumed that before 1890 the supply of free land constituted a barrier against social unrest. The opportunity to go West and begin life over again furnished a means of escape to the industrial laborer and so prevented the accumulation of industrial discontent. The logical corollary of this argument was that the industrial disturbances which came after 1890 were due to the closing of the frontier.

In recent years scholars have subjected some of these theories and the related historical material to a searching analysis. They show that after 1865, with the increasing importance of machinery on the farms, it would have been difficult if not impossible for the average industrial laborer of the East to raise the capital necessary to undertake farming in the West. The migration that settled this particular West was not from factory to farm but from eastern farm or from European farm to western farm. They also called attention to the extensive labor troubles in the East during the 1870's and 1880's before the frontier was "closed." More important still, the farmers were having hard times of their own during these same two decades, and this agricultural depression was accompanied by an actual increase of the unemployed in the cities. Unemployed industrial laborers were financially unable to turn to the farm for relief. On the contrary the reverse was true; the bankrupt farmer went to the town.

Indians and Railroads

Indian Wars

Throughout the greater part of American history the westward movement of the whites had been accompanied by the elimination or removal of the Indians, and the settlement of the trans-Mississippi West furnished no exception. The traditional attitude of the average American pioneer toward the Indian was simple; the red men had no rights which the whites were bound to recognize. The slogan of the frontier, "the only good Indian is a dead Indian," was no empty phrase. On their side the Indians were not unprotesting victims. War was their normal mode of behavior.

In this last struggle it made no difference to the whites that the Indians were living on lands set apart for them and guaranteed to them "forever" by act of Congress. The rapid advance of the whites carried them beyond legal boundaries and, if the Indians were using lands which the whites desired, the Indians had to give way. The period of hostilities lasted from 1865 to 1890, although the worst of the wars were over by 1877. These contests cost the United States government $22,000,000, to say nothing of the loss of life. The struggle was not conducted under the rules of regular warfare, and there were no great campaigns with large bodies of troops engaged, fighting for specific territorial objectives. It was rather a long-drawn-out guerilla contest, consisting of surprise attacks and rapid retreats.

The chief factors in the defeat of the Indians were the overwhelming numerical superiority of the whites, the irresistible advance of the pioneers, and the relentless pressure of the forces of the regular army. A contributing factor was the destruction of the buffalo herds. These animals had furnished the plains Indians with food, clothing, skins for their tepees, harness, and strings for their bows. By 1887 most of the buffalo had been killed.

In Jackson's administration the federal government had begun the policy of establishing Indian territories west of the Mississippi River. In 1869 President Grant advised Congress to abandon this system and to put the Indians on large reservations. This policy was adopted, and the Indians on the reservations were placed under the jurisdiction of a Board of Indian Commissioners. The Commission worked to civilize the Indians and achieved a fair degree of success in doing so. Then in 1871 Congress ended the old custom of making treaties with the Indian tribes. During the next few years conditions improved steadily for those Indians who remained at peace. On the reservations they were protected by the army and provided with supplies by the federal government.

The Dawes Act

In 1887 Congress passed the Dawes Act, which provided for the distribution of land to individuals. The head of a family might have 160 acres, and unmarried adults could have eighty acres each. To prevent the recipients of this bounty from selling or mortgaging their land, the title remained in the hands of the federal government for a period of twenty-five years. Indians who accepted the land, and who gave up the tribal mode of life, were to be given citizenship. The provisions of this law were not mandatory, but the Indians were encouraged to avail themselves of these new advantages. The Dawes Act enabled some of the Indians to adopt the white man's mode of life, and many of them have become self-supporting citizens. Because of these changes, the Indian population is now showing a definite increase. In 1492, according to the estimates of competent anthropologists, the Indians in the region of the present United States numbered about 846,000. According to the census of 1920, there were 244,437 Indians in this country; in 1930 there were 332,397, and in 1940 333,969.

Another factor in the building of the West was the construction of the transcontinental railroads. Their effect was twofold; they brought the pioneers back into direct connection with the East, and they opened wide areas of new country to other settlers. Then there is no more vivid illustration of the rapidity with which the West was brought into touch with mechanized civilization than the building of the railroads. It was not until 1858 that organized stagecoach traffic connected the Missouri River with California; only eleven years later the combined Union Pacific and Central Pacific Railroads provided through railroad service to California.

Pacific Railroads

On the eve of the Civil War William H. Russell started a faster mail service to the Pacific, the Pony Express. He had stations built at ten-mile intervals, supplied them with horses and riders, and began service in April 1860. The riders of the Pony Express made the trip from St. Joseph to California in ten days. For some eighteen months they carried the first class mail and abandoned the business only when the first transcontinental telegraph line was completed in 1861. The overland mail coach line ran until 1869 when the railroad was finished.

Reference has already been made to the terms of the two Pacific Railroad bills passed by Congress. According to the acts of Congress the road had to be completed by 1876, otherwise the whole line would be forfeited to the United States government. The Central Pacific began work at once and had a few miles in operation by 1864. The Union Pacific was slow in getting under way; it did nothing except lobby until after the enactment of the second bill in 1864. By 1865 the Union Pacific had built forty miles. Both companies had to contend with extraordinary handicaps. In the Platte valley the Union Pacific encountered no topographical obstacles, but the country provided no timber or stone for bridges and trestles. To add to the difficulties construction was carried on at the height of the Indian wars, and the construction gangs had to be ready at all times to exchange their picks and shovels for guns. The Central Pacific had to build through the mountains; it had to import all the iron from the eastern United States or from Europe. To secure the necessary labor it imported Chinese coolies from Asia.

In 1866, partly because of slow progress, Congress decreed that each road might keep on building until they met. The point in this legislation was that the land grants were much larger for construction in the mountains than through level country. By 1868 construction was going on at a surprising rate, and for a time it looked as though the roads would not meet at all but would actually pass each other. Congress stopped that rivalry by specifying the place of meeting: Promontory Point, not far from Ogden, Utah. In 1868 the Central Pacific built 360 miles of track, the Union Pacific 425. During the last sixteen months, the roads averaged two and one-half miles of track for every working day.

On May 10, 1869, locomotives from the East and West faced each other at Promontory Point, at the ends of the two lines. The ceremony of completing the great project was accompanied by appropriate celebrations all over the United States. The two rail heads were joined and the last spike driven was solid gold. The event deserved celebration. The building of the road was the greatest engineering feat yet undertaken in the United States.

Even though the record was marred by corruption and graft, and even though the road had to be largely rebuilt—before twenty years had passed Edward H. Harriman laid new rails, straightened the curves, and reduced the grades—it was a great achievement. The road gave access to millions of acres of farm land and reduced the cost of shipping both products and supplies. It led to the formation of new states, and it furnished a physical bond of union which tended to bring all sections closer together.

The successful completion of the Union Pacific encouraged other adventurers to attempt additional lines. Jay Cooke planned the Northern Pacific, to run from Lake Superior to Puget Sound. By June 1873 construction had reached Bismarck, on the Missouri River, a distance of 450 miles. Then the panic of 1873 put Jay Cooke into bankruptcy and temporarily stopped work on the road. Later Henry Villard took over the project, and in 1883 the road was finished. In 1885 the Canadian Pacific reached the coast, and in 1893 James J. Hill's Great Northern linked Minneapolis with the coast. Before the panic of 1873 intervened, the Missouri Pacific connected St. Louis with Kansas City, the Kansas Pacific connected Kansas City with Denver, and the Atchison, Topeka, and Santa Fé ran to New Mexico. In 1884 the Southern Pacific linked together various lines to give through service from New Orleans to California. By 1909 the United States had seven separate transcontinental railroad lines, and Canada had three.

The Grange

As the West and the transcontinental railroads developed together, many farmers discovered that the prosperity they had counted on did not arrive.

Farmers' Troubles

The greater the increase in the number of western farmers, the more wheat, corn, and hogs they produced, and the lower was the price. There were other difficulties. Sometimes grasshoppers attacked grain fields by the square mile, leaving nothing but stubble in the wheat field or short bits of cornstalks elsewhere. In 1874 grasshoppers ruined most of the crops in Minnesota, Kansas, and Nebraska. Blizzards in winter might kill off the stock, while tornadoes and hail ruined crops in the summer.

Farmers complained bitterly over high railroad rates, over excessive charges by commission merchants, and over high interest rates. In addition there were high prices on almost everything the farmer had to buy, especially on textiles, sewing machines, and farm machinery. Many of these machines were sold on commission by agents, a method of marketing which certainly did not help the farmer. Again, most manufacturers were protected against foreign competition by the high tariff. This national policy was of no value to the farmer.

Finally there were taxes. In those days the principal source of revenue for state and local government was the general property tax. The farmer's property consisted almost entirely of real estate and heavy machinery, something in plain sight, which could not be concealed from the assessors.

Farmers therefore were taxed up to the limit of their possessions. Businessmen, on the other hand, could invest their money in securities, and they could easily conceal their assets from the assessors.

The logical method for securing relief from this combination of grievances was cooperative action. The first comprehensive attempt to organize the farmers was undertaken by a small group of federal employees in Washington, D. C., led by Oliver Hudson Kelley. In December 1867 he announced the formation of the Patrons of Husbandry, better known as the Grange. Kelley held a position in the Bureau of Agriculture—the Department was not created until 1889—and his duties carried him over the country, particularly in the South and West. From his observation of the farmers he became convinced that something ought to be done to help them solve their problems. He believed that membership in a great fraternal order devoted to the farmers and their problems would be most helpful. The Patrons of Husbandry was the result. It was a secret society with a formal ritual and the related hocus-pocus which exercises such a charm on the American mind. The first local chapter, or Grange, was founded in Washington, D. C., as Kelley put it, "by a number of distinguished Agriculturalists"; the founders, however, were not farmers but government clerks. This very fact tended to make the farmers suspicious. But Kelley was full of faith in his project. In 1868 he resigned his government job and devoted all his time to building up the Grange.

The Grange

Kelley published a circular (September 1868) in which he explained the purpose of his new order. "Its grand object is not only general improvement in husbandry, but to increase the general happiness, wealth and prosperity of the country." Even at this early date Kelley saw the possibility of using the Grange to oppose the corporations. One of his objectives, he said, was "to protect its members against the combinations by which their interests are injuriously affected." One of Kelley's friends and coworkers, W. W. Corbett of the *Prairie Farmer* of Chicago, emphasized this latter purpose:

> It seems to me that we, as an Order, have a work to perform in the war that is to be waged in this country, at no distant day, by the people, against the monstrous monopolies that are overshadowing us. Railroad, Insurance Companies, Warehouse and Telegraph Companies, are crushing the life out of the producing classes.

In the course of two years the order had grown to the number of thirty-seven local Granges; by 1870 it had spread to nine states, and by 1872 the local chapters numbered 1150. By this time the Patrons of Husbandry had attained the prestige which goes with a nation-wide movement, and with prestige came opposition. The growth of the order alarmed local storekeepers and commission merchants. They tried to have the banks foreclose the mortgages of farmers who joined. This effort at repression convinced the farmers that they needed the Grange to protect themselves from predatory interests, and they joined in larger numbers than ever. Another factor in this growth was the drop in prices and farm income which attended the panic of 1873. The Grange reached its peak in growth in 1874, with a total enrollment of 1,500,000 members, distributed in 21,967 Granges. Although the order was strongest in the West and South, it had branches in all but four states.

Granger Program

The general objectives of the Patrons of Husbandry were defined in a formal declaration of the National Grange in 1874. First of all was the aim to "develop a better and higher manhood and womanhood among ourselves," and to make homes more comfortable and more attractive. Then came a call for reducing expenses, to buy less and to produce more, for the purpose of making the farms self-sustaining. Then the order hoped: "To discountenance the credit system, the mortgage system, the fashion system, and every other system tending to prodigality and bankruptcy."

With reference to corporations, particularly railroad corporations, the declaration announced that the Grange was not hostile to railroads, canal companies, or to "any corporation that will advance our industrial interests." But the Grange was opposed to "such spirit and management of any corporation or enterprise as tends to oppress the people and rob them of their just profits. We are not enemies to capital, but we oppose the tyranny of monopolies." In asserting the nonpolitical character and purpose of the order, the National Grange pointed out that every member had a right to influence his own political party for good. "It is his duty to do all he can in his own party to put down bribery, corruption, and trickery; to see that none but competent, faithful, and honest men . . . are nominated for all positions of trust."

Although this statement of aims was couched in general terms, it could not conceal the announced purpose of the Grange to put commission men, wholesalers, and retail storekeepers out of business. Cooperative buying was sure to bring lower prices. The Grangers knew that the local dealer made a profit of $100 on every reaper he sold, and on every threshing machine; that he averaged $60 profit on each wagon and tried to make at least $30 on each sewing machine. Cooperative buying by the Grangers brought about a reduction of at least 30 percent on the prices of this kind of machinery. The Grange tried to organize commission houses in order to free the farmers from dependence on the regular dealers. Then they went into the business of manufacturing, principally of agricultural machines. By 1874 the Grange had added insurance, gristmills, meat-packing establishments, grain elevators, and retail stores to its list of cooperative agencies. If they could find the right sort of leadership, financial ability, and executive talent they might go far.

Although the formal declaration of purpose and the actual program of Grangers emphasized the broad range of its purposes, the order came to be closely identified with the movement for subjecting the railroads to public control. The earlier state laws for regulating the roads are often referred to as Granger laws, and the cases involving these laws which came before the Supreme Court are usually referred to as the Granger cases. This activity bordered so closely upon politics that the farmers found it desirable to organize separate farmers' parties. The Grange itself was officially nonpartisan, but such parties as those in the Middle West in 1873 and 1874—Independent, Reform, Anti-Monopoly, Farmers', for example—were hardly more than the Grange in disguise.

The Grange, which still flourishes, had its period of greatest political and economic activity in the middle 1870's. Between 1874 and 1880 the number of local chapters dropped from more than 20,000 to 4000. The reasons for the decline varied in different sections, but some of the factors are fairly evident. In certain cases the members had expected too much from the organization; they rushed into it under the impression that it would prove to be a panacea for all their economic ills. When the order failed to measure up to expectations, they dropped out in disgust. In some cases, too, the local Granges owed their origin not so much to any insistent local demand as to the organizing power of the national officers. When the enthusiasm of these officials ceased to operate, the Grange disappeared. A more important reason for the decline might be found in the unsatisfactory outcome of the experiments in cooperative enterprise. Granger cooperatives did not supplant the regular commission dealers, partly because the dealers had more capital behind them, partly because they had the benefits of greater experience. Granger retail stores were not successful in driving out the better local merchants. In attempting to operate factories for the manufacture of farm machinery the Grangers soon found themselves in competition with a well-organized, liberally financed, and none too scrupulous monopoly.

Decline of the Grange

Even though its ambitious program of cooperative enterprise was not successful at the time, the Grange was far from being a failure. It aroused the interest of the farmers, got them out of their ruts, and showed them some of the possibilities in organized activity. The "agrarian crusade" which the Grangers started lasted down through the eighties and early nineties, reaching its climax in the Populist movement of 1896.

Chapter 28

RAILROADS, INDUSTRIAL ORGANIZATION, AND PUBLIC REGULATION

Foundations of Business Enterprise

Business Trends

OF all the influences which have formed the modern United States, none has been so pervasive and so far-reaching as the combination of forces known collectively as business enterprise. Business has transformed the life of the laborer, the office worker, the manufacturer, the financier, the fisherman and the sailor at sea, the professional man, and the farmer; the role of the housewife has been changed as radically as that of her husband. Economic doctrines have been made over, and a whole social philosophy has been revised. There is scarcely a social or economic problem of the present day which can be intelligently examined without reference to this background of business development.

The term "big business" is often used to cover the various phases of this development; the term is satisfactory if its meaning is understood. There was much more involved than the mere transition from small factories to large, from partnerships to corporations, from individual companies to trusts and holding companies, from assets measured in thousands to assets measured in billions, from a social structure in which the individual was at least influential to one in which corporations and the government dominate the people whom they are supposed to serve.

In some respects the development of corporations is the most significant aspect of American business. Fifty years ago James Bryce wrote:

> No invention of modern times . . . has so changed the face of commerce . . . as the creation of incorporated joint-stock companies. America, though she came latest into the field, has developed these on a grander scale and with a more refined skill than the countries of the Old World. Nowhere do trading corporations play so great a part in trade and industry; nowhere are so many huge undertakings in their hands; nowhere else has the method of controlling them become a political problem of the first magnitude.

Some economists describe our present organization as a pecuniary system, and the description is valid in so far as our life is bound up with money, prices, and credit. The influence and power wielded by those in charge of our economic activities depend on their control of vast financial resources. The money and credit lying at the base of the structure have been derived from productive industry, from far-flung marketing systems, sometimes from the monopoly made possible by effective corporate control. Here we have a combination of modern technology, business organization, and financial machinery, which taken together constitute the bases of our modern life. To here

Commentators are fond of calling the present era the age of machines, and machines are the material symbols of modern life. The period since the Civil War has seen a bewildering increase in both the number and the variety of these symbols. The first Pullman sleeping car, the "Pioneer," was put into service in 1865, and by 1879 the Pullman Company was making them on a quantity basis. Dining cars came into use in 1867. The first safe deposit vaults were used in Boston just after the Civil War. Passenger elevators, first used in Paris in 1853, were introduced in this country shortly after the Civil War. Although the first Atlantic cable had been laid before the war, the insulation was faulty, and the line was not ready for continuous service until 1866. The first clumsy typewriter was put together in 1867, but it was not until 1878 that the improved machine, with both capital and small letters, was ready for use. The telegraph, in general use before the Civil War, was applied to a new device, the stock market ticker, introduced in 1867. The telephone was invented in 1876, and in 1878 the first central switchboard was in operation. By 1880, eighty-five cities and towns had installed telephone exchanges; twenty years later the United States had more than 800,000 telephones in use, and in 1930 more than 20,000,000. The first electric dynamo, or generator, was made available in 1867. In 1878 Thomas A. Edison invented the incandescent lamp, and in 1879 Brush invented the electric arc light. Two years later the United States had thirty-eight stations for generating electric power; by 1888 this number had increased to 600, and by 1898 to more than 3000. In 1887 the city of Richmond, Virginia, had two miles of electric trolley car track in operation. In the course of the next ten years more than 800 communities had provided themselves with electric trolleys. These are a few of the discoveries and inventions which have been conspicuous in the development of modern business in the United States. The mechanical equipment in all lines of work was constantly being improved so that manufacturers were faced with the expensive problem of obsolescence. Machinery was outmoded long before it was worn out, and the manufacturer had to provide himself with new equipment or see his competitors run away with his business.

New Machines

In the transition of the United States from the simple economy of pre-Civil War days to the complex closely integrated social and economic structure which we know today, the railroads made great contributions. Their history is not a record merely of feats of successful engineering—although without that there could have been no railroads—it is a tale of mechanical improvement and farsighted management, and also a story of financial juggling, bribery, and ruthless competition, to say nothing of the unexpected intrusion of banking interests into the field of railroad transportation.

Modern Railroads

In 1861 the railroad mileage of the whole country totaled 30,635. The rolling stock consisted of approximately 100,000 freight and passenger cars and 1000 locomotives. The number of employees engaged in operation and maintenance was not more than 150,000, and the annual pay roll was $90,-000,000. The ownership of this property was vested in hundreds of small companies, each serving a limited area. Although New York and Chicago were connected by railroad, through service had not been established. Passengers had to change trains where one line stopped and another began. It was impossible to use the rolling stock of one road on all lines because there was no standard gauge; at the time of the Civil War there were eight different gauges on the important roads. The Erie used a gauge of six feet. The present gauge of four feet, eight and one-half inches was not adopted until after the Civil War.

In 1915, when railroad construction practically ceased in the United States, the country had 253,789 miles of main line track. The rolling stock included 2,397,377 freight and passenger cars and 66,500 locomotives. There were approximately 2,000,000 employees, with a total annual pay roll of some $3,000,000,000. Long before the railroad system of the country was finished there were important mechanical improvements which greatly increased both the speed and the safety of transportation by rail. In 1868 the air brake was invented. Soon afterward the automatic block signal came into use. The next improvement was the automatic coupler, a device which simplified the work of making up trains and which minimized the danger to the train crews. In the passenger cars steam heat took the place of coal stoves, and gas lights superseded oil lamps. Electric lights did not become universal on the trains until 1918. Pullman parlor and sleeping cars came into general use after the Civil War.

American railroads were built to meet conditions in the United States, and these conditions have imparted distinctive characteristics to the roads. The greater part of the freight traffic, probably 75 percent, consists of bulky commodities: coal, iron and steel, lumber, petroleum, grain, and livestock. This kind of freight required heavy rails and heavy rolling stock. Again, the United States is a "country of magnificent distances." This circumstance makes high speed desirable, and speed at low cost. Steel rails made it possible to run heavier and faster trains. In 1863 the Pennsylvania Railroad imported steel rails from England. They proved to be ten to fifteen times more durable than iron. By 1880 one fourth of the railroad mileage of the United States had steel rails. Increasing traffic and higher speeds made double tracks necessary on the most heavily used roads.

Mechanical improvements were accompanied by far-reaching changes in management and operation. Short, independent lines went through a process of partial integration to form the trunk lines and the great systems which we have today. Neither the New York Central nor the Pennsylvania systems were planned and constructed as units. On the contrary, the original pieces of which they are made were put together by farsighted builders. By 1884 the roads between New York and Chicago had been integrated into five trunk lines, and two more were in the process of construction. But the work was done without any systematic plan. No attempt was made to

Integration

study the problem as a whole, and no guiding principle was adopted to determine which roads should be consolidated.

Mechanical improvements and consolidation cost money. The chief sources of funds were the sale of stocks and bonds, federal land grants, and gambling on the stock exchange. Business of all kinds was undergoing an unparalleled expansion, with new mines, new industries, new banks, as well as new railroads. Most of this activity was undertaken by corporations, and the corporations turned out a steady stream of new securities. Because of the uncertain prospects of many new enterprises, their stock certificates were subject to wide fluctuations in price; this condition made for active speculation. There were no restrictions on corporate capitalization; the tendency was to put the figure far in advance of actual investment—that is, to base it on prospective future earnings instead of current value. Partly through the sale of watered stock and partly from the profits of spectacular deals on the market the promoters found the money to build the railroads.

Railroads and Business

Commodore Vanderbilt

In some respects the greatest of the railroad barons was Cornelius Vanderbilt, popularly known as the Commodore. At the age of sixty-eight, when most men contemplate retirement, Vanderbilt decided to quit steamboats, a business which had given him a fortune of $11,000,000, and to go into railroading. In 1862 he bought a controlling interest in the New York and Harlem Railroad running from Forty-second Street in New York City to Brewster, New York. The stock cost him $9 per share. Next, by means which have been described as devious, he secured from the city government the charter for a streetcar line, running from Forty-second Street to the Battery. This franchise promised to be so profitable that all of Vanderbilt's holdings became more valuable in the eyes of watchful speculators. New York and Harlem stock moved up to $90 a share. Members of the city government then planned to sell the New York and Harlem short, and to annul the charter for the streetcar line. In the meantime the Commodore had quietly bought up all the stock in sight, so that he had the market cornered. When the shorts came to buy, in order to fill their contracts, Vanderbilt had it all. He sold New York and Harlem to them at $179 per share. Later he gave the legislators at Albany a beating; they too had sold Harlem short, and they too had to come to the Commodore on their knees. He sold them the stock they wanted at $285.

Ventures like this brought in money, several million dollars, so that the Commodore could broaden the scope of his operations. He bought the Hudson River Railroad, running from New York to Albany, and then the New York Central, running from Albany to Buffalo. In 1869 the New York legislature passed a bill permitting him to combine all his roads into the New York Central System. He took advantage of this opportunity to issue a stock dividend of 80 percent. The original capitalization of his roads had been $55,000,000; this new stock brought the total up to $99,000,000. These and other issues watered the stock of the New York Central to the extent of $5000 per mile. Vanderbilt used his profits in improving his property. Subsequently the New York Central was extended by the purchase of lines running to Chicago, Cincinnati, and St. Louis in the West, and to Boston in the East. Equipment and service were greatly improved.

Vanderbilt was an excellent example of the railroad builder. He put money into the New York Central and made it one of the best roads in the country. A different type of railroad baron was Daniel Drew of the Erie. The Erie was a potentially profitable, 500-mile road, connecting New York harbor on the Jersey side with Buffalo. It had fallen upon hard times before the Civil War, but in 1865 it could show receipts of $16,500,000. In 1857 Daniel Drew became treasurer and managing director of Erie. He was a former stock drover, innkeeper, moneylender, and operator in the stock market.

War with the Erie

In 1867 Commodore Vanderbilt decided to put an end to competition between his road and the Erie by buying the Erie. Control of the Erie had passed from Drew to Jay Gould and James Fisk, the two financiers already referred to in connection with the attempted gold corner of 1869. Fisk was a genial, unscrupulous speculator. According to report, each one of Gould's ventures diminished the sum total of integrity in business. These were the two men whom Vanderbilt would have to beat in order to secure control of the Erie.

The attempt to buy Erie was almost hopeless. The more stock Vanderbilt bought, the more Gould and Fisk issued. Between June and October 1868, these two gamblers with other people's money increased the capital stock by $23,500,000. When Vanderbilt got an injunction from Judge Barnard ordering the directors of Erie to return the newly issued shares to the road's treasury, Gould and Fisk got a counterinjunction from a judge in Binghamton to prevent Barnard from interfering with their management of the Erie. When Judge Barnard ordered the arrest of Fisk and Gould for contempt of court, the two men took refuge in Jersey City.

After a short stay in New Jersey Gould left for Albany, carrying $500,000 in greenbacks with him. The legislature was in session, with a bill pending to legalize the recent heavy increase in Erie stock. Gould established connections with the legislature. So too did a representative of the New York Central. For the period of this sojourn at Albany the Erie books carried an account for "legal expenses" amounting to $1,000,000. Ordinary senators received $15,000 apiece. The majority leader was clever enough to get $75,000 of Vanderbilt money, and then $100,000 from Gould. The bill for legalizing the issues of Erie stock became law.

By this time Vanderbilt had a block of Erie stock in the neighborhood of 100,000 shares, and the Erie group had over $4,000,000 of Vanderbilt's money. The Commodore called off the fight. But instead of dealing directly with Gould, he preferred to negotiate with Drew, who was still a power in the Erie, and the two men worked out a treaty of peace. The Erie directors paid Vanderbilt $2,500,000 outright in consideration of his readiness to abandon his plan for buying the Erie. Then they gave him $1,000,000 for half of his Erie stock. They also gave him $1,250,000 in bonds.

This episode of the Erie war is given, not because it is typical of all railroad practices of the day but because it illustrates so many aspects of big business. Although the property belonged to the stockholders, their rights and interests were ignored. The directors did as they pleased, risking millions, loading the property with debts. The state legislature could be made to serve the purposes of the railroad managers. Perhaps not every man had his price, but there were many who did, and the railroads had no difficulty in finding who they were and no hesitation in meeting their terms.

Ruinous Competition

Even though one puts the most charitable interpretation upon railroad methods, they still appear to have been unduly expensive. Opportunities for manipulating the stock market and prospects of gain through federal land grants had resulted in the incorporation of too many railroad companies and the construction of too much track. By 1890 American railroads were in deep financial difficulties. In 1876 40 percent of all American railroad bonds were in default. By 1879 sixty-five railroad companies, with a total capitalization of $234,000,000, were in the hands of receivers. In the course of six years following the panic of 1873 European investors in American railroads suffered losses of $600,000,000 as a result of bankruptcies and fraudulent practices.

Under prevailing standards the roads which served a given area, New York to Chicago for example, could have only one policy: cut-throat competition. The result was a series of rate wars, in which charges to the shippers showed wide variations. In 1869 rates on heavy freight between New York and Chicago fluctuated from a low of $5 per ton to a high of $37.60. From New York to St. Louis the range of fluctuation was from $7 to $46. For a short time the Erie advertised a rate of $2 per ton from the Atlantic seaboard to Chicago, and with no advance warning raised the rate to $37 per ton. While the rates between competing points were often below cost, the roads tried to recompense themselves by imposing excessively high charges between points where there was no competition. This meant charging considerably more for short hauls than for long. Another consequence of unrestricted competition was a wide variation in the rates charged to individual shippers.

When the directors found competition too costly, they would get together and agree to stop it. Rival roads would form a traffic pool and divide profits on a pro rata basis. In 1877 four of the roads operating between New York and Chicago—the New York Central, the Erie, the Pennsylvania, and the Baltimore and Ohio—formed such a pool. Under this arrangement, the Central and the Erie each received 33 percent of the profits, the Pennsylvania 25 percent, and the Baltimore and Ohio 9 percent.

As time went on the corruption of lawmakers with railroad money became a serious problem. The activities of Huntington, Durant, and Ames at Washington, already described in connection with the affairs of the Union Pacific, and of Jay Gould at Albany would serve to show what the railroad managers were doing to and with the government. These were not isolated instances but examples of common practices. Having firsthand knowledge of the way laws were made, railroad magnates used the laws when they were helpful and flouted them if they were in the way. "Law!" roared Commodore Vanderbilt on one occasion. "What do I care for law! Hain't I got the power?" And again, when he was informed that his plans for the New York Central were plain violations of the laws of his state, he replied: "My God, John, you don't suppose you can run a railroad in accordance with the statutes of New York, do you?" Railroads were a powerful factor in the growth of the modern United States. They were also a major problem.

Industrial Resources

As a factor in American development, industry was just as important as the railroads. Although industrial development had gone far in the United States before the Civil War, nevertheless as late as 1880 agriculture was still the chief source of national wealth. During the next two decades the United States became a great industrial nation. By 1914 the industrial output of the United States equaled that of France, Germany, and Great Britain combined. The increase in the number and size of the factories led to the growth of a class of factory employees—a class in which the majority of its members remained tied to the mills for generation after generation. The presence of this large body of industrial workers is only one of a number of complex problems growing out of the new economic system.

This great industrial development was made possible by an unusual combination of circumstances. In the first place there had to be a demand for goods—that is, a market. The demand was provided partly by the rapid increase in population. Farmers and industrial workers alike needed a variety of supplies in rapidly expanding volume. At the same time the introduction of new technical and mechanical improvements made possible a change in the standard of living, and this change created demands for household plumbing, heating, and lighting. New houses were always needed to take care of the increasing population, and new factories were an important part of the expanding industrial system. Continued new construction provided a growing market for building materials, equipment, and machinery. This was also the era of railroad and street railway construction. Rails and rolling stock called for other vast quantities of raw materials, and their production kept employees busy. American economic life therefore was geared to two important factors: a rapidly increasing population, and a rapidly expanding industrial system.

As for natural resources, the United States has been unusually fortunate in the possession of generous supplies of almost all the materials needed in modern industry. Minerals, metals, fibers, and fuel are found or raised here in abundance, while agricultural facilities have been more than abundant. During the nineteenth century the United States could always buy the raw materials not raised here, for example rubber and tin.

Next to raw materials comes labor because human beings are necessary to run the machines. The workers were provided, partly by the natural increase in population, and partly by heavy immigration from Europe. The people were of excellent quality: energetic, full of initiative, skillful and apt in the use of tools and machines. It is significant that practically all modern mechanical contrivances have originated in western Europe and in the United States.

After raw materials and labor comes management, which includes engineering skill, business enterprise as shown in the organization of factories and in the acquisition and manipulation of markets, and financial talent, that quality which makes it possible for some people to manage the complex machinery of money and credit. This genius for administration and executive direction is essential to the growth of large-scale enterprise. American businessmen have shown marked ability in this field.

Combinations of Capital

Carnegie and Steel

The development of industry and of big business in the United States depended in part on the rise of new enterprises, the most important of which, in this period, were steel and petroleum. The art of making steel was old enough, but the process of producing it was slow and expensive. By 1850 ironmasters succeeded in developing a new process for making steel. In the United States William Kelly experimented with a method of removing the carbon from iron, but he never made his converter commercially successful. In England, however, Henry Bessemer, working with the same type of converter, was making cheap steel before 1860. Before the end of the Civil War a steel plant in Michigan used the Bessemer process, and by 1875 there were a dozen plants in the United States manufacturing steel by the new method. The new process made steel as cheap as cast iron.

William Kelly and Alexander Holley were among the first Americans to utilize the Bessemer process in this country, but they did not put the production of steel into the realm of big business. That honor was reserved for Andrew Carnegie. Carnegie began his career on the railroad, and by 1863 he had reached the post of division superintendent on the Pittsburgh division of the Pennsylvania. In 1863 Carnegie added to his railroad interests the manufacture of axles for railroad cars. Then he added iron bridges, iron rails, and locomotives. In 1865 he resigned from the railroad and devoted himself entirely to his iron works.

From his experience in manufacturing iron Carnegie knew of the advantages of the Pittsburgh area. Here were ample supplies of iron ore, coal, and limestone together with excellent transportation facilities, both by rail and water. He began work on a new steel plant at Braddock, just outside of Pittsburgh. Between 1875, when the new plant was finished, and 1879, the production of steel in the United States increased from 375,000 tons to 929,000, and Carnegie had more business than any of his rivals.

It would be hard to overestimate the importance of steel in the development of the modern, highly mechanized industrial society in the United States. The abundance and low price of the metal revolutionized railroad transportation and structural engineering. Steel replaced iron on the tracks and in the rolling stock of the railroads. For the future all large buildings would have steel frames; the skyscraper would have been impossible without structural steel. All machines, both for the factory and for the farm, were made of steel. The steel mills gave employment to thousands of American workmen. American industry became inseparably bound up with steel, and Andrew Carnegie was the major contributor to the new enterprise.

Carnegie's Philosophy

Under the circumstances Carnegie could easily look upon himself as a philanthropist contributing to the well-being of the whole world. He was furnishing the raw material for industry and doing it at low cost; directly and indirectly he provided employment for hundreds of thousands of workers. If a mechanized society is a good thing, the captains of industry who helped to develop it were public benefactors. They possessed the genius required for bringing to a focus the resources—material, financial, and human—which were needed in successful industry. They provided the qualities of management, of executive talent, without which no business could thrive.

Nor is it surprising that the captains of industry should have been interested in profits. They grew up in a society trained to admire the virtues which brought success upon the frontier: self-reliance, initiative, the ability to get results. And on the frontier the rewards of success were, in the first instance, private and individual not social. What a man made was his own. Great industrialists like Carnegie did something more than make two jobs grow where there had been only one. They created hundreds of thousands of jobs where there had been none. From the point of view of industrial leaders it was not the laborers who created the J. Edgar Thompson Steel Works, it was Andrew Carnegie. Again it was Carnegie's ability and aggressiveness which kept his costs low and sold more steel. Carnegie had started with as few resources, apparently, as any workingman. If he happened to be more successful than the great majority of his fellows, he was inclined to attribute his good fortune to an act of God and to make the most of it. The theory that the rewards of ability and hard work belonged to society rather than to the individual rested upon assumptions which Carnegie never admitted.

Petroleum

Almost of equal importance was petroleum. The personification of this enterprise was John D. Rockefeller. As in the case of steel, the petroleum industry rested upon one of the natural resources, almost worthless in its natural state. It required the interposition of the manufacturer and distributor to make it usable. Opportunity in its raw state had been there for untold thousands of years, but a peculiar combination of factors was needed to enable anybody to profit from it.

Before 1855 manufacturers were producing illuminating oil from both coal and petroleum, and the name "kerosene" was already in use. Chemists were investigating the oil of western Pennsylvania. The first problem was to procure it in sufficient quantity to make it pay. To this end Colonel E. L. Drake was put to work on what seemed like the foolish enterprise of sinking an oil well. In the summer of 1859 Drake succeeded; his first well yielded twenty-five barrels per day. As reports of the find spread, prospectors flocked into Pennsylvania as they had to California ten years before, and what had been a sparsely settled countryside was soon dotted with camps and derricks. As new wells were sunk, villages, towns, and even cities sprang up like the silver towns on the Comstock Lode.

Refined petroleum furnished a superior quality of lubricating oil, something vitally necessary in the rapidly growing industrial world. And even more important, it provided an illuminating oil far superior to whale oil or candles, and one that could be sold at a low price. Since electricity had not yet been put to practical use, kerosene was a boon to every family within reach of transportation facilities. Refineries were established at New York City, Philadelphia, Pittsburgh, and Cleveland, Ohio. Here then was the beginning of another vast enterprise.

Standard Oil

In 1859, the year made memorable by Drake's success, John D. Rockefeller of Cleveland went into the produce commission business. Even in his youth his capacity for making money was apparent, and he saved enough to enable him to invest in profitable enterprises. Unlike millions of other young men, he did not serve in the army. In 1865, at the end of the Civil War, Rockefeller went into the petroleum business. He knew nothing of the technicalities of refining oil, but he was a shrewd judge of human nature, and he had an uncanny faculty for selecting the right men as associates. In 1870 Rockefeller, Flagler, and Andrews were the most successful refiners in the country. In the course of five years their firm had accumulated $1,000,000 in capital, and they gave employment to more than 1000 men. This year they had themselves incorporated as the Standard Oil Company of Ohio.

At that time Rockefeller and his associates were concerned only with the process of refining. But the refineries stood at the strategic center of the petroleum business. Crude oil was of no value except to the refiners, and the wholesale dealers had no source of supply except the refiners. If any concern could secure a monopoly of refining, it could name its own terms with the producers and name the price to the consumer. Rockefeller established such a monopoly. First of all he secured control of the refineries in Cleveland. In the Cleveland area Rockefeller offered his rivals cash for their properties or stock in the Standard Oil Company. Those who took stock never regretted their bargain; those who refused to sell found it impossible to compete with the Standard. It took Rockefeller just three months to acquire the refineries of Cleveland. As his firm expanded, Rockefeller secured more favorable terms from the railroads than those of his rivals.

Rockefeller's purpose was the stabilization of a business which had been utterly unregulated. Before his day producers of crude petroleum had indulged in the wildest competition, and the resulting fluctuations in price from one day to the next had a range of 100 percent. Furthermore the competing companies could never provide a steady flow of business for the railroads. But with all the refineries in the hands of a single company, and with this company tied up with the railroads, unified management could easily regulate both output and shipments. There were undeniable advantages to the various parties concerned, even to the public, because unrestricted competition is unduly expensive. Having brought order and regularity to the refining business of Cleveland, Rockefeller next acquired control of the refineries in the producing regions of Pennsylvania and in Philadelphia. By 1878 Rockefeller and his associates had acquired control of 80 percent of the refineries in the United States; for practical purposes the monopoly of this branch of the oil business was complete.

In 1879 the oil companies associated with Rockefeller had a market value of more than $50,000,000, although the invested capital was only $3,500,000. In 1882 these companies, thirty-nine in number, were reorganized into the Standard Oil Trust. The process was simple. Stockholders in the affiliated concerns turned in their shares and received in their place, on a pro-rata basis, trust certificates in the new organization. The management of the Trust was vested in a board of nine trustees, with Rockefeller at the head. The collection of companies therefore became practically one great company. The Trust was capitalized at $70,000,000.

With the refineries and the facilities for transporting petroleum under their control, the Standard Oil interests began to acquire the wholesale distributing agencies. In New York there were great storage stations maintained by the New York Central and the Erie railroads. These were taken over by the Standard Oil Company. The various distributing stations in the United States were practically all brought under the same highly efficient control. One last branch of the business remained, that of the retail dealer, and the Standard set out to control this.

Fresh Beef

The advantages of unified control over formerly competing business units were too obvious to be overlooked by the businessmen, and so too were the advantages of large-scale organization. Other types of business were quick to take it up, particularly the meat-packing industry. Here again was something new in American life, something made possible by developments during and after the Civil War. The custom of using the western plains as free pastures for beef cattle and the invention of the refrigerator car came at about the same time, and there were business leaders capable of turning the new opportunities to profitable account. Then the building of the railroads, particularly in Iowa, Nebraska, and Kansas, brought the cattle country into close touch with the packers. Because of its location and rapidly growing railroad facilities, Chicago became the greatest meat-packing center in the country. In 1865 the state of Illinois incorporated the Union Stockyards, 345 acres in area, for the accommodation of shippers of livestock. In 1867 Philip Armour and Brothers entered the meat business in Chicago. Two years later the first refrigerator carload of fresh western beef was sent from Chicago to New York. In 1875 Gustavus F. Swift went into the meat business in Chicago, making a specialty of shipping fresh beef to the East. A year later the packers began to ship fresh beef to Europe.

In the meat business the packers were in a strategic position similar to that of the refiners in the petroleum field. They were the only buyers of the raw material and the only sellers who could supply the public. During the 1880's the leading packers established an effective domination over the meat business of the whole country. Then, after the manner of the Standard Oil Company, they used their power to secure favorable rates or rebates from the railroads. Many of the smaller packing houses sold out to the larger ones under compulsion. Thanks to these advantages, the "beef trust," or pool, was able to stabilize meat prices and also to fix the prices paid to the cattlemen. The leading packers divided the cattle country into districts, and each buyer agreed to operate only in his district. The producer therefore had only a single market, and he could take the price offered or keep his cattle.

Regulation under State Law

Fear of Monopoly

Even the foregoing brief survey shows that after the Civil War a new power was developing in American life—the power of organized wealth. Corporations and trusts seemed to dominate American business, and to affect the well-being of the ordinary citizen. Certain necessities of life, such as kerosene, meat, and coal, were in the hands of monopolies. Add to these such widely different types of commodities as whisky, tobacco, chewing gum, wire nails, barbed wire, farm machinery, electrical goods, all of which were subject to monopolistic control, and it becomes plain that the organized industrialists touched the American people at most important points in their daily affairs. In a decision of a case concerning the Diamond Match Company, the supreme court of the state of Michigan pointed out the consequences of monopoly:

> Indeed, it is doubtful if free government can long exist in a country where such enormous amounts of money are allowed to be accumulated in the vaults of corporations, to be used at discretion in controlling the property and business of the country against the interest of the public and that of the people, for the personal gain and aggrandizement of a few individuals.

There was nothing new in the theory that certain types of business must be conducted in such a way as to meet the needs of the public and that the government possessed the authority to see that they did so. In England government regulation of wharves and inns had long been an established practice because wharves and inns were bound up with public welfare; it required no stretch of logic to put railroads in the same category. In 1839 the state of Rhode Island established the first regulatory commission, and four other New England states followed before 1860. In 1869 the Illinois legislature passed a law providing that railroad rates must be "just, reasonable, and uniform," but in doing so the lawmakers made no provision for enforcement. As subsequent experience proved, it was easier to pass laws of this sort than to enforce them. In 1870 the new state constitution authorized the legislature to regulate the railroads. Armed with this new authority, the legislature established a schedule of maximum rates for both freight and passenger service and at the same time created a board of commissioners to make the rates effective. Iowa and Wisconsin passed similar laws providing for maximum rates and for the establishment of regulating commissions. Minnesota did the same thing.

State Regulation

In the West these experiments with public regulation of rates developed into a contest between the railroads and the farmers. The only organized agency through which the farmers could work was the Grange, therefore these regulatory measures were known as Granger laws. In such a contest the railroads possessed certain advantages. They had money and they had no scruple in using it. They could hire lawyers skilled in the art of getting around the law. They could also manipulate the service in such a way as to penalize prominent Grangers and to discourage the reformers.

During this same period there were experiments with state regulation of other types of business which because of its character and purpose was definitely connected with the welfare of the public. In 1869 the legislature of Illinois passed a law which declared all grain elevators to be public warehouses and subjected them to state regulation. The law provided for a standard schedule of fixed charges for these elevators. It also required the railroads to deliver grain to the elevator to which the farmer consigned it at the time of shipment. The reason for this law was to be found in the practices of the elevators in Chicago. Controlled by a monopoly, they had disregarded the farmers and favored the railroads.

In the same year the legislature of Louisiana had passed an important regulatory measure dealing with the slaughterhouse business. This law created a corporation and gave it authority to prepare meat for consumption in New Orleans and the neighboring parishes. It also prohibited the establishment of any other slaughterhouses within the limits of New Orleans. The corporation might grant to other persons the privilege of slaughtering animals in its houses on payment of a reasonable fee.

Both the Illinois and the Louisiana statutes were attacked in the courts by the interests affected, and in each case the plaintiffs held that the attempt at regulation was a violation of the Fourteenth Amendment, in that the laws deprived the plaintiffs of rights and property without due process of law. In Illinois the plaintiff argued that the grain-elevator business was no a public calling and, consequently, that it lay outside the range of the police power of the state. In a second line of attack the plaintiff held that even if the business were public in character, the function of regulating rates belonged to the judicial branch of the government and not to the legislature, so any statute for fixing rates was invalid.

Supreme Court Approval

The federal Supreme Court handed down its decision in the Slaughter-house Cases in 1873. This decision was one of the earliest in which the Court attempted to define the scope and purposes of the Fourteenth Amendment, and it is one of the most important of the earlier decisions with reference to the power of the state to regulate business. In this instance the Court made short work of the argument that such regulation violated the Fourteenth Amendment. The learned justices declared that "the one pervading purpose" of the three reconstruction Amendments was to bring about "the freedom of the slave race, the security and firm establishment of that freedom, and the protection of the newly-made freeman and citizen from the oppressions of those who had formerly exercised unlimited dominion over him." The Court denied that the purpose of the Fourteenth Amendment was to transfer to the federal authorities the protection of privileges and immunities of its citizens. It necessarily followed, as the Court made plain, that the due process clause of the Fourteenth Amendment did not apply to this case: ". . . under no construction of that provision that we have ever seen, or any that we deem admissible, can the restraint imposed by the State of Louisiana . . . be held to be a deprivation of property within the meaning of that provision."

The Illinois law subjecting the grain elevators of the state to public regulation was also upheld by the Supreme Court. In the Slaughter-house Cases the chief point at issue had been the applicability of the Fourteenth Amendment. In the case of *Munn* v. *Illinois* the Court went at length into the regulatory powers of the states, and it did so with such convincing logic that their authority to regulate business seemed firmly established. The Court held that the question before it was simply whether the legislature of Illinois could fix maximum charges for the services of the elevators in the state. The Court argued that the basic principle of government authorized the enactment of laws requiring the citizens to use their property in such a way as not unnecessarily to injure others. The government had full authority to regulate "the manner in which each shall use his own property, when such regulation becomes necessary for the public good." The Court cited the long-established power of the English government, under the common law, to regulate the business of "ferries, common carriers, hackmen, bakers, millers, wharfingers, innkeepers, &c., and in so doing to fix a maximum of charge to be made for services to be rendered." The Fourteenth Amendment did not alter this time-honored principle.

Then the Court made the statement which is always quoted in any discussion of the problem of government regulation of business:

> Property does become clothed with a public interest when used in a manner to make it of public consequence, and affect the community at large. When, therefore, one devotes his property to a use in which the public has an interest, he, in effect, grants to the public an interest in that use, and must submit to be controlled by the public for the common good.

The power to regulate common carriers came from the same source. According to the Court, the elevators in Chicago were so managed that they might constitute a virtual monopoly; their business was one in which the public had "a direct and positive interest." Finding the power to regulate unquestionable, the Court held that the imposition of maximum charges came logically within the scope of legislative action.

A Change of Mind

Decisions of the Supreme Court are not permanent and irrevocable. At the time they are made they are final in the sense that there is no appeal from them save by the cumbersome procedure of amending the Constitution. But the personnel of the Court is subject to change, and new justices bring different social philosophies to bear on given problems. The letter of the Constitution remains unchanged, but new decisions reverse older ones. Thus the principle of state regulation, upheld in the Munn case, was overruled by the Supreme Court itself.

In changing its mind the Court took cognizance of a peculiar piece of sophistry. In 1882, in arguing the San Mateo County Case before the Supreme Court, Roscoe Conkling implied that in framing the Fourteenth Amendment the committee purposely so worded it as to include corporations within the scope of its meaning. He maintained that the Supreme Court had erred in its decision in the Slaughter-house Cases when it limited the intent of the amendment to the Negroes. Conkling did not specifically say that the committee had consciously and purposely included corporations within the purpose of the amendment. He believed that the members had done so, and in doing so, he said, they had "builded better than they knew." Neither the journal of the committee nor the debates in Congress give any direct intimation that the framers intended to include corporations. If they had done so, Conkling would have been the first to make use of such evidence. Lacking proof of real character, he fell back on the notion that the members accomplished a purpose which none of them avowed. Conkling could have established his point much more easily by citing a formal opinion of Chief Justice Taney in 1839, in which he declared that a corporation is a person.

In 1882 the Supreme Court was not prepared to accept Conkling's argument, but in 1886, when the question came up again, it did so unanimously In the Santa Clara County Case Justice Waite declared flatly:

> The Court does not wish to hear argument on the question whether the provision in the Fourteenth Amendment to the Constitution, which forbids a State to deny to any person within its jurisdiction the equal protection of the laws, applies to these corporations. We are all of the opinion that it does.

In 1889 the Court went even further, and in the Minnesota Rate Case it laid down the rule that a state statute restricting railroad rates did deprive the company of property without due process of law. The responsibility for passing on the reasonableness of railroad charges therefore lay not with the legislature but with the courts.

In 1894, in *Reagan* v. *the Farmers' Loan and Trust Company,* the Court again held that the question of the reasonableness of rates imposed by a state commission was a matter properly subject to review by the courts. And in 1897 the Court passed on the constitutionality of a Nebraska statute for regulating railroad rates. In this decision, *Smyth* v. *Ames,* the Court flatly held that the Fourteenth Amendment did apply. The Court also laid down the principle that in determining rates the fair value of the property must be the determining factor.

Regulation by the Federal Government and the Banks

Interstate Commerce Act

Although the history of railroad development in the United States pointed to the need of public regulation, it must be admitted that the efforts of the individual states were not satisfactory, and in the nature of things they could not be satisfactory. Each state acted by itself, with no attempt to bring the various regulatory measures into harmony. For corporations engaged in interstate business this multiplicity of laws made for inevitable confusion. Furthermore, the individual state commissions, interested primarily in protecting the farmers against exorbitant charges, found it difficult to reconcile their needs with the necessity of the railroads for making profits. The commissioners were not all interested in the reasonableness of the rates, nor for that matter were the railroads. It was not reasonableness but profits which concerned them. And even if the managers had been genuinely interested in reasonable rates, it would have been difficult to figure out a basis for determining them. The failure of the states to solve the problem created the setting for the next experiment in regulation—that by the federal government.

In 1887, two years before the Court's decision in the Minnesota Rate Case, Congress had passed the Interstate Commerce Act for the purpose of subjecting the railroads to federal control. This measure came as the response to a long-continued demand. As early as 1874 the national House of Representatives had passed the McCrary bill, providing for the creation of a federal railroad commission, with power to impose maximum rates, investigate complaints, and institute proceedings against the railroads. The bill passed the House by the narrow margin of 121 to 116, with representatives from the highly industrialized Atlantic states voting heavily in the negative. The Senate did not act upon the measure. Between 1881 and 1883 twenty-seven different railroad bills were introduced in Congress. The Senate appointed a committee to investigate the problem, and this body reported: "It is the deliberate judgment of the Committee that upon no public question are the people so nearly unanimous as upon the proposition that Congress should undertake in some way the regulation of interstate commerce." The Senate decided to yield to popular pressure, and the Interstate Commerce Act was passed.

The Interstate Commerce Act declared that all railroad rates must be "reasonable and just," and it prohibited discriminations in rates. It prohibited lower charges for long hauls than for short, "over the same line in the same direction under similar circumstances and conditions," and it prohibited pools. Railroads were required to keep open for public inspection their schedules of rates, and they were forbidden to make any changes in these schedules without giving ten days' notice. Deviations from the published rates were forbidden. Persons who considered themselves damaged by any railroad might bring suit directly or might appeal to the Interstate Commerce Commission, for which the measure provided. The Commission, originally of five members, would hold office for terms of six years. On complaint of the injured party, or directly on its own initiative, the Commission could conduct an investigation into the affairs of any railroad, and the Commissioners were given power to compel the companies to produce their books. The law gave railroad officials the right to appeal from the Commission's ruling to the federal courts.

Problems of Enforcement

The Interstate Commerce Act had certain weaknesses which made its enforcement difficult. The individual shipper who found himself the victim of unfair practices or discrimination could not successfully prosecute the railroad directly because of the expense involved. Furthermore, the provision in the law giving courts the right to review all decisions of the Commission tended to strip the Commission of real power. As time went on the Commission became more and more an office where information about the roads was kept on file, and the roads carried on their business as though the law had never been passed.

In general the Interstate Commerce Act was so drawn as to make it peculiarly ineffective, and it remained ineffective for fifteen years. The prohibition of pools was easily evaded. Instead of relying upon a formal written contract, railroad executives who wished to combine could use the gentlemen's agreement. A formal contract could be brought into court as evidence, but a verbal arrangement was not subject to this handicap. As for discriminations in rates, they were made as before, and the only difficulty was a little extra bookkeeping. The charges for all shippers were uniform, as the law prescribed, but the roads could pay rebates to favored shippers. The act in question did not forbid rebates.

Control by Bankers

With the system of state regulation broken down, partly through its own inherent ineffectiveness, and partly through adverse decisions of the Supreme Court, and with federal regulation failing to develop as planned, railroad executives seemed free to follow their own devices. At this point a new and more effective control appeared—that imposed upon the roads by the investment bankers. Originally bankers had received deposits, made loans, and dealt in bills of exchange. But when the banker added to these customary functions that of disposing of stocks and bonds, he became interested in the quality of what he sold. In other words, the business must be discreetly managed and it must be so conducted as to make it pay. When the banker became interested in selling stocks and bonds, he had a direct interest in the management of the company itself. Consequently some of the bankers assumed an active responsibility in the management of corporate affairs. The most famous banking firm engaged in this kind of enterprise was Morgan, Drexel and Company, later J. P. Morgan and Company.

Morgan's interest lay in the stabilization of business. He was interested in regularity of operation because that meant regularity of profits and freedom from expensive competition. One of his first ventures into this new field came in connection with a threatened war between the New York Central and the Pennsylvania railroads. The Vanderbilt interests had taken over the Philadelphia and Reading, and they planned to use it as the nucleus of a new system in the Pennsylvania's own territory, the South Pennsylvania. At the same time Pennsylvania interests were building the West Shore, which ran along the west side of the Hudson River and thence westward, through New York Central territory. Morgan called the two parties together for a conference and insisted on a settlement of the rivalry. As a result of his efforts, the New York Central bought the West Shore and the Pennsylvania took over the South Pennsylvania. Having put an end to competition in both fields, Morgan proceeded to stabilize both lines. He cut down bonded indebtedness and capitalization. The bonded debt of the West Shore was cut in half.

Effective stabilization necessitated the regulation of rates, and, when the Interstate Commerce Commission proved ineffective, Morgan himself decided upon a policy of regulation. He and a group of bankers issued a "Private and Confidential Circular" to the heads of the railroad systems. These officials came together early in 1889. Morgan impressed upon them the absolute necessity of maintaining "public, reasonable, uniform and stable rates." Most of the railroad executives came around to Morgan's proposals. The railroads agreed to end their rate wars, and the bankers agreed not to promote the sale of rival securities. In the course of the next ten years Morgan acquired control over twelve of the great railroad systems of the country; altogether these lines had well over 55,000 miles of track, and a combined capitalization of more than $3,000,000,000. He took over the management of the coal-carrying roads of Pennsylvania and imposed what he regarded as a fair schedule of charges. Through the control of banks, insurance companies, railroads, and industrial concerns, the Morgan firm became one of the most powerful factors in the economic affairs of the country.

Having tried their hand at regulating railroads, the American people tried to regulate the trusts. By the end of 1890 the legislatures of twenty-seven states and territories had laws aimed at the destruction of monopolies.

During the Presidential campaigns of 1880 and 1884, third parties popularized the demand for effective regulation of the trusts. And in 1888 the Republican party declared its opposition

> . . . to all combinations of capital, organized in trusts or otherwise, to control arbitrarily the condition of trade among our citizens, and we recommend to Congress and the state legislatures . . . such legislation as will prevent the execution of all schemes to oppress the people by undue charges on their supplies, or by unjust rates for the transportation of their products to market.

Sherman Anti-Trust Act

Congress met the demand for legislation against the trusts with the Sherman Anti-Trust Act (1890) or, officially, "An ACT to protect trade and commerce against unlawful restraints and monopolies. . . ." This famous measure declared illegal "Every contract, combination in the form of trust or otherwise, or conspiracy, in restraint of trade or commerce." Every person who should make any such contract, or engage in any such combination or conspiracy was made liable to punishment by fine or imprisonment, or both. Monopolists were also made liable to similar punishment. Federal district attorneys, under the direction of the attorney general, were empowered to institute proceedings against offenders. The law does not define the meaning of the word "trust." The term "restraint of trade" was not defined nor was the word "monopoly." It would be difficult for juries to find defendants guilty when there was no way of determining what offense, if any, had been committed. The omissions and ambiguities of the law must have been intentional because lawyers know how to be exact and precise when they care to be. When the bill was introduced into the House, the chairman of the Judiciary Committee made the following observation: "Now just what contracts, what combinations in the form of trusts, or what conspiracies will be in restraint of trade or commerce, mentioned in the bill, will not be known until the courts have construed and interpreted this provision." That is to say, the chairman of the Judiciary Committee of the national House of Representatives admitted on the floor of the House that he had no idea of the meaning of the measure he asked the House to pass. The lawmakers therefore chose to make a law whose meaning they themselves deliberately refused to define. Something had to be done to offset the clamor of the public, loudly demanding a federal antitrust law, hence the law.

Olney's Attitude

In 1893 President Cleveland appointed Richard Olney of Massachusetts attorney general. Olney had already appeared as one of the attorneys for the "whisky trust" against the government. At the time of his appointment he was the legal advisor of the Chicago, Burlington, and Quincy Railroad. His first thought was the Burlington, and he wrote the president of the line for advice: "Among other things that I want to find out is where I am going to stand with my present clients. I am not a millionaire and cannot take any office of the sort without a good deal of pecuniary sacrifice—just how much I should like to ascertain." The president of the road urged

Olney to accept. "It shall make no difference in our relations except such as you may think it expedient to make." Three months after he entered his new office, Olney wrote that Boston money would be forthcoming to effect the repeal of the Sherman Anti-Trust Act.

With a salaried representative of big business presiding over the Department of Justice, there was little likelihood of any effort to invoke the Sherman Anti-Trust Act. Olney was in office for two years, and during that time no suits were started. The federal district attorney at Los Angeles did commit the blunder of starting suit against the Southern Pacific Railway, but Olney ordered the suit dismissed. Before he left office, the suit against the Sugar Trust, in the case of the *United States* v. *the E. C. Knight Company,* reached the Supreme Court. In this case the Court upheld the Sugar Trust, and the attorney general welcomed the decision.

Olney's successor was Judson Harmon, who was genuinely interested in prosecuting monopolists. During his term, and with his active support, suit was started against the Addystone Pipe and Steel Company. The issue in this case was the legality or illegality of a price-fixing pool covering the sale of cast-iron pipe. This case was decided first in the circuit court, with Justice William Howard Taft presiding, and the decision was upheld by the Supreme Court. Here the Court decided unanimously in favor of the government, and the Sherman Act was upheld. This was the only significant decision in favor of the government in an antitrust suit during the first ten years of the law's history.

Chapter 29

THE PROBLEM OF INDUSTRIAL LABOR

National Labor Unions

Factory Workers

The transition of the United States from the status of a relatively simple agricultural and mercantile community to that of the greatest industrial nation of the world was bound to have far-reaching effects on the mode of life and on the economic position of the factory worker. In the first stage of industrial growth, as in the textile area of New England in the first half of the nineteenth century or in the South in the last third, the mills provide a new mode of making a living. The factory pay roll brings more money into the community. In general the workers were recruited from the younger generation of the farms and villages. Even though the wages seemed low when judged by the standards of older industrial societies, they were so much velvet to the first group. The mill girls of Lowell in the 1840's did not consider themselves oppressed nor did the sons and daughters of the upland farmers of North Carolina in the 1900's. Such employees could always leave the factory and return to what they had known—and be worse off for doing so. But by the time the third or fourth generation of factory workers came along, the picture had changed, and many factory employees had no resource but the mills. Even though individual members rose to levels higher than that of the wage earner, the class of factory employees tended to become permanent.

After the Civil War industrial workers increased rapidly in numbers. In 1860 only 16 percent of the American people lived in urban communities—urban meaning towns of 8000 or more people. By 1900 the percentage of the urban population had increased to 40. In 1859 the total number of industrial wage earners in the United States was 1,311,000; fifty years later the figure had mounted to 6,615,000. But the wage earner was not alone; generally he had a family, the members of which were all involved in the tangle of problems which beset him. In 1910 the number of people engaged in manufacturing was approximately equal to the number engaged in agriculture, but by 1920 the industrial population was the larger.

Trade Unions

There had long been a realization that the impact of industrialism upon a rural society would create difficulties, and some efforts had been made to meet them. During the administration of Andrew Jackson labor organizations and strikes had become a part of the American scene. After the Civil War experiments with labor organizations became more impressive. By 1872 there were nearly 300,000 members of trade unions in the United States. Of the thirty or more unions, the most important were those of the building trades, the printers, the shoemakers, and the locomotive engineers. Not only were the laborers organizing to protect their interests, but some of them were looking into the economic philosophy of labor. In 1865 a machinist of Boston, Ira Steward by name, published a pamphlet in which he advocated the theory of high wages for all workers in industry. High wages, he argued, should be accompanied by shorter hours, and shorter hours should be secured by law. His plea was founded on the doctrine that high wages would increase buying power. Shorter hours were necessary to enable the laborer to enjoy the products of industry.

In November 1865 efforts were made in Boston to create a National Labor Party. In the following year W. H. Sylvis attempted to organize a nation-wide federation of those labor organizations, local, state, and national, which had already been formed. His National Labor Union, as Sylvis called it, held its first convention in 1866. Sylvis also demanded the eight-hour day, guaranteed by law. By 1868 the National Labor Union had a membership of 600,000. Then came a rapid decline, and after 1872 the organization ceased to have any influence. Its leadership had been confined to social reformers rather than laborers.

Knights of Labor

The real beginning of the movement to bring about a nation-wide organization of all laborers began in 1869 with the formation of the Noble Order of the Knights of Labor. Its founder, Uriah Stephens, a garment cutter of Philadelphia, proposed a secret society, open to laborers with no discrimination between crafts. The only restrictions on membership were based upon what Stephens considered moral grounds. Participation in honorable toil was the test: "no one who either sells or makes a living, or any part of it, by the sale of intoxicating drinks, either as manufacturer, dealer, or agent, or through any member of his family, can be admitted . . . and no lawyer, banker, professional gambler, or stockbroker." Secrecy was needed, he held, to protect members from retaliatory action by employers. After ten years' experience, however, all attempts at secrecy were abandoned. Starting with a membership of eleven garment cutters in 1869, the Knights by 1886 had a membership of more than 700,000.

In 1878 the Knights held their first general assembly and framed their constitution. Referring to the "recent alarming development and aggression of aggregated wealth," they called for a check "upon its power and upon unjust accumulation." They aimed "to secure to the toilers a proper share of the wealth that they create; more of the leisure that rightfully belongs to them . . . more of the benefits, privileges, and emoluments of the world." They advocated the establishment of cooperative enterprises and the enactment of laws designed to safeguard the health and safety of workers engaged in mining, manufacturing, or building. They hoped to secure the abolition of contract labor and the prohibition of the labor of all children under fourteen years of age. They advocated the eight-hour day for the purpose of giving laborers "time for social enjoyment and intellectual improvement."

Under the leadership of Terence V. Powderly, who succeeded Stephens as grand master in 1878, the Knights rapidly attained a position of national importance. In addition to their demands for better wages and shorter hours, they embarked, after the manner of the Grange, upon an ambitious series of cooperative enterprises. By 1887 they had over fifty factories and workshops and eleven newspapers. But in these experiments the Knights of Labor encountered the same difficulties which had weakened the Grange. They could not compete with established industrial concerns. The resulting losses proved embarrassing and led to a decline in membership. In 1886 there was an epidemic of strikes, over 500 in number, and although the Knights were not involved in all of them, the general public held them responsible for the general unrest. At the same time the Haymarket episode in Chicago (see page 450) resulted in an outburst of antiunion feeling. By 1894 the Knights of Labor had ceased to be important.

The A.F. of L.

Before the Knights had begun to decline, a new organization appeared which was destined to dominate the field of American labor for more than forty years. This was the American Federation of Labor, started in 1881 and reorganized in 1886. The founder of the American Federation, and the head of it until his death in 1924, was Samuel Gompers. Gompers and his followers were strongly opposed to the formation of a political labor party, and they insisted that the road to well-being for labor did not lie through legislation. The Federation advocated collective bargaining, trade agreements, or, in extreme cases where peaceful negotiation failed to bring results, the strike. In its first general convention, that of 1884, the Federation proclaimed its reliance on the forces of organized laborers rather than on lawmakers. Demands for shorter hours, supported by a nation-wide federation, would be "far more effective than a thousand laws, whose execution depends upon the good will of aspiring politicians or sycophantic department officials." In his annual report for 1911 Gompers warned his associates against yielding "control over working relations to legislative and administrative agents" because, when they did so, they "strip themselves bare of means of defense; they can no longer defend themselves by the strike. To insure liberty and personal welfare, personal relations must be controlled only by those concerned." He asked aid only for gains which laborers could not obtain through their own efforts, for example employers' liability laws.

The American Federation is built upon the principle of cooperative action among organized craft unions—in other words, the skilled laborers. Stephens and Powderly believed in bringing together all the workers, but Gompers put his reliance upon the aristocracy of labor. As time went on, the building trades became the most important group in the Federation. In the Federation each separate union had full control over its own affairs, but it had the support of the Federation in matters affecting the interests of labor as a whole. The membership of the Federation increased gradually, reaching the 70,000 mark by 1889. By 1900 it had 548,321 members.

The Federation is a union of unions. Individuals join the Federation only as members of some duly constituted unit, not as separate workers. In 1936 it was made up of 111 national and international—that is, American and Canadian, not European—unions and 32,906 local unions. All these member unions send delegates to the annual convention, which operates as the supreme authority for the Federation as a whole. The convention chooses eleven national officers, who form an executive council. The cost of this simple organization is met from the membership fees, which Gompers kept low; he did not believe in making membership a financial burden.

Attitudes toward Organized Labor

Socialist Parties

For the period between 1865 and 1900 socialism of the type advanced by Karl Marx had little influence on American labor. It is of course true that both Sylvis and Stephens sometimes spoke and wrote in terms suggestive of socialism, although they had no connection with European socialist organizations. Edward Bellamy's *Looking Backward* was a plea for a socialist state, although he was not a follower of Marx. The influence of Marxian ideology in America was slight, and it was confined largely to groups of immigrants of German origin. The First International, organized in 1864, attracted almost no attention in the United States.

The exceptions to these general statements serve to emphasize the indifference of American labor leaders to Marxian philosophy. In 1874 some of the more radically minded leaders organized the Social Democratic Working-men's party. Two years later the Working-men's party was organized, and in 1877 this organization changed its name to the Socialist Labor party. But the dominant influence in this first Socialist party was foreign rather than American. During the 1870's, the Socialist Labor party never reached a membership of more than 2600.

After 1890 the fortunes of the Socialist Labor party were taken over by Daniel De Leon, a radical Marxist. The most obvious result of his efforts was the elimination of all moderates and non-Marxians from membership. Driven from home, the outcasts in 1897 formed the Socialist party. The Socialist party has never been entirely Marxist in its doctrines, and it has become the advocate of a number of policies such as the shorter working week, prohibition of child labor, minimum wage laws, social security legislation, and, in particular, of measures designed to bring about a more genuine political democracy, such as the initiative, referendum, and recall. The Socialist party was largely American in its membership and in its philosophy. Its members have served in state legislatures and in Congress and as mayors of cities.

Opinions on Labor

The attitude of the American people toward the labor movement was on the whole unsympathetic. Down to 1842 labor unions had been described as conspiracies and punished as such under the common law. In 1842, in deciding the case of *Commonwealth* v. *Hunt,* Justice Shaw of the Massachusetts court proclaimed the legality of labor organizations and specifically admitted their right to strike. But in the 1880's, following an almost nation-wide series of strikes, the courts revived the doctrine of conspiracy. The general feeling was illustrated in the contemptuous comment of an Illinois newspaper concerning the proposed eight-hour day: "One most consummate piece of humbuggery ever suggested in connection with the labor question is the so-called 'eight hour movement.' The thing is really too silly to merit the attention of a body of lunatics. . . . No legislative body on earth can properly have anything to do with the subject."

In spite of this attitude one legislature had already done something toward securing one major objective of the unions, and this legislature was the Congress of the United States. In 1868 this body passed a law declaring that the standard day's work for government employees should be eight hours. Another federal law was passed in 1885, making it illegal for employers to import laborers under contract. This practice had been sanctioned by Congress in 1864, and it threatened to flood the country with underpaid laborers from Europe. The Knights of Labor and the Department of Justice endeavored to see that the new measure was enforced. Some of the state legislatures had begun to pass laws for the protection of the factory workers. In 1866 Massachusetts adopted an eight-hour law for minors between the ages of fourteen and eighteen. Additional measures provided for factory inspection and for safeguarding workers from dangerous machinery.

Problem of Strikes

The aspect of trade unionism which attracted most attention was the strike. And because the strike tended to interrupt orderly procedure, strikers were often hailed as troublemakers, interested in stirring up industrial warfare solely from an inherent love of violence and disorder. The attitude of the conservative financial interests toward strikes was defined by Henry Clews, one of the most prominent stockbrokers in New York. Writing in 1886 with reference to the strike against the Western Union Telegraph Company, one of Jay Gould's concerns, and the strikes on the Gould railroads, Clews described Gould as "a public benefactor in the bold and successful stand which he has maintained against strikers." Clews found the strike a challenge to the American economic system. "To the employer, it is a question whether his individual rights as to the control of his property shall be so far overborne, as to not only deprive him of his freedom, but also to expose him to interferences seriously impairing the value of his capital." He accused the Knights of Labor of assailing "the most sacred and inalienable rights of the employer." Their demands, he declared, "are so utterly revolutionary of the inalienable rights of the citizen, and so completely subversive of the social order, that the whole community has come to a firm conclusion that these pretensions must be resisted to the last extremity of endurance and authority." Clews condemned the strikers on the Gould roads, but nowhere in his book did he condemn Gould's systematic looting of the properties which he managed.

During the years before 1900 strikes were called for the purpose of maintaining existing wage scales, or for gaining shorter hours, or in rarer cases to force recognition of the union. On the basis of figures, between 1881 and

1900, 41 percent of the strikes were for higher pay, 26 percent for shorter hours. In the cities the average daily rate of pay was $2; in many of the smaller towns $1 a day was the accepted rate for semiskilled and sometimes for skilled labor. The average working day was ten hours in length, from seven in the morning to six at night, with one hour out at noon. If the custom of the Saturday half-holiday had been adopted, the employees went to work at six-thirty instead of seven, in order to put in at least a fifty-eight-hour week. But some men had to put in even longer days. On the horsecars in New York City the drivers were kept on the job from twelve to sixteen hours per day; so too were drivers for hotels and livery stables. Women in the dry-goods stores worked from seven-thirty in the morning to nine or ten at night.

Government and Strikes

Railroad Strike

In 1877 the United States had experience with its first labor struggle on a national scale—the strike of the railroad employees. In many cases the men on the trains worked only four days a week, and their wages ranged from less than $30 to slightly more than $40 per month. The New York Central paid its firemen $1.58 per day, but the average pay per month was only $41.08. In 1875 the Brotherhood of Locomotive Engineers had won two strikes, and because of this success other trainmen organized. The railroad managers in turn were determined to break up the union. During June and July 1877 most of the railroads east of the Mississippi River announced wage cuts of 10 percent. For the employees on the Baltimore and Ohio this was the fourth cut in seven years. On July 18, 1877, the B. & O. train crews went on strike, and the disturbance quickly spread to most of the railroads in the East. In a few days 100,000 men were involved. Then the strike spread over fourteen states, as far west as Kansas and as far south as Texas. On the B. & O. the strikers refused to permit new crews to move freight trains. In the cities there were large numbers of unemployed, some of whom were not indisposed to violence. The railroads attributed all disturbances to the unions, while the members claimed that the violence was caused by irresponsible idlers and tramps. The governor of Maryland called out the state militia, and on the appeal of the governor President Hayes sent federal troops into West Virginia. In Baltimore the mob drove the militia into the railroad station. Then rioters set fire to the station, the city police had to rescue the militia, and federal troops rescued both the militia and the police.

On the day following the riot at Baltimore the mob broke loose at Pittsburgh, set fire to railroad buildings, plundered the freight offices and stores, destroyed machine shops and roundhouses, a grain elevator, and the Union Station. The destruction included 2000 freight cars and 125 locomotives. The governor called out the entire state militia, but the detachment sent to Pittsburgh was overwhelmed by the mob and driven into the woods outside the city. As in the case of Baltimore, federal troops restored order. Because of urgent pleas of the governors, President Hayes sent troops into four states. The strike lasted only two weeks, and the employees were badly beaten.

Haymarket Affair

In 1886, following the economic depression of 1884, there was another epidemic of strikes, over 500 in the first few months. As in 1877, this epidemic began on the railroads, at first in the Southwest. It soon spread over Texas, Missouri, Kansas, and Illinois, and tied up 6000 miles of railroads. This strike lasted seven weeks and, as before, the strikers lost. Then Chicago became the center of a series of violent labor conflicts. First the men in the building trades went on strike and next the freight handlers. On May 3 there was a contest between strikers and strikebreakers at the McCormick Reaper works; the police fired on the rioters, and four persons were killed. On May 4 there was a meeting in Haymarket Place called to protest against the "atrocious attack of the police in shooting on our fellow workmen." Some of the addresses were made by anarchists whose violent doctrines led the police to order the crowd to disperse. At this point someone in the crowd threw a bomb, and others in the crowd fired on the police. The outcome of the Haymarket riot was seven killed and sixty wounded.

On July 8, 1886, eight anarchists were arraigned for trial. At the trial itself the presiding justice ruled that it was not necessary for the prosecution to prove that the defendants were actually guilty of throwing the bomb or even that they were actually present at the scene of the riot. If the testimony showed that they had advocated violence they could be found guilty. In spite of the want of proof, all eight were found guilty of murder. Seven received death sentences, and one a long prison term. On November 11, 1887, four of the victims were hanged. In the interval following the trial one had committed suicide. Two others succeeded in having their sentences changed to imprisonment for life. Six years later Governor Altgeld pardoned the three who were still in prison, on the ground that they had been convicted on insufficient evidence.

Carnegie and Pullman Strikes

One of the most famous strikes in American history came in 1892, at the Homestead plant of the Carnegie Steel Company. Henry Frick, president of the Carnegie Company, was opposed to organized labor. Many of the employees were members of the Amalgamated Association of Iron and Steel Workers. They were finding fault with the twelve-hour shift. Frick determined to break the union. He hired Pinkerton detectives to make a careful study of the steel works, and he had 300 of these private detectives stationed in and around the plant. When Frick refused to make new contracts with the Amalgamated, the employees went on strike. Frick planned to replace the strikers with nonunion employees, and he announced that the plant would reopen on July 6. On that morning the Pinkerton guards had a pitched battle with the strikers, as a result of which the strikers took possession of the plant. They were driven out by federal troops. The contest lasted until November 20 when the men acknowledged defeat.

In 1894 another crisis developed in connection with the strike of the Pullman employees. These workers lived in the company town of Pullman, outside Chicago. The company provided the workers with houses, water, and gas. The rates charged were considerably higher than in Chicago, so that the cost of living in Pullman was higher than in other communities. Wages per man averaged $600 per year. In case of any reduction in wages, rents and other living costs remained at the original figure.

In May 1894 the Pullman Company announced a wage cut of 20 percent, necessary, so the announcement said, because of the unfavorable business situation. A committee of employees interviewed the officials and asked for the restoration of the former scale of wages. The company not only refused to grant the request but discharged three members of the committee. Then the majority of employees, nearly 85 percent, went on strike, and the company locked out the few who were willing to remain at work. Four thousand Pullman employees were members of the recently established American Railway Union, which at the time had a total membership of 150,000. The Railway Union requested the Pullman Company to submit the issues involved to arbitration, but the company refused to arbitrate. Then the union ordered its members not to handle trains with Pullman cars attached, and the strike spread to twenty-seven states.

Cleveland against Altgeld

Eugene V. Debs, the president of the union, instructed the strikers to avoid violence, and the men always claimed that they did so. But violence occurred, and the General Managers' Association, which represented twenty-four western railroads, held the union responsible. It is also possible that neither party to the strike was directly responsible for the violence. The depression had thrown thousands out of work, and the World's Fair of 1893 had left a lot of jobless men stranded in Chicago. These people would have been enough to account for some of the disturbances. Olney, the federal attorney general, was ready to exert the full power of the national authorities to break the strike. And he was not acting simply as the disinterested agent of the public. His connection with the Chicago, Burlington, and Quincy Railroad put him on the side of the employers. Olney asked President Cleveland to authorize the use of injunctions and to send federal troops into Chicago. Cleveland, apparently without any investigation of the merits of the dispute, gave Olney his complete support. He found justification for his assertion of federal authority on the ground that the strike interfered with the mail service.

On July 2 the Department of Justice secured a sweeping injunction against Debs and other union officials, prohibiting any and all union activities in connection with the strike. Then, before any serious disorder and without any request from the state government of Illinois, President Cleveland sent federal troops into Chicago to uphold the injunction. Debs and his associates were arrested.

In connection with the use of the United States army in Chicago there was some interesting correspondence between Governor Altgeld and President Cleveland. The governor opposed Cleveland's policy. Altgeld declared that the government of the state of Illinois was well prepared to take care of any emergency. The law had been fully enforced, and every man guilty of violating it had been brought to justice. The railroads were paralyzed, Altgeld continued, not because of violence but because the companies could not find crews to operate their trains. The managers wished to conceal this fact from the public, so they made a great outcry over violent obstructions. The governor admitted that, in a very few cases where the railroad companies had attempted to run trains with green crews, mobs had interfered, but these disturbances were so few as to be insignificant. Newspaper accounts of violence, he went on, "have in many cases been pure fabrications, and in others wild exaggerations."

Law against Justice

In the meantime Debs and his fellow union officers had been arrested on two different counts: violating the injunction—that is, for contempt of court—and the criminal charge of obstructing the mail. The question of the applicability of the Sherman Act came up, and Olney thought it might be used. The United States circuit court for the northern district of Illinois held that the issue of the injuction against Debs was justified under the Sherman Anti-Trust Act. When placed in jail for contempt of court, Debs applied to the Supreme Court for a writ of habeas corpus, which was denied. In upholding the injunction, and in denying Debs's application for the writ, the Supreme Court based its argument not on the Sherman Act but on the broader ground that the government of the United States possessed full authority to prevent forcible interference with interstate commerce and with the transportation of mail. Although the criminal charges against Debs were dropped, he was imprisoned for contempt of court. Cleveland's assertion of federal authority over Governor Altgeld's protests showed a readiness to uphold the processes of law by the surprising method of violating these very processes.

Chapter 30

PATTERNS OF CITY LIFE

Urban Problems

THE rise of the United States to its position as the greatest industrial nation in the world and the recruiting of millions of factory employees necessarily brought about an increase in urban population. Here was a significant trend in American life with important consequences for the future. By 1900 one third of the American people lived in cities, and in 1930 one half. Furthermore by 1930 almost one third of the total population of the nation lived in cities of 100,000 or more inhabitants. Or to illustrate the trend in another way, in the hundred years from 1790 to 1890 the total population increased sixteen times, but the urban part of it increased 139 times.

Rise of the City

In the eastern states and even in the Middle West the rural sections showed an absolute as well as a relative loss to the cities. Illinois and Ohio both showed a drop in rural population. In Pennsylvania, between 1880 and 1890, more than 40 percent of the townships showed a decline in population; in New England 60 percent of the rural areas showed a loss, while in New York two thirds of the rural sections declined in population. Not all the people who moved away from these farming areas went to the cities, although many of them did. Some went to newer farms in the West.

In northern New England the abandoned farm became a memorial of what had been an active, self-reliant community. By 1890 Maine had 3300 abandoned farms, New Hampshire, 1300, and Vermont, 1000. With the decline of population and the decrease in the number of farms under cultivation, scores of little villages lost their means of support. In every farming area there were business centers, each with a country store, blacksmith shop, gristmill, sawmill, and a church or two. The village might also include a woodworking shop, or possibly a small textile mill. While not entirely self-sufficing, these communities had been able to take care of themselves, but they could not survive the loss of population. And there was a loss of quality here as well as of numbers. The drift away from the farms and the villages carried the most active part of the population.

The cities grew rapidly because the city was so intimately related to the new economic structure of big business. Because of the availability of labor, transportation facilities, and the ever-necessary banks, most of the factories were located in the cities. And in cases where the factories themselves were not so located, the selling agencies were. A woolen mill located in central Massachusetts would probably buy its raw material from a dealer in Boston and sell its product through a commission house in New York. The railroads had both offices and repair shops located in the cities. The largest banks were in the cities, and so too were the great insurance companies. The nerve center of big business of the 1890's was the stock exchange, and the exchange that set the standard for all smaller imitators in other cities was the New York Stock Exchange.

Urban Classes

The population of the city had its groups and classes, not necessarily permanent because individuals were constantly moving up and down the scale, but always clearly defined. At the top were the moneyed aristocrats; the business executives, bankers, lawyers, and merchants; along with them the relatively few heirs to great wealth who did no work. Next came the white-collar employees—workers in the offices and stores; on the same social plane, but frequently with a higher financial rating, were the skilled workers in building trades and in industry. After them came the mass of unskilled laborers. At the bottom of the list were the outcasts of one type or another, the drifters, incompetents, social misfits, and "bums." In a class by themselves were the professional criminals. These gradations were to be found in most of the large cities.

The accumulation of property and the concentration of wealth in the cities furnished the means for promoting not only riches but culture. With larger incomes and higher tax rates the cities could provide better schools than those in the country. City churches could attract the most eminent clergymen; some of those fortunate enough to receive "calls" from the larger places easily reconciled themselves to the necessity for confining their sermons to theology. Communicants in these "best" churches did not look to their ministers for instruction in economic matters but for spiritual enlightenment. There was no question about the superiority of city newspapers. They carried more news, and their editorials were significant contributions to the thought of the day. The great libraries were found in the city, and the public library was becoming more and more necessary as an educational institution. Altogether the city provided means for the training of both children and adults, means which were not duplicated in the country. In addition to the institutions named there were the museums, both of fine arts and archaeology and of natural history. To these opportunities for self-development should be added the social contacts made possible in the city. In spite of the stories of poor country boys who became famous, a large proportion of eminent men of the United States had their start in the city, not in the country. All this is true, but the advantages of the city were not available to all its inhabitants. Cherry Street and Mulberry Bend in New York of the 1890's would not have been chosen as ideal spots for bringing up a family.

Streets and Transit

Problems confronting the cities were serious, and many of them were due to the unexpectedly rapid increase in population. With any concentration of population, the problem of public health immediately becomes pressing. If the growth occurs slowly, the community has a chance to adjust itself to new demands, but where the increase is rapid, as it was in many American cities from 1870 to 1890, problems develop faster than ability to deal with them. Every city needed an adequate water supply and an adequate sewerage system, but many American cities of this period lacked both. Adequate housing was also unavailable. Here were problems beyond the range of comprehension of ordinary city officials. To solve them the services of experts in medicine and engineering were badly needed.

One of the immediate needs resulting from increased congestion was that of better streets. In most cities the streets were not paved. In many cases the streets had been laid out to serve only a small community; when the town became a city the streets were far too narrow. During the 1880's cities began to put down asphalt and brick paving, and they used macadamized surfaces for streets in the residential sections. But it required years to complete the work. In 1890 for example, Chicago, with 2048 miles of streets, had paved a total of only 629 miles. By the end of the century, however, the surfaces of the streets had undergone real improvement.

Engineers found the cities a remarkable field for the exercise of their talents and ingenuity. The poorer inhabitants found themselves separated by ever-increasing distances from their work, while the well-to-do found it desirable to move away from the more crowded areas. The problem of urban transportation therefore called for immediate action. In New York the need had been obvious for some time, and as early as 1832 a corporation tried the experiment of a street railway line using horsecars, but for various reasons the line did not pay. Twenty years later, however, New York did have a successful streetcar line in operation, and in 1855 Philadelphia had her first horsecars ready for traffic. By the end of the Civil War horsecars had become familiar sights in all the larger cities.

But the horsecar was none too rapid, and before long it added to the traffic jams in the crowded streets. The next improvement therefore looked toward the removal of rapid transit facilities from the streets. In 1867 construction was begun on New York's first elevated railway, the Ninth Avenue line, running from the Battery north to Thirtieth Street. This enterprise was finished and opened for traffic in 1870. Boston tried to speed up traffic in its busiest section by putting the streetcars underground instead of overhead, and the first American subway was opened there in 1897.

Neither horses nor steam locomotives proved satisfactory in urban rapid transit, and experimenters were busy with other types of power. In 1873 San Francisco introduced the cable car. But the greatest improvement in urban rapid transit came with the invention of the electric trolley car. In 1870 the first practicable electric generator was made available, so that power could be produced for commercial purposes. In 1887 Richmond, Virginia, began the use of electric street railways, and in the next twenty-five years the electric railway spread in amazing fashion. Not only the cities but small towns as well had electric car lines, and in thickly settled areas the interurban trolley competed for business with the established steam railroad.

The development of means for rapid, inexpensive transportation in the cities enabled the inhabitants to keep up with their work. For the businessmen instantaneous communication was if anything even more important, and this was made possible by the telephone. Alexander Graham Bell transmitted his first telephone message in 1876, but for the next few years the instrument was hardly more than an interesting scientific curiosity. To make it practicable there had to be a central switchboard, to connect subscribers with each other. This device was perfected in 1885, and from that time the telephone facilities of the country spread with surprising rapidity.

City Government

Problems attendant upon rapid urban growth were inevitably reflected in municipal government. Here administrative experience and skill developed slowly, much more so than schemes for turning public funds into private gain. Few city officials had either the desire or the ability to make efficiency their goal, and even where the desire was present many incumbents in office found themselves swamped with responsibilities too numerous for them to handle. To make matters worse, prominent citizens in the communities, the leaders in business enterprise, were too deeply involved in the pursuit of wealth and the management of their own concerns to bother themselves with affairs at city hall.

Municipal Graft

The growth of the cities thrust unprecedented difficulties upon the authorities and also opened up equally unprecedented opportunities for gain. When the perquisites of office made salaries look ridiculously small, corruption was inevitable. This was the era when the cities were building new streets and paving their old ones, installing new water works and sewerage systems, letting contracts for street railways and lighting facilities, building new hospitals, jails, courthouses, and in general doing everything to enable the city to cope with its responsibilities. The buying of supplies and the letting of contracts could be made extremely profitable to the officials in charge. All that was needed was collusion between officials and contractors, and the bills could be padded to almost any amount.

In writing the *American Commonwealth* James Bryce came to this discouraging conclusion: "There is no denying that the government of the cities is the one conspicuous failure of the United States. . . . The faults of the State governments are insignificant compared with the extravagance, corruption, and mismanagement which mark the administrations of most of the great cities." In 1877 a committee of the New York legislature submitted a report dealing with the problems of municipal government. The report refers to "the elaborate systems of depredation which, under the name of city government have from time to time afflicted our principal cities." The members of this committee found that municipal offices were frequently held by men who had little or no fitness for their places. They secured their places by corrupt means and they practiced corruption throughout their public careers. As this same report explained: "Animated by the expectation of unlawful emoluments, they expend large sums to secure their

"THAT'S WHAT'S THE MATTER."

Boss TWEED. "As long as I count the Votes, what are you going to do about it? say?"

Courtesy, New York Public Library

Cartoon by Thomas Nast, published in *Harper's Weekly,* October 7, 1871. Juggling election returns was one source of Tweed's power.

places, and make promises beforehand to supporters and retainers to furnish patronage or place. The corrupt promises must be redeemed."

For fifteen or twenty years after the Civil War American cities saw their debts piling up to unprecedented figures, but they could not see any proof that this indebtedness contributed to well-being. During this era the cities paid out money enough to construct all the public works needed for a century to come, but the public works were not there. The New York report referred to above concluded: "the larger part of the city debt represents a vast aggregate of moneys wasted, embezzled, or misapplied."

Tweed Ring

The most widely known corrupt city government of this era was that managed by the Tweed Ring of New York. The Ring was the small group of leaders which dominated Tammany Hall, and Tammany Hall was the organization in charge of the Democratic party in New York. William M. Tweed had risen to fame before the Civil War. He had entered politics by way of the prize ring and the saloon, at a time when neither occupation enjoyed the blessings of respectability. In 1851 he became a member of the city government which was popularly known as the "Forty Thieves." In 1863 he became chairman of the general committee of Tammany Hall. By 1869 the Ring was comfortably entrenched in power. Tweed himself was street commissioner and member of the state senate. A. Oakey Hall, a lawyer by profession, was mayor of New York. "Slippery Dick" Connolly was comptroller, and Peter B. Sweeney was treasurer of both New York City and New York County. Governor Hoffman was on friendly terms with the Ring, and so too were Justices Barnard and Arthur Cardozo. This combination was in full control of the city's funds; the governor could be counted on to veto any undesirable bill, and with two judges under their control the Ring felt reasonably safe from any attack.

Tweed could always count on a majority of the voters. Tammany Hall was more than a political organization. It was a social club and a philanthropic agency. It was the business of every district leader of Tammany Hall to know the circumstances of every family in his jurisdiction. In case of hard times the needy Democrats could count on Tammany for food, fuel, or clothing. If the wild son of the family became involved in difficulties with the law, the precinct captain could intercede in his behalf with the district attorney. If somebody needed a job, the captain would have one at his disposal. Then the Hall gave magnificent picnics at no cost to the faithful. Why should the citizens not vote right on election day?

When Tweed was at the height of his power, New York had approximately 130,000 voters, more than half of whom were under definite obligations to the Hall. Some were tied up by means of public offices or public employment of one kind or another. Others had received contracts for supplying goods or services to the city. Every saloonkeeper received his license from the city, and what the city gave the city could take away. Then there were always some voters embarrassed by suspended sentences or indictments awaiting trial. They needed the services of the Hall's trained workers, and the dictates of self-interest bound them firmly to the organization. By such ties as these—gratitude, self-interest, hope, and fear—Tweed and his associates kept the voters in line.

The official function of the Tweed Ring was to govern New York City; its unofficial purpose was to enrich itself. Next came the responsibility of looking after the "boys." From this angle the Ring might be described as an enterprise dedicated to public plunder. With Tweed and his friends there were no fine-spun distinctions between legitimate and illegitimate graft. Between 1869 and 1871 the bonded debt of the city rose from $36,293,000 to $97,287,000, and this increase was accompanied by an addition to the short-term indebtedness of $20,000,000. Much of this money found its way into the private fortunes of the leaders of the party.

The classic example of large-scale graft was provided by the erection of the new courthouse for New York County. Designed in 1868 to cost $250,-

000, the actual cost was nearly $15,000,000, much of which went to the Ring. A few of the individual items are illuminating. The bill for carpets was $300,000, and most of the carpets bought for the courthouse appeared in the new Metropolitan Hotel, opened by Tweed's son. Lumber dealers received $460,000 for material worth not more than $48,000. One contractor received $1,149,874.50 for repairing fixtures before the building was finished.

Fall of the Ring

The members of Tammany Hall counted on their chief for fair treatment, but not even the Tweed Ring could satisfy everybody. And it was one of the dissatisfied jobholders, a man named O'Brien, who brought about the ruin of Tweed's organization. O'Brien had a friend in the auditor's office, and the friend copied off some of the figures from the courthouse account. O'Brien then used this evidence in an attempt to blackmail his superiors into giving him a better job. Failing in this enterprise, he turned the figures over to *The New York Times*. On July 8, 1871, the *Times* accused the members of the Ring of wholesale corruption. Then Thomas Nast, famous cartoonist, launched a long-continued attack upon Tweed. This really hurt. As Tweed put it, the newspaper articles did him no damage among his constituents because few of them could read, but, he declared wrathfully, "they can't help seeing them damn pictures." In September 1871 some of the outraged citizens arranged for the appointment of an investigating committee, and this body prepared to publish proof of corruption.

The revelations of the investigators were too convincing to be ignored, and the Ring had to dissolve. On November 20, 1871, Connolly resigned his office of comptroller. Five days later he was arrested and released under bond of $1,000,000. Connolly spent some time in jail; upon his release he jumped his bond and sought refuge in Europe. He prudently took $6,000,000 with him. On December 16, 1872, Tweed himself was arrested, but the obliging Justice Barnard fixed his bail at the nominal figure of $5000. After two trials Tweed was found guilty and sentenced to a fine of $12,000 and to imprisonment for twelve years. At the end of a year he was out again, but a new arrest followed, and this time his bail was set at $3,000,000. Unable to furnish it he stayed in jail for a time, then escaped and followed Connolly to Europe. But he was eventually apprehended in Spain and brought back; not long afterward he died in Ludlow Street jail. So ended the Tweed Ring but not Tammany Hall.

By 1874 Tammany Hall had restored its control over the government of New York City. For a time the leaders were careful to refrain from the kind of open plunder which had brought about the collapse of the Tweed Ring, but they still found it possible to make politics a paying profession. In 1886 Richard Croker became boss of Tammany. Croker's associates made their money from the systematic licensing of organized vice and crime. Gambling houses, over 600 of them, paid $1500 apiece every month. Poolrooms paid $300 per month and houses of prostitution were assessed at the rate of $25 to $50 per month for each inmate. Then the members of the police force paid for their appointments, and those who were promoted paid for the advance in rank.

During this same period Philadelphia experienced the same type of misgovernment which afflicted New York. Tweed's counterpart in the Quaker City—not a Democrat but a Republican—was James McManes. He and his associates dominated all departments of the city government, and they were closely connected with the Republican managers in the state legislature at Harrisburg. The police force was made up of the adherents of the McManes faction; all candidates for city offices were nominated and managed by McManes; all policies were decided upon by the same dictatorial ruler. He and his group collected a percentage of all sums paid out for goods and services and, like Croker in New York, they levied tribute on organized vice.

Disease and the Public Health Movement

One of the most obvious aspects of city life during the latter part of the nineteenth century was the striking contrast between rich and poor. City

Slums

inhabitants with adequate incomes were able to enjoy the material and intellectual resources of their environment. As for the very wealthy, their revenue seemed almost fabulous. Not many rich men could pile up a fortune of nearly $100,000,000, as Commodore Vanderbilt did, but there were other large fortunes in New York. By way of contrast, the cities could also display their slums, where unfortunate American citizens lived in squalid poverty. At the close of the Civil War, New York City alone had 100,000 people living in the slums, in tenements which were unfit for human habitation. Crowded together on narrow streets, with no open space around them, they were lacking in facilities for lighting and ventilation, while sanitary facilities were simply nonexistent. In New York fully one fifth of the slum dwellers lived in cellars. Other cities also had their slum areas, possibly not as extensive but every bit as terrible.

The slums were an almost inevitable accompaniment of changing conditions in the United States: the rapid growth of industrialism and the drift of population into the urban areas. Immigrants, social misfits, and the very poor had to live somewhere, and the only places open to them were the slums. During the late 1860's there was no organized social service, no adequate arrangement for poor relief, and, worse yet, no feeling that the community had any obligation to care for the needy. American traditions rested on a philosophy of personal independence and of individual responsibility, on a belief that a man's misfortunes were solely of his own making.

This indifference of the well-to-do could not last forever; in fact, they soon had incontestable proof that the slums were their problem. Poverty

Urban Disease

was not contagious but disease was, particularly the kind that flourished in uncleanliness. The slums were literally hotbeds of disease. Epidemics of cholera, typhus, smallpox, and typhoid carried off thousands of patients annually. Although these major communicable diseases had been afflicting mankind for centuries, no one knew precisely how they were spread or how they could be prevented or cured. Cholera could race over whole continents, and the communities affected were powerless against its attack. In India there were century-old reports of this dread disease. During the early part of the nineteenth century it was endemic throughout all Asia. From the Far East Asiatic cholera spread to Russia, thence, in 1831, to England and France. In the following year it struck Quebec and New York City. Obviously the scourge was contagious, and observers noted some connection between its onset and the presence of filth or the lack of proper sanitation.

This lesson of the early nineteenth century might have been used to save American cities of later periods from epidemics of disease, but mankind forgets. Conditions in some of the most important cities proved that even the most elementary rules of cleanliness were ignored. Philadelphia took its water supply from the Delaware River and emptied its sewers into the same stream. In New York the sewers poured into the North and East Rivers so that the waterfront became a source of pollution for the whole city. In both New York and Philadelphia filth and garbage were allowed to collect in the streets. These conditions were not confined to the North. Memphis, for example, was built on lowland close to the river, with no facilities for drainage and with almost every facility for spreading contagion. New Orleans had the reputation of being one of the most unhealthful cities in the land. There could be only one consequence of such conditions. In 1865 Philadelphia had more than 770 deaths from typhoid and 300 more from typhus. In the following year cholera carried off nearly 1000 in Philadelphia alone. In 1871 the unfortunate city had an epidemic of smallpox, with 2000 deaths. In 1873 Memphis suffered from the ravages of three epidemics at once: yellow fever, smallpox, and cholera.

Public Health

This prevalence of disease furnished the incentive for the first public health campaign. And because disease and poverty seemed inseparably connected, any drive for public health had to deal with living and working conditions, with tenement house reform, and with more sanitary factories. As early as 1848 the recently organized American Medical Association became concerned over the state of public health in the larger cities of the United States. In 1850 the Massachusetts Medical Association sponsored an investigation of public health problems in that state. The investigators compiled statistics which proved beyond doubt that there was a definite relationship between unsanitary living conditions and communicable disease.

At the close of the Civil War the need of an effective policy of public health was even more evident than before, and the larger cities were driven to action. The health service in New York City was reorganized, and in 1866 the city created a municipal board of health. Within four years this board prohibited people from living in cellars, and it ordered the owners of tenement houses to make their buildings fit to live in. Then it undertook to rid the city of rats in order to diminish the danger of another outbreak of cholera. These orders, however, were not effectively enforced. It insisted upon the building of new sewers, emptying out in the harbor far enough away so that they were no longer a menace. The next step in promoting public health was taken in Massachusetts with the appointment of a state board of health. During the next decade nineteen states took similar action. In the beginning these state boards were empowered merely to investigate and to make recommendations, and they were hampered by lack of funds. In its first year the state board of health of North Carolina received an appropriation of exactly $100.

In this warfare against disease the boards of health could accomplish something by enforcing standards of cleanliness, by removing the more obvious accumulations of filth, and by arranging for unpolluted water supplies. But by far the most significant contribution to this campaign was the discovery that most disease is caused by microorganisms, known collectively as germs or bacteria. Like other discoveries in science, this was no sudden burst of inspiration on the part of any one worker but rather the composite product of many minds. Even in the eighteenth century there were physicians who argued that invisible organisms probably carried disease from person to person. In 1790 Dr. Benjamin Rush of Philadelphia suggested to his medical students that insects might be responsible for carrying certain types of fever. At the time there was no means of proving the truth of this assumption because there were no microscopes sufficiently powerful to make scientific demonstration possible. After 1830 the microscope was improved. In 1833 one investigator actually found the trichina spiralis in the human body, and in 1847 another found the same organism in raw pork. The next step, easily taken, showed how this organism could be transferred from one to the other, and the cause of trichinosis was made plain. By the middle of the nineteenth century physicians were discussing the possibility that cholera and yellow fever might be propagated by somewhat similar organisms.

Bacteriology

All this preliminary investigation had been done when Louis Pasteur began his experiments with microorganisms and boiling water. In 1858 he showed that bacteria did not develop in sterile water. Pasteur's subsequent investigations demonstrated unmistakably the relationship between germs and disease. And yet, in spite of the scientifically valid proof which he presented, he had to contend with the bitter opposition of the superstitious and the ignorant. Had Pasteur been compelled to work alone, stupidity might have triumphed, but other scientists joined in compiling an impressive body of evidence on his side. In time this became so convincing in character that only the willfully blind could venture to dispute it. In 1864 Joseph Lister, working in Glasgow with Pasteur's methods, showed that wounds could be made sterile and that infection could be prevented. During the 1870's Pasteur in France and Koch in Germany, working independently, obtained cultures of anthrax bacilli and by means of it gave the disease to healthy animals. Then they completed their demonstrations by proving that new cultures could be secured from the animals they had infected. During the 1880's the bacteriologists isolated the organisms of cholera, tuberculosis, pneumonia, diphtheria, typhoid, and tetanus. In a series of experiments and investigations carried on between 1899 and 1901 three American physicians, Walter Reed, James Carroll, and J. W. Lazear, showed that yellow fever was carried from person to person by one specific type of mosquito. Even before their work was finished another type of mosquito was found to be the responsible agent in spreading malaria.

Modern Hospitals

In laying bare the causes of disease the bacteriologists revolutionized medical practice. Before these discoveries physicians had been compelled to work in the dark because nobody knew precisely how mankind came by his ills. In addition to creating a new theory and practice of medicine, the discoveries of Pasteur, Lister, and their associates made over the hospitals. In former times the prevalence of infection had made some hospitals places of terror. Instead of being looked upon as places of recovery, they were believed to be, and often were, short cuts to death. But with the adoption of elementary principles of sanitation hospitals were freed from their old dangers. Surgery was robbed of its greatest dangers when antisepsis became a part of surgical routine.

While bacteriology made one great contribution to the development of the modern hospital, the nursing profession made another. In the United States the rise of trained nursing as a profession dates back only to the Civil War. The war had hardly begun when Dorothea Dix, previously known for her humanitarian work in behalf of prisoners and the insane, volunteered for nursing service. Following the example set by Florence Nightingale in the Crimean War, Miss Dix organized groups of nurses for work in the military hospitals. Her services were so valuable that she was given the title of superintendent of United States army nurses.

The work of the war nurses proved so valuable that plans were made to continue it in times of peace. Beginning in 1873 Bellevue Hospital in New York offered regular training courses for nurses. Similar training could be secured at the New Haven Hospital in Connecticut and at the Massachusetts General Hospital in Boston. In the course of time the larger hospitals throughout the country provided similar instruction. By the opening of the present century American hospitals had become models for the whole world. In 1876 the great Johns Hopkins Hospital was opened in Baltimore. Because of its admirable facilities and its organization it was long conspicuous as the best hospital in the United States. In 1893 the Johns Hopkins Medical School was established in connection with the hospital. It was the first medical school in this country to have a full-time teaching staff.

In any list of the most conspicuous developments in the changing practice of medicine, high place should be given to the discovery of anesthesia. Relief from pain along with antisepsis freed the patient of all terrors in surgical procedures and also made it possible for the surgeons themselves to attempt operations which would have been unthinkable in the old days. As early as 1800 an English scientist, Sir Humphry Davy, suggested that gas might be used to allay pain, and there is a report that in 1828 a surgeon in London actually used gas. Three years later chloroform was made available, and its use in surgery was proposed, but for the time there were no practical results. During the 1840's, "the anesthetic effects of ether became a matter of popular knowledge." The first physician to use it was Dr. Crawford W. Long of Georgia, but he did not publish any report of his success. In 1846 Dr. W. T. G. Morton, a Boston dentist, gave a demonstration of the use of ether as an anesthetic. This proof that ether could be safely used was given in the Massachusetts General Hospital, and reports of the demonstration were widely circulated. After that time its use became common.

These discoveries in the fields of bacteriology and medicine led to a notable improvement in the health and physical well-being of the American people, particularly those in the urban areas. In these same areas, and elsewhere too for that matter, there were other developments of a most unscientific character, frequently urged as a desirable substitute for scientific medicine. Healers of all kinds professed to rely upon the virtues of water, vegetable remedies, electricity, magnetism, plain simple sunshine, or even the operation of the mind upon matter. Every prophet had his following. Then in the 1870's Andrew T. Still of Kansas gave osteopathy to the world. It may be said that the claims made for this procedure were not always susceptible to scientific demonstration.

Popular Remedies

In a category by themselves were the manufacturers of proprietary medicines. They promised to cure all the ills of the human race with their vegetable compounds, sarsaparillas, tonics, blood purifiers, or liver pills. The sale of these alleged remedies ran into the figures of big business. Most of the manufacturers followed substantially the same schemes for victimizing the public. They would put out vividly written circulars in which they described the ordinary sensations of human beings as symptoms of disease. Then they argued convincingly that their specific remedy would cure that or any other ill. Their statements were fortified with "testimonials," supposedly written by grateful customers.

Additional Problems

Social Service

Improvements in cleanliness, sanitation, water supply, and the care of disease combined to bring about a degree of betterment among the poor of the cities, but their lot was still far from enviable. Additional help was needed if the newly arrived immigrants and other underpaid workers were to develop into good American citizens. For the children particularly it was essential to provide facilities for wholesome recreation and for manual training. Working mothers needed help with their children during the day, and those without jobs needed assistance in finding work. Even more important was the need for wholesome meeting places, where people could spend their leisure in reasonable peace and comfort. In part these various demands were met by the social center or settlement house. The best-known of these institutions was Hull House in Chicago, founded in the midst of a foreign colony. Hull House set out to supplement the work of the nine churches and missions in this area and to combat the influence of the 250-odd saloons which provided meeting places for the men of the neighborhood. Hull House was opened in 1889, and in the course of the following six years fifty similar social centers were started in other cities.

To many of the reformers of the late nineteenth century the one great obstacle in the way of improvement among the poor was liquor, and the saloon which dispensed it was held up as the symbol of endless iniquities. It is not surprising therefore that the campaign to raise urban standards of health and well-being should have been accompanied by a widespread attack on alcohol. The temperance movement had made considerable headway before the Civil War, but during this struggle many of the gains were lost. The advocates of temperance did not give up, and even before the Civil War had entirely closed they renewed their drive against alcohol. The incorporation of the New York State Temperance Society in March 1865 was one manifestation of renewed interest. In 1869 temperance workers organized a political party devoted to a crusade against liquor, the National Prohibition party, formally launched at a convention held in Chicago. Its objective was the enactment of laws to make sales of liquor illegal.

Temperance

Five years after the Prohibition party began its work, a group of earnest women founded the Woman's Christian Temperance Union, with local branches in almost every town in the United States. The W.C.T.U. planned to achieve its results by means of education. The members insisted that children in the United States should receive instruction on the subject of alcohol. They were so successful that before the end of the nineteenth century all but two states had laws requiring scientific instruction on the subject of temperance in the schools. But in many cases the education given was far from scientific; ardent teachers set out to frighten their charges rather than to instruct them. Nevertheless the temperance movement went on, with the children of primary age enrolled in the Cold Water Army, while those in high school joined the Loyal Temperance Legion. All signed the pledge which bound them to abstain forever from the use of alcohol as a beverage. But in spite of these efforts the liquor business continued to flourish.

In fact the liquor business and its disreputable accompaniment, the saloon, flourished so vigorously that it almost dominated the scene. No description of important social patterns of the late nineteenth-century American life could be complete or even satisfactory without some mention of this hardy problem. During the 1880's, before organized prohibition had made inroads upon these establishments, saloons were an adjunct—but not an ornament—to every town and city in the land.

According to the census of 1880 there were 492 cities and towns in the

United States, each with a population of 5000 or more. The people in these cities maintained and presumably supported approximately 8000 drinking places. To keep the saloons supplied there had to be breweries and distilleries, which were in themselves substantial business enterprises. In 1860 the liquor business accounted for an investment of $29,000,000; by 1870 this had increased to $67,000,000 and by 1880 to the impressive figure of $193,000,000.

Urban Crime

As for the criminal centers of the larger cities, the saloons were an integral part of their existence; crime and liquor were inseparably linked, each contributing to the success of the other. Every critic of the saloon emphasized its alliance with crime. So too every account of the problems of the city must contain some reference to crime. Every civilized community has its individuals who cannot or will not conform to established standards of laws and morals. During the last three decades of the nineteenth century crime assumed a new importance, particularly in urban life. Between 1880 and 1890 there was an increase in the prison population, running as high as 50 percent. In the course of twenty years there was an increase of 400 percent in the number of murders. And the most notorious centers of crime were the leading cities in the United States. Geographical location seemed to have no bearing on the problem, because in this respect San Francisco and Chicago were as famous as New York.

Boys who grew up in the poorer tenement districts of Cherry Street and Mulberry Bend in New York had ample opportunity to come in contact with professional criminals and to acquire the experience necessary to make them accomplished practitioners in the art. Organized gangs of pickpockets and hold-up men operated wherever police protection was inadequate, and this condition seemed general in all large cities. Bank robbers had their headquarters in New York and used the whole country as their field. These groups preyed upon anybody and everybody within their reach.

Then there was another group of criminals who specialized on the inexperienced and those who were ignorant of the ways of the city. These were the gamblers, who of course had their regular patrons but counted heavily on small-town tourists who came to the city to see life. These visitors to the city did see life, and they paid heavily for the privilege. "Honest" houses were rare. If the game was roulette, the wheel was wired so that the operator could safeguard the interests of the house. If it was poker, there were various methods which made the guest wonder at his losses. Then there were the small-time operators, whose specialty was the shell game, or possibly three-card monte. For the special benefit of out-of-town visitors, one Reed Waddell ran a profitable gold-brick swindle, which netted him $250,000 in the short space of ten years. In this same class were the vendors of "green goods," or counterfeit money.

The causes of this concentration of crime in the cities were to be found in part in the influences of the slums and in the ease with which the unscrupulous could extract money and valuables from the careless and unwary. In some of the cities criminals were left unmolested by the police, provided crimes were restricted to specified geographical limits. Again criminals bought immunity from the police themselves or from important city officials or from party leaders. It was easier and infinitely more profitable for the police to work with the criminals than to break up their operations. So the criminals and their protectors preyed on the public, while the taxpayers and the respectable element suffered.

Chapter 31

CHANGING SOCIAL PATTERNS

Religion and Science

For this colorful period of American history between 1865 and 1900 it would be difficult to name any aspect of social life which was not undergoing rapid and far-reaching alteration. New conditions called for adjustments in thought and action, and the clash between old habits and new ideas gave rise to controversies lasting until the present day. Sometimes the newly established principles were revolutionary in character, especially in religion and in education. In this particular period developments in scientific thought profoundly affected both fields.

In external appearance the modes of religious belief and practice in the United States had undergone no change for generations. The orthodox

Religious Conditions

denominations with their creeds and rituals were accepted without question by the majority of people. To be sure Unitarianism had made serious inroads on the Congregational Church of New England, but the second generation of Unitarians had lost some of the zeal of their fathers. The "better people" still went to church and believed what they were taught; or if doubts were corrupting the purity of their faith, most persons kept such unsettling notions to themselves. Not only individual behavior but also numerous state laws still bore testimony to the persistence of orthodox beliefs. Seven states in the South barred from public office any candidate who questioned the existence of God. Pennsylvania did the same and, in addition, required officeholders to profess belief in a future life, with rewards for virtue and punishment for sin. In some states unbelievers were excluded from the witness stand and the jury box. Most of the states still had laws for the punishment of "blasphemy or profane swearing." The majority of states prohibited unnecessary labor and secular amusements on Sunday.

Although the American people were still conventionally religious there were signs of a revolt against orthodoxy. During the agitation against slavery some of the leading abolitionists had included the orthodox churches in their indictment, because these denominations would not join in the abolitionist crusade. Then some of those who began by expressing dislike of the attitude of the churches toward slavery proceeded from that point to examine their doctrinal foundations, and here they soon found other grounds for attack.

Among those who entered the field of religious controversy by way of abolitionism was Gerrit Smith of New York, one of the more prominent

Agnosticism

leaders of the non-Garrisonian group. He reached the conclusion that many of the basic religious beliefs were not only unsound but positively evil, exerting a harmful influence on all serious thinking. Specifically, Smith questioned the doctrine of the immortality of the soul, and denied that divine power would or could impose eternal punishment upon man. He declared that the devil was nothing but "a mere myth." Hell was a figment of the imagination. The Trinity was "a disgusting and abhorrent monster." The doctrines of immaculate conception, apostolic succession, and election all were lacking in logic and reason. He attacked the concept of the fall of man, declaring it to be "not only destitute of proof but at war with nature and reason." Having disposed of most of the fundamental principles of the orthodox creeds—to his own satisfaction at least—he proceeded to demolish the miracles.

Smith argued that people remained in bondage to doctrinal theology, not because of its truth but because "they are not yet sufficiently courageous to overcome habits of submission to authority nor sufficiently enlightened to desire to overcome it." The situation called for a new system of education, something designed to lift men "up out of their superstitious credulity into a healthy skepticism." To this end Smith urged young men to study science and nature instead of theology. He argued that the churches stood in the way of an enlightened educational system. Instead of being "the infallible teacher of mankind," as they professed to be, churches were blinding the eyes of mankind to the light of science, and science was truth. Smith's published writings on the subject of religion appeared at irregular intervals between 1865 and 1874. Alone and by themselves they would have had no significance, but they reflected a definite trend in American thought, a trend toward skepticism and heresy.

During the 1880's Robert G. Ingersoll became famous as the great agnostic of his day. Like Smith he denied the infallibility of the Bible, and he ridiculed the belief in Hell. He was more widely known than Smith, but the doctrines of the two men had much in common. Both professed to believe in "the true religion," and both believed that science would lead the inquirer to the true religion. Ingersoll gloried in the epithet of agnostic, and he devoted his time to assaults upon orthodox religion. "For the vagaries of the clouds the infidels propose to substitute the realities of earth," he declared; "for superstition, the splendid demonstrations and achievements of science; and for theological tyranny, the chainless liberty of thought."

There seems to be no method of measuring the influence of the agnostics on the general run of people. Statistics of church membership are not conclusive because even some members were unbelievers. Bryce reported that in the larger cities there were "a good many people . . . who have virtually abandoned Christianity." Unbelief was evident too in the smaller cities. In New York City he concluded that with the exception of the Roman Catholics "the bulk of the humbler classes are practically heathen to the same extent as in London, or Liverpool, or Berlin.

If this controversy over religion had been confined to the realm of faith and dogma, theologians would have had no difficulty in meeting it. They rested their case on the principle of revealed religion and on the Bible as the medium of revelation. But when the findings of scientists discredited the literal truth of the story of creation as told in the Bible, theologians found themselves deprived of one main support for their arguments. About the middle of the nineteenth century new concepts in the field of natural science brought about a reorientation. Naturalists in Europe had been working toward the theory of evolution, and in 1859 Charles Darwin published the *Origin of Species,* in which he developed at length his evidence in support of the doctrine of evolution. It would be difficult to name any one piece of work which has exerted more profound influence on both scientific and religious thought than this. For those who accepted Darwin's conclusions the whole picture of the world and man's place in it had to be altered.

Darwinian Theory

The doctrine of evolution was spread over the United States partly through the influence of English lecturers, Thomas Huxley and Herbert Spencer for example, and partly through the active efforts of American leaders. John Fiske, philosopher and historian, was especially persistent in his determination to make the American people realize what was going on in the realm of learning. The best-known advocate of the Darwinian philosophy in the United States was Andrew D. White, president of Cornell University. In a series of lectures published under the impressive title *A History of the Warfare of Science with Theology in Christendom,* he attacked the churches because of their long-continued opposition to freedom of thought. Although a deeply religious man himself, White had no liking for reactionary theologians, and he accused them of trying to fetter the human intellect. They in turn realized as clearly as he did that discoveries in the field of science ran counter to numerous theological doctrines, and they tried to save their dogma by condemning the new learning. White, on the other hand, found the discoveries of science a safer guide than what he called the "vast masses of myth, legend, marvel, and dogmatic assertion" of clerical belief. He acted on the principle that honest investigation could never damage the truth. If certain teachings could not survive the analysis of scientific procedure, so much the worse for the teachings.

White drew heavily on the conclusions of students in the fields of anthropology and comparative religion. They showed that the beliefs of the Hebrews were not peculiar to that race but were the heritage of widely divergent primitive peoples. What men had hitherto supposed to be a body of divinely revealed truth was in substance nothing but the efforts of superstitious, ignorant savages to explain the mysteries of the world around them. Churchmen found White even more dangerous than Ingersoll.

Any concept so revolutionary as the doctrine of evolution was bound to stir up the theologians to bitter rejoinder, and they were almost unanimous in their condemnation of Darwin and his work. They found support for their position among some of the most learned scientists of the United States. Professor Agassiz of Harvard was perhaps the outstanding leader

MATTHEW B. BRADY took hundreds of action photographs during the Civil War. (Right) Brady's photograph of A. R. Waud, one of the best- known war correspondents, sketching the battle of Gettysburg for ***HARPER'S WEEKLY.*** *(Below) Professor Lowe in the "car" of his balloon, going aloft to observe Confederate forces during the battle of Fair Oaks. Balloons were first used for war observations by the French in 1794; Union forces used them considerably in 1861 and 1862. (Copyright, L. C. Handy Studios)*

"Dam Your Soul. The Horrible *Sepulcre* and Bloody Moon has at last arrived. Some live to-day to-morrow *"Die."* We the undersigned understand through our Grand *"Cyclops"* that you have recommended a big Black Nigger for Male agent on our nu rode; wel, sir, Jest you understand in time if he gets on the rode you can make up your mind to pull roape. If you have anything to say in regard to the Matter, meet the Grand Cyclops and Conclave in Den No. 4 at 12 o'clock midnight, Oct. 1st, 1871. When you were in Calera we warned you to hold your tounge and not speak so much with your mouth or otherwise you will be taken on supprise and led out by the Klan and learnt to stretch hemp. Beware. Beware. Beware. Beware.

(signed) "Philip Isenbaum, *Grand Cyclops;* John Bankstown, Esau Daves, Marcus Thomas, Bloody Bones. You know who. And all others of the Klan."

IN 1879 Albion W. Tourgee published anonymously A FOOL'S ERRAND, a novel describing the setting and activities of the Ku Klux Klan during Reconstruction, and in 1880, under his own name, THE INVISIBLE EMPIRE, a description of the Klan at work, based on evidence collected by a congressional committee. Subsequently the two were published in a single volume, including these illustrations. (Above) A Klan notice to an intended victim. (Below) The Masked Sentinel. Tourgee (1838-1905) was a "carpetbagger," public official, novelist, and from 1866 to 1875 judge of the Superior Court of North Carolina. His book had a wide sale, and he was described by one enthusiastic reviewer as "the chief of American writers."

in the campaign against evolution. As early as 1845 he had written: "I find it impossible to attribute the biological phenomena which have been and still are going on upon the surface of our globe, to the simple action of physical forces. I believe they are due, in their entirety, as well as individually, to the direct intervention of a creative power." For the benefit of those scientists who were working toward the views that Darwin developed, Agassiz declared: "The idea of a procreation of new species by preceding ones is a gratuitous supposition opposed to all sound physiological notions." He admitted that there seemed to be some sort of relationship between species, but he explained that this "connection between them becomes evident only when they are considered as a whole emanating from a creative power, the author of them all." Agassiz never altered his beliefs. When he reviewed the *Origin of Species* in 1860 he characterized the Darwinian concept as "a scientific mistake, untrue in its facts, unscientific in its method, and mischievous in its tendency." According to Agassiz, Darwin had departed widely from scientific methods and he "frequently overstepped the boundaries of actual knowledge and allowed his imagination to supply the links which science does not furnish." Without being aware of it, Agassiz himself had done the same thing. His doctrine of divine creation was not a concept which he had discovered through application of the scientific method.

Agassiz against Darwin

Many of the older natural scientists followed Agassiz and refused to accept the theory of evolution. On the other hand Asa Gray, colleague of Agassiz at Harvard, defended Darwin, and his influence helped to offset the influence of Agassiz. Younger scientists were much more responsive to Darwin's reasoning, and they had more influence over later generations of scholars. With the help of philosophers on one side and teachers of natural science on the other, Darwin's teachings became a definite part of American thought.

New Ideas in Education

Developments in the field of science were not the only influences which affected education. The system of higher education had undergone little change for many years, and in some respects it bore a much closer resemblance to the program of the Middle Ages than to that of today. The college catalogues of the 1860's show how heavily the curriculum was loaded with classics, mathematics, and philosophy and how little attention was paid to science, modern languages, history, and the social sciences.

State of the Colleges

The inadequate curriculum was not the only drawback in the colleges. Many members of the faculty were called upon to teach courses in such broad areas that effective preparation was out of the question. The professor at Columbia who taught mental and moral philosophy, political economy and history, English literature and logic may have been an extreme case, but even so specialization was anything but the rule. In some respects it may have been fortunate that library facilities were poor because the students had no way of discovering the inadequate training of their teachers.

In the smaller colleges work in science was carried on largely without laboratories; students therefore failed to acquire more than a secondhand acquaintance with their subject. Nevertheless the foundations of modern scientific work had been started even before the Civil War. By the middle of the century Asa Gray at Harvard had established a lasting reputation as one of the leading botanists. Also at Harvard Agassiz taught his students the principles and methods of research in zoology. At Yale Willard Gibbs in physics and Benjamin Silliman in chemistry were training students in accordance with sound principles and at the same time making international reputations for themselves. But these men were the exception.

Modern Education

By 1900 college curricula in general as well as the individual courses had undergone a transformation. At Harvard the new president, Charles W. Eliot, who entered office in 1869, broke old traditions. He raised the entrance requirements and so brought together a group of students able to profit from college work. Then he encouraged the faculty to broaden the curriculum. The work in science was extended and the laboratory method became general. New courses were provided in political economy and international law. History was given a place in keeping with its importance. English literature and modern literature and modern languages were placed on a level of importance with the classics.

The inclusion of so many new subjects in the curriculum made it difficult for the faculty to lay down specific course requirements for the degree. Early in the nineteenth century Harvard had adopted the elective system, and President Eliot worked for the extension of this principle. "The elective system," he wrote, "fosters scholarship, because it gives free play to natural preferences and inborn aptitudes and makes possible enthusiasm for a chosen work." By 1884, one half the work of the freshman year at Harvard was required, the rest was elective.

Eliot also believed that the proper place for professional training in the universities was at the graduate level. It was due largely to his insistence that the law and medical schools were put on a graduate basis, and he did the same with engineering. He also encouraged the development of special courses leading to the Ph.D. With these changes Harvard was transformed into a modern university.

Another program of educational reform was carried through under the direction of Andrew D. White, president of the newly founded Cornell University. Cornell was launched with the help of the federal government which, under the Morrill Act, granted the institution almost 1,000,000 acres of land. Ezra Cornell himself, a wealthy New York businessman, contributed $500,000, and Cornell selected White for the presidency. The institution opened in 1868 with 400 students and a carefully picked faculty. It offered a broad curriculum with special emphasis on the sciences, political science, and history, and with facilities for vocational and professional training in agriculture, veterinary work, and medicine. In some respects White outdid Eliot in experimenting with new ideas. Not only was the attempt made to combine practical training with the so-called liberal arts, but the new university was supposed to be closely integrated with the public school system of the state of New York.

Perhaps the most daring innovation of the White regime at Cornell was the introduction of coeducation. At the time this policy was not entirely new; Oberlin and Berea had adopted it, and so too had Iowa and Wisconsin. The East, however, looked askance at the notion of trying to educate men and women in the same institution. After two years' experience with the system White was more than ever convinced of its soundness. He wrote that the authorities had encountered no difficulty whatever. On the contrary, he found that "Good order has been increased, the standard of scholarship has been steadily raised." The system of entrance examinations proved to be an effective barrier in keeping out what he described as the "flippant and worthless boarding school misses." Furthermore, the "presence of the young women, even in comparatively small numbers, in the midst of our young men, in the halls, recitation rooms, etc., has an absolutely certain effect in checking all tendencies to rowdyism and bad language."

One more notable advance in higher education came with the founding of the Johns Hopkins University at Baltimore. Opened for work in 1876 under the direction of President Daniel Coit Gilman, Hopkins devoted itself solely to graduate instruction. Gilman brought together a notable group of scholars in economics, political science, international law, and history, and graduate students found the quality of instruction equal to the best that Europe had to offer. The medical school was perhaps even more famous than the graduate school, and men trained under the Hopkins faculty were welcomed in other institutions.

So great was the interest in education that the number of colleges increased rapidly. In the West every state had its state university, equipped to offer students almost everything available in both formal and vocational training. Several of the larger religious denominations established colleges and universities. During this period, too, wealthy benefactors provided for the establishment of new colleges for women. Before the Civil War, there were several women's colleges in the South but only one in the North. Vassar was opened in 1865. Ten years later Smith and Wellesley were opened to students. In 1885 Bryn Mawr was founded, and three years later Mount Holyoke became a college. "Harvard Annex," opened in 1879, acquired the more dignified name of Radcliffe College in 1894. All the state universities in the West were coeducational, so that before the close of the century women found ample opportunities for higher education.

These changes in the field of higher education were far-reaching in their importance; those in the secondary school field were if possible of even greater significance. According to Dr. Charles H. Judd:

Secondary Schools

> Since 1875 the educational system of this country has undergone a transformation. Better equipped elementary schools have been erected; free secondary schools have been established in large numbers; public normal schools for the training of teachers have been organized by the states; and the opportunities for college education have been enlarged and made accessible to young people from all classes of society.[1]

Among the notable changes in the secondary school field has been the increase in enrollment. This has been due in part to the increase in population, but perhaps even more to the decrease in the employment of children in industry. From 1870 to 1910 the percentage of children gainfully employed showed a definite increase, but in the next few years the figure took a sharp drop. In 1898 the public school population of the United States amounted roughly to 15,000,000, an increase of more than 63 percent in twenty years.

The increase in enrollment is only part of the story, and by itself it would call for little more than a mere mention. The really significant change occurred in the curriculum. Toward the end of the nineteenth century the course of study was built around the Greek and Latin classics. In addition there were courses in French and German, in algebra and geometry. in physics and chemistry, and in history. Beyond these nine subjects the high school offered little or nothing. The primary purposes of the high school was to prepare students for college; having accomplished this, its responsibilities stopped. Before the end of the century the schools began to include vocational training, bookkeeping, or accounting as it came to be called, and other training for business. In addition to the vocational courses the number and variety of courses in the liberal arts was greatly increased.

Although a great deal of sentimental emotionalism has been expended on the "little red schoolhouse," it is plain now, and it had become plain before 1900, that the old, single-room, ungraded school was no longer suited to American needs. Numbers of great men had received their first training in such schools, but they seem to have gone ahead in spite of, not necessarily because of, the influence of the school. Because of strong convictions on this subject, teachers and superintendents urged the substitution of the central or consolidated graded school for the old ungraded institution. The first state to take action was Massachusetts; in 1882 the district system was abolished and arrangements were made for transporting children in the rural areas to the village or town schools. This change made it possible for the school boards to provide better trained teachers, and by so doing to make the difference between rural and city schools somewhat less obvious.

[1] *Recent Social Trends,* p. 325.

The Library and the Press

At the present time one of the most important factors in the education of both youths and adults is the public library. Between 1875 and 1900 the number of public libraries containing 1000 or more volumes, increased from 2000 to approximately 5400. But the libraries could not remain unaffected by the ferment of change which was sweeping the United States, and improvements soon appeared. The American Library Association was organized in 1876 at Philadelphia. New methods of classification and cataloguing were developed; one of the most significant improvements was the inauguration of the Dewey decimal system, which greatly simplified the problems of cataloguing and shelf arrangement. In 1881 Andrew Carnegie began a series of gifts for buildings for public libraries. According to his terms the city would furnish the site and contract to maintain the library itself. By 1900 he had given away approximately $10,000,000 for this purpose, and this amount was increased to $60,000,000 by the time of his death in 1919.

Adult Education

In spite of its relatively rapid extension the public library could influence only a minority of the American people. Throughout this period, the one great purveyor of information and news was the press. In this respect the needs of the readers were generously provided for. Among weekly magazines specializing on current happenings and public affairs, *Harper's Weekly* remained one of the most satisfactory. Along with this was *The Independent,* ably edited and widely read. At the close of the Civil War Lawrence Godkin started *The Nation,* a weekly which professed to interpret the news. After 1890 *The Literary Digest* made an effort to summarize editorial opinion as expressed in leading newspapers. In 1893 a new magazine, *The Outlook,* made its appearance. Its purpose was to interpret current events. Under Lyman Abbott *The Outlook* had a widespread influence on American opinion.

For readers who preferred a more careful analysis of current affairs the publishers provided a number of monthly journals. The *North American Review* continued to fulfill its function of giving its patrons articles on public matters by the best writers available. In 1886 *The Forum* made its appearance. A few years later Dr. Albert Shaw launched *The American Monthly Review of Reviews,* which contained a judicious summary of the news as well as special articles.

Toward the end of the century a number of monthly magazines were published with the policy of combining good fiction with ably written articles on questions of the day. Easily the most famous in this group was *The Ladies' Home Journal.* Founded in 1883 by Cyrus H. K. Curtis, this newcomer in the field of monthly periodicals really arrived when Edward W. Bok became its editor in 1889. Bok gave his readers stories by the best writers, readable and interesting articles, and in addition he and his contributors supplied valuable information on the building and management of the home. In 1893 S. S. McClure put out the first number of *McClure's Magazine,* which emulated *The Home Journal,* and at the same time did considerably better in its articles on current problems in American government and politics.

Americans had been a newspaper-reading people ever since colonial days. The appearance of the large number of weekly and monthly reviews did not discourage the reading of newspapers; if anything it increased interest in the press. In the twenty years before 1900 the number of daily papers published in the United States rose from 971 to 2226, and the number of weeklies from 9000 to 14,000. Almost one half the world's total of newspapers was published in the United States. Only the most remote communities were beyond the reach of some sort of newspaper. If the increase in the number of papers brought about more intense competition among the publishers, the rivalry for readers tended to make the papers livelier and more entertaining.

Pulitzer and Hearst

A new era in American journalism began in 1883 when Joseph Pulitzer bought the New York *World* from Jay Gould. At the time the *World* had a circulation of 15,000; in the space of fifteen years Pulitzer built it up to more than 1,000,000. He developed a series of features designed to appeal to a variety of different readers. For those who resented the powers of organized wealth and of corrupt politics, Pulitzer embarked upon a vigorous campaign for reform. He demanded a new policy of taxation for the purpose of placing the cost of government on those financially able to bear it. To this end he called for taxes on incomes and on large inheritances.

To attract attention Pulitzer made use of the screaming headline, and he always played up the sensational. The person who read a murder story in the *World* had all the lurid details spread out fully before him. In 1893 Pulitzer gave his readers the first colored supplement to the Sunday paper. He ran the first colored comic, the famous "Yellow Kid." The promoter of the new journalism was fully alive to the fact that interests of newspaper readers varied widely, and he set out to reach them all. The figures for the *World's* circulation show that he succeeded.

In 1895 a competitor appeared, determined to beat Pulitzer in his race for the greatest circulation. The newcomer was William Randolph Hearst, fresh from California. After a brief sojourn at Harvard—brief because of the insistence of the authorities there—Hearst had gone back to California. His father bought the San Francisco *Examiner,* and the youthful William Randolph gained his first experience on this paper. Then he bought the New York *Journal,* which had been a relatively inconspicuous morning newspaper. It became the New York *Evening Journal,* and henceforth it was anything but inconspicuous. Sensationalism brought readers, readers who were none too critical if the reporters in their enthusiasm sometimes disregarded the principle that news stories should have some relation to actual facts. Because the "Yellow Kid" was one of Pulitzer's assets, Hearst too must have his own "Yellow Kid," so the two papers ran the strip, drawn by different artists. Hence the term "yellow journalism," which the more sedate readers applied to both these lively sheets.

Throughout the earlier history of newspaper publishing each editor and owner had gathered his own news. In 1892 the first of the great news services was organized, the Associated Press. This was neither a newspaper nor a publishing firm but an arrangement for cooperative reporting. The Associated Press was a club formed by a group of papers, the purpose of which was to provide information on all important happenings; only members of the group were allowed to use the material furnished by the service. By pooling their resources the member papers were able to get wider coverage at considerably less cost to themselves.

Sport: Exercise, Entertainment, or Big Business?

In the somewhat simpler patterns of American life which had served the American people prior to the Civil War there had been ample time and opportunity for maintaining contacts with the world out of doors. Industrial development and the rise of the city altered these patterns and barred city dwellers from outdoor life. The human being, however, is a peculiarly adaptable organism, and he contrives to find compensation for his losses. Of all these mechanisms of compensation, the most popular and the most far-reaching is modern organized sport. There never has been a time in recorded history when there was not some kind of sport available, and it would appear that urban development in the ancient world gave a great impetus to sport, as it did in the nineteenth century. But in the United States the development of sport coincided in time with the rise of big business, and present-day sport has taken on many of the attributes of business enterprise. The records show that organized sport became important after the Civil War. The first football team in the United States was organized in 1862. In 1866 the opening of the American Jockey Club's new Jerome Park marked a new era in horse racing. In 1886 the first country club was opened in the United States. Fresh air camps for the poorer children and the beginnings of the playground movement were the products of the 1870's and 1880's.

Early Baseball

Of all American games incomparably the greatest is baseball; for proof, if proof is needed, look at the records of attendance at the professional games since 1869. Baseball affords abundant opportunity for both the strategy of team play and the exhibition of a high degree of individual skill on the part of the players. The game has a long history; in fact, games involving the use of a ball are probably older than recorded history. It is said that one of the treasures in the British Museum is an Egyptian ball more than 3000 years old. This ball is stuffed with papyrus waste and covered with leather. The cover is sewn in the same fashion as that on a modern baseball. English boys played ball of a sort, and by 1820 American boys were playing town ball, a game which might be regarded as one of the ancestors of baseball.

In addition to town ball there were one old cat, two old cat, and three old cat. Four old cat had four bases and eight players on a side. Out of these games came modern baseball.

In 1839 Abner Doubleday, a civil engineer of Cooperstown, New York, laid out plans for a diamond-shaped field, each side being ninety feet in length. He also proposed rules for baseball which limited the players to eleven men on a side. His rules provided for retiring the side after three outs, and also ended the practice of putting the runner out with a thrown ball. In 1845 some players in New York City organized the Knickerbocker Baseball Club, the first formally recognized team in the United States. They used the Doubleday rules, with one important exception: their team had nine men, stationed as they are at the present time. In the course of the next few years similar teams began playing in several cities and towns, and in 1858 the National Association of Baseball Players was organized, with twenty-five teams represented. The rules committee of this Association limited the game to nine innings, except in case of a tie. In 1865 there were nearly 100 teams represented at the convention of the Association.

By 1865 the game was so well developed that the National Baseball Club of Washington, D. C., made a tour of five states and played nine games. They lost only one, to the Forest City Club of Rockford, Illinois; Albert G. Spalding, then seventeen years of age, pitched for the winning team. In 1870 the Forest City team played fifteen games in the East and lost only two games. During these years the players were all amateurs, in the sense that they received no direct compensation for their play. In 1869, however, the Cincinnati Red Stockings went professional, and their example was soon followed in other cities. In 1876 the present National League was organized with four western and four eastern teams. In 1882 a rival appeared in the American Association; the new league tried to attract customers away from the older circuit by cutting the admission charge to 25 cents. Instead of injuring business the existence of two leagues seemed to stimulate it, and when in 1883 the winners in each league arranged for a post-season contest, the first "world's series," interest and excitement reached a new high. In 1903 the American League was organized.

Modernizing the Game

As the game developed, changes were made in the rules and in the equipment of the players, all of which served to speed up the game and to make it even more interesting for the spectators. At first the batter had the privilege of swinging away at the ball until he made a hit or fouled out, but in 1875 the umpire was empowered to call strikes and balls, and the number was fixed at three and four, respectively, as at present. Also in the early years the pitcher was restricted to an underhand delivery. In 1884 restrictions on the pitcher's delivery were removed—and pitching became a real science. The curve ball was used as early as 1866 by Edmund Davis, an undergraduate at Princeton, and by Arthur Cummings of the Brooklyn team.

In professional baseball the difference between winning and losing teams was quickly reflected in the gate receipts, so every team played to win. In these contests it soon became evident that there were other factors in addition to skillful pitching and heavy hitting that accounted for victories, factors which were entirely within the rules. This was "inside baseball," a system of strategy in which rival managers tried to outsmart each other. The development of successful team play called for cooperation, and a given situation in the game called for a particular type of play. The manager, watching developments either from the bench or from his own position in the game, could tell the other players what to do.

Professional baseball means that the game had become a form of business, and the players were not the only ones to make money from it. With the advent of organized baseball there came the franchise, the owner of which had a monopoly of big league ball in his territory. His investment in the park and in the players is always a substantial sum. And the owners have their staffs of assistants who depend on the game for a living. The managers are highly paid experts whom the owner cannot neglect. Then there was a large group of athletes, newspaper correspondents, and businessmen, all of whom derived their living from the game. Railroads and hotels had their share of the business as the various teams moved from city to city on their scheduled tours. In this category of business interests there should be some mention of the professional gamblers who made their living by betting on the games and by running pools for amateur gamblers.

Still another branch of big business which has an active influence in the build-up of the game is the daily press. Newspaper publishers and editors were quick to discover that a good sporting page would appeal to many readers. So in addition to carrying the box scores and full descriptive accounts of the games, the papers published pages of interesting personal news about the players themselves, their likes and dislikes, special talents, superstitions, antagonisms, love affairs, in fact everything which would attract the attention of rabid followers of the game. All this publicity, the best advertising in the world, is given free because it promotes circulation. Other business enterprises have to pay for their publicity.

Football

Next to baseball in popularity as a spectator sport stands football, another game with its roots reaching far back into the past. Historians find evidence of football of a sort in the days of ancient Sparta and of imperial Rome. During the Middle Ages the Italians played something that resembled football with twenty-seven men on a side. At the same time Englishmen played football, a variation of the old Rugby game but with considerably more latitude in the matter of roughness.

After 1660 football became popular in the English schools and colleges, and American students subsequently tried their hand at the game. In the 1860's a new type of football became popular, something like association football. In 1862 Gerrit Smith Miller, grandson of the famous abolitionist, organized the Oneida Football Club. Miller at that time was a student at Dixwell's Latin School in Boston. This was the first recognized football team in the United States. The game played by the Oneida Club bore little resemblance to the modern game. The rules prohibited running with the ball; the players were expected to kick it or advance it by dribbling, as in modern basketball. The first intercollegiate football game was played by Princeton and Rutgers in 1869, with teams of twenty-five men on a side. Six years later representatives from Columbia, Harvard, Princeton, and Yale formed an intercollegiate football association.

The real growth of the modern game began in 1878, with the appointment of Walter Camp to the rules committee of the intercollegiate group. In 1880 he persuaded his colleagues to reduce the number of players to eleven on a side, and two years later the rule was adopted allowing the team with the ball three downs in which to make five yards. At the end of that decade Camp selected the first all-American team, made up entirely of players from Harvard, Princeton, and Yale.

The greatest development in American baseball came with the advent of the professional players and the businessmen who put up the funds; football on the contrary developed first as a game played by undergraduate students. This is not to say that it continued upon an entirely amateur basis. Perhaps the most extreme case of early professionalism was furnished by one of the leading state universities in the Middle West in 1893; seven men on the team had never even registered as students. "Ringers" and tramp athletes were far too common. In 1896 the Western Intercollegiate Conference was organized to eliminate some of these evils, and it raised ethical standards in football on more than one campus.

During the present century the game has become inseparably bound up with big business, even though the players, theoretically, are still on an amateur basis. Great concrete stands, seating 70,000 people, take care of the spectators—not infrequently at a price of $3 or $5 per ticket. Football requires even more paraphernalia than baseball, so the manufacturers have an interest in it. Then the professional coaches and their assistants depend upon the game for their living. Also the newspapers and the professional gamblers have attached themselves just as firmly to intercollegiate football as to professional baseball.

Because of this combination of factors football has developed into a form of large-scale entertainment for the masses rather than a game played for its own sake. The newspapers are partly responsible for this exaggerated emphasis, inevitably so because of their tendency to give the undergraduate entertainers who play the game the same sort of publicity which they give to professional entertainers in baseball. Then the professional coaching system is partly responsible. In the last analysis the coach's hold on his job depends on turning out winning teams, and the tangled situation in which he is involved compels him to do what is necessary to win. Once he begins to lose, alumni—who want winning teams—start a drive for a new man. As a result, the games are more often than not a battle of wits between rival coaches. This fact is, of course, played up by the newspapers, who knew how to give credit where credit is due. In recent years professional, big league football has approached baseball in popularity.

The Manly Art

The other great spectator sport of the late nineteenth century, apart from horse racing, was the prize fight. In those days, however, prize fighting, unlike baseball and football, was not on the list of respectable amusements. Part of this ill repute may have come from the fact that the first prize fighters in the United States were slaves. At the opening of the nineteenth century the heavyweight champion of this country was a freed Negro. Furthermore rules were few, and they were not designed to make the sport either scientific or uplifting. The fighters counted more on brute strength than on skill. Men fought without gloves, and a contest which stopped short of thirty, or in some cases fifty, rounds was hardly worth while. Contestants and spectators alike represented the seamy side of American life. At the close of the Civil War every state in the Union had a law prohibiting prize fights, and the bouts which were fought, like the modern sport of cockfighting, had to be carried on in secluded spots.

During the 1880's something happened. Either prize fighting attained an unaccustomed odor of respectability, or American taste sank to the fighter's level. In any case the sport began to attract a new clientele. At the same time in England the Marquis of Queensberry was instrumental in introducing new rules for the boxers. Each round was to be limited to three minutes, with a minute's interval for rest between rounds. When a fighter was knocked down the new rules provided for a count of ten in which he might get back on his feet. Under these rules the contestants were required to wear five-ounce padded gloves; also certain types of blows were ruled out. These rules did not begin to influence prize fighting in the United States until after 1890. But in spite of the evil reputation which the sport had acquired in the past, there were numbers of people who liked to see a good fight, and in the 1880's a fighter appeared who helped to bring respectability to the ring. This newcomer was John L. Sullivan of Boston, the popular hero of his generation. In 1882 he won the heavyweight championship by defeating Paddy Ryan and kept the title for ten years. His greatest fight came in 1889, when he defeated Jake Kilrain in a contest which ran to seventy-five rounds. This was the last big fight in which the contestants used their bare knuckles. Sullivan won a purse of $20,000 and a diamond belt, given by that great authority on sport and the theater, the old *Police Gazette*.

In 1892 Sullivan had to surrender his title to a new rival, James J. Corbett, known to his contemporaries as Gentleman Jim. Corbett was the first American heavyweight to fight under the Marquis of Queensberry rules. After Corbett came Bob Fitzsimmons and then James Jeffries. These men helped to raise the sport to a new level of respectability, so that in the present century prize fights are attended by the "best" people. The press and the professional gamblers also give due attention to prize fighting, as they do to baseball and football.

Horse racing is another sport for the spectators, and it too has an ancient origin. It was probably old in the days of the chariot races in ancient Rome. During the colonial period of American history horse racing was popular in the South; in the North, Newport, Rhode Island, was famous for its fast horses. During the first half of the nineteenth century racing attained wide popularity in North and South alike. However, in parts of the East those ubiquitous parasites, the gamblers, gave the sport a reputation almost as bad as that of prize fighting.

Horse Racing

The Civil War interrupted horse racing, but once the war was over several new race tracks were opened. One of the most famous was Jerome Park, in Westchester County, New York, operated by the American Jockey Club. The founders were William R. Travers and Leonard W. Jerome, prominent stockbrokers. They prohibited the sale of liquor at the park in order, as they said, to make the place respectable for ladies, and they did something in the way of discouraging professional gambling. Racing became popular, and it received the sanction of widespread approval, but the problem of the gamblers remained.

The Bicycle

The spectator sports provided entertainment and recreation of a sort, but they furnished exercise only to the participants. Sports for the individual were less spectacular, but from the standpoint of health and physical well-being they were more desirable than the contests of opposing teams. During the 1880's and 1890's bicycling seemed ideally adapted to this need. After the Civil War the old high-wheel bicycle became popular. The devotees organized local clubs, and there was even a magazine devoted to their interests, the *Bicycling World*. In 1880 a national convention of cyclists, meeting at Newport, Rhode Island, founded the League of American Wheelmen. The League worked "to promote the general interests of bicycling, to ascertain, defend, and protect the rights of wheelmen, and to encourage and facilitate touring."

In 1888 the "safety" bicycle of the modern type was put on the market, and interest in riding became nearly universal. By 1900 manufacturers were turning out new machines at the rate of 1,000,000 per year. Men, women, and children all learned to ride. During the 1890's roads outside the towns and cities had a characteristic "snake path" along one edge, where hundreds of "wheels" had made a smooth course for the enthusiasts. When women began to ride they became acutely conscious of the problem of dress; the long, full skirts of that era did not lend themselves to much activity out of doors. They began to argue that they could wear short skirts or even knickers without loss of "feminine dignity and modesty."

Golf and Tennis

Among games for the participant which provide exercise, call for a high degree of skill, and furnish the incentive for keen competition there is nothing like golf. There seems to be no record of the date of the earliest formally laid out course, but there was one at St. Andrews, Scotland, in 1552, and the St. Andrews Club, the oldest golf club, dates back to 1754. During the latter part of the eighteenth century golf had its devotees in both South

Carolina and Georgia. Then for some reason there was a lapse of interest, and the first modern golf club was started at Yonkers, New York, in 1888. During the early 1890's several new courses were laid out in this country. The first golf tournament in this country was played at Newport in 1894. The winner turned in a score of 188 for thirty-six holes. For some time golf was a game for the rich because the only courses were those of private country clubs and membership fees were high. The game carried an added amount of disrepute because of the theory that nobody played it except old men, "dudes," and "sissies." The game did not become generally popular until after the turn of the century.

Like numerous other games, tennis can trace its beginnings back to the Middle Ages, but its modern form is of comparatively recent origin. In the United States an approach toward the modern game was played at Nahant, Massachusetts, and at Newport, Rhode Island, in 1874. During this period few players paid much attention to such inconsequential matters as the size of the court, the height of the net, or the rules in general. But in 1881 the United States Lawn Tennis Association was organized, and its officials standardized the game. The first international match—between English and American players—was held in 1897. In 1900 one of the American champions, Mr. Dwight F. Davis (later Secretary of War) gave the Davis cup as a prize for the winner of such contests. Although local and international tennis matches have on occasion attracted large crowds, tennis has never been a great spectator sport like baseball or football. On the contrary, it has been primarily a game for the players themselves.

The idea of making special provision for wholesome recreation and outdoor life for the city children was slow in taking hold. In 1877 the Reverend Willard Parsons of Sherman, Pennsylvania, arranged to send a few of the poorer children into the country for short vacations. His proposal was taken up by newspapers, businessmen's associations, and philanthropic agencies, and the plan of fresh air funds took hold. The first experiment with special playgrounds for poorer children was tried in Boston, where in 1885 one of the welfare societies provided "sand gardens." Although the need for opportunities for wholesome play became more and more obvious, the cities were slow to provide adequate facilities. As late as 1910 only 180 cities—7½ percent of all the cities in the United States—had public playgrounds. The penalty for this neglect was evident in the increasing problems of juvenile delinquency. In the long run the cost of taking care of the maladjusted was considerably greater than the cost of playgrounds.

To provide facilities for play in the winter for those who did not enjoy snow and ice, private schools and colleges built gymnasiums. These had apparatus for exercise and space for playing certain indoor games, of which basketball became the most popular. For the city youth outside the range of colleges, the Y.M.C.A. performed a similar service. In recent years basketball, both amateur and professional, has attained nation-wide popularity, equal to that of baseball and football.

Chapter 32

POLITICAL ORGANIZATION AND POLITICAL ISSUES, 1877-90

Party Machines

Republican Supremacy

EXCEPT for Cleveland's two terms, the Republicans held the Presidency from 1861 to 1913. There were several reasons for this record. The Republican party had won the Civil War. Republicans had formulated the policy for financing the war, a policy which shifted more than two thirds of the cost to future generations and which gave a good profit to contemporary investors. To the manufacturers the Republican party gave the protective tariff; the manufacturers upheld the party. The Republican party gave away the public domain with a generosity never before equaled in any country. Millions of acres went to the railroad companies, while lumber and mining companies contrived to get possession of millions more. Natural resources of incalculable value were made available for exploitation, with little regard for immediate needs and with no regard whatever for future generations. Western farmers owed their cheap land and their railroads to the same generous Republican party, so for years western farmers supported eastern businessmen in politics.

State Bosses

Republican political leaders gave considerable thought to matters of organization. The party and its workers had to be held together, discipline maintained, and the relationship between the party and its financial supporters made profitable to both sides. Because of these considerations the state party leaders found themselves possessed of remarkable authority. They managed the party, and they served as the connecting link between the party and the government on one hand and between the party and certain business interests on the other. The state leader was more important than the state governor, but he was not elected by the voters nor was he responsible to them. Furthermore, he was under no constitutional or legal restrictions because his status was provided for merely by custom, not by law.

One of the best known and most successful of these professional politicians was Thomas Collier Platt of New York. In his *Autobiography,* written in 1910, he included the following comment on his political activities: "Right here it may be appropriate to say that I have had more or less to do with the organization of the New York legislature since 1873." Actually, he named the speaker of the assembly and dictated the appointment of the committees. All appointments in the state civil service had to be submitted to him for approval. He supervised the legislative program. Republican governors and legislators alike knew that cooperation with Platt was the prerequisite to political advancement. Any ill-advised independent action would end the career of the man who tried it. Discipline could be enforced because the leader controlled nominations for elective office.

In Pennsylvania, to cite one more example, the Republican organization was controlled for several years by Senator Mathew M. Quay, political heir of the Camerons and predecessor of Boies Penrose. If possible, Quay was even more powerful in his own state than Platt was in New York. In 1898 John Wanamaker, merchant and Republican, tried unsuccessfully to drive Quay out of office. As one means of discrediting the Senator, Wanamaker explained how the machine maintained its authority. Wanamaker declared that Quay maintained an organized system of terrorism to prevent individuals from deserting the party ranks. Every voter was carefully watched by local representatives of the party and at the first sign of disloyalty he was called sharply to account:

> If he is the employee of a corporation, he is threatened with discharge; if he is a merchant he is boycotted; if he is a clerk, the head of the firm is notified that he must be suppressed; if he is interested in a corporation, the company's interests are threatened; if he is a director or stockholder in a bank, large customers are found to threaten the withdrawal of their business; if he is a physician, good patrons object; if he is a lawyer, his clients are given orders and threaten to leave him; if he is a preacher, members of his congregation protest; if a man daring to be independent of political dictation is in debt, he is threatened by those who hold his obligations.

Invisible Government

In 1915 Elihu Root made a speech on the subject of "invisible government." "What is the government of this State? What has it been during the forty years of my acquaintance with it? The government of the Constitution? Oh, no; not half the time, or half way." Mr. Root went on to explain that the government of his state had

> . . . presented two different lines of activity, one of the constitutional and statutory officers of the State, and the other of the party leaders. . . . Mr. Platt ruled the State; for nigh upon twenty years he ruled it. It was not the Governor; it was not the Legislature; it was not any elected officers; it was Mr. Platt. . . . The party leader is elected by no one, accountable to no one, bound by no oath of office, removable by no one. . . . The invisible government proceeds to build up and maintain its power by a reversal of the fundamental principle of good government, which is that men should be selected to perform the duties of the office; and to substitute the idea that men should be appointed to office for the preservation and enhancement of the power of the political leader.

National Organization

The party organization had various branches, each of which was responsible for a specified type of work. In each state there was a central committee, with the party leader or "boss" in charge. These men looked after the details of party organization, and they had charge of both state and local campaigns. For national elections there was the national committee, composed of one member from each state. The chairman of the national committee had the responsibility of directing the Presidential campaign, always in cooperation with the state leaders. In 1866 the Republicans added a new unit, the Congressional Campaign Committee, consisting of one member from each state. This new agency was created to look after the nomination and election of Congressmen. Its functions gave it a close relationship with the national committee and with the state committees. Here was an excellent device for maintaining party discipline. The Congressman who was inclined to be independent would not secure another nomination.

In Congress the party had arrangements for controlling the course of legislation. In the House there was the Rules Committee, which appointed all other committees; the same committee drew up the legislative calendar. A measure which the Rules Committee did not like might never appear on the calendar at all, or it might be put so far down on the list that it would never be reached. A similar committee performed a like function in the Senate.

The cohesive factor which held this complex organization together was the spoils system. The local worker might become postmaster or customs collector or federal district attorney, and from any one of these jobs he might move into his state legislature or into Congress, possibly into the United States Senate itself. The Senate was in some respects the most important unit in the whole organization because it had the deciding voice in distributing federal patronage.

In considering prospective appointees the Senate had worked out a principle known as senatorial courtesy. This meant that a nominee for an office in any given state could not be confirmed unless he had the endorsement of the Senators from his state—provided the Senators belonged to the majority party. The President would comply with the "recommendation" of the proper Senators; the Senate would confirm appointments which were properly made. Thus the principles of invisible government which Elihu Root described in New York operated on an even larger scale in national politics.

Politics and Business

In this political system the leaders were not responsible to the people, but they were sometimes responsible to businessmen who found it convenient to maintain political connections. All corporate business was carried on under a state charter, the conditions of which were determined by legislative action. Members of legislatures could be induced to enact desirable statutes or to amend undesirable ones. When railroad managers wanted anything from the government, either state or national, they paid for it. Some of the industrial leaders were not far behind. Even if they did not openly bribe legislators, they established connections with political leaders and exerted a definite influence on party policy. In 1905, when Charles Evans Hughes was investigating the great life insurance companies, Mr. Thomas Collier Platt himself testified that for a period of fifteen years he received an annual fee of $10,000 from the Equitable Life Assurance Society. Its purpose was to make sure of Platt's good will toward the Equitable. Hughes also found that some of the companies contributed regularly to the Republican party. In the Presidential campaign of 1888 John Wanamaker was treasurer of the Republican National Committee. He sent out the following communication to manufacturers: "How much would you pay for insurance upon your business? If you were confronted by from one to three years of general depression by a change in our revenue and protective measures affecting manufactures, wages, and good times, what would you pay to be insured for a better year?" In making contributions under these conditions the businessmen felt that they were paying for definite results.

The United States Senate was an important link in the political relationship between the government and the party machinery; it also served as the tie between government and the business interests. Here were to be found men of wealth and power. In 1889 the two Senators from Michigan were spokesmen for great lumber companies; one Senator from Ohio represented railroads, another the Standard Oil Company; Senator Aldrich from Rhode Island, a wholesale grocer himself, looked out for the textile interests of his constituents. These Senators and others were big businessmen in their own right. Associated with them were prominent corporation lawyers. In 1900 there were twenty-five multimillionaires in the Senate; they controlled the committees and managed the business of the upper house.

This intimate relationship between business, politics, and government was a recognized factor in the American system. Its importance was admitted and taken as a matter of course. One of the best general statements concerning the alliance was made by William Howard Taft:

> This was not all of it brought about by direct corruption, but much was effected through more insidious influence, and by furnishing the funds that political exigencies in important electoral contests called for. The time was, and we all know it, when in many of the directorates of the great corporations of the country, orders for the delivery of delegates in a convention and of members of the legislature for purposes of corporate control were issued with the same feeling of confidence in their fulfillment as an order for the purchase of machinery or the enlargement of the pay-roll.

Hayes and Reform

An Independent President

The foregoing material will give some idea of the guiding principles of American politics of the late nineteenth century and of the conditions under which political operations were carried on. Additional information may be gathered from a survey of some of the Presidential campaigns, and from an analysis of some of the major issues of this period. The closing of the Grant administration and the inauguration of President Hayes in 1877 ended the era of executive sanction of malfeasance in office. Whatever his intentions may have been, Grant had made it possible for a host of adventurers to extract illicit gains from the government. After his time—at least until 1921—every President was honest and interested in respectable government. Hayes had been in public life long enough to understand how the

Republican organization had humiliated Johnson and dominated Grant, and he was determined to assert his independence. But in making this decision Hayes ignored the fact that the American system of government is a party government and that the party is the connecting link between executive and legislature. For satisfactory results they must work together. Although Hayes had been nominated by the Republican leaders and put into office by the strictly partisan vote of a majority of the Electoral Commission, he had not actively sought the nomination. He had made no promises—the Wormley agreements had been arranged by the party leaders—and he announced that he would serve for only one term. In making up his Cabinet he ignored the advice of the party leaders and defied their power. Hayes successfully demonstrated his independence, but he did violence to the factor which brings success at the polls: party solidarity.

In formulating his southern policy Hayes again ignored party allegiance and party needs—with one conspicuous exception which involved him in difficulties. In his inaugural he urged fair treatment for both whites and Negroes; this was a new note because hitherto the Republicans had been concerned only with the interests of the Negroes. According to his interpretation of the Constitution, the federal government had no right to maintain troops in any state except under conditions which did not at the time prevail. Then he expounded the doctrine that the Negroes would enjoy greater security under the supervision of the better white element in the South than under corrupt carpetbaggers. By this time Republican governments survived in only two southern states: South Carolina and Louisiana. That in Florida had already collapsed. By the end of April 1877 Hayes removed the troops, and the Republican officeholders retired to private life. Federal military control of southern politics and government came to an end, and for the future southern whites were left in undisputed control.

Adverse criticism of this policy poured in upon Hayes from two sources: former abolitionists and Republican political leaders. Friends of the Negroes accused Hayes of sacrificing the freedmen. The directors of the Republican party had logical reasons for condemning the President. The votes of the three southern states had been essential in the process of counting Hayes into office. At the next election the leaders would have to find enough votes to compensate for this loss. Even though Hayes had no interest in a second term, his party associates wished to keep the White House for a Republican, and they felt that Hayes owed them something. They had given him the Presidency, and he had no right to ignore them.

Civil Service Reform

Hayes also antagonized Republican leaders by his approval of civil service reform. Ever since President Washington's day the question of the patronage had troubled both dispensers and would-be recipients. Appointments were made on the basis of political favoritism, and the frank acceptance of the spoils system kept the incumbents uneasy. The spoils system inevitably made for inefficiency, sometimes for downright corruption. In 1870 President Grant had raised the issue, and in his second annual message he called attention to the need for an improved method of making appointments. In March 1871 Congress professed a desire to help the President in this particular difficulty. A rider attached to one of the appropriation bills empowered the President "to prescribe rules and regulations for the admission of persons into the civil service of the United States as will best promote the efficiency thereof." In the summer of that year, acting under authority given in this law, Grant appointed a commission, with George William Curtis as chairman, to investigate conditions in the civil service.

The men selected for this purpose worked so effectively that in December 1871 Grant was able to submit to Congress the rules which they had framed. The President promised to enforce them, and he asked Congress for further legislation so that the system thus adopted might be made permanent. The rules themselves provided for a proper classification of positions in each branch of the civil service, for appointments to the lowest grades on the basis of competitive examinations, and for promotions from lower to higher grades also on the basis of competitive examinations. The levying or paying of political assessments was forbidden. On April 16, 1872, Grant issued an executive order declaring that the "utmost fidelity and diligence will be expected of all officers in every branch of the public service." All this sounded as though the President was interested in reform. But it soon became apparent that when the desires of such spoilsmen as Butler and Conkling ran counter to these lofty principles, Butler and Conkling prevailed. Congress cut down the appropriation for the civil service commission and then stopped it entirely. For the Grant administration the issue of civil service reform was closed. Public interest, however, was kept alive by the National Civil Service Reform League.

The increase of corruption in Grant's second term demonstrated still more vividly the need of civil service reform, and President Hayes made a determined effort to establish the policy. He felt that the law of March 3, 1871, which had become obsolete under Grant, might be revived and enforced. Then on June 22, 1877, he had sent to all civil service officials an executive order which had been drawn originally for the Treasury Department.

> No officer should be required or permitted to take part in the management of political organizations, caucuses, conventions, or election campaigns. Their right to vote and to express their views on public questions, either orally or through the press, is not denied, provided it does not interfere with the discharge of their official duties. No assessment for political purposes, on officers or subordinates, should be allowed. This rule is applicable to every department of the civil service. It should be understood by every officer of the general Government that he is expected to conform his conduct to its requirements.

To one not directly involved in politics this order seemed praiseworthy and necessary. Moralists and idealists both welcomed it with enthusiasm. Politicians, on the other hand, were inclined to look upon it either with amused contempt or with rage. With a stroke of the pen Hayes would have compelled every prominent Republican worker in the country to retire from active politics or to resign the office which gave him his living.

Attacking the Spoilsmen

After providing for better methods of appointments and for separating the incumbents in office from the turmoil of political campaigns, the President attempted to improve the personnel, particularly in the larger customhouses. Investigation of these offices revealed an astonishing degree of "official ignorance, inefficiency, and corruption." Through "errors" in the accounts the government was losing $1,500,000 annually; officials were taking fees and bribes. The staff of the customhouse in New York was overmanned to the number of 200. Hayes ordered the dismissal of useless clerks and endeavored to introduce efficient business methods.

In spite of Hayes's order, Alonzo B. Cornell, naval officer at New York, ostentatiously kept his place as chairman of the Republican State Committee. At the Republican state convention in September 1877 Platt openly ridiculed the President's policy, and on the same occasion Conkling himself gave voice to the epigram which seems destined to reward him with eternal fame: "When Dr. Johnson said that patriotism was the last refuge of a scoundrel, he was unconscious of the then undeveloped capabilities and uses of the word 'Reform'!"

According to Hayes, responsibility for evils in the customhouse at New York rested with the collector, Chester A. Arthur, and on his associate Cornell. When they refused to abandon their political activities, Hayes demanded their resignations. Upon their refusal to leave voluntarily, the President removed them and eventually appointed Merritt and Burt to the posts. This dispute over the spoils system was one of the major causes of the long controversy between the President and his Republican associates in Congress.

Bland-Allison Act

In the account of Grant's administration in a previous chapter there is a brief summary of the contest between the advocates of "sound money" and the inflationists. The resumption of specie payments in 1879 was counted on to end the contest over money, but this hope was not realized. From 1879 almost to 1900 there was continual agitation over the monetary problem. Commodity prices, particularly of farm products, were declining slowly. At the same time the volume of business operations was expanding rapidly. Both conditions called for an increase in the quantity of money in circulation; the farmers wanted it to help raise prices, and some businessmen felt that there was not money enough in circulation to keep pace with increasing business needs.

One group insisted that the monetary needs of the country could be met by the issue of more paper, and in 1876 they organized a political party, the Independent National, or Greenback, party to promote their cause. In their first platform the Greenbackers explained that their work was made necessary by "a ruinous policy which the Republican and Democratic parties refuse to change." They demanded the immediate repeal of the Resumption Act of 1875 in order to "stop the present suicidal and destructive policy of contraction." They believed that interest-bearing notes of the federal government would furnish the best money ever devised. In 1880 they urged the substitution of legal tender currency for bank notes because they opposed banks. They also demanded the free coinage of silver.

When Congress met in December 1877 the inflationists had a majority in the House. They proceeded to pass bills not only to repeal the Resumption Act but also to provide for the free and unlimited coinage of silver at the ratio of 16 to 1. This proposed ratio overvalued silver because at that rate the bullion value of a silver dollar was only 93 cents. In the Senate the inflationists could not pass the House bill, but they did force a compromise. This measure, the Bland-Allison Act, restored the silver dollar at the ratio of 16 to 1. But instead of granting free coinage it gave a subsidy to the silver producers. The law required the Treasury to purchase not less than $2,000,000 worth and not more than $4,000,000 worth of silver every month and to coin this into dollars. Hayes vetoed the bill, but Congress passed it over his veto.

The Bland-Allison Act remained in effect from 1878 to 1890. During this interval the Treasury bought the minimum amount of silver as provided by law, at a total cost of $286,930,333; this metal was minted into $378,000,000. In the course of eleven years the bullion value of the silver dollar dropped from 93 to 71 cents; by 1893 it was down to 60 cents; and in 1894 it went to 49. Presidents Arthur and Cleveland both warned the country of the dangers of inflation, but no real harm seemed to come. The Treasury always stood ready to redeem the silver dollars at par. The Bland-Allison Act failed to satisfy the inflationists. Silver-mining interests labored under the delusion that the government owed them a market for their product because overproduction was reducing its price.

Garfield and the Patronage

Election of 1880

One important political result of Hayes' administration was the determination of the Republicans to restore discipline. To do so they needed a President whom they could trust. The one man in the party best suited to their needs was Ulysses S. Grant, and they undertook to force his nomination for a third term. In doing so they ignored a resolution of the House of Representatives, adopted in 1875, for the purpose of blocking such a move. By a vote of 234 to 18, the House had declared that the two-term precedent "has become, by universal concurrence, a part of our republican system of government, and that any departure from this time-honored custom would be unwise, unpatriotic, and fraught with peril to our free institutions."

When the Republican convention of 1880 opened, Grant had more delegates than any other candidate, but he lacked the necessary majority. Although the anti-Grant delegates—"Half-Breeds" as they were called—were numerous enough to control the convention if they could unite, they had not agreed upon any one nominee. In these circumstances it was good strategy for the opposition to aim at the defeat of Grant; eventually they might find an acceptable candidate. For the Grant men, or "Stalwarts," on the other hand, the proper strategy was to attach to their side an appreciable number of delegates from the opposition. This they attempted to do, under Conkling's leadership, by forcing the convention to adopt the unit rule; under this device the majority of each state delegation could control the vote of a possible minority. Then the anti-Grant minorities in the various delegations would all be enrolled on the Grant side.

Thanks to the efforts of James A. Garfield, then acting as manager for John Sherman, the opposition rejected the unit rule. When the balloting began, Grant's actual strength was shown to be slightly over 300 votes; on the last ballot, the thirty-sixth, he still received 306. On this last ballot the majority went to Garfield, who at the beginning had not been considered a candidate. With the idea of mollifying Conkling, the convention gave the Vice-presidential nomination to Chester A. Arthur of New York, one of the mainstays of the Conkling machine. The Democrats nominated General Winfield Scott Hancock of Pennsylvania.

Garfield and the Stalwarts

In 1876 the Republicans had won the presidency by the majority of a single electoral vote. In 1880 they were certain to lose nineteen votes which had been counted for them in 1876, those of Florida, Louisiana, and South Carolina. To win they must have New York and possibly Indiana, neither of which they had carried in 1876. The vote in these states was proverbially close, and it would go to the party with the larger funds, the better organization, and the more energetic workers. The procedure of making Garfield President therefore would consist in holding the normally certain Republican states and in winning Indiana and New York. If the Garfield managers could enlist the Conkling "Stalwarts," they might hope to carry both these states—New York because of the hold of the machine on the voters, Indiana by means of funds which the New York regulars knew how to raise. But these gentlemen in New York were in no mood to furnish either votes or money for Garfield. Conkling himself was sore and disgruntled almost to the point of willingness to let Hancock win. While his associates were not quite so bitter, they needed encouragement. The circumstances were pointed out to Garfield by the Republican leaders. Stephen W. Dorsey wrote bluntly: "I insist that a conference with Governor Cornell and Senator Conkling is an absolute essential to success in this campaign."

At first Garfield was unwilling to meet the New York leaders fearing that he would be called upon to make disagreeable bargains about patronage. But the urgency was great, and the futility of attempting to carry the country without the help of New York was plain. Garfield yielded to pressure, and on August 5, 1880, he had a long conference in New York City with some of the "Stalwarts," particularly Levi P. Morton, Crowley, Arthur, and Platt. Conkling himself refused to attend. Because of conflicting evidence it is difficult to determine precisely what happened at this meeting. Before the conference Garfield had declared that "there shall be no surrender to any unreasonable demands." After the conference Garfield declared emphatically that he was free and unhampered. Subsequently, the "Stalwarts" claimed that Garfield had promised to consult with the New York organization and to comply with their wishes in making federal appointments in New York. The "Stalwarts" held that Garfield made promises regarding the patronage in return for assurances of their support. There are some facts which should be considered in connection with this alleged bargain. Garfield attended the New York conference, knowing in advance what the "Stalwarts" wanted from him; at the gathering, according to his biographer, he said enough to create an atmosphere of good feeling; after the conference the "Stalwart" leaders, hitherto suspicious and indifferent, plunged into the campaign with genuine fervor; throughout the campaign Garfield unhesitatingly accepted their support.

To help raise money the Republican leaders, in flat violation of Hayes's executive order, had called upon federal civil service employees for contributions, usually on the basis of 2 percent of their salaries. Garfield not only did not oppose this practice of mulcting the job holders but approved it in writing. In a letter dated August 23, 1880, written to J. A. Hubbell, chairman of the congressional campaign committee, Garfield wrote as follows: "My dear Hubbell. Yours of the 19th. received and contents noted. Please say to Brady [second assistant postmaster general] that I hope he will give us all the assistance possible. I think he can help effectually. Please tell me how the departments generally are doing. As ever yours, J. A. Garfield." Garfield carried both Indiana and New York and consequently won the election.

Garfield did not approve of Hayes's policy of civil service reform; in fact he characterized it as "a wretched business."

> No phase of it would stand the schoolmasterish examinations and the absurd attempt to get on without the aid of Congressmen in making selections. I believe in party government, and that the spirit and doctrines of the Republican party should prevail in the Executive departments. But I do not wish to do anything which will alienate the doctrinaires from our support.

Break with Conkling

In making up his Cabinet Garfield gave particular offense to Conkling. For the State Department he selected one of Conkling's bitter enemies, James G. Blaine. For the Treasury, after a good deal of fruitless negotiation, he appointed not a New York financier but a Westerner, William Windom of Minnesota. Conkling was displeased and disgusted but not hopelessly alienated by Garfield's Cabinet selections; he was still on speaking terms with the President, as a conference between the two men on March 20 clearly shows. Then came another appointment which brought the final break. On March 22 Garfield sent to the Senate the names of nine appointees to places in New York, all of which Conkling had approved.

But, on the very next day he sent in an additional list which made Conkling furious. The most important item in this list was the nomination of W. S. Robertson as collector of the port of New York. Robertson had defied Conkling at the Republican convention and had in consequence become one of the leaders of the "Half-Breeds." When the Senate seemed inclined to embarrass Garfield by confirming Conkling's friends and rejecting all the other names, Garfield countered suddenly by withdrawing all the nominations except Robertson's. Thereupon the two Senators from New York, Platt and Conkling, both resigned.[1]

In order to give Robertson the collectorship, Garfield had to dismiss General Merritt, an able, competent, honest official, whose term had nearly two years to run. There had been no reason to find fault with Merritt's administration of the customhouse, and there could be no pretense that Robertson would make a better collector. Vice President Arthur wrote: "Garfield has not been square, nor honorable, nor truthful with Conkling . . . [he] has broken every pledge made to us."

Star Route Frauds

Although Garfield's dealing with Conkling and the "Stalwarts" showed muddled thinking, perhaps even lack of respect for political pledges, nevertheless he could move decisively when he had to deal with actual corruption in the government. During Hayes's administration a scandal known as the Star Route frauds had developed in the Post Office Department. The postal officials were all Republicans, and some of them had been actively connected with Garfield's own electoral campaign. For some reason Hayes had remained ignorant of these activities—or indifferent to them—and the responsibility for ending the corruption fell to Garfield. He had been in office only five days when he became convinced that "there had been wilful waste of the public money and gross corruption." Because of this belief he ordered James, his new postmaster general, to conduct a searching investigation and to turn over any evidence of guilt to the Department of Justice. How Garfield could learn so much about the situation in five days while Hayes could learn nothing in two years is one of the riddles of the time.

The Star Routes were mail routes, chiefly in the West. Because of peculiar local conditions, the second assistant postmaster general was allowed to increase the contractors' compensation without letting new contracts. This arrangement enabled a corrupt official, in collusion with equally corrupt Treasury employees, to arrange for substantial payments to dishonest contractors. Taking advantage of this situation, according to the evidence presented by James, one group of contractors had secured 134 of these Star Routes. These they got by making bids below the actual cost of carrying the mail. Then with the help of Thomas W. Brady, second assistant post-

[1] After resigning from the Senate Conkling and Platt both went to Albany to urge the New York legislature to vindicate them by re-electing them. Platt's chances were killed when some of his opponents discovered evidence of a lapse of private morals on his part. Later on he was re-elected to the Senate.

master general, they were granted heavy increases. In nineteen contracts in this group Brady had increased the annual compensation from $41,145 to $448,670. It was estimated that for the total of 134 routes served by these contractors, the government had been defrauded of $5,000,000.

The individual chiefly interested in these contracts was Stephen W. Dorsey, Garfield's friend and campaign manager in Indiana. In spite of this embarrassing relationship Garfield insisted that the guilty persons be brought to trial, and attorney general McVeagh began proceedings against them. Brady, who was allowed to resign instead of being removed, tried to implicate Garfield by publishing the Hubbell letter, hoping to prove by it that Garfield knew of Brady's misdeeds. Garfield had been willing enough to levy upon the civil service employees for campaign purposes, but there is no evidence to show that when he wrote the letter he knew of Brady's dishonesty in handling Star Route contracts.

Some of this corrupt Star Route money found its way into the Republican campaign fund and so helped to elect Garfield in 1880. Dorsey himself stoutly refused to admit any moral turpitude, feeling perhaps that the cause of Republican success was sacred enough to justify these drafts upon the Treasury. One Washington newspaper, frankly admitting that the Republicans had bought their majority in Indiana, expressed interest as follows: "We have no small curiosity to see how an administration which is the result of state buying in October will proceed in May to reform the man who handled the money." The accused parties, including Brady and Dorsey, were indicted in 1882, but the first trial was inconclusive. At a second trial all offenders but one were found "not guilty as indicted."

President Arthur against the Stalwarts

Garfield had been inaugurated on March 4, 1881. Four months later he was fatally wounded by an assassin; although he lived for ten weeks after the shooting, he was incapable of attending to any public affairs. On September 19, 1881, Chester A. Arthur became President. At first the accession of this professional politician seemed little less than a national calamity. Reformers remembered him as the deposed collector of the port of New York and as the dispenser of spoils for the "Stalwarts." But President Arthur surprised his enemies and disappointed his friends. He brought to his office a combination of administrative ability, sound wisdom, and high character. His annual messages reveal an intelligent understanding of public questions, while his veto messages were able and carefully reasoned. His elevation to the presidency raised him above the range of petty jobbery which interested the politicians and which had interested him at the customhouse.

During his administration President Arthur found a surplus in the federal treasury. The problem had arisen before, during the Jackson administration. In providing for revenue Congress had never made any effort to correlate income and expenditure. The chief source of income was the tariff, but the rates were determined with an eye to protection rather than revenue. Receipts, therefore, were governed by considerations having no direct relation to a logical fiscal policy, so that there were often striking discrepancies between income and outgo. In 1880 the treasury report showed a surplus of $68,000,000; in 1881, of $100,000,000; in 1882, of $145,000,000.

Treasury Surplus

In his first annual message Arthur advised Congress to reduce revenue, partly by removing some internal revenue taxes, partly by revising the tariff. In his second annual message he referred to the matter again, warning Congress and the country of the danger of "extravagant expenditure, which, as experience has taught, is ever the bane of an overflowing treasury." Congress, however, showed more interest in spending the money than in reducing the income. There were several outlets through which money could be spent in the districts, the chief of which were appropriations for public buildings, pensions, and river and harbor improvements. During the decade before Arthur's accession the provisions for river and harbor improvements had been increasingly liberal. Standing at about $4,000,000 in 1870, the figure rose to $6,648,517 for 1875, to $9,000,000 in 1880, and to $11,450,000 in 1881. The bill for 1882 called for $18,743,875 on this account. There were appropriations in it applying to nearly 500 different places. Arthur vetoed this bill of 1882, but Congress passed the measure over his veto.

Garfield's struggle with the "Stalwarts" before and after his election had attracted nation-wide attention. Then his assassination by an insane "Stalwart" dramatized the whole issue of civil service reform and made legislative action inevitable. President Arthur was in favor of civil service reform, and in his first annual message to Congress he suggested the principles which might be embodied in law. He believed that "the rules which should be applied to the management of the public service may properly conform in the main to such as regulate the conduct of successful private business." These principles he stated as follows:

> Original appointments should be based upon ascertained fitness. The tenure of office should be stable. Positions of responsibility should, so far as practicable, be filled by the promotion of worthy and efficient officers.

Arthur questioned the feasibility of applying an educational test to all prospective appointees because such a method might "exalt mere intellectual proficiency above other qualities of equal or greater importance." At the same time, he added, if Congress should consider it advisable to adopt the scheme of competitive examinations he would sign the bill.

The Pendleton Act

In December 1882 the Senate passed the Pendleton Act for civil service reform, and the House followed early in January 1883. This measure provided for the appointment of a civil service commission of three members, not more than two of whom were to be affiliated with the same political party. These commissioners and the President were authorized to formulate rules for carrying the act into effect. These rules must provide for the testing of prospective appointees by means of competitive examinations. The law declared that no official should be obliged to make any political contributions and made it illegal for the officials themselves, and for Representatives and Senators, to solicit or receive assessments from civil servants.

The law itself placed none of the offices in the classified service; discretion in this matter was left to the President. Arthur applied the new system to three groups of subordinate employees: those in the departments at Washington, those in the larger customhouses, and those in some of the larger post offices. As a result, about 14,000 officials out of a total of 110,000, or about 12½ percent, were placed in the classified service. Succeeding Presidents made additions to the list, and by 1915 nearly 61 percent of the positions were covered by the rules. There has been no fundamental change since that time. This new arrangement relieved the President of considerable embarrassment in filling minor places. Appointment to the higher positions still remained the prerogative of the President—of course, with the consent of the Senate; these places could still be used as political rewards.

The Tariff

The third great issue of this period, ranking in importance with civil service reform and silver, was the tariff. During the Civil War the protective principle had been generously extended to compensate manufacturers for the heavy taxes which they had to pay. Once these high levels were established, advocates of tariff reform found it difficult to win congressional support for any reduction. Outside of Congress there was an increasingly insistent demand for a change, and in response to it President Arthur appointed a commission to investigate the problem. The President invited a number of prominent leaders in business and politics to serve on the commission, but all of those on his original list declined to serve; the only Republicans left were advocates of high protection. Of the nine members all were protectionists and some of them were directly connected with protected industry.

The commission submitted its report on December 4, 1882. In view of the economic interests of the members themselves, this document was a surprise. The members agreed that a reduction in tariff rates was demanded "not by a mere indiscriminate popular clamor, but by the best conservative opinion of the country." Such a reduction would be conducive to general prosperity. Thereupon the commission recommended a new tariff measure, providing for an average reduction of 20 percent, but with reductions in some cases amounting to 50 percent.

Congress refused to make even the moderate changes proposed by the commission. The Senate prepared a tariff bill, which it added as an amendment to a House measure for the reduction of internal revenue duties. The House also prepared a bill. Neither of these followed the recommendations of the commission. After some discussion, and after some sharp parliamentary practice, a tariff act was framed by a conference committee and passed. This has been described as "the mongrel bill of 1883." Many duties were raised, especially on the higher grades of woolen goods and on iron ore. Some rates were lowered, but in no instance was the principle of high protection even threatened, and the high level of duties established during the Civil War was retained. So ended the experiment with tariff reform in the Arthur administration.

Blaine for President

Like the great majority of his predecessors Arthur desired a second term, and on the strength of his record his ambition was justifiable. He would do nothing, however, to conciliate the disgruntled "Stalwarts" of New York, and he would not manipulate patronage in order to get control of the party machinery. Then there was a new factor which operated against him. By the time of the early 1880's business interests had a clear conception of their relationship with the government, and they wanted a nominee who would be well disposed toward them. Arthur had shown a moderate interest in tariff reform, but the Republican leaders wanted not tariff reform but higher rates. In the Republican convention of 1884, held in Chicago, Foraker of Ohio defined the economic creed of his party: "We not only want a man who is a pronounced Republican, thoroughly tried in the crucial tests of experience, but we want also a man whose very name will allay instead of exciting the distrust that disturbs the industrial interests of the country. . . . There is one thing in which our platform reminded us today he must not believe, and that is a substantial reduction of the duties on iron and steel and wool."

For their candidate in 1884 the Republicans nominated James G. Blaine, long known as both the beneficiary and the protector of certain railroad promoters. Just before the election Blaine gave assurance of his sympathetic consideration for the business interests of the country. At a "millionaire dinner" in New York, with 200 wealthy Republicans present, Blaine attributed the prevailing prosperity in business solely to the Republican policies: "I am sure, gentlemen, that the Republican party is not arrogant nor over-confident when it claims to itself the credit of organizing and maintaining the industrial system which gave to you and your associates in enterprise the equal and just laws which enabled you to make this marvellous progress." He referred particularly to the policies of "sound money" and the high tariff. "If these policies are to be reversed you will have to recast your accounts and review your ledgers."

Grover Cleveland

The Democrats also met in Chicago where they nominated Grover Cleveland of New York. He was known as a successful mayor of Buffalo, and later as the governor of New York, elected in a supposedly Republican state by the enormous majority of 190,000. In office he had revealed the qualities of honesty, fearlessness, and aggressiveness rather than of tact. Cleveland was nominated as a reformer and a fighter. There were other considerations fully as convincing as these. Numerous Republicans were profoundly displeased with the nomination of Blaine. They were ready to vote for any desirable Democratic nominee, particularly for Cleveland. This situation led to the "Mugwump Revolt." Such influential journals as the *New York Evening Post* and *The New York Times,* the *Springfield Republican,* and the *Nation* led the attack upon Blaine.

Sober-minded citizens observed the progress of the campaign with growing anxiety. The party platforms were not enough different to attract voters either way; as a matter of fact platforms were forgotten and principles were lost in a contest in indecency. The Democrats and their "Mugwump" allies rang the changes on the "Mulligan Letters." They talked seriously of the moral issues involved in the campaign and congratulated themselves on the obvious virtues of their own candidate.

Who spoiled the picture is not known. But some Republican dug up the story, the truth of which Cleveland frankly admitted, that ten years earlier he had become the father of an illegitimate son. Here was a lapse in private virtue to offset Blaine's irregularities in finance. The "Mugwumps" were troubled. On September 4, 1884, the *Independent,* the most influential journal among the reformers, declared that the election of Cleveland "would argue a low state of morals among the people."

Clergymen in particular pointed to Cleveland as a monster of evil. Endeavoring to weaken this attack, the Democrats enlisted the services of the Reverend Henry Ward Beecher in defense of their candidate. It so happened, however, that Beecher had only recently been involved in court proceedings on a charge of undue intimacy with the wife of one of his own parishioners. The spectacle of Beecher defending Cleveland was almost as damaging as the original revelation of Cleveland's own error. But it fell to a Republican clergyman, speaking on behalf of Blaine, to make Cleveland's election a certainty.

Burchard's Blunder

On October 29, 1884, Blaine received a delegation of clergymen at the Fifth Avenue Hotel in New York. At this gathering the Reverend Samuel D. Burchard won undying fame for himself and defeat for his candidate by observing: "We are Republicans, and don't propose to leave our party and identify ourselves with the party whose antecedents have been rum, *Romanism,* and rebellion." This tactless speech alienated hundreds of Roman Catholics in New York, voters who, ordinarily Democratic, had been prevailed upon to support Blaine. After this episode they returned to their own party. Another important factor in the New York vote was the weather on election day; it rained and the strongly Republican up-state vote was small. Again, up-state New York was Conkling's bailiwick, and he made no attempt to win support for Blaine. Cleveland won the election with a popular plurality over Blaine of 23,005 votes and with 219 electoral votes to 182 for Blaine. The Democrats were jubilant. For the first time since Buchanan's days they would have their man in the White House.

From Cleveland to Harrison

President Cleveland was interested in tariff reform, but he contributed nothing to any real understanding of the problem. His messages contain no information about the effect of the tariff on American industry. He urged Congress to change the rates in such a way that established industrial interests would be neither injured nor destroyed. Manufacturers who had built up their business under the tariff should not, he said, suddenly be deprived of its support. Then too, in revising the tariff, it was necessary to safeguard the position of the American laborer. In many ways the President's arguments might have been used by the high protectionists themselves. Cleveland found a surplus in the Treasury, and a surplus was undesirable. The principal source of federal revenue was the tariff, therefore he would reduce the tariff. Here was the gist of his argument in his annual message of 1887.

Cleveland and the Tariff

After the message the chairman of the Committee of Ways and Means, Roger Q. Mills, introduced a new tariff bill. The bill did provide for lower duties; the average level was reduced from 47 to 40 percent. But the measure was not satisfactory. The treatment of protected industries was not consistent. Industries in Democratic states were left untouched, while those in Republican states carried the burden of the reduction. Furthermore, the lower duties on some commodities would have been almost certain to result in increased imports, and thus to defeat the President's purpose of reducing revenue. But the Mills bill passed the House. The Republican majority in the Senate insisted upon the maintenance of the protective system, and they substituted a new bill for the Mills measure, which the Senate eventually adopted; neither became law, and the tariff remained unchanged until 1890. The net result of Cleveland's repeated demands for tariff reform were not economic but political. The Republican party, seeing their policy of high protection threatened, made the tariff their leading issue in the campaign of 1888.

Cleveland agreed with Arthur in opposing the congressional tendency to spend public money for local or private advantage, partly for buildings, partly for Civil War pensions. He vetoed a number of bills for federal buildings. Cleveland was even more strongly opposed to the waste of public funds in paying pensions than in erecting buildings, and his policy of economy brought him widespread unpopularity. In the past Congress had been liberal with the veterans. The general pension acts made it possible for every deserving veteran, or veteran's widow, to secure a pension. But there were thousands of aspirants to this kind of federal bounty who had no justifiable claim to it. For exceptional cases Congress fell into the habit of passing special acts to take care of those who had failed to qualify under the general laws. These private pension bills were subjected to the most superficial inspection and were passed in bundles of several hundred at a time. This legislation reeked with fraud. Private acts corrected the record of deserters to enable them to secure pensions; they gave pensions to unscrupulous reprobates who had enlisted solely to get bounties, and who had then deserted. They gave pensions to scheming women who inveigled veterans into marriage ceremonies.

Pension Frauds

For the veteran in need, afflicted with ills traceable to military service, Cleveland had abundant sympathy; for impostors and false claimants he had profound contempt. To place them on the pension rolls, side by side with men who had suffered in the war, was, he declared, an insult to every honest veteran. Cleveland felt that the veterans themselves would agree with him and would help to purge the rolls of male mendicants and female schemers. Cleveland's pension commissioner tried to drop from the rolls the names of all who had secured pensions through misrepresentation. Cleveland himself attempted to check some of the fraud at the source by vetoing those private bills which showed that the proposed beneficiary was attempting to cheat the government.

In January 1887 Congress passed the Dependent Pension Act which gave a pension to every veteran of ninety days' service or over, unable to earn his living by manual labor, no matter when or how the disability had been incurred. Cleveland vetoed the bill, arguing that it would encourage further "dishonesty and mendacity." The vote on the motion to pass the bill over the veto fell short of the necessary two thirds, so Cleveland felt that he had prevented at least one raid upon the Treasury.

Republican Tactics

As the Presidential campaign of 1888 approached, the Democrats found themselves in a comfortable position, in the sense that there was no disagreement over candidates. Cleveland was none too well liked by his party, but he had no competitor and was renominated. The Republicans nominated Benjamin Harrison of Indiana. The Republicans had carried Indiana with difficulty—and with bought votes—in 1880; they lost it in 1884. In 1888 the state was still in the doubtful column. Something more than moral suasion was needed to give Harrison the electoral votes of his own state. In October 1888 W. W. Dudley wrote from Republican headquarters in New York: "Divide the floaters into blocks of five and put a trusted man with the necessary funds in charge of these five and make him responsible that none get away and that all vote our ticket."

Throughout the contest the Republicans emphasized the necessity of maintaining the protective tariff. To bring additional odium on the policy of tariff reduction they represented it as a policy fostered by British interests. Their purpose was to detach enough Irish voters from the Democratic party to elect Harrison. In this effort the Republicans made effective use of the slow-witted British minister of the day, Sir Lionel Sackville-West. In September this diplomat received a letter from Pomona, California, dated September 4, signed C. F. Murchison. The writer said that he was an Englishman by birth but a naturalized citizen of the United States. He asked the minister which candidate, Cleveland or Harrison, would better serve the interests of Great Britain. Sir Lionel unwisely replied that he thought Cleveland's election would be the greater help to Britain. Fifteen days before the election the Republicans published this correspondence. The Murchison letter was a clever fabrication and Sir Lionel was caught off his guard, but the trick was done. Cleveland was discredited as a friend of England. Cleveland demanded the recall of the offending minister and, when that was refused, dismissed him.

The returns for the popular vote as given in various tabulations do not agree. One set gives Cleveland the larger popular vote: 5,560,329 to 5,439,853 for Harrison; another gives Cleveland 5,536,242, and Harrison 5,440,708. The electoral vote stood at 233 for Harrison, and 168 for Cleveland. Harrison carried New York and Indiana by such narrow margins that they can probably be best explained in terms of the effective use of a substantial campaign fund and of Tammany's refusal to work for Cleveland.

Tariff and Silver

When Congress met, the Republicans planned to make good their campaign pledge to raise the tariff. Thomas B. Reed of Maine, the new speaker, gave the chairmanship of the Committee of Ways and Means to William McKinley of Ohio. McKinley believed in high protection. But when the new bill was ready, western Republicans refused to vote for it until their eastern colleagues should agree to a new silver bill. Western Republicans were demanding the free and unlimited coinage of silver at the ratio of 16 to 1.

The result of this contest was the Sherman Silver Purchase Act of 1890. It did not provide for free coinage, but it required the Treasury to buy 4,500,000 ounces of silver every month—virtually the total output of the mines beyond the amount used in industry and the arts. Experience under the Bland-Allison Act proved that the people would not carry silver dollars because of their bulk. To get around this difficulty the Sherman Act provided for the issue of treasury notes against the market value of the bullion, the notes to be redeemable in gold or silver coin.

The Sherman Silver Purchase Act and the McKinley tariff went through as parts of a logrolling arrangement. The McKinley Act raised duties, in some instances high enough to make them prohibitive. Then to make sure of a reduction in revenue the framers of the bill removed the duty on raw sugar and at the same time gave a bounty of 2 cents a pound to domestic producers of sugar. The increase in duties on certain agricultural products was noteworthy, especially so in the case of barley, potatoes, and eggs.

Concerning the general character of this McKinley tariff there could be no uncertainty: it was the highest tariff act ever passed in the United States; concerning its effect one cannot be dogmatic because too little is known. Some retail dealers raised prices at once in anticipation of higher wholesale prices; others urged their customers to buy freely because of prospective rises in price. Enacted only a month before the congressional elections of 1890, the bill itself and the resulting rise in prices immediately became campaign material. At the time many voters did not want a high tariff, and they were tired of Republican leadership. Throughout the West and South the farmers had organized to secure redress of their grievances, and they proceeded to punish the party in power.

MANY of his contemporaries considered Joseph Keppler a superior cartoonist to Thomas Nast. (Left) In PUCK, May 25, 1881, Keppler satirized Roscoe Conkling's resignation from the Senate, the result of Conkling's quarrel with Garfield over federal patronage in New York. Conkling is the large balloon in process of exploding. His colleague, Thomas Collier Platt, also resigned, thereby winning imperishable fame as "Me too." Keppler shows Platt deflating without even an explosion. (Below) By 1888, two years before Congress passed the Sherman Anti-Trust Act, the American people and the reformers were seriously worried over the vast power of some new business enterprises. Keppler (PUCK, March 7, 1888) shows how the leading trusts—sugar, oil, steel, and others—were inseparably connected with the protective tariff, untouched since the Civil War. (Courtesy, New York Public Library)

THIS photograph of the first silver smelter in the United States—at Alma, Colorado—was taken in 1882. Colorado and Nevada produced most of the silver mined in the United States. (Courtesy, New-York Historical Society, New York City)

The first electric streetcars appeared in Richmond, Virginia, in 1887. The first "fleet" included cars 1 through 12. This hitherto unpublished photograph of cars 6 and 12 shows the motorman with his hands on the controls and the conductor on the rear seat. On the open car the seats were reversible, so that it was unnecessary to turn the car around at the end of the line. All electric cars had controls at both ends. (Courtesy, Sprague Collection, New York Public Library)

Chapter 33

THE CHALLENGE OF THE WEST, 1890-96

Farmers in Politics

THE contest between eastern and western Republicans over the McKinley Tariff and the Sherman Silver Purchase Act was part of a far-reaching struggle. Farming interests were making a concerted effort to wrest the control of the federal government from the business interests. This major objective lay behind the demand for free silver, and it explains the rise of the Farmers' Alliance and the Populist party. From 1890 to 1896 this "agrarian crusade," and the counterdrive of the businessmen against it, dominated American politics.

Farmers Alliance

By 1890 western farmers were becoming desperate. The great industrial development of the period was bringing wealth to the financiers and manufacturers and higher wages to urban workers. Farmers on the other hand had never recovered from the panic of 1873. In fact their situation seemed to be growing worse. They still suffered from low prices for farm products, high prices for manufactured goods, high taxes, high interest rates, and high transportation costs. The circumstances called for cooperative action. The Grange had failed to meet expectations, and a heavy decline in membership left the order weak and ineffective. The Farmers' Alliance took its place. This organization planned to "unite the farmers of the United States for their protection against class legislation, and the encroachments of concentrated capital and the tyranny of monopoly."

The Alliance protested against absentee land ownership, against the national banks, and against short selling of commodities on the exchange. The members also protested against the ownership of land by the railroads. The Alliance looked to free silver as the means of saving the farmers. As the farmers became more and more determined in voicing their complaints, professional politicians found it expedient to court their favor. The local leader who had a tie to the soil began to exploit it, and those who were lacking in such an asset joined farmers' organizations. A congressman from Texas boasted that he "became a member of the Order of Patrons of Husbandry, and took an active interest in advocating the cause of progress among his fellow laborers." One from Georgia announced that since 1886 he had "devoted his time exclusively to agricultural interests, and is a member of the Farmers' Alliance," and another from South Carolina reported himself as a "member of all the organizations in his State designed to benefit agriculture."

The Farmers' Alliance demanded free silver, and its members and friends described the Sherman Silver Purchase Act of 1890 as nothing but a fraud.

When they found prices going up under the influence of the McKinley Tariff, they turned against the Republican party. The congressional elections of 1890 became a great political revolt. All through the West the farmers gathered for political rallies in churches, schools, public halls, wherever they could find room. Among the more conspicuous leaders was a woman lawyer, Mrs. Mary Lease, famous for her advice to the farmers to raise less corn and more hell. In many places the Alliance captured the local Democratic organizations and nominated pro-farmer candidates for Congress. When the returns came in, it was found that the Republicans held 88 seats in the House, while the Democrats had 231; many of these were pledged to the Alliance. The Alliance itself sent eight representatives to Washington. Success in this contest provided abundant encouragement for these rebellious farmers. They lost no time in making plans for an even more impressive victory two years later.

Election of 1892

During the interval between the congressional elections of 1890 and the Presidential campaign of 1892 the Farmers' Alliances and the Knights of Labor met in national convention at Omaha and organized the People's Party of America. The Populists hoped to wrest control of the national government from the hands of eastern businessmen and to restore the West and South to power. The Populist platform of 1892 reveals the purposes of these crusaders. The Populists demanded government ownership of the railroads, government loans to farmers at low rates of interest, free coinage of silver at the ratio of 16 to 1, a graduated income tax, postal savings banks, government ownership of telegraph and telephone lines, shorter hours for labor, restriction of immigration, popular election of United States senators, and the initiative and referendum. For their candidate they nominated James B. Weaver of Iowa, a veteran fighter in the cause of free silver and inflation.

The Republicans professed to see little cause for alarm in this western uproar. In their platform they told the voters that "the most glorious chapter of history is the record of the Republican Party." They endorsed the principle of high protection as embodied in the McKinley Tariff and prophesied that this policy "will eventually give us control of the trade of the world." They adopted a straddle plank on the currency by demanding the use of both gold and silver as standard money. They nominated Harrison for the second time. This blindness to the major political trend cost them the election.

The Democrats denounced the Republican tariff as "a fraud, a robbery of the great majority of the American people for the benefit of the few" and as "the culminating atrocity of class legislation." They followed the Republicans, however, in refusing to advocate free silver and in calling for bimetallism. For their nominee they selected Grover Cleveland. In the election Cleveland won, with 277 electoral votes to 145 for his Republican opponent. The Populists polled more than 1,000,000 popular votes, and they secured 22 electoral votes.

The Panic of 1893

Widespread Bankruptcy

Even before Harrison left office in March 1893, signs of a new industrial and financial crisis were at hand. Ever since 1879 the Treasury had kept a surplus of $100,000,000, known as the gold reserve, for redeeming greenbacks. Harrison left this fund gravely impaired and banking interests became uneasy. In the course of a few months a major economic depression settled down upon the country. The first indication of trouble had appeared in the stock market when the Philadelphia and Reading Railroad became bankrupt. This was in February 1893. Once the crash began, it became general and far-reaching. Before the end of the year more than 570 banks had failed; by October more than 8100 commercial failures had occurred. In the course of the year 25 percent of the railroad capitalization of the country went into the hands of receivers. The production of coal and iron fell off sharply, and factories went on short time or closed entirely. In some cases there were attempts to use the unemployed in mass demonstrations of protest. The most famous instance was the march of "Coxey's army." In the spring of 1894 "General" Jacob Coxey started from Ohio for Washington, D. C., to demand federal appropriations for public works. When the "army" reached the national capital some of the officers were arrested for walking on the grass, and the great demonstration ended in failure.

Among the more important of the causes of the depression was the continuance of hard times among the farmers. American industry at the time depended largely upon the domestic market for its prosperity, so the decline of rural purchasing power was bound to affect the mills. Of all the stimuli which operate to keep business functioning at a profitable level, confidence is perhaps the most important, and several untoward developments combined to destroy confidence. It may well be that the election of a Democratic President was one of these. Another was the excessive expenditures of the federal government for public buildings, rivers and harbors, and pensions. In financial circles this waste of funds raised questions as to the ability of the Treasury to meet its obligations. This growing instability of the Treasury was accompanied by reports of world-wide financial disturbances. The Argentine Republic had already become insolvent, and it was known that European governments were trying desperately to increase their gold reserves. European investors were selling their American securities and taking gold in exchange.

"Sound Money"

President Cleveland believed that the basic cause of the depression lay in the financial and monetary policies of the federal government, so he attempted to put the nation's currency on a more solid basis. When the panic came the country had some $346,000,000 in greenbacks outstanding. Silver dollars or silver certificates in circulation amounted to $316,716,652. Although in 1894 the intrinsic value of the silver dollar had dropped to 49 cents, these so-called dollars were still exchangeable for gold at par. In addition there were the Treasury notes issued under the Sherman Purchase Act of 1890, amounting to $147,000,000. Altogether this collection of what some people called "cheap money" amounted to $809,716,652, and the holders of it had the right to present it to the Treasury and to receive gold in return. But the Treasury never kept any such amount of gold on hand. Ordinarily, as pointed out above, it tried to maintain a reserve of $100,000,000, but in 1893 the figure dropped first to $95,000,000, then to $70,000,000; by 1895 it was down to $41,000,000. In the face of this situation people who could afford it began to hoard gold.

The bankers themselves were responsible for the hoarding of gold. They realized that gold would command a substantial premium if the United States should abandon the gold standard so they prepared to profit from the change. The surest method of putting a stop to this hoarding was for the Treasury to take possession of the gold supply, but this policy was not adopted. Cleveland believed in "sound money," and he insisted that government credit must be upheld by maintaining an adequate gold reserve, by paying both interest and principal of the public debt in gold, and by ending the drain upon the Treasury. He called Congress in special session for August 1893 to repeal the Sherman Silver Purchase Act. With the help of eastern Republicans the President eventually had his way, and the repeal passed the Senate in October. But in achieving this success he nearly wrecked his party. The debate on repeal was both long and bitter. In the course of the debate a young representative from Nebraska, William Jennings Bryan by name, assumed the leadership of a free silver movement.

Economic Problems

The Gold Standard

With the Sherman Act out of the way, Cleveland next tried to replenish the gold reserve. According to law, the secretary of the treasury might sell bonds for this purpose. Two separate bond issues in 1894 brought in more than $117,000,000 in gold, but this amount was quickly exhausted. Some of the buyers of the bonds got their gold from the Treasury in the first place, thus starting what Cleveland called the endless chain. The emergency seemed to call for drastic remedies, and early in 1895, with the President's approval, the Treasury entered into an agreement with a banking syndicate headed by J. P. Morgan and Company. The bankers agreed to provide the Treasury with a specified amount of gold, at least half of which was to be procured in Europe. The agreement went through, and the bankers bought bonds with the gold. They paid the Treasury at the rate of 104½ and then sold the bonds to the public at prices ranging from 112 to 119. On this one transaction the bankers' profits amounted to more than $5,000,000. Cleveland's opponents looked upon this profit as evidence that the administration had made an unholy alliance with the hated powers of Wall Street. Why, they asked, could not the government itself have sold the bonds at the higher figure directly to investors and so taken the profit itself? They overlooked the obvious answer that ordinary investors had no gold. In the course of two years the Treasury increased the national debt by more than $262,000,000, chiefly to maintain the gold reserve and to uphold the gold standard. In trying to keep all money at par with gold the President stored up political trouble for himself and for his party.

During this same time when he was having so much difficulty with the gold reserve the President became involved in the Pullman strike in Chicago. His insistence upon the use of federal troops convinced many laborers that the President was hostile to their best interests. By 1895, therefore, Cleveland had lined up both organized labor and the organized farmers against himself.

Although the state of the Treasury made heavy demands upon Cleveland's thought and time, it was not the chief concern of his second administration. Ever since 1887 he had been hoping for tariff reform. On entering office the second time he put his friends in Congress to work on a new measure, and by December 1893, when the President submitted his annual message, the Committee of Ways and Means had a tariff bill all drawn. As first prepared this Wilson bill—named for William L. Wilson, chairman of the Committee—met with Cleveland's enthusiastic approval. Lumber, coal, iron, wool, and sugar were on the free list, and the duties on textiles were reduced. There was a provision for an income tax, something which the organized farmers had been demanding for several years. In the Senate the Wilson bill was transformed into a new measure. Over 630 amendments were made, many of them of vital importance. Coal, iron ore, and sugar were restored to the dutied list. This Wilson-Gorman Act became law without the President's signature. The income tax was retained.

Judicial Usurpation

Cases involving the constitutionality of the income tax soon came before the Supreme Court. In its first opinion the Court held that the tax on income from land was unconstitutional because it was a direct tax and consequently forbidden by the Constitution. The tax on incomes from certain types of bonds was disposed of in the same way. The Court found itself unable to agree on other types of income; at this time one Justice was ill. The case was argued over again, and the final decision in the case of *Pollock v. the Farmers' Loan and Trust Company* was handed down in May 1895. At this time the Court held that the income tax as a whole was a direct tax and therefore unconstitutional. Justice Jackson, who had been absent on the previous occasion, now upheld the tax, but one of the other judges who had originally upheld the tax changed his mind and found it unconstitutional. His vote gave the opposition a majority of one. Thus an act of Congress was set aside by the vote of one judge who changed his mind.

This decision against the income tax was one of three decisions at this time, all of which made it appear that the Supreme Court had committed itself to the protection of corporate interests. During the Harrison administration the government started proceedings against the E. R. Knight Company, a branch of the Sugar Trust. In 1895 the Court held that the

Sherman Act struck only at "combinations, contracts, and conspiracies to monopolize trade and commerce," while the defendants were concerned with the business of sugar refining. This business, in the opinion of the Court, "bore no direct relation to commerce between the States."

Later in the same year the Court handed down its decision in the Debs case, which grew out of the injunction against officials of the American Railway Union in the Pullman and railroad strike. The Court found that the issue of the injunction was justified by the Sherman Anti-Trust Act of 1890. In other words the strike was a combination in restraint of trade, and the federal government had full power to suppress such a conspiracy.

Presidential Campaign of 1896

Farmers against Business

In the meantime the Populist revolt was making more headway than ever, and enthusiasm for free silver became more vociferous. In 1894 William H. Harvey published a booklet entitled "Coin's Financial School"; because of the prevailing frenzy this bundle of economic fallacy acquired the prestige of holy writ. Almost everybody in the West read it and reread it, and familiarity with it strengthened the conviction that silver inflation was the one thing needed to restore good times. Coupled with this fervor for silver was the determination to check the power of the industrial and financial magnates of the East. If something were not done soon to bring the railroads, corporations, and banks under control, their grip on the national government would become permanent.

The executive committee of the Populist party found the issues clearly drawn:

> There are but two sides in the conflict that is being waged in this country today. On the one side are the allied hosts of monopolies, the money power, great trusts and railroad corporations, who seek the enactment of laws to benefit them and impoverish the people. On the other side are the farmers, laborers, merchants, and all others who produce wealth and bear the burdens of taxation. The one represents the wealthy and powerful classes who want the control of the Government to plunder the people. The other represents the people, contending for equality before the law, and the rights of man. Between these two there is no middle ground.

McKinley and Hanna

Such was the general background of the Presidential campaign of 1896. The Republican leaders of the East could see little in this situation except an unjustified attack upon established business principles. Their first problem was to find a candidate who was reasonably sound on the issues of business and finance and at the same time well regarded in the West. Among the available possibilities were former President Harrison, who was eminently sound on both currency and tariff; Thomas B. Reed, former speaker of the House, equally sound but undesirable because of his uncompromising conservatism; and William McKinley of Ohio, a nationally known advocate of high protection. McKinley had been somewhat unpopular after the tariff of 1890 had raised prices, but his popularity was restored after the panic of 1893. The Republicans had prophesied a panic if the Democrats should win in 1892. The Democrats did win, the panic came, and the Republicans made capital out of the sequence. Also McKinley had posed as a "bimetallist," and therefore he could stand in the West as a friend of silver and in the East as an advocate of the gold standard.

McKinley was fortunate in having the support of Marcus Alonzo Hanna, a prominent businessman of Cleveland, Ohio. Hanna believed that the primary function of government was to assist business, and he was convinced that the country needed McKinley as President. In 1895 he retired from active business to make McKinley the next Republican nominee. Being a good strategist, Hanna realized that his safest course would be to pledge a majority of delegates in advance of the convention. He began in the South. The actual Republican vote there was negligible, but southern machines still had their full delegations in the national convention. Out of a total of 906 delegates the southern Republicans contributed 244; they were hand-picked and easily controlled. Hanna had assurances that most of them would vote for his candidate.

In the meantime Hanna was directing a campaign in the press to convince the voters that there was a genuine popular demand for McKinley. The Republican papers called attention to the widespread unemployment and hard times of the preceding few years and argued that all these difficulties were due to the choice of a Democrat for President. McKinley was advertised as the "advance agent of prosperity," and workingmen were promised a "full dinner pail."

The Republican convention met at St. Louis on June 16, but as early as May 1 Hanna had enough delegates to nominate McKinley on the first ballot. McKinley received 661 votes, considerably more than the necessary majority. In their platform the Republicans called unreservedly for sound money. They opposed measures calculated to debase the currency, including of course the free coinage of silver, except by international agreement. They appealed to the veteran vote by denouncing the Cleveland administration for its policy of reducing pensions. But this enthusiastic commendation of eastern business policy was not endorsed by all Republican delegates. When the platform was adopted Senator Teller of Colorado headed thirty-four silver delegates as they seceded from the convention.

Free Silver

The Democrats met at Chicago on July 7. Once the Republicans had committed themselves to the gold standard, the Democrats were left with the choice of endorsing this stand, thereby inviting almost certain defeat, or of adopting a platform which would bring to their side the Populists and allied forces of western discontent. It was a hard choice, and for the conservative eastern delegates who still controlled the national committee it was peculiarly bitter. They would lose in any case. When the delegates assembled it was plain that the silver interests had a majority. They rejected

David B. Hill of New York, the national committee's choice for temporary chairman, and put in a silver man. Then they proceeded to settle the question of contesting delegations by seating the silver advocates. It was by this means that William Jennings Bryan of Nebraska won a place in the convention. For weeks before the convention, Bryan had been maneuvering to win the nomination for himself.

In their platform the Democrats declared themselves "unalterably opposed to monometallism, which has locked fast the prosperity of an industrial people in the paralysis of hard times." They demanded the free and unlimited coinage of silver at the ratio of 16 to 1, and they insisted that the standard silver dollar should be full legal tender. When the conservative eastern delegates submitted compromise resolutions, they were voted down. A resolution commending "the honesty, economy, courage, and fidelity of the present Democratic administration" met the same fate.

In these proceedings the convention had been characterized by the wildest excitement. The silver majority brought into the convention hall the accumulated fervor of years of agitation, and whenever the issue was clearly drawn they voted heavily against the conservatives. In the words of the Democratic but conservative *New York World:* "Lunacy having dictated the platform, it was perhaps natural that hysteria should evolve the candidate." At this juncture Bryan appeared on the platform, all set for the speech which would bring him the nomination. A few extracts may serve to give some idea of the subject matter of this speech, but they cannot begin to convey any notion of the hypnotic effect of Bryan's masterful oratory.

We stand here representing people who are the equals before the law of the largest cities in the state of Massachusetts. When you come before us and tell us that we shall disturb your business interests, we reply that you have disturbed our business interests by your course. . . .

There are two ideas of government. There are those who believe that if you just legislate to make the well-to-do prosperous, their prosperity will leak through on those below. The Democratic idea has been that if you legislate to make the masses prosperous, their prosperity will find its way up and through every class that rests upon it.

You come to us and tell us that the great cities are in favor of the gold standard. I tell you that the great cities rest upon these broad and fertile prairies. Burn down your cities and leave our farms, and your cities will spring up again as if by magic. But destroy our farms, and the grass will grow in the streets of every city in this country.

Having behind us the producing masses of this nation and the world, supported by the commercial interests, the laboring interests, and the toilers everywhere, we will answer their demand for a gold standard by saying to them: You shall not press down upon the brow of labor this crown of thorns, you shall not crucify mankind upon a cross of gold.

The speech made Bryan the undisputed leader of the silver contingent, and on the fifth ballot he received the nomination. When the Populists met for their convention, they found that Bryan and the Democrats had run away with their issues, so they gave Bryan their own nomination. Thus the western interests secured their platform and their leader, and they launched their campaign to overwhelm the business interests and "gold bugs" of the East. Bryan carried his cause directly to the people. In fourteen weeks he made four long journeys, in the course of which he visited twenty-nine states and traveled 13,000 miles. During this tour he made 600 speeches.

Campaign Methods

Mark Hanna became chairman of the Republican national committee. He established two national headquarters, one in Chicago, the other in New York. He hired a staff of 1400 speakers and sent campaigners into every doubtful district in the country. He distributed tons of campaign documents. In addition to all this he utilized the small-town and country newspapers, supplying them with all the stereotyped material they would use. Campaign emblems in the form of banners, posters, and celluloid buttons were distributed by the carload. For those who looked upon a Presidential campaign as a glorified circus, Hanna and his lieutenants arranged for mass meetings, torchlight processions, band concerts, and rallies.

Hanna considered it undesirable to send McKinley on a speaking tour in competition with Bryan; instead he arranged to bring the people to the candidate. This part of Republican strategy became known as the front porch campaign. McKinley remained quietly at his home in Canton; there he received visiting delegations from all parts of the country. Groups from various walks of life—business, manfacturing, churches, Civil War veterans, almost anybody in fact—would be organized to make the pilgrimage to Canton. The chairman of the visiting delegation would make a speech, and McKinley would reply. Both talks were duly reported in the press.

Hanna himself planned these meetings, supervised the local workers, and raised the necessary funds. Altogether he collected almost $3,500,000, the greater part of which came from New York. The financial leaders of the country were ready to spend heavily to save the country from Bryanism and free silver. There were other methods, perhaps even more effective but considerably less regular. Dealers placed orders, providing for cancellation in case the Democrats should win. Manufacturers notified their employees that the plants would close indefinitely if McKinley were defeated. McKinley received 7,111,607 votes, Bryan 6,509,052; of the electoral vote, McKinley had 271, Bryan 176. In comparison with the narrow margins in the preceding campaigns, this was an overwhelming victory.

Chapter 34

FOREIGN AFFAIRS—LATIN AMERICA, SPAIN, AND THE FAR EAST

A Dynamic Foreign Policy

CHANGING patterns in American life and lively political contests did not absorb all the attention of the people and their government. During the last quarter of the nineteenth century the United States moved far along the road toward world power. There were various factors in the development of a dynamic foreign policy. One of the most important of these was the desire for possessions overseas, a desire which ultimately brought Hawaii, Puerto Rico, and the Philippines into the hands of the United States.

During the Grant administration the United States Navy had become interested in the project of establishing a naval station at the harbor of

Samoa Pago Pago in Samoa. Although this enterprise failed to secure executive approval, Grant did go so far as to send an American commissioner to Samoa. Then there followed a melodramatic story in which representatives of the United States in Samoa became deeply involved with German trading interests. In 1877 one of the Samoan chiefs came to Washington to arrange for the carrying out of an agreement made some time before with Admiral Meade. Early in 1878 a treaty was signed, by virtue of which Samoa practically ceded the harbor of Pago Pago to the United States. During this same time Germany and Great Britain were also seeking commercial and political concessions in the islands. In 1880 the consular agents representing the three powers joined in establishing a protectorate over Samoa. Although Great Britain and the United States both refused to accord any official status to this arrangement, it became the chief factor in the government of Samoa. So the United States found itself administering a valuable port in the South Seas, and, more important still, involved in a virtual alliance with Great Britain and Germany for the purpose of governing the whole Samoan group.

By 1886 rivalry of the three powers in Samoa became serious. German agents were promoting German interests at the expense of the United States. Later, during this same summer, German representatives in Samoa made themselves practically masters of the islands, without, however, being able to quell native uprisings. In 1887 and 1888 American warships were sent to Samoa, and in 1888 Congress appropriated $500,000 to protect American interests there. At the end of Cleveland's first term war seemed almost certain. There were three German, three American, and one British warship in Apia harbor. The climax came in less than two weeks after Cleveland left office: on March 16, 1889, a hurricane destroyed the German and American ships and so ended the immediate danger of war. In Harrison's administration a conference of representatives from Great Britain, Germany, and the United States met in April 1889 at Berlin. There the delegates formulated a tripartite agreement whereby the three powers guaranteed the neutrality of the islands and established a protectorate over the Samoan government.

While this contest was going on in Samoa, other American interests were becoming increasingly concerned over the Hawaiian Islands. Hawaii was peculiarly well suited to the production of sugar, and American capital found profitable employment in the field. As the production of sugar increased, Hawaii became dependent upon the United States for a market. In 1875 the two governments signed a treaty in accordance with which the United States admitted Hawaiian sugar free of duty and the Hawaiians promised not to give their islands to any third power.

Hawaii

In January 1893 a group of Americans overthrew Queen Liliuokalani and established a provisional government. The new authorities at once sent commissioners to the United States to urge annexation, and in the meantime they asked the American minister at Honolulu to assume a protectorate over the islands in the name of the United States. He did so. Marines were landed and the United States flag raised. President Harrison approved the proposal for annexation, and at his direction the new secretary of state, John W. Foster, drew up a treaty for this purpose. But the Senate delayed action and when Cleveland re-entered office he had the treaty returned to him. This move blocked annexation for several years. On July 4, 1894, the revolutionists proclaimed the establishment of an independent Hawaiian republic. Five weeks later, much against his will, Cleveland accorded it formal recognition. In the summer of 1898 the United States annexed Hawaii.

The broader range of interest in foreign affairs was bound to include Latin America. As secretary of state under Garfield, James G. Blaine tried to formulate a vigorous Latin American policy, looking toward cooperation among the American republics. With Garfield's approval he issued invitations to all the republics of the Western Hemisphere to send delegates to a Pan-American congress. Upon Garfield's death Blaine resigned his post. His withdrawal, combined with war between Chile and Peru, delayed the congress until 1889 when, under Harrison, Blaine again became secretary of state. The invitations to the Latin American governments were renewed, and in October Blaine had the satisfaction of opening the first Pan-American congress and of presiding over its deliberations. During the interval from October 1889 to April 1890 it held seventy sessions.

Latin America

The congress devoted itself to the discussion of matters of common interest to all the Americas. It considered proposals for an American customs union and for uniform customs regulations; uniform laws covering copyrights and patents; the adoption of a uniform system of weights and meas-

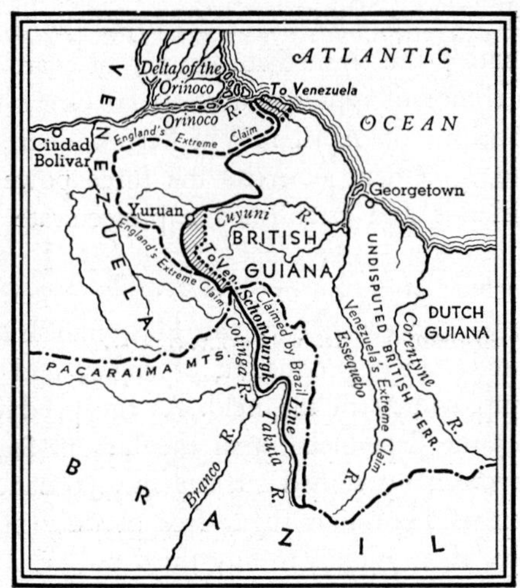

Map 15. The Venezuelan Boundary Dispute

ures; and an agreement regarding a common silver coinage. Most important of all, the congress advocated arbitration of international disputes. The specific results of the congress were negligible because the proposals were not adopted by the governments concerned. But after the meetings were over the Bureau of American Republics—now the Pan-American Union—was established in Washington.

During his second term Cleveland became involved in a dispute over the boundary of Venezuela. This controversy had started in 1814. In that year Great Britain had secured from the Dutch certain South American provinces in the vicinity of the Essequebo River, which thenceforth were known as British Guiana. Venezuela was directly west of this British colony. Between these two territorial units no precise boundary line had ever been agreed upon. Venezuela asserted a claim to all the territory west of the Essequebo River, a claim which would have deprived Great Britain of three quarters of British Guiana. Great Britain claimed the whole Essequebo basin, including the region on both sides of the Yuruari River.

Venezuela

In 1840 the British government sent Robert Schomburgk, an English engineer, to survey the boundary. He made a careful study of Dutch documents, to determine the exact limits of their holdings, and then marked out a boundary line. In proposing this line to the Venezuelans the British government based its arguments on such substantial facts as actual occupation and unimpeded holding by the Dutch. In arguing against the validity of the Schomburgk line the Venezuelan authorities could find no better evidence than mere unsupported assertions. In 1876 Venezuela attempted unsuccessfully to draw the United States into the dispute. Then the Venezuelans proposed arbitration, but the British would not agree because the Venezuelans had declined earlier offers of a settlement. In February 1887

Venezuela broke off diplomatic relations with England, accusing that government of "acts of spoliation." For the next eight years nothing was done.

In 1895 President Cleveland transferred Richard Olney from the Department of Justice to the State Department. Cleveland's second term was going badly. The administration had won for itself the bitter hatred of western and southern farmers and of laborers everywhere. It is an old trick in statecraft to divert attention from domestic ills by taking up a vigorous foreign policy. Cleveland and Olney therefore took up the Venezuela boundary dispute.

With Cleveland's approval, Olney prepared a statement of the case which the American minister, Bayard, was instructed to lay before the British government. This Olney note of July 20, 1895, still occupies a unique place in American annals. Olney protested against the enlargement of British Guiana at the expense and in defiance of Venezuela, thereby assuming, with no specific proof, that the British had already violated the Monroe Doctrine. Olney then declared, with no justification, that the Monroe Doctrine had the full status of international law. Next he proceeded to define the position of the United States:

Olney's Dictum

> The United States is practically sovereign on this continent, and its fiat is law upon the subjects to which it confines its interposition. Why? It is not because of the pure friendship or good will felt for it. It is not simply by reason of its high character as a civilized state, nor because wisdom and justice and equity are the invariable characteristics of the dealings of the United States. It is because, in addition to all other grounds, its infinite resources combined with its isolated position render it master of the situation and practically invulnerable as against any or all other powers. . . . Being entitled to resent and resist any sequestration of Venezuelan soil by Great Britain, it is necessarily entitled to know whether such sequestration has occurred or is now going on. [Unless the British government should consent to submit the entire matter to arbitration] the transaction will be regarded as injurious to the interests of the people of the United States as well as oppressive in itself. . . . The honor and welfare of this country are closely identified [with the Monroe Doctrine].

This communication can best be understood as a device for playing upon the emotions of the American people rather than as an attempt to formulate the points at issue. The assumption that England was occupying Venezuelan soil was lacking in any support except the unsubstantiated claims of Venezuela. Olney's theory that the Monroe Doctrine applied to disagreements over boundary lines was refuted by American authorities. The notion that the Doctrine was law had no basis in either history or law. And yet, President Cleveland called this Olney note "the best thing of the kind I have ever read."

Although Olney had asked for a reply before Congress convened in December, the British took their time, and the reply was not at hand. Cleveland informed Congress that the dispute between Venezuela and Great Britain had reached an acute stage and that it was necessary to make a definite statement concerning "the interest and policy of the United States." This had been done, he said, in a dispatch sent to London in the preceding July. The United States was opposed to "a forcible increase by any European power of its territorial possessions on the continent," therefore the administration was bound to protest against the extension of the area of British Guiana "in derogation of the rights and against the will of Venezuela."

Salisbury against Olney

In their belated reply the British authorities endeavored to meet Secretary Olney's contentions. Lord Salisbury denied that the Monroe Doctrine was applicable to the Venezuelan dispute. With reference to arbitration, Lord Salisbury declared that the only parties competent to decide whether or not it was "a suitable method of procedure . . . are the two parties whose rival contentions are in issue. The claim of a third nation, which is unaffected by the controversy, to impose this particular procedure on either of the two others, cannot be reasonably justified, and has no foundation in the law of nations." Lord Salisbury made it plain that the British government did not accept the Monroe Doctrine. Lord Salisbury then declared that his government was "not prepared to admit that the interests of the United States are necessarily concerned in every frontier dispute which may arise between any two of the states who possess dominions in the Western Hemisphere." He also said flatly that his government could not consent to arbitrate the British claim to any of the territory lying east of the Schomburgk line.

Secretary Olney found this British reply unsatisfactory, and President Cleveland then laid the matter before Congress. The President asked for authority to appoint a commission to investigate and report upon the matter. Upon the submission of the report it would "be the duty of the United States to resist by every means, as a willful aggression upon its rights and interests, the appropriation by Great Britain of any lands" which the investigation might show to be the property of Venezuela. "In making these recommendations I am fully alive to the responsibility incurred and keenly realize all the consequences that may follow." In other words, war with Great Britain might result from the President's policy.

The British, however, had no intention of going to war with the United States, so they agreed to arbitrate the dispute. On November 12 Secretary Olney and Sir Julian Pauncefote approved the draft of a treaty between Great Britain and Venezuela. The United States and Great Britain were each to choose two members of a tribunal of arbitration and the four so selected were to choose the fifth member. This tribunal was commissioned to determine the location of the boundary line between Venezuela and British Guiana. The tribunal handed down its award in October 1899. With two exceptions, the most important of which gave Venezuela territory at the mouth of the Orinoco River, the tribunal's findings coincided with those of Robert Schomburgk sixty years earlier. In comparison with her exaggerated claims, the territory which Venezuela received east of this line was negligible.

These various episodes, combined with plans for a larger American navy, resulted in considerable talk about an "aggressive" foreign policy. Early in 1895 Dr. Albert Shaw, editor of the *Review of Reviews,* explained that although no group or party in the United States was ambitious for conquest, "the annexation of Hawaii, the undivided control of the Nicaragua Canal, the acquisition of a strong naval station in the West Indies, and the emphatic assertion of certain principles regarding European interference in the affairs of Central and South America would form a very moderate and reasonable American policy." Dr. Shaw's magazine was widely read in the United States, and he had considerable influence upon American opinion. Several prominent members of the United States Congress went even further than Dr. Shaw.

Rebellion in Cuba

The young assistant secretary of the navy, Theodore Roosevelt, was actually belligerent. In a speech delivered at the Naval War College at Newport he extolled the martial virtues: "No triumph of peace is quite so great as the supreme triumphs of war. The courage of the soldier, the courage of the statesman who has to meet storms which can be quelled only by soldierly virtues—this stands higher than any quality called out merely in time of peace." Again, late in 1897, before the controversy between the United States and Spain had reached its final stage, Roosevelt demanded war, first in the interest of the Cubans, and "second, the benefit done to our people by giving them something to think of which isn't material gain, and especially the benefit done our military forces by trying both the Army and Navy in actual practice." The war that Roosevelt and his associates wanted actually came in 1898. The immediate occasion was a new rebellion in Cuba.

American Interests

Many Americans were interested in Cuba. Cuban producers of sugar found their market in this country. American merchants provided Cuba with flour, lumber, farm implements, and machinery for the manufacture of raw sugar. American banks and American investors furnished both credit and capital. In 1893 the combined import and export trade between the United States and Cuba amounted to more than $100,000,000. These economic connections were not responsible for American intervention in Cuba, but they help to explain American interest in news from Cuba.

By 1895 there was a sharp drop in this trade—to $65,000,000—and the Cubans found themselves in the depths of an economic depression. In part the troubles were world-wide, and all commodity prices fell. But every community felt some local or special effect of the major depression; in Cuba the sugar business almost collapsed. The drop in prices and the reduction in demand by themselves would have been enough to cause hardships. In

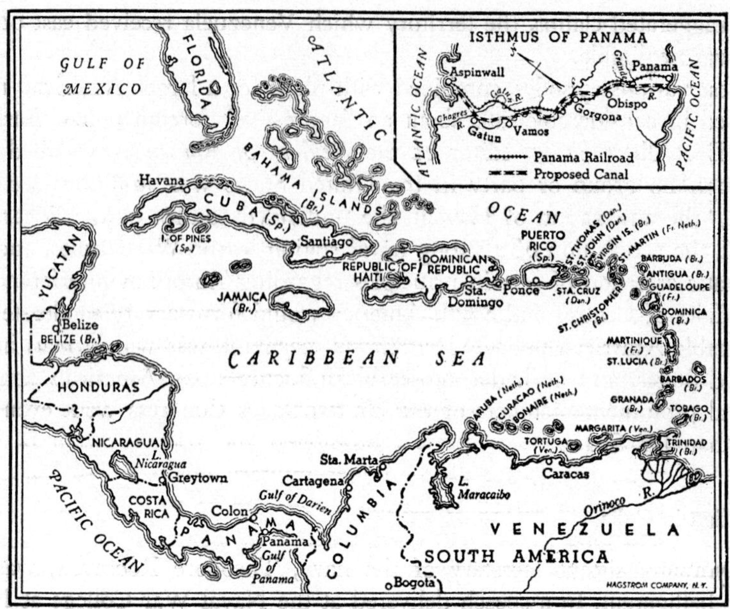

Map 16. Cuba and Puerto Rico

addition to these adverse factors Cubans had to adjust themselves to a change in the American tariff. The Wilson-Gorman Act of 1894 imposed a duty of 40 percent on raw sugar. Then the Spanish authorities retaliated with new duties on goods coming into Cuba from the United States. In 1895 sugar planters temporarily discontinued operations and discharged their employees. In this year Cuban rebels renewed their struggle for independence, and the ranks of the unemployed furnished recruits for the Cuban army.

Almost at the start the rebellion made news. On March 8, 1895, a steamship under American registry, the *Alliança,* was fired upon by a Spanish gunboat off the coast of Cuba. Although the captain of the *Alliança* seems to have been at fault, American newspapers described the affair as a deliberate attack upon the American flag. At the very beginning therefore the Spaniards were represented as hostile to this country. Once the American people came to believe that Spain was wrong, they were even more strongly convinced that the Cuban rebels were right.

In September 1895 the Cuban rebels acquired a new ally. In that month William Randolph Hearst made his debut in the newspaper field of New York. Hearst's forte was sensationalism, and he aimed to fill his readers with burning convictions of Cuban virtue and Spanish depravity. If the news suited his purpose, he used it; if the actual reports needed embroidery to make them more vivid, he supplied the trimmings; if there was no news he permitted—some say he ordered—his reporters to manufacture stories out of nothing but their own vivid imaginations.

Planned Starvation

The rebellion soon developed into two rival policies of devastation. Even before the outbreak of war pillaging and banditry had been prevalent on the island. The revolutionists planned to finish what the depression had begun. General Gomez announced that he would disorganize the economic life of Cuba. His men burned sugar cane fields in order to drive the people into the towns, which he planned to starve by cutting off supplies. He warned all persons not to travel on the railroad and threatened them with destruction in case they ignored his command.

In order to counteract these measures the Spanish authorities adopted a similar policy. Early in 1896 General Valeriano Weyler took command, proclaimed martial law, and threatened severe punishment for all who might be caught destroying property. In October 1897 he proclaimed a policy of reconcentration, requiring all people in the rural areas to move into the fortified towns. Then he prohibited the transportation of provisions from place to place except under military guard. These two programs of devastation served to complete the ruin of Cuban economic activity. Between 1894 and 1896 the sugar crop fell from 1,050,000 to 200,000 tons annually and the production of tobacco from 450,000 bales to 50,000.

American newspapers ignored the acts of devastation committed by the rebels but they promptly nicknamed Weyler "the Butcher," and complained bitterly over his uncivilized methods of warfare. Additional grounds for complaint came when his concentration camps developed into hotbeds of disease. Then, when the papers learned that hundreds of American citizens were impounded in these camps, the outcry against Spain was redoubled in intensity. The papers did not explain that these Americans were of Cuban origin.

Spanish-American Diplomacy

The authorities at Washington soon found themselves confronted with a tangle of problems. Cuban sympathizers in this country tried to organize filibustering expeditions to help the rebels. Out of a total of seventy-one such ventures, twenty-seven contrived to avoid all obstacles and to effect a landing in Cuba. American officials stopped thirty-three before they could leave port, while storms and the Spaniards accounted for the others. The government of the United States was meticulously correct in its official attitude.

President Cleveland stubbornly resisted efforts designed to bring about American intervention in Cuba, but he would have been glad to see the Spaniards make an effort to improve conditions there. In 1896 he offered his services in the interest of a settlement of existing difficulties. He suggested reforms in the system of Cuban government and complete autonomy for the Cubans in all domestic affairs. The Spanish authorities curtly informed him that Cuba already enjoyed "one of the most liberal political systems in the world." Spanish refusal even to discuss possible arrangements for a settlement prevented the President from continuing his efforts.

When William McKinley became President in 1897 the demand for American intervention in Cuba was well developed. The new President, however, did not share the belief of many of his political associates that the dictates of humanity required the United States to go to war. On the contrary he made an effort to settle the Cuban troubles by diplomacy. In June 1897 the State Department sent to Madrid a formal protest against the Spanish policy in Cuba and a demand that the war be brought to an end. The note made it plain that if the Spanish officials could not restore peace and order intervention by the United States would become inevitable.

Before the summer of 1897 was over developments in Spain gave new hope to McKinley. The conservative premier, Señor Canovas, was assassinated, and a liberal ministry under the leadership of Sagasta came into power. Sagasta removed General Weyler from his command and announced a policy of autonomy for Cuba. General Blanco, Weyler's successor, promised to put an end to the concentration system. McKinley then urged Congress to give the new Spanish regime time enough to make its policy effective.

Unfortunately conditions in Cuba did not improve. The rebels denounced the offer of autonomy, and their generals declared that anybody who proposed it would be shot. They wanted independence, and they would not consider anything short of this until all hopes of American intervention had disappeared. Cuban conservatives also vehemently opposed autonomy because it would leave them at the mercy of the revolutionists. They preferred Spanish rule to local firing squads.

Demands for Intervention

As for the war party in the United States, one of its most belligerent leaders was the assistant secretary of the navy, Theodore Roosevelt. He was determined not to miss a war if he could help it, and he believed—rightly as the event proved—that he and his kindred spirits could break down McKinley's resistance. In September 1897 Roosevelt wrote Senator Lodge about a recent conversation with the President: "I gave him a paper showing exactly where all our ships are, and I also sketched in outline what I thought ought to be done if things looked at all menacing about Spain, urging the necessity of taking an immediate and prompt initiative if we wished to avoid the chance of some serious trouble, and of the Japs chipping in." Roosevelt also gave McKinley full instructions as to the proper stations for the units of the fleet, and then added: "Meanwhile, our Asiatic squadron should blockade, and if possible take, Manila." Here was a new but important development in connection with this proposed war to free the oppressed Cubans; imperialists could make the war serve as an excuse for seizing territory on the other side of the globe. To make sure that this Oriental enterprise would be properly handled, Roosevelt wished to have Commodore George Dewey appointed to the command of the Asiatic squadron. Dewey got the assignment and early in December 1897 sailed for the Far East. On February 17 he arrived at Hong Kong.

By January 1898 the American attitude toward the Cuban problem was clearly defined. The new Spanish policy of autonomous government for Cuba was a failure from the start because it had so few supporters in Cuba.

In the United States there was a widespread conviction that Spain was incapable of ending the conflict in Cuba and that the Cubans needed American help. The more extreme newspapers like the *New York Journal* and the *Chicago Tribune* were loud in their demands for intervention. Sober-minded editors condemned the sensationalism of these dailies, but even the conservatives became convinced that the United States must intervene. They put it on the ground of high moral obligation. President McKinley, Speaker Reed, Secretary Long of the Navy Department, and other prominent Republican leaders believed that Spanish power over Cuba could be ended by diplomacy. Most of the press disagreed with the President and held that war alone would drive Spain out of Cuba.

In January 1898 also Spanish loyalists in Havana broke out in armed demonstrations against the officials of the recently installed autonomous government. This uprising revealed still further the weakness of the Spanish authorities and also called attention to the danger to Americans residing in Havana. The United States government sent the battleship *Maine* to Havana, partly to protect American interests, partly as a warning to Spain. The tense situation was getting worse. Then in February 1898 two episodes occurred which made war inevitable.

Spanish-American War

On February 9 the *New York Evening Journal* published a letter written two months earlier by Señor Dupuy De Lôme, the Spanish minister to the United States. The Spanish diplomat described McKinley as "weak and a bidder for the admiration of the crowd, besides being a common politician who tries to leave a door open behind himself while keeping on good terms with the jingoes of his own party." The letter was a private communication to a friend in Havana, and it had not been designed for publication. Furthermore it had been stolen. The unhappy minister cabled his resignation to Madrid before the State Department could demand his recall, but the damage was done. Newspaper readers were convinced that the uncomplimentary reference to McKinley revealed a deep-seated hatred of the United States, and they assumed that this hatred was universal among the Spanish people.

De Lôme Letter

Less than a week later, while the people were still excitedly talking about the De Lôme letter, a violent explosion sent the American battleship *Maine* to the bottom of Havana harbor. The explosion occurred shortly before ten o'clock in the evening, and it resulted in the death of two officers and 264 members of the crew. The city of Havana went into mourning. Theaters and places of business were closed, flags were hung at half mast, and prominent citizens were prompt and earnest in their expressions of regret and sympathy. On February 17 the victims were given the honors of a public official funeral. To the war party in the United States these protestations were taken as evidence of nothing but base hypocrisy. Americans generally

Remember the "Maine"

jumped to the conclusion that the Spaniards had purposely destroyed the battleship, and "Remember the *Maine*" became the slogan of the day.

The Navy Department appointed a court of inquiry to investigate the disaster. Although the members of this official body were supposed to give out no information, and although every effort was made to keep the report secret until the President should submit it to Congress, the press kept the public fully informed of the progress of the investigation. The report went to Congress on March 28, 1898, but every newspaper reader knew in advance what the findings would be. The court of inquiry declared that the destruction of the *Maine* was not due to negligence of officers or crew. The disaster was due to the explosion of a submarine mine, which bent the bottom plates of the ship inward and upward. Following the external explosion, two of the forward magazines within the ship blew up.

Since that time no additional information has come to light. In 1911 the Navy Department raised the hulk for further examination, but nothing of importance was discovered. To this day no one in the United States knows who was responsible for the explosion. Cuban insurgents had the only rational motive for doing it in order to bring about intervention in their cause, but it is impossible to explain how they could have contrived the explosion. Spanish officials, on the other hand, had no rational motive for plunging their country into war with the United States, but there was abundant evidence of irrational hatred of the United States among some of the younger Spanish loyalists in Havana. Circumstantial evidence pointed then, and it still points, to subordinate Spanish officers.

Was War Necessary?

In spite of McKinley's own desire for peace, the administration was being pushed toward war. Early in March, following an important conference at the White House, Representative Cannon of Illinois, chairman of the House Committee on Appropriations, introduced a bill providing $50,000,000 for defense. On March 18 Senator Proctor of Vermont made a speech in which he described Cuba as he had seen it on a recent visit. Senator Proctor was conservative in outlook, restrained in manner, not given to emotional display. His speech, given simply and quietly with no attempt at oratorical fervor, made a nation-wide impression. It tended to clinch the conviction that the United States must drive Spain out of Cuba.

On March 27, 1898, the State Department sent an ultimatum to Madrid, demanding an immediate amnesty, the end of the concentration policy, and a promise that, if the Spanish government should be unable to come to satisfactory terms with the insurgents by the following October 1, President McKinley should be recognized as the arbiter between the opposing forces in Cuba. These demands put the Spanish cabinet in a difficult dilemma. Refusal to accede to the President's terms would mean certain war with the United States; on the other hand, acceptance of the demands would almost certainly precipitate a revolution at home. In these circumstances the safest course was to play for time. Concessions therefore came grudgingly and slowly. First came the promise to abandon the concentration camps and next the offer of an armistice. Then the Spanish government guaranteed an amnesty to the rebels. After several more efforts to stave off the inevitable, the Spaniards gave in. On April 10 Woodford, the American minister at Madrid, cabled that in his opinion Spain was prepared to settle the Cuban problem by creating an autonomous government or by granting complete independence or by ceding the island to the United States. Assuming that the Spanish authorities had spoken in good faith—an assumption which had little to support it—McKinley's negotiations had resulted in a brilliant diplomatic victory.

McKinley had won a victory over the Spanish government, but he had not won the American press. The papers became more and more bitter over the President's procrastination. Conservative editors who, with McKinley, believed that Spain would before long give the United States full powers in Cuba were howled down. Each additional step toward a settlement by diplomacy was characterized as one more manifestation of McKinley's lack of courage. When Senator Stephen B. Elkins issued a statement expressing approval of peace, the *Chicago Tribune* came out with the heading: "Elkins a Poltroon," and in its editorial comment the paper declared that the Senator's statement "stinks with foulblooded indifference to the honor, dignity, and manhood of his country."

When the administration failed to recommend war immediately after the publication of the report on the *Maine*, prominent congressmen began to introduce declarations of war. The more belligerent members held special caucus meetings and threatened to repudiate both Speaker Reed and President McKinley. The *Chicago Tribune's* Washington correspondent reported that "there is a raging torrent of indignation pouring from the Capitol." Congress reflected the bulk of opinion throughout the country. The American people were going to have war, and if the President should stand in their way they would repudiate him. McKinley's only course was to yield.

Declaration of War

On April 11 he sent his war message to Congress. He justified his request for authority to intervene in Cuba on the ground that the disorder and violence on the island were a constant menace to the peace of the United States. The President referred to the destruction of the *Maine* as "a patent and impressive proof of a state of things in Cuba that is intolerable." The only hope of relief lay in what he called the "enforced pacification" of Cuba. "In American interests which give us the right and the duty to speak and to act, the war in Cuba must stop." He concluded with a request for authority to intervene.

On receipt of the President's message both houses of Congress plunged into a week's debate, not on the issue of war or peace but on the wording of the formula of the declaration. The House proposed to empower McKinley to intervene for the purpose of securing peace and establishing a stable and independent government on the island. The Senate talked in terms of independence for the Cubans. Then Senator Teller offered a resolution declaring that the United States had no intention of exercising dominion over

Cuba but was interested only in securing independence for the people. The vote on the resolution was 311 to 6 in the House and 42 to 35 in the Senate. The people and the press had their way. McKinley and his associates always felt that the war was unnecessary. After the close of the war Secretary Long summed up their attitude: "I honestly believe that if the country and Congress had been content to leave the matter in his [McKinley's] hands, independence would have come without a drop of bloodshed, as naturally as an apple falls from a tree."

Military Preparation

When the war began the regular army of the United States consisted of 28,183 officers and enlisted men. The various detachments of this force were scattered over the country in small posts, for the most part in the West. Only veterans of the Civil War had ever seen more than one regiment in one place. In addition there were the state militia forces, numbering approximately 100,000, but they were of little immediate value. Many of these state soldiers were poorly drilled, and they lacked essential supplies. Many of the officers were as innocent of any knowledge of the art of war as the men.

General Miles, who commanded the United States army, urged that the whole force be assembled at Chickamauga Park, near Chattanooga, where the men could be properly equipped, drilled, and instructed. Furthermore, General Miles warned of the danger of a campaign in Cuba before October, partly because of yellow fever, and partly because of the large Spanish army on the island. But these plans for beginning active operations six months after war was declared were abruptly changed on receipt of inspiring news from the opposite side of the world. On May 1 Commodore Dewey had sailed into Manila Bay and destroyed the Spanish fleet there. On the very next day the newspapers reported that President McKinley "has determined that the fighting shall be vigorously enforced. . . . The bugbear of the yellow fever scourge is to be ignored, and the Spaniards are to be ejected from Cuba before midsummer if American soldiers can drive them out." On May 8 the President ordered the army to proceed to Cuba and capture Havana.

When the War Department called for volunteers, more than a million men responded. Among them was the erstwhile assistant secretary of the navy, Theodore Roosevelt. He resigned in May and accepted a commission as lieutenant-colonel of a regiment of volunteer cavalry. The colonel was Leonard Wood. The regiment was composed of widely different types of Roosevelt's friends: aristocratic members of the Harvard Club in New York and cowpunchers and outlaws from the West. The colonel of this outfit—popularly known as the "Rough Riders"—had acquired some familiarity with army life, but only as a member of the medical corps; the lieutenant-colonel was a complete novice with only four days of training with his troops.

At the mobilization camps for the national guard and the volunteers there was serious confusion and inefficiency. If possible, there was even more bewilderment at Tampa, the port of embarkation for Cuba. General Shafter—sixty-three years of age, over 300 pounds in weight—who had been selected to lead the invasion of Cuba, wrote that the volunteer regiments were coming into Tampa without blankets, tents, camp equipment, and in some cases without uniforms, in others without arms. Roosevelt and the Rough Riders reached Tampa early in June, and the lieutenant-colonel wrote to his friend Senator Lodge of conditions there. The inadequate transportation facilities were so badly jammed that it took twelve hours for the regiment to move nine miles. Supplies of all kinds were accumulating, with no one in a position to know where they were to be stored or how they might be distributed.

Cuban Campaign

On June 14 the first transports left Tampa for Cuba, carrying 16,000 men and eighty-nine newspaper correspondents. On June 22-23 they landed on the southern coast of Cuba not far from Santiago. The American forces set out to capture the hills which protected the city, and on July 1 they were successful. According to the records of the War Department, San Juan Hill, the key position, was captured by an infantry regiment of the regular army under command of Colonel Hawkins. Hawkins still remains unknown to fame, but the newspapers hailed Roosevelt as the "hero of San Juan Hill." In the meantime the Spanish fleet, which had put into Santiago harbor in May, attempted to escape. The ships came out on the morning of July 3, and the American naval force destroyed them all. With the fleet gone and American forces in command of all approaches to the city on land, the Spanish commander could do nothing but surrender, and terms of his capitulation were signed on July 16.

Even before the end of the campaign in Cuba the summer rains had begun, overland transportation had become almost impossible, and American troops were afflicted with malaria; worse yet, there was a prospect of an outbreak of the dreaded yellow fever. The situation was so dangerous that General Shafter begged Secretary Alger to move the troops to a more healthful location. On August 3, 1898, Alger sent word to transfer the army to Montauk Point, Long Island. On the same day Theodore Roosevelt told his fellow officers that the only way to be sure of action was to make a stir in the newspapers, so he prepared a letter for publication. The general officers also gave out a letter for the press, declaring that American forces were incapacitated with malaria and that yellow fever could not be avoided. These distressing reports appeared in the papers and so informed the American public—to say nothing of the enemy—that the army was helpless. The papers also conveyed the impression that Roosevelt had saved the troops from destruction by forcing Alger to transfer them to Long Island. The record shows that he did nothing of the kind.

When the war started, the prevailing opinion was that its purpose was to free the suffering Cubans from Spanish tyranny. But the dispatch of Commodore Dewey to the Far East seemed to have little if any relation to this alleged objective; some persons had more ambitious ends in mind.

Henry Cabot Lodge was one of these large-minded Americans. Writing to Roosevelt in May, before the invasion of Cuba, Lodge explained:

The Philippines

> The one point where haste is needed is the Philippines, and I think I can say to you, in confidence but in absolute certainty, that the administration is grasping the whole policy at last. Porto Rico is not forgotten and we mean to have it. Unless I am utterly and profoundly mistaken the administration is now fully committed to the large policy that we both desire.

The day after Lodge wrote to Roosevelt, the newspapers announced that the administration had decided to seize Puerto Rico and the Philippines. These territories "had come to be looked on as an essential recompense to the United States for its expensive intervention." As early as May 9 the *Chicago Tribune* advocated the policy of keeping the whole Philippine group.

The sudden termination of hostilities in Cuba threatened to deprive some parts of the American army of any chance for glory, so the officers worked rapidly in their plans for seizing Puerto Rico. On July 21 General Miles landed there, and by the time the armistice was signed he had completed the conquest. In the Philippines the situation was considerably more complicated. In 1896 some of the inhabitants, under the leadership of Aguinaldo, had risen in rebellion against Spain. This struggle came to an end in December 1897 when the Spanish officials promised to pay Aguinaldo $800,000 if he would make peace and leave the islands. Actually they paid him only half the promised amount, and they ignored their promises to introduce reforms in the government. This violation of the terms of peace gave Aguinaldo an excuse for resuming his rebellion. In April 1898 the American consul at Singapore had a conference with Aguinaldo, following which the Filipino leader prepared to renew his war for independence. On May 24 he issued a formal proclamation promising independence to the Filipinos. By the time American reinforcements reached the Philippines, Aguinaldo became "aggressive and even threatening toward our army."

While Aguinaldo was showing increasing resentment toward the United States, Spanish army officers were not only friendly but cordially cooperative. In fact, they even agreed to help the Americans by keeping the insurgent forces out of Manila. On August 12, the Spaniards surrendered to General Merritt, but the Filipino rebels were not allowed to enter the city.

Peace and the Dependencies

Treaty of Paris

On August 12, at Washington, representatives of France acting in behalf of Spain and of the United States signed the preliminary terms of peace. These provided that Spain should surrender all claims to Cuba and that she should cede Puerto Rico to the United States. Concerning the Philippines the two governments agreed that the United States should occupy and hold "the city, bay, and harbor of Manila pending the conclusion of a treaty of peace which shall determine the control, disposition, and government of the Philippines." It was arranged to have commissioners from the two governments meet at Paris to draw up the final terms. For this work President McKinley appointed Secretary of State William R. Day, Senators Davis and Frye, Republicans, and Senator Gray, Democrat, together with Whitelaw Reid, of the New York *Tribune*. They began work on October 1.

The real problem at Paris was what to do with the Philippines. Concerning Cuba and Puerto Rico the official mind was made up; the first would become independent, and the second would become a dependency of the United States. But President McKinley found it difficult to convince himself that the Philippines were in the same category with Puerto Rico, and until he arrived at a decision no specific instructions could be drawn for the American commissioners. Lodge and the imperialists, however, had no doubts on the subject, and their point of view found adequate and abundant expression in the press. Not only the rabidly pro-war papers such as the *Chicago Tribune* but conservative religious journals like the *Congregationalist* of Boston approved the policy of keeping all the Philippines.

In the first instructions to the American delegation, drawn by Secretary Day with McKinley's approval, the commissioners were directed to keep in mind the purpose and spirit which had led the country into war. This was not territorial aggrandizement but "obedience to the dictates of humanity." Then the document went on to explain that although the United States had gone into the war

> . . . without any original thought of complete or even partial acquisition, the presence and success of our arms at Manila imposes upon us obligations which we cannot disregard. . . . We cannot be unmindful that, without any desire or design on our part, the war has brought us new duties and responsibilities which we must meet and discharge as becomes a great nation on whose growth and career from the beginning the Ruler of Nations has plainly written the high command and pledge of civilization. Incidental to our tenure in the Philippines is the commercial opportunity to which American statesmanship cannot be indifferent. It is just to use every legitimate means for the enlargement of American trade.

In October 1898 the President made a speaking tour through the Middle West in the course of which he became convinced that the American people really wanted the Philippines. Subsequently he explained that he asked both Republican and Democratic political leaders for light on the subject and got none, whereupon he prayed for divine guidance. This came promptly. God told him, so he said, that the United States could not give the Philippines back to Spain. The islands could not be turned over to any European power or to Japan because such a course, in view of the delicately balanced situation in the Orient, would precipitate grave international complications. The Filipinos themselves were not capable of self-government. Obviously, therefore, there was only one thing for the United States to do and that was to keep the whole archipelago. On October 26 the State Department at Washington sent word to this effect to the commissioners at Paris. The State Department authorized its agents to offer Spain a substantial sum of money, and the commissioners tendered $20,000,000. The Spanish agents accepted, and on December 10, 1898, the treaty of peace was signed. The United States consequently became the owner of Puerto Rico, the Philippines, and the island of Guam.

After the treaty was signed there still remained one obstacle to the fulfillment of imperialist ambitions. Democrats in the Senate effected a working agreement with some anti-imperialist Republicans, among whom Lodge's colleague Senator Hoar was conspicuous, and for a time it looked as though this combination might prevent ratification of the treaty. But the fears of the imperialists were quieted when, on February 6, 1899, the Senate ratified, but with only a single vote to spare.

Freedom for Cuba

Even before the war was officially finished, President McKinley and his advisers took charge of the new dependencies. By force of circumstances the War Department at Washington assumed the duties of a colonial office, operating directly under the President. On January 1, 1899, the Spanish authorities turned Cuba over to the United States. Shortly before that date President McKinley had appointed Major General John R. Brooke to the command of the American forces there. The Cubans were in dire need of immediate help. Economic life had been interrupted almost everywhere, and in some sections it had practically died out. The combination of lawlessness, poverty, and disease was responsible for widespread suffering. The first task of the United States therefore was to make the island a fit place to live in and to restore the people to such a condition of strength, health, and moral responsibility that they could look after their own affairs. So the army fed the starving, cared for the sick, introduced some of the attributes of sanitation, and in general performed the functions of a regular government. In the course of this process of making the island safe for the habitation of civilized human beings, Major Walter Reed made his significant discovery that yellow fever was not transmitted directly from person to person and that one particular type of mosquito was the guilty agent.

Thanks to this assistance rendered by the army, the Cubans were able to resume work on their plantations and to pick up the broken threads of commerce. New roads and schools were built, public buildings repaired and improved, and the orderly routine of civilized living was gradually restored. Before the work was finished General Leonard Wood succeeded General Brooke; like his predecessor he established an enviable record as an administrator. In the course of two years reconstruction had been carried far enough so that the United States could prepare to withdraw. In November 1900, under General Wood's direction, the Cuban voters elected delegates to a constitutional convention. This body drafted a constitution for the republic of Cuba. But the authorities at Washington had no intention of permitting the new government to exercise its authority to the detriment of the United States. McKinley's secretary of war, Elihu Root, explained that the United States would "require from the Cubans guarantees for the conduct of their government" sufficient "to prevent the island from falling into the hands of any other nation so that the United States would not be placed in a worse position than before by reason of turning Spain out of the island." In the furtherance of this policy of putting the republic under leading strings, the Congress of the United States adopted a set of regulations, and the War Department compelled the Cuban constitutional convention to incorporate these resolutions in the new frame of government.

These provisions—known collectively as the Platt Amendment because they first appeared officially as an amendment to the army appropriation bill of 1901—defined the relationship between Cuba and the United States. In brief, they prohibited the Cubans from bartering away their independence and from incurring any debt large enough to lead to complications with foreign powers. The Cubans were also required to continue the system of sanitation which had already been installed in their cities. They were to grant the United States harbor facilities for naval and coaling stations, and they were to permit the United States to intervene, forcibly if necessary, in order to maintain an efficient, independent government. Considerably against their will, the Cubans accepted the Platt Amendment unconditionally. Then, after their new government was in operation, they were required to embody the same provisions in a treaty with the United States. The amendment remained in effect until 1934.

A Colonial System

The status of Puerto Rico was entirely different from that of Cuba. In wresting this island from Spain the United States had no thought of giving the people independence. From the beginning the imperialists planned to keep it as a colonial dependency of the United States. In October 1898 the American army took possession and held the place as a conquered province. After the army had administered Puerto Rico for a year and a half, Congress worked out a system of civil government. This Foraker Act of April 1900 described the Puerto Rican people as citizens not of the United States but of Puerto Rico "and as such entitled to the protection of the United States." They were to have a governor and an executive council of eleven members, all to be appointed by the President of the United States, subject to approval by the Senate. At least five members of this council were to be Puerto Ricans. Practically all administrative authority was centered in the governor and council. Then there was to be an elective assembly of thirty-five members chosen by the Puerto Rican voters. The council and the assembly made up the legislature. Statutes enacted by this body were subject to annulment by the Congress of the United States.

The newly created government was an almost exact duplicate of the system in operation in the British North American royal colonies of the seventeenth and eighteenth centuries. In 1917 Congress passed a new measure, the Jones Act, which made the inhabitants of Puerto Rico citizens of the United States. This law also provided for an elective upper house in place of the one formerly appointed by the President. But the appointment of the governor still remained the prerogative of the President.

In Puerto Rico the transition from Spanish to American control was effected with a minimum of inconvenience and with no disorder. The Philippines, on the other hand, proved far more difficult to administer. The islands supported a population of more than 7,000,000, ranging in color from black through brown and yellow to white. But the white contingent was small, numbering not more than 15,000. The majority of the natives were supposedly Christian in religion, but there were some Mohammedans; also various forms of Oriental heathenism still flourished there. In some islands of the group the level of civilization was primitively low. Geographically the group consisted of more than 3000 islands, most of which were small. Of the nine largest each measured 10,000 or more square miles. Luzon, the largest, was nearly 41,000 square miles in area.

Philippine Dependency

With the surrender of Manila by the Spaniards and the beginning of peace negotiations between the United States and Spain, Aguinaldo became threatening. By the end of December 1898, according to General Otis, the insurgents were in full possession of every position of importance in the Philippines except the city of Manila. Furthermore Aguinaldo publicly announced his intention of attacking the American forces. He tried subsequently to recall this indiscreet boast, but in doing so he issued a formal protest against the "intrusion of the United States government on the sovereignty of these islands." In the meantime McKinley had instructed Otis to occupy the strategic positions in the islands; Otis answered that any attempt to do so would precipitate immediate war. McKinley in turn sent word that he did not want war with the insurgents.

The choice between war and peace did not rest with the President of the United States unless he should withdraw the American troops. On the evening of February 4, 1899, four Filipino soldiers approached an outpost near Manila and refused to obey the sentry's order to halt. The sentry opened fire, and his action immediately brought a return fire from a Filipino detachment. This exchange of shots began a general engagement in which both sides lost heavily. So began the war for the conquest of the Filipinos, a struggle which was not finished until April 1902. In the summer of 1900 the Filipino army was virtually broken up, and in the following winter Aguinaldo was captured. For the remaining part of the struggle the Filipinos carried on intermittent guerilla warfare.

Even before the outbreak of the war President McKinley had begun to prepare for the establishment of civil government in the Philippines. Early in 1899 he appointed a commission of five members to investigate and report on the problem. McKinley's first Philippine commission concluded that the Filipinos were not ready for self-government. A second commission, officially appointed April 7, 1900, went out to take actual charge of the Filipino government. This body, with William Howard Taft as chairman, included Dean C. Worcester, Luke I. Wright, Henry C. Ide, and Bernard Moses. It

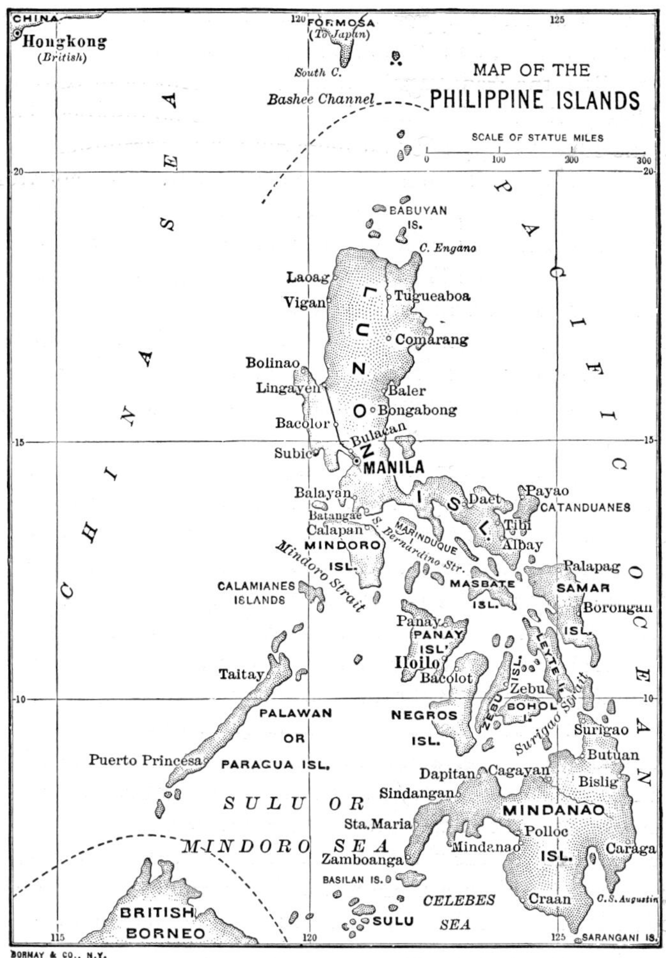

Map 17. The Philippine Islands

was to cooperate with the military governor and both were under the direction of Elihu Root, secretary of war. According to their instructions, drawn by Secretary Root, they would begin to organize local government in the country districts and in the towns and then proceed to the establishment of the larger administrative units in the provinces. Until conditions should warrant further changes, the central government would consist of the military governor as executive head, with the commission as a legislative body and advisory council.

As was the case in Cuba, the President's authority to govern the islands was originally derived from his position as commander in chief of the army. Congress confirmed him in his new power. Acting under this power McKinley and Taft proceeded as rapidly as circumstances would permit to substitute civil for military rule in the Philippines. In June 1901 the President directed Taft to take over the executive authority hitherto exercised by the military officials, except in those regions still in rebellion. On July 4, 1901, Taft was formally inaugurated as the first American civil governor of the Philippines.

After Taft's inauguration Congress passed a law providing for a regular system of colonial government for the islands. This measure went into effect on July 1, 1902. It provided for the offices of governor, vice governor, and four heads of departments, all to be appointed by the President with the advice and consent of the Senate. This section put an end to the uncontrolled authority of the President over the administration of the islands. Following the precedent set in the act for Puerto Rico, the inhabitants of the Philippines were declared citizens of the Philippine Islands; as such they were entitled to the protection of the United States. Provision was next made for the creation of a legislature. The Philippine Commission became the upper house; the lower was elected by the Filipino voters. The first election was held on July 30, 1907, and in the following October representative government was put in operation. But it was a significant if not a disquieting fact that the party of independence, or the Philippine nationalists, won a majority of seats in the lower house.

Hawaii

The acquisition of the Philippines furnished new arguments for annexing Hawaii, and so helped bring to a conclusion the work which Cleveland had interrupted when he withdrew the treaty of annexation in 1893. McKinley approved of Harrison's policy; as early as June 1897 he had a new treaty ready for submission to the Senate. But the opponents of annexation were still numerous, and in 1898, when the prospect of securing a favorable two-thirds vote upon the treaty proved hopeless, the administration changed its tactics and followed the precedent of the Texan case—to annex the territory by a joint resolution of Congress. This resolution McKinley signed on July 7, 1898. It described the islands as "a part of the territory of the United States" but did not include them within the limits of the American customs regulations. On April 30, 1900, an act of Congress gave to the islands the normal territorial form of government and brought them within the scope of the federal Constitution. The Hawaiians became citizens of the United States.

The Open Door

Rivalry in China

Although the United States was acquiring new territorial possessions in the Far East, it was for a time threatened with the loss of valuable commercial privileges in that part of the world. Ever since the establishment of American independence the commercial advantages of China had been utilized by American merchants. In 1844 the Chinese government had granted to the United States "most favored nation" privileges in Chinese ports. For fifty years these advantages had remained open to the American merchants. Then, at the very moment when the United States stood on the verge of new greatness, it appeared that these valuable concessions in China would be taken away, not by the Chinese but by those foreign governments which had for a year or more been engaged in the policy of extracting territorial leases from the Chinese. Following the lead of Russia, Germany, Japan, France, and England all engaged in this rivalry over the possession of strategic positions on the Chinese coast and over the extension of their spheres of influence in the interior. A continuance of this process threatened to exclude Americans from trade with China.

Although the British government was as much involved as any other in the violation of the territorial integrity of China, British leaders had no illusions regarding the ultimate results of the process. With a few more grants of territory to nations bent on monopolizing their own possessions, British mercantile interests would find themselves restricted to the comparatively narrow area of their own spheres in China. What the British wanted in China was not territory but trade; on this issue they found a common cause with the United States. In March 1898, while both Cabinet and House of Commons insisted that the principle of free commerce in China must be upheld, the British foreign office confidentially invited the United States to cooperate with the British in maintaining the principle. This was the situation out of which developed the doctrine of the "open door" in China.

John Hay

The credit or responsibility for proclaiming this "open door" policy went to John Hay, secretary of state under McKinley and Roosevelt. But Hay was in no sense the originator of the idea. As early as 1843 Secretary of State Daniel Webster announced that the United States could not remain on friendly terms with China "if greater privileges or commercial facilities should be allowed to the subjects of any other Government than should be granted to the citizens of the United States." In March 1898 the British government made it plain that British treaty rights and commercial freedom would be upheld in China. Lord Charles Beresford, a friend of John Hay, referred to these very aims as "the policy of the open door." British and American newspapers used the same term. When Secretary Hay was preparing his definition of this country's policy regarding China, he had the advice of W. W. Rockhill, an adviser in the State Department, and of an Englishman, Alfred E. Hippisley.

Hay's announcement of the policy appeared in the form of a note, dated September 6, 1899, and addressed to the governments of Great Britain, Russia, and Germany, and also in a second note sent to France, Italy, and Japan. He asked these governments to respect all open ports in China, to recognize all established interests within the special spheres of influence, to enforce only the Chinese tariff, and to make no discrimination in port charges and railroad rates. The British government accepted the proposal, and the other governments expressed sympathy with it. Secretary Hay then announced that the United States would consider the acceptance by each power as "final and definitive."

Chinese patriots, however, for a time interfered with the effective execution of the policy. In June 1900, with the poorly concealed approval of the Chinese government, they began a vigorous attack upon the foreigners in Peking (now Peiping). The German minister was murdered, and the other foreign officials were besieged in the British legation. American troops participated in an international expedition which went up from Tientsin to their relief. Through the whole affair of this Boxer rebellion, Secretary Hay endeavored to moderate the demands of the powers and to maintain the principle of the "open door."

Chapter 35

BIG BUSINESS AND THE DRIVE FOR REFORM

Return of Prosperity

THE dramatic and spectacular activities of war and foreign policy bulked large in the newspapers and in the contemporary thought of the McKinley-Roosevelt era, but the changes going on within the United States itself were even more important in their direct effects upon the American people. By 1897 the country was recovering from the recent depression. The belief that good business and Republican policies were not only inseparable but synonymous had become part of the dogma of economics and politics in some quarters and, fallacious though it was, the mere belief operated powerfully in business circles. The Republicans had promised to restore the high tariff, and many businessmen needed nothing more than this assurance to inspire them with hope and confidence.

Dingley Tariff

The new Republican majority lost no time in restoring the tariff wall. McKinley called Congress in special session for March 15, 1897, but the leaders could not wait even for the session to open. The Republican caucus made Reed the speaker, and Reed appointed his committees before Congress met. Furthermore, the Committee of Ways and Means, with Nelson Dingley as chairman, had a tariff bill all drawn before March 15. Although this bill covered 163 printed pages it passed the House in two weeks. The Republicans had approved the bill and therefore did not care to discuss it, and the Democrats were so completely muzzled by the majority that they were given no opportunity for debate. Although the Senate examined the bill more carefully and made more than 800 amendments, the high rates were consistently upheld. The Dingley tariff became law at the end of July.

The Dingley Act raised the rates to a new high level. The duty on raw wool, taken off by the Wilson-Gorman Act, was restored. To compensate the manufacturers, duties on manufactured woolens had to be advanced. On most woolen goods the tariff rate was more than 100 percent of the price. The rates on silk and linen were equally high, but those on cotton were more moderate. On heavy metals the rates were not exorbitant, but on certain types of manufactured cutlery the protection was ample. For example, an ordinary 25-cent pocket knife imported from Germany carried a duty of 30 cents.

The improvement in business conditions convinced the friends of protection not only that their policy was sound but also that it was the cause of the upturn. The American people entered upon a period of good times that continued until 1907. Manufacturers, merchants, and financiers alike profited

Business Activity

from the growing volume of business. Even laborers and farmers shared in the improvement. In 1899 prices in the iron and steel trade more than doubled and the textile industry was almost as prosperous. Better industrial conditions at home added to urban buying power and so, according to Republican reasoning, contributed to the welfare of the farmers. This domestic demand was supplemented by heavy European purchases of American foodstuffs, particularly wheat. Evidence of these better days was seen in the increase of deposits in savings banks, in the payment of farm indebtedness, in the erection of new buildings, and in higher wages for industrial workers.

The causes of recovery were evident. The United States was still growing—in population, farming, industry, transportation, and both foreign and domestic trade. There was a heavy demand for both capital and consumers' goods. During the depression this demand had been interrupted, and private citizens and business firms alike put off the purchase of needed supplies. Once confidence returned consumers rushed forward with their orders, hoping to secure the necessary supplies before prices went too high. Then the buying wave sent prices up, and buyers laid in additional goods to guard against further price rises. Besides this normal demand, the Spanish-American War was responsible for additional business. Then, too, there was a sudden and unexpected increase in the world's supply of gold, and this helped to force prices still higher.

The increase of gold stocks deprived the advocates of free silver of their strongest argument, and in doing so made it safe for the Republicans to pass the long-delayed gold standard law. In 1900 Congress made the gold dollar the standard unit of value and provided that all other forms of American money in circulation should be redeemable in gold. The country still had in circulation approximately $968,000,000 in Civil War greenbacks, silver dollars or silver certificates, and silver notes issued under the Sherman Act of 1890. The law also set apart a fund of $150,000,000 to be used in redeeming this money.

Businessmen and politicians had so regularly repeated the dogma that Republican success at the polls made for economic prosperity that they came to believe it themselves. McKinley's election for a second term in 1900 therefore inspired the business world with confidence, and this confidence immediately found expression in a wave of business activity. Speculation, "promotion"—that is, the launching of new combinations of capital—and reckless watering of stock furnished the *motif* of this new era.

In the world of big business there were operations on a scale that made the activities of Congress look almost insignificant in comparison. American industrialists and financiers joined forces to create business enterprises greater and more powerful than any hitherto known. In discussing them the people still talked loosely about trusts, but by 1900 the trust was already a thing of the past. In its place was to be found the holding company, an organization which had all the advantages of the trust but which was less vulnerable before the law.

Business Enterprise

Whenever business is good, investors and speculators will buy quantities of securities, particularly common stocks. In the first three months of 1899 business on the New York Stock Exchange was greater by 15,000,000 shares than in the corresponding three months of 1898. The new holding companies had peculiar advantages for marketing securities. For one thing the investment banker had come into the picture; it was his business to sell securities. Then there was the promoter. His function was to consolidate individual concerns into holding companies. In the course of such a transaction everybody profited; wealth was actually created out of thin air. Take, for example, a company known as the Consolidated Steel and Wire Company. Some time after its formation it was taken over by the American Steel and Wire Company of Illinois. The holder of a single $100 share of stock in Consolidated Steel and Wire received, at no extra cost to himself, securities in the new company worth $350. Subsequently American Steel and Wire of Illinois was absorbed by American Steel and Wire of New Jersey, and the stockholder found himself in possession of securities priced at $490. In 1901 American Steel and Wire of New Jersey was absorbed by the United States Steel Corporation, and the same stockholder then found himself the owner of stock in United States Steel with a par value of $564.37. Thus the process of forming holding companies made $100 grow into considerably more than five times that amount. The investor had not put a single additional penny into the enterprise, and the owners had put in nothing more in plant or equipment.

Manufacturing Securities

The most spectacular illustration of business methods of that day was provided by the men who organized the United States Steel Corporation. The background of this episode is both complex and entertaining. The Carnegie Steel Company had developed into a prosperous concern. Carnegie himself was a genius at organization, and he availed himself of the services of the best technical experts in the business. The combination was bound to succeed. Carnegie had no watered stock in his enterprise, and he operated on a policy of low costs. His company produced most of the crude and heavy steel used in the United States—that is, steel bars, rails, and armor plate. By 1899 Charles M. Schwab, Carnegie's right-hand man, made the assertion that the Carnegie Company could manufacture steel rails for less than $12 per ton, while English manufacturers could not get their figure under $19. What is true of rails, Schwab continued, "is equally true of other steel products. *As a result of this, we are going to control the steel business of the world.*"

In the meantime J. P. Morgan and Company had helped to promote and finance a number of companies engaged in the manufacture of steel products. Altogether there were eight of these manufacturing companies, including the American Bridge Company, the Structural Steel Company, the

American Steel and Wire Company, the National Tube Company. Because of the Morgan interest in the sale of new securities, these companies were generously capitalized. With assets of $19,000,000, National Tube was capitalized at $80,000,000. However, National Tube was an excellent investment, paying 17 percent on the higher capitalization. National Tube could do this because it controlled 90 percent of the steel pipe business of the country. The dividends actually amounted to $13,600,000 annually; figured at the same 17 percent rate on the actual investment, they would have been only $3,230,000. The other seven concerns were capitalized in about the same fashion.

For several years these Morgan enterprises bought their raw material from Carnegie. Then Morgan helped to finance a new concern, the Federal Steel Company of Illinois, which competed with Carnegie in making heavy steel. Again, as in so many of the Morgan enterprises, the difference between the book value and the actual capitalization of Federal Steel was striking: $56,000,000 of actual assets, $200,000,000 of outstanding stock. Because of this heavy overload of water, the Morgan interests were handicapped in any price war with Carnegie.

United States Steel

The various Morgan manufacturing companies transferred their orders from the Carnegie company to the new Federal Steel Company. Thereupon Carnegie threatened to go into the manufacturing business himself. An industrial war between two such powerful captains as Morgan and Carnegie would have been costly to the point of disaster. There was only one course possible for Morgan and that was to buy Carnegie out. On December 12, 1900, there was a now famous dinner party in New York given in honor of Charles M. Schwab, president of the Carnegie Steel Company. At the dinner Schwab explained how the future of the steel business might be made even more brilliant than the past. He envisioned a vast merger of interests: Carnegie, Federal, the eight manufacturing companies, the great ore deposits of the Lake Superior region, and shipping lines on the Great Lakes. The result of the dinner was the greatest financial deal ever transacted in the United States up to that time. On April 1, 1901, the formation of the United States Steel Corporation was announced to the world. This was the first billion-dollar corporation. For its services in helping to launch this enterprise, J. P. Morgan and Company received nearly $75,000,000, an amount just about equal to the national debt in 1783.

The actual number of consolidations brought about during this period was impressive in itself, while the figures for their capitalization ran to astronomical proportions. In the ten years prior to 1897, eighty-six new industrial combinations were formed, and in each case the capitalization was $1,000,000 or more. The total capitalization of this group ran up to $1,414,000,000. From 1898 to 1904, 276 new combinations were formed. The capitalization of the largest concern in this group, the United Steel Corporation, almost equaled the total for the eighty-six companies organized before 1897.

The American people were concerned because many of these great corporations were monopolies, and the business methods of monopolies were looked upon with disfavor. The American Tobacco Company fused into itself some 250 companies. Starting with a monopoly of the cigarette business, the company suppressed all efforts at competition. It bought patents on cigarette machines, not necessarily for its own use but merely to prevent anybody else from using them. Then it branched out into other lines of the tobacco business and eventually took over a substantial portion of it.

Morgan Policies

Because of the wide range of his business interests, Mr. J. P. Morgan became the symbol of financial power. He had his own bank, and he became intimately connected with such national banks as the First National, Liberty, and Chase of New York. He became a power in some of the great life insurance companies, notably the New York Life, the New York Mutual, and the Equitable Life Assurance Society. These companies invested over $50,000,000 per year, and the new relationship made it convenient and easy for them to buy their securities from J. P. Morgan and Company. Morgan directors occupied places of prominence and power on the boards of all these corporations, railroad, industrial, and financial. By 1900 J. P. Morgan and Company controlled nearly one half of the railroad mileage of the United States.

The Morgan ideal of stabilization and maintenance of prices rested upon the principle of monopolistic control; competition therefore was a menace, something to be eliminated by any means which would not involve trouble with the law. The complete history of the Morgan financial empire has not yet been written, but one chapter was written in the reports of the Interstate Commerce Commission and in the quotations of the New York Stock Exchange. This is the story of the New Haven Railroad; and the investors in New Haven stock did not find it good reading.

The New Haven railroad provides service between New York and Boston through some of the most thickly settled industrial areas in the United States. It had been a profitable road, and its stock was looked upon as one of the best investments in the world. In 1903 Morgan made Charles S. Mellen president of the New Haven Railroad and ordered him to unify all transportation facilities throughout New England. By 1907 the New Haven Railroad had acquired control of the Boston and Maine, which served most of northern New England. Four years later the Rutland came under the same management. During the same time the New Haven Railroad bought trolley lines in Massachusetts, Rhode Island, and Connecticut, and shipping lines in Long Island Sound. Hitherto the financial management of the New Haven had been conservative and safe; under the Morgan-Mellen regime the New Haven became a synonym for recklessness. By 1914 the New Haven was bankrupt, and Mellen and his fellow directors were indicted for misuse of the road's funds. The Interstate Commerce Commission accused these men of "loose, extravagant and improvident management," of bribing legislators, of subsidizing the press, and of unscrupulous manipulation of the stock market to maintain the price of New

Haven stock. Their policy made the stock practically worthless, and the company had to be reorganized.

Economic and Social Problems

The "Money Trust"

It was not irresponsible reformers and doctrinaire idealists who ruined the financial structure of what had been one of the most profitable railroads in the country but some of the most prominent businessmen in the United States. The records of business enterprise afforded other examples of the flagrant misuse of other people's money. The operations of the Diamond Match Company in suppressing competition have already been described. Reports of the concentration of wealth were so alarming and the power of its holders so impressive that in 1912 the national House of Representatives ordered its Committee on Banking and Currency to investigate the whole situation. The committee was instructed specifically to find out whether a "money trust" existed. The committee reported that if by a "money trust" it was meant that

> . . . an established and well-defined community of interest between a few leaders of finance which has been created and is held together through stock holdings, interlocking directorates, and other forms of dominion over banks, trust companies, railroads, public-service and industrial corporations, and which has resulted in a vast and growing concentration of money and credit in the hands of a comparatively few men—your committee has no hesitation in asserting as a result of its investigation up to this time that the condition thus described exists in this country today.

In 1912, the year of the House committee's report on the money trust, Congress authorized the appointment of a Commission on Industrial Relations to investigate business enterprise in the United States. The commission's report, submitted in 1915, furnishes an abundance of material on the problems of concentrated wealth. The commission found that the "final control of American industry rests, therefore, in the hands of a small number of wealthy and powerful financiers," and that the "concentration of ownership and control is greatest in the basic industries upon which the welfare of the country must finally rest." In most cases each great industry was dominated by some one large corporation or by an equally effective combination brought about by the ownership of stock. Although these great corporations had large numbers of stockholders, the few controlling individuals owned a majority of the stock. In 1911 the United States Steel Corporation had nearly 100,000 stockholders, but 1500 of them held 57 percent of the stock, and actual control "rested with a single private banking house"—that is, with J. P. Morgan and Company.

The commission went on to warn the people that the power represented in this concentration of wealth was being used "for the endowment of colleges and universities, by the creation of funds for the pensioning of teach ers, by contributions to private charities, as well as through controlling or influencing the public press." The commission also warned of the development of a "degree of control over the teachings of professors in our colleges and universities which constitutes a most serious menace." Then the report cited the cases of two college teachers who had lost their positions presumably because they had testified before the commission and because their testimony was displeasing to certain representatives of great wealth who controlled the policy of these educational institutions.

Here was the popular formula covering business enterprise in the early years of the twentieth century. American business was big business, and it was becoming steadily bigger and more powerful. This formula provided talking points for reformers of all kinds. People in general never questioned the reliability of the stereotype. And yet it was open to serious question. The total fortunes of the Vanderbilts, the Rockefellers, the Harrimans and their fellow multimillionaires did not amount to more than 2 percent of the national wealth. As for the concentration of industry, there was far less of it than popular reformers admitted. The great holding companies like United States Steel were impressive, but they did not include by any means all of American industry. As late as 1919, the most heavily industrialized sections of the country still had a total of 175,220 manufacturing plants, with an output valued at $44,775,324,000. As late as 1929 60 percent of the retail trade of the United States, amounting in value to more than $30,000,000,000, was handled by 1,300,000 independent storekeepers and dealers. Not all American business was big, and there was still room for the independent manufacturer and retailer. But the stereotype was easier to grasp than the facts, and the stereotype therefore had greater influence in shaping public opinion.

Labor Problems

The integration of industry and the concentration of financial power absorbed the attention of the leading manufacturers, bankers, and businessmen. They were engaged in making big business still bigger, and necessarily in making it pay. This work was important, vitally important, and they believed that the immediate welfare of the country and its future progress depended upon their success. If they should fail in their vast enterprises millions of wage earners and members of working families would find themselves suddenly thrown out of their jobs. And yet, these captains of industry and masters of finance rarely thought of their obligations in terms of the social and economic problems of their individual employees.

The report of the Commission of Industrial Relations declared that the labor policy of each great industry was in almost every case determined by the leading corporations in that industry. The commission found that the Morgan-First National Bank group alone dominated corporations with 785,499 employees, while the six recognized financial groups controlled literally millions of workingmen. The commission held that most of the "industrial dictators" were "totally unconcerned with regard to the working and living conditions" of their employees. Management, however, was sufficiently interested to adopt and enforce vigorous non-union policies. "In order to prevent the organization of employees for the improvement of working conditions, elaborate systems of espionage are maintained by the large corporations which refuse to deal with labor unions, and the employees suspected of union affiliations are discharged." The commission characterized the labor conditions in these great corporation-controlled industries as "a menace to the welfare of the Nation."

The specific grievances of the laborers were insufficient wages, excessively long working days, inadequate housing, and general insecurity. It is true that in many of the towns and smaller cities industrial employees were able to meet expenses, provided they could count on regular employment. But they had no title to their jobs and actual experience convinced them that unemployment was always around the corner. Even when they had regular work their income stood in sharp contrast to the fortunes of the great industrialists and bankers. Possibly the very facts of this contrast tended to increase discontent. Then, to make the discrepancy between the incomes of rich and poor even more striking, there were the slums and sweatshops of the cities. These last resorts of the down-and-out were not typical of living conditions of American workingmen, but they stood as a grim reminder of what surely had happened to the most unfortunate.

The refusal on the part of business leaders to look seriously into problems of wages, employment, and living conditions might be considered one of the major calamities of the time. Collectively these men had more direct experience with economic affairs than anyone else in the country, and this fund of experience should have been of incalculable value. But the possessors of economic power refused to assume responsibilities which are inseparably connected with that very power, so the American people sought other leadership.

Socialism in the United States

The problems of industrial workers, particularly the unskilled urban workers, were so pressing that they caught the attention of reformers and uplifters long before the industrial magnates admitted that any problems existed. Unfortunately, many reformers and uplifters lacked practical experience. Possessed of excellent intentions and inspired by exalted idealism, they sought formulas of economic salvation for the workingmen. Their aim was to give industrial workers a larger share of the abundance which great natural resources and highly developed technical skill had presented to the world. Among the most widely publicized reformers in this group were the socialists.

The word "socialism" was coined in the early part of the nineteenth century apparently by Robert Owen. In spite of Owen's own personal influence and in spite of the efforts made by other humanitarians, the principles of socialism were slow to find followers in the United States. American political thought before the Civil War shows little or no trace of socialist influence, and there was no appreciable body of socialist opinion here until after 1900. In 1874 a group of socialists organized the Social Democratic Workingmen's party; three years later they changed their name to the Socialist Labor party. Further evidence of American interest in socialism appeared in the early 1890's, when J. H. Wayland began to publish the *Appeal to Reason*. In 1897 a group of socialists who found fault with the Socialist Labor party organized the Social Democratic party; four years later it became the Socialist party. According to their platforms, these two Socialist parties agreed upon the basic dogma of their faith.

What is Socialism?

Nonsocialists find it difficult to discover precisely what is meant by socialism and impossible to determine how socialists would operate their politico-economic system once they should succeed in founding it. Even the socialists themselves are not agreed on the first point, and they carefully refrain from committing themselves on the second. One of the most widely known British socialists, George Bernard Shaw, defined socialism as "the complete discarding of the institution of private property . . . and the division of the resultant public income equally and indiscriminately among the entire population." Other socialists, especially in the United States, have declared that socialism would actually protect private property in some cases, even land where the farmer worked for himself. Other definitions are phrased in general terms. One of the older editions of the *Encyclopaedia Britannica* suggested the following: "Socialism is that policy or theory which aims at securing by the action of the central democratic authority a better distribution, and in due subordination thereunto a better production, of wealth than now prevails." The *New International Encyclopedia* defines socialism as "an ideal economic system in which industry is carried on under social direction and for the benefit of society as a whole." The inauguration of a socialist regime would involve "a thoroughgoing reconstruction of society through political action," and "a changed attitude toward property." Norman Thomas, a prominent American socialist, explained that socialists advocate "the public or social ownership and control of land, natural resources and the principal means of production and control of goods." Under socialism economic processes would be operated and directed for use instead of profit. Once socialism was fully established, the authority of government as we now know it would disappear.

All socialist thought reflects to a greater or less degree the influence of Karl Marx and the *Communist Manifesto*. This criticism of the capitalistic order, largely the work of Marx, was published in 1848. Here one finds the classic terminology of socialism and an analysis of its doctrines. Marx held that society was divided into two classes—the bourgeoise and the proletariat—whose interests were irreconcilable; these classes would continue their struggle until the proletariat would triumph.

American Socialism

American socialists advocated public ownership of all industries controlled by monopolies or trusts and of all railroad, telegraph, and telephone systems, all public utilities, all mines and oil wells. Socialists promised to satisfy the needs and even the wants of the working classes, and in doing so they took pains to contrast their own promises with the "failures" of capitalism. "Capitalism is already struggling to its destruction," as their platform of 1900 put it. "It is no longer competent to organize or administer the work of the world, or even to preserve itself." In 1908 they argued that "the capitalists are powerless to regulate production for social ends. Industries are largely conducted in a planless manner." The only remedy for economic and social ills was socialism, "under which industry will be carried on for the common good and every worker receive the full social value of the wealth he creates." Under socialism it is intended "that society in its collective capacity shall produce, not for profit, but in abundance to satisfy human wants; that every man shall have the inalienable right to work, and receive the full equivalent of all he produces."

The student who wishes to learn precisely how the socialists would operate their new economy if they get it will be somewhat puzzled. Socialist literature is notably wanting in clarity at this vital point. On the face of the record, socialists are not constitution-makers but specialists in doctrine. Norman Thomas admitted that the working principles of the socialist political and economic system have never been worked out, even on paper. A former American socialist, Mr. John Spargo, writing in 1906, made the interesting statement that "it would be absurd, and contrary to Socialist principles, to attempt to give detailed specifications of the Socialist state." Evidently, then, the failure to reduce socialism to the form of an exact constitution is due not to oversight but to design.

The American people have not responded enthusiastically to the appeals of the socialists. In 1900 Debs, on the Socialist Presidential ticket, received 94,864 votes, while Malloney on the Socialist Labor ticket polled 33,432. Four years later, the Debs vote increased to 402,895, but Corregan, the Socialist Labor candidate, received only 33,490. In 1908 Debs showed a slight gain over the preceding election, with 420,890, but Gilhaus of the Socialist Labor ticket dropped to 14,021. But in 1912, the year of unusual political excitement, Debs ran his vote up to 901,873, and Reimer on the other ticket got 29,259.

To the nonsocialist the most serious weakness of socialism is the concept itself. It is not a set of principles derived from the actual experience of mankind but a collection of a priori theories. For the sake of argument one may accept in full the socialist indictment of capitalism and agree that it has not brought a decent mode of living for the unskilled workers. But it is not so easy to accept their conclusion that socialism will accomplish what capitalism has failed to effect. The belief that socialism will work miracles is an act of pure faith. It is in fact a religion expressed not in the familiar terms of theology but in those of economics and politics. Like most acts of faith its dogma is highly simplified. A religion which promises prosperity and abundance to all the underprivileged of this world is bound to raise hopes and win converts. Socialists, of course, consider this interpretation as sheer nonsense. They insist that Marxian socialism, far from being a set of abstractions, a mere dream, is scientific and that society organized in accordance with socialist principles would be founded on science.

The primary purpose of the socialists, in fact the only reason for their party's existence, was to promote the well-being of the masses of workingmen. But the vote for Debs at the various Presidential elections shows that the laborers of the United States had not accepted socialism. By 1905 there were approximately 25,000,000 laborers in this country, most of whom voted Republican or Democratic. The American Federation of Labor refused to have anything to do with socialism; it preferred to continue the use of trade union methods—that is, collective bargaining, with the strike as a last resort—and it preferred to avoid the burden of attempting to organize the workers into a separate political party. It is true that in the constitution of 1919 even the American Federation endorsed the Marxian doctrine of the conflict of classes. But 1919 was a year of widespread unrest, marked by more than 3000 strikes in the United States. Even so, and in spite of this preamble, the Federation made no attempt to alter its aims or its methods. It still remained what it had been, an organization of skilled laborers or a sort of labor aristocracy.

Radical Unionism

Most socialists and some labor leaders lost respect for the Federation because of its persistent conservatism, and in 1905 some of these leaders tried to launch a new labor organization, the Industrial Workers of the World. In June of that year a group of idealists, radical socialists, and radical labor men called together an Industrialists' Convention at Chicago. The more conspicuous members were Eugene V. Debs, Daniel DeLeon, not a laborer but a socialist "intellectual," and William D. Haywood, a labor leader accused by some persons of preferring dynamite to the sober methods of the A.F. of L. DeLeon described the meeting of the convention as a turning point in American history. The convention decided that unionism on the craft basis was rendered obsolete by altered industrial conditions, and it proclaimed the one big union idea, a vast group in which all laborers, skilled and unskilled, could work together for their common aims.

At the time of its formation the I.W.W. proclaimed: "There is but one bargain that the I.W.W. will make with the employing class—*complete surrender of all control of industry to the organized workers.*" But the I.W.W. was never a large organization; in 1912 it may have had 5000 members. Even in the days of unrest following World War I when it received considerable unfavorable publicity, the membership of the I.W.W. probably never exceeded 60,000. The organization appealed most strongly to unskilled workers in the lower wage groups, particularly to those in eastern textile factories and in lumber camps and wheat fields of the West.

Social Legislation and the Supreme Court

The socialists and their more radical allies of the I.W.W. planned to improve the condition of industrial workers by a thoroughgoing reorganization of the economic and political system, and they advocated revolution as a means to this end. However, there were other reformers who had some appreciation of the difficulties involved in the effort to create a new society and believed that at least a measure of improvement could be effected by the more orderly process of legislation. For twenty years and more William Jennings Bryan and the Populists had warned the country of the dangers involved in the acts and purposes of masters of capital. Other leaders joined in the warnings, notably Robert M. La Follette of Wisconsin, Theodore Roosevelt, and, somewhat belatedly, Woodrow Wilson.

These major prophets were assisted by journalists, teachers, politicians, and even some of the clergy. Starting with the basic assumption that the dominant figures in the business world were endowed with more power than could safely be entrusted to any set of men, the reformers evolved a philosophy or doctrine which taught that such great wealth and power must be brought under the control of the state. In their zeal and enthusiasm they presented an oversimplified picture of a situation actually so complex that human beings are still baffled in their efforts to understand it. According to the liberals of the days before World War I, there were three parties to be considered: the public, big business, and the government. The government according to their theory would act as arbiter between the other two and also, if necessary, as the protector of the public against the depredations of big business. These friends of the people attributed the overgrown powers of big business to the unwise reliance of almost everybody on what they regarded as the outmoded economic doctrine of *laissez faire;* they proposed to scrap the doctrine and to substitute for it the theory of the public interest. For the future, businessmen should no longer pursue their policies unhampered by any restraint; they must be placed under the powers of the law and under the watchful eye of administrative units of the government. Government would then see that wealth served the people, and that the people were masters of wealth. This at least was the dogma of nonsocialist reformers at the opening of the twentieth century.

Philosophy of Public Interest

In general these reformers called for regulatory legislation. More specifically they called for laws to protect laborers from the ordinary hazards of employment and from excessive hours of work. When considered collectively, the body of state laws dealing with social security made an impressive showing. First on the list were workmen's compensation acts, designed to transfer the costs of industrial accidents from the injured employees and their families to society itself. Years of experience with the industrial system had shown that laborers ran a constant risk of being hurt by machines and that in many cases the accident could not be traced to any specific

Social Legislation

cause; it was simply one of the consequences of the job. Laws, however, never develop rapidly enough to meet changing conditions, and the laws dealing with industrial accidents were not only obsolete but peculiarly burdensome to the employee. The law assumed that all injuries were due to the carelessness of the individual himself or to the "contributory negligence" of his fellow employees. The employer had no responsibility in the premises. In case of injury, therefore, the workingman had to bear the full cost of medical care in addition to the loss of wages while he was absent from the factory. In case he lost his life the burden fell on his family. If the accident were due to carelessness or negligence on the part of the employer, the burden of proof rested with the workman. To recover damages he would have to sue his employer and bring witnesses to court who could convince a jury that the employer was in the wrong. In a contest of this sort, even if he could afford to go to court, the employee was always at a disadvantage.

Workmen's compensation acts provide for a system of insurance, the cost of which is placed on the employer. He, of course, adds this cost to his overhead, thus passing it on to the consumer or the general public. In case of injury resulting in temporary loss of employment, the worker receives weekly payments, and the insurance company pays the doctor and hospital bills. In case of permanent disability the injured man will receive regular weekly benefit payments running for a specified number of years. In case the accident results in the death of the worker, the insurance company pays a specified sum to his widow or heirs. Thus the cost of accidents is distributed widely, and the financial burden does not fall heavily on any one family. Maryland passed the first of these workmen's compensation acts in 1902. By 1929 all but four states had such laws on their statute books.

Another aim of the social reformers was to limit the hours of work for women and children, and to prevent entirely the employment of children under the age of fourteen. Any survey of working conditions showed that such laws were imperatively needed. In 1900 there were more than 2,500,000 women wage earners under the age of twenty-five, and most of them were actually below twenty-one. At this time only four states prohibited the employment of women at night, and not half the states prohibited night work by children. In 1875 Massachusetts provided for a ten-hour working day for women, and the state courts upheld the law. In 1908 the United States Supreme Court upheld a similar law of the State of Oregon. By 1930 forty-four states had passed laws of this type.

In the case of children the reformers endeavored to prohibit employment in industry of all children under the age of fourteen and to require such children to spend a specified number of days in school. In general, state laws also prohibit the employment of children at night. But it is one thing to put laws on the statute books and a very different thing to enforce them. Even in the most progressive states enforcement has lagged behind the expressed purpose of the laws. In 1928 the Labor Department of New York investigated charges that children were being employed in violation of the law and the findings were not pleasant. Nearly 1500 boys and girls, many of whom were under the legal age limit, were found to be working in factories, and an additional 2700 in stores.

Because of the violation of the child labor laws in some states and because of the refusal of a few states to enact any legislation on the subject, there has been a long-continued effort to secure a federal child labor law or, more effective still, a child labor amendment to the federal Constitution. In 1906 Senator Beveridge of Indiana proposed such an amendment, the terms of which would prohibit the shipment in interstate commerce of goods produced in mines or factories employing child labor. The proposal was not favorably received, and ten years later Congress passed a law with substantially the same provisions. In 1918 the federal Supreme Court declared this act unconstitutional. In 1919 Congress tried again, this time with a law imposing a heavy tax on the products of factories which employed children. Again the Supreme Court annulled the measure on the ground that the proposed use of the taxing power was not warranted by the Constitution. In 1924 Congress approved the draft of a proposed amendment to the Constitution, giving the federal government power "to limit, regulate, and prohibit the labor of persons under eighteen years of age." Up to the present time (1949) the proposal has not been approved by the necessary three fourths of the state legislatures.

Still another social experiment in this era was concerned with minimum wages for women. Massachusetts passed the first law for this purpose in 1912; this measure authorized the appointment of a minimum wage board, with authority to suggest but not to prescribe minimum wages for women. Employers who failed to comply with the recommendations found themselves in danger of unpleasant notoriety. In the main the law was effective, although some firms dismissed their low-grade employees on the ground that they were not worth the minimum wage. The next year eight states enacted minimum wage laws; several others followed, and in 1918 Congress passed one for the District of Columbia. Most of these differed from the Massachusetts law in that the minimum named was mandatory.

The Supreme Court and Reform

In 1923, in the case of *Children's Hospital* v. *Adkins,* the federal Supreme Court declared the District of Columbia measure unconstitutional. The act in question provided that women's wages in the District must be sufficient at least to "maintain them in health and to protect their morals." The Court held that the measure violated the due process clause of the Fifth Amendment. The opinion explained: "We cannot accept the doctrine that women of mature age require or may be subjected to restrictions upon their liberty of contract which could not lawfully be imposed in the case of men under similar circumstances."

The first attempts to fix a statutory limit to the length of the working day for men were nullified by the Supreme Court. The most famous case of this sort was that of *Lochner* v. *New York,* decided in 1905. The New York legislature had limited the hours of labor in bakeries to not more than sixty hours per week and not more than ten per day. The Court held that bakeries were not particularly unhealthful places of employment; consequently the limitation of hours was not "a legitimate exercise of the police power of the state, but an unreasonable, unnecessary, and arbitrary interference with the right and liberty of the individual to contract, in relation to labor." Such limitation might, so the Court reasoned, "seriously cripple the ability of the laborer to support himself and his family." In 1917, however, the Supreme Court gave its approval to an Oregon law limiting the day's work for factory employees to ten hours, and in the same year it upheld the federal Adamson Law, which made the eight-hour day the basis for figuring wages on the railroads. As the need of governmental protection for certain types of workingmen became more evident, the courts became more willing to give a broad interpretation to their doctrine of the police power.

During the early years of the twentieth century the Supreme Court handed down other decisions which aroused the wrath of organized labor. In 1908, in the Danbury Hatters' case, officially known as *Loewe* v. *Lawlor,* the Court found the United Hatters' Union guilty of conspiracy in restraint of trade. The union had tried to bring about a boycott against the D. E. Loewe Company. This action, the Court held, was a violation of the Sherman Anti-Trust Act. The company won its suit for damages against the members of the union, and individual members had to pay.

Another case involving the boycott started in 1907, when the Bucks Stove and Range Company sued the American Federation of Labor. One of the Federation's unions had launched a boycott against the Bucks concern. As in the Danbury Hatters' case, the point at issue was whether members of a labor union could lawfully urge the public to stop using a given product. In 1908 the Supreme Court issued a permanent injunction which prohibited the union from circulating any kind of appeal to the public not to use Bucks products. President Gompers of the American Federation called this decision "the most sweeping invasion of the liberty of the press and of the right of free speech that ever emanated from an American court." From that time on the unions worked for legislation designed to restrict the use of injunctions to what labor leaders regarded as legitimate purposes.

Reforming the Government

If social and economic reforms were to be brought about by action of the government, government itself needed to be reformed. Voters had to be freed from danger of bribery; legislatures needed independence from corrupt businessmen and political bosses; and the people wanted more power over legislatures and courts of justice.

For the voter the problem was to make himself honest and to set himself free from the domination of corrupt leaders; the method was ballot reform. According to established custom, party managers furnished the ballots, and the voters marked them in the open. It was therefore easy for the buyer of votes to make sure that his adherents delivered the goods. In 1890 the State of Massachusetts introduced a modification of the Australian ballot. Under this new arrangement the ballots were printed and distributed by the government instead of by the political party, and the government provided booths into which the voters retired to mark their ballots in secret. The secret ballot was supposed to discourage bribery by making the voters independent. By 1900 most of the states had introduced some form of secret voting.

Political Reform

Having thrown safeguards around the voter the next step was to change the method of nominating candidates for elective office. Custom had assigned this important function to caucuses and conventions in which theoretically every voter could participate. Actually, however, nominations were made by the inner ring of the party organization, the "bosses" and the "machines." The men who rose in public life were the men who worked in harmony with the leaders; reformers could not get the endorsement of the leaders and without this endorsement a political career was impossible.

To weaken the hold of the professional politicians and to give the voters some influence in the selection of candidates, reformers proposed the direct primary. This is virtually a preliminary election, held within the party, at which the party members vote for their candidates. Under this arrangement a citizen who may have been unable to secure the endorsement of the machine can get his name on the ballot provided he has a substantial following. All he has to do is to secure a specified number of signatures to a petition asking for his nomination. One of the first advocates of the direct primary was Robert M. La Follette of Wisconsin, and Wisconsin adopted the system in 1904. Other states soon followed.

Another sore spot in the American scheme of government was the United States Senate, the members of which were intimately tied in with the widely criticized state machines on the one hand and with various big business interests on the other. As the mainspring in the system of federal patronage, the Senate had become one of the symbols of political corruption. During the era of agitation in the early 1890's the Populists demanded the direct popular election of United States Senators, and in 1893 a resolution calling for an amendment to the federal Constitution for this purpose was introduced in the Senate itself. But opposition was strong and the people were slow to move. The proposed amendment—the Seventeenth—did not pass Congress until 1912, and it did not become effective until 1913. Since that time the Senators have been chosen by popular vote. Their rating in integrity would seem to be just as high as before, perhaps higher. Senators no longer buy their seats in the Senate, as Senator Addicks of Delaware declared that he did: "I've bought it; I've paid for it; I am going to have it. It has cost me $140,000."

In their eagerness to make government more responsible to the people, the reformers spent considerable time on the processes of lawmaking. Somewhat after the manner of the United States Senate, the state legislatures had become tightly enmeshed in the tangle of corrupt politics and closely allied with "predatory" business enterprise. According to the reformers these state legislators overlooked the interests of the people and ignored their demands. Even though these bodies had not gone quite so far as the municipal common councils in violating the proprieties of democracy they went far enough to distress thoughtful observers.

To break the hold of the bosses and to make the people their own lawmakers, reformers demanded the twin device of the initiative and the referendum. The referendum means simply the reference of any measure to the voters for their decision. The initiative has been defined as "the right of a certain percentage of the voters, usually five to ten per cent, to propose a law, ordinance, or constitutional amendment for action by the legislature or decision at the polls or both." By these devices an aroused public could bring about the enactment of any measure in spite of legislative opposition. When effectively used, this machinery would give the people mastery over a recalcitrant legislature, and arguments against the weapons were based on grounds having no relationship to the effectiveness of the devices.

Advocates of popular government urged the adoption of still another device for strengthening the power of the voters, which they named the recall. The idea was simple. Any elective official, and this included judges in the majority of states, could be removed from office by those who had put him in, namely, the voters. Whenever such an official proved incompetent or corrupt, the voters could demand what might be called an election in reverse; a majority of those voting could put the man out before his term expired. As in the case of the initiative and referendum the recall would not be used indiscriminately; it was designed rather as a weapon in reserve, a constant reminder that unfaithfulness to the people might terminate a political career. Some reformers suggested that the recall might be applied to judicial decisions instead of to the judge himself, particularly in cases where state judges declared statutes unconstitutional.

Votes for Women

These proposals for reform were subjected to careful analysis, and they furnished material for serious discussion. And this very discussion accentuated one more shortcoming in the American political system. With so much talk about democracy and the rights of the people to control their own government, somebody was bound to call attention to the obviously undemocratic character of the American electorate. If the principles of democracy and the consent of the governed had any real meaning, why were women left out of the picture? They formed approximately 50 percent of the adult population and they enjoyed the advantages of education on a par with the men. By virtue of numbers and training, therefore, they could demand rights at the polls. Furthermore, so many women had become self-supporting in business and the professions that they had an additional claim to the vote. This of course was not a new issue. The state of

New Jersey had allowed women to vote in the latter part of the eighteenth century, although this right had subsequently been taken away. During the middle of the nineteenth century leading reformers, men and women alike, kept up a continuous agitation for women's votes. Logically the demands of the women were so sound that they were unanswerable. Wendell Phillips stated the case clearly: "One of two things is true: either woman is like man—and if she is, then a ballot based on brains belongs to her as well as to him. Or she is different, and then man does not know how to vote for her as well as she herself does." The antisuffragists could do little more than argue that women ought not to vote because they never had.

Every reform movement must have organization, and the suffragists began with two. The American Society tried to win votes for women by working through and upon the state governments, while the National Society worked for a suffrage amendment to the federal Constitution. In 1890 these separate organizations united under the name of the "National American Woman Suffrage Association." In the East women won the right to vote in the election of school officials; by 1898 thirteen states had granted this restricted suffrage. The territory of Wyoming had permitted women to vote in general elections, and in 1890 when the territory became a state the new constitution provided for women's suffrage. Before the end of the decade Colorado, Utah, and Idaho gave votes to women. Even in the face of these gains the men who had monopolized politics for so long still held back, and it was not until 1919 that the suffrage amendment at last received the approval of Congress. The process of ratification took more than a year, but in August 1920 the Nineteenth Amendment was put into effect.

"Muck-rakers"

The preceding brief analysis of economic and social theories and reforms furnishes the setting for the early years of the twentieth century. It was a time of appraisal, with a share of adverse criticism and an abundance of devices for making a better country. Every era of reform has its particular group of writers: William Lloyd Garrison and John Greenleaf Whittier for the abolitionist crusade; Henry George, Edward Bellamy, and Henry D. Lloyd for the 1880's and 1890's; and for the first few years of the new century there was the group to which Theodore Roosevelt applied the term "muck-rakers." They were concerned with the seamy side of American public life, especially with economic and political affairs. Interest was so widespread that the cult of exposure became financially profitable to authors and publishers alike.

The most conspicuous promoter of this literature of exposure was Mr. S. S. McClure, founder, owner, and general manager of *McClure's Magazine*. McClure prided himself on his success in securing the ablest writers of the day, and he had a keen appreciation of the value of the current interest in public affairs. He encouraged Ida M. Tarbell to undertake her investigation of the Standard Oil Company, and, beginning in November 1902, he published her history of this company in his magazine. Lincoln Steffens had already published the first of a series of articles entitled "The

Shame of the Cities." In these he described the underworld of municipal government. Some people were shocked at the discovery that corruption, waste, and scandalous contempt for the rights of the people were so widespread. Another McClure author, Ray Stannard Baker, turned his attention to the financial practices and political connections of the great railroad corporations.

Other writers shouldered this same responsibility of telling the American people how sordid they had become. David Graham Phillips showed how some members of the United States Senate were acting as representatives of big business. In *Munsey's Magazine* Thomas Lawson, hitherto better known as a gambler in the stock market than as a writer, put out a series of articles entitled "Frenzied Finance." He explained at some length how he and his kind played and rigged the market. In *Collier's Weekly* Samuel Hopkins Adams attacked the fraudulent practices of the manufacturers of patent medicines. He was ably assisted in this work by Edward Bok in *The Ladies' Home Journal.* Then Upton Sinclair published a novel, *The Jungle,* which he had written as a piece of propaganda for socialism. Merely as a socialist tract the book would probably have had a limited circulation, but in the course of it the author put in a few peculiarly vivid descriptions of the meat-packing houses in Chicago, and the book immediately became famous. Another book of the time, *How the Other Half Lives,* written by Jacob Riis, gave the American people a disquieting insight into the slums of New York.

In 1905 a different type of exposure proved even more disconcerting. Charles Evans Hughes was put in charge of an investigation into the affairs of the great life insurance companies of New York. He brought out quantities of evidence to prove that the officials in charge of these companies used some of the funds entrusted to their care to promote the prosperity of certain investment bankers and to pay liberal gratuities to prominent political leaders. Policyholders had been defrauded of money which belonged to them. The Hughes investigation did have valuable results because the companies could not stand publicity of that sort. They mended their ways and their business practices became respectable.

Chapter 36

THE DOMESTIC AND FOREIGN POLICIES OF THEODORE ROOSEVELT

IN the midst of these discussions of big business, socialism, and political reform Theodore Roosevelt was suddenly raised to the Presidency of the United States. In his own day admirers and foes alike looked upon him as something unique; one prominent foreign visitor referred to the two great natural phenomena in the United States: Niagara Falls and Theodore Roosevelt. He certainly stirred the imagination of the people as few Presidents had done before. And yet his extraordinary popularity would seem to have been due not so much to his constructive achievements as to his abounding energy, his uncanny facility in putting current thoughts into words that carried the ring of oracular wisdom, and a capacity for showmanship never before known in the White House. Most important of all, he became the personification of reform, the champion of political and economic righteousness.

"What Manner of Man"

Roosevelt's name was already well known. He had served in the New York Assembly, and subsequently President Harrison made him chairman of the federal Civil Service Commission. In 1895 he became police commissioner of New York City. Two years later President McKinley made him assistant secretary of the navy, while Roosevelt made himself agitator extraordinary in demanding war against Spain. After the war, he was elected governor of New York. As governor, Roosevelt advocated laws designed to bring the corporations more definitely under public regulation, and in doing so he incurred the ill will of some outstanding leaders in both business and politics. They concluded that he must not be allowed to run for a second term. The proper place for him, they reasoned, the place where he could do the least harm, was the vice-presidency on the ticket with McKinley. Thomas Collier Platt undertook to sell the idea to Roosevelt. He soon learned what Platt had in mind and outlined his discovery to his friend Lodge: "The big moneyed men with whom he [Platt] is in close touch and whose campaign contributions have certainly been no inconsiderable factor in his strength, have been pressing him very strongly to get me put in the Vice-Presidency, so as to get me out of the State."

Republican Reformer

Roosevelt announced that he would not take the vice-presidency, but when he found that his friends from the West wished to give him the nomination as a compliment he changed his mind. At this point he ran into the opposition of Mark Hanna. Hanna's feelings were revealed in his outburst to some of the delegates: "Do whatever you damn please! I'm through! Everybody's gone crazy! What's the matter with all of you? Here's this convention going headlong for Roosevelt for Vice-President. Don't any of you realize there's only one life between that madman and the Presidency?" In spite of Hanna's disapproval, however, the convention gave Roosevelt the nomination.

The Republican platform endorsed McKinley's work in legislation, in war, and in peace-making; it attributed the great wave of prosperity to Republican policies and took pains to inform the American people

> . . . of the fact that the menace to their prosperity has always resided in Democratic principles, and no less in the general incapacity of the Democratic party to conduct public affairs. . . . [The] country's prosperity when Democratic success at the polls is announced halts and ceases in mere anticipation of Democratic blunders and failures.

In this campaign of 1900 the Democrats attempted to make an issue of imperialism. They denounced the Foraker Act for Puerto Rico "as a bold and open violation of the Nation's organic law and a flagrant breach of National good faith." Then the Democratic platform continued: "We condemn and denounce the Philippine policy of the present Administration." They demanded independence for the Philippines. Along with imperialism they attempted to revive the issue of free silver. Bryan received the unanimous vote of the convention. Adlai E. Stevenson of Illinois was his running mate. In the election McKinley won a more substantial victory than that of 1896.

McKinley's Successor

The second term opened satisfactorily. Western discontent, which had been a disturbing factor in American life for more than twenty-five years, disappeared—for the time being—as the long depression gave way to unprecedented prosperity. Conditions abroad seemed as satisfactory as they were at home. McKinley was justified in looking forward to four years of peace and comfort. On September 5 he delivered a speech at the Pan-American Exposition at Buffalo. On this occasion he showed how his experience in office had liberalized his political thinking. Formerly an isolationist and an advocate of high protection, he now urged international cooperation and reciprocity. The next day the President held a public reception in Buffalo. Through the carelessness of the secret service officer, a young fanatic, Leon Franz Czolgosz, came close enough to fire two revolver shots directly at McKinley. Eight days later he died, the third Presidential victim of assassination. Theodore Roosevelt became President.

Mark Hanna's worst fears had been realized. "I told William McKinley," he said, "it was a mistake to nominate that wild man at Philadelphia. . . . Now look, that damned cowboy is President of the United States!" But Hanna was unduly alarmed. Roosevelt had a keen understanding of politics and he knew that he could not afford to antagonize the powerful interests which controlled his party. Even before his inauguration as Vice President he had begun to cultivate the men who might help him. On the day of McKinley's death George Dunn, chairman of the New York State Republican Committee, and Douglas Robinson, Roosevelt's brother-in-law, sent him an urgent letter, strongly advising him to assure the country that he did not plan any change in policy. In response to this letter Roosevelt made the famous announcement, which most of his contemporaries had assumed to be his own: "I wish to state that it shall be my intention and endeavor to continue, absolutely unbroken, the policy of President McKinley."

Roosevelt might make overtures to the conservatives, but he could not change his nature. McKinley had been quiet and dignified. Roosevelt, on the other hand, was noisy and boisterous. In the course of a few weeks the new President put an end to the atmosphere of genial placidity which had surrounded McKinley. Even the Cabinet meetings, hitherto models of quiet dignity, now became, according to Secretary Long of the Navy, "as good as a circus."

Roosevelt's Philosophy

Roosevelt looked upon himself as the leader of his party and of the whole country. He would, he declared, be "full president" for three years. Furthermore, he had a keen appreciation of the power inherent in his office, and he was determined to exercise this power. "My belief was," he wrote, "that it was not only his [the President's] right but his duty to do anything that the needs of the Nation demanded unless such action was forbidden by the Constitution or by the laws."

Other Presidents had fallen into difficulty either because they could not work harmoniously with their party organizations—Johnson, Hayes, or Cleveland for example—or because, after the manner of Grant, they were willing to surrender their prerogatives to the party, thereby sacrificing all claim to leadership. Roosevelt was not one of these. "I intend to work with my party," he declared, "and to make it strong by making it worthy of popular support." He comprehended clearly the place of political ties in the general structure of American government. In the last analysis, cooperation with the party depended upon executive handling of the patronage, a problem which more than one President had failed utterly to solve. Roosevelt's policy in this respect was satisfactory. In making appointments, he declared, he would select Republicans if good ones were available; if not he would take the best Democrats he could find. More important still Roosevelt wrote: "The Senators and Congressmen shall ordinarily name the men, but I shall name the standard, and the men have got to come up to it."

Big Business and Labor

Theodore Roosevelt's popularity with his contemporaries can be explained not so much by what he did as by his manner of doing it. He had a keen sense of the theatrical and he made himself the central figure in dramatic situations. Even his daughter observed that he had to be the bride at every wedding and the corpse at every funeral. The circumstances of his time confronted him with a list of issues growing out of the power of corporate wealth and the intrusion of investment bankers into the fields of industry and transportation. Roosevelt dealt with some of these issues so as to make himself famous, but not in such a way as to relieve his successors from the burden of trying to find solutions for the very same problems.

Trust Buster

In his first annual message he developed his theories with reference to the relation between the trusts and the government. Great fortunes and great corporations were natural products of changing conditions, he argued; new methods were necessary, particularly when business enterprises were being conducted upon a world-wide scale. But however inevitable the trusts were and however much a phenomenon of a new age, their rise had been accompanied by serious evils. He proposed, therefore, neither the destruction of existing trusts nor the prohibition of new ones but governmental supervision and regulation. To this end he asked for publicity concerning the doings of great corporations. More specifically, he proposed the establishment of a Department of Commerce and Industries, the head of which should sit in the Cabinet.

As Roosevelt saw this problem of the corporations, the method of control was not the major issue; the real question was whether the federal government had power to control them at all. In the Knight case the Supreme Court had held that the United States had no Constitutional authority to regulate manufacturing because manufacturing was not commerce. A trust therefore could legally control distribution by its monopoly of production. Unless the decision in the Knight case could be reversed, the administration was helpless. Roosevelt and Attorney General Knox tried to find a corporation which could be successfully prosecuted. They decided that the Northern Securities Company would serve their purpose.

The Northern Securities Company was a holding corporation organized to unite certain railroads in the Northwest. The formation of this company put an end to a spectacular contest in American railroad history. J. P. Morgan and Company had entered the railroad field, and among its lines was the Northern Pacific running west from St. Paul. Then Morgan joined forces with James J. Hill of the Great Northern. South of these lines was the Union Pacific running west from Omaha, which had recently been rebuilt by Edward H. Harriman. None of these roads had direct access to Chicago, but they all connected with the Chicago, Burlington, and Quincy which did have a Chicago terminal. The Northern Pacific bought the C. B. and Q., whereupon Harriman started to buy a controlling interest in the Northern Pacific. The Hill and Morgan interests entered the market to safeguard their control, and in 1901 the price of Northern Pacific rose to $1000 per share.

This battle plunged the stock market into wild confusion. Then the leaders in the fight arranged a settlement. Harriman was taken on as one of the directors of the Northern Pacific; the parties organized the Northern Securities Company to control the Northern Pacific, the Great Northern, and the Burlington. This concern received its charter from New Jersey in November 1901, just a few weeks before Roosevelt's message on the trusts went to Congress. Late one afternoon in the following February, Attorney General Knox announced that the government would prosecute the Northern Securities Company for violation of the Sherman Act.

In 1904, after favorable decisions in the lower courts, the United States Supreme Court decided that the Northern Securities Company had been formed in violation of the Sherman Act. This was a 5 to 4 decision, nevertheless it was a victory for the administration. Roosevelt had at last demonstrated the power of the government over the forces of "predatory wealth," and J. P. Morgan, the symbol of vast financial power, had been compelled to yield. Roosevelt, the hero of San Juan Hill, acquired a new title: "the trust buster." With the lapse of time both the brilliance and importance of the victory have worn off. Four Justices of the Supreme Court opposed the decision on grounds of law, and most economists regarded it as futile. Certainly there was no evidence that the railroads separated and went their own way. In the course of his Presidency, Theodore Roosevelt and the Department of Justice instituted twenty-five suits against corporations. Even granting that this was the proper method of attack, the number was relatively small. Roosevelt's successor Taft, in his single term, started almost twice as many. Furthermore, Roosevelt did practically nothing in the way of building up a staff in the Department of Justice for handling antitrust business. In 1903, however, Congress did provide for the establishment of the Department of Commerce and Labor, in which there was a Bureau of Corporations. This Bureau gathered information about corporations, some of which was available for use later on when the Federal Trade Commission began its work.

Hepburn Act

In dealing with the railroads Roosevelt emphasized two measures of reform. Early in 1903 Congress passed and Roosevelt approved an amendment to the Interstate Commerce Act designed to make the prohibition of rebates really effective. There still remained the complex issue of the regulation of rates. As a result of judicial decisions the Interstate Commerce Commission had lost virtually all influence over rate schedules. In his annual message of 1904 Roosevelt asked for legislation to restore the Commission's authority. On June 29, 1906, he signed the Hepburn Act which enabled the Commission to fix maximum rates and which extended the Commission's jurisdiction over express companies, sleeping-car companies, and pipe lines. This measure saved the Commission from threatened oblivion and established the principle of federal regulation. Under the next two Presidents additional laws increased still further the powers of the Commission.

Roosevelt's procedure in dealing with the strike of the anthracite coal miners in 1902 illustrated his methods. Most of the anthracite mines were owned and operated by the coal-carrying railroads, such as the Lehigh

Valley, the Lackawanna, and the Philadelphia and Reading. These roads were directed by J. P. Morgan and Company. The railroads had acquired control of the mines by methods subsequently regarded as illegal. The workers in the mines found company policies burdensome and tyrannical. Wages were too low for decent living. In 1901 the average for each anthracite miner was $560 per year. Employment was irregular and the occupation itself was hazardous. Then the miners complained of the paternalistic system which the companies imposed upon them. They had to live in company houses, buy their provisions at company stores, employ company physicians, all at rates fixed arbitrarily by the company. Charges for these goods and services, so the men said, were higher than those prevailing in other communities. In this arbitrary system the individual miner was helpless. In an effort to improve their condition the employees joined the United Mine Workers then under the leadership of John Mitchell. In 1900 they went on strike, but that was a Presidential campaign year and the Republican Party could not afford to have its chances put in jeopardy by industrial warfare. Mark Hanna induced the operators to yield, and the men called off the strike.

Anthracite Mining

Early in 1902 Mitchell presented the demands of the miners for higher wages, greater freedom in living conditions, and formal recognition of the union. The operators refused even to meet the representatives of the union. In May Mitchell asked the operators to submit the dispute to arbitration. George F. Baer of the Philadelphia and Reading acted as spokesman for the operators:

> Anthracite mining is a business and not a religious, sentimental, or academic proposition. The laws organizing the companies I represent in express terms impose the business management on the president and directors. I could not if I would delegate this business management to even so high and respectable a body as the Civic Federation. Nor can I call to my aid as experts in the mixed problem of business and philanthropy the eminent prelates you have named.

Negotiations having failed, the miners began their strike. The strike continued through the summer, and as cooler weather approached people in the northeastern section of the country became alarmed over the rising price of coal. Ordinarily selling for $5 per ton, anthracite advanced to $14; by October 1 dealers were charging $25 or in some cases $30. Schools began to close for lack of fuel and there were prospects of real suffering. The mayor of New York and the governor of Massachusetts urged President Roosevelt to intervene. It so happened that 1902 was a congressional campaign year, and the strike affected the political situation. Henry Cabot Lodge of Massachusetts warned the President that in the coming election the rise in the price of coal would cost the Republican party badly needed votes.

Coal Strike

Roosevelt tried first to approach the operators through Mark Hanna, who had been successful in a similar venture two years earlier; this time, however, the operators would not listen. Then, following a suggestion made by

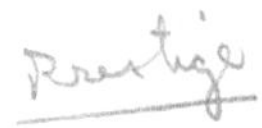

Murray Crane, Republican leader of Massachusetts, the President asked representatives of the operators and the miners' union to meet at the White House on October 3. At this gathering he urged the resumption of work in the mines. The miners agreed to return to work, pending an investigation by a commission which the President should appoint, and they promised in advance to accept the award of such a commission, provided the operators also would agree. This at first the operators emphatically refused to do. Roosevelt determined to appoint a commission anyway and, if necessary, to force a resumption of mining by the use of federal troops. The operators decided to yield and announced their willingness to abide by the findings of the commission. The men resumed work on October 23.

The commission submitted its proposals on March 21, 1903. The miners received a 10 percent advance in wages. For the future, disputes between operators and miners should be submitted to a board of conciliation. The operators were to be free to hire both union and nonunion labor. Both parties were to be bound by this award for a period of three years. The settlement of the strike brought increased popularity to the President, but it resulted in no general solution of the problems of organized labor.

The Voters Approve

Campaign of 1904

Up to this point in dealing with business enterprise and with organized labor Roosevelt had displayed skill in meeting situations of the moment. In the judgment of posterity he never went beyond that point. But his dramatic methods brought wide contemporary acclaim, and politically this was important. His own contemporaries who admired him, not posterity, would cast ballots in the coming Presidential election of 1904. On the other hand, many leaders in the Republican party, particularly those representatives of business enterprise who provided campaign funds, were convinced that the President was a traitor to the cause. They had no sympathy with the growing demand for restrictions on business, and they looked back regretfully to the days of McKinley, Cleveland, and Harrison, when the federal regulatory laws were allowed to rest quietly within the statute books.

By 1903 local leaders and local newspapers were demanding the nomination of Roosevelt for a second term; at the same time the conservatives were hunting for a more orthodox Republican. These anti-Roosevelt cohorts found their leader in the chairman of the Republican National Committee, Mark Hanna. Hanna was in a receptive mood, and had he lived he might have become the Republican nominee. His sudden death early in 1904 plunged the conservatives into confusion because there was no one else in the party strong enough to oppose Roosevelt; as a result, the President was nominated for a second term.

The Democrats found it difficult to make headway against Roosevelt's personal popularity, and their national convention revealed a spirit of defeatism and discouragement. Their strongest candidate was William Jennings Bryan, but he had behind him the discredit of two defeats. Then there was a comparatively new aspirant for the Democratic Presidential nomination, the prominent newspaper publisher William Randolph Hearst. He had already served one term in Congress, and he had the backing of his own eight papers in five cities. He posed as a radical, a friend of organized labor, and an opponent of corporations. In the convention he received 200 votes. Passing over both Hearst and Bryan, the convention gave the nomination to the conservative Judge Alton B. Parker of New York.

The campaign was uneventful and Roosevelt's election was assured. In the course of the contest the Democrats tried to make capital out of the charge that the Republicans were financed by big business. Up to this point the charge was true; there was nothing new or unusual in it. But Judge Parker introduced a new element when he accused Cortelyou of blackmailing the corporations into making contributions. His point was that Cortelyou, as secretary of commerce and labor, had acquired considerable information as to the misdeeds of big business and that he used his knowledge as a means of compelling them to pay generously for protection against prosecution. No evidence in support of this aspect of the Democratic charge has ever come to light. As for funds themselves, both parties accepted them, the only difference being that the Republicans were more fortunate in the amounts received. When the Democrats accepted $250,000 from August Belmont, they could not consistently condemn such gifts on grounds of principle.

Roosevelt indignantly denied that Cortelyou was practicing blackmail and declared the charges against him to be "unqualifiedly and atrociously false." In 1907 new light was thrown on this question of campaign contributions. A former employee of E. H. Harriman published a letter written by Roosevelt to Harriman during the campaign of 1904. Roosevelt, according to Harriman, had invited Harriman to visit him in Washington and then had urged him to help raise funds to carry New York. Roosevelt's reply would suggest that Harriman touched a tender spot: "Any such statement is a deliberate and wilful untruth—by rights it should be characterized by an even shorter and more ugly word. . . . I never requested Mr. Harriman to raise a dollar for the Presidential campaign of 1904." Critics pointed out that Roosevelt's denial did not exactly fit Harriman's charge. Harriman was talking in terms of the Republican campaign in New York. Roosevelt did not deny that he had asked for help to carry New York. He denied that he had asked for contributions for the Presidential campaign.

But all this talk about campaign contributions had been lost on the ordinary voters. They liked Roosevelt and they said so with votes. Roosevelt won the election with a popular vote of 7,628,785, larger than McKinley's in 1900 by more than 400,000. Parker, on the other hand, received only 5,084,442. He had 1,250,000 fewer votes than Bryan received in 1900. Parker carried nothing but the solid South, plus the two border states of Kentucky and Maryland.

By 1905, when Roosevelt was inaugurated for his second term, the people had learned that he looked upon government as a dynamic, constructive agency designed to promote national well-being. Further evidence of this same attitude may be seen in two laws of 1906, the Pure Food and Drug Act and the Meat Inspection Act, both of which had the President's support. The first of these measures was a protest against the business methods, particularly the advertising policies, of manufacturers of proprietary medicines. By 1900 the patent medicine business had reached a volume of $59,611,355. In some cases these alleged remedies were harmless; in others they contained habit-forming drugs such as opium, cocaine, or alcohol. In their zeal to increase sales the advertisers made statements which were grossly deceptive. There was no law against selling "cures"—which were certain to do the taker more harm than good—and the only legal concept which had any bearing on the problem was *caveat emptor*—let the buyer beware.

Public Welfare

In 1905, President Roosevelt became interested in the fight against the medicines. He thought that Congress had power to prohibit interstate traffic in adulterated or harmful foods and drugs. In 1906 a bill for this purpose was introduced. This measure was designed to prohibit the sale in interstate commerce of certain harmful products and to compel the manufacturers to declare on the label the presence of specified dangerous drugs; it was not designed to prohibit misleading or false statements in advertising. In their campaign against the measure the manufacturers and some of their friends resorted to statements almost as false as many of the claims made in behalf of their products. In spite of unscrupulous opposition, the bill became law.

The Meat Inspection Act had a somewhat similar purpose, that of protecting consumers from injurious products. Some of the meat-packing establishments were not careful to maintain proper standards of cleanliness. Instead of welcoming investigations of their plants in the interests of convincing the public that such charges were untrue, some of the packers tried to silence the critics. Then a sensational book appeared which seemed to furnish proof that the critics were right. In 1906 Upton Sinclair published *The Jungle,* a novel supposedly based upon the experiences of a recently arrived immigrant; actually it was diatribe against the meat packers. There were some lurid passages in it. The author described an alleged incident, the gist of which was that one workman fell into a large vat and that his remains eventually reached the consumers in the form of pure lard. Before bringing out the book the publishers sent a trained investigator to Chicago to find out how bad conditions were. He reported that they were even worse than the book implied. Then President Roosevelt appointed the Neill-Reynolds Commission to conduct an official investigation. Their findings were just as specific as Sinclair's. When the packers endeavored to prevent the enactment of a meat inspection law, Roosevelt sent excerpts of this report to Congress: "We saw meat shovelled from filthy wooden floors, piled on tables rarely washed, pushed from room to room in rotten box carts, in all of which processes it was in the way of gathering dirt, splinters, floor filth, and the expectoration of tuberculous and other diseased workers."

Senator Beveridge of Indiana introduced the bill providing for federal inspection of the packing houses, but Congress refused to pass the measure in its original form. However, a substitute was introduced in the House and it became law. This provided for inspection at the cost of the government. It decreed that all meat shipped in interstate commerce must be derived from animals free from disease and that the packing houses must maintain minimum standards of cleanliness.

Conservation

In this second term Roosevelt took up the complex issue of conservation of natural resources and made almost a religion of it. Conservation was the logical outcome of the too liberal land policy which the federal government had embarked upon during and after the Civil War. In its excessive liberality the federal government had opened opportunities to land speculators, lumber companies, and mining syndicates. At practically no cost to themselves these corporations had secured control of vast resources to the lasting detriment of the country at large. In 1891 Congress had attempted to stop further losses of this sort by an act which authorized the President to set apart forest lands as public reservations. Under this measure the first steps were taken in a policy of conservation. By 1910 there were 149 national forests, containing altogether about 193,000,000 acres. Of this total President Roosevelt had set apart 126,000,000 acres.

In October 1903 the President appointed a commission to investigate and report on existing laws with reference to the public domain and to recommend such changes as were necessary to effect the transfer of agricultural lands to actual settlers. This commission submitted two reports. In the second, made in 1905, it recommended that the government retain the title to all minerals, including coal, oil, and phosphate, in lands still subject to disposal. Then the right to exploit these resources could be leased profitably instead of being thrown away. Legislation embodying these recommendations, however, was not enacted until Taft became President.

In his annual message of 1907 Roosevelt gave Congress an elaborate analysis of the whole problem of conservation. He made it clear that a continuance of the older policy of stripping land, forests, and mines in the interest of immediate private profit would bring untold damage to later generations. In place of the former schemes of reckless exploitation he urged "a planned and orderly development of our resources." His recommendations included such matters as river improvements and flood control. For the lower Mississippi levees would be needed to keep the river where it belonged. He pointed out that "utilization of waterways and water-power, forestry, irrigation, and the reclamation of lands threatened with overflow, are all interdependent parts of the same problem."

Before delivering this message he had appointed a commission to investigate the inland waterways of the country, and the commission in turn had recommended a national convention for the study of the whole problem. Out of these proposals came the conference on conservation held in Washington, D. C., in May 1908. Among the delegates were the governors of the various states. The conference endorsed the proposals which Roosevelt had made in his annual message and urged Congress and the state legislatures to pass laws covering the whole program. In the following July Roosevelt appointed a national conservation commission of forty-nine members, with Gifford Pinchot as chairman. This body made a general inventory of natural resources of the United States: minerals, water rights, and forests. Two months before he left office Roosevelt laid this report before Congress, but action had to be deferred until the next administration.

Theodore Roosevelt had been fortunate in coming to the Presidency when the economic development of the United States was bringing widespread prosperity. But in 1907 a panic followed by a depression hit the world of business. Like the earlier depressions this one was not merely local but world-wide. From places as far apart as Egypt, South America, and Japan came the same story of falling prices, collapse of credit, and increase in bankruptcies. The setback in 1907 has been described as a "bankers' panic." But the depression which followed was not confined to bankers. The curve of business expansion was no longer upward and there was no significant recovery until 1915 when World War I brought European orders for American products. Nevertheless, the shock of the depression was not so severe as those of 1873 and 1893, and it did not weaken the hold of the Republican party on the voters.

"My Policies" Abroad

Theodore Roosevelt was just as deeply interested in foreign policy as in domestic affairs, and in this foreign field he found, or took, considerable freedom to act as he pleased. He defined his guiding principle in a letter to Taft with reference to intervention in Cuba in 1906 under the Platt Amendment:

> I should not dream of asking the permission of Congress. . . . It is for the enormous interest of this government to strengthen and give independence to the executive in dealing with foreign powers. . . . Therefore the important thing to do is for a president who is willing to accept responsibility to establish precedents which successors may follow even if they are unwilling to take the initiative themselves.

Roosevelt followed this principle in dealing with matters whether in Latin America or the Far East.

The first major problem to claim his attention was the proposed Panama Canal. Here was a project with a complex history and at the same time one of vital importance for the future. Even before the Spanish-American War President McKinley had appointed a commission to investigate and report on an isthmian canal. After the war the removal of foreign interests and the actual construction of the canal became major factors in American commercial and strategic policy. The building of the canal in turn gave rise to new problems of defense, and in solving these the United States became the greatest power in and around the Caribbean.

Isthmian Canal

For practical purposes American interests in an isthmian canal dated back to the settlement of the Oregon boundary and the acquisition of California in President Polk's administration. In 1846 the United States and New Granada—the name was subsequently changed to Colombia—signed a treaty under which the United States guaranteed the "perfect neutrality" of the Isthmus of Panama for the purpose of keeping transit open. The United States also guaranteed to New Granada all rights of property and of sovereignty which she "has and possesses there." This treaty was still in force at the time of the revolution in Panama in 1903. In 1855 an American corporation built the Panama Railroad to connect the Caribbean with the Pacific. Between 1848 and 1903 United States troops, with the consent and approval of Colombia, intervened on the Isthmus on seven different occasions. Before 1903, however, American intervention had always helped Colombia.

In 1850 the governments of the United States and Great Britain had signed the Clayton-Bulwer Treaty. The treaty declared that neither the United States nor Great Britain would ever obtain or maintain exclusive control over the proposed ship canal which might be constructed over any one of three routes: Panama, Nicaragua, or Tehuantepec in Mexico. Other governments might be admitted to this partnership provided they agreed to these terms.

In 1878 a French company, headed by de Lesseps, the builder of the Suez Canal, secured a concession from Colombia allowing it to build a Panama Canal. The French company began construction in 1881, but after a short time it became involved in financial difficulties and stopped work, although its concession had several more years to run. So far the canal existed only in imagination. Then the Spanish-American War and the dramatic voyage of the battleship *Oregon* around Cape Horn called attention once more to the need of the waterway. In March 1899 Congress authorized President McKinley to appoint a commission to investigate and report on the various routes. At the same time the State Department began negotiations with Great Britain for the purpose of abrogating the Clayton-Bulwer Treaty.

Early in 1900 John Hay and Sir Julian Pauncefote signed the draft of a new treaty, permitting the United States alone to build the canal, provided that ships of all nations were left free to use the canal in peace and war alike and that toll charges were uniform. This first draft prohibited the United States from fortifying the canal. This arrangement did not give the United States the freedom which seemed necessary, and the Senate refused to ratify the document. After further negotiations Secretary Hay secured more satisfactory terms. This new Hay-Pauncefote Treaty expressly abrogated the Clayton-Bulwer Treaty and gave the United States sole power to build, operate, and control the canal. Because the second draft omitted the clause which prohibited fortifications, the United States assumed that all necessary fortifications could be built. The treaty safeguarded British interests by providing that: "The canal shall be free and open to the vessels of commerce and of war of all nations observing these Rules, on terms of entire equality, so that there shall be no discrimination against any such nation . . . in respect of the conditions or charges of traffic, or otherwise." The embarrassing partnership with Great Britain was ended, and the United States was free to proceed on its own account.

Colombia and Panama

The next step was to decide upon a route. The New Panama Canal Company, a French corporation, still owned the right of way across Panama. At first this concern demanded too high a price for its property, but when it came down to $40,000,000, Congress authorized the Panama route. Then it became necessary to make arrangements with Colombia. After negotiations lasting several months, the Colombian representative, Herran, and Secretary Hay signed a treaty. This was early in January 1903. By this Hay-Herran Treaty, Colombia was to cede to the United States a strip of land across the Isthmus thirty miles in length and six miles in width. Over this zone the United States would have exclusive administrative control, in perpetuity, except in the two terminal cities of Panama and Colón. The price agreed upon was $10,000,000 in gold and, beginning nine years after the date of ratification, an annual payment of $250,000. The United States Senate ratified this arrangement on March 17, 1903.

But in Bogotá there was intense opposition, and on June 10, 1903, the agent of the French New Panama Canal Company received official notice that the document probably would not be ratified. This was accompanied by an intimation that should the company pay to Colombia the sum of $10,000,000 ratification might be secured. President Maroquin summoned a special session of Congress to consider the treaty. This body asked for $15,000,000 instead of $10,000,000 from the United States. When neither the New Panama Canal Company nor the United States would pay the sum proposed the Congress unanimously rejected the treaty.

Panamanian leaders were deeply disturbed over this rejection of the treaty, and they talked about a revolution against Colombia. Secretary Hay and President Roosevelt liked the idea. During this period Roosevelt had conversations with some of the interested parties, notably Philippe Bunau-Varilla. These prospective revolutionists learned of the President's determination to send warships to the Isthmus. Roosevelt did not instigate the revolution because he did not have to; the Panamanians did that. He gave no specific promises of help to the revolutionists, but he did say enough to assure them that he would not allow Colombian authorities to suppress an uprising in Panama.

Two weeks before the expected uprising the Navy Department ordered three gunboats to the Caribbean. Their commanders were instructed to maintain free and uninterrupted transit over the Panama Railroad and necessary to occupy the line of the railroad itself. Neither Colombian nor insurgent forces were to be allowed to land within fifty miles of Panama. These orders were carried out. On November 3 the revolt came; on the next day the republic of Panama proclaimed its independence; and two days later the United States recognized the new nation. Colombian sovereignty over the Isthmus was at an end.

Panama and the Canal

The new republic at once named Philippe Bunau-Varilla its envoy to the United States, and on November 18 he signed a treaty with Secretary Hay. Panama ratified it on December 2, 1903, and the United States Senate did likewise on February 23, 1904. The United States pledged itself to maintain the independence of the republic of Panama and in return received a perpetual lease, with complete administrative control, of a zone ten miles in width and the right to intervene in Panama itself at any time if necessary to preserve order. The United States agreed to pay $10,000,000 in gold and after nine years $250,000 annually during the life of the treaty. In April 1904 Congress appropriated the $10,000,000 and gave the President executive authority over the Canal Zone. An act of May 9, 1904, placed the powers of government over the Zone and responsibility for constructing the Canal in the Isthmian Canal Commission.

Instead of letting the contracts for constructing the Canal to private engineering firms, the job of building was put in the hands of engineers of the United States Army. In 1908 Colonel G. W. Goethals took charge of the work of construction and also of the management and government of the Canal Zone. The earlier work of Dr. Walter Reed had shown how to eliminate yellow fever. Under the efficient administration of Dr. W. E. Gorgas the Canal Zone was made as free as possible from disease. The actual construction work took approximately seven years, from 1907 to 1914. The first commercial ship went through the Panama Canal in August 1914.

Alaska Boundary

The abrogation of the Clayton-Bulwer Treaty and the signing of the Hay-Pauncefote Treaty made the United States the supreme power in the Caribbean. This change indicated a high degree of friendliness in the relations between Great Britain and the United States. Occasionally this friendliness was disturbed as it had been in the dispute over the Venezuela boundary. In Roosevelt's administration it was again disturbed, this time over the boundary between Canada and Alaska. In 1825 the British and Russian governments had agreed by treaty that the boundary of southern Alaska should follow the mountain crests in such a way as to leave in Russian hands a strip of coastal territory thirty miles in width. The point at issue was whether this line should run around the various deep inlets along that coast, or whether it should cut squarely across them. In 1867 the Russian title passed to the United States. Subsequently the Canadians insisted that the boundary did not conform to the sinuosities of the coast line.

In February 1899 the British government proposed that the disagreement be submitted to arbitration. At first Secretary Hay refused to consider the suggestion. He and President McKinley, he wrote, were "so sure of our case that we are not willing to put it in jeopardy before some chance arbitration." He did, however, at last consent to a modified form of arbitration. Then Great Britain argued that the Alaskan boundary should be submitted to arbitration on a principle identical with that in the case of Venezuela. Hay replied that the two disputes were not similar. The Canadian claim was new, while the Venezuelan boundary had been in dispute for sixty years. The parts of the coast involved in the dispute had been in the unquestioned possession of Russia or the United States, and American settlements had been made at the head of some of the inlets with no protests from Canada.

After some further discussion and after Theodore Roosevelt became President, the two governments reached an agreement providing for the submission of the question to a mixed tribunal of six members, three from the United States, two from Canada, and one from England. However, Roosevelt declared that the Canadian claim had "the scantest possible warrant in justice"; he insisted that there was no room for doubt on the main issue and that the tribunal ought to decide in favor of the United States. Evidently the British government agreed with Roosevelt rather than with the Canadians because in October 1903 the tribunal upheld the American contention on all important points. Lord Alverstone, the English member, voted with the three members from the United States.

The Hague Conferences

The idea of arbitration as a substitute for war had long found favor in American eyes, and at the close of the century there seemed to be a good prospect of making the policy effective. In 1899 the Czar of Russia made a move toward international action in behalf of peace. His government invited the nations represented at St. Petersburg to send delegates to a meeting at The Hague, and in doing so it outlined certain topics for discussion. Among other matters the Czar urged the desirability of limiting armaments, prohibiting the use not only of new types of weapons or munitions, but also of submarines. The last item on the list was a proposal for general arbitration.

Secretary Hay wrote the instructions for the American delegates at The Hague. Concerning limitation of armaments, Hay called attention to the fact that American forces were so small in comparison with those of European powers that the United States was in no position even to discuss the question. Then Hay expressed the opinion that the proposals for making war less destructive or less terrible were "lacking in practicality." He found the proposal for a more effective plan of arbitration the most promising subject of discussion, and he instructed the American delegates to submit a plan for an international tribunal and to use their influence to secure ratification of the plan.

The most important results of this first Hague Conference was the adoption of "The Convention for the Pacific Settlement of International Disputes." According to this agreement the governments concerned would submit their disputes to arbitration. To this end the conference established an international tribunal or panel of judges. Each of the twenty-six signatory powers was allowed to name four members of this tribunal, each to serve for a term of six years. These judges never convened as a single body and none of them came together except on special call. In case governments wished to submit any question to the tribunal, they would draw up a special agreement, defining the terms at issue. Then they might select any number of judges from the whole panel to act as a board of arbitration.

Within the next five years thirty-three treaties were signed by various governments for the purpose of putting the Hague Convention into effect. No government, however, bound itself unconditionally to submit all of its disputes to arbitration. The treaties were careful to provide that only such questions should be submitted as did not involve the vital interests, independence, or national honor of the parties concerned.

The government of the United States signed several of these limited arbitration treaties, but when they were submitted to the Senate for ratification this body insisted that the special agreements to be drawn in the case of each dispute must also be submitted to the Senate. Roosevelt and Hay disagreed with the Senate on this point and refused to take up the subject of the Senate's amendment with the other powers.

The partial failure of this first effort to provide a rational means for the settlement of international differences stimulated the friends of peace to further efforts. In 1906 the Czar of Russia proposed another conference at The Hague, and in June 1907 delegates from forty-six governments came together there. The Russian government also proposed certain subjects for discussion. Among these were the problems of naval warfare: the bombardment of cities, the use of torpedoes, the status of private property on the seas, neutral rights, and the question of contraband of war. The Czar also urged that improved methods of arbitration be adopted. Elihu Root, who had succeeded John Hay as secretary of state, instructed the American delegates to work for the establishment of a permanent judicial tribunal to deal with international difficulties. He also emphasized the desirability of an agreement designed to prevent the use of force in the collection of foreign debts.

The conference worked out a plan for a new international tribunal, to be composed of fifteen judges, one each from the eight leading world powers and seven from the smaller nations. The judges from these smaller powers would be chosen in accordance with the principle of rotation. According to Root's plan, these members of the court were to be judicial officers who would decide cases in accordance with the principles of international law.

In the matter of collecting debts the conference adopted a formula whereby the governments agreed to "take no military or naval action to compel the repayment of such debts until an offer of arbitration has been made by the creditor and refused or left unanswered by the debtor" or until the dispute should have been submitted to arbitration and the debtor had refused to comply with the decision of the board of arbitration. The chief advocate of this formula or doctrine was Luis M. Drago of Argentina.

Concerning limitation of armament, nothing at all was accomplished. Following this conference, Secretary Root revived the arbitration treaties and secured their approval by the Senate.

New Responsibilities

The American government soon found that the prospect of having the Panama Canal altered the whole policy of the United States toward the Caribbean. Hitherto revolution there had not directly affected the United States, and the financial relations between Latin American governments and European bankers had been of no concern. By 1902, however, all this had begun to change.

Roosevelt Corollary

In 1902 relations between Venezuela and eleven other governments reached a critical stage. Venezuela was deeply in debt and instead of making an effort to meet her obligations she seemed inclined to repudiate them. For two years before the crisis the British government exhausted the resources of diplomacy in an effort to bring the Venezuelan authorities to terms, and in the face of Venezuelan resistance and stubbornness the British notes became steadily more menacing. The German government, on the other hand, while equally insistent upon a settlement, proposed that the points at issue be submitted to arbitration, preferably to the Hague Tribunal. The Venezuelans were no more responsive to the moderate overtures of Germany than to the blunter demands of Great Britain. By the end of December 1901 the German government concluded that coercion alone would bring results. In keeping with the international amenities which prevailed in those days and with one eye on the Monroe Doctrine, the German government assured the United States "that under no circumstances do we consider in our proceedings the acquisition or the permanent occupation of Venezuelan territory." Secretary Hay replied that the Monroe Doctrine was designed to prevent any territorial aggrandizement at the expense of any American power. But the United States, he continued, "do not guarantee any State against punishment if it misconducts itself, provided that punishment does not take the form of the acquisition of territory by any non-American power."

Subsequently Germany and Great Britain decided to act together in applying pressure upon Venezuela, and both governments again assured the United States that they had no intention of seizing territory. Late in December 1902 the two European governments instituted a blockade of Venezuelan ports. Roosevelt expressed hope that the controversy might be peaceably settled and at last the Venezuelans yielded. The dispute was then submitted to the Hague Tribunal.

The affair in Venezuela, along with similar financial difficulties in other Latin American governments, seemed to call for a new definition of the Monroe Doctrine. Roosevelt endeavored to meet the need. In his annual message of 1904 he laid down the dogma subsequently known as the

Roosevelt corollary of the Monroe Doctrine. He assured his Latin American neighbors that the United States wanted only "to see the neighboring countries stable, orderly, and prosperous."

> If a nation shows that it knows how to act with reasonable efficiency, and decency in social and political matters, if it keeps order and pays its obligations, it need fear no interference from the United States. Chronic wrongdoing, or an impotence which results in a general loosening of the ties of civilized society, may, in America, as elsewhere, ultimately require intervention by some civilized nation, and in the Western Hemisphere the adherence of the United States to the Monroe Doctrine may force the United States, however reluctantly, in flagrant cases of such wrongdoing or impotence, to the exercise of an international police power.

This warning was designed to forestall any further intervention of European powers in Latin American affairs. If intervention were necessary, the United States would do the intervening.

Financial Guardianship

Although Roosevelt did not mention any particular government in this part of his message, he was thinking of Santo Domingo. The financial affairs of this island republic had been allowed to drift into serious confusion, and by 1904 both France and Italy were threatening to force a settlement. Financial confusion was accompanied by political incapacity. In 1904 Secretary Hay instructed the American minister to Santo Domingo to find out whether the government would permit the United States to take charge of the customhouses and to assist in clearing up the debts. In as much as this request for information was equivalent to an order, the Dominican authorities could do nothing but comply. Early in 1905 therefore the United States and Santo Domingo signed a formal agreement under which the United States took over the administration of the customhouses. The purpose was to apply 45 percent of the customs receipts to the payment of current expenses and to use the balance in meeting past obligations. Furthermore, the United States was prepared to give any assistance necessary for restoring credit, preserving order, increasing the efficiency of the government, and advancing the welfare of the people. Under this grant of power the United States assumed control of Dominican finance.

This agreement with Santo Domingo, like all treaties, had to be submitted to the Senate, and the Senate refused to ratify. Thereupon Roosevelt announced that the agreement was effective by virtue of his executive proclamation. The Senate held out for two years but in 1907 gave its approval. This assumption of responsibility for the financial good behavior of the Latin American powers made the United States the guardian of the Caribbean. And, as the Panama Canal moved toward completion and afterward, our government made it plain that neither financial nor political shortcomings would be tolerated in that region.

In his second term, Roosevelt was called upon to deal with one of the crises in Cuban affairs for which the Platt Amendment had been specifically framed. Following an armed uprising in the summer of 1906 the Cuban president announced that he would resign. Roosevelt sent Secretary of War Taft and Assistant Secretary of State Robert Bacon to Cuba to effect a settlement of the controversy. By that time Cuban factions were already aroused to the point of anarchy. Roosevelt ordered the establishment of a provisional government, supported by American troops, under the direction of Secretary Taft. It took three years to bring about a restoration of order and to secure the degree of harmony essential to the proper functioning of a Cuban government. Then in January 1909 the Americans withdrew and restored the administration to the Cubans themselves. Subsequently American forces were sent back to Cuba for brief periods, once in 1912 and again in 1917. On the latter occasion they stayed until 1922.

Peace of Portsmouth

During 1904 and 1905 Roosevelt pursued a foreign policy with reference to Europe and the Far East which was the most extraordinary ever undertaken by an American President. In 1904 Japan started war with Russia. During the first part of the war he wrote letters expressing full sympathy with Japan. In the latter part he worked earnestly to bring the war to a close. In April 1905, he had repeated interviews with the Japanese, Russian, British, French, and German representatives in Washington, all in the interests of peace. By June both Japan and Russia agreed to begin negotiations. Late in July the Russian and Japanese commissioners arrived in the United States, and on August 5 Roosevelt received them formally aboard the *Mayflower* at Oyster Bay. On August 8 the conference began work in Portsmouth, New Hampshire. During the negotiations Roosevelt played an important part, working for moderate terms. In September the Treaty of Portsmouth was signed, and the terms were substantially what Roosevelt had proposed in the beginning. Roosevelt and the world at large looked upon the treaty as one of the greatest achievements in his career.

In the meantime, Roosevelt had been engaged secretly in two other separate, though closely related, negotiations. One culminated in the "agreed memorandum" or the "secret pact with Japan." The other ended in the Algeciras conference on Morocco. In connection with the "agreed memorandum," not only the negotiations but the results were kept concealed until after Roosevelt's death. In 1905 Roosevelt was concerned over the attitude of Japan toward the Philippine Islands; his fears were laid at rest by the "memorandum." On July 29, 1905, Count Katsura, the prime minister, then in charge of Japanese foreign relations, had an interview with Secretary Taft in which the two men discussed the Philippines, Korea, and the general question of maintaining peace in the Far East. The substance of this conversation was reduced to writing and subsequently endorsed as authentic and correct by Roosevelt himself.

In this "memorandum" Count Katsura declared that the only interest of the Japanese in the Philippines was to have the islands governed by a strong and friendly power; that they did not wish to see them under native misrule or in the hands of some European power unfriendly to Japan. The

Japanese, Katsura pledged, harbored no aggressive designs upon the Philippines. In return for this promise, Roosevelt approved the establishment of Japanese suzerainty over Korea. This highhanded arrangement ignored any rights which the Koreans may have thought they possessed.

Pact with Japan

With reference to the Far East in general, Count Katsura said that the maintenance of peace "forms the fundamental principle of Japan's international policy." In his opinion the best means of establishing this principle would be a "good understanding" between Japan, the United States, and Great Britain. He realized that a formal alliance with the United States would be impossible, but in view of the common interests of the two countries he felt that "some good understanding or an alliance in practice" might be made, which would be as effective as a formal alliance. Taft replied that not even an informal agreement could be made without the consent of the Senate, but that he was sure the people of the United States were so fully in sympathy with the Far Eastern policy of Great Britain and Japan that "whatever occasion arose, appropriate action of the government of the United States, in conjunction with Japan and Great Britain, for such a purpose could be counted on by them quite as confidently as if the United States were under treaty obligations to take [it]."

On August 12, just two weeks after this interview, the Anglo-Japanese alliance was formally renewed, with the avowed object of maintaining peace in the Far East. The *Kokumin,* a Japanese newspaper generally regarded as the official organ of the government, announced with reference to the Anglo-Japanese Treaty that in fact "it is a Japanese-Anglo-American alliance. We may be sure that when once England became our ally, America also became a party to the agreement."

Gentlemen's Agreement

These friendly relations with Japan were not destined to last long. In 1906, the year after the acceptance of the "secret pact," the school board in San Francisco ruled that Japanese were not entitled to instruction in the city's public schools. Had it been merely a question of Japanese children, the problem would have been less difficult, but Japanese adults as well as children were entering the primary schools in order to learn English. To make the situation worse, the Hearst newspapers were busily prophesying war between the United States and Japan. The Japanese government protested against the action of the city of San Francisco on the ground that it was a violation of her treaty rights with this country. Roosevelt was disturbed and apparently exasperated at both sides. He announced that "all of the forces, military and civil, of the United States" would be used if necessary in order to uphold the treaty rights of Japan. But Roosevelt did not make war upon California. Instead the United States and Japan joined in the "gentlemen's agreement" of 1907. Japan promised to refuse passports to Japanese laborers intending to emigrate to the United States, and the United States undertook to have San Francisco revoke her objectionable rule. The matter was settled by providing separate schools for the Japanese.

During this interval there was considerable talk of war, but the Japanese were not ready. Once the threat of war was over, Roosevelt decided to send the American navy on a voyage around the world. In doing so he had a double purpose, first to impress the Japanese with a demonstration of American strength, and second to give the navy some publicity at home. Late in 1907 the fleet sailed from Hampton Roads. In the following October the officers and men were cordially welcomed in Japan. In spite of the fears of some extremists the fleet returned home in safety.

Conference at Algeciras

In this same busy second term Roosevelt found occasion to participate in the conference held at Algeciras, Spain, for the purpose of settling problems connected with Morocco. In 1904 Great Britain and Spain agreed to give France a dominant voice in Morocco. This arrangement was far from pleasing to Kaiser Wilhelm of Germany, who resented this assumption of superior power by his rivals. He endeavored to upset the agreement and to secure for his own government a share in the management of Moroccan affairs. In this plan for enhancing German prestige the Kaiser felt the need of foreign help and turned to Roosevelt. The President was somewhat startled at this invitation to join the Kaiser in his Moroccan policy and at first he refused to cooperate. Later he did agree to send American delegates to an international conference at Algeciras, where the issue could be settled.

The conference met on January 16, 1906, with representatives of thirteen governments present;[1] it remained in session until April 7. The resulting Treaty of Algeciras, consisting of 123 articles, dealt with such matters as police regulations, revenue and taxation, public works, and governmental reforms in general. The delegates from the United States signed the treaty, with a reservation setting forth that their government had no direct political interest in Morocco except to secure equality of commercial opportunity for all, and that the United States would assume no obligation or responsibility for enforcing the agreement.

Theodore Roosevelt had a clear understanding of the growing importance of the United States in world affairs, and he also had a strong urge to increase this importance. After he left office he had a tendency to exaggerate the significance of what he had accomplished. This tendency, however, should not blind anyone to the reality of his achievements.

[1] Germany, Austria, Great Britain, France, the United States, Belgium, Holland, Italy, Spain, Portugal, Russia, Sweden, and Morocco.

Chapter 37

THE PROGRESSIVE REVOLT

WHILE Theodore Roosevelt was President, the Republicans seemed to be safely entrenched in their control of the federal government. Four years after the end of his administration the Democrats came into power. This sudden collapse of Republican strength occurred in Taft's administration, and Roosevelt was partly responsible for the collapse. In 1908 Roosevelt's admirers urged him to run for a third term. He refused to do so, but he did pick his successor. Roosevelt's choice was William Howard Taft, secretary of war, and Taft received the nomination.

Taft and the Tariff

Election of 1908

The Republican platform of 1908 pledged the party to a continuance of Roosevelt's policies. Then it made a promise on a subject Roosevelt had ignored: the tariff. The platform called "unequivocally for a revision" to be brought about by a special session of Congress immediately after the next inauguration. In making the new schedules the proper guide should be the difference in the costs of production at home and abroad. Although the platform itself did not promise a revision downward, Taft did so in his own campaign speeches.

The Democrats gave William Jennings Bryan his third chance. Their platform accused the Republicans of unparalleled extravagance, both in expenditures and in an unnecessary increase in the number of federal officeholders. It accused the speaker and the Rules Committee of the House of Representatives of ruthless suppression of the rights of the opposition. Then the Democrats emphasized the relationship between the Republican party and the great business interests and called attention to the financial support which corporations were giving the Republicans. In the constructive portions of their platform the Democrats included an impressive list of laws which they would enact in the interests of social justice. They would reduce the tariff; they would compel banks to guarantee depositors against loss; they would prohibit interlocking directorates in corporations; they would enact a general employers' liability act.

Taft won with a plurality of 1,269,906 votes over Bryan. Below the level of the popular vote for President, however, there were numerous indications of growing Democratic strength. In five states where the electoral vote went to Taft, Democratic governors were elected. In several others Taft ran far ahead of winning Republican governors. It would appear that Taft had secured his impressive plurality partly because of Roosevelt's prestige;

if anything should happen to make the Taft administration unpopular, this undercurrent of Democratic strength would cause serious trouble in the next Presidential campaign. In addition to this rise in Democratic stock, there was another source of possible trouble. Roosevelt had been undeniably popular, but he had antagonized many influential people in his own party, particularly the businessmen. He had been able to hold the reformers and the business interests together; a leader less skillful in the art of politics might see the two factions move far apart.

In the course of his four years as President, Taft lost many of the followers of Theodore Roosevelt. Trouble began with the appointment of his Cabinet. No one could have questioned the President's right to appoint his own Cabinet if he had made no pre-election promises to the incumbents in office. When Taft began his campaign for the Presidency he resigned his post as secretary of war. Roosevelt appointed Luke Wright of Tennessee, a former associate of Taft on the Philippine Commission, with the understanding that Taft would continue him in the office. Taft gave Roosevelt the impression that he would be glad to retain any members of the Roosevelt Cabinet who wished to stay. Roosevelt passed on this assurance. But when Taft announced his new Cabinet, only two of the Roosevelt group were on the list, and Wright was not among them. Adverse criticism of the new President began at once and increased ominously as time went on.

Taft's inaugural was a clear statement of aims and policies but with nothing in it to inspire emotion among the reformers. The continuance of the Rooseveltian policies would be "a most important feature" of the new administration. To make the reforms permanent and at the same time to promote stability and security in business circles, further legislation would be necessary. Taft therefore urged a reorganization of the Department of Justice, of the Bureau of Corporations, and of the Interstate Commerce Commission, so that a definite policy regarding business might be established. He went on to recommend changes in the monetary and banking laws of the country in order to secure a more elastic banknote circulation. Taft also emphasized the need of a new tariff law with lower rates.

Payne-Aldrich Tariff

For the first achievement of his administration the President planned a new tariff bill; in accordance with the promise in the platform he summoned Congress in special session on March 15, 1909. The chairman of the Committee of Ways and Means, Sereno E. Payne, had a bill already prepared. It placed wood pulp, hides, flax, and iron ore on the free list. Duties on iron, steel, and lumber were heavily reduced. There were less drastic reductions on numerous other commodities. Some rates were raised. The bill provided for free trade between the United States and the Philippines. In general the revision was downward. After less than a month of debate the measure passed the House on April 9, 1909, by a vote of 217 to 161.

In the Senate, the Payne bill was taken in hand by Nelson W. Aldrich, a thoroughgoing protectionist. Under his guidance duties were restored on coal, iron ore, and hides and raised on numerous other articles. Aldrich so completely dominated the Senate Committee on Finance, which made the amendments, that neither Democrats nor liberal Republicans had any voice in the proceedings. The final details of the bill were worked out in a conference committee. During this stage the protectionist lobby made determined efforts to retain the high rates of the Senate. On July 29 Taft announced his refusal to sign the bill unless it should provide for free hides and for low duties on ore and coal. Because of his insistence the conference committee decided to agree with the President. The reformers, however, found the general level of rates so high that they regarded the law as a violation of campaign promises. Instead of giving Taft credit for mitigating the evils of the Aldrich program, they insisted that he should have vetoed the measure.

The Payne-Aldrich Tariff brought about no real change in the industrial situation in the country, but it did have a profound influence on politics. In the course of the debate in the Senate a number of middle western Republicans, imbued with the reforming spirit of the Populist era, had attempted to compel Congress to comply with the spirit of the party pledge. Failing to get a revision downward, they had voted against the bill. These insurgent Republicans believed that Taft had been beaten by the protected interests or, worse still, that he had actually joined forces with them.

In an attempt to reconcile the insurgents and to justify the administration's stand on the tariff, President Taft made a direct appeal to the people. On September 17, 1909, at Winona, Minnesota, he entered upon an elaborate defense of the new measure. He showed that of the 2024 dutiable items in the Dingley Tariff of 1897, the new act left 1150 unchanged. Of the others there were decreases in 654 items and increases in 220. These increased rates affected articles of common consumption valued at $878,756,074, whereas the decreased rates applied to goods worth $4,951,878,575. There was, the President declared, a substantial downward revision on articles entering into general use. Even the notorious Schedule K dealing with woolens had been left unchanged; he personally thought these rates should have been reduced, but any attempt to do so would have resulted in the defeat of the whole measure by the woolen interests. He argued that the welfare of the Republican party and of the country required him to overlook the defects of the act and to sign it; a veto would have demoralized the party. Taft's arguments failed of their purpose, and the process of party disintegration went rapidly on.

Increasing Unpopularity

Events combined to make the summer of 1909 uncomfortable for the new President. The controversy over the tariff would have been enough to disturb the equanimity of anyone, even so genial a person as Taft. But in addition to this he found himself involved in a tangle of disputes over the policy of conservation. One of Roosevelt's last acts had been an executive order withdrawing from entry certain lands in Montana and Utah, aggregating about 1,500,000 acres. Ballinger, Taft's secretary of the interior, revoked the order on the grounds that it had no authorization in law. Roosevelt held that he could do things not expressly forbidden by statute. Taft and Ballinger argued that the President lacked authority to withdraw lands from entry by executive proclamation alone; authorization from Congress was necessary. But Taft found that neither law nor reasoning could make any impression upon Ballinger's critics; they believed that Roosevelt's whole policy of conservation was in jeopardy. Charges were soon being made that the public resources were in danger of monopoly by power trusts and lumber companies. Additional weight was given to these charges in the summer of 1909, when Gifford Pinchot, chief forester in the Department of Agriculture, declared the charges to be true.

Ballinger Affair

At this point a curious story got into circulation and, although in its main implications it was utterly lacking in truth, it ruined Ballinger's reputation and contributed to the loss of Taft's popularity. Prior to his appointment as secretary of the interior, Ballinger, as an attorney, had had some bit of legal business in connection with a claim to certain public lands in Alaska. These claims were apparently valid, and Cunningham, the claimant, believed that he had complied with all the terms of the law. Then a young clerk in the Department of the Interior, Louis R. Glavis, spread the story that the Cunningham claims included coal deposits of incalculable value and that there was a vast plot, engineered by Guggenheim and J. P. Morgan with the support of Ballinger, to get control of the Cunningham property along with other mineral wealth in Alaska and to cheat the American people out of resources of untold wealth.

Glavis and Mark Sullivan wrote up the story, and *Collier's Weekly* published it. Ordinarily when reputable journalists, as these men were, enter upon a course of character assassination, they take some pains to verify their allegations, but in this assault upon Ballinger they made no effort to get at the facts. Then the irrepressible Pinchot, also without any investigation, gave his endorsement to the Glavis tale, and Ballinger was pilloried as the Cabinet's representative in this great conspiracy to defraud the public.

The controversy became so acute that in August 1909 the President called a meeting of his Cabinet at his summer home in Beverly, Massachusetts. After due deliberation he concluded that the charges of Glavis had no justification in fact, that Ballinger was innocent of any wrongdoing, and that Pinchot had been unwise in trying to validate the charges. Taft therefore upheld his secretary and dismissed Glavis. Pinchot, however, continued his attacks upon Ballinger and, in violation of a specific rule prohibiting government officials from corresponding with Congressmen in such matters, he appealed to Senator Dolliver. There remained for the President no alternative but to dismiss the chief forester, which he did on January 7, 1910. The whole episode infuriated the Rooseveltians. At that time Taft knew that Ballinger was innocent. In more recent years historical investigators have told the whole story and they agree with Taft.

Actually both Ballinger and Taft were friendly to the cause of conservation. Roosevelt had made his contributions to the cause in the absence of legislation. Taft was determined to embody the policy in law and so make it mandatory on his successors. To this end, in December 1909 at the opening of the first regular session of Congress, Secretary Ballinger proposed a comprehensive series of new laws to secure, among other things, a new classification of the public lands and to make it possible to dispose of timber and coal rights separately from the soil. The next month Taft laid these proposals before Congress. As a result nine separate bills embodying Ballinger's recommendations were introduced. All nine became law. In June 1910 Congress enacted another measure, authorizing the President to withdraw land from entry by means of an executive proclamation. Again in March 1911 the President approved the Appalachian Forest Reserve Act. But in this same month Secretary Ballinger resigned; his important work in reconstructing the land laws of the nation was completed; and, although an investigation by a congressional committee had brought exoneration, the clamor of his detractors had become intolerable.

Conservation Program

This episode was typical of the whole administration of President Taft. His intentions were good, his sense of the country's needs was sound, and his proposals, many of which Congress adopted, were essential to the continued effectiveness of the Rooseveltian reforms. But Taft's methods and manners were not Roosevelt's. People who had become accustomed to Roosevelt's boisterous advocacy of popular measures concluded that in Taft's case the absence of noise meant inaction. The country saw and heard Pinchot's denunciations of Ballinger. But the country was exceedingly ill informed with reference to the important constructive legislation which had been obtained.

In dealing with transportation and the trusts, Taft followed the course which Roosevelt had already marked out, but, as in the case of conservation, he aimed at administrative reforms and additional legislation to make the policies more effective. Then, in a special message of January 7, 1910, he laid before Congress recommendations drawn by Attorney General Wickersham, designed to carry still further the principle of government regulation of transportation and industry. Congress proved amenable to suggestion and passed a new railroad law. This Mann-Elkins Act extended the jurisdiction of the Interstate Commerce Commission over means of communication as well as transportation; it empowered the commission to suspend newly announced rates for a period of not over ten months, pending an investigation, and to institute proceedings on its own initiative; it revived the long- and short-haul clause. Also, to hasten the settlement of appeals from the Interstate Commerce Commission, it created the Commerce Court.

Railroads and Trusts

Concerning the trusts, Taft agreed with Roosevelt that it was not size but intention and method that rendered certain corporations obnoxious; those innocent of violations of the law ought to be free to pursue their business unhampered by fear of prosecution. In order to make clear the distinction between "good" and "bad" trusts, Taft advocated federal incorporation. His theory was that law-abiding corporations would voluntarily seek the benefits of federal incorporation; those which refused to do so would immediately become objects of suspicion; if necessary they could be prosecuted without disturbance to the whole business structure of the country. There was, however, one drawback to this plan. The profits of even the "good" trusts were in some cases so excessive that they could risk no publicity. Business therefore found fault with the proposal, and Congress failed to take action.

During the Taft administration, following prosecution by the Department of Justice, the Supreme Court ordered the dissolution of the Standard Oil Company. As a result thirty-eight companies, theoretically independent, were substituted for the one. The most important feature of this Standard Oil decision was the Court's enunciation of "the rule of reason." The Court held that the Sherman Anti-Trust Act was so broad in its application that it forced the courts to exercise discretion in interpreting it. The Court consequently argued that the "standard of reason which had been applied at the common law . . . was intended to be the measure used for the purpose of determining whether in a given case a particular act" had violated the statute.

Justice Harlan did not agree with his colleagues, and in a dissenting opinion he accused the Court of altering an act of Congress by judicial interpretation. He found that the Court was usurping some of the functions of the legislative branch of the government. "The courts," he said, "have nothing to do with the wisdom or policy of an act of Congress. Their duty is to ascertain the will of Congress, and if the statute embodying the expression of that will is constitutional, the courts must respect it. They have no function to declare a public policy, nor to *amend* legislative enactments. . . ."

Taft showed his interest in constructive legislation by giving his support to the postal savings law, which made it possible for people of limited means to deposit their savings, at interest, in the post offices. This measure, passed in 1910, was looked upon as a means of protecting the poorer people against improperly managed banks. Then in 1912, also with Taft's approval, Congress provided for a parcel post system. Again the reformers approved because this measure relieved the farmers from dependence on the express companies.

Another policy in which the President was interested—considerably more so than many of his party associates—was tariff reciprocity with Canada. Taft's chief interest was to provide a wider Canadian market for exports from the United States. To secure these advantages the United States must be prepared to offer concessions to the Canadians. According to his plan the United States would either reduce or abolish entirely duties on wood pulp, paper, rough lumber, and some manufactured goods, while Canada would offer reasonable rates on agricultural implements and some other manufactures from the United States. In January Taft submitted a proposal for this purpose. The House of Representatives passed the bill which the President desired, but the conservative Republicans in the Senate were able to prevent a vote. After the elections of 1910 had given the House a Democratic majority and had weakened the Republican hold on the Senate, Taft called the new Congress in special session. Then, with Democratic help, the measure passed. Taft signed it on July 26, 1911. In the meantime the Canadian administration which favored reciprocity was overthrown, and the new government rejected the measure, largely because of widespread popular fear that it might lead to the annexation of Canada by the United States.

Speaker Cannon

During the Taft administration the same leaders who urged tariff reform tried to weaken the Republican party organization. This effort took the form of an attack upon Speaker Cannon. Under "Uncle Joe" the speakership had been used to muzzle not only the Democratic opposition but also any Republicans whose independence was a source of concern to the party regulars. The speaker dominated the Rules Committee, which controlled procedure in the House and which also made up the legislative calendar. By neglecting to give a bill a place on the calendar or by putting it so far down on the list that it would never be reached, the Rules Committee could determine what would and what would not be discussed in the House. Furthermore, thanks to the power of recognizing members who wished to speak, the speaker could silence those members of whom he disapproved. As he grew older, Cannon became more and more intolerant of any deviation from party regularity. As he interpreted his position he was responsible for party discipline. Loyal Republicans obeyed his orders. Those who disagreed with him were ipso facto disloyal. He denied them committee assignments and refused to let them speak in the House.

In the special session of Congress which met in March 1909 a combination of dissatisfied Republicans and regular Democrats introduced a motion providing for an increase in the membership of the Rules Committee and for making it elective. The motion also provided that the speaker should appoint committees only as instructed by the House. This motion did not pass, but in the regular session which met the following December the House voted to increase the membership of the Rules Committee from five to ten, to exclude the speaker from membership, and to give to the House power to elect the Committee. In the following year, 1911, the new Democratic majority vested the appointment of most of the House committees in the Committee of Ways and Means. This controversy served to dramatize the contest between liberals and conservatives; it was one of the steps in the rise of the Progressive movement.

Theodore Roosevelt's Return to Politics

The New Nationalism

During the congressional elections of 1910 the Republican party was weakened still further. In New York Henry L. Stimson was running for governor on a progressive Republican platform, advocating direct primaries and opposing the "old guard" or conservatives in his own party. Theodore Roosevelt returned from a hunting trip in Africa and a tour of Europe just in time to take part in the campaign. He supported Stimson, and so he was put in the position of defying the conservative leaders of his party. At this time he wrote privately that he was "bitterly disappointed with Taft," but at the same time he found fault with "the wild irresponsible folly of the ultra-Insurgents. . . ." And again privately, he wrote that he would probably support Taft for a second term in 1912. His purpose was to restore party unity, but his efforts merely antagonized conservative Republicans.

Some of his campaign speeches took Roosevelt completely out of the middle of the road. At Osawatomie, Kansas, he developed a philosophy which he called the new nationalism. On this occasion he argued that for the future fortunes should be gained only

> so long as the gaining represents benefit to the community. This, I know, implies a policy of a far more active governmental interference with social and economic conditions in this country than we have yet had, but I think we have got to face the fact that such an increase in governmental control is now necessary. Every man holds his property subject to the general right of the community to regulate its use to whatever degree the public welfare may require.

Here was the doctrine of public interest with a vengeance, and the conservative press was shocked. But newspaper criticism seemed to urge Roosevelt on to even greater radicalism. He had already begun to demand the recall of judicial decisions, and he went on to plead for a federal income tax law, for additional labor legislation, and for direct primaries. President Taft, still standing on the Roosevelt policies of 1908, was left far behind.

These mid-term elections of 1910 were an almost nation-wide protest against conservative Republicanism. A number of states which were normally Republican chose Democratic governors, and in the national House of Representatives the Democrats secured a majority of fifty-five votes. In the Senate there was a nominal Republican majority of ten, but several of the western Senators were of the Insurgent variety and they voted with the Democrats. For the first time in sixteen years the Democrats found themselves in control of Congress, and they promptly began preparations for the coming Presidential campaign of 1912.

While the Democrats were working to carry the next Presidential campaign for their own party, the Insurgent Republicans undertook to capture the Republican organization. Only by this means, they asserted, could the Democrats be prevented from sweeping the country. In an effort to bring progressive Republicans together on a common ground, Robert M. La Follette of Wisconsin and certain kindred spirits launched the National Progressive Republican League. This was in January 1911. In their Declaration of Principles, the Progressives defined their object as "the promotion of popular government and progressive legislation."

La Follette and his supporters were disturbed over the attitude of Theodore Roosevelt. He refused to join the Progressive League and he would not pledge support to La Follette. Eastern Progressive Republicans preferred Roosevelt to La Follette, and Roosevelt seemed to be seeking the nomination for himself. Should he do so, he might divide the Progressive vote and so block the course of reform. In February 1912 La Follette gave a new turn to the political picture by a speech in Washington, D. C., before a gathering of newspaper publishers. The Senator seems to have been tired out, not to the point of exhaustion because he talked for two hours and a half, but so tired that he lacked discretion. He began to repeat whole passages of his speech. This display convinced some of the Progressives that Senator La Follette was in no condition to conduct a vigorous campaign. The time had come for the former President to make public his decision; he had already made it privately.

"My Hat Is in the Ring"

In an attempt to probe public opinion as to his candidacy, Roosevelt resorted to the time-honored expedient of the trial balloon. He and some of his friends in the *Outlook* office drew up a letter and arranged to give it to the press over the signatures of seven Republican governors. The letter, dated February 10, declared that in the opinion of the seven governors a large majority of Republican voters favored Roosevelt as the next Republican nominee. They urged him to make an early statement as to whether, "if the nomination for the presidency comes to you unsolicited and unsought, you will accept it."

Roosevelt replied under date of February 24: "I will accept the nomination for President if it is tendered to me, and I will adhere to this decision until the convention has expressed its preference." In taking this step Roosevelt assumed leadership of the Progressives and so ended La Follette's chances of securing the nomination. Roosevelt's decision to enter the contest was equivalent to a formal denunciation of Taft; it was at the same time a challenge to the President to fight for his rights as leader of the Republican party.

For several years reformers had been urging the direct primary as an improved method of nominating candidates for public office, and in 1912 Roosevelt tried to apply this device both to the selection of delegates to the national convention, and also to the naming of the candidates themselves. Laws already adopted provided for some form of Presidential primary in twelve states.[1] In the primary vote in these states Roosevelt ap-

[1] California, Illinois, Maryland, Massachusetts, Nebraska, New Jersey, North and South Dakota, Ohio, Oregon, Pennsylvania, Wisconsin.

peared to be the overwhelming favorite; on the face of the returns he was. But the primary vote was hardly more than 50 percent of the vote in the following November elections, and Taft was partly justified in his claim that the primary vote was in no sense indicative of the majority in the Republican party. Roosevelt carried the primaries in both Illinois and Pennsylvania, but in the following November in these two states Taft polled 50 percent more votes than Roosevelt. However, these primary states accounted for 388 delegates to the Republican national convention, and of this total Roosevelt received 281, Taft received 71, and La Follette 36.

Republican Convention

The Republican national convention met at Chicago on June 18. Before the delegates came together the national committee met to settle contests in several state delegations. There were 1078 delegates to the convention, and there were alleged contests over more than 200. Some of the contests were genuine, others were manufactured to create an impression of Roosevelt's strength. Many of the contests were in the delegations from the southern states, where the Republican party had few voters. The Taft delegates from these states had at least the virtue of regularity; the Roosevelt contestants lacked even this asset. Taft and Roosevelt both ignored the real issue that the states in question were not rightfully entitled to any representation. But the convention machinery was controlled by the Taft forces and most of the contests were settled in his favor.

During this preliminary dispute Roosevelt remained at home, following the contest in the papers. What he read inspired him to new outbursts of wrath. He characterized the seating of the Taft delegates at Chicago as "a fraud as vulgar, as brazen, and as cynically open as any ever committed by the Tweed regime in New York forty years ago." After this he had to go to Chicago to protect his interests. The night before the convention opened he delivered a rousing speech, full of evangelical fervor: "We fight in honorable fashion for the good of mankind; fearless of the future, unheeding of our individual fates, with unflinching hearts and undimmed eyes; we stand at Armageddon, and we battle for the Lord."

The first business of the convention was the choice of a temporary chairman; for this post the Taft delegates supported Elihu Root, while the Rooseveltians united on Francis E. McGovern. Root won. Taft received a majority on the first ballot. Roosevelt accused the national committee and President Taft of fraud and declared that the convention had overridden "the legally expressed will of the people" and that it had substituted "a dishonest for an honest majority." Immediately after the nomination of Taft, the Roosevelt delegates and a large following met in another building and gave their nomination to Roosevelt. He advised them to go home, sound out their constituents and friends, and then, if they found evidence of popular support, they could call another convention and nominate a Progressive candidate upon a Progressive platform.

The Roosevelt forces found what they were looking for, and on August 5 the Progressive convention assembled at Chicago. That gathering still remains unique in American political history. There were 2000 delegates, most of whom had never taken active part in politics before and all of whom were aroused to a pitch of lofty enthusiasm for Roosevelt. The delegates sang such soul-stirring hymns as "Onward, Christian Soldiers," the "Battle Hymn of the Republic," and the "Doxology." When Roosevelt appeared on the platform he was cheered continuously for more than an hour. He was nominated by acclamation without the formality of a ballot.

Progressive Revolt

The Progressive platform explained the origin of the new party: "The conscience of the people, in a time of grave national problems, has called into being a new party, born of the nation's sense of justice." The Progressives charged the old parties with surrender to "corrupt interests, which use them impartially to serve their selfish purposes." The Progressives promised to put an end to "invisible government," and to "dissolve the unholy alliance between corrupt business and corrupt politics." Their platform called for an impressive list of reforms, including the direct primary, the short ballot, the initiative, referendum, and recall, votes for women, the eight-hour day, the prohibition of child labor, the establishment of a separate department of labor, federal supervision of corporations, and a lower tariff.

The Progressive movement was in part the product of vigorous idealism in American politics, a demand for a new democracy suited to the needs of a great industrial society. In the eyes of his followers, Theodore Roosevelt was the ablest exponent of this idealism. Roosevelt himself was moved by the same kind of zeal. Human motives, however, are rarely simple, and there seems to have been a generous portion of personal ambition in Roosevelt's idealism. Furthermore, while most of the delegates to the Progressive convention at Chicago were idealists, many of them without previous political experience, there were also a few professional politicians, men who had fallen out with their regular organizations and who joined the Progressive movement in order to rehabilitate their fortunes.

The Democrats and Woodrow Wilson

Rise of Wilson

The Democrats followed this warfare with enthusiastic attention. The Republican party was split wide open, with the organized machine on one side and a popular leader supported by hysterical enthusiasts on the other. The Republicans were giving the Presidency to the Democrats. With this certainty of success the Democratic nomination acquired remarkable value, and a number of candidates announced their willingness to serve their country. Most of them have long since been forgotten, but the two leading rivals, Champ Clark and Woodrow Wilson, had more than ordinary significance. Champ Clark of Missouri, speaker of the House of Representatives, was a good illustration of the party worker who had come to the front by virtue of ability and undeviating loyalty to the organization. He knew his constituents, he was familiar with politics, and he had displayed interest in reform.

The successful candidate, Woodrow Wilson, became a leader of world-wide significance, and for this reason something needs to be said about his dramatic entrance into politics. Unlike Champ Clark, Woodrow Wilson was not a professional politician. He had achieved eminence as a professor of political science and public law and as the president of Princeton University. In academic circles he was known as a lecturer and writer, but he seemed to have no "contacts" with any political value. Why then did Wilson enter politics?

The answer to this question is to be found in a peculiar combination of circumstances. For one thing, the situation at Princeton was becoming increasingly uncomfortable for the president. Wilson had contrived to antagonize important interests there: undergraduates, alumni, many of the faculty, and the board of trustees. There were charges of a broken promise to Dean West of the graduate school, charges made by responsible parties and never satisfactorily refuted. The climax to this combination of troubles came in 1910 with the announcement of a substantial gift of money for the graduate school. The condition attached to the gift was one that Wilson could not accept: this new endowment was to be administered exclusively by Dean West. At the same time the gift was so large that the president could not refuse it. His only course therefore was to resign.

It so happened that in this very year of 1910 the Democratic party of New Jersey had a gubernatorial campaign on hand. For the past fifteen years the Democratic candidates for this office had consistently lost, and this record of failure was beginning to tell on the prestige of the state boss James Smith. The time had come for him to pick a winner. Furthermore his candidate must have the qualities collectively known as window dressing. The nation-wide unrest which found expression in the Progressive movement was felt in New Jersey, and liberal Democrats were insistently demanding a change of leadership. Something had to be done to satisfy them or they might desert the party. One of Smith's friends and neighbors was George Harvey, editor of *Harper's Weekly,* then a Democrat. For two years he had been trying to make Woodrow Wilson President of the United States, and it was he who urged Smith to give Wilson the Democratic nomination for the governorship. The story is a long one, but Smith followed Harvey's advice. After some urging Wilson consented to run, and in July he made a public announcement of his candidacy. At the Democratic state convention Wilson received the nomination on the first ballot.

In addition to the complexities on the campus at Princeton and to the efforts of George Harvey and James Smith, there was another factor in Wilson's decision to enter politics—his own private ambition. In a letter written several years previously, Wilson had expressed his disappointment with academic life and in particular with his inability to enter upon a public career. He welcomed the chance to enter active politics. The New Jersey Democrats were able to present a new type of candidate, and the widespread political unrest gave him a chance. Wilson carried the state by a plurality of 49,000; in the preceding Presidential campaign Taft had received a plurality of more than 80,000.

In the campaign Wilson had run as a progressive Democrat, when progressivism consisted in large measure of a demand for government regulation of business enterprise. And yet Wilson's own conversion to this brand of progressivism was a new departure. As recently as 1907 he had written that attempts to bring about federal regulation of corporations were based on a theory "compounded of confused thinking and impossible principles of law." Government control, he said, was merely "taking the power away from the people and putting it into the hands of political discontent." As governor of New Jersey, however, Wilson took control of his party's majority in the legislature and drove through a series of drastic laws for regulating corporations. His efforts in the most trust-ridden state in the Union attracted wide attention, and the former college president was widely talked of as a promising candidate for President of the United States.

Baltimore Convention

Fortunately for Wilson's political ambitions, his friends did more than talk. The Democratic national convention would not be any one-man show like James Smith's convention at Trenton, and there were several candidates actively at work. To be successful, a candidate would need to enter the convention with a substantial block of pledged delegates. In New York William F. McCombs became the local manager for Wilson and undertook the task of securing Wilson delegates. His efforts were ably supplemented by Josephus Daniels in North Carolina and by William Gibbs McAdoo in Georgia. Before the convention opened, Wilson's friends had collected 300 delegates.

The Democratic national convention of 1912 met at Baltimore. At the start open rivalry developed between the liberal and conservative factions of the party, with William Jennings Bryan taking the leadership of the liberals. Bryan was not a candidate for the nomination, but he was determined to prevent any conservative from running off with the prize. The balloting began on June 28 and lasted until July 2. On the first ballot Clark received 440 votes, Wilson 324, with the others divided among several aspirants.

Sure of a substantial minority for their candidate, the Wilson delegates proceeded to make Clark's nomination impossible. As one of the Texan delegates, Thomas W. Gregory—later attorney general of the United States—told the story: "In these circumstances the Wilson people made airtight agreements with a sufficient number of delegates instructed for candidates other than Clark, to the effect that under no conditions would any parties to the agreement vote for Clark." Because of the two-thirds rule then in force, this agreement killed Clark's chances. On the forty-sixth ballot Wilson won the nomination. By that time Bryan had thrown his support to Wilson.

For his campaign manager Wilson selected McCombs, who had already demonstrated his capacity for successful political work. In both the preliminary campaign and in the election itself Roosevelt and Taft merely ruined each other's chances and gave the election to Wilson. Roosevelt carried six states and Taft only two; their combined electoral vote was 96. Wilson carried all the other states, with an electoral vote of 435. On the surface the victory was impressive. But Wilson carried only thirteen states by virtue of Democratic strength; the others came to him solely because of the Republican schism. In the popular vote, Wilson ran behind Bryan's vote in 1908 and in 1896. Of the total popular vote for all candidates Wilson received a fraction more than 41 percent. The same schism which gave the Presidency to the Democrats also gave them control of Congress; they had a majority of 144 in the House and of 6 in the Senate.

Election of Wilson

What sort of man was this new President? He was born in Virginia, the son of a Presbyterian minister. He spent the greater part of his boyhood in Georgia and South Carolina. William Allen White refers to his connection with a baseball team, the Lightfoots; the business meetings of this team were "characterized by much nicety of parliamentary procedure." Brought up in a church which emphasized the rule of law, the boy carried over this concept of law and order even in matters of play. As he moved on in public life Wilson never lost his religious faith nor the intensity of conviction which accompanied it. His first year at college—he entered Davidson College, North Carolina—was interrupted by ill-health. Then he went to Princeton and graduated. For a time he tried his hand at law, and then he entered the graduate school at Johns Hopkins to study political science. He was never physically strong and often the victim of indigestion, evidently the result of his high-strung nervous temperament. In subjects which interested him he displayed a remarkable intensity of conviction, and, especially as he grew older, considerable impatience with opposition.

Robert E. Annin, one of the numerous Wilson biographers, reported a revealing conversation between Wilson and his campaign manager. After the election McCombs called on the President-elect. Wilson went straight to the point: "Before we proceed I wish it clearly understood that I owe you nothing." Somewhat taken aback, McCombs ventured to refer to his work both before and after the Baltimore convention. Wilson is said to have replied: "God ordained that I should be the next President of the United States. Neither you nor any other mortal could have prevented that." One can never understand Woodrow Wilson without taking these temperamental traits into account.

Chapter 38

WILSON'S POLICIES AT HOME AND IN LATIN AMERICA

WOODROW WILSON entered the presidency with positive ideas, derived from a long study of American government and politics. In his book, *Congressional Government,* and in numerous essays and speeches he had analyzed the fundamental weakness of the federal system. In part, as he saw it, the trouble was want of leadership; in part too extensive diffusion of responsibility. To remedy these difficulties the President should make himself the undisputed head of his party and of his administration. Then he could select policies and supervise the process of legislation.

"The New Freedom"

Politics and Reform

During his first term Wilson found favorable conditions for the development of this dynamic leadership. In making up his Cabinet, he selected local or national politicians who had helped him win the nomination. He realized that Bryan must be secretary of state. The "peerless leader" was still a power in the party, with a greater personal following than that of any other Democrat. The certain advantages of having this influence on the side of the administration more than outweighed the possible dangers attendant on Bryan's lack of training for the post. In filling the other Cabinet positions, Wilson's criterion was loyalty—that is, evidence of effective work during the preceding campaign. McAdoo of Georgia, Daniels of North Carolina, and Burleson of Texas all had been most helpful, and they were rewarded with Cabinet posts: McAdoo in the Treasury, Daniels in the Navy, and Burleson as postmaster general. McReynolds of Tennessee, who became attorney general, carried the endorsement of Colonel House. Bryan found places for "deserving Democrats" in the foreign service. Furthermore, the President and his advisers found a large number of vacancies to be filled in the Civil Service. Twenty-five hundred nominations, sent to the Senate by Taft in the latter part of his term, had been left without action by the Democratic majority in order to give the new President a good start with the patronage. In return for these appointments the administration demanded and received loyal support.

In his inaugural Wilson gave clear expression to his belief that the Democratic party had a mandate from the country to effect political and economic reform. The efficacy of this mandate was not weakened by the knowledge that a majority of the American voters did not want him for President. The temper of the country was "progressive" and he was the stronger of the two "progressive" candidates, therefore he was the leader properly accredited for the work. The American nation, he said, would use the Democratic party "to interpret a change in its own plans and point of view. . . . We have made up our minds to square every process of our national life again with the standards we so proudly set up at the beginning. . . . Our work is a work of restoration." The policies to be altered, he declared, were first the tariff, next banking and currency, and then the "industrial system which, take it on all sides, financial as well as administrative, holds capital in leading strings, restricts the liberties and limits the opportunities of labor." Agriculture should be encouraged by the application of modern science and through the medium of better credit facilities; waterways should be developed, waste places reclaimed, and forests protected; then the government should be "put at the service of humanity."

The new administration hoped to reform the existing economic order and the first step would be a revision of the tariff. This was logical because the Payne-Aldrich schedules had made high protection appear more than ever a symbol of the predatory rich. A new tariff bill became the chief interest of the special session of the 63d Congress which Wilson summoned to meet on April 8, 1913. On this occasion, instead of explaining his views in a message as his predecessors had been doing for over a hundred years, he revived the practice begun by Washington and appeared before Congress in person. He urged speedy action in order that the burden laid upon the people by the Payne-Aldrich Act might be lightened and that business might not suffer disturbance from uncertainty and delay.

Underwood Tariff

Under the direction of Oscar W. Underwood, chairman of the Committee of Ways and Means, the House passed a new measure on May 8. The Senate proceeded in more leisurely fashion, and its deliberations were constantly subjected to the pressure of interests desiring favorable treatment. These activities became so troublesome that the President issued a special warning: "Washington has seldom seen so numerous, so industrious or so insidious a lobby. . . . The government in all its branches ought to be relieved from this intolerable burden and this constant interruption to the calm progress of debate." In spite of the lobby the Senate completed its work, and on October 3 the Underwood Tariff went into effect. While not a free-trade measure, the new law did reduce the general level of duties. The free list was extended to include raw wool, sugar, iron ore and pig iron, lumber, and numerous manufactured articles. The rates on manufactured woolens and cotton goods were cut in half. This was the most sweeping change downward since the Civil War.

Banking Reform

The second item on the Wilson program was the Federal Reserve Act, dealing with banking and currency reform. Because of the importance of this whole subject, Wilson again went before Congress on June 13, 1913, to outline his own views and to urge speedy action. Fortunately the time was ripe for such a measure. In 1907 the Aldrich-Vreeland Act had provided for the appointment of a National Monetary Commission to investigate and report on the problem of banking and finance. After five years' work, under the able leadership of Senator Nelson W. Aldrich, the commission laid its report before Congress. This was in 1912, when because of the political situation no important legislation could even be considered. But a vast amount of accumulated information on the subject had been made available for the new administration. President Wilson, Secretary McAdoo, Senator R. L. Owen, Representative Carter Glass, and a number of prominent bankers all participated in framing the Federal Reserve Act. Congress passed the measure in December 1913.

This law created the Federal Reserve Board of seven members, including the secretary of the treasury. It provided for the establishment of twelve regional Federal Reserve Banks. These dealt only with member banks and with the federal government, not with the general public. They became depositories of federal funds, and they carried portions of the reserves of member banks. They were authorized to make loans and to issue federal reserve notes, the volume of which could expand and contract under the pressure of the prevailing needs of business. These notes were secured partly by gold, partly by commercial paper.

Curbing the Trusts

With the tariff and banking problems out of the way, President Wilson next laid before Congress the long-standing puzzle of the trusts. In his first annual message he had declared that the time had come to remove legal uncertainties then so evident in the business world. On January 20, 1914, he followed this initial suggestion with a more elaborate explanation of his trust program. This program involved no attack upon business, he declared, and it called for no drastic reorganization. But laws were needed to prevent interlocking directorates among the great corporations in banking, industry, and transportation. The financial operations of the railroads should be brought under the regulation of the Interstate Commerce Commission. The meaning of the Sherman Anti-Trust Act ought to be defined precisely, so that businessmen might know what practices were permitted and what were not. Then, for the guidance of American business in general, he asked for the creation of a Federal Trade Commission.

Congress responded to this request with two measures: The Federal Trade Commission Act of September 1914 and the Clayton Anti-Trust Act of the month following. The commission, of five members, was empowered to investigate corporate practices and, where these were illegal, to order readjustments in business methods. Only when these orders were ignored would the commission carry the matter to the federal courts. The Clayton Act prohibited discrimination in prices where discrimination would be productive of monopoly, and it carefully limited interlocking directorates. Then, in the interests of organized labor, the act went on to exempt from the operation of the antitrust laws all farmer and labor organizations not conducted for profit; to restrict the use of injunctions in labor disputes; and to legalize such practices as strikes and picketing.

In the mid-term congressional elections of 1914 the Democratic majority in the House was reduced but not wiped out, and the program of reform continued. In 1915 Wilson signed the Seamen's Act, which had been put through Congress largely under the influence of Senator La Follette. The purpose of this measure was to provide more liberal regulations for sailors. Deserters could no longer be punished by imprisonment; corporal punishment was prohibited; any seaman could demand up to 50 percent of the wages due him whenever the vessel on which he was employed was in a safe harbor. The law also provided that 75 percent of the crew must be able to understand the language in which orders were given. Of the deck hands at least 65 percent had to qualify as able seamen, and a substantial number of these had to be able to handle lifeboats. Finally there were various provisions imposed in the interests of safety, together with minute regulations covering standards of food and living quarters.

Sailors and Farmers

In the following year, 1916, Congress passed the Federal Farm Loan Act, establishing the Federal Farm Loan system, under the direction of a five-member board appointed by the President. The secretary of the treasury was one of the members. The law provided for the establishment of twelve federal land banks. Each bank was capitalized at $750,000. They could lend money to farmers at not more than 6 percent interest.

Another extension of federal authority in 1916 came with the enactment of the Adamson Act for the railroads. This measure was the direct result of the demand of four groups of railroad employees for increased wages. The Brotherhoods of Engineers, Firemen, Trainmen, and Conductors asked for an eight-hour day, with no reduction in wages, and for an increase of 50 percent in pay for all work over eight hours. When these demands were first submitted in March 1916 the railroad refused to agree. In June an offer of arbitration by the roads was rejected by the Brotherhoods. At this point President Wilson himself took the matter in hand, and on August 16 invited fifteen railroad presidents to come to Washington for a conference. In a public statement he recommended the adoption of the eight-hour day, because it "now undoubtedly has the sanction of the judgment of society in its favor and should be adopted as a basis for wages even where the actual work to be done cannot be completed within eight hours." Because of the lack of adequate data for determining the financial effects of the proposed wage increases, Wilson proposed that the demand for a higher rate of pay for overtime and the request of the railroads for increased rates be postponed, pending the results of an investigation. This first effort at mediation failed, and on August 28 the Brotherhood chiefs ordered a strike to begin on Labor Day, September 4.

Adamson Law

The outlook was so threatening that Wilson appeared before Congress on August 29 with a series of proposals designed to avert the strike and to bring about a constructive settlement of the whole dispute. He emphasized the seriousness of the crisis, pointing out that 400,000 men would go on strike and that their action would probably paralyze the freight service of the entire country. Then he proposed that the eight-hour day be adopted. Next he would appoint a small commission to make a careful study of both costs and conditions of work under the new arrangement. The Brotherhoods were willing to accept this plan, but the railroad executives refused. Having failed in this part of his plan, Wilson turned to Congress with specific recommendations for an enlargement and reorganization of the Interstate Commerce Commission and for the establishment of the eight-hour day as the legal basis of work and of wages for all train crews. Finally, he asked for a law empowering the President to assume control of any or all of the railroads of the country, if military exigencies should make such a step necessary, and to draft the requisite train crews and executives into national service. Bills were at once introduced to make this program effective, and on September 2 the Adamson Law was passed. This gave the employees the eight-hour day but with only pro rata pay for overtime; it also authorized the appointment of the fact-finding commission. The rest of the program was abandoned in spite of the President's earnest request for action. The proposed strike was called off and the crisis was averted. The Brotherhoods achieved their victory partly by the use of threats and partly with the help of the federal government. Wilson found justification for this attitude in two considerations: first, he was firmly convinced of the inherent justice of the eight-hour day; second, the foreign situation, both in Mexico and in Europe, was so critical that a great labor dispute had to be avoided. It is hardly just to compare Wilson's handling of the threatened railroad strike with Roosevelt's course during the anthracite strike in 1902. Roosevelt had no such threat of foreign war on his hands, and he did nothing to avert the coal strike: he merely effected a settlement after the strike had continued for six months.

Philippine Problem

The spirit of reform was not confined to the limits of the United States; it flowed out to the Philippines, and it came conspicuously into play in foreign relations. Wilson's first annual message explained his plans with reference to American dependencies, where, he said, the United States was in the position of a trustee. These territories, "once regarded as mere possessions, are no longer to be selfishly exploited; they are part of the domain of public conscience. . . . We must administer them for the people who live in them." For Puerto Rico and the Hawaiian Islands he proposed a more generous measure of self-government; but for the Philippines this would not be enough. "We must hold steadily in view their ultimate independence, and we must move toward the time of that independence as steadily as the way can be cleared." Even before Congress started its regular session he gave the Filipinos a majority in the upper house of their legislature, and he announced his intention of putting the islands as far as possible under native control. This policy was carried out by the new governor general, Francis Burton Harrison. In 1916 Congress passed the Jones Act, the purpose of which was to provide for still more self-government for the Filipinos and to prepare them for independence.

The Mobile Doctrine and Mexico

President Wilson and Secretary Bryan were both interested in world peace. The President gave full approval to Bryan's "cooling-off" treaties. These provided that all questions, including even those affecting national honor or the vital interests of the country, which might fail of diplomatic adjustment should be submitted to an international commission for investigation and report. The report must be made within one year; during this interval the parties to the agreement bound themselves to make no military or naval preparations whatever and to refrain from any hostile acts unless actually threatened by some third party. By December 1914 this peace plan had been embodied in treaties with thirty governments. Europe, however, was involved in a war which, contrary to the many hopeful expectations of that day, wrecked the cause of peace for more than one generation.

Ending Dollar Diplomacy

Wilson's administration ostentatiously repudiated the foreign policy of Taft and Secretary Knox—the policy known as dollar diplomacy. Directed primarily at Latin America, secondarily at China, the purpose had been to promote the economic development of these regions by means of loans. American banks would assist in the process, and the State Department would endeavor to guarantee the banks against loss. Taft endorsed the policy in his first annual message. American bankers were encouraged to participate in a loan to the Chinese government. When adverse critics complained that this support of business enterprise would involve the United States in serious difficulties, Secretary Knox defended the policy with almost evangelical fervor:

> If the American dollar can aid suffering humanity and lift the burden of financial difficulty from states with which we live on terms of intimate intercourse and earnest friendship, and replace insecurity and devastation by stability and peaceful self-development, all I can say is that it would be hard to find better employment.

President Wilson did not approve of governmental support for American capitalists abroad. He objected to the participation of American bankers in the proposed loan to China because the conditions of the loan would put definite responsibility upon the government of the United States.

Wilson paid considerably more attention to Latin America than to the Far East. He had not been in office a week when he notified the diplomatic agents in Latin American countries that he was opposed to revolutions there and that he was not interested in promoting the economic interests of any special group. Later, in a speech at Mobile, he announced that the future would be very different from the past. "These States lying to the south of us . . . will now be drawn closer to us by innumerable ties, and, I hope, chief of all, by the tie of a common understanding of each other." Then he pointed out the undesirable features of the grant of special concessions to foreign capitalists, and he promised "an emancipation from the subordination . . . to foreign enterprise." The United States would be the first to assist in this process of emancipation.

President Wilson was interested not only in safeguarding the Latin American states from economic penetration, but also in bringing about a more cordial relationship between the peoples of North and South America. In this matter he had the assistance of his unofficial adviser, Colonel House of Texas. "The opportunity to weld North and South America together in closer union is at your hand," the Colonel wrote. House was interested in a plan to establish a league of American states which would furnish the mechanism necessary for the peaceful settlement of disputes. He hoped that all American republics could be prevailed upon to enter such a league. In doing so they would give "mutual guarantees of political independence under republican forms of government and mutual guarantees of territorial integrity." House interviewed the representatives of the three leading South American powers: Argentina, Brazil, and Chile; he found the first two favorable, but Chile was not interested.

Pan-American Pact

These plans were being matured during 1914 at a time when the European war tended to submerge almost all other interests. In spite of this difficulty, in 1915 Colonel House completed his plan for a Pan-American pact, and early in the following year Wilson explained the main features of it in an address to the Pan-American Scientific Congress. The first article was a guarantee of territorial integrity and of political independence under a republican form of government. Article II included the principle of the Bryan cooling-off treaties, with the proviso that after investigation the dispute would be submitted to arbitration. Article IV provided that the contracting parties would not permit the departure of military or naval expeditions aimed at the overthrow of any party to the pact; they also agreed to prevent the exportation of arms and munitions if they were to be used by rebels against any established government. This was as far as the pact went. The continued opposition of Chile and the difficulties between Mexico and the United States prevented further action. The pact has historical significance because it included many of the ideas subsequently incorporated in the Covenant of the League of Nations.

In Mexico Wilson found a problem, holding over from the Taft administration, which imposed a severe strain on both his idealism and his patience. A revolution which had started in 1910 was still in progress. The causes of this uprising were both old and complex, reaching back far into the past. The population included a substantial majority of Indians. Political power, on the other hand, was in the hands of the small white minority of Spanish descent. Theoretically a republic with a constitution modeled on that of the United States, Mexico had never enjoyed popular government. During the first years of its history as an independent state, the country had been the prey of revolution after revolution, with as many as eighty presidents in the first seventy-five years.

Revolt against Diaz

In 1877 the early revolutionary era of Mexican history came to an end.

The new President, Porfirio Diaz, more dictator than constitutional official, restored order and attempted to develop some of the natural wealth. Instead of encouraging the Mexicans themselves to undertake this responsibility, Diaz offered liberal concessions to foreigners. He promised a government strong enough to guarantee the safety of investments and held out the inducement of large profits. At the time this policy of foreign exploitation was justified on the ground that Mexicans lacked the needed capital. Large numbers of foreigners entered Mexico and many of them stayed. They operated ranches, built railroads, developed mines and petroleum fields, and took charge of business generally. The majority of these outsiders came from Germany, England, and the United States. Then, in order to strengthen himself at home, Diaz encouraged his Mexican supporters to build up great estates for themselves. He furnished the land, or more accurately he compelled the Indians to provide it. Before 1890 most of the Indians had lived in communal villages, with ownership of the land vested in the villages. Diaz expropriated these communal properties and deprived the Indians of their best holdings. Having no way of making a living except on the land, the Indians became peons on the great estates. By this means Diaz bought the support of a new landowning class, but in doing so he created widespread unrest.

In 1910 Diaz was elected President for his eighth term. In the campaign Francisco Madero tried to run against him, but the dictator would not tolerate any opposition. Thwarted in his effort to obtain the Presidency by election, Madero turned to revolution. In 1911 Diaz resigned, whereupon Madero was chosen President. In its beginning this revolt had been largely political, but Madero brought in an economic issue. He promised to restore the expropriated lands to the peasants. Almost at once the peons rose in all parts of Mexico, and the political rebellion of a comparatively small ruling class developed into a great social upheaval.

Those who had profited from the Diaz regime refused to give up their estates without a fight, and they found a champion in General Victoriano Huerta. He led a rebellion against Madero, and in February 1913 he became provisional President of Mexico. Five days later Madero was shot, apparently by Huerta's command, certainly with his approval. Huerta then set up a military dictatorship and planned to continue the policies of Diaz. The followers of Madero accused Huerta of the murder of their leader, and under the leadership of Carranza and Villa they continued the revolution. By 1913 civil war had become chronic in Mexico, and some of the fighting was carried on so close to the border of the United States that American citizens were endangered. In this contest many of the larger property owners gave their support to Huerta. Such was the situation when Woodrow Wilson became President of the United States.

This tangle in Mexico introduced Wilson to the intricacies of foreign policy. The outgoing Taft administration had not accorded recognition to the Huerta regime, although it probably would have done so had there been any expectation that Wilson would not. For nearly a hundred years it had been customary to recognize the Latin American governments actually in power and discreetly to ignore both the means by which they had been established and the moral character of the personnel composing them. To be sure, the United States had refused recognition to the Emperor Maximilian, but he was a foreigner; there had been no exception in the case of a bona fide Latin American ruler. The leading European governments recognized Huerta, but Wilson would not. With him precedent carried no weight if it ran counter to the established principles of public and private morals, as it did with Huerta. He believed that the new ruler of Mexico was an unprincipled scoundrel, a murderer, and an unconstitutional despot. To his obvious unfitness as a man and to the tyrannical character of his government there was the added weakness of his inability to establish control over all parts of the country.

Watchful Waiting

Although he had no intention of recognizing Huerta as ruler of Mexico, Wilson was at first not content with a merely negative policy. The United States, he declared, had a definite duty to perform. He therefore offered the assistance of the United States not to Huerta but to Mexico in the interests of orderly government and peace. To this end in August 1913 he sent John Lind, former governor of Minnesota, to Mexico with proposals for a settlement. In taking this step the President endeavored to convince the Mexicans that he and his government were acting solely in the interests of Mexico. "We are seeking to counsel Mexico for her own good, and in the interest of her own peace, and not for any other purpose whatever." He proposed therefore an immediate end of hostilities and an early election in which Huerta should not be a candidate. All parties should agree to abide by the results of the election.

The Lind mission was a failure. Huerta and his associates refused to retire to private life. Consequently, Wilson said, the United States must wait for a change in Mexico itself. But, in waiting, he would advise all Americans then in Mexico to leave the country, and he would prohibit all parties in Mexico from receiving arms and munitions from the United States. In the meantime he hoped for the establishment in Mexico of a "just and ordered government founded upon law." The salvation of the country depended upon the acceptance of "honest constitutional government."

In his first annual message to Congress in December 1913, Wilson again discussed the Mexican tangle, the "one cloud upon our horizon."

> There can be no certain prospect of peace in America until General Huerta has surrendered his usurped authority in Mexico; until it is understood on all hands, indeed, that such pretended governments will not be countenanced or dealt with by the Government of the United States. We are the friends of constitutional government in America; we are more than its friends, we are its champions.

There were some surprising implications in this Wilsonian argument, implications which sovereign states cannot accept. Wilson virtually assumed the right to pass moral judgment on the government of an independent nation. Because that government did not square with his standards, he believed that he had the right to order its dissolution and to work for its overthrow.

Limited Intervention

In spite of opposition at home and abroad, the much criticized Huerta showed surprising tenacity in his hold upon the Mexican government, and Wilson's policy of "watchful waiting" continued on into 1914. Then a new development threatened to involve the two countries in war. On April 9, 1914, Huerta's representatives at Tampico arrested a few American bluejackets who had landed at the port for supplies. Although Huerta himself promptly ordered their release and expressed regret for the incident, Admiral Mayo, in command of the American squadron in those waters, demanded an additional apology in the form of a salute to the American flag. When Huerta refused to meet these terms, President Wilson supported the admiral and on April 20 laid the matter before Congress. While deprecating the prospect of war, he intimated that armed conflict was possible. But in case fighting should ensue, he declared, the United States would not be at war with Mexico but only with Huerta and the purpose of the struggle "would be only to restore to the people of the distracted republic the opportunity to set up again their own laws and their own government." The President then asked Congress for authority to use the armed forces of the United States "to obtain from General Huerta and his adherents the fullest recognition of the rights and dignity of the United States." That night American marines landed at Vera Cruz, and within another twenty-four hours the city was occupied by American troops.

At this point, when it seemed that war with Mexico was inevitable and that even Huerta's Mexican foes approved his defiance of the United States, three Latin American governments, the Argentine Republic, Brazil, and Chile, offered their services in the interests of peaceful settlement. Both Wilson and Huerta agreed to arbitration, and in May 1914 an agreement was signed, providing for the establishment of a provisional government in Mexico. Although Mexican factions themselves prevented this agreement from going into effect, the intervention of the South American powers averted war between Mexico and the United States.

On July 15, 1914, Huerta resigned. He could hold on no longer because he found it impossible to borrow money. On August 20 Venustiano Carranza entered Mexico City in triumph; on November 23, 1914, Wilson withdrew the American troops from Vera Cruz. But unfortunately Mexico was no nearer peace than before. Pancho Villa led a revolt against Carranza; between September 1914 and February 1915 Mexico City changed hands six times. During this interval Wilson at one time seemed ready to recognize Villa. However, Carranza gradually emerged far enough in front so that a conference of Latin American powers, meeting at Wilson's invitation decided to recognize him. This step was taken in October 1915, and diplomatic relations between the United States and Mexico were resumed. In 1916 there were additional difficulties due to Villa's raids in the United States. These led to punitive expeditions into Mexico, which were unproductive of any satisfactory results. After this the European war tended to crowd Mexican affairs into a less conspicuous place.

Panama Canal Tolls

Wilson's success in driving Huerta out of Mexico was not entirely the result of his long dissertations on constitutional government, but in part the result of the withdrawal of British support. English officials found it hard to appreciate the distinction between Huerta and Carranza, and, unlike Wilson, they did not consider themselves champions of constitutional government in regions other than their own. Consequently the British were as ready to recognize Huerta as Diaz; neither his moral character nor his theories of government disturbed them in the slightest. But the British were greatly interested in another question, that of Panama Canal tolls, and they were willing to let Wilson have his way with Huerta if in return he would meet British demands on the tolls issue. The possibility of bracketing these two unrelated matters was discussed at various times by Ambassador Page, Colonel House, Sir William Tyrrell, and President Wilson.

Here was a question which delighted the hairsplitting legalist. Under the Clayton-Bulwer Treaty Great Britain was a partner of the United States in the proposed isthmian canal. In the Hay-Pauncefote Treaty Great Britain gave up her privileged position, but in doing so she received a formal guarantee of equality of treatment in using the canal. In 1912, in preparation for the opening of the Panama Canal, Congress provided for a uniform toll charge of $1.25 per ton for all vessels except those engaged in the coastwise trade of the United States; these were to be given free use of the Canal. President Taft approved the bill. His argument was simple: "We own the Canal. It was our money that built it. We have the right to charge tolls for its use." He admitted that these charges must be uniform, but he put the coastwise shipping of the United States in a category by itself and justified its exemption on the ground that foreign governments subsidized their shipping.

Elihu Root denied the right of this government to grant the exemption. He argued that there was a parallel case under the Treaty of Washington of 1871, which gave Americans equal rights with the Canadians in using Canadian canals. When the Canadian government attempted to grant lower toll charges to Canadian vessels, President Cleveland had objected and the rates were made equal for all vessels. The British government formally protested against the law of 1912 on the ground that it was a violation of the Hay-Pauncefote Treaty.

The Democratic platform of 1912 approved the exemption of American coastwise shipping, and so too did Wilson himself at first. Subsequently he looked into the matter a little, and after his inauguration he advocated repeal of the exemption. On March 5, 1914, Wilson appeared before Congress and asked for a repeal of the tolls provision. He put this request on two grounds: the inherent justice of the proposal and the necessity of supporting the foreign policy of the administration. "I shall not know how to deal with other matters of even greater delicacy and nearer consequence if you do not grant it to me in ungrudging measure." This cryptic message aroused great curiosity at the time, a curiosity not dispelled until the publication of the Page letters and the House papers. They showed that he had reference to the Mexican muddle. In response to the President's request—virtually a command—the House voted the repeal on March 31; the Senate did not act until June 11. Opposition to Wilson was strong, and he was compelled to exert his power to the utmost.

The Conquest of Haiti

In his handling of the Mexican problem President Wilson met with adverse criticism from two groups: professional diplomats and foreign property owners in Mexico. Both looked to the United States for the protection of their interests and both were disappointed. But Wilson did prevent the United States from going to war with the distracted country, and for this part of his program he received no little praise. During this same period Wilson was drawn into a policy in Haiti which seemed to be based upon very different principles from those which he advocated in his speeches and also from those carried out in Mexico. Had his Haitian policy been discussed in the press it would undoubtedly have stirred up an interesting controversy, but for various reasons the public knew almost nothing about the venture in Haiti until after the end of World War I.

Formerly a French colony and later a Negro republic, Haiti had seen its share of revolution. During the early part of the present century conditions became worse. Between 1911 and 1915 the small republic had six presidents. One of these, President Simon, had granted concessions to investors or adventurers in Haiti, and there seemed to be considerable difficulty over these grants. Among the bona fide investors the National City Bank of New York was the most conspicuous; it had an interest in the National Bank of Haiti. Among the adventurers James P. McDonald held a high place. He had received a concession allowing him to build a railroad from Port au Prince to Cape Haitien, from south to north directly across the island. The whole story is long, involved, and more than peculiar. Reduced to its lowest terms, if such a thing is possible, it appears that the National City Bank had influence enough with the authorities at Washington to enlist their services in behalf of the National City Bank's interests in Haiti.

Problem of Haiti

Toward the end of 1914 Secretary Bryan wrote a letter to the United States minister in Haiti which might well have been written by the most ardent advocate of dollar diplomacy:

> Capital will not flow into Haiti except upon exorbitant terms and for speculative profits unless there is an assurance of peace and orderly government. . . . Our obligation to the American people requires that we shall give all legitimate assistance to American investors in Haiti, but we are under obligations just as binding to protect Haiti . . . from injustice or exploitation at the hands of Americans.

Not long afterward Bryan wrote to President Wilson with reference to the necessity of keeping Mole St. Nicholas out of foreign hands, and then he suggested that the time had come for the United States to define its policy toward Haiti. Bryan pointed out that the native government had been under French or German influence and that if such influence continued American interests were sure to suffer. In the following July 1915 United States marines were landed on the island.

American Intervention

In this summer of 1915 there was a presidential election scheduled for Haiti. Admiral Caperton announced his support of Dartiguenave, and Dartiguenave was elected. All accounts emphasize the fact that United States marines were present when Congress elected the new incumbent. Next the State Department instructed its representative in Haiti to secure a new treaty which would give the United States power over the supposedly independent republic. This proposed treaty would put the United States in control of the Haitian customs service, on terms similar to those already established in the other republic on the island, Santo Domingo. Then the United States would be authorized to appoint a financial adviser, who would draw up the budget and audit expenditures. Next there would be a Haitian constabulary, under the command of officers appointed by the President of the United States. The United States would exercise control over policies of sanitation and public works. In addition the United States would receive the right to intervene in Haiti in order to preserve Haitian independence or to maintain a government adequate for the protection of life, liberty, and property. This treaty would remain in effect for ten years and would be renewable for ten years more at the request of either party.

The Haitian government was allowed no discretion in this matter. The State Department announced that it would not recognize Dartiguenave until the Haitian Congress should authorize the negotiation of this treaty. When opposition developed, Admiral Caperton proclaimed martial law and announced that he was "vested with the power and responsibility of government in all its functions." A few days later he reported that "the treaty situation at present looks more favorable than usual. This has been effected by exercising military pressure at propitious moments in negotiations." During September, under instructions from Washington, Caperton occupied the customhouses. Then he withheld all funds from the Haitian government and prohibited the payment of any government salaries; payments would be resumed after the treaty was approved, he declared. The Haitian Congress ratified the treaty in November, and the United States Senate gave its approval early in 1916. There is no indication that the Haitian legislature accepted the new treaty voluntarily.

Disputes between the Haitian president and his Congress led to further complications, the result of which was the election of a so-called constituent assembly, scheduled to meet in January 1917. When the delegates came together they were presented with a constitution and ordered to ratify it. The Haitian Assembly refused to do so, partly because it gave foreigners the right to own land and partly because it carried a provision for ratifying all acts of the American occupation. General Cole dissolved the assembly. In June 1918 the constitution was submitted to the voters in a referendum or plebiscite. Major Williams instructed his officers that it would be desirable to have the constitution adopted, and marines supervised the voting. The vote was overwhelmingly in favor of ratification. The new constitution went into effect, and Haiti became temporarily a dependency of the United States. The system of control was thorough and complete. The government of the United States was represented by a minister and by an officer of the navy. Under them was the commandant of the marines. Next came the financial adviser and the receiver of customs. The State and Navy Departments at Washington shared supervisory powers. The American regime in Haiti was an absolute despotism, upheld by military force.

The Occupation

Beginning in 1916 the commandant of marines decided that the native population could never be properly controlled until all parts of the country were made easily accessible. To this end new roads had to be built. The officers of the occupation discovered an old Haitian law which compelled the inhabitants to work on roads; this law was revived, extended in scope, and put into effect. In 1918 there was a revolt against the system of forced labor on the roads, and the marines had to restore order. But the uprising continued until the summer of 1920, and during that time ugly stories of atrocities began to reach the American press. Reports as to the number of Haitians killed during this rebellion differ widely. The Haitians claimed that the number was 3500; Marine Corps records put it at 3250; an investigating committee of the United States Senate cut the figure to 1500. The marines suffered only slightly, with not more than fifteen casualties. In 1921 the United States Senate began its investigation of alleged atrocities in Haiti, but this body found no evidence of indiscriminate cruelty.

There is no question that the marines carried out their assignment, which was to suppress opposition to the American occupation; furthermore the marines themselves were not responsible for the assignment, so it was unjust to find fault with them or their methods. But the Senatorial investigators from the United States ignored the most important consideration—that is, that the United States had no legal right to enter an independent republic, force its government to accept an objectionable treaty, impose upon it a new constitution, subject the inhabitants to forced labor, and then govern the country under a military despotism. Such enterprises are not provided for in the Constitution of the United States, nor do they find endorsement in the speeches of Woodrow Wilson.

In 1922 former Secretary of State Lansing wrote an explanation of the Haitian policy of his government: "There was good reason to believe that in the years 1913-1914 Germany was ready to go to great lengths to secure the exclusive customs control of Haiti and also to secure a coaling station at Mole St. Nicholas." But the United States occupied Haiti, not in 1913-1914, but in 1915, and in that year Germany at least was in no position to undertake any colonial ventures in the Caribbean. President Wilson himself never gave any explanation.

Protecting the Panama Canal

The real explanation would seem to be that somebody in the administration thought that the occupation was necessary for reasons of naval strategy. Then the apologists for the administration pointed to the many constructive achievements of the occupation: good roads, schools, public works, sanitary engineering, and the economic and political reorganization of the country. These results were accomplished, it is true, but only at the cost of a flagrant violation of the Constitution of the United States. Civil government was not re-established in Haiti until 1931, and complete independence was not restored until 1934.

Control of the Caribbean

Other developments which occurred in the Caribbean during this same period show that the conquest of Haiti was part of a comprehensive plan to give the United States complete domination of all approaches to the Panama Canal. Santo Domingo had come under the financial guardianship of the United States in 1905. In 1916 revolutionary disturbances led to a military guardianship as well; before the end of that year the United States dissolved civil government and put Santo Domingo under a military despotism like that in Haiti. This continued until 1924.

In this same year of 1916 President Wilson added a third protectorate to the growing list. The Senate at last ratified the Bryan-Chamorro Treaty with Nicaragua which had been signed in 1914. Under the terms of this agreement, in return for $3,000,000, Nicaragua granted to the United States all rights necessary for the construction and maintenance of a canal across the country. In addition the United States secured, under lease, the Corn Islands in the Caribbean and a naval base on the Pacific coast of Nicaragua. Until 1925 American marines encouraged the inhabitants in the habits of peace and of loyalty toward the United States.

Again in 1916, when the Latin American policy of the United States took such a practical turn, the government carried through the project, seriously considered some years earlier, of buying the Danish West Indies. A treaty with Denmark calling for the sale of the islands for $25,000,000 was duly ratified by the United States Senate in September 1916, and in the following March the formal transfer of title took place.

A glance at a map of the Caribbean will show how this policy made the United States the dominant naval power in the West Indies. The naval station at Guantanamo, Cuba, controls the passage between Cuba and Haiti into the Gulf of Mexico. Haiti, Santo Domingo, and St. Thomas all have excellent facilities for naval stations. In addition, the rights in Nicaragua gave the United States the superior position on the Gulf coast of Central America. The Panama Canal, opened for traffic in 1914, was heavily fortified.

Perhaps the best way of giving coherence to this account of American penetration into the Caribbean would be to treat it as the policy of safeguarding both the Canal itself and the approaches to it. In this connection it is necessary to note the Lodge resolution, announced in 1911. Reports were current that a Japanese syndicate was negotiating for the purchase of land in Lower California. The United States objected because the proposed purchase included Magdalena Bay, potentially valuable as a naval station. The resolution reads:

> . . . when any harbor or other place in the American continents is so situated that the occupation thereof for naval or military purposes might threaten the communications or the safety of the United States, the Government of the United States could not see without grave concern the actual or potential possession of such harbor or other place by any Government, not American, as to give that Government practical power of control for naval or military purposes.

This resolution passed the Senate by a vote of fifty-one to four.

As time went on the policy of protecting the Canal acquired an importance equal to that of the Monroe Doctrine itself. Revolutionary disturbances or financial weakness in the Caribbean might lead to intervention by outsiders, and such intervention would be a threat to the safety of the Canal. Republican and Democratic secretaries of state, regardless of party, explained how they stood with reference to protecting the Canal and the Caribbean. In August 1923 Secretary of State Hughes said:

> I believe that the sentiment of the American people is practically unanimous that in the interest of our national safety we could not yield to any foreign power the control of the Panama Canal, or the approaches to it, or the obtaining of any position which would interfere with our right of protection or would menace the freedom of our communications.

Payment to Colombia

In the complex maze of contradictory declarations and activities which made up the Latin American policy of the United States, one more incident deserves mention, the effort to mollify Colombia for her loss of the Isthmus of Panama. The people there had never forgiven the United States for recognizing the republic of Panama. They still valued their former canal rights alone at something more than $50,000,000; for Panama itself they could not fix any definite value. President Taft tried to settle the question before he left office. but his efforts resulted in failure. Then Wilson and

Bryan took the matter up, with the result that in June 1914 a treaty was signed and submitted to the Senate. Without specific mention of Theodore Roosevelt's assistance in creating the republic of Panama, the treaty expressed regret for anything which had interrupted cordial relations between the two countries. Then the treaty provided for the payment of $25,000,000 to Colombia, and it gave Colombians certain preferential rights in the use of the Canal. Colombia in turn was to accord formal recognition to Panama. The treaty was referred to the Senate Committee on Foreign Relations, and there it slept for five years. In 1919 it was reported out, with one impressive amendment: Article I, which had contained the expression of regret, disappeared entirely. The friends of Theodore Roosevelt were still numerous, and they had angrily condemned the first article as a reflection on his integrity. Two years later, in the Harding regime, the Senate ratified the amended treaty, and the United States paid Colombia the $25,000,000. During the debate in the Senate there were more references to the value of Colombian petroleum fields than to matters of Panama Canal history.

Chapter 39

AMERICAN NEUTRALITY IN WORLD WAR I

First Effects on the United States

FROM the summer of 1914 to the end of his second term, President Wilson's policies were shaped largely by World War I and by the problems connected with it. The causes of this war belong to the field of European history, and they are too complex even to summarize here. In the background there was a combination of wrongs of the past, real or alleged, which kept alive a chronic feeling of bitterness and hate. Then there was another tangle of conflicting imperialistic interests in colonies and in trade. There was a policy known as Pan-Germanism, a plan to put Germany in control of Europe, and there was a system of rival alliances, designed to preserve peace. The members of these rival groups continued to build up their armaments, military and naval, and every new increase brought a new surge of fear. Any one of a number of forces might have wrecked the unstable structure of European peace; what actually did so was the murder of an Austrian archduke in the hitherto little-known Bosnian town of Sarajevo.

American Attitude

On August 4, 1914, President Wilson issued a proclamation of neutrality warning Americans not to enlist in the services of the belligerent powers, and warning the belligerent governments against using American soil as a base for hostile activity. The proclamation announced that "while all persons may lawfully and without restriction by reason of the aforesaid state of war manufacture and sell within the United States arms and munitions of war," they could not carry such articles on the high seas without running the risk of capture. Two weeks later the President followed this official declaration with a plea to all influential leaders of public opinion, urging them to promote "the true spirit of neutrality," which, as he explained, was neutrality in thought as well as in action.

At the beginning of the struggle the attitude of the government of the United States was officially correct; this was a matter of legal status. Impartiality of opinion or attitude, however, was something very different, and the bulk of opinion in the United States was never impartial; in the East particularly the people were strongly sympathetic with the Allies and strongly opposed to Germany and Austria. This was true of President Wilson himself. Spring-Rice, the British ambassador, reported that Wilson favored the British side and that he would regard a dispute between England and the United States as "the crowning calamity." American newspapers condemned the efforts of Austria to force a settlement upon Serbia and condemned the

Austrian government as the aggressor. They gave wide publicity to Sir Edward Grey's last-minute efforts to prevent war and to the refusal of the German government to cooperate in these efforts. When the German armies invaded Belgium the American press described the attack as one more proof of German aggression.

British Propaganda

This belief that Germany was the aggressor affected the whole concept of the war. Furthermore, it greatly simplified the task of Allied propagandists; all they had to do was to prevent the Americans from changing their mind. German propagandists, on the other hand, could never overcome this initial attitude. When the war began, most of the facilities for transmitting news to America lay with the British. They owned and controlled the cables. Most of the European news published in the American papers came by way of London. The head of the London bureau of *The New York Times* was an Englishman, and so too were most of his assistants. In these circumstances American convictions on the subject of the war received a strong British bias. British authorities, however, were not satisfied with this favorable situation. They were determined to strengthen still further this sympathy with the Allies, and they influenced American opinion by means of a great propaganda organization, Wellington House, with Sir Gilbert Parker in charge. As he himself described his position: "Practically since the day war broke out between England and the Central Powers I became responsible for American publicity." Parker's own words give some idea of the range of his work.

> Among other things, we supplied three hundred and sixty newspapers in the smaller states of the United States with an English newspaper which gave a weekly review and comment on the affairs of the war. We established connection with the man in the street through cinema pictures of the army and navy, as well as through interviews, articles, pamphlets, etc. . . . Besides an immense private correspondence with individuals, we had our documents and literature sent to great numbers of public libraries, Y.M.C.A. societies, universities, colleges, historical societies, clubs and newspapers.

Among the factors responsible for strengthening the conviction of German villainy, one of the most important was the report of German atrocities in Belgium. The German invasion of Belgium had already aroused a feeling of horror in the United States. According to reports sent over from England, German soldiers were guilty of the brutal murder of noncombatants, of assaults upon women, and cruel torture of women and children. It so happened that a group of American newspaper correspondents, men of known integrity, were with the German army in Belgium. Their first information of the alleged atrocities came to them by way of English newspapers, and in the interests of accuracy they cabled a report of their own findings: "In spirit fairness we unite in declaring German atrocities groundless as far as we were able to observe. . . . Numerous investigated rumors proved groundless." What these American correspondents overlooked was the fact of the invasion itself. That was a crowning atrocity beside which any mere assaults upon individuals looked absurdly insignificant.

To furnish proof of the aggressive designs of the German leaders, investigators went through the prewar writings of German historians, military men, and publicists and extracted from them statements illustrative of German philosophy and policy. This evidence seemed to prove not only that the Germans had been plotting the war for years but that in doing so they had been counting on ruthlessness and terrorism to give them a victory over their more humane opponents. Among these Germans who were made to give testimony against the German cause was the eminent historian Heinrich von Treitschke, who had died in 1896. As professor of history at the University of Berlin he had been in a position to reach an influential group of students. In a series of lectures on politics and statecraft he had popularized the Hegelian concept which exalted the state as an entity superior to the individuals who composed it and superior also to those principles of equity and fairness which were supposed to regulate the affairs of men. Treitschke also had written and spoken of Germany's mission to rule the world, a mission which could be carried out only by means of war.

Germany and War

Another writer drawn upon to testify against Germany was General Friedrich von Bernhardi, author of *Germany and the Next War*. When the war began this book was translated into English and widely circulated in both England and the United States. Bernhardi advocated war both as a means of making Germany great and as a biological necessity. To be effective, he argued, war must reach the civilian population. He wrote of the great destiny of the German people and declared: "We can fulfill it only by the sword. . . . Might is at once the supreme right, and the dispute as to what is right is decided by the arbitrament of war. War gives a biologically just decision, since its decisions rest on the very nature of things."

For a brief period the war brought about serious economic reverses for the United States. European investors rushed to turn their American securities into cash, and the resulting deluge of selling forced down prices. To prevent the demoralization of the security market the New York Stock Exchange closed at once and did not reopen for free trading until April 1915. Merchants engaged in foreign commerce saw their business stopped. The German and Austrian markets were lost at once, and the British soon put effective obstacles in the way of American trade with neutral ports of Europe. Next to England, Germany had been the largest buyer of American cotton, and cotton growers at first suffered heavily from the war.

Earlier wars, notably those from 1793 to 1815, had opened remarkable opportunities for neutral merchants. At the same time the belligerent governments had interpreted international law largely as they pleased, so that they had been able to impose restrictions on neutral shipping. The only way to prevent similar difficulties from arising in 1914 and later would be to have the belligerent powers come to a formal agreement on principles of maritime law governing neutral trade. Such an agreement was impossible.

The British, with their superior navy, were determined to prevent supplies from reaching Germany. On August 20, 1914, the British government issued the first of a long series of orders in council defining their policy on neutral trade. This decree announced that conditional contraband would be seized, even though it was en route to a neutral port. Our government registered no effective protest against this policy.

Neutral Trade

In November the British government announced that the North Sea was a military area; for the future all shipping in this area would be subject to British regulation. Ships could enter the area only through the Straits of Dover and could proceed only in lanes defined by the British. All shipping, regardless of ownership or destination, would be subjected to careful examination. This procedure was equivalent to a blockade of Dutch and Scandinavian ports, a blockade which had no warrant under any interpretation of international law. The British justified it on the ground of necessity. British authorities also found justification for their policy in the doctrine of continuous voyage, developed by the United States Supreme Court during the American Civil War. The situations were not parallel because the doctrine as originally evolved applied only to contraband, while the British seized noncontraband as well.

Wilson and the Allies

Secretary Bryan sent a protest against the war zone order, but it was entirely ineffective. The British continued to confiscate cargoes as they pleased. To be sure, they paid for what they took, but at prices which they determined; the merchants complained that the Germans would have paid more. On March 1, 1915, the British government made its policy somewhat more definite, but not more legal, by announcing that it would prevent all commodities, contraband and noncontraband alike, from reaching Germany either directly or through neutral ports. Again the attitude of the United States was one of sympathetic acquiescence. In July 1915 Secretary Lansing wrote:

> Germany must not be permitted to win this war or to break even, though to prevent it this country is forced to take an active part. This ultimate necessity must be constantly in our minds in all our controversies with the belligerents. American public opinion must be prepared for the time, which may come, when we will have to cast aside our neutrality and become one of the champions of democracy.

President Wilson himself had this same conception of neutrality. In these circumstances the State Department would make no effective protests against British violations of international law. It is true that in October 1915 Wilson wrote a note for Lansing to sign which did characterize British policy in strong terms. This document declared that "Great Britain cannot expect the United States to submit to such manifest injustice or to

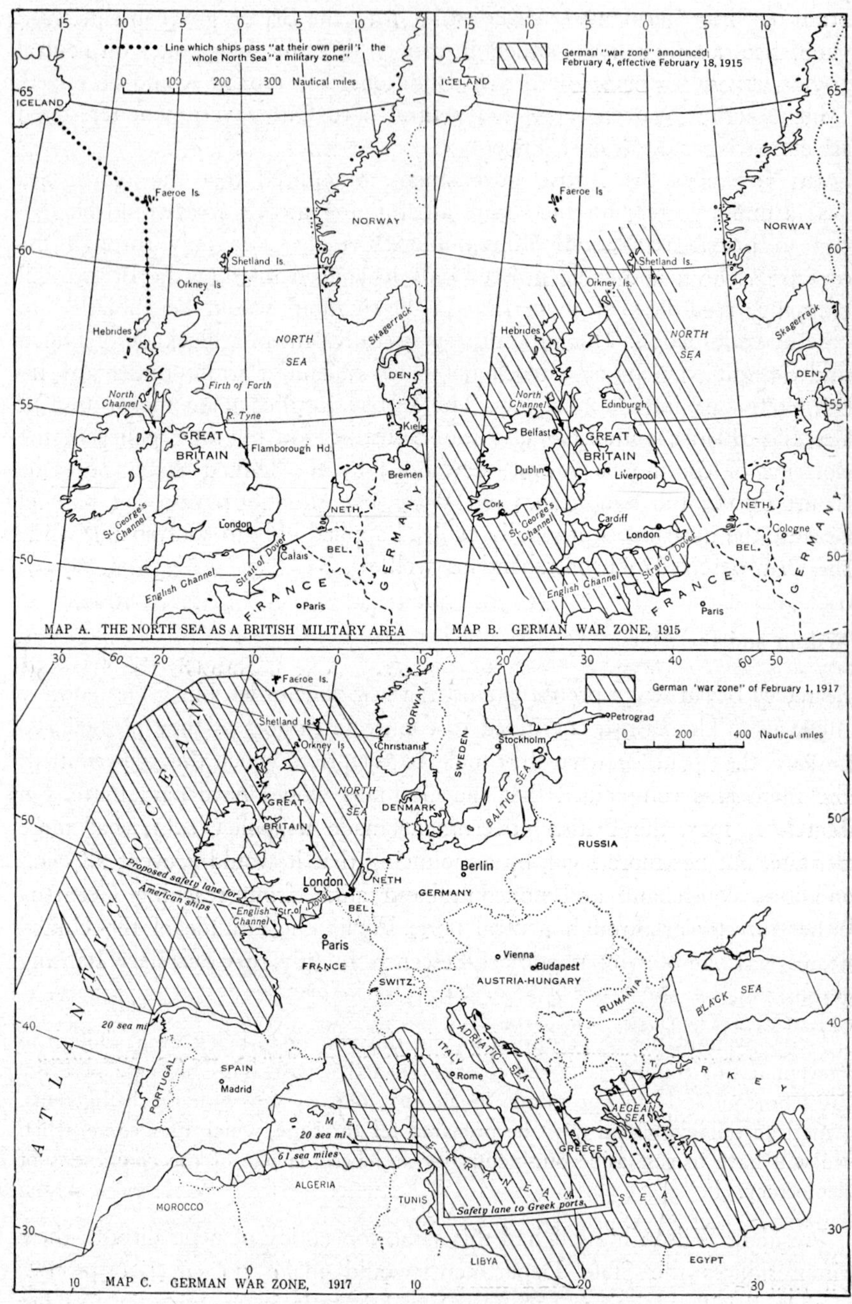

Map 18. The Maritime War Zones, 1914-17

permit the right of its citizens to be so seriously impaired." The note went on to say that "the United States maintains the right to sell goods into the general stock of a neutral country, and denounces as illegal and unjustifiable any attempts of a belligerent to interfere with that right."

British regulations were exasperating but not harmful. The Allies themselves needed American supplies, and Allied orders soon brought a great boom in business. The first few months of the war showed that victory would probably depend upon the quantity of ammunition available. British factories could not possibly furnish enough, and the neutral governments of Europe imposed an embargo on munitions. The only source left was the United States.

Wartime Prosperity

There was nothing in international law to prevent American manufacturers from selling all the war materials the belligerents were able to buy. Of course such materials were contraband, and belligerent powers were legally entitled to seize shipments consigned to enemy ports. English naval vessels did seize cargoes destined for Germany. Germany, on the other hand, found her navy confined to her own home waters by the superior British fleet and so was unable to intercept cargoes bound for England or France. President Wilson's proclamation of neutrality admitted the legality of the trade in contraband; this doctrine was reaffirmed by Secretary Bryan: "a citizen of the United States can sell to a belligerent government or its agent any article of commerce which he pleases." Even Bernstorff, the German ambassador, admitted that the trade was legal.

American manufacturers found this wartime trade very profitable. The DuPont Company furnished the Allied powers with 40 percent of their explosives used in the war, and DuPont's total wartime profits were more than $260,000,000. One of the copper companies, Calumet and Hecla, paid dividends of 800 percent on its par value. The steel manufacturers did not make so much money, but their wartime trade was profitable. For example, Bethlehem Steel showed a profit of $43,000,000 in 1916. Even the farmers shared in this growing volume of business. In 1913 the United States exported wheat to the value of $89,936,428, but in 1915 the wheat exports were valued at $333,552,226. Altogether the period from 1914 to 1917 was a time of unprecedented prosperity for the United States. Prices, wages, and profits reached new levels.

The great bulk of this wartime trade was carried on with the Allies. Many people of German origin objected to the trade on this ground; so too did some Irish, who hated to have the English get any help. Some other Americans had misgivings as to the justice of wartime trade which materially helped one belligerent and seriously injured the other. These critics felt that there was something wrong with the neutrality which made so one-sided an arrangement possible. They had friends in Congress, and these Congressmen were ready to stop the trade with the Allies. In December 1914 one bill and three resolutions were introduced in Congress, all aiming at the prohibition of the munitions trade.

These proposals alarmed the British ambassador. He argued that an embargo would be advantageous to a government such as Germany, which had been plotting war, and that it would be injurious to France and England, which had not expected war. He even held that an American embargo would be unneutral. These arguments of Spring-Rice were reinforced by additional arguments submitted by Sir Edward Grey. President Wilson reaffirmed his original stand that the trade was legal, and Secretary Bryan gave Spring-Rice definite assurance that Congress would not adopt any embargo.

Allied purchases of war materials in the United States soon raised the question of methods of payment. Russia, France, and England combined were not selling goods in international trade on a scale sufficient to finance these purchases, so some form of credit became essential. At the beginning of the war, Bryan and Wilson both agreed that no encouragement should be given to the sale of bonds of the belligerent governments. But pressure for loans increased with Allied orders, and by 1915 the administration ceased to oppose the sale of Allied bonds here. By April 1917 American investors had bought Allied bonds to the amount of $2,506,591,377. The American economic system was geared to the Allied cause. Allied purchases of food and war materials were the essential factor in American economic prosperity, and the American people advanced the funds to make these purchases possible. Economic developments therefore intensified American friendliness for the British side.

House-Grey Memorandum

Almost from the start President Wilson had a strong desire to act as mediator in the war. The first definite expression of this desire, in terms of policy, came early in 1915. The President and Colonel House decided that the Colonel should undertake a trip to Europe and explain Wilson's readiness to act as an intermediary through whom the belligerents might exchange views as to the best way of ending the war. As they saw it, peace when it came must be founded upon a new world order of friendliness and good will. In February House conferred with Sir Edward Grey and found that he was favorably disposed toward such a new world order. The new system would be built upon a great international understanding dedicated to permanent peace.

By October 1915 Colonel House was considering an elaborate scheme. He advocated some sort of understanding with the Allies under which the United States might intervene in the war for the purpose of bringing it to a successful conclusion. Once this arrangement with the Allies had been concluded, House would inform Germany that the United States might enter the war. The authorities at Berlin were not to be informed that the United States had made an agreement on the subject with the Allies. Grey replied that the Allied governments could not bind themselves until they knew precisely what House had in mind, so House returned to London to tell them. The outcome of this visit was the House-Grey memorandum.

Colonel House visited the three principal capitals, Berlin, Paris, and London. At Berlin he seems to have said little. At Paris on the other hand, House assured Cambon and Briand that "the lower the fortunes of the Allies ebbed, the closer the United States would stand by them." Two days later, as he reported to Wilson, he amplified his assurance by saying that, if the Allies should win substantial victories in the spring or summer, the United States would not feel compelled to act, but "in the event that the tide of war went against them or remained stationary, you would intervene." Again, on February 10, 1916, writing from London, House gave Wilson a summary of his talks with Sir Edward Grey:

> We finally agreed that it would be best for you to demand that the belligerents permit you to call a conference for the discussion of peace terms. We concluded this would be better than intervention, and it was understood, though not definitely agreed upon, that you might do this within a very short time—perhaps soon after I returned. [Then came the significant disclosure.] The Allies will agree to the conference, and, if Germany does not, I have promised for you that we will throw in all our weight in order to bring her to terms.

This understanding was put into definite form, dated February 22, 1916, and sent on to President Wilson. There are two parts to this House-Grey memorandum. First, whenever England and France thought that the time was suitable, Wilson would propose a conference to put an end to the war. "Should the Allies accept this proposal, and should Germany refuse it, the United States would probably enter the war against Germany." The second part provided that if the proposed conference should meet and should fail to bring about peace, the United States "would probably leave the Conference as a belligerent on the side of the Allies, if Germany was unreasonable." The word "probably" in the second part was inserted by President Wilson to make it consistent with the first section. It is significant that House had made the pledge unconditional.

According to House, the President paid him a high compliment upon his work: "It would be impossible to imagine a more difficult task than the one placed in your hands, but you have accomplished it in a way beyond my expectations." And on March 8, the President himself wrote the cablegram which House sent to Grey, reporting Wilson's approval. On April 6, 1916, Wilson sent the following suggestion to Sir Edward Grey: "Since it appears probable that this country must break with Germany on the submarine question unless the unexpected happens . . . I beg to suggest that if you had any thought of acting at an early date on the plan we had agreed upon, you might wish now to consult with your allies with a view to acting immediately." Wilson therefore sent House off in the first place; he followed the negotiations; he gave his endorsement to the memorandum; and he tried to persuade Grey to act upon it. The American people never heard of the House-Grey memorandum until the war was over; they did not have the slightest hint that the administration was committed in any such fashion. Only a few months later American voters supported the President in his campaign for re-election, and they did so partly on the supposition that he had kept the country out of war, a supposition which he encouraged. During the first half of 1916, therefore, Wilson's policy toward the American people was not one of complete candor. He did not consider it necessary to take them into his confidence and he did not trust them.

More British Restrictions

In the summer of 1916 even Wilson became disgusted with highhanded British methods in interfering with legitimate American trade. In 1914 the British government drew up lists of individuals who were suspected of having commercial relations with Germany. At first these lists were kept secret, but in 1916 some of the names were published, and certain American firms were on the list. Then it became apparent that the published lists contained only a few of the firms actually blacklisted. Individual businessmen or business firms whose names were on these black lists were not allowed to use British cable services, British banks, or British ships. Wilson unburdened himself in a letter to House: "I am, I must admit, about at the end of my patience with Great Britain and the Allies. This black list business is the last straw. I have told Spring-Rice so. . . . Both he and Jusserand think it is a stupid blunder. I am seriously considering asking Congress to authorize me to prohibit loans and restrict exportations to the Allies."

The State Department sent a note of protest, but it was not so sharp in tone as those which had been sent to Germany. Congress also authorized the President to withhold clearance papers from any ships which should refuse American cargoes because of the black list or which should in any way discriminate against the commerce of American citizens, but the President never took advantage of this grant of power. At this same time, in September 1916, Congress passed the largest naval appropriation bill in American history. By this time, however, the development of war industries had gone so far and the prosperity resulting from them had become so general that any effective protest against England had become impossible. An embargo would have been a powerful weapon to use in compelling British recognition of American rights, but it would have had too many undesirable repercussions in the United States.

The British furnished additional ground for complaint in their policy regarding mail. Neutral ships were forced into British ports for examination and search, and the search extended to all mail, both parcel post and sealed letters. Letters which for any reason whatever happened to arouse the suspicions of the censor were held up indefinitely. Important papers were lost, and with the papers went business opportunities. Again the British authorities merely ignored American protests. Sir Edward Grey knew that his government could go to great lengths in suppressing neutral trade, and he was prepared to go just as far as he could, short of actual war with the United States.

"Strict Accountability"

German Policy

Wilson's policy and attitude toward Germany were very different from his policy toward England. In one case he practically approved long-continued violations of international law without calling the British government sharply to account; in the other he delivered an ultimatum at the start, and he repeatedly demanded changes in German policy and threatened war in case of refusal. When the German government at last ignored his threats, he had put himself in such an extreme position that war was the only escape. The Germans had some appreciation of the value of American good will, and like the British they attempted to cultivate it by means of propaganda. In this effort they were notably unsuccessful, partly because their invasion of Belgium had intensified feeling against them, partly because their methods were less skillful than those of the British. The German ambassador, Bernstorff, wrote that German newspaper work was never suited to the American point of view. And he added: "The same may be said of most of the German propaganda which reached America in fairly large quantities since the third month in the War."

Even if the propaganda had been ably handled, it would have been nullified by activities of German agents in this country. The publicity given to them in the American press confirmed the belief that the Germans were dangerous. Certain prominent Germans in New York were arrested, tried, and convicted of supplying fuel and provisions to German raiders off the coast. Captain Boy-Ed, German naval attaché, was in charge of German activities in New York, many of which were carried on in violation of American laws. German agents falsified passports in order to get reservists back to their own country. One German attempted to destroy a railroad bridge in Canada; another was caught in a scheme to blow up part of the Welland Canal in Canada. Altogether sixty-seven individuals were convicted in American courts of violations of American laws.

As the munitions industry developed German agents tried to interrupt both the manufacture and the sale of war materials to the Allies. They fomented strikes in American factories; they started fires in munition plants; and they were accused of placing bombs on ships so that the cargoes would be destroyed at sea. This activity was carried on with the knowledge and approval of the Austrian and the German diplomatic officials at Washington. In 1916 the Austrian ambassador Dumba was so unfortunate as to have one of his important letters intercepted. In it he described plans for causing strikes in American plants, by means of which "we can disorganize and hold up for months, if not entirely prevent, the manufacture of munitions in Bethlehem and the Middle West." This activity led to Dumba's recall. At about the same time the State Department demanded the recall of von Papen and Boy-Ed, the German military and naval attachés.

The most important cause of friction between the American and German governments and the ultimate cause of the entrance of the United States into World War I was the use of submarines against merchant shipping.

Submarine Warfare

Early in February 1915, by way of retaliation against previous British action, the German government declared the waters around Great Britain and Ireland a war zone and announced that enemy merchant vessels would be destroyed. Neutral ships would run grave risks if they should attempt to navigate these waters.

President Wilson's response to this warning was prompt and decisive. He warned the German government that if their submarines should

> destroy on the high seas an American vessel or the lives of American citizens, it would be difficult for the Government of the United States to view the act in any other light than as an indefensible violation of neutral rights. . . . The Government of the United States would be constrained to hold the Imperial German Government to a strict accountability for such acts of their naval authorities and to take any steps it might be necessary to take to safeguard American lives and property and to secure to American citizens the full enjoyment of their acknowledged rights on the high seas.

In this note Wilson took a position from which he never receded, a position which made the continuance of peace contingent upon the action of the German government.

In March 1915 a German submarine sank the *Falaba,* a British ship, and one American citizen lost his life. The resulting outcry in the American press was indicative of the intense anti-German feeling in this country. The sinking was described as "a crime against humanity," as "barbarism run mad," as "an atrocity against which the civilized world should protest with one voice." A few weeks later word was received of the attack upon an American ship, the *Cushing,* by a German seaplane, but no lives were lost. On May 1, 1915, a German submarine torpedoed but did not sink an American oil tanker *Gulflight;* two members of the crew were drowned, and the captain died of heart failure. The *Gulflight* was the only American ship torpedoed by German submarines before diplomatic relations with Germany were broken in February 1917. The German government described the attack as an "unintentional mistake" and promised full reparation. Shortly afterward the German chancellor Bethmann-Hollweg wrote to the chief of staff of the German navy that submarine warfare was creating serious complications with neutral governments, and he insisted that attacks upon neutral vessels be scrupulously avoided. The navy did not agree with this view, but American ships were not attacked again until 1917.

The "Lusitania"

These early outbursts were nothing compared with the storm over the sinking of the British liner *Lusitania.* This crime occurred on May 7, 1915, off the coast of Ireland. The total loss of life was 1153 and included in this total were 114 American citizens. There were several circumstances connected with the sinking which aroused additional wrath in this country.

About a week before the *Lusitania* sailed, the German embassy published in American newspapers a formal warning to prospective passengers:

> Travellers intending to embark for an Atlantic voyage are reminded that a state of war exists between Germany . . . and Great Britain . . . that the zone of war includes the waters adjacent to the British Isles; that, in accordance with the formal notice given by the Imperial German Government, vessels flying the flag of Great Britain or any of her allies are liable to destruction in those waters; and that travellers sailing in the war zone in ships of Great Britain or her allies do so at their own risk.

After the disaster Ambassador von Bernstorff sent a note to the State Department expressing regret at the loss of life.

At this time Secretary Bryan argued that British ships and cargoes could not be made immune to attack merely because neutrals ventured to take passage on them. He believed that American citizens should refrain from sailing on belligerent-owned vessels, not merely in the interest of their own personal safety but for the more important cause of protecting the government from danger of war. President Wilson, however, did not agree with Bryan; he wrote that American citizens had every right to rely on the assurance given in the strict-accountability note. "We defined our position at the outset and cannot alter it,—at any rate so far as it affects the past."

On May 13 the United States government sent the first of a series of *Lusitania* notes. This document emphasized the right of American citizens to take passage on belligerent-owned ships, and it called attention to the obligation of the American government to protect American citizens in the exercise of this right. The note characterized submarine warfare as in conflict with all "rules of fairness, reason, justice, and humanity which all modern opinion regards as imperative," and it warned that the United States

> must hold the Imperial German Government to a strict accountability for any infringement of those rights. . . . The Imperial German Government will not expect the Government of the United States to omit any word or act necessary to the performance of its sacred duty of maintaining the rights of the United States and its citizens and of safeguarding their free exercise and enjoyment.

The note demanded reparation and, although there was no time limit included, it was virtually an ultimatum. In spite of the plain language of the document the German authorities were inclined to overlook its significance. The German reply to the first *Lusitania* note promised reparation for the *Gulflight*. Then it went on to describe the *Lusitania* as a belligerent ship, carrying a heavy cargo of munitions; on this ground they held that the destruction was justifiable. This response did not satisfy Wilson, and he wrote that Germany missed the essential point in the argument: "that England's violation of neutral rights is different from Germany's violation of the rights of humanity." The President insisted on the dispatch of another note to Germany. Secretary Bryan proposed that an equally stiff protest be sent to England. When some of the Cabinet members objected to the proposal, Bryan accused them of being unneutral. Wilson again opposed Bryan. After further exchanges, Bryan refused to sign the second *Lusitania* note and resigned. The President then appointed Robert Lansing to succeed Bryan as secretary of state.

"Arabic" Pledge

The second *Lusitania* note denied the German argument that the ship had been armed and that she carried explosives. Again the German reply was unsatisfactory. Before the dispute over the *Lusitania* had been settled, a new crisis arose. On August 19, 1915, a submarine sank the *Arabic,* outward bound from England. Two Americans were reported drowned. By this time the danger of war between Germany and the United States was real, and Bernstorff gave the so-called *Arabic* pledge: "Liners will not be sunk by our submarines without warning and without safety of the lives of non-combatants, provided that the liners do not try to escape or offer resistance." This promise removed the immediate danger of war, and the outcome was regarded as a diplomatic triumph for the President.

Not fire without warning

Wilson had insisted that merchant ships must not be attacked without warning and that the rules covering naval operations on the surface of the seas must apply also to submarine warfare. He had made it plain that the German government must accede to his demands or face war with the United States. For the time being Germany preferred to yield. Then the Allies, or more particularly Great Britain, increased the perplexities of the American government by arming their merchant vessels. Theoretically this armament was defensive, and the armed vessels retained their status as merchant ships; on this ground limited armament had the sanction of international law. In September 1914 the United States government had announced that merchant ships armed for defense would not be treated as ships of war. Before the inauguration of submarine warfare this principle seemed sound, but it soon became apparent that armament which was defensive against surface craft became offensive against submarines. Early in February 1915 the British admiralty ordered merchant vessels to ram submarines if escape was impossible; before the end of the month merchantmen were instructed to fire on submarines. This order and the action resulting from it transformed the armed merchant ships into ships of war.

Armed Merchant Ships

The armed-ship policy created a peculiar problem for Wilson. He had insisted upon immunity from attack for all merchantmen, and he had warned Germany of dire consequences if she ignored his demands. At the same time he could not promise immunity to British ships of war. Secretary Lansing prepared a statement to the effect that an armed merchant ship should be treated as a ship of war, by belligerents and neutrals alike. In January 1916 this proposal was submitted to the representatives of the Allied governments. Ambassador Page reported from London that Sir Edward Grey was shocked and that his "surprise and dismay are overwhelming."

Colonel House was also shocked. He was just completing the negotiations leading to the House-Grey memorandum, and the introduction of this armed-ship controversy might wreck his work. He sent an urgent cable to Lansing: "There are so many other issues involved in the controversy concerning armed merchantmen that I sincerely hope you will be able to hold it in abeyance until I return. I cannot emphasize too strongly the importance of this." Lansing at once notified the Allied governments that if they should fail to accept his proposal, the American government would not insist upon it. In other words the State Department would disregard the presence of arms on merchant ships and would continue to treat them as though they were not armed. Actually this meant that armed British merchant ships could attack German submarines with complete impunity, but German submarines could not attack armed British merchantmen without risking war with the United States.

Gore-McLemore Resolutions

Several days before Lansing drafted his proposal to the Allies, Senator Gore introduced a bill designed to prevent Americans from obtaining passports if they were planning to travel on belligerent ships. Later he introduced another bill demanding that American trade in noncontraband be protected against the illegal restrictions of the Allies. These two bills brought the whole question of neutrality up for discussion. In the House, Representative McLemore introduced a resolution warning Americans not to travel on armed ships of the belligerents. These congressional measures ran directly counter to the administration's policy. President Wilson therefore threw the whole strength of the administration against his Democratic partners in Congress. He declared that he would keep the United States out of war if possible, but that German policy might make it impossible for him to do so. If Germany should restrict or deny American rights, he would have no choice but to hold her to account.

Wilson informed Congress that the Gore-McLemore proposals must not pass. Senator Gore then introduced another, so phrased as to put the administration on record:

> Resolved, That the sinking by a German submarine without notice or warning of an armed merchant vessel of her public enemy, resulting in the death of a citizen of the United States would constitute a just and sufficient cause of war between the United States and the German Empire.

This resolution was laid on the table. A few days later the McLemore resolution was tabled in the House. Thus in spite of the disapproval of the leaders in his own party, the President clung to his position that Americans were free to take passage on the armed ships of the Allies.

"Sussex" Pledge

On March 25, 1916, the French passenger steamer *Sussex* was torpedoed in the English Channel. There were Americans on board, but no American lives were lost. The vessel herself was badly damaged but was able to make port. Secretary Lansing and Colonel House both wished to break off relations with Germany, but Wilson decided to give Germany one more warning. He authorized House to inform von Bernstorff that "we were at the breaking point and that we would surely go into the war unless some decisive change was made in their submarine policy."

Again the German government yielded to Wilson's threat, as it had done after the *Arabic* affair. In a note dated May 4, 1916, Wilson was informed that the German government "is prepared to do its utmost to confine the operations of war for the rest of its duration to the fighting forces of the belligerents." The pledge stated that no more merchant ships would be sunk "without warning and without saving human lives, unless these ships attempt to escape or offer resistance." This promise, however, was not absolute but conditional. By way of return or compensation the German government expected the United States to demand changes in the policy of the Allies, so that neutral trade would no longer be restricted by illegal interference. The *Sussex* pledge was therefore accompanied by the statement that unless the United States should be successful in securing these concessions from the Allies, "the German government would then be facing a new situation in which it must reserve to itself complete liberty of decision." Secretary Lansing and the President then collaborated in preparing a new message to Germany. This explained that the United States "cannot for a moment entertain, much less discuss, a suggestion that respect by German naval authorities for the rights of citizens of the United States upon the high seas should in any way or in the slightest degree be made contingent upon the conduct of any other Government affecting the rights of neutrals and non-combatants." On the same day the German government expressed regret at the attack upon the *Sussex* and offered reparation for American citizens who had been injured.

Preparedness and Politics

Moves toward Defense

During the first half of 1916 the United States had been on the verge of war. If the House-Grey agreement did not bring the United States in, the German submarine policy might have done it. In addition to these two forces at work there was the conviction that German aggressiveness, the German will to rule, had caused the war in Europe and that the United States might be selected as the next victim. These factors and others created a demand for preparedness to make this country safe from attack. Colonel House was using these arguments on Wilson before the end of 1914. At first the President was most unresponsive. By December 1914, however, there was so much talk of preparedness that Wilson had to refer to it in his annual message to Congress, but he still insisted that no immediate action was needed.

Wilson's views on this subject seemed shortsighted even to some of his friends, notably to Colonel House; to many of his political opponents they seemed absurd. Various agencies were at work in an effort to break down the President's resistance and to induce Congress to enlarge the appropriations for the army and navy. In December 1914 a group of prominent Republicans in New York organized the National Security League, the primary purpose of which was to sell preparedness to the American people. In 1915 the press and the moving pictures were drafted for this same cause. Hudson Maxim published a book, *Defenceless America,* which had a wide sale. In it the author prophesied the invasion of America by a "foreign foe."

Then the *Saturday Evening Post* published a long serial story entitled "America Fallen," in which the eastern cities of the United States were conquered by a foreign army. This invading force was so overwhelming that it encountered practically no opposition. It occupied the country, levied fines up to the limit of all money within reach, and grabbed the leading citizens of each city as hostages. The same theme was developed in the movies, in *The Battle Cry of Peace.*

By the end of 1915 Wilson himself became a convert to the cause of preparedness. In a speech at New York he announced his purpose to prepare, "not for war, but only for defense." The United States, he said, was justified in such preparation in order "to vindicate our right to independent and unmolested action by making the force that is in us ready for assertion." He announced that plans already made called for an increase in the regular army, for the training of a force of "citizen soldiers," and for improvements in the National Guard. The program also called for a larger navy. Wilson repeated the substance of this speech in his next message to Congress, and in the early part of 1916 he went on a speaking tour in behalf of preparedness. By February he was calling for "incomparably the greatest Navy in the world." By the summer of 1916 Congress had passed bills for the increase of both army and navy. It could hardly have been mere coincidence that the President's urgent pleas for preparedness accompanied and followed the negotiation of the House-Grey memorandum.

Republican Policy

This complex of issues, domestic and foreign, furnished the setting for the Presidential campaign of 1916. The Democratic promises of reform, made in 1912, had been carried out in constructive legislation; in ordinary circumstances this alone would have furnished ample material for appeals to the voters. But the times were not ordinary, and the voters had become greatly excited over foreign policy. In this field the administration was sure of its own ground, but it had been unable to convince its opponents of the soundness of its measures. Some people found fault with Wilson's method in dealing with Mexico. Others felt that he had been notably inept in his negotiations with England and Germany. Still others condemned Wilson for having done so little in connection with preparedness.

The Republican national convention was called to meet on June 7 at Chicago, and the Progressives held their convention at the same time and place. Both factions were tired of their quarrel, or at least they realized that without reunion a Republican victory was impossible. Theodore Roosevelt was still available, and he was ready to forgive his foes of the Old Guard; he would even accept their ballots to secure the nomination. The Old Guard, however, was in no mood to forgive Roosevelt. These men could not forget the epithets which he had showered upon them in 1912, and while they were prepared to welcome the Progressives back into the fold they would not nominate Roosevelt. Finding that his own nomination was impossible, Roosevelt suggested the name of Henry Cabot Lodge. Lodge, however, was no more satisfactory to the Progressives than Roosevelt was to the conservatives. The convention at last nominated Charles Evans Hughes, one of the associate justices of the Supreme Court, and Roosevelt promised to support him. Hughes resigned from the Court and began his campaign.

The Republican platform called for a restoration of the high tariff and characterized the Underwood Act as "a complete failure in every respect." As for foreign affairs, the Republicans called for "a strict and honest neutrality between the belligerents in the great war in Europe." They charged that the Wilson administration "has destroyed our influence abroad and humiliated us in our own eyes." They advocated a strong army and navy, but in this particular they did not differ greatly from the Democrats. The platform was silent on the problem of the so-called "hyphenated Americans"—in other words, the pro-Germans. Then there was a general condemnation of Wilson's policy in Mexico.

"He Kept Us out of War"

The Democrats met in St. Louis, and Wilson was nominated without opposition. The platform made much of the party's record of constructive legislation. It advocated an army and navy strong enough to protect American rights and to make the nation safe from attack. Concerning the "hyphenates" the Democrats were considerably more outspoken than the Republicans, and they voiced their objections to German interference in the munitions trade. In the course of the campaign the president of the American Truth Society, Jeremiah O'Leary, asked Wilson for a statement of his views on foreign affairs, and in doing so he implied that if the statement were not satisfactory the members of his organization would vote for Hughes. Wilson's reply was characteristic: "I would feel deeply mortified to have you or anybody like you vote for me. Since you have access to many disloyal Americans and I have not, I will ask you to convey this message to them."

The Democratic platform contained a slogan which the party played up during the campaign: "Wilson kept us out of war." Wilson himself accused his Republican opponents of advocating war, and he intimated that a vote for him was a vote for peace; Democratic campaign speakers made much of Wilson's success in keeping the United States out of war. Neither platform nor speakers mentioned the House-Grey memorandum, nor did any Democrat point out that the United States had avoided war simply because Germany had yielded to Wilson's threats.

The Democratic campaign was conducted with considerably more skill than the Republican. In their eagerness to win, the Republicans and their candidates talked in noncommittal terms. This hedging, especially on the issue of the "hyphenates," antagonized many who would normally have voted Republican. Nevertheless, Hughes might have won the election had it not been for a bad blunder in California. Hiram Johnson, who had been the vice-presidential candidate on Roosevelt's Bull Moose ticket in 1912, was running for the United States Senate on the Republican ticket. Hughes visited California, but he did not recognize Johnson's existence. Johnson carried the state by 300,000, while Hughes lost it by 3773. Had he carried California, he would have won the election. Actually he came so close to winning that the early postelection editions of some newspapers announced that he had won. Wilson had a plurality of the popular vote, receiving 9,128,837, while Hughes received 8,536,380. Wilson's electoral vote was 277 and Hughes's 254. The Democrats retained control of the Senate, but neither party had a majority in the House; the Democrats, however, succeeded in retaining control of the organization.

Chapter 40

THE POLICIES OF WAR

From Peace to War

Efforts for Peace

WITH the election out of the way the administration was free onc more to devote its attention to foreign affairs. The United State was still at peace, thanks to the German government's *Sussex* pledge, bu nobody knew better than President Wilson that war was inevitable shoul the German authorities change their minds. A renewal of submarine attack on passenger vessels would make the United States a partner in the allianc against Germany. In 1916 the Germans made one more effort at negotiatio before they brought the United States into the war. In August of that yea Chancellor Bethmann-Hollweg informed Bernstorff that his governmen would be glad to have President Wilson act as mediator in a formal bi for peace. Bernstorff talked the proposal over with Colonel House, wh replied that Wilson could do nothing until after the election.

In December 1916 Wilson told House that the time was propitious for a attempt to secure peace. A few days afterward the German government in formed Grew, the American chargé d'affaires, that the Central Powers woul be glad to begin negotiations. This announcement from Berlin proved em barrassing to the President because he did not wish to appear as an agent o Germany. At the same time Wilson had become impatient with England' violations of neutral rights. He was therefore in a mood to be severe wit that country. House, on the other hand, urged Wilson to refrain from an statements which might offend the Allies.

On December 18, 1916, Wilson addressed a note to the European govern ments, in which he observed that, so far as they had been stated, the wa aims of both sides seemed to be much alike. The President then asked th belligerents to define their specific terms. The note aroused a storm of pro test in England. It is reported that King George actually wept at the sug gestion that British objectives were on a par with those of the enemy. Th German government was not much happier than the British. Officials i Berlin would have preferred to begin direct negotiations with the Allies and their idea seems to have been that Wilson would merely arrange th preliminaries for direct discussions. His attempt to force the belligerents int a formal definition of their terms prior to a peace conference they charac terized as "meddling."

Wilson's note to the belligerents did not bring peace, and the impossi bility of getting the two sides together in a conference made the renewa of submarine warfare almost certain. But the discussion had called attentio to the necessity of some sort of world organization to be established afte the war, and Wilson determined to emphasize this policy before anyone could forget it. It will be recalled that Colonel House had already talked over this project with Sir Edward Grey. On January 22, 1917, the President addressed the United States Senate. At this time he informed the world that governments had been brought appreciably nearer to "the discussion of the international concert which must thereafter hold the world at peace." He took it for granted that peace must be followed by some "concert of power which will make it virtually impossible that any such catastrophe should ever overwhelm us again." Then the President went on to outline the conditions under which the United States would join "a League for Peace." "It will be absolutely necessary that a force be created as a guarantor of the permanency of the settlement," a force so much stronger than that of any single nation or combination of nations that no government would venture to defy it. At this time therefore he seemed to visualize the League of Nations as a superpower. He went on to explain that for the future the principle of the balance of power must give way to that of "a community of power; not organized rivalries, but an organized common peace." Then he followed with a phrase which again made the Allies frantic: ". . . it must be a peace without victory." He wanted a peace between equals, so that there would be no resentment, no accumulation of bitterness to serve as the cause of another war, and because only a peace between equals could last. Again he called for a peace which should recognize the principle that "governments derive all their just powers from the consent of the governed." Then he added other principles such as the freedom of the seas and limitation of armaments.

Planning the Future

The refusal of the Allies to accept a Germany victory ended the prospect of a negotiated peace in 1917. But Bernstorff did submit to Wilson, in the strictest confidence, an outline of the peace terms which would satisfy Germany. She was willing to give France a part of Alsace. On the east, Germany would want some sort of buffer state to protect her from Russia. The Allies would have to restore some of the German colonies, so that Germany would have colonial possessions "compatible with the size of her population and the importance of her economic interests." French territories occupied by Germany during the war would be restored, "on condition that certain strategic and economic modifications of the frontier be allowed, as also financial compensation." Germany would surrender Belgium, provided that Belgium would give definite guarantees for the safety of Germany. Then followed proposals regarding the freedom of the seas and commercial agreements to be arranged at the close of the war. The communication closed with the statement that the German government would discontinue submarine warfare when "we are completely assured that the President's efforts will lead to a peace that would be acceptable to us."

As late as January 1917, therefore, the German government was still assuming that it had won the war and that it could dictate the terms of peace. This assumption rested on the military situation, which at the time was favorable to the Central Powers. During the preceding summer, in the battle of Jutland, the German navy had inflicted serious losses on the British fleet, and the great British offensive on the Somme front had been stopped with terrific losses for the British. Russia was already beaten, although the full realization of this fact had not yet dawned upon the Allies. The Germans seemed justified in their belief that the renewal of unrestricted submarine warfare would force the British to surrender. These calculations were sound in all respects save one: they did not allow for the strength which the United States might exert nor the speed with which American help could be made effective in Europe.

Break with Germany

For more than two years before the United States entered the war, President Wilson had been laying down two contradictory policies. There was first his desire to keep the United States out of the conflict. Even though this interest had been temporarily submerged during the House-Grey negotiations, it had been revived during the campaign of 1916, and it was strengthened by his growing impatience with British violations of American rights. But along with the desire for peace was the determination to uphold American rights against Germany, a policy which had been pointedly defined in various notes. During the first crises which grew out of submarine warfare the President was saved from the consequences of his threats only because the German government chose to yield to his demands. If and when the German authorities should choose to defy the United States, Wilson could do nothing but hold them to a strict accountability, and strict accountability meant war. At any time the German government might bring this precarious situation to an end.

On January 31, 1917, Bernstorff announced that on the following day the German navy would resume unrestricted submarine warfare. This fateful policy had been under consideration for months, particularly after September 1916. The Kaiser issued the necessary order on January 9, 1917, and Bernstorff learned of the decision on January 19. During the interval Wilson and his advisers had received several intimations that merchant vessels would be subject to attack. Early in October Bernstorff informed the State Department that "the constellation of war has taken such a form that the German Government foresees the time at which it will be forced to regain the freedom of action that it has reserved to itself in the note of May 4th last." Just one week later Joseph Grew, the American chargé d'affaires at Berlin, wrote to Colonel House: "Our Government should therefore be fully prepared for an eventual resumption of the indiscriminate submarine warfare against commerce." The American answer was sharp and decisive. On February 3, 1917, the United States severed diplomatic relations with Germany.

The "Wilful" Men

The first result of the German announcement was to keep shipping in port, so that the flow of goods to Europe was suddenly interrupted. But the factories were still sending their products to the Atlantic seaboard, and congestion there soon became unbearable. Wilson proposed to place naval guns and gun crews on American merchant vessels, so that they might protect themselves from submarine attacks. The President explained to Congress that he probably had authority to take this step without additional legislation, but in such a crisis he liked "to feel that the authority and the power of Congress are behind me in whatever it may be necessary for me to do." And the President continued: "No one doubts what it is our duty to do. We must defend our commerce and the lives of our people in the midst of the present trying circumstances with discretion but with clear and steadfast purpose." The bill giving the President the desired power passed the House by the impressive vote of 403 to 13. The measure had the support of a substantial majority of the Senate, but the rules of that body permitted a minority to prevent the transaction of business. Under the leadership of Senator La Follette a determined group filibustered against the bill and prevented it from passing. Wilson was not the man to suffer defeat in silence, and he paid his respects to his opponents: "The Senate of the United States is the only legislative body in the world which cannot act when the majority is ready for action. A little group of wilful men, representing no opinion but their own, have rendered the great government of the United States helpless and contemptible." Then the President issued an order to arm the ships in spite of the Senate.

The British in the meantime were watching the development of anti-German feeling in the United States with an enthusiasm easily understood; in fact they did their best to intensify it. In January the British authorities had picked up the German message to Mexico which subsequently acquired fame as the Zimmermann note. They gave a copy of it to Colonel House, and he in turn gave it to Wilson. On March 1, 1917, the note was published in the American newspapers. Zimmermann informed the Mexican government of the intention to resume submarine warfare, but he said that his government still hoped that the United States would remain neutral. In case this hope failed, Zimmermann desired an alliance with Mexico. "We shall give general financial support, and it is understood that Mexico is to reconquer the lost territory of New Mexico, Texas and Arizona. The details are left to you for settlement." The note went on to urge the Mexicans to attempt to induce the Japanese to join in this alliance.

Declaration of War

Following the break in diplomatic relations, the administration waited for some "overt act" on the part of Germany. On March 18, 1917, three American ships were sunk with the loss of fifteen lives. The long-expected crisis had come, and at the next Cabinet meeting, held two days later, the whole Cabinet favored war. The President called Congress to meet in special session on April 2, and on that date he appeared before the two houses and delivered his war message. Wilson justified this war as a means of social betterment. In the wave of disillusionment which followed the war, the message was held up to scorn and ridicule. In 1917, however, the President's words were regarded as a true reflection of American idealism.

In calling the country to arms, Wilson referred to German cruelties; to

> the wanton and wholesale destruction of the lives of non-combatants, men, women, and children, engaged in pursuits which have always, even in the darkest periods of modern history, been deemed innocent and legitimate. Property can be paid for; the lives of peaceful and innocent people cannot be. The present German submarine warfare against commerce is a warfare against mankind. It is a war against all nations. . . . The challenge is to all mankind.

Faced with the choice of yielding to intolerable wrong or of fighting to vindicate the right, the President had no hesitation or uncertainty; "we will not choose the path of submission and suffer the most sacred rights of our Nation and our people to be ignored or violated. The wrongs against which we now array ourselves are no common wrongs; they cut to the very roots of human life."

Although Wilson found the immediate cause of the war in unrestricted submarine warfare, he envisioned an objective far broader than the mere suppression of such illegal activity. Our object, he declared, "is to vindicate the principles of peace and justice in the life of the world as against selfish and autocratic power and to set up amongst the really free and self-governed peoples of the world such a concert of purpose and of action as will henceforth ensure the observance of those principles." Then came the declaration which gave the American forces a holy cause to fight for:

> We are glad, now that we see the facts with no veil of false pretense about them, to fight thus for the ultimate peace of the world and for the liberation of its peoples, the German peoples included: for the rights of nations great and small and the privilege of men everywhere to choose their way of life and of obedience. The world must be made safe for democracy. Its peace must be planted upon the tested foundations of political liberty. We have no selfish ends to serve. We desire no conquest, no dominion. We seek no indemnities for ourselves, no material compensation for the sacrifices we shall freely make.

In addition to the various factors already described which account for the entrance of the United States into World War I, there was still one more which carried considerable weight: the fear that if Germany should win, she would attack the United States. Colonel House emphasized this danger as early as August 22, 1914: "Germany's success will ultimately mean trouble for us." During 1915 and 1916 Ambassador Gerard in Germany called attention to the same danger; "unless these people are made pretty sick of war, they will attack us later, probably by way of an infringement of the Monroe Doctrine in Brazil or Mexico." And again he quoted the Kaiser as saying: "America had better look out after this war." After the United States entered the war, Gerard insisted that "we are not only justly in this war, but prudently in this war. If we had stayed out and the war had been drawn or won by Germany we should have been attacked." *The New York Times* expressed the same belief: "Do we know what a German victory means for us here in the United States? We know it with full entirety and conviction. It means either that we buy freedom from molestation by perpetual poltroonery, or that within a few years we shall be engaged in a new war for independence against an incomparably more formidable foe."

Organizing an Army

Selective Service

Following the President's appeal for war Congress approved a resolution declaring that Germany had already made war upon the United States. The Senate passed the resolution on April 4 by a vote of 82 to 6; the House followed on April 6 with a vote of 373 to 50. Having declared war, Congress settled down to the task of preparing for it. The first need was an army. The Hay Act of 1916 had provided for a slight increase in American forces, but nothing had been done to make it effective, and it could not begin to supply the numbers needed for modern warfare. In previous struggles the United States had relied upon volunteering; this was true in the Civil War until 1863. In 1917 Secretary of War Baker and the general staff decided that conscription should be adopted at once, and on April 5, 1917, a bill for this purpose was laid before Congress. The Democratic speaker, the floor leader, and even the chairman of the House Committee on Military Affairs all opposed the bill. In spite of this opposition the Selective Service Act passed the House by a vote of 397 to 24 and the Senate by a vote of 81 to 8; it went into effect on May 18.

The Selective Service Act made all males between the ages of twenty-one and thirty-one liable to military service and required them to register with local draft boards. A total of 4557 registration districts was provided for, with a local board in charge of each district. On June 5, 9,586,508 men registered and received their draft numbers. In the first draft, held on July 20, 1,374,000 were called out. Each one received orders to report to his local draft board for examination or to establish his right to exemption. According to the law, all executive, legislative, and judicial officials of the federal government and of the states were exempted from the obligation to serve. Ordained clergymen and students in recognized theological schools were exempt, and also the members of regular religious denominations which prohibited their members from going to war. Men with dependents were given deferred classification equivalent to exemption. The President was authorized to grant exemption to county and city officials and to employees in arsenals and in essential private industry.

Basic Training

To give these prospective soldiers the needed training, the government constructed great training camps in various parts of the country; by November 1918 there were thirty-seven of these camps, each capable of caring for thousands of men. As fast as one group completed its minimum training it was shipped to France and another lot of recruits came in. Each camp had its own water supply, sewage system, heating plants, recreation halls, and of course the necessary barracks and mess halls. The first camps were ready for occupancy early in September, and the process of transforming civilians into soldiers began at once.

The American people had never known anything quite like these training camps. Here were herded together representatives from every rank and station in American life, aristocrats and commoners, college graduates and unskilled laborers, the refined and the vulgar, rich and poor, church members and pagans, good citizens and gangsters, bank clerks, brokers, and professional gamblers—it would be impossible to name any sector of American life which was not represented. In camp the men were put into uniform, assigned to barracks and mess halls, and put through the rudiments of military drill. They ate the same food, enjoyed the same shows, swore at the same buglers and top sergeants—not in the presence of the sergeants, however—saluted the same officers, froze their fingers on the same rifle ranges, and sang the same songs.

For the duration of the war 26,000,000 men registered or volunteered, and nearly 4,000,000 were enrolled in the army. Of this total more than 2,000,000 went overseas, and 1,300,000 saw active fighting. Nearly 49,000 were killed in action, and nearly 57,000 were killed by disease—1918 was the year of the great epidemic of influenza, which attacked soldiers and civilians alike. The number of wounded ran up to 237,135; some of these recovered, some were disabled for life. In other words, of those who went into action, more than one fifth had their names entered on the casualty lists.

"The Yanks Are Coming"

Once the men were trained, the next problem was to ship them to France and to keep them supplied with food, clothing, and military equipment. Here was a task which in extent and complexity was absolutely without parallel in previous history. Troops had been transported overseas before but never in such vast numbers. Even in normal times it would have been difficult to find shipping to carry so many men in such a short time; in war when the Germans had actually sunk 4,000,000 tons of shipping during the first half of 1917, the obstacles might well have seemed insuperable. Fortunately the Allies learned how to overcome the menace of the submarine and new building helped to compensate for some of the losses. In 1916 Congress had provided for the creation of the United States Shipping Board with authority to buy, lease, or charter ships. Subsequently the Emergency Fleet Corporation was established to supervise the building of ships in the United States. Under the direction of these two bodies the American people undertook the job described as "building a bridge to Berlin." When the war began the facilities for building ships in the United States were limited and in comparison with the need almost feeble. New shipyards were built—the one at Hog Island near Philadelphia was the largest in the world—and the start was made toward restoring the merchant marine of the United States. For a time progress was disappointingly slow, partly because of the nature of the task, partly because of administrative quarrels. By March 1918 the yards could boast of only two ships actually in service. Then the new vessels began to come down the ways, and on July 4 of that year the yards launched ninety-five ships. When the armistice was signed in November, the yards had delivered 496 ships.

The real test of efficiency for the American merchant marine came with the transportation of men and supplies to France. Of the more than 2,000,000 men sent over, 46 percent went in American vessels, 49 percent in British. But American ships carried 95 percent of the supplies, and the American navy provided 83 percent of the convoy service. The bridge therefore was built, and a substantial portion of it was American—but it did not reach to Berlin.

The consignments of troops and equipment were landed at friendly French ports, which had to be partly rebuilt for the purpose. Because American troops were assigned to the southern section of the front, they used the harbors on the French part of the Bay of Biscay, particularly Brest, St. Nazaire, La Rochelle, La Pallice, and Bassens. Here the harbors had to be dredged, new piers constructed, storage warehouses erected, and barracks put up to house the men. In addition to all this work, the French railroads had to be rebuilt, and additional terminal tracks laid down. Even new telegraph and telephone lines were necessary. Headquarters for the supply services were established at Tours, and the general headquarters of the American army was located at Chaumont; at both these places construction had to be completed before the army could be properly handled.

Army Supplies

In view of the efficiency of American industry, the people expected the United States to provide the troops with all necessary military equipment. These hopes were encouraged by the press and by the War Department. It was common talk that before the end of 1917 there would be 20,000 American airplanes in France, and American imagination was equally active in picturing generous quantities of other military necessities. When these hopes were not realized, disappointment was deep and complaint was bitter. In the pages of the *Outlook* and the *Metropolitan Magazine,* former President Theodore Roosevelt carried on a continuous attack upon Wilson and the administration. Senator Chamberlain of Oregon, of the Committee on Military Affairs, charged that the American military system had not only broken down but that it had "almost stopped functioning." He found the cause for this deplorable state of affairs in the "inefficiency in every bureau and in every department of the government of the United States." President Wilson informed the public that Senator Chamberlain's attack on the War Department was "an astounding and absolutely unjust distortion of the truth."

After the war was finished it became plain that while the American army received all the fighting material that it needed, not by any means all of it came from American factories. Up to November 11, 1918, all the light artillery, both 3-inch and 6-inch guns, together with all the ammunition which they used, were supplied by the French. Most of the heavy guns were French. The French also provided the Americans with all their tanks and with 80 percent of the airplanes. Roosevelt, Chamberlain, and their associates were right in saying that American industry was not meeting the needs of the American army in France; Secretary of War Baker was also right in his reply that the American army had everything it needed

Organizing the People

Industry, Food, and Fuel

In its effort to gear American productive effort to the abnormal demands of war, the administration subjected manufacturers to an unprecedented degree of regimentation. In 1916, as part of its program of preparedness Congress had provided for the creation of the Council of National Defense This body included the secretaries of war, navy, interior, agriculture, commerce, and labor. Associated with these high government officials was an advisory commission of seven members, each having some special understanding of a specific branch of economic activity. The Council with its advisory commission was authorized to make recommendations regarding industry and transportation in so far as these matters related to the war More specifically, they would increase the quantities of all products needed by civilians or by the army, allocate supplies of raw materials to essential industries, and make sure that unnecessary delays were eliminated. Practically the Council had dictatorial powers over American industry. Daniel Willard, president of the Baltimore and Ohio Railroad, was put in charge of transportation and communication. Howard Coffin, an automobile manufacturer, took charge of manufacturing, with special reference to munitions. Julius Rosenwald, of Sears, Roebuck and Company, had charge of supplies, particularly clothing. Bernard M. Baruch looked after minerals, metals, and raw materials; early in 1918 he became the managing director of American industry. Samuel Gompers of the American Federation of Labor had oversight of labor problems. Here was a program of national planning introduced into American industry and continued throughout the war.

In the Lever Act, passed in the summer of 1917, Congress extended the policy of centralized control over food and fuel. To make this measure effective. President Wilson appointed two commissioners or administrators, one for food and one for fuel. For the first Wilson selected Herbert Hoover of California, already famous as the administrator of Belgian relief. His general policy was to encourage the production of food so that there would be ample supplies both for the American people and for their friends in Europe. Regular farmers were persuaded to increase their output, and everybody who had access to a plot of ground was urged to plant a garden. In 1917 the price of wheat advanced to $3.45, a price which was extremely pleasing to the farmers but alarming to the consumers. Thereupon the government fixed the price at $2.20 and agreed to buy all the wheat grown in the United States. Even this price was well above normal, and there was a marked increase in the acreage planted—with a corresponding rise in the price of farm lands and an increase in the volume of farm mortgages. Incidentally the price of cotton went up, but that was not a food product and the government made no attempt to limit the price. In addition to increasing the production of foodstuffs, the Food Administration imposed regulations against hoarding. To make sure of enough for all parties concerned, certain commodities, in particular wheat flour and white sugar, were rationed. Housewives were trained in the art of home canning, so that the products of the small gardens could be made to go as far as possible.

For the Fuel Administration the President appointed Harry A. Garfield, son of the former President. His chief responsibility was to increase the output of coal and to make sure that essential industries received their needed supplies. Measures of economy, such as "heatless Mondays" and daylight saving, were adopted so that the great war machine could be properly served. There were state and local fuel administrators to carry the work down into the industrial areas.

The great increase in business caught the railroads in a state of unpreparedness, due in part to rapidly rising labor costs and in part to the inflexibility of rate structures imposed by the Interstate Commerce Commission. But uninterrupted service to the seaboard was one of the essential requirements of wartime; consequently in December 1917 the federal government took over the management of the roads for the duration of the war. William G. McAdoo, secretary of the treasury, was placed in charge of the United States Railroad Administration. Under his management the railroads were practically integrated into a single system, with common use of both terminals and rolling stock.

Wartime Labor

In order to keep the American industrial system smoothly at work and to provide for the uninterrupted flow of manufactured goods from factories to the seaboard, one of the essential requirements was an adequate labor supply. To assure this the government had to make special efforts because the general situation encouraged unrest among the workers. During the era of heavy war orders from the Allies, employers had been bidding against each other for laborers; the firm with the best wage scales could get the needed help. Then, too, wages were rising with the cost of living, so that laborers could demand concessions from their employers; labor unrest and strikes often accompany increased business activity. Employers, on the other hand, perturbed by the rapid increase in money wages, showed resentment at what they regarded as the selfishness of the wage earners. During the five-year period from 1915 to 1920 money wages doubled, although real wages advanced only 10 percent.

The prominent place given to Samuel Gompers on the advisory board of the Council of National Defense showed that the administration was alive to the needs of industrial employees. The Selective Service Act provided for the exemption from military service of workers in essential industries. Then, to prevent excessive turnover in the various plants, employment managers were appointed, whose duty it was to assign men to jobs for which they were best fitted, to maintain cordial relations between employees and management, and in general to make the workers realize and appreciate their responsibilities in the job of winning the war.

While every effort was made to prevent labor differences from reaching an acute stage, the government could not expect complete success. The officials were determined, however, not to let differences develop into strikes. In 1917 a War Labor Conference Board was established, succeeded the following year by the National War Labor Board. Under the direction of Frank P. Walsh and William Howard Taft, this board prepared to solve labor troubles by mediation. In the various industrial centers there were local committees, acting under the board, with authority to summon representatives of both parties to a dispute before them. If the local committee could not effect a settlement, the trouble would be referred to the board. In the meantime Congress prohibited both strikes and lockouts for the duration of the war and guaranteed the right of collective bargaining to the workers. Congress also prohibited employers from discharging men on account of their union activities and union members were forbidden to use unfair methods in campaigning for new members. By these various methods, disturbances were kept at a minimum.

Finance

In some of the earlier wars of the United States the problem of raising money had been peculiarly difficult. Those struggles had been preceded and accompanied by periods of economic depression, so that ordinary sources of income were partly closed. The era of World War I stands out in sharp contrast to these earlier periods. Probably no government ever entered a war with better financial prospects than the United States in 1917. Thanks to war orders, the American people found themselves in the midst of a great economic boom, with industry and agriculture alike showing heavy profits. This situation made heavy taxation and heavy loans possible, but, more important still, it put the people in the proper frame of mind for carrying the financial load.

Congress authorized increases in the income tax until the normal rate on incomes up to $4000 stood at 6 percent. From there the rate increased gradually until it reached 65 percent on million-dollar incomes. Then there were excess profits taxes and corporation taxes. The people became accustomed to a variety of internal revenue taxes—on long distance telephone calls, telegraph messages, express and freight way bills, and even on railroad tickets. Wartime expenditures continued after the armistice until the autumn of 1919. Between 1917 and October 1919 federal taxes brought in a yield of approximately $11,280,000,000, an amount unprecedented in American history.

For this country the total cost of the war was $22,272,000,000 exclusive of the loans made by the United States to several European governments. If these are added, the total cost was close to $32,610,000,000. The difference between income from taxes and total expenditure was made up by borrowing. Seven different bond issues yielded $29,500,000,000. To dispose of these bonds the Treasury put on a series of high-pressure salesmanship campaigns. With the help of newspaper publicity, posters, mass meetings, addresses by noted celebrities from the government and from the stage and

screen, people with money to invest were continually reminded that the government could use their funds and pay good interest. In most instances the buyers took the bonds voluntarily, but Americans who refused to buy were held up as disloyal citizens.

The combined tasks of creating an army and providing for its support were directed toward the major program of fighting the Germans. But according to the precepts of modern warfare it is important to hate the enemy, hence the emphasis on the twin agencies of propaganda and censorship. Fortunately for the purposes of propaganda, certain concepts concerning the war had already been firmly planted in the American mind; President Wilson had utilized them in his war message. Here was a holy war, a war to end war, a war to make the world safe for democracy, and a war to create a new world order. The very simplicity of these beliefs made them effective devices for the propagandists; they became the molds in which mass opinion was shaped.

Propaganda

The war had hardly been declared when the journalist George Creel found himself at the head of the Committee on Public Information. Appointed on April 14, 1917, this committee included, in addition to Mr. Creel, the secretaries of state, war, and navy. Its primary purpose was to sell the war to the people and to create and maintain the right attitudes. News from the various government departments, including the War Labor Board and the Council of National Defense, all came out through the Committee on Public Information. Papers cooperated with the committee, both in withholding material which lacked Creel's approval and in publishing the thousands of news stories emanating from his office. Furthermore, the committee issued its own paper, from which the local press could get not necessarily all the news which was fit to print but the news which was safe to print.

In addition to its work with the press, the committee went into the publishing business. It printed a number of books, the Red, White, and Blue pamphlets; included in this list were one on "The President's War Message, and the Facts behind It"; another was "Conquest and Kultur" with the subtitle "Aims of the Germans in Their Own Words." This was no mere casual space filler. It was a compilation of excerpts from German writings of all kinds, carefully selected to bring out the essential villainy of German designs for conquest. Seventy-five million copies of these books were circulated in the United States and additional millions abroad.

Propagandists in those days had to operate without the help of the radio, but there were other devices for getting the spoken word across to large groups of people. The committee enlisted the services of 75,000 volunteer speakers, known as the "Four Minute Men." They appeared on the stages of theaters and motion picture houses in more than 5000 different communities, and they delivered a total of 755,190 speeches. They reached an audience estimated, all told, at 300,000,000 people. Only the blind and the deaf could escape this all-pervasive activity, and even they must have felt the spirit of the times. The committee cost less than $5,000,000. The real cost was not in money but in the enforced sacrifice of independent judgment and of intellectual integrity.

Censorship

The Committee on Public Information could deal with the positive policy of creating and maintaining opinion; for the negative policies of suppressing unwanted opinions additional legislation was needed. In his war message Wilson had warned: "If there should be disloyalty, it will be dealt with with a firm hand of stern repression," and Congress showed no hesitation in supporting the administration's threat. On June 15, 1917, the Espionage Act became law. It provided for the punishment of any who should acquire information about American defenses which might be given to the enemy as well as for those who actually conveyed such information. Penalties were also imposed on all who should attempt to cause insubordination or mutiny among the enlisted men and upon any who should attempt to obstruct enlistment or recruiting. The postmaster general was empowered to close the mails to written or printed matter which he considered to be a violation of any of the preceding sections. This measure did not become obsolete at the close of the war.

In October 1917 Congress passed the Trading with the Enemy Act, one purpose of which was to prevent any written or printed material from entering or leaving the country if such material might give aid or information to the enemy. All mail which crossed the borders was examined by censors. Then in May 1918 Congress enacted the much more stringent Sedition Act, which put an end to what little there was left of freedom of speech or of the press. This measure prohibited "the saying or doing of anything with intent to obstruct the sale of United States bonds, except by way of bona fide and not disloyal advice"; it prohibited the use of "disloyal, profane, scurrilous, or abusive language, or language intended to cause contempt, scorn, contumely, or disrepute as regards the form of government of the United States," or the Constitution, the flag, or the uniform of the army or navy. The act also prohibited language intended to curtail production of war materials and language in support of the enemy. Generous powers of censorship were conferred upon the postmaster general. This measure was repealed in 1921. With the help of these measures the Department of Justice sent some 2000 men and women to prison for terms running up to twenty years. Eugene V. Debs was sent up for ten years. The federal prisons at Atlanta and Leavenworth acquired a miscellaneous population of zealots whose ideas of freedom of speech were ill suited to the exigencies of the war. Conformity became an indispensable virtue.

Members of Congress retained their Constitutional rights of free speech, and so too did Theodore Roosevelt. He gave vent to his hatred of Wilson in a series of blistering articles in the *Outlook*, in the *Metropolitan Magazine*, and in his book, *The Foes of Our Own Household*. But Roosevelt was a privileged character, so widely popular that the administration could not afford to make him a martyr and so vehemently patriotic that nobody could call him pro-German. Less fortunate critics paid the penalty, particularly if they had been connected with socialists or other radical groups.

Victory over Germany

For commander in chief of the American forces in France, Wilson selected Major General John J. Pershing. In June Pershing proceeded to France, and on July 4 he reviewed the troops of the 1st Division in Paris. After these first troops had arrived, the next American contingents sent over were engineers and construction men to prepare for handling and transporting the large American Army on its arrival. As late as March 1918 there were only 250,000 American troops in France, and of this total more than half were technical men at work on port facilities and lines of communication. Then the new army came over at the rate of 10,000 men every day for five solid months. In little more than a year after the declaration of war it was possible for American troops to enter active fighting in sufficient numbers to turn the scale of the conflict.

Final German Offensive

By March 1918 the German leaders realized that American war preparations were proceeding more rapidly than their own submarine campaign. Destructive as that had been, it had failed to crush England. With the prospect of large-scale American military movements, the Germans were compelled to try their last resource: an attack along the whole line with their whole available force before the American armies should become too large. On March 21 the German divisions began an advance on a fifty-mile front south of Cambrai. Their immediate objective was to separate the English and French armies, turn the English lines back toward the coast, and then—so they hoped—push on toward Paris. After a week of desperate fighting, during which the German advance averaged six miles a day, the drive was checked. The determination of the Germans to stake everything on this spring campaign induced the Allies to appoint a general in chief, and Ferdinand Foch became the supreme commander.

For four months after the beginning of the drive the Germans remained on the offensive. On April 9 their divisions moved against the British in the Lys Valley west of Lille. Although their advance was slower than their first drive in March, they carried it far enough to threaten the British supply system. On May 27 they struck again, between Rheims and Soissons, pushing the Allied line back to Château-Thierry. A few more dents like this would have brought the Germans to Paris.

On May 28 the American 1st Division captured Cantigny, a little village west of Montdidier. On May 31 a part of the 3rd Division helped block the German advance at Château-Thierry. These exploits were small in themselves, but they showed what the American troops could do in action. On July 15 the Germans struck for the fourth time, along the line from Château-Thierry to the edge of the Argonne Forest. This proved to be the last German offensive. By August 4 Foch had straightened out his line

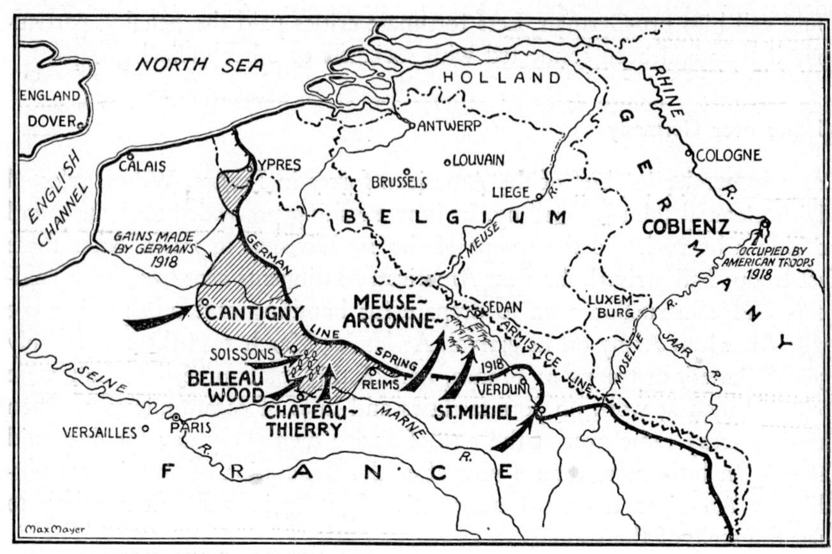

Map 19. Where the American Army Fought in France

west of Rheims, thereby relieving the danger of an attack upon Paris. On August 8, English forces began to push the Germans back toward Montdidier, and by August 18 they had eliminated the dangerous German salient in that sector. American troops assisted in both these counterattacks.

By September there were enough American troops ready so that Pershing could organize an American field army. On September 12, in cooperation with French troops, the Americans attacked the Germans in the St. Mihiel salient east and south of Verdun. In two days' fighting the Germans were driven out, and the Allied line straightened again. The Germans had now passed the peak of their power, and Foch had troops enough to strike often and hard. From this time on to the armistice in November the German troops were in retreat.

On September 26, with nine American divisions in action, the battle of the Argonne was begun. The region itself with its ravines, river valleys, hills, and woods made the advance difficult and offensive operations next to impossible. This battle lasted forty-seven days, with fighting going on continuously. Before this campaign had been under way a week the Central Powers began to disintegrate. Bulgaria withdrew from the war on September 30 with an unconditional surrender. On September 14, 1918, Austria asked for a conference to discuss possible peace terms; after a crushing defeat on the Piave, Austria signed an armistice on November 3. On October 4, the German government had requested a formal statement of the terms of peace, professing a desire to accept Wilson's program of the "Fourteen Points."

Before replying to this request, President Wilson tried to find out how genuine the proposal was and to what extent the government reflected popular opinion. He made it plain that he at least would not consider an armistice as long as the Germans remained on Belgian and French territory. On October 12 the German government agreed to evacuate the occupied territory. Having received satisfactory assurances regarding this withdrawal and regarding the representative character of the German government, President Wilson laid the correspondence before the Allies. On November 9 the Hohenzollerns abdicated and fled to Holland.

Armistice, 1918

On November 11 the German authorities signed an armistice, the terms of which had been drawn up by Marshal Foch. This called for a cessation of hostilities and for the immediate evacuation of occupied territories, including Alsace-Lorraine. Other sections were designed to render Germany powerless to renew the war. She must surrender thousands of heavy guns, machine guns, and airplanes, as well as locomotives, railroad cars, and automobiles. With these must go all the German submarines and the greater part of the German surface navy. German troops were to be withdrawn from all German territory west of the Rhine, and Allied troops were to occupy this region and the territory on the other side near the main bridges, at Mayence, Coblenz, and Cologne. With the signing of the armistice Germany ceased to exist—temporarily—as a military or naval power.

The signing of the armistice brought a pitch of emotional exaltation. The war was over, and not merely the war but the evils out of which it had grown. A new era, the regime of peace and good will, had at last arrived. In a special message to the American people President Wilson put the prevailing feeling into words: "My Fellow Countrymen: The armistice was signed this morning. Everything for which America fought has been accomplished. It will now be our fortunate duty to assist by example, by sober, friendly counsel, and by material aid in the establishment of just democracy throughout the world." The President believed what he said. So too did the millions of Americans who took part in the nation-wide celebration on that first Armistice Day.

Although the Germans professed a desire to accept peace in accordance with Wilson's ideals, they had shown no idealism in imposing terms on their own victims. In 1918 they had conquered Russia and compelled the government to accept the humiliating peace of Brest-Litovsk. Russia surrendered her Baltic provinces: Esthonia, Livonia, Lithuania, and Courland; in addition she was forced to yield Finland, Poland, the Ukraine, and even Russian Armenia. With her territory and population reduced by approximately 25 percent, the Russians were completely cut off from the Baltic except for the old capital of the Czars, which they renamed Leningrad. At the same time the Germans received important commercial privileges in Russia.

Some two months later Rumania capitulated to Germany and gave up territory, strategic mountain passes, and control of her agriculture and her petroleum fields. This treaty of Bucharest was so drawn as to give Germany an economic stranglehold upon the country. Some years later one writer observed that in comparison with these two treaties imposed by Germany, the Peace of Versailles looked like an exercise in brotherly love. But the spirit of vengeance was not confined to Germany. France and Great Britain were determined to break German power and to secure territorial gains.

Conflicting Ideas of Peace

Secret Treaties

Before the United States entered the war and consequently before President Wilson could have any official concern with proposed terms of settlement, the Allied governments had already worked out the main outlines of their new maps of Europe and the Near East. These arrangements were concealed for a time in what became known as the secret treaties. The Bolsheviki made these documents public before they made their abject surrender at Brest-Litovsk, and shortly afterward enterprising newspapers in the United States published the English texts in full.

It is not necessary to go into the details of all these documents. Their general purpose was illustrated in the Treaty of London, signed April 26, 1915, which defined the rewards to be given to Italy in return for her entrance into the war on the side of the Allies. England, France, and Russia promised her Trentino, the southern Tyrol, part of the Dalmatian coast, Avlona in full and a protectorate over Albania, various islands in the Adriatic, the Dodecanese islands, an equal share in the division of Turkey, and compensation in Africa in case France and Great Britain should enlarge their colonial holdings there. Another agreement promised Constantinople and the straits to Russia—a gain which Russia lost by walking out on the Allies—and another provided for the return of Alsace-Lorraine to France. Still another gave England and France a free hand in fixing the western boundary of Germany and gave Russia similar freedom on the eastern border.

President Wilson read and commented upon an unofficial version of the Treaty of London within a month after it was signed. Before the end of April 1917 Balfour discussed with Wilson the terms of all the secret treaties except those made with Japan, and there is nothing in the record to suggest that Wilson made any objection to these arrangements. On May 18, 1917, the British secretary of state for foreign affairs sent copies of the actual texts of these secret treaties to Wilson. During 1918, before the end of the war, Wilson received further information concerning them. By the time the armistice was signed therefore he was as well acquainted with their terms as any of the European statesmen. Yet, on August 19, 1919, President Wilson asserted that he knew nothing of these secret treaties until he went to Paris.

There were other manifestations of the deep-seated inability of the Europeans to arrive at any settlement based upon those principles of good will which the President was advocating. Clemenceau's memory carried him back to the Franco-Prussian War and to Bismarck's famous threat to bleed

France white; the French premier welcomed the opportunity to apply the same treatment to Germany. In England David Lloyd George, characterized even by his friends as slippery and by his opponents as a wild man, was making threats about hanging the Kaiser and dismembering Germany.

For all these demands for a punitive, vindictive peace Wilson showed complete disregard. On January 8, 1918, in an address to the Senate of the United States, he had announced his program for world peace; as he himself put it, "that program, the only possible program, as we see it, is this." Then he gave a list of the Fourteen Points. The first five of these dealt with matters of interest to the whole world; the next eight had to do with the settlement of war issues and of boundaries in the case of specifically named countries; the last called for the establishment of a league of nations. In his introduction the President announced that the "day of conquest and aggrandizement is gone by," a "happy fact," he said, which was "clear to the view of every public man whose thoughts do not still linger in an age that is dead and gone." What he demanded, on behalf of the United States, was "that the world be made fit and safe to live in."

The Fourteen Points

Point 1 called for "Open covenants of peace, openly arrived at," and the end of private international understandings and secret diplomacy. Point 2 read: "Absolute freedom of navigation upon the seas, outside territorial waters, alike in peace and war, except as the seas may be closed in whole or in part by international action for the enforcement of international covenants." Next came the demand for the removal of "all economic barriers and the establishment of an equality of trade conditions" among all nations which should accept the peace. Number 4 called for the reduction of armaments. Number 5 proclaimed: "A free, open-minded, and absolutely impartial adjustment of all colonial claims, based upon a strict observance of the principle that in determining all such questions of sovereignty the interests of the populations concerned must have equal weight with the equitable claims of the government whose title is to be determined." Point 6 dealt with Russia, a country with which Wilson and many other liberals then had considerable sympathy. He made a plea for the evacuation of all Russian territory, for the cooperation of all nations in securing to Russia the opportunity to work out her social and economic problems in her own way, and for "a sincere welcome" for her into the society of free nations.

Point 7 called for the evacuation and restoration of Belgium. "Without this healing act the whole structure and validity of international law is forever impaired." In Point 8 Wilson demanded the restoration of Alsace-Lorraine to France, so that "the wrong done to France by Prussia in 1871" may be righted. Point 9 was brief: "A readjustment of the frontiers of Italy should be effected along clearly recognizable lines of nationality." In Point 10 he urged that the dependent peoples of Austria-Hungary be "accorded the freest opportunity of autonomous development." In Point 11 he urged the restoration and evacuation of the occupied Balkan states and a settlement of Balkan problems "by friendly counsel along historically established lines of allegiance and nationality." Point 12 provided for the dismemberment of Turkey, with guarantees for both the Turkish portions and for the non-Turkish sections to be separated from the Ottoman Empire. Point 13 provided for the restoration of the Polish nation to include "the territories inhabited by indisputably Polish populations. The new Polish state must have "a free and secure access to the sea." Finally, in Point 14, came the climax to the system: "A general association of nations must be formed under specific covenants for the purpose of affording mutual guarantees of political independence and territorial integrity to great and small states alike."

Opposition to Wilson

These Fourteen Points were proclaimed to the world without consultation with the Allies, and in obvious contradiction to the secret treaties. Here was a clash of policies destined to cause serious friction. When the Germans announced their readiness to accept peace on the basis of the Fourteen Points, the question arose at once as to whether or not the Allied governments were bound by this program. Clemenceau said flatly that, in as much as his government had not been consulted in advance and had never endorsed the Points, France was under no obligation to recognize them. Lloyd George said that nobody was bound then, but unless reservations were made before the signing of the armistice the Allies would be bound. Thereupon Lloyd George said that his government would not accept the second point in any circumstances, even though refusal to do so would result in a separate peace with Germany. France and England reserved to themselves "complete freedom on this subject when they enter the Peace Conference." The Allies also reserved the right to exact full reparation from Germany for all damage done to the civilian population of the Allies by land, sea, or air. In other particulars the Allies accepted the Fourteen Points.

In proclaiming the Fourteen Points as the basis of peace for the Allied and Associated nations the President assumed a position of leadership which had never been officially accorded, and the heads of the governments in Europe had no intention of surrendering their prerogatives to him. However willing they may have been to recognize his grasp of moral principles—and they questioned his infallibility even in this field—they never admitted his right to instruct them in matters of policy or statecraft. Clemenceau, especially, had little patience with Wilson; he found him merely an evangelical doctrinaire. "This man Wilson with his Fourteen Points!" the French Premier is reported to have said. "God was content with Ten." And in somewhat similar vein an unnamed member of the British Parliament was quoted as saying: "The worst of President Wilson is that he talks like Jesus Christ and acts like Lloyd George."

Chapter 41

PEACE AND ITS PROBLEMS

When the war came to an end Wilson did not have proof of official support in Europe; worse still, the congressional elections of November 1918 proved that he had lost the support of a majority of the American voters. His predicament was in part the result of tactlessness. On October 24, 1918, he chose to define the issue for the people, and to appeal for support on this issue. In this plea he said: "If you have approved of my leadership and wish me to continue to be your unembarrassed spokesman in affairs at home and abroad, I earnestly beg that you will express yourselves unmistakably to that effect by returning a Democratic majority to both the Senate and the House of Representatives." Then he went on to find fault with the Republicans: "At almost every turn since we entered the war they have sought to take the choice of policy and the conduct of the war out of my hands and put it under the control of instrumentalities of their own choosing." He admitted that the Republicans had been prowar, but he blamed them because they had also been antiadministration. "The return of a Republican majority to either house of the Congress would, moreover, be interpreted on the other side of the water as a repudiation of my leadership." He admitted that he was the servant of the people, and he expressed his readiness to yield to their wishes—an admission which he promptly forgot. After this, if the voters should turn against him, it would be plain that they did not approve of his leadership. During the campaign speakers urged the voters to uphold the President. A favorite Democratic poster depicted a gravely troubled Wilson with the slogan: "He needs, God knows, our help." But the leaders were not content with moral suasion alone. They went into shipyards and ordered employees to vote Democratic.

Congressional Election

attempt to interfere!

In spite of the President's effort to win support by making foreign policy a political issue, the administration lost the elections. The Republicans came out with a majority of two in the Senate and of forty-five in the House. It may be that Wilson's plea to the voters was not the cause of this Democratic defeat; but that is beside the point. The President had asked for an endorsement, thereby calling the attention of the whole literate world to the issue, and the voters failed to respond to his plea. For good reasons or for bad, the voters had shown in the only way open to them that they preferred different leadership. Theodore Roosevelt took particular delight in emphasizing Wilson's loss of support: "Our allies and our enemies and Mr. Wilson himself should all understand that Mr. Wilson has no authority whatever to speak for the American people at this time. His leadership has just been emphatically repudiated by them." However, Wilson was still President.

The Conference at Versailles

American Commissioners

A more pliant leader than President Wilson might have acquiesced in the situation and have recognized Republican supremacy, but Wilson's mind did not work in that groove. Opposition served to make him stubborn. He made it plain that no matter what might transpire in Congress, he was still the chief executive, in charge of foreign policy. When Congress assembled in December he informed that body that the Allies had accepted the Fourteen Points as the basis of peace and that they wanted him to come to Europe to assist in making the treaty. He was going to Europe as head of the American delegation. In making up the American commission, he appointed Robert Lansing, secretary of state, General Tasker H. Bliss, military expert, Colonel House of Texas, former Presidential agent and envoy extraordinary, and Henry White, a Republican in retirement, onetime American ambassador to Italy and to Germany. White had the benefit of broad experience in diplomacy.

President Wilson arrived in Europe on December 13, 1918. During the month's interval between his landing and the opening of the peace conference he made a tour of Allied capitals, meeting everywhere popular ovations such as no American had received abroad since the days of Benjamin Franklin. It seemed that all the nationalist groups or submerged races of Europe which longed for recognition and self-determination looked to Wilson for help; the homage they paid him was a measure of the intensity of their hopes. Here was compensation for the unfavorable attitude of his own people. In addressing the French Chamber of Deputies, he announced: "The nations of the world are about to consummate a brotherhood which will make it unnecessary in the future to maintain those crushing armaments which make the people suffer almost as much in peace as they suffered in war." There was, however, one consideration which Wilson overlooked: those cheering audiences in Europe could not ratify the treaty of peace. That would still remain a function of the Senate of the United States.

The conference opened formally at Versailles on January 18, 1919, with delegations present from thirty-two different governments—twenty-seven states and five British dominions. The defeated powers were conspicuous by their absence. All told there were seventy commissioners, too large a group to undertake the intricacies of treaty-making. After coming together for the opening, the whole group met only five times thereafter; these plenary sessions were put on largely for purposes of show.

Writing the Treaty

Until the middle of February the actual work on the treaty was carried on by a small group known as the Council of Ten, composed of the head of the delegation and the foreign secretary of each of the five leading powers: Japan, Italy, France, Great Britain, and the United States. This group met daily, discussed problems, listened to reports made by various experts, and tried to formulate specific provisions of the treaty. Progress, however, was slow, and the working body soon became the Council of Three, consisting of Clemenceau, Lloyd George, and Wilson. They drafted the Treaty of Versailles.

Actually the function of the Council of Three was not as simple as that last statement sounds. The council did put the treaty into its final form. But these men could not conduct all the investigations needed to make rational decisions possible. Out of the groups of experts provided by the various governments the council appointed a series of commissions to investigate and report on the more important problems, for example on Poland, on Rumania, on reparations, and on responsibility for the war. Other problems went to committees. The commissions and committees collected evidence and submitted their findings to the council. When the council took up a specific report, the members of the commission were present to provide additional information. Then in the light of this evidence the council would formulate the article in the treaty. In some cases it is said that the commissions put their conclusions into the form of a tentative article for the treaty; if so, this material was always subject to review by the council. With reference to the attitude of the members of the council toward this work of the experts, two American historians attached to the American group, Professors Haskins and Lord of Harvard, made this statement: "Certainly none of the chief delegates was more eager for the facts of the case than was the President of the United States, and none was able to assimilate them more quickly or use them more effectively in the discussion of territorial problems."

From President Wilson's point of view the most important article in the treaty was the one including the Covenant of the League of Nations. The Covenant was drawn up by a commission composed of representatives from fourteen different governments with Wilson as chairman. This body had its first meeting on February 3, and it completed the first draft of the Covenant on February 14. This evidence of speed furnished ground for the critics to complain that the work must have been carelessly done. While there may have been some basis for this charge, it should be remembered that Wilson's commission did not start from scratch. Several tentative drafts of a covenant were already in existence, and they were all before the commission. Of these the more important were the ones drawn by Lord Robert Cecil, by General Jan Smuts, and by Wilson himself in consultation with Colonel House. Much preliminary work therefore had been completed before the appointment of Wilson's commission.

Powerless Germany

Since the greater part of the Treaty of Versailles dealt with matters beyond the range of the direct interests of the United States, the provisions may be briefly summarized. One of the primary purposes was to punish Germany. She had to admit full responsibility for starting the war. If Germany had started the war, it was logical to make her pay for damages to Allied interests. The Germans were therefore required to pay $5,000,000,000 in gold before May 1, 1921, and whatever additional sums the Reparations Commission might assess upon her. This amount was subsequently fixed at $31,680,000,000 and then reduced to $26,000,000,000. Still later it was cut to $714,000,000. The victorious powers were disappointed in their expectations of making Germany pay the cost of the war.

The territorial provisions were severe in their effects upon Germany. She lost all her colonies in Africa, the South Seas, and in China. These were distributed among the members of the British Empire and Japan. She was required to restore Alsace-Lorraine to France and to turn over her Polish provinces to the newly established government of Poland. The German provinces on the left bank of the Rhine were demilitarized, and the Germans were forbidden to establish or maintain fortresses there or to conduct military maneuvers in that region. To complete the process of rendering Germany powerless, the Treaty reduced the German army to 100,000 men and abolished the system of compulsory service which had been in operation for more than one hundred years. The Germans were also forbidden to manufacture or import arms, munitions, or other materials for war. Then the German navy was limited to six battleships.

The League of Nations

President Wilson considered the making of a new international system as the most important function of the peace conference, so important that it more than offset the provisions of a punitive peace. The primary purpose of the Covenant was to establish an agency for handling international affairs and for promoting the common interests of the civilized world. The Covenant provided for the immediate organization—that is, after ratification of the Treaty—of the three essential organs of the League: the Council, the Assembly, and the Secretariat. As originally formed the Council was composed of representatives of the five leading victorious powers: Japan, Italy, France, Great Britain, and the United States; they would have permanent membership in the Council. In addition, there would be four additional representatives, chosen from other members of the League, on the principle of rotation. The Council therefore became the agent of the great powers.

The Covenant

The Assembly was made up of representatives of all members of the League. Each member government was entitled to three assemblymen, but no government could have more than one vote. All the Allied and Associated powers were made members at the start, and membership was offered to most neutrals. Additional members might be admitted by two-thirds vote of the Assembly. The Secretariat was the European name for a permanent office staff or civil service. This body kept the records and handled routine work. At the height of the League's prestige this body numbered nearly 700.

One of the primary functions of the League was, as the Covenant put it:

"to promote international cooperation and to achieve international peace and security." As a means of achieving this objective the Covenant provided for limitation of armaments. When a program of limitation should be worked out and approved by the League and then accepted by the individual governments, each member contracted not to increase its armaments without the consent of the League. This provision of the Covenant never became effective.

Another means of limiting the possibility of war was a guarantee of security to all members of the League. Article X was designed for this purpose. Members of the League undertook to respect and preserve as against external aggression the territorial integrity and existing political independence of all members. In case of threatened aggression, the Council was authorized to "advise" upon means for fulfilling this obligation. President Wilson called Article X "the very heart of the covenant. Without it the league would be hardly more than an influential debating society." The President also explained that while the engagement under this article constituted "a very grave and solemn moral obligation," it was nevertheless only a moral, and not a legal, obligation. "It is binding in conscience only, not in law."

So far as the actual text of Article X is concerned, the President's interpretation seemed simple. But there were rumors that Wilson had made verbal commitments under Article X, commitments which went far beyond the text. These rumors eventually reached the United States Senate. According to report the President had told his colleagues at the peace conference that any threat to alter by force the boundaries arranged in the treaty would bring immediate action:

> . . . when the decisions are made the Allied and Associated powers guarantee to maintain them . . . there underlies all of these transactions the expectation on the part—for example—of Roumania, and of Czechoslovakia and of Serbia that, if any covenants of this settlement are not observed, the United States will send her armies and her navies to see that they are observed.

When Senator Spencer of Missouri brought this statement to the attention of the Senate, Secretary Tumulty declared: "Senator Spencer's statement is absolutely and unqualifiedly false." President Wilson repeated Tumulty's assertion: "I reiterate the denial. The statement you made was false." The publication of the records proved that Senator Spencer had correctly quoted the President.[1]

In view of these official explanations of Article X as given in Paris, there was bound to be uncertainty as to the real meaning of the Covenant and the responsibilities which the United States would assume under it. With this explanation of the nature of Article X in mind, it is easy to understand the

[1] The quotations in the two preceding paragraphs were taken from Robert E. Annin, *Woodrow Wilson,* pp. 312, 351. Quoted by permission of the publishers, Dodd, Mead and Company.

complaints of those who argued that the President introduced new elements of controversy into a dispute already marked by serious misunderstanding.

Article XI explained that any threat of war was a matter of concern to every member of the League, and that in case of such threat the League would take action deemed necessary in the circumstances. Articles XIII and XV bound the members to submit their disputes to arbitration or to the Council. If the Council should make a unanimous decision, apart from the parties to the dispute, the members were bound not to make war upon the state complying with the award. Article XVI provided that, if any member should go to war in violation of the Covenant, the members should sever commercial relations with the offending party. Concerning the troublesome issue of colonial dependencies, a system of mandates would be established, so that the more highly developed governments would be placed in the position of guardians over the less advanced. This device was worked out for the special benefit of the former German colonies. Instead of being given outright to the victors, certain specified victorious governments would hold mandates over the dependencies. The mandatory powers were supposed to be responsible to the League for the proper administration of their wards. Even here there were exceptions in favor of the South African Union and of Japan.

In February 1919, before the whole treaty had been completed, President Wilson returned temporarily to the United States to sign the bills passed by the current session of Congress. He carried the first draft of the Covenant with him. The draft was criticized by both friends and opponents of the League, and some of the objections raised seemed so helpful to Wilson that after his return to Paris in March he had them embodied in the Covenant. Four of these amendments seemed specially important. One called for recognition of the Monroe Doctrine. Another provided that any member might withdraw from the League upon giving two years' notice, provided it had complied with its international obligations. The third gave notice that domestic questions were to be excluded from the jurisdiction of the League, while the fourth made the acceptance of mandates optional with any government.

Aid for France

Upon the completion of the Treaty representatives of the German government were invited to sign it; they did so under protest. After the completion of the work of the conference of Versailles, President Wilson took the Treaty back to the United States. As a matter of fact, Wilson carried back not one treaty, but two; the second one, however, never emerged from the Senate Committee on Foreign Relations. This second treaty provided for a triple alliance consisting of France, England, and the United States. The preamble declared that unprovoked aggression by Germany against France would violate the Treaty of Versailles and that such aggression would be regarded as a hostile act against all the signatory powers of the Treaty of Versailles. Article I declared that if the guarantees in the Treaty of Versailles failed to protect France, the United States and Great Britain should "be bound to come immediately to her assistance" in the event of unprovoked aggression. Article III required the Council of the League to approve this treaty, and Article IV required Wilson to submit it to the Senate along with the Treaty of Versailles. He did so, but the Senate never ratified it.

Before taking up the contest over the Treaty in the United States, it may be well to make one or two general observations, which were often overlooked in the heat of the contest. One has to do with the nature or character of the League itself. It was about as harmless an international organization as one could imagine. Far from being a superstate as some alarmists chose to call it, it was hardly the influential debating club which Wilson said it would degenerate into without Article X. The powers of the Assembly were carefully restricted and those of the Council largely advisory. Again in the Covenant the words "advise," "suggest," and "recommend" occur, instead of the words which might imply power to act directly. The League as such had no powers. Power still remained where it had been—in the hands of individual member governments. In all important matters the Council had to agree unanimously to make any action effective. Any one of the permanent members therefore had an absolute veto on any proposal or measure which its government disapproved. The League was never anything but a group of member governments, and they rarely agreed on significant matters of political policy. In no circumstances could the League take the initiative in promulgating any new policy.

Superpower or Debating Club

Wilson believed in the League because he thought the people and the governments of the world were united in their desire to put international relations upon a basis of logic and reason. Had this desire been strong and general, the League would have played a real part in world affairs. Wilson's mistake lay not in his basic premises but in thinking that the governments everywhere were prepared to adopt them, in believing that his views must prevail simply because they were right.

The Senate and the League

During the few days in February 1919 when Wilson was in Washington, the Republican leaders perfected their strategy for dealing with the Treaty and the League. On Sunday morning, March 2, 1919, Senator Brandegee of Connecticut called upon Senator Henry Cabot Lodge, chairman of the Senate Committee on Foreign Relations. Senator Brandegee was interested in having the Senate make a declaration that the proposed League of Nations could not be approved by the Senate. He was not particularly concerned with a formal vote; what he wanted was the endorsement of more than one third of the Senate. Brandegee and Lodge then went to see Senator Knox and asked him to draft the proposed announcement. Knox did so, and Senator Lodge undertook to bring the proposal to the attention of the Senate. This he did just before midnight on March 3.

Republican Strategy

The first part of this Republican warning to the President called his attention to the Constitutional provision which gave the Senate power "to advise and consent to, or dissent from, the ratification of any treaty of the United States," and which makes it clear that "no such treaty can become operative without the consent of the Senate expressed by the affirmative vote of two thirds of the Senators present." Next the resolution explained that while the Senate would be glad to have the nations of the world "unite to promote peace and general disarmament," it was the opinion of the Senate that "the constitution of the League of Nations in the form now proposed to the Peace Conference should not be accepted by the United States." When objections were made to the introduction of the document itself, Senator Lodge named thirty-seven senators who would have voted for it. The resolution and these names went into the record.

Here was a threat much more specific in character than the November elections had been; the Republican party would demand at least a negative voice in peace-making; the treaty must satisfy them or there would be no ratification. Again Wilson refused to yield. The very next evening he made a speech at the Metropolitan Opera House in New York, in the course of which he hurled back a challenge to those who should venture to oppose his program: "When that Treaty comes back, gentlemen on this side will find the covenant not only in it, but so many threads of the Treaty tied to the covenant, that you cannot dissect the covenant from the Treaty without destroying the whole vital structure."

On July 10, 1919, the Senate received the full text of the Treaty of Versailles. On July 14 it was referred to the Senate Committee on Foreign Relations. To facilitate their study of the document and to satisfy themselves as to the nature and extent of Wilson's verbal promises at Paris, the committee asked the President for permission to examine his records of the meetings of the Councils of Ten and of Four. Wilson peremptorily refused. His refusal made it possible even for honest men to believe that he was concealing matters of vital importance.

At this point the President made his only gesture toward meeting the majority halfway. He invited the members of the Senate Foreign Relations Committee to a conference at the White House and there gave them some of his views on the Treaty. His statements did not satisfy the Senators. Furthermore, to these very Senators who were already suspicious of the President's good faith, Wilson made his denial concerning his knowledge of the secret treaties. Here again they had evidence which refuted his assertion. The auspices were not favorable for a satisfactory exchange of views. With reference to the proposed reservations Wilson told the Committee: "There can be no reasonable objection to such interpretations accompanying the act of ratification provided they do not form a part of the formal ratification itself. Most of the interpretations which have been suggested to me embody what seems to me the plain meaning of the instrument itself." But he went on to insist that if these reservations were included in the ratifying resolution, long delays would be inevitable.

Appeal for Support

Following this conference with the leaders of the Senate on September 3, the President began a series of speeches in which he planned to take his case directly to the people. He delivered his first address at Indianapolis, and his last at Pueblo. At Pueblo he suffered a serious physical collapse which kept him out of active life for months. If he had been able to complete his tour he might possibly have aroused public opinion in favor of the League, but there was no certainty of this. One definite proof of the attitude of the voters had been given in November 1918.

As chairman of the Senate Committee on Foreign Relations, Senator Lodge submitted his first report on the Treaty on September 10, 1919. After calling attention to the President's refusal to turn over essential documents to the committee, Lodge commented unfavorably upon the Covenant:

The Lodge Reservations

> The Committee believes that the league as it stands will breed wars instead of securing peace. They also believe that the covenant of the league demands sacrifices of American independence and sovereignty which would in no way promote the world's peace but which are fraught with the gravest dangers to the future safety and well being of the United States.

Lodge evidently was making veiled references to Wilson's verbal promise to send American forces to protect boundary lines in the Balkans. In answer to the argument that if the United States should adopt reservations, she might be excluded from the League, Lodge declared that such a course would be impossible. Other governments could not retaliate against the United States, because this country had asked nothing from the war and had received nothing from it. "The other nations will take us on our own terms for without us their league is a wreck and all their gains from a victorious peace are imperilled."

Senate Republicans differed in their motives, but they were united in their demands for reservations. There were fifteen Senators, according to Lodge, who would not vote for the Treaty in any circumstances but who would vote for some reservations in order to defeat the Treaty. Others favored the principle of reservations but were not agreed as to the most desirable type. It was Lodge's purpose to frame a set of reservations which would command the vote of every Republican senator, regardless of motive. Also, as Lodge himself explained:

> There was another object which I had very much at heart, and that was that if we were successful in putting on reservations we should create a situation where, if the acceptance of the treaty was defeated, the Democratic party, and especially Mr. Wilson's friends, should be responsible for its defeat, and not the opponents of the treaty who were trying to pass it in a form safe for the United States.

Here was Lodge's own admission that partisanship rather than principle influenced his action.

On November 6, 1919, Senator Lodge submitted his committee's resolution to ratify the Treaty, which included fifteen reservations. The resolution stated that the process of ratification should not be considered as complete until the reservations had been accepted by the Allied and Associated powers. These reservations dealt with a variety of matters. Number one announced that in case of withdrawal the United States should be the sole judge as to whether its international obligations had been fulfilled. Furthermore, notice of withdrawal might be given by a concurrent resolution of the Congress—which would not require executive approval. The second announced that the United States would assume no responsibility and would take no action under Article X except in so far as Congress should authorize it. The third disclaimed any obligation to accept a mandate for the United States except under specific authorization of Congress. Next the United States was declared to have the final voice in determining what questions lay within its exclusive jurisdiction. The fifth placed the Monroe Doctrine and questions arising under it entirely outside the range of League action. The sixth withheld the approval of the United States for the transfer of Shantung to Japan. The seventh provided that no person should be authorized to represent the United States in any meeting or session directly connected with the League until Congress should specifically provide for the appointment. Next, with reference to the powers of the Reparations Commission, the eighth reservation denied that the commission could exercise any control over American trade except as specifically provided by Congress. The ninth put the control of American appropriations for League purposes into the hands of Congress. The tenth was designed to safeguard American rights under any plan for limitation of armaments. The next three did not seem particularly significant. The fourteenth announced that the United States should not be bound by any decision or action of any branch of the League in which any member together with its dominions should have more than one vote. This was aimed at Great Britain and the dominions. As Franklin D. Roosevelt pointed out—and subsequently explained that he had not meant it that way—the United States actually controlled as many votes in the Assembly as did Great Britain. Cuba, Haiti, Santo Domingo, Nicaragua, and Liberia, for example, might have been subject to control by the United States in this one respect even more completely than was the case with Canada or Australia and Great Britain. The fifteenth and last was an expression of sympathy for a free Ireland.

Refusal to Ratify

Shortly before the ratifying resolution was submitted to a vote, President Wilson—still too ill to take an active part in public affairs—wrote to Senator Hitchcock and urged all Democrats to vote against Lodge's reservations: ". . . in my opinion the resolution in that form does not provide for ratification, but rather for the nullification of the treaty. I sincerely hope that the friends and supporters of the treaty will vote against the Lodge resolution of ratification." This message was binding on all members of the Democratic party who had any interest in a political future or in patronage, and it contributed heavily to the defeat of the Treaty.

In one way or another the Treaty came to a vote on three different occasions, and on no one of these could the necessary two-thirds vote be mustered. On November 19, 1919, the vote was taken on the ratifying resolution, including the Lodge reservations; this stood 39 in favor, 55 against. Only 5 Democrats voted for the ratifying resolution, while 42 voted against. Then the friends of the treaty carried a vote to reconsider, and Senator Underwood moved for unconditional ratification of the Treaty. One Republican and 37 Democrats voted in favor, while 46 Republicans and 7 Democrats voted against. In the actual vote on the Treaty therefore the Wilson supporters could muster only 38 affirmative votes; they needed 64. Then the first session of the 67th Congress came to an end. In the next session, on March 19, 1920, the ratifying resolution with the Lodge reservations again came to a vote; this time the figures were 49 in the affirmative and 35 in the negative. On this occasion the Democrats divided almost evenly: 23 in the affirmative, 24 in the negative. This vote of March 19 ended the contest, and the Senate returned the Treaty to the President.

At the time each side blamed the other for the defeat of the Treaty. Possibly the President could have saved his Treaty by endorsing the Lodge reservations. To have done so would have involved no real loss to the League; the only loss would have been in the matter of executive prestige. If this view be taken, Wilson himself killed his great project. Those who take the other side insist that if Wilson had surrendered on this point, Lodge would have devised some other scheme to prevent ratification. This may be true, but the burden of proof is on those who make the assertion. At least Lodge voted for the reservations, and if the 41 Democrats who voted against the resolution had voted for it, there would have been an affirmative vote of 81, more than enough to ratify. The adverse vote in the Senate was probably an accurate index to public opinion. For various reasons the American people did not want to enter the League of Nations.

There were numerous reasons for opposition to Wilson's program. First there was Wilson himself. More than any other American he had become the symbol of the war, and in turning away from war the people turned away from him and his works. Some of the antagonism toward him may have been due to the campaign pledge of 1916: he kept us out of war. Again, some people hated Wilson personally. His manner antagonized numerous influential persons. Then there were Republicans who opposed Wilson and his party simply because they considered the Democrats always wrong. Republican leaders such as Lodge, who were too intelligent to accept this notion of Democratic ineptitude, were prepared to discredit Wilson and his party on the eve of the coming Presidential election. Their attack upon the Treaty and the League therefore might be attributed to the strategical necessities of party politics.

Again, some of the opposition seems to have been due to an honest desire to hold the United States aloof from the complex tangle of European political affairs. The League was branded an entangling alliance, and all the veneration for the founding fathers was aroused and directed against something new and strange. The more moderate members of this group would doubtless have been satisfied with reservations, but the extremists, or isolationists, would have nothing to do with the League. Still others professed to regard the League as a British invention, cleverly designed to promote British influence and power at the expense of the United States. Others were grieved over Wilson's failure at Paris—that is, his sacrifice of ideals. This group opposed the Treaty of Versailles because of its inherent weaknesses and because it contained the causes of future trouble.

Postwar Readjustments

When the Senate rejected the Treaty of Versailles, it left the United States officially at war with Germany. The armistice had merely stopped hostilities and disarmed Germany; it did not restore peace. In May 1920 Congress tried to clear up this anomalous situation by passing the Knox peace resolution. This repealed the declaration of war and proclaimed the war at an end. Next it provided that all German property, public and private, which had come into the possession of the United States because of the war, should be retained by the United States until peace should be arranged. The Knox resolution also announced that this government "does not waive any of the rights, privileges, indemnities, reparations or advantages to which it and its nationals have become entitled under the terms of the armistice . . . or under the Treaty of Versailles."

Peace with Germany

As might be expected, President Wilson vetoed the resolution, and he expressed his opinion of it in no uncertain terms: "I have not felt at liberty to sign this joint resolution because I cannot bring myself to become party to an action which would place ineffaceable stain upon the gallantry and honor of the United States." Here the matter was dropped for the duration of Wilson's term; for some purposes the United States was still officially at war, for other purposes she was at peace.

When Warren G. Harding became President he found it desirable to speed up the process of making peace. On April 12, 1921, in a special message to Congress, he called attention to the problem. On July 2, 1921, Congress passed a joint resolution declaring the war at an end, and reserving to the United States "all rights, privileges, indemnities, reparations, or advantages" to which she was entitled by virtue of her participation in the war or as a result of the armistice or which she would have gained under the Treaty of Versailles. In the following August Germany and the United States signed a separate treaty of peace, containing the same guarantees, which was duly ratified. On January 1, 1922, diplomatic relations between the two governments were resumed, and the war was completely over.

To the casual reader of newspapers the process of ending the war was to be observed in making the armistice and the Treaty of Versailles and in the bitter contest between the President and his Republican opponents in the Senate. This domestic struggle was intense while it lasted, but once it was over the people counted upon a quick return to normal conditions. But the transition from war to peace was less simple than most people imagined; the mere ending of hostilities and the restoration of diplomatic relations proved to be the easiest part of the tangled problem. The patterns of behavior of a people at war are widely different from those of peace, and the substitution of one for the other cannot be brought about merely with the turn of the clock.

Postwar Confusion

To make matters even more difficult, the administration at Washington, Congress, and, to a certain extent, the people had become accustomed to Wilson's energetic leadership from the White House; during the latter part of his administration, however, this leadership was withdrawn. Just before he left for France the President had told Congress that the problem of reconstruction would not be especially difficult and that his services would not be necessary. The people, he said, "know their own business, are quick and resourceful at any readjustment, definite in purpose, and self-reliant in action. Any leading strings that we might seek to put them in would be hopelessly tangled, because they would pay no attention to them and go their own way." If this announcement meant anything, it meant that the administration would offer neither suggestion nor assistance to American businessmen in their efforts to extricate themselves from the machinery of war. Next, Wilson's long absence from Washington made effective guidance impossible, and his subsequent illness practically removed him from the scene. This last situation was obvious to the newspaper correspondents. For example the *Boston Herald* of April 21, 1920, carried a long account under the heading: "Pitiful Stagnation at Capital Follows President's Illness." The article opened with the statement: "The executive machinery of the United States government is today in a condition of utter stagnation." This observer believed that without effective leadership serious economic difficulties would develop. "For a limited period," he continued, "the farms, mines and factories of the country can pour raw materials and machinery into the vacuum the war created in Europe. Once this vacuum is satisfied, and the disparity in exchange will hasten that time, the European market for American goods will close tightly." The time had come for the Department of Commerce and other federal agencies to give serious thought to an almost inevitable postwar economic crisis. The government, however, showed little concern with economic affairs.

American Legion

Some of the essential moves toward peace could go on in spite of Wilson's preoccupation with his proposed new international organization. The work of demobilizing the army began soon after the signing of the armistice; by May 1919 nearly half the enlisted men in this country were retired to private life. By January 1920 the whole expeditionary force had returned from Europe, with the exception of 17,000 men left with the army of occupation in Germany. For the government it was a comparatively simple matter to discharge the soldiers, but it was not so easy for them to return to their former places in civil life or to find new openings. In cases where former employers were willing to take the veterans back, new incumbents had to be dropped. Eventually the government found jobs for about a quarter of the total; the rest of them found jobs for themselves or remained unemployed. This was true of those who came out whole and uninjured. For the permanently disabled the government provided hospitalization; it gave vocational training to those who could be rehabilitated. Here again, however, the number actually trained included hardly more than 25 percent of the total number of disabled.

As one means of assisting themselves during this baffling period of readjustment and of promoting their interest in the future, military leaders planned for a veterans' organization. Precedents for this course had been provided by the Grand Army of the Republic, which had long been famous for its interest in the political and economic problems of the Civil War veterans. Even before the war was over some of the younger American officers in France had started the American Legion. After the armistice the organization was completed, and on November 11, 1919, the Legion held its first national convention. According to its constitution the Legion was founded to "uphold and defend the Constitution of the United States, to maintain law and order, to foster 100 per cent Americanism, and to preserve the memories and incidents of the Great War." Not stated, but probably not forgotten, was the possibility that an organization of 4,000,000 young men, scattered throughout the villages, towns, and cities of the United States, might have political value.

The Bonus

From the beginning the founders of the Legion realized that, once the war had become a thing of the past, many of the veterans would lose interest in the organization. To induce the men to join and to hold them once they had joined, some material incentive would be needed. Again the history of the G.A.R. pointed the way. Congress had been more than generous in providing pensions for veterans of the Civil War and for their widows. Beginning in 1920 the Legion launched its campaign for a soldiers' bonus.

Representatives of the Legion appeared before the Republican national convention of 1920 and demanded support for the bonus. The Republicans refused to endorse the demand, but on the other hand their platform contained no expression of disapproval. In the Democratic convention the Legion made a similar effort, and a large number of delegates seemed inclined to yield. Opposition to the bonus, however, was strong, and Carter Glass of Virginia used his influence successfully to put the convention on record against the proposal. The Democratic platform praised the army for its achievements and the soldiers for their heroism and patriotism. These qualities, so the platform read, "constitute a sacred heritage of posterity, the worth of which can never be recompensed from the treasury and the glory of which must not be diminished by any such expedients."

Failure in the two great national conventions did not end the demand for the bonus; the advocates merely transferred their pressure to Congress. In the course of 1920 one hundred bonus bills were introduced in the House of Representatives. When the new Republican administration under President Harding entered office demands for the bonus were renewed, but when Harding addressed the Senate in opposition, there seemed to be little prospect of Republican support. Harding, however, let it be known that he could see logic in the argument for a bonus, and Congress passed a bill. This measure provided for cash payments to veterans, with a maximum of $500 per veteran for service in the United States and $625 for service abroad. For those veterans who were willing to take a deferred payment instead of cash, the bill provided for a paid-up endowment insurance policy, under which a man entitled to $500 in cash would receive $1690 at the expiration of twenty years. President Harding killed the measure with a veto on the ground that Congress had made no provision for raising the revenue needed to pay the bonus. But in 1924 another measure was passed, over President Coolidge's veto, the most important provision of which was the insurance feature described above. In 1931, over Hoover's veto, Congress passed a measure which permitted veterans to borrow up to 50 percent of the maturity value of their bonus allowances. And in 1936, over the veto of President Franklin D. Roosevelt, Congress passed another measure providing for the immediate payment of the full amount of the bonus. By the summer of 1937 the federal government had paid out approximately $12,000,000,000 to veterans of World War I. This total included the bonus payments and the various other amounts on account of hospitalization, rehabilitation, and the administration of the Veterans' Bureau.

The Veterans' Bureau was created under an act of Congress in August 1921 for the purpose of consolidating the various agencies which dealt with the veterans and their problems. The national headquarters were in Washington, but there were fourteen district branches in different parts of the country. During the Harding administration the Bureau had a staff of nearly 17,000 employees, handling a budget of $500,000,000 per year. The Bureau had charge of work concerned with medical aid, financial assistance to needy veterans, problems of insurance, hospitalization, rehabilitation, and vocational training.

Another postwar problem had to do with the return of the railroads to their owners. During the period of government management expenses had increased substantially without a corresponding increase of revenues. The roads remained in government hands for almost two years, and during this period the government incurred losses on their account amounting to $594,000,000. Here again President Wilson had no specific policy to recommend, and other parties concerned found it difficult to agree. The members of the Railroad Brotherhoods urged a continuance of government operation as a permanent policy; McAdoo, the first director general, and his successor, Walker D. Hines, both approved a plan under which the roads would have continued under government operation for a period of five years after the war. The Interstate Commerce Commission was content merely to point out a number of possible solutions of the problem. The railroad companies

Esch-Cummins Act

or their representatives advocated immediate return to private hands, but with more government supervision and regulation.

The policy adopted provided for a return to private ownership. In March 1920 President Wilson signed the Esch-Cummins Act, which restored the roads to private hands. The law enlarged the Interstate Commerce Commission from a membership of nine to eleven and gave this administrative agency supervisory control over new security issues, maximum and minimum rates, use of terminal facilities, and arrangements of car service. The law also authorized the consolidation of the whole railroad system of the country in case of another war. Furthermore, the law guaranteed the roads a return of 6 percent to be figured on the estimated value of the properties. Of this return, one half of 1 percent was to be set apart for improvements. Then the government gave the roads $200,000,000 and provided for generous government loans to them in the future. To meet the needs of the employees, the same law created the Railway Labor Board with nine members, three of which would represent the companies, three the employees, and three the public. Under the law all disputes over hours of work, wages, or conditions of employment had to be submitted to this board. Thus the Interstate Commerce Commission had full control of the revenue of the roads, while the Labor Board had equally far-reaching authority over one of the most important factors in operating costs, that of wages. This division of administrative authority was perhaps the weakest feature of the law. Other aspects of abnormal wartime activity were ended with fewer complications.

Chapter 42

POLITICAL PROBLEMS OF THE 1920'S

ONCE the Treaty of Versailles was defeated, Republican leaders made plans to win the Presidential election of 1920. In the campaign they hoped still further to discredit President Wilson. In the words of Henry Cabot Lodge, keynote orator of the Republican national convention of 1920: "Mr. Wilson and his dynasty, his heirs and assigns, or anybody that is his, anybody who with bent knee has served his purposes, must be driven from all control, from all influence upon the government of the United States." The Republican platform called attention to the "inexcusable failure to make timely preparation" for the war and to the heavy costs which necessarily resulted from this lack of foresight. Also, according to the platform: "The outstanding features of the Democratic Administration have been complete unpreparedness for war and complete unpreparedness for peace."

Harding for President

Campaign of 1920

This Chicago convention of 1920 had an impressive list of candidates for the nomination. Among the leading contestants were General Leonard Wood, heir to the mantle of Theodore Roosevelt; Frank O. Lowden, former governor of Illinois; Senator Hiram Johnson of California; Herbert Hoover of California; and Calvin Coolidge of Massachusetts. And finally there was United States Senator Warren Gamaliel Harding, a newspaper editor from Ohio. In the beginning Harding himself had no thought of the Presidency and certainly no desire for it. But he had a political counselor who already had groomed him for other offices, Harry M. Daugherty, and in 1919 Daugherty began to steer Harding toward the White House. After various interviews, Harding consented to the use of his name. Then Daugherty set out to get promises from state committees and prospective delegates that they would make Harding their second, third, or fourth choice after the better known contestants were put out of the running. By February 1920 he felt safe enough to make the following prophecy:

> I don't expect Senator Harding to be nominated on the first, second, or third ballots, but I think we can afford to take chances that about eleven minutes after two, Friday morning of the convention, when fifteen or twenty weary men are sitting around a table, someone will say, "Who will we nominate?" At that decisive time the friends of Harding will suggest him and we can afford to abide by the result.

Harding won the nomination.

In their list of possible candidates the Democrats were less fortunate than the Republicans. President Wilson had not encouraged the rise of strong leaders, and in spite of his illness there was ground for thinking that he might like the nomination himself. At the Jackson Day dinner in January 1920 he had declared: "Personally, I do not accept the action of the Senate of the United States as the decision of the nation. I have asserted from the first that the overwhelming majority of the people of this country desire the ratification of the treaty." Then he proposed to make the coming campaign "a great and solemn referendum" on this issue. This issue did not appeal to any person endowed with political sense, and consequently the Democratic convention was sunk in discouragement. The candidate chosen was another newspaper man from Ohio, James M. Cox. He had once beaten a Republican candidate for the governorship, but he was not a figure of national prominence. The voters could not be expected to rally to an unknown candidate running on a dead issue. The Democratic platform praised Wilson and the League and condemned the Republicans for their failure to ratify the Treaty. It denied the Republican charges of inefficiency in preparation for war, and it blamed the Republicans for the delay in the return of normal conditions.

Republican Landslide

In the election Harding scored a plurality of nearly 7,000,000 popular votes, with 404 electoral votes; Cox got 127. The Democrats carried only one state outside the solid South, Kentucky, and that was balanced by their loss of Tennessee. Furthermore, the Republicans gained a majority of 165 in the House and of 24 in the Senate. The tremendous Republican plurality was not due to confidence in Harding because there was no basis for confidence; the voters wanted to express their hostility to Wilson. In the great agricultural areas of the Middle West and the Northwest the farmers hated Wilson because of the restrictions placed on the price of wheat during the war. The Germans in these regions voted against Wilson because they disapproved of the Treaty of Versailles; so too, for the same reason, did some of the Irish in the East. Over and above these local objections to Wilson, however, there was an evident swing toward the Republican side. This may have been the result of superior campaigning. Publicity in the last analysis is a matter of money, and the Republicans had money. The Republican National and Congressional Campaign Committees collected and spent over $8,100,000, and in addition they incurred a deficit of $1,600,000. The Democrats paid out less than a quarter of the Republican total.

Harding's Cabinet included representatives of widely diverse interests in the Republican party. For secretary of state the President picked Charles Evans Hughes; for the Treasury, Andrew W. Mellon, a well-known Pittsburgh millionaire; for the Department of Commerce, Herbert Hoover. These three were men of national reputation and of demonstrated talent. In the second group might be placed John W. Weeks, secretary of war, a former banker from Massachusetts; H. C. Wallace, in Agriculture; Edwin Denby, in the Navy Department; James J. Davis, Labor; and—possibly in this group—Will Hays, the postmaster general. These were not so well known as the first three except Hays, and they were hardly up to the level of the others in point of ability. In a third group stood the attorney general, Harry M. Daugherty, and the secretary of the interior, Albert B. Fall, former Senator from New Mexico. Fall's misuse of his official position eventually landed him in prison.

Harding never had any understanding of national or international affairs. He did at times endorse one policy or oppose another, but there was always traceable the influence of a Cabinet member or of someone who told the President what to say. Harding's inaugural announced that the United States would have no part in the League of Nations. He urged the development of commerce with Latin America. In connection with foreign trade, he felt that a higher tariff was imperative. He advocated administrative efficiency, lower taxes, sound commercial practices, elimination of unnecessary governmental interference in business, and industrial peace. His administration, he said, would be pledged to service. "Service is the supreme commitment of life. I would rejoice to acclaim the era of the golden rule and crown it with the autocracy of service. I pledge an administration wherein all the agencies of the government are called to serve and even promote an understanding of government purely as an expression of the popular will."

Foreign Policy

In the formation of foreign policy the initiative lay with the secretary of state. According to rumor, President Harding stood in awe of his keen-minded foreign minister, and there is no record that Secretary Hughes was ever invited to the poker games in which the President and his intimates found relaxation. Hughes provided an asset of respectability in an administration which before long acquired a decidedly unsavory reputation.

In dealing with, or rather in not dealing with, the recently established Bolshevik government in Russia, Hughes followed the precedent established during the Wilson administration. The United States would not accord diplomatic recognition to the new regime. In March 1921 Hughes rejected a proposal for opening commercial relations. If the Russian government was prepared to change its policy so as to provide proper securities for commercial intercourse, the United States would be glad to see proof of it. Without such evidence "this government is unable to perceive that there is any proper basis for considering trade relations." Hughes also complained of the undercover activities of Russian agents in this country.

Washington Conference

During the 1920's people believed that the really great, constructive achievement of the Harding administration was the conference on limitation of armament. Credit for this conference went to Secretary Hughes, although Senator William E. Borah had already given a decided impetus to the movement. In December 1920 he had introduced a resolution asking the

President to call a conference to adopt plans for limiting naval construction. In the following May, again under Borah's influence, the proposed resolution was appended to the naval appropriation bill, which became law in July. Subsequently, long after the conference was over, it appeared that the British government had a major part in initiating it.

Secretary Hughes had a comprehensive policy in mind. If fear and jealousy could be removed from the Far East, where international friction almost threatened another war, limitation of armament would almost automatically follow. Both the United States and Japan were engaged in elaborate naval building programs, with Japan in the difficult position of attempting something which her strategic situation seemed to make essential but which her resources were too limited to warrant. Then too, the United States was none too well pleased with the Japanese attitude toward China. It appeared that Japan was bent upon establishing an effective hegemony over China to the detriment of all Occidental powers. Next there was the problem of the Anglo-Japanese alliance, strongly opposed by the British dominions and the United States.

Secretary Hughes endeavored to remove these causes of bitterness. While the Borah resolution was still pending in Congress, the secretary of state took up the proposal and privately secured the approval of the leading governments of the world. Then, on August 11, 1921, he issued formal invitations. There was a little diplomatic sparring over the acceptance of the invitation, particularly with Japan, but no insuperable obstacles were raised anywhere; on November 12, 1921, the delegates convened in Washington.[1]

President Harding opened the conference. Then Secretary Hughes proceeded to lay before the conference definite proposals for restricting the navies of the world. First, he urged that, for a period of ten years, all capital shipbuilding plans be suspended, even to the extent of abandoning work on vessels actually under construction; next that the strength of the navies in service should be limited by scrapping certain specified ships; then that the ratio of naval strength prevailing at the time should be preserved; and finally that capital ship tonnage be taken as the measure of naval strength. The honesty of purpose of the administration was proved by the willingness to sacrifice a position of assured supremacy for one of equality with Great Britain. According to Hughes's proposal, the United States would scrap fifteen ships of the existing fleet and fifteen under construction

Three Treaties

The proposal was put into treaty form, which left the tonnage of capital ships of the United States, Great Britain, and Japan in the ratio of 5-5-3, and the treaty was duly ratified by the powers concerned. According to this apportionment of naval strength France received a ratio of 1.75. The French accepted it under protest, and they insisted upon complete freedom in the

[1] The American representatives were Secretary Hughes, Henry Cabot Lodge, Elihu Root and Oscar W. Underwood. The other governments represented were England, France, Japan Italy, China, Belgium, Portugal, and Holland.

building of auxiliary craft, including cruisers, destroyers, and submarines. Secretary Hughes had hoped to effect an agreement on these vessels too, but the determined stand of France prevented action. Competition therefore was still possible in lighter craft. In connection with the abandonment of capital ship construction an agreement was effected whereby the United States, Great Britain, and Japan stopped most of the work on fortifications and naval bases in the Pacific.

While the conference was in session representatives of the United States, Great Britain, France, and Japan signed the Four Power Treaty, which undertook to safeguard existing rights in the Pacific islands. In case of any controversy over these possessions, the four powers agreed to meet in a joint conference for discussion, and, it was hoped, for a settlement of the dispute. Next, if the rights of any of the signatories should be threatened by any other power, the contracting parties agreed to communicate with each other and to act together. The primary purpose of the Four Power Treaty was the termination of the Anglo-Japanese Alliance.

Then the conference accepted a Nine Power Treaty for the purpose of defining the rights of China and of protecting the country from aggression. The governments agreed to respect the independence and territorial integrity of China and to recognize the principle of equality of opportunity there for all nations in commercial and industrial development—in other words, to preserve the Open Door. Perhaps the most important problem in connection with China was officially beyond the scope of the conference—the question of Shantung. This former German "sphere" in China had been transferred to Japan. Nevertheless, Secretary Hughes was instrumental in persuading Japan to yield public control of the province to China; the important economic concessions there, however, still remained in Japanese hands. These treaties were all ratified by the United States Senate. At the time and for several years thereafter, the work of the Washington Conference was hailed as a triumph in the cause of peace. Subsequent events proved that it was a triumph for Japan. As a result of the three treaties she became the dominant power in the Far East.

Secretary Hughes hoped that if the United States could not join the League of Nations, she might at least join the World Court. This body had been created by the League in December 1920. To safeguard the rights of his government Hughes proposed four reservations: that adhesion to the Court involved no legal relationship on the part of the United States to the League of Nations or the assumption of any obligations under the Covenant; that the United States be allowed to participate on terms of equality with other governments in the election of judges of the Court; that the United States would pay a fair share of the expenses of the Court; and finally that no amendment be made to the statute founding the Court without the consent of the United States. President Harding approved this policy, but the Senate never gave its assent.

From Harding to Coolidge

In domestic policies Harding's concept of service was simple. He wanted everybody to be happy. He had promised to utilize the "best minds" of the Republican party and to call upon them both to plan and to execute important policies. These best minds, however, did not appear in subordinate positions. When President Harding entered office, he found about 240,000 federal positions outside the classified civil service. These were all available for political use. Furthermore he made numerous exceptions to the civil service rules, thereby creating additional patronage for party workers. In some departments, notably in the foreign service, the appointments were excellent. The Departments of Commerce and Agriculture likewise were able to secure good men. But apart from these three Harding's record in connection with appointments is a sorry one. Before he had been in office two years the National Civil Service Reform League, at its forty-second annual meeting, described his record in these words: "It is doubtful if, since the passage of the United States Civil Service Law in 1883, there has been a more insistent effort made on the part of party spoilsmen to overthrow the merit system in the Federal civil service than has been made in the last year and a half."

During the latter part of Harding's brief career in the White House, and particularly after his death, stories of malfeasance and corruption multiplied fast. Some of these had to do with one Jesse Smith, a friend of Attorney General Daugherty, who had a desk but no office in the Department of Justice. Then a congressional committee investigated the administration of the Veteran's Bureau under Colonel Forbes. Forbes was Harding's own personal selection for this important post. Of the total annual budget which Congress provided for the Bureau, at least half was devoted to sheer graft. Forbes was convicted of corruption and sent to a federal prison.

Teapot Dome

The crowning piece of criminality in public office was furnished by Albert B. Fall, secretary of the interior, in leasing the naval oil reserves. In 1912 two naval oil reserves had been set apart in California. In 1915 the smaller but more famous Teapot Dome reserve was set apart in Wyoming. The purpose of the federal government was to preserve this oil in the ground until conditions should make it difficult for the navy to buy its supply in open market. In April 1921 Secretary Denby announced that the Navy Department was going to surrender control of the reserves. Then, on May 31, Harding issued an executive order transferring the administration of the reserves from the Navy Department to the Interior. The original draft of this order was written by Fall. Although the reserves had been placed under the jurisdiction of the Navy Department by an act of Congress, Fall and Harding made the change on their own responsibility. Then Fall promptly leased the California reserves to his friend, Edward F. Doheny. In April 1922 he leased the Teapot Dome field to another friend, Harry

F. Sinclair. These leases were made secretly, on terms which were financially unfavorable to the government and destructive of the principle of conservation.

On hearing rumors of these extraordinary proceedings, certain Senators, among them La Follette of Wisconsin, raised vigorous protests. In June 1922 Harding transmitted to the Senate a letter from Fall explaining the leases; accompanying this was a letter signed by Harding himself but written by someone else, in which the President assumed full responsibility for what had been done. "I think it is only fair to say in this connection that the policy decided upon and the subsequent acts have at all times had my entire approval." The degree of Harding's comprehension of what had gone on will probably never be known.

In transferring the oil reserves from the Navy to the Department of the Interior, Fall and Harding both laid themselves open to the danger of impeachment. Other aspects of the transaction were even more reprehensible. For ten years Fall had been in such straitened circumstances that he could not pay his taxes. Then after making these oil leases he suddenly showed signs of unusual affluence. By the end of 1922 he had spent nearly $200,000 in improvements on his property in New Mexico. Subsequent investigations proved that he had received $233,000 from Sinclair and $100,000 from Doheny. These were the amounts paid by the lessees for privileges of enormous value; Doheny testified that he expected to make $100,000,000 out of the California fields.

The full truth concerning these transactions was not brought out until 1924 after Fall had resigned from the Cabinet and Harding was dead. During the Coolidge administration the leases were canceled by order of the federal courts, "by reason of the fraud and conspiracy of Secretary Fall and Mr. Doheny." On October 25, 1929, Fall was convicted of bribery and sentenced to a year's imprisonment plus a fine of $100,000. He was so successful in keeping his case before the courts, however, that he did not enter prison until July 1931.

Raising the Tariff

Republican leaders had never been satisfied with the Underwood Tariff Act of 1913, and once they recovered control they planned for a new law. First they passed a temporary measure and then worked out the complex details of a whole new tariff. The regular measure, known as the Fordney-McCumber Tariff, went into effect in September 1922. It raised the level of rates on manufactured goods to 25 percent above that even of the much criticized Payne-Aldrich Act of 1909, and it imposed high duties on various agricultural products. President Harding's characterization of the measure as the greatest work in tariff history was balanced by the comment of the *Wall Street Journal,* which condemned the act as "one of the most selfish, short-sighted and extravagant laws of the kind ever enacted."

By the summer of 1923 the burden of the Presidency was becoming too heavy for Harding. Corruption was revealed in many official quarters; trusted friends upon whom the President had relied for advice proved undependable and false. Partly to escape from these growing embarrassments, Harding and a few friends planned a trip to Alaska. On the return journey Harding became ill in California and on August 2 he died suddenly. His death brought two curious reactions. First there were stories that the President had not died a natural death but that he had been poisoned or that he had committed suicide. The real cause was a coronary embolism. The other reaction was an expression of exaggerated sympathy in the press. Charity probably requires a statement that Harding himself was not directly to blame for the misfortunes of his administration. But even though acquitted of corruption he cannot escape the charge of vast incompetence.

Coolidge as President

Harding's death put Calvin Coolidge in the Presidency. On hearing the news he is said to have remarked: "I think I can swing it." Early in the morning of August 3, 1923, in his father's home at Plymouth, Vermont, he took the oath of office as President of the United States. Coolidge announced his intention of carrying out Harding's policies, and he asked for the cooperation of all who had been associated with his predecessor. As Vice President and regular attendant at Cabinet meetings, Coolidge must have known of some of the weaknesses of Secretaries Daugherty and Denby. Even so, he planned to keep these two men in his Cabinet. But Republican leaders in the Senate knew that these two liabilities must be disposed of before the coming Presidential campaign. On February 11, 1924, the Senate practically ordered Coolidge to demand Denby's resignation. At first Coolidge refused, but before the end of March he complied with the order. Coolidge was left in an embarrassing dilemma. Either he had knowingly and purposely kept an incompetent official in office for nearly eight months and then let him go only because of political pressure, or he had sacrificed an able man merely to satisfy the Senate. Denby was no weaker in March 1924 than he had been three years earlier, and certainly no weaker than he had been in August 1923. On March 1, 1924, the Senate appointed a special committee to investigate Attorney General Daugherty and the Department of Justice, and before the end of the month Daugherty resigned, also at Coolidge's request.

Throughout his adult life Calvin Coolidge had been interested primarily in politics. Then having been elevated to the Presidency not by an election in his own right but through the death of his predecessor, he desired a chance to prove that the people really wanted him as their President. And he had political friends just as eager to help him as he was anxious to be elected. Among these was William M. Butler of Massachusetts, who made sure of enough delegates in the Republican national convention to nominate his chief and who managed the campaign itself. Coolidge received the nomination without difficulty.

Election of 1924

The Democrats had not recovered from their terrific slump in 1920, and for the time being the factional cleavage in the party had become more acute. For years the solid South had provided a substantial nucleus of votes in return for which, under the Wilson administration at least, it had received its due reward in patronage. On the other hand, the Democratic party in the North, largely urban, had not received recognition commensurate with its strength. In 1924 this element demanded its turn. For their candidate northern Democrats presented the able, popular governor of New York, Alfred E. Smith. Although born and raised on the lower East Side and trained in the political school of Tammany Hall, Governor Smith had gone far beyond the range of the ordinary city politician. At Albany he had displayed outstanding ability, ability conceded even by his Republican opponents. He and his admirers set out to capture the Democratic nomination. The auspices seemed favorable because the convention was scheduled to meet at Madison Square Garden in New York.

Democratic forces from the South and West, on the other hand, were united in support of William Gibbs McAdoo, son-in-law of President Wilson, former secretary of the treasury and director of the railroads during World War I. The convention opened on June 23 and lasted until July 10, the longest national convention ever held in this country. For one hundred ballots the Smith and McAdoo delegates voted stubbornly, and neither candidate could reach the necessary two-thirds majority. Then the two leaders gave up the struggle. On the 103d ballot the nomination went to John W. Davis of New York.

Senator La Follette had been nursing Presidential ambitions since 1912 when Theodore Roosevelt ruined his chances for the Progressive nomination. In 1924 he attempted to capitalize on the prevailing liberal and socialistic agitation and to run on a third ticket. He announced that the American people ought to have the chance to join a new party, because of "the failure of the two old parties to purge themselves of the influences which have caused their administrations repeatedly to betray the American people." If the voters should repudiate these old parties, he went on, "we shall then witness . . . the beginning of a new era in the life of the American people." His platform advocated the election of all federal judges, federal control of the meat-packing industry, public ownership of railroads and of hydroelectric plants, a deep waterway from the Great Lakes to the sea, a government marketing agency to assist the farmers, use of the full power of the national government to crush monopoly, heavy income and excess profits taxes, adequate laws to permit laborers to organize effectively, and the abolition of injunctions in labor disputes.

In the election Coolidge polled a popular vote of 15,718,789; Davis received 8,378,962, and La Follette 4,822,319. Although the greater part of La Follette's strength came from the West, he received more than 1,000,000 votes in the four eastern states of Massachusetts, New Jersey, New York, and Pennsylvania. In his own state of Wisconsin he was the leading candidate. Of the electoral vote Coolidge received 382, Davis 136, and La Follette 13. The Republicans also won substantial majorities in both houses of Congress.

The six years of Coolidge's career as President happened to coincide with a decided upswing in economic prosperity—for all except the farmers—

and the era was sometimes described as the Coolidge boom. For the President this circumstance served both to justify and to strengthen the simple economic philosophy which he had absorbed on his father's farm in Vermont, at Amherst College, and in his political career. Briefly he was the embodiment of rugged individualism and of *laissez faire*. He believed in the virtues of hard work and economy, in individual opportunity, and in freedom of business enterprise. Under his guidance the Federal Trade Commission ceased to interfere with business morals.

A Collection of Unsolved Problems

Among the various problems that Coolidge inherited from his predecessor were the debts owed to the United States by most of the governments of Europe. During World War I and after the armistice these governments had borrowed from us to the amount of $10,338,000,000. More than $3,260,000,000 of this amount had been lent since the armistice. Great Britain had been the heaviest borrower, with a total of $4,277,000,000; France and Italy ranked second and third. Capacity to pay, however, by no means equaled the readiness to borrow, and by 1921 the principal of the debt was increasing because of arrears of interest. The debtor nations felt that the peculiar circumstances of the war put these immense sums in a category apart from ordinary financial obligations. The Allies had participated in a common cause, so the argument ran, and these financial obligations represented each country's contribution to that cause. It was only fair, they said, to pool the costs of the enterprise on a basis of what each party could pay. Or, as M. Clemental, of the French government, put it:

War Debts

> If one abandons juridical grounds and considers the problem from the higher points of view of cooperation and equity, strict justice would seem to require the general pooling of war expenditures and their division among the Allies proportionally to the riches of each nation and without consideration for special engagements which the exigencies of the moment imposed.

If the United States had the same sort of interest in the war or responsibility for it as the powers of Europe, and if all parties involved were obliged to contribute all they could, this French theory might hold. The basic premises, however, were unsound. As President Coolidge very aptly put it: "Whatever assistance we may have given to finishing the War, we feel free from any responsibility for beginning it."

While European political leaders were advocating cancellation on one ground, economists arrived at the same conclusion but by a different line of reasoning. They argued that the debts could not be paid without seriously upsetting the economic stability of both Europe and the United States. These arguments in behalf of cancellation made little impression on the American people. President Coolidge reflected the common view with his characteristic comment: "Well, they hired the money, didn't they?" The

United States government insisted upon a settlement, and the British were the first to come to terms. They agreed to a plan whereby they would make a cash payment of $4,128,085 to the United States; then they would issue bonds to this government, to the amount of $4,600,000,000, with interest at 3.5 percent; this principal would be paid in installments over a period of sixty years. Thus the British undertook to pay to this country, by the year 1997, installments amounting all told to $11,105,000,000. Adjustments were made with the other debtors whereby the rate of interest was cut in proportion to estimated ability to pay.

As might have been expected, these debts were never paid. Repayments on account from all debtors reached a total of $2,628,000,000 in 1932, and then—except for payments made by Finland—they stopped. After default became a settled policy, Congress passed the Johnson Act prohibiting further loans to governments which failed to meet their financial obligations to the United States. This measure became inoperative in March 1941 with the enactment of the Lend-Lease Act.

Philippine Unrest

Among the specific problems of the Coolidge administration the Philippine Islands threatened for a time to be the most embarrassing. In those dependencies the long-standing desire for independence had been strengthened when President Wilson encouraged Governor Harrison to turn over important powers and responsibilities to the Filipinos themselves. Under Harrison the Filipino leaders had created a Council of State which included the departmental secretaries, the speaker of the House, and the president of the Senate. The purpose was to create a system of parliamentary government in which the American governor would become a figurehead. President Harding, on the other hand, tried to restore the lost prestige and power of American officials in the Philippine government, and he found the means for doing so in the Jones Act, which had been passed in 1916. This measure had made the departmental secretaries responsible to the governor and had given him an absolute veto over all Filipino legislation. The Jones Act also reserved to the Congress of the United States power to annul any act of the Filipino legislature within six months of its enactment, even though it had been signed by the governor. President Harding prepared to use these powers. He appointed General Leonard Wood as governor. Coolidge came on the scene when the contest between Governor Wood and the Filipinos had reached a dramatic climax.

On October 17, 1923, the Philippine legislature, in joint session, unanimously adopted a resolution demanding the recall of Governor Wood and the appointment of a Filipino as governor. On October 18, the secretary of war, John W. Weeks, under whose immediate jurisdiction the Philippines lay, sent the following vigorous message to Governor Wood: "You are entitled to the support of the Administration and shall have it. . . . The veto power granted to the Governor-General is applicable to all legislation whether it be local or otherwise." Following this exchange, the Philippine Senate and House of Representatives drew up a series of resolutions which charged Governor Wood with illegal, arbitrary, and undemocratic practices. As a result, the legislature declared, it had become necessary for the Filipinos "to take all needful steps, and to make use of all lawful means within our power to obtain the complete vindication of the liberties of the country now violated and invaded." Furthermore, the resolutions continued, the existing situation "once more demonstrates that the immediate and absolute independence of the Philippines, which the whole country demands, is the only complete and satisfactory settlement of the Philippine problem."

President Coolidge's reply, sent on February 21, 1924, aimed to convince the Filipinos that the authorities at Washington could rule them better than they could govern themselves. After questioning the truth of the assertion that the Filipino demand for independence was unanimous, Coolidge enlarged upon the benefits which the Filipinos derived from the connection with the United States. Then he informed the members of the independence group that they were not ready for independence "either in wealth or experience." The Filipinos did not agree, but they were powerless.

During this same era, Puerto Ricans sought additional privileges of self-government. Thereupon the President pointed out the value of their connection with the United States. In January 1928 the president of the Puerto Rican Senate and the speaker of the Puerto Rican House sent a message to Coolidge, complaining of the humiliating status of their country. They asked that Puerto Rico be made a "free state." On February 28, 1928, Coolidge replied. These Puerta Rican messages, he said, "seem to be based largely on a complete misunderstanding of concrete facts." The present government of Puerto Rico was more liberal than any the people had ever known; the people had greater control over their own affairs and less interference from without.

Caribbean Problems

In dealing with the Caribbean Coolidge made no striking contributions to American policy. During his administration Haiti remained where Wilson had put it, subject to the autocratic, military rule of the United States. In Santo Domingo, on the other hand, there was a change of status. In September 1924 Coolidge removed the marines, and the government was restored to the inhabitants. This renunciation of the white man's burden in one place was soon followed by a substantial increase of the load in another.

Shortly after Coolidge entered the White House the political situation in Nicaragua became even more unstable than usual. During a civil war between Liberals and Conservatives, the administration at Washington proclaimed an embargo on the shipment of arms to either faction, and at the same time it tried to settle the dispute by a conference. The conference ended in failure. On December 23, 1926, marines were landed in Nicaragua, to "protect American and foreign lives and property." Then the embargo on arms was removed, larger forces were sent in, and before the end of January 1927 there were fifteen American naval vessels in Nicaraguan waters, with a force of 4500 men ready for action. By 1928 American forces had restored order and peace. This activity in Nicaragua was justified on the ground that it was necessary to protect the Panama Canal.

President Coolidge and Secretary of State Kellogg also had difficulties with Mexico over the social and economic policy of the Mexican government. In the new constitution of 1917 there were articles designed to re-establish the Mexican title to land and to petroleum fields which had been lost through overgenerous grants of invaluable concessions or through sale at nominal prices to foreign owners. Under this constitution and the laws passed to carry it into effect, ranchers and oil companies were threatened with the loss of their properties. These foreign owners appealed to their respective governments, and the United States tried to protect American citizens. The State Department held that these owners could not be deprived, without adequate compensation, of titles which they had acquired prior to May 1917. In 1925 the Mexican Congress passed laws to validate the seizure of foreign-owned property. Secretary Kellogg protested vigorously but ineffectively. In 1938 Mexico expropriated foreign-owned oil properties.

Havana Conference

Although the Coolidge administration insisted upon its right to use force in Nicaragua and to instruct the Mexicans upon the subject of the law of real property, it also participated in policies looking toward peaceful cooperation among all American governments. On January 16, 1928, President Coolidge delivered the opening address at the 6th Pan-American Conference, which met at Havana. Because of recent events in Haiti and Nicaragua, Latin American writers and speakers had complained of the dangers of American imperialism. Coolidge tried to reassure them with a discussion of the political ideals of his country.

> It is among the republics of this hemisphere that the principle of human rights has had its broadest application, where political freedom and equality and economic opportunity have made their greatest advance. [These advantages rested on a foundation of self-government and democracy.] We are thoroughly committed to the principle that they [the people] are better fitted to govern themselves than anyone else is to govern them. . . . It is better for the people to make their own mistakes than to have someone else make the mistakes for them.

On this occasion it would have been tactless to mention Haiti, and the President concluded with the remark that "All nations here represented stand on an exact footing of equality."

One of the most important discussions at this conference centered on this very issue that Coolidge discussed so glibly, that of equality among the nations. Some of the Latin American delegates wished to give substance to this abstract theory by introducing into the proposed code of international law the following declaration: "No state may intervene in the internal affairs of another." If Coolidge had really meant what he said about self-government and equality and if these principles really did lie at the foundation of the foreign policy of the United States, this government could have had no legitimate objection to ratifying the declaration. But American hegemony in the Caribbean might require intervention, and Coolidge had no intention of surrendering this right. Consequently Charles Evans Hughes, the leader of the American delegation, opposed the declaration so vigorously that it was dropped. The United States also opposed the establishment of a Pan-American court of justice to have jurisdiction over differences which might arise between American governments. The United States insisted upon her own exclusive right to decide any question involving what she considered to be her interests in the Caribbean area.

Immigration

Coolidge's problems in the foreign field were not confined to Latin America. In 1924 the Japanese threatened to make trouble over our new immigration policy. In 1921 an emergency immigration act had been passed, providing for a quantitative limitation; the duration of this measure was subsequently extended to July 1, 1924. In his first annual message, December 1923, Coolidge expressed his approval of the restrictive principle already adopted, and asked for more nearly permanent legislation upon the subject.

> American institutions rest solely on good citizenship. They were created by people who had a background of self-government. New arrivals should be limited to our capacity to absorb them into the ranks of good citizenship. America must be kept American. For this purpose, it is necessary to continue a policy of restricted immigration. . . . I am convinced that our present economic and social conditions warrant a limitation of those to be admitted.

Congress agreed with the President and passed the Johnson-Lodge Immigration Act of 1924. The law continued the principle of numerical restriction, limiting the annual intake from any given country to 2 percent of the immigrants from that country already here according to the census of 1890. To minimize confusion and hardship the bill provided for the selection of immigrants at the source instead of at immigrant stations at the United States. And most important of all, it provided for the exclusion of aliens who are not eligible for naturalization—in other words, the Japanese.

From 1907 to 1924 Japanese immigration to this country had been held in check by means of the "Gentlemen's Agreement," a semiformal understanding under which the Japanese government itself promised to withhold passports from Japanese laborers intending to embark for the United States. This method had been reasonably effective. If the sole purpose of this legislation had been restriction, the Japanese problem could have been safely left to the working of the "Gentlemen's Agreement" plus the quota principle. There were, however, some members of Congress who wished to put the Japanese in their place.

Japan's Hurt Feelings

The Japanese were quick to show their resentment. Two days before the House adopted the measure, Secretary of State Hughes sent a letter to the chairman of the Senate Committee on Immigration, enclosing a note of protest from the Japanese ambassador Hanihara. He made no effort to keep within the bounds of ordinary diplomatic phraseology. "I realize, as

I believe you do, the grave consequences which the enactment of the measure retaining that particular provision would inevitably bring upon the otherwise happy and mutually advantageous condition between our two countries."

On the advice of Secretary Hughes the Senate Committee on Immigration had already decided to continue the "Gentlemen's Agreement" and to put Japan under the quota principle. Then came the Hanihara letter. On April 14 Senator Lodge declared that the letter was "improper." It has, he said, "created a situation which makes it impossible for me to support the pending amendment. . . . I never will consent to establish any precedent, which will give any nation the right to think that they can stop by threats or compliments the action of the United States when it determines who shall come within its gates and become part of its citizenship." On this same day, by a vote of 76 to 21 the Senate defeated the amendment which would have continued the "Gentlemen's Agreement," and on the next day it voted to exclude the Japanese. The law went into effect on July 1, 1924.

Ambassador Hanihara tried without avail to repair some of the damage. On April 17 he wrote another letter to Secretary Hughes in explanation of the first. "I had no thought," he said, "of being in any way disagreeable or discourteous and still less of conveying a veiled threat." The truth of this assertion might be questioned. Diplomatic officials of those days knew perfectly well what was meant by the term "grave consequences," and Hanihara was an experienced diplomat. The Japanese professed to be deeply hurt by this measure. Some of their newspapers even urged war.

Kellogg-Briand Pact

Although the government of the United States had refused to join the League of Nations and although it insisted upon its right to dominate the Caribbean, our officials showed considerable interest in one of the prevailing enthusiasms of the day. This was the establishment of world peace by wishful thinking. Following World War I there was an assumption that the days of international banditry were over, that no government harbored aggressive designs against its neighbors. Not even the increasing evidence of Japanese bitterness against the United States and the failure to bring about further limitation of armaments weakened this belief.

The crowning illustration of this faith in the power of wishes was afforded by the world-wide acceptance of the Kellogg-Briand Pact or Pact of Paris. In April 1927 Aristide Briand, French foreign minister, committed his government to the negotiation of a treaty which should outlaw war between the United States and France. At first the deep significance of this suggestion seemed lost upon all Americans except President Nicholas Murray Butler of Columbia University, who sent a communication concerning it to *The New York Times*. In July 1927 Ambassador Herrick had a conference with Secretary Kellogg on the subject. In December 1927 Secretary Kellogg discussed the matter with the Senate Committee on Foreign Relations. Senator Borah of Idaho had been interested in outlawing war for some time, and he urged that Briand's program be extended to include other governments. Secretary Kellogg promptly transmitted to Briand the proposal that the leading world powers join in "a declaration renouncing war as an instrument of national policy."

On February 6, 1928, a Franco-American treaty of arbitration was signed, the preamble of which condemned war as an instrument of international policy; the treaty itself provided for the settlement of all differences of whatever character by peaceful means. On April 13, 1928, the United States asked the governments of Great Britain, Germany, Italy, and Japan to approve treaties for outlawing war. In the first article of the proposed draft, the contracting parties "condemn recourse to war for the solution of international controversies, and renounce it as an instrument of national policy." Then they bound themselves never to resort to any but peaceful means for the settlement of disputes. In June 1928 Kellogg submitted the treaty to fourteen governments, and on August 27, 1928, all of them signed it. Forty-eight more nations were then invited to join the movement. On January 15, 1929, the pact was ratified by the United States Senate by a vote of 85 to 1.

Hoover and the Election of 1928

Coolidge's Withdrawal

By 1927 politically minded people were speculating as to Coolidge's plans for the next Presidential campaign. For some time Coolidge let them guess and said nothing. Then, one hot summer afternoon, August 2, 1927, during his vacation in South Dakota, the President distributed typewritten slips of paper with the message: "I do not choose to run for President in 1928." Thus President Coolidge announced his withdrawal from politics. Three days later he amplified his announcement by saying that he would retire from the White House on March 4, 1929. Speculation was still rife, both among those who hoped that he would run again and among those who feared that he might. To stop the discussion, Coolidge issued the following: "My statement stands. No one should be led to suppose that I have modified it."

In spite of all this, experts in politics still continued to insist that Coolidge's declarations were nothing but sham and pretense and that he wished to have the nomination come to him in the form of a mandate. Some insisted that he expected such a demand and that he was bitterly disappointed when it failed to come. There were even some with lively imaginations who pictured him as the mythical "man on horseback" and who saw in his continuance in office a grave menace to our republican form of government. On January 31, 1928, Senator Robert M. La Follette, the younger, of Wisconsin, inspired by the history of the days of President Grant, introduced a resolution, declaring that it was

> . . . the sense of the Senate that the precedent established by Washington and other Presidents of the United States in retiring from the Presidential office after

their second term has become, by universal concurrence, a part of our republican system of government, and that any departure from this time-honored custom would be unwise, unpatriotic and fraught with peril to our free institutions.

To his first resolution La Follette coupled another advising President Coolidge to take due notice of this warning and to govern himself accordingly. On February 7 the Senate debated the La Follette resolutions and three days later adopted the first; the specific warning to Coolidge did not pass. All the prominent Democrats in the Senate voted for the anti-third-term resolution.

With Coolidge out, the way was opened for the secretary of commerce, Herbert Hoover, former director of war relief in Belgium and later Food Administrator under the Wilson administration. An engineer by profession, Hoover had never sought elective office before, but he had competent political help and he appealed strongly to the American people. Arthur Krock of *The New York Times,* writing from the convention in Kansas City, reported: "Wall Street did not want Hoover . . . the Farm Bloc did not want Hoover. . . . The elder politicians did not want Hoover." The people, however, did want Hoover. Only one ballot was cast; out of the total of 1084 votes, 837 went to Hoover. Senator Charles Curtis of Kansas received the nomination for the vice-presidency.

In his acceptance speech Hoover promised a continuance of economic prosperity:

One of the oldest and perhaps the noblest of human aspirations has been the abolition of poverty . . . we in America today are nearer to the final triumph over poverty than ever before in the history of any land. The poorhouse is vanishing from among us. We have not reached the goal, but, given a chance to go forward with the policies of the last eight years we shall soon, with the help of God, be in sight of the day when poverty will be banished from this nation. There is no guaranty against poverty equal to a job for every man. This is the primary purpose of the policies we advocate.

Campaign against Smith

The Democrats held their convention at Houston, Texas, and this time the urban contingent prevailed over southern and rural opposition. Alfred E. Smith, who had been denied the nomination four years previously, was triumphantly nominated on the first ballot. Smith's nomination brought the issue of religion into the campaign. He was a Roman Catholic, and many Protestants, hating Catholicism with all the bitterness of the sixteenth century, vowed that the White House was no place for a Roman Catholic. Some Protestant church officials urged their people to vote against Smith. In addition to the disparaging statements which were put into print, stories circulated orally which were designed to injure Smith's reputation; most of these were palpably untrue. This "whispering campaign" was widespread; how damaging it may have been no one can say. Smith's admirers were not affected by it, except in so far as it tended to strengthen their admiration, while those who believed the stories would never have voted for him anyway.

The normal course for those who did not like Smith would have been to vote the Republican ticket. Voters in the Solid South, however, were in a difficult predicament. Most of them hated the very name Republican—to which they customarily attached the adjective "black"—because of its association with the Civil War and Reconstruction. As a way out of the difficulty, in Georgia for example, ballots were provided with a list of electors labeled "Hoover Democrats." Thus the voters who cared to do so could vote for Hoover without voting Republican.

Nearly 75 percent of the voters went to the polls. Hoover carried forty states with 444 electoral votes, while Smith carried the other eight with 87 electoral votes. The popular vote stood at 21,429,109 for Hoover, 15,005,497 for Smith. Hoover broke the Solid South for the first time since Reconstruction; he carried Florida, North Carolina, Texas, Virginia, and all the border states: Kentucky, Maryland, Missouri, Tennessee, and West Virginia.

Prosperity and Tariff

In his inaugural President Hoover interpreted the election as an expression of the determination of the American people to continue business under private enterprise with as little government regulation as possible. He also referred to his favorite theme of prosperity. His purpose would be to "establish more firmly stability and security of business and employment and thereby remove poverty still further from our borders." Eight months thereafter the country had entered upon the depression.

Hoover called Congress to meet in special session, beginning April 15, 1929, to pass a new tariff law. Much to the President's disgust, Congress spent fourteen months in the drafting of this measure. In 1930, when it was at last finished, the Hawley-Smoot Act raised the rates on manufactured goods above the much criticized Fordney-McCumber measure. Then it increased heavily the rates on farm products. Its authors at least were proud of their work. Representative Hawley told the country: "A protective tariff creates prosperity, and in that economic condition all participate." This assertion was flatly contradicted by the prevailing widespread depression, which had begun in 1929.

Chapter 43

THE MAD DECADE

THE years between World War I and the advent of the New Deal have sometimes been labeled the "mad decade." It was a time of protest, disillusion, inquiry, experiment. Old traditions were under attack. Writers and artists were trying to discover or to create new standards in literature, in painting, and in life. Puritanism and Victorianism became labels of reproach, symbols of ways of living and thinking which emancipated moderns found hateful. Some of the postwar writers went in heavily for the new psychology, as one critic put it, according to the gospel of St. Freud. Others took their cue from the new sociology and emphasized the evil influence of a repressive environment. So-called "proletarian writers" made the dogma of Karl Marx their guide in both literature and literary criticism.

Literature and Art

Spirit of Disillusion

A few samples will serve to illustrate trends in American literature of the 1920's and 1930's, where the same trends were continued. Much of the writing had only contemporary significance and the books now are rarely disturbed on the library shelves. The spirit of disillusion was particularly evident in books about World War I. There was a feeling that the American people had been tricked into World War I and that our losses in money and men were nothing but useless sacrifice. These writers held that all talk about high ideals—"make the world safe for democracy"—was stupidity or nonsense or, worse yet, designed to cover up selfish ambitions. In *What Price Glory?* Laurence Stallings and Maxwell Anderson gave theater patrons a vivid touch of the "realism" of war with its filth, profanity, and lack of heroism. In *A Farewell to Arms* Ernest Hemingway taught the same lesson in a different setting.

The spirit of disillusion influenced even the writing of history. If human beings were so lacking in fundamental decency as modern writers said they were, there never could have been any greatness among men. Some historians began to "debunk" history. For example Rupert Hughes told his readers that most of what they thought they knew about George Washington was wrong.

It became fashionable to "debunk" American life as well as American history. The special targets were the small town and the rural areas. They were held up as hideous illustrations of the barrenness of American life. In *Spoon River Anthology* Edgar Lee Masters described life as he thought he saw it in a small midwestern town. According to Masters there was no decency in the people there, nothing but horror and cruelty. Writing in prose instead of verse, Erskine Caldwell in *Tobacco Road* described life in the South. His characters lived on a level considerably lower, morally and intellectually, than blooded hogs. John Steinbeck wrote of the Southwest and West. *Of Mice and Men* describes two wanderers hunting for work. In *Grapes of Wrath* Steinbeck professed to follow the misfortunes of farmers, driven out of Oklahoma by drought and poverty, on their way to California. In *Winesburg, Ohio,* and in *Many Marriages* Sherwood Anderson found his characters completely lost in frustration and futility.

Even one of the greatest American novelists of recent years, Sinclair Lewis, dealt largely in satire. In most of his work there was a tendency to ridicule or scorn both people and customs. In *Main Street* Lewis described conditions in the average small town of the Middle West. As he saw them, the people in Gopher Prairie were dull, bored, lacking in intellectual interests or emotional enthusiasm. Their type of life with its unchanging customs and traditions ruined the human beings who were so unfortunate as to have to stay there. The book stirred the wrath of readers in towns of the type described. These people argued that Lewis had drawn an incomplete picture, that he missed all the finer qualities which redeemed these communities.

In *Babbitt* Lewis professed to describe the everyday, commonplace existence of the businessman of the medium-sized city. Like *Main Street,* it was brilliant satire, and there were "Babbitts" in every city. But there were also plenty of businessmen as intelligent even as Sinclair Lewis. In drawing his characters, Lewis showed something familiar, but without the redeeming qualities which most people have. *Elmer Gantry* portrayed the soulless minister. Here religion was held up to ridicule and attack more bitter than anything since the *Age of Reason* of Tom Paine. *Dodsworth* was a manufacturer whose business had been so absorbing that he had forgotten how to live. *Arrowsmith* had more kindly qualities, dealing with the heroism of doctors pioneering in new fields.

Historical Novels

In general the novels of Willa Cather stood out in sharp contrast with those of Sinclair Lewis. In *My Antonia* and earlier in *O Pioneers!* she gave us characters who possessed the qualities which Lewis missed. Her people seemed just as real as Babbitt and his wife Myra. In *Shadows on the Rock* she did an artistic bit of historic description of early days in Quebec. And yet even Willa Cather wrote some bitter descriptions of small-town life.

Contemporary novelists described almost every aspect of American life. Edna Ferber's *Show Boat* recorded the interests and experiences of the old theatrical stock companies on the western rivers—and by so doing gave the stage a fine play and the radio an idea which has not been entirely exhausted yet. In *So Big* Miss Ferber described the growth of Chicago, typical of the great cities of the Middle West. Dorothy Canfield Fisher gave us scenes from sections as far apart as Kansas and Vermont.

During these years historical novelists tried to bring back the spirit of earlier times. Samuel Hopkins Adams told the story of Peggy O'Neal in

The Gorgeous Hussy. He gave a vivid picture of Jackson's administration. A somewhat different type of historical novel appeared in the works of Walter Edmonds. In *Erie Water* and *Rome Haul* he gave vivid pictures of life on the Erie Canal. In *Drums Along the Mohawk*, Edmonds dealt with life on the frontier of upstate New York during the American Revolution.

Margaret Mitchell's *Gone with the Wind* was a realistic story of the Civil War and reconstruction, written by a southerner. Miss Mitchell showed how the war and its aftermath worked on the characters and emotions of those who were caught in its storm. A widely popular best seller was Hervey Allen's *Anthony Adverse*. The plot and the characters ranged in time over three generations and in place from Europe to the West Indies, to Africa, back to Europe, and then to America. *Anthony Adverse* was fiction on a vast scale, in the heroic manner, touching on the whole list of human experience and feelings.

Poets and critics also tried to describe America. Of the poets, Robert Frost might be looked upon in some respects as the spiritual successor to Whittier. His theme was the countryside of northern New England. Carl Sandburg has shown America at work, on the farms and in the mills. Edwin Arlington Robinson has used verse as a means of inquiry into the problems of life and work. In a class by himself was Stephen Vincent Benét, who revived the epic, or heroic narrative poem, and applied it to an American theme. *John Brown's Body* was a story of both events and of human feeling of Civil War days. There is excellent verse in it, and sound history too.

For readers who liked to find evidence of thinking and of plot or intelligent planning in literature, a new type of "stream of consciousness" writing brought severe shocks. The most eminent leader in this school was Gertrude Stein, whose writings made no sense whatever to orthodox readers. She was, however, almost an object of worship among those American writers of the new era who chose to live in Paris. In some respects there is no better manifestation of the "mad decade" than the incomprehensibilities of Gertrude Stein.

Literature of the years following World War I helps to explain why some Americans were so alarmed over communism. There were communists among the writers, men and women who thought Karl Marx had found the way to universal understanding. These people judged American life by Marxian standards and found it all wrong. Life was good or bad depending on its loyalty or lack of it to Marxian ways. A book was good or bad depending on its attitude toward Marxian doctrine. Much of the literary criticism and comment was a direct reflection of Marxian philosophy.

Modern Art

If some writers of the 1920's were in a fog, some artists wandered around and worked in an atmosphere of chaos. These were the cubists, who believed that everything in art could be reduced to straight lines, angles, and geometrical figures. Along with them, but in a more complete chaos, were the futurists and surrealists. These people threw splashes of color on canvas and professed to see meaning in what they had done. It made little difference how their pictures were hung, because they were completely bewildering no matter how you looked at them. One puzzled critic put his feelings into a lecture which he entitled: "Are These Moderns Crazy, or Am I?" The more charitable commentators explained that the artists were merely striving to find their way in a new world. They looked upon cubism and surrealism as advanced, new forms.

Futurism apparently had its start among the fascists in Italy, who did their best to destroy civilization. F. T. Marinetti, a believer in the new art and the new barbarism, described it as "the battle cry of all the innovators, of the intellectual free lances of the world; it is the love of the new; the impassioned art of velocity, the systematic defamation of the antique, the old, the slow, the erudite and the professionals. . . . It is a box of dynamite for all the venerated ruins." Some futurists were people who wanted to be artists but who would not go through the long, hard work needed to learn the principles of drawing and painting. Others were rebels against established customs and standards. Cubists and futurists attracted attention, as undisciplined children always do, because they made a lot of noise.

Fortunately these eccentric rebels who specialized in splashes of color were not typical of American artists. There were men and women who broke away from conventional rules, but who worked with meaning and purpose which will make their pictures live. John Steuart Curry has made the West, past and present, come to life. His greatest work is in the murals in the capitol building at Topeka, Kansas. The central panel of John Brown is an unforgettable portrayal of a famous fanatic. Thomas Hart Benton, Grant Wood, and Doris Lee have given us vivid colorful scenes from American life, both town and country.

The "Red" Menace

American Communists

Proletarian literature was not the only cause of worry over communism. Because of Bolshevik claims that the alleged destruction of capitalism in Russia had brought immeasurable gains—claims entirely unsupported by evidence—like-minded agitators sought to destroy capitalism here; then the control of all instruments of transportation and production could be put into the hands of the workers. After the formation of the Bolshevist government American socialists divided into two groups, with the left wing working for close cooperation with Moscow. In 1919 the American branch of the Communist party was organized at Chicago, and its members advocated the destruction of the American constitutional and economic system. Although the State Department withheld recognition from the new regime in Russia, the Bolshevist authorities sent Ludwig C. A. K. Martens to this country to direct revolutionary activities here.

In addition to the Communist party itself, there were affiliated organizations trying to spread subversive influences. The Trade Union Educational League was created for the purpose of "boring from within" among labor unions to make them agents of communism. Some of the leaders of the Industrial Workers of the World were frankly communist. The Communist party and its affiliates may have had a total membership of perhaps 100,000. They were admired and encouraged by numerous "liberals" who professed to look to Russia for the regeneration of the world. These friends of Russia, characterized as "pinks" or "parlor Bolsheviks" to distinguish them from the real "Reds," exerted considerable influence, particularly in literary and even in some university circles.

During the year 1919 there were a number of outrages attributed to communist agitators. In April a bomb was found in the mail of Mayor Ole Hanson of Seattle; the mayor had made himself conspicuous by opposing communist agitators in his city. On the very next day a parcel post package was delivered at the home of Senator Hardwick in Atlanta, Georgia; the package exploded in the hands of the servant. Senator Hardwick had taken the position that undesirable foreign agitators should be denied admission in the United States. When the newspapers reported on the explosion at Senator Hardwick's home, a clerk in the New York post office recognized something very familiar in the description of the package; he had put sixteen similar packages aside and held them for insufficient postage. When opened they were found to contain bombs. Among the addressees were some of the most prominent men in the country; Attorney General Palmer, Postmaster General Burleson, Justice Holmes, J. P. Morgan, and John D. Rockefeller, Sr. Two months later Attorney General Palmer's house in Washington was badly damaged by a bomb. More than a year later, on September 16, 1920, there was a terrific explosion at the corner of Broad and Wall Streets, New York; thirty people were killed outright, and several hundred more were injured. This corner was directly opposite the offices of J. P. Morgan and Company, and the Morgan establishment was badly damaged. The men responsible for these explosions were never discovered.

If these efforts to destroy isolated Americans by violence had been the only evidence of subversive activity, the American people might have become enraged but not necessarily alarmed. Other activities, however, gave grounds for apprehension. In Seattle, Washington, a strike of the workers in the shipyards was expanded, in accordance with communist technique, into a general strike which almost paralyzed economic activities throughout the city. Here the I.W.W. was responsible. Then on Armistice Day the American Legion parade in Centralia, Washington, was fired upon, and four men were killed. Again the I.W.W. was held responsible.

Economic Disturbances

Further evidence of widespread unrest in this same year of 1919 was found in an epidemic of strikes throughout the country and in the proof that communists were using some of them for their own purposes. According to the Department of Labor, there were 3374 separate strikes in this one year, with more than 4,000,000 workers involved. Among the more spectacular of these was the great strike of the steel workers, lasting from September 1919 to January 1920, during which 350,000 employees left work.

There was no question that the workers suffered genuine grievances. Nearly half the employees were working on twelve-hour shifts, and 25 percent of them worked seven days per week. The average length of the working week for all employees in the steel mills was sixty-eight and one half hours. But the leader of the strike was a communist, William Z. Foster. He defined the purpose of the strike in communist terms—that is, to put the workers in full control of the steel mills. This aspect of the strike attracted wide attention, so much so that it served to conceal the actual grievances. In the words of one historian, the steel strike "was, without question, the most terrific battle between capital and labor and the most disastrous defeat for organized labor in the twentieth century."

While the steel strike was in progress the United Mine Workers, numbering 425,000, went out on strike. They demanded a reduction of the working week to thirty hours, together with a 60 percent increase in wages. This latter demand they justified partly on the ground of high living costs, partly on the excessive profits taken by the mine owners. The owners, however, insisted that any increase in wages must result in higher prices for coal. When the strike threatened to interfere with both industrial production and with railroad transportation, President Wilson interfered. The President urged the miners to remain at work while a special commission investigated the problem. Officials of the union refused to comply with his request. The President then characterized the strike as both unjustifiable and unlawful and, further, as "a grave moral and legal wrong against the government and people of the United States." Technically the United States was still at war, so the government invoked the emergency powers granted under the Lever Act. Attorney General Palmer secured an injunction which prohibited the United Mine Workers from giving any support to the strike. The wartime Fuel Administration was revived, and troops were sent into the mining areas. A second injunction required the officials to call off the strike within three days; under vehement protests the union complied. Then, following further investigations, the miners were awarded an advance in wages of 27 percent, but the working week was not shortened.

Boston Police Strike

These two strikes were particularly important, not only because of the number of workers involved and the wide area affected but because they were both concerned with economic processes essential to the established industrial system. Another strike, directly concerning only 1500 men and a single city, Boston, Massachusetts, attracted nation-wide attention. The members of the Boston police force complained that their salaries were too low to meet the heavy increase in the cost of living. They asked for higher pay, and they also wanted the city to provide their uniforms. To give point to their demands they formed a union and received a charter from the American Federation of Labor. Under Massachusetts law the Boston police were under the direction of a commissioner appointed by the governor; Commissioner Curtis refused to approve the demands of the men, and he denied their right to organize under the A.F. of L. Early in September the commissioner suspended the patrolmen who had secured the Federation's charter, and then practically the whole police force went out on strike. For one night the city of Boston was the scene of disorder and looting, but this was confined to the downtown area. Residential areas were not affected. On the afternoon following the strike the mayor had militia forces on patrol duty, and the danger of serious lawlessness was over.

Samuel Gompers, president of the American Federation of Labor, urged Governor Calvin Coolidge to revoke the orders of the commissioner and to restore the suspended policemen. Coolidge, however, gave his support to the commissioner, and telegraphed a reply to Gompers which became famous: "There is no right to strike against the public safety by anybody, anywhere, any time." President Wilson praised Coolidge, and on the strength of this episode Coolidge became a political figure of national importance. Then the police commmissioner organized a new police force, recruited largely from veterans of World War I. Not a member of the old force was ever reappointed.

Conservative Reaction

Restricting the Reds

In the United States, government authorities find it difficult to deal with attacks upon the established order, partly because of the constitutional guarantees of freedom of speech and of the press and partly because advocates of a new order, Communists, for example, can always masquerade as honest liberals. Attorney General Palmer in his annual report showed that hundreds of periodicals of the foreign language press in this country were advocating a forcible change in our form of government. He believed that there were 2500 dangerous agitators actively at work here. On November 7, 1919, acting under orders of the secretary of labor, federal agents in various parts of the country arrested more than 250 conspicuous radical agitators. Other radicals were under detention in New York, charged with entering the country in violation of immigration laws. Then the Attorney General hit upon the notion of shipping some of these unwanted troublemakers to Russia. Under his orders 249 of them were loaded on the transport *Buford,* henceforth nicknamed the "Soviet Ark," and consigned to their spiritual home. This action had its ironic aspects, especially so when it transpired that some of the loudest agitators found Russia even more distasteful than the United States.

In view of their long-continued advocacy of revolution as the approved method of bringing economic and political change, American socialists could hardly be surprised to find themselves classed with the Reds and treated accordingly. Postmaster General Burleson closed the United States mail to a single issue of a socialist journal, the *Masses,* and then refused to allow it regular mailing rates on the ground that it had ceased to be a periodical. In New York City soldiers and sailors attacked a socialist mass meeting. Mayor Hylan of the same city prohibited the display of the socialist emblem, the red flag. Victor Berger, elected to Congress in Wisconsin, was refused admission. In New York the legislature appointed the Lusk Committee to investigate radical and subversive activity and propaganda for the purpose of protecting school children from dangerous doctrines. In April 1920 the same legislature voted to exclude five Socialist assemblymen on the ground that they were members of "a disloyal organization composed exclusively of perpetual traitors." *The New York Times* characterized the expulsion as patriotic and declared: "An immense majority of the American people will approve and sanction the Assembly's action." On the other hand the New York Bar Association, under the leadership of Charles Evans Hughes, published a formal protest against the expulsion.

Teachers' Oaths

Because of some specific evidence and a great deal of vague fear that teachers in schools and colleges had become infected with radicalism, state legislatures passed laws requiring teachers to take oaths of loyalty. The first appeared in Rhode Island in the war year of 1917; the others came later, evidently springing from some common source. The Rhode Island law required every teacher in the state to pledge allegiance to the United States, to the state of Rhode Island, and to the American public school system; he must uphold the constitutions of his state and of the nation. Then the teacher must promise "to protect the school rights of my pupils, to conserve the democracy of school citizenship, to honor public education as a principle of free government, to respect the profession of education as a public service, and to observe its ethical principles and rules of professional conduct." He must promise to teach principles of loyalty to the government, and public officials, "honor to the flag, obedience to law and government."

By 1936 twenty-two states had enacted teachers' oath laws. The oath required in New York, in a law passed in 1934, was much shorter than the Rhode Island measure: "I do solemnly swear (or affirm) that I will support the Constitution of the United States of America and the Constitution of the State of New York, and that I will faithfully discharge, according to the best of my ability, the duties of the position of . . ." The Georgia law of 1935 perhaps defined most clearly the real purposes of this type of legislation. There the teacher promised to "refrain from directly or indirectly subscribing to or teaching any theory of government or economics or of social relations which is inconsistent with the fundamental principles of patriotism and high ideals of Americanism."

Why should any patriotic teacher have hesitated to subscribe to these principles? Certainly not because of the principles, but rather because of the ulterior motives of the promoters of these oaths and more particularly because of the unwarranted implication that as a class teachers were disloyal. It would be difficult to find a more loyal or patriotic group of American citizens than the teachers in our schools and colleges. They resented the notion that they were untrustworthy and opposed the oath bills on this account. Still other opponents of this type of legislation did not like some of the individuals and organizations who sponsored it. Then there was the added consideration that in the case of patriotic teachers the oaths were useless. In the few cases where teachers believed in overthrowing the American social and political order, such an oath would have not the slightest restraining influence. The oaths were unnecessary in the vast number of cases and futile in the isolated instances where action was really needed.

The New Klan

One of the most important factors in creating unrest and uneasiness was the Ku Klux Klan. This was not the southern organization of post-Civil War days brought back to life, but a new creation. The name, the costume or uniform, and the principle of secrecy were taken over from precedents of that earlier troubled era, and so too were the methods of suppressing dissent. The new Klan seems to have had its inception in an intensified wave of hostility toward Negroes, which followed the showing of D. W. Griffith's famous film *The Birth of a Nation*. The Klan's founder was William J. Simmons of Atlanta, Georgia. He had secured a charter from the legislature of Georgia in 1916. During its earlier career the Klan failed to take hold, and when the war ended it could boast of only a few hundred members. Then Edward Y. Clarke hit upon the scheme of sending out recruiting officers and paying them on a commission basis. The membership fee was $10.00, and the solicitors, known as Kleagles, kept $4.00 out of each $10.00. By 1925 the Klan had a membership of 5,000,000 men.

According to its constitution the Ku Klux Klan aimed to unite

> white male persons, native-born Gentile citizens . . . to cultivate and promote patriotism toward our Civil Government . . . to maintain forever white supremacy; [and, among other things,] to conserve, protect, and maintain the distinctive institutions, rights, privileges, principles, traditions and ideals of a pure Americanism.

Actually the Klan was devoted to the encouragement of prejudice—prejudice of whites against Negroes, of Gentiles against Jews, and of Protestants against Catholics. Dressed in their long, white, flowing robes, announcing their presence by a giant flaming cross on some conspicuous hill, the Klansmen worked to establish what they called Americanism. For those individuals who failed to meet with their approval they applied coats of tar and feathers. Sometimes they went further and subjected their victims to violence or serious torture. Or they might fall back on economic pressure and boycott. Then the Klan went into politics, to control both nominations and elections; it dominated politics and government in California, Arkansas, Indiana, Ohio, Oklahoma, Oregon, and Texas, and for a time it was influential in Louisiana, Massachusetts, and New York.

It was not so plain during the 1920's, but it is abundantly clear now that the Klan closely resembled those political structures which fastened dictatorships all over Europe. In the beginning the fascists in Italy and the nazis in Germany were political parties, operating in secrecy, setting themselves above both government and the law, ignoring established rights in order to promote their own brand of tyranny, and steadily increasing their strength by acts of violence. That the Klan did not go so far here as its counterparts did in Europe was perhaps due to the force of long-established traditions opposed to lawless tyranny.

Sacco and Vanzetti

Anyone who attempts to review the tangled story of social change and public opinion during the decade of the 1920's is bound to be impressed, first, with the extent of ill-defined fear aroused by the Reds and, second, with the uncertain groping for adequate defenses against the danger. This state of mind sometimes resulted in activity bordering on the hysterical. An internationally famous trial in the suburban town of Dedham, Massachusetts, can be understood only in the light of the prevailing confusion. In April 1920 a paymaster of South Braintree was murdered. Two weeks after the murder the authorities arrested two Italian radicals, Sacco and Vanzetti, and the grand jury indicted them on a charge of first degree murder. After a much criticized trial, the jury found them guilty. Repercussions of the conviction were amazing. Outside the Boston area Americans had paid little attention to the trial. In Europe, on the other hand, radicals had followed the case with intense interest, and on the report of the conviction these European agitators staged a series of demonstrations. A bomb was even set off in the residence of the American ambassador in Paris.

Following these demonstrations counsel for the convicted men and a large number of sympathetic friends began a campaign for a new trial. They called attention to the notoriously hostile atmosphere of the courtroom at Dedham where the trial had taken place; spectators, jury, prosecuting attorney, and even the presiding justice, Webster Thayer, made no attempt to conceal their antagonism to the accused. Testimony was accepted from witnesses of notoriously unreliable character, and the prosecuting attorney was accused of rigging the evidence. Evidence that Vanzetti had been miles away from South Braintree at the time of the murder was ignored. A member of the state police, testifying as an expert on firearms, explained, under carefully framed questions, that the markings on the bullet found in the murdered man's body "were consistent with" markings on bullets fired from Vanzetti's pistol. Vanzetti, by the way, explained that as a traveling fish peddler he carried a gun for his own protection. After the trial the state policeman explained that he answered as he did because of the way the question had been put. Had he been asked the straight question as to whether or not the bullet had been fired from Vanzetti's gun, he would have been obliged to answer no. Members of the court and some of the newspapers seemed to proceed on one of two possible assumptions: the men were necessarily guilty because they were radicals, or, even if innocent of the murder, they deserved to die because of their radicalism.

Efforts of the friends of the accused resulted in delaying the death sentence until 1927. After the men were sentenced Governor Fuller of Massachusetts appointed a special commission, with President Abbott Lawrence Lowell of Harvard at its head, to review the trial and to advise him with reference to a widespread demand that the convicted men be pardoned.

This commission went back over the case and reported that on the basis of the evidence before the Court the conviction was just. The governor decided not to pardon the men, and in August 1927 they were executed.

Religion and Morals

In every period of social turmoil, when the security afforded by settled modes of thought and behavior seems to be imperiled, conservatives who try to defend established principles are accused of intolerance and intransigeance; on the other hand, all who show interest in change are branded as dangerous radicals. This principle, made abundantly clear in disputes over economics and politics, was demonstrated once more in theology. Here the controversy between liberals and conservatives resulted in another court proceeding, one which attracted more attention in the United States than the Sacco-Vanzetti case.

During the 1870's and thereafter, the Darwinian concept of evolution and the philosophy which developed from it had tended to undermine belief in the accepted account of Creation as reported in the book of Genesis. Roman Catholics were not affected by this debate, but the various Protestant evangelical denominations were divided into two factions. In 1910 these two groups received new names, and the old controversy was revived and intensified. In that year Protestant churches circulated millions of copies of a little book entitled *The Fundamentals, A Testimony to the Truth.* These fundamentals, described as basic and essential in all Christian belief, were the virgin birth, the physical resurrection of Christ, the second coming of Christ, the doctrine of the atonement, and the divine origin and absolute inerrancy of the Bible. From this time on the two great factions in Protestantism were known as Fundamentalists and Modernists.

Fundamentalism

Fundamentalism was looked upon as a challenge to modern scientific thought, and the Fundamentalists pointed to the doctrine of evolution as the root of all theological errors of the day. The clash extended beyond the churches because the Fundamentalists called upon state governments to uphold their position; they demanded laws to prohibit teaching of the doctrine of evolution. Bills for this purpose were introduced in more than twenty legislatures. In Oklahoma, Mississippi, and Tennessee the bills became laws. The Tennessee statute provided that

> it shall be unlawful for any teacher in any of the universities, normals and all other public schools of the State, which are supported in whole or in part by the public school funds of the State, to teach any theory that denies the story of the Divine creation of man as taught in the Bible, and to teach instead that man has descended from a lower order of animals.

According to the Fundamentalists, such laws were necessary to protect children and youths from doctrines which would undermine religious faith and so destroy the possibility of eternal happiness. The proponents justified the measures on the ground that taxpayers should decide what the public schools ought to teach.

This Tennessee law came before the state courts in a case involving John T. Scopes, a teacher of biology in the high school of Dayton. The case originated from the mixed motives of a desire to test the constitutionality of the law, and in the words of the leading actors in the drama, "to put Dayton on the map." A group of young men, including Scopes himself, meeting in a drugstore in the town, made arrangements to have Scopes caught in the act of teaching evolution. Then he had to be arrested. His arrest took place on May 9, 1925, and at once and for weeks thereafter Dayton became one of the most famous places in the United States. William Jennings Bryan, who had retired from politics and was dividing his time between selling Florida real estate and proclaiming Fundamentalism, offered his services to the prosecution. The Civil Liberties Bureau of New York provided Scopes with three of the ablest lawyers in the country: Clarence Darrow, Dudley Field Malone, and Arthur Garfield Hays. The trial was set for July 1925. Here at last the contest between the Fundamentalists and the Modernists had been brought into the open.

Scopes Case

Before the trial, more than one hundred newspaper correspondents went to Dayton and twenty-two telegraph operators came to handle the business. The court opened with prayer. The indictment stated that Scopes "did unlawfully, wilfully teach in the public schools . . . certain theory and theories that deny the story of the Divine Creation of man as taught in the Bible, and did teach instead that man has descended from a lower order of animals." The state's attorney general accused Scopes of teaching a doctrine which was "undermining the faith of Tennessee's children and robbing them of their chance of eternal life."

The course of the trial was marked by bitter intolerance on both sides. Accusing Darrow of aiming "to slur at the Bible," Bryan proclaimed his determination "to protect the word of God against the greatest atheist and agnostic in the United States." Darrow in turn spoke scornfully of what he called Bryan's "fool religion." He was determined, he said, "to show up Fundamentalism" and "to prevent bigots and ignoramuses from controlling the educational system of the United States."

The jury at the Dayton courthouse found Scopes guilty as charged, and the judge imposed a fine of $100. Then the defense carried the case on appeal to the state supreme court. In 1927 it upheld the constitutionality of the antievolution law, but it let Scopes off with no penalty. The trial settled nothing—except perhaps that it might be unwise to teach evolution in Tennessee. The basic issue—that is, the truth or falsity of a given proposition in theology—could not be determined in a court of law.

Following the trial at Dayton the Fundamentalists organized two societies to spread their cause throughout the country: these were the Supreme Kingdom and the Bible Crusaders of America. Then the campaign against evolution was carried beyond the public school area into the colleges and universities but without appreciable success. In 1926 the Southern Baptist Convention adopted the following resolution and so aligned itself more clearly than ever on the side of the Fundamentalists: "This convention accepts Genesis as teaching man was a special creation of God and rejects every theory, evolutionary or otherwise, which teaches that man originated or came by way of lower animal ancestry."

That type of conservatism which tolerates no change in established customs was given another field for action during the 1920's in a campaign for dress reform. It was not the clothing of men which attracted attention and inspired adverse comment; it was that of the women, particularly of the younger generation. The issue was stated clearly in a "Tract on Modern Dress Reform," with the subtitle: "As It Was in the Days of Sodom." According to the author, who chose to remain anonymous: "The shocking attire worn by some women on the street, in public assemblies, and even in church, has led the writer to start this dress reform movement in the attempt to safeguard our rising generation, by creating a public sentiment against these immoral tendencies." The evil tendencies were described in detail, with the general conclusion: "Surely it is a sad comment on the awful drift of the times, when we look at the ordinary dress worn by women today, and remember that even a harlot would not have been permitted to wear such attire on the streets only a few years ago." President Murphree of the University of Florida entered the campaign. He announced that the "low-cut gowns, the rolled hose and short skirts are born of the Devil and his angels, and are carrying the present and future generations to chaos and destruction." A group of prominent dowagers in New York urged the formation of a society to oppose the prevailing fashions which they said were characterized by "an excess of nudity." Even *The New York Times* entered the campaign with a declaration that "the American woman has lifted her skirts far beyond any modest limitation," and this too when skirts were only a mere nine inches from the floor! The YWCA also launched a national campaign against "immodest dress."

Dress Reform

The author of the tract submitted a "Dress Reform Pledge," designed to end the dangers inherent in the prevailing fashions. The signers bound themselves as follows: "I promise to abstain from all appearance of immodest dress—such as: Low neck—Exposing back and chest. Short sleeves —Less than three-quarter length. Short skirts—above shoe tops. Thin gauzy waists, exposing the skin." In Philadelphia a "Dress Reform Committee" of prominent citizens sent out a questionnaire to a thousand representative clergymen, asking them to submit their views with reference to proper dress for women. Then the Committee designed a "moral gown," a garment endorsed by ministers of fifteen different denominations. This "moral gown" was of loose fit, with sleeves reaching below the elbows, and with the hem of the skirt not more than seven and one-half inches from the floor.

After the manner of the Fundamentalists, the advocates of dress reform turned to the state legislatures for support. In 1921 the legislature of Utah debated a bill which provided fine and imprisonment for women who should appear on the street with skirts higher than three inches above the ankle. In Virginia someone proposed a bill forbidding any woman from wearing either blouse or evening gown which should reveal "more than three inches of her throat." In Ohio the reformers would have prescribed a two-inch limit. The Ohio proposal went even further. It would have prohibited the sale of any "garment which unduly displays or accentuates the lines of the female figure," and it also prohibited any "female over fourteen years of age" from wearing "a skirt which does not reach to that part of the foot known as the instep." But the women continued to wear what they liked, and by 1927 skirts reached only to the knees.

Prohibition and Racketeering

The most ambitious and by far the most comprehensive of these efforts to make people virtuous by law was the experiment with nation-wide prohibition. Here was a social experiment of magnificent proportions. Like the anti-Red, antievolution, and antirevealing-dress laws, the legislation against liquor was derived from a theory of general welfare; it was the duty of the government to protect the people from anything injurious. There was nothing new in the opposition to alcohol, but there was something new in the efficient direction of the drive and in its temporary success.

Eighteenth Amendment

The effective agent in making nation-wide prohibition a reality was the Anti-Saloon League. First launched in 1893, this body soon spread its direct influence over thirty states and acquired a mailing list of 500,000 persons. Its membership was drawn largely from the Protestant evangelical churches, those dynamic bodies which had played such an important part in the drive for moral reform during the 1830's. The Anti-Saloon League differed from other temperance organizations, the Women's Christian Temperance Union, for example, in two important particulars. Instead of relying on voluntary effort, it recruited an impressive staff of paid workers. Also, instead of devoting itself to the methods of education and moral suasion, it went directly into politics. The League was nonpartisan and it threw its support to any candidate who would pledge himself to endorse the program of the League. By 1914 a majority of members of the national House of Representatives were avowed supporters of the League.

The campaign to end the liquor traffic began in earnest in 1913. Working first to capture the states, in the course of four years the League had secured some sort of antiliquor law in twenty-six; local option laws restricted the sale of liquor in several others. Then the entrance of the United States into World War I strengthened the cause of the prohibitionists. It was argued that more than $1,000,000,000 was tied up in the liquor business which in no way contributed to the cause of winning the war. The makers of malt and distilled liquors used 100,000,000 bushels of grain at a time when the Allies were hard pressed for food. Again the liquor business employed thousands of able-bodied men who could be used more advantageously in war industries or in the army. The enemy in the war was Germany, and many of the brewers were of German origin; it was a patriotic duty to deprive them of their business.

Introduced in Congress in 1917, the Eighteenth Amendment passed the Senate by the substantial vote of 65 to 20, and the House by 282 to 128. Although the House did not vote until December 1917, so that the proposal could not be submitted to the states until after that date, Mississippi had ratified it by January 8, 1918. Inside of fourteen months the necessary three fourths of the states had acted favorably, and in the end all but two states, Connecticut and Rhode Island, ratified the Amendment. The measure was proclaimed in effect on January 16, 1920, one year after ratification. It remained in effect until its repeal in December 1933.

The Eighteenth Amendment prohibited the manufacture, transportation, and sale of alcoholic liquor for use as beverages. The Amendment also provided that Congress and the several states should have concurrent power to enforce this article by appropriate legislation. Precisely what this section meant was never satisfactorily determined. Even the best constitutional lawyers could not agree whether the provision was mandatory or merely permissive. Not all states passed measures of enforcement and some of those which did so repealed them before the experiment came to an end.

To make the Eighteenth Amendment effective Congress, in October 1919, enacted the so-called Volstead Act, passed over President Wilson's veto. This measure defined intoxicating beverages as any which contained more than one half of 1 percent of alcohol; then it laid down regulations with reference to the manufacture and sale of alcohol for industrial, ecclesiastical, and medicinal purposes. It also permitted the manufacture and sale of beer, provided the alcoholic content was reduced to one half of 1 percent.

Lack of Enforcement

With the ratification of the Eighteenth Amendment and the passing of the Volstead Act, members of the Anti-Saloon League considered the battle won. Events proved that they were unduly optimistic. At first responsibility for enforcement was put in the hands of the Prohibition Bureau, a branch of the Treasury Department. Under Harding's associates, enforcement was directed in part to the enrichment of the officials in charge. In 1925 a director of prohibition was appointed, but by that time the facilities for producing and distributing illicit liquor had already outrun the capacity of the government to deal with the offenders. In 1930 the machinery of enforcement was transferred from the Treasury to the Department of Justice but with no gain in efficiency. Part of the fault lay with Congress, which would never appropriate money enough to provide a sufficiently large staff of officials. But the basic difficulty was the attitude of the American people. They went into the experiment in a moment of exalted enthusiasm. This enthusiasm cooled rapidly, and as it cooled some people missed their liquor.

Under prohibition the licensed dealer was replaced by the bootlegger, while the speakeasy succeeded the legally operated saloon. Distilled spirits became popular and the pocket flask became common. During the first months of prohibition some individuals devoted their spare time to practical aspects of the study of chemistry, the results of which were at least alcoholic if not appetizing. But the making of home brew or bathtub gin was a messy business, and the amateurs were soon replaced by professionals. Some of the stuff sold was sheer poison. One commentator wrote: "There are those still alive in America who can recall a period in the nation's history when it took years, instead of just one night, for a man to drink himself to death. That day is gone. The Demon Rum has been abolished. In its stead Americans now drink hair tonic, sheep dip, coffin varnish, and other inoffensive beverages."

As time went on the quality of illicit liquor seems to have undergone improvement. At least the Wickersham Commission reported in 1930:

> With the perfection and discovery of new methods of distilling alcohol, the illicit distillery has become for the time being the chief source of supply. In consequence . . . a steady volume of whisky, much of it of good quality, is put in circulation at cheap prices. . . . The improved methods, the perfection of organization, the ease of production, the cheapness and easy accessibility of materials, the abundance of localities where such plants can be operated with a minimum risk of discovery, the ease with which they can be concealed and the huge profits involved, have enabled this business to become established to an extent which makes it very difficult to put to an end.

Because the liquor dealers operated outside the law, it was possible for enterprising gangsters to take charge of the bootleg industry in given localities and to control the business in their own interest. Bootleg liquor sometimes sold at the rate of $10 per bottle, perhaps even more. The actual cost of making whisky, including labor, materials, and overhead, was perhaps 20 cents per gallon. If this gallon were sold at retail, drink by drink in the speakeasy, at the rate of 50 cents per drink, the return might be as high as $40. It is not surprising that rival gangsters fought bitterly for the control of such profitable enterprises.

By 1930 it was evident that prohibition had failed to solve the liquor problem. The preliminary report of the Wickersham Commission helped to explain why, and the final report, submitted in 1931, showed that many thoughtful Americans favored repeal. When the Presidential campaign of 1932 came around, the issue of repeal almost took precedence over the depression, and both major parties had to announce a policy. The Democrats came out strongly for repeal of the Eighteenth Amendment and the Volstead Act. Under President Hoover's influence the Republican party, on the other hand, proposed a new amendment to the Constitution, a curious wet-dry affair described by one writer as "a logical and constitutional monstrosity whose provisions would have been even more unworkable than the Eighteenth Amendment." According to this program, the Republicans would submit an amendment

Repeal

the provisions of which, while retaining in the Federal Government power to preserve the gains already made in dealing with the evils inherent in the liquor traffic, shall allow States to deal with the problem as their citizens may determine, but subject always to the power of the Federal Government to protect those States where prohibition may exist and safeguard our citizens everywhere from the return of the saloon and attendant abuses.

In 1933 the Twenty-first Amendment repealed the Eighteenth, and the "noble experiment" was over.

Prohibition failed of its objective—that is, to put an end to the use of liquor for beverage purposes—because a substantial portion of the American people did not favor this objective. Another factor which helped strengthen the demand for repeal was the desire to turn some of the profits from the lucrative liquor business into revenue for the government. The demand for repeal came to a climax in the depth of the depression when the need for revenue was acute. So the desire to impose state and federal taxes on a flourishing business supported other causes working toward repeal.

Crime Wave

Still another consideration strengthening the movement for repeal was the alarming relationship between the illicit liquor business and crimes of violence, particularly homicide. Carried on outside of the protecting forces of the law, the liquor business was subject to attack by criminals who victimized each other. Manufacturers and dealers therefore provided their own form of protection, a form which necessarily depended upon violence. Then, as pointed out above, enterprising spirits in various localities took charge of the liquor business and built up profitable monopolies. These monopolies were maintained by the expedient of killing off rivals. Sometimes the successful promoter would arrange for an alliance with the police and perhaps with higher authorities, so corruption of government and crimes of violence went together.

The most famous illustration of this system was afforded by Al Capone and his gang. In 1920 Capone went to Chicago to assist a prosperous beer king. In the short interval of three years the newcomer had ousted the former leader and had taken full charge of the liquor business in Chicago. He had a gang of 700 thugs working for him, all provided with weapons, including machine guns. Between 1920 and 1930 there were more than 500 gangster murders in Chicago, murders which went unpunished. The Capone outfit provided the liquor for most of the speakeasies in Chicago, estimated at 10,000 in number. According to some guesses the gang took in $60,000,000 annually. Here was a new and sinister force in America, a force which if carried to its logical end might disrupt the political structure. Finally federal agents succeeded in bringing Mr. Capone to trial, not on charges connected with the liquor business nor with the murders which were a necessary part of his system but simply because he had falsified his income tax returns. For this offense he spent nine years in a federal prison in California.

Closely connected with these organized liquor gangs and continuing for some years after repeal was another form of organized crime known as the racket. Racketeers levied tribute upon honest businessmen. The operator and his agents would visit the places of business in a specific line—dry cleaners, for example. The proprietors were invited to pay the racketeer regular sums for "protection." The sum demanded might be large, so large that the victim would refuse to pay. Then the racketeer would subject the recalcitrant to violence and his place of business to partial or complete destruction. The racketeers were safe from prosecution, partly because any victim who reported to the authorities would be killed, partly because the racketeers were in league with local political party leaders or even with public officials so that they were safeguarded against prosecution. In 1929 there were probably seventy-five separate rackets in Chicago. In New York the situation became so bad because of the interrelations of racketeers and influential politicians that the governor appointed a special district attorney to uncover evidence against the rackets and to break them up. The appointee was a young lawyer by the name of Thomas E. Dewey.

Chapter 44

ECONOMIC PROBLEMS OF THE 1920'S

Hard Times for Agriculture

CHANGES in the patterns of social life in the United States gave rise to uneasiness and sometimes resulted in restrictions on freedom, but they did not really injure people. Economic changes on the other hand culminated in the most serious depression this country had ever known. The farmers were the first sufferers. Circumstances beyond their control restricted their markets, cut their prices, and plunged them by the thousand into bankruptcy. With half the population living in rural areas and the other half partly dependent on rural buying power, the troubles of the farmers became a national problem.

Wartime Prosperity

It will be recalled that once World War I was under way the Allied powers began to buy increased quantities of foodstuffs from the United States. When this country entered the struggle the government put immediate pressure upon the farmers to increase their output. They did so and thus helped to create the postwar problem in agriculture. Between 1910 and 1920 the total farm acreage increased from 878,798,325 to 955,883,715. Between 1915 and the peak in 1921 the acreage devoted to wheat alone was increased by 3,227,000. This increase in acreage was accompanied by a rise in the value of farm lands and farm property from a total of $41,000,000,000 in 1910 to $78,000,000,000 in 1920. This increased investment in farming was accompanied by a substantial rise in the value of farm products. The following table gives some idea of this advance.

ANNUAL VALUE OF FARM PRODUCTS IN BILLIONS OF DOLLARS

Year	Value	Year	Value
1900	5	1917	19.33
1905	6.25	1918	22.5
1910	9	1919	23.75
1915	10.75	1920	18.33
1916	13.5	1921	12.5

Farmers in most lines were subjected to a double urge to increase production—governmental pressure and rising prices—and they responded as the wheat farmers did. In 1914 the acreage planted to cotton was 53,500,000; in 1919 the figure was 75,500,000. From 1914 to 1919 the number of beef cattle on the farms increased from 36,000,000 to 45,000,000. For several years before the war the price of wheat had averaged about $1.06 per bushel; in 1919 it sold for $2.58 on the farm, or $2.78 in the market. From 1900 to 1914 the price of cotton had averaged slightly more than 13 cents per pound; early in 1921 the price stood at 40 cents. At the peak, corn sold for $2.00 a bushel, oats for $1.00. In South Dakota, good farm land sold at better than

$300 per acre. Between 1914 and 1919 the buying power of farmers more than doubled. In one newly settled section of Montana, homesteaders who got their land for nothing began to raise wheat, and they made a yield of twenty to forty bushels per acre; this meant an average gross return of $60 per acre. For a time everybody was rich.

Postwar Bankruptcy

In 1921 this brief era of magnificent prosperity came to an abrupt end. The price of wheat dropped from its high level to 90 cents, cotton to 20 cents; then it gradually slid down to 6. From 1920 to 1921 the buying power of farmers was cut almost in half. From this latter year, and for the rest of the decade, on the basis of any rational accounting system, large numbers of farmers were losing money. In 1924 the Department of Agriculture reported that 600,000 farmers were bankrupt, and of this number 230,000 lost their land to their creditors; others kept their land because the creditors did not know what to do with it. The volume of farm mortgages had increased from $3,320,470,000 in 1910 to $9,241,390,000 in 1930. As for the bankers who loaded themselves up with farm paper at high valuations, they failed by the hundred. By 1924 in Minnesota, Montana, and the two Dakotas 550 banks had failed; in the state of Montana alone one third of the banks had failed, and the end was nowhere in sight.

The causes of this crash were partly domestic in origin, partly foreign. The abnormal increase in acreage would necessarily have forced a readjustment after the war. After the crash farmers were inclined to forget that much of this increase had been voluntary on their part in an effort to make money from the high prices; they attributed the whole thing to government urging and then blamed the government when the bottom dropped out. But there were other causes, less obvious perhaps but even more significant and more disturbing for the future.

In Europe the wheat-growing nations soon resumed production. At the same time some of the newer countries in the Western world, Argentina and Canada for example, increased their output. These various countries could produce wheat more cheaply than the United States. In 1923 the wheat-exporting countries of the world had a surplus, over and above the total annual requirements of the wheat-importing countries, amounting all told to 350,000,000 bushels. Under these conditions prices had to come down.

If the population of the United States had continued to increase at the rate maintained during the last forty years of the nineteenth century, the people might have caught up with increased agricultural productivity. This, however, was not the case. The natural increase was declining in rate while the new policy of restricted immigration cut off an appreciable potential increase from Europe. At the same time improved agricultural methods made it possible to increase the yield per acre without increased cost, so a smaller area of land was needed to raise food for the nation. Still another factor operated to cut down demand. Farmers were turning from horses and mules to tractors so the demand for fodder actually declined. In the South the falling price of cotton marked the end of prosperity.

For these economic ills the farmers, in addition to blaming the government because it had encouraged them to take on additional land during the war, also blamed the Federal Reserve Board because of its policy of deflation after 1920. The Reserve banks had rediscounted farm paper, as they were allowed to do under the Federal Reserve Act of 1913. When the Federal Reserve officials realized how the security behind this paper was shrinking in value, they ordered the loans called. This policy put both the farmers and their local bankers into bankruptcy. Farmers believed that a little delay would have saved the banks.

If the government was responsible for the troubles of the farmers—which was not the case—the logical remedy was governmental action. In the summer of 1921, therefore, a coalition of Democratic and Republican members of Congress tried to help the farmers. This was the Farm Bloc, and it included perhaps twenty Senators and one hundred Representatives. Even though the Bloc was a minority, it was able to exert substantial influence on congressional policy. Behind the Farm Bloc in Congress there was the organized power of the American Farm Bureau Federation, backed by 1500 county farm bureaus. The Farm Bloc compelled Congress to pass the Agricultural Credits Act, providing for the establishment of twelve intermediate credit banks. These new banks were authorized to discount farmers' notes which had been taken by local banks and to lend on the security of livestock, growing crops, and farm equipment. The law also provided for still another set of lending agencies, the National Agricultural Credit Corporations, to be operated as private enterprises. If credit could save the farmers, they would have been restored to prosperity. But credit, even low-cost credit, could not help.

Farm Bloc

The basic troubles, however, were falling prices and narrowing markets; loans could not solve these problems. As the product of a Vermont farm, Coolidge felt that he knew something about the problem. In his first annual message he suggested that the difficulties of the farmers might be ameliorated by reducing taxes, by providing cheaper transportation facilities and fertilizers, and by a more general diversification of crops. Farmers' organizations might be helpful in securing these benefits. Then, early in 1925, he appointed an unofficial agricultural commission to suggest specific means of agricultural relief, and he spent some time in discussing the question with the agricultural committees of both houses of Congress. On January 28, 1925, he sent to Congress a proposal drawn by his agricultural commission. In the main this program called for a further development of farmers' organizations to promote cooperative selling and for the creation of a Federal Cooperative Marketing Board. This proposed federal board might adjust production to fluctuating market conditions and thus stabilize prices. Then he hoped that the farmers themselves would organize "stabilization corporations" for each major agricultural commodity. These corporations, working with the federal board, would remove surplus stocks from the market. To finance this experiment he proposed that Congress authorize

Plans for Recovery

the Treasury to advance a revolving fund of $100,000,000 from which the board could make advances to the "stabilization corporations." In his last annual message Coolidge was still advocating this same plan of regulated selling.

In the meantime the congressional program for farm relief was embodied in the McNary-Haugen bill. This measure had the backing of a substantial majority in Congress and also of such groups as the National Live Stock Producers' Association and the American Wheat Growers' Association. The bill aimed to protect the producers of cotton, wheat, corn, rice, hogs, and tobacco against low prices and against too severe fluctuations in the market. It provided for a Federal Farm Board of twelve members, to be appointed by the President, and for the appropriation of a revolving fund of $250,000,000, to be advanced, at the discretion of the Board, to the cooperative corporations in charge of the major crops. These loans would be used to dispose of the seasonal surplus in excess of domestic needs. According to the promoters, it would be possible to secure a satisfactory domestic price on some farm products; the surplus could be sold abroad for what it would bring. The most distinctive feature of the measure was the "equalization fee," from the proceeds of which the original revolving fund would be repaid and a permanent working capital could be secured. The amount of this fee would be determined and apportioned by the Federal Farm Board, and it would be paid, at the board's order, upon the transportation, processing, or sale of the commodity concerned. Coolidge vetoed this bill. He could see no value, he wrote, in having the people hire farmers to raise crops which neither they nor anybody else wanted.

The Farm Board

In Hoover's administration, Congress created a Federal Farm Board and granted to it a revolving fund of $500,000,000. The board was empowered to organize cooperative marketing associations and "stabilization corporations." As defined in the law itself, the general purpose was "to promote the effective merchandising of agricultural commodities in interstate and foreign commerce, and to place agriculture on a basis of economic equality with other industries." The stabilization corporations were authorized to buy wheat and cotton in the market, in quantities large enough to maintain an even price level.

President Hoover sponsored the policy and signed the bill which Congress passed. Then he appointed Alexander Legge, president of the International Harvester Company, as the chairman of the Farm Board. The board began its operations in the fall of 1929, the most inauspicious time for any such experiment. The effort to maintain an even price level lasted approximately one year, and the board bought 330,000,000 bushels of wheat and 1,319,800 bales of cotton. During this period commodity prices were tumbling all over the world, and in the United States the price of wheat dropped from $1.00 to 60 cents. The board lost half the sum turned over to it from the Treasury. This effort to maintain domestic prices at figures above the world level resulted in abject failure.

Industry and the "New Era"

It might be expected that an eight-year depression in agriculture would have been reflected almost at once in all forms of business activity, and ordinarily that would be the case. In the 1920's, however, except for a brief setback in 1921, American business underwent an impressive expansion; industry and finance both profited heavily during the very time when the farmers were falling into bankruptcy. A variety of factors made this anomalous condition temporarily possible.

Industrial Prosperity

For a matter of fifty years in the United States general economic prosperity had been associated with the degree of activity of the heavy industries: iron and steel and building materials. Between 1922 and 1928 these industries flourished. They provided the raw materials used by certain new industries and in the spectacular expansion of the more familiar activities of building construction and roadmaking. Opportunities for employment were generous, wages were good, money was plentiful, and optimism over the future became positively fantastic. At the same time foreign trade was unusually profitable—as long as the American people continued to lend money to the Europeans so that they could buy American goods.

Among the relatively new industries the making of automobiles seemed best to typify the traditional American qualities of inventiveness, mechanical ingenuity, daring, and business sense. At the turn of the century there were perhaps 8000 automobiles in use in the United States; these were high-priced cars beyond the financial reach of ordinary buyers. In 1905 the number of passenger cars and trucks reached the figure of 25,000 and in 1910, 187,000. Then production really went forward: nearly 1,000,000 in 1915, 2,333,000 in 1920, almost 4,500,000 in 1925. This was the peak of production until 1935. The figures for automobiles registered in the United States increased steadily from 9,231,941 in 1920 to 26,501,443 in 1929. The country had become automobile conscious.

Before the depression of 1929, the automobile factories themselves gave direct employment to 375,000 people. Employment in related lines, however, was even more impressive. In the manufacture of accessories and supplies and in the service occupations of selling, garage work, and filling stations an estimated 3,700,000 found jobs. How much business there was in the running of roadside restaurants, tourist cabins and homes, no one can tell, but directly and indirectly the number of people who depended on the automobile for support must have come close to 5,000,000. Then too there were the employees engaged in building the new hard surface highways, the mileage of which in 1937 reached the figure of 371,424.

Another great business enterprise which reached a high point of development by 1929 was the motion picture. Thomas A. Edison developed the first successful kinetoscope, a device for showing snapshots taken in rapid succession on a continuous film. The first motion pictures exhibited were simple affairs, one of the favorites being a train which seemed to run directly into the audience. In 1903 the first movie drama, *The Great Train Robbery,* was put on the screen. By 1905 the five-cent movie theater or nickelodeon had become a familiar institution. The early pictures were all silent. In 1927 the first sound pictures were tried out, and then Warner Brothers abandoned the silent film and produced talking pictures. Colored pictures were introduced in 1929.

The public responded enthusiastically to the movies. By 1930 attendance at the motion picture theaters reached the total of 100,000,000 paid admissions every week, and there was room enough in these theaters to seat one tenth of the whole American population at one time. By 1939 the film industry represented an investment in this country alone of well over $2,000,000,000. Although it did not provide a market for heavy raw materials, the motion picture industry kept a lot of money in circulation.

The third great new industry was radio. In 1895 Guglielmo Marconi transmitted and received wireless signals over a short distance. In 1901, at Newfoundland, he received a wireless message sent across the Atlantic. In 1915 voices were transmitted from the United States to France, and in 1920 Station KDKA at Pittsburgh began regular broadcasting. Hitherto radio had been merely a competitor of the telegraph and cable; commercial broadcasting made it a magnificent device for entertainment. By 1922, 60,000 homes in the United States had radios; in 1929 the number had increased to 9,000,000 and ten years later it stood at 27,500,000.

In this summary of economic expansion during the 1920's one other factor should be included, that of building construction. This was the era of ambitious suburban developments, of new apartment houses, new hotels, new office buildings, and incidentally of new winter resorts for the Florida boom. Here the work was overexpanded, particularly in the matter of hotels and office buildings. These new structures attracted guests and tenants away from the old establishments, with the result that both lost money. Building construction and automobile manufacturing both began to decline in volume before the summer of 1929.

One more business attracted nation-wide attention at the time, not because it was new but because of the methods of some of its promoters. In the production of electric power there was a twentyfold increase in output during the twenty years prior to 1929; this was impressive, but not nearly so impressive as the piling up of holding companies and the sales of worthless securities.

The New Era

Business statistics for the 1920's show precisely what happened with reference to certain kinds of economic activity. But no figures can begin to reveal the state of mind which accompanied this activity. To call it buoyant optimism would be an extreme understatement. Political leaders told the people that a new era had arrived, an era in which there was no further need for the old virtues of thrift and economy and in which old economic notions had no place. American business had reached a new status, not permanent but everchanging and changing always in the same direction—steadily upward. The day of business reverses had passed forever. For the future there would be nothing but a record of increasing production, expanding consumption, greater wealth, more money to spend. Investments which multiplied under the old, slow principles of compound interest were outmoded; one so-called investment corporation put out a fifteen-minute daily radio broadcast under the appealing caption of "Compounding Capital." Not only businessmen but professional men, servant girls, even retired ministers talked about their investments and how their "estates" were building up at phenomenal rates. And almost everybody believed the story. That is one reason why the crash, when it came, had such profound emotional effects. Depressions had been relegated to the scrap heap, along with other antiquated aspects of the old economy; they just couldn't happen any more.

Accompanying this state of mind were certain phenomena which for a time gave an additional stimulus to business activity. When the American people became automobile conscious, obliging dealers encouraged prospective customers to buy on the installment plan. Dealers in other devices took their cue from the automobile salesmen, and the consumer could buy anything on the installment plan: electric refrigerators, furniture, even clothing—not to mention the houses bought on shoestrings. By 1929, 15 percent of all retail sales in the United States were on the installment basis, and outstanding installment paper reached the total of $6,000,000,000.

To stimulate buying still further, dealers resorted to advertising on a scale never known before. For 1927 alone the total advertising budget amounted to more than $1,500,000,000. The advertisers drew upon all the resources of modern psychology. Pictures, slogans, countless pages of printed matter kept up continuous appeals to all the known human emotions—particularly ambition, fear, snobbishness, and vanity. Combined with advertising was a high-pressure selling campaign, with every device to speed up the salesman and to break down what the business psychologists called "sales resistance."

Integration

Business enterprise made several impressive contributions to the history of this era. The trend toward concentration, long evident in industry and in transportation, was carried on with new and striking results. Manufacturers of automobiles, rubber, moving pictures, even food products, all sought additional advantages in consolidation. Between 1928 and 1929 there were more than 1200 mergers affecting some 4000 concerns. In the field of retail business, especially in the selling of groceries, tobacco, and drugs, the chain store became common, so common that by 1930 20 percent of the retail business had been taken over by the chains. In the electrical utility field the independent operating companies were brought together in groups of holding companies, some logically put together, some arranged in fantastic patterns with not one but several layers of holding companies above the operating companies. The holding companies owned stock in operating companies and in each other, so that assets and liabilities became hopelessly confused,

The process of integration in the various lines was accompanied by considerable corporate reorganization and by the formation of new holding companies. All this activity furnished the opportunity for the issue of quantities of new securities. In fact, some of the reorganization or integration was effected for the primary purpose of putting out these securities. Some of the utility magnates got their money for buying additional operating companies by the simple expedient of selling stock in new holding companies. The success of such a policy was made possible by the large number of speculators who would snap up anything that purported to be a stock certificate; they never thought to inquire what did or did not lie behind the paper in the way of assets or of able and honest management. The market was always going up, and they could always sell for more than they paid.

The Harding, Coolidge, and Hoover administrations gave full approval to prevailing practices in business. Orders of the Federal Trade Commission decreased in number. Most important of all, the Commission gave encouragement to the various trade associations in their efforts to develop what they called codes of fair practice. In 1925 the Supreme Court itself gave its approval to the trade associations. Thanks to the friendliness of both executive and judicial branches of the national government, these associations increased in number until by 1927 there were perhaps 1000 of them. Some of them were old and well known such as the National Association of Wool Manufacturers. Every major industry had its association.

The codes of fair practice represented an effort on the part of the associations to regulate business from within, so that regulation by the government would be unnecessary. So far as the public could tell this regulation most frequently took the form of agreements to regulate prices; in other words they might have been considered conspiracies in restraint of trade. But the Supreme Court had absolved them from any such stigma.

As for new security issues, these amounted, in 1923 and 1924, to $8,000,000,000 or $9,000,000,000, and in 1929 to nearly $15,000,000,000. Some of this investment went into productive channels—that is, plant or equipment. But more of it went into holding company stock, some of which, instead of promoting production, proved to be a positive drain on the resources of operating or manufacturing concerns. Also some of the investment was in foreign securities, German or South American. These assets subsequently froze so hard that they never thawed out.

Malpractice in Business

It goes without saying that the majority of American businessmen were honest, as honest as the general run of their fellows; it also goes without saying that there always have been unscrupulous businessmen. Inevitably the doings of this class attract more attention than their respectable colleagues, particularly from the press and also from historians. Wickedness always has had a stronger appeal than virtue both for writers and for the reading public. The misdeeds of American businessmen have furnished considerable entertainment to their fellow countrymen, even when these same countrymen complain bitterly at the way they have been treated. In 1933 Ferdinand Pecora, counsel for the Senate Committee on Banking and Currency, carried on a searching investigation into financial practices and business methods of the era before 1929. His findings still serve to illustrate the seamy side of American business, not the shortcomings of the little fellows but the depredations of big bankers and executives.

Mr. Pecora proved that operators of Wall Street pools rigged prices on the Exchange and that they received direct help from officials of the companies whose stock was being manipulated. He explained how some bank officials so far forgot their trust as to trade in the stock of their own banks, and he proved that they made substantial fortunes for themselves. Then he showed how the promoters of some holding companies pyramided these companies, piling one on another, and how they plundered the companies they created. It was not that these men needed additional money because they already had all they could use, but the piling up of fortunes had become a game, the principal rule of which was that anything goes and the object of which was to make the highest possible score.

The playing field for this remarkable game was the New York Stock Exchange, once described by John T. Flynn, a writer on economics, as "the great American debt machine." Among the implements used were the investment bankers and the stockbrokers. Once a stock was listed on the big board these agents helped to unload it on the speculating public. After the crash those who had suffered losses blamed corporation executives, investment bankers, and brokers for selling poor quality stuff. They forgot how eager they had been to buy, how they would snap up any new issue without making the slighest attempt to evaluate the assets behind it. In the circumstances the dealers would have been superhuman if they had paid any more attention to quality than their customers did. There may have been sound psychology behind the old legal principle of *caveat emptor*—let the buyer beware. Why should the government protect the fool from the consequences of his own folly?

The Great Bull Market

In this remarkable stock market jamboree of the 1920's there were several distinctive characteristics. First was the heavy increase in the volume of trading.

Stock Trading in Millions of Shares

Year	Shares	Year	Shares
1920	223	1925	452
1921	171	1926	449
1922	260	1927	576
1923	237	1928	920
1924	282	1929	1124

The drop in 1921 was of course connected with the brief depression of that year. The rise from 1925 on was the Coolidge boom. This volume of trading was both cause and effect. People speculated in stocks because prices were going up, and prices were going up because so many people were speculating in stocks.

The increase in the price level of common stocks was the second striking characteristic of the great bull market. Again the table tells the story, this time in terms of common stock averages for 1926, the index number of which is fixed at 100:

June 1924	65.6
June 1925	85.1
June 1926	96.9
June 1927	114.
June 1928	148.2
June 1929	191.
September 1929	216.1

This means that anyone who had invested one thousand dollars in an average assortment of industrials and utilities in June 1924 would have seen his investment more than double by September 1929. Had he invested his money in Radio Corporation of America in 1928, by September 1929 it would have grown to $6430. Other favorite issues showed equally impressive gains. In practically every case, however, this advance was in price only; it had nothing to do with values. Prices were determined by the rising market and by the certainty that you could always sell any stock at a better price. This made the market look like fairyland; it was—in the sense that once in it people cut loose from rational behavior.

The third striking characteristic of the great bull market was the phenomenal increase in brokers' loans. These represented money which brokers lent their customers to enable them to buy stocks, usually on margin. If you had $1000 you could have bought stocks to that amount with your own money. But it was more profitable to take your own $1000, put it with $3000 more borrowed from your broker, and buy $4000 worth. After the market went up, as it was sure to do, you could sell out, take your profit on the whole transaction, and pay back the loan, plus the brokers' commission. Gambling with other people's money was immensely profitable.

In 1922 the total volume of brokers' loans stood at something under $1,000,000,000, but in 1926 the figure was close to $3,000,000,000. In 1928 it reached $6,500,000,000, and in 1929 it went to more than $8,500,000,000. It has been estimated that in 1929 more than 1,000,000 speculators were trading on margin, while between two and three as many more were buying and selling stocks, not for investment but for profits on the rising market. These margin traders knew that in case the market should decline, their brokers would immediately demand additional margin to cover the drop; if the traders could not meet the demand, the brokers would sell them out. But there was no need to worry over this merely theoretical possibility because stocks could not go down. The administration gave its blessing to the bull market; both President Coolidge and Secretary Mellon declared publicly that stock prices were not too high and that their current high level was merely an illustration of the prevailing good times. Businessmen and some of their economists gave support to this doctrine by talking about the new era in economics. And the investment trusts which seemed to be springing up everywhere were supposed to exert a determining influence on the market. They held such great quantities of securities in their portfolios that they could not afford to let the market drop, and furthermore they could trade in such heavy volume that they could always check any tendency toward a decline. If readers of the present generation argue that people could not have been so stupid as this account makes them appear, the answer is that these things did happen and that these beliefs were widely held. They look silly enough when subjected to the test of rational thinking, but rational thinking has no place in fairyland. The time for rational thinking came when fairyland blew up.

Course of the Depression

Stock Market Crash

For the first few months of the Hoover regime prosperity seemed secure. It is true that the automobile business and the building construction industry had slowed down appreciably, but the bull market was still going strong. On September 3, 1929, prices on the New York Stock Exchange hit their all-time high. Allied Chemical and Dye went to 354½, and American Tel. and Tel. passed 300; among the more highly speculative issues there was Auburn Automobile, which hit 498. It seemed that the market was entering upon another and even more pleasing demonstration of its onward and upward career. But in October there was a new demonstration, and this time it was not onward and upward. On October 24 the number of shares bought and sold on the Exchange hit a new record: 12,894,650 shares. Hitherto 5,000,000 shares in one day had been looked upon as phenomenal. Sales to the number of 12,000,000 could mean only one thing, and that was panic. Prices broke and speculators went crazy. They had to sell before the bottom dropped out. When the market closed Allied Chemical had dropped to 218, American Tel. and Tel. to 204, and Auburn Auto fell to 120. Five days later brought a still more impressive deluge of selling: 16,410,030 shares. At least the records show that much, but the market dropped so fast that some business was never recorded. The ticker was hours behind the actual sales, and nobody could tell what prices were at any time.

By November 13 listed securities had undergone a decline in prices amounting all told to more than $30,000,000,000. The great bull market was over. Speculators could no longer count on selling their paper for a higher price than they had paid, and the traders had to stop gambling with other people's money. In a single week brokers' loans dropped from the peak of over $8,500,000,000 to hardly more than $1,000,000,000. Prices had broken so fast that brokers sold out their customers with no warning; there was no time to call for additional margin. Paper fortunes vanished like dreams. Men who had retired with securities enough to give them and their families a comfortable living for life waked up to find themselves without a nickel. The brokers' offices still did some business because the shorts were cleaning up as quotations went steadily down, but the volume of business was small. There was a brief recovery in 1930, and the former "investors" who could put their hands on a little money came back into the game. But the hope of continued upturn was illusory, and the market moved slowly down toward the dismal depths of 1932. Then you could buy the former fancy leaders for a song.

Decline in Business

The stock market crash was neither the cause of the depression nor the depression itself; it was merely proof that the country—and the world too—had entered upon the downswing of an economic cycle. Additional proofs came in rapid, discouraging order. Banks began to close their doors. Even in the best days of the Coolidge boom, in 1928, the United States could record 491 bank failures. But in 1930 bank failures numbered 1345; in 1931 there were 2298. In some cases banks failed because of dishonest management. Their executives had become infected with the ethics of the gamblers in the market. Others had to close their doors because their portfolios were full of "frozen assets." This paper represented money lent at the inflated values of 1928; there was no possible way to get the money back. In other cases businessmen failed and so could not meet their notes.

As the depression gradually spread over the country manufacturers had to curtail operations or close their shops entirely. Orders were no longer coming in. Farmers could not buy more than bare necessities because of their long-continued hard times. Urban workmen in many cases could not buy because they were on part time or entirely out of jobs. Many white collar workers could not buy because they had drained themselves of resources in too much installment dealing or because they had lost their shirts in the crash of the stock market. This does not mean that business stopped and that nobody bought goods; business operations were nevertheless so curtailed that bankruptcies were inevitable. The following table shows the fluctuations in industrial production:

January 1928	100
October 1929	130
January 1930	90
January 1931	80
January 1932	60
March 1933	35
August 1933	80
December 1933	60

For the greater part of 1932 the average was approximately 50. As for bankruptcies, each year from 1921 to 1929 there had been an average of 21,616 commercial failures—not including banks. Bankruptcies for the depression years were numbered as follows:

1929	22,909
1930	26,355
1931	28,285
1932	31,822
1933	20,307

If foreign trade had continued in normal volume the depression would not have been so destructive, but Europe was having its economic troubles too. In fact, some economists trace the beginning of the whole decline to the financial crisis in Austria and southeastern Europe. President Wilson's policy of self-determination had broken up not only the old Austro-Hungarian Empire but also the delicately balanced economic structure in the Danube valley. From that quarter the depression spread like an epidemic to all parts of the world. Furthermore, with the advent of the depression here, American investors stopped lending money to Europe, thereby depriving Europe of the means for buying American goods. Again the figures tell the story. In 1929 exports from the United States had been valued at $5,240,000,000; in 1931 they had dropped to $2,423,000,000.

American citizens who had shown no interest in business indexes, foreign trade, stock market activity, or economic affairs could not help being interested when the depression came directly home to them. They felt the impact in the form of loss of jobs. By the end of 1930 there were probably 7,000,000 people out of work. At the depth of the depression in 1932 unemployment ran to more than 12,000,000, and some estimates put it as high as 15,000,000.

Because of popular beliefs regarding the relationship of prosperity and Republican politics—beliefs which Hoover himself and his associates had helped to strengthen—the depression inevitably gave rise to widespread, bitter criticism for the Hoover regime. To be sure Hoover had safeguarded his promises of continued good times with the reservation—"with the help of God"; but the public put the blame on the President and not on the Deity. The first results of this feeling appeared in the congressional elections of 1930, before the depression had begun to hit bottom. At this time the voters ended Republican control of the Senate; technically the new Senate showed forty-eight Republicans, forty-seven Democrats, and one independent, but the Republicans could not control the upper house. In the House of Representatives the new alignment showed 220 Republicans and 214 Democrats, but the Democrats won control of the organization and put in John N. Garner of Texas as speaker. In the elections of 1932, as will be seen below, the Democrats scored a smashing victory.

Economic Cycles

It is easier to describe what happened during the depression than to give a satisfactory explanation of its causes. The depression was world-wide. It is true that the Hawley-Smoot Tariff did result in further losses of American foreign trade, and to this extent the tariff policy figured slightly in the picture. But the depression would have come anyway, regardless of American tariff acts. The most satisfactory explanation of the depression of 1929 and of other depressions in the past is simply that they are part of the economic cycle and consequently are just as normal as periods of prosperity. The history of economic development in the United States provides logical support for this argument. Under any system of free enterprise producers turn out goods a little ahead of demand. Sooner or later a saturation point is reached and consumers stop buying. Hence we have the upturns and downswings of the cycle. Usually the slackening in demand and in the production of heavy goods precedes the onset of actual depression, sometimes by several months.

The practices of the boom era were partly responsible for the gravity of the downswing in 1929. By widespread installment buying people had drawn heavily upon their surplus of the future. Thus they had nothing available to serve as a cushion against the drop. Again the "investors" in stocks had bought their paper at high prices and sold it at low; the difference between the figures represented dead loss to them. Because of these factors many families had no savings available for an era of hard times. This lack of reserve buying power made the situation worse.

At the time of the depression there was a lot of talk about overproduction as a cause of the depression. This explanation is satisfactory provided one keeps the meaning of the term in mind. We have probably never had overproduction in this country in terms of desire; we have simply had more goods than people could afford to buy under conditions prevailing at a certain time. Given the means to pay, almost every family in this country could buy more of something than it actually does. This is true particularly of families in the low income groups. Of course we had overproduction when the depression threw people out of work, but we never have had production enough to give every family an abundance of both necessities and luxuries. The fallacy in attributing the depression to the simple formula of overproduction alone is well illustrated in the following comment:

> We have too much wheat, so the farmers are being pauperized and the unemployed of the cities are standing in line and begging for bread, while thousands upon thousands of poor Chinese are starving to death. We have too much wool, therefore no one can get a new suit of clothes. We have a vast oversupply of building material, so the unfortunates are without shelter and must sleep in the parks.

The writer might have also added that we had too much cotton, so the southern farmers who raised it could not have new overalls. Overproduction therefore is simply another way of saying lack of buying power.

Economic Fallacies

Another favorite theme of commentators on the depression was technological unemployment. This meant that improved machinery was reducing the need for human labor, cutting down the number of jobs, and therefore throwing men out of work. There was an element of truth in the formula. There is no question that machines for making cigars displaced hand labor and that machines for making electric light bulbs and rubber tires, for example, had become so efficient that the amount of hand labor required actually diminished. In this sense there had been technological unemployment ever since the eighteenth century. The complaints of the hand spinners who were thrown out of work by the jenny and the mule in 1790 were no different in principle from complaints from other types of workers in 1930.

Improved machines have always affected individual types of employment. What is overlooked in the easy acceptance of the technological unemployment formula is the easily demonstrable fact that down to 1929, in spite of the vast technological improvements throughout all forms of industry, the number of jobs in industry or directly connected therewith had steadily increased. While men were being thrown out of work in specific instances, opportunities for employment had always increased.

In recent years figures have sometimes appeared in print which purported to show an actual decline of jobs in the United States between 1919 and 1929. These figures were accompanied by the conclusion that opportunities for employment were on the decline. The figures of the census of 1920 and 1930 indicate nothing of the sort. The census of 1920 reported the number of gainfully employed as 41,614,248; the census of 1930 showed the gainfully employed as 48,829,920. In 1920 these gainfully employed made up 39.4 percent of the total population, in 1930 they made up 39.8 percent. Here certainly was no decline in opportunity for employment. There was a drop in the number of gainfully employed after 1930, but the trend in employment turned sharply upward again in 1940-42. Even in the category of manufacturing and mechanical industries, where the absolute decline in employment is alleged to have taken place, the census figures show a positive increase in the number of jobs: 12,831,879 in 1920, 14,110,652 in 1930.

In 1933 Mr. Simeon Strunsky, of *The New York Times,* who succeeded far better than most of us in keeping his intellectual balance during the trying times of the depression, gave a vivid illustration of the fallacies in the formula of technological unemployment. Taking the printing press as typical of the machine which displaces hand labor, he demonstrated the havoc wrought by this device. His analysis deserves quotation.

To grasp what Gutenberg's invention has done to displace human labor and promote social collapse, let us imagine today's Sunday issue of *The New York Times* got out in manuscript form, with professional medieval penmen doing the work now performed by compositors, engravers, stereotypers and press operators. The *Times* today would comprise, roughly, one million words, counting text and pictures as words. A copyist working steadily with pen and ink would do well to average twenty-five hundred words an hour, or twenty thousand words in a working day of eight hours. It would, therefore, take fifty scriveners one day to produce one copy of this paper. To turn out the more than 750,000 copies of which today's issue consists we would need 37,500,000 working eight hours. That would be, as we say in engineering, 300,000,000 man-hours.

Actually, today's *Times,* thanks to Messrs. Gutenberg, Mergenthaler and their successors, was produced by about one thousand typesetters, engravers, stereotypers and press operators in about sixteen hours. . . . This is a total of 16,000 man-hours. The invention of printing has therefore enabled one man to do the work that required about 19,000 men once upon a time. After that, it remains only to recall the evil wrought by this enormous displacement of labor, by the wholesale relegation of medieval scribes to the scrap heap.[1]

[1] *The New York Times,* Jan. 28, 1933.

For a time President Hoover and his associates in the government refused, publicly at least, to believe that the slump was anything more than a slight, temporary interruption of the progress onward and upward. In January 1930 the President assured the country that the trend of business was upward; in March he prophesied that the difficulties would be over in two more months. When the two months had elapsed he told the people the worst was over. In the same January of 1930 Secretary Mellon could see "nothing in the present situation that warrants pessimism."

Fighting the Depression

By the end of 1930, however, federal officials realized fully the need of something more effective than phrase making. President Hoover recommended an impressive program of public works to provide employment and to create a market for raw materials. His plan included road building, the construction of public buildings, and improvements for airways. Then he recommended the granting of more generous credits to both farmers and businessmen. In January 1932 Congress authorized the establishment of the Reconstruction Finance Corporation, with a capital stock of $500,000,000 paid out of the Treasury of the United States. The RFC was authorized to lend federal money to businessmen in trouble. This category included almost all types: industries generally, insurance companies, banks, and railroads. The RFC checked the course of deflation and prevented many bankruptcies. By June 30, 1939, it had made loans to the impressive total of $13,340,745,394.67. At the time of its establishment many pessimists declared that most of the RFC loans would turn out to be nothing but gifts, that the borrowers would never be able to repay. This has not been the case, and of the loans made before 1940, 74 percent were repaid. The RFC was the Hoover administration's most impressive weapon for combating the depression.

The depression affected the federal government in two ways. Revenue declined rapidly, while the attempt to mitigate the effects of the depression added to expenditure. In 1930 federal revenues amounted to a total of $4,177,941,702; in 1932 the total had dropped to $2,005,725,437. Expenditures for the same two years were $3,994,152,487 and $5,153,644,895, respectively. At the time it was difficult to deal with this increase in debt. Any increase in income taxes might have restricted private expenditures still further. Increased government expenditures seemed essential to make up for the lack of private expenditure. The administration decided to wait for the return of normal times before attempting to balance the budget.

Chapter 45

THE NEW DEAL

THE Presidential election of 1932 came in the depths of the depression, and on the basis of previous experience the party in power was marked for defeat. In these circumstances neither platforms nor candidates would have much effect on the outcome. The Republicans held their national convention in June at Chicago, and the delegates plainly revealed their discouragement. President Hoover received the nomination on the first ballot. He forced the renomination of Vice President Curtis. Then he drove through the wet-dry plank on prohibition which has already been referred to.

The platform outlined the President's efforts to deal with the depression and praised his leadership. It promised economy, the maintenance of the gold standard, and new banking laws to protect depositors. Concerning farm relief, the platform called attention to the party's achievements in providing tariff protection to the farmers, and in establishing the Federal Farm Board, which, so the platform alleged, "has many achievements of merit to its credit."

Nomination of Roosevelt

Because of the certainty of Republican defeat, the Democratic nomination was a prize of real value and there were numerous contestants for it. Among the leaders were Alfred E. Smith, who wanted another chance, John N. Garner of Texas, Governor Albert C. Ritchie of Maryland, James A. Reed of Missouri, and above all others, Governor Franklin D. Roosevelt of New York. His name caught popular attention, while his campaign manager, James A. Farley, had succeeded in pledging a large number of delegates in advance of the convention. On the fifth ballot Roosevelt received the nomination.

The Democratic platform was short and pointed. It attributed the depression to "the disastrous policies pursued by our government since the World War, of economic isolation," and of promoting the consolidation of business. It promised immediate and drastic reduction of government expenditures, and the maintenance "at all hazards" of a sound currency. It went back to the Cleveland policy of a tariff for revenue but added a new policy, that of reciprocal trade agreements with individual governments. It advocated federal grants to the states for unemployment relief and an expansion of the public works program. Then it promised unemployment and old-age security legislation to be brought about by state action. For the farmers it promised refinancing of mortgages and the control of crop surpluses. For national defense it pledged an adequate navy. For depositors in the banks and for investors it promised adequate banking laws and protection for buyers of securities. It promised independence for the Philippines. Then came the plank on prohibition: "We favor the repeal of the Eighteenth Amendment."

The Second Roosevelt

One of Roosevelt's political assets was his unusually pleasing voice. To take full advantage of this he spent part of September and October on an extensive speaking tour, from Albany to the Pacific coast and back. In a series of addresses he touched upon the problems of farm relief, silver, the railroads, the tariff, and public utilities. Some of his most effective speeches dealt with the subject of federal expenditures and the need for economy. At Pittsburgh on October 19 Roosevelt characterized the Hoover administration's record as "the most reckless and extravagant . . . of any peacetime government anywhere at any time." He promised economy, financial reform, and a balanced budget. Again at St. Louis Roosevelt told his audience: "It is my pledge and promise that this dangerous kind of financing shall be stopped and that rigid governmental economy shall be enforced by a stern and unremitting administration policy of living within our income." In the election Hoover polled 15,575,474 popular votes, but he carried only six states: Maine, New Hampshire, Vermont, Connecticut, Delaware, and Pennsylvania. Roosevelt received a popular vote of 22,314,058, with 472 electoral votes. This political overturn gave the Democrats full control of both houses of Congress.

Republican Eclipse

In the last session of the 72nd Congress both houses passed the resolution for repealing the Eighteenth Amendment. Then Congress took up the question of Philippine independence. The Hawes-Cutting measure provided for the establishment of a Philippine commonwealth, which would be completely independent after twelve years. Hoover vetoed the measure because he believed that under the terms of the law the United States was not meeting its obligations either to the Filipinos or to the world at large, to say nothing of the American people. The Philippine legislature also refused to accept the Hawes-Cutting Act. In 1934, under the Roosevelt administration, Congress passed a second measure, the Tydings-McDuffie Bill. The chief changes were that American military posts were to be removed and arrangements with reference to American naval bases were to be settled by subsequent negotiations between the United States and the Philippines. The Filipinos approved the new law.

From its opening in 1929 to its dismal close on March 4, 1933, the Hoover administration had suffered reverse after reverse. Then at its very end, when the first signs of economic recovery were appearing in the troubled world, a banking panic precipitated a new crisis. Although there had been banking difficulties in Nevada in the preceding November, the real storm broke loose in Detroit, Michigan. On February 14, 1933, the governor proclaimed an eight-day "banking holiday." This meant that no checks could be cashed and no withdrawals permitted. Ten days later the governor of Maryland announced a three-day banking holiday. Shortly after four o'clock in the morning of March 4, Governor Lehman closed all the banks in New York State. The governor of Illinois acted immediately thereafter. By noon of that day every state government in the union had placed restrictions on banking operations. In these circumstances Franklin D. Roosevelt was inaugurated for his first term.

Starting the New Deal

As Roosevelt began his inaugural the confident note in his voice cheered people by the million. There was nothing to fear, he said, but fear itself. He urged action to end unemployment, to aid the farmer, and to bring about economy in the federal government. As for the banks and brokers: "There must be a strict supervision of all banking and credits and investments; there must be an end to speculation with other people's money, and there must be provision for an adequate but sound currency." He would urge all these matters upon Congress. Should the legislature fail to respond, he would ask for executive power "to wage a war against the emergency, as great as the power that would be given to me if we were in fact invaded by a foreign foe." Even more than his words, the new President's manner inspired widespread confidence.

On March 5 President Roosevelt issued a proclamation keeping all the banks closed until further notice. Then he called Congress in special session to meet on March 9. One-half hour after Congress opened, Roosevelt sent a special message calling for immediate action. A bill designed to deal with the banking crisis was introduced immediately after the message, and before eight o'clock that same day the measure was on its way to the White House for the executive signature.

So the New Deal began. It has been a topic of bitter controversy ever since. Its defenders find in it proof of the inevitability of historical forces. They consider the various measures to have been the logical, coherent product of social and economic evolution. Its foes found it a hit-or-miss congeries of badly planned measures, something compounded, as H. L. Mencken put it, of "false diagnoses and quack remedies." Both sides argued with all the fervor of medieval theologians talking about determinism and free will. In general the New Deal aimed at recovery, relief, and reform, but the administration did not begin with a prepared program. In fact, according to Frances Perkins, Secretary of Labor, there never was a program. The New Deal was merely a purpose and a method. The purpose was to promote the economic well-being of the American people through the instrumentality of the federal government and—after one lone gesture toward economy—to achieve this aim with borrowed money, if necessary.

This first measure of the New Deal validated the President's previous proclamation with reference to money and the banks and gave him power to regulate transactions in credit, currency, gold, silver, and foreign exchange. Then the law provided for the appointment of federal managers for banks which were strong enough to resume business but so weak that they could not stand alone.

One of the first objectives of the New Deal was to raise prices. The immediate result, so it was hoped, would be a diminution of the load of indebtedness. At the same time rising prices would stimulate buying and so start the wheels of business once more. Then the accompanying industrial revival would provide more jobs. The direct rise in prices was to be effected by devaluation of the dollar. The next step would be help for agriculture. Farmers were to receive additional assistance through a program of voluntary crop limitation, which in itself would result in higher prices through scarcity. The plan also called for federal benefit payments to all farmers who would cooperate. Industrial laborers would be helped with a shorter work week, with minimum wage and maximum hour laws, together with a broad program of social security. To bridge the gap until this machinery could be put in motion the program of public works would be expanded. Then home owners and farm owners in trouble with their mortgages would be pulled out of their difficulties with federal funds. At the same time the bankers and security dealers would be put under restrictions.

By way of prelude, before the main program could get under way, Roosevelt asked Congress for two measures designed to make good two specific pledges in his party's platform. One was the Economy Act, the other a bill to modify the Volstead Act. In the first of these measures Congress made a drastic cut in payments to veterans of both the Spanish-American and the World Wars. All federal salaries were also cut, up to a maximum of 15 percent. It was hopefully estimated that this measure would reduce federal expenditures by $900,000,000 each year. This Economy Act of 1933 was the first—and also the last—effort made to reduce federal expenditures. Sometime thereafter the advocates of spending gained ascendancy in the administration. The modification of the Volstead Act raised the permissible alcoholic content of beverages from one half of 1 percent to 3.2 percent, thereby making possible the manufacture and sale of something more nearly akin to real beer. On April 7, 1933, the date named in the law, this new beverage went on sale, legally in twenty-one states and illegally but openly in many others.

Industry, Labor, and Agriculture

The Blue Eagle

Of all New Deal legislation the measure which best typified the purposes of the administration was the National Industrial Recovery Act. This law gave the President power to set up machinery for a "great cooperative movement throughout all industry" to bring about increased employment, to reduce the length of the working week, to provide higher wages, to prevent unfair competition, and to put an end to overproduction. One section suspended the antitrust laws, while another authorized the making of codes of fair competition. Section *7a* guaranteed to labor the right to organize. Manufacturers liked the experiment because it prohibited price cutting and legalized agreements to maintain prices. The President liked it because it

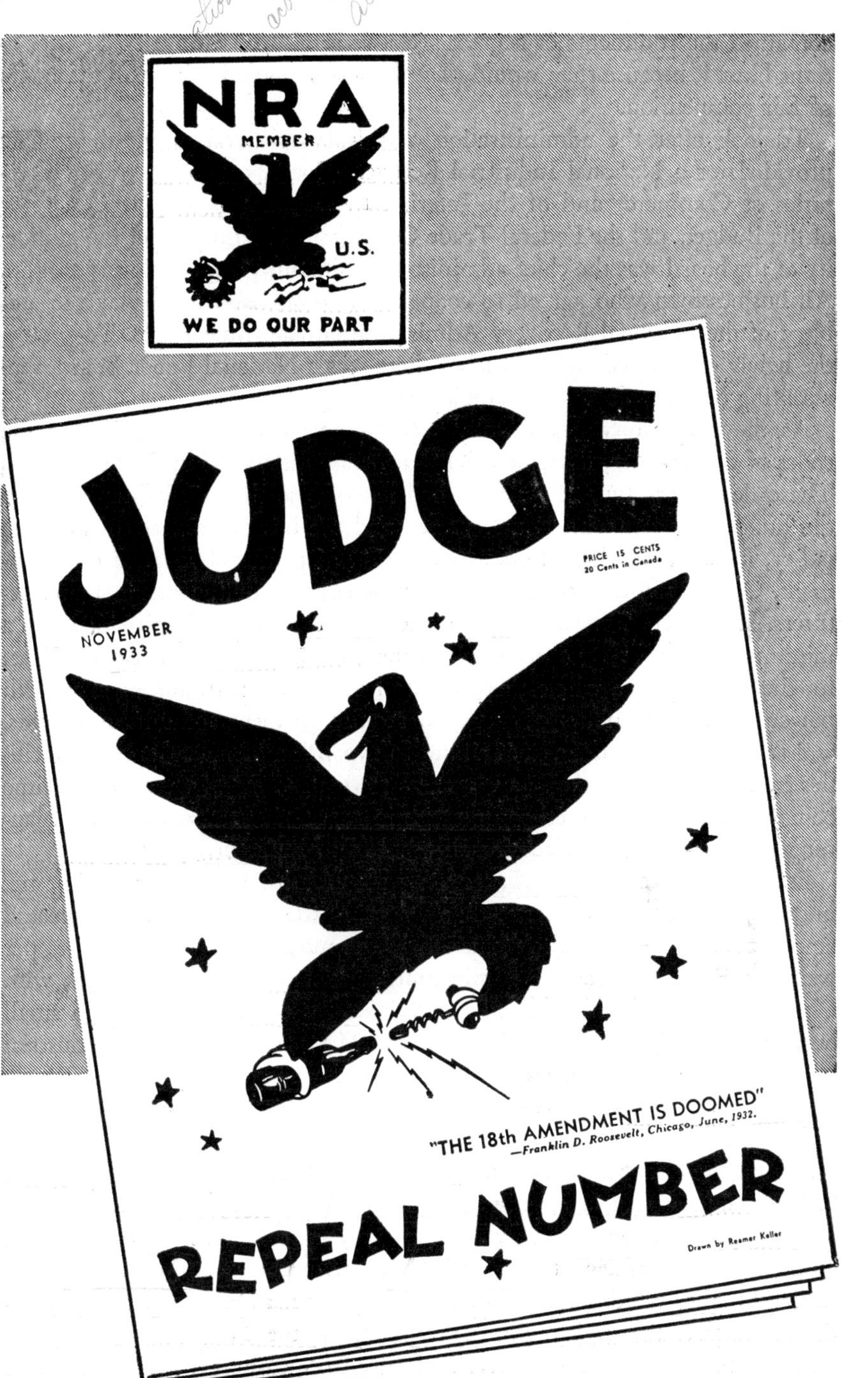

When repeal of the Eighteenth Amendment was assured, the NRA Blue Eagle was put to a new use by one of the humorous magazines of the day.

contained the rudiments of a great social reform. The various trade associations liked it because they would play the leading role in drafting the codes of fair competition.

To look after the administration of this complicated program the law provided for a National Industrial Recovery Board, composed of the secretaries of Commerce and of the Interior, the attorney general, the director of the Budget, and the Federal Trade Commission. Acting under the authority of the board was the chief administrator himself, General Hugh Johnson. All businessmen who agreed to cooperate were allowed to display the emblem of the National Recovery Administration: the Blue Eagle. To protect the newly established rights of labor there was a National Labor Board, representing both employers and employees.

As the program was gradually worked out, with the adoption of the codes of fair practice, it seemed that business underwent important changes. The codes—every type of business had its code, so they were numbered by the hundred—dealt with hours, wages, and the broader aspects of business policy, including such matters as expansion of plant and change of equipment. One of the first codes to be completed, that of the cotton manufacturers, set the maximum working week at forty hours. It provided for a minimum wage of $13.00 per week in the North, $12.00 in the South. Then for the industry as a whole there was to be a central planning agency, with power to alter the hours of work, to require uniform accounting systems, and to regulate all matters pertaining to expansion of manufacturing facilities in the industry. Because agreements to regulate prices were for the time being no longer considered conspiracies in restraint of trade, this same planning agency could fix prices for all types of manufactured cotton.

Enthusiasm over the law lasted only six months. Prices were going up, undeniably, but they rose faster than wages. Furthermore, the only increased employment came from the reduction in the number of working hours per week. In February 1934 the administration appointed a special board, with Clarence Darrow as chairman, to investigate the effect of the law on small business enterprises. The board reported in May that the National Industrial Recovery Act encouraged monopoly and handicapped small business. Worse still, there was little increase in employment. In May 1934 the unemployed still numbered 10,616,000.

In 1935 the Brookings Institution published its conclusions regarding the NIRA. These expert economists found that the law and its administrators had actually retarded recovery. In May 1935 the federal Supreme Court brought the experiment to an end. In the Schechter Poultry Case Chief Justice Hughes handed down the opinion of a unanimous court. The decision held that the code-making provisions of the NIRA constituted an unwarranted transfer of legislative authority from Congress to the President. Next, the Court held that the determination of hours and wages in local industries is not connected with interstate commerce and consequently the federal government had no power to legislate on such matters. Finally the

Court held that there had been no emergency serious enough to warrant these departures from the Constitution.

Wagner Act

When the Recovery Act was annulled, the friends of organized labor tried to save the major principles of Section 7a. To take its place Congress passed the Wagner-Connery Labor Relations Act. This measure declared that it was the policy of the United States to safeguard interstate commerce by giving encouragement and protection to organized labor. The new law prohibited employers from interfering with or from attempting to control any labor organization or from refusing to bargain collectively with their employees. The law created a National Labor Relations Board of three members, with power to determine what union represented a majority of employees in any given plant. Under the law employees might register complaints against unfair actions of their employers. The Board could issue orders to employers, and these orders were to be enforced if necessary through the courts.

Employers complained that the law discriminated against them, on the ground that their employees were given a distinct advantage over them in the matter of collective bargaining. With the support of the law and the board, labor unions could compel employers to take cognizance of complaints. For the first time in history the employer was left without means of negotiation with his employees in case they did not care to negotiate. Employers also attacked the law on the ground that it was unconstitutional, but on April 12, 1937, the Supreme Court found the law constitutional. This decision, by the way, stood almost in direct reversal of the principle on which NIRA had been declared unconstitutional.

The CIO

With this proof of strong government support, labor leaders hoped to extend their influence into wider fields, particularly in the heavy industries such as the steel mills and the mass-production plants of automobile manufacturers. Some of the leaders believed that the principle of organization by crafts was unsuited to these great plants, and they advocated organization by industries. Mr. John L. Lewis of the United Mine Workers felt that the American Federation of Labor was not giving proper encouragement to this type of organization. Late in 1935 he and some other leaders formed the Committee for Industrial Organization to promote the principle of industrial unionism. Mr. Lewis and his aides then forced employers in the steel and automobile fields to come to terms with his new C.I.O. unions. In November 1938, having broken with the A.F. of L., the organization changed its name to the Congress of Industrial Organizations, and Mr. Lewis became president of the Congress.

In June 1938 Congress attempted to make permanent whatever gains had occurred. In the Wages and Hours Act provision was made for the gradual increase of the minimum wage until it should become fixed at 40 cents per hour in all industries. The bill provided for a maximum working week of 44 hours for the first year, and this was to be gradually reduced to 40. All overtime work would be paid for at the rate of time and one half. And the same law prohibited the shipment in interstate commerce of all goods produced by child labor.

The AAA While one congressional committee was working on the plan to revive industry and another helped labor, still another was struggling with the difficult problem of agriculture. The result was the companion measure of the NIRA, also passed in 1933, the Agricultural Adjustment Act. The primary purpose of this measure was to raise the prices of the major agricultural products. The method was the application of the principle of scarcity—that is, to prevent the raising of surplus crops. The bill covered the following seven products: wheat, cotton, corn, hogs, dairy products, tobacco, rice, and sugar. Producers of these crops were asked voluntarily to reduce their normal output by 15 percent—in the case of cotton, 33 percent. Then the government would make benefit payments for that part of the crop not produced. For example, if a wheat farmer ordinarily raised 1000 bushels, he would be asked to raise only 850 bushels. For the 150 bushels which he refrained from raising, he would receive benefit payments at the rate of 28 cents per bushel. The cotton planters were asked to plow under every third row of the crop which was already started when the law went into effect. Then with smaller crops the price would rise, so the farmers would profit both ways. To provide funds for these benefit payments, the Treasury would collect processing taxes from industrialists who transformed the raw material into a finished product. Flour millers, for example, would pay the processing tax on wheat. For the three years during which the AAA was in effect the government made benefit payments to the amount of approximately $2,000,000,000.

Early in 1936, by a vote of six to three, the Supreme Court declared the AAA unconstitutional. According to the decision: "The act invades reserved rights of the States. It is a statutory plan to regulate and control agricultural production, a matter beyond the powers delegated to the Federal Government." Payments to the farmers were stopped at once. But the Soil Conservation Act had been passed the year before, and benefit payments were renewed under it. But the collection of processing taxes came to an end, and later the Supreme Court ordered the return of all those which had been paid. In March 1936 President Roosevelt signed a new measure designed "to provide for the protection of land resources against soil erosion and for other purposes." Among the other purposes was a continuance of benefit payments. Then in 1938, after the change in personnel of the Supreme Court had brought advocates of a different social philosophy into power, Congress passed a new Agricultural Adjustment Act. In addition to continuing benefit payments, this measure authorized the Treasury to lend money at rates fixed by the administration to those farmers who might wish to turn their crops over to the government for security. Then, if the market price should rise above the amount of the loan, the farmer could reclaim his crop and sell it at the higher price. If the price dropped or remained the same the government would keep possession of the crop. The direct effect of the New Deal's agricultural program was to increase substantially the income of farmers.

Economic Reform

Monetary Policy

Inseparably connected with the NIRA and the AAA in the New Deal program was the monetary policy, designed like the others to bring prosperity by raising prices. The difference was that while the first two measures would operate indirectly, the third would work directly and at once; at least the monetary experts said that it would. This monetary policy seems to have originated in widely different quarters. Some farmers were calling for inflation for the purpose of raising prices. At this point the silver interests in Congress saw a chance to create an artificial market for their commodity by unloading it on the government at fancy prices. Then the advocates of a managed currency attributed many of our economic ills to the fixed value of the gold dollar and to the high price of gold. By keeping the value of the dollar in step with fluctuations in the price structure, so they argued, violent economic upheavals could be prevented. They also had a hand in formulating the government's new policy. The opponents of the notion of a managed dollar promptly tried to discredit it by dubbing it the "rubber dollar," or in the more picturesque phraseology of Al Smith, the "baloney dollar."

The policy or policies adopted might be described as a hodgepodge of many of the proposals submitted. On March 5, 1933, in order to put a stop to further hoarding of gold, the government took over control of the supply of gold. In April 1933 the United States left the gold standard, and two months later the gold clause was canceled in all public and private contracts. Then the AAA contained a monetary section which authorized the President, at his discretion, to issue up to a maximum of $3,000,000,000 in Treasury notes, to reduce the gold content of the dollar by not more than 50 percent, to fix the ratio of silver to gold, and to provide for the unlimited coinage of silver. In the summer of 1933 the Treasury began progressively to raise the price of gold, on the theory that any change in the price of gold would be at once and automatically registered in a corresponding change in all commodity prices. Before the end of the year the President authorized the Treasury to buy all the silver mined in the United States at the price of 64½ cents per ounce—that is, 50 percent above the market price. Early in 1934 the President reduced the gold content of the dollar from 23.22 grains to 15⅕21, and so fixed the value of the new gold dollar at 59 cents in terms of the old.

The policies described above were accompanied by a number of others, the ramifications of which reached into almost all aspects of American economic life. For the reform of banking, Congress in 1933 passed the Glass Act, which created the Federal Deposit Insurance Corporation; this agency insured all deposits up to $5000. The same measure prohibited banks from engaging in both deposit and investment business. It permitted branch banking except in those states where local laws prohibited the practice. In 1935 the Glass-Steagall Act changed the name of the body in control of our banking system from the Federal Reserve Board to the board of governors of the Federal Reserve System. Then the board was given full control of open-market operations—that is, of the wholesale buying and selling of government securities.

The prominence of the stock exchange in the depression, combined with the feeling of large numbers of people that they had been fleeced by the brokers, was bound to lead to federal action. So in 1933 Congress passed the Securities Act, which prohibited both persons and corporations from selling any securities in interstate commerce unless such securities had been previously registered with the Federal Trade Commission. Corporations desiring to register securities must give information under oath regarding the condition of the business and the character of the assets behind the securities. Penalties provided for making misleading or false statements were severe. In 1934 another law created the Securities and Exchange Commission, which took over the responsibility of registration and the granting of permission to issue new securities. The new commission was also empowered to license the stock exchanges of the United States, and the same law gave the Federal Reserve Board control over margin trading.

Home Mortgages

In its efforts to provide relief from embarrassing ills the government could not overlook the urban home owners of the country. Many of them had bought their property under mortgages at valuations in keeping with the flush days of the great bull market. When the crash came numerous owners could no longer meet their interest payments, and they could not extricate themselves from debt by selling their holdings because there was no demand. At the same time the banks, building and loan associations, insurance companies, and private citizens who held these mortgages were in distress because they were no longer realizing the income to which they were legally entitled and which their own commitments made necessary. They encountered the same difficulties in selling as the owners did, and if they took over property under foreclosure they were left with the problem of managing it at a time when it was generally unprofitable. The real estate business had become stuck on a dead center.

The administration's answer to the puzzle was the Home Owners' Loan Corporation, established under authority of an act of Congress in June 1933. The HOLC was created not to make new mortgage loans but to take over those where the owners were unable to meet their obligations; mortgage holders turned over the paper to the HOLC and received in exchange bonds of the new organization. Thus the HOLC was an agency for relieving distressed mortgageholders as well as distressed owners.

Additional legislation provided further federal funds to be lent for repairs, alterations, and upkeep of property, and still other funds for new construction. Altogether the federal government became the greatest single factor in the real estate business. Then in 1937 Congress passed the National Housing Act, creating the United States Housing Authority. The purpose of this new enterprise was to provide federal loans to municipalities for the building of new housing for people in the low income groups. These loans were made to run for sixty years with interest at 3 percent. The new structures were to be built in what had been slum areas, and the old buildings had to be cleared away as part of the slum clearance project.

Of all the Rooseveltian projects looking toward economic betterment one of the most practical was the Civilian Conservation Corps. The purpose was to provide constructive, healthful, out-of-door work for unemployed young men. According to the law authorizing the camps, not more than 300,000 men were to be enrolled at any one time, and the maximum period of enrollment was not to be longer than two years. The men were assigned to camps which were located in various parts of the United States. The members of the corps were put to work at planting trees, removing underbrush, providing safeguards against forest fires, constructing small dams for water control, building bridges and fences, and in general improving forest properties throughout the United States.

The CCC

Apart from the program of relief, no major project of the New Deal led to more argument than the Tennessee Valley Authority and its policies. The beginning of this enterprise goes back to World War I. In 1917 Congress authorized the construction of power plants at Muscle Shoals, Alabama, on the Tennessee River. These plants would provide power to be used in the manufacture of nitrates which were needed by the munitions makers. Two of these nitrates plants were completed in 1918. By that time the war was over, and the nitrates needed for fertilizer and other purposes could be procured elsewhere more cheaply than at Muscle Shoals. It looked as though the government's $145,000,000 investment would have to be charged off as one more item of dead loss. But work on one of the main dams on the Tennessee River, the Wilson Dam, was completed in 1925. The government continued to run the power plant and sold the power to the Alabama Power Company.

TVA

The original project had included plans for other power plants, and in 1928 Congress passed a bill to complete the whole program. President Coolidge vetoed the bill, and three years later President Hoover vetoed a similar measure. Both of these executives were opposed to putting the government into the power business in competition with private enterprise, and there the matter rested until the next administration.

President Roosevelt entered office with a different outlook. In his own state of New York he had come to look upon the electrical utilities as a problem which could be solved only through the application of governmental authority. He had found fault with their charges, their business methods, and, in particular, with their efforts to influence public opinion. He was willing to put the government into competition with the utilities, and he believed that in such competition the government could manufacture

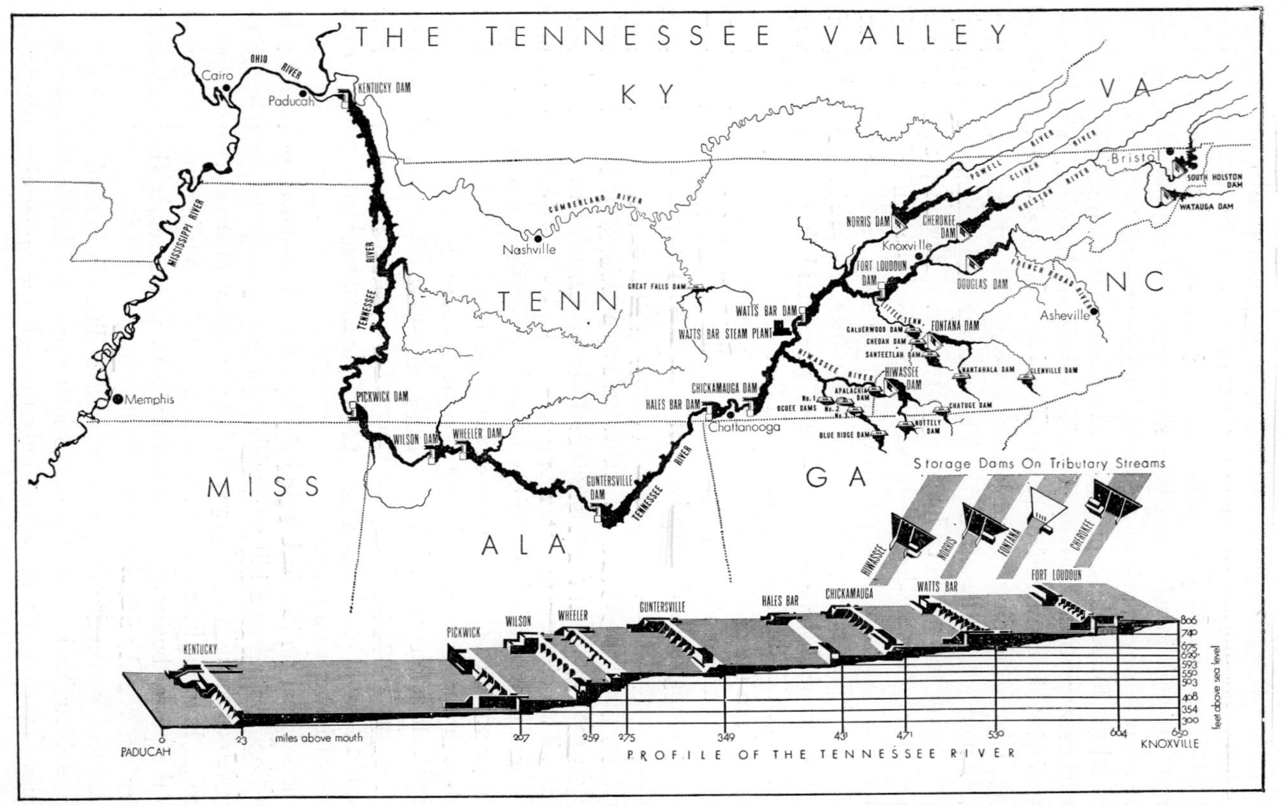

Started in 1933, this great project was completed by 1945.

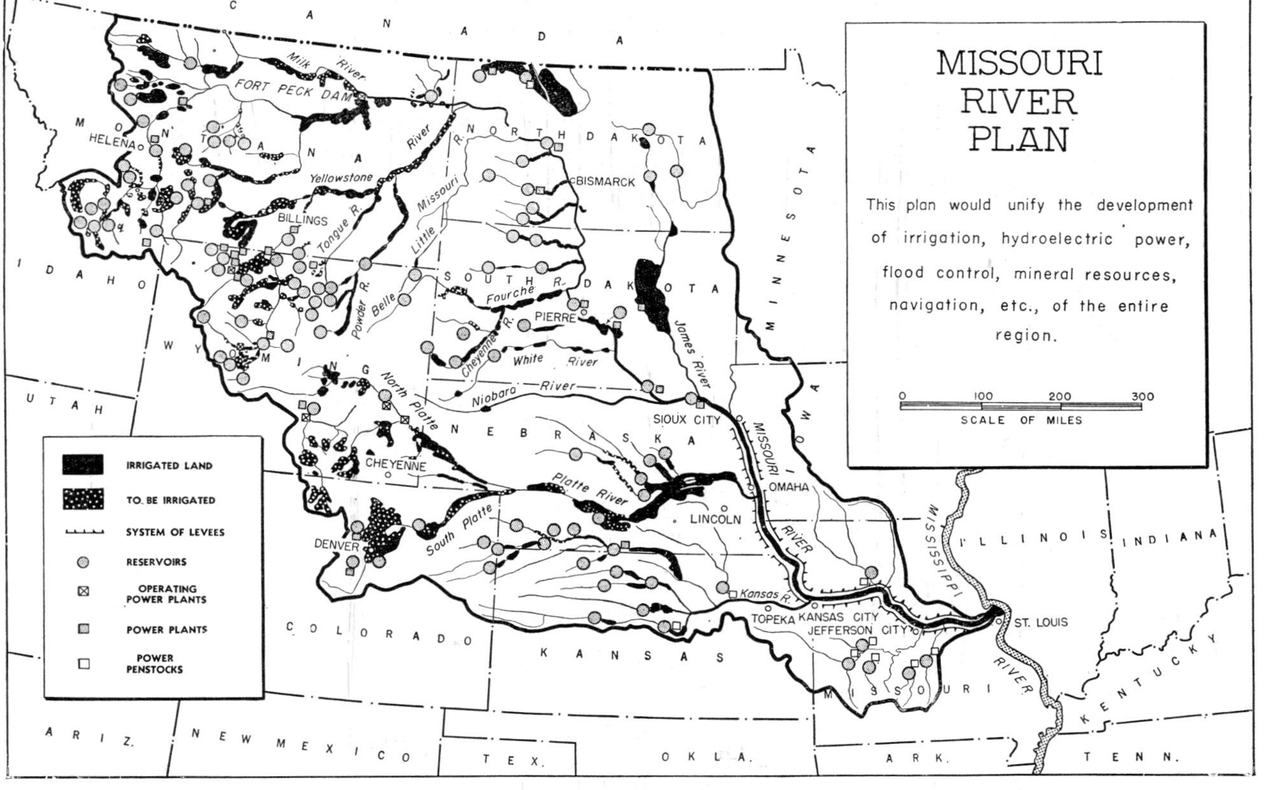

This plan, approved by Congress in 1944, is largely in the blueprint stage.

and sell power at rates well below those charged by the private companies. A government plant therefore might be regarded as a "yardstick" for measuring charges to consumers in the electrical utility field.

The manufacture of electric power was only part of the program. The Tennessee valley includes an extensive area, 41,000 square miles in extent, made up of parts of eight states lying between Virginia and the Mississippi River. Within this region there is some excellent farm land, and also land where the soil has been exhausted by unscientific agricultural methods. There are business centers and industrial towns and cities, and, by way of contrast, thousands of miles of virgin forest. Much of the region was within reach of navigable rivers or rivers which could be made navigable. Here was a relatively compact territorial unit, suitable for a wide diversity of economic interests, which might be made into a great laboratory of social and economic planning. Justification for the experiment could be found in the urgent need of systematic work in the interest of flood control, in the equally urgent need of comprehensive efforts to check further erosion and to remedy damage already done. Then the necessary construction work would provide employment.

In the spring of 1933 Congress created the Tennessee Valley Authority, with a board of three in charge. The TVA went immediately to work on the dams needed to complete the program of flood control. And of course each of the major dams was a source of hydroelectric power. Up to the end of 1939 the TVA had completed five major dams on the Tennessee River and its tributaries, and there were four more under construction. Also in 1939 TVA bought extensive properties of the Tennessee Electric Power Company, one of the subsidiaries of the Commonwealth and Southern. This purchase gave the TVA five additional power plants. In February 1936 the Supreme Court upheld the constitutional right of the TVA to sell electric power, primarily on the ground that the manufacture of power was incidental to the major work of controlling floods, improving navigation, and preventing erosion. This right was confirmed in a second decision in January 1939.

In the program of relief the Democrats began with public works projects which had been started during the Hoover administration. In the Roosevelt regime the Public Works Administration was created, under the direction of Harold Ickes, secretary of the interior. Through this agency the national government financed some enterprises directly and made grants to states, cities, or even private corporations for others. By June 1934 the PWA had allocated $3,300,000,000 for a total of 15,673 different construction projects.

Relief

To provide immediate employment another agency, the Federal Emergency Relief Administration, joined the rapidly increasing list of alphabetical units. Congress turned over $250,000,000 to the FERA for grants to those states which would make additional relief appropriations on the basis of three state dollars for each federal dollar. An additional $250,000,000 was appropriated for help to states which could appropriate nothing for relief. The next unit organized to provide relief was the Civil Works Administration, established in November 1933. Under the leadership of Harry L. Hopkins, CWA put men to work on roads, parks, playgrounds, and drainage projects. Four million men were given employment, at wages averaging $15 for a thirty-hour week.

In spite of these devices, by 1935 the unemployed still numbered close to 10,000,000, and there were probably 5,000,000 directly on relief. These last, with their dependents, probably included close to 20,000,000 people. In his message to Congress in January 1935, President Roosevelt analyzed the problem and tried to reach a solution. Specifically he proposed to turn the estimated number of 1,500,000 unemployables back to the states and local welfare agencies. For the able-bodied persons in actual need of work the government must provide jobs, The projects undertaken were to compete as little as possible with private enterprise. The President suggested that men might be put to work on slum clearance, rural electrification, and elimination of grade crossings.

Following the message, Congress created still another agency, the Works Progress Administration—later renamed the Work Projects Administration—with Harry L. Hopkins in charge. The WPA began to function at once, and it provided funds for a variety of projects, many of which were designed for unemployed in the white collar class—writers, artists, actors, and musicians—as well as for laborers. From January 1933 to June 1939 the federal government paid out in direct relief, grants to states for relief, and work projects in various categories the sum of $17,868,804,000. From June 1933 to June 1940 the United States debt increased from $22,538,672,164 to $45,000,000,000. The greater part of this increase was due to the cost of relief.

Social Security

Even after the establishment of the alphabetical agencies the administration of relief was on none too systematic a basis, and there was no national policy or administrative body to provide safeguards against the normal, inevitable hazards of illness, unemployment, or old age. In 1935 Congress sought to meet this need by enacting the Social Security Law. This comprehensive measure was really a collection of ten related programs, all to be administered under a Social Security Board. The best-known part of this measure, and the only part administered entirely by the federal government, has to do with old-age and survivors' insurance. Under this law and its amendment of 1939, provision is made for monthly benefit payments to retired employees and to their surviving dependents. The amount of each monthly payment or pension is figured on the basis of the average monthly wages earned during the period of employment. The maximum monthly pension payment, however, was set at $85. To provide funds for the payment of these pensions employers and employees both paid a tax of 1 percent of the worker's wages, up to wages of $3000 in any one year; earnings above $3000 were not subject to this specific tax. The Social Security Board was required to keep a detailed record of the earnings of every employee eligible for this old-age pension.

In addition to this broad program of old-age insurance, the Social Security Act provided for old-age payments to those in need, even though they have accumulated nothing under the pay-roll tax. These payments were made to the states, and the states provided twice the amount paid by the federal government. The other parts of the social security program were financed jointly by the states and the national government. These other matters covered were: the blind; dependent children; maternal and child welfare; maternal and child health; crippled children; child welfare; public health; and vocational rehabilitation.

Politics and Elections in the New Deal

The outstanding political characteristic of the New Deal was the continuing popularity of President Roosevelt. In 1936 his renomination for a second term was a foregone conclusion. The Democratic platform found abundant reasons for pride in his record, approval of his policies, and confidence in a new philosophy of government. For the future, the Democratic party would emphasize the principles of power at the top level and national authority as opposed to states' rights: "the test of a representative government is its ability to promote the safety and happiness of its people."

Election of 1936

As the election of 1936 approached, the Republicans found themselves in a quandary. Their leaders did not like the New Deal, but the people did, and they would probably say so with votes. Former President Hoover described the Democratic program as "a cold-blooded attempt by starry-eyed boys to infect the American people by a mixture of European ideas, flavored with our native predilection to get something for nothing." Campaign strategy, however, seemed to force the Republicans to promise even greater benefits than those delivered by the New Deal. Certainly this was the gist of the Republican platform and also the main theme of the speeches of Alfred M. Landon, the candidate. In this contest of promises of federal largesse, the Democrats already had the position and the advantages of professionals. Why should the voters turn them out and trust to a lot of amateurs? The figures tell the story. In the popular vote Roosevelt received 26,484,229, Landon, 17,469,771. The Democrats won the electoral votes of all but two states, Maine and Vermont, and they registered gains in both houses of Congress.

Recession of 1937

The Presidential campaign of 1936 was accompanied by a marked improvement in industry and business. For this improvement, up to August 1937, the administration assumed full credit. "We planned it that way," the President proclaimed. Then in August a decline set in, which, while it lasted, was actually sharper than that of 1930-32, although fortunately it did not continue so long. In nine months industrial production lost two thirds of the advance made under the New Deal.

The causes of the decline have been attributed in part to heavy purchase of raw materials on a rising market during 1936 and 1937 and to the lack of buying power to take up the product. Manufacturers therefore had to curtail their operations. This industrial decline increased unemployment and so decreased buying power still further. Then, during the first part of 1937 the administration cut down its expenditures for relief and curtailed its borrowing. The advocates of heavy spending and lending attributed the recession to this one factor. In any case the spenders had the full support of the President. On April 2, 1938, Roosevelt publicly announced the renewal of the spending program, and in a radio address a few days later he informed the people that he was asking Congress for $3,000,000,000 for relief and public works.

Attack on Supreme Court

During the interval between the election of 1936 and the announced triumph of the heavy spenders the President went through a fight with Congress in which he suffered his first major defeat. In January 1937, after his second inauguration, he announced to the reporters at one of his press conferences that he was going to remake the Supreme Court, partly because it had stood in the way of New Deal reforms. The essential provisions of the President's plan for the Supreme Court called for the appointment of one additional judge for each member of the court who had reached the age of seventy, who had held his position for at least ten years, and who should refuse to resign. Under this arrangement the Supreme Court might be increased to a total of fifteen.

In this controversy Democrats joined with Republicans in administering a reprimand such as few Presidents have suffered at the hands of the Senate. On June 14, 1937, the Senate Judiciary Committee submitted its report on the President's proposal. Seven Democrats and three Republicans signed the report, and it had the support of the majority of Senate Democrats. This report characterized the plan as "a needless, futile and utterly dangerous abandonment of our constitutional principles." After several weeks of debate, the Senate returned the bill to the committee. However, as his friends put it, the President lost the battle but he won the war. The Court began to approve new laws. Then some of the justices resigned and some died, so in a few years the Court had a majority of Roosevelt appointees.

In the Congressional elections of 1938, for the first time in ten years, the Republicans showed a definite gain at the polls. They raised their membership in the Senate from fifteen to twenty-three, and in the House from eighty-eight to 170. The number of Republican state governors was raised from five to eighteen. In view of the trends in the preceding elections this shift was almost revolutionary. The Republicans felt that they could now begin to rehabilitate their shattered organizations in the states, and several leaders in the party began to show a lively interest in the Republican nomination for the Presidency in 1940.

For months the leading Republican contestant was Thomas E. Dewey, the racket-smashing district attorney of New York City. Another leading contestant was Senator Robert A. Taft of Ohio, son of former President William Howard Taft. Senator Taft had the experience in both state and national affairs which Dewey lacked, and he had the political advantage of coming from the Middle West. One other possibility stood in a class by himself, a man who had never sought nor held public office, a newcomer in the party, one who had made no preliminary campaign to round up delegates. This was Wendell L. Willkie, president of the Commonwealth and Southern Corporation. Early in 1939 a few influential journalists mentioned Willkie as a Presidential possibility. Arthur Krock of *The New York Times* pointed to Willkie as a possible nominee as early as February 23, 1939. General Hugh Johnson saw the same sign of promise. On May 26, 1940, after a tour through the Middle West, Turner Catledge of *The New York Times* wrote: "The stock of Wendell L. Willkie as a Presidential possibility is rising precipitately in certain quarters, although the great question remains as to whether he can translate this reaction into convention delegates this late in the race." By June 24, when the convention opened, Willkie had risen to second place in popularity. On the sixth ballot he received the Republican nomination. For the first time in years the party had a candidate who really took hold of the imagination of the people. For the vice-presidency the Republicans nominated Senator McNary of Oregon.

Election of 1940

World War II had begun almost a year before, and the Republican platform went on record against involvement in foreign war, but it advocated a defense adequate to protect the United States and "also efficiently to uphold the Monroe Doctrine." As for the victims of aggression in Europe, the party advocated such help "as shall not be in violation of international law or inconsistent with the requirements of our own national defense." The Republicans undertook to solve unemployment by giving encouragement to private industry. They would help the farmers with policies designed to "establish and maintain an equitable balance between labor, industry, and agriculture" and also by reducing the costs of production. Until these new policies could restore prosperity to the farmers, the Republicans would provide benefit payments. In its major provisions the platform bore a close resemblance to that of the Democrats.

For various reasons President Roosevelt decided to overlook the two-term tradition and to accept the nomination again, if the convention should agree. He received it on the first ballot. For his running mate the delegates followed Roosevelt's suggestion and nominated Henry A. Wallace, secretary of agriculture. The Democratic platform pledged the American people against participation in foreign wars: "we will not send our Army, naval or air forces to fight in foreign lands except in case of attack." But like the Republicans they would defend the Monroe Doctrine. They would provide the victims of aggression in Europe with "all the material aid at our command, consistent with law and not inconsistent with the interests of our own national self-defense." Continued help was pledged to the farmers to protect them from the evil of low prices.

The issues in this campaign of 1940 were simple and with certain outstanding exceptions there was little difference between the policies of the two candidates. Their foreign policy was the same: keep out of war unless attacked and give all possible help to Great Britain. Both candidates favored a strong program of national defense, including selective service for the army. Willkie charged that the administration's work in this field had proceeded much more slowly than necessary. Again both candidates were interested in the welfare of organized labor and of the farmers. Willkie gave formal assurances that none of the social security policies of the New Deal would be revoked. The two candidates parted company on the subjects of federal finance and business enterprise. Willkie disapproved of the President's willingness to increase the public debt, his attitude toward business, and his economic philosophy. The Republican candidate promised to cut down federal expenditures and to encourage production under a system of private enterprise.

Interest in the election brought out the heaviest vote ever cast in the United States. Roosevelt received 27,243,466 popular votes, while Willkie got 22,304,755. Roosevelt carried thirty-eight states, with 449 electoral votes, Willkie 10 states,[1] with 82 electoral votes. Roosevelt's plurality, 4,914,713, was the smallest he had received but nevertheless ample to keep him in office. Willkie's vote exceeded Hoover's of 1932 by 6,000,000, and Landon's of 1936 by nearly 5,000,000. There was no substantial change in the House of Representatives. In the Senate, however, by one of those strange results which our electoral system makes possible, the Republicans gained three seats.

Election of 1944

Up to 1944 there had been only one Presidential election held when the United States was actually at war. This was in 1864. In 1944 the Democrats were more strongly convinced than ever that President Roosevelt was the "indispensable man." Having broken the old tradition against a third term in 1940, there was no reason why they should fear a fourth term, so Roosevelt received the nomination. Because of differences within the Democratic party, Henry Wallace was dropped as the vice-presidential candidate, and Senator Harry S. Truman of Missouri was given the place.

The Republicans nominated Governor Thomas E. Dewey of New York. Following Roosevelt's example of 1932, Dewey made a campaign tour as far as the Pacific Coast and back. In his speeches he urged an economic policy so much like the New Deal that some voters professed to see no difference. As the event proved it was poor political strategy for Dewey to run on the issues popularized by his opponents. Furthermore Dewey's verbal attacks upon President Roosevelt antagonized some people. The most important factor in the campaign, however, was the war, and it worked to the advantage of the party in power. Roosevelt's electoral vote fell off somewhat over 1940: 432 in 1944 as against 449. Dewey received 99, which compared favorably with Willkie's 82. In the popular vote in 1944 Roosevelt received 25,603,152 and Dewey 22,006,616.

[1] Maine, Vermont, Indiana, Michigan, Iowa, North Dakota, South Dakota, Nebraska, Kansas, Colorado.

Chapter 46

FOREIGN POLICY—FROM THE GOOD NEIGHBOR TO PEARL HARBOR, 1933-41

General Conditions

PRESIDENT ROOSEVELT entered office in what seemed to be an era of international peace and good will. Although the United States had not joined the League of Nations, she had shown a readiness to cooperate with it. All the important governments of the world had accepted the Kellogg-Briand Pact, which outlawed war as an instrument of national policy. In 1925 and 1926 the countries of western Europe put into effect the Locarno Treaties by which Germany, Belgium, France, Italy, and Great Britain agreed to guarantee existing boundaries. Germany signed arbitration treaties with France, Poland, Czechoslovakia, and Belgium by which these governments undertook to settle disputes by peaceful means. The various governments appeared ready to forget past differences and to devote themselves to civilized pursuits. Large numbers of people, particularly in the United States, accepted this concept of world affairs as not only settled but permanent.

Every idyllic picture must have its proverbial cloud on the horizon, but in this case it seemed even smaller than a man's hand. In 1931 and 1932 the Japanese had conquered Manchuria and transformed it into the puppet state of Manchukuo, but few Americans expected the Japanese to make further conquests. Secretary of State Stimson did warn of danger, and he was prepared to support the League of Nations in a protest. The other threat to peace had not even attained the dimensions of a visible cloud. In January 1933 President von Hindenburg of Germany appointed a new chancellor, Adolf Hitler. Nobody in America realized then that in seven years' time Hitler would destroy civilization throughout western Europe and substitute for it a system built upon terrorism, violence, and almost irresistible force.

Roosevelt defined the guiding principles of his foreign policy in his first inaugural of March 4, 1933:

> In the field of world policy I would dedicate this Nation to the policy of the good neighbor—the neighbor who resolutely respects himself and, because he does so, respects the rights of others—the neighbor who respects his obligations and respects the sanctity of his agreements in and with a world of neighbors.

This brief quotation has a double value. It illustrates Roosevelt's skill in hitting upon the peculiarly apt phrase. It also provided an easily remembered name for a popular policy.

Cooperation with Latin America

For Latin America Roosevelt found the basis for a new policy already laid down by President Hoover. Before his inauguration Hoover had made a good-will tour of the nations to the south, and after his inauguration he made a definite bid for their friendship by reversing some of the Wilson and Coolidge policies. In 1930 he ordered an investigation into affairs in Haiti. Following this investigation he authorized the establishment of a provisional government under Haitian auspices. Next came the election of a Haitian legislature, the first since 1915. In 1931 Haiti adopted a new constitution and elected a president. Thus after sixteen years Haiti was restored to its former status as an independent republic. President Hoover also ordered the withdrawal of the marines from Santo Domingo.

The Good Neighbor

Roosevelt began where Hoover left off and carried the policy of respecting Latin American rights much further. In December 1933, at the Pan-American Conference meeting at Montevideo, Secretary of State Hull gave formal approval to the doctrine that "no state has the right to intervene in the internal or external affairs of another." The President himself reaffirmed this action in an announcement (December 28, 1933): "The definite policy of the United States from now on is one opposed to armed intervention." In August 1934, at the end of nineteen years of military domination by the United States, the marines were called home from Haiti. Then the United States formally surrendered the rights of intervention, which had been given by treaty, in Haiti and in Nicaragua. Shortly before this, a new treaty with Cuba put an end to the Platt Amendment. In 1936 the United States surrendered its treaty right to intervene in the Panama Republic.

Roosevelt's policy of the good neighbor created a new era in the relations between the United States and Latin America. Having accomplished so much in dispelling suspicion and creating good will in its place, President Roosevelt and Secretary Hull tried to provide for cooperation in all matters of foreign policy which might affect the American governments. In January 1936 the President sent out invitations to another conference, to meet the following December at Buenos Aires. Earlier conferences of this sort had been called Pan-American. But the very term was associated with the old doctrine of North American supremacy and so was distasteful to the Latin Americans. Roosevelt's new invitation asked the governments to send delegates to an Inter-American Conference. The tactful change in name seems to have been appreciated.

At the conference delegates from twenty-one governments adopted a Convention for the Maintenance, Preservation, and Reestablishment of Peace, which provided for consultation whenever the peace of America might be threatened. The conference also adopted a Declaration of Principles of Inter-American Solidarity and Cooperation, which called for cooperative policy in case of danger. For the future, disputes were to be settled by conciliation, arbitration, or "through the operation of international justice." If these documents with high-sounding names seemed hazy and indefinite in content, like the Kellogg-Briand Pact, nevertheless they were the product of joint action, and they reflected a new, friendly attitude on the part of Latin America toward the United States.

In the autumn of 1938 the governments of the world suddenly waked up to a realization of what Hitler's terrorism had in store for them. By the capitulation at Munich, France and Great Britain yielded to Hitler's demand for Czechoslovakia. This Franco-British experiment in abject appeasement was alarming. Following the tragedy at Munich there was another Inter-American Conference, which met in December 1938 at Lima, Peru. In the past both cultural ties and geographical position bound the Latin Americans more closely to Europe than to America, and every conference of American nations had to take this connection into account. At this time there seemed to be even greater interest than ever in fascist Italy and nazi Germany. In the circumstances there could be no forthright statement of principle or policy; any attempt to force one upon the conference would have shown how far apart the delegates really were. The declaration of Lima, which was at last produced, reaffirmed the faith of the American peoples in individual liberty and in international law and suggested some sort of united action in case aggression from Europe should threaten any American power. The delegates also approved Secretary Hull's eight-point program, known as the Declaration of American Principles. These were in brief a reaffirmation of the doctrine that peace rested on respect for national integrity, international law, and treaties made in accordance therewith. The Declaration contained a mildly adverse complaint against armed force as an instrument of policy. There was no definite guarantee that all American governments would combine to oppose an extension of European totalitarianism to the New World.

Lima

By the summer of 1940, when Hitler had all western Europe except the British Isles under his control, Secretary Hull arranged for another conference, to open on July 20 at Havana. Again representatives of the twenty-one republics came together, this time in the face of grave danger. Hitler's influence in some of the governments was apparent, and he was sending out assurances that he had no aims in Latin America—assurances which meant the reverse of what they said. Here was one problem for the conference. In connection with the major issue of the Hitler menace, there were the closely associated matters of the status of the Dutch and French colonies in the Caribbean area and the problem of German trade with Latin America. As a safeguard against further German penetration of the Western world, Secretary Hull submitted a plan for a comprehensive Inter-American trade agreement or cartel under which the United States would buy Latin American products. American dollars would be put into direct competition with German schemes of barter. At last the real test had come.

Havana

Could the United States count on genuine cooperation and support in Latin America?

On July 29, 1940, the conference at Havana reached an agreement with reference to the provisional administration of colonies of any European power which might be endangered by German conquests in Europe. In case of threat of a transfer of such colony or colonies from one European power to another, the American republics would arrange to establish "regions of provisional administration." The provisional administration would have a dual purpose: to contribute to the safety of the American republics and to promote the well-being of the regions themselves. Responsibility for administering these regions would be delegated to an emergency committee composed of one member from each of the twenty-one American republics; this committee would be ready to function as soon as two thirds of the governments had appointed their members, and it would meet at the request of any of the signers of the resolution. In case of sudden emergency, any of the American republics, acting singly or together, should have the right to act in defense of itself or of the continent.

To give the foregoing policy the proper legal basis, the conference adopted a formal convention. This declared, among other things, that "the American republics would consider any transfer or attempt to transfer sovereignty, jurisdiction, possession or any interest or control in any of these regions to another non-American State as contrary to American sentiments, principles and rights of American States to maintain their security and political independence"; then the legal accord continued to the effect that the American republics would not "recognize nor accept such transfer or intent to transfer" territory or control. The economic accord arrived at was general in terms, stressing the advantages of a system of free commerce and expressing hope that such a system could be made world-wide. In the meantime the American republics would encourage inter-American trade. The original proposal of a great cartel for the handling of American products was not approved.

The agreement reached on the question of European holdings in the New World was, of course, a reaffirmation of the Monroe Doctrine, but with this important difference. The Monroe Doctrine had been unilateral, and it contained within itself no mechanism of enforcement; the Havana agreement was multilateral, including all twenty-one republics, and it provided for a definite system of enforcement—definite in the sense that its effectiveness depended entirely on the readiness of the governments concerned to take action. At the start the arrangement held out greater promise than the League of Nations, because the twenty-one republics were all faced with a common danger and the bond of self-interest might well be strong enough to force them to act. Here at last was the inter-American union which Bolivar had envisioned at the original Panama Congress and which Woodrow Wilson and Colonel House had suggested prior to 1917. The United States Senate ratified the Havana Convention.

Attitudes toward Europe

London Conference

Roosevelt's first venture into European affairs was considerably less promising than his experiments in Latin America. Beginning in 1932 a committee representing the governments of Belgium, France, Germany, Italy, Great Britain, the United States, and six smaller states selected by the League of Nations had begun work on the agenda for an international conference on economic affairs. Because of the attitude of the United States, the coming conference was barred from debating such matters as reparations, war debts, or tariff policies. But the conference still had such important topics of discussion as foreign exchange, the problem of prices, world trade, and stabilization of currencies. The conference was scheduled to meet at London, and President Roosevelt showed lively interest in it. However, the President and Secretary Hull found it difficult to agree on instructions to the American delegates. The delegates themselves were not in agreement, and after they reached England the President upset some of the plans which had been made. The President had called for stabilization of currencies; subsequently he refused to approve any plan for stabilization.

The conference assembled in June 1933 with 168 delegates present, representing sixty-six governments. The course of the conference revealed either lack of preparation or fundamental inability to agree on common objectives. Provisional plans for stabilizing currencies were thrown into confusion when Roosevelt's secretary of the treasury, Woodin, announced that reports of stabilization coming from London had no foundation in fact, and that any agreement on the subject if reached at all would be reached in Washington, D. C. Nobody could forecast the President's next change in mind, and there was no object in working out agreements at London only to have them repudiated at Washington. The great conference at London therefore accomplished little.

Limitation of Armament

During the Harding-Coolidge-Hoover era the prevailing enthusiasm for peace and the belief that peace was attainable merely through the good intentions of one party had been accompanied by tentative and gingerly steps toward limitation of armaments. This policy was logical enough, provided the premises on which it rested were sound. In view of all the talk about peace, it was to be expected that President Roosevelt should make his contribution to a better world. On May 16, 1933, he sent a statement to the executives of fifty-four governments, urging them to work for the abolition of all offensive weapons. Then all governments would agree not to increase their armaments, and they would enter into pacts of nonaggression. Most important of all, they would bind themselves not to send any armed forces beyond their own frontiers and peace would be established for all time.

Although addressed to most of the leading governments of the world, the Roosevelt message was designed primarily for Adolf Hitler, who had just given notice that Germany would ignore the limitations imposed upon her by the Treaty of Versailles and rearm as she saw fit. Hitler told his hand-picked *Reichstag* that Germany did not want war, would not make war, and desired only to protect her own borders. Germany was also prepared to disarm completely if only her neighbors would do the same. These assertions stood in direct contradiction to statements in Hitler's own book *Mein Kampf*. He had not only outlined a comprehensive program which would have been impossible of realization without war, but he had explained with amazing frankness that any promises made were merely a means to an end. Mendacity was a principle of statesmanship.

So little was accomplished in limiting armaments that it is almost a waste of time to mention it. In 1930 Japan, Great Britain, and the United States had agreed to prolong their naval holiday for another six years and to extend the limitation to destroyers, submarines, and cruisers. In 1934, however, Japan announced that after 1936 she would no longer observe the Washington Treaty of 1922. Then a naval conference met at London in 1935 with Japan, Italy, France, Great Britain, and the United States participating. The Japanese delegates soon withdrew, and without Japanese cooperation there was no opportunity for effective work. In March 1936 France, Great Britain, and the United States signed the London Naval Treaty, prohibiting for six years the construction of cruisers and battleships and placing limitations on the size of other classes of fighting ships. By that time plans for rearmament were attracting more attention than plans for peace.

Recognition of Russia

Among the unsettled questions which Roosevelt inherited was the problem of Soviet Russia. From 1917 when the Bolsheviki established their "dictatorship of the proletariat" to 1933 the United States had officially ignored the existence of the new regime. At first recognition was withheld because there was no proof of stability in the communist government. Later, when stability had been achieved, disapproval of Russian policies prevented recognition. Part of the communist dogma was world revolution. Therefore the communist rulers, who rigorously suppressed all nonconformists in Russia, took advantage of the privileges of free speech and free press elsewhere to spread their propaganda into many parts of the world. In the United States they found a following among some labor leaders and also among the "intelligentsia," particularly in the fields of literature and journalism. Taking their orders from Moscow, American communists made themselves a public nuisance in the United States.

Admitting that communist propaganda had been a source of trouble in this country, Roosevelt nevertheless felt that diplomatic relations should be resumed with the Soviet Union. It was one of the most important countries of the world, and recognition need not imply approval of communism. In December 1933, after prolonged negotiations, recognition was accorded and formal diplomatic relations were renewed. In return, and as a specific condition of recognition, the Russian government gave a formal promise not to carry on any more propaganda in the United States. Although they gave it, the Bolsheviks had little intention of complying with it. According to their way of reasoning, their government never had been concerned with propaganda in this country; such work had been carried on by the American Communist party, which had no connection with the Soviet government. Although the public received no official inkling of it, there was another reason for the recognition of Russia. Russia was opposed to further Japanese aggression in the Far East, and recognition of Russia by the United States might deter the Japanese from further ventures. The futility of this latter notion was demonstrated in July 1937 when the Japanese entered upon their war for the conquest of China.

Reciprocal Trade Agreements

In the meantime Secretary of State Hull, although aware of these disturbing trends—to the extent that any public officials were fully aware of them—proceeded to work on a plan to bring back better economic conditions by the peaceful encouragement of world trade. Because of the intense nationalism of the dictatorships and particularly because of the alarming spread of militarism, it is remarkable that any policy founded upon peace and sanity should have had any success whatever. But there was still room for decency in international affairs, and Hull's program of reciprocal trade agreements stood out as one element of rationality in a world rapidly going mad.

The policy of Secretary Hull was designed to deal with the high tariff of the United States and with the import quotas and export controls adopted by European governments. Democratic leaders in the Roosevelt administration realized that the American tariff could not be safely reduced so long as foreign restrictions remained in effect. At the same time, the secretary of state firmly believed that economic prosperity and foreign trade were inseparable. Briefly, then, his aim was to lower individual tariff items in return for corresponding concessions by other governments. Under his influence in June 1934 Congress passed the Reciprocal Trade Agreements Act; since that time the measure has been regularly renewed. This law gave the President authority to negotiate trade agreements with foreign countries, under which American tariff rates on specified items would be reduced by not more than 50 percent. In no case, however, was any item to be added to or removed from the free list. Concessions granted to any one government automatically went into effect with all others with which the United States had most-favored-nation agreements. By 1939, 68 percent of American foreign trade was covered by reciprocal trade agreements.

Anarchy and War

By 1935 there were signs of an abandonment of the concept of a world united in a League of Nations and dedicated by Locarno Treaties and the Kellogg-Briand Pact to peace through collective action. Japan had successfully defied the doctrine in her conquest of Manchuria, and the only penalty she suffered was a mild reprimand administered by the League. The United States expressed disapproval of the Japanese policy and withheld recognition from Manchukuo. This expression did not alter the situation in the Far East, and its only result was to create Japanese ill will.

In the meantime, Mussolini, leader of fascist Italy, had watched developments in the Far East with more than ordinary interest. He was faced with a domestic situation that was rapidly getting out of hand, and he knew that there was nothing like a "vigorous" foreign policy to divert popular attention from the shortcomings of government at home. If Japan could forcibly reorganize China without suffering any worse penalty than mere words, he too might add to Italian possessions. In 1935 he attacked and conquered Ethiopia. Again, as in the case of Japan, the United States proclaimed herself the guardian of the moral law. In August 1935, before the war began but in anticipation of it, Congress adopted a joint resolution of neutrality, imposing an embargo on materials of war and authorizing the President to prohibit American citizens from taking passage on belligerent ships. In October, after the outbreak of war, the President issued a proclamation in accordance with the congressional resolution. By so doing the United States abandoned the doctrine which she had upheld ever since the eighteenth century, the doctrine of freedom of the seas.

Neutrality

In his annual message of January 1936 President Roosevelt defined the role of the United States in these terms: "through a well-ordered neutrality to do naught to encourage the contest, through adequate defense to save ourselves from embroilment and attack, and through example and all legitimate encouragement and assistance to persuade other nations to return to the ways of peace and good will." In accordance with the President's recommendation, Congress adopted new neutrality resolutions, which declared an embargo on the export of "arms, ammunition, and implements of warfare" to all belligerents and which required the registration and licensing of all munitions manufacturers in the United States. But when the League of Nations began to consider the application of economic sanctions to Italy, the United States would give no promise of cooperation.

In 1936 Hitler announced that the Treaties of Locarno were void and that his forces would reoccupy and fortify the Rhineland. Neither France nor Great Britain did more than talk, and their refusal to act gave tacit approval to Hitler's spectacular repudiation of another section of the Treaty of Versailles. Here he was acting in accordance with a precept laid down in *Mein Kampf;* in a policy of aggression, one should proceed by successive steps, each more extreme than its predecessor but each one just short of provocation to war. Then the opponents who acquiesced in the first step will find it difficult to oppose succeeding ones.

In 1937, when the Japanese entered upon the conquest of China, Congress passed a more formal neutrality law, by which the export of arms, implements, and munitions of war was prohibited. The measure also prohibited the sale of securities of a belligerent country in the United States; it prohibited the transportation of war materials in American ships and the travel of Americans in belligerent ships. All these prohibitions became mandatory when the President found that a state of war existed. The President might also invoke a cash-and-carry provision, in accordance with which foreign buyers of nonmilitary commodities in the United States might be required to pay for their purchases on delivery in this country and to transport their purchases. The President signed this measure, subsequently stating that he did so with regret.

Growing Dangers

For a brief period there was hope of action against these aggressors. In October 1937 President Roosevelt suggested a quarantine to protect the civilized part of the world from war. A few weeks later representatives of nineteen governments, including Russia, Great Britain, and the United States, met in conference at Brussels to discuss the situation in the Far East. At first President Roosevelt favored an agreement with Great Britain and Russia to block Japan, but before the conference met he changed his mind. The conference followed the League in condemning Japanese action in China, but it went no further. The Japanese showed their resentment in December by deliberately sinking the American gunboat *Panay* in the Yangtze River.

In the spring of 1939, after Hitler had taken possession of Austria and Czechoslovakia and was preparing to seize Poland, President Roosevelt sent a plea for peace to both Hitler and Mussolini. Referring to widespread fear of more wars, the President claimed the right to speak because of the effect of such wars upon all mankind. He called Hitler's attention to his power to avert war and then asked him if he would give assurance for the present and for the future that he had no aggressive designs upon any of the nations of Europe and the Near East. If Hitler would give such assurance, the President would transmit the news to the governments concerned and would endeavor to secure similar pledges of good intentions toward Germany. If such reciprocal assurances could be given, the President continued, he would then arrange for a conference to discuss such important matters as limitation of armament and the removal of barriers in the way of world trade. "I hope that your answer will make it possible for humanity to lose fear and regain security for many years to come."

Less than two weeks later Hitler replied to the President, and at the same time his foreign office made it plain that Germany would re-annex Danzig and would subject Poland to such degree of control as German authorities considered desirable. Specifically in reply to the President, Hitler announced his readiness to give assurances to the governments concerned, provided they asked for them and would also give similar assurances to him. He always had advocated the settlement of disputes without resort to arms, he said. As for German aggression, "I would ask him to name the States which are threatened with aggression and to name the aggressor in question. It will then be possible to refute these monstrous general accusations by brief statements." Even then few people realized what a monumental liar Hitler was

He was determined to make the Germans supreme in Europe: "Today we rule the Fatherland, tomorrow we rule the world"; and while he was willing to take all he could get merely by a show of force, he was ready to put his force to work.

Congress wound up its work in August 1939 and before doing so it had appropriated the sum of $1,614,000,000 for military and naval defense. Sums for this purpose were growing larger, but apart from the quarantine speech the President gave no public intimation that he considered the United States in any special danger. On September 1, 1939, Germany began a new world war by sending her armies into Poland. Roosevelt called Congress in special session to meet on September 21, not to provide for additional defense but to repeal that part of the Neutrality Resolution of 1937 which imposed an absolute embargo on the export of arms and munitions. His purpose in urging repeal was to throw open to the Allies the great industrial resources of the American people. Then the expansion of our industrial plants made necessary by war orders could be utilized in improving the defensive position of the United States itself. The President expressed hope that the United States would be able to keep out of the war.

World War II

The new Neutrality Act, passed in November 1939, prohibited American ships from carrying commodities of any sort to belligerent ports. But belligerents were permitted to buy materials of all kinds in the United States, provided they acquired title to them before shipment and provided they looked after the transportation themselves. American citizens were forbidden to travel on any ship belonging to any belligerent, and American ships were forbidden to carry arms. By this means it was expected that American producers and manufacturers might transact business with the Allies without involving the United States in danger of war.

Once the war started, German armies overwhelmed Poland with amazing speed and efficiency. Then early in the winter Russia, after futile negotiations for territory near Leningrad, attacked Finland, and by sheer overwhelming mass the Red Army forced the small country to capitulate. Later Finland joined Germany in making war on her old enemy, Russia, and still later she joined the Allies in war against Germany. But the war in the West seemed to have reached a standstill, with the French behind their Maginot Line and the Germans protected by the West Wall. Action on the sea and in the air continued, but elsewhere there was so little sign of life that some commentators began to call it a "phoney war." Then, in the midst of this lull, news began to pour into the United States, and it convinced everybody that the war was no longer "phoney." On April 9, 1940, German troops occupied Denmark without a struggle and began their conquest of Norway. Before they finished this assignment they drove rapidly across the Netherlands and Belgium and invaded France. In June Italy entered the war, and on June 25 France signed the terms which left her not only defenseless but stripped of her industrial area and all her seaports. The fall of France was the inevitable result of the capitulation at Munich.

Plans for Defense

The rapid westward sweep of the German forces was full of sinister meaning for the United States. Should the British be defeated—and in the spring of 1940 Hitler had good reason for his boasts that she would—the Western Hemisphere might be open to the invader. To some of the American people and to President Roosevelt the danger appeared so obvious that immediate action became imperative. On May 16, 1940, the President addressed Congress and the nation at large on the subject of national defense. "These are ominous days," he said, "days whose swift and shocking developments force every nation to look to its defenses in the light of new factors." Then after pointing out the easy accessibility of even the Middle West to attack from the air, he asked Congress for $1,000,000,000 for defense in addition to appropriations already made. In particular he emphasized the necessity for far greater strength in the air, and he asked for an annual production of planes numbering at least 50,000. On May 31 the President asked for still another billion, and Congress began its unprecedented appropriations for military and naval purposes. By December 21, 1941, two weeks after Japan had attacked the United States, congressional appropriations for defense and for war had reached the figure of more than $70,000,000,000. For purposes of comparison it may be recalled that for World War I the direct cost to the United States was $22,272,000,000.

On June 20, 1940, Congress began consideration of the Burke-Wadsworth bill, providing for selective service for the army in time of peace. Six weeks later Secretary of War Stimson made an earnest plea for the enactment of the measure: "If there is any lesson which has been thoroughly proved by history throughout the life of our nation, it is that the only safe and effective way to meet a great war emergency is by the timely creation of a selective compulsory system for raising our armies." In spite of the threatening situation in Europe and in spite of the reasonableness of Secretary Stimson's argument, there was considerable opposition to the measure, and the debate upon it showed that not even all Congressmen had become aware of the danger. One member was quoted, but not named, in *The New York Times* as follows: "I still find it difficult to have much concern about an imminent invasion of the United States if Germany is victorious." In mid-September 1940, however, the measure became law. Under its terms men within the age limits of 21 to 35 were made liable for military service for one year.

Keeping War from Our Shores

Just previous to this, in the interest, as he said, of "national solidarity in a time of world crisis," President Roosevelt made two important changes in his Cabinet. For secretary of the navy he named Frank Knox, and for secretary of war he selected Henry L. Stimson. Both men were prominent Republicans; Stimson had served in two Cabinets, first as secretary of war under President Taft and then as secretary of state under President Hoover. Some Democrats found fault with the appointments on partisan grounds, while some Republicans accused the two men of treachery to their own party. Again there was opposition because both Knox and Stimson were advocates of intervention in the war.

In the summer of 1941, because of the increasingly threatening situation, the War Department asked Congress to make two amendments to the Burke-Wadsworth Act; the first, to remove the limit of one year on the length of service; the second, to end the ban on service overseas. Congress passed the first, but only by the narrowest possible majority: 203 to 202; permission to send the men overseas could not be secured until after the Japanese attack.

Helping Britain

According to the President's conviction, readiness for war consisted not only in provision for an army, navy, and air force but in the existence of factories equipped to turn out the needed materials for war. Congressional opposition to plans for an adequate army indicated that appropriations could not be secured for essential munitions and other equipment. Without American orders for such equipment and supplies, American maunfacturers were not likely to devote their old plants to war production or to build new ones to provide goods needed for war. However, even if orders could not be secured from our own government, they might be secured from England.

The policy which gradually developed was a revolutionary departure in American foreign policy and an undeniable violation of old principles of international law. Hitler, however, had destroyed the foundations of international law, thereby making it impossible for any government to conduct its affairs under the old concepts. For the future President Roosevelt would not leave the responsibility of arming Hitler's enemies to private manufacturers and merchants. Instead the United States government itself would undertake the work. On September 3, 1940, President Roosevelt informed Congress that he had arranged to furnish Great Britain with fifty destroyers, described as "over age." In return the British government gave the United States leases on certain sea and air bases in the Western Hemisphere. These leases were to run for ninety-nine years. The British also promised not to surrender or scuttle their navy. The bases in question were located on the following British possessions in the Western Hemisphere: Newfoundland, Bermuda, Bahama Islands, Jamaica, St. Lucia, Trinidad, British Guiana, and Antigua. The President made his announcement merely "for the information of the Congress," not to give that body the opportunity of taking action upon the matter.

Lend-Lease

Partly perhaps because of the irregularity of the method and partly because of uninformed criticism, the President decided to seek congressional sanction for a much more comprehensive program of aid to Britain. In the course of a press conference on December 17, 1940, the President explained that, because of the Johnson Act of 1934 and the Neutrality Act, aid to the enemies of Hitler was small in quantity. He advocated some sort of mortgage sale, so that the British could get the goods without being compelled to pay in advance. A few days later, in a "fireside chat," he declared that the

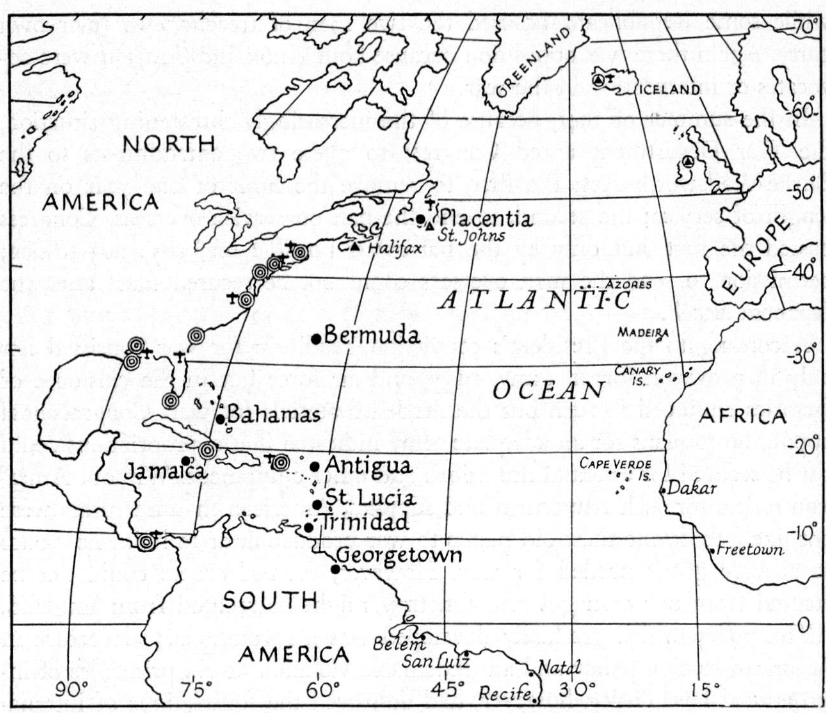

From Bemis, *Diplomatic History of the United States*

Old bases, home waters. New air bases, home coasts.
British bases. British-American bases later established, 1941.
The new bases, 1940.

Map 20. United States Naval Bases

United States must become the arsenal of democracy. To give added emphasis to his proposal he warned the American people of the increasing danger to them. On January 6, 1941, the President appeared personally before Congress with a plea for greater help for the foes of Hitler. Repeating his warning of grave danger, he prophesied that, whenever the dictators should decide to make war upon the United States, they would not wait for any warlike act on our part or for any declaration of war on their own. Then he asked Congress to provide for "an all inclusive national defense" and to guarantee full support to all nations engaged in war against Hitler. Such was the origin of the Lend-Lease Act, introduced in Congress on January 9, 1941, as H.R.1776, providing for all-out aid to Britain. It authorized the manufacture and transfer of war supplies to Britain and her associates, with no limit on the quantity and with no immediate provision for payment. When the bill passed—March 11, 1941—Congress provided $7,000,000,000 to finance the program. President Roosevelt explained that the measure was of vital importance to our own program of defense.

There was no point in manufacturing goods for Britain only to have them sent to the bottom of the Atlantic by German submarines; the completion of the President's policy called logically for additional naval protection for American cargoes. To facilitate this work the United States arranged for the establishment of United States naval bases in Greenland and Iceland. Then, objecting to the term "convoy," the President authorized an American naval and air patrol of the Atlantic for the protection of American cargoes. On May 27, 1941, the President proclaimed a state of unlimited emergency and announced: "We will not hesitate to use our armed forces to repel attack." Just two days earlier the German admiral, Raeder, announced that any American naval assistance to the British would bring immediate retaliation by Germany.

Atlantic Charter

In August 1941 Prime Minister Winston Churchill and President Roosevelt met at sea off Newfoundland and talked over the whole question of supply for the democracies. At the same time the two statesmen made public an eight-point program for peace. This Atlantic Charter bound the two powers to refrain from any aggrandizement, territorial or other, following the war. They promised that no territorial changes would be made unless these were approved by the people directly concerned. The third point called for the right of all peoples to choose the form of government under which they lived and proclaimed the right of the occupied countries to a restoration of independence. Then the two leaders endorsed a proposal to give access to essential raw materials to all states. Next, they called for better labor standards and for social security. For the sixth point, they called for a peace which, after the destruction of nazi tyranny, would afford safety to all nations. The seventh point promised freedom to use the high seas without hindrance, while the eighth recommended some limitation of armament. The Lend-Lease Act and the Atlantic Charter amounted to an alliance between the United States and Great Britain.

During the second half of the year 1941 hardly a week passed without some incident which brought the United States closer to an actual "shooting war." On September 1, speaking at Hyde Park, the President issued a new warning: "I know that I speak the conscience and determination of the American people when I say that we shall do everything in our power to crush Hitler and his Nazi forces." Then he urged the American people to exert themselves to the utmost in order to destroy "the forces of insane violence" which Hitler had turned loose. This speech was a fitting prelude to news which came in before the end of that week. In the preceding May a German submarine had torpedoed and sunk an American merchant ship, the *Robin Moor,* flying the American flag in the South Atlantic. The passengers and members of the crew took refuge in lifeboats, hundreds of miles from land. The German government ignored suggestions that apologies and reparation were in order. The *Robin Moor* was a merchant vessel not a warship, but sooner or later there was bound to be an attack upon some unit of the United States Navy. On September 4 the Navy Department gave out the following dramatic announcement: "The U.S.S. Destroyer *Greer,* en route to Iceland with mail, reported this morning that a submarine had attacked her by firing torpedoes which missed their mark. The *Greer* immediately counter-attacked with depth charges. Results are not known."

President Roosevelt soon reported more German attacks, and then issued a sharp warning:

> In the waters which we deem necessary for our defense, American naval vessels and American planes will no longer wait until Axis submarines lurking under the water, or Axis raiders on the surface of the sea, strike their deadly blow—first. . . . But let this warning be clear. From now on, if German or Italian vessels of war enter the waters, the protection of which is necessary for American defense, they do so at their own peril. . . . The sole responsibility rests upon Germany.

Although the administration had begun preparation for war in earnest in 1940, the country was not ready when war came. For the lack of adequate preparedness the responsibility rests partly upon the isolationists, those Americans who for one reason or another tried to prevent the administration's measures from being adopted. If the administration seemed dilatory and remiss, it must be remembered that the United States is a democracy and that the President cannot move too far against the demands of the people, no matter whether these demands are wise or stupid. Many of the President's opponents could not free themselves from traditional beliefs, and they were unable to comprehend the meaning of events in Europe. They still talked as though the United States were in complete control of its own destinies, entirely free to choose peace if the people so desired.

Isolationism

Many individuals of earnest purpose and excellent intentions advocated peace because war is evil. They failed to understand that peace is a condition which can be established and maintained only with considerable effort; sometimes, because of the aggressiveness of outsiders, it cannot be maintained at all. Some clergymen and church members were particularly active in spreading this notion that war could be avoided merely by wishful thinking. College students also took an active part in this sentimental drive against war. The Oxford pledge, binding signers not to go to war under any circumstances whatever, originated in England and soon became popular in this country. On May 15, 1940, 300 students at Harvard sent an anti-war petition to President Roosevelt; they informed him that "never under any circumstances will they follow in the footsteps of the students of 1917." At about the same time a so-called "Christian committee" at Yale sent a petition to President Roosevelt urging him to keep the United States out of war; this petition had 1486 signatures. Another group of undergraduates at Yale sent in a petition urging American help for Great Britain, but this had only 700 signatures.

In September 1940 this opposition to war was institutionalized through the creation of the America First Committee. This organization advocated an impregnable defense for the United States, so its leaders declared, but it opposed every step in preparedness. In little more than a year the America First Committee acquired a membership of close to 1,000,000. Among the leaders of this organization were General Robert Wood, a prominent businessman, and other honest persons. But the America First Committee also included some German agents and pro-nazi workers. Some of the most prominent speakers in the campaign to block the President's program were actually German agents. Miss Laura Ingalls, well-known flier, was arrested by the FBI on the charge of serving as a German agent. In February 1942 she was found guilty. In the middle of August 1941, when the administration was trying to persuade Congress to remove the limit of one year on service for the "selectees" and to authorize their use outside the limits of the Western Hemisphere, the America First Committee led the opposition.

Japan and Pearl Harbor

Japanese Aggression

As we know now, and as we should have known earlier, Germany was not the only foreign power which might decide the issue of peace or war for the United States; Japan might take a hand. Parts of the Atlantic Charter, particularly Points 2, 3, 6, and 8, had a direct bearing upon Japanese aggression in China as well as upon German aggression in Europe. Should this Charter go into effect, the Japanese would find themselves deprived of their puppet state of Manchukuo and denied all gains from their long war for the conquest of China. Furthermore, the Japanese realized the certain effect of the Lend-Lease program in strengthening the United States.

During the 1930's Japan had grown steadily more hostile to the Western powers. In Manchukuo the Japanese effectively closed the Open Door, insisting at the same time that they had not done so. By 1938 they were crowding non-Japanese economic activities out of China. In July 1939 the United States served notice that the American-Japanese commercial treaty signed in 1911 would be abrogated in January 1940. Then in September 1940 President Roosevelt announced an embargo, effective October 16, on the exportation of any more scrap iron and steel to Japan. During 1940 and 1941, although Japanese protests had been partly responsible for the failure to fortify Guam, the United States did improve its defenses at Midway and Wake Islands, increased the forces in Hawaii and the Philippines, and concentrated a considerable portion of its naval strength in the Pacific.

As the campaign in China dragged on without prospect of Japanese victory, the Japanese broadened the range of their ambitions. On November 3, 1938, the Japanese premier, Prince Konoye, proclaimed the establishment of the new order in East Asia. In the summer of 1940, the Japanese announced the formation of the "Greater East Asia Co-prosperity Sphere." On September 27, 1940, at Berlin representatives of Germany, Italy, and Japan signed a new treaty of alliance. The Japanese agent in this enterprise was one Saburo Kurusu, destined later to win eternal notoriety in the United States. The purpose of this treaty was to bind the members of the alliance to come to the assistance of any one of the three in case of war with any outside power. Furthermore, the two European partners recognized the supremacy of the Japanese in eastern Asia, while Japan recognized the supremacy of the Axis in Europe. The Vichy government gave the Japanese the privilege of moving troops into French Indo-China, and Japanese forces immediately took possession. Although Secretary of State Hull professed to make light of this predatory bargain, it was aimed at the United States. On October 4 Prince Konoye issued the following threat: "If the United States refuses to understand the real intention of Japan, Germany, and Italy and persists in challenging those powers . . . there will be no other course open to it than to go to war." By this time the Japanese made it clear that their new policy called for Japanese domination not only of Manchuria, China, and Indo-China but of Burma, Malaya, the Philippines, Hawaii, and the western coasts of America. While these Japanese intentions were made public, few people in the United States could bring themselves to believe that the Japanese had a fragment of the power needed to realize their design.

Read in the light of the events of December 7, 1941, Japanese threats against the United States made in 1940 and later take on grim significance.

Threats of War

On October 4, 1940, the Japanese foreign minister, Matsuoka, gave an interview to the press: "I fling this challenge to America. If she in her contentment is going to stick blindly and stubbornly to the status quo in the Pacific, then we will fight America." The United States, he continued, "must recognize the New Order in the Far East or face the responsibility for war in the Pacific and in the entire world." And again, in the same interview: "Americans must see the spirit of the tripartite pact which is clearly aimed at them." In December, 1941, the American magazine *Time* quoted part of a letter written by Admiral Yamamoto early in 1941 and published by Domei, the Japanese news agency. The significant part of the letter ran: "Any time war breaks out between Japan and the United States, I shall not be content merely to capture Guam and the Philippines and occupy Hawaii and San Francisco. I am looking forward to dictating peace to the United States in the White House at Washington."

By way of response to these belligerent warnings, the British and American governments announced that they were cooperating in the Far East, and American forces in Hawaii received additional reinforcements. Early in 1941 the Navy Department at Washington arranged for the creation of separate Atlantic, Pacific, and Asiatic fleets. Other announcements of British and American reinforcements in the Far East were made public, and in the summer of 1941 President Roosevelt ordered an embargo on aviation gasoline for Japan and announced the freezing of Japanese credits in the United States. By this time reports were coming out of Japan of orders for complete mobilization and of the meeting in July of an imperial conference, the eighth since 1894. These reports were accompanied by others indicating that Japanese forces in Indo-China were being greatly increased and that Japanese troops were threatening Thailand. During August both the British and the American governments warned Japan against further aggressive moves, and on August 24 Prime Minister Churchill announced: "We shall of course range ourselves unhesitatingly at the side of the United States." In November Churchill warned the Japanese that if they should attack the United States, Great Britain would come to American aid "within the hour."

Final Negotiations

On October 17, 1941, a new Cabinet entered office in Japan; these officials, led by Premier Tojo, were all strongly pro-Axis, and they represented the most belligerent faction in the Japanese army. Tojo's policy was simple and definite: "The national policy calls for a successful settlement of the China incident and the establishment of the Greater East Asia Co-prosperity Sphere as a contribution to world peace." On November 4 Premier Tojo despatched Saburo Kurusu on a special mission to the United States to give this government "a last opportunity to make amends for past aggression."

In theory Kurusu was to assist the Japanese ambassador, Admiral Nomura, in negotiations which had begun during the preceding March. At that time President Roosevelt and Secretary Hull were willing to discuss matters with the Japanese, but they insisted that both governments agree in advance upon certain basic principles; negotiations could then proceed within the limits of these principles. Both parties would recognize the inviolability of the territorial integrity and sovereignty of all nations, and agree to a policy of noninterference in the internal affairs of other countries. Next came the principle of equality, including equality of commercial opportunity. Fourth on the list was a pledge to accept the methods of cooperation and conciliation for the prevention of disputes and for the settlement of disputes already in existence. The Japanese never accepted these principles.

Subsequent developments proved that the Japanese had no intention whatever of negotiating on the basis of any terms except their own. In November the new premier, General Tojo, announced that the United States must agree to send no further help to the government of General Chiang Kaishek and to leave China entirely "free to deal with Japan." Next the Western powers must end their policy of "military encirclement" of Japan. Then the United States must recognize Manchukuo, restore the commercial treaty of 1911, and remove all restrictions upon Japanese economic activity. On November 26 Secretary Hull submitted a basis for agreement between the two countries, but again this was predicated upon the complete withdrawal of Japan from China. Premier Tojo announced bluntly that the American terms were not acceptable to Japan. American and British policies in the Far East must be revised to fit the new situation. On December 2 President Roosevelt appealed directly to the Emperor Hirohito, asking particularly about heavy Japanese troop concentrations in Indo-China. No direct reply ever came.

The two Japanese agents in Washington did not reply to Secretary Hull's note of November 26 until the afternoon of December 7, at 2:20 o'clock, Washington time. At 1:20 Washington time—that is, at 7:50 A.M. Hawaiian time—the Japanese began their attack upon Pearl Harbor. The communication which they presented to Secretary Hull was in keeping with Japanese official character: "The Japanese Government," so this amazing perversion of the truth ran, "has always maintained an attitude of fairness and moderation, and did its best to reach a settlement, for which it made all possible concessions. . . . On the other hand, the American Government . . . caused an undue delay in the negotiations."

Pearl Harbor

Secretary Hull's oral response to the Japanese note of December 7 endeared him to every American: "In all my fifty years of public service I have never seen a document that was more crowded with infamous falsehoods and distortions—infamous falsehoods and distortions on a scale so huge that I never imagined until today that any Government on this planet was capable of uttering them." Obviously all Japanese professions of willingness to negotiate were nothing but a screen to disguise their last-minute preparations for their attack on Pearl Harbor. Documents captured during the war proved that the Japanese began to plan the attack on Pearl Harbor in September and by November everything was ready.

On December 8 President Roosevelt addressed a joint session of Congress to ask for a declaration of war against Japan: "Yesterday, Dec. 7, 1941—a date which will live in infamy—the United States of America was suddenly and deliberately attacked by naval and air forces of the Empire of Japan." In less than an hour after the President delivered his war message, the Senate unanimously passed a declaration of war. The House followed shortly after, with a vote of 388 to 1. The lone dissenter was Representative Jeannette Rankin of Montana who had been one of the minority in April 1917. Never before in American history had the American people gone to war with such impressive evidence of unanimous approval. Hitler and Mussolini also declared war on the United States. Congress responded promptly, this time with unanimous votes in each chamber.

The Japanese attack at Pearl Harbor was a serious setback for the United States. Thanks to detailed maps and plans in their possession, the attacking forces wiped out hangars, airfields, and runways and destroyed most of the American planes. Of the eighty-six naval vessels at anchor, every one was put out of commission. Losses in personnel, killed, wounded, and missing, reached the figure of 4575. For the time being, the Japanese had naval superiority of four to one over the United States in the Pacific.

These losses need not have occurred. According to evidence compiled by the Roberts Investigating Commission, the American commanders at Hawaii had known for months that war was imminent and that it would start without warning. Plans had been made to cope with the danger, but the commanding officers failed to put the plans into effect. Equipment was not abundant but was ample enough to have prevented serious damage.

In its conclusions the Roberts report found that the authorities at Washington had fulfilled their obligations. The commanders at Hawaii had prepared plans which, if used, would have been adequate. But the commanders had failed to confer at the most critical time, and their separate actions were not adequate. The report stated that

> It was a dereliction of duty on the part of each of them not to consult and confer with the other respecting the meaning and intent of the warnings and the appropriate measures of defense required by the imminence of hostilities. [The commanders were taken completely by surprise.] Each failed properly to evaluate the seriousness of the situation. These errors of judgment were the effective causes for the success of the attack.

Chapter 47

VICTORY OVER GERMANY AND JAPAN

Early Defeats and First Successes

Organizing for War

The American people were left in no doubt that the war was on. After December 7 Japanese submarines appeared off California, but they did relatively little damage. On the other hand, German submarines established a blockade of the Atlantic Coast. Ranging from the Gulf of St. Lawrence to the Gulf of Mexico and the Caribbean they destroyed shipping at the rate of two ships per day. For the first time since the Napoleonic Wars the United States as a whole suffered some of the consequences of a blockade. Because of enemy action the American people were cut off from the sources of supply of rubber, tin, hemp, and quinine. Atlantic coastwise shipping was so disrupted that east coast ports could not get their normal supply of petroleum. Imports from South America were seriously curtailed, with resulting shortages in such widely used commodities as bananas and coffee.

Fortunately the lessons learned at Pearl Harbor were turned to immediate account. President Roosevelt ordered a unified command for Hawaii and for the Canal Zone. Then in March 1942 he ordered a thoroughgoing reorganization of the army. At the top he appointed General Marshall, who continued as chief of staff. Under him were three generals, one in charge of ground forces, one in charge of air forces, and one in charge of supply. So far as the army command was concerned, these four men were made responsible for winning the war. For the first time in the United States the air force received the recognition which modern warfare demands. Furthermore, the high commands of both army and navy in Washington began to work together.

Although the United States was not ready for war when the Japanese attacked Pearl Harbor, our armed forces were relatively much stronger than in 1917. By December 1941 the United States army, including the air force, had reached the figure of 1,750,000 officers and men. With the exception of small units garrisoned in Iceland and at other posts in the Atlantic, and a few thousand men in the Philippines, the greater part of this army was receiving training in the United States. Part of the force was being prepared for combat service, while the other part had charge of the training programs and camps.

Thanks to plans already adopted and in operation before the war began, the army was prepared for a rapid increase in size. By the middle of May 1942 nearly 26,000,000 men below the age of 45 had registered for possible military service. By the end of 1943 the War Department planned to have an armed force numbering more than 10,000,000. Nearly one tenth of the population of the United States would be needed for the various services.

The United States entered upon the greatest program of naval expansion in its history. By 1945 the American navy had become larger than all the navies of the United Nations combined. In 1942 the total personnel, including officers and men of the navy and the marine corps, totaled under 500,000. Two years later the total was 3,632,381. Before the end of the war the figure passed 4,000,000.

In World War II the United States organized women's branches in the armed forces. These were the Women's Army Corps, known as the WACS, the Women's Reserve of the United States Naval Reserve, called the WAVES, the SPARS in the Coast Guard, and the Women's Reserve in the Marine Corps. There was also the Women's Auxiliary Ferrying Squadron, which flew planes from factories to airfields. Nurses and women physicians received commissions in both the army and the navy.

The field of action in which these armed services would be used covered the globe. By contrast, the battle area of World War I was relatively small, that of the American Civil War almost tiny. In World War II American forces served in Iceland, Greenland, and the Aleutians in the north, in the Near East, in Africa, Sicily, Italy, all of western Europe except Spain and Portugal, and in Germany. They moved from Australia across the reaches of the Pacific and its islands to Tokyo and from India to China. It took time to organize and supply all this fighting power, but once it was ready the professional armies of Germany and Japan were no match for it.

Japanese Conquests

Because of the incompleteness of our preparation and because of Japanese readiness, the first part of the war was a series of defeats for us. During that time we were close to disaster. The Japanese attacked the Philippines shortly after their raid at Pearl Harbor. They had plans of conquest stretching over a line 7000 miles from their home islands. Plans and equipment were ready, the result of preparations covering several months. The schedule was impressive. On December 8 they occupied Thailand, or Siam, to have a base of operations against Malaya and the great British naval base at Singapore. Four days later they occupied Guam, and on the 24th they took Wake Island. The next day they occupied the British-controlled city of Hong Kong. On January 2, 1942, they occupied Manila. American forces withdrew to the Bataan Peninsula and then to the island fortress of Corregidor. There they held out until May 6. By that date Japanese forces were in full possession of all the Philippine Islands. Early in January 1942 Japanese troops landed on Borneo and Celebes for the conquest of the Netherlands Indies. On January 20 they invaded Burma. They landed troops on the Malayan Peninsula and worked south toward Singapore. The British sent a naval detachment, including two of their best battleships, the *Prince of Wales* and the *Repulse,* to reinforce Singapore. The two big ships had practically no anti-aircraft artillery, so the Japanese easily destroyed them. On February 15 Singapore surrendered. By March 19 the Japanese had seized Java and

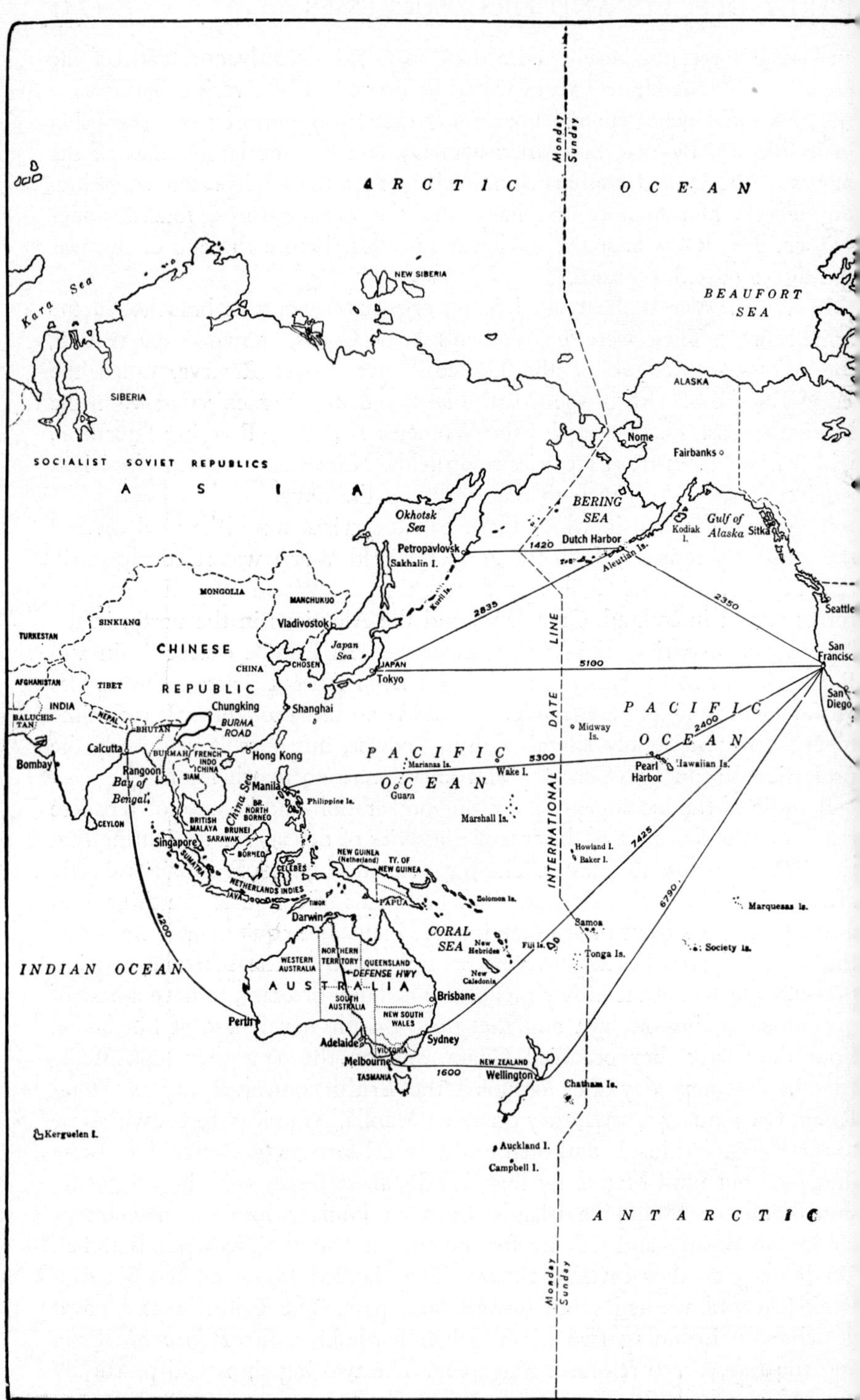
ARCTIC OCEAN
Monday
Sunday
Kara Sea
NEW SIBERIA
BEAUFORT SEA
ALASKA
SIBERIA
Nome
Fairbanks
SOCIALIST SOVIET REPUBLICS
ASIA
BERING SEA
Okhotsk Sea
Gulf of Alaska
Kodiak I.
Sitka
Dutch Harbor
Petropavlovsk
1420
Sakhalin I.
Aleutian Is.
2350
MONGOLIA
MANCHUKUO
Kuril Is.
2835
Seattle
SINKIANG
Vladivostok
TURKESTAN
CHINESE
Japan Sea
San Francisco
CHINA
CHOSEN
JAPAN
5100
AFGHANISTAN
TIBET
REPUBLIC
Tokyo
San Diego
INDIA
Chungking
NEPAL
Shanghai
PACIFIC OCEAN
BALUCHISTAN
BHUTAN
BURMA ROAD
Midway Is.
2400
Calcutta
Hong Kong
INTERNATIONAL DATE LINE
Bombay
BURMAH
FRENCH INDO CHINA
Rangoon
SIAM
PACIFIC OCEAN
Marianas Is.
5300
Wake I.
Pearl Harbor
Hawaiian Is.
Bay of Bengal
Manila
Guam
China Sea
Philippine Is.
BR. NORTH BORNEO
Marshall Is.
CEYLON
BRITISH MALAYA
BRUNEI
SARAWAK
Singapore
BORNEO
SUMATRA
CELEBES
Howland I.
Baker I.
7425
NEW GUINEA (Netherland)
TY. OF NEW GUINEA
NETHERLANDS INDIES
JAVA
TIMOR
PAPUA
Solomon Is.
Marquesas Is.
Darwin
6790
4200
CORAL SEA
Samoa
New Hebrides
Fiji Is.
Tonga Is.
Society Is.
NORTHERN TERRITORY
QUEENSLAND
WESTERN AUSTRALIA
DEFENSE HWY
INDIAN OCEAN
New Caledonia
AUSTRALIA
Brisbane
SOUTH AUSTRALIA
NEW SOUTH WALES
Perth
Adelaide
Sydney
VICTORIA
Melbourne
NEW ZEALAND
TASMANIA
1600
Wellington
Chatham Is.
Kerguelen I.
Auckland I.
Campbell I.
ANTARCTIC
Monday
Sunday

Map 21

ELLESMERE ISLAND
GREENLAND
FRIDTJOF NANSEN LAND
SVALBARD (Spitzbergen)
GREENLAND SEA
BARENTS SEA
DEVON I.
BAFFIN BAY
VICTORIA ISLAND
BAFFIN ISLAND
x Magnetic Pole
Davis Strait
Denmark Strait
ICELAND
Reykjavik
NORWAY
SWEDEN
FINLAND
Murmansk
Archangel
UNION OF
DOMINION OF CANADA
Hudson Bay
Julianehaab
700
Bergen
Leningrad
BRITISH ISLES
SCOTLAND
North Sea
DENMARK
Baltic Sea
ESTONIA
LATVIA
LITHUANIA
EAST PRUSSIA
Moscow
RUSSIA
N. IRELAND
IRISH FREE STATE
WALES
ENGLAND
London
NETHERLANDS
BELGIUM
GERMANY
Berlin
POLAND
Kharkov
NORTH
LABRADOR
2610
FRANCE
UKRAINE
Odessa
Rostov
Aral Sea
Caspian Sea
UNITED STATES
Great Lakes
NEWFOUNDLAND
St. Johns
Halifax
SWITZERLAND
HUNGARY
RUMANIA
Chicago
Boston
New York
Washington
ITALY
YUGOSLAVIA
BULGARIA
Black Sea
SPAIN
Corsica
Sardinia
ALBANIA
Sicily
GREECE
TURKEY
ARMENIA
AMERICA
Azores
PORTUGAL
Gibraltar
NORTH ATLANTIC OCEAN
TANGIER
ALGERIA
Crete
Cyprus
SYRIA
PERSIA
Charleston
Bermudas
Madeira
MOROCCO
TUNISIA
Mediterranean Sea
IRAQ
MEXICO
3820
Canary Islands
RIO DE ORO
LYBIA
EGYPT
TRANSJORDAN
PALESTINE
KUWAIT
Gulf of Mexico
Bahama Is.
CUBA
WEST INDIES
HAITI
STO. DOMINGO
AFRICA
ARABIA
OMAN
BRITISH HONDURAS
JAMAICA
PUERTO RICO
HONDURAS
Caribbean Sea
Cape Verde Islands
Dakar
FRENCH WEST AFRICA
ANGLO-EGYPTIAN SUDAN
Red Sea
ERITREA
ADEN
GUATEMALA
SALVADOR
NICARAGUA
COSTA RICA
PANAMA
Trinidad
SENEGAL
GAMBIA
PORTUGUESE GUINEA
FR. GUINEA
NIGERIA
Sokotra
3730
VENEZUELA
BRITISH GUIANA
SURINAM
FRENCH GUIANA
SIERRA LEONE
IVORY COAST
TOGOLAND
FRENCH SOMALILAND
BR. SOMALILAND
ITALIAN EAST AFRICA
Panama Canal
COLOMBIA
LIBERIA
GOLD COAST COLONY
DAHOMEY
CAMEROONS
FRENCH EQUATORIAL AFRICA
Galapagos Is.
1870
7810
RIO MUNI
GABON
BELGIAN CONGO
UGANDA
KENYA
ITALIAN SOMALILAND
ECUADOR
BRAZIL
PERU
SOUTH AMERICA
Natal
KABINDA
TANGANYIKA TERRITORY
Zanzibar
ANGOLA
NYASALAND
BOLIVIA
RHODESIA
MADAGASCAR
Mauritius
PARAGUAY
Rio de Janeiro
BRITISH SOUTH WEST AFRICA
BECHUANALAND
MOZAMBIQUE
Réunion
Gonstrah I.
ARGENTINA
SWAZILAND
BASUTOLAND
UNION OF SOUTH AFRICA
Valparaiso
URUGUAY
SOUTH ATLANTIC OCEAN
Cape Town
Buenos Aires
Cape of Good Hope
CHILE
Falkland Is.
South Georgia
Str. of Magellan
Cape Horn
OCEAN
South Orkneys
South Shetlands

World War II

Sumatra, the heart of the colonial empire of the Netherlands. In the first five months of the war the Japanese conquered 1,327,796 square miles of land, with a population of 118,640,000. With these conquests they gained possession of rich resources of tin, petroleum, and natural rubber.

With the major Pacific islands in their hands, the victorious Japanese next moved against Australia. They had strong bases along the northern shore of New Guinea, a powerful naval base at Rabaul in New Britain, and they were building bases in the Solomon Islands. General Douglas MacArthur had been ordered out of Corregidor before the surrender to take charge of the defense of Australia. The situation looked black. Nevertheless, in spite of Japanese successes and disasters for the Allies, MacArthur kept up magnificent courage. When he pulled out of the Philippines, he proclaimed his faith in victory in these simple words: "I came through and I will return." He did—in October 1944.

Doolittle's Raid

On April 18, 1942, Colonel James Doolittle led a squadron of American bombers over Japan to bomb Tokyo. When the pilots took their planes off from the carrier *Hornet,* they knew they could not return to the ship. They did drop their bombs on Tokyo and Yokohama. Some of the pilots landed in China, some on Russian territory in eastern Siberia, some in Japanese-controlled China. The Japanese executed the men who fell into their hands. At the time of the raid the value seemed to be largely moral. But later information showed that it frightened the Japanese into important defensive measures. They were so afraid of a large-scale air attack that they took their large carrier fleet out of the Indian Ocean and kept it in home waters. They also kept a large number of land-based planes on Japanese islands. This concentration of air strength in Japanese home areas made possible the American landing on Guadalcanal and helped to account for Japanese naval defeats near the Solomons.

Coral Sea and Midway

The first defeat inflicted on the Japanese came early in May 1942 in the naval battle of the Coral Sea off the northeast coast of Australia. The Japanese and American fleets were 100 miles apart, and all the fighting was done by carrier-based planes. The battle lasted four days. The Japanese lost twenty ships, including two carriers. The United States lost the carrier *Lexington.* Here at last was an interruption of Japanese successes, and it proved prophetic of things to come. Once the United States navy began to strike, Japanese losses became more and more impressive.

Early in June 1942 the Japanese sent a great fleet of battleships and troop transports into the central Pacific. They were planning to land forces in the Aleutians and at Midway. American pilots sighted the Japanese force west of Midway, and the Battle of Midway began. When it was over after three days of fighting, the score showed eighteen, probably twenty Japanese ships sunk. The list included four carriers, with all their planes and most of their crews, two heavy cruisers, several destroyers, and one transport. Three other transports were heavily damaged. Navy reports made at the time emphasized heavy Japanese losses in personnel. Later report showed that the Japanese lost nearly all of their best naval fliers. The Japanese did not occupy Midway, but they did land troops on three islands of the Aleutian group: Attu, Agattu, and Kiska. As long as they remained, they were a threat to Alaska, but after an occupation lasting a year American forces drove them out in May 1943.

Two months after the Battle of Midway, the Americans struck their first counterblow against the Japanese. In August 1942 marines went ashore on Guadalcanal in the Solomon Islands. This island, of which most Americans had never heard before, had great strategic value. The Japanese needed it if they were to attack Australia. By the same token the Americans needed it to block further Japanese conquests. The Japanese made desperate and repeated efforts to dislodge the small force, but the Americans held on. Fighting on land continued until February 9, 1943, when the Japanese withdrew their troops. During these months the Japanese did their utmost to land reinforcements and to destroy American ships. Their efforts resulted in bitter fighting between American and Japanese fleets, particularly off the Solomons and at the battle of Santa Cruz. The greatest naval engagement of the war up to that time was fought off Guadalcanal from November 13 to 15, 1942. Japanese losses were twenty-eight ships sunk, with eight more heavily damaged. Included in the list of ships sunk were eight Japanese transports, with an estimated 30,000 troops. The United States Navy lost two cruisers and six destroyers. The American victory off Guadalcanal furnished an excellent measure of Japanese naval strength and skill. The Japanese were bitter, able fighters, and no American officer who took part in these engagements had any reason to scorn the fighting ability of these enemies. But in their general strategy the Japanese overestimated their own strength and greatly underestimated that of their foes. By the end of November 1942 the Japanese had suffered heavy losses on all types of ships: 243 sunk and 259 damaged. They still had large numbers of craft left, but they were not strong enough to clear the Americans out of the Pacific. At the end of the first year of war against the United States the Japanese saw their career of conquest stopped. For the remaining three years they learned some of the bitter lessons of defeat.

Guadalcanal

While the navy was proving its superiority over the Japanese off the Solomons, General MacArthur started his land offensive. Late in September 1942 he began to move against the Japanese on New Guinea. The Japanese had crossed the Owen Stanley Mountains and were within thirty miles of Port Moresby. By November they were driven back across the mountains. This campaign for New Guinea lasted on into 1943. By the end of that year Allied forces had all of eastern New Guinea under control, and the Japanese were driven out of the Solomons. Japanese threats to supply lines to Australia were over, and the Japanese themselves began the long, bitterly contested retreat which took them from the South Pacific back to Japan. American forces were set for an island-hopping campaign that ended in Tokyo.

Victory over Germany

At the start of the war, the general plan, or strategy, of the United States was simple. First, build up American factories so that we could supply most of our own needs, with substantial quantities left over for Russian and British forces. Next, concentrate on the defeat of Hitler in Africa and in Europe; for this work General Dwight D. Eisenhower was appointed supreme commander of Allied forces. Third, destroy the naval and military power of Japan. Because of the impossibility of fighting one major war in the Pacific and another in Africa and Europe at the same time, victory in the Pacific had to wait for victory over Germany.

In 1942 British and American leaders decided to strike the first common blow against Germany, not in Europe but in northern Africa. Such an expedition would require uninterrupted supplies of materials and men to be sent both from the British Isles and from the United States. Before this supply service could be made effective, German submarines had to be cleared from the Atlantic Ocean. In June 1942 the Germans destroyed 111 United Nations ships in the Atlantic. Submarines operated off our own coast, in the mouth of the St. Lawrence, in the Gulf of Mexico, and even in the mouth of the Mississippi River. In the first ten months of 1942 the Germans destroyed more than 500 ships. Then this threat to our supply lines was almost ended. From October 1942 to the end of the war, German submarines did relatively little damage. Only eleven ships were lost in October.

African Campaign

During 1940 and 1941 British and German forces had struggled for the control of North Africa, but neither side had been able to win a decisive victory. The Germans, however, had come close to it. In the summer of 1942, led by Field Marshal Rommel, they drove eastward to within sixty miles of Alexandria, Egypt. In October, however, the British General Montgomery won a brilliant victory at El Alamein and once more drove the Germans westward.

On November 7, 1942, a great British and American force under General Eisenhower landed on the coasts of Morocco and Algeria. Up to that time this was the largest single sea-borne expedition ever undertaken. It required 500 transports to carry the men and 350 naval vessels to guard them. But the landing was successful. Then Montgomery and General Eisenhower drove toward each other for a junction. The Germans were able to bring in reinforcements, so it was May 1943 before the combined British and American armies could finish the job of defeating Italian and German armies in Africa.

During this same winter of 1942-43, in eastern Europe, Russian forces gave the Germans their first setback. After starting his undeclared war against Russia, Hitler had driven his forces to within sight of Moscow. At the end of the fighting in 1941 the German dictator told his people that Russia was so badly beaten she would never fight again. The next year

German forces reached Stalingrad on the Volga River. But Stalingrad marked the end of their advance. The Russians made a brilliant defensive stand and then, in 1943, began to push the enemy back toward his own borders.

After the invasion of Africa was under way, Churchill and Roosevelt met at Casablanca, Morocco, to talk over plans for the future. At that time they announced that the enemy powers must surrender unconditionally. Almost a year later, Stalin, Churchill, and Roosevelt met at Teheran, in Iran. The chiefs of staff "concerted plans for the destruction of the German forces. . . . No power on earth can prevent our destroying the German armies by land, their U-boats by sea, and their war plants from the air." The three powers made good on this grim prophecy.

Sicily and Italy

The forces of the United Nations had not invaded Africa for the sake of Africa. American and British leaders, particularly Winston Churchill, wanted the northern coast as a base of operations against Europe. On July 10, 1943, the Allies invaded Sicily and conquered the island in a little over one month. On July 25, antifascist Italians started a revolution against Mussolini and made him a prisoner, but the Germans rescued him. By that time Italy had been occupied by German forces so completely that it was a German province. The Italian Marshal Badoglio set up a new government and joined the United Nations, but German troops hung on until 1945.

Early in September 1943 General Montgomery and General Clark landed in Italy and began a drive toward Rome. Because of the weather, the natural obstacles of geography, and the Germans, the invaders did not capture Rome until June 1944. As one followed the newspaper accounts of the battles in Italy, progress seemed discouragingly slow. But even before Rome was taken, the Americans and British captured valuable airfields, which they used in intensive bombing of Germany. During 1943 and 1944, United Nations commanders carried on an almost continuous air assault upon Germany. The major objectives were industrial areas and transportation systems. If German sources of guns, munitions, airplanes, ball bearings, synthetic oil, and synthetic rubber could be even partly interrupted, her powers of defense would be seriously weakened. Furthermore, this continuous bombing seriously weakened German transportation facilities. Throughout the war, United Nations planes dropped nearly 2,500,000 tons of explosives on Germany; they destroyed nearly 41,000 German planes, about half of them in combat. The British and American air forces lost 26,715 planes. One important factor in German defeat was this steady pounding from the air.

Landing in Normandy

On June 6, 1944, General Eisenhower's combined British, Canadian, and American forces landed on the beaches of Normandy. This was "D-Day," the news for which the world had been waiting. This successful landing started a full-size drive against Germany from the west. Men and supplies were carried across the English Channel in 3200 transports and landing craft. Overhead was a great protecting "umbrella" of 8000 airplanes. Once the beaches were secured, men poured ashore. In the next 100 days, 2,500,000 invading soldiers landed in France.

General Marshall's report gives a vivid picture of the obstacles which the invaders had to overcome:

> German defenses on all beaches were formidable; they consisted first of bands of underwater obstacles designed to break up formations of landing craft; mines were freely used to make these obstacles more lethal. The beaches themselves were heavily mined and strung with wire. Concrete pillboxes and gun emplacements were sited to deliver withering crossfire along the beaches. All exits leading inland from the beaches were blocked by anti-tank walls and ditches, mine fields and barbed wire. Further inland, mortars and artillery were sited to deliver indirect fire on the beaches.

It took General Eisenhower's combined armies a few weeks to establish themselves in Normandy, secure their supply lines, and land the needed equipment. On July 25 American troops under General Bradley broke through the German lines at St. Lô. Once out in the open, Bradley and Patton showed the Germans something about fast-moving war, the kind the Germans called *blitzkrieg*. The campaign which followed the break-through had few parallels in boldness and speed. Just one month after the victory at St. Lô, a French force entered Paris. By that time the Germans had lost nearly 500,000 men, and the surviving units had to abandon most of their equipment. Early in October American forces crossed the German border into Aachen. In November forces advancing toward the north captured Antwerp in Belgium and turned it into a great supply base. The next major objective was to cross the lower Rhine in the neighborhood of Arnheim, Holland. In this attempt the Americans and British used air-borne forces in numbers never before tried. They were successful in effecting a landing, but heavy concentrations of German troops prevented the crossing of the Rhine.

In December 1944, acting on direct orders of Hitler himself, General von Rundstedt made a last desperate effort to break Eisenhower's line and drive back to the coast. **Battle of the Bulge** Attacking south of Aachen, on a forty-mile front running from Monschau to Echternack, the Germans actually crashed through. The resulting struggle is known as the Battle of Ardennes, or the "Battle of the Bulge." But in January 1945 the German advance was stopped, and the enemy did not reach the Channel. The Germans killed hundreds of American troops, and they held up the schedule for a large-scale advance into Germany by some six weeks. But their offensive power was gone. Having tried and failed, there was nothing left for the Germans but retreat and destruction. They could still put up a stubborn fight, costly to our side, but they could not win. And, while they were struggling to hold back Eisenhower and his men in the west, the Russians were coming in steadily from the east. Here was one of the most effective squeeze plays in the history of warfare, with the Germans caught squarely between two irresistible forces

For the first time since Napoleon's day, 125 years earlier, the Germans were subjected to war on their own soil.

During World War I and afterward, some military experts expressed the opinion that Allied forces would never be able to cross the Rhine. The question cannot be settled for World War I because no one tried. As Eisenhower's troops approached the Rhine, the same question was raised. Could the invaders cross the river into the heart of Germany? They could. Early in March they occupied Cologne on the left bank. And then came one of the breaks which generals dream about and rarely see. Some twenty miles south of Cologne, at the town of Remagen, a small American advance force came upon the Ludendorff Bridge, intact and almost unguarded. Over they rushed and soon had a base on the right bank. Two weeks later another American force crossed the Rhine at Oppenheim, south of Mainz. By this time, Eisenhower was ready for his final drive to end the war in Europe.

Crossing the Rhine

As the war moved toward its end in Europe, Stalin, Churchill, and Roosevelt met at Yalta in Russia early in 1945 to agree upon the policy for handling a beaten Germany. They decided to set up a central control commission at Berlin, composed of the top military commanders. Responsibility for administering German affairs would be shared by Russia, France, Great Britain, and the United States, each controlling a clearly defined zone or area. The leaders at Yalta announced that German war industries, the German military class, and the German general staff would be destroyed. The war criminals would suffer "just and swift punishment." Then, so the victors announced, "Germany will never again be able to disturb the peace of the world." The meeting at Yalta also provided for a conference of United Nations, to meet at San Francisco in the spring of 1945, to prepare a charter for a formal United Nations organization.

By this time there was no hope of escape for Germany. Russian forces were moving directly toward Berlin from the east, while others were coming from the south by way of Hungary and Czechoslovakia. In the west British and American forces captured the great Ruhr industrial area and then began to fan out, south toward Austria, north toward the ports of Wilhelmshafen and Hamburg, and east toward Berlin. In April 1945 American and Russian forces met on the left bank of the Elbe River. The final collapse soon came. On April 29 Mussolini was killed, and German forces in Italy surrendered unconditionally. On May 1 Hitler committed suicide. On May 2 the Russians entered Berlin. On May 6 the Germans surrendered unconditionally. Formal terms were signed at Berlin on May 9, and the fighting in Europe was finished.

The Germans used to boast that they could make war pay, and for a time they did. In Poland alone they had seized property worth $2,400,000,000. Norway, Holland, Belgium, and France furnished even greater and more valuable quantities of loot. The Germans stole machinery from factories, livestock from farms, and gold from banks and public treasuries. They forced conquered peoples by the thousand into slave labor in Germany.

War was profitable for the Germans as long as they were winning. But they had to keep on winning. When they lost the war, they lost some of their captured and stolen profits. Worse still, in defeat they faced a world upon which they had deliberately piled cruelty, terrorism, and systematic massacre, and the world was not likely to forget. Nine or ten million persons had been killed, another 10 million disabled for life. Hundreds of thousands of helpless civilians had been tortured, starved, and murdered in German concentration camps. During the latter part of the war, when they knew they could not win, the Germans let loose their flying bombs, V-1 and V-2, against England. These bombs killed 145,000 English civilians. With this record spread on the pages of history, the Germans asked for peace. Many, perhaps most, of the Germans expressed no regrets over starting the war. The only thing they regretted was their failure to win.

Destruction of Japanese Power

Long before the overwhelming defeat of Germany had been achieved, American forces began to speed up the war against Japan. In November 1943 Generalissimo Chiang Kai-shek, Churchill, and Roosevelt met at Cairo, Egypt. Meetings of Churchill and Roosevelt always meant bad news for the enemy. This time the conference announced that after unconditional surrender, "Japan shall be stripped of all the islands in the Pacific which she has seized or occupied since the beginning of the first World War in 1914, and that all the territories which Japan has stolen from the Chinese . . . shall be restored to the Republic of China. . . . Korea in due course . . ." would become free and independent.

Drive against Japan

General Marshall outlined the major plan for crushing the Japanese: "Japan could best be defeated by a series of amphibious attacks across the far reaches of the Pacific. Oceans are formidable barriers, but for the nation enjoying naval superiority they become high-roads of invasion." In August 1943, after an Allies' conference at Quebec, General MacArthur was ordered to continue operations along the coast of New Guinea and to reach the Philippines by the fall of 1944. Americans would capture bases in the Gilbert, Marshall, and Mariana Islands, so that by the spring of 1945 we could seize a base in the Ryuku group at the very door of Japan. This was the process known as "island hopping." In accordance with this major plan, operations went rapidly forward. With complete naval superiority and far more than equal air power, land forces seized the islands as needed. Each single operation was a hard test for the Australian, New Zealand, and American forces involved. Fighting in the steaming hot jungles called for endurance as well as courage, but the troops met every test. In fact, they were so successful that the chiefs of staff decided to send MacArthur into the Philippines in October 1944 instead of December, as originally planned.

MacArthur's first objective was the island of Leyte, between the larger islands of Mindanao and Luzon. The great American landing force was spotted by Japanese fliers, but the men got ashore. MacArthur announced, dramatically: "I have returned." The Japanese decided to risk practically their whole remaining navy to prevent the Americans from occupying the Philippines. In a great naval engagement, lasting six days, American naval units "virtually eliminated Japan as a sea power." Early in January MacArthur made another successful landing, this time on Luzon itself. On February 23, 1945, MacArthur's men completed the occupation of Manila. Early in March they recaptured Corregidor, where American forces had surrendered in May 1942.

Before plans could be completed for invading Japan, two island bases were needed, Iwo Jima in the Volcano group and Okinawa in the Ryukyu Islands. Iwo Jima was taken with no more than normal Japanese resistance. But on Okinawa the enemy put up a terrific fight, knowing that their own home islands would be the next objective of the victorious Americans. The campaign on Okinawa lasted from the end of March to June 21, 1945, and it cost the lives of 39,000 American fighting men. The Japanese lost 109,629 killed. Thanks to this victory, the way to Honshu Island and Tokyo was at last open.

Atom Bomb

During the latter part of July, President Truman—President Roosevelt had died on April 12, 1945—met with the heads of the Russian and British governments at Potsdam, near Berlin. The conference decided upon the major political and economic principles which would guide the occupation forces in Germany. The conference also issued another warning to Japan, calling for unconditional surrender.

As plans for invading Japan were completed, the army prepared to try an experiment. For years American and British scientists had been working on a new type of explosive, using the principle of atomic fission or splitting the atom. Tests in New Mexico showed that the bomb had terrific destructive power. On August 5, 1945, an American plane dropped one atomic bomb on Hiroshima. Five days later another was dropped on Nagasaki. Hiroshima had a population of 343,000. Sixty percent of the city was wiped out. One third of Nagasaki was destroyed. The military authorities have never made public the size of these two bombs, but a B-29 was used to carry the bomb. A single atomic bomb had destructive power equal to the normal bomb loads of 2000 superfortresses.

Between the dates when the two bombs were dropped, the Soviet Union declared war on Japan. The Red army occupied Manchuria and northern Korea. By this time the Japanese were through. Before the atomic bombs opened a new era of destructiveness, the "Sons of Heaven" had seen our superfortresses flying over their cities. They knew from bitter experience what ordinary bombs could do, and they wanted no more. On August 10, 1945, the Japanese government offered to surrender. Four days later they did surrender unconditionally.

On this memorable occasion Emperor Hirohito made a remarkable broadcast to his people. It had always been Japan's purpose, he said, to "strive for the common prosperity and happiness of all nations." In going to war it had been "far from our thought either to infringe upon the sovereignty of other nations or to embark upon territorial aggrandizement." Unfortunately, so the emperor said, after four years "the war situation developed not necessarily to Japan's advantage, while the general trends of the world have all turned against her interest." So, out of consideration for everybody's welfare, these Japanese humanitarians decided to ask for an end of the war.

Japanese Surrender

General MacArthur ordered Japanese envoys to go to Manila, where they would be informed of the terms. On August 27 American soldiers began to land in Japan. Three days later General MacArthur himself went ashore at Yokohama. On September 1 the Japanese envoys formally signed the documents of surrender. The ceremony took place on the newest and largest American battleship, the *Missouri*. General MacArthur had charge of this momentous meeting. General Wainwright, who had remained in command at Corregidor in 1942 and who had been a prisoner of war of the Japanese until the surrender, was present at the signing. In the surrender document the Japanese representatives put their names to the following statement: "We hereby proclaim the unconditional surrender to the Allied powers of the Japanese imperial general headquarters and of all Japanese armed forces." On September 5 and 7 American forces entered Tokyo, and the occupation of Japan was really started. Admiral Yamamoto did not dictate terms of peace in the White House or anywhere else. Yamamoto was dead.

Production for War

In World War II the costs were heavy—in both money and men. In 1945 alone our government spent more than $90,000,000,000. Estimates for the total financial cost of the war to us run up as high as $500,000,000,000. Part of the funds needed came from taxation, part from borrowing. The Treasury put on drives for six great war loans, which brought in a total of close to $109,500,000,000. Income taxes reached the highest level in American history. Thirteen million men and women were enrolled in the various branches of the armed forces. Merely to equip, train, and send this vast force where it was needed required immense quantities of supplies and shipping.

War Production Board

Warfare in the 1940's required more machines of all kinds than any earlier war, so production was equally important with military and naval campaigns. Thanks to the Lend-Lease Act, American production enterprises had already been greatly expanded. To speed them up still further, President Roosevelt appointed the War Production Board, with Donald M. Nelson as chairman. It was the board's responsibility to provide factories and machinery for production, procure raw materials, and distribute these materials where they were most needed. So far as possible, existing factories were converted from ordinary peacetime work to war production. Great new factories were built and equipped with modern machinery. By the end of 1943 the building part of the job was done. The plants could turn out a steady stream of munitions, guns, motor vehicles, landing craft, airplanes, and ships.

The responsibility of setting up new plants was too big for ordinary private enterprise, so the federal government used its vast resources. For plant expansion from 1940 to 1944, private investment amounted to more than $7,500,000,000. United States government investment, on the other hand, amounted to nearly $16,000,000,000. The war put the government into business on a far greater scale than ever before.

For purposes of comparison it may be recalled that in World War I, up to November 11, 1918, all the light artillery for American forces, both three-inch and six-inch guns, plus all the munitions they used, were supplied by the French. Almost all of the heavy guns were French, as were 80 percent of the airplanes. The French provided the Americans with all the tanks they used. In that war our allies provided the essential equipment. In World War II American factories made a new record. Production of war materials became one of the marvels of modern times. The scope of this work can be seen from a few figures. By the end of 1943 the output of airplanes reached a new high level, 8800 in a single month. For that year the plants turned out a total of 86,000 planes. In 1940 American producers had delivered only 6000. The story of ships was almost as remarkable: in 1941, a total of 103; in 1943, a total of 1750. No country in the world could equal this volume of production. Germany and Japan could not even approach it. Our overwhelming superiority in equipment was a major factor in the destruction of the enemy powers.

No one should get the idea that machines took the place of men in war. It took millions of workers to produce the machines, so many millions that unemployment disappeared. During the war the problem was to find men and women to fill the jobs. Furthermore, the use of machines by the armed forces required large numbers of men. The big B-29 bombers did efficient work over Japan. They may have convinced the Japanese that war at home was far less enjoyable than their own killing of defenseless Chinese. But every B-29 carried a crew of several men, and large ground crews were needed to keep the planes flying. General Marshall said that it took twelve officers and seventy-three men in the immediate combat zone to keep one B-29 in the air. In warfare, as in industry, more machines called for more men.

Rationing

Conversion of the whole American industrial plant to war needs was bound to have important effects on civilian life. As President Roosevelt put it in 1942, "this enormous program is dislocating industry, labor, agriculture, and finance. It is disrupting, and will continue to disrupt, the normal manner of life of every American family." First came the halt in all building construction not needed in the war effort, next the end of production of automobiles for civilian use. In normal times of peace the American people had bought 3,300,000 new cars every year. During the war they bought practically none. Other familiar consumers' goods soon disappeared from the stores: radios, washing machines, electric refrigerators, electric and gas ranges, vacuum cleaners, typewriters. The use of wool for civilians was cut in half. After a time, such ordinary goods as men's shirts and underwear were as scarce as collectors' items.

To provide for the fair distribution of necessities, a nation-wide system of rationing was worked out under the Office of Price Administration. First on the list were automobile tires. Gasoline and fuel oil soon followed. Rationing was extended to include shoes and many articles of food, particularly meat, butter, sugar, and most canned goods. Little coupons from the ration books and round paper tokens, known as "points," were as necessary as money if you wanted to buy anything on the rationed list.

Price Control

Under ordinary conditions the widespread and increasing shortage of consumers' goods would have resulted in a sharp rise in prices. Foreseeing this danger, the administration planned for comprehensive price control. In April 1941, months before we entered the war, President Roosevelt provided for the establishment of the Office of Price Administration. A few months later he urged Congress to pass a general price-control law. Congress found it hard to agree on the terms of such a measure, and the proposed bill did not become law until January 1942, after we entered the war. *The New York Times* described this act as the "tattered remnant" of the administration's original bill. It provided for a single administrator with power to place an upper limit, or "ceiling price," on all commodity prices except farm products. And even prices on these commodities could be restricted under certain conditions, with the approval of the secretary of agriculture and if they tended to rise above certain levels. For most farm products the level was 110 percent of "parity"; "parity" was the purchasing power of the farmer's dollar from 1909 to 1914. Senator Brown of Michigan, who had been partly responsible for the measure, prophesied that the bill would prevent "excessively high prices, gross profiteering, maintain a reasonable price relationship and by stopping the upward curve of prices will be a potent factor in preventing after-the-war collapse." The news weekly, *Time,* was less enthusiastic: "The Price-Control Bill had been messed up to the point of insanity. In all the 153 years of Congress there had been few bills more politically manhandled, or so potentially dangerous to the national welfare." *The New York Times* called the measure "the most brazen sort of class legislation." In signing the measure, President Roosevelt expressed dissatisfaction with the arrangement for farm prices.

In April 1943 President Roosevelt directed the price administrator not to increase prices on major items in the cost of living, to put ceiling prices on many items not before covered, and to reduce prices which were too high. This became known as the "hold the line" order. Between May 1943 and December 1944 the cost of living advanced only about 1 percent. Between May 1942 and May 1943 the advance had amounted to 9 percent.

It was a simple matter to impose price ceilings on consumers' goods already manufactured and in warehouses and retail stores. Partly for this reason OPA was effective during the war. New goods for civilians were not being produced, and most factories were busy with war orders. On goods already produced there was no problem of costs and no question of profits as an incentive. After the war, with wages up and productive efficiency down, manufacturers complained that OPA left them no profits. Without profits they could see no point in taking the risks of production. The problem of price control after the war is referred to in Chapter 49.

War Labor Board

To make the machinery of production move smoothly, there had to be uninterrupted cooperation between management and employees. Differences and disagreements could not be permitted to result in idleness and strikes. The era of defense had been marked by a number of labor troubles, some of them so serious that the federal government had to intervene. Soon after Pearl Harbor President Roosevelt called a conference of representative leaders from labor, industry, and the government for the purpose of working out an effective labor policy. He wanted an agreement to end strikes and lockouts for the period of the war, and he urged the adoption of policies to guarantee industrial peace.

It was difficult to reach a satisfactory solution, but the conference ended its work on December 23, 1941. The conference agreed to ban all strikes and lockouts for the duration of the war and to submit disputes to arbitration. Then, following the precedent of World War I, President Roosevelt issued an executive order creating the new National War Labor Board. As defined by the President, the board's function was to adjust disputes and to prevent strikes and lockouts, so that war production might go on continuously: "the national interest demands that there shall be no interruption of any work which contributes to the effective prosecution of the war." The order prescribed the procedure to be followed in case disputes should develop. First the parties in difficulty resorted to "direct negotiations or to the procedures provided in a collective bargaining agreement." Should these negotiations fail, the disputants had to notify the conciliation commissioners of the Department of Labor. The secretary of labor would then certify the dispute to the War Labor Board.

On February 23, 1942, Wendell L. Willkie declared: "There is no need . . . to point out the preposterously ineffectual manner in which the Government's labor policy—if anything so vacillating can be called a policy—has been handled. The country is well aware of it." Two days later Senator Byrd of Virginia called upon Congress to adopt a comprehensive labor policy in the interest of full-time production. As "a first and important step" in that direction, Senator Byrd demanded the removal of Secretary of Labor Perkins. He charged that she had shown "inefficiency, ineptness, and incapacity to meet her duties," and he complained because

> after nine years of incompetence, and in the face of the greatest emergency this country has known, when labor troubles constitute a weak link in our chain of

national defense, Miss Perkins is continued in office. . . . She has given no leadership in the solution of defense strikes, and our national welfare would be promoted by her removal.

Both of these complaints may have resulted from a report on strikes during the month of January 1942, issued by the National Association of Manufacturers. During that month there were sixty-eight strikes, forty-three of which were concerned with war production. These involved 15,512 employees, and they resulted in 661,976 lost man-hours. This lost time would have been sufficient to produce four 170-foot submarine chasers. Many of these strikes were "critical" in the sense that they affected the production of essential parts for planes, artillery, and machine tools. In spite of President Roosevelt's plea for uninterrupted production and in spite of pledges by both CIO and A.F. of L., strikes still occurred. In 1942 there were almost 3000 strikes, but they involved fewer than 1,000,000 workers. In 1944 there were more than 4000 strikes, involving 2,115,637 workers. Nevertheless, the total man-hours lost by strikes was but little compared to the vast number of hours put in by workers everywhere.

In addition to dealing with strikes, the War Labor Board tried to maintain the existing level of wages. This was done by applying the "little steel formula," which limited wage increases to 15 percent. This arrangement was applied first to wages in the steel companies not tied up with "big steel" —that is, the United States Steel Corporation.

Greatly increased farm production was needed to meet the heavy demands of the armed forces and to supply our allies. Nor was there any prospect that this great demand for food would cease with the close of the war. It would be some time before war-torn and occupied areas of Europe and Asia, whose people had been ill fed for years, would be in a position to feed themselves. Increased wartime production goals in agriculture had to be met with no increase in the number of workers and in the face of equipment shortage. The Agricultural Adjustment Agency guided and helped farmers in meeting the wartime quotas by means of acreage allotments and crop conservation, and it encouraged farmers to increase production by means of parity payments and subsidies. The farm yield of 1942 was the greatest in American history, and in 1944 even this record was surpassed.

Domestic Problems

With the coming of war the President automatically came into possession of that broad authority known as the war power. This authority is derived in part from the President's status as commander in chief of the armed forces and in part from precedent, experience, and the needs of a specific situation. President Lincoln made wide use of these war powers, the most notable instance being the Emancipation Proclamation. Wilson's administration also fell back on this convenient formula that the government may

Censorship

do various things in time of war which it may not do in time of peace. In December 1941 Congress gave President Roosevelt power to reorganize government departments at his discretion. Then Congress authorized the establishment of censorship, the seizure of enemy property, and the letting of war contracts without competitive bidding. The granting of these specific powers did not mean that the President was prohibited from resorting to other powers if circumstances so required. In time of war the constitutional principle followed was one of broad construction, not only of laws and the Constitution but of established customs.

Ever since the American Revolution every war has had its problems of public opinion and of the press; World War II had the added problem of the radio. The Constitution, with its guarantees of free speech and a free press, does not help the executive in dealing with this question, or collection of questions. The publication of any information which might be of service to the enemy must be prevented. But this broad rule leaves many matters in doubt. What sort of information is helpful to the enemy? In World War II, for the first time, the publication of weather reports and maps, except for very limited areas, was forbidden. If the publication of certain types of facts could be forbidden, what about opinions? Too much adverse criticism of the government might be regarded as giving aid and assistance to the enemy. So, too, might the publication of accounts of mistakes or blunders of high officials. Here were real problems, and they were never completely solved.

Then there was the closely related problem of propaganda. To what extent should the government endeavor to create favorable opinions regarding the war and toward official policies relating to the war? During World War I Congress had passed an Espionage Act and then a much more drastic Sedition Act. At the same time, President Wilson created the Committee on Public Information, which not only decided what might be published but sometimes went pretty close to manufacturing news for the press.

Shortly after Pearl Harbor, President Roosevelt announced the inauguration of an extensive system of censorship, designed to prevent important information from reaching the enemy. As director of censorship the President appointed Mr. Byron Price, up to that time executive editor of the Associated Press. Mr. Price received authority over the press, radio, cables, and both outgoing and incoming mail. Mr. Price was able to count on the cooperation of both press and radio. He asked them not to divulge certain types of information until it could be of no service to the enemy.

After the establishment of Mr. Price's office or bureau, the authorities at Washington took additional steps in the work of dealing with opinion, and planned for a drastic system of censorship. In 1942, after various experiments, President Roosevelt created the Office of War Information and put Elmer Davis in charge. Mr. Davis said that he would try to "give the people a clear, complete and accurate picture" of the events of the war. His office had general oversight of the publication of news about the war by both press and radio. It also kept up a continuous stream of propaganda directed to enemy countries.

The problem of criticism of the administration in time of war is always difficult to handle. At the start Attorney General Biddle had advocated a liberal policy toward such critics; he warned the people against "witch hunts"—that is, the persecution of any who might hold unpopular opinions. But the quantity of dangerous writing and speaking soon compelled Mr. Biddle to change his mind. Because of the system of propaganda worked out and applied by the Germans, every government had to be constantly on the watch to protect itself against traitors at home.

Disloyalty at Home

World War II gave rise to two descriptive terms: "ideological warfare" and "fifth column." The first is an attack upon basic beliefs and convictions; the second refers to the agents who make this attack. Both terms referred to enemy activity carried on within the limits of a given country, in advance of and in preparation for possible invasion. Fifth columnists circulated enemy propaganda and carried on activities designed to give the enemy a preliminary grip on the country. These enemy agents may have been aliens, or they may have been disloyal citizens. Someone aptly described fifth-columnists as termites that bore from within.

Fifth columnists did not work at random but in accordance with a carefully drawn plan. They tried to break down the spirit of resistance and destroy the will to fight. Once people lost confidence in themselves and their cause, conquest would become easy. In 1940 large numbers of French people had been filled with defeatism even before the army collapsed. Again, these fifth columnists tried to undermine popular confidence in the existing government. Another objective was to destroy confidence in possible allies. In general, ideological warfare created discord and controversy among the people; it tended to keep them confused and divided on current issues. Fifth columnists fought countless shrewd ideological battles. Their clever operations were in striking contrast to the blundering, stupid efforts of German propaganda agents in World War I.

During the first part of 1942 evidence concerning such work in the United States was brought to light in numerous periodicals. The beginning of this campaign in the United States can be traced back to 1933, the year that Hitler came to power in Germany. The German Ministry of Propaganda prepared a document entitled "General Instructions Concerning German Propaganda Action in the Two Americas." This program was supposed to be kept secret, but the general staff of the French Army secured a copy of it, so it got into circulation. This document described the course which German agents would follow in building up a strong body of pro-nazi opinion in the United States. It explained how trained investigators were sent over here to discover issues over which the American people were divided. Other agents were then put to work to strengthen these divisions.

The worst of these nazi organizations was the German-American Bund, of which Fritz Kuhn was the leader. There were also American organizations with American leaders working openly for the nazi cause. Among the better known was the Christian Front, under the leadership of Mr. George W. Christians of Tennessee. On January 1, 1942, Christians put out a "plan" for agitation during the war, the purpose of which he said was "to finish the demoralization and disintegration of the existing order and create a REIGN OF TERROR." He published quantities of subversive propaganda. In the same category with Mr. Christians was Mr. William Dudley Pelley, publisher of the *Galilean* and founder of the pro-nazi organization of the "Silver Shirts." After the war came to the United States, Pelley published a line of pro-nazi, seditious, defeatist propaganda. He held the administration responsible for our getting into the war, and he urged the voters

> to rectify the New Deal diplomatic blunder and bring the war to a graceful conclusion with as little further loss to American territory and sovereignty as may be contrivable . . . The prospects are that the war will be brought to a fairly swift close, the moment the anti-Nazi fire eaters can be excused politically from power. And that is a consummation devoutly to be wished.

Pelley was the man who proclaimed: "The time has come for an American Hitler and a pogrom." Another pro-nazi rabble rouser was Robert Noble, who proclaimed his admiration for Germany and for Hitler: "I am for the Axis powers because they are the liberators of the world." After the publication of these statements, Noble, Pelley, and Christians were arrested under orders of Attorney General Biddle.

Enemy Aliens

Another major problem of the war was to be found in the large number of enemy aliens, and, in the case of the Japanese, of American-born citizens who also held citizenship in Japan. Because of the Japanese record of dishonesty and the nature of the attack on Pearl Harbor, Americans had every reason to be suspicious of the Japanese. In theory, the policy of our government toward enemy nationals was simple. Those who had resided here for a long time and who had become loyal Americans should not be made to suffer for the misdeeds of their own government. On the other hand, enemy agents were to be interned, and enemy plotters and criminals were to be severely punished. In the main, this is the policy which the administration started to follow.

When the war began there were approximately 1,124,000 enemy aliens residing in the United States. On the Pacific Coast there were 112,553 Japanese, of whom 40,899 were born in Japan. The great majority of these were in California. The Californians were worried over these people. Up to April 16, 1942, the FBI had arrested 8010 enemy aliens: 4443 Japanese, 2440 Germans, and 1127 Italians. Also in 1942, the War Department advised the Department of Justice to arrange for the removal of all aliens from areas vital to defense in the regions of San Francisco and Los Angeles. All Japanese, citizens and aliens alike, were moved out of the prohibited areas into concentration camps.

In putting Japanese residents into concentration camps, the government violated constitutional rights. But the problem was a hard one, and the emergency was serious. Early in 1942 the balance between defeat and victory was still delicate, and it might tip either way. The ruling class in Japan had behaved in such a way as to give all Japanese an evil reputation. This was not deserved in all cases, but it was easy to understand. Our government had not forgotten how the Japanese had lied out of the *Panay* affair, and the treacherous attack on Pearl Harbor was still fresh in everybody's mind. Because of the unprincipled record of Japanese officials, entirely innocent American citizens of Japanese ancestry had to suffer. Many of these American-born Japanese served with distinction in our armed forces during the war.

Most Americans who stayed at home found something to do on the "home front." During the early part of the war, in fact before we entered, the Office of Civilian Defense worked out plans to protect our cities against enemy bombing raids. Volunteer watchers were on duty night and day, with orders to report any strange plane to the nearest "filter center." Every city block had air raid wardens and deputies. Cities experimented with "blackouts" in preparation for possible air raids. Fortunately no enemy bombers came within range, but in 1942 nobody could afford to overlook the danger of attack. The Red Cross trained thousands of people in first aid, and, under the direction of the Red Cross, hospitals established and maintained blood banks for use in case of enemy attacks. Most of the people went into these efforts with remarkable enthusiasm. They wanted to do something in the war effort.

Death of Roosevelt

During the latter part of the war it became clear that President Roosevelt was not well. His pictures made him look older than his years, and in his talks over the radio he sounded tired. His trip to Yalta in February 1945 left him almost exhausted. He died suddenly early in April 1945 when the victory for which he had worked so long was almost in sight. Newspapers paid high tribute to his leadership in international affairs. One editor said: "More than any other President a world upheaval of unparalleled gravity has made him a world figure never to be forgotten or ignored in the story of our times." Harry Truman was the seventh Vice President called upon to become the nation's chief executive. He announced that our foreign policy of cooperation with the United Nations would be continued: "I want the entire world to know that this direction must and will remain—unchanged and unhampered!"

End of Isolationism

In World War II the policy of the United States was a long way removed from isolationism. What the rest of the world did affected us, and what we did affected the world. Whether we liked it or not did not matter. This situation was not new. Forty years earlier Theodore Roosevelt pointed out that we could not avoid playing a part in world affairs. Our choice was not simply to play or not to play; it was to play the part badly or to play it well. The course of World War II gave new emphasis to what Theodore Roosevelt had stated so clearly. Just before World War II isolationists had argued that we could and should keep entirely free from foreign quarrels. Interventionists argued that we could not keep clear of such disputes, that we had to intervene to protect our own interests. For the future the United States was destined to take an increasingly important part in world affairs.

Chapter 48

ONE WORLD—OR TWO?

DURING World War II the nations opposed to the Rome-Berlin-Tokyo Axis had achieved a remarkable degree of unanimity in action. Of course there had been differences of opinion over policies; these were inevitable. But there had been complete agreement on the main purpose, victory, and at least a practical agreement on strategy in winning the war. Then, before the war ended, Allied statesmen became convinced that victory alone was not enough. The practice of acting together had worked miracles in defeating the enemy; there was obvious need to continue the practice during the coming years of peace. This need was vividly demonstrated in Wendell L. Willkie's popular book, *One World*. If all governments were prepared to cooperate, and if they were all united in a common desire for peace, a world organization would make postwar cooperation both easy and efficient. This time, so people believed, there would be no such collapse as that which followed World War I.

The United Nations

President Roosevelt devoted one fifth of his last inaugural address, on January 20, 1945, to this subject of world organization.

> We learned lessons—at a fearful cost—and we shall profit from them. We have learned that we cannot live alone, at peace; that our well-being is dependent on the well-being of other nations—far away. We have learned that we must live as men, not ostriches, nor dogs in the manger. We have learned to be citizens of the world, members of the human community. In the days and years that are to come, we shall work for a just and honorable peace, a durable peace, as today we work and fight for a total victory in war.

When Roosevelt spoke, work toward this goal of world organization was already well started. In October 1943 the foreign secretaries of the Big Three powers, Molotov of Russia, Eden of England, and Hull of the United States, meeting at Moscow, had given approval on the part of the nations they represented to the policy of world union. They pledged that "their united action . . . will be continued for the organization and maintenance of peace and security." Furthermore, "they recognize the necessity of establishing at the earliest practicable date a general international organization . . . for the maintenance of international peace and security."

World Unity

A month later the United States Senate, by the impressive vote of 85 to 5, approved the Moscow Declaration. Our government, so the Senate pledged, would join in establishing and maintaining an "international authority with power to prevent aggression and to preserve the peace of the world." This action seemed to provide full guarantees of continued cooperation. The United States would not pull out as we had done in 1919. Also in 1943, Stalin, Churchill, and Roosevelt, meeting at Teheran, gave further endorsement to the Moscow Declaration.

In the second half of 1944 representatives of the great powers met at Dumbarton Oaks near Washington, D. C. Their purpose was to draw up and agree upon the framework of a new international organization which would preserve the good points of the old League of Nations while avoiding its weaknesses. Several other key decisions regarding the project were made by Stalin, Churchill, and Roosevelt at the Yalta Conference in February 1945.

At Yalta plans were made for a great conference of all governments that had declared war upon the Axis. The conference would meet at San Francisco, and it would draw up the formal charter of the United Nations. With abundant proof of worldwide approval of the program, 300 official delegates from 50 governments came together in sessions that lasted from April to June 1945. The United States was represented by a distinguished commission that was headed by the new secretary of state, Edward M. Stettinius, and included leading legislators of both political parties as well as other prominent citizens. President Truman opened the proceedings with a radio address: "You members of this conference are to be the architects of the better world."

United Nations Charter

Speaking for the Soviet Union, Foreign Commissar Molotov gave unqualified approval: "An international organization must be created . . . having the means for military protection of the security of nations. We will fully co-operate in the solution of this great problem." These expressions of harmony and good will seemed to guarantee lasting solidarity on the part of the Allied powers. Under these favorable auspices the delegates completed work on the Charter.

In building the United Nations the conference adopted many of the proposals agreed upon at Dumbarton Oaks. For the general discussion of any problem in international affairs there was the General Assembly, in which every member government had one vote. The powers of the Assembly would be limited largely to making recommendations. This body would meet regularly once every year. The most important branch of the United Nations would be the Security Council. This body would have five permanent members: France, China, the Soviet Union, Great Britain and the United States. The Assembly was authorized to elect six additional, but nonpermanent, members of the Council to serve for two years.

The Council received authority to investigate and to act upon disputes in the international field. Its first effort would be in the interest of a peaceful settlement. Should this effort fail, the Council could use pressure, either economic or, in serious cases, actual force. Each one of the five great powers was called upon to appoint military experts to serve on the general staff of the United Nations, and member governments were expected to keep "a quota of forces readily available." The Security Council could then use this force against aggressors.

To make sure of needed action in case of sudden emergency the Charter decreed that "The Security Council shall be so organized as to be able to function continuously. Each member of the Security Council shall for this purpose be represented at all times at the seat of the Organization." If the Assembly should ever discover any threat to the peace of the world, it was required by the Charter to turn the matter over to the Security Council. But the Council could also act on its own initiative without waiting for the Assembly. These provisions seemed to guard against the most glaring weakness in the League of Nations, which had no authority to use force.

Up to this point the United Nations looked like an effective organization. But there was a joker in the Charter which threatened to put the United Nations Organization on the same level of weakness with the old League. In making preliminary plans for the new order at Yalta, Stalin, Churchill, and Roosevelt had agreed that the Security Council could take no action involving the use of force without unanimous approval of the permanent members. In other words, any one of the Big Five could veto any proposal for action. At San Francisco this issue of the veto was subjected to long and vigorous discussion. The smaller powers argued strongly against it; but the great powers insisted that the pledge given at Yalta must be honored, and they had their way.

To complete the organization there was an Economic and Social Council, composed of representatives from eighteen member governments. Members of this body were to be elected by the Assembly for three-year terms. Then there was a Trusteeship Council, to include governments which had held mandates over dependent areas under the League of Nations. Russia and China had held no mandates, but they were made members of the Trusteeship Council. The Charter also provided for a new International Court of Justice with headquarters at The Hague. A secretariat was set up to keep records, run the office, and handle routine business. Many activities of the United Nations, especially those concerned with public welfare, would be carried on by separate organizations. These are something like the federal commissions in our own government, such as the Interstate Commerce Commission. They are created by the General Assembly. Among the better known of these bodies are the International Labor Organization (ILO) and the United Nations Educational, Scientific and Cultural Organization (UNESCO). For a permanent home the United Nations selected New York City, and, thanks to the generosity of John D. Rockefeller, Jr., a large site was secured on Manhattan Island.

Russia Ends Cooperation with the West

During and immediately after World War II many Americans convinced themselves that the One World ideal was feasible and that the Soviet Union

"You'll git over it, Joe. Oncet I wuz gonna write a book exposin' th' Army after th' war, mysel

BILL MAULDIN'S drawings of Willie and Joe, battle-scarred G.I.'s of World War II, were widely popular with servicemen abroad and civilians at home. (Copyright 1944 United Feature Syndicate, Inc.)

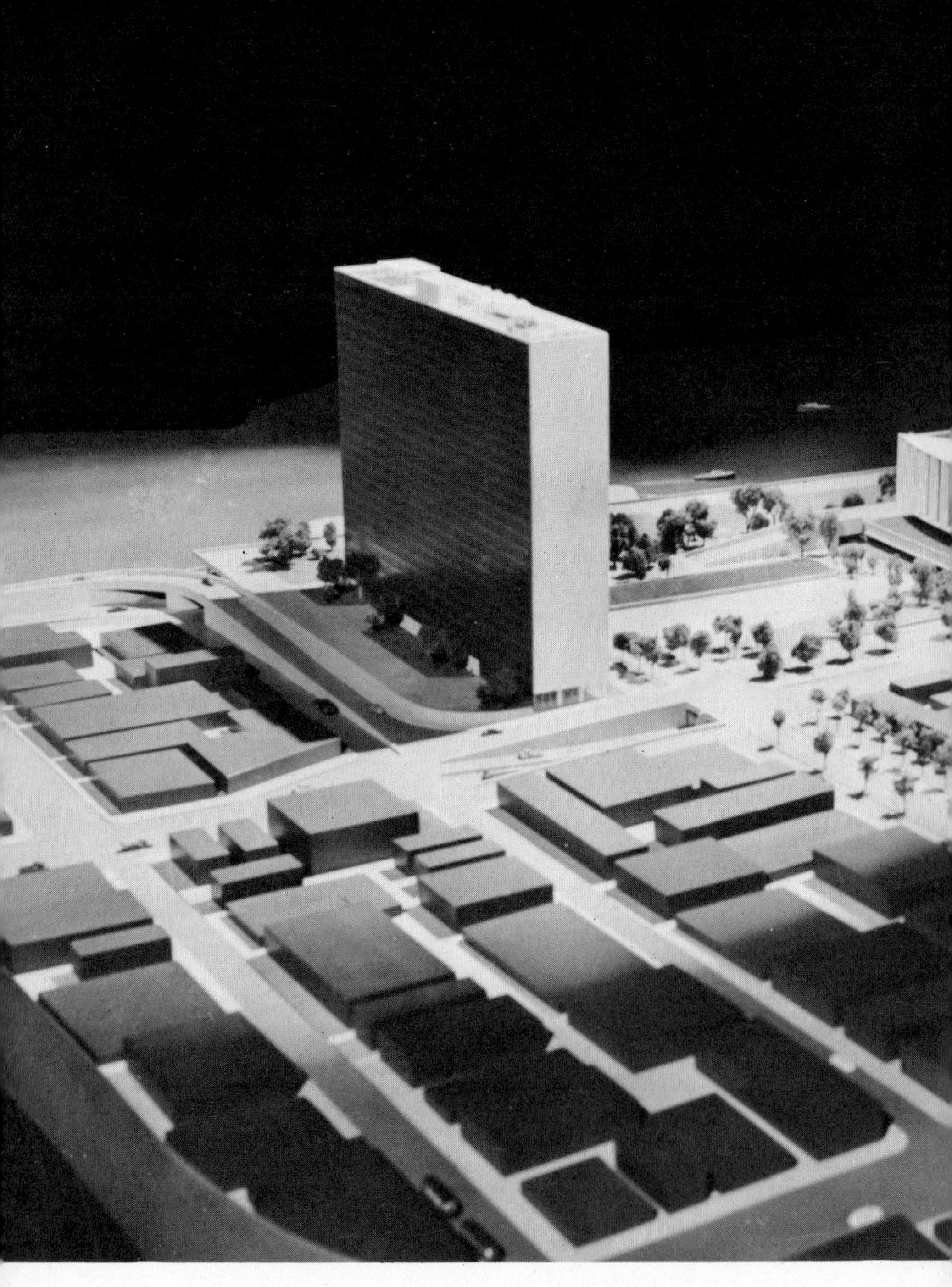

THE Architect's model of the United Nations' permanent home to be erected near the East River Drive in New York City. (Courtesy, United Nations)

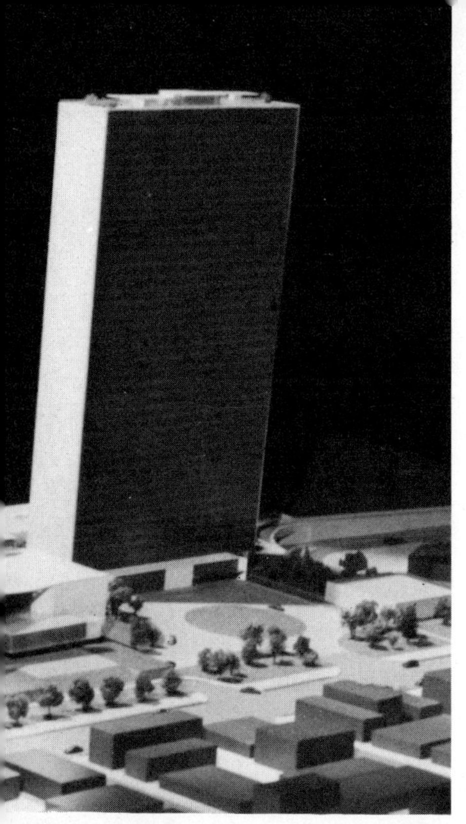

FLEET Admiral Chester W. Nimitz signing the documents which marked the defeat of Japan. The ceremony took place, September 2, 1945, on the U.S.S. MISSOURI. General Douglas MacArthur, with his arm around Admiral William E. Halsey, stands directly behind Admiral Nimitz. Rear Admiral Forrest Sherman stands near Admiral Nimitz, and representatives of the Allied powers look on. (Official U. S. Navy photograph)

THE financial capital of the nation—Wall Street in 1834 (Courtesy, New-York Historical Society, New York City) and Wall Street today (Ewing Galloway)

would support it. In the enthusiasm of the common war effort against the Axis powers it was too easily assumed that the Kremlin had abandoned its plans for world revolution and that Stalin was a good fellow, with whom we could make agreements. Roosevelt himself wrote that he had "a hunch that Stalin . . . doesn't want anything but security for his country, and I think that if I give him everything I possibly can and ask nothing from him in return, *noblesse oblige,* he won't try to annex anything and will work with me for a world of democracy and peace." The concept of *noblesse oblige,* however, was unknown to the Soviet rulers. The record in both Europe and Asia before 1941 and after 1945 shows that the optimism of the Roosevelt administration was based on a failure to understand the full purposes of Russian policy.

Divorce of the Powers

Russian cooperation with the West ceased before the end of 1945, and with it died the hope for any immediate realization of the One World ideal. The nations became divided into two sharply separated groups, communist and non-communist, with the Soviet Union reverting to Lenin's policy of world revolution. The Kremlin was undoubtedly encouraged in its decision by American demobilization. The United States armed forces were so reduced in numbers and strength that we could no longer talk convincingly to Stalin.

The divorce of the powers began early in 1945, when victory was assured but before the war ended. At Yalta, in addition to promising support for the United Nations, Stalin had also promised democracy, self-government, and civil rights for the peoples of eastern Europe. Events soon proved, however, that these words meant very different things in the communist and non-communist vocabularies. The Yalta Conference was hardly finished when Andrei Vishinsky, a high Soviet official, went to Bucharest, the capital of Rumania, and gave the king two hours and five minutes to establish a communist government. The king protested but complied. When someone told Vishinsky that his methods would not be approved by the Western powers, the reply was a clear reflection of the Russian attitude: "Let the sparrows twitter."

Although the United States did not recognize the new Rumanian regime established in defiance of the Yalta agreements, President Roosevelt did not protest to Stalin, because the war was still going on. However, this forbearance ended when news came that a communist government was also being imposed upon Poland. On April 1, 1945, both Roosevelt and Churchill sent protests to Stalin, but these were fruitless. Even before his death on April 12, 1945, Roosevelt had become seriously concerned over the hostile attitude of the Kremlin rulers.

Before the end of the San Francisco Conference President Truman became so alarmed by the growing evidence of Russian aggression that he sent Harry Hopkins on a special mission to Moscow. Hopkins told Stalin frankly that the millions of Americans who had approved Roosevelt's policy toward Russia were gravely disturbed by recent developments; if the course of events should remain unchanged, these same people would oppose any further attempts at Soviet-American cooperation. Hopkins reported that the major reason for American uneasiness was the Russian policy toward Poland, which was an obvious violation of the Yalta Declaration. Stalin, in turn, explained that his government did not like the American attitude toward Poland and the recent termination of Lend-Lease. The only definite result of this mission was the arrangement for another meeting of the Big Three to be held at Potsdam.

The Iron Curtain

Early in 1946 Winston Churchill, speaking at Fulton, Missouri, recognized the change that was materializing and warned his audience of the growing dangers of Soviet aggression. Then, in his vivid style, he showed how the communists were drawing an "iron curtain" across Europe, from the Baltic to the Adriatic. At the time, people who still clung to the hope that the Soviet Union was a friendly power felt that Churchill had maligned an ally. Events of the next several years, however, emphasized the significance and accuracy of Churchill's grim prophecy.

Between 1945 and 1948 communist forces tightened their grip upon central and eastern Europe. Not only Rumania and Poland but Bulgaria, Yugoslavia, Hungary, and Albania fell under the control of pro-Russian governments. Western opinion was particularly shocked early in 1948 by a communist seizure of power in Czechoslovakia, long regarded as one of the most humane and democratic states of Europe.

In these so-called satellite countries the helplessness of the individual in the face of tyrannical government was vividly illustrated. The rulers broke the back of opposition groups by condemning their leaders to slave labor camps or even executing them. Communists themselves were not immune from their own terror. Both in the Soviet Union itself and in the satellites there were frequent "purges," during which communist leaders, once mainstays of the party, might find themselves suddenly out of favor. Imprisonment or execution was the fate of hundreds condemned on flimsy charges of spying for the West or of "nationalist-rightist deviation," that is, insufficient loyalty to the Kremlin.

Russian Provocation

As long as the victims of this tyranny were nationals of the "iron curtain" countries, the United States could criticize only on general principles. But when American citizens suffered imprisonment or harassment, the government felt compelled to protest. One such case involved Robert Vogeler, an American businessman in Hungary, arrested on charges of sabotage and espionage in November 1949 and not released until April 1951 despite State Department remonstrances. A second American victim was William Oatis, an Associated Press correspondent, whom the government of Czechoslovakia arrested on charges of espionage early in 1951 and sent to prison after a farcical trial. Oatis finally gained his freedom in May 1953.

Even more serious in American eyes was a series of plane incidents. In April 1950 an American navy plane, flying over the Baltic, disappeared with a loss of ten men. The Russians admitted firing upon it, but claimed that it had been reconnoitering over Russian territory; the Americans denied this and protested that the plane had been attacked over the open sea. Unsuccessful in getting satisfaction in this dispute, the State Department had another frustrating experience the next year when another American plane wandered off its course into Hungary and was compelled to land by *Russian* fliers. Accused of "violation of the frontier with criminal intent," four American airmen were sentenced to three months in jail or a fine of $120,000. The State Department decided to pay the fine in order to get the men home. Critics condemned the administration for submitting to blackmail, but few were prepared to support the only apparent alternative—to use American force to halt these indignities. Such a course might precipitate a third World War, and the United States was not willing to assume such an awesome responsibility.

In addition to these episodes a number of similar plane incidents occurred both in Europe and off the coast of Asia in the Pacific. To exasperated Americans Russia seemed to be resorting to a policy of deliberate pin-pricks. By isolated acts of violence the communists would provoke the United States into sharp notes of protest and minor economic reprisals, but the Soviet Union would carefully relax its pressure before the situation deteriorated to the point of actual hostilities.

Soviet Imperialism

Stalin's decision to end cooperation with the West was not unnatural in view of communist history. The alliance against Hitler had been strictly a marriage of convenience, and, once the Nazi menace was ended, the Soviet leader could see no purpose in continuing the arrangement. He returned to the philosophy which Lenin had developed and which Stalin himself had consistently upheld—except during the brief interval of World War II. Lenin had warned: "As long as capitalism and socialism exist, we cannot live in peace. In the end, one or the other will triumph, a funeral dirge will be sung either over the Soviet Republic or over world capitalism." As for methods, Lenin put into words the policy which communists have followed consistently ever since his day: "We have to use any ruse, dodge, trick, cunning, unlawful methods, concealment, veiling of the truth. . . ." Stalin gave full endorsement to Lenin. In his book, *Foundations of Leninism,* published in an English translation in New York in 1939, the Russian dictator described his plans with as much detail as Hitler had done in *Mein Kampf.*

The determination to spread communism throughout the world was not the only driving force in Soviet policy. For 300 years before the revolution Czarist Russia had followed a program of expansion, toward the Far East, toward the Dardanelles, and toward the Balkans. Stalin revived this imperialist policy. Under this double sanction of communism and Russian imperialism the Soviet Union gave the Western world ample reason to fear for its own survival. The danger was multiplied by the fact that Communist parties throughout the world accepted blindly the leadership of Moscow. Faithful party members in each country were available for use as spies and saboteurs in the interest of Russia.

American Military Policy after World War II

Soviet expansionism was encouraged by a power vacuum after World War II. Germany, Japan, and Italy lay crushed in defeat; England and France had been exhausted by their efforts to achieve victory. Only the United States possessed a potential of power adequate to hold Russia in some kind of check. But for several years postwar cutbacks in the armed forces made the American counter-balance dangerously weak.

Rapid demobilization was a policy popular with the general American public. Soldiers and sailors long separated from home were eager to resume civilian life as soon as possible, while lonesome parents and wives were of course even more impatient to have the boys brought back from overseas. The Truman administration, not yet fully alerted to the Soviet threat in 1945, did its best to hasten the homecoming.

By the spring of 1946 it became obvious that the demobilization was going too fast and too far. The Air Force, which had boasted a wartime strength of 2,500,000 men and 85,000 planes had been reduced to 165,000 men and 9,000 planes. General Eisenhower, now Chief of Staff, warned that the Army did not have one single division properly trained and equipped. The contrast with some 200 divisions available to the Soviet Union was startling.

Restoring The Armed Forces

The Truman administration now sought to repair the damage by slowing down the rate of discharges and asking Congress to extend the draft. Such proposals, however, were unpopular, and a firm policy of rearmament did not become feasible until 1948. In June of that year Congress passed a new selective service act. It provided for the registration of all men between the ages of 18 and 26. Inductions would begin with those of 19 and over. Those called up would remain in active service for 21 months and would remain in the reserve for five years. This measure was in effect when the Korean war began in 1950. The law was extended with somewhat different provisions in 1951 and again in 1955.

President Truman asked Congress repeatedly to authorize a policy of universal military training. Early in 1952 a bill was under debate, providing for six months training for all physically and mentally fit 18-year-old young men to be followed by seven and one-half years in the reserve. The measure was strongly opposed by organized farmers, organized labor, educational authorities, and various church groups. Particularly sensitive to such pressures in an election year, Congress quietly killed the bill.

Unifying the Forces

As part of the policy of rebuilding the nation's defensive strength, Congress—in 1947—passed the National Security Act to bring the army, navy, and air force together in a single National Military Establishment. The head of this unified organization was given the title of Secretary of Defense and a place in the Cabinet. Under him were three secretaries, one for the army, one for the navy, and one for the air force; they did not have cabinet rank. Associated with these four top officials were the Joint Chiefs of Staff, with a chairman appointed by the President.

Unification of the armed forces was much easier to achieve on paper than in actuality. Within the new organization the services wrangled angrily. Particularly bitter were the fights between the navy and the air force, each proudly confident that it provided the nation's chief shield of defense. The navy demanded large appropriations for aircraft carriers; the air force contended that carrier-based air power had become outmoded and that every available dollar should go for long-range bombers. Such controversies made life miserable for the first two secretaries of defense, James V. Forrestal and Louis A. Johnson. President Truman partially quieted the situation by appointing the highly-respected General Marshall to the secretaryship in 1950. Behind the scenes, however, the rivalries continued, and as late as 1956 during the secretaryship of the Republican Charles E. Wilson new inter-service controversies were being aired before the public.

Attempts at Peacemaking

War Crimes Trials

In this atmosphere of hostility between the communist and non-communist worlds the problem of formulating peace terms for the powers defeated in World War II was naturally difficult. On one point only was there speedy agreement: the Axis leaders responsible for plotting aggression and violating the rules of war should be punished. At the Conference of Foreign Ministers at Moscow in 1943, Eden, Molotov, and Hull had agreed that the principal enemy leaders, those responsible for the war, should be treated as criminals. In November 1945 an international military tribunal, meeting at Nuremberg, put twenty-one prominent Nazis on trial. Hitler and Goebbels had already committed suicide. The trial lasted ten months and revealed a sickening record of crimes and atrocities. Of the defendants ten were hanged, seven were given prison terms, and three were acquitted. Goering would have been hanged, but cheated the gallows with a last-minute suicide. Later several Japanese leaders, including the war premier General Tojo, were tried and executed.

Blueprints for Peace

The Yalta Conference of February 1945 had laid down certain guiding principles for dealing with the defeated powers. Stalin, Churchill, and Roosevelt agreed that Germany would be divided into four occupation zones, respectively allocated to the Russians, British, French, and Americans. An Allied Control Commission with headquarters at Berlin would coordinate policy. Berlin itself would lie within the Russian occupation zone, but would be divided into four sections, each under the control of one of the Allied powers. Important decisions were also made for the exaction of reparations, the dismantling of German war industry, and the demilitarization of the country. This Yalta blueprint was implemented at the Potsdam Conference of July 1945 where Attlee, Stalin, and Truman made more detailed plans for the occupation. They also decided upon a plan of procedure for further peacemaking. A Council of Foreign Ministers, representing Russia, France, England, and the United States, would work out terms first for

Problems of Peace-making

Italy, Finland, Hungary, Bulgaria, and Rumania, then for Germany and Austria. After the great powers had reached agreement, the draft treaties would be considered in larger conferences where the defeated powers and the small nations would have their say.

From the beginning the peacemaking machinery operated only with much noisy clashing of gears. Each local issue became involved in the larger struggle for power between East and West. In drafting the Italian treaty, for example, the hardest problem was Trieste, an important Adriatic port demanded by both Italy and Yugoslavia. Since Yugoslavia was under communist control and Italy was gravitating toward the non-communist bloc, the Trieste issue obviously reflected the whole clash of interest between the two worlds. Fortunately, in this instance, a compromise solution was found through partition of the territory in question. After many months of wearisome negotiation treaties with Italy and the smaller powers were finally signed in February 1947.

The Council of Foreign Ministers found the drafting of treaties for Germany and Austria much more difficult. The Ministers worked on this problem in Moscow for seven weeks in March and April 1947. But they were unable to come to any agreement whatever on reparations, boundaries, economic policies, or a form of government for Germany. Later attempts to draft a treaty were similarly futile. The real difficulty was that each side feared a peace treaty that would tip the world balance of power toward its rival. If Germany became a western type democracy, the Soviet Union's dominant position in central Europe would be threatened; if, on the other hand, a situation were created that opened the way to a communist seizure of power over the entire country, the rest of Europe would lie at the mercy of the new Berlin-Moscow alignment.

The Austrian problem was less difficult, because Austria was a very small country and hence much less important as a pawn in the diplomatic game. Actually the powers were in substantial agreement on the terms of an Austrian treaty as early as 1949, but Russia obstructed the final signing by insisting that the German treaty must be completed first. Finally, however, the Soviet Union gave in on condition that Austria should be neutralized. On this basis a treaty restoring sovereignty to Austria and ending the occupation was signed on May 15, 1955.

The United Nations in a Divided World

Efforts to Enforce Peace

Amidst growing evidence of mutual suspicion between East and West the United Nations had been attempting to operate. The first General Assembly met at London in January 1946, and the Security Council began to function continuously in New York the following March. Immediately the new organization was confronted with problems arising out of the world struggle for power. When the Security Council persisted in considering complaints of Russian interference in Iran, Andrei Gromyko, the Soviet delegate, walked out of the Council Chamber to demonstrate his displeasure. The Russians did, however, pull their troops out of Iranian territory. To optimists this seemed to indicate that the United Nations might exert great influence through focusing world attention on dangerous situations. Pessimists, however, minimized the part played by the United Nations; they were sure that the Russian retreat in Iran was only a tactical withdrawal and that the communists would not hesitate to move forward again when the time seemed ripe.

A second troublesome problem for the United Nations arose out of the Palestine question. Millions of Jews throughout the world shared the Zionist dream of restoring a Jewish national state in the historic homeland, but the Arabs of the area bitterly opposed this project. United Nations efforts to find an acceptable compromise were unavailing. When the Republic of Israel brought the issue to a head by proclaiming its independence in 1948, it soon became involved in war with its Arab neighbors. The first United Nations mediator sent out to try to put an end to the fighting was assassinated, but the second, Ralph J. Bunche, an American Negro, was successful in getting the belligerents to accept an armistice in 1949. For this achievement Bunche received the Nobel Peace Prize the next year. Unfortunately, however, the Palestinian armistice was not followed by a definitive peace treaty. Frequent border clashes threatened to bring about a revival of full-scale war between the Jews and the Arabs.

Although the United Nations enjoyed modest success in many of its nonpolitical activities such as the study of international economic problems, the promotion of cultural exchange, the control of trade in narcotics, and emergency aid for afflicted children in backward areas, the weakness of the organization's peace-enforcing machinery was obvious. The work of the Security Council was repeatedly halted by Russian obstructionism in the form of bitter invective, boycotts, and vetoes. The general staff and military force called for in the United Nations Charter could not be formed.

Atomic Disarmament

From the beginning the United Nations attempted to formulate a program for international disarmament, but the difficulty of achieving this in a divided and suspicious world was tremendous. The controversy centered on the atomic bomb, the terrible destructiveness of which had been demonstrated in the closing weeks of World War II. In 1946 the United States proposed a plan for effective international control. This plan, largely the work of Bernard Baruch, provided for the creation of an "International Atomic Development Authority" as a unit of the United Nations. This Authority would have control of all known supplies of uranium, thorium, and other fissionable materials; it would also have authority to inspect any country in the world, free from interference by the local government and from possible interruption by veto, to find out whether unauthorized bombs were being made. Once the Authority was duly established and formally recognized, Great Britain and the United States would turn over to it all their knowledge of the bomb and would destroy all existing bombs.

The Russians refused to agree to the Baruch plan. They wanted to ban the atomic bomb by treaty, but they would not concede the necessity of unrestricted inspection. Whenever the subject came up, they flatly refused to permit any non-Russian inspection of Russian industrial facilities. In 1948 the seriousness of the deadlock on disarmament became even more obvious with President Truman's announcement that the Soviet Union was known to have developed its own atomic bombs and that the United States intended to push forward with the development of a still more formidable weapon, the hydrogen bomb.

In 1950 after the outbreak of the Korean war, weaknesses in the United Nations Charter were somewhat rectified through the Assembly's adoption of the so-called Acheson Plan, proposed by the American Secretary of State. If effective action by the Security Council were blocked by veto, the Acheson Plan provided that the Assembly might be called into special session to deal with the situation. The Assembly—where the veto did not apply—could set up special commissions of investigation and could recommend to the member states collective measures to check aggression.

The Truman Doctrine and the Marshall Plan

Help for Free Nations

Since the United Nations could not guarantee peace in a divided world, the United States felt it necessary to develop a positive policy of its own for preventing the further extension of communism in Europe. In 1947 the danger spot was Greece, where the anti-communist government in power was threatened by communist rebel warfare in the north. The rebels were receiving active military support from Albania, Bulgaria, and Yugoslavia. To make matters worse, the Greek people were suffering from a devastating economic depression, and the British government, which had been providing some assistance, announced that it could do nothing more. Without help from somewhere Greece might be added to the growing list of Soviet Union satellites.

In March 1947 President Truman asked for, and subsequently received, Congressional authority to grant $300,000,000 to Greece and $100,000,000 to Turkey, which was also in jeopardy. His purpose was to use American resources to strengthen friendly nations so that their governments could withstand communist pressure. As Truman put it:

> One of the primary objectives of the foreign policy of the United States is the creation of conditions in which we and other nations will be able to work out a way of life free from coercion. . . . I believe that it must be the policy of the United States to support free peoples who are resisting attempted subjugation by armed minorities or by outside pressures.

In answer to critics who accused the administration of by-passing the United Nations, President Truman declared that his government would step out, if and when the United Nations should find his policy "unnecessary and undesirable."

Help for Greece and Turkey was not the only sign of American interest in rebuilding Europe. Congress had already provided many millions of dollars for relief in Italy, Austria, China, and even in Poland, and made generous loans to France and England. However, help of this sort could be useless, particularly if given with no systematic policy behind it, and if the recipients were under no obligation to reciprocate by helping themselves. In June 1947 Secretary of State Marshall clarified the policy of the United States in these significant words:

European Recovery

> Our policy is not directed against any country or doctrine, but against hunger, poverty, desperation and chaos. Its purpose should be the revival of a working economy in the world so as to permit the emergence of political and social conditions in which free institutions can exist. Such assistance I am convinced must not be on a piecemeal basis as various crises develop. . . . The initiative I think must come from Europe. . . . The program should be a joint one, agreed to by a number, if not all, the European nations.

The British and French governments promptly went to work on economic recovery programs for their countries and invited the Soviet Union to join. The Russians would have none of it. They condemned the Marshall Plan as another scheme of "capitalist imperialism." With complete disregard of communist tactics in the seizure of power in other countries, the Soviet authorities blandly declared that "internal economic affairs are to be decided by the sovereign people themselves. . . . Other countries should not interfere in these internal affairs."

Congress approved the Marshall Plan and announced its readiness to appropriate funds, up to $5,000,000,000 annually until 1952. This policy of American cooperation became known as the European Recovery Program, shortened to ERP. Even the immediate results were favorable. Because of renewed hope in France, a series of communist-inspired strikes failed completely. Communists lost the crucial 1948 elections in Italy. By 1950 results in the economic field were evident. In the cooperating countries—16 altogether—production was lifted to pre-war levels or above.

In President Truman's inaugural address of January 20, 1949, at the beginning of his second term, he proposed still further economic measures to combat the spread of communism. In what became known as his Point Four program, Truman urged the extension of American technical and financial assistance to underdeveloped areas in Asia, Africa, and Latin America. Congress eventually made modest appropriations for this purpose and some encouragement was given to private investment, but the Point Four program was never developed as wholeheartedly as the European aid proposals had been.

The West Rebuilds Its Defenses

Closely related to the Marshall Plan was a new policy toward western Germany. No real European economic recovery could be achieved until this region, the most heavily industrialized on the continent, was restored to productivity. To promote German recovery and to create a new barrier to the spread of communism, Great Britain, France, and the United States agreed in 1948 to merge their occupation zones into a new West German state, to be organized on a federal basis. The western democracies felt justified in following this policy, because the Soviet Union had stubbornly obstructed all efforts to draft a German peace treaty or to coordinate occupation policies.

The Soviet government angrily denounced the new policy as a violation of the Potsdam Agreement. As a drastic countermeasure, the Russians in June 1948 started a blockade of Berlin. They closed all waterways, highways, and railroads leading into the city from the west. This move threatened the inhabitants of the French, British, and American zones of the city with starvation. By way of protest the Western powers called attention to the Potsdam Agreement, which gave all the occupying powers equal rights in Berlin. President Truman declared that the right to occupy a sector of the city necessarily carried with it the right of transportation, and he said this principle had been clearly understood at Potsdam.

Blockade and Air Lift

Representatives of the Western powers announced that they were staying in Berlin. To save the city from economic collapse and starvation the British and Americans started an air lift to fly essential supplies into their zones of the city. Carrying cargos of food and coal, the planes landed at the rate of about 5,000 tons per day. While considerably short of normal needs, the airlift shipments saved the city. At the same time the Western powers shut off all the eastbound transportation from their own zones to the Russian area, so the communists suffered some of the consequences of a counter blockade.

Thanks to the air lift, the Russian blockade failed of its purpose. The Western powers did not abandon their sectors of Berlin, and the Germans in these sectors became more anti-Russian than ever. Nevertheless, the situation was full of danger. The thoughtless act of some subordinate official or even some sheer accident might suddenly change the "cold war" into a "hot" one. Consequently, there was widespread relief when, in May 1949, after 328 days, the Russians finally called off the blockade.

German Republic

The Russians also failed to force the Western powers to give up their plans for the establishment of a West German state. In May 1949 a German constituent assembly completed work on a constitution for the so-called Federal Republic of Germany. Under Chancellor Konrad Adenauer the new government began to function in September 1949. Until 1952 Adenauer and his colleagues were directed by an Allied Control Commission, headed by John J. McCloy of the United States. With a population of 47 million, and with most of the old German industrial areas within its borders, this German Federal Republic was potentially the strongest power in western Europe. By way of retaliation the Russians set up the "German Democratic Republic" in their own zone and announced that it was the only lawful government for the whole of Germany. Although this new Soviet satellite had a population of only 18 million, its heavily armed "People's Police" made it a threat to West Germany so long as the latter state remained unarmed.

The vulnerability of West Germany reflected the military weakness of all western Europe. In case of war the Soviet Union's 200 divisions augmented by additional forces from the satellite states could overrun the whole continent within a few weeks. Steps to strengthen the defenses of the West were initiated in 1949 with the signing of the North Atlantic Treaty. This defensive alliance linked twelve governments: Belgium, Canada, Denmark, France, Great Britain, Iceland, Italy, Luxembourg, the Netherlands, Norway, Portugal, and the United States. All agreed that an attack upon any one of the contracting parties would be considered as an attack upon all and that all the governments would join in resistance. The Kremlin promptly denounced the treaty as an aggressive move against the Soviet Union and as a violation of the United Nations Charter.

NATO

To provide the military force necessary for collective defense, a North Atlantic Treaty Organization, soon shortened to NATO, was established with headquarters at Paris. General Dwight D. Eisenhower was appointed to the post of supreme commander of the NATO army, planned as an integrated force with component units from the various member states. After Eisenhower resigned this post in 1952 to enter the Presidential campaign at home, he was succeeded by another American, General Matthew B. Ridgway. The prominent position of the United States in the new alliance was dramatic evidence of how far the nation had moved from its isolationist position of the 1920's and 1930's.

The problem of the military defense of western Europe like that of economic recovery hinged on Germany. So long as West Germany remained demilitarized, all the rest of Europe was exposed. But France, remembering vividly German aggresssion in 1914 and 1940, bitterly opposed all proposals for the rearmament of her ancient enemy. Several years of delicate negotiations were required before this opposition could be overcome. In 1952 West Germany made a significant step forward, when military occupation by the United States, Great Britain, and France was formally ended and the Bonn government was restored to almost complete sovereignty. The Western powers were permitted, however, to continue to keep troops in West Germany as a deterrent to Soviet aggression.

Finally, on March 5, 1955, new international treaties were signed, restoring full sovereignty to West Germany, permitting her to have an army of 500,000 men, and admitting her to membership in NATO. West Germany thus became the fifteenth member of the alliance, Greece and Turkey having previously joined in 1951.

Although necessary, the military expenditures of the NATO powers placed a heavy burden upon the budgets of the western European countries—a burden that might endanger the still weak economies of these nations. To help its allies meet these extraordinary expenses, the United States made large grants. Appropriations for military assistance soon exceeded those for economic aid. Between October 1949 and December 1953 the United States shipped $7,700,000,000 in arms and other military equipment to its fellow NATO powers and to other anti-communist governments throughout the world. In 1951 the Mutual Security Administration was created to administer both the military assistance and economic aid programs.

Japan and the Philippines

The problems of postwar reconstruction were not confined to Europe. Some of the most critical issues developed in the Far East, where communist imperialism was particularly difficult to hold in check.

The administration of defeated Japan proved far less troublesome than that of Germany. This more favorable state of affairs was due in part to the absence of separate zones of occupation, in part to the forceful personality and administrative ability of General Douglas MacArthur, who had been appointed military governor of Japan at the close of World War II. To be sure, he held his position subject to the advice of two commissions, one with representatives of eleven governments, the other of four. But MacArthur managed to have his own way, and he was remarkably successful in winning the confidence and support of the Japanese people.

The New Japan

The policy of the administration was to transform Japan from an aggressive, militaristic despotism into a peaceful democracy. Under MacArthur's watchful eye the Japanese drew up a new constitution. The Emperor retained his throne, but he was required to have the advice and approval of the cabinet for all his official acts. The Diet, elected by universal suffrage, was to control the cabinet and to make all laws. The new constitution renounced war and prohibited the maintenance of an army, navy, or air force. Even the Emperor approved the new democracy. He urged his subjects to drop the "false conception that the Emperor is divine and that the Japanese people are superior to other people and fated to rule the world."

With the new government in operation, MacArthur, for the most part, freed the press, the schools, and the theater from censorship. He encouraged workers to form and join labor unions. He gave all the encouragement he could to economic recovery, so that the Japanese might become self-supporting. A far-reaching system of land reform was designed to break up feudal controls. As a result of these measures, MacArthur felt that communism ceased to be an issue in Japan. As for most other American observers, they found conditions in Japan as compared with other conquered areas, generally satisfactory. MacArthur had his critics, but they had to admit that Japan had made amazing progress since the war.

Japanese Peace Treaty

Just as the Soviet threat in Europe had encouraged measures to create a new balance of power by restoring sovereignty to West Germany, so similar fear of communist expansion in Asia convinced the United States that a strong Japan should be recreated. Over Soviet objections the American State Department lined up support among the other nations for a Japanese peace treaty. To emphasize the bipartisanship of this policy, the Truman administration employed John Foster Dulles, a leading Republican expert on foreign affairs, as its agent in the preliminary negotiations. The Soviet Union refused to join in this peacemaking effort, and China—with two governments disputing the right to speak for the nation—was not invited.

The formal peace conference was held at San Francisco in September 1951. Forty-nine nations signed the treaty of peace, recognizing Japan as a sovereign power and providing for the withdrawal of all foreign *occupation* troops within ninety days after the treaty went into effect. Japan could, however, make separate agreements with outside powers to station armed forces within her border, to defend her from attack. The treaty restricted Japanese territory to her own home islands. All claims to Korea, Formosa, the Kurile Islands, and Sakhalin were renounced. The Soviet Union denounced the method by which peace was being made and sent Andrei Gromyko to San Francisco to protest against it. Heavily outnumbered, Gromyko failed even in his effort to slow down the majority. The treaty went into effect in April 1952.

The principal objective of the Japanese peace treaty was to create a strong defensive outpost against communism in the Far East. United States armed forces were kept in Japan under the terms of a special administrative agreement signed between the two governments in February 1952. In the long run, however, Japan could not be rendered secure from Russian attack unless the Japanese were enabled to provide for their own defense. The United States accordingly urged the rearmament of its former enemy. Ironically, the provision of the Japanese constitution of 1946 prohibiting the maintenance of armed forces now proved embarrassing. Some Japanese politicians favored an amendment to permit the rebuilding of the army; others opposed this. Without changing the constitution, the Japanese government in 1953 made provisions for an enlarged National Defense Force and entered into agreements with the United States for military assistance grants. The two nations signed a mutual defense pact the following year.

Philippine Independence

A second anti-communist bastion in the Far East was the Republic of the Philippines. In these islands, which had been under American rule since 1898, the United States had a chance to show how American ideals could be put into actual practice. After V-J Day the Filipinos went ahead with their plans for establishing an independent state, plans which the Japanese had interrupted in 1942. On July 4, 1946, President Truman issued a special proclamation, announcing the entrance of the Philippine Republic into the family of nations; on behalf of the United States he announced the withdrawal and surrender "of all rights of possession, supervision, jurisdiction, control or sovereignty" over the islands, and he recognized "the independence of the Philippines as a separate and self-governing nation."

Grateful to the United States for thus fulfilling its pledge made several years before, the Filipinos gladly entered into close relations with their former rulers. Under a 99-year agreement made in 1947 the United States was permitted to retain military and naval bases in the islands. The two nations also signed a mutual defense pact in 1953.

The Rise of Red China

In sharp contrast to these favorable developments in Japan and the Philippines was the failure of American efforts to bring peace and unity to war-ravaged China. Even before the conflict with Japan began in 1937 China had for a decade been troubled by civil war between the Chinese Nationalist government of Chiang Kai-shek and the Chinese communists. Chiang had kept the upper hand but he had never been able to crush the rebels completely. During the war with Japan the communists, well established in North China, kept up a small scale struggle with Chiang at the same time that they fought against the Japanese invaders. When World War II ended, China was on the winning side, but victory did not bring strength. On the contrary, the Nationalist government was so badly weakened by war and internal dissension that it was unable to restore order. Communists took advantage of this weakness to start their campaign for the conquest of all China.

Unfortunately for Chiang, decisions made at the Yalta Conference had the effect of strengthening the position of his enemies. At this time—

Yalta and China

February 1945—it appeared that many months of war would be required to defeat Japan. No one knew how close to collapse the Japanese already were or how decisive the atomic bomb would be. For this reason Roosevelt and Churchill were in a mood to make wide concessions to bring Russia into the Far Eastern war. They promised that after victory the Soviet Union would receive the Kurile Islands, the southern half of Sakhalin, a lease of Port Arthur, control of Dairen, and a voice in managing the two principal railroad lines of Manchuria. The terms of this agreement were temporarily concealed from Chiang Kai-shek.

Since 1945 there has been bitter controversy over this episode at Yalta. Roosevelt's supporters emphasize the military considerations that motivated him and contend that nothing was given to Stalin that the latter could not have taken for himself in any case. On the other hand, critics argue that it was a mistake to encourage the Russians to enter the war against Japan and a betrayal of friends to grant Stalin rights that belonged more properly to China. Regardless of the merits of the case, the Russians promptly took control of the areas allotted to them at Yalta.

With Japan beaten, and with the Russians firmly established throughout Manchuria, the Chinese communists stepped up the tempo of their war against Chiang Kai-shek. The United States provided Chiang's government with some three billion dollars' worth of arms and equipment between 1945 and 1949, but the effort was a futile one. Many influential Nationalists were so corrupt and inefficient that most of these American arms were easily captured by the communists.

Failure of U.S. Policy

Both inside and outside the government the formulation of a sound American policy was made more difficult by widespread misunderstanding of the nature of Chinese communism. The followers of Mao Tse-tung were depicted as really not communists at all but as determined agrarian reformers. They were contrasted favorably with the corrupt hangers-on who surrounded and dominated Chiang Kai-shek.

In an attempt to restore peace President Truman sent General George C. Marshall as special envoy to China late in 1945. American policy was to replace the one-party Chiang dictatorship with a fusion government that would include not only the Nationalists and the communists but also more democratic political elements from the center. For several months Marshall tried to mediate among the various Chinese groups, but he eventually had to give up the effort and return home in December 1946.

The Chinese civil war raged on until 1949 when the communists gained control of the whole mainland of China and Chiang Kai-shek's Nationalist government had to retire to the island of Formosa. What was the United States to do now? Should it increase its support to the Nationalists, even to the extent of sending American forces to help defend Formosa and launch a counter-offensive against the mainland? Or should the United States follow the example of Great Britain in recognizing the victorious Chinese communist government? President Truman and Secretary of State Acheson decided upon a middle course between these two alternatives. Concluding that further aid to Chiang was hopeless, they cut him off for the time being. At the same time, however, they refused to recognize the Chinese communist government and blocked its admission into the United Nations. The extent to which China had fallen under Soviet influence was revealed in 1950 when Russia signed an alliance with communist China and agreed to restore to the new satellite Port Arthur, Dairen, and various other rights acquired from Japan.

Obviously these developments were highly distasteful to Americans. For well over a century the policy of the United States in the Far East had emphasized political independence, territorial integrity, and free trade for China. From 1931 to 1941 American opposition to Japan's actions in Manchuria and China was based on the simple ground that Japan had violated these principles. In the period immediately following World War II, the Soviet Union proved itself far more successful than Japan had ever been in taking over China, and the United States found itself frozen out of this part of the mainland of Asia. Republicans blamed this defeat on the ineptness of Roosevelt, Truman, and Acheson. The Democrats argued that, given the failure of the Chinese Nationalist government to hold the loyalty of its own people, there was no way that the communist victory could have been prevented except through an all-out war in which large American forces would have been involved.

War in Korea

Background

The small country of Korea, liberated in 1945 after thirty-five years of Japanese rule, became a crucial battleground between the communist and non-communist worlds. After the liberation Korea north of the 38th parallel was occupied by Russian forces, and south of that line by Americans. Although both the occupation and the division of the country were supposed to be temporary, Russian obstructionism blocked United Nations efforts to establish a unified government for the entire country. The result was that in Korea, as in Germany, two governments were established. North of the 38th parallel was the communist "People's Democratic Republic of Korea"; south of the parallel was the "Republic of Korea," established under United Nations auspices. By the summer of 1949 the Soviet Union and the United States had both withdrawn their occupation troops, but each continued to aid the particular Korean government which it favored.

This uneasy balance of power was broken on June 24, 1950, when heavy communist forces from North Korea crossed the 38th parallel and converged on Seoul, the South Korean capital. The South Koreans were poorly prepared to defend themselves: they had an army, but no equipment—no tanks, no airplanes, no artillery. Their communist attackers, on the other hand, had a large and well-trained army and possessed abundant equipment for modern war, including a supply of Russian tanks. As the moral backer of South Korean independence, the United States was under obligation to protect the republic from conquest, but the United State had no armed forces in Korea; the nearest ones were in Japan. To bring reinforcements from the continental United States across the Pacific would require approximately a month.

United Nations Policy

In spite of the odds, Secretary Acheson and President Truman decided to oppose the communists. At two o'clock on the morning of June 25, they agreed to call on the Security Council of the United Nations for immediate action in Korea. That very afternoon the Council met and demanded the withdrawal of the North Korean forces. Two days later President Truman announced that the United States would give air and naval support to South Korea. At the same time he made an important change in American policy toward Formosa. Since communist seizure of the island would endanger American forces engaged in Korea, the United States Seventh Fleet was ordered to neutralize the area and prevent both communist attack on the island and Nationalist operations against the mainland. On this same June 27 the Security Council called upon members of the United Nations to give military assistance in repelling the North Korean aggressors. On June 3[illegible] General MacArthur recommended the use of United States ground forces in Korea, and Truman approved. These details show that the United States took the initiative in deciding on the use of force and that the United Nations endorsed these decisions. Shortly afterward General MacArthur was named commander-in-chief of the United Nations forces in Korea.

The early Security Council resolutions condemning the communist invasion were made possible only by the fact that the Soviet Union was boycotting the Council in protest against its refusal to seat communist China and could not, therefore, exercise a veto. In August Russia abruptly reversed this policy. Returning to the Council, Jacob Malik, the Soviet representative, used every available means to block the transaction of business and to attack the United States for what he called a "gross and overt aggression" against the Korean people. Warren A. Austin, the American representative, denounced, in turn, Malik's "total and unabashed perversion of the facts."

Military Operations

While this battle of words continued at United Nations headquarters, a grim war of bombs and bullets was being fought in Korea. At first the North Koreans enjoyed all the advantages of superior power. American troops, who made up most of the United Nations army, were outnumbered, often as much as four to one in a given area. Furthermore these Americans were young and entirely without battle experience. They had been trained for occupation duties in Japan, not for actual war. Inevitably they were compelled to fall steadily back, trading space for time, and sometimes lives for time. The Americans were dependent on one port, Pusan, in the southeast. The strategy of the invaders was to drive the Americans back upon Pusan, in hope of forcing their surrender or driving them out of the country in a small scale Dunkirk. The Americans had unquestioned air superiority, which proved helpful when weather permitted its use, but air power alone could not stop the communist advance.

So the first three months of the war consisted of nothing but setback and retreat for the United Nations forces. Then, on September 15, General MacArthur began a daring offensive, with a surprise landing at Inchon, a full hundred miles behind the North Korean lines. In three weeks time the the allied forces advanced to the 38th parallel. On October 7, by a vote of 47 to 5, with eight countries abstaining, the United Nations Assembly authorized MacArthur to carry the war into North Korean territory and thus prepare the way for unifying the country. By November 21 United Nations patrols had advanced almost to the Manchurian border. On November 24, General MacArthur launched the final offensive, which he hoped would end the war.

China Enters the War

So far as the North Koreans were concerned, they were completely beaten. But on November 25 an army of Chinese communists, fully equipped, crossed the Manchurian border and began an entirely new war. For weeks there had been reports of heavy Chinese concentrations along the frontier. Moreover, when the question of authorizing MacArthur to cross the 38th parallel had been under debate in the General Assembly, the delegate from India had bluntly warned that this step would cause communist China to enter the war. Unfortunately neither General MacArthur in the field nor his superiors in Washington had taken these warnings seriously.

Caught completely off balance, with their advance units far beyond their bases of supply, the United Nations troops were flung into a bitter retreat.

In five weeks they were back at the 38th parallel and before the end of January 1951 their lines were a full seventy miles below the border. The retreat during early December was described in the press as "one of the worst military defeats in United States history." But this time the United Nations forces were stronger and better equipped than in the early weeks of the war. Before the end of the winter of 1950–51 they had recaptured Seoul, and by early April they were once more across the 38th parallel. Between spring and early summer the opposing forces seesawed back and forth with no decisive gains by either side. In this fighting the Chinese used Russian artillery, tanks, and jet fighter planes. By the end of the summer of 1951 the United Nations forces had established a defense line across the narrow waist of the peninsula, most of it north of the 38th parallel. Thereafter, except for air fighting, military activity consisted largely of patrols, while the main attention was given to long drawn out negotiations for an armistice.

Apart from the fighting, the most dramatic event of the war was President Truman's dismissal of General MacArthur. On April 11, 1951, Truman relieved the general of his authority in the Far East and named General Matthew B. Ridgway as his successor. Because of a power failure, Truman's order to the general did not reach him until after he heard the news unofficially in a radio news report. The dismissal was sudden and abrupt, so abrupt that MacArthur could not even make a farewell address to his men. The method of the recall was unprecedented.

MacArthur Dismissed

MacArthur's dismissal was the climax of several months of friction between the Truman administration and the strong-minded general. Truman and Acheson wanted to limit the Asiatic war to Korea, avoiding any widening of the conflict that might involve the United States in fighting for years in the vast terrain of China. Any such larger war, they believed, would be likely to bring in the Soviet Union, thus precipitating World War III. General MacArthur, on the other hand, wanted a free hand to bomb enemy bases across the Manchurian frontier. He also disapproved Truman's policy of neutralizing Formosa and advocated active support to Chiang to encourage the opening of a new front on the China mainland.

If these disagreements had been confined to official communications, they might not have been too serious. But MacArthur repeatedly made public his criticism of the Truman policies. These defiant statements, made in violation of explicit orders, angered the President, because they violated the American principle that the military is subordinate to the civilian branch of the government. They also embarrassed our relations with the English and the French, who feared that the aggressive commander would push them into a general war. The final straw was a letter from MacArthur to Representative Joseph W. Martin, the Republican minority leader, made public on April 5, 1951. In words strongly critical of both his own government's policy and that of England and France, the general argued that the communist conspirators had "elected to make their play for global conquest" in Asia and that Europe's salvation therefore lay in a decisive victory in the chosen battlefield.

The publication of MacArthur's letter to Martin was followed a week later by the general's recall. This disciplining of one of the great military heroes of American history was highly unpopular with large sections of the American public. San Francisco and other cities gave stirring ovations to the general upon his return. On April 19 MacArthur delivered an eloquent address before a joint session of Congress, repeating his criticisms of current policy and declaring that "in war there is no substitute for victory."

MacArthur's call for bold measures received many cheers, but Truman's more cautious views continued to dominate actual American policy. Even among Republicans MacArthur's appeal was more to the heart than to the head. After the inauguration of President Eisenhower in 1953 the new administration ignored the MacArthur program and followed a policy of limiting the Korean war and seeking a compromise settlement, essentially similar to that formulated by Truman and Acheson.

The Korean Armistice

By the summer of 1951 the Korean war had moved into a deadlock, where decisive victory for either side was impossible unless large new forces were committed to the conflict. Some kind of truce to stop the futile struggle was obviously needed, but many months of frustrating negotiations were required to accomplish this.

Truce Talks

As early as January 1951 the General Assembly of the United Nations had recommended an immediate cease-fire with safeguards to prevent either side from building up its forces during the ensuing peace negotiations. Russia, however, opposed this resolution and continued to block peace efforts until June when she abruptly changed her tactics. On June 23 Jacob Malik, the Soviet deputy foreign minister, in a speech over the UN radio, proposed that the belligerents in Korea agree to a cease-fire along the 38th parallel.

Malik's suggestion met a favorable response, and on July 10, 1951, truce negotiations were begun at Kaesong, a town lying near the battlefront in western Korea. Since the war was still in progress except in the area of Kaesong itself, there were acrimonious charges and counter-charges of violations of the neutral zone. So bitter did these become that the negotiations were completely suspended from August 23 to October 25, 1951. Eventually the talks were resumed at Panmunjom, six miles to the southeast of Kaesong in a district more easily neutralized.

The renewed negotiations proceeded at an exasperatingly slow pace. The communist leaders often seemed more interested in gaining a propaganda advantage than in making peace, and the United Nations representatives had to defend themselves against sharp verbal attacks. But real issues were also at stake. One of these was to determine just where the truce line should be drawn. The communists wanted to restore the 38th parallel boundary, but the United Nations commanders insisted on the line that they were actually holding somewhat farther to the north and more easily defended. Eventually the communists conceded this point and agreed that the truce line should follow the battleline whenever hostilities ceased.

Even more difficult was the problem of exchanging prisoners of war. The United Nations held some 125,000 prisoners; the communists about 13,000. The communists insisted that all prisoners held by both sides should be repatriated; the United Nations, fearful of reprisals against non-communists, refused to return Koreans and Chinese who did not want to go home. Talks broke down on the prisoner issue in October 1952 and were not resumed until the communists finally accepted a face-saving compromise on March 30, 1953. Negotiations at Panmunjom were reopened in April, and after three months of further bargaining a truce was finally signed on July 27, 1953.

Truce Agreement

The agreement provided for an immediate cessation of hostilities and for the withdrawal of armed forces from a demilitarized zone 2½ miles wide along the truce line. Each side promised not to take advantage of the armistice to build up its armed forces within Korea. To police these provisions it was agreed that there should be a Neutral Nations Supervisory Commission with power to make inspections on both sides of the line. Democratic Sweden and Switzerland and communist Poland and Czechoslovakia were the four neutral nations represented on this Commission. All prisoners who wished to be repatriated were to be exchanged within the next few weeks; those disinclined to go home were to be turned over to the custody of a Neutral Nations Repatriation Committee, which would give representatives from the two sides an opportunity to try to persuade them to change their minds. But the prisoners were not to be coerced, and those refusing repatriation were eventually to be set free and helped to find sanctuary.

During the final negotiations of the truce the United Nations representatives had almost as much trouble with Syngman Rhee, the South Korean President, as with the communists. Rhee, who had devoted his life to the cause of Korean independence, was bitterly opposed to an armistice that would leave the northern half of the country under communist control. In June 1953 he imperiled the truce negotiations by ordering South Korean guards to open the stockades and release some 27,000 North Korean prisoners-of-war, whose future was still under discussion at Panmunjom. Later he threatened that South Korea might carry on the war alone if the truce were signed. The United States had to warn Rhee that he could expect no help if he violated the armistice; on the other hand, South Korean fears were partially assuaged by a mutual defense treaty with the United States, signed October 1, 1953.

After the completion of the "Big Switch" under which the prisoners consenting to voluntary repatriation were exchanged, those who had refused to go home were turned over to the Neutral Nations Repatriation Commission, as stipulated in the armistice. The non-communist world took satisfaction in the fact that the number who refused to return to communist China and

North Korea was much larger than that from the other side who declined to go home. About 22,500 Chinese and North Koreans declined repatriation; of these only 333 changed their minds during the explanation period. On the other side, 359 of the United Nations troops refused repatriation, and 8 of these decided to return as a result of the interviews. Only 22 American soldiers refused to go home; most of these probably feared prosecution and punishment for collaborating with the enemy while they were prisoners-of-war. In view of the evidence that the communists had made strong efforts to brainwash and indoctrinate the prisoners in their hands, this was a good record. Even among the Americans who elected to stay with the communists, several later regretted their decisions and returned home, reconciled to accepting whatever their punishment might be.

The Korean armistice merely stopped the fighting; the division of the country and the international rivalries which had caused the war in the first place still continued. At the Geneva Conference on Far Eastern Affairs in the spring of 1954 the agenda included the Korean problem. The anti-communists presented a plan for Korean unification based upon free elections under UN supervision; the communists rejected UN supervision and insisted upon the withdrawal of all foreign troops as a precondition to elections. Stalemated on this basic issue, the discussions inevitably ended in failure.

The truce was observed so far as open hostilities were concerned, but a bloodless contest to control the Korean destiny continued. The Czech and Polish members of the Neutral Nations Supervisory Commission were accused of using their positions to spy on defense activities in South Korea, while they were blocking any effective steps to prevent a build-up of the communist air force in North Korea. In June 1956 the Supervisory Commission was ordered to leave South Korea by the UN commander. Such incidents made it obvious that the Korea problem had not really been solved and that serious trouble might once again break out in that unhappy little country.

Why the War?

In view of the indecisive results of the Korean war, had the sacrifice been worth-while? South Korea itself had suffered over a million casualties, while fifteen other United Nations countries lost over 150,000 more. The contribution of the United States was particularly heavy, since 33,417 American servicemen lost their lives and more than 103,000 were wounded. The communist North Koreans and Chinese suffered much greater casualties, and Korea, both north and south, was devastated and impoverished.

Yet supporters of the United Nations policy offered two powerful arguments in justification of their course. First, if the free world had not struck in behalf of South Korea, the communists would have had no obstacle whatever in the way of their complete conquest of the whole Far East, including even Japan. They had to be checked somewhere. Because they chose to attack in Korea, Korea became the logical place to stop them. Second, the United Nations effort in Korea was a campaign in behalf of morality against international brigandage. Without this moral effort the Western world could have made no plea anywhere for help against aggression. In spite of the losses suffered by the United Nations in the field, the moral gain was worth the cost. The validity of these arguments depended upon future developments. If communist imperialism in the Far East should prove to have been permanently checked, the cost of the Korean war would be a small price for such vast gains.

By 1953 the One World dream of Wendell Willkie and Franklin Roosevelt had been shattered by hard post-World War II realities. Two rival worlds had emerged instead. The issue had now become whether the noncommunist world could preserve its freedom and civilization against the intrigue and aggressiveness of the communist world. Both in Europe and the Far East the free world seemed to have gained a measure of security, but the balance of power was still perilously uncertain.

Chapter 49

THE TRUMAN YEARS

During the eight years of the Truman administration domestic affairs tended to be overshadowed by foreign problems. Yet issues of great importance were before the country. The New Deal program had been interrupted by the outbreak of World War II. What would happen after the war? Would the voters demand new reforms and welfare activities, involving the government in a still greater role in economic affairs? Or would there be a reaction against such policies and a trend toward increased individualism? Neither point of view gained effective control of the government during the immediate postwar years.

Truman and His Advisers

When Roosevelt's sudden death made Harry S. Truman President of the United States on April 12, 1945, the nation was barely acquainted with its new leader. Truman had been a typical American Vice President in that his party had chosen him for second place on the ticket not so much because he was clearly of Presidential calibre as because his nomination would please certain elements within the party. The professional politicians had favored Truman because of his years of faithful service to Boss Tom Pendergast's Kansas City machine; organized labor had supported him because of his record of consistent support for the New Deal. Although Truman's early career had been that of a plodding politician rather than that of a potential leader, he had gained stature during ten years in the Senate. During the war he had done particularly good work as chairman of a special committee to investigate the national defense program.

As President, Truman demonstrated both strong and weak points of character. In dealing with a succession of international crises more serious than most other Presidents have had to meet, Truman showed an ability to make prompt decisions and to act boldly, a strong sympathy with oppressed peoples both at home and abroad, and a sturdy determination to fight for what he thought was right. On the other hand, Truman resented criticism and was often guilty of petty displays of temper and imprudent statements. Although he was personally honest, he was not always able to impose strict standards of probity upon his subordinates.

Changing Personnel

Like other Vice Presidents who have succeeded to the Presidency, Truman began by asking his predecessor's cabinet members to continue in their offices. Within a few months, however, significant changes occurred. Figures prominent in Washington circles since early New Deal days retired, and a new group of men, closer to Truman personally, became the key figures in the administration. Because of the critical international situation the President made several changes in the State Department. James F. Byrnes, a former Senator from South Carolina and Justice of the Supreme Court, served as Secretary of State from 1945 to 1947. He was followed by General George C. Marshall, who held the office until 1949, when he was succeeded by Dean Acheson. Acheson was one of the most controversial members of the administration. Although he did outstanding work in founding the North Atlantic Treaty Organization and in taking other measures to combat Soviet imperialism, the Republicans accused him of being "soft" on communism and not acting vigorously enough to prevent Red aggression in China and Korea. Other advisers upon whom Truman leaned heavily were John F. Snyder, a St. Louis banker, who became Secretary of the Treasury in 1946, and Fred M. Vinson of Kentucky, who served in various important posts during the first year of the Truman administration and then became Chief Justice of the Supreme Court in 1946.

Two of the most influential men among the old New Deal group quarreled publicly with the President. The first to go was Harold Ickes, the Secretary of the Interior, who resigned in protest against what he regarded as the undue influence in the administration of Edwin M. Pauley, a wealthy California oil operator. The second to leave was Henry A. Wallace, the former Vice President whom Roosevelt had appointed Secretary of Commerce shortly before his death. Wallace was asked to resign in 1946 after he had made a public speech implicitly criticizing Secretary of State Byrnes for "getting tough" with Russia. Wallace became the hero of a dwindling number of Americans who believed that friendly cooperation with the Soviet Union was still possible. Even he, however, became disillusioned with this policy after the Korean war began.

The Fair Deal

Although Truman dropped the old pilots and took on new ones, he still attempted to sail the ship by the Rooseveltian compass. During his first year in the White House, the new President sent to Congress what came to be known as his "Fair Deal" program. This called for higher minimum wages, increased social security coverage to include health insurance, public housing, laws to prevent racial discrimination in employment, and assistance to farmers and small businessmen. With a few subsequent additions these continued to be the domestic goals of the Truman administration during the next eight years.

In contrast with Roosevelt's New Deal, only a small part of Truman's Fair Deal was ever enacted into law. There were several reasons for this. One was the political alignment in Congress. Although the Democrats theoretically controlled Congress for six of the eight years between 1945 and 1953, conservative sentiment was strong in both parties, and social legislation was often blocked by an alliance of Republicans and southern Democrats. Nor was there any strong demand for the Fair Deal from the general public. Economic conditions were generally good, and fear of communism had supplanted fear of want as the prevailing mood. Moreover, many of the specific reform proposals aroused a determined and effective opposition. The

South was opposed to any federal interference on the racial issue, while the American Medical Association waged an expensive and successful campaign to defeat Truman's proposal for national health insurance, which most doctors feared as a step toward socialized medicine.

Despite these obstacles a modest domestic program was achieved. Federal minimum wage standards were raised from 40 to 75 cents an hour; the social security system was enlarged to cover farm and domestic workers, self-employed persons, and college professors; and federal funds for public and private housing were provided. In getting Congressional support for his foreign policy, moreover, Truman was usually successful. The large appropriations needed for the Marshall Plan and military assistance programs were readily provided, as were the heavy expenditures required for rearmament and for the prosecution of the Korean war.

Governmental Reorganization

Conservatives and liberals both agreed on the need for increasing the efficiency of government operations. In 1947 Congress unanimously passed a law providing for a Commission on Organization of the Executive Branch of the Government to be composed of six Republicans and six Democrats with former President Hoover serving as chairman. The Hoover Commission employed 300 experts to study the actual functioning of the government and to propose reforms that would promote efficiency and economy of operation. In 1949 Congress passed a Reorganization Act authorizing the President to prepare specific proposals for carrying out the recommendations of the Hoover Commission. Such plans were to go into effect unless disapproved by Congress. Under this procedure President Truman was able to reform many of the antiquated procedures of the government. Still further reforms were made after Eisenhower became President.

Important changes affecting the Presidency were also enacted. At President Truman's recommendation a new Presidential Succession Act was passed in 1947, providing that in case the President and Vice President were both removed by death or other cause the Speaker of the House of Representatives would act as President. Next in succession would be the President pro tempore of the Senate and then the cabinet officers in order of rank. In 1951 the Twenty-second Amendment was added to the Federal Constitution. This provided that no person should be elected to the office of President more than twice, and that no person who had held the office of President for more than two years of a term to which some other person had been elected should be elected to the office of President more than once. The amendment had originated four years earlier in the Republican-controlled 80th Congress as a belated rebuke to Roosevelt's rejection of the two-term tradition. Its passage by the requisite three-quarters of the states had resulted from the support of Republican and southern Democratic legislators. Although Truman was specifically exempted from the provisions of the new amendment, its passage was undoubtedly intended to discourage any third-term aspirations on his part.

Industry and Labor

For industry the first major task after World War II was reconversion, changing factory procedures from production for war to production for peace. On the physical side this process called for new machine tools. On the human side it meant finding jobs for the millions of former servicemen, retraining old employees, and breaking in the new ones. While the process of reconversion was going on, the administration worried over the possibility of an economic depression. Experts at Washington remembered the slight setback of 1921 and the disastrous collapse of 1929, both of which, so economists said, were related to the end of World War I.

Some of the nation's leading economists believed that increased government planning was required to prevent future depressions and to maintain the full employment that had characterized the war economy. A so-called full employment bill, strongly urged by the New Deal Democrats, would have authorized a board of economists to draw up a national production and employment budget, showing how much government spending would be required each year to supplement private investment and guarantee full employment for all able-bodied workers. Conservatives opposed this, because they feared that it would lead to a regimented economy. Eventually in February 1946, Congress passed a watered-down Employment Act which provided for an annual "economic report" to be prepared by a board of three economists and stipulated in somewhat vague terms that government policy should be coordinated to maintain "maximum employment."

Seeking Stability

The government's newly assumed responsibility for maintaining employment proved to be unimportant in the immediate postwar situation. Instead of the feared depression, a period of unprecedented prosperity set in. Because of the war millions of American families had been unable to get the new refrigerators, cooking stoves, oil burners, plumbing supplies, and automobiles that they needed. Many months of full production were required to supply these accumulated demands. As for capital goods, in addition to machine tools for the factories, the American people needed new houses, literally by the million. Every state in the union was behind in its highway construction, with some of the thickly populated Eastern states badly off in this respect. Even as late as 1952 New York State was twenty years behind in modernizing its highways.

The cold war with Russia also stimulated the economy. The Truman and Marshall Plans and the military assistance program required large quantities of goods, while the demands of rearmament at home and the Korean war brought heavy orders for aircraft and other military equipment. For better or worse, the country was in a booming guns-and-butter economy, with factories straining to supply both military and civilian demands. High wages, high profits, and high prices were the almost inevitable results.

In this postwar industrial picture labor occupied a most conspicuous place. In comparison with workers abroad American employees were fortunate.

From the early years of American industry, management has invested heavily in mechanical power and in labor-saving machines, both of which make for high productivity for the individual worker. Processes of production have become steadily more efficient, to the advantage of both management and labor. The workers themselves were well trained, energetic, and—except when on strike—ready to work. As a result of these various factors, during roughly the first half of the twentieth century, real wages of industrial workers in this country had trebled. At the same time industries had adopted the forty-hour week as standard.

Labor and Inflation

During World War II most factories were so short of help that workers put in four to eight hours of overtime, in some cases more. This overtime had been paid for at the rate of time and a half, so weekly take-home wages were high. With the end of the war management decided that it could get along without hiring overtime help. The workers responded with a demand for forty-eight hours' pay for a forty-hour week; such a raise, they insisted, was necessary to maintain their standard of living. When employers argued that they could not pay this increase without raising prices on their products, the unions and the administration both contradicted them. The authorities at Washington contended that wages could go up without affecting prices.

Unions in the mass production industries determined to enforce their demands with strikes. The first of these, against General Motors, began in November 1945. In January 1946 the steel workers struck. Other unions followed, and 1946 proved to be the most active year for strikes in American history. Over four million workers took part in these drives for higher pay. Labor won this first round. But prices went up too, so the higher wages were partly offset by the rising cost of living.

The country was caught, in fact, in an inflationary spiral. Rising prices created a chronic demand for higher wages; higher wages, in turn, contributed to higher costs and still further price rises. The Truman administration tried to combat the situation by advocating a continuance of war-time price controls. But the nation was tired of these. The National Association of Manufacturers engaged in a huge advertising campaign to sell the message that the best way to combat inflation was to remove controls. Higher prices, the NAM argued, would stimulate production, and the law of supply and demand would then have a chance to operate. With consumers crying for goods, manufacturers demanding a free hand to fix their own prices, and organized labor asking for higher wages, price control was doomed. The Republican victory in the Congressional election of 1946 was interpreted as an indication that the nation wanted to return to a free economy, and in December 1946 President Truman announced the end of most controls except those on rents. With restraints removed the inflationary spiral climbed higher and faster. During the Korean war there was a partial return to price control, but the measures taken were not very successful.

Under these conditions labor was not long satisfied with its gains of 1946.

Particularly in the mass production industries, mining, and transportation labor leaders followed a policy of forcing periodic pay increases, plus social benefits such as pensions and insurance. Although some of these gains were made without work stoppages, strikes continued to be frequent.

Labor and Public Opinion

Public opinion on the labor issue was influenced by the frequency of the strikes and what sometimes seemed to be arrogant behavior on the part of the union leaders. When the railroad engineers and trainmen struck in May 1946, all but the most necessary traffic was halted for two days. The strike was finally abandoned when President Truman threatened to draft the workers into the army to get the trains running again.

The public was even further antagonized by the tactics of John L. Lewis, the head of the United Mine Workers, who was at the height of his power in the immediate postwar years. Lewis was reputed to have compared himself with other labor leaders in these colorful words: "When I see any of them, I feel like a mastiff dog stalking down the street while a puny Pekingese pup skulks well behind, eating of my leavings." Even during World War II Lewis gained a reputation for calling out his men whenever he saw fit, regardless of consequences to the country at large. He carried this lordly attitude even farther during the postwar years. In 1947 his defiance of a federal court injunction brought down upon him and his union a fine of $710,000; in 1949 they had to pay an additional $1,420,000. Lewis's aggressiveness was unpopular with the general public, but it won many advantages for his men, including not only one of the highest wage scales in the country but annual pensions for retired miners, health and welfare benefits, and better safety conditions.

The almost five thousand strikes of 1946 created a strong demand for a change in the laws. Employers blamed many of their difficulties on what they regarded as the pro-labor bias of the Roosevelt and Truman administrations. They complained particularly of the Wagner Act of 1935, which they considered to be unfair in that it prohibited employers from interfering in any way with the right of their employees to organize and to bargain collectively but did not forbid union activity that might injure the employer. As interpreted by the courts, the Wagner Act made it impossible for an employer to talk to his employees on the subject of labor relations. The National Association of Manufacturers took the lead in demanding a new federal labor-relations law that would be less one-sided.

Taft-Hartley Act

President Truman sympathized in some degree with this demand for legislation. He made recommendations for changes in the law that would encourage the delay of strikes through "cooling-off periods" and the appointment of fact-finding commissions. But Congress felt the need for stronger measures. When the Republicans gained control of both houses in the election of 1946, they interpreted their victory as a mandate from the voters to frame a new labor law. After five months of deliberation, Congress passed the Taft-Hartley Labor-Management Relations Act in June 1947. Although the measure went through both houses with heavy majorities, Truman vetoed the bill on the grounds that it contained "seeds of discord" which would plague the nation for years to come. Congress ignored this protest and passed the bill over the veto. Most of the Republicans and most of the southern Democrats supported it.

The Taft-Hartley Act amended the Wagner Act and restored to employers certain rights which had been taken away in the earlier law. It outlawed the closed shop but permitted a union shop, if a majority of employees in a given plant voted for one. It permitted the limited use of injunctions, to halt strikes which might threaten public health or safety. Under its provisions, employers were allowed to sue unions for violation of contract or for participating in strikes which were merely jurisdictional; they might talk directly to their own employees about labor matters. Employees who took part in an unauthorized strike might be dismissed. To gain benefits under the law, union officials were required to take an oath that they were not communists.

Union leaders were bitterly opposed to the new law. Although divided on other issues, such men as William Green of the A.F. of L., Philip Murray of the C.I.O., and John L. Lewis of the Mine Workers made common cause in condemning what Green called "slave labor legislation." Having failed to prevent the passage of the law, the leaders carried on a long campaign to try to secure its repeal. Their opportunity seemed to have arrived after the election of 1948 when the Democrats, pledged to repeal in their national platform, regained control of Congress. Even Senator Taft, one of the fathers of the controversial law, now favored some modification of it. But Congress was too much divided on the issue to decide just what changes should be made and the result was that nothing at all was done. In 1951, however, the act was amended to permit negotiation of union-shop agreements without special vote of the workers.

Actually the Taft-Hartley Act weakened the unions much less than their leaders had feared or employers may have hoped that it would. The federal law was less damaging to the organized labor movement than some of the thirty state laws pushed through at about the same time. Many of these prohibited the union shop: their supporters called them "right to work" laws; labor leaders complained that they were really "right to scab" laws, designed to permit the discriminations against union workers that the Wagner Act had forbidden.

Communist Problem

The anti-communist oath required by the Tart-Hartley Act was the result of two factors: a growing awareness of the danger of communism and fear of communist influence in some of the unions, particularly within the C.I.O. Although the central organization of the C.I.O. had never been sympathetic to communism, some of the member unions had been infiltrated, especially during the early days of the movement when help from any quarter had been welcome in organizing the mass production industries. But the communists could not be kept within the limits of legitimate labor activity; their ultimate program called for revolution, and they were prepared to use the labor movement in their plot to overthrow the government. For this reason they became not only a nuisance but a positive danger. By 1949 C.I.O. president Philip Murray felt strong enough to act. One after another communist-controlled unions were expelled from the organization, and rival unions under moderate leadership were chartered.

Despite the frequency of strikes, there was evidence that labor-management relations were entering a new and milder phase. Both on the side of the employers and of the unions there were fewer resorts to violence than there had been during the 1920's and 1930's. A hopeful landmark was achieved in the new form of contract agreed to by General Motors and the United Automobile Workers in 1950 after a period of collective bargaining, in good faith and without a strike. The contract included the standardized provisions for pensions and welfare insurance, with a provision for an annual wage increase. It continued the so-called "escalator clause," widely adopted in 1948, linking wages to the cost of living. Then came the most significant feature of the new contract. It was to run for five years, with no provision whatever for reopening by either side. This was the longest contract in recent industrial history, and it looked like a triumph for both sides. Instead of the customary prospect of an annual strike, here was a mutual pledge of industrial peace for five years. Later in 1950 the Ford workers signed a similar contract.

New Kind of Contract

Critics of President Truman charged that in his desire to avoid recourse to the procedures of the disliked Taft-Hartley Act, he sometimes resorted to action of doubtful legality. In 1952, while the Korean war was in progress, the President attempted to prevent a threatened steel strike by ordering government seizure of the steel mills. He based his action, not on any specific statute, but upon what he claimed was the inherent power of the Chief Executive under the Constitution to take necessary action in a national emergency.

Steel Strike of 1952

The Presidential seizure raised a constitutional issue of grave importance. The steel companies appealed to the federal courts, and the issue was finally decided by the Supreme Court in June 1952. By a 6 to 3 decision the Court ruled that Truman's seizure of private property without authorization by Congress was illegal and a violation of the Constitution.

As soon as the steel mills were turned back to private control, the feared strike occurred. The workers were out over seven weeks and defense production was seriously curtailed before the issues were finally compromised by the two sides. As usual, the cost of the new contract was passed on to the consumers in the form of higher prices.

Communists in the United States

Among the numerous postwar problems of the Truman administration, one of the most troublesome was the Communist party. After World War I, when communism was still new, American members and their sympathizers had aroused considerable fear, but at that time they were hardly more than a minor nuisance. In 1945 and after, the situation was entirely different. By that time the Soviet Union had become the strongest power in Europe and Asia. Because of the apparently friendly attitude of Russia during the war, many Americans found it hard to believe that communists might be dangerous. A little reading of communist literature was enough to prove the contrary. The Communist party proclaimed that its objective was to establish communism throughout the world and urged the use of revolution, terrorism, and sabotage as means to achieve this end. Although the number of party members in the United States was never large, even a few communists, strategically located in critical government agencies or in defense industries, might endanger national security. In 1947 President Truman attempted to meet the problem by ordering a loyalty check of all government employees and the dismissal of any found to have subversive affiliations.

Smith Act Prosecutions

The administration also took steps to weaken the Communist party. In 1948 the twelve top party leaders in the United States were indicted on charges that their activities had violated the Smith Act of 1940, which made it unlawful to "advocate, abet, advise, or teach the duty, necessity, desirability, or propriety of overthrowing or destroying any government in the United States by force or violence." William Z. Foster, the head of the party, was not tried because of a bad heart, but the trial of the other eleven began in January 1949 and continued for nine weary months. After resorting to exasperating obstructionism, the defense based its principal case on the contention that the party was peaceful in its aims and did not advocate the use of violence. This the jury refused to believe, and all the defendants were found guilty and sentenced to fines and prison terms. When the case eventually came before the Supreme Court, the convictions were affirmed in an important decision, upholding the constitutionality of the Smith Act. The law did not violate the First Amendment, in the opinion of Chief Justice Vinson, who said: "Overthrow of the Government by force and violence is certainly a substantial enough interest for the Government to limit speech." In dissenting opinions Justices Black and Douglas argued that the Smith Act did violate the First Amendment. The government's success in this case led to the arrest and conviction of a number of other Communist party leaders.

Congressional Inquiries

Despite this activity on the part of the administration many Congressmen and Senators were not satisfied that communism was being attacked with sufficient energy. The House Committee on Un-American Activities and various Senate committees conducted extensive investigations into alleged communist infiltration, not only into the government, but into labor unions, the amusement world, schools, colleges, and even churches. Public opinion was sharply divided on the value of these congressional investigations. Many Americans, thoroughly alarmed by the communist menace, regarded Red-hunting legislators like Martin Dies of Texas, J. Parnell Thomas of New

Jersey, and Senator Joseph McCarthy of Wisconsin as patriots engaged in a great work. Others accused these men of being publicity-seeking politicians, attempting to capitalize on the fear of communism to advance their own fortunes. The investigating committees were criticized for damaging men's reputations with unfounded charges, not permitting accused persons to cross-examine the witnesses against them, and jeopardizing constitutional liberty by interrogating witnesses on their political and social beliefs. At their best, the investigations exposed dangers to national security that were difficult to deal with through regular law-enforcement channels; at their worst, they injured innocent individuals and planted hysterical fears in the minds of the general public.

Perjury Trials

The House Committee on Un-American Activities initiated the chain of events that eventually led to a prison term for Alger Hiss, a former State Department official who had been present in a minor capacity at the Yalta Conference and had played a somewhat more important role in the San Francisco Conference. When Hiss denied before a grand jury certain charges that had been made against him, he was indicted for perjury. At his first trial the jury disagreed, but after a second trial Hiss was found guilty in January 1950 and sentenced to five years imprisonment. The principal witness against him had been Whittaker Chambers, an editor of *Time* magazine and a former member of the Communist party, who accused Hiss of having been a fellow-member and of having copied secret State Department documents for transmission to the Soviet Union. The conviction of so prominent a figure, who had enjoyed the confidence of Secretaries of State and Justices of the Supreme Court, was highly upsetting to national confidence.

Somewhat similar to the Hiss case was the case of William Remington, a former Commerce Department official, who was indicted for perjury after denying that he had been a communist engaged in espionage. Remington's first conviction was set aside upon appeal, but he was found guilty a second time in 1953 and sentenced to prison, where he died following an assault by fellow-prisoners. Judith Coplon, a Justice Department clerk, was found guilty of passing secret documents to a Soviet agent, but the verdict was set aside because of irregularities in her trial.

Rosenberg Case

Far more serious than the Hiss, Remington, and Coplon cases was the case of Julius and Ethel Rosenberg. The Rosenbergs, husband and wife, were accused of being part of a communist spy ring that had managed to obtain vital information about the atomic bomb, while it was still in its developmental stage during World War II. The transmission of these secrets to Russia was supposed to have helped that country to develop its own bomb much sooner than it could otherwise have done so. Convicted of espionage in 1951, the two Rosenbergs were sentenced to death, while two of their accomplices, Morton Sobell and David Greenglass, were given long prison terms. As might have been expected, the communists organized mass demonstrations both within the United States and in foreign capitals to protest against what they described as a gross miscarriage of justice. The plight of the Rosenbergs also gained some sympathy from non-communists, who did not deny that the defendants had had a fair trial but who thought that the death penalty was too harsh. Pope Pius XII himself forwarded an appeal for clemency to President Eisenhower. But the President refused to interfere, saying that the Rosenbergs might "have condemned to death tens of millions of innocent people" by increasing the chances of atomic war. The two were executed in Sing Sing Prison on June 19, 1953.

Senator McCarthy

The politician who provoked the greatest controversy over the communist issue was Senator Joseph McCarthy of Wisconsin. In 1950 McCarthy startled the country with the charge that there were "at least fifty-seven" communists in the State Department. In later speeches he repeated the accusation with bewildering variations in the numbers. Challenged to prove his charges before a special Senate committee under the chairmanship of Senator Millard E. Tydings of Maryland, McCarthy was unable to name a single Communist party member in the State Department, but he did make serious accusations against Professor Owen J. Lattimore, who had never been a member of the department but had served as an occasional consultant on Far Eastern affairs. Lattimore, McCarthy asserted, was Russia's "top espionage agent in America." Hurrying home from a United Nations mission in Afghanistan, the professor made a complete denial of these charges. In their report, Senator Tydings and the Democratic majority of the committee were severely critical of McCarthy, describing his charges as "the most nefarious campaign of half-truths and untruths in the history of this Republic." The Republican minority on the committee conceded that the Wisconsin Senator had failed to prove his case but criticized the investigation of the State Department as superficial.

The Lattimore case was far from ended. McCarthy had his revenge by helping the Maryland Republicans to defeat Tydings for re-election in November 1950. Tydings was hurt by charges that he had been guilty of whitewashing the Truman State Department. The local Republican organization even resorted to a faked photograph purporting to show the Senator, who was actually a conservative Southern Democrat, in chummy conversation with Earl Browder, a well-known communist. In 1952 Lattimore was hauled before another Senate committee for interrogation. On the basis of alleged discrepancies in his testimony he was indicted for perjury. He was never brought to trial, however; Federal Judge Luther Youngdahl dismissed several counts of the indictment, and the government's case was so weak on the remaining charges that Attorney General Herbert Brownell decided to drop the prosecution.

The communist issue was a bitterly controversial one. President Truman accused the Republicans of using charges of communist infiltration into the government as a "red herring" to divert attention from the real issues before the country. Many liberals agreed with him and denounced all such harping on the communist issue as "witch hunting." This point of view, however, was severely shaken by the Hiss case and similar exposures. In the enc alarm over the communist issue reacted against the Democrats and helpe the Republicans to win their victory of 1952. But if the administration Demc crats were guilty of minimizing the communist problem, the Republican sinned in the opposite direction by exaggerating the menace and chargin that the Democrats had allowed communist cells to honeycomb th government.

Preoccupation with the issue of domestic communism also characterize many of the state governments. State loyalty oaths, legislative investigatin committees, and sedition trials were the order of the day.

Changing Social Patterns

Problems of Minorities

Communist party activity among minority groups drew sharp attentio to an old problem. For a good many years these groups had been the victim of discrimination on account of race, color, or religion. Individuals in thes groups had been tempted by plausible communist promises of equality anc power. The most effective way of ending their affiliation was to end the dis crimination. Fair treatment of minority groups would also give the lie t anti-American propaganda among the yellow and black peoples of Asia anc Africa. Quite apart from the communist problem, many Americans wantec to end discrimination because they believed it contrary to democratic ideals To this end, President Truman asked for new laws against lynching anc against poll taxes. Northern Democrats, particularly in the cities, urgentl supported his program. Southern Democrats, on the other hand, opposed it Acting in concert with Republicans, they prevented Congress from takin any action whatever.

The Supreme Court, however, indicated that it could act in this field i Congress could not. In June 1950 the Court handed down three unanimou decisions. One ordered the University of Texas to admit a Negro student t the state university law school, on the ground that he could not get treat ment equal to that of white students in the state's special law school fo Negroes. The second ordered the University of Oklahoma to permit a Negr student in the graduate school of education to associate with the whit students. The third ordered the Southern Railroad to end its discriminatio against Negroes in its dining cars.

Although some progress was made in integrating graduate and profes sional schools in the South following these decisions, southern white opinio was still bitterly opposed to any general leveling of racial barriers. B improving Negro elementary and secondary schools the southerners hopec to preserve "the separate but equal" doctrine which the Supreme Court hac hitherto accepted.

In states where there had been no tradition of racial segregation, such a New York, the problem of removing the worst features of discriminatio seemed easier. In that state a law against discrimination in employment o account of race, color, or religion went into effect in 1945. And in spite of filibusters in the United States Senate and angry resolutions in southern legislatures and conventions, the years after the war saw remarkable changes in race relations. For one thing the issue became national, with widespread interest in fair treatment of minority groups. The Supreme Court outlawed white primaries and some poll tax laws, so that large numbers of Negroes at last received the right to vote. Court decisions banned some, though not all, restrictions on housing and in labor union membership. Opportunities for employment in government at all levels—local, state, and national—were increased. Public opinion became far more generous than it had been in recognizing achievements such as those of the great scientist, George Washington Carver, and of musicians like Roland Hayes and Marian Anderson. Furthermore public opinion has become widely intolerant of insulting epithets and labels suggestive of inferiority.

This improvement in attitudes toward minority groups might be regarded as evidence of a broadening democracy in the United States. Further evidence of this trend might be found in the rapidly growing student bodies in American colleges and universities. In earlier years higher education had been regarded as the privilege of the fortunate few. Then after World War I there had been a substantial increase in the numbers attending college. After World War II this increase in enrollment was even more impressive. For the year 1939–40 there were almost 1,500,000 students in institutions of higher learning. In 1949 the total was nearly 2,500,000. The Korean war resulted in a slight drop, but by 1954 total enrollment was again around the 2,500,000 level. Part of the increase was due to the higher income of industrial workers, part to the feeling that every young person capable of doing the work was entitled to some training beyond high school.

College Enrollment

For a time one major factor in this growth was the Servicemen's Readjustment Act, popularly known as the G.I. Bill of Rights. As originally passed in 1944, the law promised government aid in completing educational careers interrupted by induction into the armed forces. After the end of the war, the law was amended to provide educational opportunities for all veterans, regardless of age. A veteran might enter school or college at any time within four years of his discharge. The government undertook to pay tuition and moderate allowances for living costs. With their wide experience, greater maturity, and serious purpose these veterans were excellent students. Up to 1954 a total of 7,800,000 veterans of World War II had availed themselves of these educational benefits. By a law passed in 1952 Korean war veterans enrolled in schools and colleges were promised benefits ranging from $110 to $160 a month, according to the number of their dependents.

Partly as a result of these veterans' programs, there was a widespread demand for additional federal help for education, particularly in the schools of less prosperous or less populous states. Congress gave considerable attention to the problem, but action was cut off when the religious issue was brought in. There were acute differences of opinion as to whether or not federal funds should be used to provide assistance to students in parochial as well as in public schools, with the result that Congress did nothing.

The democratic trend in American civilization was also evident in new methods for the mass sale of books. The Book-of-the-Month Club and the Literary Guild, both founded in 1926, had pushed their memberships to over a million each by 1946. The success of these ventures in selecting an outstanding book each month and selling it by mail was so great that many other book clubs were organized. Even more extraordinary was the development of a vast market for cheap paper-bound books, which were sold in drug stores and news stands.

Literature

Popular taste in literature ran in divergent channels. Mystery stories continued to be popular, but were now characterized less by cleverness of plot than by toughness and violence. On the other hand, novels with religious themes like Lloyd Douglas's *The Robe* and Thomas Costain's *The Silver Chalice* were outstanding best-sellers, as were also non-fiction works dealing with religious themes like the books of Norman Vincent Peale and Fulton J. Sheen. The need for reassurance or escape in an age of anxiety was also reflected in the vogue of books on popular psychology and true adventure stories. Fiction, to the dismay of some critics, moved toward a realism and frankness that sometimes bordered on the pornographic. But there were still fine novels like Herman Wouk's *The Caine Mutiny* and Ernest Hemingway's *The Old Man and the Sea,* whose appeal lay in worthy themes and sensitive writing.

Science

The impact of science was felt on every phase of American life. The nuclear physicists, whose work had seemed too difficult and theoretical to interest the general public before the days of the atomic bomb, were now believed to hold the key to future developments both sinister and hopeful. The same energy that could wipe out whole cities might in a peaceful world be used to provide power for industry and transportation or to attack malignant disease. Research in electronics provided innovations almost as remarkable. Radar made it possible to detect approaching planes when they were still 150 miles distant; it warned ships at sea of icebergs or other dangers to navigation; it kept plane crews informed of the terrain over which they were flying. Electronics also gave the nation television, a new form of mass entertainment whose cultural impact was even greater than that which the movies and radio had had a generation before. Television usually seemed to pitch its programs at a low intellectual level. On the other hand better recording methods made possible by electronics and new high-fidelity equipment created a tremendous market for classical as well as popular recorded music.

Applied science made major contributions to the home as well as to industry. Synthetic fibers were made widely available for both clothing and decorative fabrics. Plastics took the place of the more expensive wood and metal for many household articles and gadgets. Household heating from floors or baseboards promised new comfort and economy of fuel.

Research in the field of medicine brought improvements in technique and discoveries of new drugs and remedies. New methods of blood transfusion made possible the maintenance of blood banks, ready for instant use. To the sulfa drugs, well known before the war, there was added penicillin, an almost miraculous help in certain types of infection. Streptomycin, another new drug, was being used effectively to combat tuberculosis. Another discovery, aureomycin, proved to be a cure for virus pneumonia, hitherto beyond the reach of medical science. New types of anesthesia made surgery easier for the patient, and surgeons adopted the new procedure of putting their patients back on their feet days earlier than had been customary.

Organized Crime

During 1950 and 1951 an investigating committee of the United States Senate conducted a nation-wide study of crime, gambling, and the corrupt relationship between politicians and the underworld. Senator Estes Kefauver of Tennessee served as chairman. Because many of the sessions of the investigation were broadcast by television, Senator Kefauver became nationally known, a factor of some importance in his race for the Democratic nomination for the Presidency in 1952. In the course of a year the committee examined more than five hundred witnesses, including political leaders, gamblers, and racketeers. Professional gamblers throughout the nation were found to have a total gross income of some twenty billion dollars, on which they paid only a tiny fraction of income taxes. Gamblers maintained close relations with political leaders. They evaded prosecution by bribing public officials. The committee found that "organized crime" carried on "extensive operations in interstate commerce . . . in violation of the laws of the United States."

Moral Laxity

The attitude that anything goes if you can get away with it was not confined to the ranks of professional criminals. A postwar let-down in moral standards was evident both in government and in business. Even the university world had its scandals. During 1951 it was revealed that college basketball players from seven different institutions had been taking bribes from professional gamblers to throw games or manipulate the scoring. Even more deserving of censure than these young men were certain athletic directors and other college officials who connived at falsifying records to permit unqualified students to play on their teams and who otherwise violated the rules regarding the recruitment and subsidization of athletes. At historic West Point, 90 cadets, including some of the most prominent football players, had to be dropped for cheating in 1951.

Postwar Politics

Of all the patterns of American life, next to those of earning a living, politics still stands supreme. A national election commands the attention of everyone old enough to talk and read. Not every citizen exercises his privilege of voting, but politics over the radio and television and in the press occupies much of his attention even if the polling place does not.

After World War II the first political test came in the Congressional elections of 1946. At the time there was considerable adverse criticism of the

Democratic party and of President Truman. The administration was blamed for the long series of strikes, the high cost of living, the housing shortage, and the high taxes. Out of this situation the Republicans evolved a lively campaign slogan: "Had enough? Vote Republican." Many voters did so; the Republicans won control of the new 80th Congress with a majority of 58 in the House and 6 in the Senate.

80th Congress

In the first session of the new Congress the major issues were labor, and the high cost of government with consequent high taxes. The Republicans redeemed their pledge to do something about labor by passing the Taft-Hartley Act. They did something for economy by reducing the federal budget by more than three billion dollars, although in so doing they antagonized many Westerners by cutting down expenditures for reclamation and so-called public power projects. They had promised to reduce income taxes, and they passed a bill for this purpose. President Truman vetoed it on the grounds that it would contribute to inflation and would benefit large taxpayers more than small. In the next session Congress passed a new tax reduction bill over a veto. Many Democratic members turned against the President on these issues of labor and income taxes.

Campaign of 1948

Victory in the Congressional elections of 1946 and the redemption of campaign pledges formed the basis for Republican hopes in the Presidential campaign of 1948. They also found ground for optimism in the general situation at home and abroad. Since 1932 the Democrats had been able to capitalize on the depression, the growing menace of Hitler's Germany, the war threats of Japan, and the war itself. By 1948 the depression had long since disappeared—ended by the Democrats, so Truman assured the voters. Germany was defeated and helpless; Japan had become a docile democracy. Furthermore the Democrats no longer had the magic of Roosevelt's name to guarantee victory.

Both major parties choose Philadelphia for their national conventions because of the superior facilities for television there. The Republicans met first. For candidates they had Harold Stassen of Minnesota, who had delivered the keynote speech in the same city when the Republicans had nominated Wendell Willkie in 1940; Senator Robert A. Taft of Ohio, Republican floor leader in the Senate; Governor Earl Warren of California; and Governor Thomas E. Dewey of New York, the 1944 nominee. On the third ballot Dewey was nominated unanimously; Governor Warren was given the second place on the ticket. The platform upheld the European Recovery Program and the foreign policy of the administration, as the Republicans in Congress had done. In domestic affairs the platform promised economy and reduction of the national debt.

A number of prominent Democrats were convinced that Truman could not win or were opposed to the President on other grounds. Before the convention opened this faction tried to find another candidate. James Roosevelt, Mayor O'Dwyer of New York, and Boss Hague of Jersey City, with supporters from 25 states, were sure that they could draft General Eisenhower.

The general assured them that they could not: "I will not, at this time, identify myself with any political party, and could not accept nomination for any public office." After this failure to win Eisenhower the anti-Truman drive collapsed for lack of a candidate, so the President won the nomination on the first ballot. For second place the convention named Senator Alben W. Barkley. A strong platform committed the party to work for civil rights legislation and other Fair Deal objectives.

Third Party

The campaign of 1948 was not simply a two-party contest. Early in the spring Henry A. Wallace, who had broken with Truman on the issue of foreign policy, had announced that he would run on a third ticket, with a running mate of his own selection, Senator Glen H. Taylor of Idaho. The Wallace supporters met in convention, and adopted a name for their party, Progressive—somewhat lacking in originality, but reminiscent of a former popular leader. Wallace and Taylor were duly nominated. The Progressives called for peace and friendship with Russia. The Communist party named no candidate of its own in 1948, but endorsed the Progressive ticket. This proved to be the kiss of death for the Wallace campaign; many liberals who might otherwise have supported him became convinced that, although Wallace himself was not a communist, the new party was dangerously under communist influence.

During the Democratic convention thirty-five southern delegates had walked out as a gesture of disapproval of the party's stand on civil rights. In the middle of July these States' Rights Democrats, soon christened Dixiecrats, met in convention at Birmingham, Alabama. There they nominated a fourth candidate, Governor J. Strom Thurmond of South Carolina. Their aim was to keep the names of Truman electors off the ballots in as many states as possible. So the Truman organization faced the loss of votes in the North to the Progressives and in the South to the Dixiecrats.

Truman's Campaign

Although the Republicans believed that a Dewey victory was certain and many Democrats privately agreed with them, President Truman refused to concede that his cause was hopeless. He based his campaign on the charge that the Republican-controlled 80th Congress was a "do-nothing" Congress which had failed to curb inflation and to pass welfare legislation. In an attempt to drive home the point he called Congress into special session and challenged the Republicans to make good on their campaign promises. When the session, as was natural under the circumstances, accomplished little or nothing, Truman cited this failure as additional evidence that the 80th Congress was the worst in the history of the federal government. The President proved to be a tireless campaigner, visiting every section of the country and making scores of short, informal speeches in what came to be known as his "give 'em Hell" style. The voters enjoyed these pungent attacks.

By contrast Dewey's campaign was a tame affair. He phrased his speeches in very general terms. He promised economy and a more efficient organization of the federal government. He would put able men into key public offices. But somehow the Republican candidate failed to arouse the voters. He avoided specific issues and his hearers found him cold and distant. He anc his advisers took a Republican victory for granted. So too did the so-callec experts in public opinion, the poll-takers. They all predicted a sweep for the Republicans.

But the experts were wrong. The popular vote was very close with Tru man receiving about 24,000,000 ballots to Dewey's 22,000,000, but the margir in the electoral college was decisive: Truman had 303 electoral votes, Dewey 189, and Thurmond 39. Wallace, who ran fourth in the popular vote, dic not carry a single state. The Democrats also won control of both houses o Congress. A favorite occupation after the election was to attempt to explair why the Democrats had won this unexpected victory. Among the reasons of fered were: Republican overconfidence and failure to vote, Dewey's negative campaign, Truman's vigorous speeches, the American political tradition tha Presidential candidates unsuccessful in a first campaign never win in a second, and the coming-of-age of a generation of voters who had known only Democratic leadership. A factor of obvious importance was the suspi cion in the Middle West that the Republicans were cold to the needs of the farmer. This helped the Democrats to carry such states as Iowa, Wisconsin and Minnesota.

81st Congress

For his second term Truman asked Congress to enact an elaborate Fai Deal program. He urged repeal of the Taft-Hartley Act, a higher minimun wage, enlarged social security, and federal aid to education. He repeatec his earlier requests for price control, federal aid to housing, rent control, anc more public power projects. And he continued to antagonize the South by his demands for a civil rights program and the American Medical Associa tion by his plea for national health insurance and an enlarged public healtl program. But the Democratic 81st Congress was almost as conservative a the Republican 80th had been. During its first two months the new Congres passed only one major bill, and this was to raise the President's salary tc $100,000 and gave him an additional $90,000 tax-free expense account. Late Congress passed new laws to raise the minimum wage level and to broader social security benefits. Price control came after the Korean war made i essential. The 81st Congress did prove itself more liberal than the 80th in the field of immigration. A law passed in 1948 to permit the admission of 205,000 displaced Europeans—victims of Nazi and communist oppression—had beer so restrictive and discriminatory that only 140,000 had been able to enter the country under its provisions. The more liberal law enacted in 1950 allowec 415,000 to come in.

Midterm Elections

The Congressional elections of 1950 were hotly contested. The Republi cans, stung by their defeat in 1948, waged a vigorous campaign. They chargec that Democratic blundering was responsible for the communist victory ir China and the unnecessary Korean war. They implied that the State Depart ment was manipulated by communists and that the New Deal and the Fai Deal had been leading the country down the road to socialism. The Demo crats fought back energetically, claiming that their policies had already aved western Europe from communism, were winning in Korea, and had ealt vigorously with the country's domestic needs. Truman took up his ravels again and made many characteristic speeches. At Butte, Montana, he eclared: "The Taft-Hartley law hangs over the head of labor, threatening o destroy the gains of fifteen years." At St. Louis: "Any farmer who votes or the Republican party is voting against his own interests and ought to have is head examined."

In the elections the Democrats retained control of Congress, but with ma- orities reduced to 2 in the Senate and 36 in the House. The Republicans ook particular satisfaction in the results of several contests. In Ohio Senator 'aft won a smashing re-election victory, despite an all-out drive by the 'ruman administration and organized labor to defeat the man most promi- ently associated with the Taft-Hartley Act. In Maryland the Republican ohn M. Butler defeated Senator Tydings—a victory that greatly increased enator McCarthy's prestige in Republican party circles. And in California Governor Warren won re-election by decisively defeating James Roosevelt, DR's son, while Richard M. Nixon, who had gained prominence on the House Un-American Affairs Committee during the Hiss case, won election n the Senate over Helen Gahagan Douglas, a prominent liberal Democrat. On the whole, the election results were a serious setback to organized labor's ttempt to enlarge its political influence. Optimistic Republicans announced hat the balloting indicated enough anti-Truman sentiment to guarantee a Republican victory in 1952.

Corruption in Washington

The Republicans found campaign material for the future in a series of evelations concerning graft and corruption in high federal circles. In 1949 here was an investigation of the so-called "five-percenters"—peddlers of olitical influence who undertook to obtain government contracts for small usinessmen for a fee. More serious were the reports which began to circu- ate concerning the Reconstruction Finance Corporation. The RFC had een started in Hoover's administration, to bolster up American business uring the great depression. The Democrats continued the RFC when hey took over in 1933. For several years it operated as a successful and horoughly honest government lending agency, particularly under the man- gement of Jesse Jones. After World War II, however, rumors spread that he RFC was making loans which no honest banker would dare even to onsider, and that these loans could be secured by working through the right eople in Washington.

During 1951 a Senate investigating committee, headed by Senator J. Wil- iam Fulbright of Arkansas, a Democrat, reported on some RFC activities. The committee found that a small group in Washington with connections in he White House staff had used its influence with some of the RFC direc- ors to get loans for friends or clients. In this way the American Lithofold Corporation of St. Louis, an advertising firm, had received loans of more han half a million dollars, even though the RFC had three times rejected arlier applications. The Lustron Corporation of Columbus, Ohio, maker of prefabricated homes, had received an RFC loan of $37,500,000 despite it insolvent condition. The government lost $32,000,000 on the Lustron deal The RFC scandals involved Merl Young, the husband of a White Hous stenographer, who had received favors to the amount of $125,000, and othe persons close to the President himself. William L. Boyle, chairman of th Democratic National Committee, resigned his post following revelation that he had taken a profitable part in the Lithofold Corporation's affairs.

President Truman made the mistake at first of minimizing the importanc of these disclosures, even to the point of characterizing one of Fulbright' early reports as "asinine." But the administration soon became convinced tha something must be done to restore public confidence, and the RFC was ac cordingly reorganized with a single director taking the place of the forme board.

During 1951 and 1952 Congressional investigators uncovered case afte case of maladministration in the Bureau of Internal Revenue. In the cours of a year 190 employees, including 7 of the top collectors, resigned or wer discharged. The pattern of behavior was fairly clear. Collectors accepte bribes to drop cases of fraud. Some taxpayers were subjected to extortior under threat of prosecution if they did not meet the demands. Then ther was considerable petty graft. Early in January 1951 the collector at Bosto was convicted of bribery, and the following March the collector at St. Loui was found guilty on similar charges. The collector at New York was di missed. Inside of a year his successor was dropped because of irregularitie in his own income tax returns. In March 1952 the Bureau was reorganize The 64 collectors, who had been political appointees, were dropped. In thei place there would be 25 regional collectors, under Civil Service rules. Th ramifications of the tax scandals were still being exposed long after Truma left office. In June 1956 Matthew J. Connelly, who had been Truman's ap pointments secretary, and T. Lamarr Caudle, who had been an Assistan Attorney General until Truman dismissed him, were found guilty of havin conspired to help a defendant accused of tax evasion.

The basic difficulty running through these scandals was the generally lo level of morality in government. Similar periods of corruption, it will b recalled, had followed the Civil War and World War I. The Democrats ha charge of the investigations and brought out an impressive array of damag ing facts. They wanted a housecleaning before the Presidential campaig got started. The Republicans argued that real reform could not be achieve unless the party in power were thrown out. They took particular pains t emphasize Truman's loyalty to his appointees and associates. Such misplace loyalty, they held, was unbecoming in his office.

Republican Convention

The leading contenders for the Republican Presidential nomination i 1952 were Senator Taft and General Eisenhower. Taft's long record of op position to the New and Fair Deals had made him a great hero to Republi can conservatives. He was also strongly supported in the Middle and Fa West by the so-called nationalist faction of the party, a faction suspicious o close ties with Europe and favoring an "Asia first" foreign policy. The more liberal elements in the party who favored moderate social reform and a strongly internationalist foreign policy found their ideal candidate in the popular General Eisenhower. Eisenhower, who had refused to allow his name to be presented to either convention in 1948, took a different position in 1952. In January he announced that he would accept a Republican Presidential nomination, but that he would not desert his NATO command to campaign for delegates. In June he retired from the army to enter politics more actively.

On the eve of the Republican convention, which met in Chicago in July, Taft had a slight advantage in the number of pledged delegates. Many of these, however, came from the South where Republican electoral votes were ordinarily non-existent. Ever since the end of Reconstruction the Republican party in those states, as *The New York Times* put it, "has existed for one purpose only—to deliver delegates at the convention in return for patronage." Taft also had control of the National Committee and the Committee on Credentials. The situation was reminiscent of that in 1912, when Senator Taft's father had controlled the party machinery and used it, with disastrous results for himself.

As usual, one of the first problems before the convention was that of contested delegations. All told, there were over 90 contested seats, but the most significant were 38 from Texas and 17 from Georgia. In both states the Eisenhower camp claimed that their man had been the choice of the rank-and-file members, but the state committees had arbitrarily named Taft delegations. The Republican National Committee and the Committee on Credentials voted to seat the Taft men.

Eisenhower's managers raised a loud howl of protest. In their effort to overrule these pro-Taft decisions, they gained an important tactical victory with the adoption of a new convention rule. Hitherto all delegates seated by the Committee on Credentials had been allowed to vote on all contests but their own. The new rule barred from voting on any contest delegates from states where more than one-third of the Committee had opposed the majority. Then, when the convention itself took up the Georgia case, on appeal from the decision in the Committee on Credentials, the delegates voted 607 to 531 to seat the Eisenhower group. The Taft men surrendered on Texas without a vote. Victory for Eisenhower in these contests marked the end of Taft's hopes. On the first ballot—changed as state after state jumped on the band wagon—Eisenhower got 845 votes. To assuage a little of the bitterness of the nationalist wing of the party, the Vice-Presidential nomination was given to Senator Richard M. Nixon of California.

The Republican platform called for collective security for the world as its general foreign policy. On civil rights the party emphasized the duty of each state "to order and control its own domestic institutions," but it also called for the use of federal power in case of need. The farm plank demanded full parity prices for all farm products, adequate storage facilities on the farms, together with commodity loans and ample credit. This farm plank was straight New Deal, the kind of "me too" strategy which Taft had sc often deplored. As for labor, the platform endorsed the Taft-Hartley Act but expressed a willingness to accept reasonable modifications.

Democratic Convention

The Democrats also held their convention in Chicago. For the first time in twenty years there was deep uncertainty over the prospective nominee Truman had announced several months before that he did not wish to run again. Vice President Barkley was seriously considered for a time, but he withdrew from the race when the C.I.O. announced that it considered the popular "veep" too old for the job. Senator Kefauver had entered the preferential primaries and picked up more pledged delegates than any other candidate, but the Tennessee Senator's investigations had made him unpopular with both the President and the professional politicians. Senator Russell of Georgia was too much the sectional candidate of the South to have any real chance for the nomination, while the strongly pro-New Deal Averell Harriman was not well known to the general public despite his many years of experience in government and diplomacy. The first two ballots demonstrated that neither Senator Kefauver nor any of the other avowed candidates could gain a majority. On the third ballot the convention swung to Governor Adlai E. Stevenson of Illinois, an able state executive who had stated that he did not wish to be a candidate but had acknowledged that nobody could refuse a genuine draft. The Vice-Presidential nomination went to Senator John Sparkman of Alabama, a conciliatory gesture toward the Southern wing of the party which was once again threatening a walk-out on the civil rights issue.

In their platform the Democrats pledged themselves to continue international cooperation and to enact new measures of social welfare. They called once more for the repeal of the Taft-Hartley Act and for a continuation of farm price supports. For civil rights they wanted action at all levels of government to end racial discrimination.

Campaign of 1952

Stevenson's keen sense of humor and his eloquent and candid discussion of the issues endeared him to many of the nation's intellectuals, the group derisively called "egg heads" in 1952. But the Democratic candidate was less successful in gaining the support of the rest of the American public Actually his assignment was an almost impossible one. The Republicans had an unusually attractive candidate. Although Eisenhower had spent his adult life as a professional soldier, he had neither the imperious manner nor the dogmatism that characterized some generals. Sunny in disposition, kindly and obviously sincere, he inspired more enthusiastic loyalty than any Republican candidate since Theodore Roosevelt.

Stevenson was also handicapped by having to defend the Democratic record. Although the Truman administration had many notable achievements to its credit, particularly in the field of foreign affairs, it was nevertheless vulnerable to attack. In the recent revelations of graft and corruption the Republicans found ample material for condemning "the mess" in Wash ngton. The Korean war was in a particularly frustrating stage during the ruce negotiations of 1952, and this added sting to Republican attacks on Truman-Acheson "bungling" in the Far East. It also paid dividends to charge he Democrats with "softness" on the issue of domestic communism.

In mid-September the Democrats livened up the campaign with a dislosure that Senator Nixon's friends in California had raised a fund of ome $18,000, which he used to meet expenses in connection with his work n Washington. But these charges boomeranged. Nixon's television speech efending himself proved to be an effective bit of sentimentality, while the Republicans made the plausible claim that Nixon's subsidy was no worse han certain gifts from private sources that Governor Stevenson had used o help key Illinois state executives to remain in public service. Historians ointed out that the friends of Daniel Webster had come to the aid of that otorious debtor in somewhat similar fashion in earlier years.

Although Presidents in office had never before campaigned actively for heir would-be successors, Truman traveled extensively, making speeches or the Democratic ticket. But he was unable to repeat his success of 1948. 'articularly in his attacks upon Eisenhower, the President probably hurt tevenson more than he helped him.

The Presidential election was a landslide victory for the Republicans. Eisenhower received a popular vote of nearly 34,000,000. He carried 39 states vith 442 electoral votes. Stevenson received over 27,000,000 votes, but carried nly 9 states—not one outside the South—with 89 electoral votes. Even in the itherto solid south Eisenhower carried Florida, Oklahoma, Tennessee, Texas, and Virginia. The Republicans also won control of both houses of Congress, although by narrow margins. Eisenhower was stronger than his arty.

The Republican sweep was primarily a tribute to the general's extraorinary popularity. Other factors also had their influence. Many voters beeved that it was time for a change. One party had been in power too long or its own good. The labor leaders had publicly endorsed Stevenson, but ney could not deliver the labor vote. The Western farm states had reurned to their traditional Republicanism. However various the causes, the lection marked the end of an epoch. Twenty years of Democratic control of ne federal government had come to a close.

Chapter 50

EISENHOWER AND THE REPUBLICANS

WHEN the Republicans assumed power in January 1953, many change followed. The transition was most obvious on the personal side. Me prominently associated with the New Deal and the Fair Deal disappeare from the Washington scene and quietly slipped into private employmen New men, recruited largely from the world of business, assumed the ke positions of government. At the policy level, however, the change was les abrupt. Although the Eisenhower administration took certain measures tha liberal Democrats condemned, there was no wholesale reversal of New Dea policies. Indeed Eisenhower disappointed Republican conservatives by hi acceptance of most of the basic measures of the 1930's and 1940's. In the fiel of foreign policy the new President moved with especial caution. New me appeared in the State Department and in American embassies abroad; pub lic statements gave American policy a somewhat different emphasis. Yet fo the most part the administration built upon the foundations that Truma and Acheson had laid.

Eisenhower as Leader

Eisenhower's strong preference for the "middle of the road" displease both progressives and conservatives. But these critics could not deny th President's extraordinary popularity with the general public. In his avoidanc of extreme measures Eisenhower appeared to be fulfilling the wishes of great majority of his fellow-countrymen. Enjoying unprecedented pros perity and weary of the political excitement of the previous twenty years these Americans put their trust, not in the Republicans as a party, but in th President as a person.

The Eisenhower Team

Eisenhower's leadership was exerted differently from that of such popula predecessors in the White House as the two Roosevelts or Wilson. Thes men had emphasized the need for the President to be a strong party leade to formulate legislative programs and to push them through Congress, t seize upon key domestic issues and dramatize them. Their conduct of foreig policy had been similarly vigorous. Each had been in reality his own Sec retary of State, strongly guiding the nation toward the place in the worl which he had envisioned for it.

By contrast, Eisenhower assumed the role of active leader only on infre quent occasions. In his army career he had excelled not so much in originat ing brilliant strategy as in assembling a highly competent staff and in achiev ing an excellent collaboration of effort. He was accustomed to delegat responsibility and to leave subordinates a free hand in carrying out thei ssignments. As President, Eisenhower followed the same line of conduct. 1ore than any of his immediate predecessors, he was able to free himself f much of the killing routine of the office by appointing a strong White Iouse staff, headed by former Governor Sherman Adams of New Hamp-ıire, who held the rank of Assistant to the President. Similarly Eisenhower laced heavy responsibility upon such key advisers as Vice President Nixon, ıe Cabinet members, and the National Security Council. The President's nusual delegation of duties occasioned some criticism; even before his ill-esses he was occasionally characterized as a "part-time" executive who found surprisingly large number of hours for golf. But his admirers defended the 'isdom of the President's dependence upon competent subordinates for rdinary executive business while he conserved his energy for major deci-ons. Politically Eisenhower reaped impressive dividends by disassociating imself from these delegated responsibilities. When things went wrong, the nhappy cabinet officer involved had to stand the brunt of criticism rather ıan the President himself.

In dealing with Congress Eisenhower followed a similarly modest con-ept of the President's function. He came to the White House with a deep spect for the separation of powers and liked to describe himself as a Constitutional President." Although he recommended measures in his ıessages and occasionally used his influence to help bills that he favored or block those that he opposed, his intervention was rarely dramatic. Par-cularly during the early months of his administration, he seemed to assume ıat Congress should act for itself with a minimum of executive interfer-nce. When he learned that not much of his program was likely to be en-cted into law without White House pressure, he changed his tactics, utiliz-ıg press conferences, radio-TV appearances, and personal appeals to the gislators to greater advantage.

Eisenhower's original cabinet was jocularly described as composed of nine millionaires and a plumber." Although there may not have been ıat number of millionaires by actual count, the appointees included an un-sually large proportion of big business leaders and corporation lawyers. Charles E. Wilson, president of the General Motors Corporation, became ecretary for Defense, and George M. Humphrey, a wealthy coal and steel ıagnate from Ohio, became Secretary of the Treasury. John Foster Dulles, ıe new Secretary of State, was a leading Wall Street lawyer, while Herbert rownell, the Attorney General, was another New York lawyer and close 'iend of Governor Dewey. The "plumber" was Martin P. Durkin, presi-ent of the AFL plumbers' union, whom Eisenhower unexpectedly named s Secretary of Labor despite the fact that he was known to be a Democrat nd a supporter of Stevenson in the 1952 election.

The heavy preponderance of businessmen among the Eisenhower ap-ointees occasioned some adverse criticism. Secretary Wilson made a bad art by showing reluctance to divest himself of his General Motors stock oldings as required by law. When interrogated by a Senatorial committee on possible conflicts of interest between the government and the corporatic he had so recently headed he commented that he thought "what was goc for the country was good for General Motors and vice versa." This was n the last occasion upon which Wilson's fondness for blunt statement was prove embarrassing to the administration. Secretary of the Treasury Hun phrey avoided this kind of trouble and gained wide respect as one of tl ablest men in the Eisenhower team.

Factional Differences

During the early years of the administration the scars left by the Eise hower-Taft fight for the 1952 nomination were still visible. Senator Ta publicly rebuked the President-elect for the Durkin appointment, which l considered "incredible" since the new Secretary was a "Truman Democrat known to favor repeal of the Taft-Hartley Act. In this and in other matte Taft felt that Eisenhower had not shown a proper deference for the conserv tive wing of the party. Despite such momentary displays of irritation tl Senator proved himself a loyal lieutenant of the man who had disappointe his hope of reaching the White House himself. For six months Taft worke manfully at the task of improving relations between the two factions of tl party. It was, therefore, a serious blow to the administration when Ta died in July 1953 after a short illness.

Other conservative Republicans showed less loyalty than Taft. Senat McCarthy was the most painful thorn in the President's side, but Senato like Jenner of Indiana, Bricker of Ohio, and Dirksen of Illinois also fe free to oppose administration measures—particularly in the field of foreig policy. Indeed Eisenhower was so disturbed by the obstructionism of th faction that late in 1953 he discussed with his intimates the feasibility organizing a new party that would be dedicated to his own ideals and wou appeal to what he called the "progressive moderates." But the President w sufficiently a realist to recognize the almost insuperable obstacles confrontir American third-party movements. He therefore confined himself to tl more practical objective of winning over rank-and-file Republicans to h program. In this he had a substantial success. As it became more and mo clear that the renomination of the popular President in 1956 was essential Republican victory, open rebellion against his leadership became rare. M Carthy and others who persisted in beating their own drums found then selves parading with only a handful of followers.

Administering the National Domain

The Republican administration departed most strikingly from the Dem cratic policies of the preceding twenty years in the field of natural resource Whereas Roosevelt and Truman had fought to retain federal control these resources and had encouraged public power and other governmen sponsored projects, Eisenhower favored turning over much of this contr to the states with the development of the resources left as far as possible private enterprise.

The new policy achieved an early victory in an act of Congress, signed by ıe President on May 22, 1953, transferring to the coastal states all rights to ıe oil, natural gas, and other resources lying within their historic off-shore mits. The Roosevelt and Truman administrations had argued that these ff-shore reserves ought to belong to the entire nation; the state governments oncerned had denied this federal claim and insisted that the underseas esources lying off their coasts belonged to them. In 1947 and 1950 the Su-reme Court ruled in favor of the federal government, but the states coun-ered this defeat by instituting a campaign to get Congress to transfer the ff-shore title to them. President Truman twice vetoed Congressional bills or this purpose.

Offshore Oil

In the 1952 campaign Eisenhower pledged himself to support the claims f the states. The political advantage of doing this was obvious, since it elped the Republicans to carry not only California but Democratic Texas s well. Undoubtedly, however, Eisenhower was taking a position that he ncerely believed to be right and in accordance with his basic respect for ates' rights.

In the new Congress the bill to transfer the off-shore resources to the ates was opposed by Democrats like Senator Lister Hill of Alabama and epublican independents like Senator Wayne Morse of Oregon. These men rgued that the federal government should keep its title and devote the oil oyalties to national defense and aid to education. But the bill had powerful ipport. Although only three states—California, Texas, and Louisiana—ould immediately benefit, legislators from the other 17 coastal states tended favor a measure that would confirm state ownership of whatever of value ight be discovered off their coasts in the future. Many legislators from e interior states also supported the bill as a step toward limiting federal uthority.

The conservationists were given some consolation in a subsequent act onfirming the federal title to off-shore resources lying beyond the historic oastal limits—3 miles in most instances and 10½ miles in the case of Texas. ccording to some estimates, 80 per cent of the underwater oil was thus tained under federal control.

The Eisenhower administration also modified federal policy toward the ectric power industry. Under Roosevelt and Truman the federal govern-ent had built large multipurpose dams in many sections of the country nd had given preference to municipalities and cooperatives in the purchase f the power generated at these sites. President Eisenhower accepted what ad already been done and even favored a few new projects like the Upper olorado River dam and the Frying Pan-Arkansas River tunnel. In princi-le, however, he favored a reduction of federal activity in this field in favor what he called a "partnership policy." As formulated by Secretary of the iterior Douglas McKay, the new policy stressed the primary responsibility f "the people locally"—that is, the states, municipalities, and private com-anies. The federal government, McKay said, should act only in those rare

Power

cases where the needed hydroelectric projects were too large or complex fc local means to supply. In accordance with this philosophy, the Republica 83rd Congress reduced appropriations for existing Federal power author ties and refused to sanction new ones.

The McKay power policy was symbolized by the Hell's Canyon issu Public power advocates insisted that this important power site on the Snak River at the Idaho-Oregon boundary should be harnessed with a hig multipurpose dam built by the federal government; private power interes opposed this with a plan for three small dams to be constructed by a priva utilities company. Reversing the policy of the Truman administratio McKay withdrew government opposition to the private power plan, an the Federal Power Commission approved it. In 1956 the Democratic Co gress tried to reopen the question with a bill authorizing the federal dam, bu the measure was defeated in the Senate with the White House taking much more active role than usual.

Dixon-Yates

Although the private power advocates were successful on Hell's Canyo they took a bad beating in the complicated affair of the Dixon-Yates co tract. To meet the huge power demands of the Atomic Energy Commissio the TVA faced the need to increase its generating capacity, but the Republ can Congress refused to authorize the building of steam plants which woul have nothing to do with the control of navigable rivers. Instead the AE signed a contract with a private syndicate headed by Edgar H. Dixon an Eugene A. Yates. The Dixon-Yates combine was to build a steam generatin plant in Arkansas to supply the city of Memphis across the Mississippi Riv in Tennessee. This would lessen the load upon the TVA system and allo it to supply the AEC without building new plants.

The Dixon-Yates contract was vigorously criticized. The fact that it w made by the AEC instead of by TVA aroused suspicion that this was th first step in a campaign to undermine all the public power agencies. Th contract furthermore appeared to have been somewhat secretly negotiate without public bids. Citizens of Memphis feared that they would have pay higher rates under the new arrangement.

The Eisenhower administration, troubled by the unexpected heat of th controversy, was probably relieved by the decision of the city of Memph to provide for its own needs by building a municipal generating system. B still more serious trouble lay ahead. When its contract was cancelled, th Dixon-Yates combine demanded compensation for work already undertake Meanwhile, however, a Congressional investigation had cast serious dou on the legality of the whole transaction. It was revealed that one of th government's principal advisers in negotiating the contract had also bee advising the Dixon-Yates group. The AEC used this conflict of interest ground for holding the contract void and refusing to pay. As a final chapt in the unfortunate affair, the Dixon-Yates combine brought suit against th government for $3,500,000.

The private versus public power controversy was also involved in Eisen-ower's proposals for modifying the Atomic Energy Act of 1946. This im-ortant law, passed during the Truman administration, had vested full ontrol over both the military and civilian development of atomic power in he Atomic Energy Commission. Eisenhower wanted Congress to amend his law to permit the AEC to license private agencies to develop nuclear nergy for peaceful uses. The Atomic Energy Act of 1954 gave the President nost of what he wanted, but contained safeguards, insisted upon by the ublic power advocates, to prevent private monopoly of atomic patents and uclear-generated electricity. The two sides disputed over the results of the ew policy. Champions of private enterprise claimed that the peaceful de-elopment of atomic energy was making satisfactory progress under the artnership principle; public power advocates asserted that private capital vas not really interested in developing atomic power to compete with exist-ng installations and that the United States was falling behind England and ther countries in this important field.

Democrats, eager to condemn what they called the "giveaway" policies of he administration, pointed an accusing finger at a number of other cases in vhich the Republicans were alleged to have allowed private lumbering and nining companies to encroach upon the national forest and wildlife re-erves. But the issue was far from clear-cut because the Democrats them-elves had not been consistent defenders of the national domain. Democrats rom Texas and Louisiana had been conspicuous in the fight to transfer the ff-shore oil to the states, and President Eisenhower would not have been ble to defeat the Hell's Canyon bill without the help of eight Democratic otes in the Senate.

Natural Gas Bill

Democrats from Arkansas, Texas, and other natural gas-producing states lso took a leading part in trying to get Congress to exempt natural gas oing into interstate pipelines from price regulation by the Federal Power Commission. The bill was hotly contested with legislators from the heavily rbanized states demanding continued federal regulation to protect con-umers. Rumors that the oil and gas companies were spending over a million ollars in lobbying for the measure were dramatized when Senator Francis . Case, a Republican from South Dakota, revealed that John M. Neff, an il-company lawyer, had contributed an unsolicited $2,500 to Case's campaign und in the expectation that the Senator would vote for the bill. Case re-urned the money and voted against the bill. Despite this episode the bill vas passed in February 1956 with 22 Democrats and 31 Republicans voting or it, and 31 Democrats and 14 Republicans opposing it. President Eisen-ower vetoed the measure with a message indicating that he approved its urpose but could not sanction the "arrogant" manner in which private per-ons had been seeking "to further their own interests." The President's veto urther weakened the effectiveness of Democratic attacks upon the "give-ways."

Peace and Prosperity

The Republicans' proudest boast was that they gave the country "peace and prosperity." They took particular satisfaction in laying the bogy that had served the Democrats since the Hoover administration—the idea that unemployment and hard times would inevitably follow a Republican return to power.

In September 1953 the Eisenhower administration had reason to fear that a depression was in the making. Among the danger signals were a decline in the stock market, a falling off in residential building, declining farm prices, and an increasing number of business failures. One cause for the recession was the decline in military spending that followed the Korean armistice; another was believed to be the conservative "hard money" policy that Secretary of the Treasury Humphrey had been following.

Recession of 1953

The administration took quiet measures to arrest the decline without alarming the country. The Federal Reserve Board eased its credit restrictions and certain tax reductions, due to occur on December 31, 1953, under existing law, were allowed to take place even though it would end all immediate prospects for the Republicans to achieve their goal of a balanced budget.

The recession lasted about six months. During this time the Democrats condemned the administration for not taking more vigorous measures. Walter Reuther of the CIO and other labor leaders demanded a large public works program to combat rising unemployment. President Eisenhower resisted this pressure, but he did order that such a program should be put in readiness for use if it became necessary.

By May 1954 the economic skies began to brighten, and the country soon returned to a condition of high prosperity. Conservatives attributed this speedy recovery to business confidence that the government was in friendly hands and would not become involved in rash experiments. Liberals claimed that the Eisenhower team, borrowing more than it cared to acknowledge from the New Deal book, had arrested the economic decline with deficit spending, easy credit measures, and an announced readiness to resort to public works whenever the situation became sufficiently serious.

Budget Balancing

The balanced budget that the Republicans failed to achieve in their first year in office did not actually materialize until 1956. Out of power, the Republicans had attributed the perennial deficit to Democratic wastefulness and had assumed that a balanced budget would be readily accomplished. In 1953 they applied themselves vigorously to chopping away at the last budget submitted by Truman just before he left office. Department appropriations were reduced, and the government payroll that had climbed to 2,600,000 persons by 1952 was cut to 2,400,000 by 1954.

Despite honest effort the Eisenhower administration discovered no easy method to balance the budget. Since two thirds of government expenditure were for national defense, really substantial savings could only be made in this area. Under the administration of Secretary of Defense Wilson th defense budget was in fact so reduced that the Democrats accused the Re-publicans of putting their zeal for a balanced budget above national secu-rity. But even these cuts were not sufficient to reduce total expenditures to the $60 billion level that had been the Republican goal. When the budget finally moved into the black in July 1956, it was at a level around $66 billion, and the balance was achieved largely through the unprecedentedly large revenues brought in by prosperity.

Whether the Eisenhower administration could make any further reduc-ion in government costs appeared to depend on the international situation and future defense needs. Government expenditures for non-military pur-poses seemed more likely to go up than down, as the Republicans developed heir own program for ecomonic expansion.

Seaway

In May 1954 Congress authorized the joint United States-Canada St. Lawrence Seaway project. This plan to provide a waterway by which ocean-going vessels could pass directly from the Great Lakes to the Atlantic Ocean had been advocated for thirty years, but had been blocked by the opposition of railroads, ocean ports, and coal and power companies—all of whom be-lieved that the Seaway would injure their interests. By 1954 this opposition had weakened, as the demands of national defense—and particularly the need to bring iron ore from Labrador and other new sources to the mid-western steel mills—had grown. In the end, the decisive event was a warn-ing from Canada that she intended to build the Seaway alone unless the United States acted without further delay. Congress stipulated that the American part of the project should be built by a government corporation, which would raise $105 million by selling its bonds to the United States Treasury. The cost to the federal government was kept relatively low by urning over the construction and control of the hydroelectric installations on the Seaway to the New York State Power Authority and the Ontario Hydro-Electric Commission. This decision to turn the power development over to the state was, of course, thoroughly consistent with Eisenhower's partnership policy."

If federal expenditures for the Seaway were kept at a minimum, the same ould not be said for the highway-building program authorized by Congress n 1956. By promising to pay 90 per cent of the cost to the states of building 1,000 miles of modern superhighways over the next sixteen years, the fed-ral government committed itself to the expenditure of almost $33,500,000,000. The Republicans had wanted to finance this with government bonds, but the Democratic Congress insisted upon a pay-as-you-go policy and raised fed-ral excise taxes on gasoline and tires.

Although conservatives were disappointed that the Republicans had not een able to impose a Coolidge-like economy upon the government, they ook satisfaction in other developments. The Eisenhower administration ook prompt steps in 1953 to end the economic controls imposed during he Korean war. This freeing of private enterprise was not followed by any ramatic jump in prices. For three years indeed the Eisenhower boom was characterized by a substantially stable price level, giving the Republicans plausible case for claiming that they had halted the postwar inflation. Thi case was somewhat weakened by developments in 1956 when the familia inflationary symptoms of rising prices, higher wages, and a growing volum of debt were once again evident. In 1954 the Republicans gave further com fort to the conservatives by reducing excise and income taxes. The new law granted special tax relief to stockholders and businessmen in conformity wit the philosophy that tax legislation should be so written as to encourag rather than hamper investment.

Agriculture and Labor

Although most businessmen were enthusiastic in their praise of the Eiser hower administration, spokesmen for agriculture and labor were more cau tious. They gave the President credit for sincerity and good intentions, bu they criticized his dependence on advisers from the world of business.

Farm Problems

During the 1952 campaign Eisenhower promised that the goals of hi farm policy would be "full parity in the market place" and a minimum c government regulation. Whether satisfactory agricultural prices could i fact be maintained without substantial government intervention proved t be one of the great problems of the Eisenhower administration. The Pres dent appointed as his Secretary of Agriculture Ezra Taft Benson, a conserva tive Utah businessman, even more eager than Eisenhower to reverse wha he thought to have been the unhealthy direction of Democratic farm policy

The farm policy debate that became bitter under Eisenhower had begu under Truman. The system of price supports, initiated during the 1930' and extended during the war to encourage production, depended upon variety of devices such as government loans on stored crops, marketin quotas, and direct government purchase of agricultural surpluses. The air of the policy was to maintain prices in terms of "parity." (Parity was a thec retical price level, designed to give farmers the same purchasing power the had enjoyed in normal years, especially the period 1909 to 1914.) Price sup ports were criticized on the grounds that they were expensive to the taxpaye forced the consumer to pay unreasonably high prices, and jammed goverr ment storehouses with unwanted wheat, corn, cotton, potatoes, and butte

The Brannan Plan, proposed by Truman's Secretary of Agriculture, woul have abandoned price supports on perishable crops and substituted a syster of direct subsidies to the farmers. Price supports for nonperishable crop would have been continued but with a revised formula for calculating parity The Brannan Plan was rejected on the grounds that it would be less effectiv and more expensive than the existing program. Instead Congress passed th Agriculture Act of 1949, providing that basic crops would be supported a 90 per cent of parity through 1950, not less than 80 per cent for 1951, an between 75 and 90 per cent thereafter. Perishable commodities were to b protected with flexible supports.

The gradual transition to a system of flexible supports for the basic crops, tipulated in the Act of 1949, was not actually carried out. Fearing a sharp ecline in farm prices, Congress extended the 90 per cent of parity supports rough 1954.

Eisenhower Policy

When Eisenhower came to office, therefore, his hands were tied for the ext two years. But the administration was determined to get rid of rigid rice supports as soon as the old law ran out. Benson believed that rigid upports encouraged overproduction and created an ever-more serious prob- em in disposing of the government-held surplus. Flexible supports would llow the law of supply and demand to operate. When commodities were eing over-produced, a cut in the support price would encourage a conver- ion of acreage to more profitable crops.

After a sharp fight the administration gained Congressional approval for exible supports in the Agriculture Act of 1954. The government was em- owered to fix the price supports for the basic commodities between 82½ er cent and 90 per cent of parity in 1955 and between 75 and 90 per cent ereafter.

The Eisenhower-Benson program had won an important but dangerous ictory. If flexible supports improved the farmer's position, the administra- on's course would be justified. If, on the other hand, the new policy should rove injurious to agriculture, the political results for the Republicans ight be disastrous. Unfortunately the experiment was made at a time of lling farm prices. The decline had begun during Truman's last months in ffice and continued throughout the first three years of the Eisenhower ad- inistration. Total net farm income declined from $14,300,000,000 in 1952) $11,300,000,000 in 1955. The parity ratio which had stood at 100 in 1952 ink to 81 by March 1956. Benson argued convincingly that the decline in 953 and 1954 should not be charged against his policies, since the rigid rice support system was still in effect, but the decline of 1955 was much ore serious to the administration's prestige. When hog prices collapsed om $20 to $11 per hundred pounds in the fall of 1955, politically-minded epublicans became thoroughly alarmed and pressured the reluctant Secre- ary into a pork-purchasing program.

Debate over the farm problem reached a new crisis in the spring of 1956. Iaunting memories of the 1920's warned that a drastic decline in the farmer's urchasing power might undermine the whole economy and drop the coun- y from prosperity to depression. The Democrats, who had won control f Congress in the 1954 elections, seized upon the issue and passed a farm ill which would have restored rigid 90 per cent of parity supports. Eisen- ower showed courage by vetoing this measure in an election year. But he lso showed political astuteness by fixing support prices for wheat, cotton, nd corn at 82½ per cent for another year instead of the 75 per cent which he act of 1954 would have permitted. He also used administrative action to ive generous support to dairy prices.

After the controversial Democratic bill had been disposed of, Congress by a bipartisan vote accepted Eisenhower's soil-bank plan. The new act ap propriated $1,200,000,000 to pay farmers for taking land out of cultivation an provided other benefits to alleviate the agricultural situation.

During the summer of 1956 the signs of farm revolt seemed to be subsid ing. Agricultural prices moved upward a little, and the farmers looked for ward to government payments from the soil-bank fund. Political analyst still found Eisenhower personally popular in the farm-belt states. But th President's apparent success had not been a clear-cut victory for free enter prise. The government was still deeply involved in agricultural affairs. In deed some unkind critics pointed out that Eisenhower's soil-bank pla looked suspiciously like Roosevelt's original AAA under a different name.

Labor

Secretary of Labor Durkin believed that his principal responsibility wa to obtain a modification of the Taft-Hartley Act. By September 1953 he ha worked out a program of 19 amendments to the law which he believed wer acceptable to the President. In the end, however, probably warned by rum blings of conservative displeasure, Eisenhower refused to go along. Durki resigned, and in the bitter controversy that followed over whether the Whit House had or had not broken its word, all hope of a friendly accommodatio between the administration and organized labor appeared to be lost.

Despite this unpromising start, Eisenhower did not get into any reall serious difficulty with labor. Although the union leaders criticized what the considered to be the pro-management decisions of the reconstituted Na tional Labor Relations Board, most of them conceded the fairness of Jame P. Mitchell, the Secretary of Labor appointed to succeed Durkin. Mitchel was a labor-relations expert from the ranks of management, but he prove to be energetic in enforcing the minimum wage laws and in administerin the department. In 1956 Eisenhower recommended raising the Federa minimum wage from 75 to 90 cents an hour. The Democratic Congress out bid him by raising the hourly minimum to $1.00, and the President signe the bill. The administration also suggested minor amendments to the Taft Hartley Act, but Congress, well aware of the difficulty of satisfying bot management and labor, took no action.

Actually, labor was prospering. Except for the automobile industry and few others that had to cut back because of overproduction, employment was a a high level and wages continued to improve. Collective bargaining took plac with relatively few serious strikes. In 1955 the automobile industry accepte a new principle in the so-called "guaranteed annual wage." Somewhat mis leadingly named, the guaranteed annual wage in the form adopted wa merely an extension of the unemployment insurance system. Special com pany funds were built up from which workers laid off during slack time would be paid benefits supplementary to those made under the state un employment system.

Although labor's political influence declined under the Eisenhower ad ministration, its solidarity was increased with the ending of the feud whic had separated the AFL and the CIO since 1938. On December 5, 1955, th wo federations were merged under the name "American Federation of Labor and Congress of Industrial Organizations (AFL-CIO)." George Meany of the AFL became president of the new organization, and Walter Reuther of the CIO became vice president in charge of the industrial department.

Health and Welfare

In April 1953 Mrs. Oveta Culp Hobby, a charming Texan, was sworn in as the first Secretary of the Department of Health, Education and Welfare—a new cabinet post whose creation symbolized the expanding functions of government. Mrs. Hobby, naturally conservative anyway, was careful to quiet any suspicion that the new department intended to move in the direction of socialized medicine or federal control over education.

Welfare Legislation

Despite this conservative bias the administration was eager to make a record in the field of welfare legislation. In 1954 Congress liberalized the Social Security system by extending coverage to self-employed farmers, religious workers, and other groups. Old-age pensions were increased in amount, and less stringent rules regarding the amounts which pensioners might earn were adopted. As the 1956 election approached, the Social Security Act was again amended. This time the Democrats took the lead, over Eisenhower's opposition, in lowering the eligibility age for women to 62 and making disabled workers eligible at 50.

On other federal programs Eisenhower persisted in the middle of the road. Instead of the 135,000 units of public housing per year proposed by the Democrats in 1956, Eisenhower advocated 35,000 units a year, and Congress bowed to his wishes. The administration recommended the principle of government reinsurance for private health insurance plans but was not able to push the matter through. Such a program went too far for the American Medical Association and not far enough for the advocates of compulsory health insurance. The President also proposed federal aid to the states for public school construction, but this much needed measure was lost because of Southern fear that federal aid might be used to force racial integration in the schools.

In April 1955 public announcement was made of the proven effectiveness of a new polio vaccine, developed by Dr. Jonas E. Salk. The news that one of the most dreaded of children's diseases could now be prevented was greeted with the ringing of church bells and other evidences of public jubilation. Parents swamped doctors with requests for the immediate inoculation of their children. Unfortunately the release of the vaccine for general use was marked by great confusion. Some 71 of those first inoculated contracted the disease. The public, which had accepted the vaccine with such enthusiasm, now became afraid of it, and the government suspended its release for a period. Eventually most of the trouble was traced to a single manufacturer, and new standards of testing and control restored public confidence.

The Department of Health, Education and Welfare was sharply criticize for underestimating the dimensions of the Salk vaccine problem and makin inadequate preparations for its release to the public. In July 1955 Mrs. Hobb resigned—professedly to care for her husband, who was seriously ill. The nev Secretary was Marion B. Folsom, an administrator much more ambitious t gain credit for the administration in the welfare field.

The Civil Rights Issue

President Eisenhower showed strong sympathy for the Negro's demand fo job equality. The first Negro to serve on the White House staff and the fir Negro to hold a sub-Cabinet post were both Eisenhower appointees. Th President also ordered the abolition of all segregation within Federal nav bases and similar installations—completing the integration of the arme services that had begun under Roosevelt and Truman.

On May 17, 1954, Chief Justice Earl Warren, former governor of Californi whom Eisenhower had appointed to succeed Chief Justice Vinson, delivere

Integration

one of the most important decisions in the history of the Supreme Cour State laws requiring Negro children to attend separate public schools we declared to be violations of the Fourteenth Amendment, which stipulates th no state shall "deny to any person within its jurisdiction the equal protectio of the laws." By this unanimous action the Court set aside the "separate b equal" doctrine under which segregation laws had been allowed to stan since 1896. "Separate educational facilities," declared Warren, "are inherent unequal."

Although the Court was uncompromising in its rejection of segregation, was moderate in the rules that it laid down for implementing the new pri ciple. Reserving decision on this aspect of the problem for a year's furth study, it finally stipulated that the local authorities were to be charged wi responsibility for integrating the public schools and that the federal distri courts were to see that this was done. The local authorities were to be r quired to make "a prompt and reasonable start," but were to be allowed "a ditional time" for dealing with the difficulties of particular local situ tions.

In the border states the Supreme Court was taken at its word, and ste were at once taken to integrate the schools. President Eisenhower hop that the capital city of Washington might provide a model for the rest the South, and prompt action to abolish school segregation there was a cordingly taken. Similar progress was achieved in states like Maryland, Del ware, West Virginia, and Missouri.

Elsewhere in the South, however, the anti-segregation decision was m with hostility and defiance. Here and there long somnolent chapters of t Ku Klux Klan sprang to life again with hooded paraders and burnir crosses. More common were the new "Citizens Councils," organized in ov a hundred Southern communities. These attempted to perpetuate wh supremacy by a variety of means, including the use of economic reprisals against Negroes who were active in the campaign for equal rights. Some states amended their school laws to permit abolition of the public schools and the payment of tuition fees to private segregated schools or made other provisions for circumventing integration. In a curious twentieth-century revival of doctrines once associated with Jefferson and Calhoun, some state legislatures affirmed the right of the states to "interpose" to arrest the enforcement of federal policies considered by the legislatures to be unconstitutional.

The most unfortunate consequence of the excitement aroused by the segregation issue was an outbreak of Southern violence. Two white men charged with the kidnapping and brutal murder of Emmett Till, a 14-year-old Negro boy who had allegedly made disrespectful remarks to a white woman, were acquitted by Mississippi juries despite strong evidence of their guilt. When a federal court ordered the University of Alabama to admit a young Negro woman named Autherine Lucy to graduate study, the campus was the scene of such mob demonstrations that the University authorities felt it necessary to exclude Miss Lucy from classes in order to protect her life. Later the trustees expelled the young woman on the grounds that she had been guilty of improper conduct in accusing the University of complicity in the riots.

Although the Southern Negroes showed restraint in not returning blow for blow, they did demonstrate a renewed determination to insist upon their rights. In protest against the seating rules enforced on Southern buses, the Negroes of Montgomery, Alabama, conducted a non-violent but highly effective boycott of the buses. This episode led to similar movements elsewhere in the South.

Eisenhower's proposals for new civil rights legislation were less extensive than Truman's had been but ran into the same kind of difficulty in Congress. An administration bill to establish a Civil Rights Division in the Department of Justice and to empower the Attorney General to initiate civil suits against groups depriving persons of their civil rights passed the House in 1956, but was buried in committee in the Senate.

Problems of Internal Security

Loyalty Programs

In April 1953 President Eisenhower established a new employee security program by executive order. In contrast with Truman's policy, government employees were to be dismissed not merely if they were found to be disloyal but if they constituted a security risk for any other reason such as drunkenness, drug addiction, or immoral conduct. At the end of the first four months of the new check the administration announced that 1,456 persons had been removed from the federal payroll. Republicans asserted that these figures proved that the Democrats had been lax on the security issue, but the Democrats retorted indignantly that they were being made the victims of a "numbers game" under which dismissals for unreliable conduct were being lumped together with a relatively few cases of subversion to give the public the impression that the number of communists infiltrating the government had been much larger than it actually was.

The most prominent victim of the President's security program was Dr. J. Robert Oppenheimer, who had directed the Los Alamos laboratories when the first atomic bombs were built. Oppenheimer, now an adviser to the Atomic Energy Commission, was accused of associating with communists and obstructing the development of the hydrogen bomb. By a vote of 2 to 1 an investigating board reached the paradoxical conclusion that he was "a loyal citizen" but that, nevertheless, his security clearance should be withdrawn because of his indiscreet conduct. The AEC affirmed this decision in a 4 to 1 ruling. The merits of this case, involving one of the world's greatest scientists, became a matter of sharp controversy.

Many men less prominent than Dr. Oppenheimer found themselves suspended from government service and compelled to defend themselves on security charges. In 1956 the Bar Association of the City of New York issued a report upholding the need for a government security program but condemning such unfair procedures as suspending accused employees without pay, entertaining vague and trivial charges, and denying accused employees the right to face and cross-examine their accusers.

McCarthy Inquiries

While the Eisenhower administration was under attack from one side for being too drastic in its security measures, it was assaulted on the other flank for being too lenient. Senator McCarthy, who became chairman of the Senate Permanent Investigations Sub-Committee in the 83rd Congress, busied himself in a variety of activities embarrassing to the administration. For many months President Eisenhower tried to avoid any open break with McCarthy and ordered his subordinates to cooperate with the Senator's investigations.

This attempt at appeasement failed in 1954 when McCarthy's inquisitorial campaign found a target in the Army. Trying to pin responsibility for the promotion and honorable discharge of Major Irving Peress, an Army dentist accused of communist activities, McCarthy summoned General Ralph Zwicker before his committee. When the Senator found Zwicker's answers unsatisfactory, he berated him viciously, declaring that he was "not fit to wear that uniform." Indignant at the way in which a veteran officer with a fine combat record had been treated, Secretary of the Army Robert Stevens announced that the Army would not cooperate further in the investigation of the Peress affair. Later Stevens weakened under pressure from McCarthy's Republican colleagues on the committee and promised to supply the names of those involved in Peress's promotion.

Still smarting from this encounter with McCarthy, the Army retaliated by circulating a secret document charging that the Senator and Roy Cohn, the committee counsel, had been threatening the department in an attempt to get special privileges for the recently drafted Private David Schine, a chum of Cohn's and a former consultant to the committee. When these accusations leaked out to the press, there was an immediate demand that the investigators should be themselves investigated. Instead of referring the Army's charges and McCarthy's counter-charges to some other committee not involved in the controversy, the Permanent Investigations Sub-Committee itself conducted hearings. McCarthy temporarily turned over his chairmanship to Senator Karl Mundt of South Dakota.

For thirty-six days the televised hearings provided the public with an extraordinary spectacle that featured histrionic lawyers, evasive witnesses, and irrelevant speech-making by the committee members. The results of the investigation were not very satisfactory to either of the parties. The Republicans on the committee exonerated McCarthy of serious misconduct, while the Democratic minority criticized him for condoning Cohn's improper activities. Secretary of the Army Stevens and his subordinates were roughly treated in both reports. Cohn resigned from his post as committee counsel.

Despite the indecisive outcome of the Army-McCarthy scuffle, the episode tarnished the Wisconsin Senator's reputation and steeled the resolution of certain of his Senate colleagues to call him to book. The responsibility for filing formal charges of improper conduct against McCarthy was taken by Senator Ralph E. Flanders, a Vermont Republican, Senator William Fulbright, an Arkansas Democrat, and Senator Wayne Morse of Oregon, a former Republican who had broken with the Eisenhower administration, first called himself an Independent, and later became a Democrat. A special committee of three Republicans and three Democrats under the chairmanship of Senator Arthur Watkins of Utah was appointed to investigate these charges.

In refreshing contrast to the earlier circus Senator Watkins, a conservative Republican with experience as a federal judge, conducted the new hearings in a dignified and orderly fashion. The committee recommended censure of McCarthy, basing its findings largely on his contemptuous defiance of an earlier Senate committee that had attempted to investigate certain financial transactions that appeared to involve McCarthy's political integrity. When the issue came before the full Senate in December 1954, the harsh word "censure" was dropped in favor of the slightly milder term "condemn." With this qualification the motion to condemn Senator McCarthy was carried by a vote of 67 to 22.

President Eisenhower indicated his approval of the McCarthy condemnation by publicly praising Watkins for doing a "splendid" job. The Wisconsin Senator retaliated by apologizing to the American people for having advocated Eisenhower's election. The condemnation marked a turning-point in the McCarthy story. Although he still had thousands of loyal admirers throughout the nation, his power within the Republican party tended to decline as Eisenhower's rose. The Senator suffered a further blow when Democratic victory in the Congressional elections of 1954 cost him his committee chairmanship.

Meanwhile Congress had continued to strengthen the laws dealing with subversion. Persons convicted of conspiring to overthrow the government by force were deprived of their citizenship. The death penalty was extended to the crime of peacetime espionage. The Democrats, seeking to refute the favorite Republican charge that they were soft on the loyalty issue, took the lead in passing an act in 1954 formally outlawing the Communist party.

The New Look in Foreign Policy

In January 1954 Secretary of State Dulles made an important speech defining the different emphasis which the Eisenhower administration was developing in foreign policy. The United States, Dulles declared, would in the future depend less upon "local defensive power" and place primary reliance upon "a great capacity to retaliate instantly by means and at places of our own choosing." The "massive retaliation" concept, as this was called, implied that the United States intended to avoid Korea-type wars in which the communists had the advantage of choosing the battleground; instead, the government hoped to deter such local aggressions by the threat that the United States would strike back with nuclear weapons against the communist homelands. Dulles's speech aroused considerable misgivings among America's European allies, who saw in it a threat that any small war might become a big one involving the most terrible weapons.

Closely related to the massive retaliation concept was a revised defense policy. As new chairman of the Joint Chiefs of Staff, the President chose Admiral Arthur W. Radford, who had been a critic of Truman's defense policy. Radford opposed excessive dependence on perimeter defense—that is, the stationing of large bodies of American troops in forward positions in Asia and Africa; he believed instead that American power should be largely concentrated in strategic reserve in or near North America. This would mean a substantial reduction in the Army and some reduction in the Navy, while principal reliance was placed upon the Air Force. The mainstays of American defense would be long-distance bombers, nuclear weapons, and guided missiles.

New Defense Policy

President Eisenhower favored the new defense policy not only because it seemed to his experienced mind sound on its merits but because it would permit a reduction in the defense budget. Heavy dependence on nuclear weapons would save money and give greater security, or as one wag expressed it, provide "a bigger bang for a buck." In accordance with this policy the defense budget was cut from $43,700,000,000 in 1953 to $35,600,000,000 in 1956, while total armed forces were reduced from 3,402,783 to 2,814,632 during the same period.

The new policy did not escape sharp criticism. General Matthew B Ridgway, Army Chief of Staff, opposed the cuts in ground forces vigorously while he was still in service and still more so after his retirement. The military budget, he charged, "was not based so much on military requirements or on what the economy of the country could stand, as on political considerations." His argument was that rapid Soviet progress in nuclear armament would soon wipe out the American advantage in that department and leave ground forces, in which the Soviets had a great superiority, as the decisive factor in any future war.

Even though the Air Force was the favorite son in the new defense policy, Senator Stuart Symington of Missouri and other Democratic legislators accused the administration of allowing the development of American air power to lag behind Russian. In 1956 Congress took the unusual step of voting $900,000,000 more for aircraft production and research than Secretary of Defense Wilson had asked for.

Republican Nationalism

President Eisenhower's independence in the field of foreign policy was threatened by a powerful wing of his own party. Senator John W. Bricker of Ohio was the author of a proposed Constitutional amendment which would make invalid any treaty that dealt with matters reserved by the Constitution to the states unless the treaty provisions were accepted by the state legislatures and would give Congress the power to regulate all executive agreements with foreign nations. Behind these proposals lay, for one thing, a revived isolationism that looked with suspicion on the United Nations and other international agencies, which it was feared might sponsor treaties prejudicial to states' rights. Extremists took as their slogan: "Get the U.S.A. out of the United Nations! Get the United Nations out of the U.S.A.!" Even more strongly, the Bricker amendment reflected dislike for recent Presidential agreements like that of Yalta and Potsdam. For the alleged sins of Roosevelt and Truman, Bricker wanted to tie the hands of future Presidents.

Eisenhower vigorously opposed so radical a change in the Constitutional system. "We cannot hope," he declared, "to maintain peace if we shackle the Federal Government so that it is no longer sovereign in foreign affairs." The Bricker amendment in its most drastic form was decisively defeated in 1954, but a moderate substitute, sponsored by Walter George, veteran Senator from Georgia, came within one vote of the necessary two-thirds in the Senate. Thirty-two Republicans, including Senator William F. Knowland of California, the majority leader, deserted the President to vote, along with 28 Democrats, for the George amendment; while 14 Republicans and 17 Democrats upheld the President.

Soviet "New Look"

An event of unforseeable consequences for the American future was the death of Josef Stalin on March 5, 1953. His immediate successor in power was Georgi Malenkov, whose rotund figure and apparent good humor gave a basis for cautious optimism that Russian policy toward the West would become less hostile. In February 1955 a shift of power within the ruling group resulted in Malenkov's resignation and the elevation of Marshal Nikolai Bulganin to the Premiership. Even more powerful than Bulganin appeared to be Nikita S. Khrushchev, the boss of the Russian Communist party. Whether this turn of the wheel would soften or toughen Soviet foreign policy was not at first apparent, but over the course of the next few months the Soviet Union seemed to be tending toward a more moderate course. Within Russia Stalin's crimes were denounced by the new leaders, the party dictatorship became somewhat less onerous, and some cultural exchange with the West was again permitted. In the field of foreign policy the Russians were still seeking to extend their influence but appeared to rely less on force than on trade and economic penetration. Just how the United States should respond to these changes in the Russian situation posed difficult problems for the Eisenhower administration.

Difficulties in Asia and Africa

China Policy

Since Truman's Far Eastern policy had been a favorite target for Republican criticism, it was natural for the Eisenhower administration to stress the corrective steps that it was taking. On February 2, 1953, the new President announced that he was rescinding Truman's order neutralizing Formosa. He asserted that for the Seventh Fleet to be under orders both to protect Formosa from communist assault and to prevent Formosa's use as a base for Nationalist attacks on the mainland was to require the United States "to serve as a defensive arm of Communist China." The Seventh Fleet was "no longer to be employed to shield Communist China."

This "unleashing" of Chiang Kai-shek gave joy to the Asia-first faction among the Republicans and dismayed England and France, who feared that it might be preliminary to an American-backed Nationalist invasion of the China mainland. Both the joy and the dismay were superfluous, because the change in American policy was more verbal than real. The Chinese Nationalists were too weak to take the offensive, and Eisenhower was no more willing than Truman to provide American troops for such an adventure.

Insofar as the unleashing of Chiang served any purpose, it was in the war of nerves. By deneutralizing Formosa, offering vague hopes of liberation to the satellite nations, and stockpiling atomic arms, Eisenhower and Dulles sought to impress Communist China and Russia with the serious consequences that might follow further communist aggression. Unfortunately these tactics sometimes seemed to jar the nerves of America's allies more than those of her enemies.

The Eisenhower administration's most notable achievement in foreign affairs was to gain the Korean armistice that had eluded Truman and Acheson.[1] Although disappointing to those Americans who wanted the vigorous MacArthur policy to be employed, the ending of the Korean war brought a vast sense of relief to the general public and contributed greatly to the Presidents' popularity.

Indo-China

The Korean chapter was barely closed before a new threat of communist expansion became critical. For over seven years French armies in Indo-China had been struggling against a communist-dominated rebel faction called the Vietminh. In the spring of 1954 the war reached a crisis with the Vietminh siege of the French fortress of Dienbienphu, the key to control of all northern Indo-China.

The Eisenhower administration was most reluctant to see the communist

[1] See Chapter 48.

win another victory. A French defeat, it was feared, might lead to the extension of communist control over all southeast Asia. The United States had been giving material aid to the French in the form of money, B-26 bombers and other forms of equipment, and Air Force technicians to service the planes. When it became obvious that this would not be enough, the question arose as to whether the United States should attempt to save Dienbienphu by striking against the Vietminh forces with its own planes. Admiral Radford favored such intervention, but General Ridgway and President Eisenhower opposed it. While the administration hesitated, Dieubienphu fell to the communists.

French reverses in Indo-China led to a French cabinet crisis. The new premier, Pierre Mendès-France, was determined to stop the drain on French resources by making an armistice. Dulles opposed this and sought to build up a united front against the communists. But the Geneva Conference convened to discuss the Indo-China situation resulted in a diplomatic defeat for the United States. On July 21, 1954, the war was halted on the basis of an agreement to partition Indo-China into communist and non-communist zones. The hopes of the Eisenhower administration to bring about a different result had been defeated by the war-weariness of the French, the reluctance of the British to run the risks of provoking general war, and the reluctance of the American public to jump from the Korean frying pan into the Indo-China fire. The fact that the Vietminh were a colonial people rebelling against foreign rule made the prospect of large-scale intervention on the side of the French particularly unpopular with many sections of American opinion.

SEATO

The United States attempted to salvage some of its lost prestige by lining up a new bloc of nations to oppose further communist aggression in the area. The Southeast Asia Treaty, signed September 8, 1954, had the support of eight countries—the United States, Great Britain, France, Australia, New Zealand, Philippine Republic, Thailand, and Pakistan. As a demonstration of anti-communist solidarity, the Southeast Asia Treaty Organization (SEATO) was seriously weakened by the determination of India and Burma to pursue a policy of neutrality without commitment to either the communist or the anti-communist bloc.

Formosa Problem

In the fall of 1954 the focal point of tension shifted to the Formosa Straits when the Chinese Communists began bombarding Quemoy, a Nationalist-held island only five miles from the mainland. Did the United States's pledge to defend Formosa extend to the off-shore islands? Senator Knowland and others of the nationalist wing tried to get the President to make such a commitment, but he declined to do so. Indeed when the communists moved into the barren Tachens, two hundred miles north of Formosa, the administration limited its aid to helping the Nationalist forces to evacuate the islands.

At the same time, however, Eisenhower reiterated his determination not to permit a communist seizure of Formosa and the Pescadores. In a mutual security treaty, signed December 1, 1954, the United States gave a formal pledge to assist in the defense of these islands if Nationalist China were the victim of an unprovoked attack. On January 29, 1955, this pledge was strengthened by a Congressional resolution authorizing the President to use military force, if necessary, for the defense of Formosa and the Pescadores. Whether the United States would also fight to prevent communist seizure of Quemoy and the other off-shore islands was left purposely vague.

Attempts to arrange a cease-fire between the two Chinas through the United Nations failed, but tension over the Formosa question gradually eased as Communist China relaxed its pressure for the time being. Although the United States continued to deny diplomatic recognition to Communist China, representatives of the two governments did carry on informal discussions in Geneva on the question of exchanging prisoners. Some Americans held by the Chinese thereby gained their freedom, but the negotiations were not sufficiently successful to result in any fundamental change in the relations of the two governments.

The Struggle for Peace

The cornerstone of American foreign policy, as bequeathed from Truman to Eisenhower, was the North Atlantic Treaty Organization. Just how strong this chain would prove in a crisis was conjectural. One of its weakest links was France. Beset by colonial difficulties and divided in internal politics, the French followed a faltering course. The declining power of this ally made the United States eager to build up the strength of West Germany as a more effective barrier to Russian expansion. But France continued to fear her ancient enemy and to interpose obstacles to German rearmament.

NATO Problems

Secretary Dulles exhibited his impatience with France by warning that continued obstructionism on her part might compel "an agonizing reappraisal" of basic American policy. "Agonizing reappraisal," like other blunt phrases coined by Dulles, antagonized foreign public opinion. The French interpreted it as a threat to cut off American aid unless they yielded to American wishes on the German issue. To underline their independence of such dictation, the French long delayed and finally, in August 1954, rejected the European Defense Community plan, which they themselves had originally proposed. President Eisenhower deplored this as a "major setback" to American foreign policy.

Patient diplomacy on the part of Anthony Eden, the British foreign secretary, repaired the damage. In October 1954 a West European Union was organized to include both West Germany and Italy as well as Great Britain, France, and the so-called Benelux countries (Belgium, Luxemburg, and the Netherlands). This permitted the rearmament of West Germany and its admission to NATO under conditions that were reassuring to France.

Despite this salvaging of NATO, the actual military strength of the alliance was far from impressive. The new German army still existed largely on paper, while French troops continued to be tied up in the colonies. At the same time the Eisenhower cuts in American ground forces and rejection of the theory of perimeter defense tended to reduce rather than strengthen American garrisons in Europe. For these and other reasons the NATO forces never achieved the number of divisions that had originally been planned.

What American foreign policy obviously needed was challenging new ideas that would reflect the changed situation brought about by the death of Stalin and shifts in Soviet tactics. President Eisenhower attempted to make one such contribution in his so-called "atoms-for-peace" proposal of December 8, 1953. In a dramatic appearance before the General Assembly of the UN Eisenhower recommended the establishment of an International Atomic Energy Agency to develop the peaceful uses of atomic energy with uranium and other fissionable materials contributed by the United States and other powers. The idea encountered opposition both from suspicious Russians and American nationalists fearful of all new forms of internationalism. Consequently, the plan was not adopted in the shape that Eisenhower had proposed. But progress of a modest sort was made. The United States entered into between twenty and thirty bilateral treaties with foreign countries for cooperation in atomic research. In August 1955 an International Conference on the Peaceful Uses of Atomic Energy was held at Geneva with both the United States and the Soviet Union participating.

Geneva Conference

Although Winston Churchill had suggested a new meeting of the Big Four as early as May 1953, memories of Yalta and Potsdam made such a "summit conference" seem unwise to Eisenhower until two years later when the Soviet Union seemed to be entering upon a more reasonable course of action. On May 10, 1955, the French, British, and American governments invited the Russians to meet with them "to remove the source of conflict between us." Four days later the Soviet Union accepted. As a result, the Big Four—President Eisenhower, British Prime Minister Sir Anthony Eden, French Premier Edgar Faure, and Soviet Premier Bulganin—met, together with their advisers, at Geneva in July 1955. Eisenhower was at his best in this kind of man-to-man exchange. Attempting to reassure the Russians that NATO was a purely defensive alliance, the President declared: "The United States will never take part in an aggressive war." Bulganin replied: "We believe the statement."

To provide a way out of the long deadlock over disarmament, Eisenhower proposed his so-called "open-skies" plan. The great powers, he urged, should remove the fear of surprise attacks by exchanging complete blueprints of their military establishments and allowing each other full opportunity for aerial photography over all territories. Like the earlier atoms-for-peace proposal, the open-skies plan failed to bring concrete results, because the Russians raised fatal objections. Eisenhower's conduct at Geneva had its greatest importance in giving the lie to oft-repeated charges that the United States was a war-mongering power—a libel that the communists themselves sometimes seemed to believe.

American public opinion, prone to swing too easily from troughs of pessimism to peaks of optimism, exaggerated the accomplishments of the Summit Conference. Subsequent negotiations revealed that the powers were still far apart on key issues like German unification and disarmament. It was evident that the cold war was not yet over, but that it had entered a new phase in which the weapons would be chiefly propaganda and economic penetration—weapons which the new masters of the Kremlin appeared to wield with alarming skill.

Conflict in the Middle East

Middle Eastern Conflicts

The United States found itself uncomfortably involved in a series of crises in the Middle East. The fundamental problem here was an upsurge of nationalism with consequent resistance to all forms of colonialism. Greeks were rebelling against British rule on the island of Cyprus; Arabs were contesting French authority in Morocco and Algeria; Egypt was trying to overthrow the last vestiges of British and French control over the Suez Canal. These issues were perplexing to the Eisenhower administration. On the one hand, there was American dislike for imperialism and a desire to avoid antagonizing the oil-rich Arab world. On the other, there was a wish not to weaken the strategic position of Britain and France, America's principal allies. Naturally the communists found this situation entirely to their liking. By selling arms to Egypt, promising economic aid to the Arab countries, and supporting the Arabs against the Israelis in the UN, they steadily extended Soviet influence at the expense of the West.

This Middle Eastern volcano erupted dangerously in 1956. The focal center of trouble was Egypt, where for four years Premier Abdel Gamal Nasser had been following an aggressively nationalist policy. The Eisenhower administration, desperately trying to attach the Arab world to the anti-communist side in world politics, persisted for a long period in a policy of appeasement toward Nasser. In 1954 the United States urged a somewhat reluctant Britain to evacuate its troops from the Suez Canal zone. When Nasser made arms deals with the Soviet bloc in 1955, the Eisenhower administration refused to counter this move by selling arms to Israel. Instead the United States and Britain made a new attempt to buy Nasser's friendship with an offer to help Egypt finance the building of a high dam on the Nile River to relieve the country's desperate need for more irrigation and power.

When Nasser persisted in his policy of provocation toward Israel and flirtation with Russia, Britain and the United States abruptly shifted to a tougher policy. In July 1956 the two governments notified Egypt that their offer to help with the dam project was withdrawn. Nasser's reaction was prompt. On July 26 he announced the nationalization of all the property and assets of the Suez Canal Company, in which the British government and private French investors held most of the stock.

Egyptian seizure of the Suez Canal was a profound shock to the western world, since much of Europe's oil as well as other vital shipping passed through this strategic waterway. The British and French governments wanted to send troops to maintain international control, but the Eisenhower administration strongly opposed the use of force. Instead the question was first submitted to a conference of foreign ministers at London. Eighteen of the twenty-two participating nations approved a Dulles-proposed plan for internationalizing the canal, but Nasser refused to accept it. Failing in this, the American Secretary of State next promoted the organization of a Suez Canal Users Association. Dulles's policy was to divert shipping from the canal and otherwise exert economic pressure upon Egypt, until Nasser either altered his policies or was overthrown.

But the American policy was increasingly resented by England and France, who blamed Nasser for their mounting difficulties in the Middle East and North Africa. The Israelis felt that the Egyptian government was stirring up the Arab world against them and threatening the very existence of their nation. On October 29, 1956, the situation reached a crisis with an Israeli invasion of Egyptian territory in the Sinai Peninsula. The next day Britain and France dispatched ultimatums to Israel and Egypt, demanding that the belligerents keep out of the Suez area and accept Anglo-French occupation of key points along the canal. When Nasser said no, British and French planes began bombing Egyptian airfields, preparatory to actual invasion by paratroopers and landing forces. By November 6 about one quarter of the canal area was under the control of the invaders.

The Eisenhower administration strongly disapproved of this resort to force. The outbreak of hostilities was especially untimely, since it damaged the moral prestige of the West at the very moment when the Soviet Union was shocking world opinion by the brutal repression of an anti-communist revolt in Hungary. The United States made prompt use of the machinery of the United Nations in an attempt to restore peace. Although British and French vetoes prevented action by the Security Council, the Assembly was called into special session on November 2 and by a vote of 64 to 5 accepted an American-proposed resolution calling for an immediate cease-fire. At first Britain, France, and Israel rejected this UN order, announcing their determination not to stop before gaining their minimum objectives.

On November 6, however, the British and French governments abruptly reversed their policy. Three considerations apparently motivated them. One was the pressure of the American government; a second was divided opinion at home—particularly in England, where Prime Minister Eden's conduct had provoked bitter criticism in Parliament and hostile demonstrations in the streets. The third and most decisive factor was an ominous threat of Russian intervention on behalf of Egypt. Premier Bulganin's proposal for joint Russian-American action was sharply rejected by President Eisenhower, who called upon the Soviet Union to live up to its own UN responsibilities by withdrawing its forces from Hungary.

Thus by dramatic coincidence, November 6, the day of the American

Presidential election, was also the day when all the Middle Eastern belligerents agreed to a cease-fire. The next UN steps were to get the invaders to agree to withdraw their forces from Egyptian territory and turn over the policing of the canal district and the Sinai Peninsula to an international army made up of units contributed by the smaller nations. Israel was reluctant to agree to this arrangement, but gave in under the insistence of the other powers.

Was this a victory for UN principles? Only time would tell whether the shaky armistice could be transformed into a durable peace. There was disturbing evidence that the real gainer had been the Soviet Union, which had shrewdly made its gesture of support to Egypt at the very moment when the whole Arab world was aroused against the West. Also favorable to the communist side was the breakdown, at least temporarily, of the solidarity between the United States and the European democracies.

Political Crosscurrents

Congressional Elections 1954

In the 1954 Congressional elections the Democrats made a determined effort to recover the losses that they had suffered in 1952. They based their campaign on accusations that the Republican administration had been giving away national resources, injuring the farmers by unsympathetic policies, and doing less than it should to combat unemployment. President Eisenhower entered the campaign to defend his policies and to warn that the election of a Democratic Congress might lead to "cold war" and "chaos" in the relations of the two branches of government. Vice President Nixon aroused Democratic resentment by his attacks upon certain candidates in the Midwest and Far West, whom he accused of being "almost without exception members of the Democratic party's left wing clique which . . . has tolerated the Communist conspiracy in the United States."

The election was a victory for the Democrats, who won 232 seats in the House as compared with 203 for the Republicans. In the Senate the new alignment was 49 Democrats to 47 Republicans. Although disappointed by this setback, the Republicans took consolation in the thought that the peculiar rhythm of American politics commonly resulted in even greater losses for the party in power in the mid-term elections. The Democrats had, in fact, done less well in the Congressional contests than in the election of state governors where they had won unexpected victories in states like New York, Pennsylvania, and Maine.

The events of 1954 underlined the Republican party's unusual dependence upon President Eisenhower. If he ran for re-election in 1956, the Republicans would almost certainly win; if he decided to retire to his farm at Gettysburg, Pennsylvania, they would probably lose.

The President's second term intentions were still in doubt when the nation was stunned by the news that he had suffered a "moderate coronary thrombosis" on September 24, 1955, while on vacation in Denver, Colorado. Fortunately, no major crisis arose during the three months of the President's illness and convalescence, and routine business was smoothly handled by the Eisenhower team. Vice President Nixon presided over Cabinet meetings, but his role appeared to be less influential than Presidential Assistant Sherman Adams, who remained close to Eisenhower and decided what matters should come to the patient's attention as he gradually regained his strength.

Eisenhower's Illness

At first, all but the most optimistic Republicans assumed that the President's heart attack had made it unthinkable that he should run for re-election. But in February 1956 Eisenhower's doctors gave out reassuring news. Their patient's recovery, they announced, had been excellent; he was probably good for "five to ten years" more of active service. On February 29 Eisenhower publicly announced his willingness to accept a second nomination.

On June 8, however, the President again became a hospital patient. This time the trouble was an intestinal obstruction caused by a condition known as ileitis. An emergency operation was performed, and once more the country waited nervously for the outcome. Would the fact that he had suffered a second serious illness in nine months cause the President to change his mind? The reply was no: on July 10 Eisenhower reaffirmed his decision to run again.

Whether the voters would be willing to elect a 66-year old candidate with this record of recent illnesses was still a question. Democratic hopes were kindled, and aspirants for the Presidential nomination began a feverish search for delegates. Senator Estes Kefauver of Tennessee carried several of the early primaries, but he was hopelessly handicapped by the continued hostility of the professional politicians and the opposition of conservative leaders in the South who disliked his liberalism on civil rights and other issues. As Kefauver's prospects darkened, those of Adlai Stevenson, the 1952 nominee, steadily improved. Stevenson's moderation made him particularly acceptable to Democrats who wanted to avoid party factionalism. A third hopeful was Governor Averell Harriman of New York. If Kefauver or Stevenson were unable to win a majority, the prospects for Harriman or some other candidate looked promising. The possibility of such a deadlock was greatly reduced, however, shortly before the Convention, when Kefauver withdrew and asked his supporters to vote for Stevenson.

Democratic Convention

At the Democratic Convention held in Chicago in August 1956, former President Truman tried to head off the Stevenson band wagon by announcing his support of Harriman. But this maneuver came too late to be effective, and Stevenson was nominated on the first ballot, receiving 905½ votes to Harriman's 210. The real excitement came in the choice of a Vice-Presidential candidate. Departing from precedent, Stevenson expressed no preference and left the decision to the Convention. On the second roll call Senator Kefauver received the nomination, barely beating out Senator John Kennedy of Massachusetts.

The Democratic party platform advocated fixed farm price supports at 90 per cent of parity, denounced the Republicans for permitting the "pillaging" of natural resources by private interests, promised "defensive weapons" for Israel, and condemned the Eisenhower administration for ineptness in foreign policy. On the explosive civil rights issue the Democrats were cautious, recognizing the importance of the Supreme Court's decision on segregation but rejecting "all proposals for the use of force."

The only question for the Republicans to decide was whether or not to renominate Vice President Nixon. Nixon was unpopular not only with Democrats but with many independents and Republicans as well because of his connection with the nationalist wing of the party and because of the alleged unfairness of his tactics in earlier campaigns. Believing that the President's age and recent illnesses made the Vice-Presidential nomination of particular importance, some Republicans thought that some less controversial figure should be selected to run with Eisenhower. The President refrained from indicating his own wishes in the matter until April 26, when he stated that he would be "delighted" to have Nixon again on the ticket.

Stassen and Nixon

This seemed to settle the question until it was reopened a month before the Republican Convention by Harold Stassen, the President's Adviser on Disarmament. Stassen announced that certain private polls had indicated that a ticket headed by Eisenhower and Governor Christian Herter of Massachusetts would run at least 6 per cent better than an Eisenhower-Nixon ticket. This attempt to launch a Herter boom aroused the angry opposition of Republican National Chairman Leonard Hall and other conservative leaders. Stassen found himself outmaneuvered at every point. Governor Herter not only declined to cooperate, but accepted an invitation to place Nixon's name in nomination at the Convention. Stassen continued to question the expediency of renominating Nixon but in the end gave up the fight and made one of the seconding speeches.

Republican Convention

The Republican Convention, which convened at San Francisco on August 20, demonstrated Eisenhower's complete dominance of the party. Eisenhower and Nixon were unanimously renominated, and a party platform fully endorsing the administration's policy was adopted. On civil rights the Republicans went somewhat farther than the Democrats by asserting that the party accepted the Supreme Court's decision that segregation must be "progressively eliminated." The high point of the Convention came when the President flew to San Francisco to make his acceptance speech before a wildly enthusiastic audience.

The issue of the President's health faded in importance as Eisenhower's public appearances gave apparently satisfactory evidence that he was vigorous enough to carry on with his duties. The Republican strategy was simple: convince the voters that they were "happy" and that the nation's peace and prosperity proved the success of the administration. "We Like Ike" was a slogan even more captivating than in 1952.

Against this strong Republican position Stevenson and Kefauver fought manfully but ineffectually. The Democratic candidates traveled widely, hoping by personal contact with the voters to convince them that the Republicans were guilty of false optimism. They were particularly critical of the

Dulles foreign policy, charging that the United States was alienating its friends and failing to check the Soviet Union's growing influence in Asia and Africa.

Stevenson provoked a significant controversy by advocating that the United States take the lead in trying to get an international agreement banning hydrogen bomb tests. He argued that continued explosion of these weapons involved a hazard to the health of all mankind and possible danger to future generations. By working to end the tests the United States would take a positive step toward reducing international tensions and would improve its moral standing in the world. No risk would be involved, since any Russian violation of the agreement could be immediately detected. Eisenhower sharply opposed Stevenson's proposal. He contended that to ban the tests without an adequate inspection system would endanger national security. Since scientific opinion was divided on the technical aspects of the problem, most voters appeared to be baffled by the issue and inclined to accept the judgment of the President in view of his military experience.

Campaign of 1956

The outbreak of war in the Middle East gave Stevenson a final opportunity to question the wisdom of Eisenhower's foreign policy. Five days before the election the Democratic candidate delivered a strong indictment of what he called the demonstrated "bankruptcy" of the administration's policy. Ironically, however, the crisis appeared to help rather than hurt the President. Public opinion polls indicated that thousands of voters shifted to Eisenhower during the last days of the campaign in the belief that the safest course of action in the gathering storm was to keep the experienced pilot at the helm. More than ever, politics became reduced to a matter of simple trust in an individual.

When the ballots were counted on November 6, it was found that Eisenhower had exceeded his triumph of 1952. He had received over 34 million votes to Stevenson's 25 million. The electoral count was even more decisive: 457 for Eisenhower to 74 for Stevenson. Once again Eisenhower had broken into the formerly Solid South to carry not only Florida, Virginia, Texas, and Tennessee, but even Louisiana. His margin of victory was the greatest since Franklin Roosevelt's sweep of 1936.

But the President's triumph was a personal one. In other contests both for state and federal office the Democrats more than held their own. The Democrats slightly increased their strength in the House of Representatives by winning 235 seats to 200 for the Republicans.[1] In the Senate the Democrats retained the narrow edge that they had won in the 1954 election. The new division was 49 Democrats to 47 Republicans. Particularly disappointing to the Republicans was the defeat of former Secretary of the Interior Douglas McKay, who had resigned from Eisenhower's Cabinet to run against former Republican, now Democratic, Senator Wayne Morse of Oregon.

[1] One of the successful Democrats died the day after the election, reducing the number of Democratic seats to 234. Several of the contests were extremely close, raising the possibility that the division might be slightly different after recounts had been completed.

Not since 1848 had a victorious Presidential candidate failed to carry his party to victory in at least one branch of Congress. That this had happened in the 1956 election was all the more amazing because of the decisiveness of the Eisenhower sweep. The results were further confirmation of the fact that the President enjoyed to an extraordinary degree the affection and trust of the nation, but that this popularity did not extend to his party.

Triumph of Eisenhower

What the nation appeared to want was, first and most important, peace—if this could be honorably preserved—and, second, a policy of gradual progress at home. Eisenhower was liked because he was equally opposed to radical change and to reaction. To give a "middle-of-the-road" Republican President a "moderate" Democratic Congress was not, therefore, altogether inconsistent.

SELECTED READINGS

General Bibliography: There are several comprehensive works on the history of the United States; these are generally available in college and university libraries.

Bibliographies:

Allison, W. H., and others, *A Guide to Historical Literature,* New York, 1931. Section X deals with the United States, but it is brief.

Channing, E., A. B. Hart, and F. J. Turner, *Guide to the Study and Reading of American History,* Boston, 1912.

Winsor, J., *Narrative and Critical History of America,* 8 vols., Boston, 1884-1889.

General Histories:

Bemis, S. F., editor, *American Secretaries of State and Their Diplomacy,* 10 vols., New York, 1927-29. The outstanding history of American foreign relations.

Channing, E., *History of the United States,* 6 vols., New York, 1905-25. Invaluable, though sometimes exasperating; general survey from the colonial period to 1865.

Gabriel, R. H., editor, *Pageant of America, A Pictorial History of the United States,* 15 vols., New Haven, 1923-29. Comprehensive political and social history, 1783-1865, with a wealth of illustrations.

Hart, A. B., editor, *The American Nation: A History from Original Sources by Associated Scholars,* 28 vols., New York, 1904-18. This work, largely political, deals with American history from the European background to 1917. Each volume has a helpful bibliography.

Johnson, A., editor, *Chronicles of America,* 50 volumes, New Haven, 1918-21. Both political and social.

McMaster, J. B., *History of the People of the United States, from the Revolution to the Civil War,* 8 vols., New York, 1883-1913; vol. 9, covering Lincoln's administration, New York, 1927.

Schlesinger, A. M., and D. R. Fox, editors, *History of American Life,* 12 vols., New York, 1927 ff. A cooperative social history. Each volume has a bibliography.

General Reference:

Johnson, A., and D. Malone, editors, *Dictionary of American Biography,* 20 vols., New York, 1928. A remarkable collection of biographical data.

Seligman, E. R. A., editor, *Encyclopaedia of the Social Sciences,* 15 vols., New York, 1930.

Collections of Sources:

Commager, Henry S., editor, *Documents of American History,* 2d ed., 2 vols. in 1, New York, 1940.

Werfel, H. R., R. H. Gabriel, and S. T. Williams, editors, *The American Mind,* New York, 1937.

Chapter 1. The First English Colony

In addition to the general works already cited, the following are particularly valuable for the period covered in this chapter:

Geography:

Paullin, C. O., *Atlas of the Historical Geography of the United States,* Washington, 1932.

Spanish Background:

Merriman, R. B., *The Rise of the Spanish Empire in the Old World and the New,* 3 vols., New York, 1918-26.

The English Colonies and Virginia:

Andrews, C. M., *The Colonial Period of American History,* 5 vols., New Haven, 1934.
Bruce, P. A., *Economic History of Virginia in the Seventeenth Century,* 2 vols., New York, 1895.
——, *Institutional History of Virginia in the Seventeenth Century,* 2 vols., New York, 1910.
Osgood, H. L., *The American Colonies in the Seventeenth Century,* 4 vols., New York, 1904-07.
Wertenbaker, T. J., *Virginia under the Stuarts,* Princeton, 1914.
——, *Planters of Colonial Virginia,* Princeton, 1922.

Chapter 2. New Colonies—New England to Georgia

Adams, J. T., *The Founding of New England,* Boston, 1921.
Andrews, M. P., *A History of Maryland,* New York, 1929.
Ashe, S. A., *History of North Carolina,* 2 vols., Greensboro, 1908, 1925.
Calder, I. M., *The New Haven Colony,* New Haven, 1934.
Clark, G. L., *A History of Connecticut,* New York, 1914.
Coulter, E. M., *A Short History of Georgia,* Chapel Hill, 1933.
Flick, A. C., editor, *History of the State of New York,* Vols. I & II, New York, 1933.
McCrady, E., *South Carolina under the Royal Government,* New York, 1899.
Morison, S. E., *Builders of the Bay Colony,* Boston, 1930.
Palfrey, J. G., *History of New England,* 5 vols., Boston, 1858-90.
Root, W. T., *The Relations of Pennsylvania with the British Government, 1696-1765,* New York, 1912.

Chapter 3. Economic and Social Life in the Colonies

In addition to the general histories, the following special studies are especially valuable:

Bidwell, P. W., and J. I. Falconer, *History of Agriculture in the Northern United States, 1620-1860,* Washington, 1925.

Bruce, P. A., *Social Life in Virginia in the Seventeenth Century,* Richmond, 1907.
Dunbar, S., *History of Travel in America,* Vol. I, Indianapolis, 1915.
Fisher, S. G., *Men, Women, and Manners of Colonial Times,* 2 vols., Philadelphia, *c.* 1890.
Gray, L. C., *History of Agriculture in the Southern United States to 1860,* 2 vols., Washington, 1933.
Johnson, E. R., *History of Domestic and Foreign Commerce of the United States,* 2 vols., Washington, 1915.
Parrington, V. L., *The Colonial Mind,* New York, 1927.
Phillips, U. B., *American Negro Slavery,* New York, 1918.
Sweet, W. W., *The Story of Religion in America,* New York, 1930.
Savelle, Max, *Seeds of Liberty,* New York, 1948.
Weeden, W. B., *Economic and Social History of New England, 1620-1789,* 2 vols., Boston, 1890.

Chapter 4. American Government and British Policy

The works of Andrews, Channing, and Osgood, already cited, have material on this subject. The following studies are more highly specialized:

Barnes, V. F., *The Dominion of New England,* New Haven, 1923.
Beer, G. L., *The Origins of the British Colonial System, 1578-1660,* New York, 1908.
——, *The Old Colonial System, 1660-1754,* 2 vols., New York, 1912.
Burns, J. F., *Controversies between Royal Governors and Their Assemblies,* Villanova, 1923.
Dickerson, O. M., *American Colonial Government,* Cleveland, 1912.
Greene, E. B., *The Provincial Governor,* New York, 1904.
Harlow, R. V., *History of Legislative Methods before 1830,* New Haven, 1917.
Labaree, L. W., *Royal Government in America,* New Haven, 1930.
Osgood, H. L., *The American Colonies in the Eighteenth Century,* 3 vols., New York, 1904-07.

Chapter 5. The Background of the Revolution

For the history of France in America, by far the most readable and complete account is in Francis Parkman, *Works,* 12 vols., Boston, 1893. The general histories, already cited, have convenient summaries. A more recent general account, much shorter, is G. M. Wrong, *The Rise and Fall of New France,* New York, 1928. For English problems and policy, see:

Alvord, C. W., *The Mississippi Valley and British Politics,* 2 vols., Cleveland, 1917.
Beer, G. L., *British Colonial Policy, 1754-1765,* New York, 1907.
Freeman, D. S., *George Washington,* Vols. 1 and 2, New York, 1948.
Gipson, L. H., *British Empire before the American Revolution,* 7 vols. to date, New York, 1936.

McCormac, E. I., *Colonial Opposition to British Imperial Authority during the French and Indian War,* Berkeley, 1911.

Chapter 6. The Rise of American Opposition

In addition to the general histories, there is an almost endless number of works on the American Revolution. The following list is brief and selective:

Davidson, P., *Propaganda and the American Revolution,* Chapel Hill, 1941.

Fisher, S. G., *Struggle for American Independence,* 2 vols., Philadelphia, 1908.

Lecky, W. E. H., *The American Revolution,* New York, 1912. Chapters selected from the author's *History of England in the Eighteenth Century,* 8 vols.

McIlwain, C. H., *The American Revolution: A Constitutional Interpretation,* New York, 1923.

Miller, John G., *Origins of the American Revolution,* Boston, 1943.

Schlesinger, A. M., *Colonial Merchants and the American Revolution,* New York, 1918.

Schuyler, R. L., *Parliament and the British Empire,* New York, 1929. This study effectively demolishes McIlwain's major premise.

Trevelyan, G. O., *Early History of Charles James Fox,* new ed., London and New York, 1908.

——, *The American Revolution,* new ed., 4 vols., New York, 1905-12.

——, *George the Third and Charles Fox,* 2 vols., London and New York, 1912-14. The above three works are a comprehensive history of the Revolution from the point of view of the English Whigs.

Van Tyne, C. H., *History of the Founding of the American Republic,* 2 vols., Boston, 1922, 1929.

Chapter 7. The Break with Great Britain

In addition to works cited for the preceding chapter, the following are illuminating:

Becker, C. L., *The Declaration of Independence,* New York, 1922.

Carter, C. E., editor, *The Correspondence of General Thomas Gage,* 2 vols., New Haven, 1931, 1933.

French, Allen, *The First Year of the American Revolution,* Boston, 1934.

Mackenzie, F., *Diary,* 2 vols., Cambridge, 1926. An interesting account of conditions in America by a British officer.

Murdock, H., *The Nineteenth of April 1775,* Boston, 1925.

Chapter 8. Military Operations and the French Alliance

Military Affairs:

Adams, C. F., *Studies Military and Diplomatic,* New York, 1911.

Alden, J. R., *The American Revolution, 1775-1783,* New York, 1954.

Anderson, T. S., *The Command of the Howe Brothers during the American Revolution,* New York, 1936.

Curtis, E. E., *The Organization of the British Army in the American Revolution,* New York, 1926.

Hatch, L. C., *The Administration of the American Revolutionary Army,* New York, 1904.

Knollenberg, B., *Washington and the Revolution,* New York, 1940.

Miller, John C., *Triumph of Freedom,* Boston, 1948.

Nickerson, H., *The Turning Point of the Revolution,* Boston, 1928.

Diplomacy:

Bemis, S. F., *The Diplomacy of the American Revolution,* New York, 1935.

Corwin, E. S., *French Policy and the American Alliance of 1778,* Princeton, 1916.

Monaghan, F., *John Jay, Defender of Liberty,* New York, 1935.

Perkins, J. B., *France in the American Revolution,* Boston, 1911.

Van Doren, C., *Secret History of the American Revolution,* New York, 1941.

——, *Benjamin Franklin* New York, 1938.

Chapter 9. Revolutionary Problems and the Treaty of Peace

For the peace negotiations see the references under Diplomacy, Chapter 8.

Abbott, W. C., *New York in the American Revolution,* New York, 1929.

Barck, O. T., Jr., *New York City during the War for Independence,* New York, 1931.

Bolles, A. S., *The Financial History of the United States,* New York, 1879.

Burnett, E. C., *The Continental Congress,* New York, 1941.

Hockett, H. C., *The Constitutional History of the United States,* Vol. I, New York, 1939.

Jameson, J. F., *The American Revolution Considered as a Social Movement,* Princeton, 1926.

Jensen, M., *The New Nation,* New York, 1950.

McLaughlin, A. C., *A Constitutional History of the United States,* New York, 1935.

Nevins, A., *The American States during and after the Revolution, 1775-1789,* New York, 1924.

Sumner, W. G., *The Financier and Finances of the American Revolution,* 2 vols., New York, 1892.

Van Tyne, C. H., *The Loyalists in the American Revolution,* New York, 1902.

Chapter 10. Foreign and Economic Problems, 1783-89

The best general account of this period is in the first volume of McMaster, *History of the People of the United States.*

Abernathy, T. P., *Western Lands and the American Revolution,* New York, 1937.

Bemis, S. F., *Pinckney's Treaty,* Baltimore, 1926.

Hinsdale, B., *The Old Northwest,* New York, 1888.

Jacobs, J. R., *Tarnished Warrior, the Story of Major-General James Wilkinson,* New York, 1938.
Paxson, F. L., *History of the American Frontier,* Boston, 1924.
Roosevelt, T., *The Winning of the West,* 6 vols., New York, 1900.
Turner, F. J., *The Frontier in American History,* New York, 1920.
Whitaker, A. P., *The Spanish-American Frontier, 1783-1795,* Boston, 1927.

Chapter 11. The Federal Constitution

All the standard works have material on the Constitution, and there is a long list of special studies. The following have special interest:

Beard, C. A., *An Economic Interpretation of the Constitution of the United States,* New York, 1913. This book stirred the wrath of William Howard Taft.
Beveridge, A. J., *The Life of John Marshall,* Vol. I, Boston, 1916.
Farrand, M., *Records of the Federal Convention,* 3 vols., New Haven, 1911. Vol. 4, New Haven, 1937.
The Federalist. Essays written by Hamilton, Jay, and Madison. A convenient collection is the edition by Dawson, New York, 1897. These essays together provide the most comprehensive analysis of the Constitution ever written.
Hockett, H. C., *The Constitutional History of the United States,* Vol. I, New York, 1939.
Kelly, A. H., and W. A. Harbison, *The American Constitution: Its Origins and Development,* New York, 1948.
Warren, C., *The Making of the Constitution,* Boston, 1928.

Chapter 12. Federalist Policies

The standard works deal extensively with this period and the special studies are numerous. The following are merely samples:

Bemis, S. F., *Jay's Treaty,* New York, 1923. A full account of the issues involved in making the treaty.
Beveridge, A. J., *The Life of John Marshall,* 4 vols., Boston, 1916. The best account of the *X Y Z* affair.
Bowers, C., *Jefferson and Hamilton,* Boston, 1925. A vivacious history of the period.
Ford, H. J., *Rise and Growth of American Politics,* New York, 1898. A convenient summary of party history.
Minnegerode, M., *Jefferson, Friend of France,* New York, 1928. This gives Genêt's side of the Genêt Affair.
Schachner, N., *The Founding Fathers,* New York, 1954.
Stanwood, E., *History of the Presidency,* 2 vols., Boston, 1928. Contains party platforms and figures for all Presidential elections from 1788 to 1924.

Chapter 13. Jeffersonian Democracy

Adams, H., *History of the United States during the Administrations of Jefferson and Madison,* 9 vols., New York, 1889-91 (reprinted in 3 vols.,

1929). Particularly good on foreign relations and in all respects by far the best account of the years from 1801 to 1817.

Beard, C. A., *Economic Origins of Jeffersonian Democracy,* New York, 1915. Full of information, but somewhat tiresome.

Bowers, C., *Jefferson in Power,* Boston, 1936.

Lyon, E. W., *Louisiana in French Diplomacy,* Norman, Okla., 1934.

Schachner, N., *Aaron Burr,* New York, 1937.

——, *Thomas Jefferson,* 2 vols., New York, 1951.

Chapter 14. Neutral Trade and the War of 1812

The works already cited may be supplemented by numerous special studies:

Brant, I., *James Madison, the President, 1809-1812,* Indianapolis, 1956.

Elliott, Charles W., *Winfield Scott,* New York, 1937.

Mahan, A. T., *Sea Power in Its Relation to the War of 1812,* 2 vols., Boston, 1905.

Morison, S. E., *The Life and Letters of Harrison Gray Otis,* 2 vols., Boston, 1913.

Pratt, J. W., *The Expansionists of 1812,* New York, 1925.

Roosevelt, T., *The Naval War of 1812,* New York, 1882.

Schurz, C., *Henry Clay,* 2 vols., New York, 1898.

Sears, L. M., *Jefferson and the Embargo,* Durham, 1927.

Chapters 15 and 16. The American System: Industry, Cotton, and Foodstuffs; Transportation

Industry:

Callender, G. S., editor, *Selections from the Economic History of the United States,* Boston, 1909. The selections themselves are valuable, and the editor's comments are particularly illuminating.

Clark, V. S., *History of Manufactures in the United States,* rev. ed., 3 vols., New York, 1929.

Commons, J. R., editor, *Documentary History of American Industrial Society,* 11 vols., Cleveland, 1910-11.

Johnson, E. K., *History of Domestic and Foreign Commerce of the United States,* 2 vols., Washington, 1915.

Stephenson, G. M., *History of American Immigration,* Boston, 1926.

Transportation:

Cutler, C. C., *Greyhounds of the Sea: The Story of the American Clipper Ship,* New York, 1930.

Dunbar, *History of Travel in America,* 4 vols., Indianapolis, 1915.

Meyer, B. H., editor, *History of Transportation in the United States before 1860,* Washington, 1917.

Spears, J. R., *The Story of the American Merchant Marine,* New York, 1918.

Agriculture:

In addition to the works of Bidwell, Gray, and Phillips, cited in Chapter 3, see:

Hutchinson, W. T., *Cyrus Hall McCormick,* 2 vols., New York, 1930, 1935.
Phillips, U. B., *Life and Labor in the Old South,* Boston, 1929.

Chapter 17. American Politics, 1816-29

The standard works devote considerable attention to this period. For specific information on major topics:

Bemis, S. F., *John Quincy Adams and the Foundations of American Foreign Policy,* New York, 1949.
Beveridge, A. J., *John Marshall,* Vol. IV, Boston, 1916.
Dangerfield, G., *Era of Good Feelings,* New York, 1951.
Perkins, D., *The Monroe Doctrine, 1823-1826,* Cambridge, 1927.
Warren, C., *The Supreme Court in American History,* rev. ed., 2 vols., Boston, 1932.

Chapter 18. From Jackson to Tyler

Bassett, J. S., *The Life of Andrew Jackson,* rev. ed., 2 vols. in 1, New York, 1916.
Bowers, C., *The Party Battles of the Jackson Period,* Boston, 1922.
Catterall, R. C. H., *The Second Bank of the United States,* Chicago, 1903.
Fish, C. R., *The Civil Service and the Patronage,* New York, 1905.
Fuess, C. M., *Daniel Webster,* Boston, 1930.
James, M., *Andrew Jackson,* 2 vols., New York, 1933-37.
Schlesinger, A. M., Jr., *The Age of Jackson,* Boston, 1945.

Chapter 19. The Era of Reform

Adams, G., and E. Hutten, *The Mad Forties,* New York, 1942.
Barnes, G. H., *The Anti-Slavery Impulse, 1830-1844,* New York, 1933.
Bestor, A. E., *Backwoods Utopias,* Philadelphia, 1949.
Bleyer, W. G., *Main Currents in the History of American Journalism,* Boston, 1927.
Brooks, V. W., *The Flowering of New England,* New York, 1936.
——, *The World of Washington Irving,* New York, 1944.
Commager, H. S., *Theodore Parker: Yankee Crusader,* Boston, 1936.
Curti, M. E., *The American Peace Crusade,* Durham, 1929.
Galpin, W. F., *Pioneering for Peace,* Syracuse, 1933.
Garrison, W. P., and F. J. Garrison, *William Lloyd Garrison,* 4 vols., New York, 1885-89.
Harlow, R. V., *Gerrit Smith,* New York, 1939.
Hinds, W. A., *American Communities and Cooperative Colonies,* Chicago, 1908.
Mott, F. L., *A History of American Magazines,* 3 vols., Cambridge, Mass., 1938.
Parrington, V. L., *Main Currents in American Thought,* 3 vols. reprinted in 1, New York, 1939.
Post, Albert, *Popular Freethought in America, 1825-1850,* New York, 1943.

Stanton, E. C., and others, *History of Woman Suffrage,* 6 vols., New York, 1887-1922.
Tyler, A. F., *Freedom's Ferment,* Minneapolis, 1944.

Chapter 20. Territorial Expansion

Bailey, T. A., *A Diplomatic History of the American People,* rev. ed., New York, 1942.
Barker, E. C., *The Life of Stephen F. Austin,* Dallas, 1925.
Bemis, S. F., and others, editors, *American Secretaries of State and Their Diplomacy,* 10 vols., New York, 1927-29.
——, *A Diplomatic History of the United States,* New York, 1936.
McCormac, E. I., *James K. Polk,* Berkeley, 1922.
Quaife, M. M., editor, *The Diary of James K. Polk,* 4 vols., Chicago, 1910.
Rippy, J. F., *The United States and Mexico,* rev. ed., New York, 1931.
Smith, J. H., *The Annexation of Texas,* New York, 1911.
——, *The War with Mexico,* 2 vols., New York, 1919.

Chapter 21. Politics and Slavery, 1850-57

From this chapter on through reconstruction the standard work is still J. F. Rhodes, *History of the United States from the Compromise of 1850,* 9 vols., New York, 1893-1922. For a briefer summary, see:

Craven, A., *The Repressible Conflict, 1830-1861,* Baton Rouge, 1939. Covers this period from the Southern point of view.
Nevins, A., *Ordeal of the Union,* New York, 1947.
Nichols, R. F., *The Disruption of American Democracy,* New York, 1948.
Randall, J. G., *The Civil War and Reconstruction,* Boston, 1937.

For Douglas:

Johnson, A., *Stephen A. Douglas,* New York, 1908.
Milton, G. F., *The Eve of Conflict: Stephen A. Douglas and the Needless War,* Boston, 1934.

Chapter 22. The Road to Secession

In addition to the works previously cited, the following are enlightening:

Beveridge, A. J., *Abraham Lincoln, 1809-1858,* 2 vols., Boston, 1928.
Davis, J., *Rise and Fall of the Confederate Government,* 2 vols., New York, 1881.
Dumond, D. L., *The Secession Movement,* New York, 1931.
Nevins, A., *Emergence of Lincoln,* 2 vols., New York, 1950.
Randall, J. G., *Lincoln the President,* New York, 1945.
Villard, O. G., *John Brown, 1800-1859,* Boston, 1910.

Chapter 23. Military Activities, 1861-65

Writings on the Civil War are voluminous. For reliable single-volume general accounts there are:

Channing, E., *History of the United States,* Vol. 6, New York, 1925.

Eaton, C., *A History of the Southern Confederacy,* New York, 1954.

McMaster, J. B., *History of the People of the United States during Lincoln's Administration,* New York, 1927.

Rhodes, J. F., *History of the Civil War,* New York, 1917.

Military Affairs:

Buell, C. C., and R. U. Johnson, *Battles and Leaders of the Civil War,* 4 vols., New York, 1884-88.

Catton, B., *Stillness at Appomatox,* New York, 1953.

——, *This Hallowed Ground,* New York, 1956.

Eisenschiml, O., and R. Newman, *The American Iliad,* Indianapolis, 1947.

Freeman, D. S., *Robert E. Lee,* 4 vols., New York, 1934.

——, *Lee's Lieutenants,* 3 vols., New York, 1940.

Sandburg, Carl, *Abraham Lincoln: The War Years,* 4 vols., New York, 1939.

Shannon, F. A., *The Organization and Administration of the Union Army,* 2 vols., Cleveland, 1928.

Chapter 24. War Problems, Foreign and Domestic

For foreign problems, Bailey, Bemis, and Rhodes all have convenient summaries. In addition:

Adams, E. D., *Great Britain and the American Civil War,* 2 vols., New York, 1925. An exhaustive study.

Callahan, J. M., *Diplomatic History of the Southern Confederacy,* Baltimore, 1901.

Jordan, D., and E. J. Pratt, *Europe and the American Civil War,* Boston, 1931.

Owsley, F. L., *King Cotton Diplomacy,* Chicago, 1931.

Nonmilitary Problems:

Coulter, E. M., *The Confederate States of America, 1861-1865,* Baton Rouge, 1950.

Fite, E. D., *Social and Industrial Conditions in the North during the Civil War,* New York, 1910.

Randall, J. G., *Constitutional Problems under Lincoln,* New York, 1926.

Chapter 25. Reconstruction

For the general subject of reconstruction Rhodes is still indispensable.

In addition:

Bowers, C. G., *The Tragic Era,* Boston, 1929. Sharply critical of congressional policy.

DeWitt, D. M., *The Impeachment and Trial of Andrew Johnson,* New York, 1903. Covers legal and constitutional issues.

Dunning, W. A., *Reconstruction, Political and Economic,* New York, 1907.

Oberholtzer, E. P., *History of the United States since the Civil War,* 5 vols., New York, 1917-39.

Winston, R. W., *Andrew Johnson, Plebeian and Patriot,* New York, 1928. A judicious treatment of Johnson.

Ku Klux Klan:

Lester, J. C., and D. L. Wilson, *The Ku Klux Klan: Its Origin, Growth and Disbandment,* New York, 1905.
Tourgee, A. W., *A Fool's Errand,* New York, 1876.

There are excellent studies of reconstruction for the separate states:

Coulter, M. J., *Civil War and Readjustment in Kentucky,* Chapel Hill, 1926.
Davis, W. W., *Civil War and Reconstruction in Florida,* New York, 1913.
Eckenrode, H. J., *Political History of Virginia during Reconstruction,* Baltimore, 1904.
Ficklin, J. R., *History of Reconstruction in Louisiana through 1868,* Baltimore, 1910.
Fleming, W. L., *Reconstruction in Alabama,* New York, 1905.
Garner, J. W., *Reconstruction in Mississippi,* New York, 1901.
Hamilton, J. G. de R., *Reconstruction in North Carolina,* New York, 1914.
Lonn, E., *Reconstruction in Louisiana after 1868,* New York, 1918.
Patton, J. W., *Unionism and Reconstruction in Tennessee,* Chapel Hill, 1934.
Ramsdall, C. W., *Reconstruction in Texas,* New York, 1910.
Simkins, F. B., and R. H. Woody, *South Carolina during Reconstruction,* Chapel Hill, 1932.
Thomson, C. M., *Reconstruction in Georgia,* New York, 1915.

For a recent general survey of Southern history, the most comprehensive and satisfactory treatment, with an extensive bibliography, is F. B. Simkins, *The South Old and New, 1820-1947,* New York, 1947.

Chapter 26. President Grant

For the political history of the Grant administration Oberholtzer and Rhodes provide abundant information. Important aspects of this period are covered in:

Blaine, J. G., *Twenty Years of Congress,* 2 vols., Norwich, Conn., 1884.
Eckenrode, H. J., *Rutherford B. Hayes,* New York, 1930.
Flick, A. J., *Samuel Jones Tilden,* New York, 1939.
Haworth, P. L., *The Hayes-Tilden Disputed Presidential Election of 1876,* Cleveland, 1906.
Hesseltine, W. B., *Ulysses S. Grant, Politician,* New York, 1935.
Nevins, A., *Abram S. Hewitt,* New York, 1935.
——, *Hamilton Fish, the Inner History of the Grant Administration,* New York, 1936. This is particularly good on foreign policy.

Chapter 27. Development of the West

Branch, E. D., *The Cowboy and His Interpreters,* New York, 1926.
Buck, S. J., *The Granger Movement,* Cambridge, 1913.
Clemens, S. L. (Mark Twain), *Roughing It,* 1872.
Glasscock, C. B., *The Big Bonanza,* Indianapolis, 1931.
Leupp, F. E., *The Indian and His Problem,* New York, 1910.
Osgood, E. S., *The Day of the Cattleman,* Minneapolis, 1929.

Paxson, F. L., *History of the American Frontier,* Boston, 1924.
——, *The Last American Frontier,* New York, 1910.
Riegel, R. E., *America Moves West,* rev. ed., New York, 1947.
——, *The Story of the Western Railroads,* New York, 1927.
Turner, F. J., *The Frontier in American History,* New York, 1920.

Chapter 28. Railroads, Industrial Organization, and Public Regulation

Adams, C. F., and H. Adams, *Chapters of Erie,* Boston, 1871.
Brandeis, L. D., *Other People's Money,* New York, 1914.
Clews, H., *Fifty Years in Wall Street,* New York, 1908.
Corey, L., *The House of Morgan,* New York, 1930.
Jones, E., *Trust Problem in the United States,* New York, 1927.
Josephson, M., *The Robber Barons,* New York, 1935.
Lane, W. J., *Commodore Vanderbilt,* New York, 1942.
Myers, G., *History of the Great American Fortunes,* rev. ed., New York 1936.
Nevins, A., *John D. Rockefeller,* 2 vols., New York, 1940.
Pyle, J. G., *Life of James J. Hill,* 2 vols., New York, 1917.

Major Judicial Decisions:

Warren, *The Supreme Court,* cited above.

Chapter 29. The Problem of Industrial Labor

Adamic, L., *Dynamite: The Story of Class Violence in America,* London 1934. An account of the major strikes between 1865 and 1929.
Browne, W. R., *Altgeld of Illinois,* New York, 1924.
Commons, J. R., and others, *History of Labour in the United States,* 4 vols. New York, 1918-35.
Dulles, F. R., *Labor in America,* New York, 1949.
Gompers, S., *Seventy Years of Life and Labor,* New York, 1925.
Powderly, T. V., *Thirty Years of Labor,* Columbus, 1889.

Chapter 30. Patterns of City Life

The best general accounts of urban development are:

Bryce, J., *The American Commonwealth,* rev. ed., 2 vols., New York, 1891 Vol. II deals extensively with urban problems.
Nevins, A., *The Emergence of Modern America,* New York, 1927.
Schlesinger, A. M., *The Rise of the City,* New York, 1933.

City Government:

Lynch, D. T., *"Boss Tweed": The Story of a Grim Generation,* New York 1927.
——, *The Wild Seventies,* New York, 1941.
Myers, G., *History of Tammany Hall,* New York, 1901.
Steffens, L., *The Shame of the Cities,* New York, 1904.

Slums:

Riis, J., *How the Other Half Lives,* New York, 1891.
Woods, R. A., and others, *The Poor in the Great Cities,* New York, 1895.

Health and Medicine:

Cushing, H., *The Life of Sir William Osler,* 2 vols., London, 1925.
Fulton, J. F., *Harvey Cushing,* Springfield, Ill., 1946.
Shryock, R. H., *The Development of Modern Medicine,* Philadelphia, 1936.

Chapter 31. Changing Social Patterns

Religion:

Clark, J. S., *The Life and Letters of John Fiske,* 2 vols., Boston, 1917.
Dakin, E. F., *Mrs. Eddy,* new ed., New York, 1930.
Garrison, W. E., *The March of Faith,* New York, 1933.
Hopkins, C. H., *The Rise of the Social Gospel in American Protestantism,* New Haven, 1940.
Milmine, G., *The Life of Mary Baker G. Eddy*, Boston, 1919.
Rowe, H. K., *The History of Religion in the United States,* New York, 1924.
Will, A. S., *Life of Cardinal Gibbons,* 2 vols., New York, 1922.

Education:

Cubberly, E. P., *Public Education in the United States,* Boston, 1914.
Curti, Merle, *Social Ideas of American Educators,* New York, 1935.
Thwing, C. F., *History of Higher Education in the United States since the Civil War,* New York, 1906.

Art:

Isham, S., *The History of American Painting,* New York, 1927.
Tallmadge, T. E., *The Story of American Architecture,* New York, 1927.

Sports:

Farnol, J., *Famous Prize Fights,* Boston, 1928.
Spalding, A. G., *America's National Game,* New York, 1911.
Weyand, A. M., *American Football,* New York, 1926.

Chapter 32. Political Organization and Issues, 1877-90

Glasson, W. H., *Federal Military Pensions in the United States,* New York, 1918.
Gosnell, H. F., *Boss Platt and His New York Machine,* Chicago, 1924.
Howe, G. F., *Chester A. Arthur, a Quarter-Century of Machine Politics,* New York, 1934.
McElroy, R., *Grover Cleveland,* 2 vols., New York, 1923.
Nevins, A., *Grover Cleveland,* New York, 1932.
Noyes, A. D., *Forty Years of American Finance,* New York, 1909.
Peck, H. T., *Twenty Years of the Republic,* New York, 1906.

Platt, T. C., *Autobiography of Thomas Collier Platt,* New York, 1910.
Smith, T. C., *Life and Letters of James A. Garfield,* 2 vols., New Haven, 1925.
Stanwood, E., *American Tariff Controversies in the Nineteenth Century,* 2 vols., Boston, 1903.
Stewart, F. M., *The National Civil Service Reform League,* Austin, 1929.

Chapter 33. The Challenge of the West, 1890-96

Some of the works cited for Chapter 32 contain material on this subject. For additional material:

Bryan, W. J., *The First Battle,* Chicago, 1896.
Buck, S. J., *The Granger Movement,* Cambridge, 1913.
Croly, H., *Marcus Alonzo Hanna,* New York, 1912.
Hicks, J. D., *The Populist Revolt,* Minneapolis, 1931.
Sullivan, M., *Our Times: The United States, 1900-1925,* 6 vols., New York, 1926-35. Although the opening date is 1900, Vol. 1 includes a good account of the campaign of 1896.
Werner, M. R., *Bryan,* New York, 1929.

Chapter 34. Foreign Affairs—Latin America, Spain, and the Far East

In addition to the works of Bemis and Bailey, already cited, there is an abundance of material on American foreign relations.

Bau, M. J., *The Open Door Doctrine in Relation to China,* New York, 1923.
Chadwick, F. E., *The Relations of the United States and Spain,* 3 vols., New York, 1909-11.
Cortissoz, R., *The Life of Whitelaw Reid,* 2 vols., New York, 1921.
Dennett, T., *Americans in Eastern Asia,* New York, 1922.
——, *John Hay,* New York, 1933.
Dennis, A. L. P., *Adventures in American Diplomacy, 1896-1906,* New York, 1928.
Fairbank, John K., *The United States and China,* Cambridge, 1948.
Forbes, W. C., *The Philippine Islands,* 2 vols., Boston, 1928.
James, H., *Richard Olney,* Boston, 1923.
Long, J. D., *The New American Navy,* 2 vols., 1903.
Millis, W., *The Martial Spirit,* Boston, 1931.
Pratt, J. W., *Expansionists of 1898,* Baltimore, 1936.
Pringle, H. F., *Theodore Roosevelt,* New York, 1931.
Reinsch, P. S., *Colonial Administration,* New York, 1905.
Rippy, J. F., *Latin America in World Politics,* rev. ed., New York, 1938.
Roosevelt, T., *The Rough Riders,* New York, 1919.
——, and H. C. Lodge, *Selections from the Correspondence of Theodore Roosevelt and Henry Cabot Lodge,* 2 vols., New York, 1925.
Ryden, G. H., *The Foreign Policy of the United States in Relation to Samoa,* New Haven, 1933.
Wilkerson, M. M., *Public Opinion and the Spanish-American War,* Baton Rouge, 1932.

Wisan, J. E., *The Cuban Crisis as Reflected in the New York Press, 1905-1898,* New York, 1934.
Worcester, D. C., *The Philippines, Past and Present,* 2 vols., New York, 1914.

Chapter 35. Big Business and the Drive for Reform

Allen, F. L., *The Lords of Creation,* New York, 1935. A readable and reliable history of business enterprise in the United States from 1900 to 1935.
Bradford, E. S., *Principles of Commission Government in American Cities,* New York, 1911.
Corey, L., *The House of Morgan,* New York, 1930.
Filler, L., *Crusaders for American Liberalism,* New York, 1939.
Hendrick, B. J., *The Life of Andrew Carnegie,* 2 vols., Garden City, 1932.
Hillquit, M., *History of Socialism in the United States,* New York, 1910.
Howe, F. C., *Wisconsin, an Experiment in Democracy,* New York, 1912.
Jones, E., *The Trust Problem in the United States,* New York, 1927.
McCarthy, C., *The Wisconsin Idea,* New York, 1912.
Moody, J., *The Truth about the Trusts,* New York, 1904.
Spargo, John, *Socialism,* New York, 1906.
Schwarzschild, L., *The Red Prussian,* New York, 1947. An incisive analysis of Karl Marx and his theories, one of the most effective presentations of the fallacies in Marxian ideology.
Seager, H. R., and C. A. Gulick, Jr., *Trust and Corporation Problems,* New York, 1929.
Stanton, E. C., and others, *History of Women Suffrage,* 6 vols., New York, 1881-1922.

Chapter 36. The Domestic and Foreign Policies of Theodore Roosevelt

For this period, Mark Sullivan, *Our Times, 1900-1925,* 6 vols., is indispensable. The various volumes of "Mr. Dooley" (Finley Peter Dunne) can be read with profit as well as amusement. There are several general summaries of American history in the twentieth century:

Barck, O. T., Jr., and N. M. Blake, *Since 1900,* New York, 1947.
Dumond, D. L., *America in Our Time,* New York, 1947.
Wish, H., *Contemporary America,* New York, 1945.

For this period and after, see also:

Bowers, C. G., *Beveridge and the Progressive Era,* Boston, 1932.
Jessup, P. C., *Elihu Root,* 2 vols., New York, 1938.
Pringle, H. F., *The Life and Times of William Howard Taft,* 2 vols., New York, 1939.
——, *Theodore Roosevelt,* New York, 1931. By far the best biography of Roosevelt.

The literature on foreign affairs, in addition to Bemis and Pringle, is abundant.

Bemis, S. F., *The Latin American Policy of the United States,* New York, 1943.

Dennett, T., *Roosevelt and the Russo-Japanese War,* New York, 1925.
Griswold, A. W., *The Far Eastern Policy of the United States,* New York, 1938.
Hill, H. C., *Roosevelt and the Caribbean,* Chicago, 1927.
Mack, G., *The Land Divided,* New York, 1944. The best account of the Panama Canal.

Chapter 37. The Progressive Revolt

For the Taft administration, the most satisfactory general accounts are in Pringle's biographies of Roosevelt and Taft and in Mark Sullivan's *Our Times, 1900-1925.* The literature on Wilson and his times is abundant. Of the shorter biographies:

Annin, R. E., *Woodrow Wilson,* New York, 1924. Adversely critical.
Dodd, W. E., *Woodrow Wilson and His Work,* New York, 1932. Eulogistic.

Of the more elaborate works:

Baker, R. S., *Woodrow Wilson, Life and Letters,* 8 vols., Garden City, 1927-38. The authorized biography.
Daniels, J., *The Wilson Era,* 2 vols., Chapel Hill, 1946. The story from the point of view of an admiring Cabinet member.
Link, A. S., *Wilson, the Road to the White House,* Princeton, 1947. The first volume of a new, more objective biography.
Paxson, F. L., *American Democracy and the World War,* 3 vols., Boston, 1936-48. A judicious account.
Seymour, C., *The Intimate Papers of Colonel House,* 4 vols., Boston, 1926-28. This does not undervalue House's influence.

Chapter 38. Wilson's Policies at Home and in Latin America

In addition to the works already cited, the following deal with special topics:

Blaisdell, T. C., Jr., *The Federal Trade Commission,* New York, 1932.
Glass, C., *An Adventure in Constructive Finance,* Garden City, 1927.
Hackett, C. W., *The Mexican Revolution and the United States,* Boston, 1926.
Jones, C. L., *Caribbean Interests of the United States,* New York, 1916.
Kemmerer, E. W., *The A B C of the Federal Reserve System,* Princeton, 1938.
Montague, L. L., *Haiti and the United States, 1900-1935,* Durham, 1940.
Notter, H., *The Origins of the Foreign Policy of Woodrow Wilson,* Baltimore, 1937.
Rippy, J. F., *The United States and Mexico,* New York, 1926.

Chapter 39. American Neutrality in World War I

Most of the works dealing with Woodrow Wilson have material on American foreign policy from 1914 to 1917. The following list supplements the one already given:

Baker, N. D., *Why We Went to War,* New York, 1936.
Gerard, J. W., *My Four Years in Germany,* New York, 1920.
Hendrick, B. J., editor, *The Life and Letters of Walter Hines Page,* 3 vols., Boston, 1924-25.
Lansing, R., *War Memoirs,* New York, 1935.
Millis, W., *The Road to War,* Boston, 1935.
Seymour, C., *American Neutrality, 1914-1917,* New Haven, 1935.
Tansill, C. C., *America Goes to War,* Boston, 1938.
Von Bernstorff, J. H., *My Three Years in America,* New York, 1920.

Chapter 40. The Policies of War

Paxson's second volume is the best general account of American participation in World War I. In addition to the general works on Wilson, see:

Baruch, B., *American Industry in the War,* New York, 1941.
Clarkson, G. B., *Industrial America in the World War,* Boston, 1923.
Palmer, F., *Newton D. Baker: America at War,* 2 vols., New York, 1931.
Pershing, J. F., *My Experiences in the World War,* 2 vols., New York, 1931.
——, *Annual Report,* U. S. War Department, 1918.

Public Opinion:

Creel, G., *How We Advertised America,* New York, 1920.
Laswell, H., *Propaganda Technique in the World War,* New York, 1927.
Mock, J. R., and C. Larson, *Words That Won the War,* Princeton, 1940.
Peterson, H. C., *Propaganda for War,* Norman, Okla., 1939.

Chapter 41. Peace and Its Problems

Armistice:

Rudin, H., *Armistice 1918,* New Haven, 1944. The authoritative account

Peace Negotiations:

Bailey, T. A., *Woodrow Wilson and the Lost Peace,* New York, 1944.
Baker, R. S., *Woodrow Wilson and World Settlement,* 3 vols., Garden City, 1922.
Birdsall, Paul, *Versailles Twenty Years After,* New York, 1941.
Miller, D. H., *The Drafting of the Covenant,* 2 vols., New York, 1938.
Nicolson, H., *Peacemaking, 1914,* New York, 1939.
Temperley, H. W. V., *A History of the Peace Conference of Paris,* 6 vols., London, 1920-24.

Defeat of the Treaty in the U. S.:

Bailey, T. A., *Woodrow Wilson and the Great Betrayal,* New York, 1945.
Fleming, D. F., *The United States and the League of Nations, 1918-1920,* New York, 1932. Completely uncritical.
Lodge, H. C., *The Senate and the League of Nations,* New York, 1925.

Transition from War to Peace:

Mock, J. R., and E. Thurber, *Report on Demobilization,* Norman, Okla. 1944.

Chapter 42. Political Problems of the 1920's

The best general account of the 1920's is found in Mark Sullivan, *Our Times* Vol. 6. For Harding, a good general analysis is S. H. Adams, *Incredible Era: The Life and Times of Warren Gamaliel Harding,* Boston, 1939; for the oil scandals M. E. Savage, *The Story of Teapot Dome,* New York, 1924; for immigration Wittke, C., *We Who Built America,* New York, 1939.

Coolidge

Fuess, C. M., *Calvin Coolidge,* Boston, 1940.
White, W. A., *A Puritan in Babylon,* New York, 1938.

Foreign Affairs, in addition to Bailey and Bemis:

Buell, R. L., *The Washington Conference,* New York, 1922.
Dulles, F. R., *The Road to Teheran: The Story of Russia and America 1781-1943,* Princeton, 1944.
Moulton, H. G., and L. Pasvolsky, *War Debts and World Prosperity,* New York, 1932.
Shotwell, J. T., *War as an Instrument of National Policy,* New York, 1929.
Stuart, G., *Latin America and the United States,* New York, 1938.

Chapter 43. The Mad Decade

Allen, F. L., *Only Yesterday,* New York, 1931.
Beach, J., *American Fiction, 1920-1940,* New York, 1941.
Chaffee, Z., Jr., *Freedom of Speech,* Boston, 1930.
Frankfurter, F., *The Case of Sacco and Vanzetti,* Boston, 1927.
Mecklin, J. M., *The Ku Klux Klan: A Study of the American Mind,* New York, 1924.
Merz, C., *The Dry Decade,* Garden City, 1931.
Shipley, M., *The War on Modern Science,* New York, 1927.

Chapter 44. Economic Problems of the 1920's

Barber, H. L., *The Story of the Automobile,* Chicago, 1927.
Berle, A. A., Jr., and G. G. Means, *The Modern Corporation and Private Property,* New York, 1933.
Gee, W., *The Social Economics of Agriculture,* New York, 1942.
Glover, J. G., and W. B. Cornell, editors, *The Development of American Industries,* New York, 1932.
Hansen, A. H., *Fiscal Policy and Business Cycles,* New York, 1941.
Hunt, E. E., *An Audit of America,* New York, 1930.
Lescarboure, A. C., *This Thing Called Broadcasting,* New York, 1930.
Seldes, G., *The Years of the Locust,* Boston, 1933.
Strunsky, S., *The Living Tradition: Change and America,* New York, 1939.
Thorp, M. F., *America at the Movies,* New Haven, 1939.

Chapter 45. The New Deal

Interpretations of the New Deal have been and are controversial, but for Roosevelt's point of view, see *The Public Papers and Addresses of Franklin D. Roosevelt,* 9 vols., New York, 1938-40. Among the mass of books on the subject, the following have real value:

Andrews, J. B., *Labor Laws in Action,* New York, 1938.
Burns, J. M., *Roosevelt, The Lion and the Fox,* New York, 1956.
Hansen, A. H., *Full Recovery or Stagnation,* New York, 1938.
Harris, H., *Labor's Civil War,* New York, 1940.
Johnson, H. S., *The Blue Eagle from Egg to Earth,* Garden City, 1935.
Lilienthal, D. E., *TVA: Democracy on the March,* New York, 1944.
London *Economist,* Editors of, *The New Deal: An Analysis and Appraisal,* New York, 1937.
Lyon, L. S., and others, *The National Recovery Administration,* Washington, 1935.
Perkins, F., *The Roosevelt I Knew,* New York, 1946.
Ramsay, M. L., *Pyramids of Power: The Story of Roosevelt, Insull and the Utility Wars,* Indianapolis, 1937.
Rauch, B., *The History of the New Deal,* New York, 1944.
Robinson, E. E., *The Roosevelt Years, 1933-1945,* Philadelphia, 1955.
Rosenfarb, J., *The National Labor Policy and How It Works,* New York, 1940.
Schlesinger, A. M., *The New Deal in Action,* New York, 1939.
Wecter, D., *The Age of the Great Depression, 1924-1941,* New York, 1948.

Chapter 46. Foreign Policy—From the Good Neighbor to Pearl Harbor, 1933-41

There is a vast amount of source material in S. S. Jones and D. P. Myers, editors, *Documents on American Foreign Relations,* 6 vols., Boston, 1939.

Latin America, in addition to the works of Bemis and Stuart:

Buell, R. L., "The Hull Trade Program and the American System," World Affairs Pamphlet No. 2, 1938.
Hull, C., *Memoirs,* 2 vols., New York, 1948. Covers all aspects of foreign policy from 1933 to 1945 from the point of view of Roosevelt's secretary of state.
Schuman, F. L., and G. Soule, "The Foreign Policy of the New Deal," World Affairs Pamphlet No. 3, 1938.

Russia:

Lovenstein, M., *American Opinion of Soviet Russia,* Washington, 1941.

Hitler's Policy:

Hitler, A., *Mein Kampf,* New York, 1939. The most illuminating volume.
Shirer, W. L., *Berlin Diary, 1934-1941,* New York, 1941. By an able radio commentator.
Tolichus, O. D., *They Wanted War,* New York, 1940. A simplified account.

Japan:

Buss, C. A., *War and Diplomacy in Eastern Asia,* New York, 1941.

Davis, F., and E. K. Lindley, *How War Came,* New York, 1942. A dramatic story of the final events before Pearl Harbor.

Grew, J. C., *Ten Years in Japan,* New York, 1944. The United States ambassador's account.

Morison, S. E., *The Rising Sun in the Pacific, 1931-April 1942,* Boston, 1948.

Millis, W., *This Is Pearl!,* New York, 1947. A full account of relations with Japan during 1941.

Beard, C. A., *President Roosevelt and the Coming of War, 1941,* New Haven, 1948. Shows how a gifted historian can ignore quantities of evidence in order to indict Roosevelt.

Chapter 47. Victory over Germany and Japan

The definitive history of American participation in World War II has not been written. The best single volume to date is F. T. Miller, *History of World War II,* Philadelphia, 1945.

Official Summary:

Marshall, G. C., H. H. Arnold, and E. J. King, *War Reports,* New York, 1947.

European Campaign:

Butcher, H. C., *My Three Years with Eisenhower,* New York, 1946.

Eisenhower, D. D., *Report by the Supreme Commander . . . on the Operations in Europe,* Washington, 1946.

——, *Crusade in Europe,* Garden City, 1948.

Authoritative Naval History:

Buchanan, A. R., editor, *The Navy's War: A Mission Completed,* New York, 1946.

Morison, S. E., *History of United States Naval Operations in World War II,* Boston, 1947. This work will be completed in thirteen volumes.

Industrial Production:

Goodman, J., editor, *While You Were Gone: A Report on Wartime Life in the United States,* New York, 1946.

Nelson, D., *Arsenal of Democracy: The Story of American Production,* New York, 1946.

Chapter 48. One World—or Two?

Chase, E. P., *The United Nations in Action,* New York, 1950. Covers the first five years of the UN.

Clay, L. D., *Decision in Germany,* New York, 1950. Aspects of American policy.

(2) Each House may determine the rules of its proceedings, punish its members for disorderly behavior, and, with the concurrence of two thirds, expel a member.

(3) Each House shall keep a journal of its proceedings, and from time to time publish the same, excepting such parts as may in their judgment require secrecy; and the yeas and nays of the members of either House on any question shall, at the desire of one fifth of those present, be entered on the journal.

(4) Neither House, during the session of Congress, shall, without the consent of the other, adjourn for more than three days, nor to any other place than that in which the two Houses shall be sitting.

SECTION VI

(1) The Senators and Representatives shall receive a compensation for their services, to be ascertained by law, and paid out of the Treasury of the United States. They shall in all cases, except treason, felony, and breach of the peace, be privileged from arrest during their attendance at the session of their respective Houses, and in going to and returning from the same; and for any speech or debate in either House, they shall not be questioned in any other place.

(2) No Senator or Representative shall, during the time for which he was elected, be appointed to any civil office under the authority of the United States, which shall have been created, or the emoluments whereof shall have been increased, during such time; and no person holding any office under the United States shall be a member of either House during his continuance in office.

SECTION VII

(1) All bills for raising revenue shall originate in the House of Representatives; but the Senate may propose or concur with amendments as on other bills.

(2) Every bill which shall have passed the House of Representatives and the Senate, shall, before it become a law, be presented to the President of the United States; if he approve he shall sign it, but if not he shall return it, with his objections, to that House in which it shall have originated, who shall enter the objections at large on their journal, and proceed to reconsider it. If after such reconsideration two thirds of that House shall agree to pass the bill, it shall be sent, together with the objections, to the other House, by which it shall likewise be reconsidered, and if approved by two thirds of that House, it shall become a law. But in all such cases the votes of both Houses shall be determined by yeas and nays, and the names of the persons voting for and against the bill shall be entered on the journal of each House respectively. If any bill shall not be returned by the President within ten days (Sundays excepted) after it shall have been presented to him, the same shall be a law, in like manner as if he had signed it, unless the Congress by their adjournment prevent its return, in which case it shall not be a law.

(3) Every order, resolution, or vote to which the concurrence of the Senate and House of Representatives may be necessary (except on a question of adjournment) shall be presented to the President of the United States; and before the same shall take effect, shall be approved by him, or being disapproved by him, shall be repassed by two thirds of the Senate and House of Representatives, according to the rules and limitations prescribed in the case of a bill.

SECTION VIII

(1) The Congress shall have power to lay and collect taxes, duties, imposts, and excises, to pay the debts and provide for the common defense and general welfare of the United States; but all duties, imposts, and excises shall be uniform throughout the United States;

(2) To borrow money on the credit of the United States;

(3) To regulate commerce with foreign nations, and among the several States, and with the Indian tribes;

(4) To establish an uniform rule of naturalization, and uniform laws on the subject of bankruptcies throughout the United States;

(5) To coin money, regulate the value thereof, and of foreign coin, and fix the standard of weights and measures;

(6) To provide for the punishment of counterfeiting the securities and current coin of the United States;

(7) To establish post offices and post roads;

(8) To promote the progress of science and useful arts, by securing for limited times to authors and inventors the exclusive right to their respective writings and discoveries;

(9) To constitute tribunals inferior to the Supreme Court;

(10) To define and punish piracies and felonies committed on the high seas, and offenses against the law of nations;

(11) To declare war, grant letters of marque and reprisal, and make rules concerning captures on land and water;

(12) To raise and support armies, but no appropriation of money to that use shall be for a longer term than two years;

(13) To provide and maintain a navy;

(14) To make rules for the government and regulation of the land and naval forces;

(15) To provide for calling forth the militia to execute the laws of the Union, suppress insurrections, and repel invasions;

(16) To provide for organizing, arming, and disciplining the militia, and for governing such part of them as may be employed in the service of the United States, reserving to the States respectively the appointment of the officers, and the authority of training the militia according to the discipline prescribed by Congress;

(17) To exercise exclusive legislation in all cases whatsoever, over such district (not exceeding ten miles square) as may, by cession of particular States, and the acceptance of Congress, become the seat of the government of the United States, and to exercise like authority over all places purchased by the consent of the legislature of the State in which the same shall be, for the erection of forts, magazines, arsenals, dock-yards, and other needful buildings; and

(18) To make all laws which shall be necessary and proper for carrying into execution the foregoing powers, and all other powers vested by this Constitution in the government of the United States, or in any department or officer thereof.

SECTION IX

(1) *The migration or importation of such persons as any of the States now existing shall think proper to admit, shall not be prohibited by the Congress prior*

to the year one thousand eight hundred and eight, but a tax or duty may be imposed on such importation, not exceeding ten dollars for each person.[7]

(2) The privilege of the writ of habeas corpus shall not be suspended, unless when in cases of rebellion or invasion the public safety may require it.

(3) No bill of attainder or ex post facto law shall be passed.

(4) No capitation, or *other direct, tax* shall be laid, unless *in proportion to the census* or enumeration hereinbefore directed to be taken.[8]

(5) No tax or duty shall be laid on articles exported from any State.

(6) No preference shall be given by any regulation of commerce or revenue to the ports of one State over those of another: nor shall vessels bound to, or from, one State, be obliged to enter, clear, or pay duties in another.

(7) No money shall be drawn from the Treasury, but in consequence of appropriations made by law; and a regular statement and account of the receipts and expenditures of all public money shall be published from time to time.

(8) No title of nobility shall be granted by the United States: and no person holding any office of profit or trust under them, shall, without the consent of the Congress, accept of any present, emolument, office, or title, of any kind whatever, from any king, prince, or foreign State.

SECTION X

(1) No State shall enter into any treaty, alliance, or confederation; grant letters of marque and reprisal; coin money; emit bills of credit; make anything but gold and silver coin a tender in payment of debts; pass any bill of attainder, ex post facto law, or law impairing the obligation of contracts, or grant any title of nobility.

(2) No State shall, without the consent of the Congress, lay any imposts or duties on imports or exports, except what may be absolutely necessary for executing its inspection laws: and the net produce of all duties and imposts, laid by any State on imports or exports, shall be for the use of the treasury of the United States; and all such laws shall be subject to the revision and control of the Congress.

(3) No State shall, without the consent of Congress, lay any duty of tonnage, keep troops, or ships of war in time of peace, enter into any agreement or compact with another State, or with a foreign power, or engage in war, unless actually invaded, or in such imminent danger as will not admit of delay.

ARTICLE II

SECTION I

(1) The executive power shall be vested in a President of the United States of America. He shall hold his office during the term of four years, and, together with the Vice President, chosen for the same term, be elected, as follows:

(2) Each State shall appoint, in such manner as the legislature thereof may direct, a number of electors, equal to the whole number of Senators and Representatives to which the State may be entitled in the Congress: but no Senator or Representative, or person holding an office of trust or profit under the United States, shall be appointed an elector.

[7] Obsolete provision.

[8] Modified by Amendment XVI.

The electors shall meet in their respective States, and vote by ballot for two persons, of whom one at least shall not be an inhabitant of the same State with themselves. And they shall make a list of all the persons voted for, and of the number of votes for each; which list they shall sign and certify, and transmit sealed to the seat of the government of the United States, directed to the president of the Senate. The president of the Senate shall, in the presence of the Senate and House of Representatives, open all the certificates, and the votes shall then be counted. The person having the greatest number of votes shall be the President, if such number be a majority of the whole number of electors appointed; and if there be more than one who have such majority, and have an equal number of votes, then the House of Representatives shall immediately choose by ballot one of them for President; and if no person have a majority, then from the five highest on the list the said House shall in like manner choose the President. But in choosing the President, the votes shall be taken by States, the representation from each State having one vote; a quorum for this purpose shall consist of a member or members from two thirds of the States, and a majority of all the States shall be necessary to a choice. In every case, after the choice of the President, the person having the greatest number of votes of the electors shall be the Vice President. But if there should remain two or more who have equal votes, the Senate shall choose from them by ballot the Vice President.[9]

(3) The Congress may determine the time of choosing the electors, and the day on which they shall give their votes; which day shall be the same throughout the United States.

(4) No person except a natural-born citizen, or a citizen of the United States, at the time of the adoption of this Constitution, shall be eligible to the office of President; neither shall any person be eligible to that office who shall not have attained to the age of thirty-five years, and been fourteen years a resident within the United States.

(5) In case of the removal of the President from office, or of his death, resignation, or inability to discharge the powers and duties of the said office, the same shall devolve on the Vice President, and the Congress may by law provide for the case of removal, death, resignation, or inability, both of the President and Vice President, declaring what officer shall then act as President, and such officer shall act accordingly, until the disability be removed, or a President shall be elected.

(6) The President shall, at stated times, receive for his services a compensation, which shall neither be increased nor diminished during the period for which he shall have been elected, and he shall not receive within that period any other emolument from the United States, or any of them.

(7) Before he enter on the execution of his office, he shall take the following oath or affirmation: "I do solemnly swear (or affirm) that I will faithfully execute the office of President of the United States, and will, to the best of my ability, preserve, protect, and defend the Constitution of the United States."

SECTION II

(1) The President shall be commander in chief of the army and navy of the United States, and of the militia of the several States, when called into the actual service of the United States; he may require the opinion, in writing, of the principal

[9] Superseded by Amendment XII.

officer in each of the executive departments, upon any subject relating to the duties of their respective offices, and he shall have power to grant reprieves and pardons for offenses against the United States, except in cases of impeachment.

(2) He shall have power, by and with the advice and consent of the Senate, to make treaties, provided two thirds of the Senators present concur; and he shall nominate, and by and with the advice and consent of the Senate, shall appoint ambassadors, other public ministers and consuls, judges of the Supreme Court, and all other officers of the United States, whose appointments are not herein otherwise provided for, and which shall be established by law: but the Congress may by law vest the appointment of such inferior officers, as they think proper, in the President alone, in the courts of law, or in the heads of departments.

(3) The President shall have power to fill up all vacancies that may happen during the recess of the Senate, by granting commissions which shall expire at the end of their next session.

SECTION III

He shall from time to time give to the Congress information of the state of the Union, and recommend to their consideration such measures as he shall judge necessary and expedient; he may, on extraordinary occasions, convene both Houses, or either of them, and in case of disagreement between them, with respect to the time of adjournment, he may adjourn them to such time as he shall think proper; he shall receive ambassadors and other public ministers; he shall take care that the laws be faithfully executed, and shall commission all the officers of the United States.

SECTION IV

The President, Vice President, and all civil officers of the United States, shall be removed from office on impeachment for, and conviction of, treason, bribery, or other high crimes and misdemeanors.

ARTICLE III

SECTION I

The judicial power of the United States shall be vested in one Supreme Court, and in such inferior courts as the Congress may from time to time ordain and establish. The judges, both of the Supreme and inferior courts, shall hold their offices during good behavior, and shall, at stated times, receive for their services a compensation, which shall not be diminished during their continuance in office.

SECTION II

(1) The judicial power shall extend to all cases, in law and equity, arising under this Constitution, the laws of the United States, and treaties made, or which shall be made, under their authority;—to all cases affecting ambassadors, other public ministers, and consuls;—to all cases of admiralty and maritime jurisdiction;—to controversies to which the United States shall be a party;—to controversies between two or more States;—*between a State and citizens of another State;* [10]—between citizens of different States;—between citizens of the same State claiming lands

under grants of different States, and *between a State, or the citizens thereof, and foreign States, citizens, or subjects.*[10]

(2) In all cases affecting ambassadors, other public ministers, and consuls, and those in which a State shall be party, the Supreme Court shall have original jurisdiction. In all the other cases before mentioned, the Supreme Court shall have appellate jurisdiction, both as to law and fact, with such exceptions, and under such regulations, as the Congress shall make.

(3) The trial of all crimes, except in cases of impeachment, shall be by jury; and such trial shall be held in the State where the said crimes shall have been committed; but when not committed within any State, the trial shall be at such place or places as the Congress may by law have directed.

SECTION III

(1) Treason against the United States shall consist only in levying war against them, or in adhering to their enemies, giving them aid and comfort. No person shall be convicted of treason unless on the testimony of two witnesses to the same overt act, or on confession in open court.

(2) The Congress shall have power to declare the punishment of treason, but no attainder of treason shall work corruption of blood, or forfeiture except during the life of the person attainted.

ARTICLE IV

SECTION I

Full faith and credit shall be given in each State to the public acts, records, and judicial proceedings of every other State. And the Congress may by general laws prescribe the manner in which such acts, records, and proceedings shall be proved, and the effect thereof.

SECTION II

(1) The citizens of each State shall be entitled to all privileges and immunities of citizens in the several States.

(2) A person charged in any State with treason, felony, or other crime, who shall flee from justice, and be found in another State, shall, on demand of the executive authority of the State from which he fled, be delivered up, to be removed to the State having jurisdiction of the crime.

(3) *No person held to service or labor in one State, under the laws thereof, escaping into another, shall, in consequence of any law or regulation therein, be discharged from such service or labor, but shall be delivered up on claim of the party to whom such service or labor may be due.*[11]

SECTION III

(1) New States may be admitted by the Congress into this Union; but no new State shall be formed or erected within the jurisdiction of any other State; nor any State be formed by the junction of two or more States, or parts of States, without the consent of the legislatures of the states concerned as well as of the Congress.

[10] Limited by Amendment XI.

[11] Superseded by Amendment XIII so far as pertains to slaves.

(2) The Congress shall have power to dispose of and make all needful rules and regulations respecting the territory or other property belonging to the United States; and nothing in this Constitution shall be so construed as to prejudice any claims of the United States, or of any particular State.

SECTION IV

The United States shall guarantee to every State in this Union a republican form of government, and shall protect each of them against invasion; and, on application of the legislature, or of the executive (when the legislature cannot be convened), against domestic violence.

ARTICLE V

The Congress, whenever two thirds of both Houses shall deem it necessary, shall propose amendments to this Constitution, or, on the application of the legislatures of two thirds of the several States, shall call a convention for proposing amendments which, in either case, shall be valid to all intents and purposes, as part of this Constitution, when ratified by the legislatures of three fourths of the several States, or by conventions in three fourths thereof, as the one or the other mode of ratification may be proposed by the Congress; provided *that no amendment which may be made prior to the year one thousand eight hundred and eight shall in any manner affect the first and fourth clauses in the ninth section of the first article;* [12] and that no State, without its consent, shall be deprived of its equal suffrage in the Senate.

ARTICLE VI

(1) All debts contracted and engagements entered into, before the adoption of this Constitution, shall be as valid against the United States under this Constitution, as under the Confederation.

(2) This Constitution, and the laws of the United States which shall be made in pursuance thereof; and all treaties made, or which shall be made, under the authority of the United States, shall be the supreme law of the land; and the judges in every State shall be bound thereby, anything in the constitution or laws of any State to the contrary notwithstanding.

(3) The Senators and Representatives before mentioned, and the members of the several State legislatures, and all executive and judicial officers, both of the United States and of the several States, shall be bound by oath or affirmation to support this Constitution; but no religious test shall ever be required as a qualification to any office or public trust under the United States.

ARTICLE VII

The ratification of the conventions of nine States shall be sufficient for the establishment of this Constitution between the States so ratifying the same.

[12] Obsolete provision.

AMENDMENTS

AMENDMENT I[13] 1791

Congress shall make no law respecting an establishment of religion, or prohibiting the free exercise thereof; or abridging the freedom of speech, or of the press; or the right of the people peaceably to assemble, and to petition the government for a redress of grievances.

AMENDMENT II 1791

A well regulated militia, being necessary to the security of a free State, the right of the people to keep and bear arms shall not be infringed.

AMENDMENT III 1791

No soldier shall, in time of peace, be quartered in any house, without the consent of the owner, nor in time of war, but in a manner to be prescribed by law.

AMENDMENT IV 1791

The right of the people to be secure in their persons, houses, papers, and effects, against unreasonable searches and seizures, shall not be violated, and no warrants shall issue, but upon probable cause, supported by oath or affirmation, and particularly describing the place to be searched, and the persons or things to be seized.

AMENDMENT V 1791

No person shall be held to answer for a capital or otherwise infamous crime, unless on a presentment or indictment of a grand jury, except in cases arising in the land or naval forces, or in the militia, when in actual service in time of war or public danger; nor shall any person be subject for the same offence to be twice put in jeopardy of life or limb; nor shall be compelled in any criminal case to be a witness against himself, nor be deprived of life, liberty, or property, without due process of law; nor shall private property be taken for public use, without just compensation.

AMENDMENT VI 1791

In all criminal prosecutions the accused shall enjoy the right to a speedy and public trial, by an impartial jury of the State and district wherein the crime shall have been committed, which district shall have been previously ascertained by law, and to be informed of the nature and cause of the accusation; to be confronted with the witnesses against him; to have compulsory process for obtaining witnesses in his favor, and to have the assistance of counsel for his defense.

AMENDMENT VII 1791

In suits at common law, where the value in controversy shall exceed twenty dollars, the right of trial by jury shall be preserved, and no fact tried by a jury shall be otherwise re-examined in any court of the United States than according to the rules of the common law.

[13] In strict legal language the Amendments are known as "Articles," but in order to avoid confusion with the Articles of the original Constitution and in conformance with general usage they are listed as "Amendments" here. The date is that of when they were declared ratified.

AMENDMENT VIII 1791

Excessive bail shall not be required, nor excessive fines imposed, nor cruel and unusual punishments inflicted.

AMENDMENT IX 1791

The enumeration in the Constitution of certain rights shall not be construed to deny or disparage others retained by the people.

AMENDMENT X 1791

The powers not delegated to the United States by the Constitution, nor prohibited by it to the States, are reserved to the States respectively, or to the people.

AMENDMENT XI 1798

The judicial power of the United States shall not be construed to extend to any suit in law or equity, commenced or prosecuted against one of the United States by citizens of another State, or by citizens or subjects of any foreign State.

AMENDMENT XII 1804

The electors shall meet in their respective States, and vote by ballot for President and Vice President, one of whom, at least, shall not be an inhabitant of the same State with themselves; they shall name in their ballots the persons voted for as President, and in distinct ballots the persons voted for as Vice President, and they shall make distinct lists of all persons voted for as President, and of all persons voted for as Vice President, and of the number of votes for each, which lists they shall sign and certify, and transmit sealed to the seat of the government of the United States, directed to the president of the Senate;—the president of the Senate shall, in the presence of the Senate and House of Representatives, open all the certificates, and the votes shall then be counted;—the person having the greatest number of votes for President, shall be the President, if such number be a majority of the whole number of electors appointed; and if no person have such majority, then from the persons having the highest numbers not exceeding three on the list of those voted for as President, the House of Representatives shall choose immediately, by ballot, the President. But in choosing the President, the votes shall be taken by States, the representation from each State having one vote; a quorum for this purpose shall consist of a member or members from two thirds of the States, and a majority of all the States shall be necessary to a choice. And if the House of Representatives shall not choose a President whenever the right of choice shall devolve upon them, before the fourth day of March next following, then the Vice President shall act as President, as in the case of the death or other constitutional disability of the President.—The person having the greatest number of votes as Vice President, shall be the Vice President, if such number be a majority of the whole number of electors appointed, and if no person have a majority, then from the two highest numbers on the list, the Senate shall choose the Vice President; a quorum for the purpose shall consist of two thirds of the whole number of Senators, and a majority of the whole number shall be necessary to a choice. But no person constitutionally ineligible to the office of President shall be eligible to that of Vice President of the United States.[14]

[14] Modified by Amendment XX.

Amendment XIII 1865

Section 1. Neither slavery nor involuntary servitude, except as a punishment for crime whereof the party shall have been duly convicted, shall exist within the United States, or any place subject to their jurisdiction.

Section 2. Congress shall have power to enforce this article by appropriate legislation.

Amendment XIV 1868

Section 1. All persons born or naturalized in the United States, and subject to the jurisdiction thereof, are citizens of the United States and of the State wherein they reside. No State shall make or enforce any law which shall abridge the privileges or immunities of citizens of the United States; nor shall any State deprive any person of life, liberty, or property, without due process of law; nor deny to any person within its jurisdiction the equal protection of the laws.

Section 2. Representatives shall be apportioned among the several States according to their respective numbers, counting the whole number of persons in each State, excluding Indians not taxed. But when the right to vote at any election for the choice of electors for President and Vice President of the United States, Representatives in Congress, the executive and judicial officers of a State, or the members of the legislature thereof, is denied to any of the male inhabitants of such State, being twenty-one years of age, and citizens of the United States, or in any way abridged, except for participation in rebellion, or other crime, the basis of representation therein shall be reduced in the proportion which the number of such male citizens shall bear to the whole number of male citizens twenty-one years of age in such State.

Section 3. No person shall be a Senator or Representative in Congress, or elector of President and Vice President, or hold any office, civil or military, under the United States, or under any State, who, having previously taken an oath, as a member of Congress, or as an officer of the United States, or as a member of any State legislature, or as an executive or judicial officer of any State, to support the Constitution of the United States, shall have engaged in insurrection or rebellion against the same, or given aid or comfort to the enemies thereof. But Congress may by a vote of two thirds of each House, remove such disability.

Section 4. The validity of the public debt of the United States, authorized by law, including debts incurred for payment of pensions and bounties for services in suppressing insurrection or rebellion, shall not be questioned. But neither the United States nor any State shall assume or pay any debt or obligation incurred in aid of insurrection or rebellion against the United States, or any claim for the loss or emancipation of any slave; but all such debts, obligations, and claims shall be held illegal and void.

Section 5. The Congress shall have power to enforce, by appropriate legislation, the provisions of this article.

Amendment XV 1870

Section 1. The right of citizens of the United States to vote shall not be denied or abridged by the United States or by any State on account of race, color, or previous condition of servitude.

Section 2. The Congress shall have power to enforce this article by appropriate legislation.

Amendment XVI 1913

The Congress shall have power to lay and collect taxes on incomes, from whatever source derived, without apportionment among the several States, and without regard to any census or enumeration.

Amendment XVII 1913

The Senate of the United States shall be composed of two Senators from each State, elected by the people thereof, for six years; and each Senator shall have one vote. The electors in each State shall have the qualifications requisite for electors of the most numerous branch of the State legislature.

When vacancies happen in the representation of any State in the Senate, the executive authority of such State shall issue writs of election to fill such vacancies: *Provided,* That the legislature of any State may empower the executive thereof to make temporary appointments until the people fill the vacancies by election as the legislature may direct.

This amendment shall not be so construed as to affect the election or term of any Senator chosen before it becomes valid as part of the Constitution.

Amendment XVIII 1919

Section 1. After one year from the ratification of this article the manufacture, sale, or transportation of intoxicating liquors within, the importation thereof into, or the exportation thereof from the United States and all territory subject to the jurisdiction thereof for beverage purposes is hereby prohibited.[15]

Section 2. The Congress and the several States shall have concurrent power to enforce this article by appropriate legislation.

Section 3. This article shall be inoperative unless it shall have been ratified as an amendment to the Constitution by the legislatures of the several States, as provided in the Constitution, within seven years from the date of the submission hereof to the States by the Congress.

Amendment XIX 1920

Section 1. The right of citizens of the United States to vote shall not be denied or abridged by the United States or by any State on account of sex.

Section 2. Congress shall have power, by appropriate legislation, to enforce the provisions of this article.

Amendment XX 1933

Section 1. The terms of the President and Vice President shall end at noon on the 20th day of January, and the terms of Senators and Representatives at noon on the 3rd day of January, of the years in which such terms would have ended if this article had not been ratified; and the terms of their successors shall then begin.

Section 2. The Congress shall assemble at least once in every year, and such meeting shall begin at noon on the 3rd day of January, unless they shall by law appoint a different day

[15] Repealed by Amendment XXI.

Section 3. If, at the time fixed for the beginning of the term of the President, the President elect shall have died, the Vice President elect shall become President. If a President shall not have been chosen before the time fixed for the beginning of his term, or if the President elect shall have failed to qualify, then the Vice President elect shall act as President until a President shall have qualified; and the Congress may by law provide for the case wherein neither a President elect nor a Vice President elect shall have qualified, declaring who shall then act as President, or the manner in which one who is to act shall be selected, and such person shall act accordingly until a President or Vice President shall have qualified.

Section 4. The Congress may by law provide for the case of the death of any of the persons from whom the House of Representatives may choose a President whenever the right of choice shall have devolved upon them, and for the case of the death of any of the persons from whom the Senate may choose a Vice President whenever the right of choice shall have devolved upon them.

Section 5. Sections 1 and 2 shall take effect on the 15th day of October following the ratification of this article.

Section 6. This article shall be inoperative unless it shall have been ratified as an amendment to the Constitution by the legislatures of three fourths of the several States within seven years from the date of its submission.

AMENDMENT XXI 1933

Section 1. The eighteenth article of amendment to the Constitution of the United States is hereby repealed.

Section 2. The transportation or importation into any State, Territory, or possession of the United States for delivery or use therein of intoxicating liquors, in violation of the laws thereof, is hereby prohibited.

Section 3. This article shall be inoperative unless it shall have been ratified as an amendment to the Constitution by conventions in the several States, as provided in the Constitution, within seven years from the date of submission hereof to the States by the Congress.

AMENDMENT XXII 1951

Section 1. No person shall be elected to the office of the President more than twice, and no person who has held the office of President, or acted as President, for more than two years of a term to which some other person was elected President shall be elected to the office of the President more than once. But this Article shall not apply to any person holding the office of President when this Article was proposed by the Congress, and shall not prevent any person who may be holding the office of President, or acting as President, during the term within which this Article becomes operative from holding the office of President or acting as President during the remainder of such term.

Section 2. This article shall be inoperative unless it shall have been ratified as an amendment to the Constitution by the legislatures of three fourths of the several States within seven years from the date of its submission to the States by the Congress.

INDEX